2

欧洲藏汉籍目录丛编

Catalogues of
Ancient Chinese Classics
in Europe

❦

张西平 主 编

谢 辉 林发钦 副主编

SPM
南方出版传媒
广东人民出版社
·广州·

文化公所
Hall de Cultura

A Catalogue of the Wade Collection of Chinese and Manchu Books in the Library of the University of Cambridge

剑桥大学图书馆威妥玛文库汉、满文书籍目录

A CATALOGUE

OF THE

WADE COLLECTION

OF

CHINESE AND MANCHU BOOKS

IN THE LIBRARY OF THE

UNIVERSITY OF CAMBRIDGE

BY

HERBERT A. GILES

M.A.; LL.D. (ABERD.)

PROFESSOR OF CHINESE IN THE UNIVERSITY OF CAMBRIDGE

CAMBRIDGE

AT THE UNIVERSITY PRESS

1898

L. C.

PREFATORY NOTE.

The following pages contain a "shelf catalogue" of the Chinese and Manchu books presented to the University Library at Cambridge by the late Sir Thomas Francis Wade, K.C.B., G.C.M.G., formerly Her Majesty's Minister at Peking, Professor of Chinese in the University from 1888 to his death in 1895, and Fellow of King's College.

The following letter addressed to the Vice Chancellor by Sir Thomas Wade contains his own description of the collection.

CAMBRIDGE, 11 October, 1886.

SIR,

The less formal communications which have earlier passed between us on the subject, will have prepared you for the receipt of a request, in official shape, that I may be allowed to present to the University a collection of Chinese literature brought together during a residence in China extending over many years. Pending its acceptance, I have been enabled by your kind permission to house it in the University Library, and I had hoped by this time so to have redistributed it as to render its inspection possible. Although I have been most liberally dealt with as to space, however, the arrangement of the books, necessarily requiring an acquaintance with the Chinese written character, and hence devolving on me single-handed, has taken longer than I had anticipated.

The collection will in certain departments require to be gradually subsidised. It contains very little, for instance, relating directly to Buddhism; much less to Taoism, or Islamism. There is, on the other part, as will happen in collections unsystematically made, a certain amount of redundancy. Still, when all that is superfluous or imperfect has been deducted, there will be found in the departments of Confucian philosophy, both of the earlier and later schools; of Archæology; History and *reliquiæ* of public men; Geography, topographical and political; Law and Administration; Poetry and Belles Lettres; enough to satisfy the needs of an advanced student of the language.

The Legal and Official division, as might be expected in the library of a man whose functions have been so largely those of an official interpreter as mine, is as full as any interpreter could desire.

There are besides the above a considerable number of works to a certain extent encyclopædic, which, for want of a more descriptive term, we are wont to speak of as Miscellanies. These are often, in effect, sectional libraries, not of original matter, but useful as redeeming useful texts from oblivion.

There is likewise a fair proportion of Manchu translations of good Chinese works, and a few Mongolian works. Of the last, very few. I doubt indeed that there are more of these than a dictionary or two in Manchu and Mongolian, or in those two languages and Chinese. Of Chinese Dictionaries arranged according to the rhyme, for the use of poets and composers, which are, in effect, repertories of quotations from the best authors; or in categories of subjects; or under the keys or roots of the several characters; or under other systems which I need not here pause to explain, there is a respectable provision.

Lastly, I have added some works by foreign hands in English, French, or other languages, of which the University Library may not impossibly contain duplicates; books of travel or history; grammars and dictionaries of Manchu, Mongolian, or Tibetan; such works in short as I have found it expedient, without pretension to acquaintance with all the languages in which they may be written, to have within reach for occasional reference.

The circumstances which have induced me to offer this collection, more particularly at this juncture, to the University of Cambridge, I will detail in a separate letter. It will for the moment suffice to say that, while presenting it as a free gift, I press for but one condition, namely that, for the rest of my life, I be allowed free access to it, and that, so long as my powers of mind and body permit, I be constituted its special curator or guardian.

The difficulty considered of finding a man who has not only the inclination but the leisure, to occupy himself with such a charge. this will not I feel sure be regarded an unreasonable prayer, and, assuming it granted, I shall then urge the prescription of very strict regulations in regard to the use of the collection which will have become the property of the University. The destruction of books in China during the twenty years of disorder consequent upon the late rebellion was terrible. Large libraries have since been destroyed by fire, in the capital and elsewhere. That which I am now tendering to the University includes little if anything that it will be absolutely impossible to recover, and both natives and foreigners are at this moment reprinting industriously. Still, replacement of works or volumes, shonld any be lost or abstracted, would be slow and troublesome, and the cost of some of the works in the collection, for which, after years of waiting, I have been tempted to give almost fancy prices, was when I left China in 1882, still daily rising.

These considerations will, I trust, excuse my anxiety, should I appear excessive, to see the integrity of the collection sufficiently guaranteed. I feel that the matter may safely be left in the hands of the University authorities responsible.

I have the honor to be, Sir,

Your most obedient Servant,

THOMAS FRANCIS WADE.

This collection was formed during a residence of forty years in the East by judicious selection of the best editions of the best works in the most important branches of Chinese literature; and the result is a comprehensive library admirably suited to the needs of any ordinary student. For even although Buddhism, Taoism, some of the fine arts such as music and painting, and several of the sciences such as botany and medicine, can scarcely be said to be adequately represented, still, much may be found on those and kindred subjects in the various great encyclopædias with which the library is so well supplied.

A rough classification, adopted by the donor to suit the room at his disposal, has been allowed to stand, and the books are therefore in the actual order in which he left them. In view however of any difficulties of search likely to arise from such arrangement, alphabetical lists both of the titles of the works and of the names of the authors have been added as a supplement to the Catalogue.

The classification is as follows:

A. Chiefly devoted to editions of the Classics and to exegetical works upon various portions of the Confucian Canon, but containing also the writings of Taoist philosophers, various Buddhist *sûtras* etc. etc. [175 works in 478 vols.]

B. Under the heads of History, Biography, and Statutes, this section contains (B 734) a complete and uniform edition of the Twenty-two Dynastic Histories of China in 227 large volumes, the splendid encyclopædia of Ma Tuan-lin (489), with its prototype (476) and subsequent enlargements (527 and 629), the Mirror of History (961), the Statutes of the present dynasty (261), the Penal Code (134), various collections of reprints, etc. etc. [291 works in 2038 vols.]

C. The chief feature of this the Geographical section is the Imperial Geography (85) in 24 large vols. Here is also to be found (114) the oldest printed book in the University Library. [56 works in 263 vols.]

D. This section contains a few of the leading novels, some plays and essays, and a good collection of anthologies, including three volumes (146—148) of specimens from the writings of the poetesses of the present dynasty. [85 works in 312 vols.]

E. Besides a beautiful and valuable edition of the Imperial Dictionary of K'ang Hsi (225), this section comprises many works of especial value to the general student, such as the great literary Concordance (265), the descriptive Catalogue of the Imperial Library (143), and several important encyclopædias. [110 works in 481 vols.]

F, X, and **Y.** Among the "Miscellaneous" books in these sections may be mentioned a rare collection of pamphlets (F 35) issued by the T'ai-p'ings during their great rebellion, and the first 12 volumes of a military encyclopædia (F 124) published in 1599. [47 works in 405 vols.]

Z. This section contains various translations of religious and scientific works; among them a facsimile copy of the New Testament in Chinese (40) as presented to the Empress-Dowager of China on her 60th birthday by the missionary body, and a copy of Euclid (41) partly translated by Matteo Ricci in 1607 and finished by A. Wylie in 1857. [32 works in 41 vols.]

G. This section is for students of the Manchu and Mongol languages, and contains in addition to translations of the Chinese Classics several useful handbooks for beginners. [87 works in 286 vols.]

Total: 883 works in 4304 volumes.

The cost of printing the catalogue has been defrayed out of a fund subscribed by some of Sir Thomas Wade's friends.

HERBERT A. GILES.

Cambridge: October, 1898.

前　言

　　以下几页包含一份由已故威妥玛爵士（Sir Thomas Francis Wade）向剑桥大学图书馆所赠汉文和满文图书的"书架目录"。威妥玛爵士曾荣获高级巴思勋章、圣米迦勒及圣乔治勋章，生前担任女王陛下驻北京大臣，1888年至1895年去世前一直担任剑桥大学汉学教授，兼任国王学院研究员。

　　下文是威妥玛爵士写给剑桥大学副校长的一封信，其中包括他本人对这些藏书的描述。

剑桥，1886年10月11日

校长阁下：

　　以前我们曾就此事进行过非正式的交流，这将有助于您为即将收到一份正式请求做好准备：我可能获准向剑桥大学捐赠一批中文文献藏品，这些文献为本人旅居中国多年期间所购得。在该请求获得批准前，承蒙您恩准，将这些书籍存放于剑桥大学图书馆。我希望到目前为止已对这批藏品进行了重新分类，以便进行必要的检查。尽管在空间方面我获得了最大的自由，但是，书籍布置工作需由熟悉中国文字的人员完成，因此该项工作已移交我一人处理后，所花费的时间超出了我的预期。

　　这批藏书中的某些类别今后需要逐渐补充。例如，直接与佛教相关的图书很少，直接与道教或伊斯兰教相关的图书更少。另一方面，与其他非系统性藏书一样，这批藏书中有一些是多余的。即便如此，在剔除多余或有瑕疵的书籍之后，这些书籍仍然可以纳入多个类别，包括：儒家哲学（早期和晚期学派）；考古；历史和公众人物遗迹；地理学、地形学和政治学；法律和行政管理；诗歌和纯文学。它们足以满足高级语言学生的学习需求。

　　不出所料，对于像我这样主要担任官方翻译的人来说，藏书中包含很多法律和官方文献，可以满足所有需求。

　　除上述书籍外，藏书中还有大量在某种程度上类似百科全书的图书，由于缺乏更准确的词来描述这类书籍，我们常常称之为"杂录"（Miscellanies）。实际上，杂录往往像分门别类的图书馆，虽然没有原始材料，但有助于提醒人们回忆某些被遗忘的有用文本。

　　这批藏书中还有一定比例的经典汉文著作的满文译本和数量极少的蒙文著作。我真的怀疑，只有一两本满文和蒙文字典或者满、蒙、汉文字典。除此以外，还有按照音韵编排的汉语字典，方便诗人和作家使用，实际上，这些字典有的是名家的语录汇编，有的按主题分类，有的按几个汉字的关键词或字根分类，有的按其他体系分类（在此无需赘述这些体系），此类图书的数量相当可观。

最后，我还在藏书中加入了一些由外国作家用英文、法文或其他语言创作的部分作品，剑桥大学图书馆也许没有这些图书的副本。藏书中还有关于旅游或历史书籍以及满文、蒙文或藏文的语法书和字典，总之，我发现这些图书可以应急，无需通晓创作这些书籍所用的所有语言，可供偶尔查阅。

至于捐赠这批藏书的原因，特别是此时向剑桥大学捐赠这批图书的原因，我将在另一封信中详述。目前只要说这是一批免费礼物即可，我只有一个条件，那就是，在我有生之年，能够获准免费阅读这些书籍，而且，只要我的心智和体力允许，请指定我担任这些藏书的特别监护人或保护人。

很难找到一个乐意并且有时间负责此项工作的人，但我敢肯定，这不是一个荒唐的愿望。如果我的条件获得批准，我会要求针对这批藏书的使用作出极为严格的规定，而这批藏书将成为剑桥大学的财产。最近发生的叛乱之后，中国经历了二十年的动荡，期间书籍受损情况令人触目惊心，首都及其他地方的大量藏书被焚。现在我打算向剑桥大学捐赠的这些藏书中包括少量完全无法修复的书籍，目前中国人和外国人都在努力再版重印。尽管如此，如果要替换丢失或被盗的书籍或单册是一个漫长而繁琐的过程，而且这批藏书中部分书籍的价格不菲，1882年我离开中国时被劝说以近乎昂贵的价格购买这些图书，多年之后，这些书籍的价格依然节节攀升。

请原谅我的焦虑，正是这些原因使我急于看到这批藏书的完整性能得到充分保障。我认为，此事应交由剑桥大学校方处理更为可靠。

校长阁下，很荣幸成为
您最顺从的仆人，
威妥玛

这批藏书是我在东方国家旅居四十年间收集的，精心挑选了中文文献最重要门类最出色著作的最佳版本；因此，它们完全能够满足任何普通学生的需求。尽管佛教、道教和音乐、绘画等部分纯艺术图书以及植物、医药等学科的图书很难称得上丰富，但是，在这一批藏书中数量众多的各种百科全书类图书中可以找到以上及相关类别的主题。

为适应自己的房间，捐赠者对这些图书进行了粗略的分类，因此，这些图书的实际顺序与捐赠者交付时的顺序一致。不过，考虑到这种排列方法可能会给查找图书带来困难，因此本《目录》还附有按照书名和作者姓名字母顺序排列的清单。

分类如下：

A．主要为各个版本的经典以及对儒家经传各部分的注疏作品，还包括道教哲学家的著作以及各种佛经等。〔共175部，478册。〕

B．这一部分的条目为历史、传记、法规，包括（B 734号）一套版本统一的中国二十二史

（227人册）、马端临编写的一流百科全书（《文献通考》）（489号）及其蓝本（《通典》）（476号）和续篇（527号和629号）、《资治通鉴》（961号）、当朝法规（261号）、《刑律》（134号）、不同系列的再版重印本等。〔291部，2038册。〕

C．地理类图书，主要是24大册的《皇舆表》（85号）以及（114号）剑桥大学图书馆中最古老的印刷图书。〔56部，263册。〕

D．该条目中包括几部重要的小说、一些戏剧和散文以及大量文集，其中包括三册（146–148号）当朝女诗人的代表作。〔85部，312册。〕

E．除了一套版本精美珍贵的《康熙字典》（225号），该条目还包括很多对普通学生特别有价值的著作，例如《艺文类聚》（265号）、《四库全书总目提要》（143号）和几部重要的百科全书。〔110部，481册。〕

F．X．Y．这几个条目中的"杂录"书籍包括太平天国运动发行的一批罕见小册子（F 35号）以及1599年出版的军事百科全书（F 124号）的前12册。〔47部，405册。〕

Z．该条目包含宗教和科学著作的不同译本；其中包括一本中文《新约》的摹写本（40号），这是传教士使团献给慈禧太后六十大寿的礼物，此外还包括一套中文《几何原本》（Euclid）的副本（41号），利玛窦（Matteo Ricci）1607年翻译了该书的一部分，剩余部分由伟烈亚力（A．Wylie）1857年翻译完成。〔32部，41册。〕

G．该条目的书籍适合学习满文和蒙古文的学生，除了中文经典的满文和蒙文译本，还包括对初学者非常有用的手册。〔87部，286册。〕

总计：883部，4304册。

此《目录》的印刷费由威妥玛爵士的部分朋友出资设立的一个基金支付。

翟理斯（Herbert A. Giles）

剑桥：1898年10月

（管宇译，彭萍校）

CATALOGUE OF
THE WADE LIBRARY

CHINESE

A. *Classics and Philosophy.*

A 1. 六 經 圖 定 本

Liu ching t'u ting pên

A description of the various articles etc. mentioned in the Six Classics, with numerous illustrations, by 王皜 Wang Kao. [Incorrectly labelled 大昜象數 *Ta i hsiang shu*, which is the title of § I.] 1740. 28.5cm.

A 2—3. 讀 昜 口 義

Tu i k'ou i

A work on the Canon of Changes, by 楊一夔 Yang I-k'uei (T. 南雪), who dated his MS. 1794. 1852. 27.5cm.

A 4. 爻 物 當 名

Hsiao wu tang ming

A work on the Diagrams, by 黎遂球 Li Sui-ch'iu (T. 美周), first published in 1635. 1818. 28cm.
G. W.

THE WADE LIBRARY

A 5. 易 漢 學

I han hsüeh

The Canon of Changes as interpreted under the Han dynasty, by 惠棟 Hui Tung (T. 松崖), edited by 畢沅 Pi Yüan, who died in 1797. *No date.* 29cm.

A 6—7. 易 經 來 註 圖 解

I ching lai chu t'u chieh

A commentary on the Canon of Changes, with diagrams, by 來瞿唐 Lai Chü-t'ang. 1598. 23cm.

A 8. 周 易 傳 義 合 訂

Chou i ch'uan i ho ting

An exegetical work on the Canon of Changes, published by order of the Emperor Ch'ien Lung, who contributed a preface, under the superintendence of 朱軾 Chu Shih. 1737. 27cm.

A 8a.

Another copy, inferior paper, without title-page.

A 9. 易 義 闡

I i shan

Explanation of the Canon of Changes, by 韓松 Han Sung (T. 雪亭). 1789. 25.5cm.

A 10. 易 經 本 意

I ching pên i

The meaning of the Canon of Changes. [Title-page missing.] *No date.* 26.5cm.

A 11. 易 經 大 全 會 解

I ching ta ch'üan hui chieh

Commentaries on the Canon of Changes, edited by 來爾繩 Lai Erh-shêng (T. 木臣) whose preface is dated 1681. 1719. 27cm.

A 13. 易 經 離 句

I ching li chü

Phrases from the Canon of Changes, explained by 李盤 Li P'an for the use of teachers. 1819. 26cm.

A 15. 李 氏 易 傳

Li shih i chuan

A commentary on the Canon of Changes, by 李鼎祚 Li Ting-tsu of the T'ang dynasty, edited by 盧見曾 Lu Chien-tsêng. 1756. 24.5cm.

A 16. 禹 貢 山 川 地 理 圖

Yü kung shan ch'uan ti li t'u

Geographical identifications in connection with the engineering labours of the Great Yü who died B.C. 2197, with sketch maps, by 程大昌 Ch'êng Ta-ch'ang of the 12th cent. A.D. [MS. copy, without title-page, preceded by extract from the Imperial Catalogue.] 1773. 29 × 18cm.

A 17—18. 尚 書 古 文 疏 證

Shang shu ku wên su chêng

Verifications of the ancient text of the Canon of History, by 閻若璩 Yen Jo-chü (T. 百詩), preceded by 朱子古文書疑 Chu tzŭ ku wên shu i, which gives the views of Chu Hsi, by his son 閻詠 Yen Yung. 1704. 25cm.

A 19—20. 尚 書 今 古 文 注 疏

Shang shu chin ku wên chu su

Commentary on the ancient and modern texts of the Canon of History, by 孫星衍 Sun Hsing-yen. 1815. 24.5cm.

A 21. 書 經 體 註

Shu ching t'i chu

The Canon of History, with a running commentary. Reprint of the work by 范紫登 Fan Tzŭ-têng. See A 75. 1824. 27cm.

4

THE WADE LIBRARY

A 22. 詩 經 精 華

Shih ching ching hua

The essence and beauty of the Canon of Poetry, by 薛嘉穎 Hsieh Chia-ying. 1825. 27cm.

A 23—24. 詩 故 考 異

Shih ku k'ao i

Various readings and interpretations of the Canon of Poetry, by 徐華嶽 Hsü Hua-yo, whose preface is dated 1816. 1832. 24cm.

A 25. 春 秋 體 註 大 全 合 參

Ch'un ch'iu t'i chu ta ch'üan ho ts'an

The Spring and Autumn Annals, with running commentary. Reprint of the work of 范紫登 Fan Tzǔ-têng, edited by 周熾 Chou Ch'ih (T. 旦林), and accompanied by the commentary of 胡安國 Hu An-kuo. 1711. 26.5cm.

A 26. 左 氏 辯 例

Tso shih pien li

On the usages in Tso's commentary on the Spring and Autumn Annals, by 馬驌 Ma Su. *No date.* 25.5cm.

A 27. 呂 氏 春 秋

Lü shih ch'un ch'iu

The so-called Spring and Autumn of Lü, attributed on insufficient grounds to 呂不韋 Lü Pu-wei of the 3rd cent. B.C., edited by 黃甫龍 Huang-fu Lung and 沈兆廷 Shên Chao-t'ing, with preface from 方孝孺 Fang Hsiao-ju who died in 1402. *No date.*

27cm.

A 27a.

Another edition. Edited by 畢沅 Pi Yüan. 1789. 29 × 18cm.

A 28.　　　春 秋 說 畧
Ch'un ch'iu shuo lüeh

A commentary on the Spring and Autumn Annals, by 郝懿行 Shih (*or* Hao) I-hang, 1757—1825. Completed in 1795 and dated by the author 1805.　1827.　　　　　　　　　　　　27cm.

A 29.　　　春 秋 鈔
Ch'un ch'iu ch'ao

Notes on the Spring and Autumn Annals, by 朱軾 Chu Shih. 1736.　　　　　　　　　　　　　　　　27cm.

A 29a.

Another copy, common paper.　　　　　　　　　26cm.

A 30.　　　公 穀 傳
Kung ku chuan

The commentaries of Kung 羊 Yang and Ku 梁 Liang on the Spring and Autumn Annals, synoptically arranged by 姜兆錫 Chiang Chao-hsi.　1740.　　　　　　　27cm.

A 32.　　　晏 予 春 秋
Yen tzŭ ch'un ch'iu

The Spring and Autumn Annals of the philosopher Yen, a collection of historical notes attributed on insufficient grounds to 晏嬰 Yen Ying of the 6th cent. B.C.　1789.　　　　　29 × 18cm.

A 33—35.　　　儀 禮 節 畧
I li chieh lüeh

A commentary on the Decorum Ritual, by 朱軾 Chu Shih. 1719.　　　　　　　　　　　　　　　　27cm.

A 36—39.　　　左 傳 快 讀
Tso chuan k'uai tu

Reprint of a commentary on the *Tso chuan*, by 李駿嵒 Li Chün-yen.　1850.　　　　　　　　　　26.5cm.

A 40.　　爾　雅　啟　蒙
Erh ya ch'i mêng

A guide to the study of the *Erh Ya* or so-called Literary Expositor,
by 沈兆霖 Shên Chao-lin.　1852.　　　　　　　25cm.

A 41.　　爾　雅　註　疏
Erh ya chu su

The *Erh Ya*, or so-called Literary Expositor, with commentary by
郭璞 Kuo P'o, A.D. 276—324, edited with notes by 邢昺 Hsing
Ping, A.D. 932—1010. *No date.*　　　　24.5 × 19cm.

A 42.　　儀　禮　鄭　氏　注
I li chêng shih chu

A re-issue of the Decorum Ritual, with commentary by 鄭康成
Chêng K'ang-ch'êng of the Han dynasty, as published under the
Sung dynasty.　1814.　　　　　　　　　28.5cm.

A 43.　　翻　宋　本　禮　記
Fan sung pên li chi

Reprint of the Sung dynasty editions of (1) the 禮記注 *Li chi
chu* Book of Rites with commentary by 鄭康成 Chêng K'ang-ch'êng
of the Han dynasty, and (2) the 禮記釋文 *Li chi shih wên*
Explanation of the Book of Rites by 陸元朗 Lu Yüan-lang who
died A.D. 625. [番 for 翻 on label.] 1806.　　　28.5cm.

A 44.　　禮　記　讀　本
Li chi tu pên

The Book of Rites, with commentary, being a reprint of the work
by 鄭康成 Chêng K'ang-ch'êng. [禮記旁訓 on label.] 1844.
　　　　　　　　　　　　　　　　　　　26cm.

A 45—47.　　禮　記　纂　言
Li chi tsuan yen

The Book of Rites, with commentary by 吳澄 Wu Ch'êng,
A.D. 1247—1331, edited by 朱軾 Chu Shih. 1727.　　26cm.

A 47*a b*****.**

Another copy, white paper. 27cm.

A 48—49. 禮 記 庭 訓

Li chi t'ing hsün

The Book of Rites, with commentary, by 潘炳綱 P'an Ping-kang. 1791. 27cm.

A 50—51. 禮 記 體 註

Li chi t'i chu

The Book of Rites, with running commentary, by 范紫登 Fan Tzŭ-têng, to which is added the 禮記集說 *Li chi chi shuo* of 陳澔 Ch'ên Hao, A.D. 1261—1341, edited by 徐文初 Hsü Wên-ch'u. 1766. 27cm.

A 54. 大 戴 禮 記

Ta tai li chi

The Book of Rites according to the text of 戴德 the Elder Tai. 1718. 27cm.

A 55.

Another copy, common paper. 26cm.

A 56. 呂 氏 四 禮 翼

Lü shih ssü li i

A work on the proprieties, by 呂坤 Lü K'un (T. 叔簡), A.D. 1536—1618, being a short popular supplement to the Book of Rites. 1719. 27cm.

A 57. 禮 記 說

Li chi shuo

Notes on the Book of Rites, by 楊秉杷 Yang Ping-pa. 1818. 25cm.

A 58. 大 戴 禮 記 補 註

Ta tai li chi pu chu

The Book of Rites according to the Elder Tai, with commentary, edited by 孔廣森 K'ung Kuang-sên. 1794. 28cm.

THE WADE LIBRARY

A 59—60. 日 講 易 經 解 義
Jih chiang i ching chieh i

The Canon of Changes explained, for daily use. Edited by Imperial command, with a preface from the Emperor K'ang Hsi, by 牛鈕 Niu Niu, 孫在豐 Sun Tsai-fêng, and 張英 Chang Ying, assisted by many scholars. 1683. 26cm.

A 61—62. 日 講 書 經 解 義
Jih chiang shu ching chieh i

The Canon of History explained, for daily use. Edited by Imperial command, with a preface from the Emperor K'ang Hsi, by 庫勒納 K'u Lo-na and 葉方藹 Yeh Fang-ai, assisted by many scholars. 1680. 26cm.

A 63—67. 日 講 春 秋 解 義
Jih chiang ch'un ch'iu chieh i

The Spring and Autumn Annals explained, for daily use. Edited under Imperial instructions, with prefaces from the Emperors K'ang Hsi (in whose reign it was begun) and Ch'ien Lung, by 庫勒納 K'u Lo-na, 李光地 Li Kuang-ti, and many scholars. 1737. 26cm.

A 68—70. 日 講 禮 記 解 義
Jih chiang li chi chieh i

The Book of Rites explained, for daily use. Edited under Imperial instructions, with preface from the Emperor Ch'ien Lung, by 張廷玉 Chang T'ing-yü and others, as originated by the Emperor K'ang Hsi. 1747. 28cm.

A 71—74. 日 講 四 書 解 義
Jih chiang ssŭ shu chieh i

The Four Books explained, for daily use. Edited by Imperial command, with a preface from the Emperor K'ang Hsi, by 陳廷敬 Ch'ên T'ing-ching and other scholars. [Several pages missing.] 1677. 24.5cm.

A 75. 詩 經 體 註 衍 義

Shih ching t'i chu yen i

The Canon of Poetry explained, with the commentary of Chu Hsi, by 范紫登 Fan Tzǔ-têng whose preface is dated 1687, edited by 顧且巷 Ku Ch'ieh-an. See A 21. *No date.* 27cm.

A 76.

Another edition of A 5. *No date.* 24cm.

A 77—80. 四 書 講 義 尊 聞 錄

Ssǔ shu chiang i tsun wên lu

The Four Books explained, with extracts from all the great commentators, by 戴鋐 Tai Hung (T. 景亭). 1729. 27.5cm.

A 81—82. 四 書 補 註 備 旨

Ssǔ shu pu chu pei chih

The Four Books, with commentaries etc., by 鄧林 Têng Lin (T. 退巷). Preface by 杜定 Tu Ting, dated 1779. 1818. 26cm.

A 83—85. 四 書 章 句 集 註

Ssǔ shu chang chü chi chu

The Four Books, punctuated according to Chu Hsi, with commentaries and preface by Chu Hsi dated 1189, edited by 陳宏謀 Ch'ên Hung-mou, 1695—1771. [Label inaccurate.] *No date.* 26cm.

A 86. 四 書 集 註 補

Ssǔ shu chi chu pu

The Four Books, with Chu Hsi's commentary and additions, edited by 王復禮 Wang Fu-li. 1819. 27.5 × 20.5cm.

A 87—90. 四 書 講 義 困 勉 錄

Ssǔ shu chiang i k'un mien lu

The Four Books, explained from various sources by 陸隴其 Lu Lung-ch'i (T. 稼書). 1699. 25.5cm.

A 91—92. 四 書 考 異

Ssŭ shu k'ao i

On the discrepancies in the Four Books, by 翟灝 Chai Hao (T. 晴江), edited by 杭世駿 Hang Shih-chün. 1799. 24cm.

A 93—94. 四 書 口 義

Ssŭ shu k'ou i

The Four Books explained, by 方柔如 Fang Jou-ju (T. 樸山). 1788. 24cm.

A 95—96. 四 書 考 輯 要

Ssŭ shu k'ao ch'i yao

Important points in the Four Books, discussed by 陳宏謀 Ch'ên Hung-mou. 1771. 25.5cm.

A 97—106. 四 書 玩 註 詳 說

Ssŭ shu wan chu hsiang shuo

The Four Books explained, with voluminous notes and commentaries, by 冉覲祖 Jan Chin-tsu (T. 永光), and a preface by 張英 Chang Ying. 1687. 23.5cm.

A 107—108. 四 書 翼 註 論 文

Ssŭ shu i chu lun wên

The Four Books, with commentary and excursus, by 張甄陶 Chang Chên-t'ao (T. 惕菴). 1746. 23.5cm.

A 109—113. 四 書 本 義 匯 參

Ssŭ shu pên i hui ts'an

The real meaning of the Four Books, with commentaries, by 王步青 Wang Pu-ch'ing. 1745. 25cm.

A 114. 蘇 批 孟 子

Su p'i mêng tzŭ

Notes on Mencius, by 蘇洵 Su Hsün, father of the famous poet Su Tung-p'o, A.D. 1009—1066, edited by 趙大浣 Chao Ta-kuan. 1815. 27 × 16cm.

A 115. 二 論 啟 幼 引 端

Erh lun ch'i yu yin tuan

The Discourses of Confucius, explained for beginners, by 劉忠
Liu Chung (T. 藎侯). 1820. 23cm.

A 116—117. 四 書 典 林

Ssŭ shu tien lin

Phrases in the Four Books, illustrated and explained by passages
from the remainder of the Confucian Canon etc., arranged in categories,
by 江永 Chiang Yung. 1735. 25cm.

A 118. 四 書 古 人 典 林

Ssŭ shu ku jen tien lin

A dictionary of the personages mentioned in the Four Books, by
江永 Chiang Yung. 1749. 22cm.

A 119. 四 書 典 制 彙 編

Ssŭ shu tien chih hui pien

A dictionary of the usages and ceremonial in the Four Books, by
胡掄 Hu Lun (T. 應麟). 1732. 24cm.

A 120. 四 書 摭 餘 說

Ssŭ shu chih yü shuo

Essays on the Four Books, by 曹之升 Ts'ao Chih-shêng (T.
寅谷). 1830. 24cm.

A 121. 此 木 軒 四 書 說

Tz'ŭ mu hsien ssŭ shu shuo

Essays on the Four Books, by 焦袁熹 Chiao Yüan-hsi (T.
廣期), written between 1689 and 1700. 1744. 24cm.

A 122—123. 周 易 折 中

Chou i chê chung

The Book of Changes viewed impartially, edited under Imperial
instructions, with a preface from the Emperor K'ang Hsi, by 李廣地
Li Kuang-ti. 1715. 27cm.

THE WADE LIBRARY

A 124—126. 書 經 傳 說 彙 纂
Shu ching ch'uan shuo hui tsuan

The Canon of History, with commentaries and exegetical notes (illustrated), edited under Imperial instructions, with a preface from the Emperor Yung Chêng, by 王頊齡 Wang Hsü-ling and other scholars. 1730. 28cm.

A 127—131. 詩 經 傳 說 彙 編
Shih ching ch'uan shuo hui pien

The Canon of Poetry, with commentaries and exegetical notes (illustrated), edited under Imperial instructions, with a preface from the Emperor Yung Chêng, by 王鴻緒 Wang Hung-hsü and other scholars. 1727. 25.5cm.

A 132—135. 春 秋 傳 說 彙 纂
Ch'un ch'iu ch'uan shuo hui tsuan

The Spring and Autumn Annals, with commentaries and exegetical notes, edited under Imperial instructions, with preface from the Emperor K'ang Hsi, by 王掞 Wang Shan. 1721. 28cm.

A 136—143. 儀 禮 義 疏
I li i su

The Decorum Ritual explained, with commentary. [Title-page etc. missing.] *No date.* 29.5 × 20.5cm.

A 144—149. 周 官 義 疏
Chou kuan i su

The official Ritual of the Chou dynasty, explained with commentary, edited under Imperial instructions, with preface from the Emperor Ch'ien Lung dated 1748, by 鄂爾泰 O-êrh-t'ai, 張廷玉 Chang T'ing-yü, 朱軾 Chu Shih, and others. 1754. 25.5 × 18cm.

A 150—158. 禮 記 義 疏
Li chi i su

The Book of Rites explained, with commentary, issued by Imperial command. (No title-page.) *No date.* 25cm.

A 159. 孝 經 注 解
Hsiao ching chu chieh

The Canon of Filial Piety, with commentary and explanation, the former and preface by the Emperor Ming Huang, A.D. 713—756, the latter by 司馬光 Ssŭ-ma Kuang, 1009—1086, together with notes by 范祖禹 Fan Tsu-yü. 1847. 27cm.

A 160. 孝 經
Hsiao ching

The Canon of Filial Piety, edited and annotated by 朱軾 Chu Shih, to which is added the 三本管窺 *San pên kuan k'uei*, being a collation of the ancient and modern texts etc. 1720. 27cm.

A 161—162. 三 經 四 書 正 文
San ching ssŭ shu chêng wên

Standard texts of the Confucian Canon, consisting of the Canon of Changes with preface by 程頤 Ch'êng I, A.D. 1033—1107, and the Canon of History with preface by 蔡沈 Ts'ai Ch'ên, 1167—1230. *No date.* 34 × 23cm.

A 163. 爾 雅 音 圖
Erh ya yin t'u

The Erh Ya, or so-called Literary Expositor, with preface and commentary, by 郭璞 Kuo P'o, A.D. 276—324. 1801. 35 × 25cm.

A 164—165. 四 書
Ssŭ shu

The Four Books, with preface and commentary, by 朱熹 Chu Hsi, the former dated A.D. 1189. *No date.* 33 × 21cm.

A 166. 國 語
Kuo yü

Historical notes on the feudal period, attributed to 左丘明 Tso-ch'iu Ming, with preface and commentary by 韋昭 Wei Chao, 3rd cent. A.D., edited by 宋庠 Sung Hsiang, who died in 1064. *No date.* 30cm.

A 167.

家 語
Chia yü

The Family Sayings, attributed to Confucius' but probably the work of 王肅 Wang Su, who died A.D. 256, edited by 茅坤 Mao K'un, with preface from 王世貞 Wang Shih-chêng. 1599.

26.5cm.

A 168.

夏 小 正 攷 注
Hsia hsiao chêng k'ao chu

The Calendar of the Hsia dynasty, with commentary by 畢沅 Pi Yüan. See A 224. 1783.

29 × 18cm.

A 169.

四 書 合 講
Ssŭ shu ho chiang

Harmony of the Four Books, with Chu Hsi's commentary and preface by 翁復克 Wêng Fu-k'o. Printed from metal types. See A 298. 1827.

32 × 18.5cm.

A 170—171.

四 書 補 註 附 考 備 旨
Ssŭ shu pu chu fu k'ao pei chih

The Four Books, with commentary, etc., by 鄧林 Têng Lin (T. 退巷), whose preface is dated 1736, edited with additions by 仇滄柱 Ch'iu Ts'ang-chu. *No date.*

29 × 18cm.

A 172—173.

Another edition, dated 1832.

A 174.

批 黙 四 書 讀 本
P'i tien ssŭ shu tu pên

The Four Books, punctuated and annotated in red, with the commentary of Chu Hsi. 1827.

30 × 17.5cm.

A 175—176.

聖 諭 像 解
Shêng yü hsiang chieh

Anecdotes bearing upon the Sacred Edict of the Emperor K'ang Hsi (see A 354), with numerous full-page illustrations, by 梁延年 Liang Yen-nien, whose preface is dated 1681. 1856.

29cm.

A 177—179.
Another copy, thick paper. 31 × 19.5cm.

A 180—217. 十 三 經
Shih san ching

The Thirteen Classics, with commentaries by various scholars, edited, with preface from the Emperor Ch'ien Lung, by 鄂爾泰 O-êrh-t'ai and 張廷玉 Chang T'ing-yü. 1747. 28.5cm.

A 218. 聖 諭 廣 訓
Shêng yü kuang hsün

The Sacred Edict of the Emperor K'ang Hsi, with Amplification and Paraphrase. (Mounted.) 1724. 27 × 20cm.

A 219—223. 古 論 大 觀
Ku lun ta kuan

Essays by early writers on philosophy, government, religion, etc., edited by 陳繼儒 Ch'ên Chi-ju (T. 眉公) of the 18th cent. *No date.* 28cm.

A 224. 夏 小 正
Hsia hsiao chêng

Reprint of works on the Calendar of the Hsia dynasty, a section of the 大戴禮 Ritual of the Elder Tai. See A 168. 1821. 28cm.

A 225. 古 聖 賢 像 傳畧
Ku shêng hsien hsiang chuan lüeh

Portraits and brief biographical notices of ancient worthies, ranging from 倉頡 Ts'ang Chieh, the fabled inventor of writing, 28th cent. B.C., down to the end of the 16th cent. A.D., by 顧沅 Ku Yüan (T. 湘舟). See A 232. 1830. 26.5cm.

A 226—230. 闕 里 文 獻 考
Ch'üeh li wên hsien k'ao

A work on the family of Confucius, his descendants, disciples, and commentators, by 孔繼汾 K'ung Chi-fên of the 69th generation, completed in 1697 and edited by 孔昭煥 K'ung Chao-huan of the 71st generation. See A 237. 1762.   26.5cm.

A 231. 聖 廟 志 輯 要
Shêng miao chih chi yao

Chief features of the Confucian Temple, with an account of the sacrificial worship, dances, songs, etc. performed there, illustrated, by 高維嶽 Kao Wei-yo and others. *No date.*   25.5cm.

A 232. 聖 廟 祀 典 圖 考
Shêng miao ssŭ tien t'u k'ao

Portraits of Confucius, his disciples, and chief exponents whose tablets stand in the Confucian Temple, by 顧沅 Ku Yüan. See A 225. 1826.   26cm.

A 233. 孔 子 集 語
K'ung tzŭ chi yü

A collection of the utterances of Confucius, from all sources, apocryphal and canonical, by 孫星衍 Sun Hsing-yen. *No date.* 24cm.

A 234. 聖 蹟 圖
Shêng chi t'u

Scenes connected with the lives of Confucius and Mencius, with illustrations. *No date.*   26cm.

A 235—236. 曲 阜 縣 志
Ch'ü fu hsien chih

Topography of the District of Ch'ü-fu in the 兗州 Yen-chou Prefecture of Shantung, the site of the ancient State of 魯 Lu in which Confucius was brought up, by 潘相 P'an Hsiang. 1774. 25cm.

A 237. 闕 里 志
Ch'üeh li chih

An account of Ch'üeh-li, the village in modern Shantung, where Confucius was brought up, with illustrations, by 孔衍瑪 K'ung Yen-mei, a descendant of the Sage in the 65th generation. 1694. 24cm.

A 238—255. 十 三 經
Shih san ching

The Thirteen Classics, with the commentary of 王弼 Wang Pi,
3rd cent. A.D., edited by 金蟠 Chin P'an. 1640. 25cm.

A 256—262. 十 一 經 音 訓
Shih i ching yin hsün

The Eleven Classics, with interlinear commentaries, prefaces by
楊國楨 Yang Kuo-chêng, 林則徐 Lin Tsê-hsü (the famous
"Commissioner Lin") and others, edited by 劉師陸 Liu Shih-lu.
1831. 26cm.

A 263—269. 四 書 五 經 正 文
Ssŭ shu wu ching chêng wên

The authorised text of the Four Books and the Five Classics, with
the correct sounds given along the headline. *No date.* 25 × 13cm.

A 270—273. 毛 詩 疏
Mao shih su

The Canon of Poetry according to the text of 毛萇 Mao Ch'ang,
with notes by 鄭玄 Chêng Hsüan, A.D. 127—200, and commentary
by 孔穎達 K'ung Ying-ta, A.D. 577—648. 1630. 23cm.

A 274. 古 經 解 鈎 沉
Ku ching chieh kou ch'ên

The difficulties in the Confucian Canon explained, by 余蕭客
Yü Hsiao-k'o. *No date.* 25cm.

A 275—280. 經 義 述 聞
Ching i shu wên

The meaning of the Confucian Canon, by 王引之 Wang Yin-chih,
whose preface is dated 1797. 1817. 24cm.

G. W. 2

A 281—282.   陔　餘　叢　考

Kai yü ts'ung k'ao

Miscellaneous essays and notes on classical and historical subjects, by 趙翼 Chao I, A.D. 1727—1814.   1790.   24cm.

A 283—284.   百　子　金　丹

Po tzŭ chin tan

Selections from the writings of various philosophers, arranged under categories, by 郭偉 Kuo Wei (T. 士俊).   1743.   19.5cm.

A 285—287.   日　知　錄

Jih chih lu

Notes, classical and historical, by 顧絳 Ku Chiang, A.D. 1612—1681, edited by 潘耒 P'an Lei.   1695.   24 × 17cm.

A 288—295.   傳　家　寶

Ch'uan chia pao

A guide to conduct and morals, for both sexes, by 石成金 Shih Ch'êng-chin (T. 天基. H. 惺齋) whose preface is dated 1739. [Leaf 2 of the author's biography is missing.]   1843.   24cm.

A 296—297.   檀　几　叢　書　餘　集

Fan chi ts'ung shu yü chi

Essays and extracts from various scholars of the Ming and Ch'ing dynasties, compiled by 張潮 Chang Ch'ao and 王晫 Wang Cho, including some of their own, being a supplement to a previous work under the same title which was published in 1659. *No date.* 26cm.

A 298—299.   四　書　合　講

Ssŭ shu ho chiang

Harmony of the Four Books, with Chu Hsi's commentary, printed at Ningpo from metal types. See A 169.   1879.   20cm.

A 300—301. 東 山 經 觧
Tung shan ching chieh

The Five Classics, with commentary, by 周封魯 Chou Fêng-lu, known as Tung-shan. 1860. 12 × 10cm.

A 302—304. 四 書 味 根 錄
Ssǔ shu wei kên lu

The Four Books, with commentary. 1837. 17 × 12cm.

A 305. 四 書 典 腋
Ssǔ shu tien yeh

A collection of miscellaneous notes on the Four Books, by an author whose pen-name is 松軒主人 the Master of the Pine-tree Pavilion. [*T'ien* for *tien* on label.] 1873. 12.5 × 9cm.

A 306—307. 十 三 經 策 案
Shih san ching ts'ê an

Exegetical notes on the Thirteen Classics, by 王謨 Wang Mo (T. 仁圃). 1808. 18 × 12.5cm.

A 308—310. 七 經 精 義
Ch'i ching ching i

The essential meaning of the Seven Classics, by 黃淦緯 Huang Chin-wei, of which only six appear to have been treated, namely, the Canon of Changes, the Book of Rites, the Canons of Poetry and History, the Spring and Autumn, and the Decorum Ritual. [Vol. II should be vol. I.] 1835. 17cm.

A 311—324. 四 書 五 經 大 全
Ssǔ shu wu ching ta ch'üan

The full text, with commentaries, of the Four Books and Five Classics. 1711. 26cm.

A 325. 易 經 全 書
I ching ch'üan shu

Manuscript copy of the Canon of Changes. 1854. 24 × 19cm.

A 326. 四 書
Ssŭ shu

Manuscript copy of the Four Books. 22 × 18cm.

A 327. 小 學 集 註
Hsiao hsüeh chi chu

The Little Learning, a handbook for the young, by 朱熹 Chu Hsi, A.D. 1130—1200, with various commentaries, issued by Imperial command, with a preface from the Emperor Yung Chêng. 1734.

27.5 × 19cm.

A 328. 朱 文 端 公 文 集
Chu wên tuan kung wên chi

The collected essays of 朱軾 Chu Shih, A.D. 1666—1736. *No date.* 26cm.

A 329. 小 學 集 解
Hsiao hsüeh chi chieh

The Little Learning, with the explanations of various scholars, edited by 張行孝 Chang Hsing-hsiao, being a reprint of the edition of 1731. 1847. 26cm.

A 330. 大 象 圖
Ta hsiang t'u

Cosmogony, with illustrations, followed by 穀語 *Ku yü*, three essays on the value of life and some of its obligations. *No date.* 27cm.

A 331—340. 朱 子 全 書

Chu tzŭ ch'üan shu

The complete works of Chu Hsi, published by Imperial command, with a preface from the Emperor K'ang Hsi, and edited by 李廣地 Li Kuang-ti and other scholars. 1713. 26cm.

A 341. 朱 高 安 行 述

Chu kao an hsing shu

The career of 朱軾 Chu Shih, A.D. 1666—1736, the famous statesman and writer, by his sons. [*Kao-an* is the name of his birthplace.] *No date.* 26cm.

A 342—343. 性 理 綜 要

Hsing li tsung yao

Essays on philosophical, historical, and literary subjects, annotated or written by 詹淮 Chan Huai whose preface is dated 1415 and is preceded by a preface from the Emperor Yung Lo. Edited by 陳仁錫 Ch'ên Jen-hsi. 1632. 28cm.

A 344. 性 理 易 讀

Hsing li i tu.

Philosophical essays, with notes, by an author whose pen-name is 志遠主人 *Chih yüan chu jen.* 1852. 29 × 17cm.

A 345. 性 理 精 義

Hsing li ching i

Digest of the great philosophical compendium 性理大全書 *Hsing li ta ch'üan shu*, of the Ming dynasty, published by Imperial command, with preface from the Emperor K'ang Hsi, by 李光地 Li Kuang-ti and other scholars. 1717. 25cm.

A 346.

Another edition, white paper. 1850. 28cm.

A 347—349. 宋 學 士 全 集

Sung hsüeh shih ch'üan chi

Complete collection of the miscellaneous writings of 宋濂 Sung Lien, A.D. 1310—1381, joint author of the History of the Yüan Dynasty, edited by 彭始摶 P'êng Shih-t'uan. 1709. 25cm.

A 350—352. 甘 泉 文 集

Kan ch'üan wên chi

The collected writings of 湛若水 Chan Jo-shui, who was 91 in A.D. 1556, with original prefaces from 1580. 1681. 26.5cm.

A 353. 温 公 家 範

Wên kung chia fan

Rules for domestic life, by 司馬光 Ssǔ-ma Kuang the historian, A.D. 1019—1086, edited by 朱軾 Chu Shih. 1719. 27cm.

A 354. 聖 諭 廣 訓 衍

Shêng yü kuang hsün yen

The Sacred Edict of the Emperor K'ang Hsi, with preface by the Emperor Yung Chêng. Each maxim is followed by the Amplification of Yung Chêng, and by the Paraphrase of 王又樸 Wang Yu-p'u. [The label has only the last 3 characters.] 1724. 27cm.

A 354a.

Another copy. [The label has only the last 2 characters.] 26cm.

A 354b.

Another edition, same date, of the Edict and Amplification, but with a different Paraphrase printed separately at the end. 27cm.

A 355.

彥 氏 家 訓
Yen shih chia hsün

A work on family life and education, by 彥之推 Yen Chih-t'ui, A.D. 531—595, edited by 朱軾 Chu Shih. [Reprint of the edition of 1574.] 1719.   26.8cm.

A 356.

Another copy, white paper.   26.8cm.

A 358.

幼 學 故 事 尋 源 詳 解
Yu hsüeh ku shih hsün yüan hsiang chieh

A handbook of historical and mythological allusions, also known as the 成語考 Ch'êng yü k'ao (see B 36) by 邱濬 Ch'iu Chün, A.D. 1420—1495, edited by 楊應象 Yang Ying-hsiang. [The original work is attributed on title-page to 程允升 Ch'êng Yün-shêng.] *No date.*   24.5cm.

A 359.

Another edition, with supplement and illustrations. [The title-page is slightly varied, and the work is attributed to Ch'êng Yün-shêng, no mention being made of Ch'iu Chün.] 1796.   26cm.

A 360.

Another edition of A 359. 1796.   26cm.

A 361.

藝 林 彙 考
I lin hui k'ao

A work on Dress and Food, by 沈自南 Shên Tzǔ-nan (T. 留侯). *No date.*   26cm.

A 363—364.

大 學 衍 義
Ta hsüeh yen i

The Great Learning, illustrated from history by 眞德秀 Chên

Tê-hsiu whose preface is dated 1234, and edited by 陳仁錫 Ch'ên Jen-hsi in the 17th cent. according to the text of 楊廉 Yang Lien whose introduction is dated 1522. *No date.* 25cm.

A 365—372. 大 學 衍 義 補
Ta hsüeh yen i pu

The same work, published with additions by 邱濬 Ch'iu Chün in 1488, and edited by Ch'ên Jen-hsi. *No date.* 25cm.

A 373—375. 大 學 衍 義 輯 要
Ta hsüeh yen i ch'i yao

The same work, edited by 陳弘謀 Ch'ên Hung-mou. 1737. 25cm.

A 376—398. 十 子 彙 函
Shih tzŭ hui han

The writings of the Ten Taoist Philosophers, 老子 Lao Tzŭ, 列子 Lieh Tzŭ, 莊子 Chuang Tzŭ, 荀子 Hsün Tzŭ, 管子 Kuan Tzŭ, 韓非子 Han Fei Tzŭ, 楊子 Yang Tzŭ, 淮南子 Huai-nan Tzŭ, 文子 Wên Tzŭ, and 鶡冠子 Ho Kuan Tzŭ, with commentaries by various scholars. 1804. 28cm.

A 399. 道 德 經 釋 義
Tao tê ching shih i

The *Tao Tê Ching* explained, with a chapter on the various readings, attributed to the famous Taoist philosopher 呂嵒 Lü Yen of the 8th cent. A.D., edited by 牟目源 Mou Mu-yüan, and followed by the 常清經 *sûtra* of Perpetual Purity and the 金玉經 *sûtra* of Gold and Jade, the latter being attributed to Lü Yen. 1809.
28 × 16cm.

A 400. 墨 子 十 五 卷 目 一 卷
Mo tzŭ shih wu chüan mu i chüan

The Remains of the philosopher Mo Tzŭ, 5th cent. B.C., edited by 畢沅 Pi Yüan. 1784. 29cm.

A 401—405.　歷 代 神 仙 通 鑑

Li tai shên hsien t'ung chien

Lives of the Saints of Taoism, with numerous illustrations, by 徐道 Hsü Tao. 1700.　　　　　　　　　　　　　25.5cm.

A 406—407.　佛 本 行 集 經

Fo pên hsing chi ching

The Life of Buddha, translated from the original *sûtra* by 闍那崛多 *Gñ*ânagupta, A.D. 587, and published by Imperial command, with preface from the Emperor Yung Lo dated 1412. *No date.* 24.5cm.

A 408—409.　妙 法 蓮 華 經 台 宗 會 義

Miao fa lien hua ching t'ai tsung hui i

The *sûtra* of the Lotus of the Good Law, or *Saddharmapundarîka sûtra*, originally translated by Kumarajiva, with the explanations of 台宗 T'ai Tsung, edited by 藕益 Ou I. [Abbreviated title on label.] *No date.*　　　　　　　　　　　28.5cm.

A 410—411.　南 本 大 般 涅 盤 經

Nan pên ta pan nieh p'an ching

The Southern *Mahâparinirvâna sûtra*, translated about A.D. 420 by 曇無讖 Dharmaraksha, and revised some ten or twenty years later by the priests 慧嚴 Hui Yen and 慧觀 Hui Kuan, aided by the famous poet 謝靈運 Hsieh Ling-yün. *No date.* 28.5cm.

A 412.　　一 切 經 音 義

I ch'ieh ching yin i

The sounds and meanings of the terms used in the Buddhist Canon, by the priest 玄應 Hsüan Ying, about A.D. 649. [First character wanting on label.] *No date.*　　　　　28.5cm.

A 413—415. 開 元 釋 教 錄

K'ai yüan shih chiao lu

Bibliography of Buddhist works published between A.D. 67 and 730, numbering 1142 in all, by the priest 智升 Chih Shêng. *No date.* 28.5cm.

A 416. 教 乘 法 數 摘 要

Chiao shêng fa shu tsê yao

Selections from the Numerical Categories of the Buddhist Canon, originally compiled about A.D. 1430 by the priest 圓瀞 Yüan Ching. *No date.* 26cm.

A 417. 金 剛 經 初 學 指 南

Chin kang ching ch'u hsüeh chih nan

Guide to the study of the Diamond *Pragnaparamita sûtra*, with commentaries by 呂祖 Lü Tsu and 盧慧能 Lu Hui-nêng, edited by 張起莘 Chang Ch'i-hsin, and first published in 1736. 1829.

25 × 14.5cm.

A 418—419. 佛 法 金 湯 徵 文 錄

Fo fa chin t'ang chêng wên lu

A Buddhist Miscellany, by 姚希孟 Yao Hsi-mêng (T. 孟長). 1634. 26cm.

A 420—421. 彙 纂 功 過 格

Hui tsuan kung kuo ko

A Taoist work on moral and social obligations, reprinted and issued by 胡鳴玉 Hu Ming-yü. 1758. 27cm.

A 422. 正 教 眞 詮

Chêng chiao chên ch'üan

A work on the Mohammedan religion, by 王岱興 Wang Tai-yü, with prefatory notes of various dates, the earliest being 1642. 1795. 25cm.

A 423.

禪 門 日 誦
Ch'an mên jih sung

Extracts from the Buddhist *sûtras*, for daily reading by priests. [The full title is 諸 經 日 誦 朝 時 功 課 集 要.] 1841. 26cm.

A 424.

儒 門 法 語
Ju mên fa yü

A handbook of utterances by various eminent scholars on the morality of Confucianism, by 彭定求 P'êng Ting-ch'iu. 1834. 24.5cm.

A 425.

翻 譯 各 義 集 選
Fan i ming i chi hsüan

Technical phrases in Buddhist literature, arranged under 45 headings, and apparently taken from the work of the priest 法雲 Fa Yün, who wrote in A.D. 1151. *No date.* 26cm.

A 426.

老 子 道 德 經 攷 異
Lao tzŭ tao tê ching k'ao i

The text of the *Tao Tê Ching*, critically examined by 傅奕 Fu I, A.D. 554—639, edited by 畢沅 Pi Yüan. 1781. 29 × 18cm.

A 427.

太 上 混 元 道 德 眞 經
T'ai shang hun yüan tao tê chên ching

The text of the *Tao Tê Ching*, elucidated by the commentaries of the 八仙祖 Eight Immortal Patriarchs, and edited by 王符 Wang Fu. 1851. 28cm.

A 428—438.

皇 朝 經 世 文 編
Huang ch'ao ching shih wên pien

A collection of the essays of authors under the present dynasty, compiled by 賀長齡 Ho Ch'ang-ling. 1825. 26.5cm.

A 439—450.

Another edition, with supplement. 1851.　　26.5cm.

A 451—452.　東　華　錄
　　　　　　　Tung hua lu

A short history of China from the beginning of the present dynasty in the middle of the 17th cent. down to the year 1735, by 蔣良騏 Chiang Liang-ch'i. 1765.　　24cm.

A 453—454.　聖　武　記
　　　　　　　Shêng wu chi

A descriptive account of the military operations carried on under the present dynasty, by 魏源 Wei Yüan. 1822.　　24cm.

A 455—456.　恭　壽　堂　奏　議
　　　　　　　Kung shou t'ang tsou i

A collection of Memorials to the Throne, presented by 韓大中丞 Governor Han. *No date.*　　26 × 19cm.

A 457—460.　歷　代　名　臣　傳
　　　　　　　Li tai ming ch'ên chuan

Biographies of eminent officials, from about B.C. 200 to A.D. 1300, by 朱軾 Chu Shih and 蔡世遠 Ts'ai Shih-yüan. 1729.　25.5cm.

A 461—465.　禮　部　則　例
　　　　　　　Li pu tsê li

The Regulations of the Board of Rites, with diagrams, issued under Imperial command by a commission of scholars presided over by 文孚 Wên-fu. 1820.　　24 × 18cm.

A 466—469.　儀　禮　節　畧
　　　　　　　I li chieh lüeh

An abridgement of the Decorum Ritual, with explanatory notes, by 朱軾 Chu Shih. 1719.　　25cm.

A 470—474. 五 車 韻 瑞
Wu chü yün jui

A dictionary of phraseology, arranged according to the rhymes, the leading characters being also given in the Lesser Seal script, by 凌稚隆 Ling Chih-lung (T. 以棟). 1592. 26cm.

A 475—478. 經 文 易 書 etc.
Ching wên i shu etc.

The text of the Five Classics and Four Books, with commentaries, each vol. labelled according to its contents. [Mounted, 4 pages on each leaf.] 1836. 27 × 32cm.

B. *History, Biography, Statutes, etc.*

B 1—4. 博 古 圖
Po ku t'u

Illustrations of ancient sacrificial vessels, tripods, vases, mirrors, etc., being a reprint of the original work of 王黼 Wang Fu, 12th cent. A.D., edited by 黃曉峰 Huang Hsiao-fêng. 1752. 31cm.

B 5. 考 古 圖
K'ao ku t'u

A supplementary work to the above, by the editor Huang Hsiao-fêng. 1752. 31cm.

B 6. 萬 寶 全 書
Wan pao ch'üan shu

A handbook of general information, arranged according to categories, edited with supplement by 毛煥文 Mao Huan-wên. 1749. 23.5cm.

THE WADE LIBRARY

B 7. 鑑 撮

Chien ts'o

A summary of Chinese history from the fabulous times of the Three Emperors, about B.C. 3000, to the establishment of the present dynasty in the 17th cent., being a reprint of the original work by 曠敏本 K'uang Min-pên of 岣嶁 Kou-lou in Hunan. 1818.

27 × 20cm.

B 8—10. 歷 代 統 紀 表

Li tai t'ung chi piao

The chronology of the Twenty-four Dynastic Histories of China, arranged by 段長基 Tuan Ch'ang-chi. 1817. 30cm.

B 11. 歷 代 疆 域 表

Li tai chiang yü piao

The frontier tribes under the various dynasties, arranged in tabular form, with maps, by 段長墓 Tuan Ch'ang-chi. 1815. 30cm.

B 12. 歷 代 沿 革 表

Li tai yen ko piao

The subdivisions of the empire under the various dynasties, with the names in vogue at each period, arranged in tabular form, by 段長墓 Tuan Ch'ang-chi. 1815. 30cm.

B 13. 續纂外藩蒙古回部王公表

Hsü tsuan wai fan mêng ku hui pu wang kung piao

Supplement to the Register of nobles of the feudatory States and Mongol tribes, compiled by 慶桂 Ch'ing-kuei and other high officials. 1812. 34cm.

B 14.

Another edition, edited by 潘世恩 P'an Shih-ên and others. 1849. 38cm.

B 15. 宗 室 王 公 功 績 表

Tsung shih wang kung kung chi piao

Register of the meritorious services of nobles of the Imperial Clan in direct male line from the founder of the present dynasty, compiled under Imperial orders by 傅恒 Fu-hêng, 劉統勳 Liu T'ung-hsün, and others. 1764. 34cm.

B 16—23. 吏 部 則 例

Li pu tsê li

Regulations of the Board of Civil Office, compiled under Imperial orders by 文孚 Wên-fu, 松筠 Sung-yün, and others. 1824. 25cm.

B 24. 處 分 則 例 圖 要

Ch'u fên tsê li t'u yao

The system of official punishments, arranged in tabular form, by 蔡逢年 Ts'ai Fêng-nien. 1859. 26cm.

B 25—28. 吏 部 處 分 則 例

Li pu ch'u fên tsê li

Regulations for the punishment of officials under the Board of Civil Office. 1820. 26cm.

B 29—34. 牧 令 書

Mu ling shu

Essays on a variety of subjects, political, agricultural, moral, social, etc., by writers of the present dynasty, compiled by 徐棟 Hsü Tung (T. 致初). 1838. 23.5cm.

B 35. 保 甲 書

Pao chia shu

A work on the tithing system, by 徐棟 Hsü Tung (T. 致初). 1848. 23.5cm.

B 36.

成 語 考
Ch'êng yü k'ao

A well-printed edition of the original work on which A 358 is based. *No date.* 22cm.

B 37.

Another edition, with supplement. 1845. 24cm.

B 38.

庸 吏 庸 言
Yung li yung yen

The official Proclamations of 劉衡 Liu Hêng (T. 簾舫), beginning with his famous oath against bribery when appointed magistrate of the 巴 Pa District in Ssüch'uan. 1845. 25.5cm.

B 39—40.

福 惠 全 書
Fu hui ch'üan shu

A guide to the duties and responsibilities of official life, by 黃六鴻 Huang Liu-hung (T. 思湖). 1694. 23cm.

B 41—50.

戶 部 則 例
Hu pu tsê li

The Regulations of the Board of Revenue, edited by 潘世恩 P'an Shih-ên and others. 1838. 26.5cm.

B 51—52.

長 蘆 鹽 法 志
Ch'ang lu yen fa chih

History of the salt monopoly at Ch'ang-lu in Chihli, by 顏檢 Yen Chien and other high officials. 1805. 28cm.

B 53—54.

江 蘇 海 運 全 案
Chiang su hai yün ch'üan an

Record of official documents referring to the sea-transport of tribute rice to Kiangsu, edited by 陶澍 T'ao Chu. 1826. 25.5cm.

B 55—59. 戶 部 漕 運 全 書
Hu pu ts'ao yün ch'üan shu

The grain-transport system, as organised and carried on under the Board of Revenue, published by Imperial command under the superintendence of 潘世恩 P'an Shih-ên and others. 1844. 29cm.

B 60—63. 漕 運 則 例 纂
Ts'ao yün tsê li tsuan

Regulations for the system of grain-transport to the capital, by 楊錫紱 Yang Hsi-fu. 1769. 26.5cm.

B 64—72. 禮 部 則 例
Li pu tsê li

The Regulations of the Board of Rites, issued under Imperial order by 特登額 T'ê-têng-ê (President) and others. 1844. 27.5cm.

B 73—76. 大 清 通 禮
Ta ch'ing t'ung li

Ceremonial observances under the present dynasty, being a reprint of the work by 來保 Lai Pao, 陳世倌 Ch'ên Shih-kuan, and others. 1841. 26cm.

B 77—79. 學 政 全 書
Hsüeh chêng ch'üan shu

Complete record of Imperial Edicts bearing upon the duties and functions of Education Officials under the present dynasty, compiled by 恭阿拉 Kung-o-la and others, and based upon the earlier work of 魏晉錫 Wei Chin-hsi. 1812. 24.5cm.

B 80—83. 科 場 條 例
K'o ch'ang t'iao li

Regulations for conducting the great competitive examinations, issued

G. W.

by an Imperial Commission which included the well-known names of 曾國藩 Tsêng Kuo-fan and 瑞麟 Jui-lin. 1852. 27.5 × 19cm.

B 84—91. 皇 朝 禮 器 圖 式
Huang ch'ao li ch'i t'u shih

The sacrificial vessels, official dresses, musical instruments, and civil and military paraphernalia, of the present dynasty, with illustrations, issued under an Imperial Commission, with preface by the Emperor Ch'ien Lung, dated 1759. 1766. 28.5cm.

B 92—95. 兵 部 則 例
Ping pu tsê li

Regulations of the Board of War, issued under an Imperial Commission headed by the President 伯麟 Po Lin. 1823. 24.5 × 18cm.

B 96—100. 中 樞 政 考 八 旗
Chung shu chêng k'ao pa ch'i

The organisation and administration of the Manchu forces under the Eight Banners, issued under an Imperial Commission. 1825. 24.5 × 18cm.

B 101—106. 中 樞 政 考 綠 營
Chung shu chêng k'ao lü ying

A similar work on the Chinese army. 1825. 24.5 × 28cm.

B 107—108. 英 法 俄 美 條 欵
Ying fa o mei t'iao k'uan

Treaties between China and England, France, Russia, and the United States. 1860. 27cm.

B 109—111. 五 軍 道 理 表
Wu chün tao li piao

List of places, with their distances from various provincial centres, to which criminals may be banished for military service, issued under an Imperial Commission. 1809. 24 × 18cm.

B 112. 三 流 道 理 表
San liu tao li piao

List of places, with their distances from various provincial centres, to which criminals may be banished for life. 1811. 24cm.

B 113. 名 法 指 掌
Ming fa chih chang

An easy guide to the administration of justice, by 沈辛田 Shên Hsin-t'ien. 1743. 22.5cm.

B 114—133. 刑 案 匯 覽
Hsing an hui lan

A collection of leading criminal cases, compiled by 鮑書芸 Pao Shu-yün, followed by a supplement in 4 vols. 1834. 25cm.

B 134—147. 大 清 律 例 按 語
Ta ch'ing lü li an yü

The Penal Code, consisting of the fundamental criminal laws of the present dynasty together with such by-laws, subject to alteration, as have been added from time to time, edited with notes by 黄恩彤 Huang En-t'ung. 1847. 23.5cm.

B 148—155. 粤 東 成 案 初 編
Yüeh tung ch'êng an ch'u pien

Record of criminal cases, to be used as precedents, tried in the province of Kuangtung, edited by 朱樗 Chu Yün (T. 雲木).
1828. 23cm.

B 156. 粤 東 省 例 新 纂
Yüeh tung shêng li hsin tsuan

The by-laws of the province of Kuangtung, edited by 黄恩彤 Huang En-t'ung, with a preface by the famous Viceroy 耆英 Ki-ying. 1846. 26.5cm.

B 157—158. 工 部 則 例
Kung pu tsê li

The Regulations of the Board of Works, edited by 松筠 Sung-yün and other high officials. 1798. 24.5cm.

B 159. 居 官 日 省 錄
Chü kuan jih hsing lu

A work on the duties and obligations of officials, by a Red Girdle, or member of a collateral branch of the Imperial family, named 烏爾通 Wu-êrh-t'ung (T. 潤泉). 1873. 25cm.

B 160. 資 治 新 書 全 集
Tzŭ chih hsin shu ch'üan chi

A work on the various departments of the administration and the details connected with each, for the use of officials. 1663. 25cm.

B 161—164. 農 政 全 書
Nung chêng ch'üan shu

An agricultural encyclopædia, by the famous statesman and Jesuit convert, 徐光啓 Hsü Kuang-ch'i, A.D. 1562—1634, first published by Imperial command in 1640. 1843. 28cm.

B 165—166. 吾 學 錄 初 編
Wu hsüeh lu ch'u pien

A guide to the duties of officials on a variety of subjects connected with the administration, by 吳榮光 Wu Jung-kuang, Viceroy of the Two Hu. 1832. 26cm.

B 167. 金 湯 借 箸 十 二 籌
Chin t'ang chieh chu shih êrh ch'ou

A work on the organisation of military forces, arranged under twelve sections, such as *Readiness, Drill, Commissariat, Arms*, etc., by 李盤 Li P'an (T. 小有) of the Ming dynasty. *No date.* 28.5cm.

B 168—170. 武 備 制 勝
Wu pei chih shêng

A work on the art of war by land and sea, with diagrams, by 茅元儀 Mao Yüan-i of the 17th cent. [In manuscript.] 1843. 27cm.

B 171—172. 東 漢 會 要
Tung han hui yao

A history of the institutions of the Eastern Han dynasty, A.D. 25—220, by 徐天麟 Hsü T'ien-lin, whose preface is dated 1226. 1822. 24cm.

B 173—174. 西 漢 會 要
Hsi han hui yao

A history of the institutions of the Western Han dynasty, B.C. 206—A.D. 25, by 徐天麟 Hsü T'ien-lin of the 13th cent. *No date.* 28cm.

B 175—180. 唐 會 要
T'ang hui yao

A history of the institutions of the T'ang dynasty, A.D. 618—906, by 王溥 Wang P'u, whose preface is dated 961. 1774. 28cm.

B 181—182. 五 代 會 要
Wu tai hui yao

A history of the institutions of the Five Dynasties, A.D. 907—960, by 王溥 Wang P'u. [In manuscript; no preface.] *No date.* 27.5cm.

THE WADE LIBRARY

B 183—192. 元 朝 典 章 綱 目
Yüan ch'ao tien chang kang mu

The Institutes of the Yüan or Mongol dynasty, founded A.D. 1206. [In manuscript; preface wanting.] *No date.* 28cm.

B 193—226. 大 明 會 典
Ta ming hui tien

The Institutes of the Ming dynasty, founded A.D. 1368, with Imperial prefaces dated 1503, 1509, and 1576, compiled by a Commission under the presidency of 申 時 行 Shên Shih-hsing. 1576. 25.5cm.

B 227—230.

Another edition, with the same prefaces, issued under the superintendence of 張 京 元 Chang Ching-yüan. 1621. 27cm.

B 231—235. 天 下 一 統 志
T'ien hsia i t'ung chih

A geography of the empire, first published in 1461, with preface of that date from the Emperor 英 宗 Ying Tsung of the Ming dynasty. 1849. 28cm.

B 236—243. 廣 博 物 志
Kuang po wu chih

A compendium of information on a variety of subjects, arranged under categories, with preface dated 1608, by 董 斯 張 Tung Ssŭ-chang (T. 退 周), being an extension of the work attributed to 張 華 Chang Hua of the 3rd cent. A.D. 1761. 25cm.

B 244. 考 古 類 編
K'ao ku lei pien

A dictionary of literary and political institutions, arranged under categories, by 柴 紹 炳 Ch'ai Shao-ping (T. 虎 臣) and 姚 廷 謙 Yao T'ing-hsien (T. 平 山). 1726. 26cm.

B 245—254. **歷 代 紀 事 年 表**
Li tai chi shih nien piao

A chronology of the Chinese dynasties from the reign of the mythical Emperor Yao, B.C. 2356, down to the close of the Yüan dynasty in the 14th cent. A.D. 1715. 26cm.

B 255. **紀 元 編**
Chi yüan pien

A handbook of chronology, from about B.C. 200 to the 17th cent. A.D., with list of year-titles assumed by usurpers, and a chapter on the chronologies of Cochin China, Japan, and Central Asian kingdoms, by **六 承 如** Liu Ch'êng-ju. [With it is bound up the **讀 史 論 略** *Tu shih lun lüeh*, being notes on the study of history, by **杜 紫 綸** Tu Tzŭ-lun, 1875.] 1831. 26cm.

B 256.

Manuscript Index to the Statutes of the Ming and Ch'ing dynasties. 32cm.

B 257—260. **大 清 會 典**
Ta ch'ing hui tien

The Institutes of the Ch'ing or Manchu-Tartar dynasty, issued by Imperial command. [Preface etc. wanting; will be found in B 2013—2038.] *No date.* 33cm.

B 261—341. **大 清 會 典 事 例**
Ta ch'ing hui tien shih li

The Statutes of the Ch'ing or Manchu-Tartar dynasty, supplemented by the various edicts which have been published in connection with the general working of the system, issued under an Imperial Commission, with preface from the Emperor Chia Ch'ing. 1818. 32cm.

B 342. **大 清 會 典 白 文**
Ta ch'ing hui tien po wên

Manuscript copy of the text of the Institutes of the present dynasty. See B 257. 30 cm.

B 343. 爵 秩 全 覽
Chüeh chih ch'üan lan

Tables of rank and precedence of the Imperial family and officials generally. 1860. 29cm.

B 344—347. 大 清 會 典
Ta ch'ing hui tien

The Statutes etc.; see B 257. [Five pages of preface by the Emperor Ch'ien Lung wanting.] 1764. 28cm.

B 348—369. 大 清 會 典 則 例
Ta ch'ing hui tien tsê li

The Statutes of the Ch'ing or Manchu-Tartar dynasty, with additional regulations, compiled by Imperial command. 1748. 28cm.

B 370. 大 清 律
Ta ch'ing lü

The fundamental and unalterable laws of the present dynasty, punctuated and annotated in red ink, with preface from the Emperor Shun Chih, dated 1646. 1707. 30cm.

B 371—376. 大 清 律 例
Ta ch'ing lü li

The Penal Code, etc., see B 134, being a new and revised edition with all amendments and additions. 1845. 27cm.

B 377. 律 例 便 覽
Lü li pien lan

A handy guide to the Penal Code, see B 134, by 蔡逢年 Ts'ai Fêng-nien. 1859. 26cm.

B 378. 洗 冤 錄 集 證
Hsi yüan lu chi chêng

Reprint of "Instructions to Coroners," the famous work on medical jurisprudence, written by 宋慈 Sung Tz'ŭ in the period A.D. 1241—1253, with explanations and verifications, punctuation etc. in red and blue ink. 1843. 28cm.

B 379—382. 大 清 律 例

Ta ch'ing lü li

The Penal Code etc., see B 134. 1802. 29cm.

B 383—385. 刑 部 比 照

Hsing pu pi chao

Precedents from the archives of the Board of Punishments, with illustrative cases, by 許槤 Hsü Lien. 1834. 16.5 × 12.5cm.

B 386—390. 說 帖 類 編

Shuo t'ieh lei pien

A magistrate's handbook, with recorded decisions and illustrative cases, by 戴敦元 Tai Tun-yüan (T. 金溪). 1835. 18.5cm.

B 391—392. 吏 治 懸 鏡

Li chih hsüan ching

A guide-book for those entering upon official duties, arranged under eight sections, by 徐文弼 Hsü Wên-pi, edited by 石岩傅 Shih Yen-fu and others. *No date.* 17.5 × 12cm.

B 393—397. 鹿 州 全 集

Lu chou ch'üan chi

The complete works of 藍鼎元 Lan Ting-yüan, with portrait and preface to edition of 1721. 1730. 17 × 12cm.

B 398—399. 資 治 新 書

Tzŭ chih hsin shu

A guide to correct administration by officials, by 李漁 Li Yü (T. 笠翁), first published in 1663. *No date.* 17.5cm.

B 400—401.   搢 紳 全 書

Chin shên ch'üan shu

List of (vol. I) civil and (vol. II) military officials in active service
in the empire of China, arranged under the posts occupied. [Popularly
known as the "Red Book," from the colour of the original wrapper.]
1891.   19.5cm.

B 402.   依 樣 葫 蘆

I yang hu lu

A guide to the composition of official letters, petitions, etc., by a
writer whose pen-name was 畏壘山人 the Hermit of Wei-lei.
1813.   17cm.

B 403.   尺 牘 類 選

Ch'ih tu lei hsüan

Specimens of elegantly written letters, to serve as models, selected
by 陳世熙 Ch'ên Shih-hsi. 1812.   20cm.

B 404—405.   福 惠 全 書

Fu hui ch'üan shu

A general guide to official duties and ceremonial etiquette, by
黃六鴻 Huang Liu-hung. [One leaf of *Index* misplaced in binding.]
1694.   22cm.

B 406—406a.   鑑 撮

Chien ts'o

An epitome of history from the earliest ages down to the accession
of the Emperor Tao Kuang in 1821, by 曠敏木 K'uang Min-mu.
1839.   22.5cm.

B 407—415.   歷 代 職 官 表

Li tai chih kuan piao

A chronological record of the various official posts for the administration of the empire, with their names and some account of the duties attached to them under previous dynasties, edited by 阿桂 O-kuei and other high officials, with a poetical preface by the Emperor Ch'ien Lung. 1780.   26cm.

B 416.   史　詮
Shih ch'üan

Explanations of the 史記 *Shih Chi* or Historical Record of 司馬選 Ssŭ-ma Ch'ien, by 程一枝 Ch'êng I-chih (T. 巢爻). [吏 for 史 on label.] 1579.   27.5cm.

B 417—418.   西　夏　書　事
Hsi hsia shu shih

A history of the Western Hsia State from A.D. 881 to 1232, by 吳廣成 Wu Kuang-ch'êng (T. 西齋). 1825.   25.5cm.

B 419.   關　中　金　石　記
Kuan chung chin shih chi

A collection of inscriptions on tiles, stone tablets, and bronzes, dating from about B.C. 220, found in the province of 陝西 Shensi, by 畢沅 Pi Yüan. 1781.   27.5cm.

B 420.   中　州　金　石　記
Chung chou chin shih chi

A collection of inscriptions (see B 419) found in Honan, by Pi Yüan. 1786.   29cm.

B 421.   晉　書　地　理　志
Chin shu ti li chih

Notes on the geography of the History of the Chin dynasty, by 畢沅 Pi Yüan. 1784.   29cm.

B 422. 十 六 國 疆 域 志
Shih liu kuo chiang yü chih

The frontiers of the Sixteen States, by 洪亮吉 Hung Liang-chi.
1798.   25cm.

B 423. 東 晉 疆 域 志
Tung chin chiang yü chih

The frontier under the Eastern Chin dynasty, A.D. 317—420, by
洪亮吉 Hung Liang-chi. 1796.   25cm.

B 424. 三 國 疆 域 志
San kuo chiang yü chih

The frontier under the Three Kingdoms, A.D. 220—265, by 洪
亮吉 Hung Liang-chi. 1781.   25cm.

B 425. 三 元 甲 子 萬 年 書
San yüan chia tzŭ wan nien shu

An official calendar from A.D. 1626 to 1855. *No date.*   25cm.

B 426. 萬 年 書
Wan nien shu

An astrological almanac, printed in black and red. *No date.*   28cm.

B 427. 文 獻 通 考 紀 要
Wên hsien t'ung k'ao chi yao

Extracts from the *Wên hsien t'ung k'ao* by 馬端臨 Ma Tuan-
lin, see B 489. [Title-page and preface wanting.] *No date.*   27cm.

B 428. 文 獻 通 考 節 貫
Wên hsien t'ung k'ao chieh kuei

Articles from the *Wên hsien t'ung k'ao* of 馬端臨 Ma Tuan-lin,
see B 489, by 周宗濂 Chou Tsung-lien. 1750.   25cm.

B 429—475. 通 志
T'ung chih

A history of China from about B.C. 2800 to A.D. 600, by 鄭樵 Chêng Ch'iao, A.D. 1108—1116, issued by Imperial command, with a preface from the Emperor Ch'ien Lung. 1749. 29cm.

B 476—488. 通 典
T'ung tien

A cyclopædia of information on the various departments of official administration, (namely, *Political Economy, Literary Degrees, Government Offices, Rites, Music, Military and Naval, Geography* and *National Defences*), from the earliest ages down to the 8th cent. A.D., by 杜佑 Tu Yu, who died A.D. 812, issued by Imperial command, with a preface from the Emperor Ch'ien Lung. 1747. 29cm.

B 489—526. 文 獻 通 考
Wên hsien t'ung k'ao

A cyclopædia of the same class as the *T'ung tien* (see B 476), upon which it was based, but much enlarged and supplemented by five additional sections, namely, *Bibliography, Imperial Lineage, Appointments, Uranography,* and *Natural Phenomena*, by 馬端臨 Ma Tuan-lin of the 13th cent. A.D., issued by Imperial command, with a preface from the Emperor Ch'ien Lung. 1748. 29cm.

B 527—546. 續 通 典
Hsü t'ung tien

A supplement to B 476—488, bringing the work down to modern times, issued under an Imperial Commission. 1783. 28cm.

B 547—628. 續 通 志
Hsü t'ung chih

A supplement to B 429—475, bringing the work down to the end of the Ming dynasty, A.D. 1644, issued under an Imperial Commission. 1785. 28cm.

B 629—672.　　續 文 獻 通 考
Hsü wên hsien t'ung k'ao

A supplement to B 489—526, bringing the work down to the end
of the Ming dynasty, A.D. 1644, issued under an Imperial Commission.
[Vol. IX is wrongly numbered 218/219, instead of 28/29.]　1784.　28cm.

B 673—686.　　皇 朝 通 典
Huang ch'ao t'ung tien

A further supplement to B 527—546, giving details for the present
dynasty, compiled by order of the Emperor Ch'ien Lung and published
about 1790.　*No date.*　　　　　　　　　　　　　　　28cm.

B 687—693.　　皇 朝 通 志
Huang ch'ao t'ung chih

A cyclopædia of political, archæological, and scientific information
in reference to the present dynasty, issued by Imperial command
about 1790.　*No date.*　　　　　　　　　　　　　　28cm.

B 694—730.　　皇 朝 文 獻 通 考
Huang ch'ao wên hsien t'ung k'ao

A cyclopædia of political and governmental information in reference
to the present dynasty, issued by Imperial command about 1790.
No date.　　　　　　　　　　　　　　　　　　　　28cm.

B 731.　　通 鑑 輯 覽
T'ung chien chi lan

A synopsis of the *History* by 司 馬 光 Ssŭ-ma Kuang (see B 961),
edited under Imperial command by 劉 統 勳 Liu T'ung-hsün and
others, with a preface from the Emperor Ch'ien Lung.　1767.　30cm.

B 731a—737a.　　易 知 錄
I chih lu

An epitome of Chu Hsi's revision of the Mirror of History (see

B 1029—1053), brought down to the close of the Yüan dynasty in 1368, by 吳乘權 Wu Shêng-ch'üan (T. 楚材). [A supplement containing the Ming dynasty will be found in B 1228—1229.] 1711.
17.5cm.

B 739ª. 明 鑑 易 知 錄
Ming chien i chih lu

Supplement to the above, containing the Ming dynasty, by the same author. [Vol. I missing.] *No date.* 17cm.

B 740ª—741ª. 都 察 院 奏 摺
Tu ch'a yüan tsou chê

Memorials to the Throne from the Court of Censors. [In manuscript.] 1842. 17cm.

B 742ª—743ª. 上 諭
Shang yü

A collection of Imperial Edicts. 1842. 17cm.

B 744ª—749ª. 春 明 夢 餘 錄
Ch'un ming mêng yü lu

A description of the sights and monuments of Peking, by 孫承澤 Sun Ch'êng-tsê. *No date.* 17cm.

B 750ª—751ª. 教 匪 案
Chiao fei an

Memorials and Rescripts on the suppression of a dangerous secret society and armed rising in 1813. [In manuscript.] *No date.* 17cm.

B 752ª—756ª. 剿平三省邪匪方畧
Ch'ao p'ing san shêng hsieh fei fang lüeh

An account of the suppression of rebels in three provinces during the year 1796, by 慶桂 Ch'ing-kuei and others. [In manuscript.] *No date.* 18cm.

B 757a. 平 定 粤 匪 紀 略
P'ing ting yüeh fei chi lüeh

An account of the suppression of the rebels in Kuangtung and Kuangsi between 1850 and 1864. 1870. 16cm.

B 758a.

Another copy. [The supplement has been wrongly bound up between chapters 2 and 3.]

B 759a—770a. 滿 洲 名 臣 傳
Man chou ming ch'ên chuan

Biographies of eminent Manchu officials, issued by Imperial command. *No date.* 15.5cm.

B 771a. 逆 臣 傳
Ni ch'ên chuan

Biographies of rebellious officials, the first of whom is 吳三桂 Wu San-kuei who died A.D. 1678. *No date.* 14.5cm.

B 772a—779a. 漢 名 臣 傳
Han ming ch'ên chuan

Biographies of eminent Chinese officials under the present dynasty. *No date.* 16cm.

B 780a. 宗 室 王 公 傳
Tsung shih wang kung chuan

Biographies of Imperial clansmen under the present dynasty. *No date.* 15cm.

B 732. 歷 代 史 總 論
Li tai shih tsung lun

A summary of Chinese history from the earliest ages down to about 1845, issued by command of the Emperor of Japan, with preface and poem from his own hand, the latter printed in red. 1847. 27.5cm.

B 733. 史 記 索 隱
Shih chi so yin

An exegetical work on the Historical Record of 司馬遷 Ssǔ-ma Ch'ien (see B 734 and 1068), by 司馬貞 Ssǔ-ma Chêng of the 8th cent. A.D. *No date.* 29.5cm.

B 734—950. 二 十 四 史
Erh shih i shih

The Twenty-four Dynastic Histories of China, covering a period from the earliest ages down to A.D. 1643, issued under an Imperial Commission headed by 鄂爾泰 O-êrh-t'ai and 張廷玉 Chang T'ing-yü, with a preface from the Emperor Ch'ien Lung. 1747. 28cm.

B 951. 西 藏 碑 文
Hsi tsang pei wên

Inscriptions in Tibet, followed by Memorials to the Throne on the administration of government in Tibet. 1851. 28.5cm.

B 952. 孟 忠 毅 公 奏 疏
Mêng chung i kung tsou su

The Memorials to the Throne of 孟喬芳 Mêng Ch'iao-fang, A.D. 1595—1654. *No date.* 29.5cm.

B 953—954. 普 法 戰 記
P'u fa chan chi

A history of the Franco-Prussian war of 1870, dictated by 張宗良 Chang Tsung-liang and written in Chinese by 王韜 Wang T'ao. 1873. 28cm.

B 955. 總 理 衙 門 咨 行 洋 務
Tsung li ya mên tzǔ hsing yang wu

Communications from the Tsung-li Yamên on foreign affairs between 1860 and 1865. *No date.* 24cm.

G. W. 4

B 956.　　　同　治　奏　議
　　　　　　　　　　T'ung chih tsou i

Selected memorials to the Throne during the reign of T'ung Chih,
1860—1874.　1875.　　　　　　　　　　　　　　　　　26cm.

B 957—960.　　　列　女　傳
　　　　　　　　　　Lieh nü chuan

Biographies of eminent women, based upon the original work of
皇甫謐 Huang-fu Mi who lived A.D. 215—282, by 汪庚 Wang
Kêng, with full-page illustrations by 仇英寶 Ch'iu Ying-shih.
1779.　　　　　　　　　　　　　　　　　　　　　　　29.5cm.

B 961—993.　　　資　治　通　鑑
　　　　　　　　　　Tzŭ chih t'ung chien

A history of China, popularly known as "The Mirror of History,"
from the 4th cent. B.C. to the 10th cent. A.D., by 司馬光 Ssŭ-
ma Kuang whose memorial to the Throne on completion of his work
is dated 1084, edited with commentary and corrections of the text
(see last vol.) by 胡三省 Hu San-hsing in 1285, and republished,
with preface from 王磐 Wang P'an, by 胡克家 Hu K'o-chia.
1816.　　　　　　　　　　　　　　　　　　　　　　27.5cm.

B 994—1009.　　　通　鑑　輯　覽
　　　　　　　　　　T'ung chien chi lan

A history of China from B.C. 2953 to the beginning of the 17th
cent. A.D., issued under an Imperial Commission headed by 傅恒
Fu-hêng, with a preface from the Emperor Ch'ien Lung. 1767. 27cm.

B 1010.　　　遺　史　世　記
　　　　　　　　　　I shih shih chi

Historical notes extending from the 8th cent. B.C. to the establishment of the Ming dynasty in 1368; anonymous. [Sections I—VIII

only; the biographies as given in Index are wanting. 吏 for 史 on label.] *No date*.　27cm.

B 1011.　　　史　懷
Shih huai

Historical notes covering a period from the 7th cent. B.C. to the middle of the 3rd cent. A.D., by 鍾惺 Chung Hsing of the Ming dynasty. [吏 for 史 on label.] *No date*.　26.5cm.

B 1012.　　歷　代　建　言
Li tai chien yen

Historical notes covering a period from B.C. 2255 to about A.D. 1640; anonymous. [Manuscript.] *No date*.　26.5cm.

B 1013—1023.　續　資　治　通　鑑
Hsü tzü chih t'ung chien

A supplement to the History of Ssŭ-ma Kuang (see B 961), from A.D. 960 to 1368, by 畢沅 Pi Yüan. 1801.　29cm.

B 1024.　　補　續　羣　輔　錄
Pu hsü ch'ün fu lu

Identifications of famous men who have been classed in numerical groups, by 吳運焜 Wu Yün-hun, based upon the work of 陶元亮 T'ao Yüan-liang of the 4th cent. A.D. [The first two characters on label are transposed.] 1788.　24cm.

B 1025—1028.　通　鑑　綱　目　三　編
T'ung chien kang mu san pien

A history of the Ming dynasty, A.D. 1368—1644, prepared by order of the Emperor Ch'ien Lung to take the place of the 明紀綱目 *Ming chi kang mu*, by 張廷玉 Chang T'ing-yü. 1775.　27.5cm.

B 1029—1053.　　資 治 通 鑑 綱 目

Tzŭ chih t'ung chien kang mu

A revision of the Mirror of History (see B 961—993) by 朱熙 Chu Hsi, edited by 陳仁錫 Ch'ên Jen-hsi (T. 明卿), with a preface from the Emperor Hsien Tsung dated 1474. [Subdivided into 前編, 正編, and 續編.] 1767.　　26.5cm.

B 1054—1065.　　錢陝園考訂綱目

Ch'ien chih yüan k'ao ting kang mu

The History by 朱熙 Chu Hsi (see B 1029), revised and edited by 錢選 Ch'ien Hsüan (T 枚一) whose preface is dated 1698, and posthumously printed. *No date.*　　28.5cm.

B 1066—1067.　　史 記 節 畧

Shih chi chieh lüeh

An abstract of the Historical Record of 司馬遷 Ssŭ-ma Ch'ien (see B 734 and 1068), by 穆文 Mu Wên (T. 熙敬). [吏 for 史 on label.] 1579.　　28cm.

B 1068—1071.　　孫 月 峰 批 史 記

Sun yüeh fêng p'i shih chi

The Historical Record of 司馬遷 Ssŭ-ma Ch'ien (see B 734), annotated by Sun Yüeh-fêng, and edited by 馮元仲 Fêng Yüan-chung. [吏 for 史 on label.] 1636.　　27cm.

B 1072—1076.　　史 記 評 林

Shih chi p'ing lin

Commentaries on the Historical Record of 司馬遷 Ssŭ-ma Ch'ien, including that of 司馬貞 Ssŭ-ma Chêng, one of whose prefaces is dated A.D. 736, edited by 陳明卿 Ch'ên Ming-ch'ing. [吏 for 史 on label.] *No date.*　　25.5cm.

B 1077—1080.   三　國　志
San kuo chih

The History of the Three Kingdoms, A.D. 220—280, by 陳壽 Ch'ên Shou who died in 297, with commentary by 裴松之 P'ei Sung-chih and preface dated A.D. 429. 1887.　　　　27.5cm.

B 1081—1082.   逸　周　書　補　注
I chou shu pu chu

The institutions of the Chou dynasty, 12th to 3rd cent. B.C., with commentary by 孔晁 K'ung Ch'ao of the 晉 Chin dynasty, 4th cent. A.D. and additional commentary by 陳逢衡 Ch'ên Fêng-hêng. 1825.　　　　24cm.

B 1083.

An earlier edition of the above, without the additional commentary. 1786.　　　　24.5cm.

B 1084—1089.   五　代　史　記　注
Wu tai shih chi chu

The New History of the Five Dynasties, A.D. 907—959, by 歐陽修 Ou-yang Hsiu, who died in 1072, with commentary by 彭元瑞 P'êng Yüan-jui. 1815.　　　　29cm.

B 1090—1097.   三　朝　北　盟　會　編
San ch'ao pei mêng hui pien

History of the period between A.D. 1117 and 1163, with special reference to the invasion of the 金 Chin Tartars, by 徐夢莘 Hsü Mêng-hsin. [Manuscript.] *No date.*　　　　25cm.

B 1098—1101.   明　鑑
Ming chien

A history of the Ming dynasty, A.D. 1368—1644, compiled by an Imperial Commission. 1818.　　　　27.5cm.

B 1102—1105. 明 季 北 略
Ming chi pei lüeh

An account of the fall of the Ming dynasty, by 計六奇 Chi Liu-ch'i, whose preface is dated 1671. *No date.* 27cm.

B 1106—1109. 明 季 稗 史 彙 編
Ming chi pai shih hui pien

An account of the last struggles of the representatives of the Ming dynasty, by 顧絳 Ku Chiang, who died 1681, and others. *No date.* 27cm.

B 1110. 大 明 文 武 官 兵 俸 餉
Ta ming wên wu kuan ping fêng hsiang

The salaries of civil and military officials under the Ming dynasty, A.D. 1368—1644. [Manuscript.] *No date.* 29.5cm.

B 1111—1126. 明 史 藁
Ming shih kao

A history of the Ming dynasty, with Edict of the Emperor K'ang Hsi ordering its preparation, printed in red ink and dated 1697, by 王鴻緒 Wang Hung-hsü. 1714. 28cm.

B 1127—1130. 八 旗 滿 洲 氏 族 通 譜
Pa ch'i man chou shih tsu t'ung p'u

An account of the Manchu-Tartar tribes, originated by the Emperor Yung Chêng, and completed under the Emperor Ch'ien Lung who furnished a preface. 1734. 27.5cm.

B 1131. 咸 豐 十 年 上 諭
Hsien fêng shih nien shang yü

Imperial Edicts on foreign affairs during the year 1860. [Manuscript; marked "Shih Lu" on label.] 25.5cm.

B 1132—1133. 東 華 錄

Tung hua lu

A history of the present dynasty down to the year 1735, by 蔣 良騏 Chiang Liang-ch'i (T. 千之). 1765. 25cm.

B 1134—1135. 聖 武 記

Shêng wu chi

An account of the military operations of the present dynasty, by 魏源 Wei Yüan who died in 1856. 1844. 25.5cm.

B 1136. 鎮 撫 事 宜

Chên fu shih i

A collection of pamphlets on keeping frontier nations, such as Russia and Tibet, in peaceful subordination, by 松筠 Sung-yün who died in 1835. 1823. 27cm.

B 1137—1141. 平 定 教 匪 紀 畧

P'ing ting chiao fei chi lüeh

An account of the 天理會 T'ien li hui rebellion in 1813 and its final suppression in 1816, published by order of the Emperor Chia Ch'ing. *No date.* 28cm.

B 1142. 上 諭 八 旗

Shang yü pa ch'i

Imperial Edicts addressed to the Eight Manchu Banners between 1723 and 1736 by the Emperor Yung Chêng. *No date.* 25.5cm.

B 1143. 上 諭 旗 務 議 覆

Shang yü ch'i wu i fu

Reports by the Boards on Edicts referring to the Eight Manchu Banners. *No date.* 25.5cm.

B 1144—1147. 吳 文 節 公 遺 集
Wu wên chieh kung i chi

The State papers, letters, and poems, of 吳文鎔 Wu Wên-jung, who committed suicide in 1854 when as Viceroy of Hu-Kuang he was overwhelmed by the T'ai-p'ing rebels. 1857. 25cm.

B 1148. 曾 文 正 公 文 鈔
Tsêng wên chêng kung wên ch'ao

Essays by the famous Viceroy Tsêng Kuo-fan, who died in 1872, edited by 黎庶昌 Li Shu-ch'ang, his secretary and later on Minister in Madrid and Tokio; with portrait. 1873. 24.5cm.

B 1149. 諭 求 直 言
Yü ch'iu chih yen

An Edict calling for plain-spoken advice, issued by the Emperor Tao Kuang, with replies from Kiying, Tsêng Kuo-fan, and other high officials. [The "Chao" on label should be "Yü".] 1850. 26cm.

B 1150.

Another copy. [The 詔 on label should be 諭.]

B 1151. 蘇 文 忠 奏 議
Su wên chung tsou i

Memorials to the Throne on various subjects, by 蘇軾 Su Shih, who died A.D. 1101. 1813. 29cm.

B 1152. 粵 東 奏 稿
Yüeh tung tsou kao

Memorials to the Throne from Kuangtung, 1847—1850, by 耆英 Kiying, 葉名琛 Yeh Ming-shên, known as "Governor Yeh," and others. [Manuscript.] 24cm.

B 1153—1156. 紀 氛 記 畧

Chi fên chi lüeh

Memorials relating to the T'ai-p'ing rebellion, A.D. 1850—1862.
[Manuscript.] 25cm.

B 1157. 舌 擊 編

Shê chi pien

The official reports of 沈儲藥 Shên Ch'u-kao during the years
1853—1854, on military operations against the T'ai-p'ing rebels. 1859.
22.5cm.

B 1158. 乞 留 各 奏

Ch'i liu ko tsou

Memorials to the Throne in 1860, by 僧格林沁 Sêng-ko-lin-
sin and others. [Manuscript.] 22 × 12cm.

B 1159—1170. 通 鑑 紀 事 本 末

T'ung chien chi shih pên mo

A rearrangement of the Mirror of History of 司馬光 Ssǔ-ma
Kuang (see B 961), by 袁樞 Yüan Shu who died A.D. 1205,
edited by 張溥 Chang P'u who died in 1641, with the old prefaces,
the earliest being dated 1258. 1685. 25cm.

B 1171—1176. 續資治通鑑紀事本末

Hsü tzǔ chih t'ung chien chi shih pên mo

A continuation of the above work down to the end of the Mongol
dynasty in the 14th cent. with supplement. [Manuscript.] *No date.* 23cm.

B 1177—1180. 讀 史 綱

Tu shih kang

A guide to the study of history, from the earliest ages down to
the 13th cent. A.D., by 左廢 Tso Ch'ien, edited by his son 左昊
Tso Hao. 1691. 22.5cm.

B 1181—1185.   宋 元 紀 事 本 末
Sung yüan chi shih pên mo

A history of the Sung and Mongol dynasties on the plan adopted by Yüan Shu (see B 1159), by 馮琦 Fêng Ch'i, edited by 張溥 Chang P'u, who died in 1641. *No date.*   25.5cm.

B 1186—1191.   明 鑑 紀 事 本 末
Ming chien chi shih pên mo

A history of the Ming dynasty, in continuation of the above, by 谷應泰 Ku Ying-t'ai. 1658.   25.5cm.

B 1192—1197.   續 後 漢 書
Hsü hou han shu

A continuation of the History of the Later Han dynasty, in which the Minor Han, A.D. 221—265, is considered as the legitimately ruling House of the three rival kingdoms, by 蕭常 Hsiao Ch'ang of the Sung dynasty. [Omit 蕭 on label.] 1841.   24cm.

B 1198—1199.   兩 漢 雋 言
Liang han tsun yen

A dictionary of ancient phraseology, arranged under categorical headings, by 林越 Lin Yüeh (T. 次) of the Sung dynasty, edited by 凌迪知 Ling Ti-chih. 1576.   25cm.

B 1200—1204.   遼 史 拾 遺
Liao shih shih i

A history of the Liao dynasty or Kitan Tartars, A.D. 907—1125, supplemented by notices from over 300 writers whose works had not been previously used, by 厲鶚 Li O who graduated in 1720. 1821.   24cm.

A 1205—1212. 繹 史
I shih

A history of China from the earliest ages down to the end of the Ch'in dynasty, B.C. 206, with illustrations, by 馬驌 Ma Su. 1670. 26 × 19 cm.

B 1213—1216. 尚 史
Shang shih

Ancient history, covering a period from about B.C. 2700 to B.C. 200, by 李鍇 Li Ch'ieh, whose preface is dated 1745. 1805. 24.5cm.

B 1218—1229. 易 知 錄
I chih lu

An epitome of Chu Hsi's revision of the Mirror of History, by 吳乘權 Wu Shêng-ch'üan. [Sections 1 and 2 are missing. The figures on labels refer to the number of Chinese vols bound up together. For a complete edition down to the Yüan dynasty, see B 731a—737a. In vols 1228, 1229, is included part of the work catalogued as B 1025—1028, dealing with the Ming dynasty.] 1711. 25cm.

B 1230—1231. 讀 史 鏡 古 編
Tu shih ching ku pien

Lessons from history, by 潘世恩 P'an Shih-ên who died in 1854. 1824. 25.5cm.

B 1232. 歷 代 名 儒 傳
Li tai ming ju chuan

Biographies of eminent Confucianists, by 朱軾 Chu Shih and 蔡世遠 Ts'ai Shih-yüan. 1729. 27cm.

B 1232a. 歷 代 循 吏 傳
Li tai hsün li chuan

Biographies of virtuous officials, by the same authors. 1729. 26.5cm.

B 1233. 鑑 畧 四 字 書
Chien lüeh ssŭ tzŭ shu

Historical memoranda, arranged in verses of 4 characters by 王 仕雲 Wang Shih-yün, whose preface is dated 1663. *No date.* 27cm.

B 1234. 二 十 二 史 感 應 錄
Erh shih êrh shih kan ying lu

Illustrations of the doctrine of retribution, drawn from the 22 Dynastic Histories, by 彭希涑 P'êng Hsi-su. [吏 for 史 on label.] 1846. 24cm.

B 1235—1236. 二 十 二 史 劄 記
Erh shih êrh shih cha chi

Notes on the 22 Dynastic Histories, by 趙翼 Chao I who died in 1814. 1800. 24cm.

B 1237—1238. 二 十 一 史 約 編
Erh shih i shih yo pien

Notes on the 21 Dynastic Histories, by 鄭元慶 Chêng Yüan-ch'ing (T. 芷畦), "covering a period," as stated on the title-page, "from the creation to A.D. 1644, and dealing with astronomy, geo-"graphy, government, rites, music, literature, political economy, "officials, foreign nations, military and judicial matters, Buddhism, "and Taoism." 1698. 24cm.

B 1239. 十 七 史 蒙 求
Shih ch'i shih mêng ch'iu

Allusions to the 17 Dynastic Histories, arranged in verses of four characters and accompanied by a commentary, for the use of boys, by 王令 Wang Ling (T. 逢原), with a preface by 呂誨 Lü Hui, dated 1101, in which he says that he recovered only 10 of the original 16 sections. 1829. 22.5cm.

B 1240—1271. 守 山 閣 叢 書
Shou shan ko ts'ung shu

A collection of III miscellaneous works, reprinted in uniform edition by 錢熙祖 Ch'ien Hsi-tsu, with a preface by 阮元 Yüan Yüan. The blocks of this work were destroyed during the T'ai-p'ing rebellion. [Author's name appears on label instead of title.] 1844.   28cm.

B 1272—1278. 黃 氏 叢 書
Huang shih ts'ung shu

A collection of works, reprinted uniformly by 黃丕烈 Huang P'ei-lieh, consisting of the 周禮 Chou li, 戰國策 Chan kuo ts'ê, 國語 Kuo yü, 輿地廣記 Yü ti kuang chi, 易林 I lin, 傷寒總病論 Shang han tsung ping lun, and several small works labelled "Miscellaneous." 1818.   28cm.

B 1279—1298. 藝 海 珠 塵 甲 集
I hai chu ch'ên chia chi

A collection of 165 works, reprinted by 吳省蘭 Wu Hsing-lan (T. 泉之) in 1809, and edited by his nephew 錢熙輔 Ch'ien Hsi-fu with a supplement of 42 other works. 1850.   24.5cm.

B 1299—1302.

The Supplement only of the above work. [Subdivided on labels into 2 sets of 2 vols each.]   24cm.

B 1303. 歷 代 循 良 能 吏 列 傳 彙 鈔
Li tai hsün liang nêng li lieh chuan hui ch'ao

Biographies of virtuous and able officials of all times, by 喬用選 Ch'iao Yung-ch'ien. 1844.   23cm.

B 1304.　　　　　　　鑑 撮

Chien ts'o

A short history of China from the earliest ages down to A.D. 1644,
by 曠 敏 本 K'uang Min-pên. *No date.*　　　　20 × 13.5cm.

B 1305—1306.　　　　　說 鈴

Shuo ling

A collection of reprints of short works by various authors, compiled
by 吳 震 方 Wu Chên-fang whose preface is dated 1702.　1800.

17.5 × 13 cm.

B 1307—1310.　　唐 人 說 薈

T'ang jen shuo wei

A reprint of miscellaneous writings by authors of the T'ang dynasty,
A.D. 618—907, compiled by 陳 世 熙 Ch'en Shih-hsi (T. 蓮塘).
[The title was afterwards changed to 唐代叢書, as on label,
but the work is better known as above.]　1843.　　　17 × 12cm.

B 1311.

Another copy of B 1136.　　　　　　　　　27.5cm.

B 1312.　　　　平 番 奏 議

P'ing fan tsou i

Memorials to the Throne on the pacification of the aborigines in
Kansuh, 1822—1823. *No date.*　　　　　　　30cm.

B 1313—1318.　　八 旬 萬 壽 盛 典

Pa hsün wan shou shêng tien

A memorial of the 80th year of the Emperor Ch'ien Lung and
the 55th year of his reign, compiled by 阿桂 O-kuei and other
high officials.　1792.　　　　　　　29.5cm.

B 1319—1322. 雍　正　上　諭
Yung chêng shang yü

The Edicts of the Emperor Yung Chêng, A.D. 1723—1735. 1736.
28cm.

B 1323—1350. 硃　批　諭　旨
Chu p'i yü chih

Memorials to the Throne during the years A.D. 1723—1733 of
the reign of Yung Chêng, with the Imperial interlinear annotations
("Vermilion Pencil") printed as written in red ink, and also a preface
by the Emperor. 1733. 30cm.

B 1351—1362. 太　平　廣　記
T'ai p'ing kuang chi

An encyclopædia of information drawn from the lighter literature
of China, originally designed as a supplement to the *T'ai p'ing yü
lan* (B 1385) but often regarded as an independent work, by 李昉
Li Fang and others who presented it to the Throne in A.D. 978,
edited by 談愷 T'an K'ai. 1566. 26cm.

B 1363—1378. 歷代名臣奏議
Li tai ming ch'ên tsou i

Advice to the Throne, by eminent officials of all ages, from Confucius, 5th cent. B.C., down to 趙良弼 Chao Liang-pi, 13th cent.
A.D., who after over a year's residence in Japan advised Kublai
Khan not to attack that country, compiled by 張溥 Chang P'u.
1635. 25cm.

B 1379. 碧　血　錄
Pi hsüeh lu

A Record of Blood, being notices of eminent statesmen and others
who met violent deaths, with portraits illustrating each scene, from
the 2nd cent. B.C. to the 17th cent. A.D., by 莊仲方 Chuang
Chung-fang, edited by 邵懿辰 Shao I-ch'ên. 1856. 26cm.

B 1380—1384. 明 臣 奏 議
Ming ch'ên tsou i

Selected Memorials by officials under the Ming dynasty, A.D. 1368—1644. 1781. 26cm.

B 1385—1417. 太 平 御 覽
T'ai p'ing yü lan

An encyclopædia of general information, compiled under Imperial instructions issued in A.D. 977 to 李昉 Li Fang and others, who presented it to the Throne in 983 with the title of 太平編類 T'ai p'ing pien lei which was afterwards changed by the Emperor as above; edited by 阮元 Yüan Yüan. 1812. 26.5cm.

B 1418—1424. 孔 氏 叢 書
K'ung shih ts'ung shu

A collection of reprints, not uniform in typography, of classical works by various authors. [Title-page and preface wanting.] *No date.* 27cm.

B 1425. 策 畧
Ts'ê lüeh

Notes on philosophy, the classics, history, astronomy, geography, military matters, and political economy, by 汪紱 Wang Fu (T. 雙池). 1828. 24.5cm.

B 1426—1452. 西 山 全 集
Hsi shan ch'üan chi

The complete works of 眞德修 Chên Tê-hsiu, A.D. 1178—1235, with portrait, edited under Imperial command by 楊鶚 Yang O and others; with introductory poem and preface by the Emperor Ch'ien Lung, printed in red ink. 1737. 25cm.

B 1454—1470. 三 才 圖 會
San ts'ai t'u hui

An encyclopædia of geography, ethnology, language, the arts and sciences, etc. etc., with numerous illustrations, compiled by 王圻 Wang Ch'i of the 16th cent. A.D. [Vols I, XVI, and XIX are missing.] *No date.* 26.5cm.

B 1471—1476. 培 遠 堂 偶 存 稿
P'ei yüan t'ang ou ts'un kao

The official writings of 陳宏謀 Ch'ên Hung-mou, A.D. 1695—1771, edited by a son and grandson. *No date.* 25cm.

B 1477. 手 札 節 要
Shou cha chieh yao

Selections from the private letters of Ch'ên Hung-mou; see B 1471. 1837. 23.5cm.

B 1478. 黃 門 奏 疏
Huang mên tsou su

The Memorials to the Throne of 楊雍建 Yang Hsiung-chien (T. 自西 and 以齋) whose preface is dated 1663. 1845. 25.5cm.

B 1479—1481. 恭 壽 堂 奏 議
Kung shou t'ang tsou i

The Memorials to the Throne of 韓文綺 Han Wên-ch'i, who died in 1841. *No date.* 25.5cm.

B 1482—1483. 陶 雲 汀 先 生 奏 疏
T'ao yün ting hsien shêng tsou su

The Memorials to the Throne of 陶澍 T'ao Chu, who died in 1839, with portrait. 1828. 25.5cm.

B 1484—1495. 那 彦 成 奏 議
No yen ch'êng tsou i

The Memorials to the Throne of No-yen-ch'êng, who died in 1833

G. W. 5

THE WADE LIBRARY

and whose preface is dated 1820, preceded by a funeral address from the Emperor Tao Kuang dated 1833. 1834. 24.5cm.

B 1496—1505. 皇 朝 經 世 文 編
Huang ch'ao ching shih wên pien

A collection of essays by writers of the present dynasty on literary, military, and economic subjects, compiled by 賀長齡 Ho Ch'ang-ling (T. 耦庚). 1826. 28cm.

B 1506—1508. 李 文 襄 公 奏 議
Li wên hsiang kung tsou i

The Memorials to the Throne of 李之芳 Li Chih-fang, who died in 1694, preceded by two introductory notes from the Emperor K'ang Hsi, dated 1687. *No date.* 28cm.

B 1509—1512. 葉 文 莊 公 奏 議
Yeh wên chuang kung tsou i

The Memorials to the Throne of 葉盛 Yeh Shêng, with preface dated 1452. *No date.* 28cm.

B 1513—1517. 阿 文 成 公 年 譜
O wên ch'êng kung nien p'u

A record of the life of the famous general O-kuei, who died in 1797. 1813. 28.5cm.

B 1518—1519. 秦 漢 書 疏
Ch'in han shu su

Memorials to the Throne by eminent statesmen under the Ch'in State (and dynasty) and Han dynasty, from the 4th cent. B.C. to the end of the 2nd cent. A.D., compiled by 豐雙江 Fêng Shuang-chiang. 1798. 29.5cm.

B 1520—1529.

前 漢 紀
Ch'ien han chi

The History of the Western Han dynasty, B.C. 206—A.D. 24, by 班固 Pan Ku, with commentary by 顏師古 Yen Shih-ku who died in 645, edited by 余靖 Yü Ching whose preface is dated 1035. 1537. 28.5cm.

B 1530—1536.

後 漢 紀
Hou han chi

The History of the Eastern Han dynasty, A.D. 25—220, by 范曄 Fan Yeh who died in 445, with commentary by 章懷太 Chang Huai-t'ai, edited by 余靖 Yü Ching whose preface is dated 1034. 1537. 28.5cm.

B 1537—1540.

大 臣 傳
Ta ch'ên chuan

Biographies of eminent civil and military officials, from the 2nd cent. B.C. to the 11th cent. A.D. [The label carries the title of Section I only.] *No date.* 27cm.

B 1541—1543.

歷 代 名 臣 傳
Li tai ming ch'ên chuan

Biographies of eminent officials from the 2nd cent. B.C. to the 13th cent. A.D., by 朱軾 Chu Shih and 蔡世遠 Ts'ai Shih-yüan. 1729. 27cm.

B 1544—1545.

歷 代 名 臣 傳 節 錄
Li tai ming ch'ên chuan chieh lu

Short biographies of 177 eminent officials from the 2nd cent. B.C. to the close of the Ming dynasty in A.D. 1644, compiled by 崇厚 Ch'ung-hou, Superintendent of Trade at Tientsin. 1870. 27.5cm.

THE WADE LIBRARY

B 1546. 歷 代 循 吏 傳

Li tai hsün li chuan

Biographies of virtuous officials from the 2nd cent. B.C. to the 13th cent. A.D., by 朱軾 Chu Shih and 蔡世遠 Ts'ai Shih-yüan. 1729. 26.5cm.

B 1547—1550. 二 十 二 史 言 行 略

Erh shih êrh shih yen hsing lüeh

The whole duty of man, illustrated by the lives of famous men from the Twenty-two Dynastic Histories, compiled by 過元皎 Kuo Yüan-min, and followed by two supplementary volumes in manuscript (*no date*) referring to the Ming dynasty and labelled accordingly. 1799. 28cm.

B 1551—1558. 歷 代 名 臣 言 行 錄

Li tai ming ch'ên yen hsing lu

Biographies of eminent officials, from the 3rd cent. B.C. to the 17th cent. A.D., by 朱桓 Chu Huan, whose first edition was dated 1758. 1797. 24.5cm.

B 1559. 歷 代 名 儒 傳

Li tai ming ju chuan

Biographies of eminent Confucianists, from the 2nd cent. B.C. to the 13th cent. A.D., by 朱軾 Chu Shih and 蔡世遠 Ts'ai Shih-yüan. 1729. 26.5cm.

B 1560. 漢 唐 宋 名 臣 錄

Han t'ang sung ming ch'ên lu

Biographies of eminent statesmen under the Han, T'ang, and Sung dynasties, about B.C. 200—A.D. 1200, by 李廷機 Li T'ing-chi. 1606. 27cm.

B 1561—1562. 吳 郡 名 賢 圖 傳 贊
Wu chün ming hsien t'u chuan tsan

Notices of eminent worthies of Soochow in Kiangsu, from the 6th cent. B.C. down to the present dynasty, with portraits, by 顧 沅 Ku Yüan (T. 湘 舟). 1827.　　　　27 cm.

B 1563—1610. 册 府 元 龜
Ts'ê fu yüan kuei

An encyclopædia of constitutional history, compiled under Imperial command and completed in A.D. 1013, by 王 欽 若 Wang Ch'in-jo and others, edited by 李 嗣 京 Li Ssŭ-ching. 1642.　　26 cm.

B 1611—1613. 正 文 獻 通 考 纂
Chêng wên hsien t'ung k'ao tsuan

The encyclopædia of Ma Tuan-lin (see B 489), edited in an abridged form by 葉 大 緯 Yeh Ta-wei and others. 1664.　　25 cm.

B 1614. 續 文 獻 通 考 纂
Hsü wên hsien t'ung k'ao tsuan

Supplement to the encyclopædia of Ma Tuan-lin (see B 489), by 王 圻 Wang Ch'i, first issued in 1586, by the same editors as the above. 1664.　　25 cm.

B 1615—1650. 安 溪 全 書
An ch'i ch'üan shu

The complete works of 李 光 地 Li Kuang-ti, who died A.D. 1718, consisting chiefly of annotated editions of the Classics. 1802.
25.5 cm.

B 1651—1658. 皇 清 奏 議
Huang ch'ing tsou i

Memorials to the Throne by eminent statesmen of the present dynasty. *No date*.　　24 cm.

B 1659—1660.   前 後 守 寶 錄
Ch'ien hou shou pao lu

The official correspondence of 魁聯 K'uei-lien, while acting as Prefect at 寶慶府 Pao-ch'ing Fu.   1853.   23cm.

B 1661—1662.   胡 文 忠 公 遺 集
Hu wên chung kung i chi

The literary remains of 胡林翼 Hu Lin-i, who distinguished himself as a general against the T'ai-p'ing rebels and died in 1861. 1866.   24.5cm.

B 1663.   初 使 泰 西 記
Ch'u shih t'ai hsi chi

An account of the first mission to foreign nations, in 1867, being that of 孫家穀 Sun Chia-ku (a clerk in the Tsung-li Yamên) associated with Mr. Anson Burlingame, then United States' Minister at Peking, by a writer whose pen-name is 避熱主人 *Pi-jê-chu-jen*. See B 1860.   1877.   23cm.

B 1664.   皇 朝 功 紀 盛
Huang ch'ao kung chi shêng

An account of the wars of the present dynasty, by 趙翼 Chao I who died in 1814.   1792.   24cm.

B 1665—1666.   按 黔 疏 草
An ch'ien su ts'ao

Memorials on the province of Kueichou, presented to the Throne between A.D. 1621—1628 by a Censor. (In manuscript.) *No date.*
24.5cm.

B 1667.   東 槎 紀 略
Tung ch'ai chi lüeh

Notes on the administration of the island of Formosa, by 姚瑩 Yao Jung.   1832.   25cm.

B 1668. 簷 曝 雜 記
Yen pao tsa chi

Miscellaneous essays, by 趙翼 Chao I who died in 1814. *No date.* 24.5cm.

B 1169. 鄒 忠 介 公 奏 疏
Tsou chung chieh kung tsou su

Memorials to the Throne, by 鄒元標 Tsou Yüan-p'iao. 1641. 26cm.

B 1670. 溫 公 家 範
Wên kung chia fan

The family rules of 司馬光 Ssŭ-ma Kuang, A.D. 1019—1086, edited by 朱軾 Chu Shih. 1719. 26.5cm.

B 1671. 宣 和 遺 事
Hsüan ho i shih

Reprint of a collection of historical notes and anecdotes, published during the 12th cent. A.D., edited anonymously. 1868. 28.5cm.

B 1672. 于 清 端 公 集
Yü ch'ing tuan kung chi

The literary remains of 于成龍 Yü Ch'êng-lung, a famous statesman who died A.D. 1684, with portrait, and original preface dated 1683, edited by 蔡方炳 Ts'ai Fang-ping and others. *No date.* 27cm.

B 1673—1674. 勉 益 齋 偶 存 稿
Mien i chai ou ts'un kao

Miscellaneous essays written between 1826 and 1832, by 山裕謙 Shan Yü-ch'ien. 1832. 25.5cm.

B 1675—1678. 勉 益 齋 續 存 稿
Mien i chai hsü ts'un kao

Supplement to the above, containing essays written between 1832 and 1840. *No date.* 25.5cm.

B 1679—1680. 靳 文 襄 公 奏 疏
Chin wên hsiang kung tsou su

The Memorials to the Throne of 靳輔 Chin Fu, famous for his engineering labours upon the Yellow River, who died in 1692. *No date.* 26cm.

B 1681—1683. 石雲山人奏議文集
Shih yün shan jen tsou i wên chi

The Memorials to the Throne, A.D. 1805—1835, and the literary remains of 吳榮光 Wu Jung-kuang (T. 伯榮) who graduated in 1799, edited by his brother and read for the press by his daughter. 1841. 30cm.

B 1684. 黎 襄 勤 公 奏 議
Li hsiang ch'in kung tsou i

The Memorials to the Throne of 黎襄勤公 Li (canonised as) Hsiang-ch'in kung who died in 1824, edited by his sons with a preface from 孫玉廷 Sun Yü-t'ing. 1827. 26.5cm.

B 1685—1686. 孫 文 定 奏 疏
Sun wên ting tsou su

The Memorials to the Throne of 孫嘉淦 Sun Chia-kan who died in 1753, edited by a grandson. 1805. 29.5cm.

B 1687—1688. 湯 文 正 公 遺 稿
T'ang wên chêng kung i kao

The literary remains of 湯斌 T'ang Pin, who died in 1687, with preface dated 1690, preceded by his 洛學編 *Lo hsüeh pien*, consisting of biographical notices of various scholars from about the Christian era down to his own times, with original preface dated 1673 and preface to a supplement dated 1738. *No date.*   25.5cm.

B 1689—1692.   王 陽 明 全 集
Wang yang ming ch'üan chi

The complete works of 王守仁 Wang Shou-jen who died in 1528, with portrait, edited by 俞嶙 Yü Lin.   1673.   26.5cm.

B 1693—1696.   張 公 奏 議
Chang kung tsou i

The Memorials to the Throne between A.D. 1684—1703 of 張鵬翮 Chang P'êng-ho, who died in 1725, with maps, especially a bird's-eye view of the Grand Canal, occupying 52 leaves in vol. I. 1800.   26.5cm.

B 1697—1738.   知 不 足 齋 叢 書
Chih pu tsu chai ts'ung shu

A collection of works to the number of 289, reprinted in a uniform edition by 鮑廷博 Pao T'ing-po (T. 士恭) and approved by the Emperor Ch'ien Lung in 1774.   1776.   18.5cm.

B 1739—1793.   粵 雅 堂 叢 書
Yüeh ya t'ang ts'ung shu

A collection of works to the number of 127, reprinted in a uniform edition by 伍崇曜 Wu Ch'ung-yao. See B 1849.   1853.   18.5cm.

B 1794—1815.   海 山 仙 叢 書
Hai shan hsien ts'ung shu

A collection of works to the number of 46, reprinted in a uniform edition by 葉志詵 Yeh Chih-shên. [Label inaccurate.]   1848.   19cm.

B 1816—1828.　　事 類 賦 統 編
Shih lei fu t'ung pien

A reprint, with much additional matter, of the original work of
吳淑 Wu Shu who died A.D. 1002, being a handbook of reference
to literary allusions arranged under categories, edited by 潘國珍
P'an Kuo-chên.　1869.　　　　　　　　　　　　18cm.

B 1829—1848.　　龍 威 秘 書
Lung wei pi shu

A collection of works to the number of 19, reprinted in a uniform
edition by 馬俊良 Ma Chün-liang.　1794.　　　　　　17cm.

B 1849—1850.　　彙 刻 書 目
Hui k'o shu mu

An index to classical, historical, and general literature, including
many well-known collections of reprints, etc. etc., compiled by 顧
脩 Ku Hsiu (T. 茶崖).　1799.　　　　　　　　　　19cm.

B 1851—1854.　　自 治 官 書
Tzŭ chih kuan shu

The writings, chiefly official, of 趙申喬 Chao Shên-ch'iao who
died in 1720, edited by a grandson.　1724.　　　　25cm.

B 1855.　　湖 南 奏 疏
Hu nan tsou su

Memorials to the Throne, by 盧坤 Lu K'un and others, referring
to the rising of the Hunan aborigines in 1832. [In manuscript.] *No
date.*　　　　　　　　　　　　　　　　　　　25cm.

B 1856.　　兩 廣 奏 議
Liang kuang tsou i

Memorials to the Throne from various high officials referring to the
disturbances in Kuangtung and Kuangsi during 1832. [In manuscript.]
No date.　　　　　　　　　　　　　　　　25.5cm.

B 1857. 國 朝 畫 徵 錄
Kuo ch'ao hua chêng lu

Notes on eminent painters of the present dynasty, by 張庚 Chang Kêng (T. 浦山). 1739. 25.5cm.

B 1858. 穆 天 子 傳
Mu t'ien tzŭ chuan

A narrative of the adventures of 穆王 Mu Wang, fifth sovereign of the Chou dynasty who died B.C. 946, first published in the 3rd cent. A.D. with preface by 荀勗 Hsün Hsü, stating that the work had been found in an old tomb in A.D. 281, but now regarded as a forgery of that date. 1840. 24cm.

B 1859. 咨 劄 批 駁 呈 詞
Tzŭ cha p'i po ch'êng tz'ŭ

A collection of official dispatches to subordinates, etc. [In manuscript.] *No date.* 25cm.

B 1860. 天 外 歸 帆 草
T'ien wai kuei fan ts'ao

Reminiscences of a journey to foreign countries, in verse, by 斌椿 Pin Ch'un (T. 友松) associate Envoy with Mr. Anson Burlingame in the mission of 1867. See B 1663. 1868. 26cm.

B 1861. 海 國 勝 遊 草
Hai kuo shêng yu ts'ao

Notes on a visit to foreign countries, in verse, by the same author. 1868. 26cm.

B 1862. 乘 查 筆 記
Ch'êng ch'a pi chi

Notes on the mission to foreign countries in 1867, by the same author. 1869. 26cm.

B 1863. 輶 車 雜 錄
Yao chü tsa lu

Miscellaneous State papers, by 朱軾 Chu Shih who died in 1736,
including specimen of a prayer for rain. *No date.* 26cm.

B 1864.

A manuscript copy of B 1312. 26cm.

B 1865—1866. 撫 朔 尺 牘
Fu so ch'ih tu

Letters on the pacification of Kansuh. [In manuscript; anonymous.]
No date. 24cm.

B 1867. 欽 定 廣 東 上 諭 奏 摺
Ch'in ting kuang tung shang yü tsou chê

State papers referring to Kuangtung for the year 1832. [In manuscript.
論 for 諭 on label.] *No date.* 25cm.

B 1868. 欽 定 湖 南 上 諭 奏 摺
Ch'in ting hu nan shang yü tsou chê

State papers referring to Hunan for the year 1832. [In manuscript.]
25cm.

B 1870—1876. 洪 武 實 錄
Hung wu shih lu

Official record of the founder of the Ming dynasty, who reigned
as Hung Wu, A.D. 1368—1399. [In manuscript; vol. I missing.]
No date. 29cm.

B 1877—1880. 永 樂 實 錄
Yung lo shih lu

Official record of the third Emperor of the Ming dynasty, who reigned
as Yung Lo, A.D. 1403—1424. [In manuscript.] *No date.* 29cm.

B 1881—1886. 宣 德 實 錄

Hsüan tê shih lu

Official record of the fifth Emperor of the Ming dynasty, who reigned as Hsüan Tê, A.D. 1426—1435. [In manuscript.] *No date.* 29cm.

B 1887—1902. 正 統 實 錄

Chêng t'ung shih lu

Official record of the sixth Emperor of the Ming dynasty, who reigned as Chêng T'ung, A.D. 1436—1449. [In manuscript.] *No date.* 29cm.

B 1903—1912. 成 化 實 錄

Ch'êng hua shih lu

Official record of the ninth Emperor of the Ming dynasty, who reigned as Ch'êng Hua, A.D. 1465—1487. [In manuscript.] *No date.* 29cm.

B 1913—1919. 弘 治 實 錄

Hung chih shih lu

Official record of the tenth Emperor of the Ming dynasty, who reigned as Hung Chih, A.D. 1488—1505. [In manuscript.] *No date.* 29cm.

B 1920—1928. 正 德 實 錄

Chêng tê shih lu

Official record of the eleventh Emperor of the Ming dynasty, who reigned as Chêng Tê, A.D. 1506—1521. [In manuscript.] *No date.* 29cm.

B 1929—1949. 嘉 靖 實 錄

Chia ching shih lu

Official record of the twelfth Emperor of the Ming dynasty, who reigned as Chia Ching, A.D. 1522—1566. [In manuscript.] *No date.* 29cm.

78   THE WADE LIBRARY

B 1950—1954.   隆 慶 實 錄
                          Lung ch'ing shih lu

Official record of the thirteenth Emperor of the Ming dynasty, who
reigned as Lung Ch'ing, A.D. 1567—1572. [In manuscript.] *No date.*
                                                                29cm.

B 1955—1970.   大清仁宗睿皇帝訓
                      Ta ch'ing jen tsung jui huang ti hsün

Edicts by the Emper Chia Ch'ing, A.D. 1796—1820.   1824.   32cm.

B 1971—1973.   史 畧
                           Shih lüeh

An epitome of history, from the earliest ages down to the foundation
of the Ming dynasty in 1368, by 曾先之 Tsêng Hsien-chih, with
a note by 劉基 Liu Chi who died in 1375. [吏 for 史 on label.]
No date.   33cm.

B 1974—1977.   通 鑑 節 要
                        T'ung chien chieh yao

An epitome of the Mirror of History (see B 961). *No date.*   33cm.

B 1978—1997.   高 麗 史
                        Kao li shih

A history of Korea, by 翁樹崐 Wêng Shu-k'un. [In manuscript.]
1814.   29cm.

B 1998—2002.   東 鑑
                        Tung chien

A history of eastern nations, being an account of the three States
which now form modern Korea, by 徐居正 Hsü Chü-chêng and
others who presented it to the Throne in A.D. 1485. *No date.* 33.5cm.

B 2003—2004. 高 麗 名 臣 傳
Kao li ming ch'ên chuan

Biographies of eminent Korean officials, by 公轍 Kung-ch'ê. 1822.

32cm.

B 2005—2012. 國 朝 奏 疏
Kuo ch'ao tsou su

Memorials to the Throne on various subjects, from officials of the present dynasty, edited by 朱樗 Chu Yün (T. 雲木). [In manuscript.] 1829. 28.5cm.

B 2013—2038. 大 清 會 典
Ta ch'ing hui tien

The Institutes of the Ch'ing or present Manchu-Tartar dynasty, issued by Imperial command, with a preface from the Emperor Chia Ch'ing. See B 261—341. 1818. 30.5cm.

C. *Geography, Travels, etc.*

C 1. 瀛 環 志 畧
Ying huan chih lüeh

A geography of the world, with maps, by 徐繼畬 Hsü Chi-yü. 1848. 29.5cm.

C 2.

Another edition. [Issued by the Tsung-li Yamên or Board for Foreign Affairs at Peking.] 1866. 31cm.

C 3—8. 海 國 圖 志
Hai kuo t'u chih

Geographical and general notes on foreign countries, with maps, based upon translations from foreign works collected by the famous Commissioner Lin, by 魏源 Wei Yüan, whose first edition with preface dated 1842 was issued in 1847 and consisted of sixty books, forty more being added in the present edition. 1852. 28cm.

C 9—10. 乾 隆 府 廳 州 縣 圖 志
Ch'ien lung fu t'ing chou hsien t'u chih

A topographical description of the empire during the reign of Ch'ien Lung, by 洪亮吉 Hung Liang-chi who died in 1809. 1788. 25cm.

C 11—12. 防 海 輯 要
Fang hai chi yao

The essentials of maritime defence, by 俞昌會 Yü Ch'ang-hui. 1842. 25.5cm.

C 13—16. 方 輿 紀 要 簡 覽
Fang yü chi yao chien lan

A geography of the Eighteen Provinces, by 潘鐸 P'an To. 1858. 26.5cm.

C 17—18. 霞 客 遊 記
Hsia k'o yu chi

The travels in various provinces of 徐宏祖 Hsü Hung-tsu (T. 霞客), edited by his son. 1808. 24cm.

C 19. 度 隴 記
Tu lung chi

Across the province of Shensi, being notes on the official journey of 祁雋藻 Ch'i Chien-tsao, by 董醇 Tung Shun. 1851. 25.5cm.

C 20. 甘 棠 小 志
Kan t'ang hsiao chih

An account of 邵伯 Shao-po and its environs in Kiangsu, where

the Duke of Shao administered justice under the famous pear-tree in the 11th cent. B.C., with maps, by 董醇 Tung Shun. 1855. 26cm.

C 21. 三省邊防備覽
San shêng pien fang pei lan

The frontier defences of Ssǔch'uan, Shensi, and Hupeh, by 嚴如煜 Yen Ju-i. 1822. 30cm.

C 22—23. 洋防輯要
Yang fang chi yao

The essentials in coast defences, by 嚴如煜 Yen Ju-i. *No date.* 30cm.

C 24. 苗防備覽
Miao fang pei lan

Frontier defences against the wild tribes on the borders of Kueichou, with maps, by 嚴如煜 Yen Ju-i whose preface to first edition is dated 1820. 1843. 30cm.

C 25. 綏猺廳志
Sui yao t'ing chih

An account of the aborigines in the 連州 Lien-chou peninsula, Kuangtung, with maps, by 姚東之 Yao Chien-chih. 1837. 27cm.

C 26—27. 廣東新語
Kuang tung hsin yü

A description of the province of Kuangtung, and of the manners and customs of its people, by 屈大均 Ch'ü Ta-chün (T. 翁山). 1700. 27cm.

C 28—32. 廣東海防彙覽
Kuang tung hai fang hui lan

The coast defences of the province of Kuangtung, with maps, by 盧坤 Lü K'un, who died in A.D. 1618, and others. *No date.* 26cm.

C 33—36.   粵 海 關 志
Yüeh hai kuan chih

An account of the Custom-houses in Kuangtung and Kuangsi. [In manuscript.] *No date.*   30cm.

C 37—42.   瓊 州 府 志
Ch'iung chou fu chih

The Topography of the Prefecture of Ch'iung-chou, which includes the island of Hainan, by 蕭 應 植 Hsiao Ying-chih. 1774.   25.5cm.

C 43—47.   江 北 運 程
Chiang pei yün ch'êng

The inland water-route, north of the river Yang-tsze, for the transport of rice to the capital, with maps, by 董 恂 Tung Hsün. 1860.   27cm.

C 48—55.   蘇 州 府 志
Su chou fu chih

The Topography of the Su-chou (Soochow) Prefecture in Kiangsu, with maps, by 沈 世 奕 Shên Shih-i and others. [Label inaccurate.] 1691.   26cm.

C 56—58.   上 海 縣 志
Shang hai hsien chih

The Topography of the Shanghai District in Kiangsu, with map, illustrations, bibliographical notes, and preface to the first edition dated A.D. 1504, by 李 文 耀 Li Wên-yao and others. 1750.   27cm.

C 59—68.   南 巡 盛 典
Nan hsün shêng tien

An account of four Imperial progresses between A.D. 1751 and 1765, with the poems and essays written by the way, edited by 高 晉 Kao Chin and others, with a preface from the Emperor Ch'ien Lung. 1771.   28cm.

C 69—84. 江 西 通 志

Chiang hsi t'ung chih

A topographical account of the province of Kiangsi, with maps and illustrations, by 謝旻 Hsieh Min. 1730. 28.5cm.

C 85—108. 大 清 一 統 志

Ta ch'ing i t'ung chih

A complete geographical and general description of the empire of China, compiled under Imperial instructions by 蔣廷錫 Chiang T'ing-hsi and others, with a preface from the Emperor Ch'ien Lung. 1745. 30cm.

C 109. 坤 輿 乾 鑿 度 圖

K'un yü ch'ien tsao tu t'u

An atlas of the Eighteen Provinces, edited by 顧炳章 Ku Ping-chang, with prefaces by earlier editors dated 1805 and 1846. [Bound upside down.] 1854. 31 × 22cm.

C 110—113. 職 貢 圖

Chih kung t'u

The costumes and customs of tributary countries, including the British, French, Spanish, and other western nations, with full-page illustrations, compiled under Imperial command by 永璇 Yung Hsüan and others, with an introductory poem from the Emperor Ch'ien Lung. 1761. 28cm.

C 114. 異 域 國 志

I yü kuo chih

The costumes of strange nations, including Koreans, Huns, Persians, Arabs, and many Central Asian tribes, with brief notes and illustrations, followed by 16 illustrations of birds and animals. [This work was originally referred to the 11th or 12th century, but a manuscript note on fly-leaf, dated 1796, based upon the entry in the

THE WADE LIBRARY

Imperial Catalogue (E 143), shows that it must belong to the period 洪武 Hung Wu, A.D. 1368—1398.] *No date.* 31 × 21.5cm.

C 115. 外 藩 紀 略
Wai fan chi lüeh

Notices of feudatory countries in Central Asia, with map, by 椿 園 "Ch'un-yüan." 1777. 24cm.

C 116—117. 藩 部 要 略
Fan pu yao lüeh

An account of the feudatory tribes of Mongolia, etc., by 祁韻 士 Ch'i Yün-shih. 1846. 25.5cm.

C 118—119. 新 疆 識 畧
Hsin chiang shih lüeh

An account of Chinese Turkestan, by 松筠 Sung-yün, the well-known Mongol statesman who escorted Lord Macartney's embassy to Peking in 1816 and served as Resident in Tibet. 1821. 30 × 19.5cm.

C 120. 回 疆 誌
Hui chiang chih

An account of Mahomedan countries in Central Asia, with illustrations of the costumes and map, issued in A.D. 1768 by 蘇爾德 Su-êrh-tê and 福森布 Fu-sên-pu. [In manuscript, with stamped border and facsimile drawings.] *No date.* 25cm.

C 121—122. 西 域 瑣 談
Hsi yü so t'an

Notes on Central Asian countries, by 椿園 "Ch'un-yüan," issued in 1777. [In manuscript, each leaf being folded over a leaf from a collection of poems entitled 御製詩三集 *Yü chih shih san chi,* from the pen of the Emperor Ch'ien Lung who reigned A.D. 1736—1796.] *No date.* 22.5cm.

C 123. 西 陲 總 統 事 略
Hsi ch'ui tsung t'ung shih lüeh

Notes on the administration of Chinese Turkestan, by 筠松 Sung-yün (see C 118—119.) 1809. 30cm.

C 124—135. 讀 史 方 輿
Tu shih fang yü

The geography of the empire from the earliest ages down to modern times, by 顧祖禹 Ku Tsu-yü, first published in A.D. 1667 with preface by 魏禧 Wei Hsi. 1831. 26cm.

C 136—137. 大 清 一 統 志 表
Ta ch'ing i t'ung chih piao

A chronological geography of the empire, arranged in tabular form, by 徐午 Hsü Wu. 1794. 27.5cm.

C 138—149. 畿 輔 通 志
Chi fu t'ung.chih

A history of Peking and its environs, with maps, based upon the work published in 1682, by 李衛 Li Wei and others. 1732. 27cm.

C 150. 畿 輔 義 倉 圖
Chi fu i ts'ang t'u

On the establishment of public granaries for the storage of gifts of grain against times of famine in the province of Chihli, with maps, by 方觀承 Fang Kuan-ch'êng. 1753. 29.5cm.

C 151—158. 日 下 舊 聞 考
Jih hsia chiu wên k'ao

An edition, with notes, of the archæological description of Peking and its environs published by 朱彝遵 Chu I-tsun who died in 1709, issued by command of the Emperor Ch'ien Lung. 1774. 28cm.

C 159—160. 帝 京 景 物 畧
Ti ching ching wu lüeh

The sights of Peking, by 方逢年 Fang Fêng-nien whose preface
is dated 1637. *No date.*   25cm.

C 161. 避 暑 山 莊 記
Pi shu shan chuang chi

Poems from a summer retreat, by the Emperor K'ang Hsi, with
prefatory note dated 1711, edited with commentary by 鄂爾泰
O-êrh-t'ai and others by command of the Emperor Ch'ien Lung.
1741.   26.5cm.

C 162—173. 天 下 郡 國 利 病 書
T'ien hsia chün kuo li ping shu

An historical geography of the empire, its border States, and some
Central Asian countries, with maps, by 顧絳 Ku Chiang whose
preface is dated 1662. 1831.   26cm.

C 174. 輿 圖 要 覽
Yü t'u yao lan

A concise geography of the empire, with maps, and notices of
Korea, Annam, and barbarian nations. *No date.*   25.5cm.

C 175. 皇 朝 輿 地 畧
Huang ch'ao yü ti lüeh

A concise geography of the empire under the present dynasty,
with index arranged under the rhymes and maps, by 六承如
Liu Ch'êng-ju. [Wrongly bound. The first 10 leaves should follow
leaf 45.] 1831.   21cm.

C. 176.

Another copy.   22cm.

C 177—178. 大 清 一 統 輿 圖
Ta ch'ing i t'ung yü t'u

An atlas of the empire, by 嚴樹森 Yen Shu-sên. [Section 20 missing.] 1863.   28cm.

C 179—180. 武 夷 山 志
Wu i shan chih

An account of the famous hills in the province of Fuhkien which produce Bohea tea, and the numerous antiquities of the neighbourhood, with portraits of local celebrities, by 董天工 Tung T'ien-kung (T. 典齋) who issued the first edition in 1754, edited by 羅艮嵩 Lo Liang-sung. 1846.   26.5cm.

C 181—200. 福 建 通 志
Fu chien t'ung chih

An historical and topographical description of the province of Fuhkien, with maps and illustrations, prepared under Imperial instructions by 郝玉麟 Hao Yü-lin and others. [*Tung* for *T'ung* on label.] 1737.   27cm.

C 201. 烏 石 山 志
Wu shih shan chih

A description of the sights and monuments of Wu-shih-shan, a famous hill within the city of Foochow, the occupation of which by local missionaries was the subject of a serious dispute with the Chinese authorities in 1879, by 劉永松 Liu Yung-sung. [Four vols in cloth case.] 1842.   27cm.

C 202. 閩 都 記
Min tu chi

An historical account of the capital of the Fuhkien province, known as Foochow, with six maps showing its development from the year 202 B.C., by 王應山 Wang Ying-shan. 1831.   26.5cm.

C 203—215. 盛 京 通 志
Shêng ching t'ung chih

An historical account of Shing-king, one of the Manchurian pro-vinces, with its capital at Moukden, prepared under Imperial instructions by 阿桂 O-kuei and others. 1778.   29cm.

C 216—239. 雲 南 通 志
Yün nan t'ung chih

An historical account of the province of Yünnan, based upon the work A.D. 1691, issued under Imperial instructions by 阮元 Yüan Yüan and others, with a preface from 伊里布 I-li-pu. 1831.   26cm.

C 240—242. 雲 南 備 徵 志
Yün nan pei chêng chih

A history of the administration of Yünnan, by 王崧 Wang Sung. 1831.   25.5cm.

C 243—248. 承 德 府 志
Ch'êng tê fu chih

An historical account of the Prefecture of Ch'êng-tê in Chihli, also known as 熱河 Jê-ho (Jehol), issued under Imperial instructions by 那彥成 No-yen-ch'êng and others. 1831.   27cm.

C 249—250. 天 津 府 志
T'ien ching fu chih

An historical account of the Tientsin Prefecture, issued under Im-perial instructions by 李衛 Li Wei and others, with a preface from 陳弘謀 Ch'ên Hung-mou. 1739.   24cm.

C 251—255. 天 津 縣 志
T'ien ching hsien chih

An historical account of the District of Tientsin, by the same authors and with preface as above. 1739.   23.5cm.

C 256—258. 盛 京 通 志
Shêng ching t'ung chih

An historical account of Shing-king (see C 203—215), prepared by 宋筠 Sung-yün and others from the edition of 1736. *No date.* 23.5cm.

C 259—263. 貴 州 通 志
Kuei chou t'ung chih

An historical account of the province of Kueichou, based upon an earlier work and edited by 范承勳 Fan Ch'êng-hsün and others. 1792. 36cm.

———————————

D. *Poetry, Novels, Plays, etc.*

D 1—4. 東 周 列 國 志
Tung chou lieh kuo chih

An historical novel dealing with the feudal age of China, 8th to 3rd cent. B.C., with map and illustrations, edited in 1736 by 蔡昊 Ts'ai Hao (T. 元放). 1877. 20cm.

D 5—8. 三 國 志 演 義
San kuo chih yen i

An historical novel dealing with the period of the Three Kingdoms, A.D. 168—265, with illustrations, attributed to 羅貫中 Lo Kuan-chung of the 12th cent., reprinted from the edition of 1644 which was issued by 瑞聖嘆 Jui Shêng-t'an with critical commentary by 毛宗岡 Mao Tsung-kang. [Label inaccurate.] 1877.
20cm.

D 9—12.
Another edition of the same reprint, with many more illustrations. 1889. 20cm.

THE WADE LIBRARY

D 13—14.　英 烈 傳 (or 雲 合 奇 蹤)

Ying lieh chuan (or Yün ho ch'i tsung)

An historical novel dealing with the fall of the Mongols and establishment of the Ming dynasty from A.D. 1368, with illustrations, by 徐文長 Hsü Wên-ch'ang who lived under the latter dynasty. *No date.*　　　　　　　　　　　　　　　　　　　　18.5cm.

D 15.　　御 世 仁 風

Yü shih jen fêng

Historical episodes exemplifying the virtue or wisdom of ancient rulers, with full-page illustration to each, by 金忠 Chin Chung (T. 澂恕). 1620.　　　　　　　　　　　　　　　　32.5cm.

D 16—17.　漪 園 四 種

I yüan ssŭ tsung

Four collections of short plays, entitled 五虎記 *Wu hu chi,* 三世記 *San shih chi,* 四友記 *Ssŭ yu chi,* and 雙兔記 *Shuang t'u chi,* by 姚鼐 Yao Nai. 1776.　　　　　　　26.5cm.

D 18—25.　元 曲 選 雜 劇

Yüan ch'ü hsüan tsa chi

One hundred selected plays of the Yüan or Mongol dynasty, A.D. 1280—1368, with an illustration to each, edited by 吳興臧 Wu Hsing-tsang. 1615.　　　　　　　　　　　　　25cm.

D 26—29.　審 音 鑑 古 錄

Shên yin chien ku lu

A collection of 66 short plays, each with coloured full-leaf illustration, edited by 琴隱翁 the Old Lute-Recluse. *No date.*　　29.5cm.

D 30—41.　六 十 種 曲

Liu shih tsung ch'ü

A collection of plays arranged under 60 headings, edited by 閔

世道人 a Philosopher who has seen the world. [*Chü* for *ch'ü* on label.] 1845.   25cm.

D 42—43.   玉 嬌 梨
Yü chiao li

A novel of social life, known to foreigners as "The Two Cousins," by 散人 Good-for-Nothing of 荻岸 the Reedy Bank, with illustrations, and critical commentary by 金聖歎 Chin Shêng-t'an who was executed about A.D. 1662. *No date.*   19cm.

D 44—49.   紅 樓 夢
Hung lou mêng

A novel of social life, known to foreigners as "The Dream of the Red Chamber," attributed to 曹雪芹 Ts'ao Hsüeh-ch'in of the 17th cent., with illustrations, and critical commentary by 王希廉 Wang Hsi-lien.   1832.   19cm.

D 50—52.   聊 齋 志 異
Liao chai chih i

A collection of stories, chiefly dealing with supernatural agencies, by 蒲松齡 P'u Sung-ling who was born in A.D. 1622, with commentary and exegetical notes.   1884.   20cm.

D 53—55.   金 瓶 梅
Chin p'ing mei

A novel of social life dealing with the early years of the 12th cent. A.D., attributed to 王世貞 Wang Shih-chêng who died in 1593, with illustrations, and critical commentary by 張竹坡 Chang Chu-p'o.   1695.   22.5cm.

D 56—59.

Another edition, without illustrations.   1695.   24cm.

D 60—69.   歷 代 賦 彙
Li tai fu hui

A collection of the masterpieces of all ages in the poetical-prose style known as *fu*, issued under Imperial instructions by 陳元龍 Ch'ên Yüan-lung, with a preface from the Emperor K'ang Hsi.   1706.

27.5cm.

D 70—73.

Supplement to the above.   27.5cm.

D 74.   荻 芬 書 屋 賦 稿
Ti fên shu wu fu kao

The poetical-prose compositions (*fu*) of 董醇 Tung Shun.   1859.

25cm.

D 75.   歷 朝 賦 楷
Li ch'ao fu k'ai

Models of poetical-prose (*fu*), selected and edited by 王修玉 Wang Hsiu-yü.   1786.   22cm.

D 76—81.

Another edition of D 1—4, edited by Ts'ai Hao.   1736.   25.5cm.

D 82.

A manuscript copy of D 42—43.   1855.   21.5 × 18cm.

D 83—86.

Another edition of D 44—49.   *No date.*   19cm.

D 87.   好 求 傳
Hao ch'iu chuan

A novel of social life, known to foreigners as "The Fortunate Union." Anonymous.   1863.   26.5cm.

D 88.

A tall copy of the above, on white paper.　　　　　28.5cm.

D 89—91.　　古　文　辭　類　纂
　　　　　　　　Ku wên tz'ü lei tsuan

A classified collection of elegant extracts from authors of all ages, by 姚鼐 Yao Nai. 1779.　　　　　25cm.

D 92—93.　　詳　訂　古　文　評　註
　　　　　　　　Hsiang ting ku wên p'ing chu

A collection of elegant extracts from authors of all ages, with commentaries critical and exegetical, by 過珙 Kuo Kung whose preface is dated 1703. 1840.　　　　　23.5cm.

D 94—97.　　古　文　柝　義
　　　　　　　　Ku wên hsi i

A collection of elegant extracts from authors of all ages, with the meaning explained, by 林雲銘 Lin Yün-ming (T. 西仲) whose preface is dated 1687. [折 for 柝 on label.] 1830.　　　22.5cm.

D 98.　　古　文　觀　止
　　　　　　　Ku wên kuan chih

A collection of elegant extracts from authors of all ages, with explanatory notes, by 吳乘權 Wu Shêng-ch'üan (T. 楚材), and preface to first edition dated 1695. [Leaf 1 of Index is missing.] 1868.　　　　　24.5cm.

D 99—102.　　古　文　眉　詮
　　　　　　　　Ku wên mei ch'üan

A collection of elegant extracts from authors of all ages down to the 13th cent. A.D., by 浦起龍 P'u Ch'i-lung (T. 二田). 1744.
　　　　　　　　　　　　　　　　27.5cm.

D 103—109. 古 文 約 選
Ku wên yo hsüan

A collection of elegant extracts from authors between B.C. 200 and A.D. 1100, by 果 Kuo, Prince of the 1st order. 1733. 27.5cm.

D 110—116. 古 文 淵 鑑
Ku wên yüan chien

A collection of elegant extracts from authors of all ages down to the end of the 12th cent. A.D., compiled under Imperial instructions by 徐乾學 Hsü Ch'ien-hsüeh and others, with a preface from the Emperor K'ang Hsi, and printed in black, red, yellow, and green. 1685.   30cm.

D 117—119. 昭 明 文 選
Chao ming wên hsüan

A collection of elegant extracts originally compiled by 蕭統 Hsiao T'ung, A.D. 501—531, eldest son of the founder of the 梁 Liang dynasty, with commentary by 李善 Li Shan whose introduction is dated 658, and punctuation and critical notes by 何焯 Ho Ch'uo, 1660—1722, edited by 葉樹藩 Yeh Shu-fan, and printed in black and red. 1762.   30cm.

D 120—121. 清 容 居 士 集
Ch'ing jung chü shih chi

The miscellaneous writings of 蔣士銓 Chiang Shih-ch'üan, a distinguished literary official who died in 1784, edited by 元袁枬 Yüan Yüan-chüeh. 1840.   24.5cm.

D 122—123. 四 照 堂 文 集
Ssŭ chao t'ang wên chi

The miscellaneous writings of 盧紘元 Lu Hung-yüan (T. 度災). 1663.   27cm.

D 124—126. 吳 詩 集 覽

Wu shih chi lan

The poetical works of 吳偉業 Wu Wei-yeh (T. 駿公) who
lived A.D. 1609—1671, edited by 靳榮藩 Chin Jung-fan. 1781.

25.5cm.

D 127. 甌 北 詩 鈔

Ou pei shih ch'ao

Poems by 趙翼 Chao I, who lived A.D. 1727—1814. 1791. 24cm.

D 128. 甌 北 詩 話

Ou pei shih hua

Critiques on poetry, by Chao I (see above). 1802. 24cm.

D 129. 樂 府 三 歌

Yo fu san ko

Three collections of old songs, edited by 陳本禮 Ch'ên. Pên-li
(T. 素邨), with commentary. 1811. 24cm.

D 130. 協 律 鉤 元

Hsieh lü kou yüan

A collection of old songs, edited by Ch'ên Pên-li (see above). *No*
date. 24cm.

D 131. 屈 辭 精 義

Ch'ü tz'ü ching i

The poems of 屈原 Ch'ü Yüan, B.C. 332—295, edited and explained by Ch'ên Pên-li (see above). *No date.* 24cm.

D 132. 剡 源 集

Yen yüan chi

The literary remains of 戴表元 Tai Piao-yüan (T. 帥初 and

曾伯) who flourished at the close of the 13th cent. and beginning of the 14th cent. A.D., with original preface. 1840. 24.5cm.

D 133—134. 甌 北 集
Ou pei chi

A collection of the poems of Chao I (see D 127), with original preface dated 1757. 1812. 23.5cm.

D 135. 御 賜 詩 章
Yü tz'ü shih chang

Poems by the Emperor Yung Chêng, A.D. 1723—1736, addressed to his trusted counsellor 朱軾 Chu Shih, with which is bound up the 貞女傳 *Chêng nü chuan*, or life of the eldest daughter of Chu Shih, by 蔡世遠 Ts'ai Shih-yüan, and also the 廣惠編 *Kuang hui pien*, a treatise on benevolence, by Chu Shih, dated 1721. *No date.* 26cm.

D 136. 讀 騷 樓 詩 初 集
Tu sao lou shih ch'u chi

The poems of 陳逢衡 Ch'ên Fêng-hêng, whose preface is dated 1829. 1833. 24cm.

D 137. 八 家 詩 選
Pa chia shih hsüan

Selected poems from the works of 宋琬 Sung Yüan, 曹爾堪 Ts'ao Erh-k'an, 施閏章 Shih Jun-chang, 沈荃 Shên Ch'üan, 王士祿 Wang Shih-lu, 程可則 Ch'êng K'o-tsê, 王士禎 Wang Shih-chêng, and 陳廷敬 Ch'ên T'ing-ching, representing the rival schools of the 17th cent. A.D., edited by 吳之振 Wu Chih-chên. 1672. 26.5cm.

D 138—139. 高 青 邱 詩 集 注
Kao ch'ing ch'iu shih chi chu

The poetical works of 高啓 Kao Ch'i (T. 季迪), who flourished

A.D. 1336—1374, with preface to the first edition dated 1478, edited by 金檀 Chin T'an. 1728. 28cm.

D 140. 小書巢詩課偶存
Hsiao shu ch'ao shih k'o ou ts'un

The poetical remains of 陸以莊 Lu I-chuang (T. 平泉) who died in 1827, with funeral address and epitaph by the Emperor Tao Kuang, followed by a supplement to the above and also by a collection of his 賦 *fu* poetical-prose compositions. 1847. 29.5cm.

D 141. 竹嘯軒詩鈔
Chu hsiao hsien shih ch'ao

The poetical works of 沈德潛 Shên Tê-ch'ien, A.D. 1673—1770, edited by 王汝驤 Wang Ju-hsiang. 1784. 28cm.

D 142. 江左十子詩鈔
Chiang tso shih tzŭ shih ch'ao

The poetical works of ten poets of Kiangnan, namely, 劉潢 Liu Huang, 顧宗泰 Ku Tsung-t'ai, 施朝幹 Shih Ch'ao-kan, 范雲鵬 Fan Yün-p'êng, 徐蓀坡 Hsü Hsiang-p'o, 任大椿 Jen Ta-ch'un, 葉抱崧 Yeh Pao-sung, 諸廷槐 Chu T'ing-huai, 王廷謁 Wang T'ing-o, and 王元勳 Wang Yüan-hsün, edited by 王鳴盛 Wang Ming-shêng. 1764. 27cm.

D 143—145. 歷代詩話
Li tai shih hua

Critiques of poetry ancient and modern, edited by 何文煥 Ho Wên-huan. 1770. 19.5cm.

D 146—147. 閨秀正始集
Kuei hsiu chêng shih chi

Selections from the works of the poetesses of the past two hundred

THE WADE LIBRARY

years, with biographical notes, by 完顏惲珠 Wan-yen Yün-chu (T. 珍浦), whose preface to first edition of 1831 is dated 1829. 1861.   19cm.

D 148.

Supplement to the above, first published in 1836. 1861.   19cm.

D 149—153.　　杜　少　陵　全　集
Tu shao ling ch'üan chi

The complete poetical works of 杜甫 Tu Fu, A.D. 712—770, edited with exegetical notes by 仇兆鰲 Ch'iu Chao-ao. 1693. 24cm.

D 154—157.　　李　太　白　文　集
Li t'ai po wên chi

The writings of Li Po, the famous poet, who lived A.D. 705—762, edited with exegetical notes by 王琦 Wang Ch'i (T. 琢崖). 1758.
24.5cm.

D 158.　　蘇　東　坡　文　選
Su tung p'o wên hsüan

Selections from the writings of 蘇軾 Su Shih or Su Tung-p'o, statesman, philosopher, and poet, who flourished A.D. 1036—1101, edited with exegetical notes by 閔爾容 Min Erh-jung and printed in black and red with punctuation in red and blue. [集 for 選 on label.] *No date.*   27cm.

D 159—161.　　施　註　蘇　詩
Shih chu su shih

The poems of 蘇軾 Su Shih (see D 158), with commentary by 施元 Shih Yüan of the Sung dynasty, edited by 張榕端 Chang Jung-tuan and others. 1700.   26cm.

D 162—171.　　古　詩　類　苑
Ku shih lei wan

Ancient poems, from the earliest ages down to the end of the

6th cent. A.D., classified and arranged under subject-headings, by 張之象 Chang Chih-hsiang (T. 玄超) who flourished in the 16th cent., edited by 俞顯卿 Yü Hsien-ch'ing. *No date.* 27.5cm.

D 172. 古 詩 歸
Ku shih kuei

Ancient poems, from the earliest ages down to the end of the 6th cent. A.D., chronologically arranged, by 鍾惺 Chung Hsing and 譚元春 T'an Yüan-ch'un. [A few pages missing at end.] 1617. 26cm.

D 173. 古 唐 詩 合 解
Ku t'ang shih ho chieh

Selections from the poetry of the T'ang dynasty, 7th, 8th, and 9th cent. A.D., with commentary by 王堯衢 Wang Yao-ch'ü (T. 翼雲). [古 omitted on label. Preface and Index missing, for which see D 276.] *No date.* 25.5cm.

D 174. 楚 騷
Ch'u sao

The poems of 屈原 Ch'ü Yüan, B.C. 332—295, in the ancient script known as the Lesser Seal character with the modern characters underneath, by 王稚登 Wang Chih-têng. 1601. 27cm.

D 175. 楚 辭 燈
Ch'u tz'ü têng

The poems of Ch'ü Yüan (see D 174), explained by 林雲銘 Lin Yün-ming (T. 西仲). 1697. 25cm.

D 176. 御 製 七 十 二 候 詩
Yü chih ch'i shih êrh hou shih

Poems for four seasons, by his Majesty (?) Ch'ien Lung, with a eulogistic note by 胡高望 Hu Kao-wang. *No date.* 17cm.

THE WADE LIBRARY

D 177—180. 唐　宋　詩　醇
T'ang sung shih shun

Selections from the poets of the T'ang and Sung dynasties, 7th to 13th cent. A.D., with critical notes, by the Emperor Ch'ien Lung whose preface to first edition is dated 1750, edited by 陳弘謀 Ch'ên Hung-mou and others.　1760.　　　　　17.5cm.

D 181—193. 列　朝　詩　集
Lieh ch'ao shih chi

Extracts from the poets of all dynasties, from B.C. 200 to date, by 錢謙益 Ch'ien Ch'ien-i.　1652.　　　　　25cm.

D. 194.

Manuscript of vol. XIII of the above. *No date.*　　26.5cm.

D 195—200. 名　家　詩　觀
Ming chia shih kuan

A collection of the works of famous contemporary poets, by 鄧漢儀 Têng Han-i (T. 孝威).　1672.　　　26.5cm.

D 201—202. 詩　古　微
Shih ku wei

Critiques on poetical composition, by 魏源 Wei Yüan who died in 1856.　1840.　　　　　25cm.

D 203. 古　詩　源
Ku shih yüan

A collection of ancient poems, edited with notes, by 沈德潛 Shên Tê-ch'ien whose preface to first edition is dated 1719.　1833.　23cm.

D 204. 抄　本　古　今　詩
Ch'ao pên ku chin shih

A manuscript collection of extracts from ancient and modern poets. *No date.*　　　　　23.5cm.

D 205—209.   御 選 唐 詩
                      Yü hsüan t'ang shih

Specimens of the poetry of the T'ang dynasty, 7th, 8th, and 9th
cent. A.D., selected by the Emperor Ch'ien Lung, and edited by a
commission of scholars. See D 246.   1787.   24.5cm.

D 210—211.

A continuation of the above for the 金 Chin dynasty of 女眞
Nü-chên Tartars, 12th and 13th cent.   24.5cm.

D. 212—217.

A continuation of the above for the 宋 Sung dynasty, A.D.
960—1280.   24.5cm.

D 218—225.

A continuation of the above for the 元 Yüan or Mongol dynasty,
A.D. 1280—1368. [Vol. IV missing.]   24.5cm.

D 226—236.

A continuation of the above for the Ming dynasty, A.D. 1368—1644.
                                              24.5cm.

D 237.   元 詩 選
                      Yüan shih hsüan

A selection from the poetry of the Yüan dynasty (see D 218), by
顧奎光 Ku K'uei-kuang.   1751.   26cm.

D 238—245.   宋 詩 鈔
                      Sung shih ch'ao

The poetry of the Sung dynasty, being 集 collections of the
poems of the most eminent writers, arranged chronologically with
biographical notices by 吳之振 Wu Chih-chên. [施 for 詩 on
every label.] 1671.   26cm.

THE WADE LIBRARY

D 246—275.   全 唐 詩
Ch'üan t'ang shih

A complete collection of the poetry of the T'ang dynasty (see D 205), issued under instructions from the Emperor K'ang Hsi, with preface from his Majesty, by 曹寅 Ts'ao Yin and others. 1707. 23cm.

D 276.   古 唐 詩 合 解
Ku t'ang shih ho chieh

Reprint of D 173, with preface by Wang Yao-ch'ü dated 1732. [古 omitted on label.] 1821.   25cm.

D 277—280.   唐 詩 貫 珠
T'ang shih kuan chu

Choice specimens from the poetry of the T'ang dynasty, 7th, 8th, and 9th cent. A.D., arranged under subject-headings with commentary by 胡以海 Hu I-mei (T. 變亭). 1715.   23.5cm.

D 281—283.   唐 詩 別 裁 集
T'ang shih pieh ts'ai chi

Extracts from the poets of the T'ang dynasty (see D 246), with notes by 沈德潛 Shên Tê-ch'ien whose preface is dated 1717, edited with additional notes by 俞汝昌 Yü Ju-ch'ang. 1838. 25.5cm.

D 284—285.   唐 詩 歸
T'ang shih kuei

A selection from the poetry of the T'ang dynasty (see D 246), by 鍾惺 Chung Hsing (T. 伯敬) and 譚元春 T'an Yüan-ch'un (T. 友夏). *No date.*   26cm.

D 286—290.   宋 詩 紀 事
Sung shih chi shih

The poetry of the Sung dynasty, A.D. 960—1260, in its historical

bearings, with notes and criticisms by 厲鶚 Li O (T. 太鴻).
1746. 24cm.

D 291—299. 明 詩 綜
Ming shih tsung

The poetry of the Ming dynasty, A.D. 1368—1644, including extracts from over 3400 writers arranged chronologically by 朱彝尊 Chu I-tsun who died in 1709. *No date.* 25cm.

D 300. 明 詩 別 裁 集
Ming shih pieh ts'ai chi

Extracts from the poets of the Ming dynasty (see D 226), edited with notes by 沈德潛 Shên Tê-ch'ien and another. 1739. 27cm.

D 301—308. 國 朝 正 雅 集
Kuo ch'ao chêng ya chi

The poetry of the present dynasty, comprising specimens from about 2000 poets, with biographical notices and exegetical notes by 符葆森 Fu Pao-sên (T. 南樵). 1857. 20cm.

D 309—312. 國 朝 詩 別 裁 集
Kuo ch'ao shih pieh ts'ai chi

Extracts from the poets of the present dynasty, with notes by 沈德潛 Shên Tê-ch'ien. 1759. 24.5cm.

E. *Dictionaries, Works of Reference, etc.*

E 1—7. 讀 禮 通 考
Tu li t'ung k'ao

A critical examination of the Book of Rites, by 徐乾學 Hsü Ch'ien-hsüeh who published the first edition in 1670, edited by a son with preface from 朱彝尊 Chu I-tsun. 1696. 27cm.

E 8—28. 五 禮 通 考
Wu li t'ung k'ao

A critical examination of the ceremonial observances in connection with (1) Worship and thanksgiving, (2) Marriage and festive occasions, (3) State Hospitality, (4) War, and (5) Death and mourning, by 金 匱秦 Chin Kuei-ch'in. 1751. 27cm.

E 29—30. 音 學 全 書
Yin hsüeh ch'üan shu

A comprehensive work on the sounds and rhymes, compiled from various sources by 王贈芳 Wang Tsêng-fang (T. 霞九). 1827. 27cm.

E 31—32. 同 音 字 鑑
T'ung yin tzŭ chien

A phonetic dictionary of the Chinese language, homophonous characters being grouped together under the headings of the 千字文 Ch'ien tzŭ wên Thousand Character Essay, by 朱紫 Chu Tzŭ (T. 天凝). 1811. 26cm.

E 33. 明 堂 大 道
Ming t'ang ta tao

An account of the ancestral temple of the Imperial family, by 惠棟學 Hui Tung-hsüeh. *No date.* 28cm.

E 34—36. 通 雅
T'ung ya

Notes on a variety of subjects, chiefly classical and archæological, without any specific classification, by 方以智 Fang I-chih (T. 密之) who completed the work in 1639 and dated his introduction 1643. 1666. 28cm.

E 37—52. 分 類 字 錦
Fên lei tzŭ chin

A thesaurus of phraseology, consisting of sets of two, three, and four characters, arranged under categories, issued under Imperial instructions by 張廷玉 Chang T'ing-yü and others, with preface from the Emperor K'ang Hsi. 1722.   27cm.

E 53—62.   野 獲 編
                    Yeh huo pien

A collection of essays and notes upon points connected with the Court and the administration, classified under various headings, by 沈德符 Shên Tê-fu (T. 景倩) whose preface is dated 1606, edited by 錢枋 Ch'ien Fang in 1700. 1827.   26.5cm.

E 63—66.   日 知 錄 集 釋
                Jih chih lu chi shih

Notes and essays on a variety of subjects, some of which were issued to friends in 1670, by 顧絳 Ku Chiang, also known as 顧炎武 Ku Yen-wu, edited by 黃汝成 Huang Ju-ch'êng in 1695. 1834.   26cm.

E 67—71.   授 時 通 考
                Shou shih t'ung k'ao

An encyclopædia of agriculture, issued under Imperial instructions by 陳弘謀 Ch'ên Hung-mou, 鄂爾泰 O-êrh-t'ai, and others, with preface from the Emperor Ch'ien Lung dated 1742. 1826.   26cm.

E 72.   歷 代 說 約
                  Li tai shuo yo

Notes on the Emperors of each dynasty from the "First Emperor," B.C. 259—210, to the establishment of the present dynasty in A.D. 1644, with special reference to the right of succession, by 劉曾璈 Liu Ts'êng-ao (T. 諧雲). 1832.   24 × 18cm.

E 73.   詔 求 直 言
                  Chao ch'iu chih yen

Reprint of Edicts and Memorials from the "Peking Gazette," 1850—1851. 1864.   25cm.

E 74—76. 音 學 五 書

~ *Yin hsüeh wu shu*

Five works on the Rhymes, namely, the 音論 *Yin lun*, the 詩本音 *Shih pên yin*, the 易音 *I yin*, the 唐音正 *T'ang yin chêng*, and the 古音表 *Ku yin piao*, by 顧絳 Ku Chiang, also known as 顧炎武 Ku Yen-wu. 1643.   30cm.

E 77. 釋 名 疏 證

Shih ming su chêng

A dictionary of terms, with explanations, by 劉珍 Liu Chên, also known as 劉熙 Liu Hsi, who died A.D. 126, edited with notes and original preface by 畢沅 Pi Yüan. 1789.   28cm.

E 78. 古 今 韻 略

Ku chin yün lüeh

A dictionary, arranged under the Rhymes, by 邵長蘅 Shao Ch'ang-hêng, edited by 宋犖 Sung Lao. [Section I missing.] *No date*.   28.5cm.

E 79. 花 鏡

Hua ching

A work on the cultivation of flowers, with a supplement on the rearing of birds, animals, fishes, and insects, by 陳淏子 Ch'ên Hao-tzǔ (T. 扶搖). 1783.   18cm.

E 80. 山 海 經

Shan hai ching

A geographical work assigned to the 10th or 11th cent. B.C. — its antiquity however is a disputed point — first issued by 郭璞 Kuo P'o early in the 4th cent. A.D., edited by 畢沅 Pi Yüan. 1783.

29cm.

E 81. 呂 氏 四 禮 翼

Lü shih ssŭ li i

A work upon the moral and social duties of men and women, with special reference to the importance of early training, by 呂坤 Lü K'un who died in 1618, edited by 朱軾 Chu Shih. 1699. 26cm.

E 82. 三 輔 黃 圖

San fu huang t'u

An account of the various palaces, halls, gateways, belvederes, lakes, and gardens, in the capitals of the empire since the 3rd cent. B. C., edited by 畢沅 Pi Yüan. 1784. 29cm.

E 83. 龔 文 恭 公 摺 稿

Kung wên kung kung chê kao

The Memorials of 龔守正 Kung Shou-chêng between the years A.D. 1818—1851. *No date.* 19cm.

E 84. 張 子 全 書

Chang tzŭ ch'üan shu

The complete works of 張載 Chang Tsai, A.D. 1020—1076, with commentary on the 西銘 *Hsi ming* and 正蒙 *Chêng mêng* by 朱熙 Chu Hsi, edited by 朱軾 Chu Shih. 1719. 27cm.

E 85. 經 韻 集 字 析 解

Ching yün chi tzŭ hsi chieh

A dictionary of the Classics, arranged under the Radicals, giving the rhyme, spelling, and meanings of each character, by 熊守謙 Hsiung Shou-ch'ien and 彭艮敞 P'êng Liang-ch'ang. [析 for 析 on label.] 1822. 29cm.

E 86.　　東 藩 輯 畧
Tung fan chi lüeh

Notes on Korean affairs, by 嚴從簡 Yen Ts'ung-chien. [In manuscript.] *No date.*　　26.5cm.

E 87.　　初 學 粵 音 切 要
Ch'u hsüeh yüeh yin ch'ieh yao

A Phonetic Vocabulary, in the Canton dialect, printed at the London Missionary Society's Press, Hongkong. 1855.　　20cm.

E 88—93.　　古 今 律 歷 考
Ku chin lü li k'ao

A work upon mathematics, astronomy, and music, based upon classical and historical authorities, by 邢雲路 Hsing Yün-lu (T. 士登), edited by 魏文魁 Wei Wên-k'uei. 1600.　　27cm.

E 94—95.　　十 三 經 集 字 摹 本
Shih san ching chi tzŭ mu pên

The characters in the Thirteen Classics, with their forms in the script known as the Lesser Seal, arranged in the order in which they occur, beginning with the 大學 *Ta hsüeh* Great Learning, no character appearing twice, with Index, by 彭玉雯 P'êng Yü-wên, edited by 張小浦 Chang Hsiao-p'u. 1849.　　26cm.

E 96—97.

Another copy.　　27.5cm.

E 98—99.

Another copy. [Title-page missing.]　　25cm.

E 100—122.　　十 三 經
Shih san ching

A uniform edition of the Thirteen Classics, with commentaries by the recognised authorities in each case. *No date.*　　16cm.

E 123. 韻 字 鑑

Yün tzŭ chien

A dictionary of the Rhymes, arranged according to the Radicals, by 歲徧齋主人 *Sui pien chai chu jen* (a pen name), whose preface to first edition is dated 1842. 1846. 12 × 10cm.

E 124. 正 音 彙 編

Chêng yin hui pien

Exercises in colloquial Mandarin, for the use of southerners, edited by 張玉成 Chang Yü-ch'êng and first published in 1785. 1820. 17cm.

E 125. 李 氏 音 鑑

Li shih yin chien

A work on the Rhymes, Tones, and spelling system of the Chinese language, by 李汝珍 Li Ju-chên (T. 松石), edited by 余秋室 Yü Ch'iu-shih. 1810. 17 × 13cm.

E 126. 讀 書 作 文 譜

Tu shu tso wên p'u

On the proper methods of study and the art of composition, by 唐彪 T'ang Piao (T. 翼), edited by 毛奇齡 Mao Ch'i-ling, 韓菼 Han T'an, and another, the preface of the first being dated 1709. 1816. 16cm.

E 127—142. 經 籍 籑 詁

Ching chi chuan ku

A dictionary of characters found in classical writings, arranged according to the rhymes, by 阮元 Yüan Yüan. 1812. 17.5cm.

E 143—168. 四 庫 全 書 總 目 提 要

Ssŭ k'u ch'üan shu tsung mu t'i yao

A descriptive catalogue of the Imperial Library at Peking, compiled

　　　　THE WADE LIBRARY

under instructions from the Emperor Ch'ien Lung, dated 1772, by an Imperial commission and finished in 1782, edited by 阮元 Yüan Yüan. 1795. 　　　　　　　　　　　　　　　19cm.

E 169—171.　四庫全書簡明目錄
Ssǔ k'u ch'üan shu chien ming mu lu

An abridgement of the above, issued under Imperial instructions dated 1774. *No date.* 　　　　　　　　　　19cm.

E 172.　鍾 鼎 彝 器 欵 識
Chung ting i ch'i k'uan shih

Inscriptions of various styles on ancient bells, tripods, and sacrificial vessels, by 薛尚功 Hsieh Shang-kung, edited by 阮元 Yüan Yüan whose preface is dated 1797. [*Chih* for *shih* on label.] 1882. 19cm.

E 173.　留 苑 盦 尺 牘
Liu yüan an ch'ih tu

The letters of 嚴籟 Yen Lu (T. 士竹). 1856. 　　17cm.

E 174.　留 青 新 集
Liu ch'ing hsin chi

A collection of essays and miscellaneous writings by various authors, compiled by 陳枚 Ch'ên Mei (T. 簡侯). 1708. 　19cm.

E 175.　聖 諭 廣 訓
Shêng yü kuang hsün

The Sacred Edict of the Emperor K'ang Hsi, with the Amplification by Yung Chêng and the Paraphrase. See A 354. 1818. 　17cm.

E 179.　撫 朔 尺 牘
Fu so ch'ih tu

Odd volume of letters on the pacification of Kansuh. [In manuscript; anonymous.] *No date.* 　　　　　　　　23.5cm.

E 180.   蠶 桑 輯 要
                     Ts'an sang chi yao

On the management of silkworms and mulberry-trees, with numerous
illustrations, by 沈秉成 Shên Ping-ch'êng. 1871.   25cm.

E 181.   國 語
                     Kuo yü

Historical notes on the period of the Feudal States, by 左邱明
Tso-ch'iu Ming, with the commentary of 韋昭 Wei Chao and
pronunciation by 宋庠 Sung Hsiang who died in A.D. 1064, edited
by 張一鯤 Chang I-k'un. 1806.   25cm.

E 182.

Another copy. [Title-page missing.]   24.5cm.

E 183—189.   子 史 精 華
                     Tzŭ shih ching hua

An encyclopædia of quotations from historical and philosophical
literature, arranged under categories, compiled under instructions from
the Emperor K'ang Hsi by a commission of scholars, including
張廷玉 Chang T'ing-yü, and published in the following reign.
[吏 for 史 on all the labels.] 1727.   25cm.

E 190—191.   彙 刻 書 目
                     Hui k'o shu mu

An index to standard works in Chinese literature, with authors'
names, numbers of chapters or sections, etc. etc., by 顧修 Ku Hsiu
(T. 荼厓), whose preface is dated 1799. 1870.   22cm.

E 192.   狀 元 圖
                     Chuang yüan t'u

A complete list of the *Chuang yüan*, or Senior Classics, between
the years A.D. 1371—1876, with portraits and biographical notices

of all down to the year 1607, by 沈一貫 Shên I-kuan whose first edition was published in 1609, edited to date by 饒玉成 Jao Yü-ch'êng. [The examination is now held every third year; it was irregular under the Ming dynasty and in the early years of the present dynasty.] 1875. 20cm.

E 193—194. 續　茶　經
Hsü ch'a ching

A treatise on tea and its preparation, by 陸羽 Lu Yü who died A.D. 804, followed by a supplementary work on the same subject by 陸廷燦 Lu T'ing-ts'an (T. 慢亭). 1734. 24.5cm.

E 195—200. 格　致　鏡　原
Ko chih ching yüan

An encyclopædia of the arts, sciences, and handicrafts, in the form of quotations from the standard literature, arranged under categories by 陳元龍 Ch'ên Yüan-lung. 1735. 23.5cm.

E 201. 經　傳　釋　詞
Ching chuan shih tz'ŭ

Explanations of characters in the Confucian Canon, by 王引之 Wang Yin-chih whose preface is dated 1798, edited by 阮元 Yüan Yüan. 1819. 26cm.

E 202. 經　字　異　同
Ching tzŭ i t'ung

The variants in the Confucian Canon, arranged according to their occurrence in the various books, by 張維屏 Chang Wei-p'ing. 1839. 25cm.

E 203. 通　俗　編
T'ung su pien

A thesaurus of phraseology, chiefly referring to manners and customs, superstitions, natural phenomena, etc., arranged under categories, by 翟灝 Chai Hao. 1751.   23.5cm.

E 204—206.   羣 經 字 詁
Ch'ün ching tzǔ ku

A dictionary of the words in the Confucian Canon, not including the Four Books, with exegetical notes from all the best authorities, compiled by 段諤廷 Tuan O-t'ing and edited by 黃本驥 Huang Pên-chi. 1849.   24cm.

E 207.   經 句 說
Ching chü shuo

Essays on sentences drawn from the Confucian Canon, by 吳英 Wu Ying (T. 伯和). [Page 2 of Preface missing.] *No date.*   25cm.

E 208—211.   說 文 解 字 注
Shuo wên chieh tzǔ chu

A dictionary of the Chinese language as it appeared at the close of the 1st century A.D., comprising 10,600 characters in the Lesser Seal script, with meanings and etymological notes, by 許愼 Hsü Shên who died about A.D. 120, edited with commentary by 段玉裁 Tuan Yü-ts'ai. 1808.   29cm.

E 212.   六 書 準
Liu shu chun

Illustrations of the Six Scripts or classes into which the Chinese written characters have been divided, arranged under the Tones, by 馮鼎調 Fêng Ting-tiao whose preface is dated 1660, posthumously edited by his son. *No date.*   28.5cm.

E 213—214.   說 文 解 字 通 釋
Shuo wên chieh tzǔ t'ung shih

The dictionary of Hsü Shên (see E 208), edited with explanations by 徐鍇 Hsü Ch'ieh and spelling by 朱翱 Chu Ao, followed by a reprint of the 繫傳 *Hsi chuan*, a work on the same lines by an unknown author, whose explanations have special reference to the Confucian Canon.　1839.　　　　　　　　　　　　27.5cm.

E 215—217.　　　同　文　備　考
　　　　　　　T'ung wên pei k'ao

A dictionary of the script known as the Lesser Seal, based upon the work of Hsü Shên (see E 208), with additions and notes by 王應雷 Wang Ying-lei whose prefatory remarks are dated 1539 and 1557. *No date.*　　　　　　　　　　　　28.5cm.

E 218—219.　　　經　典　釋　文
　　　　　　　Ching tien shih wên

The phraseology of the Confucian Canon and Taoist Classics explained, with pronunciation, by 陸元郎 Lu Yüan-lang (T. 德明), A.D. 550—625, edited by 陸文弨 Lu Wên-ch'ao from the edition of the Sung dynasty.　1791.　　　　　　　　　26cm.

E 220.　　　小　學　韻　語
　　　　　　　Hsiao hsüeh yün yü

Moral and social lessons for the young, in rhymed lines of 4 characters, by 羅澤南 Lo Tsê-nan who was killed in the T'ai-p'ing rebellion, and whose preface is dated 1856.　1886.　　28.5cm.

E 221.　　　五　經　文　字
　　　　　　　Wu ching wên tzŭ

A lexicographical work on the orthography and meaning of characters in the Five Classics, based upon the original stone tablets of 蔡邕 Ts'ai Yung, 2nd cent. A.D., arranged under 36 Radicals, by 張參 Chang Ts'an whose preface is dated A.D. 776, first published in 876, followed by a supplementary work embracing the Nine Classics, by 唐玄度 T'ang Hsüan-tu whose preface is dated 837. *No date.*　30cm.

E 222. 正 音 咀 華
Chêng yin chü hua

Lessons in colloquial Mandarin, for the use of Manchus and southerners, by 莎彝尊 So-i-tsun. 1853. 26.5cm.

E 223. 正 音 辨 微
Chêng yin pien wei

A vocabulary of words and phrases in colloquial Mandarin, for the use of Manchus and southerners, by 莎彝尊 So-i-tsun. 1837. 24cm.

E 224. 經 書 字 音 辨 要
Ching shu tzŭ yin pien yao

A work on the orthography and sounds of the characters in the Confucian Canon, by 楊名颺 Yang Ming-yang whose preface is dated 1830, edited by 崇綸 Ch'ung Lun. 1847. 30cm.

E 225—237. 康 熙 字 典
K'ang hsi tzŭ tien

The "Palace" edition, on white paper, of the Imperial Dictionary, containing over 40,000 characters, issued under the instructions and the personal superintendence of the Emperor K'ang Hsi by a commission of scholars, including 張玉書 Chang Yü-shu, 陳廷敬 Ch'ên T'ing-ching, 蔣廷錫 Chiang T'ing-hsi, and others, with preface from his Majesty. 1716. 26cm.

E 238—243. 執 文 通 覽
I wên t'ung lan

A dictionary of the script known as the Lesser Seal, with the various forms in which each character has appeared, arranged under the modern script, according to the Radicals, and commentary by 沙木 Sha Mu whose preface is dated 1787. 1806. 27.5cm.

E 244. 事 物 紀 原
Shih wu chi yüan

Notes on 1841 different subjects of literary, archæological, and popular interest, with special reference to origin of manners, customs, superstitions, etc., by 閻 敬 Yen Ching whose preface is dated A.D. 1448. *No date.* 26.5cm.

E 245. 事 類 賦
Shih lei fu

An encyclopædia dealing with natural phenomena, mineralogy, botany, natural history, etc., arranged under categories and written in the poetical-prose style, by 吳 淑 Wu Shu who died A.D. 1002, with preface to the edition of 1146 upon which this issue is based, edited by 華 麟 祥 Hua Lin-hsiang. 1532. 26.5cm.

E 246—247. 廣 事 類 賦
Kuang shih lei fu

An enlarged edition of the above, by 華 希 閔 Hua Hsi-min (T. 豫 原). 1699. 26.5cm.

E 248—249. 困 學 紀 聞
K'un hsüeh chi wên

Notes on classical and poetical literature, natural philosophy, etc. etc., by 王 應 麟 Wang Ying-lin who died A.D. 1296, edited by 閻 潛 邱 Yen Ch'ien-ch'iu and others. 1813. 26cm.

E 250—251.

Another edition, by 翁 元 圻 Wêng Yüan-ch'i (T. 鳳 西). 1851. 20cm.

E 252—254. 禮 書
Li shu

An account of the ceremonial usages of ancient times, including music, archery, official robes and paraphernalia, etc. etc., with numerous illustrations, by 陳祥道 Ch'ên Hsiang-tao of the Sung dynasty, A.D. 960—1260. 1804. 21cm.

E 255—257. 韻 府 萃 音
Yün fu ts'ui yin

A concise dictionary, arranged under the Rhymes and giving the sounds and principal meanings, with leading characters printed in red, by 龍伯 Lung Po (H. 青霏子). 1810. 21.5cm.

E 258. 奎 章 全 音
K'uei chang ch'üan yin

An officially-authorised dictionary of the Rhymes, containing 13,345 characters in all, issued by the Grand Secretariat. *No date.* 22.5cm.

E 259. 韻 綜 集 字
Yün tsung chi tzŭ

A vocabulary of words arranged under their Rhymes according to the Radicals, by 陳詒厚 Ch'ên I-hou. [Label inaccurate.] *No date.* 24cm.

E 260. 佩 文 詩 韻
P'ei wên shih yün

A handbook of about 10,000 characters arranged in rhyming groups under 106 finals, with sounds and meanings. *No date.* 19.5cm.

E 261—262. 蘇 氏 韻 輯
Su shih yün chi

A vocabulary of words arranged under the Rhymes and Tones, based upon the work of 沈約 Shên Yo, A.D. 441—513, and of 夏竦 Hsia Sung, A.D. 985—1051, edited by 蘇茂相 Su Mao-hsiang of the Ming dynasty. [*Yüan* for *yün* on label.] *No date.* 26 × 20.5cm.

E 263.

Another edition of E 85. [折 for 析 on label.]   1833.   26cm.

E 264.   字　類　標　韻
Tzŭ lei piao yün

A guide to the Rhymes, arranged under the Radicals, by 華綱 Hua Kang (T. 維寧) whose preface is dated 1756. See E 310. 1804.   22cm.

E 265—304.   佩　文　韻　府
P'ei wên yün fu

A concordance of all phrases in classical, historical, poetical, and philosophical literature, arranged under the Rhymes in groups of 2, 3, and 4 characters to each, issued under instructions from the Emperor K'ang Hsi by a commission of scholars including 張玉書 Chang Yü-shu, 陳廷敬 Ch'ên T'ing-ching, 李光地 Li Kuang-ti and others, with a preface from his Majesty.   1711.   23cm.

E 305—308.

Supplement to the above, by 張廷玉 Chang T'ing-yü and others. 1720.   25cm.

E 309.

Another copy of E 84, on inferior paper.   26.5cm.

E 310.

A reprint of E 264, edited by 王乃棠 Wang Nai-t'ang.   1875.
26cm.

E 311.

A reprint of E 245.   1816.   19cm.

E 312—313.

A reprint of E 246—247.   1816.   19cm.

E 314—315.

A supplement to the above, chiefly topographical. [Vol. I missing.]
No date. 19cm.

E 316—317. 幼 學 求 源

Yu hsüeh ch'iu yüan

An edition, under another name, of A 358 (see also B 36). 1847.
16.5cm.

E 318—320. 六 書 分 類

Liu shu fên lei

A dictionary of the various scripts or styles of writing, arranged
under the Radicals, by 傅賓石 Fu Pin-shih. 1705. 26cm.

E 321—324. 六 書 故

Liu shu ku

An examination into the origin and development of the art of
writing, in the form of a dictionary, the characters being grouped
under categories, by 戴侗 Tai T'ung of the 13th cent. A.D., with
preface to (?) first edition dated 1320, edited by 李鼎元 Li Ting-
yüan. 1784. 27cm.

E 325—360. 駢 字 類 編

P'ien tzŭ lei pien

A concordance to two-character phrases in classical, historical,
poetical, and philosophical literature, arranged under categories,
compiled by Imperial command by 張廷玉 Chang T'ing-yü, 蔣
廷錫 Chiang T'ing-hsi, and others, with preface from the Emperor
Yung Chêng. 1726. 25cm.

E 361.　　字　學　七　種

Tzŭ hsüeh ch'i tsung

On the orthography of the written characters, as specially required at the public examinations, by 李秘園 Li Pi-yüan, edited by 張拜泰 Chang Pang-t'ai. 1833.　　　　26cm.

E 362.　　　字　鑑

Tzŭ chien

Reprint of a work on orthography, with the characters arranged under the Rhymes, by 李文仲 Li Wên-chung, about A.D. 1322, with preface by 朱彝尊 Chu I-tsun, dated 1709. *No date.* 26.5cm.

E 363—364.　　題　解　韻　編

T'i chieh yün pien

Lines from well-known poets, arranged under the Rhymes according to the last character in each line, with explanatory notes, by 陳維屏 Ch'ên Wei-p'ing, edited by 王茂松 Wang Mou-sung. 1837.

23cm.

E 365.　　　廣　韻

Kuang yün

A dictionary arranged under the Rhymes, based upon the edition of A.D. 1008, edited by 朱彝尊 Chu I-tsun; original author unknown. 1704.　　　27cm.

E 366.　　　玉　篇

Yü p'ien

A dictionary based upon the 說文 Shuo Wên (see E 208) and arranged under 542 Radicals, by 顧野王 Ku Yeh-wang, A.D. 519—581, edited by 朱彝尊 Chu I-tsun. 1778.　　27cm.

E 367—368. 隸 辨
Li pien

A dictionary of the various forms of the *li* script, which was in use about A.D. 200—400, arranged under the Rhymes, by 顧藹吉 Ku Ai-chi whose preface is dated 1718, edited by 黃晟 Huang Shêng. 1743. 26.5cm.

E 369—370. 韻 府 羣 玉
Yün fu ch'ün yü

A dictionary of phraseology, arranged under the Rhymes, by 陰時夫 Yin Shih-fu (T. 勁弦) of the 13th and 14th cent. A.D. (his own preface is undated, but a contemporary preface bears date 1307), reprinted from the edition of 1590 issued by 王元貞 Wang Yüan-chêng (T. 孟起). *No date.* 27cm.

E 371—374. 通 藝 錄
T'ung i lu

A collection of essays on education, literature, philosophy, art, etc. etc., with illustrations, by 程瑤田 Ch'êng Yao-t'ien. 1803. 28.5cm.

E 375—418. 淵 鑑 類 函
Yüan chien lei han

An encyclopædia of general information from the earliest ages down to the establishment of the present dynasty, arranged under categories, issued by an Imperial commission of scholars, including 張英 Chang Ying, 王士禎 Wang Shih-chêng, and others, with a preface from the Emperor K'ang Hsi. 1710. 23cm.

E 419. 河 洛 精 蘊
Ho lo ching yün

A work on "the Plan of the Yellow River and the Writing of the River Lo" or the system of philosophy based upon the combinations

of the Eight Diagrams, by 江永 Chiang Yung who died in 1762.
[Title-page dated 1774.]   1785.   27.5cm.

E 420.

Another copy of A 360.   27cm.

E 421.   吳 郡 名 賢 圖
Wu chün ming hsien t'u

Portraits of eminent natives of the Prefecture of Soochow in Kiangsu,
with biographical notices, by 顧沅 Ku Yüan (T. 湘舟).   1829.
26.5cm.

E 422—424.   字 彙
Tzŭ hui

The first dictionary in which the Radicals were reduced to 214 in
number, by 梅膺祚 Mei Ying-tsu (T. 誕生) who flourished in
the 16th cent., edited by 韓荼 Han T'an.   1682.   25cm.

E 425—426.

Another edition of the above, edited by 錢𡵉 Ch'ien Chia.
1754.   27cm.

E 427—436.   五 車 韻 瑞
Wu chü yün jui

A dictionary of phraseology arranged under the Rhymes, by 凌
稚隆 Ling Chih-lung (T. 以棟).   1592.   27cm.

E 437—456.   四 庫 全 書 考 證
Ssŭ k'u ch'üan shu k'ao chêng

Corrections and verifications in the catalogue of the Imperial Library,
see E 143. [Title-page and Preface missing.] *No date.*   26.5cm.

E 457—460.   羣 芳 譜
Ch'ün fang p'u

A thesaurus of information on flower, fruit, and vegetable gardening, with details on the preparation of drugs and on the rearing of birds and fishes, by 王象晉 Wang Hsiang-chin (T. 藎臣) of the 17th cent. A.D. *No date.* 26cm.

E 461—467. 廣 羣 芳 譜
Kuang ch'ün fang p'u

A revised and enlarged edition of the above, issued under Imperial instructions by 劉灝 Liu Hao, with preface from the Emperor K'ang Hsi. 1708. 23.5cm.

E 468—480.

Another copy, on inferior paper, of E 225—237. 29cm.

E 481. 康 熙 字 典 撮 要
K'ang hsi tzŭ tien ts'o yao

The Concise Dictionary of Chinese, by Rev. J. Chalmers, LL. D., being a re-arrangement of the Imperial Dictionary under 884 Phonetics, with the illustrative quotations omitted. 1878. 29.5cm.

F. *Miscellaneous.*

F 1—16. 科 塲 條 例
K'o ch'ang t'iao li

Rules and Regulations for the public examinations, issued under Imperial instructions by 耆英 Kiying and others. 1834. 26cm.

F 17—26. 古 文 評 註
Ku wên p'ing chu

A collection of elegant extracts from authors of all ages, including the present dynasty, compiled and annotated by 過珙 Kuo Kung,

whose preface is dated 1703, and another, and edited by **曾潢**
Tsêng Huang and another.　1880.　　　　　　　　22cm.

F 27—34.　　　　　**儒　林　外　史**
　　　　　　　　　　　　Ju lin wai shih

A novel dealing with the history of the middle of the 14th cent.
A. D., by **閑齋老人** *Hsien chai lao jen* (a pen name) whose
preface is dated 1736.　1874.　　　　　　　　21cm.

F 35—71.

Thirty-four printed pamphlets of various sizes, issued by the T'ai-
p'ing Rebels between 1850 and 1864, including adaptations of the well-
known school primers **三字經** *San tzŭ ching* and **千字文** *Ch'ien
tzŭ wên*, national hymns, prayers, etc. etc. [3 duplicates.]

F 72—79.

Odd documents in manuscript referring to the T'ai-p'ing Rebellion.

F 80—88.

Copies of dispatches received from the Chinese authorities between
1841—1850. [In manuscript.]

F 89—119.

Copies of Memorials from the Six Boards to the Throne in the
17th and 18th centuries. [In manuscript.]

F 120—123.　　　　　**七　克**
　　　　　　　　　　　　Ch'i k'o

The Seven Capital Sins, by **龐迪我** P'ang Ti-wo (Didacus Pantoja)
whose preface is dated 1614, although 1643 is given on back of title-
page, edited by Bishop **湯亞立** T'ang Ya-li (?).　1798.　　27cm.

F 124—125. 登 壇 必 究
Têng t'an pi chiu

An encyclopædia devoted to military matters, including tactics, commissariat, munition of war, etc. etc., by 王鳴鶴 Wang Ming-hao. [12 vols in 2 cloth cases, containing only § 1—17 out of § 40 in all.] 1599. 26cm.

F 126—129. 七 巧 新 譜
Ch'i ch'iao hsin p'u

Four odd vols of the Chinese geometrical puzzle or tangram, forming two complete sets, dated (1) 1823, (2) no date, (3) 1826, and (4) 1815.
17cm.

F 130—133. 草 廬 經 畧
Ts'ao lu ching lüeh

Outlines of the art of war, by an anonymous writer of the Ming dynasty, the first two characters referring to the great general Chu-ko Liang, A.D. 181—234, edited by 伍崇曜 Wu Ch'ung-yao. 1850.
20cm.

F 134—138. 舌 擊 編
Shê chi pien

The official letters of 沈儲 Shên Ch'u, 1853—1854, at the outbreak of the T'ai-p'ing Rebellion. 1859. 22cm.

F 139. 輕 世 金 書
Ch'ing shih chin shu

A translation of the Imitation of Christ, by 楊瑪諾 Yang Ma-no (Emmanuel Diaz), published in 1640, edited by Bishop 湯亞立 T'ang Ya-li (?). 1800. 23.5cm.

F 140. 新 約 全 書
Hsin yo ch'üan shu

Translation of the Four Gospels and The Acts, printed at Shanghai. 1852. 13.5 × 10 cm.

F 141—142. 有 正 味 齋 尺 牘
Yu chêng wei chai ch'ih tu

A collection of letters, by 吳錫麒 Wu Hsi-ch'i. 1875. 17cm.

F 143. 太 上 感 應 篇
T'ai shang kan ying p'ien

A Taoist tract on the retribution which follows evil deeds, usually assigned to the 11th cent. A.D., author unknown, printed in red and edited together with a collection of medical recipes for family use by 梁玉成 Liang Yü-ch'êng. 1829. 17.5cm.

F 144. 萬 字 典
Wan tzŭ tien

A vocabulary of Chinese characters arranged under the usual Radicals, with a sub-arrangement under the Radicals of the remaining phonetic portions, together with sounds and leading meanings, by 布列地 Poletti (P.). *No date.* 19.5cm.

F 145. 初 學 識 字
Ch'u hsüeh shih tzŭ

A student's guide to orthography, giving the standard forms of doubtful characters as accepted at the public examinations, etc. etc., by 潘隆 P'an Lung. 1894. 16 × 13cm.

F 146. 三 字 經 註 釋
San tzŭ ching chu shih

A Christian tract, arranged in the form of the well-known Trimetrical Classic or Child's Guide to Knowledge. 1847. 17.5cm.

F 147. 營 卷
Ying chüan

A method of gambling upon the results of the public examinations, arranged upon the 千字文 *Ch'ien tzŭ wên* or Thousand-Character Essay. 1874. 17cm.

F 148.

比 卷
Pi chüan

A similar work from another establishment. *No date.* 17cm.

F 149.

天 文 地 理
T'ien wên ti li

Notes on astronomy and physical geography, followed by Christian evidences drawn from nature, translated extracts from the Bible, etc. etc., by 慕維廉 Mu Wei-lien. 1893. 20cm.

F 150.

種 痘 奇 書
Chung tou ch'i shu

A treatise on vaccination, originally printed at Canton in 1805 and lithographed in London. 1828. 22cm.

F 151.

復 傳 律 例 書
Fu ch'uan lü li shu

The Book of Deuteronomy, being Section V of a translation of the Bible, printed at Ningpo. 1846. 25cm.

F 152.

致 富 新 書
Chih fu hsin shu

A tract on Political Economy from a Christian standpoint, by 鮑留雲 Pao Liu-yün. 1827. 24.5cm.

F 153.

回 回 原 來
Hui hui yüan lai

The Mahomedans in China, being an account of the alleged introduction of Mahomedanism in consequence of a dream by the Emperor T'ai Tsung of the T'ang dynasty in A.D. 628. 1754. 26cm.

F 154.

耶 穌 聖 教 洗 禮 規 式
Yeh su shêng chiao hsi li kuei shih

Rules for the Baptism of Adults, printed at Hongkong. 1851. 25cm.

F 155.   論　復　新　之　理
Lun fu hsin chih li

The doctrine of Regeneration by Baptism, anonymous. *No date*. 26cm.

F 156.   三　寶　仁　會　論
San pao jen hui lun

An account of the London Missionary, the Religious Tract, and British and Foreign Bible Societies, by 博愛者 (?) a Philanthropist. 1819.   20cm.

F 157.   金　陸　述　累
Chin ling shu lüeh

A manifesto on the approach of the T'ai-p'ing rebels to Nanking, anonymous. 1853.   25cm.

F 158.   英　文　舉　隅
Ying wên chü yü

English for beginners, by 汪芝房 Wang Chih-fang, with a preface from the Marquis Tsêng. 1879.   25cm.

F 159.   勸　讀　聖　錄
Ch'üan tu shêng lu

A Protestant tract, advising earnest study of the Scriptures. *No date*.   24cm.

F 160 and 160a.   粵　東　同　官　錄
Yüeh tung t'ung kuan lu

Names, parentage, ages, etc., of the officials in the province of Kuangtung. [160a is undated. As it contains the name of "Governor Yeh," it must have appeared between 1848 and 1857.] 1842.   28cm.

F 161.   耶　穌　道　理　總　論
Yeh su tao li tsung lun

Christian Tracts, N°. 3, — that there is only One God; printed at Malacca, anonymous. 1841.   25cm.

F 162. 捐 輸 選 補 條 例

Chüan shu hsüan pu t'iao li

Regulations for the sale of official rank and selection for employment. 1843. 24.5cm.

F 163. 聖 會 禱 詞

Shêng hui tao tz'ü

The Book of Common Prayer, with the stamp of St. Paul's College, Hongkong, on the cover. *No date.* 26.5cm.

F 164. 出 麥 西 傳 註 釋

Ch'u mai hsi chuan chu shih

Exodus, with notes, translated by 爲仁者 Wei Jen Chê (W. Dean). 1851. 26cm.

F 164a. 四 書 補 註 附 考 備 旨

Ssü shu pu chu fu k'ao pei chih

Vol. I only of this work, containing the Great Learning and the Doctrine of the Mean, by 登林 Têng Lin of the Ming dynasty. [Book-plate at end.] 1740. 27cm.

F 165. 皇 帝 登 極 恩 詔

Huang ti têng chi ên chao

Act of Grace by the Emperor Kuang Hsü upon his accession to the throne. 1875. 40cm.

X and Y. *Miscellaneous.*

X 1—120. 通 志 堂

T'ung chih t'ang

A collection of the most famous commentaries on the Confucian Canon, edited by 徐乾學 Hsü Ch'ien-hsüeh (see Y 1—102.) 1675. 25cm.

G. W. 9

X 121.　　數　書　九　章
Shu shu chiu chang

A work on mathematics, originally written and published by 秦 九韶 Ch'in Chiu-shao in 1247, and noticeable as containing the first treatise on 天元 the Chinese system of algebra. An edition was published in 1616 by a Buddhist priest, called 清常 Ch'ing Ch'ang.　1842.　　　　　　　　　　　　24cm.

X 122.　　數　書　九　章　札　記
Shu shu chiu chang cha chi

A critical examination, by 宋景昌 Sung Ching-ch'ang, of the algebra of Ch'in Chiu-shao (see X 121).　1842.　　24cm.

X 123—125.　　竹　書　紀　年　集　證
Chu shu chi nien chi chêng

The Bamboo Annals, with Verifications, first published in 1813, by 陳逢衡 Ch'ên Fêng-hêng.　1842.　　　　　　24cm.

X 126—133.　　萬　姓　統　譜
Wan hsing t'ung p'u

A Biographical Dictionary, arranged under the Rhymes, by 凌 迪之 Ling Ti-chih.　1579.　　　　　　　　25cm.

X 134—136.　　知　新　錄
Chih hsin lu

A Miscellany of general information on a variety of subjects, by 王棠 Wang T'ang (T. 勿翦).　1717.　　　　　25cm.

X 137—138.　　日　纂　二　集
Jih tsuan êrh chi

Twenty philosophical essays, by 鄭瑄 Chêng Hsüan (T. 漢奉), popularly known as 昨非居士 the Hermit of Tso-fei. (?) 1755. 25cm.

Y 1—102. 皇 清 經 解
Huang ch'ing ching chieh

Explanations of the Confucian Canon by writers of the present or Manchu-Tartar dynasty, edited by 嚴杰 Yen Chieh, and intended to be a continuation of the *T'ung chih t'ang*, X 1—120. 1829. 25cm.

Z. Religion, Science, etc.

Z 1—5. 康 熙 字 典
K'ang hsi tzŭ tien

A 12mo edition of the Imperial Dictionary (see Z 23—29 and E 225—237) mounted on foreign paper, 2 sheets to each page. 1715.
36 × 24cm.

Z 6. 舊 約 全 書
Chiu yo ch'üan shu

The Old Testament in Chinese. Printed at the 墨 海 Mo-hai office, Shanghai. 1858. 20cm.

Z 7. 眞 道 入 門
Chên tao ju mên

Christian Manual and Sacred Chronology, by William Dean, Hongkong. 1849. 27 × 14cm.

Z 8. 內 科 新 說
Nei k'o hsin shuo

A new treatise on the medical art, by Benjamin Hobson, assisted by 管茂材 Kuan Mao-ts'ai, to which is added a medical vocabulary in English and Chinese, by the same author, who was a member of the London Missionary Society. 1858. 25cm.

THE WADE LIBRARY

Z 9. 脫 影 奇 觀

T'o ying ch'i kuan

A treatise on photography, with diagrams, based upon Dudgeon's 脫影源流 *T'o ying yüan liu*, and a preface by 崇厚 Ch'ung-hou. 1873. 27 × 16cm.

Z 10. 譚 (or 談) 天

T'an t'ien

Herschel's Outlines of Astronomy, printed at Shanghai, with a preface by A. Wylie. 1859. 30.5cm.

Z 10a.

Second edition of the above. 1874. 30.5cm.

Z 11. 西 醫 略 論

Hsi i lüeh lun

A treatise on the medical science of western nations, by Benjamin Hobson. 1857. 25cm.

Z 12. 萬 國 公 法

Wan kuo kung fa

A translation of Wheaton's International Law, by W. A. P. Martin, D.D. 1864. 29.5cm.

Z 12a.

Another copy.

Z 12b.

Another copy.

Z 12c.

Another copy.

Z 13—14. 化 學 指 南

Hua hsüeh chih nan

A work on chemistry, by 畢利幹 Billequin, of the Imperial College, Peking; with diagrams. 1873. 29.5cm.

Z 15. 重 學

Chung hsüeh

A translation of Whewell's Elementary Mechanics, by the Rev. J. Edkins and 李善蘭 Li Shan-lan; with diagrams and a preface by A. Wylie. 1867. 27 × 20cm.

Z 16. 格 物 入 門

Ko wu ju mên

Elements of Natural Philosophy and Chemistry, by W. A. P. Martin, D.D. 1868. 29cm.

Z 17.

Another copy.

Z 19. 舊 約 全 書

Chiu yo ch'üan shu

A translation of the Old Testament in colloquial. 1874. 28cm.

Z 20. 代 微 積 拾 級

Tai wei chi shih chi

A translation of Loomis' Analytical Geometry and Differential and Integral Calculus, with list of technical terms and preface by A. Wylie. [3 vols in cloth case.] 1859. 30cm.

Z 21. 代 數 學

Tai shu hsüeh

A translation of de Morgan's Algebra, with preface by A. Wylie. [2 vols in cloth case.] 1859. 23cm.

Z 22.

A compendium of the Book of Common Prayer, translated into Chinese by Dr. Morrison, 5th edition 1845 (1st edit. 1829); a Chinese and English Vocabulary, by Robert Thom, 1843; and The Chinese Speaker, by Robert Thom, 1846. [3 vols. in cloth case.]   25.5cm.

Z 23—29.   康 熙 字 典
K'ang hsi tzŭ tien

The Imperial Dictionary of the Emperor K'ang Hsi, arranged according to 214 Radicals (see E 225—237 and Z 1—5). 1715. 30cm.

Z 30.   歷 代 帝 王 年 表
Li tai ti wang nien piao

A Chronology, compiled and first published by 齊召南 Ch'i Chao-nan in 1777, with additions by 阮福 Yüan Fu. 1824. 26cm.

Z 31.   經 韻 集 字 析 解
Ching yün chi tzŭ hsi chieh

A dictionary of the rhymes in the Confucian Canon, with explanations by 熊守謙 Hsiung Shou-ch'ien. 1822.   29.5 × 17.5cm.

Z 32.   紀 元 編
Chi yüan pien

A chronological list of the Emperors of China from the beginning of the Han dynasty, B.C. 206, to the end of the Ming dynasty, A.D. 1644, with comparative tables of Annamite, Japanese, and other foreign chronologies, by 李兆洛 Li Chao-lo. 1831.   23cm.

Z 33—34.   詩 韻 合 璧
Shih yün ho pi

A work on the Rhymes, to aid in poetical composition, by 湯文潞 T'ang Wên-lu, first published in 1857. 1878.   21 × 11cm.

Z 35. 心 算 指 明

Hsin suan chih ming

A guide to Mental Arithmetic, by 何天爵 Ho T'ien-chio (Chester Holcombe). 1874. 18cm.

Z 36. 新 遺 詔 書

Hsin i chao shu

The New Testament, translated by the Rev. Dr. Morrison. [8 vols in cloth case.] 1813. 28 × 16cm.

Z 37.

A cheap edition of the above. [8 vols in cloth case.] 17 × 12cm.

Z 38. 新 約 全 書

Hsin yo ch'üan shu

Translation of the New Testament, issued from the Presbyterian Mission Press, Shanghai. 1864. 13.5cm.

Z 39. 新 約 全 書

Hsin yo ch'üan shu

The New Testament, translated into a simple style, by 楊格非 Yang Ko-fei (the Rev. G. John). 1886. 20cm.

Z 40. 新 約 全 書

Hsin yo ch'üan shu

Facsimile copy of the New Testament presented by the Missionary body to the Empress-Dowager of China on her 60th birthday. 1894. 31 × 24cm.

Z 41. 幾 何 原 本

Chi ho yüan pên

The Elements of Euclid, translated (Bks I—VI) into Chinese by

利瑪竇 Li Ma-tou (Matteo Ricci) and 徐光啓 Hsü Kuang-ch'i, the preface of the former being dated 1607, and (Bks VII—XV) by Alexander Wylie, whose preface is dated 1857, edited by 曾國藩 Tsêng Kuo-fan. 1865.   30cm.

MANCHU and MONGOL.

G. *Miscellaneous.*

G 1—21.

A translation of Chu Hsi's revision of the Mirror of History, see B 1029—1053. [Volumes 1 and 2 contain the 前編 *Ch'ien pien*, vols. 3—14 the 正編 *Chêng pien*, and vols. 15—21 the 續編 *Hsü pien*, the last seven being labelled accordingly.]   30cm.

G 22.

A translation of the Gospel of St. Matthew, with interlinear Chinese version.   30.5cm.

G 23.

A translation of the 異域錄 *I yü lu*, a work on the nations of Central Asia by 圖理琛 T'u Li-shên, with map.   30cm.

G 24.   史 部 成 語
Li pu ch'êng yü

Terms and phrases used in the Board of Civil Office, with interlinear Chinese version.   28cm.

G 25.   御 製 盛 京 賦
Yü chih shêng ching fu

A Eulogium, in the poetical-prose style, on the city of Moukden, by the Emperor Ch'ien Lung, with commentary by 鄂爾泰 O-êrh-t'ai, 張廷玉 Chang T'ing-yü, and other high officials. [Chinese and Manchu versions.] 25cm.

G 26—27.

Cheo Gurun I Fijungge Nomun, a translation of the 易經 Canon of Changes, with interlinear Chinese text. [Mounted.] 1765. 28cm.

G 28—29.

Another edition, Manchu text only. [MS. Chinese text to Preface.] 29cm.

G 30—33. 蒙 古 清 文 鑑
Mêng ku ch'ing wên chien

A Manchu-Mongol edition of G 118—153. 28.5cm.

G 34—37. 御 製 三 合 清 文 鑑
Yü chih san ho ch'ing wên chien

The above work in Manchu, Mongol, and Chinese, in parallel columns. 1780. 29cm.

G 38—39. 清 文 彙 書
Ch'ing wên hui shu

A Manchu-Chinese Dictionary, by 李延甚 Li Yen-chi. 27cm.

G 40—43.

Memorials and Decrees relating to the Eight Manchu Banners, A.D. 1723—1733. 24.5cm.

G 44—49.

The military organisation of the 八旗 *Pa-ch'i* Eight Manchu Banners. 25cm.

THE WADE LIBRARY

G 50—55.

Penalties for maladministration etc., exacted by the Board of Civil Office.   27cm.

G 56—64.

The organisation of the 綠營 *Lü ying* Chinese army, with supplementary volume.   25cm.

G 65—74.

Translation of the 五經 *Wu ching* Five Classics, with Chinese interlinear text.   25cm.

G 75.

Translation of the 四書 *Ssŭ shu* Four Books, with Chinese interlinear text.   27cm.

G 76—77.

The above work, with commentary.   27cm.

G 78.

A translation of the 朱子節要 *Chu tsŭ chieh yao*, being important essays selected from the writings of Chu Hsi, first published in 1602. 1675.   26cm.

G 79.

A translation of the 孝經 *Hsiao ching* or Classic of Filial Piety. 1728.   27cm.

G 80—81.

A translation of the 性理精義 *Hsing li ching i*, being a compendium of mental philosophy compiled by 李光地 Li Kuang-ti and others under instructions from the Emperor K'ang Hsi, and first issued in 1715.   28cm.

G 82.

A translation of the 聖諭廣訓 *Shêng yü kuang hsün* or Sacred Edict of the Emperor K'ang Hsi, with Amplification and Chinese interlinear text. See A 354. 29cm.

G 83. 遼 史 語 解
Liao shih yü chieh

A list of the Manchu and Mongol terms in the History of the Liao or Kitan Dynasty, A.D. 907—1125, with explanations. 28.5cm.

G 84.

Another copy, on white paper. 28cm.

G 85. 金 史 語 解
Chin shih yü chieh

A list of the Mongol terms in the History of the Chin or Nü-chên Dynasty, A.D. 1115—1234, arranged under categories, with explanations. 28cm.

G 85a. 元 史 語 解
Yüan shih yü chieh

A list of the Manchu and Mongol terms in the History of the Yüan Dynasty, A.D. 1260—1368, arranged under categories, with explanations. 28cm.

G 86—88.

A translation of the Four Books, with commentary and Chinese interlinear text; see G 162—167. [Imperfect.] 27cm.

G 89. 六 部 成 語
Liu pu ch'êng yü

Terms and phrases used in the Six Boards, with interlinear Chinese version. 1816. 24cm.

G 90—93. 增 訂 清 文 鑑
Ts'êng ting ch'ing wên chien

An edition of G 118—153, with supplement and Chinese interlinear translation. [Vol. 4, the binding of which is not uniform, contains Supplement.] 1771. 27cm.

G 94—98.

Another copy of the above. 28.5cm.

G 99.

Another copy of G 38—39. [Mounted.] 37.5 × 20.5cm.

G 100. 清 文 補 彙
Ch'ing wên pu hui

A supplement to the above. [Mounted.] 1786. 27.5 × 20.5cm.

G 101. 一 學 三 貫
I hsüeh san kuan

A text-book in Manchu and Chinese, arranged under categories, for the use of beginners. 1746. 29cm.

G 102—103.

Another copy of G 38—39. 27.5cm.

G 104—107.

Another copy of G 90—93. 1771. 29cm.

G 108—109.

Another copy of the above. 29cm.

G 110—111. 漢 滿 字 典
Han man tzŭ tien

An Index to all the Chinese words and phrases in the Imperial

Dictionary, arranged according to the 214 Radicals and forming with the Imperial Dictionary a complete Chinese-Manchu lexicon. [Manuscript.] 29.5cm.

G 112. 清 文 啓 蒙
Ch'ing wên ch'i mêng

A Manchu phrase-book for beginners, with interlinear Chinese version. [Mounted.] *No date.* 29 × 23.5cm.

G 113—114.

Section III of the above work, labelled "Manchu Particles," with manuscript index. [Mounted.] *No date.* 29 × 23.5cm.

G 115. 讀 史 論 畧
Tu shih lun lüeh

A translation of Desultory Notes on the study of History. 1730. 28cm.

G 116—117.

A collection of Imperial Homilies delivered by the Emperor Hung Wu of the Ming dynasty, who reigned A.D. 1368—1399. 34cm.

G 118—153. 滿 洲 清 文 鑑
Man chou ch'ing wên chien

An encyclopædia of general information, arranged under categories, published by order of the Emperor K'ang Hsi. 35cm.

G 154—157. 續纂外藩蒙古回部王公傳
Hsü tsuan wai fan mêng ku hui pu wang kung chuan

Biographical notices of the nobles of the Feudatory States and the Mongol tribes, in Chinese and Manchu, including B 13, 14. *No date.* 37cm.

G 158—161.

Translation of the 書經 *Shu ching* Canon of History; see G 65—74.
35cm.

G 162—167.

Translation of the 日講四書 *Jih chiang ssŭ shu* Four Books as edited for daily use by 陳廷敬 Ch'ên T'ing-ching and others in 1677. See G 75.   35cm.

G 168—173.

Another copy of the above.   35cm.

G 174—181.

Translation of the 三國志 *San kuo chih* History of the Three Kingdoms, A.D. 220—280, by 陳壽 Ch'ên Shou, with Chinese interlinear text. [The first seventy leaves have been supplied in manuscript.]   27cm.

G 182—184.   三 合 便 覽
San ho pien lan

A phrase-book in Manchu, Chinese, and Mongol, with the Mongol sounds written in Manchu, by 方顯 Fang Hsien, edited with additions by his son.   1780.   27cm.

G 185—190.

Translation of the 金瓶梅 *Chin p'ing mei*, see D 53—55, with Chinese interlinear text.   1708.   25cm.

G 191.

Translation of the 聖諭廣訓 *Shêng yü kuang hsün*, see G 82, with Chinese interlinear text.   27cm.

G 192—203.

Translation of the 古文淵鑑 *Ku wên yüan chien*, a collection of elegant extracts from various authors.   30.5cm.

G 204.

Top Be 'Huashabure Nirokan. 29.5cm.

G 205—207.

Translation of selected stories from the 聊齋志異 *Liao chai chih i*, see D 50—52, with interlinear Chinese version. 25cm.

G 208—210.

A manuscript copy of G 100. 24cm.

G 211.

A translation of the 西廂記 *Hsi hsiang chi*, a dramatic novel of the 14th century A.D., author unknown. 1710. 23cm.

G 212.

Another copy of the above. 22cm.

G 213—213*a***.** 清 文 啓 蒙
Ch'ing wên ch'i mêng

A guide to the study of the Manchu language, for beginners, by 舞格 Wu Ko. 1729. 25cm.

G 214.

A manuscript copy of G 38—39. 22cm.

G 215. 薛 文 清 公 要 語
Hsieh wên ch'ing kung yao yü

Translation of two homilies by 薛瑄 Hsieh Hsüan, who died in 1464, with Chinese interlinear text, edited by 谷中虛 Ku Chung-hsü. 1564. 27cm.

G 216.

Another copy of G 100. 26cm.

G 217.

Another edition of the above. [Imperfect.]　　　　25cm.

G 218.　　　戒　賭　十　則
　　　　　　　Chieh tu shih tsê

Ten objections to the vice of gambling, with Chinese interlinear
text. *No date.*　　　　　　　　　　　　　25.5cm.

G 219.

A guide to the study of Manchu, with interlinear notes. *No date.* 25cm.

G 220.　　　清　文　指　要
　　　　　　　Ch'ing wên chih yao

A reading-book with Chinese interlinear translation, followed by
supplement. [Title-page and preface missing; see G 245.]　　22cm.

G 221.　　　四　本　簡　要
　　　　　　　Ssŭ pên chien yao

A collection of forty homilies translated into Manchu with Chinese
interlinear text, with prefaces from 富明良 Fu-ming-liang and
富明安 Fu-ming-an, sons of the author, dated 1712 and 1746,
respectively.　　　　　　　　　　　　　　22.5cm.

G 222.

Manuscript copy of G 237.　　　　　　　23.5 × 13cm.

G 223.　　　吏　治　輯　要
　　　　　　　Li chih chi yao

Translation of a Guide to the duties of an official, with Chinese
interlinear text, by 通瑞 T'ung-jui and others. 1844.　　25cm.

G 224.　　三　合　吏　治　輯　要
　　　　　　　San ho li chih chi yao

The above work in Manchu, Mongol, and Chinese. 1857.　　26cm.

G 225—234.

Another copy of G 185—190.   1708.   24.5cm.

G 235.   滿 漢 註 文 成 語
Man han chu wên ch'êng yü

Selected phrases from the Canons of Changes, History, and Poetry.
[Imperfect.]   24cm.

G 236.

Another copy of G 100. [With MS. marginal corrections.] 1786. 24cm.

G 237.   滿 漢 成 語 對 待
Man han ch'êng yü tui tai

A Manchu-Chinese phrase-book for the use of students.   25cm.

G 238—244.   清 漢 文 海
Ch'ing han wên hai

A repertory of phrases in Manchu and Chinese, arranged under
the Rhymes, by 孫玉庭 Sun Yü-t'ing.   1821.   24cm.

G 245.

A complete copy of G 220.   1709.   23cm.

G 246.

Manuscript copy of the above. [No title-page.]   24cm.

G 247.   滿 漢 合 璧 三 字 經 註 解
Man han ho pi san tzŭ ching chu chieh

The Trimetrical Classic in Manchu and Chinese, with commentary.
1795.   24cm.

G. W.   10

G 248—249.   音 漢 清 文 鑑
Yin han ch'ing wên chien

Phraseology from the Manchu encyclopædia, G 118—153, with the Chinese translation in parallel columns, by 董佳 Tung Chia, whose preface is dated 1735.   1757.   23.5cm.

G 250—251.

A translation of the 小學 *Hsiao hsüeh* of Chu Hsi. [Imperfect.]
23cm.

G 252—253.

Manuscript copy of G 38—39. [Sections 1—4 missing.]   22.5cm

G 254—275.   大清仁宗督皇帝聖訓
Ta ch'ing jen tsung jui huang ti shêng hsün

Homilies by the Emperor Chia Ch'ing, A.D. 1796—1821.   30.5cm.

G 276.

Preface to G 118—153, with Chinese interlinear text.   1771.   27.5cm.

G 277.   清 文 字 彙
Ch'ing wên tzŭ hui

A Manchu-Chinese vocabulary. [In manuscript; imperfect.]   26.5cm.

G 278.

Index to G 118—153, with syllabic arrangement and reference to categories.   28cm.

G 279.

The Old Testament translated into the Mongol tongue, with a note in Russian, dated St. Petersburg, 1840, certifying that "it corresponds with the translation of these books acknowledged and used by those who profess the Protestant faith."   26.5 × 22cm.

G 280—283. 草 木 圖 說

Ts'ao mu t'u shuo

A new edition of the *Sô Mokou Zoussets*, an illustrated Japanese Herbarium, with native names and European identifications in Roman type, by 飯沼慾齋 Iinouma Yokoussai, first published in 1856. 1874. 27cm.

G 284. 譯 字

I tzŭ

A vocabulary of words to illustrate different scripts, Arabic, Manchu, Sanskrit, Tibetan, Siamese, and Burmese, arranged under categories. [Manuscript.] 1798. 28cm.

G 285. 同 文 韻 統

T'ung wên yün t'ung

A Sanskrit-Tibetan Syllabary, compiled by 傅恒 Fu-hêng and others. 1750. 28.5cm.

G 286. 蒙 文 晰 義

Mêng wên hsi i

A treatise on Mongolian, with Chinese interlinear text. 1848. 28cm.

INDEX TO AUTHORS.

Ch'ên Wei-p'ing, E 363.

Ch'ên Yüan-lung, D 60; E 195.

Chêng Ch'iao, B 429.

Chêng Hsüan, A 270; X 137.

Chêng K'ang-ch'êng, A 42; 43; 44.

Chêng Yüan-ch'ing, B 1237.

Ch'êng I, A 161.

Ch'êng I-chih, B 416.

Ch'êng K'o-tsê, D 137.

Ch'êng Ta-ch'ang, A 16.

Ch'êng Yao-t'ien, E 371.

Ch'êng Yün-shêng, A 358; 359.

Chi Liu-ch'i, B 1102.

Ch'i Chao-nan, Z 30.

Ch'i Chien-tsao, C 19.

Ch'i Yün-shih, C 116.

Chiang Chao-hsi, A 30.

Chiang Liang-ch'i, A 451; B 1132.

Chiang Shih-ch'üan, D 120.

Chiang T'ing-hsi, C 85; E 225; 325.

Chiang Yung, A 116; 118; E 419.

Chiao Yüan-hsi, A 121.

Ch'iao Yung-ch'ien, B 1303.

Ch'ien Chia, E 425.

Ch'ien Ch'ien-i, D 181.

Ch'ien Fang, E 53.

Ch'ien Hsi-fu, B 1279.

Ch'ien Hsi-tsu, B 1240.

Ch'ien Hsüan, B 1054.

Ch'ien Lung, D 176

Chih Shêng, A 413.

Chih yüan chu jen, A 344.

Chin Chung, D 15.

Chin Fu, B 1679.

Chin Jung-fan, D 124.

Chin Kuei-ch'in, E 8.

Chin P'an, A 238.

Chin Shêng-t'an, D 42.

Chin T'an, D 138.

Ch'in Chiu-shao, X 121.

Ch'ing Ch'ang, X 121.

Ch'ing-kuei, B 13; 752a.

Ch'iu Chao-ao, D 149.

Ch'iu Chün, A 358; 365.

Ch'iu Ts'ang-chu, A 170.

Ch'iu Ying-shih, B 957.

Chou Ch'ih, A 25.

Chou Fêng-lu, A 300.

Chou Tsung-lien, B 428.

Chu Ao, E 213.

Chu Hsi, A 164; 327; B 1029; 1054;
E 84.

Chu Huan, B 1551.

Chu I-tsun, C 151; D 299; E 1;
362; 365; 366.

Chu Shih, A 8; 29; 33; 45; 144;
160; 328; 341; 353; 355; 457;
466; B 1232; 1541; 1546; 1559;
1670; 1863; D 135; E 81; 84.

Chu T'ing-huai, D 142.

Chu Tzǔ, E 31.

Chu Yün, B 148; 2005.

Ch'ü Ta-chün, C 26.

Ch'ü Yüan, D 131; 174; 175.

Chuang Chung-fang, B 1379.

Chuang Tzǔ, A 376.

Ch'un-yüan, C 115; 121.

Chung Hsing, B 1011; D 172; 284.

Ch'ung-hou, B 1544; Z 9.

Ch'ung Lun, E 224.

Dharmaraksha, A 410.

Fa Yün, A 425.

Fan Ch'êng-hsün, C 259.

Fan Tsu-yü, A 159.

Fan Tzǔ-têng, A 21; 25; 50.

Fan Yeh, B 1530.

Fan Yün-p'êng, D 142.

Fang Fêng-nien, C 159.

Fang Hsiao-ju, A 27.

Fang Hsien, G 182.

Fang I-chih, E 34.

Fang Jou-ju, A 93.

Fang Kuan-ch'êng, C 150.

Fêng Ch'i, B 1181.

Fêng Shuang-chiang, B 1518.

Fêng Ting-tiao, E 212.

Fêng Yüan-chung, B 1068.

Fu-hêng, B 15; 994; G 285.

Fu I, A 426.

Fu-ming-an, G 221.

Fu-ming-liang, G 221.

Fu Pao-sên, D 301.

Fu Pin-shih, E 318.

Fu-sên-pu, C 120.

Gñânagupta, A 406.

Good-for-Nothing of the Reedy Bank, D 42.

Han, Governor, A 455.

Han Fei Tzǔ, A 376.

Han Sung, A 9.

Han T'an, E 126; 422.

Han Wên-ch'i, B 1479.

Hang Shih-chün, A 91.

Hao Yü-lin, C 181.

Hermit of Wei-lei, B 402.

Ho Ch'ang-ling, A 428; B 1496.

Ho Ch'uo, D 117.

Ho Kuan Tzǔ, A 376.

Ho T'ien-chio, Z 35.

Ho Wên-huan, D 143.

Hsiao Ch'ang, B 1192.

Hsiao T'ung, D 117.

Hsiao Ying-chih, C 37.

Hsieh Chia-ying, A 22.

Hsieh Hsüan, G 215.

Hsieh Ling-yün, A 410.

Hsieh Min, C 69.

Hsieh Shang-kung, E 172.

Hsien chai lao jen, F 27.

Hsing Ping, A 41.

Hsing Yün-lu, E 88.

Hsiung Shou-ch'ien, E 85; Z 31.

Hsü Chi-yü, C 1.

Hsü Ch'ieh, E 213.

Hsü Ch'ien-hsüeh, D 110; E 1; X 1.

Hsü Chü-chêng, B 1998.

Hsü Hsiang-p'o, D 142.

Hsü Hua-yo, A 23.

Hsü Hung-tsu, C 17.

Hsü Kuang-ch'i, B 161, Z 41.

Hsü Lien, B 383.

Hsü Mêng-hsin, B 1090.

Hsü Shên, E 208; 213.

Hsü Tao, A 401.

Hsü T'ien-lin, B 171; 173.

Hsü Tung, B 29; 35.

Hsü Wên-ch'ang, D 13.

Hsü Wên-ch'u, A 50.

Hsü Wu, C 136.

Hsüan Ying, A 412.

Hsün Hsü, B 1858.

Hsün Tzǔ, A 376.

Hu An-kuo, A 25.

Hu I-mci, D 277.

Hu Kao-wang, D 176.

Hu Lin-i, B 1661.

Hu Lun, A 119.

Hu Ming-yü, A 420.

Hu San-hsing, B 961.

Hua Hsi-min, E 246.

Hua Kang, E 264.

Hua Lin-hsiang, E 245.

Huai-nan Tzŭ, A 376.

Huang Chin-wei, A 308.

Huang En-t'ung, B 134; 156.

Huang Fu-lung, A 27.

Huang-fu Mi, B 957.

Huang Hsiao-fêng, B 1; 5.

Huang Ju-ch'êng, E 63.

Huang Liu-hung, B 39; 404.

Huang P'ei-lieh, B 1272.

Huang Pên-chi, E 204.

Huang Shêng, E 367.

Hui Kuan, A 410.

Hui Tung, A 5.

Hui Tung-hsüeh, E 33.

Hui Yen, A 410.

Hung Liang-chi, B 422; 423; 424; C 9.

Iinouma Yokoussai, G 280.

I-li-pu, C 216.

Jan Chin-tsu, A 97.

Jao Yü-ch'êng, E 192.

Jen Ta-ch'un, D 142.

Jui-lin, B 80.

Jui Shêng-t'an, D 5.

Kao Ch'i, D 138.

Kao Chin, C 59.

Kao Wei-yo, A 231.

Ki-ying, B 156; 1149; 1152; F 1.

Ku Ai-chi, E 367.

Ku Chiang, A 285; B 1106; C 162; E 63; 74.

Ku Ch'ieh-an, A 75.

Ku Chung-hsü, G 215.

Ku Hsiu, B 1849; E 190.

Ku K'uei-kuang, D 237.

Ku Liang, A 30.

Ku Ping-chang, C 109.

Ku Tsu-yü, C 124.

Ku Tsung-t'ai, D 142.

Ku Yeh-wang, E 366.

Ku Yen-wu, E 63; 74.

Ku Ying-t'ai, B 1186.

Ku Yüan, A 225; 232; B 1561; E 421.

K'u Lo-na, A 61; 63.

Kuan Mao-ts'ai, Z 8.

Kuan Tzŭ, A 376.

K'uang Min-mu, B 406.

K'uang Min-pên, B 7; 1304.

K'uei-lien, B 1659.

Kung-ch'ê, B 2003.

Kung-o-la, B 77.

Kung Shou-chêng, E 83.

Kung Yang, A 30.

K'ung Chao-huan, A 226.

K'ung Ch'ao, B 1081.

K'ung Chi-fên A 226.

K'ung Kuang-sên, A 58.

K'ung Yen-mei, A 237.

K'ung Ying-ta, A 270.

Kuo, Prince, D 103.

Kuo Kung, D 92; F 17.

Kuo P'o, A 41; 163; E 80.

Kuo Wei, A 283.

Kuo Yüan-min, B 1547.

Ma Su, A 26; B 1205.

Ma Tuan-lin, B 427; 428; 489.

Mao Ch'ang, A 270.

Mao Ch'i-ling, E 126.

Mao Huan-wên, B 6.

Mao K'un, A 167.

Mao Tsung-kang, D 5.

Mao Yüan-i, B 168.

Master of the Pine-tree Pavilion, The
  A 305.

Mei Ying-tsu, E 422.

Mêng Ch'iao-fang, B 952.

Min Erh-jung, D 158.

Mo Tzŭ, A 400.

Mou Mu-yüan, A 399.

Mu Wang, B 1858.

Mu Wei-lien, F 149.

Mu Wên, B 1066.

Niu Niu, A 59.

No-yen-ch'êng, B 1484; C 243.

O-êrh-t'ai, A 144; 180; B 734;
  C 161; E 67; G 25.

O-kuei, B 407; 1313; C 203.

Old Lute-Recluse, The, D 26.

Ou I, A 408.

Ou-yang Hsiu, B 1084.

Pan Ku, B 1520.

P'an Hsiang, A 235.

P'an Kuo-chên, B 1816.

P'an Lei, A 285.

P'an Lung, F 145.

P'an Ping-kang, A 48.

P'an Shih-ên, B 14; 41; 55; 1230.

P'an To, C 13.

P'ang Ti-wo, F 120.

Pao Liu-yün, F 152.

Pao Shu-yün, B 114.

Pao T'ing-po, B 1697.

P'ei Sung-chih, B 1077.

P'êng Hsi-su, B 1234.

P'êng Liang-ch'ang, E 85.

P'êng Shih-t'uan, A 347.

P'êng Ting-ch'iu, A 424.

P'êng Yü-wen, E 94.

P'êng Yüan-jui, B 1084.

Philosopher who has seen the
  World, A, D 30.

Pi-jê-chu-jen, B 1663.

Pi Yüan, A 5; 27a; 168; 400; 426;
  B 419; 420; 421; 1013; E 77;
  80; 82.

Pin Ch'un, B 1860.

Po Lin, B 92.

Poletti (P.), F 144.

P'u Ch'i-lung, D 99.

P'u Sung-ling, D 50.

Sêng-ko-lin-sin, B 1158.

Sha Mu, E 238.

Shan Yü-ch'ien, B 1673.

Shao Ch'ang-hêng, E 78.

Shao I-ch'ên, B 1379.

Shên Chao-lin, A 40.

Shên Chao-t'ing, A 27.

Shên Ch'u, F 134.

Shên Ch'u-kao, B 1157.

Shên Ch'üan, D 137.

Shên Hsin-t'ien, B 113.

Shên I-kuan, E 192.

Shên Ping-ch'êng, E 180.

Shên Shih-hsing, B 193.

Shên Shih-i, C 48.

Shên Tê-fu, E 53.

Tso Hao, B 1177.

Tsou Yüan-p'iao, B 1669.

Tu Fu, D 149.

Tu Ting, A 81.

Tu Tzŭ-lun, B 255.

Tu Yu, B 476.

T'u Li-shên, G 23.

Tuan Ch'ang-chi, B 8; 11; 12.

Tuan O-t'ing, E 204.

Tuan Yü-ts'ai, E 208.

Tung Chia, G 248.

Tung Hsün, C 43.

Tung Shun, C 19; 20; D 74.

Tung Ssŭ-chang, B 236.

Tung T'ien-kung, C 179.

T'ung-jui, G 223.

Wan-yen Yün-chu, D 146.

Wang Ch'i, B 1454; 1614; D 154.

Wang Chih-fang, F 158.

Wang Chih-têng, D 174.

Wang Ch'in-jo, B 1563.

Wang Cho, A 296.

Wang Fu, A 427; B 1; 1425.

Wang Fu-li, A 86.

Wang Hsi-lien, D 44.

Wang Hsiang-chin, E 457.

Wang Hsiu-yü, D 75.

Wang Hsü-ling, A 124.

Wang Hung-hsü, A 127; B 1111.

Wang Ju-hsiang, D 141.

Wang Kao, A 1.

Wang Kêng, B 957.

Wang Ling, B 1239.

Wang Ming-hao, F 124.

Wang Ming-shêng, D 142.

Wang Mo, A 306.

Wang Mou-sung, E 363.

Wang Nai-t'ang, E 310.

Wang Pi, A 238.

Wang P'u, B 175; 181.

Wang Pu-ch'ing, A 109.

Wang Shan, A 132.

Wang Shih-chêng, A 167; D 53; 137; E 375.

Wang Shih-lu, D 137.

Wang Shih-yün, B 1233.

Wang Shou-jen, B 1689.

Wang Su, A 167.

Wang Sung, C 240.

Wang Tai-yü, A 422.

Wang T'ang, X 134.

Wang T'ao, B 953.

Wang T'ing-o, D 142.

Wang Tsêng-fang, E 29.

Wang Yao-ch'ü, D 173; 276.

Wang Yin-chih, A 275; E 201.

Wang Ying-lei, E 215.

Wang Ying-lin, E 248.

Wang Ying-shan, C 202.

Wang Yu-p'u, A 354.

Wang Yüan-chêng, E 369.

Wang Yüan-hsün, D 142.

Wei Chao, A 166; E 181.

Wei Chin-hsi, B 77.

Wei Hsi, C 124.

Wei Jen Chê (W. Dean), F 164; Z 7.

Wei Wên-k'uei, E 88.

Wei Yüan, A 453; B 1134; C 3; D 201.

Wên-fu, A 461; B 16.

Wên Tzŭ, A 376.

Wêng Fu-k'o, A 169.

Wêng Shu-k'un, B 1978.

INDEX TO BOOKS.

Ch'un ch'iu shuo lüeh, A 28.

Ch'un ch'iu t'i chu ta ch'üan ho ts'an, A 25.

Ch'un ming mêng yü lu, B 744a.

Ch'ün ching tzǔ ku, E 204.

Ch'ün fang p'u, E 457.

Chung chou chin shih chi, B 420.

Chung hsüeh, Z 15.

Chung shu chêng k'ao lü ying, B 101.

Chung shu chêng k'ao pa ch'i, B 96.

Chung ting i ch'i k'uan shih, E 172.

Chung tou ch'i shu, F 150.

Erh lun ch'i yu yin tuan, A 115.

Erh shih êrh shih cha chi, B 1235.

Erh shih êrh shih kan ying lu, B 1234.

Erh shih êrh shih yen hsing lüeh, B 1547.

Erh shih i shih, B 734.

Erh shih i shih yo pien, B 1237.

Erh ya ch'i mêng, A 40.

Erh ya chu su, A 41.

Erh ya yin t'u, A 163.

Fan chi ts'ung shu yü chi, A 296.

Fan i ming i chi hsüan, A 425.

Fan pu yao lüeh, C 116.

Fan sung pên li chi, A 43.

Fang hai chi yao, C 11.

Fang yü chi yao chien lan, C 13.

Fên lei tzǔ chin, E 37.

Fo fa chin t'ang chêng wên lu, A 418.

Fo pên hsing chi ching, A 406.

Fu chien t'ung chih, C 181.

Fu ch'uan lü li shu, F 151.

Fu hui ch'üan shu, B 39; 404.

Fu so ch'ih tu, B 1865; E 179.

Hai kuo shêng yu ts'ao, B 1861.

Hai kuo t'u chih, C 3.

Hai shan hsien ts'ung shu, B 1794.

Han man tzǔ tien, G 110.

Han ming ch'ên chuan, B 772a.

Han t'ang sung ming ch'ên lu, B 1560.

Hao ch'iu chuan, D 87.

Ho lo ching yün, E 419.

Hou han chi, B 1530.

Hsi chuan, E 213.

Hsi ch'ui tsung t'ung shih lüeh, C 123.

Hsi han hui yao, B 173.

Hsi hsia shu shih, B 417.

Hsi hsiang chi, G 211.

Hsi i lüeh lun, Z 11.

Hsi shan ch'üan chi, B 1426.

Hsi tsang pei wên, B 951.

Hsi yü so t'an, C 121.

Hsi yüan lu chi chêng, B 378.

Hsia hsiao chêng, A 224.

Hsia hsiao chêng k'ao chu, A 168.

Hsia k'o yu chi, C 17.

Hsiang ting ku wên p'ing chu, D 92.

Hsiao ching, A 160; G 79.

Hsiao ching chu chieh, A 159.

Hsiao hsüeh, G 250.

Hsiao hsüeh chi chieh, A 329.

Hsiao hsüeh chi chu, A 327.

Hsiao hsüeh yün yü, E 220.

Hsiao shu ch'ao shih k'o ou ts'un, D 140.

G. W.

I li chêng shih chu, A 42.

I li chieh lüeh, A 33; 466.

I li i su, A 136.

I lin hui k'ao, A 361.

I shih, B 1205.

I shih shih chi, B 1010.

I tzŭ, G 284.

I wên t'ung lan, E 238.

I yang hu lu, B 402.

I yü kuo chih, C 114.

I yü lu, G 23.

I yüan ssŭ tsung, D 16.

Jih chiang ch'un ch'iu chieh i, A 63.

Jih chiang i ching chieh i, A 59.

Jih chiang li chi chieh i, A 68.

Jih chiang shu ching chieh i, A 61.

Jih chiang ssŭ shu, G 162.

Jih chiang ssŭ shu chieh i, A 71.

Jih chih lu, A 285.

Jih chih lu chi shih, E 63.

Jih hsia chiu wên k'ao, C 151.

Jih tsuan êrh chi, X 137.

Ju lin wai shih, F 27.

Ju mên fa yü, A 424.

Kai yü ts'ung k'ao, A 281.

K'ai yüan shih chiao lu, A 413.

Kan ch'üan wên chi, A 350.

Kan t'ang hsiao chih, C 20.

K'ang hsi tzŭ tien, E 225; Z 1; 23.

K'ang hsi tzŭ tien ts'o yao, E 481.

Kao ch'ing ch'iu shih chi chu, D 138.

Kao li ming ch'ên chuan, B 2003.

Kao li shih, B 1978.

K'ao ku lei pien, B 244.

K'ao ku t'u, B 5.

Ko chih ching yüan, E 195.

Ko wu ju mên, Z 16.

K'o ch'ang t'iao li, B 80; F 1.

Ku chin lü li k'ao, E 88.

Ku chin yün lüeh, E 78.

Ku ching chieh kou ch'ên, A 274.

Ku lun ta kuan, A 219.

Ku shêng hsien hsiang chuan lüeh,
    A 225.

Ku shih kuei, D 172.

Ku shih lei wan, D 162.

Ku shih yüan, D 203.

Ku t'ang shih ho chieh, D 173;
    276.

Ku wên hsi i, D 94.

Ku wên kuan chih, D 98.

Ku wên mei ch'üan, D 99.

Ku wên p'ing chu, F 17.

Ku wên tz'ŭ lei tsuan, D 89.

Ku wên yo hsüan, D 103.

Ku wên yüan chien, D 110; G 192.

Ku yü, A 330.

Kuan chung chin shih chi, B 419.

Kuang ch'ün fang p'u, E 461.

Kuang hui pien, D 135.

Kuang shih lei fu, E 246.

Kuang tung hai fang hui lan, C 28.

Kuang tung hsin yü, C 26.

Kuang po wu chih, B 236.

Kuang yün, E 365.

Kuei chou t'ung chih, C 259.

Kuei hsiu chêng shih chi, D 146.

K'uei chang ch'üan yin, E 258.

K'un hsüeh chi wên, E 248.

K'un yü ch'ien tsao tu t'u, C 109.

Kung ku chuan, A 30.

Kung pu tsê li, B 157.

Kung shou t'ang tsou i, A 455;
  B 1479.

Kung wên kung kung chê kao, E 83.

K'ung shih ts'ung shu, B 1418.

K'ung tzŭ chi yü, A 233.

Kuo ch'ao chêng ya chi, D 301.

Kuo ch'ao hua chêng lu, B 1857.

Kuo ch'ao shih pieh ts'ai chi, D 309.

Kuo ch'ao tsou su, B 2005.

Kuo yü, A 166; E 181.

Lao tzŭ tao tê ching k'ao i, A 426.

Li ch'ao fu k'ai, D 75.

Li chi i su, A 150.

Li chi shuo, A 57.

Li chi t'i chu, A 50.

Li chi t'ing hsün, A 48.

Li chi tsuan yen, A 45.

Li chi tu pên, A 44.

Li chih chi yao, G 223.

Li chih hsüan ching, B 391.

Li hsiang ch'in kung tsou i, B 1684.

Li pien, E 367.

Li pu ch'êng yü, G 24.

Li pu ch'u fên tsê li, B 25.

Li pu tsê li, A 461; B 16; 64.

Li shih i chuan, A 15.

Li shih yin chien, E 125.

Li shu, E 252.

Li tai chi shih nien piao, B 245.

Li tai chiang yü piao, B 11.

Li tai chien yen, B 1012.

Li tai chih kuan piao, B 407.

Li tai fu hui, D 60.

Li tai hsün li chuan, B 1232a; 1546.

Li tai hsün liang nêng li lieh chuan
  hui ch'ao, B 1303.

Li tai ming ch'ên chuan, A 457;
  B 1541.

Li tai ming ch'ên chuan chieh lu,
  B 1544.

Li tai ming ch'ên tsou i, B 1363.

Li tai ming ch'ên yen hsing lu,
  B 1551.

Li tai ming ju chuan, B 1232; 1559.

Li tai shên hsien t'ung chien, A 401.

Li tai shih hua, D 143.

Li tai shih tsung lun, B 732.

Li tai shuo yo, E 72.

Li tai ti wang nien piao, Z 30.

Li tai t'ung chi piao, B 8.

Li tai yen ko piao, B 12.

Li t'ai po wên chi, D 154.

Li wên hsiang kung tsou i, B 1506.

Liang han tsun yen, B 1198.

Liang kuang tsou i, B 1856.

Liao chai chih i, D 50; G 205.

Liao shih shih i, B 1200.

Liao shih yü chieh, G 83.

Lieh ch'ao shih chi, D 181.

Lieh nü chuan, B 957.

Liu ching t'u ting pên, A 1.

Liu ch'ing hsin chi, E 174.

Liu pu ch'êng yü, G 89.

Liu shih tsung ch'ü, D 30.

Liu shu chun, E 212.

Liu shu fên lei, E 318.

Liu shu ku, E 321.

Liu yüan an ch'ih tu, E 173.

Lo hsüeh pien, B 1687.

Lu chou ch'üan chi, B 393.

Lü li pien lan, B 377.

Lü shih ch'un ch'iu, A 27.

Lü shih ssŭ li i, A 56; E 81.

Lun fu hsin chih li, F 155.

Lung ch'ing shih lu, B 1950.

Lung wei pi shu, B 1829.

Man chou ch'ing wên chien, G 118.

Man chou ming ch'ên chuan, B 759a.

Man han ch'êng yü tui tai, G 237.

Man han chu wên ch'êng yü, G 235.

Man han ho pi san tzŭ ching chu chieh, G 247.

Mao shih su, A 270.

Mêng chung i kung tsou su, B 952.

Mêng kù ch'ing wên chien, G 30.

Mêng wên hsi i, G 286.

Miao fa lien hua ching t'ai tsung hui i, A 408.

Miao fang pei lan, C 24.

Mien i chai hsü ts'un kao, B 1675.

Mien i chai ou ts'un kao, B 1673.

Min tu chi, C 202.

Ming ch'ên tsou i, B 1380.

Ming chi pai shih hui pien, B 1106.

Ming chi pei lüeh, B 1102.

Ming chia shih kuan, D 195.

Ming chien, B 1098.

Ming chien chi shih pên mo, B 1186.

Ming chien i chih lu, B 739a.

Ming fa chih chang, B 113.

Ming shih kao, B 1111.

Ming shih pieh ts'ai chi, D 300.

Ming shih tsung, D 291.

Ming t'ang ta tao, E 33.

Mo tzŭ shih wu chüan mu i chüan, A 400.

Mu ling shu, B 29.

Mu t'ien tzŭ chuan, B 1858.

Nan hsün shêng tien, C 59.

Nan pên ta pan nieh p'an ching, A 410.

Nei k'o hsin shuo, Z 8.

Ni ch'ên chuan, B 771a.

No yen ch'êng tsou i, B 1484.

Nung chêng ch'üan shu, B 161.

O wên ch'êng kung nien p'u, B 1513.

Ou pei chi, D 133.

Ou pei shih hua, D 128.

Pa ch'i man chou shih tsu t'ung p'u, B 1127.

Pa chia shih hsüan, D 137.

Pa hsün wan shou shêng tien, B 1313.

Pao chia shu, B 35.

P'ei wên shih yün, E 260.

P'ei wên yün fu, E 265.

P'ei yüan t'ang ou ts'un kao, B 1471.

Pi chüan, F 148.

Pi hsüeh lu, B 1379.

Pi shu shan chuang chi, C 161.

P'i tien ssŭ shu tu pên, A 174.

P'ien tzŭ lei pien, E 325.

Ping pu tsê li, B 92.

P'ing fan tsou i, B 1312.

P'ing ting chiao fei chi lüeh, B 1137.

P'ing ting yüeh fei chi lüeh, B 757a.

Po ku t'u, B 1.

Po tzŭ chin tan, A 283.

Pu hsü ch'ün fu lu, B 1024.

P'u fa chan chi, B 953.

San ch'ao pei mêng hui pien, B 1090.

San ching ssŭ shu chêng wên, A 161.

San fu huang t'u, E 82.

San ho li chih chi yao, G 224.

San ho pien lan, G 182.

Ssŭ chao t'ang wên chi, D 122.

Ssŭ k'u ch'üan shu chien ming mu lu, E 169.

Ssŭ k'u ch'üan shu k'ao chêng, E437.

Ssŭ k'u ch'üan shu tsung mu t'i yao, E 143.

Ssŭ pên chien yao, G 221.

Ssŭ shu, A 164; 326; G 75.

Ssŭ shu chang chü chi chu, A 83.

Ssŭ shu chi chu pu, A 86.

Ssŭ shu chiang i k'un mien lu, A 87.

Ssŭ shu chiang i tsun wên lu, A 77.

Ssŭ shu chih yü shuo, A 120.

Ssŭ shu ho chiang, A 169; 298.

Ssŭ shu i chu lun wên, A 107.

Ssŭ shu k'ao ch'i yao, A 95.

Ssŭ shu k'ao i, A 91.

Ssŭ shu k'ou i, A 93.

Ssŭ shu ku jen tien lin, A 118.

Ssŭ shu pên i hui ts'an, A 109.

Ssŭ shu pu chu fu k'ao pei chih, A 170; F 164a.

Ssŭ shu pu chu pei chih, A 81.

Ssŭ shu tien chih hui pien, A 119.

Ssŭ shu tien lin, A 116.

Ssŭ shu tien yeh, A 305.

Ssŭ shu wan chu hsiang shuo, A 97.

Ssŭ shu wu ching chêng wên, A 263.

Ssŭ shu wu ching ta ch'üan, A 311.

Su chou fu chih, C 48.

Su p'i mêng tzŭ, A 114.

Su shih yün chi, E 261.

Su tung p'o wên hsüan, D 158.

Su wên chung tsou i, B 1151.

Sui yao t'ing chih, C 25.

Sun wên ting tsou su, B 1685.

Sun yüeh fêng p'i shih chi, B 1068.

Sung hsüeh shih ch'üan chi, A 347.

Sung shih ch'ao, D 238.

Sung shih chi shih, D 286.

Sung yüan chi shih pên mo, B 1181.

Ta ch'ên chuan, B 1537.

Ta ch'ing hui tien, B 257; 344; 2013.

Ta ch'ing hui tien po wên, B 342.

Ta ch'ing hui tien shih li, B 261.

Ta ch'ing hui tien tsê li, B 348.

Ta ch'ing i t'ung chih, C 85.

Ta ch'ing i t'ung chih piao, C 136.

Ta ch'ing i t'ung yü t'u, C 177.

Ta ch'ing jen tsung jui huang ti hsün, B 1955.

Ta ch'ing jen tsung jui huang ti shêng hsün, G 254.

Ta ch'ing lü, B 370.

Ta ch'ing lü li, B 371; 379.

Ta ch'ing lü li an yü, B 134.

Ta ch'ing t'ung li, B 73.

Ta hsiang t'u, A 330.

Ta hsüeh yen i, A 363.

Ta hsüeh yen i ch'i yao, A 373.

Ta hsüeh yen i pu, A 365.

Ta ming hui tien, B 193.

Ta ming wên wu kuan ping fêng hsiang, B 1110.

Ta tai li chi, A 54.

Ta tai li chi pu chu, A 58.

Tai shu hsüeh, Z 21.

Tai wei chi shih chi, Z 20.

T'ai p'ing kuang chi, B 1351.

T'ai p'ing yü lan, B 1385.

T'ai shang hun yüan tao tê chên ching, A 427.

T'ung tien, B 476.

T'ung wên pei k'ao, E 215.

T'ung wên yün t'ung, G 285.

T'ung ya, E 34.

T'ung yin tzŭ chien, E 31.

Tzŭ cha p'i po ch'êng tz'ŭ, B 1859.

Tzŭ chien, E 362.

Tzŭ chih hsin shu, B 398.

Tzŭ chih hsin shu ch'üan chi, B 160.

Tzŭ chih kuan shu, B 1851.

Tzŭ chih t'ung chien, B 961.

Tzŭ chih t'ung chien kang mu,
  B 1029.

Tzŭ hsüeh ch'i tsung, E 361.

Tzŭ hui, E 422.

Tzŭ lei piao yün, E 264.

Tzŭ shih ching hua, E 183.

Tz'ŭ mu hsien ssŭ shu shuo, A 121.

Wai fan chi lüeh, C 115.

Wan hsing t'ung p'u, X 126.

Wan kuo kung fa, Z 12.

Wan nien shu, B 426.

Wan pao ch'üan shu, B 6.

Wan tzŭ tien, F 144.

Wang yang ming ch'üan chi, B 1689.

Wên hsien t'ung k'ao, B 489.

Wên hsien t'ung k'ao chi yao, B 427.

Wên hsien t'ung k'ao chieh kuei,
  B 428.

Wên kung chia fan, A 353; B 1670.

Wu ching, G 65.

Wu ching wên tzŭ, E 221.

Wu chü yün jui, A 470; E 427.

Wu chün ming hsien t'u, E 421.

Wu chün ming hsien t'u chuan tsan,
  B 1561.

Wu chün tao li piao, B 109.

Wu hsüeh lu ch'u pien, B 165.

Wu i shan chih, C 179.

Wu li t'ung k'ao, E 8.

Wu pei chih shêng, B 168.

Wu shih chi lan, D 124.

Wu shih shan chih, C 201.

Wu tai hui yao, B 181.

Wu tai shih chi chu, B 1084.

Wu wên chieh kung i chi, B 1144.

Yang fang chi yao, C 22.

Yao chü tsa lu, B 1863.

Yeh huo pien, E 53.

Yeh su shêng chiao hsi li kuei shih,
  F 154.

Yeh su tao li tsung lun, F 161.

Yeh wên chuang kung tsou i,
  B 1509.

Yen pào tsa chi, B 1668.

Yen shih chia hsün, A 355.

Yen tzŭ ch'un ch'iu, A 32.

Yen yüan chi, D 132.

Yin han ch'ing wên chien, G 248.

Yin hsüeh ch'üan shu, E 29.

Yin hsüeh wu shu, E 74.

Ying chüan, F 147.

Ying fa o mei t'iao k'uan, B 107.

Ying huan chih lüeh, C 1.

Ying lieh chuan, D 13.

Ying wên chü yü, F 158.

Yo fu san ko, D 129.

Yu chêng wei chai ch'ih tu, F 141.

Yu hsüeh ch'iu yüan, E 316.

Yu hsüeh ku shih hsün yüan hsiang
  chieh, A 358.

Yü chiao li, D 42.

Supplementary Catalogue of the Wade Collection of Chinese and Manchu Books in the Library of the University of Cambridge

剑桥大学图书馆威妥玛文库汉、满文书籍目录续编

SUPPLEMENTARY CATALOGUE

OF THE

WADE COLLECTION

OF

CHINESE AND MANCHU BOOKS

IN THE LIBRARY OF THE

UNIVERSITY OF CAMBRIDGE

BY

HERBERT A. GILES

M.A.; LL.D. (ABERD.)

PROFESSOR OF CHINESE IN THE UNIVERSITY OF CAMBRIDGE

CAMBRIDGE

AT THE UNIVERSITY PRESS

1915

PREFATORY NOTE.

This supplementary collection of Chinese books has been gathered together since the year 1898.

In 1908, when a large number of valuable works came into the market, a fund was raised by private subscription, the subscribers being: —

> The Master of Emmanuel
> The Provost of King's
> Professor Sir Clifford Allbutt, K.C.B.
> Professor A. A. Bevan
> Professor E. G. Browne
> J. Y. Buchanan, Esq., F.R.S.
> Professor F. C. Burkitt
> F. J. Cobbold, Esq., M.P.
> N. C. Cohen, Esq.
> S. Gaselee, Esq.
> Professor H. A. Giles
> C. Hanbury, Esq.
> Professor Liveing
> Professor Macalister
> J. F. P. Rawlinson, Esq., K.C., M.P.
> A. E. Shipley, Esq., F.R.S.
> Professor W. W. Skeat
> Professor V. H. Stanton
> University Library
> Lady Wade

With this fund, (1) a great many gaps in the Chinese Library were filled up, and (2) some rare works were acquired.

Under the first of these heads may be mentioned Y 1ª, which is an anthology, in 401 volumes, of the prose masterpieces produced under the T'ang dynasty (A.D. 618—906), and is a companion to D 246, already on the shelves, a similar anthology of the poetical masterpieces of the same period.

Under the second head will be found D 75ª, which contains, in 24 volumes, the complete writings of the famous poet, Tu Fu (A.D. 712—770). Hitherto, the oldest printed book in the University Library has been C 114, an illustrated account of all foreign nations known to the Chinese, which dates back to the last quarter of the 14ᵗʰ century. The work here under notice dates back to the year A.D. 1204.

Some important donations have been made, of which two call for particular mention.

A large number of works, marked in this Catalogue with a dagger, were presented by Dr F. Sanger, of St John's College; and several of these are of peculiar interest as specially representing the literary activity of the province of Fuhkien, in which Dr Sanger happened to be stationed.

Those works which are marked with an asterisk were presented by Mr L. C. Taylor, of Clare College. The large majority of these form new acquisitions, the remainder being other editions of works already secured.

Over one thousand three hundred volumes have thus been added to the Library.

HERBERT A. GILES.

Cambridge: 21 June, 1915.

前　言

这批补充的中文藏书是1898年以后搜集的。

1908年，大量有价值的书籍流入市场，大学成立了一个私募基金，捐助人名单如下：

伊曼纽尔学院院长（The Master of Emmanuel）

国王学院院长（The Provost of King's）

高级巴思勋爵士克利福德·奥尔巴特教授（Professor Sir Clifford Allbutt，K.C.B.）

A. A.比万教授（Professor A. A. Bevan）

E. G.布朗教授（Professor E. G. Browne）

皇家学会会员J. Y.布嘉南先生（J. Y. Buchanan，Esq.，F.R.S.）

F. C.伯基特教授（Professor F. C. Burkitt）

下院议员F. J.葛博德先生（F. J. Cobbold，Esq.，M.P.）

N. C. 科恩先生（N. C. Cohen，Esq.）

S.盖斯利先生（S. Gaselee，Esq.）

翟理斯教授（Professor H. A. Giles）

C. 汉伯瑞先生（C. Hanbury，Esq.）

利伟因教授（Professor Liveing）

玛卡里斯特教授（Professor Macalister）

王室法律顾问、下院议员J. F. P. 劳林森先生（J. F. P. Rawlinson，Esq.，K.C.，M.P.）

皇家学会会员A. E. 西普力先生（A. E. Shipley，Esq.，F.R，S.）

W. W. 斯基特教授（Professor W. W. Skeat）

V. H. 斯坦通教授（Professor V. H. Stanton）

剑桥大学图书馆

威妥玛夫人（Lady Wade）

在该基金的帮助下，（1）填补了中文藏书的很多空白，（2）获得了一些珍稀的图书。

本目录第一个条目中值得一提的是Y 1a号图书，这是一部401册的唐代（公元618—906年）散文名作选集，与已经收藏的唐代诗歌名作选集D246号图书类似。

本目录第二个条目的D 75a号图书是著名诗人杜甫（公元712-770年）的24册作品全集。C 114号图书（《异域图志》）是迄今为止剑桥大学图书馆最古老的印刷图书，用图解的方式记录了中国人所知的其他各个国家。此书可追溯到14世纪的最后25年，本目录中的该书可以追溯到公元1204年。

部分重要捐赠中有两次捐赠值得特别提及。

这份目录中，很多图书旁边标注了剑标符号，它们都是圣约翰学院（St John's College）的F.桑格博士（Dr F. Sanger）捐赠的；其中有几本专门描述福建省文学活动的图书特别引人关注，桑格博士恰好曾被派驻福建省。

目录中标注了星号的图书由克莱尔学院（Clare College）的L. C. 泰勒先生（L. C. Taylor）捐赠。其中绝大多数是之前没有的新藏品，其他图书则是已有藏书的其他版本。

此次共向图书馆捐赠了1300册书籍。

翟理斯

剑桥：1915年6月21日

（管宇译，彭萍校）

SUPPLEMENTARY CATALOGUE OF
THE WADE LIBRARY

A 427ᵃ. 感 應 篇 and 玉 皇 寶 訓

Kan ying p'ien and Yü huang pao hsün

(*a*) The Treatise of Rewards and Punishments, wrongly attributed to Lao Tzŭ. With commentary. 1856.

(*b*) The Precepts of Yü Huang Shang Ti, a member of the Trinity of modern Taoism. [The volume also contains the 陰隲文 *Yin Chih Wên*, "The Treatise of Secret Blessing," 關聖帝君覺世真經 *Kuan Shêng Ti Chün Chao Shih Chên Ching*, "The True Canon of Kuan Ti, God of War, to Awaken the Age," and other Taoist writings.] 2 vols. in blue cloth case. 1875.   23cm.

A 427ᵇ. 列 子

Lieh Tzŭ

The remains of the mythical Taoist philosopher, Lieh Tzŭ, supposed to have lived in the 4ᵗʰ or 5ᵗʰ cent. B. C. [The labels bear the inscription 宋本列子 Sung dynasty edition of Lieh Tzŭ, and the following in Chinese is pasted on the fly-leaf opposite the first page: "It is notorious that while volumes dating from the Sung dynasty (A.D. 960—1260; *see* D 75ᵃ) rank as the oldest of printed books, many of those preserved to-day are not genuine. Now I am convinced that these volumes of Lieh Tzŭ are ancient and valuable.

G. W.   I

On opening them, the delicate colour of the paper arrests the eye, while the ink has the fragrant odour of antiquity, neither of which attributes would be present if the book were not of the Sung period."] 8 pt. in 4 vols, in blue cloth case. *No date.*   23cm.

A 427ᶜ.   楞 嚴 經 正 脈
Lêng yen ching chêng mo

The famous *Lêng yen sûtra*, first translated A.D. 1312, and generally regarded by the literati as a masterpiece. Published with commentary by the Buddhist monk 交光眞鑑 Chiao-kuang-chên-chien, with a preface by 呂崇烈 Lü Ch'ung-lieh. 10 vols in blue cloth case, 1649.   27cm.

B 382ᵃ.   漢 魏 叢 書
Han wei ts'ung shu

A collection of reprints from authors of the Han and Wei dynasties, first printed A.D. 1592. Edition of 1791. 80 vols in 4 tin boxes.   25cm.

B 382ᵇ.   玉 海
Yü hai

An encyclopaedia divided according to subjects and comprising upwards of 240 articles, compiled early in the 12th century by 王應麟 Wang Ying-lin. With eight prefaces and various appendices. 204 pt. in 120 vols, in 12 blue cloth cases. 1738.   25cm.

B 1470ᵃ.   功 順 堂 叢 書
Kung shun t'ang ts'ung shu

A collection of eighteen reprints. 24 vols, in four blue cloth cases. 1821.   25.5cm.

B 1470ᵇ.   唐 宋 詩 醇
T'ang sung shih shun

Specimens of the poetry (*see* D 200ᵃ) of the T'ang and Sung dynasties, selected by the Emperor Ch'ien Lung from the works of

李白 Li Po, 杜甫 Tu Fu, 白居易 Po Chü-i, 韓愈 Han Yü, 蘇軾 Su Shih, and 陸游 Lu Yu, and edited, with copious commentary, by a commission of scholars. With preface by Ch'ien Lung. 47 pt. in 20 vols, with silk covers, in 2 blue cloth cases. 1760.

28cm.

B 1470ᶜ.   十 國 春 秋
Shih kuo ch'un ch'iu

Annals of the ten small principalities which existed between the end of the T'ang and the beginning of the Sung dynasties, by 吳任臣 Wu Jen-ch'ên of the 17th cent. A.D. Revised by 牛奐 Niu Huan, with a preface by 魏禧 Wei Hsi (1624—1680). New edition by 周昂 Chou Ang. 116 pt. in 16 vols, in 4 blue cloth cases. 1793.   26cm.

B 1470ᵈ.   國 朝 先 正 事 畧
Kuo ch'ao hsien chêng shih lüeh

Biographies of eminent men of the late Manchu-Tartar dynasty, including famous ministers, writers on Confucianism, commentators on the classics, essayists, etc. Compiled by 李元度 Li Yüan-tu, with preface by 曾國藩 Tsêng Kuo-fan. 60 pt. in 24 vols, in a wooden box. 1869.   27cm.

D 75ᵃ.   杜 工 部 詩 (and 文) 集
Tu kung pu shih (and wên) chi

Collection of the poetical and prose works of Tu Fu, A.D. 712—770 (spoken of as Tu Kung-pu in reference to his post as secretary in the Board of Works), with collected commentaries, and prefaces by 王洙 Wang Chu (A.D. 1039), 王安石 Wang An-shih (1052), 胡宗愈 Hu Tsung-yü (1090), and 蔡夢弼 Ts'ai Mêng-pi (1204). With an appendix containing the inscription on the poet's tombstone by 元稹 Yüan Chên (779—831). 22 pt. in 24 vols, of which the last 2 pt. in 2 vols. contain the prose writings. With blue paper covers, in 4 ornamental cases. 1204.   30cm.

D 75ᵇ.　　　　　西　遊　眞　詮

Hsi yu chên ch'üan

A mythological narrative of travels in the west in search of the sacred books of Buddhism, based on the journey of the pilgrim 玄奘 Hsüan Tsang. With notes and punctuation by 陳士斌 Ch'ên Shih-pin, and illustrations. 20 vols, in 2 blue cloth cases. Preface dated 1696.　　　　　　　　　　　　　24.5cm.

D 75ᶜ.　　　　　水　滸　傳

Shui hu chuan

A romantic novel by 施耐菴 Shih Nai-an, edited with illustrations and commentary by 金聖嘆 Chin Shêng-t'an. 20 vols, in 2 blue cloth cases. 1657.　　　　　　　　　　　　　24.5cm.

D 161ᵃ—162ᵇ.　韓　昌　黎　先　生　全　集

Han ch'ang li hsien shêng ch'üan chi

The complete works of 韓愈 Han Yü, otherwise known as 韓文公 Han Wên-kung, poet, philosopher and statesman, A.D. 768—804, based upon the edition of the Sung dynasty. 1784.

25.5cm.

D 180ᵃ.　　　　　西　廂　記

Hsi hsiang chi

A romantic drama of the 14ᵗʰ cent. A.D., by an unknown author. Edited with critical notes and punctuation by 金聖嘆 Chin Shêng-t'an. Illustrated. 8 pt. in 6 vols, in blue cloth case. 1780.　　23cm.

D 180ᵇ.　　　　　琵　琶　記

P'i p'a chi

A drama, in 42 scenes, by Kao Tsê-ch'êng, first performed in 1704. With critical notes by 毛聲山 Mao Shêng-shan and 汪文蓍 Wang Wên-shih. Edited by 從周 Ts'ung Chou, with illustrations. 12 pt. in 8 vols, in blue cloth case. 1800?　　24cm.

D 200ª. 御 選 唐 宋 文 醇

Yü hsüan t'ang sung wên shun

Specimens of the prose of the T'ang and Sung dynasties, selected by the Emperor Ch'ien Lung from (*see* B 1470*ᵇ*) the works of 韓愈 Han Yü, 柳宗元 Liu Tsung-yüan, 李翱 Li Ao, 孫樵 Sun Ch'iao, 歐陽修 Ou-yang Hsiu, 蘇洵 Su Hsün, 蘇軾 Su Shih, 蘇轍 Su Chê, 曾鞏 Tsêng Kung, and 王安石 Wang An-shih, and edited, with copious commentary and a preface from the Emperor, by a commission of scholars. 58 pt. in 20 vols, in 2 pairs of wooden boards. 1738. 26.5cm.

D 200ᵇ. 蘇 文 忠 公 詩 集

Su wên chung kung shih chi

The collected poetical works of Su 軾 Shih (A. D. 1036—1101), canonised as Wên Chung, and better known as Su 東坡 Tung-p'o. With critical notes and punctuation by 紀昀 Chi Yün (1724—1805). 50 pt. in 12 vols in 2 blue cloth cases. 1835. [*See* H 36.] 28cm.

E 71ª. 滂 喜 齋 叢 書

P'ang hsi chai ts'ung shu

A collection of reprints from the P'ang-hsi Studio, comprising 54 short treatises. 32 vols, in 4 blue cloth cases. 1883. 25.5cm.

E 71ᵇ. 笑 林 廣 記

Hsiao lin kuang chi

A collection of humorous anecdotes. 2 vols in blue cloth case. 1861. 15.5cm.

E 71ᶜ. 草 字 彙

Ts'ao tzŭ hui

A handbook of "grass character" or cursive script, arranged under radicals, by 莊門熙 Chuang Mên-hsi. With the original preface, by 蔣光越 Chiang Kuang-yüeh, dated 1786. 5 pt. in 4 vols, in blue cloth case. 1886. 17cm.

E 71ᵈ. 丹 鉛 總 錄

Tan yen tsung lu

A collection of miscellaneous writings, being the compressed edition of a much more extensive production, by 楊慎 Yang Shên, whose fancy name was 升菴 Shêng-an (A. D. 1488—1529.) Originally published in 1554 by 梁佐 Liang Tso. New edition, revised by 陳愷 Ch'ên K'ai. 27 pt. in 8 vols, in blue cloth case. 1794.   16cm.

E 79ᵃ. 正 字 通

Chêng tzŭ t'ung

A dictionary of the Chinese language, arranged according to the 214 radicals, by 廖文英 Liao Wên-ying. 32 vols, in 4 blue cloth cases. 1670.   25cm.

E 87ᵃ. 字 典 考 正

Tzŭ tien k'ao chêng

A list of mistakes in the Imperial dictionary of K'ang Hsi, arranged under the radicals. Preceded by a memorial on the subject from 奕繪 I-hui and three others, dated 1831, and an Imperial edict. 8 vols, in blue cloth case. 1831.   25cm.

E 87ᵇ. 楚 辭 集 注

Ch'u tz'ŭ chi chu

The collection of poetry known as the "Elegies of Ch'u," by the famous statesman and poet, 屈原 Ch'ü Yüan (B. C. 332—295), his nephew 宋玉 Sung Yü, and others. Edited, with collected commentaries and 司馬遷 Ssŭ-ma Ch'ien's biography of Ch'ü Yüan, by 朱熹 Chu Hsi. 8 pt. in 12 vols, in 2 blue cloth cases. 1650? 26 cm.

E 177ᵃ. 夢 溪 筆 談

Mêng ch'i pi t'an

A collection of miscellanea, including dissertations on music and mathematics, by the famous art-critic 沈括 Shên Kua (A. D. 1030—1093) who called himself Mêng Ch'i Wêng, The Old Man of the Dream-Brook. Edited by 李穆堂 Li Mu-t'ang; with preface, dated 1166, by 湯修年 T'ang Hsiu-nien. 26 pt. in 6 vols, in blue cloth case. [Marked by a late owner, who bought it in 1852, as 坊肆所售絶少 "very rarely to be found in bookshops."] *No date*, but probably about 1600.   26cm.

E 177ᵇ.   河 東 全 集 錄
Ho tung ch'üan chi lu

Collected works of 柳宗元 Liu Tsung-yüan (A. D. 773—819), sometimes known as Ho-tung after his birthplace. Edited by Ch'u Hsin, and revised by Wu Wei-ch'i. With the original preface by 劉禹錫 Liu Yü-hsi, who died in 842, and biographical memoir from the New History of the T'ang dynasty by Ou-yang Hsiu and Sung Ch'i. 6 pt. in 8 vols, in a pair of wooden boards. *No date*. 26cm.

E 374ᵃ.   本 草 綱 目
Pên ts'ao kang mu

The *Materia Medica* of China, by 李時珍 Li Shih-chên of the Ming dynasty, in 52 books. Second edition. 1657. In 24 vols; vols 12 and 13 in one; 4 cloth cases. Bequeathed by Professor Alfred Newton, 1907.   26cm.

E 374ᵇ.   輟 耕 錄
Cho kêng lu

"Miscellaneous Jottings put together in the intervals of Farming," consisting of notes on the overthrow of the Mongols, and of remarks on poetry, painting, porcelain, etc., first published in 1368. With the original preface, dated 1346, in grass character. By 陶宗儀 T'ao Tsung-i. 30 pt. in 6 vols, in blue cloth case. *No date*.   24.5cm.

E 374ᶜ.   陸 宣 公 集
Lu hsüan kung chi

The collected works of the political writer 陸贄 Lu Chih of the T'ang dynasty (A. D. 754—805). With portrait of the author, biographies from the New and Old T'ang histories, and prefaces by 權德輿 Ch'üan Tê-yü (759—818), 年羹堯 Nien Kêng-yao, Viceroy of Ssŭch'uan and Shensi (1665—1726), and the Emperor 雍正 Yung Chêng. 22 pt. in 6 vols, in blue cloth case. 1723.   25.5cm.

E 481ª. 漢 言 通 用 之 法
Han yen t'ung yung chih fa

A Grammar of the Chinese Language, by the Rev. R. Morrison, 1811. Copied from the original by the Rev. W. Milne, 1813—1814. 32cm.

† E 482. 關 帝 明 聖 眞 經
Kuan ti ming shêng chên ching

The *sûtra* of Kuan Ti, the God of War, followed by various documents, such as 文帝警世寶誥 the Admonitions of the Emperor Wên Ti (Liu Hêng), etc. 1894.　　32cm.

† E 483.

Another, but differing work, with the same title. *No date.* 24cm.

† E 484. 以 文 堂
I wên t'ang

An almanac for the year 1900, showing lucky and unlucky days, giving various forms of divination, the rise and fall of tides, flags of foreign nations, and a variety of miscellaneous information. 24cm.

† E 485. 六 字 經
Liu tzŭ ching

The six-word *sûtra*, being five repetitions of the formula *Om ma-ni pad-me hum* = Glory to Manipadme! — followed by one repetition of *Na-mah A-mi-t'o-fo* = I believe in Amida Buddha! 1905. 21cm.

† E 486. 禪 門 日 誦
Ch'an mên jih sung

A collection of Buddhist liturgies, rituals, magic formulas (*dhârani*), etc., published 1792, and re-issued 1880.　　27cm.

† E 487. 三 世 因 果 經
San shih' yin kuo ching

A Buddhist *sûtra* on the doctrine of three births, the past, the present, and the future, and retribution for evil deeds in the first and second states. 1901.　　21cm.

† E 488.   道 藏 三 元 經
                Tao ts'ang san yüan ching

A Taoist *sûtra*, dealing with the three primordial powers, —God, Earth, and Man. 1890.   26cm.

† E 489—490.   性 命 圭 旨
                    Hsing ming kuei chih

An eclectic view of life, showing that Confucianism, Taoism, and especially Buddhism, are all of value in shaping man's destiny; with numerous illustrations of eminent individuals. Re-issue of a work published in 1669. *No date.*   26cm.

† E 491.   欽 定 梵 音 大 悲 咒
                Ch'in ting fan yin ta pei chou

A *Dhârani*, or magic formula, with Sanskrit sounds, to be addressed to the goddess Kuan Yin. Said to have been translated by the Buddhist priest, 玄奘 Hsüan Tsang, and its publication to have been ordered by the Emperor Ch'ien Lung in 1756. *No date.*

                                                      26.5cm.

† E 492.   相 宗 八 要 直 解
                Hsiang tsung pa yao chih chieh

Translations of 論 *shastras*, etc., by the Chinese Buddhist priest, 玄 (formerly by taboo 元 Yüan) 奘 Hsüan Tsang. Part I only. *No date.*   25cm.

† E 493.   占 察 善 惡 業 報 經 疏
                Chan ch'a shan o yeh pao ching su

Translation, by the shaman 菩提登 P'u t'i têng, of a *sûtra* on the rewards and punishments for good and evil; with explanations by the shaman, 智旭 Chih Hsü. Part II only. *No date.*   25cm.

† E 494—496.   中 學 國 文 讀 本
                    Chung hsüeh kuo wên tu pên

A collection of extracts from the prose writings of the chief authors under the T'ang, Sung, Ming, and Yüan dynasties. *No date.*   21cm.

† E 497.　　黃　庭　經　註
Huang t'ing ching chu

The *Sùtra* of the Yellow Hall, on immortality and how to attain to it, by a Taoist recluse. Re-issue in 1793 of the edition of 1673. With 陰符經 *Yin fu ching* and 金玉經 *Chin yü ching* added.

28cm.

† E 498—499.　繪　圖　監　本　易　經
Hui t'u chien pên i ching

The *I ching*, or Canon of Changes, with illustrations and rhyming mnemonic verses. 1909.

20.5cm.

† E 500.　　列　仙　酒　牌
Lieh hsien chiu p'ai

Illustrated list of Taoist "Immortals," male and female, noted for indulgence in wine. 1906.

19.5cm.

† E 501—504.　芥　子　園　畫　傳　四　集
Chieh tzŭ yüan hua chuan ssŭ chi

A guide to the art of portraiture, with pictures of ancient celebrities, men and women, by 丁臬 Ting Kao, with a supplement on ancient seals, edited by 李笠翁 Li Li-wêng. First published in 1689. 1818.

26cm.

† E 505—506.　　道　德　經
Tao tê ching

The *Sùtra* of the Way and the Exemplification thereof, supposed by some to be the work of 老子 Lao Tzŭ, but now known to be a forgery of the second cent., B.C. Edited, with exegetical notes by a 眞人 Taoist of 純陽 Ch'un-yang. Re-issue in 1805 of edition of 1690.

27.5cm.

† E 507.　金　剛　般　若　波　羅　蜜　經
Chin kang pan jo po lo mi ching

The *Vajra prajna pâramitâ sùtra*, popularly known as the "Diamond *Sùtra*" and supposed to be able by its efficacy to crush diamond. Sounds and tones marked in upper margin. Canton, 1876.   29.5cm.

† E 508—510. 銅 板 易 經 遵 註 合 講
T'ung pan i ching tsun chu ho chiang

The *I ching*, or Canon of Changes, with the standard commentary and explanations. Printed from copper blocks, and edited by 翁克夫 Wêng K'o-fu of 太末 T'ai-mo in Chehkiang. 1810.   25cm.

† E 511—526. 御 批 歷 代 通 鑑 輯 覽
Yü p'i li tai t'ung chien chi lan

A history of China from the age of Fu Hsi (B.C. 2953) to the end of the Ming dynasty (A.D. 1644), published by order of H. M. the Emperor Ch'ien Lung, with Imperial preface dated 1767. *No date*.   21cm.

† E 527—546. 論 語, 大 學, 中 庸, 孟 子
Lun yü, Ta hsüeh, Chung yung, Mêng tzŭ

The Four Books, with exegetical notes by 何晏 Ho Yen of the 3rd cent. B.C., and commentaries by 趙岐 Chao Ch'i of the 2nd cent. B.C. and by 朱熹 Chu Hsi, A.D. 1130—1200. *No date*.
      15.5cm.

E 547.   要 覽 祝 文 記
Yao lan chu wên chi

A collection of important forms for invocations, prayers, etc. MS. *No date*. Presented by Mrs. Cooper.   24cm.

† E 548.   北 斗 眞 經
Pei tou chên ching

The *Sùtra* of the Northern Bushel (the constellation of the Great Bear). 1863.   26cm.

E 549—552. 戰 守 心 法

Chan shou hsin fa

Secret methods of offensive and defensive warfare, with numerous illustrations of forts, guns, torpedoes, etc. Presented by L. C. Arlington, Esq. 1907. 30cm.

† E 553. 孝 經

Hsiao ching

The Filial Piety Classic, with notes by the Emperor Shun Chih. 1650. 32cm.

E 554—555. 愛 日 吟 廬 書 畫 錄

Ai jih yin lu shu hua lu

Books and Pictures belonging to 葛金烺 Mr Ko Chin-làng. Presented by the author. 1909. 29.5cm.

E 556. 禱 告 文 全 書

Tao kao wên ch'üan shu

The Book of Common Prayer, complete. St. Paul's College, Hongkong, 1855. 28cm.

E 557. 中 國 聖 賢 要 道 類 編

Chung kuo shêng hsien yao tao lei pien

Select Teachings from Chinese Literature. Shanghai, 1909. 21cm.

E 558. 吾 妻 鏡

Wu ch'i ching

Almanac, in manuscript, for the 5th, 6th, (7th missing), and 8th years of Japanese 建長 A. D. 1249—1255. With coat of arms, George I, and label "Munificentia Regia, 1715;" also name of former owner, with date, "Johannes Burgesini, 1632." 28.5cm.

† E 559—561.

Three odd volumes, in rare palace edition, of B 1454. 25cm.

E 562. 大 觀 本 草
Ta kuan pên ts'ao

Section III of an old Materia Medica (see E 374ª), in leather case, with University arms. *No date.* 25.5cm.

E 563. 馬 耳 可 傳 福 音
Ma êrh k'o ch'uan fu yin

The Gospel of St Mark, translated from the original [Greek]. Malacca. *No date.* 26.5cm.

E 564. 馬 太 傳 福 音
Ma t'ai ch'uan fu yin

"The Gospel of Matthew in Chinese, with explanatory notes." By William Dean. Hongkong, 1848. 28cm.

E 565. 三 國 志 傳
San kuo chih chuan

Chapters VII and VIII of Biographies of the Three Kingdoms, with illustrations at the head of each page, and University coat of arms. "Ex dono Reverendi Dris Holdsworth" on fly-leaf. *No date.* 26cm.

E 566. 西 漢 文
Hsi han wên

Extracts from the literature of the Western Han dynasty, B.C. 206—A.D. 25. [Fragment, chiefly Index.] 1633. 25cm.

E 567. 曆 法 正 宗
Li fa chêng tsung

A Chinese almanac for the year 1644 (last year of Ming dynasty), with the usual miscellaneous information and illustrations. 24cm.

E 568. 萬 家 錦 隊 滿 天 春
Wan chia chin tui man t'ien ch'un

A collection of eighteen plays, with illustrations. 1504. 24cm.

E 569. 　　新　約　全　書
Hsin yo ch'üan shu

The New Testament, complete. By Griffith John. Hankow, 1886.
20cm.

E 570. 　紅　十　字　會　救　傷　第　一　法
Hung shih tzŭ hui chiu shang ti i fa

Red Cross Society First Aid to the Wounded. By 柯士賓
Ko Shih-pin(?). London, 1897. 　　　　　　　　　　18.5cm.

E 571. 　　隨　園　全　集
Sui yüan ch'üan chi

Collected works of 袁枚 Yüan Mei, whose sobriquet was Sui
Yüan (A.D. 1715—1797). 30 works with separate title-pages, including
his collected poems and essays, his letters, and the famous cookery-
book. 110 vols, in 12 blue cloth cases. 1891. 　　　　　　19cm.

H 1. 　釋　迦　如　來　應　化　事　蹟
Shih chia ju lai ying hua chi

Scenes from the life of Shâkyamuni Buddha, consisting of illustration and letterpress on each leaf, compiled by 楊文會 Yang Wên-
hui. 4 vols. in a pair of wooden boards, 1881. 　　　　　41cm.

H 2. 　　西　清　古　鑑
Hsi ch'ing ku chien

Bronzes and other antiquities from the Hsi-ch'ing Palace: full-page
illustrations with descriptive letterpress. Issued under Imperial instructions by a commission of scholars. Pt. 1—8, in 4 vols. 1749. 41.5cm.

H 3. 　皇　清　開　國　方　畧
Huang ch'ing k'ai kuo fang lüeh

A short history of the foundation of the present Manchu-Tartar
dynasty, from 1583 to 1644 A.D., as accomplished by the three rulers
太祖高 T'ai Tsu Kao, 太宗文 T'ai Tsung Wên, and 世祖章

Shih Tsu Chang. Issued, with a preface by the Emperor 乾隆 Ch'ien Lung, under the superintendence of the famous general and statesman 阿桂 O-kuei, 梁國治 Liang Kuo-chih, 和珅 Ho-shên and others. 32 pt. in 16 vols, in 2 blue cloth cases. 1786.

40cm.

H 4. 貞 觀 政 要
Chêng kuan chêng yao

A treatise on the principles of government, illustrated by the history of the period *chêng-kuan* (A.D. 627—649), by 吳兢 Wu Ching, who died in 742. Divided into chapters, each treating of a different subject, and consisting mainly of conversations with the Emperor 太宗 T'ai Tsung and his ministers. With a preface by the Emperor 成化 Ch'êng Hua. 10 pt. in 8 vols, with yellow covers, in blue cloth case, 1465. 35cm.

H 5. 陶 淵 明 集
T'ao yüan ming chi.

Collected works of 陶潛 T'ao Ch'ien (365—427), whose personal name was originally Yüan-ming. Reproduction of 蘇軾 Su Shih's edition, with portrait of T'ao Ch'ien and Su Shih. 10 pt. in 3 vols, in blue cloth case. 1879. 31.5cm.

H 6. 戰 國 策
Chan kuo ts'ê

History of the Contending States in the feudal period preceding the unification of the empire under the First Emperor, B.C. 221. By an unknown author, with commentary by 高愈 Kao Yü, edited by 姚宏中 Yao Hung-chung of the Sung dynasty. With an additional volume of documentary records. 36 pt. in 5 vols, in blue cloth case, 1869. 30cm.

H 7. 池 北 偶 談
Ch'ih pei ou t'an

A general literary miscellany, arranged under four divisions, treating respectively of (1) Court notabilia, (2) Distinguished characters, (3) Literary compositions, and (4) Marvels. [The first part contains references to the presentation of tribute by European nations.] By 王士禛 Wang Shih-chêng (A.D. 1634—1711). 26 pt. in 12 vols, in 2 blue cloth cases. 1701.   28cm.

H 8.   泉 史 and 貨 布 文 字 考
Ch'ūan shih and Huo pu wên tzŭ k'ao

(1) A history of the coinage of China by 盛子履 Shêng Tzŭ-li, with illustrations. 1833.

(2) Inscriptions on ancient money by 馬伯昂 Ma Po-ang, with illustrations. 1842.   29.5cm.

H 9.   大 乘 妙 法 蓮 華 經
Ta ch'êng miao fa lien hua ching

The *Saddharmapundarīka sûtra*, translated by 鳩摩羅什 Kumārajīva (A.D. 397—415), and edited by the priest 道宣 Tao Hsüan. *No date.*   28.5cm.

H 10.   孝 經 傳 說 圖 解
Hsiao ching chuan shuo t'u chieh

The Classic of Filial Piety, with commentary and full-page illustrations. 1811.   27cm.

H 11.   唐 宋 詩 醇
T'ang sung shih shun

Another edition of B 1470ᵇ, with title-page showing date and critical notes by the Emperor Ch'ien Lung. Edited by 陳宏謀 Ch'ên Hung-mou and others. 47 pt. in 24 vols, in 4 blue cloth cases. 1760.   30cm.

H 12.   品 花 寶 鑑
P'in hua pao chien

Scenes from social life in Peking. 20 vols in 4 cloth cases. 1849.
17cm.

H 13. 宜 稼 堂 叢 書
I chia t'ang ts'ung shu

A collection of reprints from the I-chia Hall. 68 vols, in 8 blue cloth cases. 1842. 25 cm.

H 14. 唐 宋 八 大 家 文 鈔
T'ang sung pa ta chia wên ch'ao

Prose writings of eight famous authors of the T'ang and Sung dynasties, namely: (1) 韓愈 Han Yü (A.D. 768—824); (2) 柳宗元 Liu Tsung-yüan (773—819); (3) 曾鞏 Tsêng Kung (11th cent.); (4) 王安石 Wang An-shih (1021—1086); (5) 歐陽修 Ou-yang Hsiu (1007—1072), including his 五代史 *Wu tai shih*, History of the Five Dynasties; (6) 蘇洵 Su Hsün (1009—1066); 蘇軾 Su Shih, better known as Su 東坡 Tung-p'o (1036—1101); and 蘇轍 Su Chê (1039—1112). With critical notes by 茅坤 Mao K'un. 164 pt. in 34 vols, in 6 blue cloth cases. [F. 2 wrongly inserted after f. 16 in the first vol. of Su Shih, and a duplicate f. 10 in pt. 7 of Han Yü, before f. 1 of Ou-yang Hsiu's history.] 1631. 27.5 cm.

H 15. 古 今 圖 書 集 成
Ku chin t'u shu chi ch'êng

A volume of the largest printed encyclopaedia in the world, compiled by 蔣廷錫 Chiang T'ing-hsi and a commission of scholars under the personal superintendence of the Emperor 康熙 K'ang Hsi (1662—1722). Contains pt. 335 and 336 of the section *I shu* "Arts and Sciences," dealing with portions of the sub-headings "Eating and Drinking" and "Digestion of Food" under the main heading "Medical Science." [The vol. belongs to a copy of the best edition, excellently printed on fine white paper, of which only a very limited number were struck off, and which is now unobtainable.] 1726. 28 cm.

H 16. 帝 鑑 圖 說
Ti Chien T'u Shuo

Episodes from the lives of the Emperors of China, from Yao and
G. W.

2

Shun down to the end of the Sung dynasty. Extracts from the dynastic histories, with illustrations and explanations. Compiled by 張太嶽 Chang T'ai-yo, with preface dated 1573. 4 vols, of which the first three contain the good deeds, and the fourth the wicked deeds. In a pair of wooden boards.   31cm.

H 17.   白 虎 通 疏 證

Po hu t'ung su chêng

A treatise expressing the views of a convocation of scholars under the Eastern Han dynasty regarding various points in the classics. Edited and arranged under 44 heads by the historian 班固 Pan Ku (died A.D. 92). With commentary and confirmatory evidence by 陳樂 Ch'ên Li. 12 pt. in 6 vols., 1832.   27.5cm.

H 18.   金 壺 精 萃

Chin hu ching ts'ui

A small vocabulary explaining curious two-character phrases occurring in standard works, arranged under 4 categories. By 楊慶麟 Yang Ch'ing-lin. 2 vols, in ornamental cloth case. 1876.   30cm.

H 19.   白 氏 長 慶 集

Po shih ch'ang ch'ing chi

The works of the poet 白居易 Po Chü-i (A.D. 772—846), with a preface by his friend and contemporary 元稹 Yüan Chên. Edited by 馬元 Ma Yüan. 71 pt. in 12 vols. 1606.   26cm.

H 20.   西 域 記

Hsi yü chi

The travels of 玄奘 Hsüan (or 元 Yüan) Tsang in western countries, A.D. 629—645, in search of Buddhist books, etc. 4 vols, Japanese edition.   26cm.

H 21.   今 古 奇 觀

Chin ku ch'i kuan

A collection of forty short stories, or novelettes, written in an easy but elegant style. In 4 vols, European binding. 1730.   24cm.

H 22. 世 說 新 語

Shih shuo hsin yü

A collection of minor historical incidents from the Later Han to the Chin dynasty inclusive (2nd to 5th cent A.D.). By 王義慶 Wang I-ch'ing of the 5th cent., with extensive commentary by Liu Hsiao-piao of the 6th cent. With "postface" by 陸游 Lu Yu (1125—1209), and list of names of the personages of the period. 6 vols. 1891.   26.5cm.

H 23. 金 壺 字 考

Chin hu tzŭ k'ao

A vocabulary of two-character phrases, arranged under four categories. By 郝在田 Hao Tsai-t'ien, whose preface is dated 1873. 1888.   27cm.

✳ H 24. 金 剛 經 直 疏

Chin kang ching chih su

The Diamond *Sûtra*, correctly explained by the Buddhist priest Shih-lien (*see* A 417). 1849.   24.5cm,

✳ H 25. 字 學

Tzŭ hsüeh

A guide to the correct orthography of characters, discrimination between like forms, etc. 1876.   25cm.

✳ H 26. 二 十 四 孝 圖 說

Erh shih ssŭ hsiao t'u shuo

The Twenty-four Examples of Filial Piety. Text and illustrations. *No date.*   25cm.

H 27. 楊 鐵 崖 文 集

Yang t'ieh yai wên chi

Works of the poet 楊維禎 Yang Wei-chêng (14th cent. A.D.), compiled by 王榮絃 Wang Jung-hung. [1 vol. only, containing pts. 1 and 2 of "Ancient poetry".] 1773.   25cm.

H 28.   玉 歷 鈔

Yü li ch'ao

A description of the Ten Courts of Purgatory in the nether world, through some or all of which every erring soul must pass. With illustrations and commentary. 2 pt. in 1 vol. 1886.   24.5cm.

H 29.   官 話 指 南

Kuan hua chih nan

A Manual of Chinese conversation, by Goh Daigoro. Tokyo, 1881.

25cm.

H 30.   百 家 姓

Po chia hsing

The Book of Family Surnames. *No date.*   17cm.

H 31.   理 財 節 畧

Li ts'ai chieh lüeh

Essays on China's commerce in silk, tea, straw braid, wool, etc., with foreign countries. By F. E. Taylor, Commissioner of Customs. Shanghai, 1901.   24.5cm.

✳ H 32.   焦 山 志

Chiao shan chih

History of Chiao-shan, an island in the Yangtsze, about 3 miles to the N.E. of Chinkiang, famous for its Buddhist monastery, and known to foreigners as Silver Island. 10 vols. 1865. [Presented by L. H. Tamplin, Esq.]   25cm.

✳ H 33.   莆 風 清 籟 集

P'u fêng ch'ing lai chi

An anthology of Fuhkien poets, from the T'ang dynasty down to modern times, including specimens by Buddhist and Taoist priests, nuns, and others. Edited by a large number of scholars. 20 vols. 1772.   24.5cm.

✱ H 34. 興 化 府 志
Hsing hua fu chih

Topographical account of the Prefecture of Hsing-hua in Fuhkien.
24 vols. New edition. 1871. 24.5cm.

✱ H 35. 陳 公 文 集
Ch'ên kung wên chi

The complete works of 陳拙齊 Ch'ên Cho-chai, a distinguished
littérateur, native of Fuhkien. 4 vols. 1670. 23.5cm.

✱ H 36. 施 註 蘇 詩
Shih chu su shih

The poems of 蘇東坡 Su Tung-p'o, with commentary by
施維翰 Shih Wei-han (A.D. 1621—1683), and rare portrait of
the poet wearing agricultural labourer's hat and pattens or "clogs."
1699. [*See* 200b.] 23cm.

✱ H 37. 李 太 白 文 集
Li t'ai po wên chi

The complete poetical and prose works of Li T'ai-po (died A.D.
762). Edited by 王琦 Wang Ch'i (T. 琢崖) of the Manchu dynasty; the edition mentioned in the Imperial Catalogue. 8 vols. 17th
cent. [Title-page and part of Index missing.] 25.5cm.

✱ H 38. 陳 龍 川 集
Ch'ên lung ch'uan chi

The works of Ch'ên Lung-ch'uan, a *littérateur* of the Sung dynasty,
with portrait; first published in 1193. 8 vols. 1709. 23cm.

✱ H 39. 避 暑 山 莊
Pi shu shan chuang

The poems of the Emperor K'ang Hsi, A.D. 1662—1722, with
illustrations and Manchu translations interleaved. 1711. 26cm.

※ H 40. 白 香 山 詩 集
Po hsiang shan shih chi

The poetical works of 白居易 Po Chü-i, A.D. 772—846, with early prefaces and author's own "Record" (dated 845). 10 vols. 1703. [Table of Contents damaged.]   28cm.

※ H 41. 剖 瓠 存 稿
P'ou kua ts'un kao

The collected writings of 蕭重 Hsiao Chung (T. 遠村). 5 vols. 1834.   27cm.

※ H 42. 黃 御 史 集
Huang yü shih chi

The writings (chiefly poems) of 黃滔 Huang T'ao (T. 文江), a Censor under the T'ang dynasty (graduated A.D. 895), published by order of the Emperor K'ang Hsi, about 1700. 4 vols.   28cm.

※ H 43. 澹 軒 稿
Tan hsien kao

The remains of Tan Hsien, scholar and official, who graduated in A.D. 1430. 4 vols. 1566.   25cm.

※ H 44. 歷 朝 賦 楷
Li ch'ao fu ch'iai

Specimens of the *fu* style of poetry, from the 周 Chou dynasty, B.C. 1122—255, down to and including part of the Manchu dynasty. 8 vols. 1686.   24cm.

※ H 45. 示 我 周 行
Shih wo chou hsing

A traveller's guide, being itineraries for China Proper, showing the principal routes, with distances, between the most important towns; by 賴盛遠 Lai Shêng-yüan. 3 vols. 1774.   17cm.

✳ H 46.   增默盦詩遺集

Tsêng mo an shih i chi

Further poems by 敦尙先 (T 蘭石) Kuo Shang-hsien of 莆田 P'u-t'ien in Fuhkien. 1 vol. 1871.   25.5cm.

✳ H 47.   時　憲　書

Shih hsien shu

Chinese Official Almanac for 1840. [In bad condition.]   20.5cm.

H 48.   御　製　耕　織　圖

Yü chih kêng chih t'u

The various processes in tillage and weaving, with versified text and 46 illustrations by 焦秉貞 Chiao Ping-chên, who had studied perspective under foreign tuition, and preface by the Emperor K'ang Hsi. 1 vol. in case. 1696.

[The original work was by 樓璹 Lou Shou, published in 1210.]
36cm.

H 49.   金　石　索

Chin shih so

An illustrated collection of inscriptions of all kinds, calligraphic and pictorial, in 12 parts, six of these referring to inscriptions on metal (coins, mirrors, bells, etc.), and six to inscriptions on stone (buildings, tablets, etc.). By 馮雲鵬 Fêng Yün-p'êng. 1822.   36cm.

Y 1ᵃ.   全　唐　文

Ch'üan t'ang wên

A complete collection of the prose literature (*see* D 246) produced under the T'ang dynasty. Issued by Imperial command under the general direction of 董誥 Tung Kao and others. 1000 pt. in 401 vols, in 40 pairs of wooden boards. 1818.   26.5cm.

Z 42—43.　　　　　　體　功　學

T'i kung hsüeh

Halliburton's Physiology, translated by Philip B. Cousland. Shanghai, 1905.　　　　　　　　　　　　　26.4cm.

Z 44.

Medical Nomenclature, by the Committee of the China Medical Association. Shanghai, 1904.　　　　　　　　21.5cm.

ADDENDUM.

H 50.　　　　　　柳　文　印　義

Liu wên yin i

The complete works of 柳宗元 Liu Tsung-yüan, A.D. 773—819, including his poetry, essays, critiques, biographical and historical notes, funeral orations, inscriptions on tablets and graves, correspondence, prefaces, dedications, memorials to the Throne, sacrificial addresses, etc., etc. With preface by 陸之淵 Lu Chih-yüan, d. A.D. 1190. A very fine specimen of the art of printing under the Sung dynasty. 1167.　　　　　　　　　　　　　26cm.

INDEX TO AUTHORS.

Tu Fu, D 75[a].
Tung Kao, Y 1[a].
Wang I-ch'ing, H 22.
Wang Shih-chêng, H 7.
Wang Ying-lin, B 382[b].
Wêng K'o-fu, E 508—510.
Wu Ching, H 4.

Wu Jên-ch'ên, B 1470[c].
Yang Ch'ing-lin, H 18.
Yang Shên, E 177[c].
Yang Wei-chêng, H 27.
Yang Wên-hui, H 1.
Yüan Mei, E 581.

INDEX TO BOOKS.

Hsing ming kuei chih, E. 489—490.

Huang ch'ing k'ai kuo fang lüeh, H 3.

Huang t'ing ching chu, E 497.

Huang yü shih chi, H 42.

Hui t'u chien pên i ching, E 498—499.

Hung shih tzŭ hui chiu shang ti i fa, E 570.

Huo pu wên tzŭ k'ao, H 8.

I chia t'ang ts'ung shu, H 13.

I wên t'ang, E 484.

Kan ying p'ien, A 427ᵃ.

Ku chin t'u shu chi ch'êng, H 15.

Kuan hua chih nan, H 29.

Kuan ti ming shêng chên ching, E 482.

Kuan ti ming shêng chên ching, E 483.

Kung shun t'ang ts'ung shu, B 1470ᵃ.

Kuo ch'ao hsien chêng shih lüeh, B 1470ᵈ.

Lêng yen ching chêng mo, A 427ᶜ.

Li ch'ao fu ch'iai, H 44.

Li fa chêng tsung, E 567.

Li t'ai po wên chi, H 37.

Li ts'ai chieh lüeh, H 31.

Lieh hsien chiu p'ai, E 500.

Lieh Tzŭ, A 427ᵇ.

Liu tzŭ ching, E 485.

Lu hsüan kung chi, E 374ᶜ.

Lun yü, Ta hsüeh, Chung yung, Mêng tzŭ, E 527—546.

Ma êrh k'o ch'uan fu yin, E 563.

Ma t'ai ch'uan fu yin, E 564.

Mêng ch'i pi t'an, E 177ᵃ.

P'ang hsi chai ts'ung shu, E 71ᵃ.

Pei tou chên ching, E 548.

Pên ts'ao kang mu, E 374ᵃ.

Pi shu shan chuang, H 39.

P'i p'a chi, D 180ᵇ.

P'in hua pao chien, H 12.

Po chia hsing, H 30.

Po hsiang shan shih chi, H 40.

Po hu t'ung su chêng, H 17.

Po shih ch'ang ch'ing chi, H 19.

P'ou kua ts'un kao, H 41.

P'u fêng ch'ing lai chi, H 33.

San kuo chih chuan, E 565.

San shih yin kuo ching, E 487.

Shih chia ju lai mi hsing hua chi ch'üan p'u, H 1.

Shih chu su shih, H 36.

Shih kuo ch'un ch'iu, B 1470ᶜ.

Shih shuo hsin yü, H 22.

Shih wo chou hsing, H 45.

Shui hu chuan, D 75ᶜ.

Su wên chung kung shih chi, D 200ᵇ.

Sui yüan chüan chi, E 571.

Ta ch'êng miao fa lien hua ching, H 9.

Ta kuan pên ts'ao, E 562.

Tan hsien kao, H 43.

Tan yen tsung lu, E 71ᵈ.

T'ang sung pa ta chia wên ch'ao, H 14.

T'ang sung shih shun, B 1470ᵇ.

ERRATA IN CATALOGUE OF 1898.

P.　9, line 5 — *For* 顧 etc. *read* 顧豹文 Ku Pao-wên, whose 字 style was 且菴 Ch'ieh-an.

»　17, » 9 from foot — *For* 577 *read* 574.

»　42, » 5 » » — *For* 木 *read* 本, *for* mu *read* pên.

»　49, » 7 — *For* i *read* ssŭ.

»　52, » 3 and 9 — *For* 熙 *read* 熹.

»　53, » 8 — *For* The institutions *read* Documentary remains.

»　57, » 10 from foot — *For* 1258 *read* 1174 and 1258.

»　64, » 9 — *For* 編 *read* 總.

»　64, » 10 — *For* pien *read* tsung.

»　66, last line — *For* 1798 *read* 1558.

»　70, line 12 — *Insert* 武 *after* 朝.

»　83, » 7 from foot — *For* 國 *read* 圖.

»　89, » 5 » » — *For* 瑞 *read* 金, *for* Jui *read* Chin.

»　90, » 9 » » — *For* 吳與臧 Wu Hsing-tsang *read* 臧晉叔 Tsang Chin-shu.

»　93, » 12 — *For* 柝 *read* 析.

»　110, » 9 — *For* shih *read* chih. *Dele* "Chih for shih on label."

»　119, » 10 — *After* 傅 *insert* 世堯 Fu Shih-yao whose 字 style was, *and dele* Fu.

»　126, » 3 — *After* Hsi-ch'i *add* of the 18th cent.

[Index to be corrected accordingly.]

Catalogue of the Chinese Library of the Royal Asiatic Society

皇家亚洲学会中文文库目录

CATALOGUE

OF

THE CHINESE LIBRARY

OF THE

ROYAL ASIATIC SOCIETY.

BY

THE REV. S. KIDD.

LONDON:

PRINTED BY JOHN W. PARKER, ST. MARTIN'S LANE.

M.DCCC.XXXVIII.

ADVERTISEMENT.

The following explanatory Catalogue of the Chinese Library of the Royal Asiatic Society was drawn up by the Rev. S. Kidd, the Professor of Chinese Literature in the University College, and presented by him to the Society.

The Council of the Society are of opinion that the information which this valuable communication contains, respecting the actual compass and general character of the Literature of China, will render it highly interesting, not merely to the Chinese student, but also to the general scholar, and they have accordingly directed 500 copies to be printed, for the use of the Members.

The expense will be defrayed by an individual Member of the Society.

GRAFTON STREET,
June 1838.

启 事

　　以下《皇家亚洲学会中文藏书目录》提要由伦敦大学学院（the University College）中国文学教授S.基德牧师（Rev. S. Kidd）起草并呈交皇家亚洲学会。

　　学会理事会认为，这一有价值的《目录》所包含的信息考虑到中国文学的实际领域和一般特点，对中国学生乃至普通学者均极具吸引力，因此理事会指示印制500份供会员使用。

　　费用将由学会的某位会员承担。

格拉夫顿街（Grafton Street），

1838年6月

（管宇译，彭萍校）

CHINESE LIBRARY.

LANGUAGE.

Chuen tsze wei

A well-known Dictionary of the ancient Seal character, in six vols. This form of the character was originally written 800 years B. C.

Keang hoo chih tŭh fun yun tsŏ yaou

A Pocket-Dictionary and Letter-Writer for travellers: or, "An abridged Dictionary, arranged according to the tones,"—that is, the final sound of the character. In four vols. Two copies.

Fun yun

A Dictionary arranged according to the tones, in one vol.

Tsze wei

A Dictionary according to the primitives, in fourteen vols.

B

Yun   *ya*

A Dictionary arranged according to the tones, in five vols.

Yun *foo* *shih* *e*

A Dictionary arranged according to the tones, in twenty four vols.

E *wăn* *tung* *lan*

A Dictionary arranged according to the primitives, in thirty-eight vols. Literal title—"General Observations on Polite Literature."

Yun *tsze* *luy* *yin*

A Dictionary arranged according to the tones, in eight vols.

Lŭh *shoo*

An ancient Dictionary arranged according to the form and meaning of the character, in five vols. A standard work, to which all later lexicographers have been indebted; originally composed by Paou-she, during the dynasty Chow, about the year B. C. 1100.

Koo   *kin*   *yun*   *leŏ*

A Dictionary according to the ancient and modern laws of intonation, in five vols.

Yun   *foo*   *k'eun*   *yŭh*

" A Treasury of Rhymes and a Group of Gems." A Dictionary arranged according to the tones, in twenty vols.

Shwŏ   *wăn*

An ancient Dictionary arranged according to the form and meaning of the characters, in six vols. It was composed by Heu-shin, an officer of government during the dynasty Han, A. D. 100. The object of the work was both to preserve the original form of the character, and to trace its meaning and derivation.

E   *wăn*   *lan*

A Dictionary of the Seal character, in four vols.

Gnaou   *e*   *tsze*   *yun*

A Dictionary arranged according to the tones, in three vols.

B 2

E   wăn   pei   lan

An excellent Dictionary arranged according to the primitives, in forty-two vols. Its author, Sha-mŭh, was thirty years in completing it. It was first published in the reign of Këen-lung.

K'ang   he   tsze   tëen

A Dictionary compiled from the best authorities, by order of the late Emperor Kang-he. It occupied thirty persons five years, is arranged according to the primitives, and entitled " A Standard or Canon of the Character." Sixteen vols. 8vo., European binding.

Tsze   lin   yŭh   pëen

" A Grove of Characters and a Page of Diamonds." A Dictionary according to the primitives, in one vol.

Ching   tsze   túng

A Dictionary arranged according to the primitives, in twenty-three vols., originally published during the Ming dynasty.

Ching   tsze   tëen

A Dictionary according to the primitives, in twenty vols.; also another copy in fourteen vols.

Kwan   hwa   tsung   lun

General remarks on the Mandarin dialect, in one vol.

Tsze   e

An explanation of important words in physical and moral science, in two vols.

Tsing   wăn   ke   mung

" Tartar Literature to enlighten the Dull." A sort of vocabulary, with a Chinese interpretation, for the use of boys, in four vols.

Tung   wăn   t'sëen   tsze   wăn

" The Thousand-character Classic," according to the three forms of writing:—the Seal, or ancient character; the Running-hand, or grass character, and the Correct, or ordinary character: in two vols.

T'sëen   tsze   wăn

The Thousand-character Classic, with a commentary, in one vol. It is composed of a thousand different symbols, so arranged as to make sense without the recurrence of the same word; hence its title.

T'sëen   tsze   wăn

The same work as the two preceding, consisting of the text only, in one vol.

Tsing   wăn   hwuy

A Manchow-Tartar-Chinese Lexicon, in European binding, thick 8vo., one vol.

Mwan   Han   hŏ   peih   seuen   yaou

Valuable and important selections in the Manchow-Tartar and Chinese languages, in four vols.

Tsing   wăn   këen

The Mirror of the Manchow-Tartar language, in twenty-six vols.

Sin   lŭh   tsze   fă

A Manual of four different methods of writing the Chinese character, in two vols.

HISTORY.

Shoo   *king*

This work is the second of the " Five Classics," and the most ancient portion of Chinese History, comprising records of the first sovereigns of antiquity, who lived about the time of the Deluge, with a commentary, in twelve vols.

Koo   *wăn*   *shang*   *shoo*

The same work under another title, with a commentary, in six vols.

Shoo   *king*

The text only of the above work, in four vols.

Kang   *këen*   *ta*   *tseuen*

A complete view of General History, in thirty-four vols.

Kang   *këen*   *ming*   *ke*

A general view of History, perspicuously arranged, in four vols.

Fung　　Chow　　kang　　këen

Fung Chow's General History, in forty vols.　A work of considerable authority in China.

Se　　yang　　ke　　tung　　suh

An authentic Record of the general Customs of the Western Ocean.　The phrase　　　　Se-yang, usually denotes Europe, but it seems here to refer to Arabia and India: in twenty vols.

She　　　　ke

Historical Memorials, in twenty-four vols.

She　　ke　　tung　　këen

A complete and perspicuous survey of History, in thirty-nine vols.

Tung　　këen　　kang　　mŭh

A general History of China, by Choo-foo-tsze, the distinguished commentator on the " Four Books," in sixty-seven vols.

Tsing neih ke

An abridged account of an Insurrection, which took place in the eighteenth year of Kea-king, in two vols.

Chun tsew

Confucius's History of his own Times, containing an account of the sixth century before the Christian era: it is the last in order of the "Five Classics," and derives its title—"Spring and Autumn"—from the circumstance of its having been commenced at the former, and concluded at the latter of those seasons. It consists, with a commentary, of seventeen vols. Another copy, the text merely, in six vols.

Hwang tsing k'ae kwŏ fang leŏ

Methods and plans by which the foundation of the Imperial Tartar dynasty was laid in China, in twelve vols.

Shwŏ ling

An account of embassies from Russia, Cochin-China, Formosa, the Loo Choo Islands, and other states. Two works, the former in twelve, the latter in eight vols.

Tung   hwa   lŭh

A manuscript account of the Tartar dynasty composed by some historiographers of government, during the reign of Këen-lung, in sixteen vols. The printing of this work is a capital offence by the laws of China.

STATISTICS AND TOPOGRAPHY.

Kwang   tung   t'ung   che

A topographical and statistical work on the Province of Canton, in thirty-six vols.

Nan   Hae   hëen   che

Statistics of the district Nan Hae, in the province of Canton; in twelve vols.

Fan   yu   hëen   che

Statistics of Fan-yu, the district in which European ships anchor; in twelve vols.

Yih   tung   che

A statistical account of the whole Chinese Empire, in thirty-two vols.

Keung   *chow*   *foo*   *che*

A statistical account of the northern part of the Island, Hae Nan; in sixteen vols.

T'ae   *p'ing*   *kwang*   *ke*

" Extensive Records of general Peace and Prosperity." A sort of abstract of the different provinces of China, statistical, topographical, &c., in forty vols.: originally published in the tenth century.

Yuĕ   *tung*   *peih*   *ke*

Records relating to the Province of Canton, in four vols.

San   *kwŏ*   *che*

Statistics of the three kingdoms   *wei, shŭh, woo,* which flourished about the third century of the Christian era. This work, though generally derived from the events of that period, abounds with fiction, and must, therefore, notwithstanding its title, be regarded as a sort of historical novel. It is written with distinguished ability, and considered as a model of elegant composition in that department of literature to which it belongs. Three copies, one octavo and two duodecimo, twenty vols. each.

Ming   chin   leih   tae   tsow   e

A general collection of Statistics addressed to the Emperor by celebrated ministers of successive ages, in thirty-two vols.

Nan   Han   ch'un   t'sew

" The Spring and Autumn of Nan Han." Probably a statistical account of a district in the province of Sze Chuen, in four vols.

Nan   te   tung   heaou

" General illustrations of Nan Te," in one vol., two copies.

Han   Sung   k'e   shoo

" Extraordinary description of the dynasties Han and Sung;" or statistical and topographical illustrations of the *san-kwŏ* and *shwuy-hoo* united : in twenty vols

Hing   shwuy   kin   këen

A description of the rise, courses, productions, &c. of the celebrated rivers of China, and an account of ' the river for the transportation of grain,"—the great canal ; in forty vols.

Ta Ying kwo tung che

General Statistics of the great English Nation, by the Rev. C. Gutzlaff, in one vol.

Shwuy Hoo chuen

An historical work of the Sung dynasty, founded partly on fact and partly on fiction. Literal title, "Streams and Lawns narrated;" in twenty vols., two copies.

———

BIOGRAPHY.

———

Ming hëen lëĕ neu she sing poo

A biographical work, containing lives of eminent men and celebrated females, through successive ages; in one hundred and twenty vols.

Lëĕ neu chuen

Biographical sketches of eminent females, in eight vols.

POETRY.

———

She   king

A collection of ancient odes, originally compiled by Confucius, in four vols.   Three copies.

She   king

The same work, with a copious commentary, in seventeen vols.

T'sëen   sow   yen   she

A collection of odes, entitled the Banquet Odes of a Thousand Old Gentlemen; in thirty-six vols.

Hung   seuĕ   low   keu   chung   keŭh

The nine dramatic pieces, or popular songs of the red and white chamber, in ten vols.

Wan   show   keu   ko   yŏ   chang

Pieces of music and songs sung in the streets on imperial birth-days; in six vols.

She   yun   choo   ke

"The Pearl-Mirror of Poetical Harmony;" a collection of odes, in four vols.

Shih   urh   chung   keŭh

The twelve popular odes, or dramatic pieces, in twenty-four vols.

Lŭh   yin   ting   she

The Odes of the Green-shaded Hall, in two vols.

Leih   ung   shih   chung   keuh

Leih-ung's ten dramatic compositions, or popular odes, in eighteen vols.

She   fă   jïh   mun

An introduction to the laws of poetry, in one vol.

Shĭh   san   poo   wei   ko

Satirical songs, accompanied with thirteen broad caricatures of different persons, in one vol.

NATURAL HISTORY.

Kwang   pŏ   wŭh   che

A sort of universal history of nature,—" Every-thing that exists between Heaven and Earth;" in twenty vols.

Pun   t'saou   kang   mŭh

" A general Outline of Plants and Herbs."   This is considered the best pharmacopœia as well as botanical work in China; in forty-three vols.

Pun   tsaou   kang   mŭh   tsih   yaou

An abstract of the most important parts of a general treatise on Botany; in thirteen vols.; the three last comprising notices of herbs suitable for the human species and animals.

T'ang   jin   shwŏ   wei

The T'ang Dynasty's, or the Chinese, herbal ex-positor; in thirty-two vols.

Urh joo t'ing k'eun fang poo yuen

A treatise on the heavens, the seasons, fruit-trees, grain, vegetables, flowers, medicine, fish, &c., in which the mode of cultivating tea, bamboo, hemp, and the cotton-plant, is discussed. The fifth volume gives an account of the introduction of the cotton-plant into China in the thirteenth century, its different names, and the high value attached to it: in eighteen vols.

Urh   meaou

A description of the bamboo, its shoots, plants, &c.; in four vols.

Hwa   t'oo

"Drawings of flowers;" the first of which is *Füh   show,* "the Hand of Buddha," *i. e.* the flower of the citron, so called from its supposed resemblance to the hand; in one vol.

———————

c

MORAL PHILOSOPHY.

Sze   *shoo*

"The Four Books," consisting of the *Ta heŏ*, which contains literature suited to adults, as the title indicates; the *Chung-yung*, the constant (golden) medium; the *Shang-lun* and the *Hea-lun*, which comprise the conversations of Confucius with his disciples, his instructions to the governments of his day, his maxims, &c.; the *Shang Măng* and *Hea Măng*,—that portion of the work which was composed by Mencius, whose name it bears, and who flourished about 150 years later than his prototype Confucius, or B. C. 350. The "Four Books" are six thin volumes,—the title being derived, not from the size of the work, but from the number of the philosopher's disciples, four, who compiled their master's sayings.

Sze   *shoo*   *kwan*   *hwa*

"The Four Books," in Mandarin, in one vol.

Sze   *shoo*   *hŏ*   *keang*

The preceding Four Books, with the Commentary of *Choo-He*, and a general paraphrase composed of extracts from various commentators; in six vols.

Sze   shoo   tseih   choo

The same work as the preceding, without the paraphrase, but having the comments of Choo-foo-tsze, the well-known moral philosopher and historian, who lived in the twelfth century: in six vols.

Lun   yu   e   soo

"The Sentiments of the *Lun yu* expanded." A commentary on the first of the "Four Books;" in five vols.

Choo   foo   tsze   tseuen   shoo

The whole works of Choo-foo-tsze, the celebrated commentator on the "Four Books," moral philosopher and historian, who flourished in the twelfth century: in twenty-eight vols.

Shing   yu   kwang   heun

"The Sacred Edict." "A book of political moralities, composed by a late emperor, and paraphrased by a vice-governor of a province. On the 1st and 15th of each month, or the new and full moon, the principal officers of the province assemble in a hall, and listen to an officer of government mounted on a table, who rehearses *memoriter*, a section of this work, first in Chinese, and next in the Tartar language, for the benefit of the soldiers who attend." (Morrison.) *Translated by Dr. Milne.*

C 2

Hwang   ming   che   shoo

A work on filial piety, in twelve vols.; the title of which is, "The Imperial Ming dynasty's Book of National Regulations."

Wan   te   tseuen   shoo

The whole works of *Wăn-te,* comprising essays on the regeneration of the people, filial piety, prosperity, rewards and punishments, together with sacred edicts and other matters; in eight vols. Two copies.

Jin   săng   peih   tŭh

A work on filial piety, in two vols., entitled " Man's Life must be Read."

Fan   yih   sze   shoo

The " Four Books," translated into the Manchow-Tartar language by order of the emperor: in six vols.

Sih   keae   lŭh

Restraint of the passions recommended: in two vols.

King   foo   sin   shoo

A new book to excite the attention of the rich, in six vols.

Taou   tih   king

"The Sacred Classic of Reason and Virtue." A work of the philosophical sect of China, founded by Laou Keun tsze B. C. 500, which is much esteemed among the disciples of that school: in two vols.

Lŭh   sze   pe   keuĕ

The secret mysteries of official emolument and posterity: in one vol. Compositions partly literary and partly moral in their character. Probably a series of prize essays.

Chung   yung   kwan   hwa

The Golden Medium,—the second of the "Four Books" of Confucius, according to the Mandarin dialect; in one vol.; published at the Capital.

K'eun   chin   choo   shuh

"A Narrative of certain Worthies of the sect of Taou," in one vol. The designation especially applies to the eminent of that school, who, being denuded of their corporeal figure, become a kind of spiritual genii.

Shing   king   kwang   yih

" Sacred Classics."   A sort of metaphysical treatise on the two original powers in nature—Heaven and Earth—with moral lessons deduced from the subject ; in one vol.   Two copies.

Kwang   shen   wei   han

" Moral virtues extended."   A collection of treatises on various subjects in moral philosophy.   Published by imperial authority; in two vols.

T'seih   sew   luy   kaou

Seven Essays.   The subjects are:—Heaven and Earth ;   National Affairs ;   Righteous Principles ; Test of Truth ;   Poetry ;   Men and things ;   and Marvellous Satires : in seven vols.

Chwang   Tsze   nan   hwa

" The Southern Flowers of Chwang Tsze," a celebrated philosopher, whose works, according to the author of Notitia Linguæ Sinicæ, rank next to the " Four Books."   He is much praised for elegance of style by Premare, who often quotes him : in three vols.

Kwăn   heŏ   ke   wăn

"Laborious Learning and Digested Knowledge."
A compendium of metaphysical and moral science,
in fourteen vols.

Tsze   che   sin   shoo

A work on Political Economy, embracing a variety
of topics pertaining to the authority of the legislature, and the supposed well-being of its subjects;
the title of which may be rendered, "A new book
on things necessary for use, and good government."
Two copies having the same title, the one consisting
of *ten*, the other of *seven* vols.

Kea   paou   tseuen   tseih

"A Collection of Domestic Jewels." A work
containing a hundred negative precepts on personal
and relative behaviour, besides instructions of a miscellaneous nature suited to families. It was published in the reign of Kang He, probably by a
domestic tutor, who was a disciple of Fŭh: in
thirty-two vols.

Fŭh   hwuy   tseuen   tseih

"A complete Book of Happiness and Mercy." A
work on political morality, by the emperor Këen-
lung, and entitled Këen-lung's Government Tables:
in eight vols.

Kung   Tsze   kea   yu

"*Kung*, the philosopher's personal narrative, or domestic instructions." A record of Confucius's life and sentiments, taken from his lips by his disciples: In two vols.: two copies.

T'ae   shang   kan   ying   pëen

A well-known essay of the sect of Taou on virtue and vice, inducing rewards and punishments, entitled, "The Influence of Human Conduct on the Great Supreme,"—an epithet applied to the founder of the sect, to whom this work is attributed, although it was not known in the world until several hundred years after his time. It contains many excellent precepts, and also some medical advice, which is not uncommon in books on moral subjects. It was first published in the thirteenth century, under the patronage of the Emperor Le-tsung, who gave a million pieces of brass coin to pay for the original edition: in two vols.

Wan   shen   t'ung   kwei

All virtues have the same consummation; in two vols.

METAPHYSICS AND GENERAL SCIENCE, ARTS, &c.

Yih   *king*

The third of the "Five ancient Classics," which contains an account of the science of numbers, consisting of the *changes, combinations,* and *transmutations* that take place in nature, by the operation of which all the effects in the visible universe are produced. According to this system, chaos is divided into two parts, *light* and *darkness, perfection* and *imperfection, male* and *female,* to which powers numbers are made to correspond, in a manner not dissimilar to the Pythagorean theory of the principles of all things : in two vols.

Luy   *king*

The origin and laws of the Universe explained, with a commentary; in fifteen vols.

T'ae   *heun*   *pë̆*   *heun*

Principles relating to the origin of the universe stated and discussed, together with figures explanatory of the system : in five vols.

Luy   king   t'oo   yih

A similar work to the preceding, together with figures of the "Three Powers,"—Heaven, Earth, and Man: in six vols.

San   t'sae   t'oo   hwuy

A collection of plates representing the three great powers in nature, Heaven, Earth, and Man, under which every department of knowledge is included. A celebrated Encyclopedia published during the Ming dynasty.

T'sing   she

History of Nature, in twelve vols.

Yuen   këen   luy   han

"A profound treatise on universal science." A work published by imperial authority, on the Heavens, the Earth, the Air, and the Sea, their inhabitants, productions, and other phenomena. It also treats of political and moral duties, contains an historical account of ancient offices and titles of nobility, describes the nature of good government, and the rules whereby it may be carried into effect. The whole work comprises **153** vols.

Tsëen   k'eŏ   luy   shoo

Truth profoundly investigated in several departments:—a sort of Encyclopedia Sinensis, in sixty vols.

Sing   le   ta   t'seun

A complete system of the principles of nature, published early in the fifteenth century. This work contains a full exposition of Chinese theories on the origin of the Universe, Chaos, the Monad, Dual, and Triad powers in nature, the production of matter, mind, spirit, and organized forms of every description: in twenty vols. Also a smaller edition of the same work, in six vols., 12mo.

Lŭh   hŏ   nuy   wae   so   yen

A consecutive account of men and things within and beyond the six points—East, West, South, North, the Zenith, and the Nadir: in twelve vols.

Chow   yih   chĕ   chung

One of the chief commentaries on the Chinese Classics, published by K'ang-he towards the close of his reign: in twelve vols.

Koo   wăn   ya   ching

Elegant and accurate ancient literature, in eight vols.; published in the reign of Këen-lung.

Wăn   chang   yew   he

Literary recreations, prize essays, &c.; in four vols.

Swan   fă   tung   tsung

"A treatise on the art of numbering," arithmetic, one of the six polite arts of the Chinese; in five vols. The other five arts are, *decorum, music, archery, chariot-driving,* and *writing.*

Shan   hae   king

"The Classic relating to mountains and seas," within and beyond the limits of the empire,—east, west, south, and north: in twenty vols. It ranks next to the Classics of Confucius with the learned.

Ta   lŭh   jin

A book on fortune-telling by means of astrology, entitled the Six Astronomical Signs: in thirteen vols.

Foo   chow   kŏ   yang

A manuscript account of certain spells or charms
to which the Chinese of the sects *Fuh* and *Taou*
attach power to expel evil spirits and noxious influences. "The Foo," Dr. Morrison says, "answer to
those amulets or charms which consist in certain
words or sentences written in a particular order, and
which the Arabians called Talisman." Some of
these the Chinese wear about their persons, or paste
on the lintels and posts of their doors, as *preven-
tives* of disease and other evils. Such charms as are
curative they write on paper, which being burnt is
put into a cup of tea and drunk by the patient.
In one vol.

Wan   fă   kwei   tsung

Ten thousand laws or precepts reverting to one
point. An explanation of omens, charms, &c.: in
five vols.

Sze   k'oo   t'seuen   shoo

A catalogue of the Imperial library,—a great
national collection of books, published in the thirty-
ninth year of Këen-Lung (A. D. 1774): in eight
vols.

Keae   tsze   yuen   hwa   chuen

"Paintings of the Mustard-Seed Garden Narrated." A treatise on painting and drawing, including natural objects, those of art, &c.: in thirteen vols.

Hwa   too   yuen

A similar work to the preceding, entitled "drawings and plates connected:" in four vols.

Tëen   wăn   leih   le   ta   tseuen

A general outline of the principles of astronomy:
in six vols.

Kaou   how   mung   k'ew

A work on Astronomy, explaining the computed
distances of the Heavens from the Earth, comparative size of the Sun and this Globe, general nature
of the planetary system, and other celestial phenomena: in four vols. The author, who is a Chinese
mathematical instrument-maker, acknowledges his
obligations to the books of Europeans, published by
Imperial authority. He also gives directions for
making sun-dials and clocks, with plates. His work
was first published about the close of the last
century.

Chŭ   pih   k'ew

Twelve works of this title, of four vols. each, containing descriptions of Chinese manners, customs, ceremonies, &c. Published in the forty-sixth year of Këen-lung. From the title, "the band in white skin garments," there would appear to be allusion to bands of fencers anciently employed in Chinese courts.

Kew   wăn   chwang   kung   tseih

A general collection of themes on moral and literary subjects, in five vols.

ANTIQUARIAN RESEARCHES.

—————

Tseih   koo   tse   chung   ting   ke

A description of ancient bells, metal vases, tripods, and vessels of porcelain manufacture: in four vols.

Tseuen   che

A manuscript account of ancient coins, in two vols.

Pŏ   koo   t'oo

Drawings of ancient vessels and instruments, &c., in eighteen vols.

Koo   yŭh   t'oo

A work containing descriptions of ancient vessels, weapons, insignia, &c., with plates, in six vols.

OFFICIAL PUBLICATIONS OF THE CHINESE GOVERNMENT.

———

Ta   t'sing   tsin   shin   tseuen   shoo

A work containing a list of all the civil and military officers of the Empire, a new edition of which is published quarterly:—the Red Book of China, which furnishes rules of etiquette to be observed between members of government in their official intercourse: in sixteen vols. Also three copies of other editions, in four vols. each, designated *sew chin,* "sleeve pearls,"—a term appropriated to any small book that is thought to be valuable, from the circumstance of the Chinese carrying it in the sleeve of their garments, instead of the pocket.

She   hëen   shoo

"The Imperial Almanack." Three copies: one for the eleventh year of Yung-ching, A. D. 1733; another for the sixtieth year of Këen-lung, A. D. 1795; and two others for the twelfth and sixteenth years of Kea-king, A. D. 1807 and 1811.

D

King   chaou

The Pih-king Gazette in manuscript, containing edicts from the emperor, and communications addressed to him from the governors of the different provinces throughout the Empire.

RITES AND CEREMONIAL USAGES.

Le   ke

The fourth of the " Five Ancient Classics," in thirty-eight vols., which treats principally of the customs prevalent during the three most celebrated dynasties of China,—*Hea, Shang,* and *Chow;* but also contains rules for the observance of suitable etiquette, on civil, military, social, and religious occasions, as well as regulations adapted to private intercourse.

San   le   t'oo

Drawings for the purpose of illustrating the subjects discussed in the *Le-ke*: in two vols.

Le   shoo   kang   muh

A general description of rites and ceremonies. Incomplete.

Këen   pun   le   ke

"The Revised Original Le-ke," in ten vols. The same work as the preceding Le-ke, or "Record of Ceremonies and Rites,"—the word *Le* signifying decorum, propriety, politeness, reverence—whatever is becoming in individuals, families, or worshippers of the gods.

Chih   tŭh   luy   seuen

Select specimens of cards of congratulation, forms of condolence, invitations, addresses, expressions of gratitude, &c., &c.: in twelve vols.

Keang   low   chih   tŭh

A work similar to the preceding, in ten vols.

Chow   she   kin   wang

"Intercourse with the World in an Embroidered Purse." A work containing models for inscriptions over doors, &c.; eulogies on deceased relations; benedictions; congratulatory odes; family ceremonies; complimentary addresses; forms of bonds and covenants: also notices of the public roads of the Empire, and of the sources of the lakes on the Yangtsze-keang, one of the principal rivers of China; with other miscellaneous information of a polite and literary character: in twelve vols.

D 2

JURISPRUDENCE.

Pŏ   gnan   sin   pëen

A new compilation of cases in law, wherein the decision of an inferior court has been reversed by a superior tribunal; from the first year of Këen-lung's reign to the period of publication: in thirty-two vols.   Also another edition, in twenty vols.

Ta   tsing   hwuy   tëen   tsih   le

A collection of the laws, statutes, and by-laws, of the Chinese Empire, under the Tartar dynasty, in 121 vols.; entitled "The Collective Canons, Precepts, and Emendatory Clauses of the Great Pure (Manchow-Tartar) Dynasty.

Ta   tsing   hwuy   tëen

General statutes of the Chinese Empire, enacted under the present Tartar dynasty;—a work which contains a detailed account of the existing government in every department: in twenty-four vols.

Luh   poo   tsih   le

The laws of the six supreme courts, or boards, at *Pih-king*: these are, the Boards of Appointments, of Revenue, of Ceremonies, of the Army, of Punishments, and of Public Works: in thirty-six vols.

Hing   poo   tsih   le

The laws of the tribunal of punishments, or court of appeals at *Pih-king*, which takes cognizance of all criminal cases: in two vols.

Ta   ming   hwuy   tëen

The collective canons of the Great Ming dynasty (the general laws of the Empire at that period), which was the reigning family when the Manchow-Tartars subjugated China: in forty-eight vols.

Ta   tsing   leŭh   le

The laws of the Imperial Tartar dynasty—the Penal Code of the Chinese Empire: in twenty-four vols.; and a smaller edition in twenty vols. This work has been translated into English by Sir G. T. Staunton, Bart., &c.

Hoo   poo   tsih   le

The laws of the Board of Population, which is also the Board of Revenue arising from the People: in six vols.

Teaou   le   yŏ   pĕen

A general compilation of precepts and regulations, or Imperial declarations, ordinances, instructions, &c., collected and arranged in seventy-eight vols. The term *teaou le* signifies those additional or modifying laws which are framed by successive Emperors, in contradistinction from those denominated *leŭh*, and attributed originally to *Seaou-ho*, who lived B.C. 200. The laws of China altogether are said to be upwards of 2000 in number.

Hae   shwuy   gnan

Cases in law pertaining to the district Hae Shwŭy: in six vols.

Fă   kea   king   tĕen   luy

"The Legal Profession arousing Heaven's (the Imperial) Thunder." A work of similar character to the following: in one vol.

Fă   kea   t'ow   tan   han

A treatise on the laws. The legal profession is not allowed to be practised in China, as it is in England; but there are expositors of the law, of whom is the author of this volume, entitled "The Legal Profession penetrating the coldness of the Liver," a title founded on the Chinese notion that the liver is the seat of courage, and intended to convey a strong impression of the authority of the laws: in one vol.

Fă   yu   kin   nang

An exposition of the laws in an embroidered purse—a figurative expression for what contains excellent thoughts in an ornamented style: in six vols.

MEDICAL SCIENCE.

E   tsung   kind   këen

"The Medical Profession's Golden Mirror." A celebrated treatise on medical science, in forty vols. It was compiled during the reign of Këen-lung, about the middle of the eighteenth century, by a hundred persons, connected with the Imperial College of Physicians at Peking, and is probably the latest national publication on the subject. All existing treatises, procurable in print or manuscript, were collected by order of the Government, in aid of the design, and for the purpose of being consulted by the editors. The work was completed in four years.

T'ae   soo   mih

A medical work on the pulses of the human frame, with introductory remarks on the powers of nature, their order, subordination, &c.: in one vol.

Ling   choo   king

"The Spiritual or Intellectual Hinge," a medical work, in six volumes, attributed to   Ke-pih, an antediluvian statesman—one of three celebrated personages of that period, distinguished for their medical knowledge.

Shang han san shoo hŏ peih

A treatise on diseases arising from cold; in three parts, consisting of four vols. The title "Shang-han," injured by cold, comprehends all diseases produced by checked perspiration—especially fevers—exposure to marsh miasmata, damp air, or cold. In the former parts of this work, comprising the three first volumes, the author traces the symptoms of disease in the state of the patient's tongue, the sound of his voice, &c.; and in the last part, or fourth volume, he prescribes suitable remedies.

Hwang te nuy king soo wăn

A medical work denominated, "The plain Questions of the Emperor's Domestic Classic." This and the preceding treatise, named *Ling choo*, are considered the most ancient in China, on the causes and treatment of disease. *Yen-te* or *Shin-nung*, "the divine husbandman;" *Ke-pih*, the author of *Ling-choo*; and *Hëen-yuen*, or *Hwang-te*; formed a sort of royal society for medical purposes, in the earliest ages of the world. The present treatise is said to embody the results of certain consultations between the two last-mentioned personages on the subject of *splanchnology*; and, as well as the *Ling-choo*, to recognise the doctrine of the circulation of the blood—a theory with which modern practitioners in China are not *well* acquainted: in six vols.

Sëĕ   she   e   gnan

Sëĕ-she's collection of medical cases : in thirty-two vols.

Shang   han   san   choo

The three commentaries on the injurious effects of cold ; or fever produced by checked perspiration : in five vols.

Chin   kew   pă   tsuy   ta   ching

A work on cautery, the origin of which is ascribed to *Ke-pih,* the author of the "Intellectual Hinge." This treatise appears to refer to *actual* cautery, from the term employed in the title-page, which denotes that the operation is performed by an iron instrument. Nine different instruments are also represented by figures in the body of the work. The Chinese are, however, acquainted with *potential* cautery, effected by moxa, which they denominate gnae tsaou. The subjects in this work are arranged according to the three powers—Heaven, Earth, and Man. Its title might be rendered, " Eminently Conspicuous Instances of Success in Cautery:" in seven vols.

Chin　　kew　　tseu　　ying

Another work on the same subject, in eight vols.; both are written in Japanese as well as Chinese.

King　　yŏ　　tseun　　shoo

The whole works of *King-yŏ*, a medical writer of considerable eminence in China during the fifteenth century: in twenty-four vols.

Ling　　ching　　chĕ　　nan　　e　　gnan

A correct medical guide, founded on extensive practice; in twelve vols.

Shang　　han　　pëen　　ching　　lŭh

Records of the symptoms of fever occasioned by checked perspiration. A medical work on colds, in fourteen vols.

Chung　　tow　　k'e　　shoo

A tract on vaccination, by the late Alexander Pearson, M. D., of Canton, and translated into Chinese, with the assistance of occasional reference to the natives, by Sir G. T. Staunton, Bart., &c., &c.

E　　lin　　che　　yuĕ

A medical work, in fifteen vols. A publication of the Imperial College of Physicians at Peking.

MAPS, PLATES, DRAWINGS, &c.

Kwang   yu   ke

A new edition of large maps, in thirteen vols.; comprising also topographical and statistical details.

Kwang   yu   t'oo

Extensive maps and drawings; in four vols.

Hwang   tsing   chih   kung   t'oo

Plates of tributary offerings rendered to the Imperial Tartar dynasty; in nine vols.

Yu   che   kăng   chih

Plates of ploughing and weaving, by Imperial rescript; in one vol., quarto.

Ta   ho   ming   so   t'oo   hwuy

A general and uniform collection of plates of celebrated places; in six vols.

BUDDHISM, or THE RELIGION OF FUH.

***

Shen   mun   jih   sung   tseuen   tseih

A complete collection of daily recitatives for the use of the disciples of Fŭh (Buddha); in one vol. These and similar compositions are chanted, or read in a tone peculiar to the Buddhists, for the purpose of propitiating their deities, and procuring the pardon of sin.

Soo   fang   hwa   shen   sze

" Plain, fragrant, elegant teachers of the contemplative doctrine." A book on Buddhism, in two vols. The third character (*hwa*) is frequently used in titles of superior books of this sect; it is also a designation of China.

Hwa   yen   king

A large work of the sect of Buddha, published by Imperial authority early in the fifteenth century; probably a translation of the Boodŭ Pooranŭ, mentioned in Ward's Hindoo Mythology (Morrison). The title of the book translated literally would be, " The elegant, venerable Classic :" in sixteen vols., large 8vo.

Lăng yen ching mih soo

Lăng-yen's correct vein of thought expanded: in six vols. *Lăng* is a Tartar word; *Yen* is the same as the second character of the preceding title:—a work on Buddhism.

Lăng yen king tseih choo

General comments on the Classic *Lăng-yen*—the same title as the preceding; in five vols.

Jin tëen yen mŭh

"The Eyes of Men and Heaven." A work on Buddhism, in two vols.

Lŭh taou tseih

"The Six Ways or Doctrines;" in two vols. A work of the sect of Fŭh.

K'e sin lun

"The Origin of Faith Discussed," or according to another title, *Hwa yen tsung fă*, "The excellent, venerable, authoritative precepts." A work on Buddhism, in two vols.

Leih   seang   kaou   ching

"Successive transformations accomplished." A work of the Buddhists, published by Imperial authority: in sixteen vols.

Fŭh   mun   ting   che

The standard laws of the religion of Fŭh; in four vols.

Keae   shă   fang   săng   wăn

"Guard against Killing, and spare Life." An essay of the Buddhists on the preservation of animal life as a moral duty: in one vol.

Fŭh   ting   tsze   lŭh

A Buddhistic work with plates, representing the metempsychosis: in twelve vols.

Yŭh   leih   chaou   chuen   king   she
A work on Buddhism.

THE THREE SECTS.

Sow   shin   ke

A treatise on the gods of the Three Sects—the learned, the philosophic, and the Buddhist—with an account of the transformations peculiar to the last: in one thick vol., 8vo.

San   keaou   sow   shin

A work similar in its nature to the preceding, in three vols.; entitled "The Three Sects—that of *Confucius, Buddha*, and *Taou-sze*—investigating their deities."

Fung   shin   yen   e

A treatise on the gods of China; in ten vols.

TRANSLATIONS OF THE SACRED SCRIPTURES INTO CHINESE:—ROMAN CATHOLIC, AND PROTESTANT THEOLOGY, TRANSLATIONS, &c.

———

Sin   *wei*   *chaou*   *shoo*

The New Testament, translated by Dr. Morrison into Chinese; in eight vols., 8vo. Published A. D. 1815. Also the Epistles of James, John, Peter, and Jude, with the Apocalypse.

Shing   *king*

A translation of the Old and New Testaments, by Dr. Marshman; in five vols., 8vo. Printed with metal types at Serampore.

Shin   *tëen*   *shing*   *shoo*

The Old and New Testaments translated by Dr. Morrison: a new edition, 8vo., published A. D. 1832. Also a copy of the first edition, published A.D. 1823: in twenty-one vols.; printed with wooden blocks, or plates.

Ling   *hwăn*   *pëen*

An Essay on the Nature, Immortality, Value, and Destiny, of the Human Soul, by Dr. Milne, late of Malacca: in two vols., 12mo.

E

Chin   taou   tsze   ching

"The Truth its own Witness." A tract on the evidences of Christianity, by a Roman Catholic Missionary: in one vol. Published in the reign of *Kang-he,* A.D. 1718.

Wan   wŭh   chin   yuen

"The true Origin of all Things." Probably a Roman Catholic work: in one vol.

Shing   shoo   tsëĕ   keae

A Commentary on the Epistle to the Ephesians, by Dr. Milne; in two vols., 8vo.

Chin   shin   ching   keu

Paley's Argument for the Being of God, translated into Chinese by Dr. Morrison; in one vol. Lithographed.

The Gospel of Matthew in Manchow-Tartar; in one vol.

Shing   shang   mih   seang

Sacred Sorrow and Silent Meditation; in one small vol. A Roman Catholic work.

WORKS OF FICTION.

Hung   low   mung

"The Dreams of the Red Chamber." A novel of considerable repute in China, the style of which is colloquial in the *Pih-king* dialect: in twenty vols.; two copies.

T'aou   hwa   shen

"Peach Blossoms Expanded." A novel, in four vols.

T'ëen   yu   hwa

"Heaven's Rain and Flowers." A novel published in the reign of *Kea-king:* in thirty vols.

Te   yih   k'e   shoo

"The Most Wonderful Book." A novel, in twenty vols. Composed by a disciple of *Fang-chow's,* and published in the reign of *Kang-he.*

Fun   chwang   low

The Painted Chamber." A novel, in twelve vols.

E 2

Kin   hing   mei   chuen

"The Golden-potted Plums Narrated,"—another copy of "The Most Wonderful Book," with a different title; both works containing a description of Chinese manners and customs, especially with reference to courtships and marriage, the design of which, according to the preface, is to promote virtue, and discourage vice.

Shih   tsing   ya   tseu

"The Pleasures of a Tranquil Disposition," or the eighteen transformations of the   pǎng—a fabulous bird transformed from a fish of an immense size; several thousand Chinese miles in extent; at every frisk or leap it rises 90,000 miles, and hence it is used to denote rapid promotion (Morrison): in two copies, five vols. each.

Shin   low   che

An account of a visionary monster seen at sea, said to be like a snake with horns, and like a dragon, in the lower part of the body, having scales; sometimes assumes the form of a watch-tower. (Morrison's Dic.): in six vols.

Kin   koo   k'e   kwan

Ancient and modern wonders; in ten vols.

Haou   k'ew   chuen

"A Narrative of a Happy Courtship." This work has been translated into English under the title of "The Fortunate Union," by J. F. Davis, Esq.: in four vols.

Yuen   jin   pih   chung

The celebrated hundred comedies of the Yuen dynasty; in forty vols.

Te   pǎ   tsae   tsze

or

Tsing   tsing   tse

"Stillness and Purity perfected." A novel of the eighth grade of talent. There is a class of Chinese works of fiction designated, irrespective of the style, according to the degree of interest excited by the subject—from the *first* or *highest*, through the intermediate gradations, to the *tenth* or *lowest* degree of talent.

Te   t'seih   tsae   tsze

"The Seventh Genius." A novel of the seventh grade of talent, adorned with cuts: in six vols.

Pih   kwei   tseuen   chuen

"The White Sceptre perfectly narrated." An ancient badge of authority bestowed by the emperor on the governors of provinces. A novel of the tenth grade: in four vols.

Mow   tan   ting   hwan   hwăn

"The returning spirit of the dome of *Mow-tan*," the peonia, designated by the Chinese "the king of flowers." A novel founded probably on a belief in apparitions, which prevails extensively among the Chinese: in six vols.

T'ang   p'ing   kwei   tseuen

"The just spirit of T'ang (name of a celebrated dynasty) perfected." A novel of the ninth grade of talent: in two vols.

Kin   shih   yin   yuen

"The marriage union of *Metal* and *Stone*." A narrative of courtship and marriage between parties whose names are *kin*, "metal," and *shih*, "stone;" with remarks on the properties of these substances, as applicable to husband and wife: in six vols.

Te   sze   tsae   tsze

A novel of the fourth grade of talent; in four vols.

Taou   ke   këen   ping

Criticisms and satires; in ten vols.

Sew   seang   urh   too   mei

A work of fiction written in the colloquial style, and adorned with plates: in six vols.

Mwan   Han   se   seang   ke

" Tartar and Chinese western apartment recorded:" A comedy, the author of which is one of the six writers pre-eminently distinguished among the Chinese for natural genius and elegance of style: in four vols.

Te   san   tsae   tsze

A novel of the third grade of talent; in four vols.

Leaou   chae   che   e

A romance designated " the fortuitous narration of strange occurrences," which, it has been thought, resembles the " Fairy Queen" of Spenser. It appears to be the object of the author to depict the transitory nature of earthly things. Two copies, sixteen vols. each, 12mo.

TRAVELS, &c.

Hea   kih   yew   ke

Travels by land and by water recorded: in sixteen vols. The Chinese consider visits to the principal parts of the Empire, as necessary to complete the education of a gentleman, but do not go beyond the boundaries of their own country.

Chow   king   pei   lan

A complete tour of the Empire, or observations made in travelling by land and by water: in six vols.

Se   yew   chin   tseuen

The western traveller's correct instructor; in twenty vols.

BOOKS FOR YOUTH.

Yew   heŏ   she

Rhymes for the instruction of youth ; or, studies in poetry suited to the age of *ten* years: in one vol.

Yew   heŏ   keu   keae

Easy sentences for the instruction of youth, on miscellaneous subjects: in one vol.

Tung   yuen   tsă   tsze

Miscellaneous literature of the eastern garden—a book for children: in one vol.; two copies.

Yew   heŏ   tsă   tsze

Miscellaneous kinds of youthful instruction—a book for children: in one vol.

Shing   leŭh   ke   mung   tsŏ   yaou

Laws of sound, for the use of boys, in two parts, each containing fifteen different words to practise upon: in one vol.

Yew   heŏ   koo   sze   keung   lin

"The Coral Forest of Ancient Lore for the Instruction of Youth." An abstract of ancient learning, containing also a parallel between ancient and modern titles of office, with some of the complimentary and poetical terms applied to persons holding particular offices, together with a compendium of moral duties, designed for youth: in two vols.

MISCELLANIES.

Tuug   se   yang   kaou   mei   yuĕ

" Eastern and Western Ocean's monthly investigations, by the Rev. C. Gutzlaff." A monthy periodical on miscellaneous subjects : in one vol.

Too   săng   kung   gnan

An account of murders, suicides, and executions ; in three vols.

Tsoo   nan   she   tĕĕ

Records of literary examinations in prose and verse, for the district *Tsoo-nan* ; in one vol.

Ping   lŭh

" Military records,"—a work on the art of war ; in twenty-four vols.

Ping   yuen   sze   pĕen

The art of fortification ; in five vols.

Kin   seang   yuĕ

Monthly cuts ; in one vol.

A Catalogue of the Chinese Manuscripts in the Library of the Royal Asiatic Society

皇家亚洲学会图书馆藏中文典籍目录

A CATALOGUE

OF THE

CHINESE MANUSCRIPTS

IN THE

LIBRARY OF THE

ROYAL ASIATIC SOCIETY.

ERRATA.

————◆————

No.	6	For	*Hwa ch'ien*	read	*Hua chien.*
,,	18	,,	*K'o*	,,	*Ko.*
,,	30	,,	*Lin*	,,	*Lien.*
,,	33	,,	*tsoo*	,,	*tsu.*
,,	34	,,	棲	,,	樓
,,	47	,,	,,	,,	,,
,,	69	,,	*chung*	,,	*tsung.*
,,	73	,,	*ch'ien*	,,	*chien.*
,,	100	,,	*tsëën*	,,	*ts'an.*
,,	118	,,	No. 125	,,	No. 126.
,,	146	,,	*ch'ien*	,,	*chien.*
,,	191	,,	*che*	,,	*chih.*
,,	216	,,	故	,,	古
,,	225	,,	,,	,,	,,
,,	251	,,	245	,,	246.
,,	262	,,	*shoo*	,,	*shu.*
,,	269	,,	右	,,	古
,,	347	,,	茶	,,	茶
,,	361	,,	*pe*	,,	*pei.*
,,	424	,,	審	,,	番
,,	548	,,	*tso*	,,	*tsou.*

THE following Catalogue was compiled between 1879 and 1881 by Mr. Henry F. Holt, then Joint-Secretary of the Royal Asiatic Society, with a view to afford greater facilities of reference to the valuable Chinese Library of this Society.

The Council having decided to print the Catalogue, Mr. Giles, of the Chinese Consular Service, has been kind enough to correct the proofs. Mr. Holt's preface was as follows :—

" The plan which has been pursued has been to arrange the works in various book-cases named after China itself or after eminent persons whose names are associated with that country.

" The letters and figures which accompany the names indicate the exact position of each work in its respective case, so that no difficulty need ever be experienced by the Librarian in selecting or replacing any work which may be required, whether he be acquainted with the language or not.

"Another feature which has been introduced consists in the series of cross references which have been given. In this Library, as in others, it occurs that several works are incomplete. With a view therefore of, as far as possible, remedying this defect, references have been made to the Catalogues of the other Chinese Libraries in London, namely those of the British Museum, the India Office, and University College, Gower Street. These are respectively indicated by the letters B.M. (British Museum), I.O.C (India Office Catalogue), and L.U. (London University). By these means the Student, finding an imperfect copy of the work of which he is in search on these shelves, can tell where other and perhaps perfect copies may be found.

V   PREFACE.

" Printed copies of the Catalogue of the India Office and British Museum Libraries will be found here. That of University College is a Manuscript of 140 pages, each containing five slips. A copy of it was made by Mr. H. J. Holt, and will be found in this Library. The method of reference to it will be seen on the first page.

" Other references have also been made to Wylie (*Notes on Chinese Literature*), Cordier (*Bibliotheca Sinica*), and Mayers (*Chinese Readers' Manual*), as well as to Professor Kidd's Catalogue of this Library made in 1838. Names of translators have been added, as far as known, together with occasional notes of general literary interest.

" This Library, which contains some 5000 volumes, cannot of course compare with the national collection at the British Museum, which has four times as many. But there is good reason for believing that it is quite on a par with any other. In it almost every branch of Chinese Literature is represented, and it contains many works not to be found in any other collection in this country."

It is to be hoped that members of the Society interested in Chinese studies will, by donations either of books or money, help to make this useful collection more complete.

T. W. RHYS DAVIDS,
Secretary, R.A.S.

ROYAL ASIATIC SOCIETY,
22, *Albemarle Street,*
January, 1889.

前　言

以下《目录》由何为霖（Henry F. Holt）先生1879年至1881年间编纂。何为霖时任皇家亚洲学会联席秘书，此举旨在为学会有价值的中文藏书提供更好的参考工具。

学会理事会决定印刷该目录时，承任职于驻华使馆的翟理斯先生美意，对目录进行了校勘。何为霖先生所作的序言如下：

"我们的计划是将不同书架上以中国或与中国相关名人命名的图书进行整理。

"书名旁的字母和数字表示每本书在各自书架上的确切位置，所以，无论图书管理员是否熟悉中文，在寻找或替换某本图书时都不会碰到任何困难。

"本目录的另一个特点是可以进行交叉检索。和其他图书馆一样，这家图书馆的部分作品不够完整。有鉴于此，为了尽可能弥补这一缺陷，图书馆还提供伦敦其他中文藏书的目录检索服务，包括大英博物馆、印度事务部（India Office）以及位于高尔街的伦敦大学学院（University College，Gower Street）的藏书。这些藏书的代号分别为B.M.（大英博物馆）、I.O.C（印度事务部）和L.U.（伦敦大学）。通过这种方法，学生在这些书架上找到有缺陷的图书，可以知道去哪里找到该图书其他也许完整的副本。

"本目录还包含印度事务部和大英博物馆藏书印刷本目录。伦敦大学学院的藏书目录是一份写本，共有140页，每一页包括五张纸条。何为霖抄写的该目录中其中一份副本也收藏在此图书馆。本目录的索引方法见目录第一页。

"本目录还参考了伟烈亚力（Wylie）［《汉籍解题》（*Notes on Chinese Literature*）］、高第（Cordier）［《中国书目》（*Bibliotheca Sinica*）］、梅辉立（Mayers）［《中国辞汇》（*Chinese Readers' Manual*）］等人的成果以及基德教授1838年为本图书馆编写的目录。还添加了已知译者的姓名以及偶尔出现的一般文学主题的注解。

"本图书馆收录了大约5000册中文图书，显然无法比肩大英博物馆的国家级馆藏，后者的藏书量是本图书馆的四倍之多。但是也完全有理由相信，本图书馆依然可以媲美其他任何一家图书馆，在这里几乎可以找到各类中文文献，还能找到英国其他藏书中所没有的很多图书。"

衷心希望皇家亚洲学会各位对汉学感兴趣的成员能够积极捐献图书或资金，帮助不断完善这些有用的藏书。

T. W. 里斯·戴维斯（T. W. RHYS DAVIDS）
皇家亚洲学会秘书

亚伯马勒街（Albemarle Street）22号
皇家亚洲学会
1889年1月
（管宇译，彭萍校）

CATALOGUE

OF

CHINESE MANUSCRIPTS.

———◆———

1. 金 瓶 梅
Chin, P'ing, Mei.

"The Story of Chin, P'ing, and Mei." A Novel. A Description of Chinese manners and customs, especially with reference to Courtship and Marriage, the design of which, according to the Preface, is to promote Virtue and to discourage Vice. 2 cases, 20 vols. *Ref.* B.M. p. 11.

[*Amherst* I, A 1-2.]

2. 金 瓶 梅
Chin, P'ing, Mei.

"The Story of Chin, P'ing, and Mei." A Novel attributed to Wang Shih-ching. *Ref.* B.M. p. 11. [*Amherst* I, A 3-4.]

3. 東 周 列 國 全 志
Tung Chou lieh kuo ch'üan chih.

A History embracing the period from the Eastern Chou Dynasty, B.C. 255 to the commencement of the Chin Dynasty, B.C. 249. With illustrations. Edited by 蔡元放 Ts'ai Yüan-fang. 2 cases, 24 vols. *Ref.* B.M. p. 207.

[*Amherst* I, A 5.]

4. 太 平 廣 記
T'ai p'ing kuang chi.

"Extensive Records of General Peace and Prosperity." Being an abstract of History, Statistics, Topography, &c., of the different Provinces of China.

[*Amherst* I, A 6—11.]

B

5. 藕 黃 尺 牘
Su huang ch'ih tu.

"A Model Letter Writer."   3 vols.   1801.

[*Amherst* II, A 1.]

6. 花 箋 記
Hua ch'ien chi.

"The Story of the Flowery Note Paper."   A Novel. Edited, with Notes, by 金 聖 嘆 Chin Shêng-t'an.   4 vols. 6 chüan.   *Ref.* B.M. p. 106.   See No. 25.

[*Amherst* II, A 2.]

7. 定 鼎 奇 文 or 大 明 傳
Ting ting ch'i wên, or, Ta ming chuan.

4 chüan, 22 Hui.   No date.   [*Amherst* II, A 3.]

8. 金 石 姻 緣
Chin Shih yin yuan.

The Celestially brought about union of Chin and Shih. *Ref.* L.U. 38, 5.   See No. 114.   [*Amherst* II, A 4.]

9. 紅 梨 記
Hung li chi.

"The Red Pear Record."   One of the "Sixty Plays." 2 vols. 30 chih.   1737.   *Ref.* B.M. p. 82.   [*Amherst* II, A 5.]

10. 還 魂 記
Huan hun chi.

"The Returned Ghost." A Play.   4 vols. and 55 chih. *Ref.* B.M. p. 85.   [*Amherst* I, A 6.]

11. 辰 生 殿
Ch'ang shêng tien.

"The Palace of Longevity." A Drama. 1679.   *Ref.* B.M. p. 83.   [*Amherst* II, A 7.]

12. 紫 釵 記
Tzŭ ch'ai chi.

" The Story of the Purple Hair-pin.' One of the " Sixty Plays." 2 chüan. *Ref.* B.M. p. 221 ; L.U. 105, 4.

[*Amherst* II, A 8.]

13. 鳳 求 凰
Fêng ch'iu huang.

"The Phœnix in search of a Wife." A Novel. 2 vols. 24 chih.   [*Amherst* II, A 9.]

14. 玉 搔 頭
Yü sao t'ou.

2 chüan, and 30 chih.   [*Amherst* II, A 10.]

15. 真 鸞 交
Chên luan chiao.

2 vols.   [*Amherst* II, A 11.]

16. 奈 何 天
Nai ho t'ien.

" Seek Aid from Heaven." 2 vols. 30 chih.

[*Amherst* II, A 12.]

17. 意 中 綠
I chung lu.

" A book of hidden meanings," being good examples of phrases :—joking, punning, loose, farcical, &c. 2 vols. 30 chih.   [*Amherst* II, A 13.]

18. 南 柯 記
Nan Ko chi.

An Account of the Kingdom of Nan Ko. 2 vols. 35 chih. *Ref.* B.M. p. 127.   [*Amherst* II, A 14.]

B 2

19. 牡 丹 亭 還 魂
Mou tan t'ing huan hun.

"The Returning Spirit of the Peony Bower." 2 vols.
8 chüan.   [*Amherst* II, A 15.]

20. 巧 團 圓 傳 奇
Ch'iao t'uan yüan chuan ch'i.

"The Secret Affectionate Union." A Drama. 2 vols.
Ref. B.M. p. 133.   [*Amherst* II, A 16.]

21. 牡 丹 亭
Mou tan t'ing.

"The Story of the Peony Bower." One of the "Sixty
Plays." 2 vols. 8 chüan. *Ref.* B.M. p. 158.
      [*Amherst* II, A 17.]

22. 名 媛 詩 鈔
Ming yüan shih ch'ao.

"Odes to Celebrated Beauties." 4 vols. 6 chüan. 1803.
      [*Amherst* II, A 18.]

23. 雷 峰 塔
Lei fêng t'a.

"The Thunder-peak Pagoda." A Novel. 4 vols. *Ref.*
B.M. p. 149. Translated for the *Phœnix*, by C. Carroll
and another. Also by Julien, under the title of *Blanche et
Bleue.*   [*Amherst* II, A 19.]

24. 聖 敎 日 課
Shêng chiao jih k'o.

"Daily Religious Exercises." A Roman Catholic work
published in Chinese. It was printed in the 首善堂 the
"Hall of Supreme Goodness," within the West Gate of
Peking. 3 vols. 1800. *Ref.* B.M. p. 148.
      [*Amherst* II, A 20.]

25. 花 箋 記

Hua ch'ien chi.*

"The Story of the Flowery Note Paper." Translated by Thoms. 4 vols. *Ref.* B.M. p. 106 ; L.U. 37, 3. See No. 6.
[*Amherst* II, A 21.]

26. 琵 琶 記

P'i pa chi.

"The Story of a Lute." One of the " Sixty Plays." 6 vols. *Ref.* B.M. p. 163. [*Amherst* II, A 22.]

27. 牡 丹 亭

Mou tan t'ing.

"The Story of the Peony Bower."
[*Amherst* II, A 23.]

28. 宋 詩 別 裁

Sung shih pieh ts'ai.

4 vols. 8 chüan. 1763. [*Amherst* II, A 24.]

29. 牡 丹 亭 還 魂

Mou tan t'ing huan hun.

"The Returning Spirit of the Peony Bower."
[*Amherst* II, A 25.]

---

* This work was translated by P. P. Thoms under the title of " Chinese Courtship," in verse, Chinese and English, to which is added an Appendix treating of the Revenue of China. London, Macao, 1824, 8vo. 324 pp. See also Remusat, Mél. Asiat. II. p. 334. German, by H. Kurtz (Das Blumenblatt), St. Gatlen, 1836, 8vo.

30. Case containing the following plays :

邯 鄲 夢
I. The **Han tan mêng.**

2 vols. 30 chih.

風 箏 誤
II. The **Fêng chêng wu.**

2 vols. 30 chih.

蜃 中 樓
III. The **Shên chung lou.**

2 vols. 30 chih.

憐 香 伴
IV. The **Lin hsiang pan.**

2 vols. 36 chih.

[*Amherst* II, A 26.]

31. 南 柯 記
Nan Ko chi.

"An Account of the Kingdom of Nan Ko." 2 vols. 35 chih. *Ref.* B.M. 127.   [*Amherst* II, A 27.]

32. 牡 丹 亭
Mou tan t'ing.

"The Peony Bower." One of the "Sixty Plays." 4 vols. 8 chüan.   [*Amherst* II, A 28.]

33. 香 祖 摟 等 八 種 曲
The Hsiang tsu lou, and 7 other plays. Namely :—

2 空 谷 香 K'ung ku hsiang.

3 桂 林 香 Kwei lin hsiang.

4 第 二 碑 Ti êrh pei.

5 各 青 樹 Ko ch'ing shu.

6 臨 川 夢 Lin ch'uan mêng.

7 雪 中 人 Hsüeh chung jen.

8 四 絃 秋 Ssǔ hsien ch'iu.

1774.   [*Amherst* II, A 29.]

34. 今 古 奇 觀 續 編 十 二 樓
Chin ku ch'i kuan hsü pien shih êrh lou.

"The Twelve Chambers." A sequel to the "Wondrous Tales of Ancient and Modern Times." By 覺世 Chüo Shih. 6 vols. 1658. *Ref.* B.M. p. 101.　　[*Amherst* II, A 30.]

35. 更 豈 有 此 理
Kêng ch'i yu tz'u li.

2 vols. (with plates of subscriptions, &c.). *Ref.* L.U. 29, 4.　　[*Amherst* II, A 31.]

36. 雷 峰 塔
Lei fêng t'a.

"The Thunder-peak Pagoda." Otherwise known as the "History of the White Serpent." With a few illustrations. 4 vols. 5 chüan. 1806. *Ref.* B.M. p. 149. See No. 23.

[*Amherst* II, A 32.]

37. 二 度 梅
Êrh tu mei.

"The Story of the Two Plumes." Illustrated. 6 vols. 6 chüan. *Ref.* B.M. p. 155; L.U. 123, 2. Translated into French by A. Piry, of the Chinese Customs Service. See No. 62.　　[*Amherst* II, A 33.]

38. 漁 家 樂
Yü chia lê.

4 vols.　　[*Amherst* II, A 34.]

39. 尺 牘 類 選
Ch'ih tu lei hsüan.

The full title is 霏屑軒尺牘類選. *Fei hsiao hsien ch'ih tu lei hsüan.* "A Model Letter Writer." Compiled by 陳世熙, Ch'ên Shih-hsi. 1802. *Ref.* B.M. p. 28.

[*Amherst* 1, B 1.]

40. 聊 齋 志 異
Liao Chai chih i.

16 vols. *Ref.* B.M. p. 167; L.U. 52, 4; Kidd, p. 55.
Translated by H. A. Giles under the title of "Strange
Stories from a Chinese Studio." 2 vols. London, 1880.
[*Amherst* I, B 2.]

41. 鳳 洲 綱 鑑
Fêng Chou Kang Chien.

"The Annals of General History." By 王鳳洲 Wang
Fêng-chou. In the Great Annals, first came the *T'ung
Chien*, next the *T'ung chien kang mu*, which is a reconstruc-
tion and condensation thereof, and then the present book
which is a much more abbreviated history, extending
from *Fu Hsi* downwards. *Ref.* Wylie, p. 21; Mayers, xix.;
Kidd, p. 8. [*Amherst* I, B 3—8.]

42. 情 史
Ch'ing Shih.

"History of the Loves of Celebrities." By 詹詹 Chan
Chan. 12 vols. 24 chüan. 1784. *Ref.* B.M. p. 22.
[*Amherst* I, B 9.]

43. 文 帝 全 書 內 函
Wên Ti ch'üan shu nei han.

The complete works of Wên Ti. Comprising Essays on the
Regeneration of the People, Filial Piety, Rewards and
Punishment, Prosperity, &c. 8 vols. 1801. *Ref.* Kidd,
p. 20; Wylie, p. 16. [*Amherst* I, B 10.]

44. 封 神 演 義
Fêng shên yen i.

"The Story of the Canonised Saints." A tale regarding
the Adventures of Wu Wang (B.C. 1122) the Founder of
the Chou Dynasty, in his contest between Chou Wang,
the last of the House of Shang. 1695. *Ref.* B.M. p. 55;
Kidd, p. 48; Wylie, p. 163. [*Amherst* I, B 11-12.]

45. 玉 嬌 梨
Yü chiao li.

Commonly known as the Romance of "The Two Cousins."
Translated by A. Remusat in 1826, 2 vols. 12mo., and by
Julien in 1864 as "Les deux Cousines." 4 vols. *Ref.* Wylie,
p. 163.　　　　　　　　　　　　　　　　[*Amherst* I, B 13.]

46. 說 岳 傳
Shuo Yŏ chuan.

"Biography of Yŏ Fei." A General who served under
the Sung Dynasty.　　　　　　　　　[*Amherst* II, B 1.]

47. 況 有 江 樓 尺 牘
K'uang yu chiang lou ch'ih tu.

"Models of Rhetoric and Elegant Style." 12 chüan.
　　　　　　　　　　　　　　　　　　　[*Amherst* II, B 2.]

48. 平 妖 傳
P'ing yao chuan.

"The Story of the Pacification of the Elves and Fairies."
A Romance of the T'ang Dynasty. By 馮猶龍, Fêng
Yu-lung. 10 vols. 40 hui (1st vol. missing). 1750.
L.U. 69, 1.　　　　　　　　　　　　　[*Amherst* II, B 3.]

49. 史 記 通 鑑
Shih Chi T'ung Chien.

"The Historical Record." 4 cases, 39 vols. *Ref.* B.M.
p. 195.　　　　　　　　　　　　　　　[*Amherst* II, B 4—7.]

50. 夜 譚 隨 錄
Yeh tan sui lu.

"Evening Entertainments." A Collection of Tales.
2 vols. 12 chüan. *Ref.* B.M. p. 257.

　　　　　　　　　　　　　　　　　　　[*Amherst* II, B 8.]

51. 玉 嬌 梨
Yü chiao li.

Commonly known as the Romance of "The Two Cousins."
4 vols. *Ref.* Wylie, p.163. See No. 45.   [*Amherst* II, B 9.]

52. 玉 嬌 梨
Yü chiao li.

Commonly known as the Romance of "The Two Cousins."
4 vols. *Ref.* Wylie, p. 163. See No. 45.   [*Amherst* II, B 10.]

53. 國 語
Kuo Yü.

"The Narratives of the States."   By 左 丘 明 Tso Ch'iu
Ming.   4 vols.   *Ref.* B.M. 218.   [*Amherst* II, B 11.]

54. 雙 鳳 奇
Shuang fêng ch'i.

"The wonderful story of the two Phœnixes."   An Historical Romance founded upon events which occurred during
the Han Dynasty.   10 vols. 80 hui.   *Ref.* B.M. p. 184.
1813.   [*Amherst* II, B 12.]

55. 桃 花 扇 傳 奇
T'ao hua shan chuan ch'i.

"The Story of the Peach Blossom Fan."   A Drama.   By
孔 稼 部 K'ung Chia-pu.   *Ref.* B.M. p. 115; L.U. 100, 5.
See No. 108.   [*Amherst* II, B 13.]

56. 金 瓶 梅
Chin, P'ing, Mei.

"The Story of Chin, P'ing, and Mei."   A Novel attributed
to Wang Shih-ching.   Edited by 張 竹 坡 Chang Chu-pŏ.
3 cases, 20 vols.   1695.   *Ref.* B.M. p. 11 ; L.U. 38, 2.
                [*Amherst* II, B 14-15.]

57. 子 不 語
Tzŭ pu yü.

" Topics untouched by the Sage." 8 vols.

[*Amherst* II, B 16.]

58. 玉 堂 字 彙
Yü T'ang Tzŭ hui.

The " Jade Hall " Dictionary. Compiled by 梅應祈 Mei Ying-ch'i. 4 vols. 1676. *Ref.* B.M. p. 155; L.U. 138, 5.

[*Amherst* II, B 17.]

59. 屜 樓 志
Shên lou chih.

" The Story of the Sea Serpent." An account of a monster sometimes seen at sea, like a snake with horns, and which occasionally raises its body like a tower out of the water. 6 vols. 1804. See No. 85.

[*Amherst* II, B 18.]

60. 小 倉 山 房 尺 牘
Hsiao ts'ang shan fang ch'ih tu.

" The Complete Letter Writer, (issued from) the Mountain Home of Hsiao-ts'ang." 4 vols. 6 chüan. 1797.

[*Amherst* II, B 19.]

61. 性 理 精 義
Hsing li ch'ing i.

" The Essence of Works on Mental Philosophy." Compiled by order of the Emperor K'ang Hsi. By a Commission. *Ref.* B.M. p. 128.

[*Amherst* I, C 1.]

62. 二 度 梅 傳
Êrh tu mei chuan.

" The Story of the Two Plumes." *Ref.* B.M. p. 155; L.U. 120, 3. See No. 37.

[*Amherst* I, C 2.]

63. 獪 園
Kuai yüan.

" The Deceptive Garden." 16 sections. 1774.

[*Amherst* I, C 3.]

64. 綉 虎 尺 牘
Hsiu hu ch'ih tu.

"A Complete Letter Writer." 6 vols. 1796.

[*Amherst* I, C 4.]

65 三 國 志
San Kuo chih.

"The History of the Three Kingdoms" of Wei, Shu and Wu. 2 cases, 20 vols. [*Amherst* I, C 5-6.]

66. 新 齊 諧
Hsin ch'i hsieh.

"A new collection of Tales." Compiled by 隨 園 戲 Sui Yüan-hsi. Called the 子 不 語 Tzǔ pu yü on the margin. 12 vols. 24 chüan. 1800. *Ref.* L.U. 89, 4.

[*Amherst* I, C 7.]

67. 白 圭 全 傳
Pŏ Kuei ch'üan chuan.

"The Story of the White Sceptre." A Novel. The "Kuei," a species of sceptre, was an ancient badge of authority bestowed by the Emperor on Governors of Provinces. 4 vols. 1807. [*Amherst* I, C 8.]

68. 後 西 遊 記
Hou hsi yu chi.

"A later narrative of Travels in the West." Edited by 金 聖 嘆 Chin Shêng-t'an. 10 vols. 49 hui. 1750 (?).

[*Amherst* I, C 9.]

69. 十 二 種 曲
Shih êrh chung ch'ü.

"Twelve Popular Odes," or Dramatic Pieces. Compiled by 笠 翁 Li Wêng. 3 cases, 24 vols. *Ref.* B.M. p. 133.

[*Amherst* I, C 10—12.]

70. 警 富 新 書
Ching fu hsin shu.

"A Warning to the Rich." By 梁 天 來 Liang Tëen-lai. 6 vols. 1809. *Ref.* B.M. p. 132; Kidd, p. 21; L.U. 41, 2.

[*Amherst* I, C 13.]

71. 夜 譚 隨 錄
Yeh tan sui lu.

"Evening Entertainments." A Collection of Tales. 6 vols. 12 chüan. 1791. [*Amherst* I, C 14.]

72. 本 草 綱 目
Pên ts'ao kang mu.

"A General Outline of Plants and Herbs." This is considered the best Pharmacopœia as well as Botanical Work in China. 12 vols. and Introduction. 1801. *Ref.* Kidd, p. 16; B.M. p. 129; L.U. 128, 3. See No. 111.

[*Amherst* I, C 15.]

73. 唐 詩 合 解 箋 注
T'ang shih ho chieh ch'ien chu.

A Selection of Poems by the most Celebrated Authors of the T'ang Dynasty (A.D. 618—905). Part I. 12 chüan. Part II. 4 chüan. 1732. *Ref.* B.M. p. 238.

[*Amherst* I, C 16.]

74. 戰 國 策
Chan kuo tsê.

"The Story of the Contending States." 10 chüan. 1581. *Ref.* B.M. p. 135. [*Amherst* II, C 1.]

75. 讀 史 論 畧
Tu shih lun luŏ.

"Discourses for Regulating the Study of History."

[*Amherst* II, C 2.]

76. 姑 妄 聽 之
Ku wang t'ing chih.

"Old Wives' Tales." By 觀 奕 道 人 Kuan Yi Tao-jen. 1809. *Ref.* L.U. 44, 4.   [*Amherst* II, C 3.]

77. 粉 粧 樓 全 傳
Fên chuang lou ch'uan chuan.

"The Story of the Pavilion of Paint," with illustrations. An historical novel, in continuation of the Shuo tang chih chuan. 6 vols. 80 hui. 1806. *Ref.* B.M. p. 67.
[*Amherst* II, C 4.]

78. 醻 世 錦 囊 全 書
Ch'ou shih chin nang ch'üan shu.

"A Treasury of Information on Social Etiquette." By 鄒 景 揚 Tsou Ching-yang. 1 case, 12 vols. *Ref.* B.M. p. 220 ; Kidd, p. 35.   [*Amherst* II, C 5.]

79. 海 瑞 案 傳
Hai suy ngan chuan.

"Hai Sui's Legal Decisions." Edited by 李 春 芳 Li Ch'un-fang. 6 vols. 1606. *Ref.* Kidd, p. 38 ; L.U. 19, 3.
[*Amherst* II, C 6.]

80. 希 夷 夢
Hsi-I Mêng.

"The Dreams of Hsi-I," a Taoist Doctor. A Novel. 2 cases. 7 vols. 40 chüan. 1809. *Ref.* B.M. p. 73 ; L.U. 21, 3.   [*Amherst* II, C 7-8.]

81. 廻 文 傳
Hui wên chuan.

"The Story of a Literary Puzzle." 6 vols. *Ref.* B.M. p. 133.   [*Amherst* II, C 9.]

82. 增 智 襄 補
Tsêng chih hsiang pu.

" Aids to Increase Knowledge."

[*Amherst* II, C 10.]

83. 禪 眞 逸 史
Ch'an chên yi shih.

" A History of Buddhist Saints." 10 vols. (1st vol. missing). [*Amherst* II, C 11.]

84. 龍 圖 公 案
Lung t'u kung ngan.

" The Criminal Cases of Lung T'u, or Dragon Face," a famous Chinese judge. 5 vols. 10 chüan. 1810. *Ref.* B.M. p. 148; L.U. 58, 5. [*Amherst* II, C 12.]

85. 蜃 樓 志
Shên lou chih.

" The Story of the Sea Serpent." An account of a visionary monster seen at sea, said to be like a snake with horns, and like a dragon in the lower part of the body, having scales; sometimes assumes the form of a watchtower, whence the name (Morrison's Dictionary). 6 vols. 24 chüan. 1804. *Ref.* Kidd, p. 52. See No 59.

[*Amherst* II, C 13.]

86. 依 樣 葫 蘆
I yang hu lu.

A Descriptive Account of the various sorts of Gourds. 4 vols. 4 chüan. 1804. [*Amherst* II, C 14.]

87. 紅 樓 夢
Hung lou mêng.

" The Dream of the Red Chamber." A Novel of very considerable repute in China. For epitome, see *Journal of China Branch of the Royal Asiat. Soc.* for 1885, p. 1. 2 cases, 20 vols. 1811. *Ref.* Kidd, p. 51; B.M. p. 209; Wylie, p. 162. [*Amherst* II, C 15-16.]

88. 重 訂 廣 事 類 賦
Ch'ung ting kuang shih lei fu.

An Encyclopedia of General Information. With Notes. By 華希閔 Hua Hsi-min. 40 chüan. 1788.

[*Amherst* II, C 17-18.]

89. 今 古 奇 觀
Chin ku ch'i kuan.

"Ancient and Modern Wonders." A collection of marvellous tales, translations of many of which have appeared in the *China Review*. 10 vols. 40 chüan. *Ref.* B.M. p. 101; Kidd, p. 52. [*Amherst* II, C 19.]

90. 說 鈴
Shuo Ling.

An Account of Embassies from Russia, Cochin China, Formosa, the Loo Choo Islands, and other States. 12 vols. 1796—1821. *Ref.* B.M. p. 184. [*Amherst* I, D 1-2.]

91. 神 仙 通 鑑
Shên hsien t'ung chien.

A General Series of Biographical Notices of Taoist Divinities. By 徐 衟 Hsü Tao, &c. 5 cases, 39 vols. 1787. *Ref.* B.M. p. 173. [*Amherst* I, D 3—7.]

92. 前 西 遊 記
Ch'ien hsi yu chi.

"First part of Travels in the West." 2 cases, 20 vols. 100 hui. 1696. [*Amherst* I, D 8-9.]

93. 聊 齋 志 異
Liao Chai chih i.

"Strange Stories from a Chinese Studio." 2 cases, 16 vols. 1768. *Ref.* B.M. p. 167; L.U. 52, 4; Kidd, p. 55. See No. 40. [*Amherst* I, D 10-11.]

94. 西 遊 眞 詮
Hsi yu chên chüan.

"A Complete Narrative of Travels in the West," in search of the Sacred Books. By 邱長春 Ch'iu Ch'ang-ch'un. Illustrated. 2 cases, 20 vols. [*Amherst* I, D 12-13.]

95. 家 寶 全 集
Chia pao ch'üan chi.

"A Complete Collection of Household Jewels," being a Compendium of useful domestic and social knowledge. By 石成金 Shih Ch'êng-chin. 2 cases, 32 vols. published at Yangchow. *Ref.* B.M. p. 182. [*Amherst* I, D 14-15.]

96. 天 雨 花
Tien yü hua.

"The Rain and Flowers of Heaven" (?). A Novel, chiefly in verse. By 陶貞懷 Ta'o Chên-yüan. 3 cases, 30 vols. 1804. *Ref.* B.M. p. 200. [*Amherst* II, D 1—3.]

97. 前 紅 樓 夢
Ch'ien hung lou mêng.

"The Earlier Dream of the Red Chamber." 2 cases, 24 vols. 1791. [*Amherst* II, D 4-5.]

98. 後 紅 樓 夢
Hou hung lou mêng.

"The Later Dream of the Red Chamber." 10 vols. 32 hui. [*Amherst* II, D 6.]

99. 後 紅 樓 夢
Hou hung lou mêng.

"The Later Dream of the Red Chamber." 10 vols.
[*Amherst* II, D 7.]

C

100. 四 書 匯 叅

Ssŭ shu hui chüan.

" A Complete Set of the Four Books."　4 cases, 22 vols.

[*Amherst* II, D 8—11.]

101. 資 治 新 書

Tzŭ chih hsin shu.

" A new work on the Laws of the Empire."　By 李 笠 翁
Li Li-wêng.　7 vols.　*Ref.* L.U. 118, 1.

[*Amherst* II, D 12.]

102. 平 山 冷 燕

Ping shan lêng yen.

Translated by Stanislas Julien under the title of "Les deux
jeunes filles lettrées."　Paris, 1860.　4 vols.　1797.　*Ref.*
L.U. 68, 5; Wylie, p. 163.　　　[*Amherst* II, D 13.]

103. 山 海 經

Shan hai ching.

" The Classic of the Hills and Seas."　With Ko Pŏ's
Commentary.　Edited by 吳 夷 珩 Wu Chung-wêng.
4 vols. 18 chüan.　1667.　See No. 230.　[*Amherst* II, D 14.]

104. 六 合 內 外 瑣 言

Liu ho nei wai so yen.

" Trifles on men and things within and beyond the Six
Points "—East, West, South, North, the Zenith and the
Nadir.　Kidd, p. 27.　*Ref.* L.U. 57, 2; Kidd, p. 27.

[*Amherst* II, D 15-16.]

105. 神 天 聖 書

Shên t'ien shêng shu.

The Bible.　Translated into Chinese by R. Morrison
and Mr. Milne.　3 cases, 24 vols.　1823.　*Ref.* B.M. p. 1.

[*Amherst* I, E 1—3.]

106. 水 滸 傳
Shui hu chuan.

An historical novel.　By 施 耐 菴 Shih Nai-ngan.　The scene is laid in Honan and Shantung, and relates to the time of Hui Tsung (1101—1126) of the Sung Dynasty.　It is of a less martial character than the *San Kuo* and furnishes a greater insight into Chinese life in various phases. 2 cases, 20 vols.　1734.　*Ref.* B.M. p. 181; Kidd, p. 13; L.U. 86, 5.　See No. 120.　　　　[*Amherst* I, E 4-5.]

107. 大 清 搢 紳 全 書
Ta ch'ing chin shên ch'üan shu.

A Complete Official Directory of the Empire; the "Red Book," as it is usually called.　3 cases, 12 vols.　*Ref.* B.M. p. 164; Kidd, p. 33.　　　　[*Amherst* I, E 6—8.]

108. 桃 花 扇 傳 奇
T'ao hua shan chuan ch'i.

" The Story of the Peach Blossom Fan."　4 vols.　*Ref.* B.M. p. 115.　See No. 55.　　　　[*Amherst* I, E 9.]

109. 四 書 題 鏡
Ssŭ shu t'i ching.

A Mirror of Themes from the Four Books.　10 vols. 1807.　　　　[*Amherst* I, E 10.]

110. 三 國 志
San kuo chih.

" The History of the Three Kingdoms," of Wei, Shu, and Wu, which flourished about the third century of the Christian era.　See No. 250.　　　　[*Amherst* I, E 11-12.]

c 2

111. 本 草 綱 目
Pên ts'ao kang mu.

The "Materia Medica" of 李時珍 Li Shih-chên. 6 cases, 44 vols. 1657. *Ref.* Wylie, p. 67; B.M. p. 129; Kidd, p. 16; L.U. 128, 3. See No. 72. [*Amherst* II, E 1—6.]

112. 尺 牘 類 選
Ch'ih tu lei hsüan.

"The Model Letter Writer."   *Ref.* B.M. p. 28.
[*Amherst* II, E 7.]

113. 花 樓 衍 義
Hua lou yen i.

On the Broad Principles of Right and Justice, Liberality and Benevolence (?). 14 vols. 1814.
[*Amherst* II, E 8.]

114. 金 石 姻 緣
Chin Shih yin yüan.

The Heavenly-influenced union of Chin and Shih. *Ref.* L.U. 38, 5. See No. 8.   [*Amherst* II, E 9.]

115. 詠 物 詩 選 註 釋
Yung wu shih hsüan chu shih.

A Collection of Poetical Recitations, with Explanatory Notes. 4 vols. 8 chüan. 1800. *Ref.* B.M. p. 250.
[*Amherst* II, E 10.]

116. 詩 韻 含 英 題 解 辨 同 合 訂
Shih yün han ying t'i chieh pien t'ung ho ting.

A Copious Tonic Dictionary of poetical expressions explained and discussed." Compiled by 甘芳谷 Kan Fang-ku. 4 vols. 1775. *Ref.* B.M. p. 93.
[*Amherst* II, E 11.]

117. 籌 世 錦 囊 全 書
Ch'ou shih chin nang ch'üan shu.

"Polite Intercourse with the World." A work containing models for inscriptions over doors, eulogies on deceased relations, benedictions, congratulatory odes, family ceremonies, complimentary addresses, forms of bonds and covenants; also notices of the public roads of the Empire, sources of the lakes, on the Yang-tzŭ river, with other miscellaneous information of a polite and literary character. 6 vols. *Ref.* B.M. p. 220; Kidd, p. 35.

[*Amherst* II, E 12.]

118. 好 逑 傳
Hao ch'iu chuan.

"The Fortunate Union." A tale of Social Life. Translated under the above title by Sir John Davis. 4 vols. *Ref.* B.M. p. 103; Kidd, p. 53; Wylie, p. 163; Möllendorff, p. 22. See No. 125. [*Amherst* II, E 13.]

119. 文 帝 全 書
Wên Ti ch'üan shu.

The Complete Works of Wên Ti. 1 case, 8 vols. 1803. *Ref.* Kidd, p. 20; Wylie, p. 16. [*Amherst* II, E 14.]

120. 水 滸 傳
Shui hu chuan.

An Historical Novel. By 施耐菴 Shih Nai-ngan. The scene is laid in Honan and Shantung, and relates to the time of Hui Tsung (1101—1126) of the Sung Dynasty. It is of a less martial character than the *San kuo chih* and furnishes a greater insight into Chinese life in various phases. 2 cases, 20 vols. 75 chüan. 1734. *Ref.* R.M. p. 181; Kidd, p. 13; L.U. 86, 5. See No. 106.

[*Amherst* II, E 15-16.]

121. 粵 東 筆 記
Yüeh tung pi chi.

Records relating to the Province of Kuang-tung.   4 vols.
Ref. Kidd, p. 11.   [*Amherst* II, 17.]

122. 本 草 綱 目
Pên ts'ao kang mu.

The "Materia Medica" of China.   4 cases, 44 chüan.
1786.   *Ref.* B.M. p. 129.   See No. 72.
       [*Amherst* I, F 1—4.]

123. 十 國 春 秋
Shih kuo ch'un ch'iu.

"The Spring and Autumn Annals (*i.e.* the history) of the
Ten Kingdoms."   1—8 only out of 16 vols.
       [*Amherst* I, F 5.]

124. 字 彙
Tzǔ Hui.

A Dictionary. By 梅 鷹 祖 Mei Ying-tsu.   2 cases,
14 vols.   *Ref.* B.M. p. 155.   [*Amherst* I, F 6-7.]

125. 鑑 史 提 綱
Chien shih t'i kang.

A Collection of the most important facts in History.
4 vols.   [*Amherst* I, F 8.]

126. 好 逑 傳
Hao ch'iu chuan.*

"The Fortunate Union."   4 vols.   *Ref.* B.M. p. 103 ;
Kidd, p. 3.   See No. 118.   [*Amherst* I, F 9.]

---

* This novel has been translated into English by T. Percy, "The Pleasing
History of Hao Kiou," 1761. London, 4 vols. 8vo.   Also in German by
C. G. von Meerr, Leipzig, 1760, 8vo. French : Lyons, 1766, 4 vols. 12mo.;
and Paris, 1828, 12mo. Dutch : Amsterdam, 1767, 12mo.; Bremen,
1869, 8vo.   Sir J. Davis also made a translation, entitled as above.

127. 唐 宋 文 醇
T'ang Sung wên shun.

Examples of the highest class of literature of the periods of the T'ang and Sung Dynasties. 2 cases, 20 vols.

[*Amherst* I, F 10-11.]

128. 印 譜
Yin p'u.

An Illustrated work on Ancient and Modern Seals. 6 vols. [*Amherst* I, F 12.]

129. 小 學 正 文
Hsiao hsüo chêng wên.

"The correct text of the *Hsiao hsüo* (Learning for the Young)." 2 vols. [*Amherst* I, F 13.]

130. 法 苑 珠 林
Fa yüan chu lin.

"The Forest of the Pearls and the Garden of the Law (?)." Only 2 cases, 1—6, 19—24. *Ref.* B.M. p. 201.

[*Amherst* I, F 15-16.]

131. 通 鑑 綱 目
T'ung chien kang mu.

A General Review of History. 2 cases only, 21—30, 31—39. *Ref.* B.M. p. 45. See Nos. 165, 240.

[*Amherst* II, F 1-2.]

132. 增 補 遣 愁 集
Tsêng pu ch'ien ch'ou chi.

"A Remedy to Dispel Grief." Compiled by Chang Kuei-shêng 張 貴 勝. *Ref.* L.U. 105, 5 ; B.M. p. 13.

[*Amherst* II, F 3.]

133. 四 書
Ssǔ shu.

The "Four Books," in Manchu and Chinese. 1756.
[*Amherst* II, F 4.]

134. 萬 法 焣 宗
Wan fa kuei tsung.

"On the Doctrine of the Transmigration of Souls," or perhaps more correctly, "Of the Immortality of the Soul (?)." This is *not* a missionary work. 5 vols. *Ref.* L.U. 122, 4.
[*Amherst* II, F 5.]

135. 算 法 統 宗
Suan fa t'ung tsung.

"The Rules of Arithmetic," illustrating the principle of the Abacus. *Ref.* B.M. p. 39.   [*Amherst* II, F 6.]

136. 文 法 入 門
Wên fa ju mên.

" Elements of Composition." 2 vols.
[*Amherst* II, F 7.]

137. 論 語
The "Lun yü."

"The Confucian Analects." 2 vols. *Ref.* B.M. p. 193.
[*Amherst* II, F 8.]

138. 豆 棚 閒 話
Tou p'êng hsien hua.

2 vols.   [*Amherst* II, F 9.]

139. 一 歹 話
Yi hsi hua.

"An Evening Talk." 4 vols.   [*Amherst* II, F 10.]

140. Lung yen ching lüo.

[*Amherst* II, F 11.]

141. 二 論 啟 幼 引 端

Êrh lun ch'i yu yin tuan.

"The Beginner's Guide to the Confucian Analects."
2 vols. 4 chüan. 1795. *Ref.* B.M. p. 134.

[*Amherst* II, F 12.]

142. 時 文 筆 譜

Shih wên pi p'u.

" Essays on Modern Literature." 2 vols. 4 chüan. 1813.

[*Amherst* II, F 13.]

143. 古 文 筆 譜

Ku wên pi p'u.

" Essays on Ancient Literature." [*Amherst* II, F 14.]

144. 本 草 集 要

Pên Ts'ao chi yao.

Summary of the most important information contained in
Pên ts'ao. See No. 72. 2 cases, 13 vols.

[*Amherst* II, F 15-16.]

145. 道 德 經 解

Tao tê ching chieh.

The Canon of Tao, and the Exemplification thereof, with
exegetical notes. See No. 202. *Ref.* B.M. p. 120.

[*Amherst* II, F 17.]

146. 數 求 聲
品 字 箋

Shu ch'iu shêng,
and **P'in tzŭ ch'ien.**

" Many appeals for preferments," and "The Records of
honours conferred (?)." 4 vols. and 3 vols. in one case.

[*Amherst* II, F 18.]

147. 休 寧 縣 志
Hsiu-ning hsien chih.

Topographical Records of the District of Hsiu-ning.
Ref. Biot, p. 33.　　　　　　　　　　[*Amherst* II, F 19].

148. 正 字 通
Chêng tzŭ t'ung.

A Chinese Dictionary.　3 cases, 20 vols.　*Ref.* B.M.
p. 132.　　　　　　　　　　[*Amherst* II, F 20—22.]

149. 漢 宋 奇 書
Han Sung ch'i shu.

Statistical and Topographical Illustrations of the two
great historical novels or romantic accounts of periods
during the Han and Sung Dynasties, called the 三 國 志
San kuo chih (see No. 110) and the 水 滸 傳 Shui hu-chuan
(see No. 106).　2 cases, 20 vols.　　[*Amherst* I, G 1-2.]

150. 疇 世 錦 囊 全 書
Ch'ou shih chin nang ch'üan shu.

A Treasury of Information on social etiquette.　By 鄒
景 揚 Tsou Ching-yang.　1 case, 7 vols.　*Ref.* B.M. p. 220;
Kidd, p. 35.　　　　　　　　　[*Amherst* I, G 3.]

151. 水 滸 傳
Shui hu chuan.

3 cases, 20 volumes.　*Ref.* B.M. p. 181; L.U. 86, 5; Kidd,
p. 13.　See No. 106.　　　　　　[*Amherst* I, G 4—6.]

152. 感 應 篇
Kan ying p'ien.

"The Book of Rewards and Punishments."　*Ref.* Wylie,
p. 179.　2 vols.　　　　　　　[*Amherst* I, G 7.]

---

* *Kan ying p'ien.*　This work, which belongs to the debased Taoism
of later ages, has been translated by S. Julien under the title of "Le livre
des Recompenses et des Peines," Paris, 1835, 8vo.　*See also,* for English
translation, "Doolittle's Vocabulary," vol. ii.; *also* A. Remusat, "Le
Livres des Recompenses et des Peines," Paris, 1816.

153. 大 清 摺 紳 全 書
Ta Ch'ing chin shên ch'üan shu.

A Complete official Directory for the Empire. Four Directories, each 4 vols., come under this slip. 4 vols. *Ref.* B.M. p. 164. [*Amherst* I, G 8.]

154. 唐 人 說 薈
T'ang jen shuo wei.

"The Herbal Expositor of the period of the T'ang 唐 Dynasty," (A.D. 618, 905). 4 cases, 32 vols. *Ref.* Kidd, p. 16. [*Amherst* II, G 1—4.]

155. 今 古 奇 觀
Chin ku ch'i kuan.

Wondrous Tales of Ancient and Modern Times. By 覺世 Chüo Shih. See No. 89. *Ref.* B.M. p. 101; Kidd, p. 52. [*Amherst* II, G 5.]

156. 駁 案 新 編
Pǒ ngan hsin pien.

"Judgments reversed." A new edition of cases which have been brought before the High Court of Justice for Revision of Judgment. 4 cases, 32 vols. 1736.

[*Amherst* I, H 1—4.]

157. 綴 白 裘
Chui pǒ ch'iu.

A collection of Plays. *Ref.* B.M. p. 39.

[*Amherst* I, H 5—10.]

158. 大 清 律 例
Ta ch'ing lü li.

The Laws of the Imperial Tartar Dynasty—the Penal Code of China. 2 cases. Translated by Sir George Staunton. [*Amherst* II, H 1-2.]

159. Chi hsiu lei pao.

14 vols. [*Amherst* II, H 3-4.]

160. 四 庫 全 書
Ssǔ k'u ch'üan shu.

A Catalogue of the Imperial Library. A great national collection of books, published in the 39th year of Ch'ien Lung (*or* Kien Long). 8 vols. 1774. *Ref.* Kidd, p. 29.

[*Amherst* II, H 5.]

161. 積 古 齋 鐘 鼎 器 欵 識
Chi ku ch'i chung ting ch'i k'uan shih.

A work on ancient Bells, Tripods, &c.

[*Amherst* I, J 2.]

162. 嶺 南 叢 述
Ling nan ts'ung shu.

An Account of the Provinces of Kuang-tung and Kuang-hsi. By 登 淳 Têng Shun. 18 vols. 60 chüan. 1830. *Ref.* B.M. p. 199. [*Amherst* I, J 3-4.]

163. 春 秋 註
Chun Tsew choo.

The "Spring and Autumn" or History of the State of Lu. By Confucius. With commentary. 1790.

[*Amherst* I, J 5.]

164. 鐘 鼎 彝 器 欵 識 *
Chung ting i ch'i k'uan shih.

Facsimiles of Inscriptions on Bells, Tripods, Vases, &c., of Successive Ages, transcribed and explained. By 薛 尚 功 Shê Shang-kung of the Sung Dynasty. 4 vols. 20 chüan. 1797. *Ref.* B.M. p. 172. [*Amherst* I, J 7.]

---

* Translated by Gaubil, revised and corrected by M. de Guignes, Paris, 1770, 4to.

165. 通 鑑 綱 目

T'ung chien kang mu.

2 cases only, 1—8, 19—24. See No. 131.

[*Amherst* I, J 8-9.]

---

166. 御 製 曆 象 考 成

Yü chih li hsiang k'ao ch'êng.

Buddhism. "Successive Transformations accomplished."
A Buddhistic work, published under Imperial authority.
16 vols. 16 chüan. No date. *Ref.* Kidd, p. 47.

[*China* I, A 1.]

167. 孔 子 家 語

K'ung tzŭ chia yü.

"The Family Sayings of Confucius." These "Sayings"
are not authentic. An attempt to translate the work was
made some years ago in the *Chinese Recorder*.

[*China* I, A 2.]

168. 佛 頂 五 錄 總 目

Fŏ ting wu lu tsung mu.

Buddhism. Six vols., comprising the

枝 錄 chih lu, 1 vol.　　宗 錄 tsung lu, 1 vol.

蒙 鈔 mêng ch'ao, 4 vols.

A Buddhistic work, with plates, representing the metempsychosis. *Ref.* Kidd, p. 47.　　[*China* I, A 3-4.]

169. 陔 餘 叢 考

Kai yü ts'ung k'ao.

12 vols. 43 chüan (1st vol. missing).　　[*China* I, A 5.]

170. 霞 客 遊 記

Hsia k'ê yu chi.

"The Travels of Hsü Hsia-k'ê." 徐霞客. 16 vols. 1703.
Ref. B.M. p. 174; Kidd, p. 56.　　[*China* I, A 6.]

171. 三 教 搜 神
San chiao sou shên.

Religion.   The Three Sects.

The 三 教 源 流 聖 帝 佛 師 搜 神 記

"San chiao yüan liu shêng ti fŏ shih sou shên chi,"
is the full title of the "History of the founders of the
Three Sects—Confucianism, Buddhism, Taouism, and other
Saints and Sages."   1819.   [*China* I, A 7.]

172. 人 生 必 讀
Jen shêng pi tu.

"The moral obligations of life."   2 vols. 2 chüan.   1786.
[*China* I, A 8.]

173. 監 本 禮 記
Chien pên li chi.

The "Book of Rites" revised.   10 vols. 30 chüan.
1781. *Ref.* B.M. p. 121; I.O.C. p. 18. (10 chüan).
[*China* I, A 9.]

174. 易 經
Yi ching.

"The Book of Changes."   2 chüan.   1681.
[*China* I, A 10.]

175. 皇 明 制 書
Huang Ming chih shu.

The Imperial Ming dynasty's book of National Regulations.   12 vols. 14 chüan.   1375.
[*China* I, A 11.]

176. 書 經
Shu ching.

The Book of History.   One of the Five Classics.   *Ref.*
Wylie, Notes, 2.   See No. 263.   [*China* II, A 1.]

177. 新 遺 詔 書
Hsin I Chao Shu.

The New Testament. Translated by Dr. Robert Morrison. Also the Epistles, with the Apocalypse, in a thin separate volume. 8 vols. 8vo. 1813. *Ref.* B.M. p. 158; I.O.C. p. 56; Kidd, p. 49. [*China* II, A 2.]

178. 羣 芳 譜
Ch'ün fang p'u.

A "Herbarium," by 王象晉 Wang Hsiang-chin. Edited by 毛鳳苞 Mao Fêng-pao, and others. 18 vols. [*China* II, A 3-4.]

179. 薛 氏 醫 按
Shê shih I ngan.

A collection of medical cases by Shê Shih. This is an abridgment and commentary by Shê Shih of a work published about the year 1287 by Ch'ên Tzǔ-ming 陳自明 called 婦人大全瓦方 Fu jen ta ch'üan liang fang. It principally relates to female complaints. Each article is followed by prescriptions suitable to the ailment in question. *Ref.* Wylie, p. 79; Kidd, p. 42. 32 vols. in 4 cases. [*China* II, A 5—8.]

180. 上 下 論 上 下 孟
Shang hsia lun; Shang hsia mêng.

Part of the "Four Books," namely the Lun yü, or Analects of Confucius, and the books of Mencius. [*China* II, A 9.]

181. 幼 學 句 解
The "Yu Hsüŏ (須知 hsü chih) Chü Chieh."

"General knowledge necessary for beginners," with explanations, in 4 chüan. (2nd chüan missing). 1790. *Ref.* B.M. p. 40. [*China* II, A 10.]

182. 詩 韻 珠 璣
Shih yün chu chi.

" A Treasury of Rhymes," by 余 照 Yü Chao. 5 vols. 5 chüan. 1801. *Ref.* B.M. p. 264; Kidd, p. 15.

[*China* II, A 11.]

183. 番 禺 縣 志
P'an-yü hsien chih.

" A Topography of the district city of P'an-yü, in the province of Kuangtung. It is really the port of Canton, where foreign vessels anchor. 12 vols. in two cases. 1st vol. with Index and Illustrations missing. *Ref.* Kidd, p. 10.

[*China* II, A 12-13.]

184. 大 清 律 例
Ta Ch'ing lü li.

" The fundamental laws and subordinate statutes of the Ch'ing Dynasty," 24 vols. in 4 cases. 1646. *Ref.* B.M. p. 218; (1768), I.O.C. p. 58.

[*China* III, A 1—3.]

185. 紅 雪 樓 九 種 曲
Hung hsüeh lou chiu ch'ung ch'ü.

" The nine plays of the red snow tower." 10 vols. These " plays " or popular stories are as follows :—

1	香 祖 樓	Hsiang tsu lo, 2 vols.
2	空 谷 香	K'ung ku hsiang, 2 vols.
3	桂 林 霜	Kuei lin hsiang, 1 vol.
4	一 片 石	Yi p'ien shih, 1 vol.
5	第 二 碑	Ti êrh pei, 1 vol.
6	冬 青 樹	Tung ch'ing shu, 1 vol.
7	臨 川 夢	Lin ch'uan mêng, 1 vol.
8	雪 中 人	Hsüeh chung jen, }
9	四 絃 秋	Ssǔ hsien ch'iu, } 1 vol.

1774.

[*China* III, A 4.]

186. 清 文 彙 書
Ch'ing wên hui shu.

A Manchu-Chinese dictionary. 12 vols. 12 chüan. 1750.

[*China* III, A 5.]

187. 笠 翁 十 種 曲
Li wêng shih chung ch'ü.

Ten Plays, compiled by Li Wêng. 18 vols. *Ref.* B.M. p. 133; Kidd, p. 15; L.U. 55, 2.   [*China* III, A 6.]

188. 韻 雅
Yün Ya.

A Dictionary arranged according to the Tones. 5 vols. *Ref.* Kidd, p. 2.   [*China* III, A 7.]

189. 四 書
Ssŭ shu.

18 vols.   [*China* III, A 8—10.]

190. 臨 證 指 南 醫 按
Lin chêng chih nan i ngan.

A correct Medical Guide, founded on extensive practice. 1769. *Ref.* Kidd, p. 43.   [*China* I, B 1-2.]

191. 廣 東 通 志
Kuang-tung t'ung che.

A Topographical Account of the Province of Kwangtung. 5 cases, 36 vols. *Ref.* B.M. p. 268; L.U. 48, 4.
   [*China* I, B 3—7.]

192. 全 本 禮 記 體 註
Ch'üan pên Li Ki t'i chu.

The Book of Rites, with a collection of Comments compiled by Chin Hao. 10 chüan. 1766. *Ref.* B.M. p. 121; I.O.C. p. 19.   [*China* I, B 8.]

193 拍 案 驚 奇
P'ŏ ngan ching ch'i.

10 vols. 36 chüan.   [*China* I, B 9.]

D

194. 廣 輿 記
Kuang yü chi.

A complete Geography of the Empire of China, originally compiled by 睦應陽 Lu Ying-yang during the Ming dynasty. Reproduced under the Emperor K'ang Hsi (1662—1722) by 祭方炳 Ts'ai Fang-ping. 13 vols. 24 chüan. 1686. *Ref.* B.M. p. 148; I.O.C. p. 53; Wylie, p. 48.

[*China* II, B 1.]

195. 試 賦 麗 則
Shih fu li tsê.

4 vols. 1779. [*China* II, B 2.]

196. 時 文 備 法
Shih wên pei fa.

6 vols. 1809. [*China* II, B 3.]

197. 禪 眞 逸 史
Ch'an chên yi shih.

12 vols. 40 hui. [*China* II, B 4.]

198. 古 文 評 註
Ku wên p'ing chu.

Specimens of Ancient Authors, with commentary and notes. 10 vols. 1786. [*China* II, B 5.]

199. 音 漢 清 文 鑑
Yin han ch'ing wên chien.

1 vol. 5 chüan. 1735. [*China* II, B 6.]

200. 古 文 評 註
Ku wên p'ing chu.

10 vols. 1785. See No. 198. [*China* II, B 7.]

201. 明 文 少 題
Ming wên shao t'i.

4 vols. 1731. [*China* II, B 8.]

202. 道 德 經
Tao tê ching.

The Canon of Tao and the Exemplification thereof. Has been translated into French, English and German, by Julien, Chalmers, (1) von Strauss and (2) Plaenckner, respectively. 2 vols. No date. *Ref.* Kidd, 21 ; B.M. p. 119.

[*China* II, B 9.]

203. 金 鑑 外 科
Chin chien wai k'ŏ.

The Golden Mirror of Medicine for the cure of external complaints. By Wu Ch'ien 吳 謙. Published by Imperial Order. 10 vols. 16 chüan. 1742. *Ref.* B.M. p. 348. L.U. 37, 2.

[*China* II, B 10.]

204. 快 心 三 編
K'uai hsin san pien.

Three pleasant Stories. 6 chüan. *Ref.* B.M. p. 185 ; L.U. 45, 3.

[*China* II, B 11.]

205. 禮 記
Li Chi.

"The Book of Rites." Full title is the 全 本 禮 記 體 註 Ch'üan pên Li Chi t'i chu. There is a collection of comments compiled by Ch'ên Hao 陳 澔. Edited by Fan Tzŭ têng 范 紫 登 and others. 10 chüan. 1765. *Ref.* B.M. p. 121 ; I.O.C. p. 19. Translation by Dr. Legge will be found among *The Sacred Books of the East*.

[*China* II, B 12.]

206. 泉 志
Ch'üan chih.

"A History of Coinage" from the earliest times to the middle of the tenth century. This copy is *manuscript*. No date. *Ref.* B.M. p. 83 ; Kidd, p. 32. [*China* III, B 1.]

207. 快 心 編
K'uai hsin pien.

"A Merry Tale." 7 vols. No date. *Ref.* B.M. p. 185 ; L.U. 45, 3.

[*China* III, B 2.]

D 2

208. 色 戒 錄
Sê chieh lu.

"The Art of Continence." 1 vol. No date. *Ref.* Kidd, p. 20. [*China* III, B 3.]

209. 天 崇 欣 賞
T'ien tsung hsin shang.

5 vols. 1778. [*China* III, B 4.]

210. 詞 學 全 書
Tz'ŭ hsüŏ ch'üan shu.

7 vols. 1746. [*China* III, B 5.]

211. 昭 明 文 選
Chao ming wên hsüan.

Choice Literary Essays. Vols. 9—16 inclusive. Chüan 27—60 inclusive. [*China* III, B 6.]

212. 清 文 彙 書
Ch'ing wên hui shu.

A Manchu-Chinese Dictionary. 12 vols. 1806. [*China* III, B 7.]

213. 花 鏡
Hua ching.

3 vols. 6 chüan. 1688. [*China* III, B 8.]

214. 女 仙 外 史
Nü hsien wai shih.

"Legends of Nymphs." 20 vols. 100 hui. *Ref.* B.M. p. 133; L.U. 64, 4. [*China* III, B 9-10.]

215. 粵 中 見 聞
Yüeh chung chien wên.

"A Descriptive Account of Canton." The work is also called 說 粵 新 書 Shuo Yüeh hsin shu. 5 vols. 1801.
[*China* III, B 11.]

216. 幼 粵 故 事
Yu hsüŏ ku shih.

"First Lessons in Ancient History." 4 vols. 4 chüan. 1796. See No. 181.   [*China* III, B 12.]

217. 離 騷 經
Li sao ching.*

"Sinking into Grief." A poem in justification of the author's public character. By Ch'ü Yüan 屈原. 2 vols. 4 chüan. *Ref.* B.M. p. 102 ; Wylie's Notes, p. 181; Möllendorff, p. 20.   [*China* III, B 13.]

218. 琵 琶 記
P'i pa chi.

"The Story of a Lute." A Novel, with illustrations. *Ref.* B.M. p. 163.   [*China* III, B 14.]

219. 戶 部 則 例
Hu pu tsê li.

"Regulations of the Board of Revenue." 6 vols. 31 chüan. 1746. *Ref.* B.M. p. 34 ; Kidd, p. 38. [*China* III, B 15.]

220. 法 界 安 立 圖
Fa chieh ngan li t'u.

The Buddhist Kosmos, with illustrations, compiled by the priest 仁潮 Jen Ch'ao. 1679. *Ref.* B.M. p. 92; L.U. 13, 4.
                    [*China* III, B 16.]

221. 故 事 尋 源
Ku shih hsin yüan.

                    [*China* I, C 1.]

222. 歷 伐 名 賢 列 女 氏 姓 譜
Li tai ming hsien lieh nü shih hsing p'u.

A Biographical Account of successive generations of illustrious and virtuous women. 16 cases, 120 vols. 157 chüan. 1792.   [*China* I, C 2—9, to II, C 1—8.]

---

* *Li Sao.* Translated and published, with the original text in French, by the Marquis Hervey de Saint Denys, Paris, 1870, 8vo.

223. 高 厚 蒙 求
Kao hou mêng ch'iu.

A collection of important articles relating to Astronomical Science. The author, who is a Chinese mathematical instrument maker, admits his obligations to the works of Europeans, which have been published in Chinese by imperial authority. By 徐朝俊 Hsü Chao-chün. 4 vols. 1807. *Ref.* B.M. p. 173; Wylie, p. 99; Kidd, p. 30; L.U. 30, 2.

[*China* II, C 9.]

224. 傷 寒 辨 證 錄
Shang han pien chêng lu.

Records of The Symptoms of Fever occasioned by checked perspiration. A medical work on colds. 14 vols. 14 chüan. 1748.   [*China* II, C 10-11.]

225. 幼 學 故 事 瓊 林
Yu hsüŏ ku shih ch'iung lin.

A comprehensive account of matters relating to Antiquity, for the use of young people. By 程允升 Chêng Yün-shêng. 2 vols. 4 chüan. 1796. *Ref.* B.M. p. 40; L.U. 89, 3.   [*China* II, C 12.]

226. 一 統 志
Yi t'ung chih.

A Geographical and Statistical Account of the Empire of China. By Imperial Commission. Comprises:—1. Situation and boundaries of provinces. 2. Climate. 3. Historical notices. 4. Notable objects of a natural kind. 5. Customs and dispositions of people. 6. Cities, canals and celebrated buildings. 7. Schools and libraries. 8. Population. 9. Area. 10. Government officials. 11. Mountains and rivers. 12. Antiquities. 13. Fortresses and passes. 14. Bridges. 15. Dams. 16. Various monuments. 17. Confucian temples. 18. Taoist and Buddhist temples. 19. Eminent statesmen. 20. Famous persons. 21. Hermits. 22. Natural and artificial products. *Ref.* B.M. p. 21; I.O.C. p. 63; L.U. 131, 3.   [*China* III, C 1—4.]

227. 兵 垣 四 編
Ping yüan ssŭ pien.

"On the Art of Fortification." Stopped and emphasized in red, with printed red marginal commentaries and explanations. 5 vols. 1621. *Ref.* Kidd, p. 58.

[*China* III, C 5.]

228. 南 漢 春 秋
Nan han chu'n ch'iu.

The "Spring and Autumn Annals" (*i.e.* History) of the Southern Han dynasty.　　　[*China* III, C 6.]

229. 厦 門 志
Hsia mên chih.

"A Topography of Amoy." 1, 2. Topography. 2, 3. Civil and Military Government. 5. Shipping. 6. Intercourse with Formosa. 7. Customs and land revenues, &c. 8. Foreign marts. 9. Literature, Inscriptions. 10. A list of incumbents of office. 11. A list of literary graduates. 12, 13, 14. Biographical notices. 15. Manners and customs. 16. Antiquities. 16 sections. 1832. *Ref.* B.M. p. 50.

[*China* III, C 7.]

230. 山 海 經
Shan Hai Ching.

4 vols. See No. 103.　　　[*China* III, C 8—11.]

231. 大 清 會 典
Ta Ch'ing hui tien.

A Comprehensive description of the System of Government under the Ch'ing Dynasty (A.D. 1640—to date), being a Collection of the Laws, Statutes and Bye Laws of the Chinese Empire under the Tartar Dynasty. 20 cases, 121 vols. 180 chüan. 1747. *Ref.* B.M. p. 217; Kidd, p. 36; L.U. 40, 2. (100 chüan. 1764). I.O.C. p. 58.

[*China* I, D 1—11, to II D 1—9.]

232. 硃 批 諭 旨
Chu p'i yü chih.

"Imperial Rescripts declaring the Sovereign Will."
Imperfect: 1 case contains vols. 43—48 incl., and 1 case
vols. 107—112 incl. [*China* II, D 10-11.]

233. 左 繡
Tso hsiu.

Imperfect. Only 1 case, vols. 1—7. 7 vols. missing.
1720. [*China* II, D 12.]

234. 大 清 會 典
Ta Ch'ing hui tien.

Vols. 19—24 only. See No. 230. [*China* II, D 13.]

235. 藝 文 備 覽
I wên pei lan.

An excellent Dictionary arranged according to the Primitives. Its Author, Sha Muh, was 30 years in completing
it. 6 cases. 1798. *Ref.* B.M. p. 325; L.U. 13, 3.

[*China* III, D 1—6.]

236. 醫 宗 金 鑑
I tsung chin chien.

"The Golden Mirror of Medicine." A celebrated Treatise
on Medical Science. It was compiled by 100 persons connected with the Imperial College of Physicians at Peking.
All existing Treatises procurable in print or in manuscript
were collected by order of the Government in aid of the
design. The work was completed in four years. 5 cases,
40 vols. 1739. [*China* III, D 7—11.]

237. 欽 定 禮 記 義 疏
Ch'in ting li chi i su.

"The meaning of the Book of Rites," with explanations.
Imperfect. Only vols. 19—25 incl. See No. 205. *Ref.*
B.M. p. 121. [*China* I, E 1.]

238. 行 水 金 鑑 圖
Hsing shui chin chien t'u.

A Description of the Rise, Courses, Productions, &c., of the Celebrated Rivers of China, together with an account of the Grand Canal. 4 cases, 40 vols. 175 chüan. 1726. *Ref.* Kidd, p. 12. [*China* I, E 2—5.]

239. 神 仙 通 鑑
Shên hsien t'ung chien.

"A History of the Gods." 2 cases, 12 vols.

[*China* I, E 6-7.]

240. 通 鑑 綱 目
T'ung chien kang mu.

"A Condensation of the Mirror of History." By 朱熹 Chu Hsi and his disciples. 8 cases, 67 vols. 1803. *Ref.* B.M. p. 46; I.O.C. p. 61; Kidd, p. 8. See No. 165.

[*China* II, E 1—8.]

241. 適 情 雅 趣
Shih ch'ing ya ch'ü.

5 vols. 10 chüan. [*China* II, E 9.]

242. 史 記
Shih chi.

"The Historical Record." By 司馬遷 Ssŭ-ma Ch'ien. With a Commentary by 徐孚遠 Hsü Fu-yüan and 陳子龍 Ch'ên Tzŭ-lung. 24 vols. 130 chüan. 1806. *Ref.* B.M. p. 194; Kidd, p. 8. [*China* III, E 1—4.]

243. 史 記
Shih chi.

"The Historical Record." By 司馬遷 Ssŭ-ma Ch'ien 3 cases, 22 vols. 130 chüan. *Ref.* B.M. p. 194; Kidd, p. 8.

[*China* III, E 5—7.]

244. 類 經
Lei ching.

"Class Classics," being a compilation of the texts of two ancient medical works. 3 cases, 15 vols. 32 chüan.

[China III, E 8—10.]

245. 紅 樓 夢
Hung lou mêng.

"The Dream of the Red Chamber." By 曹雪芹 Ts'ao Hsüeh-ch'in. 8 vols. 8 chüan. 1835. *Ref.* L.U. 24, 4-5; Kidd, p. 51. See No. 88.   [*China* III, E 11.]

246. 四 書
Ssŭ shu.

The "Four Books." See No. 100.   [*China* I, F 1.]

247. 本 草 綱 目
Pên ts'ao kang muh.

See Nos. 72, 111.   [*China* I, F 2—5.]

248. 丘 錄
Ping Lu.

An Encyclopædia of matters connected with military affairs. Manuscript. 4 cases, 30 vols. 14 chüan. *Ref.* B.M. p. 204.   [*China* I, F 6—9.]

249. 佛 門 定 制
Fŏ mên ting chih.

"The established laws and formularies of the disciples of Buddha." Compiled by 詹承誥 Chan Ch'êng-Kao. *Ref.* B.M. p. 22; L.U. p. 16, 5.   [*China* I, F 10.]

250. 三 國 志
San kuo chih.

"The History of the Three Kingdoms." A romance founded on the Civil Wars of China during the 2nd and 3rd centuries. By 羅貫中 Lo Kuan-chung. 20 vols. 120 hui. 1644. *Ref.* B.M. p. 142; I.O.C. p. 54. See No. 110.

[China II, F 1-2.]

251. 四 書 直 解
Ssŭ shu chih chieh.

The "Four Books," clearly explained. 1765. *Ref.* B.M.
p. 192. See Nos. 100, 245. [*China* II, F 3.]

252. 旁 訓 詩 經 體 註 衍 義
P'ang hsün shih ching t'i chu yen i.

The Book of Odes, with Comments and Copious Interpretations. 4 vols. 8 chüan. 1687. *Ref.* B.M. p. 180.
[*China* II, F 5.]

253. 正 字 通
Chêng tzŭ t'ung.

A Dictionary arranged according to the Primitives. The
Preface to this edition is in Manchu-Chinese. 4 cases,
23 vols. 1672. *Ref.* B.M. p. 132; Kidd, p. 4; L.U. 5, 2.
[*China* II, F 6—9.]

254. 監 本 詩 經
Chien pên shih ching.

The original text of the Book of Odes. 4 vols. 1818.
Ref. B.M. p. 180. [*China* II, F 10.]

255. 聖 書
Shêng shu.

A Commentary on the Epistle to the Ephesians. By
William Milne, D.D. 2 vols. (in Chinese). Malacca. 1825
Ref. Kidd, p. 50. 1825. [*China* II, F 11.]

256. Part of the "Four Books," containing :

大 學 疏 義 Ta hsüŏ su i, 1 vol.
論 語 考 證 Lun yü k'ao chêng, 2 vols.
孟 子 考 證 Mêng tzu k'ao chêng, 1 vol.
1811. See No. 251. [*China* II, F 12.]

257. 三 國 志
San Kuo chih.

The History of the Three Kingdoms of Wei, Shu and Wu. An Historical Romance. See II, F 1-2. 2 cases, 20 volumes (second vol. missing). 1644. See II, F 1-2. See Nos. 111, 250.   [*China* II, F 13-14.]

258. 四 書 註
Ssŭ shu chu.

The "Four Books," with Commentary. See Nos. 101, 246, &c.   [*China* II, F 15.]

259. 皇 清 職 貢 圖
Huang ching chih kung t'u.

Tributory offerings rendered to the Imperial Ch'ing Dynasty. 9 vols. 1751.   [*China* III, F 1.]

260. 楞 嚴 正 脈
Lêng yen chêng mŏ.

"The true meaning of the *Lêng yen* sutra." 6 vols. *Ref.* B.M. p. 161.   [*China* III, F 2.]

261. 補 詳 字 義
Pu hsiang tzŭ i.

4 vols. 14 pëĕn.   [*China* III, F 3.]

262. 古 文 尙 書
Ku wên shang shoo.

On the Ancient Text of the Book of Historical Documents. 6 vols. 13 chüan. By 惠棟 Hui Tung. This copy is a Japano-Chinese publication, being printed with Japanese tone marks. It belonged to M. Titsingh, the Dutch writer whose autograph it bears, and is called by him So-so-Kotzu. *Ref.* B.M. p. 90; Kidd, p. 7.   [*China* III, F 4.]

263. 書 經 體 註
Shu ching t'i chu.

The Book of Historical Documents, with Comments.
4 vols. 1760. *Ref.* B.M. 114 ; Kidd, p. 7.

[*China* III, F 5.]

264. 西 樵 遊 覽 記
Hsi ch'iao yu lan chi.

4 vols. 14 chüan.   1790.   [*China* III, F 6.]

265. 刑 部 則 例
Hsing Pu Tsê Li.

"The Regulations of the Board of Punishments." 1680.
Ref. B.M. p. 34 ; Kidd, p. 37.   [*China* III, F 7.]

266. 色 戒 全 錄
Sê chieh ch'üan lu.

The Art of Continence.   2 vols. 1696.

[*China* III, F 8.]

267. 傷 寒 三 書 合 璧
Shang han san shu ho pi.

"A Treatise on Diseases arising from Colds." In three
parts, consisting of four volumes.   The title "Shang Han,"
injured by cold, comprehends all diseases produced by
checked perspirations, especially fevers, exposure to marsh,
miasmata, damp air, or cold. 4 vols. 1788. *Ref.* Kidd,
p. 41 ; Wylie, pp. 82-3.   [*China* III, F 9.]

268. 家 寶 全 集
Chia pao ch'üan chi.

"A complete collection of Household Gems." Being a
work containing precepts on personal and social behaviour,
together with instructions of a miscellaneous nature suited
to families. 4 cases, 30 vols.   1708. *Ref.* B.M. p. 182 ;
Kidd, p. 23 ; L.U. 31, 5.   [*China* III, F 10—13]

269. 羊 城 右 鈔
Yang ch'êng ku ch'ao.

"Ancient Records of the City of Rams," *i.e.* Canton. Compiled by 仇池石 Ch'iu Shih-shih. 5 vols. 8 chüan. 1806. *Ref.* B.M. p. 103.　　　　[*China* III, F 14.]

270. 四 書 合 講
Ssǔ Shu ho chiang.

The Four Books harmoniously explained, according to the Commentary of Chu Hsi 朱熹. With a Paraphrase. 4 vols. 1805. *Ref.* B.M. p. 192; Kidd, p. 18.　　See Nos. 101, 245, &c.　　　　[*China* I, G 1.]

271. 四 書 合 講
Ssǔ Shu ho chiang.

5 vols.　1730.　　　　[*China* I, G 2.]

272. 通 鑑 綱 目
T'ung chien kang mu.

See No. 132, &c.　　　　[*China* I, G 3—5.]

273. 萬 壽 衢 歌 樂 章
Wan shou ch'ü ko yǒ chang.

Pieces of Music and Songs sung in the streets on Imperial Birthdays (Kidd). 6 vols. 1790. *Ref.* Kidd, p. 14.
[*China* I, G 6.]

274. 丘 文 莊 公 集
Ch'iu wên chuang kung chi.

5 vols. 10 chüan.　1708.　　　　[*China* I, G 7.]

275. 春 秋 傳 說
Ch'un ch'iu chuan shuo.

3 cases, 19 vols. 38 chüan.　1722.

[*China* I, G 8—10.]

276. 通 鑑 綱 目

T'ung Chien Kang Mu.

"A Condensation of the Mirror of History." By 朱 熹 Chu Hsi and his disciples. 4 cases, 34 vols.

[*China* II, G 1—4.]

277. 欽 定 書 經 傳 說 彙 纂

Chin ting Shu Ching chuan shuo hui tsuan.

"The Book of Historical Documents, with a Compilation and Digest of Comments and Remarks thereon." Compiled by Imperial Commission, with a preface by the Emperor. *Ref.* B.M. p. 113. [*China* II, G 5-6.]

278. 監 本 詩 經

Chien pên shih ching.

"The original text of the Book of Odes." 1818. *Ref.* B.M. p. 180. [*China* II, G 7.]

279. 康 熙 古 文 全 集

K'ang Hsi ku wên ch'üan chi.

K'ang Hsi's Complete Collections of Ancient Literature. 3 cases, 28 vols. 1675. [*China* II, G 8—10.]

280. 監 本 春 秋

Chien pên ch'un ch'iu.

"The original text of the Spring and Autumn Annals." The full title is 芥子園重訂監本春秋 Chieh tzǔ yüan ch'ung ting chien pên ch'un ch'iu. The Chieh tzǔ yüan edition of "The Spring and Autumn Annals." 1790. *Ref.* B.M. p. 113. [*China* III, G 1.]

281. 字 彙
Tzŭ Hui.

A Dictionary arranged according to the Primitives. By 韓菼 Han T'an. 14 vols. 1705. *Ref.* B.M. p. 72; Kidd, p. 1. [*China* III, G 4-5.]

282. 康 熙 字 典
K'ang Hsi Tzŭ Tien.

4 cases, 32 vols. [*China* III, G 6—9.]

283. 詩 經 體 註
Shih Ching t'i chu.

"The Book of Odes," with a body of comments, including the commentary of Chu Hsi. 4 vols. 1687. *Ref.* B.M. p. 180. [*China* III, G 12.]

284. 篆 字 彙
Chuan tzŭ hui.

"A Dictionary of the 'Seal' Character." This form of the character dates from about B.C. 800. (Kidd). 6 vols. 1691. *Ref.* B.M. p. 155. [*Elgin* I, A 1.]

285. 天 文 曆 理
T'ien wên li li.

A complete work on Astronomy. By 徐發 Hsü Fa. 6 vols. 8 pëĕn. *Ref.* L.U. 105, 2. [*Elgin* I, A 2.]

286. 經 世 緒 言
Ching shih hsü yen.

"Heedful words addressed to mortal men." 1831. [*Elgin* I, A 3.]

287. 瓊 州 府 志
Ch'iung Chou Fu Chih.

A Topographical account of the City and Department of Ch'iung Chou, the capital of the Island of Hainan. 1774. 2 cases, 16 vols. 9 chüan. [*Elgin* I, A 4-5.]

288. 醫 林 指 月
I lin chih yüeh.

A medical work issued by the College of Physicians on the best methods of preserving health during the year. 2 cases, 15 vols. (1st vol. missing). *Ref.* Kidd, p. 43.

[*Elgin* I, A 6-7.]

289. 羅 浮 山 志
Lŏ fou shan chih.

An illustrated Topography of the Lŏ-fou hill in the Province of Kwang-tung. 2 cases, 14 vols. This hill, or rather mountain—for it is very lofty and difficult of access—is thickly covered with Buddhist monasteries. *Ref.* B.M. p. 191 ; L.U. 56, 5. [*Elgin* I, A 8-9.]

290. 適 情 雅 趣
Shih ch'ing ya ch'ü.

" Happy Thoughts to promote pleasure and amusement."

[*Elgin* I, A 10.]

291. 靈 樞 經
Ling shu ching.

A medical work which treats of internal maladies and the practice of Acupuncture. It is not actually known to have appeared earlier than the eleventh century, and it is thought to be the production of 王 冰 Wang Ping, in the eighth century, but is probable that it contains a great part of a more ancient work of a similar character. 6 vols. 9 chüan. *Ref.* Kidd, p. 40 ; Wylie, p. 78. [*Elgin* I, A 11.]

E

292. 朱 子 全 書

Chu Tzǔ ch'üan shu.

The complete works of Chu Hsi 朱熹, the famous commentator of the Sung dynasty, and founder of the modern school of Confucian exegesis. Compiled under the direction of the Emperor K'ang Hsi. 4 cases, 28 vols. 1714. *Ref.* B.M. p. 45; I.O.C. p. 49; L.U. 6, 1.

[*Elgin* II, A 1—4.]

293. 古 文 辭 類 纂

Ku wên tz'ŭ lei tsuan.

A classified compendium of ancient styles of literary composition. 2 cases, 14 vols.   [*Elgin* II, A 5-6.]

294. 雍 正 上 諭

Yung Chêng shang yü.

" Imperial Edicts." Issued during the first seven years of the Emperor Yung Chêng (A.D. 1723—36). 24 vols. 4 cases. 1729. *Ref.* B.M. p. 270. [*Elgin* II, A 7—10]

295. 素 問

Su wên.

This work, and the *Ling shu ching* (see *ante*, No. 291), are considered to be the most ancient medical treatises in China. The *Su Wên* is said to embody the results of certain consultations between the author of the *Ling shu ching* and Huang Ti, or the Yellow Emperor, and, as well as the *Ling shu ching*, to recognise the doctrine of the circulation of the blood. But there can be no doubt that its real date is many centuries later than the semi-mythological period to which it has been too enthusiastically assigned. 6 vols. 9 chüan. *Ref.* Kidd, p. 41.   [*Elgin* II, A 11.]

296. 太 玄 別 訓

T'ai hsüan pieh hsün.

Principles relating to the origin of the Universe stated and discussed, together with figures explanatory of the system. 5 vols. 1745. *Ref.* B.M. p. 251; Kidd, p. 25.

[*Elgin* II, A 12.]

297. 武 夷 山 志

Wu I shan chih.

A Topographical account of the Wu I Hills. These are the hills on the western frontiers of the Fokien province, whence comes the celebrated "Bohea" tea, that word being a corruption of "Wu I." 5 vols. 24 chüan. 1682. *Ref.* B.M. p. 250. [*Elgin* II, A 13.]

298. 淵 鑑 類 函

Yüan chien lei han.

An Encyclopædia of Universal Knowledge. Published by Imperial authority during the reign of the Emperor K'ang Hsi. A most valuable work, replete with information on all subjects. It is arranged under categories—Heaven, Earth, Man, Buddhism, Taoism, Animals, Birds, etc. etc. 20 cases, 153 vols. 450 chüan. 1710. *Ref.* B.M. p. 11; I.O.C. p. 11; L.U. 137, 1; Wylie, p. 150.

[*Elgin* I, B 1 to 11, B 10.]

299. 西 洋 記

Hsi yang chi.

"Records of the Western Ocean." An account of maritime countries and islands stretching westward from China. Illustrated throughout. 2 cases, 20 vols. 20 chüan, 100 hui. 1579. *Ref.* B.M. p. 143; Kidd, p. 8; Wylie, p. 163; L.U. 73, 5. [*Elgin* II, B 11-12.]

E 2

300. 搜 神 記
Sou shên chi.

"Handbook of Mythology." By 干寶 Kan Pao of the Chin dynasty. See No. 410. *Ref.* B.M. p. 94.

[*Elgin* II, B 13.]

301. 條 例 約 編
T'iao li yŏ pien.

A general compilation of laws and regulations, imperial declarations, ordinances, instructions, &c. Fifty-four pages are missing from 1st vol., so that the date cannot be ascertained, but it must be *circa* 1830. 8 cases, 81 vols. *Ref.* B.M. pp. 33-4; Kidd, p. 38.　　[*Elgin* I, C 1—8.]

302. 性 理 大 全
Hsing li ta ch'üan.

A complete work on Mental Philosophy. A compilation of the works of many scholars, with a preface by the Emperor Yung Lŏ (1403—1425). The present copy is wanting the preface and introduction. 2 cases, 20 vols. 70 chüan. 1597. *Ref.* B.M. p. 80; L.U. 89, 5; Kidd, p. 27; Wylie, p. 69.

[*Elgin* I, C 9-10.]

303. 四 書 人 物 備 考
Ssŭ shu jen wu pei k'ao.

An examination of the men and things mentioned in the "Four Books." By 蘗應旂 Hsieh Ying-ch'i, with notes. *Ref.* B.M. p. 172.　　　[*Elgin* I, C 11.]

304. 潛 確 類 書
Ch'ien ch'ŏ lei shu.

"An Encyclopædia." By 陳仁錫 Ch'ên Jen-hsi. Wylie says the 11th and 14th books were suppressed as having used an unguarded freedom of language respecting the Manchus. 8 cases, 60 vols. 120 chüan. 1632. *Ref.* Wylie, p. 150; B.M. p. 26; I.O.C. p. 10.

[*Elgin* II, C 1—8.]

305. 海 國 圖 志
Hai kuo t'u chih.

"A History of Foreign Countries." Compiled by 魏 源 Wei Yüan, from materials collected by the famous Commissioner Lin and himself. 2 cases. 60 chüan. 1849. *Ref.* B.M. p. 241.   [*Elgin* II, C 9-10.]

306. 儀 禮 章 句
I li chang chü.

The Decorum Ritual explained sentence by sentence.
[*Elgin* II, C 11.]

307. 易 經 大 全 會 解
Yi Ching ta ch'üan hui chieh.

" The Book of Changes, with explanatory comments by Chu Hsi, and others." Translated by Dr. Legge, *Sacred Books of the East*, vol. xvi. Into Latin, by J. Mohl, S.J., Stuttgart, 1834. *Ref.* B.M. p. 262 ; I.O.C. p. 15.
[*Elgin* II, C 12.]

308. 古 文 雅 正
Ku wên ya chêng.

" Elegant Extracts from Ancient Literature." Compiled by 蔡 世 遠 Ts'ai Shih-yüan. 2 cases, 8 vols. 14 chüan. Nanking, 1777. *Ref.* B.M. p. 207.   [*Elgin* I, D 1-2.]

309. 廣 博 物 志
Kuang pŏ wu chih.

" An Encyclopædia." A book of reference on everything that exists between heaven and earth. 3 cases, 22 vols. (1st volume missing). 1761. *Ref.* B.M. p. 222 ; Wylie, p. 150 ; Kidd, p. 16 ; L.U. 47, 5.
[*Elgin* I, D 3—5.]

310. 鍼 炙 拔 萃 大 成
Chên chiu pŏ ts'ui ta ch'êng.

This Japanese work, with its title, pronounced *Sin kiŏ pa tsi tajsi*, is a translation from the Chinese, which is "A complete account of the chief features of Acupuncture and Cautery," By 陽 靳 賢 Yang Chin-hsien. *Ref.* Kidd, p. 42; B.M. p. 254.   [*Elgin* I, D 6.]

311. 鍼 炙 聚 英
Chên chiu chü ying.

This, like the preceding, is a Chinese book printed in Japan. It has the Japanese tone-marks. Inside is written "Singio Singe" (the Japanese title). "Instructions in Acupuncture and Cautery." 8 vols. 8 chüan. 1546.

[*Elgin* I, D 7.]

312. 一 統 志
Yi t'ung chih.

"A Geography of the Empire." Compiled by an Imperial Commission. 4 cases, 30 vols. *Ref.* B.M. p. 123; L.U. 131, 3. See No. 226.   [*Elgin* I, D 8—11.]

313. 論 語 義 疏
Lun yü i su.

"The Confucian Analects." Translated under this title by Dr. Legge in vol. i of *The Chinese Classics*. Printed in Japan, with the tone-marks. This copy belonged to Titsingh, who calls it "Rongo Lukan Gisio." There is a memorandum of his in the book. 5 vols. *Ref.* B.M. p. 193.

[*Elgin* I, D 12.]

314. 傷 寒 三 書 合 璧
Shang han san shu hŏ pi.

"A Treatise on Diseases arising from Colds." *Ref.* Kidd, p. 41; Wylie, pp. 82-3. See No. 267.   [*Elgin* I, D 13.]

315. 書 畫 譜
Shu hua p'u.

6 cases, 48 vols. 100 chüan.   1710. [*Elgin* II, D 1—6.]

316. 分 類 字 錦
Fên lei tzŭ chin.

A Classified Lexicon of Elegant Expressions.   Compiled by Imperial Commission.   8 cases, 64 vols. 1722. *Ref.* B.M. p. 15.

[*Elgin* II, D 7—11, also comprising II, E 11—13.]

317. 南 海 縣 志
Nan hai hsien chih.

A Topographical account of the district of Nan-hai, in the department of Kuang-chou Fu. 2 cases, 20 chüan. 1741. *Ref.* Biot. p. 132 ; Kidd, p. 10.

[*Elgin* I, E 1-2.]

318. 都 名 所 圖 會
Tu ming so t'u hui.

In Japanese called "To mei syo to kwai."   A Japanese illustrated work, being a collection of views in the capital.

[*Elgin* I, E 3.]

319. 聖 諭 廣 訓
Shêng yü kuang hsün.

"The Sacred Edict" of the Emperor K'ang Hsi. Translated by the Rev. W. Milne under this title.   London, 1817 ; 2nd edition, Shang Hai, 1870. The Amplification, or first portion, has been translated into French by Piry, and published with the Chinese text. *Ref.* B.M. p. 94 ; L.U. 85, 2 ; Wylie, p. 71 ; Möllendorff, p. 27.

[*Elgin* I, E 4.]

320. 三 才 圖 會
San ts'ai t'u hui.

"An Encyclopædia." Vols 3, 8, 9, and 12 only. *Ref.* L.U. 72, 3.   [*Elgin* I, E 5.]

321. 太 平 御 覽
T'ai p'ing yü lan.

1807.   [*Elgin* I, E 6, to II, E 4.]

322. 韻 府 拾 遺
Yün fu shih i.

"A Supplement to the *P'ei wên yün fu.*" The latter is the great *Concordance* of all literature, arranged according to the rhymes. 4 cases, 24 vols. *Ref.* B.M. p. 230; Kidd, p. 2.   [*Elgin* II, E 5—8.]

323. 春 秋 體 註
Ch'un ch'iu t'i chu.

"The Spring and Autumn Annals." 4 vols. 4 chüan. 1711. Being the annals of the State of Lu from B.C. 722 to B.C. 484. Said to have been compiled by Confucius. Translated by Dr. Legge, vol. v of *The Chinese Classics.* See No. 275. *Ref.* B.M. p. 112.   [*Elgin* II, E 9.]

324. 二 十 二 史
Êrh shih êrh shih.

"The Twenty-two Histories." (1) 32—40; (2) 71—80; (3) 81—88; (4) 89—97; (5) 98—107; (6) 108—117; (7) 112—142; (8) 125—130; (9) 131—134; (10) 135—142; (11) 143—150; (12) 151—159; (13) 160—164. Continued in next shelf.   [*Elgin* I, F 1—13.]

325. 二 十 二 史
Êrh shih êrh shih.

"The Twenty-two Histories" (*continued*). (1) 165—171; (2) 172—179; (3) 180—187; (4) 188—194; (5) 195—202; (6) 203—210; (7) 211—218; (8) 219—227; (9) 228—234; (10) 235—242; (11) 243—250; (12) 251—262; (13) 263—272; (14) 273—283.   [*Elgin* II, F 1—14.]

326. 二 十 二 史
Êrh shih êrh shih.

" The Twenty-two Histories " (*continued*). (1) 284—295 ; (2) 296—307 ; (3) 308—317 ; (4) 318—322 ; (5) 323—329 ; (6) 330—336.   [*Elgin* I, G 1—6.]

327. 淵 鑑 類 函
Yüan chien lei han.

"An Encyclopædia." See No. 298. Arranged according to subjects. Compiled by an Imperial Commission: (7) 8—14 ; (8) 15—21 ; (9) 22—28 ; (10) 65—71 ; (11) 72—78 (continued). *Ref.* B. M. p. 11.   [*Elgin* I, G 7—11.]

328. 淵 鑑 類 函
Yüan chien lei han.

Continuation of above : (1) 79—85 ; (2) 86—92.

                         Elgin II, G 1-2.]

329. 經 世 文 編
Ching shih wên pien.

(3) 14—24 ; (4) 29—36 ; (5) 37—43 ; (6) 44—50 ; (7) 51—57 ; (8) 58—65 ; (9) 66—73. [*Elgin* II, G 3—9.]

330. 十 子 全 書
Shih tzŭ ch'üan shu.

" The complete works of the Ten Philosophers of Taoism." Imperfect. Containing only 2 cases, vols. 15—22 ; 23—30 *Ref.* B.M. p. 88.   [*Elgin* II, G 10-11.]

331. 大 和 名 所 圖 會
Ta ho ming so t'u hui.

A Japanese-Chinese work, largely illustrated. The drawings are very good. 6 vols. (first vol. missing).

                       [*Elgin* II, G 12.]

332. 曾 文 正 公
Tsêng wên chêng kung.

"An Encyclopædia of Literature."   114 vols.

                      [*Macartney* I, II.]

333. 廣羣芳譜
Kuang ch'ün fang p'u.

An enlarged edition of the "Herbarium." See Nos. 178, 417. 6 vols. 100 chüan. 1709.   [*Macartney* III, 1—6.]

334. 玉嬌梨
Yü chiao li.

"The Romance of The Two Cousins." See No. 45. 4 chüan, 20 chapters.   Printed on back is, *Te san Tsae Tsze shoo*, or "Third class work of Genius," 第三才子書, in reference to the fanciful classification under which Chinese novels have been ranged.   [*Macartney* III, 7.]

335. 水滸傳
Shui hu chuan.

By 施耐菴 Shih Nai-ngan.   See No. 106. 1734. *Ref.* B.M. p. 181.   [*Macartney* III, 8-9.]

336. 三國志
San kuo chih.

2 cases, 20 vols. 60 chüan. 1816. See No. 110. Printed on back is, *Te yih Tsae Tsze shoo*, or "First class work of Genius." See No. 334.   [*Macartney* III, 10-11.]

337. 大學 中庸
Ta Hsüo. Chung Yung.*

The "Great Learning" and "Doctrine of the Mean." The former, or part of it, is attributed to Confucius; the latter, to Tzǔ Ssǔ, grandson of Confucius.

[*Macartney* III, 12.]

---

* Translated by G. Pauthier. French, with Latin version and Chinese text. Paris, 1837. 8vo. Also by Cibot in Mem. Conc. les Chinois, i. pp. 436—459. 1776. Also by Dr. Legge, vol. i. of *The Chinese Classics.*

338. 易 經 書 經 詩 經
The Yi Ching, Shu Ching and Shih King.

For the *Yi Ching*, see No. 307. Translations of the *Shu Ching* or "Book of History," and the *Shih Ching* or "Book of Poetry," form vols. iii and iv of Legge's *Chinese Classics*. [*Macartney* III, 13.]

339.

"Bible Lessons." Being the Scripture Lessons of the British and Foreign School Society. 1832.

[*Macartney* III,14.]

340. Yüan jen pi chung.

[*Macartney* IV, 1—6.]

341. 景 德 鎮
Ching tê chên.

[*Macartney* IV, 7.]

342. 康 熙 字 典
K'ang Hsi Tzŭ Tien.

"K'ang Hsi's Dictionary." The standard lexicon of the Chinese language. Arranged (1) under 214 radicals, or classifying keys, and (2) in groups according to the number of additional strokes of which each character is composed. Compiled by the orders and under the direction of the Emperor K'ang Hsi. 6 vols. in 12 parts. 1716. *Ref.* B.M. p. 94; I.O.C. p. 6; L.U. 30,1. See No. 282.

[*Macartney* IV, 8—13.]

343. 御 纂 醫 宗 金 鑑
Yü tsuan i tsung chin chien.

"The Golden Mirror of Medicine." A Collection of Medical Works, consisting of the *Shan han lun*, and *Chin kuei yao lüeh*, by Chang Chi. Prescriptions of celebrated Physicians, Rules regarding the Pulse, &c. 1740. *Ref.* B.M. 243; L.U. 135, 4. [*Macartney* V, 2—6.]

344. 禮 記 讀 本
Li chi tu pên.

"The Original Text of the Book of Rites."   6 chüan.
(?) 1790. *Ref.* B.M. p. 121. Translated by Dr. Legge,
vols. xxvii and xxviii of *The Sacred Books of the East.*

[*Macartney* V, 7.]

345.

"Buddhist Tracts."   [*Macartney* V, 8.]

346. 射 鷹 樓 詩 話
Shê ying lou shih hua.

1851.   Printed at Foochow.   [*Macartney* V, 9.]

347. 茶 經
Ch'a Ching.

"A Treatise on the Tea Plant." 1735. *Ref.* B.M. p. 146.

[*Macartney* V, 10.]

348. 圓 天 圖 說
Yüan t'ien t'u shuo.

"A Treatise on Astronomy." By 李 明 徹 Le Ming-ch'ê,
Taoist Priest, with Illustrations.   1819. *Ref.* B.M. p. 128 ;
L.U. 137, 3.   [*Macartney* V, 11.]

349.

Herschel's outlines of Astronomy, translated into Chinese,
by A. Wylie.   [*Macartney* V, 12.]

---

350. 蜃 樓 志
Shên lou chih.

"The Story of the Sea Serpent."   4 vols.   See No. 59.

[*Pottinger,* A 1.]

351. 分 韻 撮 要
Fên yün ts'ŏ yao.

An abridged Phraseological Guide, arranged according to the Rhymes. By 虞學圃 Yü Hsüŏ-pu. *Ref.* B.M. p. 265.

[*Pottinger,* A 2.]

352. 文 章 游 戲
Wên chang yu hsi.

"Rambles in Polite Literature." Compiled by 繆蓮仙 Miu Lien-hsien. 4 vols. 8 chüan. 1803. *Ref.* B.M. p. 156; L.U. 122, 3; Kidd, p. 28. [*Pottinger,* A 3.]

353. 天 花 濺 批 評
T'ien hua ch'êng p'i p'ing.

A Novel. [*Pottinger,* A 4.]

354. 江 湖 尺 牘 分 韻 撮 要 合 集
Chiang hu ch'ih tu fên yün ts'ŏ yao hŏ chi.

See No. 383. 1803. *Ref.* B.M. p. 265; Kidd, p. 1; L.U. 33, 1. [*Pottinger,* A 5.]

355. 虞 初 續 志
Yü ch'u hsü chih.

5 vols. 10 chüan. 1802. [*Pottinger,* A 6.]

356. 好 逑 傳
Hao ch'iu chuan.

"The Fortunate Union." A copy annotated and stopped with red. See Nos. 118, 126. 4 chüan. 1787. *Ref.* B.M. p. 103. [*Pottinger,* A 7.]

357. 孔 子 家 語 原 註
K'ung tzŭ chia yü yüan chu.

"The Family sayings of Confucius." Edited, with a Commentary, by 王肅 Wang Su. 2 vols. 4 chüan. 1805. See No. 167. *Ref.* B.M. p. 229. [*Pottinger,* A 8.]

358. 十 二 樓
Shih êrh lou.

6 vols.   1658.   [*Pottinger*, A 9.]

359. 度 生 公 案
Tu shêng kung ngan.

"Collection of Criminal Cases."   3 vols.

[*Pottinger*, A 10.]

360. 畫 圖 綠
Hua t'u yüan.

"A Treatise on Painting and Drawing."   Illustrated.
4 vols.   [*Pottinger*, A 11.]

361. 東 北 遊 記
Tung pe yu chi.

"Narratives of Travels in the West and North."   Two
volumes are given to each, and every page has an illustration.   4 vols.   [*Pottinger*, A 12.]

362. 詩 法 入 門
Shih fa ju mên.

"Elements of Poetical Composition." [*Pottinger*, A 13.]

363. 重 訂 綴 白 裘 新 集 合 編
Ch'ung ting chui pǒ ch'iu hsin chi hǒ pien.

New edition of a well-known Collection of Plays.   See
No. 157.   6 cases, 48 vols.   [*Pottinger*, B 1—4.]

364. 讀 史 論 畧
Tu shih lun lüo.

"On the Study of History."   [*Pottinger*, B 5.]

365. 法 語 錦 囊
Fa yü chin nang.

6 vols.   [*Pottinger*, B 6.]

366. 西 廂 曲

Hsi hsiang ch'ü.

The Play of the "Western Chamber." 3 vols. (first vol. missing). *Ref.* B.M. p. 169. [*Pottinger*, B 7.]

367. 西 廂 曲

Hsi hsiang ch'ü.

The Play of the "Western Chamber." 6 vols.

[*Pottinger*, B 8.]

368. 天 花 藏

T'ien hua tsang.

4 chüan. 20 hui. [*Pottinger*, B 9.]

369. 靈 魂 篇

Ling hun p'ien.

"An Essay on the Nature, Immortality, Value and Destiny of the Human Soul." By Dr. Wm. Milne, late of Malacca. Presented by Rev. Dr. Morrison, 18 April, 1826. 2 vols. 1825. *Ref.* B.M. p. 166. [*Pottinger*, B 10.]

370. 紅 樓 夢

Hung lou mêng.

"The Dream of the Red Chamber." 2 cases, 20 vols. For brief notice, see No. 388. [*Pottinger*, C 1-2.]

371. 唐 平 鬼 全 傳

T'ang p'ing kuei ch'üan chuan.

"The Story of the Pacification of the Demons." A Romance of the T'ang Dynasty (A.D. 618—905). 2 vols. *Ref.* B.M. p. 118. [*Pottinger*, C 3.]

372. 十 種 曲

Shih tsung ch'ü.

By 笠翁 Li Wêng. 10 vols. (1st vol. missing). See No. 69. *Ref.* B.M. p. 133 ; L.U. 55, 2. [*Pottinger*, C 4.]

373. 三 國 志
San kuo chih.

"The History of the Three Kingdoms." 2 cases, 20 vols.

[*Pottinger, C 5-6.*]

374. 廣 善 彙 函
Kuang shan hui han.

"Moral Virtues Extended." A Collection of Treatises on Various Subjects in Moral Philosophy. Published by Imperial Authority. 2 vols.   [*Pottinger, C 7.*]

375. 三 國 志
San kuo chih.

"The History of the Three Kingdoms." An Historical Romance. 2 cases, 20 vols. See Nos. 110, 250, 257.

[*Pottinger, D 1-2.*]

376. 新 增 資 治 新 書 二 集
Hsin tsêng tzŭ chih hsin shu êrh chi.

A work on Political Economy, embracing a variety of topics pertaining to the authority of the Legislature and the well-being of its subjects. 10 vols. *Ref.* Kidd, p. 23.

[*Pottinger, D 3.*]

377. 地 理 備 考
Ti li pei k'ao.

"The Student's Manual of Geography," translated into Chinese.   [*Pottinger, D 4.*]

378. 封 神 演 義
Fêng shên yen i.

A tale regarding the adventures of Wu Wang, the founder of the Chou Dynasty, in his contest with Chou Wang, the last of the House of Shang. 2 cases, 20 vols. *Ref.* B.M. p. 55 ; L.U. 17, 4. See No. 44.   [*Pottinger, D 5-6.*]

379. 情 史
Ch'ing shih.

"History of the Loves of Celebrities." By 詹 詹 Chan Chan. 12 vols. 1806. *Ref.* B.M. p. 22; L.U. 116, 1. See No. 42. 　　　　　　　　　　　　　　[*Pottinger*, E 1.]

380. 後 說 鈴
Hou shuo ling.

The Supplementary *Shuo ling*. This latter work (see No. 90) is an Account of Embassies from foreign countries. The *Hou Shuo ling* is a later work on the same subject. 1 case, 8 vols. 　　　　　　　[*Pottinger*, E 2.]

381. 水 滸 傳
Shui hu chuan.

An Historical Novel called, "The Story of the River Banks." Imperfect. Only vols. 11—20. 20 chüan, 38—75. 1734. See, for complete copies, Nos. 106, 120, 151. *Ref.* B.M. p. 181; Kidd, p. 13; L.U. 86, 5.

[*Pottinger*, E 3.]

382. 東 周 列 國 全 志
Tung chou lieh kuo ch'üan chih.

A History embracing the period from the Eastern Chou dynasty to the commencement of the Ch'in dynasty, 800 to 221 B.C. Imperfect. Only vols. 13—24. *Ref.* B.M. p. 207; L.U. 118, 5. 　　　　　　　　　[*Pottinger*, E 4.]

383. 江 湖 尺 牘 分 韻 撮 要 合 集
Chiang hu ch'ih tu fên yün ts'o yao ho chi.

A Letter Writer for Travellers, and abridged Phraseological Guide, arranged under the Rhymes. 4 vols. 1798. *Ref.* B.M. p. 265; Kidd, p. 1; L.U. 33, 1.

[*Pottinger*, E 5.]

384. 聊 齋 志 異
Liao chai chih i.

2 cases, 16 vols. 1765. See No. 40.

[*Pottinger*, E 6-7.]

F

385. 廣 州 府 志
Kuang chou fu chih.

A Topography of Kuang-chou Fu (Canton). 12 vols. (9th vol. missing). European binding. [*Pottinger*, F 1—12.]

386. 雙 鳳 奇
Shuang fêng ch'i.

" The Wonderful Story of the Two Phœnixes." An Historical Romance founded upon events which occurred during the Han Dynasty. 7 vols. 80 hui. 1813. *Ref.* B.M. p. 184; L.U. 86, 4. See No. 54. [*Pottinger*, F 13.]

387. 檮 杌 閒 評
T'ao wu hsien p'ing.

" The Leisure Notes of a Fool." 1 case, 10 vols. 50 chüan. *Circa* 1800. *Ref.* B.M. Cat. p. 201; Kidd, p. 55.

[*Staunton* I, A 1.]

388. 紅 樓 夢
Hung Lou Mêng.

Commonly known as " The Dream of the Red Chamber." But " Red Chamber " is used figuratively in the sense of *wealth and power*, the work itself being a novel, on the grandest possible scale, dealing with the failing fortunes of a once wealthy and once powerful family. It extends to 120 chapters, filling 24 vols. 8vo. of about 120 pages to each. In the course of the story more than 400 characters are introduced, and these are delineated with such masterly skill that even this immense number scarcely creates any confusion in the reader's mind. For an epitome of the story, which abounds both in humour and in pathos, see *Journal of the China Branch of the Royal Asiatic Society* for 1885, p. 1. The story is said to have been written by 曹雪芹 Ts'ao Hsüeh-ch'in, early in the present dynasty; and in consequence of certain alleged sneers at the Manchus was placed in the *Index Expurgatorius*. But it is now sold and read freely all over the empire. 24 vols. 2 cases, 120 sections. Early in the 19th century. *Ref.* Wylie, p. 162; B.M. Cat. p. 209; Kidd, p. 51; L.U. 23, 5.

[*Staunton* I, A 2-3.]

389. 紅 樓 復 夢
Hung lou fu mêng.

"The Second Dream of the Red Chamber." By 少海氏 Shao Hai-shih. The details will be found in preceding entry. 3 cases, 31 vols. 100 chüan. 1800. *Ref.* B.M. Cat. p. 325; L.U. 25, 5.   [*Staunton* I, A 4—6]

390. 六 部 處 分 則 例
Liu pu ch'u fên tsê li.

The Rules of the "Six Boards," in Peking, in reference to the censure or punishment of officials. These are the Boards of Appointments, Revenue, Ceremonies, Army, Punishments, and Public Works. 36 vols. 4 cases (1 missing) 1809. [Chia Ch'ing, 13th year.] *Ref.* Not in Wylie or B.M. Cat.; Meyer, p. 326.   [*Staunton* I, A 7—10.]

391. 滿 漢 名 臣 傳
Man Han ming ch'ên chuan.

"The Lives of Illustrious Statesmen, Manchu and Chinese." 48 chüan are taken up by the former and 32 by the latter. The work was published during the Ch'ien Lung period (1736—96) by Imperial authority. 10 cases, 80 chüan. *Circa* 1750.   [*Staunton* II, A 1—10.]

392. 算 法 統 宗
Suan fa t'ung tsung.

About the middle of the Ming dynasty (1368—1628). 程 大位 Ch'êng Ta-wei composed this work, the main object of which is to elucidate the principle of the Abacus in its application to the rules of arithmetic. It gives a general detail of the formulæ of the Chiu Chang 九章 (see Mayer's *Chinese Reader's Manual*, p. 340, number 262), but there is little originality, and the style of composition is rugged and prolix in the extreme. The work is edited by 吳繼綬 Wu Chi-shou. 6 vols. 12 chapters. 1593. *Ref.* B.M. Cat. pp. 39 and 246; Wylie, p. 95; L.U. 92, 2.

[*Staunton* II, A 11.]

F 2

393. 金 石 姻 綠
Chin shih yin yüan.

The celestially-brought-about union of Chin and Shih.
20 chapters.   1794.   See Nos. 8, 114.   *Ref.* L.U. 38, 5.

[*Staunton* II, A 12.]

394.   禮 記 芥 子 園 重 訂 監 本 禮 記
Li Chi.   Chieh tzŭ yüan ch'ung ting chien
pên Li Chi.

The Chieh tzŭ yüan edition of the "Book of Rites," with
a collection of comments compiled by 陳澔 Ch'ên Hao,
edited by 李氏 Li Shih.   10 vols.   Nanking, 1790.   8 vols.
Ref. B.M. Cat. p. 121; I.O.C. No. 23.

[*Staunton* I, B 1.]

395.   周 禮 註 疏
Chou li chu su.

The Chou Ritual.   On the first page it is called the Chou
Li chi i 輯義; or, "A Concordance of the Chou Ritual."
6 vols. and 12 chüan.   1796.   *Ref.* Douglas, p. 50; 2 other
editions, not this one, I.O.C. No 21; L.U. 6, 5.

[*Staunton* I, B 2.]

396.   唐 律 疏 義
T'ang lü su i.

"The Laws of the T'ang dynasty (A.D. 618—905)
explained."   The work commences on the 4th year of the
Yung Hui 永徽 period of the Emperor Kao Tsu (654).
16 MS. vols. 30 chüan.   2 cases.   [*Staunton* I, B 3-4.]

397.   左 繡
Tso hsiu.

[*Staunton* I, B 5.]

398.   婺 源 縣 志
Wu yüan hsien chih.

A statistical and general account of the district town of
Wu-yüan, the name of the department and town of the
3rd order in Hui-chou Fu in the province of Kiang-nan.
2 cases, 14 vols.   *Ref.* Biot. Dict. des Villes, p. 150.

[*Staunton* I, B 6-7.]

399. 大 清 律 例

Ta Ch'ing lü li.

The fundamental statutes and subordinate laws of the Ch'ing dynasty. 20 volumes, complete. 1810. Translated by Sir G. Staunton. *Ref.* B.M. p. 218; I.O.C. p. 58; Kidd, p. 37; R.A.S., Staunton I, B 7-8; Wylie, p. 57.

[*Staunton* I, B 8-9.]

400. 儀 禮 章 句

I Li chang chü.

"The Decorum Ritual explained, sentence by sentence." 4 vols. 1798. *Ref.* B.M. 59; I.O.C. p. 19; Wylie, p. 5.

[*Staunton* I, B 10.]

401. 易 經

Yi Ching.

"The Book of Changes." Full title is, 易 經 大 全 會 解 "The Book of Changes, with explanatory comments." By Chu Hsi, Chu Fung-lin, and others. Compiled by Lai Mu-chên. The Tsung-tao-t'ang edition, 4 chüan. 1681. See No. 307. *Ref.* B.M. 262; I.O.C. p. 15; Kidd, p. 25; Wylie p. 1. [*Staunton* II, B 1.]

402. 艸 字 彙

Ts'ao tzŭ hui.

A Dictionary or collection of the cursive forms, or "Grass characters." By 石 梁 Shih Liang. It consists of facsimile copies of the handwriting of great poets and others celebrated in Chinese literary history. The characters are arranged under the radicals. No meanings are given, but the names of the writers, whose autographs are represented, are printed in the margin. In 6 vols. 1786. *Ref.* I.O.C. p. 4; L.U. 111, 2. [*Staunton* II, B 2.]

403. 易 經
Yi Ching.

"The Book of Changes." See Staunton II, C 1, and No. 307, for account and references. 2 vols. 4 chüan. 1818.

[*Staunton* II, B 3.]

404. 小 學
Hsiao hsüo.

"Learning for the Young" 4 vols. See No. 129. *Ref.* B.M. p. 46; Wylie, p. 68. [*Staunton* II, B 4.]

405. 諧 聲 品 字 箋
Hsieh shêng p'in tzŭ chien.

A Phonetic Dictionary, compiled by 虞德升 Yü Tê-shêng. There are in all 96 leading characters, the vocables under which amount to 1500, embracing more than 60,000 characters. 7 vols. 1677. *Ref.* B.M. 266.

[*Staunton* II, B 5.]

406. 遣 愁 集
Ch'ien ch'ou chi.

" Essays to Dispel Grief." A series of articles which the author considers calculated to dispel melancholy. Compiled by Chang Kuei-shêng, edited by Yü Sao and Ku Yu-hsiao. 6 vols. 12 chüan. (?) 1830. *Ref.* B.M. p. 13.

[*Staunton* II, B 6.]

407. 文 公 家 禮 正 衡
Wên Kung chia li chêng hêng.

" On Domestic Ceremonies," by Wên Kung. Chu Hsi's " Family ceremonies." Corrected, adjusted and edited by 彭濱 P'êng Pin. 4 vols. 8 chüan. 1762. *Ref.* L.U. 123, 1.

[*Staunton* II, B 7.]

408. 昭 明 文 選
Chao ming wên hsüan.

"A collection of elegant extracts from polite literature." Compiled by Prince Hsiao Tung, of the Liang dynasty. (A.D. 507—557). With a commentary by Li Shan, edited by Yeh Shu-fan. Only contains 8 vols. and 26 chüan. 16 vols. 60 chüan. 1771. *Ref.* B.M. p. 169; L.U. 124—1.

[*Staunton* II, B 8]

409. 楚 辭 集 註
Ch'u tz'ǔ chi chu.

"The Elegies of Ch'u," with a commentary by Chu Hsi. By 屈 原 Ch'ü Yüan, of the 4th century, B.C. 4 vols. 17 chüan. *Ref.* B.M. 102; Wylie, pp. 181-2.

[*Staunton* II, B 9.]

410. 搜 神 記
Sou shên chi.

"Handbook of Mythology," edited by Yang Kuang-lieh 揚 光 烈 . The original work was by Kan Pao, who lived in the early part of the 4th century. It was in 30 vols. 3 chüan. 1750. See No. 300. *Ref.* Wylie, "Notes;" B.M. Cat. p. 94.　[*Staunton* II, B 11.]

411. 爾 雅
Êrh ya.

"The Literary Expositor." Commented on by Kǒ Pǒ. This is an illustrated dictionary of terms used in the classical and other writings of the Confucian period, and is of great importance in elucidating the meaning of words. It is divided into 19 sections, each of which treats of a separate class of subjects. The authorship is attributed to Tzǔ Hsia. 4 vols. 1803. Copies of this work (large 4to) were formerly very valuable. But reproductions by the photo-lithographic process (8vo) are now sold at a cheap rate in Shanghai. *Ref.* Wylie, p. 7; B.M. p. 224; I.O.C. p. 20; L.U. 120, 5.

[*Staunton* II, B 13.]

412. 東 西 漢 全 傳
Tung hsi Han ch'üan chuan.

Chronicles of the Eastern and Western Han dynasties.

[*Staunton* II, B 13.]

413. 琴 譜
Ch'in p'u.

" The music book for the Ch'in, or Chinese zitha." 4 vols.
8 chüan. 1662. *Ref.* B.M. Cat. p. 53 (1746); L.U. (1802)
38, 3. [*Staunton* II, B 14.]

414. 選 集 漢 印 分 韻
Hsüan chi han yin fên yün.

A fine copy of a most valuable work, in which the " Seal "
forms of all the most important characters are drawn.
Arranged according to the rhymes. 1798.

[*Staunton* II, B 15.]

415. 藝 文 通 覽 序
I wên t'ung lan hsü.

[*Staunton* I, C 1—7.]

416. 韻 府 羣 玉
Yün fu ch'ün yü.

A small Encyclopædia of the period of the Yüan dynasty
(1280—1341), by 陰 時 夫 Yin Shih-fu. 20 vols. 20 chüan.
1763. *Ref.* Wylie, p. 10. [*Staunton* I, C 8-9.]

417. 羣 芳 譜
Ch'ün fang p'u.

This work is a " Herbarium," compiled by Wang Hsiang-
chin, and published about the close of the Ming dynasty.
The chief portion of the work consists of extracts from preceding authors, ancient and modern, regarding the various
productions of the garden and field, given *seriatim*, but
without much judgment in the arrangement. It is divided
into 12 parts, under the heads of: " the heavens ; the year ;
grains ; vegetables ; fruit ; tea and bamboo ; mulberry ;

hemp and grass cloth plants; trees; flowers; storks; and fish. The details relate mainly to the medical virtues of the different objects, while the remarks on cultivation are very superficial. 18 vols. 12 parts. 1708. See No. 178. *Ref* Wylie, p. 122; B.M. 234.　　　　[*Staunton* I, C 10-11.]

418. 類 經 圖 翼
Lei Ching t'u i.

The *Lei ching*, in 32 books, is the production of 張介賓 Chang Chieh-pin, a celebrated physician. The theme of the work is the two ancient books, *Su wên* 素問 and *Ling shu ching* 靈樞經 (see Nos. 291 and 295), which are dissected and arranged under twelve heads, namely, sanitary considerations; masculine and feminine principles; form of the intestines; pulse and appearance; sinews and nerves; radical and ultimate conditions; breath and taste; medical treatment; disease and sickness; acupuncture; circulation of air; pervading principles. These disquisitions, which embody the views of the author, are followed by eleven books of diagrams and auxiliary remarks. These latter are the works now catalogued. 11 chüan. 1624. *Ref.* B.M. 12; Kidd, 26; Wylie, p. 81.　　　　[*Staunton* II, C 1.]

419. 元 人 百 種 曲
Yüan jen pŏ tsung ch'ü.

The celebrated hundred comedies of the Yüan dynasty published during the reign of the Emperor Wan Li. 40 vols. 1573—1620. *Ref.* Wylie, p. 206; Kidd, p. 53.

[*Staunton* II, C 2—5.]

420. 古 文 分 編 集 評
Ku wên fên pien chi p'ing.

" Selections from Ancient Literature." 18 vols. in 2 cases. (first vol. missing).　　　　[*Staunton* II, C 6-7.]

421.

The Pentateuch (called the Shêng Ching), printed at Serampore with metallic movable characters. 1817.

[*Staunton* II, C 8.]

422. 景 岳 全 書
Ching Yŏ ch'üan shu.

The whole works of Dr. Ching Yŏ, a medical writer of considerable eminence in China during the 15th century. He was otherwise known as Dr. Chang Chieh-pin 張 介 賓 (see No. 418). 24 vols. 64 chüan. 4 cases. 1710. Medical writers. *Ref.* B.M. p. 12; Kidd, p. 43; L.U. 42, 3 (1790).

[*Staunton* I, D 1—4.]

423. 欽 定 戶 部 則 例
Chin ting Hu pu tsê li.

Regulations of the Board of Revenue and population. By Imperial command. 32 vols. 1762.

[*Staunton* I, D 5—8.]

424. 審 音 鑑 古 錄
Fan yin chien ku lu.

A very fine illustrated edition of the best novels, 14 in number.

[*Staunton* I, D 9.]

425. 新 遺 詔 書
Hsin i chao shu.

The New Testament in Chinese, translated by Robert Morrison. Serampore. 8 vols. 8vo. 1813. *Ref.* B.M. p. 2; L.U. 88, 2; I.O.C. p. 56 (1815).

[*Staunton* I, D 10.]

426. 千 叟 宴 詩
Ch'ien sou yen shih.

A Collection of Odes, laughter-moving and jovial, as befits a banquet. 36 chüan. 4 cases. 1785.

[*Staunton* II, D 1—4.]

427. 大 清 會 典
Ta Ch'ing hui tien.

Statutes of the Empire of China. A comprehensive description of the system of government under the Ch'ing, or Manchu-Tartar, dynasty. 24 vols. in 3 cases. 1764. *Ref.* B.M. p. 217.

[*Staunton* II, D 5—7.]

428. 淳 化 閣 帖 考 正
Ch'un hua kǒ t'ieh k'ao chêng.

"Revised Inscriptions of the Ch'un Hua Hall." 1848.
[*Staunton* II, D 8.]

429. 籌 海 圖 編
Ch'ou hai t'u pien.

This work, as written in 16 books by 鄭若曾 Chêng Jǒ-ts'êng, is a minute detail of the seaboard districts of China, illustrated by an extensive series of maps in the rudest style of art. The main object of the work is the discussion of plans of defence against the seafaring marauders from Japan, who proved a formidable scourge to the inhabitants of the coast during the Ming dynasty. This work appeared in 1562, and another edition in 1582. 8 vols. 13 chüan. 1624.
[*Staunton* II, D 9.]

430. 周 易 折 中
Chou Yi chê chung.

The *Chou Yi*, is the *Chou Changes*, the book being, in fact, the Yi Ching, "The Book of Changes," the *Chou Changes* being a name applied to it in reference to the texts by Wên Wang and Chou Kung. See No. 307. There is a long description of this book in Wylie, p. 2. 12 vols. in 2 cases. 1716. *Ref.* Wylie, p. 2. [*Staunton* II, D 10-11.]

431. 東 西 洋 考
Tung hsi yang k'ao.

"Chang Hsieh's (張變) account of those countries in the southern and eastern seas," which had commercial interviews with China during the period of the Ming dynasty (1368—1628). 12 chüan. 1618. *Ref.* B.M. 9; L.U. 119, 2. [*Staunton* II, D 12.]

432. 禮 記 圖 四
Li Chi t'u ssu.

An Imperial edition in 82 chüan, being 77 chüan and 5 chüan of illustrations. 5 cases. Marginally called the 禮記義疏 Li Chi i su. The meaning of "The Book of Rites." (?) 1700. *Ref.* B.M. 121. [*Staunton* I, E 1—5.]

433. 華 嚴 經
Hua yen ching.

The Chinese version of the Buddha Purvana Sutra.
Yung Lŏ, 10th year. 16 vols. 1413.

[*Staunton* I. E 6-7.]

434. 困 學 紀 聞
K'un hsüo chi wên.

" A series of Literary and Scientific critical remarks."
By 王 應 麟 Wang Ying-lin. 14 vols. in 2 cases. 1814.
Ref. L.U. 45, 5 ; 46, 2 ; Wylie, p. 129 ; B.M. 237.

[*Staunton* I, E 10.]

435. 嘯 亭 字 韻
Hsiao t'ing tzŭ yüan.

3 vols. 29 chüan. 1805. [*Staunton* I, E 10.]

436. 莊 子 南 華 經 解
Chuang tzŭ Nan hua ching chieh.

The Canon of Nan hua, by Chuang Tzŭ, explained.
Formerly known under the simpler title of " Chuang Tzŭ."
This work was re-christened as above in 742 A.D., with a
view to its establishment as a " Canon " of debased Taoism.
It contains the genuine philosophical speculations of Chuang
Tzŭ, who flourished in the 3rd century B.C., together with
much that is undoubtedly spurious. Translated by H. A.
Giles, under the title of " Chuang Tzŭ, Mystic, Moralist,
and Social Reformer." 3 vols. 3 chüan. 1722. *Ref.* Mayer's
Chinese Manual, art. 92, p. 30 ; Wylie, p. 174 ; B.M.
(inserted), 57 ; Kidd, p. 22. [*Staunton* I, E 11.]

437. 杜 工 部 集
Tu kung pu chi.

10 vols. 20 chüan. 1824. [*Staunton* II, E 1.]

438. 萬 善 同 歸
Wan shan t'ung kuei

This is a treatise on the unity of origin of every excellence; all being traced to " Buddhism in the heart." It was written by the priest 永 明 壽 Yung Ming Shou, and published, with a preface, by the Emperor, at the date mentioned.　2 vols. 6 chüan.　1734.　*Ref.* Wylie, p. 171 ; L.U. 124, 3 ; B.M. 271.　　　　　[*Staunton* II, E 2.]

439. 大 明 會 典
Ta Ming hui tien.

The Imperial Statutes of the Ming dynasty (1368—1628). 228 chüan, 48 vols.　6 cases.　1577.　*Ref.* B M. p. 157.
　　　　　　　　　　　　　　　　[*Staunton* II, E 3—8.]

440. 說 文 真 本
Shou wên chên pên.

The celebrated dictionary of the Lesser Seal character, and earliest lexicon of the Chinese language.　Compiled by 許 慎 Hsü Shên, an officer in the government service, A.D. 100.　It is a collection of all the Chinese characters then in existence, amounting to about 10,000, analysed by the author into their original picture elements, with a view of showing the " hieroglyphic " origin of the Chinese language. It was the first lexicon arranged under *radicals*, for which purpose 540 were called into use, subsequently reduced in the K'ang Hsi dictionary to the more manageable number of 214.　(See No. 342.)　An ingenious key to the 540 radicals of the *Shuo Wên*, bringing them into numerical rapport with the 214 of K'ang Hsi, and enabling the student to use the former lexicon with ease, was publised some years back by Dr. Chalmers in the columns of the *China Review*. 6 vols. in one.　1598.　*Ref.* Wylie, p. 8 ; Kidd, p. 3 ; I.O.C. p. 3 ; B.M. 74.　　　　　[*Staunton* II, E 9.]

441 御 製 增 訂 清 文 鑑
Yü chih tsêng ting ch'ing wên chien.

45 vols. in 8 cases. ［*Staunton* I, F 1—8.］

442. 東 華 錄
Tung hua lu.

An account of the reigning Tartar dynasty of China, composed by some historiographers of government during the reign of Ch'ien Lung (1736—1796). The work is a summary of events from the origin of the dynasty down to the year 1734, and is edited by 蔣 良 騏 Chiang Liang-chi. *Ref.* B.M. p. 340 ; Kidd, p. 10. ［*Staunton* I, F 9—12.］

443. 大 佛 頂 首 楞 嚴 經 隻 記
Ta Fŏ ting shou Lêng Yen Ching chi chi.

"The *Lêng Yen* Sutra." 5 vols. 10 chüan. 1734.
［*Staunton* I, F 13.］

444. 大 六 壬 大 全
Ta liu jen ta ch'üan.

A work on fortune-telling and divination by means of Astrology, and entitled the "Six Astronomical Signs." 13 vols. 13 chüan. 2 cases. 1704. *Ref.* B.M. p. 145 ; L.U. 96, 3 ; Kidd, p. 28. ［*Staunton* I, F 14, 15,］

445. 名 臣 奏 議 集 畧
Ming ch'ên tsou i chi lüeh

A general collection of Memorials addressed to the Emperor, by celebrated ministers of successive ages. 32 vols. in 8 cases. 1st and 2nd chüan missing. *Ref.* Kidd, p. 12. ［*Staunton* II, F 1—8.］

446. 聖 諭 廣 訓
Shêng yü kuang hsün.

The sixteen Maxims of the Emperor K'ang Hsi, amplified by his successor, Yung Chêng. 1725. For details, see No. 319. *Ref.* L.U. 85, 2. ［*Staunton* II, F 9.］

447. 清 文 啓 蒙
Ch'ing wên ch'i mêng.

A Manchu-Chinese Grammar. 4 vols. Translated by A. Wylie, Shanghai, 1856. [*Staunton* II, F 11.]

448. 太 素 脉
T'ai su mŏ.

[*Staunton* II, F 12.]

449. 人 天 眼 目
Jen T'ien yen mu.

"The eyes of Men and of Heaven." A Buddhist work by the priest 仁 岠 Jen Chü. 2 vols. 2 chüan. 1703. *Ref.* L.U. 28, 3 ; Kidd, p. 46 ; B.M. p. 92.

[*Staunton* II, F 13.]

450. 戒 殺 放 生 文
Chieh sha fang shêng wên.

"On abstention from taking life and releasing captive animals." By 祩 宏 Chu Hung. Canton. 1790. *Ref.* B.M. p. 48 ; L.U. 32, 3 ; Kidd, 47.

[*Staunton* II, F 14 *a*.]

451. 玉 歷 鈔 傳 警 世
Yü li ch'ao chuan ching shih.

"The Ten Courts of Purgatory," with full description of the various punishments and tortures to which erring souls are subjected during the transition state of metempsychosis. Translated by H. A. Giles, as an appendix to the *Liao Chai*. See No. 40. [*Staunton* II, F 14 *b*.]

452. 禪 門 日 誦
Ch'an mên jih sung.

"Selections for daily services." A number of devotional extracts from the Buddhist canon, by different authors. Compiled by 默 持 Mŏ Ch'ih. 1792. *Ref.* B.M. 156 ; I.O.C. p. 43 ; L.U. 81, 3. [*Staunton* II, F 15.]

453. 綠蔭庭詩鈔
Lu yin t'ing shih ch'ao.

"The Odes of the Green Shaded Hall." 2 vols. *Ref.*
Kidd, p. 15. [*Staunton* II, F 16.]

454. 瀛環志畧
Ying huan chih lüeh.

"A geographical treatise on the world." By 徐繼畬
Hsü Chi-yü. 6 vols. 10 chüan. 1848. Geography.

[*Staunton* I, G 1.]

455. 開國方畧
K'ai kuo fang lüeh.

2 cases, 12 vols. 32 chüan. 1786. [*Staunton* I, G 2-3.]

456. 古玉圖
Ku yü t'u.

An illustrated work on ancient vessels, insignia, weapons,
&c. A compilation by 王黼 Wang Fu and others. 1 vol.
1752. *Ref.* B.M. p. 326 ; Kidd, p. 32 ; L.U. 69, 4 ; I.O.C.
p. 2. [*Staunton* I, G 4 *a*.]

457. 考古圖
K'ao ku t'u.

An illustrated collection of antiquities. By Wang Fu
and others. See last entry. 5 vols. 1752. *Ref.* B.M. p. 228 ;
Kidd, p. 32 ; I.O.C. p. 2 ; L.U. 69, 4.

[*Staunton* I, G 4 *b*.]

458. 四書合講
Ssŭ shu hŏ chiang.

The Four Books, harmoniously explained, according to
the Commentary of Chu Hsi. With a Paraphrase. 6 vols.
1819. The "harmony" introduced by Chu Hsi consisted
in uniformity of exegesis. He did not, as the Han scholars
had done, interpret the same combination in various ways
merely to suit the supposed exigencies of the text. *Ref.*
B.M. p. 192. [*Staunton* I, G 5.]

459. 列 女 傳
Lieh nü chuan.

Biographical sketches of eminent women. Illustrated.
12 vols. 16 chüan. 1780. *Ref.* Kidd, p. 13.

[*Staunton* I, G 6.]

460. 四 書 合 講
Sŭ shu hŏ chiang.

The Four Books, harmoniously explained according to
the Commentary of Chu Hsi. With a paraphrase. 6 vols.
1813. See No. 458. *Ref.* B.M. p. 192.

[*Staunton* I, G 7.]

461. 農 政 全 書
Nung chêng ch'üan shu.

"The Thesaurus of Agriculture." 60 chüan. 2 cases.
1843. *Ref.* B.M. p. 175. [*Staunton* I, G 8-9.]

462. 廣 興 圖
Kuang yü t'u.

An Atlas of the Chinese Empire. Compiled by 羅 洪 先
Lŏ Hung-hsien, with the maps of 朱 思 本 Chu Ssŭ-pên.
4 vols. 2 chüan. 1579. *Ref.* B.M. 142.

[*Staunton* I, G 10.]

463. 二 妙
Erh miao.

Drawing of bamboo, &c. [*Staunton* I, G. 11a.

464. 官 子 譜
Kuan tzŭ p'u.

A series of chess diagrams. 1800.

[*Staunton* I, G 11b.]

465. 無 雙 譜
Wu shuang p'u.

Biographical Notices of Peerless Worthies. By 金 古 良
Chin Ku-liang. 1690. [*Staunton* I, G 11c.]

G

466. 東 坡 遺 意
Tung p'ŏ i i.

Posthumous Reflections of Su Shih 蘇 軾, known as the poet Su Tung-p'ŏ. 1780.   [*Staunton* I, G 11*d.*]

467. 同 文 千 字 文
T'ung wên ch'ien tzŭ wên.

" The Thousand-character Essay," according to the three forms of writing: the Seal, or ancient character; the Running-hand, or grass character; and the Clerk's, or ordinary character; in two vols. So called because it contains exactly 1000 *different* characters, arranged in intelligible though disconnected sentences. Was put together in a single night by Chou Hsing-ssŭ 周 興 嗣, a distinguished scholar of the sixth century of our era, his hair turning white under the effort. Is the second primer put into the hands of the Chinese schoolboy (see No. 520), and is studied more for the sake of its 1000 characters than for any useful knowledge they may contain. 1 case, 2 vols. 1582.

[*Staunton* I, G 12.]

468.

Algebraic geometry, with differential and integral calculus. By A Wylie, of Shanghai. Published in Chinese, in 5 vols. 1859.   [*Staunton* II, G 1.]

469. 談 天
T'an t'ien.

Herschel's Astronomy, in 5 vols. Published by A. Wylie, in Chinese. 1859.   [*Staunton* II, G 2.]

470. 博 古 圖
Pŏ ku t'u.

" An Illustrated Collection of Antiquities." Compiled by Wang Fu and others. 1752. 3 cases, 18 volumes. *Ref.* B.M. 228; I.O.C. p. 2. See Nos. 456, 457.

[*Staunton* II, G 4—6.]

471. 禮 書 綱 目
Li shu kang mu.

"A condensation of the history of Forms and Ceremonies."
By 江 永 Chiang Yung. 4 cases, 82 vols. 85 chüan. 1722.
Ref. B.M. 100. [*Staunton* II, G 7—10.]

472. 道 德 經
Tao tê ching.

"The Canon of Tao and the Exemplification thereof."
This work has been attributed, but on wholly insufficient
grounds, to the philosopher 老君 Lao Chün, or Lao Tzǔ,
of the 7th century B.C. The balance of evidence goes to
show that it was pieced together, not earlier than the second
century of our era, from the recorded sayings of Lao Tzǔ;
and padded out with mysterious utterances to suit the phase
of superstition through which the pure philosophy of Tao
was then passing. For this view of the question, see *The
Remains of Lao Tzǔ*, by H. A. Giles, Hong Kong, 1886.
For translations, see No. 202.

[*Staunton* II, G 12.]

473. 六 道 集
Liu tao chi.

"The Six Paths." A Buddhist work. By 弘贊 Hung
Tsan. 2 vols. 1682. *Ref.* B.M. 83; L.U. 58, 1.

[*Staunton* II, G 12.]

474.

Chinese Almanacs for the years 1733, 1795, 1807, 1811.
Ref. B.M. p. 60.

475. 常 活 之 道 傳
Ch'ang huo chih tao chuan.

"The Doctrines of Eternal Life." 6 chapters. 1834.

G 2

476. 創 世 傳 註 釋
Ch'uang shih chuan chu shih.

"The Book of Genesis." With Explanatory Notes. By W. Deane. Hong Kong. 1 vol. 1850.

477. 正 字 千 文
Chêng tzŭ ch'ien wên.

A Manual, showing the different forms of writing characters. 2 vols. 1820.

478. 正 字 通
Chêng tzŭ t'ung.

A Chinese Dictionary. Compiled by 廖 文 英 Liao Wên-ying. 16 vols. See No. 253. *Ref.* B.M. p. 132; L.U. 5, 2.

479. 春 秋 體 註 大 全 合 參
Ch'un ch'iu t'i chu ta ch'üan hŏ ts'an.

"The Spring and Autumn Annals." With a body of comments, and with the Commentary of Hu Ngan-kuo 胡 安 國. 1711. 4 vols. 4 chüan. See No. 323. *Ref.* B.M. p. 112.

480. 番 禺 縣 志
P'an yü hsien chih.

A Topography of the District of P'an-yü. 1 vol. 1774.

481. 霏 屑 軒 尺 牘 類 選
Fei hsiao hsien ch'ih tu lei hsüan.

"A Model Letter Writer." Compiled by 陳 世 熙 Ch'ên Shih-hsi. *Ref.* B.M. p. 28; L.U. 15, 1.

482. 福 惠 全 集
Fu hui ch'üan chi.

8 vols. 32 chüan.

483. 粉 粧 樓 全 傳
Fên chuang lou ch'üan chuan.

"The Story of the Painted Pavilion," with illustrations. An historical novel in continuation of the *Shuo tang chih chuan.* 80 chapters.

484. 海 國 聞 見 錄
Hai kuo wên chien lu.

"The Sayings and Doings of Foreign Countries." Relating chiefly to the Islands and Coasts in the Eastern and Southern Oceans. By 陳 倫 熼 Ch'ên Lun-chiung. 1 vol. 2 chüan. 1744. *Ref.* B.M. p. 27.

485. 好 逑 傳
Hao ch'iu chuan.

"The Fortunate Union." A Novel. 4 vols. 18 chapters. 1787. See Nos. 118, 126. *Ref.* B.M. p. 103; L.U. 21, 2.

486. 休 寧 縣 志
Hsiu ning hsien chih.

A General and Topographical Account of the District of Hsiu-ning, in the Department of Hui-chou Fu, in Kiang-nan. 5 vols. 1693.

487. 合 錦 廻 文
Hŏ chin hui wên.

"Collection of Cryptograms." 6 vols. 16 chüan. 1798. *Ref.* B.M. p. 135; L.U. 27, 5.

488. 護 法 論
Hu fa lun.

"On protecting Buddhism."

489. 後 唐 全 傳
Hou T'ang ch'üan chuan.

"Chronicles of the After T'ang dynasty."   1736.

490. 花 鏡
Hua ching.

By 陳淏子 Ch'ên Hao-tzŭ. One of the best books on flowers which has appeared during the present dynasty. The last book treats of rearing animals, including some species of insects.   1688.

491. 槐 軒 千 家 詩 解
Huai hsien ch'ien chia shih chieh.

"Specimens of Poetry, with explanations."   1735.

492. 凰 求 鳳
Huang ch'iu Fêng.

"The Phœnix in search of a Wife."   2 vols.

493. 灰 闌 記
Hui lan chi.

Printed in Europe; presented by Stanislas Julien, 1st March, 1833. Apparently the text from which he translated the "Cercle de Craie."   2 copies.

494. 康 熙 字 典
K'ang Hsi tzŭ tien.

K'ang Hsi's Dictionary. Imperfect. Only vols. 13 and 21—32 incl. See No. 342. *Ref.* B.M. p. 94.

495. 更 豈 有 此 理
Kêng ch'i yu tz'ŭ li.

2 vols.   See No. 35.

496. 咬 嚂 吧 總 論
Chiao liu pa tsung lun.

A Description of Java.　With maps and plates.　*Ref.* B.M. p. 177.

497. 鑑 史 提 綱
Chien shih t'i kang.

4 vols.　1808.

498. 遣 愁 集
Ch'ien ch'ou chi.

" Anti-Melancholia."　Being a series of articles on the different studies, &c., which the author considers calculated to dispel grief and melancholy.　4 vols. 12 chüan.　*Ref.* L.U, 109, 5 ; B.M. p. 13.

499. 羣 眞 著 述
Ch'ün chên chu shu.

A Record of Illustrious Persons.　1680.

500.

Chin-Kang-po-yeh-ho-lin-me Ko, i.e. the *Vadpratchedidīka Sutra,* and the *Paramatta Diamond Sutra.*

With an appendix containing the 心 經 Hsin Ching, or, in full, No-ho-po-ye-po-lo-me-hsin-ching (*Paramitahridya Sutra*).　Embroidered, and presented, by the faithful female disciple 崔 孫.

501. 經 世 緒 言
Ching shih hsü yen.

10 vols. 9 chüan.　1830.

502. 故 事 尋 源
Ku shih hsün yüan.

5 vols.

503. 古 玉 圖
Ku yü t'u.

An Illustrated Collection of Precious objects of Antiquity.
vols. 1—20 inclusive. 1779. *Ref.* B.M. p. 326. See
No. 456.

504. 獪 園
Kuai yüan.

7 vols. 16 sections. 1774.

505. 路 加 傳 福 音 書
Lu chia chuan fu yin shu.

The Gospel according to St. Luke, in Chinese. Printed
at the American Mission Press. No date.

506. 祿 嗣 祕 訣
Lu ssŭ pi chüeh.

507. 龍 圖 公 案
Lung t'u kung ngan.

2 vols. 10 chüan. 1816. *Ref.* B.M. p. 148. See No. 84.

508. 雷 峰 塔
Lei fêng t'a.

"The Story of the Thunder-peak Pagoda." Otherwise
known as the "History of the White Serpent." 8 small vols.
4 chüan. 1772. *Ref.* B.M. p. 149. See No. 23.

509. 雷 峰 塔

Another edition of the preceding. See No. 23.

510.

The Gospel of St. Matthew, in Chinese. 1st Edition.
London Missionary Society's Press, Shanghai, 1850.

511.

The Gospel of St Matthew. In Chinese, with Explanatory
Notes. By William Dean. Hong Kong, 1848.

512. 牡 丹 亭
Mu tan t'ing.

"The Story of the Peony Bower." 4 vols. See No. 21.

513. 南 柯 記
Nan ko chi.

"An Account of the Kingdom of Nan-ko," from "A Collection of Reprints of works written during the T'ang dynasty" (A.D. 618—905). 2 vols.

514. 南 北 通 曉 雜 字
Nan pei t'ung hsiao tsa tzŭ.

2 vols.

515.

The Pentateuch, in Chinese. Printed at Ningpo. 1 vol. 1846.

516. 北 宋 志
Pei Sung chih.

"The History of the Northern Sung dynasty." *Ref.* B.M. p. 165.

517. 博 古 圖
Pŏ ku t'u.

"An Illustrated Collection of Antiquities." Compiled by 王 黼 Wang Foo, and others. 2 cases, vols. 1—6, and 7—12. *Ref.* B.M. p. 228 ; I.O.C. p. 2. See No. 470.

518. 駁 案 新 編
Pŏ ngan hsin pien.

Cases which have been brought before the High Court of Justice for Revision of Judgment. New edition. 2 cases, 20 vols. See No. 156.

519. 三 禮 圖
San li t'u.

Illustrations of the Vessels, Ornaments, &c., referred to in the "Three Rituals." 2 vols. 1676. This once expensive work, reproduced by the photo-lithographic process, is now sold cheaply in Shanghai. *Ref.* B.M. p. 28 ; L.U. 71, 5.

520. 三 字 經
San tzŭ ching.

"The Three-character Classic." The first book put into the hands of a Chinese schoolboy, being a short guide to ethics, history, science, biography, etc., all in one. So called because arranged in rhyming sentences of three words to each. Composed during the Sung dynasty, by 王 伯 厚 Wang Pŏ-hou. This work, together with the *Thousand-character Essay* (see No. 467) has been translated into French by Stanislas Julien, and into English (metrically) by H. A. Giles.

521. 三 字 經 訓 詁
San tzŭ ching hsün ku.

"The Three-character Classic" explained. By 王 伯 厚 Wang Pŏ-hou, and 王 普 升 Wang Chin-shêng.

522. 三 字 經 訓 詁
San tzŭ ching hsün ku.

"The Three-character Classic," explained and copiously annotated. By 王 伯 厚 Wang Pŏ-hou.

523. 傷 寒 論
Shang han lun.

"Discourses on Catching Colds." By Chang Chi 張 機. 5 vols. 16 chüan. 1780. *Ref.* B.M. p. 8. See No. 267.

524. 禪 門 日 誦 全 集
Ch'an mên jih sung ch'üan chi.

A complete Collection of Buddhist Daily Chants. By the Priest 默 持 Mŏ Ch'ih. *Ref.* B.M. p. 156; L.U. 81, 3; I.O.C. p. 43.

525. 聖 傷 默 想
Shêng shang mŏ hsiang.

"Silent Meditations on the Sacred Wounds." A Roman Catholic work. 1 vol.

526. 聖 書 小 云
Shêng shu hsiao yün.

"Notes on the Holy Books." A Japanese and Chinese work.

527. 聖 諭 廣 訓
Shêng yü kuang hsün.

"The Maxims of the Emperor K'ang Hsi," amplified by his successor, Yung Chêng. 1724. See No. 319.

528. 贖 罪 之 道 傳
Shu tsui chih tao chuan.

"A Story illustrating the Doctrine of the Redemption." By Carl F. Gutzlaff. 2 chüan. 1834. *Ref.* B.M. p. 68.

529. 說 岳 全 傳
Shuo Yŏ ch'üan chuan.

The complete narrative of Yŏ Fei, the patriot general who served so faithfully under the Sung dynasty, and who was wrongfully put to death at the instigation of his rival, 秦 檜 Ch'in Kuei. 10 vols. 20 chüan. 80 hui. 1793. *Ref.* B.M. p. 212.

530. 新 增 資 治 新 書
Hsin tsêng tzŭ chih hsin shu.

A work on Political Economy, embracing a variety of topics pertaining to the authority of the Legislature and the well-being of the people. 7 vols. *Ref.* Kidd, p. 23.

531. 新 約 全 書
Hsin yŏ ch'üan shu.

The New Testament, translated into the Mandarin Colloquial style. Shanghai. 1856. *Ref.* B.M. p. 2.

532. 新 約 全 書

Hsin yŏ ch'üan shu.

The Delegates' version of "The New Testament." Shanghai. 1866. Executed by delegate members from the various Protestant Missionary Societies in China. The style is professedly high-class; but the result is for the most part either unintelligible or obscure. *Ref.* B.M. p. 2.

533. 性 理 精 義

Hsing li ching i.

"The Essence of works on Mental Philosophy." Compiled by a Commission, by order of the Emperor K'ang Hsi (1662—1723). 6 vols. *Ref.* B.M. p. 128.

534. 搜 神 記

Sou shên chi.

"Handbook of Mythology." By 干 寶 Kan Pao. 3 chüan. See No. 410. *Ref.* B.M. p. 94.

535. 事 類 賦

Shih lei fu.

"A Classified Literary Encyclopædia." By 吳 淑 Wu Shu. 2 cases, 14 vols. 40 chüan. 1801. *Ref.* B.M. p. 244.

536. 四 書 人 物 考

Ssŭ shu jen wu k'ao.

The Men and Things of the "Four Books," examined. 6 vols. 1739. *Ref.* B.M. p. 194.

537. 四 書 題 鏡

Ssŭ shu t'i ching.

A Mirror of Themes from the "Four Books." 16 chüan. 1744.

538. 大 學
Ta hsüŏ.

"The Great Learning" (presented by Dr. Cornwall, 4th December, 1838). 1816. *Ref.* B.M. p. 193. See No. 337.

539. 大 悲 八 十 四 尊 現 相 寶 懺
Ta pei pa shih ssu tsun hsin hsiang pao ch'an.

540. 大 乘 妙 法 蓮 華 經
Ta shêng miao fa lien hua ching.

"The Lotus-flower Sutra."

541. 大 英 國 統 志
Ta ying kuo t'ung chih.

A History of England, in Chinese. By the Rev. Charles Gutzlaff. Illustrated with portraits of the Georges.

542. 太 平 廣 記
T'ai p'ing kuang chi.

Extensive Records compiled during the reign of the Emperor T'ai Tsung. By 李昉 Li Fang. 6 cases, 40 vols. *Ref.* B.M. p. 122.

543. 代 數 學
Tai shu hsüo.

A translation of De Morgan's Algebra, made by A. Wylie, October 1859.

544. 桃 園 結 義 章 程
T'ao yüan chieh i chang ch'êng.

"By-laws of the Ancient Peach Garden Association." A thin vol. in MS.

545. 天 文 畧 論
T'ien wên lüeh lun.

"A Digest of Astronomy." By B. Hobson. Canton. 1849. *Ref.* B.M. 202.

546. 千 手 千 眼 大 悲 心 咒 懺 法
Ch'ien shou ch'ien yen ta pei hsin chou ch'an fa.

The Confessional Services of the Great Compassionate Kwan-yin, possessing a thousand hands and a thousand eyes. Edited by the Priest 竭 誠 Chieh Ch'êng. *Ref.* B.M. p. 100.

547. 靖 逆 記
Ching ni chi.

"An account of the suppression of banditti in Shen-si, and other parts, in 1813." By 蘭 簸 Lan I, the historian. 1821. *Ref.* B.M. p. 118; Kidd, p. 9.

548. 慈 雲 走 國 全 傳
Tz'ŭ yün tso kuo ch'üan chuan.

"A Complete Narrative of the Wanderings of Prince Tz'ŭ yün." An historical romance referring to events supposed to have taken place during the Sung dynasty. 8 chüan (1st missing). 1815. *Ref.* B.M. p. 221.

549. 東 西 洋 考 每 月 統 記 傳
Tung hsi yang k'ao mei yüeh t'ung chi chuan.

"A Monthly Periodical of Foreign and Domestic News." Edited by the Rev. C. F. A. Gutzlaff. Contains 1833, moons 7th, 8th, 9th, 10th, 11th, 12th, 1st, and 2nd. 1833. *Ref.* B.M. p. 164.

550. 二 度 梅 傳
Êrh tu mei chuan.

"The Story of the Two Plums." A work of fiction in the colloquial style. Illustrated. 6 chüan. 1800. See No. 37. *Ref.* B.M. p. 155; Kidd, p. 55.

551. 外 海 紀 要
Wai hai chi yao.

1828.

552. 萬 壽 盛 典
Wan shou shêng tien.

These volumes belong to a work of this name, which is a Record of a Jubilee Celebration of the 80th birthday of the Emperor K'ang Hsi. The work is in 120 chüan. It is in the library of University College, 124-5, but is minus the very volumes of plates here present. Chüan 41-42 only. 2 vols. of plates. *Ref.* L.U. 124-5.

553. 幼 學 淺 解 問 答
Yu hsüŏ ch'ien chieh wên ta.

"Easy questions and answers for young scholars." 1847.

554. 易 經
Yi ching.

2 vols. 1781. For details, see No. 307.

555. 瀛 環 志 畧
Ying huan chih lüeh.

"A Geographical Treatise on all within the circuit of the Seas." By 徐繼畬 Hsü Chi-yü. 6 vols. 10 chüan. 1848. *Ref.* B.M. p. 174.

556. 嘆 咭 喇 國 新 出 種 痘 奇 書
Ying chieh li kuo hsin ch'u chung tou ch'i shu.

"A new English Treatise on Vaccination." 1806.

557. 漁 家 樂
Yü chia lê.

"The Pleasures of Angling." 4 vols.

558. 玉 嬌 梨
Yü chiao li.

"The Romance of the Two Cousins." 4 vols. 20 hui. 1782. See No. 45.

559. 御 纂 歷 代 三 元 甲 子 編 年
Yü tsuan li tai san yüan chia tzǔ pien nien.

Chronological list of the three first Graduates at the triennial examination for the Han-lin, or Imperial Academy.

560. 粵 謳
Yüeh ngou.

Canton Songs. 1828.

561. 玉 堂 字 彙
Yü t'ang tzǔ hui.

The "Jade Hall" Dictionary. 3 vols. *Ref.* B.M. p. 155.

562. 雍 正 上 諭
Yung Chêng shang yü.

"Imperial Edicts" of the Emperor Yung Chêng (A.D. 1723—36). 24 vols. 4 cases. 1729.

GILBERT AND RIVINGTON, LIMITED, ST. JOHN'S HOUSE, CLERKENWELL ROAD, LONDON, E.C.

INDEX.

———◆———

H

H 2

430 周易折中 *Chou Yi chê chung.* Staunton II, D
  10-11, p. 75.

206 泉志 *Ch'üan chih.* China III, B 1, p. 35.

476 創世傳註釋 *Ch'uang shih chuan chu shih,* p. 84.

436 莊子南華經解 *Chuang tzǔ Nan hua ching chieh.*
  Staunton I, E 11, p. 76.

192 全本禮記體註 *Ch'üan pên Li Chi t'i chu.* China
  I, B 8, p. 33.

284 篆字彙 *Chuan tzǔ hui.* Elgin I, A 1, p. 48.

157 綴白裘 *Chui pǒ ch'iu.* Amherst I, H 5—10,
  p. 27.

499 羣眞著述 *Ch'ün chên chu shu,* p. 87.

275 春秋傳說 *Ch'un ch'iu chuan shuo.* China I,
  G 8—10, p. 46.

323 春秋體註 *Ch'un ch'iu t'i chu.* Elgin II, E 9, p. 56.

479 春秋體註大全合參 *Ch'un ch'iu t'i chu ta
  ch'üan hǒ ts'an,* p. 84.

178 羣芳譜 *Ch'ün fang p'u.* China II, A 3-4; Staunton
  I, C 10-11, pp. 31, 72.

363 重訂綴白裘新集合編 *Ch'ung ting chui pǒ
  ch'iu hsin chi hǒ pien.* Pottinger, B 1—4, p. 62.

164 鐘鼎彝器欵識 *Chung ting i ch'i k'uan shih.*
  Amherst I, J 7, p. 28.

88 重訂廣事類賦 *Ch'ung ting kuang shih lei fu.*
  Amherst II, C 17-18, p. 16.

428 淳化閣帖考正 *Ch'un hua kǒ t'ieh k'ao chêng.*
  Staunton II, D 8, p. 75.

163 春秋註 *Ch'un ch'iu chu.* Amherst I, J 5, p. 28.

232 硃批諭旨 *Chu p'i yü chih.* China II, D 10-11,
  p. 40.

409 楚辭集註 *Ch'u tzǔ chi chu.* Staunton II, B 9,
  p. 71.

292 朱子全書 *Chu Tzǔ ch'üan shu.* Elgin II, A 1-4,
  p. 50.

420 古文分編集評 *Ku wên fên pien chi p'ing.* Staunton II, C 6-7, p. 73.

76 姑妄聽之 *Ku wang t'ing chih.* Amherst II, C 3, p. 14.

262 古文尙書 *Ku wên shang shu.* China III, F 4, p. 44.

143 古文筆譜 *Ku wên pi p'u.* Amherst II, F 14, p. 25.

198 古文評註 *Ku wên p'ing chu.* China II, B 5 ; II, II, B 7, p. 34.

293 古文辭類纂 *Ku wên tz'ŭ lei tsuan.* Elgin II, A 5-6, p. 50.

308 古文雅正 *Ku wên ya chêng.* Elgin I, D 1-2, p. 53.

456 古玉圖 *Ku yü t'u.* Staunton I, G 4 *a*, pp. 80, 88.

244 類經 *Lei ching.* China III, E 8—10, p. 42.

418 類經圖翼 *Lei Ching t'u i.* Staunton II, C 1, p. 73.

23 雷峰塔 *Lei fêng t'a.* Amherst II, A 19 ; II, A 32, pp. 4, 7, 88.

260 楞嚴正脉 *Lêng yen chêng mŏ.* China III, F 2, p. 44.

40 聊齋志異 *Liao Chai chih i.* Amherst I, B 2 ; I, D 10-11 ; Pottinger, E 6-7, pp. 8, 16, 65.

205 禮記 *Li Chi.* China II, B 12 ; Staunton I, B 1 ; I, E 1—5, pp. 35, 68, 75.

344 禮記讀本 *Li chi tu pên.* Macartney V, 7, p. 60.

459 列女傳 *Lieh nü chuan.* Staunton I, G 6, p. 81.

190 臨證指南醫按 *Lin chêng chih nan i ngan.* China I, B 1-2, p. 33.

369 靈魂篇 *Ling hun p'ien.* Pottinger, B 10, p. 63.

162 嶺南叢述 *Ling nan ts'ung shu.* Amherst I, J 3-4, p. 28.

291 靈樞經 *Ling shu ching.* Elgin I, A 11, p, 49.

30 憐香伴 *Lien hsiang pan.* Amherst II, A 26, p. 6.

217 離騷經 *Li sao ching.* China III, B 13, p. 37.

I

7 定鼎奇文 *Ting ting ch'i wên.* Amherst II, A 3, p. 2.

138 豆棚閒話 *Tou p'êng hsien hua.* Amherst II, F 2, p. 24.

402 艸字彙 *Ts'ao tzŭ hui.* Staunton II, B 2, p. 69.

82 增智襄補 *Tsêng chih hsiang pu.* Amherst II, C 10, p. 15.

132 增補遣愁集 *Tsêng pu ch'ien ch'ou chi.* Amherst II, F 3, p. 23.

332 曾文正公 *Tsêng wên chêng kung.* Macartney I, II, p. 57.

233 左繡 *Tso hsiu.* China II, D 12; Staunton I, B 5, pp. 40, 68.

437 杜工部集 *Tu kung pu chi.* Staunton II, E 1, p. 76.

318 都名所圖會 *Tu ming so t'u hui.* Elgin I, E 3, p. 55.

3 東周列國全志 *Tung Chou lieh kuo ch'üan chih.* Amherst I, A 5; Pottinger, E 4, pp. 1, 65.

131 通鑑綱目 *T'ung chien kang mu.* Amherst II, F 1-2; I, J 8-9; China II, E 1—8; I, G 3-5; II, G 1—4, pp. 23, 28, 41, 46, 47.

412 東西漢全傳 *Tung hsi Han ch'üan chuan.* Staunton II, B 13, p. 72.

431 東西洋考 *Tung hsi yang k'ao.* Staunton II, D 12, p. 75.

442 東華錄 *Tung hua lu.* Staunton I, F 9—12, p. 78.

549 東西洋考每月統記傳 *Tung hsi yang k'ao mei yüeh t'ung chi chuan*, p. 94.

361 東北遊記 *Tung pei yu chi.* Pottinger, A 12, p. 62.

466 東坡遺意 *Tung p'ŏ i i.* Staunton I, G 11 *d*, p. 82.

467 同文千字文 *T'ung wên ch'ien tzŭ wên*, Staunton I, G 12, p. 82.

Descriptive Catalogue of the Chinese, Japanese, and Manchu Books in the Library of the India Office

印度事务部图书馆藏中、日、满文典籍解题目录

DESCRIPTIVE CATALOGUE

OF THE

CHINESE, JAPANESE,

AND

MANCHU BOOKS

IN THE

LIBRARY OF THE INDIA OFFICE.

COMPILED BY

THE REV. JAMES SUMMERS,

PROFESSOR OF CHINESE IN KING'S COLLEGE, LONDON.

PRINTED BY ORDER OF
THE SECRETARY OF STATE FOR INDIA IN COUNCIL.

LONDON:

1872.

PREFACE.

The collection of Chinese books, of which this little work professes to be a Descriptive Catalogue, was very gradually formed. Parcels of books were sent from time to time, about the beginning of the present century, by the members of the Factory at Canton, (then entirely under the control of the Honourable East India Company,) to the Library in Leadenhall Street. There they remained almost unnoticed for many years, and they received no addition of consequence until the labours of Professor S. Julien, in the publication of the Travels of Hiuen Tsang in India—a translation from the Chinese—excited the attention of students of Buddhism, and led the late Professor H. H. Wilson to procure from China the very voluminous Buddhist works in Chinese which constitute no inconsiderable portion of this collection. These latter however, like the original parcels, lay in dust on their shelves and quite unknown until, by the liberality of the Secretary of State for India in Council, they were ordered to be catalogued and bound, so that some idea might be obtained of their contents, and that they might be placed conveniently within the reach of enquirers. This was done upon the recommendation of the late Librarian, Dr. Fitzedward Hall, M.A.

iv

The compiler of this catalogue has only to express his sense of the imperfections attaching to his work, and to crave the indulgence of those who may use it. Orientalists only can understand fully the difficulties which present themselves to the Cataloguer of Eastern Literature. The title of a book is often untranslatable; the author's name is frequently out of sight and has to be sought for in some obscure corner or work; the date of the publication is alike often doubtful, and in the case of Buddhist Literature the identification of the Chinese title with the Sanscrit original is sufficiently troublesome. Thanks however to the labours of Professor Stanislas Julien, Rev. J. Edkins, Rev. J. Eitel, and Mr. A. Wylie the path of future explorers has been very much cleared and opened up. The Compiler is indebted also to the Rev. Samuel Beal for some corrections relating to the Buddhist books which will be found in the Table of Errata at the end of this catalogue.

London, *March*, 1872.

NOTE. The value of the vowels in the expression of Oriental words is that of the continental languages—Italian especially; J corresponds with the French J=ZH: *cheu* is the equivalent for *chow*, each vowel being sounded.

前　言

　　这份可以勉强称为叙录的小成果中包含的中文图书是逐渐收集而来的。自本世纪初期开始，广州商馆（the Factory at Canton）［当时完全处于不列颠东印度公司（the Honourable East India Company）］控制下的员工会有时会向位于利德贺街（Leadenhall Street）的图书馆邮寄图书包裹。多年来，这些书籍几乎一直默默无闻地呆在图书馆，没有受到重视，直到儒莲（S. Julien）教授为出版中文《大唐西域记》（*the Travels of Hiuen Tsang in India*）英译本所做的努力引起佛教学生的关注，并促使当时健在的H. H. 威尔逊（H. H. Wilson）教授从中国购买大量的佛学书籍，这些图书在本藏书目录中所占的比例不容忽视。然而，这些书籍和之前收到的包裹一样，在书架上尘封许久，不为人知，直到印度事务大臣（Secretary of State for India）开恩下令，这些图书才得以编目分类并进行装订，从而使书籍的内容能够为人所知，并得以安放在恰当的位置，方便查阅。这项工作是根据已故图书管理员菲茨爱德华·霍尔（Fitzedward Hall, M. A.）博士的建议开展的。

　　该目录的编纂人员意识到该目录存在瑕疵，并恳求使用者谅解，只有东方学专家才能够充分理解编纂东方文献目录会遇到怎样的困难。这些图书的书名往往无法翻译；往往没有明确标注作者的姓名，需要在某些隐蔽的角落或作品中寻找；出版日期也是如此，往往难以确定，对佛教文献而言，要确定源自梵文的中文书名又非常麻烦。儒莲（Stanislas Julien）教授、传教士艾约瑟（Rev. J. Edkins）、传教士欧德理（Rev. J. Eitel）和伟烈亚力先生（Mr. A. Wylie）的劳动成果为今后的探索者开辟了道路，扫除了障碍。该目录编纂人员还要特别感谢传教士毕尔（Rev. Samuel Beal）为佛学书籍所作的勘误工作，详见本目录最后的勘误表。

伦敦，1872年3月。

　　注：东方语言词汇元音的音值与欧洲大陆语言的音值一样——特别是意大利语；J对应法语中的J=ZH；cheu相当于chow，每个元音都要发音。

（管宇译，彭萍校）

INDEX.

———o———

*The numbers refer to the article, and not to the pages.

yi

A partial classification of the books has been made, as follows :—

I. LANGUAGE.

II. PHILOSOPHY AND RELIGION.

III. MISCELLANEOUS WORKS . . page 49

These are placed in alphabetic order, and include works on Philosophy, Religion, Law, Mythology, History, Astronomy, Chronology, Geography, Arithmetic, Medicine, Literature, etc.

LANGUAGE

---

§. I. ANCIENT INSCRIPTIONS.

1. Sung wang fu chai chung ting kw'an shi.

宋 玉 復 齋 鐘 鼎 欸 識

This is a collection of inscriptions in *facsimile*, from ancient bells and tripods, fifty nine in all, arranged chronologically. The modern reading of each inscription is given and historical remarks thereon are added.

The author's or compiler's name was *Wang fu chai* 王復 齋 of the *Sung* 宋 dynasty, (A.D. 960—1278.) Printed in a superior style in large folio. One volume. Dated 1802.

2. Sie shi chung.

薛 低 鐘

'Sie's Bells.' This is the contracted form of title. The full title runs: *Lie tai chung ting i ki kw'an shi fa tie* 歷 代鐘鼎彝器欸識法帖 i. e. 'Examples of scrolls and inscriptions on the bells, tripods, vases, and vessels of successive ages.' It is similar to the above (1), but smaller in size. Four volumes now bound in one. The author's name was *Sie shi* | 氏 or *Sie shang kung* | 尙功 The work bears date, the 2nd. year of Kiaking (A.D. 1797.)

3. Po ku t'u.

博 古 圖

'Plates of Antiquities.' The full title is *Siuen ho po k'u t'u* 宣 和 博 古 圖 i. e. 'Siuen ho's plates of antiquities' *Siuen ho* is a pseudonym for the real author.

It is an account of ancient vases, tripods and various other vessels in gold, silver and other metals, with their exact measurements and the inscriptions upon them interpreted in modern characters. There are several hundred plates of vases such as the emperors bestowed on princes, ministers, and literary men of former ages as rewards of merit. There are several prefaces by various authors of different dynasties. It is in 30 books, now bound up in three volumes.

The date of this edition is A.D. 1753.

4. Ku yu t'u   &   Kiau ku t'u.

古 玉 圖   考 古 圖

These are looked upon as divisions of the *Po ku t'u* (3.) They are printed and illustrated in a manner precisely similar to that work, but they relate to various articles not mentioned therein. 3 vols. Bound in one volume.

§. II. DICTIONARIES.

The Chinese began at a very early date to arrange the written characters of their language, and they have done so under three methods:—1. According to the f o r m; 2. According to the n a m e given to each character; 3. According to the s i g n i f i c a t i o n. They have consequently: (1) dictionaries in which the characters are arranged under the elementary —usually 214—radical forms; (2) dictionaries in which the characters are arranged under the syllables with their special intonations—usually four—by which the characters are expressed ; (3) dictionaries in which the words are classed according to their meaning under celestial, terrestial, and human objects, phenomena, actions &c. (cf. Table of Contents under 15.)

The extent to which the Chinese have gone in the making of dictionaries may be seen in a List of 218 separate works, given in the Imperial Catalogue, which list is reprinted in the *Chinese Repository*, vol. xvii. p. 433. *et seq.*

5. Shwo ꞷun chin pun.

說 文 眞 本

This is the earliest form of Dictionary according to the radical forms, which are here 540 in number.   It is in 30 books or chapters—four volumes,—now bound in one. The author's name was *Hü-shin* 許 愼 who lived about A.D. 100.   He took the ancient "*chuen·* characters, which resembled the more ancient hieroglyphic forms, and traced their origin to these latter.   The varieties are given and the significations as far as possible, with the modern forms

DICTIONARIES.

of the characters likewise. The work is chiefly valuable for the examples of the Chuen-forms which it contains. There is a duplicate, but inferior copy, of the *Shwo vun* in this Library.

6. Chuen tsz wei.

篆 字 彙

'Collection of the C h u e n characters'. A dictionary of the ancient *chuen* 篆 —commonly called the "S e a l"—characters, arranged under the 214 radicals, with the significations of each attached. Under each common modern form the "S e a l" characters are discovered in their numerous varieties. There are six volumes,—now bound in one.

7. Tsau tsz wei.

艸 字 彙

This is a dictionary,—or rather, a collection of specimens —of the cursive forms—called by the Chinese, *Tsau tsz* 草字 i.e. " grass characters ".

It consists of *facsimile* copies of the handwriting of great poets and others celebrated in Chinese literary history. The characters are arranged under the radicals; no meanings are given, but the names of the writers whose autographs are represented are printed in the margin.

It is in six volumes,—now bound in one.

Among the authors' names we notice that of *Tung p'o* 東 波 ， the eminent poet, who appears to have written very large, bold, but nearly illegible characters.

8. Tsz wei

字 彙

"Character's collected". A dictionary of the Chinese characters arranged for the first time under the 214 radicals. It is by *Mei ying tsu* 梅膺祚, who published it A.D. 1615. Previous lexicographers had arranged the characters under a greater number of radical forms; he first reduced them to 214, the number now followed always. It is said to contain 33,179 characters, with their explanations. In 14 vols, now bound in two.

The following is an abstract of its contents.

Vol. I. 1. The *Yün-pi*[a]. List to show how the characters may be correctly written. 2. *T'sung ku*[b]. List of 179 characters, with their variants in common use. 3. *Tsun shi*[c]. List of 110 characters, with their obsolete forms. 4. *Ku-kien t'ung-yung*[d]. List of 135 characters, with their ancient forms still in use. 5. *Kien tsz*[e]. List of characters which contain two or more radicals, showing under which of these radicals each character may be found in the Dictionary.

[a] 運筆 [b] 從古 [c] 遵時 [d] 古今通用 [e] 檢字

Vols. II—XIII contain the Dictionary itself.

Vol. XIV. 1. *Pien-sz*[a]. List of characters similar in form, but different in pronunciation and meaning. 2. *Sing-u*[b]. List of defective characters, such as are easily mistaken for others, with corrections, and the pronunciations and meanings of both. 3. *Yun fa*[c] *chi t'u*[d]. Table of syllables arranged under the 32 consonants, the 44 assonants, and the four tones. 4. *Yun fa*[c] *hung t'u*[e]. Table similar to the preceding by *Li kia shau*[f].

[a] 辨似 [b] 醒誤 [c] 韻法 [d] 眞圖 [e] 橫圖 [f] 李嘉紹

6　　　　　　　　　DICTIONARIES.

9.　K'ang　hi　tsz　tien.

康　熙　字　典

'Kanghi's Code or Canon of Charácters.'　A dictionary prepared and published under the direction of the Emperor Jin 仁 ("the Benevolent"), the title of whose reign was *K'ang hi,* A.D. 1662.　It was founded upon the *Ching tsz t'ung* 正字通.　It was compiled by 27 of the *literati,* members of the *Han-lin* (Imperial Academy).　In 32 vols, now bound in 8 vols., 12 mo.

Vol. I. contains: 1. List of 214 radicals; 2. List of characters difficult to find (*Kien tsz* 檢字), as in the *Tsz wei* (8. q.v.) but amplified and improved; 3. List called *Pien sz* 辨似, as in the *Tsz wei* (8. q.v.)

Vol. II., which bears the title of *Tang yün* 等韻, treats of the accents, consonants, vowels, assonants, and syllables of the Chinese language and their changes, and also a list of the characters used in the dictionary as guides to the pronunciation.　The remaining volumes (except the last two) are taken up with the dictionary itself, the characters being arranged under each radical, according to the number of strokes in each primitive (i.e. the part left after elimination of the radical). ·　A supplementary addition (*tsang* 增) is made, under each division, of those characters which were omitted in the *Tsz wei* 字彙, and the *Ching tsz tung* 正字通.　The last two volumes contain two supplements: 1. The *Pu-i* 補遺, List of characters which are not classical, though their names and meanings are known; 2. The *Pi kiau* 備考. List of characters whose significations are doubtful, or whose pronunciations and meanings are unknown.

In proceeding to describe each character, the pronunciation

of it is given by the method called *fan tsi* 反切. Two characters are given, the names of which are supposed to be known; the initial sound of the former is then added to the final or rhyming sound of the latter to form the name of the character under explanation: thus from *ting* and *mung* would arise *tung*. The names of books are given as authorities for the pronunciations so defined. The meanings are then arranged in logical order, brief extracts from classical works are cited, the name only of the work being given. Occasionally critical remarks are added.

10. Ching tsz yu pien ta tseun.

正 字 玉 篇 大 全

This is a dictionary of the Chinese characters arranged under the 214 radicals, with explanations in Japanese in the *katakana* characters. The exact pronunciations also according to the *koye* and *yomi* systems are subjoined, and the key rhyme is added to facilitate reference to the "*Gradus*." It is in oblong folio, one volume, very thick.

11. Zo syok dai kwo yeki gyok ben dai zen

增 續 大 廣 益 會 玉 扁 大 全

A Japanese dictionary of the Chinese characters, arranged like the above under the 214 radicals, but with extra comments. By *Mori Tei sai* 毛利貞齋. This is more the nature of a lexicon than a simple dictionary. It is in twelve volumes, and is now bound in four. This dictionary was first published in 1691. Several editions have appeared since, and this is one of the recent issues.

12. Chau sien wei kwo tsz wei.

朝 鮮 偉 國 字 彙

A dictionary of the Chinese, Corean, Japanese, and English languages.   It was published at Batavia in 1835 by *Philosinensis* (i. e., Rev. W. H. Medhurst, D.D.), and bears the English title: " Translation of a Comparative Vocabulary of the Chinese, Corean, and Japanese Languages:" to which is added the "Thousand - character - classic" in Chinese and Corean; the whole accompanied by copious indexes of all the Chinese and English words occurring in the work.   There is: 1. A Vocabulary of English and Corean, with references by which the corresponding terms in Chinese and Japanese may be discovered ; 2. An Index to all the Chinese characters used in the book ; 3. *Wei yü lüi kiai* 倭 語 類 解 ' Japanese assorted and explained,' which hardly agrees with the fact, for Chinese here forms the basis. All the explanations are given in Corean, both of the Chinese and Japanese words. The classification begins with *Celestial* objects, then *Times and Seasons*, and everything is classified by the method followed by the Chinese (cf. Dictionaries, 5). After this vocabulary follows : 4. The *Tsien tsz vun* 千 字 文 usually called the " Thousand-character-classic," because it contains 1000 Chinese different characters connected in meaning, which are explained in Corean, the English being also given.

13. Yu chi tsang ting tsing vun kien.

御 製 增 訂 清 文 鑑

Han-i araha nonggime toktobuha Manchu gisun-i buleku bithe.

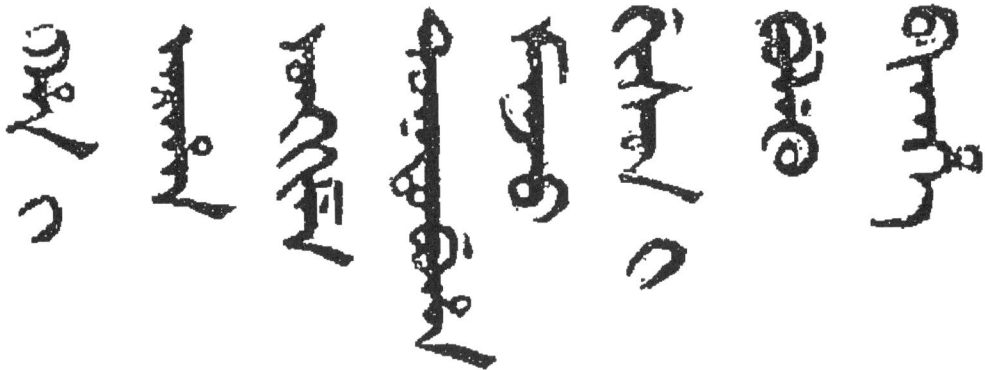

'Mirror of the Manchu Language, published by Imperial authority: augmented and revised edition.' A. D. 1772. This is a dictionary of expressions arranged according to subjects, beginning with *celestial* objects. An explanation is given in Manchu of all the Chinese and Manchu, and the pronunciation of the Manchu words in Chinese characters. There is a copious index of Manchu words, so that the work is available for students of both languages.

Long extracts respecting the origin of the Manchus and the genealogy of the present rulers of China have been translated by Julius Klaproth, and will be found in his *Verzeichniss der Chinesischen und Mandschuischen Bücher der königliche Bibliothek zu Berlin*, folio, Paris, 1822. Klaproth there gives three indexes to this dictionary.

The work is now bound in three volumes, small folio, and lettered *Manchu gisun-i buleku bithe.*

10

§ III. *ENCYCLOPÆDIAS.*

14. Tsien kio lui shu.

潛 確 類 書

This is a work of an encyclopædic nature, as it compre-hends every subject in the range of Chinese knowledge; but it treats them in a manner somewhat different from ours. Instead of long dissertations, it takes up and explains all the peculiar or technical phraseology of each subject, substan-tiating every explanation by quotations from classical authors, or the standard books to which each particular subject relates. For example, under *Buddhism* and *Buddha*, there are some 360 terms, special to these subjects, explained. Expressions used by poets, historians, and philosophers are entered and interpreted in a brief, but lucid manner. Mr. Wylie informs us that from the freedom of speech used in this work in relation to the reigning family, it has been placed in the *Index expurgatorius*, only with respect however to the chapters on the Manchus. The book is similar to the *Yuen kien lüi han* 淵鑑類函 (v. 15), which is founded upon this, and contains the same expressions, but arranged in a different way. The phrases are classified in the usual manner under: " *Heaven, Times and Seasons, Earth, Nations, Mountains, Land and Water, Dwellings, Classes of Men, Religions, Food, Furniture, Plants, and Animals.* The original work was by *Chin jin si* 陳仁錫, Historio-grapher — about A.D. 1632. In 120 chapters, now bound 15 vols.

15. Yuen kien lui han.

淵 鑑 類 函

'The Fathomless Mirror.' This is an encyclopædia compiled by order of the second Emperor of the present dynasty, and published in 1710.

It is in 450 books or chapters (*kiuen*), now bound in 32 vols.

General Table of Contents of each volume.

Vol I. bks. 1—14. Celestial objects, natural phenomena, times and seasons.

Vol. II. bks. 15—27. Times and seasons, divisions of the year, heat and cold, terrestrial objects, natural features of the land, hills.

Vol. III. bks. 28—40. Mountains, seas, rivers, imperial matters, general remarks.

Vol. IV. bks. 40—52. Court customs, rules and regulations, &c.

Vol. V. bks. 53—61. Government, residences, acts, imperial harem, regulations, instructions, relatives, appointment of officers.

Vol. VI. bks. 62—77 Appointments, government officials, names, duties, colleges, presidents, &c.

Vol. VII. bks. 78—92. Presidents of boards, their subordinates, various.

Vol. VIII. bks. 93—106. Names of various officials.

Vol. IX. bks. 107—117. Generals, governors, magistrates, guardians.

Vol. X. bks. 118—129. Appointments, names of various officers.

Vol. XI. bks. 130- 143. The same, and their various offices, and works.

Vol. XII. bks. 144—158. Statecraft, merits, crimes, punishments, ceremonials, forms, assemblies, salutations at Court, &c.

Vol. XIII. bks. 159—174. Ceremonials, duties to superiors, public worship, vessels used.

Vol. XIV. bks. 175—187. Forms, matrimonial, funeral, mourning, music, chanting, singing, dancing, &c.

Vol. XV. bks. 188—198. Instrumental music, literature, ancient poetry, history, books, dissertations, &c.

Vol. XVI. bks. 199—211. Poetry, inscriptions, collectanea, discourses, learning, writing materials, military art and service, war, arms, &c.

Vol. XVII. bks. 212—225. Assaults, seafights, war chariots, encampments, drill, commissariat.

12   ENCYCLOPÆDIAS.

Vol. XVIII. bks. 226—239. Various arms, military music and instruments, equipments, frontier lands, Corea, Japan, Yezo, Cochin China, Siam, &c.

Vol. XIX. bks. 240—256. Frontier lands, Tibet, Tartary, human affairs, relations of life, person, beautiful or deformed.

Vol. XX. bks. 257—269. Ages, slaves, parts of body, names of persons, passions, sentiments, language, &c.

Vol. XXI. bks. 270—282. Duties of life, emotions, conduct, intelligence, justice, perseverance, &c.

Vol. XXII. bks. 283- -297. Bravery, nobility, affluence, satire, reproof.

Vol. XXIII. bks. 298—309. Conversation, dialogue, congratulations, &c.

Vol. XXIV. bks. 310—324. Rewards, retributions, pride, lust, rebellion; Buddhist religion, Buddha, priests, rules of conduct; Tauist religion, genii, priests, spirits, demons, divination, healing, exorcising, &c.

Vol. XXV. bks. 325—338. The fine arts, music, books, paintings, chess, geography of the empire. metropolis, districts.

Vol. XXVI. bks. 339—350. Provinces and departments, Kwang-tung, Szchuen, &c.; dwelling places, palaces, temples; fire and heat, smoke, lamps, coal, precious metals, gold, silver, jewels, &c.

Vol. XXVII. bks. 351—364. Parks, passes, bridges, roads, Buddhist temples, productions and occupations, markets, commerce, trades, profit, &c.

Vol. XXVIII. bks. 365—374. Cloth and silks, cotton, silk, woollens, ornaments of ceremony and dress, caps, girdles, rings, seals, hour-glasses.

Vol. XXIX. bks. 375—387. Ornaments of dress, shoes, stockings, couches, mats, carpets, fans; vessels and furniture, tables, chests, baskets, pipes, dishes, cups, boats, ships, masts, sails, vehicles on wheels, carriages, axles, wheels.

Vol. XXX. bks. 388—403. Food, rice, bread, cakes, tea, drinking, eating; the five grains—corn, barley, wheat, rice, and millet; medicines—names of various medicines; vegetables, fruit.

Vol. XXXI. bks. 404—420. Fruits, flowers, grasses, trees, birds.

Vol. XXXII. bks. 421—433. Birds and beasts.

vol. XXXIII. bks. 434—450. Animals and insects.

II. PHILOSOPHY AND RELIGION.

---

§ *I. ANCIENT CHINESE CLASSICS.*

16. Yi king ta tseun.

易 經 大 全

'The classic of changes—complete.' This is the most ancient book the Chinese have. *Fuhi* 伏犧 an ancient Emperor, who is said to have lived 3000 years B. C. is the reputed author. He invented certain symbols, called the *Pa-kwa* 八卦 or "eight diagrams", as arbitrary signs of the first principles of things, and upon these he based his doctrines concerning the nature and origin of things. Everything is said to have been produced by the combination of two principles:—the active and that acted upon. These are sometimes called "the Dual powers", and everything in nature is referred to one or other of these. Primarily *Heaven* and *Earth* are the dual powers, and these are the chief of the eight diagrams. The other six are called their "children":—*mountains* and *fountains* (i. e. heavy and light), *fire* and *water* (i. e. heat and cold), *wind* and *thunder* (i. e. flexible and rigid). From these eight, sixty-four other diagrams were formed, recognizing always the two principles as before. This edition is in 20 chapters, now bound in two volumes.

By the term " classics " as applied to Chinese is to be understood the canonical books, which are held in supreme veneration by the Chinese, on account of their origin, being the productions of their ancient wise kings and statesmen; for the value of their contents, forming the code of their science and the sources of their legislative enactments; and by reason of the style in which they are written, which forms a model of dignified prose, exhaustive composition, and apt illustration.

These books have been denominated King 經 a word which in its primary sense signifies the 'warp' in the silken fabric, and which has been adopted by the Buddhist translators as a suitable equivalent for सूत्र *sûtra*,—the word which designates their standard or classic works.

Translation : "Y-King antiquissimus sinarum liber quem ex latina interpretatione P. Regis aliorumque ex societate Jesu P. P. edidit Julius Mohl. 1834, Stuttgartiæ et Tubingæ, 2 vols."

17. Yi king hwei i kiai.

易經會義解

'The meaning and elucidation of the *Yih-king*.' This is merely one of the numerous commentaries on the Yi-king, but a very good one, with explanatory notes. So numerous are the commentators on this book that there exist (according to the great catalogue of the Imperial library at Peking) 1450 works upon the Yi-king alone.

18. Shu king ta tsuen.

書經大全

'The classic of history complete.' The *Shu-king* is the most ancient book of history which the Chinese have. It comes next in point of antiquity to the Yi-king 易 經 (17). The Shu-king is fragmentary, and of a politico-religious character. It consists chiefly of a discourse between the Emperors of the *Hia* 夏 *Shang* 商 and *Cheu* 周 dynasties, and their ministers; the period in which they lived being about 1600 years in duration—from the Emperor *Yau* 堯 to *Ping-wang* 平 王 [B.C. 2355-720]. There is much of practical wisdom contained in the remarks made in the various dialogues, which renders the book well worthy of consideration. The history of "The Book" is involved in considerable obscurity. The story is that it was framed in its present shape from collected fragments of official documents by *Kung-fu-tsz* 孔 夫 子 (Confucius) about B.C. 500. It was condemned to be burnt by *Chi-hwang-ti* 始 皇 帝 "The First Emperor" who united the petty states under one rule, B.C. 220, and on the revival of literature under the Emperor *Wen-hwang-ti* 文 皇 帝 "The Literary Emperor" no copy could be found. At last an aged and blind scholar, named *Fu-sang* 伏 生 was discovered who was able to repeat the whole from memory, and subsequently on pulling down the house of Confucius, some original parts of it were found. For a further history of the book and its various commentators see "Wylie's *Notes on Chinese Literature*," pp. 2-3. and "Dr. Legge's *Chinese Classics*." This edition is in six chapters, and is now bound in two volumes.

Translations. "*Ancient China* 書 經 The Shoo-king or the Historical Classic, being the most ancient authentic record of the annals of the Chinese empire, illustrated by later Commentators. Translated by W. H. Medhurs Sen., Shanghae, 1846.

"*Le Chou-king*, un des livres sacrés des Chinois, qui renferme les fondements de leur ancienne histoire, les principes de leur Gouvernement et de leur morale; ouvrage recueilli par Confucius. Traduit et enrichi de notes par feu le P. Gaubil, missionaire à la Chine. Revu et corrigé sur le Texte Chinois, accompagné de nouvelles notes, de planches gravées en taille douce et d' additions tirés des historiens originaux, dans lesquelles on donne l'histoire des princes omis dans le Chou-king. Par M. De Guignes. On y a joint un discours préliminaire, qui contient des recherches sur les temps antérieurs à ceux dont parle le Chou-king, et une notice de l' Y-king, autre livre sacré des Chinois. Paris, 1770."

19. Shu king.

書 經

The previous remarks will apply to this edition likewise, which contains the text and the commentary by Chu-hi 朱 熹 There is a duplicate of this work in the library.

20. Shi king ta tsuen.

詩 經 大 全

The *Shi-king* is a collection of lyrical pieces, dating from the Cheu 周 dynasty (B.C. 112) to the time of Confucius. These odes, hymns, and songs, to the number of 311, were collected by the sage from a much larger number, many of which were deemed by him unworthy of a place in the collection, on account of their immoral or corrupt tendency. They are divided into four classes :—

1. *Kwo-fung* 國風 Songs which indicate popular feeling in the petty states.
2. *Siau-ya* 小雅 and *Ta-ya* 大雅 Songs of a higher cast—lofty praise or bitter satire.
3. *Sung* 頌 Hymns in praise of dead kings and others.

The songs of the Shi-king are intended to lead from the contemplation of small events and trifling circumstances, to the consideration of the great affairs of the state, and the political and moral advancement of mankind. The poetical quality of the verses varies considerably. In some there exists a noble, simple, and natural sublimity. In many of the songs the first two or three lines are plain repetitions, and they are yet striking, coming as they do from the dark ages almost prehistoric. Several extracts from the ancient Shi-king will be found, with translations, in Dr. Morrison's *Chinese Dictionary*, vol. I., and an elaborate account of the work in Dr. W. Schott's *Entwurf einer Beschreibung der Chinesischen Litteratur. Abhandlungen der Akademie der Wissenschaften zu Berlin,* 1850. This edition is now bound in two vols.

Translation. "*Confucii Chi-king* sive Liber carminum Ex Latina P. Lacharme interpretatione. Edidit Julius Mohl. Stuttgartiae et Tubingee, 1830."

21. Cheu li.

周禮

'The Ritual of the Cheu dynasty.' This is one of the three books of ceremonies upon which Chinese forms are based. It

relates the manners and ceremonies of the court in the Cheu dynasty, B.C. 1200, and is generally attributed to *Cheu-kung* 周公 the brother of the first emperor of that dynasty. The style is terse and often obscure, thus marking the antiquity of the work. It is in twelve chapters and is now bound in one volume. It forms part of the *Kiu-king* (q. v. 29.)

Translations. "The ceremonial usages of the Chinese B.C. 1121, as prescribed in the *Institutes of the Chow dynasty, strung as pearls,* or *Chow-le-kwan-choo* 周禮貫珠 being an abridgement of the *Chow-le-Classic,* by *Hoo Peih-seang* 胡必相 (designated *Mung-Chen* 夢占). Translated from the original Chinese, with notes, by William Raymond Gingell. London, 1852.

"Le Tcheou-li ou Rites des Tcheou, traduit pour la première fois du Chinois par feu Edouard Biot, avec un Table Analytique. Paris, 1851, two vols,"

22. Li ki ta ts'uen.

禮 記 大 全

This is a special edition of the *Li-ki* designated "All Complete." In thirty chapters, bound in three volumes. Another edition forms a part of the *Kiu-king* 九 經 (q. v. 29) and is in ten chapters bound up in two volumes.

Translation. "禮記 *Li-ki* ou mémorial des Rites, traduit pour la première fois du Chinois, et accompagné de notes, de commentaires et du texte original, par J. M. Callery. Turin, 1853."

23. Kien pun li ki.

監 本 禮 記

The *Li-ki* clearly and distinctly printed for school boys. Ten books, bound in three volumes.

24. Ts'uen pun li ki t'i chu.

全 本 禮 記 體 註

'Complete edition of the *Li-ki*, with full comments.' By *Fan-ki-tang* 范 紫 登 assisted by others. In ten volumes, now bound in two.

25. I li.

儀 禮

The most ancient book of Rites, the basis of the more modern *Li-ki* 禮 記. Its author is said to have been *Cheu-kung* 周 公 The subject matter of the work is the conduct of the individual under every phase of social intercourse. One of its sections, the *Hia-siau-ching* 夏 小 正 "Catalogue of the Hia dynasty," contains an astronomical evidence of 2000 years before Christ.

26. I li king chuen.

儀 禮 經 傳

The same work with annotations, and part of the *Kiu-king* 九 經. In two divisions, *nüi* 內 "interior," and *wai* 外 "exterior." The former is in 23 chapters, the latter in five chapters, and the whole is bound in three volumes.

27. Ch'un tsiu ta ts'uen.

春 秋 大 全

'The Spring and Autumn Annals.' This is an account of the *Lu* 魯 kingdom, the native country of *Kung-fu-tsz* 孔 夫 子

(Confucius), and its history from B.C. 722 to B.C. 484. This was written by the philosopher himself. The work was amplified by one of his pupils, named *Tso* 左 hence the title *Tso-chuen* 左傳 under which it is often quoted. The comments of two other scholars—*Kung-yang* 公羊 and *Kü-liang* 穀梁 are also to be found in this edition, which is designated *Ta-ts'uen* 大全 "All Complete." Thirty-seven books, now bound in three volumes.

The *Ch'un-tsiu* is also to be found under the head *Kiu-king* (q. v. 29) in two divisions, each of twelve chapters, bound in two volumes.

Translation. " Book I. of the *Ch'un-tsiu* in Chinese, with a Latin translation by Bayer, is to be found in the " *Commentaria Academice Petropolitanea,*" vol. VII., p. 398 et seq."

There is another copy of the *Ch'un-tsiu*, part of Dr. Leyden's collection in five volumes, but a different edition.

28. Er ya yin t'u.

爾雅音圖

'The words of the *Er-ya*, an ancient dictionary of classical synonyms, &c., with plates.' Three volumes, quarto, now bound in one. The commentary is by *Ko-pu* 郭璞 of the Tsin dynasty (A.D. 265—419). The *Er-ya* also forms part of the *Kiu-king* (q. v. 29).

29. Kiu king pu chu.

九經補註

The Chinese have at different periods united the various classic works of antiquity under one general title, which has changed at the caprice of the publishers—generally under the auspices of the Court—and hence they can speak of the "Five Classics," the "Nine Classics," and the "Thirteen Classics." The title above is "The Nine Classics, augmented and anno-tated." The *Yi-king, Shu-king, Shi-king, Er-ya, Hiau-king, Cheu-li, Li-ki, I-li,* and the *Ch'un-tsiu* appear to make up the "Nine Classics." The whole work is now bound under the separate heads (q. v.) in 13 volumes.

---

§ II. CONFUCIANIST WORKS.

30. Sz shu chin pun.

四　書　眞　本

'The Four Books.' By this title is meant the following works:—

1. The *Ta-hio* 大學 *lit.*, 'Great learn, or learning,' which is explained to mean the learning suited for the adult. But the Manchu translation simply translates—'Great learning.' It was composed by *Tsang-tsz* 曾子 one of the pupils of Confucius. It treats on the first principles of government, and forms the text book for school boys at a very early age, when they commit it to memory. In later years the teacher expounds its principles. Translations have been made into several European languages, by the Jesuit Missionaries and by others (v. below).

2. The *Chung-yung* 中庸 'The unchangeable middle.' This is a philosophic treatise on the "true medium," by *Tsz-sz* 子思 a relative of Confucius.

3. The *Lun-yu* 論語 'Conversations.' It contains a number of wise sayings by Confucius, at different periods of his life. They refer to questions of religion, ethics, politics, &c. The title is a misnomer, as far as anything like dialogue is concerned, for the remarks are generally of an isolated and fragmentary character.

4. *Meng-tsz* 孟子 'Mencius.' The writings of Mencius, or Meng-tsz, a disciple of Tsz-sz. Mencius died about B.C. 314, and these accounts of his ways and wanderings, and sayings, were compiled and issued by two of his disciples.

These 'Four Books' are the basis of Chinese education, and are committed to memory in the schools by boys of ten or twelve years of age. The text then forms the subject for catechetical lectures by the teachers at future stages of school life. In six volumes.

Translations. "Several translations of the *Sz-shu* have appeared. The *Ta-hio* into English, by R. Morrison D.D., London, 1812; J. Marshman, Serampore, 1814; and C. B. Hillier, Hong-kong 1851-52; into French, by G. Pauthier, Paris, 1837; and into Latin, by Bayer, in *Museum Sinicum.* 1730. The *Chung-yung*, into Latin, by Prosper Intorcetta, Goa, 1676; and subsequently into French, by Abel Rémusat, Paris, 1817. The *Lun-yu*, into German, by Wilhelm Schott, Halle, 1826; into English, by J. Marshman, Serampore, 1809. The *Meng-tsz*, into Latin, by Stanislaus Julien, Paris, 1824.

31. Sz shu ching vun.

四 書 正 文

'The correct text of the Four Books.' A school edition, having the plain text, and without any commentary, but only occasional glosses on the words.

32. Sz shu chin pun.

四 書 眞 本

'The true and original text of the Four Books.' A school edition in four volumes, now bound in one.

33. Hiau king.

孝 經

'The classic of filial piety,' said to have been recorded by a disciple of Confucius, as containing his opinions on the subject; originally in eighteen chapters, but a copy was found when the house of Confucius was pulled down, having twenty-two chapters. Many Chinese scholars doubt its genuineness, and say that the doctrines it contains are at variance with those of Confucius. This forms part of the *Kiu-king* (q. v. 29) v. Wylie's *Notes*, p. 7.

---

§ III. BUDDHIST WORKS.

The Buddhistic literature of China consists for the most part of translations of the sacred books of the Buddhists, which were written originally in the language of India—in Sanscrit, or more probably in Pali. Of these translations there were three classes, corresponding with like divisions in the originals. Even the general title of the whole in Sanscrit was transferred into Chinese. The three divisions of the Buddhist sacred books were named *Tr'pîtaka* त्रिपिटक, which the Chinese translators rendered *San-tsang* 三藏, 'the three receptacles, or collections.' The first, containing the actual words of Buddha, the *sûtra* सूत्र, was provided with an equivalent in *king* 經 'classic'; the second, relating to discipline and order, *vinaya* विनय found its counterpart in *lu* 律 'a measured composition—as in music;' the third, which entered on the discussion of abstruse doctrines of philosophy—*abhidharma* अभिधर्म was represented by the comprehensive term *lun* 論 'discourse, or discussion.'

These terms were very generally employed in translations for the *sûtra, vinaya* and *abhidharma* classes of Buddhist works. But they seem to have deviated somewhat from this rule occasionally. The *Prajnâ Pâramitâ* for example, which relates entirely to speculative philosophy, is dignified with the title of *king*, equivalent to *sûtra*, although it belongs to the *abhidharma* class.

34. Ta pan nyi po lo nu to king.

大 般 若 波 羅 蜜 多 經

This is a translation, from Sanscrit or Prakrit, into Chinese, of the *Mahâ prajnâ pâramitâ sûtra* महा प्रज्ञा पारमिता सूत्र compiled by *Kashyapa*, made by *Hiuen-ts'ang* 玄奘 the traveller to India from China, A.D., 630. It is in 600 chapters, and is now bound in 24 volumes, imperial 8vo.

This work belongs to the third class or division of Buddhistic writings, called in Sanscrit *Abhidharma* अभिधर्म, and is a system of metaphysical philosophy, written originally in Sanscrit or Pali, and translated by Imperial command. The word *prajnâ* प्रज्ञा means 'understanding,' and *pâramitâ* पारमिता said to signify according to Chinese, *tau-pi-gan* 到 彼 岸 'to arrive at *that* shore.' It is a *dharma*, the first of the nine, and contains 8000 *slokas*. Hodgson calls it a *Nyâya shâstra* or a work of a scientific character. Burnouf describes the *Prajnâ pâramitâ* '*La perfection de la sagesse—une espèce de somme philosophique où se trouve contenue la partie spéculative la plus élevée du Buddhisme*' (B. I., I. p. 68).

The *Prajnâ Pâramitâ* forms the second division of the *Ka-gyur* in Tibetan (a copy of which is deposited in the India Office Library) under the title of *Sher-ch'hin*, in twenty-one vols.

35. Fang kwang pan nyi po lo mi king.

放 光 般 若 波 羅 蜜 經

The *Prajnâ Pâramitâ sûtra* epitomised, and entitled the *Fang-kwang* or 'Light emitting.'* It is in thirty chapters, now bound in two volumes. The translation of this work from Sanscrit into Chinese was made in the third century of our era by *Chŭ-su-lan* 竺 叔 蘭 and *Wu-lo-cha* 無 羅 叉.

This edition was printed A.D. 1840 from the blocks cut in 1610, and which are still preserved at Kia-hing.

36. Mo ho po jo po lo mi king.

摩 訶 般 若 波 羅 蜜 經

A translation of the *Mahâ prajnâ pâramitâ sûtra*, in an abridged form. This is also called *Ta-pin-pan-nyi-king*

---

* There is a *Boddhisattwa* of this name, *Fang-kwang*, a picture of whom may be seen in the *Ki-tsiang-pau-tsan* 吉 詳 寶 懺 (v. 70), leaf 56, but whether this has reference to the above title or not we cannot say.

大品般若經. Translated by *Kiu-mo-lo-shi* 鳩摩 羅什 (Sans. Kumarajîva) and *Tsang-jui-tang* 僧睿 等 in *Yau-ts'in* 姚秦 In thirty chapters, eight vols., now bound in two vols.

37. Kin kang pan nyi po li mi king.

金 剛 般 若 波 羅 蜜 經

A translation of the *Prajnâ pâramitâ sûtra*, with the epithet *Kin-kang* 'Diamond,' prefixed to it, and usually known as the *Vajra Chédika*. It is an abstract merely of the great *Prajnâ pâramitâ*. In one chapter. By *Kiu-mo-lo-shi* (S. Kumarajîva). A translation into German has been made by I. J. Schmidt from the Tibetan version of this work. It is to be found in the *Mémoires de l' Académie des Sciences de St. Pétersbourg*, t. iv., p. 126.

38. Kin kang pan nyi po lo mi p'o kung lun.

般 若 波 羅 蜜 經 破 空 論

A discourse on the 'Diamond' *Prajnâ pâramitâ sûtra*, to show the vanity of things. In one chapter. By *Chi-hien* 智旭, a priest, in the Ming dynasty, A.D., 1368. Translated by *Kiu-mo-lo-shi* (S. Kumarajîva).

39. Kin kang san mei king tung tsung ki.

金 剛 三 昧 經 通 宗 記

A translation of the 'Diamond' *Sûtra* of ecstatic meditation, समाधि (S. Samâdhi), with a copious introduction and commentary by *Tsĭ-chen*. Three Chinese volumes, now bound in one.

40. Ta fang kwang fu hwa yen king.

大 方 廣 佛 華 嚴 經

By *Shĭ-cha-nan-da* 實 叉 難 陀 (Sikshananda), a priest of *Udin* (Khoten), in the *T'ang* 唐 dynasty (A.D., 618—904). In 80 chapters—32 vols.—now bound in six vols. This belongs to the 'Great development' (Mahâyâna) *sûtras*, and dates on Chinese authority, B.C. 2nd century, when *Lung-shu* 龍 舒 lived (E).

41. Ta fang kwang fu hwa yen king yau kiai.

大 方 廣 佛 華 嚴 要 解

This is the important parts of the previous work (40) explained. By *Kiai-hwan* 戒 環 a *bikshu*. In two vols.

42. Ta pan nyi pwan king.

大 般 涅 槃 經

A translation of the *Mahâ Nirvâna Sûtra* महा निर्वाण सूत्र. This work gives its name to the fifth division of the *Mahâyâna sûtras*. In 40 chapters—eight vols.—now bound in two vols. By *Tan-wu-t'sin* 曇 無 讖 (Dharmalatsin), a Brahmin of Central India. Appended are two chapters by Jana Baddala, cir. A.D., 500.

43. Nan pun ta pan nyi pwan king.

南 本 大 般 涅 槃 經

The *Mahá Nirvána Sútra*, designated *Nan-pun* or 'Southern.'

44. Miau fa lien hwa king.

妙 法 蓮 華 經

This is a translation of the सद्धर्म पुण्डरीक *Saddharma Pundaríka*, or the 'Lotus of the Good Law.' In seven chapters, three vols., now bound in one vol. By two Hindu priests, *Küi-to* 崛多 and *Ki-to* 笈多 in the *Súi* 隋 dynasty, A.D., 581—618. Besides the parables which it contains, it treats of an important point of doctrine—viz., the fundamental unity of the three means that a Buddha uses for saving a man from the conditions of his existence in this world. A translation of this work from the Sanscrit into French was made by M. Eugène Burnouf, and published in 1852, after the author's death, under the title of *Le Lotus de la bonne loi.*

45. Fa hwa hwei i.

法 華 會 義

'The meanings of words in the *Fă-hwa* 法 華 (44) collected.' The text is translated by *Kiu-mo-lo-shi* 鳩摩羅什 (S. Kumarajiva), A.D., 397—417. In 18 chapters—eight vols.— now bound in three volumes.

46. Miau fa lien hwa king tai tsung hwei i.

妙法蓮花經台宗會義

'The collected meanings of the *Tai-tsung* 台宗 (Elders of *T'ien-tai*) on the *Saddharma Pundarika*.' It is an exposition of the *Miau-fa-lien-hwa-king*, in 16 chapters or books, by *Chi-hiŭ* 智旭. It is one of the standard books of the *T'ien-tai* 天台 sect, hence the title. This school was founded by *Chi-k'ai* 知顗 in the 6th century, and had as its head-quarters a monastery named Tien-tai, in *Chĕ-kiang* 浙江 province.

47. Wei mo kie so shwo king.

維摩詰所說經

'The *sûtra* which *Wei-mo-kiĕ* uttered.' *Wei-mo-kiĕ* in old Chinese may be *Vi-ma-kit*, and according to *Matwanlin* means 'pure.' Translated by *Kiu-mo-lo-shi* 鳩摩羅什 (Sans. Kumarajîva). In three chapters, one vol. The object of the work is to show that without quitting secular life, a deep acquaintance with Buddhist doctrine may be obtained (E).

48. Pei hwa king.

悲華經

'The *sûtra* of the Lotus of Mercy.' In ten chapters, three vols., now bound in one. Translated by *Tan-wu-t'sin* 曇無讖 (S. Dharmalatsin), a Hindu of the 4th century. Buddha describes a world in the south-east, called 'the Lotusworld,' governed by the 'Lotus Buddha.' There a Bodhisattwa asks why he prefers living in this world of vice and misery; he replies, "Out of pity for its suffering inhabitants and from a desire to save them" (E).

49. Lang ka a po to lo pau king.

楞 伽 阿 跋 多 羅 寶 經

'The precious *Langkâvatâra* लंकावतार *sûtra*.' The full term is *Saddharma Langkâvatâra, i.e.,* Instruction of the Good Law given in the Island of Ceylon. It is in two vols. Translated by *Kiŭ-na-pă-tŏ-lo* 求 那 跋 陀 羅 S. *Guna Bhadra*), who lived in the Sung dynasty, A.D., 420—477. This work is similar to the *Prajnâ parâmitâ*, with a tendency to controversy.

50. Fu ting tsun shing to lo ni cheu king.

佛 頂 尊 勝 陀 羅 泥 咒 經

'*Sûtra* of Buddha's most honoured and eminent *to-lo-ni* (Dhâranî), *i.e.,* charms, invocations. Translated by *Fŭ-tŏ-po-le* 佛 陀 波 利 (S. Buddhapâli), a priest of *Ki-pin* (Cophene) in the T'ang dynasty, in the 8th cent.

There is another copy of this work in the library.

51. Ta fang kwang yuen kio siu to lo liau i king.

大 方 廣 圓 覺 修 多 羅 了 義

Sûtra of the meaning of the *Sûtra* of complete perfection.'

In one chapter. Translated by *Fŭ-tŏ-to-lo* 陀佛多羅 (S. Buddhatala) of *Ko-pin* (Cophene), in the T'ang dynasty (A.D., 618—904).

52. Yin ming ji ching li lun heu ki.

因 明 入 正 理 論 後 記

A treatise on logic, translated by *Hiuen-tsang* 玄奘 in the T'ang dynasty (A.D. 618—904). Edited by *Wu-shü-hü* 吳樹虛 of Hang-cheu 杭州, about the middle of the 18th century. Mr. Edkins translates a portion in his list, to be found in the *Journal of the Royal Asiatic Society*, vol. xvi., p. 329.

53. Ching wei shi lun sui chu.

成 唯 識 論 隨 註

This belongs to the *Abhidharma*, or metaphysical class of Buddhist works. It was translated by *Hiuen-tsang* 玄奘 in the T'ang dynasty. The original author was Dharmapara Bodhisatwa (*Hu-fă-pu-să* 護法菩薩), of Southern India. It is in ten chapters, now bound in two vols. It was founded on a Shastra by Vasu Bandhu Bodhisatwa, a native of Northern India, entitled *Wei-shĭ-san-shĭ-lun*, which was an abridgement of the fifth sect of *Yü-kia-sz-ti-lun*. Vasa Bandhu wrote within 900 years after Buddha " entered Nirvana " (E).

54. Fu pun hing tsi king.

佛 本 行 集 經

'The *sùtra* of the actions of Buddha collected.' This is a

BUDDHIST WORKS.

translation of the *Lalita vistara sûtra*, which, according to Burnouf, is *L'histoire divine et humaine du dernier Buddha, Shâkyamuni* (B. I., p. 69). In 60 chapters, 12 vols., now bound in three vols. Translated by *Chen-na-kŭ-to* 闍那屈多 (S. Chenakitta), a Hindu, in the Süi dynasty, A.D., 608—622. It belongs to the *Hĭna yâna* 'Lesser development' *sûtras*.

55. Ching wei shi lun wan shi ping ki.

成 唯 識 論 文 釋 併 記

The same as *Ching-wei-shĭ-lun* (v. 53) only with a commentary by *Wu-shü-hü* 吳 樹 盧 It is in five vols., but now bound in one.

56. Chu king ji sung.

諸 經 日 誦

'Daily chantings from all the *sûtras*.' In two vols. The first volume contains the 'Diamond' *sûtra*, *Kin-kang-king* 金 剛 經, that of *Yŏ-sz* 藥 師 (the Eastern Buddha), a section of the *Fa-hwa* 法 華; the *sûtra* of the feast of hungry ghosts; the smaller *Nirvâna sûtra*, *Niĕ-pan-king* 湟 槃 經, and magical formulæ *sûtra* of the "bloody basin." The second volume contains forms for morning and evening service according to the Buddhist ritual.

57. Chu pan king tsan chi yin.

註 般 經 懺 直 音

The correct sounds of the characters in all the *sûtras*.'

There are here the sounds, expressed by homophonous characters, of all foreign and uncommon words in twenty-two of the well known books of the Buddhists.

58. Chung lun.

中 論

This is part of the collection, entitled; *Fŭ tsang tsĭ yau* 佛 藏 輯 要 (q. v. 63). It is a treatise on the *Madhyamika,* 'middle doctrine,' the originator of which was *Nâgârjuna.* The *Chung-lun* 中 論 was, (in the original) by *Lung-shu-pu-sǎ* 龍 樹 菩 薩, and was translated by *Kiu-mo-lo-shi* 鳩 摩 羅 什 (S. Kumarajîva). It is a translation of the *Prajná múla shâstra tîka.*

59. Fa yuen chu lin.

法 苑 珠 林

This is a Buddhistic encyclopædia in 100 chapters, now bound in eight vols. It is a new edition, well printed. The compiler's name was *Tau-shi* 道 世, a doctor and Buddhist priest, who lived A.D., 668. It contains articles, both general and special, on Buddhism and subjects connected therewith, and has been frequently drawn upon for particulars about the various points of Buddhist faith and practice. The Rev. W. Milne used it in preparing his article on pagodas, printed in the *Journal of the Hong-kong Branch of the Royal Asiatic Society* (vol. v., p. 55), and M. le Professeur Stanislas Julien has translated some stories from it in his *Avadânas, Contes et Apologues Indiens.* References are continually made herein to the Buddhist classics, and quotations are given.

C

60. Fan wang ho chu.

梵 網 合 註

'Collected comments on the *Fan wang sútra.*' Translated by *Kiu mo lo shi* 鳩摩羅什 (S. Kumárajîva). The commentary is by *Chi hien* 智旭. The work belongs to the *vinaya* विनय class. This also bears the title *Fŭ tsang tsĭ yau* 佛藏輯要.

61. Fu shwo chang sheu mi tsui hwo chu.

佛 說 長 壽 滅 罪 護 諸

Sútra, translated by the priest (*çramana* श्रमण) *Fŭ tŏ po li* 佛陀波利 (S. Buddhapâli) of Cophene.

62. Fu shwo ta Mo li chi king.

佛 說 大 摩 里 支 經

'*Sútra* of the *Bodhisatwa Mo-li-chi* 摩里支 (S. Malichi) of the words of Buddha.' Translated by *T'ien-sĭ-tsai* 天息災 a priest of the west, cir. A.D. 1200.

63. Fu shwo u lan pan king.

佛 說 盂 蘭 盆 經

This belongs to the miscellaneous *sútras.* Translated in the 3d century by *Chu-fă-hu* 竺法護.

64. Fu tsang tsi yau.

佛 藏 輯 要

'The important parts of the Buddhist collection.' This is a general name attached to several books.

65. Hwa yen yuen jin lun kiai.

嚴 華 原 人 論 解

A discourse on Buddhism as compared with Confucianism and Tauism, and on the origin of mankind. The author was *Tsung mĭ* 宗密, a priest of the T'ang dynasty, and the commentator was *Yuen kiŏ* 圓覺 of the Yuen dynasty. Other scholars of the Ming and Tsing dynasties had to do with the present edition.

66. Ji ko pien mung lio kiai.

日 課 便 蒙 畧 解

'Daily lessons for young learners, brief with explanations.' By a Shaman (çramana) of the metropolis, A.D., 1730. It contains invocations, prayers, &c. One volume.

67. Ju shi tau ping sin lun.

儒 釋 道 平 心 論

A discourse respecting the three religions practised in China —viz., the *Ju* 儒, *i.e.*, the Confucianist; the *Shĭ* 釋, *i.e.*, the

BUDDHIST WORKS.

Buddhist; and the *Tau* 道 *i. e.,* the Tauist. The work is b
Liu mĭ 劉謐 a native writer, a Buddhist, who, of course
defends his own religion against the others. One volume.

68. K'ai yuen shi kiau lu.

開 元 釋 教 錄

A Buddhist bibliography, containing the names of all the
Buddhist books which were translated into Chinese from A.D.,
67 to A.D., 730, by 176 authors. The book contains in all the
names of 2278 titles; many of the books referred to are
however, lost. The author of this work was *Chi shing* 智昇
A.D., 730. The titles of the books are arranged in chronological order, and brief notices of the authors are attached to
each title. At the end of the first part there is a list of 49
catalogues of the Buddhist books. In the second part, which
is arranged in seven sections, existing originals as well as
translations are mentioned, and also other particulars relating
to the books. It is in 20 books, large 8vo size, and is now
bound in two vols. (Cf. Wylie's *Notes on Chinese Literature*
p. 116.)

69. K'ai yuen shi kiau lu lio ch'u.

開 元 釋 教 錄 畧 出

A catalogue of Buddhist books, giving the names of their
authors or translators, the dynasty under which they were published, the number of chapters, and the number of sheets which
each contains. This is a summary of the preceding work. In

20 chapters, now bound in one volume. By *Chi shing* 智昇 a *sha mun* 沙門 (Sans. çramana), cir. A.D., 730.

70. K'e king lu su.
刻 經 錄 叙

A list of prefaces respecting the engraving of the blocks for the Buddhist scriptures. They are by different authors in praise of the books and those at whose expense the great collections were published. One volume.

71. Ki tsiang pan tsan hing L
吉 祥 寶 懺 行 議

A liturgical work belonging to a class of books corresponding to the German *Buszbuch*. Mr. Edkins says they are addressed to Manjusri,* Amitâbha Buddha, and Avalokiteçvara (*Kwan-yin* 觀音), and that works of this class correspond to the Nepaulese *sûtras*, which Burnouf describes. The book contains 50 well-engraved outlines of deities and demons. One volume.

72. King tsang yo shwo.
經 藏 約 說

A collection of *sûtras*, in five Volumes, by *Fǎ t'ien* 法天;— 50 separate works, the chief of which are:—

1. *Fǔ shwǒ tang lai pien king*, 佛 說 當 來 變 經 'The *sûtra* of changes to come,' uttered by Buddha. Translated by *Chǔ fǎ hu* 竺 法 護 in the 3d century.

* *Wun-chu-n-li* 文珠師利 Manjusri Bodhisattwa.

2. *Pu să sang ti king,* 菩薩生地經 'The *sútra* of the native land of the Bodhisattvas. Translated by *Chi kien* 支兼 an *upásaka* from the Getæ country, in the 2d century.

3. *Shen hing fă siang king,* 禪行法想經 '*Sútra* of contemplation.' Translated by *An shi kau* 安世高 in the 2d century.

4. *Wăn chu sz li wăn pu ti king,* 文珠師利問菩提經 'The *sútra* of *Manjusri's* enquiries on knowledge.' Translated by *Ku mo lo shi* (Sans. Kumarajîva).

5. *Ching tsan ta shing kung te king,* 稱讚大乘功德經 'The *sútra* in praise of the merits of the *Mahâyâna* (doctrine).' Translated by *Hiuen ts'ang*

73. K'ung tsio ming wang cheu king.

孔雀明王咒經

The book of the Dhâranî of the King of Madhurâ.

One chapter in manuscript, between boards. Translated by *Kiu mo lo shi* 鳩摩羅什 (S. Kumarajîva).

74. Kwei yuen king.

歸元經

'The mirror of return to first principles '—*i.e.*, the state of rest and purity described and inculcated by the Buddhists. This is a Buddhist play of the *Tsing t'u* 土淨 (pure land) school, by *Chi tă* 智達 a priest of *Hang cheu,* 杭州, in the

17th century. Such plays are acted in Tauist temples; much of them is in the Mandarin dialect, and they consist of chantings and recitations coming alternately. The scenes are taken from the *Amitâbha sûtra*, that is, the *Wu liang sheu king* 無量壽經, which is the text book of the Tsing t'u school (Edkins, Budd. Lit. of China, in *Journal of the Royal Asiatic Society*, Vol. XVI., p. 334.)

75. Lan pan hwei tswan.
蘭 盆 會 纂

Various explanations of points in the Buddhist faith, with notes on the Pali words and Buddhistic expressions. By *Chu fă hu* 竺法護 of the Western Tsin dynasty.

76. Lan pan i kwei.
蘭 盆 儀 軌

Buddhist formula used in the investiture of priests, &c., with explanations of Pali words. This is a part of the above work (74), and forms with it one volume.

77. Lien tsung tsi yau.
蓮 宗 輯 要

'Important selections of the Lotus-school,' which is a branch of the *Tsing t'u* school; the *Amitâbha Buddha sûtra* stands first. In two volumes.

40　　　　　BUDDHIST WORKS.

78. Ling tsiu yi pin shen sz yu lu.
靈 就* 一 彬 禪 師 語 錄

The teachings of Yi pin, of the Vulture Peak† of the
Esoteric school of the Buddhists.　He belonged to the temple
of Ling tsiu.　It was compiled by his disciples at the close of
the last century.　In two chapters,—one volume.

79. Lung shu tsing t'u wan.
龍 舒 淨 土 文

'The Lung shu essay on the *Tsing t'u.*'　By Wang jǐ hiu
王日休 who says that he compiled it from the *King* 經
(*i.e.,* the Sútras) and all the records,—Chuen ki 傳記.　He
was born at *Lung shu,* hence the name prefixed to the title.
He lived under the Sung dynasty (A.D. 960—1127).　The
preface to this edition is dated A.D. 1806.　It is in two vols.
Dr. W. Schott, of Berlin, has made a translation, which may be
found in his work, *Ueber den Buddaïsmus in Hochasien und
China.*　Berlin, 1846.

80. Pe chang tsung lin tsing kwei ching i ki.
百 丈 叢 林 清 規 證 義 記

This is a modern edition of the work, called Tsing kwei.
Regulations of the Buddhist priesthood.　A collection of
Buddhist rules, with their verifications and meaning.　By Pe
Chang, a noted priest of the 8th century.　In six volumes, A.D.
1823.　In one volume.

---

* This character should have the radical 鳥 attached below.

† The "Vulture Peak" (*Ling tsiu*) was a mountain near Râjâgriha, which
was famous for its caverns, and where many ascetics lived; *v.* Eitel's *Handbook for Students of Chinese Buddhism,* 43, a.

81. Ming yin wan chi pin shen sz ch'u lu.

鵬 因 文 質 彬 禪 師 初 錄

A List, by Chi pin, a priest.　One volume.

82. Shen mun k'o sung tsi yau.

禪 門 課 誦 輯 要

A collection of six small Buddhist *sûtras*, and two other small works, prefaced by an account of the introduction of Buddhism into China.　The *sûtras*, with their translators, are :—

1. *Sz shĭ er chang king* 四十二章經 'The *sûtra* of 42 chapters.'　By *Kia yĕ mo tang* 迦葉摩騰 (S. Kâsya-pamadanga) and *Chŭ fă lan* 竺法蘭 in the Later Han Dyn. (1st century).

2. *Fŭ i kiau king* 佛遺教經 'The *sûtra* of Buddha's bequeathed instruction, or, the Last Words of Buddha.'　By *Kiu mo lo shĭ* 鳩摩羅什 (S. Kumarajîva).

3. *Pă ta jin kiŏ king* 八大人覺經 'The *sûtra* of the eight perceptions of the Great Man.'　By *An shi kau* 安世高 a *çramana* of the Later Han Dyn.　It is an epitome of principles of Buddhism—its view of human life, and the means of escaping from its evils.

4. *Yŏ sz liu li kwang ju lai pun yuen kung tĕ king* Translated by Hiuen tsang.　V. No. 97 of this Catalogue.

5. *Fŭ shwŏ a mi tŏ king* 佛說阿彌陀經 'The *Amitâbha Sûtra*, spoken by Buddha.　By Kumarajîva.

BUDDHIST WORKS.

6. *Pă shĭ pă fŭ tsan mei king* 八十八佛懺悔經 The *sûtra* of repentance of the 88 Buddhas, who are here invoked.

7. *Tsing tu wan* 淨土文 The author's name is lost.

8. *Nien fŭ yuen k'i* 念佛緣起 Introduction to the invocation of Buddha (*Amitâbha*) and Bodhisattwas, with the number of the repetitions.

83. Shi u ho shang yu lu.

石 屋 和 尚 語 錄

The prose and verse composition of the Priest, *Shĭ-ŭ* 石屋 who was a native of *Chang shŭ* 常熟 in the province of *Kiang su* 江蘇 A.D. 1273. In one volume 8vo. This edition is designated *Chi na* 支那 or 'Chinese.'

84. Shu ho t'ien t'ai san shing shi tsuen tsi.

續 和 天 台 三 聖 詩 全 集

A collection of verses by three priests of the *T'ien t'ai* 天台 monastery. Their names were Fung kan, Han shan, and Shĭ te. They lived in the 7th century, at T'ien t'ai, near Ningpo. In two vols. The preface by the Emperor Yung Ching 雍正 bears date 1733.

85. Sz tsi ta sz yi kau.

思 齊 大 師 逸 藁

A collection of tracts in prose and verse, by a Chinese Buddhist, who lived at Hangchow in the 17th century. He belonged to the Tsing-t'u school. In this title he is called the *Sz tsi ta sz*, which Mr. Edkins translates, " The even-minded teacher."

86. Shen mun ji sung.

禪 門 日 誦

Selections for daily services from all the *sútras*. A number of devotional extracts from the Buddhist classics by different authors. The full title has Chu king 諸 經 prefixed, meaning that the passages are selected from ' all the classics.'

87. Ta hwei pu kio shen sz shu.

大 慧 普 覺 禪 師 書

Oral teachings of the esoteric school. This volume is in manuscript. The date of the original is A. D. 1580. This is dated 46th year of Kien lung.

88. Ta shing chi kwan Fa mun shi yau.

大 乘 止 觀 法 門 釋 要

The subject of this is the mystic doctrine of the *Chi kwan* of the *Maháyána* school. The title reads :—" The important parts translated of the Buddhists' doctrine, entitled *Chi kwan* 止 觀 of the ' Great Development ' school. The meaning of *chi* is ' to stop,' and *kwan* is ' to observe.' " The author's name is *Chi hien* 智 旭 This edition was published in 1826.

89. Tan king.

壇 經

A work containing the teaching of *Ta mo* 達 摩 (Bodhi-dharma) who died A.D. 529 or thereabouts. By his disciples.

This appears to be the only Buddhist work by a Chinese author bearing the title of *King* 經 (*sûtra*). It belongs to the esoteric school.

90. Tsai kia liu yau kwang tsi.

在 家 律 要 廣 集

'A collection of important works, on discipline for the laity,' edited by Chi hien. It contains fifteen works, in three volumes. Noticeable are :—

1. Extract from the *Sz fun liŭ tsang* 四 分 律 藏 a short and interesting account of the first Upâsakas and Upâsikas, Buddhist Seculars. Translated about A.D. 500 by Buddhayagama, assisted by Chu fa nien.

2. *Kiai siau tsai king* 戒 消 災 經 *sûtra* for avoiding suffering by submitting to Buddhist rules.

3. *Fu shwo chai king* 佛 說 齋 經 *sûtra* of fasting. These two latter were translated by Chi kien 支 謙 an Upâsaka from the Getæ country about A.D. 200.

4. Extracts from the Fan wang king 梵 綱 經 with comments.

5. Extracts from the Upâsa kiai king 優 婆 塞 戒 經 *sûtra* of the rules of the Upâsakas. Translated by Dharma-latsus. (E.)

91. Tsing mie jen hiang tsi.

淨 業 染 香 集

A number of biographical notices of Chinese Buddhists. The author belonged to the *Ts'ing tu* school. By *Wu ling* 悟靈 A.D. 1823.

92. Tsung king lu.

宗 鏡 錄

A thesaurus of Buddhist doctrines in 100 chapters. By the priest *Chi kio* 智覺 of the Sung dynasty (A.D. 960-1127) In 50 books, now bound in three volumes.

93. Tsz pei tsan.

慈 悲 懺

A book of extracts, forming a kind of ritual or devotional work—*Bussbuch*. In one volume.

94. Tung tsung shi tsz i wan.

洞 宗 世 次 疑 問

Description of doubtful points in the succession of the *Tsau-tung* school. (E). The preface is by *Hiau tsing* 曉青.

This volume contains many notices, biographical, literary and historical of the esoteric schools and their authorship. (E).

95. Twan tsi sin yau.

斷 際 心 要

The necessary things for separating the priests' heart (from secular objects). By *Hwei hi yün* 諱希運 from Fukien province, who died A.D. 847. The preface is dated A.D. 858. In one volume.

96. U lan pan king.

盂 蘭 盆 經

This is merely another title for No. 74. (q.v.)   In one chapter.   Translated by *Chŭ fă hu* 竺法護 of the western *Tsin* 晉 dynasty, (A.D. 936.944).   In one volume. cf. 74.

97. Wei mo kie so shwo king.

維 摩 詰 所 說 經

The *sûtra* which was spoken by *Wei mo kië* 維摩詰, Mr. Edkins tells us that in old Chinese this was pronounced *Vi ma kit*, and that the name according to Matwanlin means 'pure.' The person indicated was a secular believer in Buddhism. The author's name was Kumarajîva.

98. Yi tai king yin i.

一 切 經 音 義

'The meaning of the sounds of the whole of the *sûtras*.' A glossary of the Sanscrit words, transliterated or translated, which occur in the Buddhist books from the Sanscrit, as they appear in the Chinese translations.   By *Hiuen ying* 玄應 in the 7th. century.   In 26 chapters, now bound in one volume.

99 Yo sz liu li kwang ju lai pun yuen kung te king.

藥 師 瑠 璃 光 如 來 本 願 功 德 經

A Buddhist *sûtra*, having reference to *Yŏ sz* (the Eastern Buddha).   Translated by *Hiuen ts'ang* 玄奘.

100. Yuen kio siu to lo liau i king.

圓 覺 修 多 羅 了 義 經

'The *sútra* of the *sútra* of the meaning of complete perfection.' Translated by Buddhatala 佛 陀 多 羅 of Kipin (Cophen) in Kabul.

101 Yuen tsi fa wei.

雲 樓 法 彙

A collection of the writings of *Chu hung* 株 宏 principal of the Buddhist monastery of *Yün tsi*, at *Hang cheu* 杭 州, an eminent writer of the 17th. century. It contains commentaries on the *sútras*, articles on Buddhist faith and practice, letters &c. There are also contained in it some controversial papers on the Christian religion, to which he was led by a perusal of the works of Matthew Ricci. He belonged to the *Lin tsi* 臨 齊 school. Thirteen books, now bound in two volumes.

102. Yuen tsi tsing t'u hwei u.

雲 樓 淨 土 彙 語

This is a collection of Buddhist tracts, on avoiding taking life, and on worshipping Buddha. By *Chu hung* 株 宏 of the *Yün tsi* monastery, a writer of the 17th. century, who was commonly called *Lien ch'i ta sz* 蓮 池 大 師 or 'the great teacher of the Lotus Lake.'

103. A-pi-ta-mo fa chi lun.

阿 毗 達 磨 發 智 論

This is a treatise upon knowledge arising from the *abhidharma*, the whole work is in 20 chapters, but here is unfortunately only a fragment, the 17th. and 18th. chapters. It was written by *Ka to yen ni tsz* 迦 多 衍 尼 子 (S. Katayeni putra) and translated by *Huien ts'ang*. Printed in 1637.

104. Yung ming sin fu chu.

永 明 心 賦 註

An abridgment of a larger work on the esoteric doctrine of the Buddhists, by *Yung ming* 永明 of the *Sung* 宋 dynasty; reprinted by the order of the Emperor *Yung ching* 雍正, whose preface is prefixed.

The present edition bears date 1838. In two volumes, now bound in one.

105. Wu liang i king.

無 量 義 經

The *sûtra* of infinite or immeasurable justice. In one volume. The original author was *Liu k'iu* 劉虬, the translator was *Tan mo ka to ye she* 曇摩伽陀耶舍 a *çramana* of India.

106. Yu kia she shi yau tsi.

瑜 伽 施 食 要 集

A sort of Buddhist prayer book, full of invocations to *Kwan yin* and other divinities. In the place of title page there is a plate of twenty strange characters, such as are used to express the *dharani* &c. They correspond in some degree with the *Lansha* characters used by the Buddhists in Tibet. In one volume, Imp. 8vo.

III. MISCELLANEOUS WORKS.

107. Ching hiang lie.

貞 享 曆

Astronomical calculations in Sinico-Japanese. By *Swan chi* 筭哲. The book is in manuscript on the mulberry paper of the Japanese. Seven volumes, now bound in one.

108. Ching yin tsui yau.

正 音 撮 要

'The Important Points of the True Sounds.' One of the text books for Chinese in learning Mandarin. This is several chapters from the book in Chinese and English, the latter by Robert Thom, late H.M. Consul at Ningpo. (8vo. Ningpo.) This book contains also some translations from the *Hung leu mung* 紅 樓夢 'Dreams of the Red Chamber,' a novel in the Peking dialect.

109. Chu tsz tsuen shu.

朱 子 全 書

The complete works of *Chu tsz* 朱子 the Philosopher. In sixty-six chapters, now bound in six volumes. Published by Imperial authority, and edited by *Hung-tsz-li* 熊賜履 a President of the Board of Civil Office, *Li-kwang-ti* 李光地 a President of the Board of Civil Office, *Wu-han* 吳涵 an Academician, and twelve others of the *literati*. The first twenty-five chapters treat on the "Four Books;" chapters 25-40, on the "Five Classics;" chapter 41, on Music (*Lŏ* 樂); chapters 42-48, on Metaphysics (*Sing-li* 性理); chapters 49,

50, on Cosmogony and Phænomena of Nature; chapter 51, on Demons and Spirits (*kwei shin* 鬼 神); chapters 52-57, on Doctrines and their Teachers (*Tau t'ung* 道 統.) The remaining chapters contain essays on various subjects connected with poetry and literature in general, the names of all eminent writers on ancient literature and poetry, etc.*

110. Hang hai kin chin.

航　海　金　針

'The golden needle for navigating the ocean.' The Law of Storms, by D. J. Macgowan, M.D., in three chapters, imperial octavo. Ningpo, 1853.

111. Chu tsz tsi yau.

朱　子　節　要

This is a selection of the important parts of Chu hi's works

---

* *Chu tsz* 朱子, more correctly *Chi hi* 朱熹, also known by the name *Wen kung* 文公 'Prince of Letters,' was born in the 12th century and established his reputation as one of the most thorough scholars and writers of his own or any age. His aim seems to have been to rescue the learned works of his predecessors from the oblivion of antiquity, and to make their writings something more than a dead letter by elucidating their meaning in the simplest and clearest language. By his great erudition he threw light upon the darkest passages so as to give a practical effect to their intention. His commentaries on the Classics are still the chief even now. The Chinese say that "Confucius alone understood Heaven and Chu tsz alone understood Confucius;" hence their admiration of him is extreme. Besides these extensive commentaries, he wrote numerous essays on metaphysical subjects and edited a complete history of China, and wrote a separate treatise of a philosophic kind, entitled, *Sing li* 性理 'Nature and Order,' in which he appears to make Heaven, Nature, and Fate to be the great first principles of the universe.

in Chinese and Manchu. The translation in the latter language dates 1676. In one volume. The Manchu title runs: *Chu tsi chiyeĭ yau bithe.*

121. Han kiu ch'uen.

好 逑 傳

'The Fortunate Union.' A romance in four small volumes, now bound in one. A translation of it appeared in French during the last century, and also an English version founded thereon under the title of the "Pleasing History," but the most complete translation is by Sir John F. Davis, Bart., K.C.B. late Governor of Hongkong, and forms a volume of the Oriental Translation Fund's publications.

113. Hwa ch'uen.

畫 傳

A book of instruction in drawing, arranged and classified. By *Li liĕ-ung* 李笠翁. In four volumes, now bound in two.

114. I kien chi.

夷 堅 志

'Accounts of marvels in foreign lands.' Stories of strange events, which have occured in the experience of travellers and others. In twenty volumes, now bound in five.

115. Ji ki ku sz.

日 記 故 事

'Memoranda on Ancient Affairs.' It consists of short moral

stories for children, illustrated with rude wood-cuts. The principal headings are in large type as texts on which the stories are founded. Dr. Morrison has translated the twenty-four examples of filial piety in his Chinese Dictionary (vol. i. p. 724 *et seq*).

116. Kung tsz kia yu.

孔 子 家 語

'The family traditions concerning *K'ung tsz*' (Confucius). By *Wang sŭ* 王 肅 in the 3rd century. The work is confessedly spurious, but is valued for the traditions founded on fact, which are contained therein. Two volumes, now bound in one.

117. Hien tsing ngau ki.

閒 情 偶 寄

Literary essays by *Li liĕ-ung* 李 笠 翁 A. D. 1670. They relate to Poetry and Criticism chiefly, and are based upon Chinese philosophy (*Wang tau* 王 道 the doctrines of the ancient Kings).

This author appears also to have produced a work on drawing (v. *Hwa chuen* 108.)

118. Kiun shu pi kau.

羣 書 備 考

Examinations and critical essays on literature collected.

119. Kwang tung sin yu.

廣 東 新 語

'New conversations on Kwang Tung.' The physical geography and antiquities of the province of Canton, explained in a conversational and free style. The various phænomena of nature and the productions of the earth are discussed. In ten volumes, now bound in three. By *Kü Ung-shan* 屈翁山.

120. Kwang yu ki.

廣 興 記

'Record of the Vast World.' A geographical work on the empire of China, originally compiled by *Lü Ying-yang* 睦應陽 under the Ming dynasty; reproduced under *Kang hi* 康熙 (1662-1722) by *Tsai Fang-ping* 祭方炳 In twenty-four books, now bound in three volumes.

This work was utilized by M. E. Biot in his *Dictionnaire des noms anciens et moderns des villes et arrondissements compris dans l'empire chinois.* Paris 1842.

121. Ma i siang fa.

麻 衣 相 法

A little book for the common people upon palmestry and various superstitions.

122. Pe mei sin yung t'u chuen.

百 美 新 詠 圖 傳

'Portraits and Accounts of Celebrated Beauties.' Outlines of female figures with brief descriptions. The book is very beautifully printed on white paper, and was stitched in scarlet wrappers with silk. Four volumes, now bound in one.

MISCELLANEOUS WORKS.

123. Pe kia sing kau lio.

百 家 姓 考 畧

An explanation of all the Surnames of the Chinese, their origin, local settlements, etc. This is a common school book, but the present edition has a commentary. One volume.

124. Pun tsau pi yau yuen chi.

本 草 備 要 原 始

Chinese Herbal and Materia Medica. Illustrated with wood engravings of plants, etc. By *Li Ching-yu* 李正宇 Eight volumes, now bound in two.

125. San kwo chi.

三 國 志

'History of the Three States.' A romance founded upon the history of the Three Kingdoms and the civil wars in China, which lasted nearly a century, from A.D. 168-265. In it some of the most celebrated heroes and statesmen of Chinese history figure. In twenty volumes, now bound in four.

The author's name was *Lo Kwan-chung* 羅貫中, who founded it upon a real history by *Chin-sheu* of the Tsin dynasty, A translation of a portion of it has been made into French by M. Theod. Pavie, from the Manchu version.

126. San tsz king hiun ku.

三 字 經 訓 詁

'The Three-Character-Classic with Instructions and Explanations.' This is an elementary school book composed in stanzas of three characters each, and containing the simple elements of Chinese lore in a terse form. The facts are isolated, and refer to a variety of subjects, philosophy, history, biography, etc. It was made by *Wang Pŭ-heu* 王 伯 原 about the end of the Sung dynasty (A. D. 960-1278).

There are two editions of this book in the Library; one of these is explained by a running commentary. The Chinese boy commits the whole to memory before he understands its meaning, and after he is somewhat advanced in his studies he receives an explanation of it from his teacher.

127. Shan hai king.

山 海 經

'Classic of the Mountains and Seas.' This work professes to be an account of the world, but is in reality a book of myths. It is attributed to *Pĕ yĭ* 伯 益 minister of the Emperor Shun 舜 (B. C. 2255). In the Imperial catalogue it is classed under *Siau shwo* 小 說 "Light Literature." It is in eight chapters—four volumes—now bound in one.

This edition is what is called a "sleeve edition." It was published under the supervision of *Kŏ pŏ* 郭 璞 of the Tsin 晉 dynasty and *Wu chung-hang* 吳 中 行 of the Ming 明 dynasty (1368-1647).

128. Shou shi li i.

受 時 曆 儀

A work on astronomy by a celebrated author, Ko Chung-king 郭中敬 under Koubilai Khan in the Yuen 元 dynasty (A.D. 1260-1341). This is a Japanese edition of the work. Seven volumes, now bound in one.

129. Shing king.

聖 經

A translation of the Old and New Testament by Dr. Marshman into Chinese, and printed with metallic type at Serampore, Five volumes, 8vo.

130. Sin i chau shu.

新 遺 詔 書

The new Testament translated into Chinese by Dr. Robert Morrison. The character of the style is the classical, but a too literal rendering of the original has prevented its being worthy of Chinese admiration. In eight volumes, 8vo. A.D. 1815.

131. Swan hio k'i mung.

算 學 啟 蒙

'Instructions in the laws of Arithmetic.' A Japanese school-book. By *Sung ting chu Shi ki* 松廷朱 世傑 Dated the first year of *Manji* 萬治 A.D. 1658.

132. Sz wu yuen hwei.

事 物 原 會

On the origin of things. A small pamphlet.

133. Sz ku tsuen shu mu lu.

四 庫 全 書 目 錄

Catalogue of the books in the "Four Libraries"—the Imperial Library—of Peking. This is a mere list of the names of the books, the names and dates of authors arranged, as is usual with the Chinese, under four divisions; *king* 經 'classics,' including the various annotated editions, *shi* 史 'history' and every subject connected therewith, *Tsz* 子 'philosophy,' *Tsĭ* 集 'collections,' including poetry and *belles-lettres*. Other works of imagination and fiction are not included in this catalogue at all, being looked upon by the Chinese as of too trivial a nature to form part of the national collection. It is in twenty chapters or books, and now bound in three volumes.

134. Tan kwei tang.

丹 桂 堂

A book on casting nativities, palmestry, and other similar arts. A small pamphlet, date, 1820.

185. Ta tsing hwei tien.

大 清 會 典

'Collected Ordinances of the Ta Tsing Dynasty.' Published in 1818 by order of the Emperor, who had caused the older work to be completed.

This great work contains not only the present laws and regulations, but the changes which these have undergone since the establishment of the Manchu rule in 1644. The whole work is in 920 books, under twenty-four heads, and there is a supplement in 132 books, containing subjects relating to ceremonies, etc., and concluding with a topographical account of China, with maps.

In this encyclopædia of state-forms, every office, both small and great, is described, the duties of each specified, and the changes which each office has undergone is detailed. This work is bound in two sets, one of fifteen volumes, the other of four, nineteen volumes in all. The book has frequently been drawn upon, and Father Hyacinth has availed himself of the information contained in the *Hwei tien* in his statistical description of the Chinese empire (STATISTICHESKOE OPISANIE KITAISKOÏ IMPERII Petersburg, 1842, 2 vols. 8vo.)

186. Ta tsing liu li.

大 清 律 例

'Laws of the Great Tsing Dynasty.' This is the Criminal Code of the Chinese. This is one of the later editions, of which there have been many from the time of Kang hi, 1646 to 1829.

The body of the work is arranged under the following heads : 1. General Laws ; 2. Civil Laws ; 3. Fiscal Laws ; 4. Military Laws ; 5. Laws relative to Public Works. (v. *Chinese Repository*, vol. ii. p. 10). There are two copies, one of forty-nine books, four vols., 12mo ; the other of thirty-four books, in three vols., imperial 8vo.

A very complete index of the contents of this work is given by Sir John Davis in "The Chinese" I. p. 237. A translation in full was made and published by Sir George Thomas Staunton under the title : " *Ta tsing leu lee*, being the Fundamental Laws and Supplementary Statutes of the Penal Code of China, 4to. London : 1810." A review of this appeared in the *Chinese Repository*. May 1833.

137. Ta tsing tsin shin tsuen shu.

大 清 縉 紳 全 書

The official "Red book" of the Chinese. It contains the names, titles, and offices of the mandarins in all parts of the empire, about which there is also a mass of details. The whole is arranged under the geographical divisions of the empire. The distances of the principal towns from the capital, the customs, places of education, and productions are given under each head.

138. Tang tan pi kiu.

登 壇 必 究

'Important Investigations on Military Affairs.' One volume. A work on military art and operations, illustrated with numer-

MISCELLANEOUS WORKS.

ous diagrams of weapons and artifices of war. The title relates to a peculiar custom of the Chinese emperor in conferring a commission for active service. The general's sword is laid upon a high altar, to which the officer ascends and takes it, hence the expression *tang tan* 'ascending the altar.'

139. T'ien chu shi i.

天 主 實 義

This is a work on various points of the Roman Catholic religion by Matteo Ricci in 1601. Wylie gives the following epitome of its contents under eight heads: 1. Creation and Preservation of the Universe; 2. Ignorance of mankind regarding God; 3. The difference between men and brutes, in that man has an immortal soul; 4. The difference between the soul of man and the spiritual powers, and diversity of substances in the universe: 5. Doctrines of metempsychosis and prohibition of taking life exposed, with explanations of the theory of fasting and abstinence; 6. The imperishable character of the mind, with the certainty of heaven and hell; 7. Original goodness of human nature and the peculiar tenets of Christianity; 8. An explanation of European customs, especially the celebacy of the clergy.

140. Tsien tsz wan.

千 字 文

'The Book of a Thousand Characters.' By *Cheu Hing tsz*, A.D. 550. It is a common school-book, and consists of 1,000 different characters exactly, the same word never occurring more than once. The 1,000 characters were collected by *Wang he-che* by command of an emperor of the Liang dynasty. The emperor then gave them to Cheu Hing taz, and commanded him to make an ode with them. He is said to have done so in a single night, and that his hair turned gray in consequence.

There are two editions of this little work in the Library, one contains a commentary of value.

141. T'ung kien kang mu.

通 鑑 綱 目

A General History of China, in ninety-one books. It was originally compiled under the direction of *Chu hi* 朱熹 the philosopher and commentator on the classics. A revised edition by *Chin Jin si* 陳仁錫 was published about A. D. 1630. He divided the work into three parts; *viz.*, 1. The *Tsien pien* 前編 'Former Section;' 2. *Ching pien* 正編 'Principal Section,' and 3. *Sŭ pien* 續 | 'Continuing Section.' It was reprinted in 1708, and several times since. A translation into French was made by Père Maillu, and published in twelve volumes, 4to. in 1777-84. The first part has twenty-five books; the second, sixty books; and the third, twenty-seven books; the whole being bound up in twenty-six volumes.

This work is not so much an independent production as a convenient form of the *Tung kien* 通鑑 which appeared nearly a century before, by the renowned *Sz-ma Kwang* 司馬光 The emperor *Ying tsung* 英宗 (A.D. 1064-1067) commanded the Royal Historiographer Sz-ma Kwang to compose a succinct history of China with correct chronological arrangements, and to make use of the historical works extant, and especially the annals, in preparing it. Sz-ma Kwang finished his work in 1084 and laid it at the feet of the emperor *Shin tsung* 神宗, Ying tsung's successor, who gave it the title of *T'ung kien, i.e.,* 'Complete or thorough Mirror (of Events).' It is in 294 chapters, and includes the history of a period of 1362 years, from the earliest historical period to the beginning of the Sung dynasty (A.D. 960). Facts only are related, the reader is left to form his own independent judgment upon them. Impressed with the worth of the *T'ung kien,* and wishing to increase its usefulness, *Chu hi* 朱熹 (v. p. 50) prefaced the accounts given in detail with a summary, but without in any way altering the sense of any passage. These summaries, which are printed in large characters, are followed by the detailed account and a commentary; thus the original work is enclosed as it were in a net-work, and hence the name *Kang-mu.* The full title therefore signifies: 'The Complete Mirror and Net.'

142. Tung yuen tsa tsz ta tsuen.

東 園 雜 字 大 全

A school-book of rudimentary instruction for young children, —a child's primer—containing outlines of astronomy, geography, genealogy of Confucius, arithmetic, etc., with various useful lists for Chinese boys. This is a very old edition.

143. Shang han shi yen tsing fa.

傷 寒 世 驗 精 法

The laws or methods relating to fevers. A medical work on the subject of fevers, with the Chinese method of treatment. It contains cases and prescriptions. In eight volumes, now bound in two.

144. Yĭ t'ung chĭ.

一 統 志

'A complete account' (of the Chinese empire). The title in full is *Ta tsing yĭ t'ung chĭ* 大清一統志 It is an account of every province, city, mountain, river, etc., of the empire. It was published in the year 1744 under the auspices of the emperor Kau tsung 高宗· It is in 108 chapters, now bound in six volumes, small folio.

The heads of information contained in these are: 1. Situation and boundaries of the provinces; 2. Climate; 3. Historical notices; 4. Notable objects of a natural kind; 5. Customs and dispositions of the people; 6. Cities, canals, and celebrated buildings; 7. Schools and libraries; 8. Number of inhabitants; 9. Area; 10. Government officials; 11. Mountains and rivers; 12. Antiquities; 13. Fortresses and passes; 14. Bridges, etc; 15. Dams; 16. Various monuments; 17. Confucianist temples; 18. Tauist and Buddhist temples; 19. Eminent statesmen; 20. Famous persons of both sexes; 21. Hermits; 22. Natural and artificial productions.

145. Yiu hio chĭ.

幼 學 詩

Odes for the young. One of the Chinese school-books. One volume.

146. Yu chĭ kang chĭ tu.

御 製 耕 織 圖

An Imperial edition of a work on the cultivation of the

MISCELLANEOUS WORKS.

ground and the manufacture of silk. A number of odes and plates in large quarto.

147. Yu kiau li.

玉 嬌 梨

A novel in which the private life and habits of society among the Chinese are well depicted. In twenty-four books, now bound in one volume.

Mr. Abel-Rémusat made a translation of this under the title, *Les deux Cousines*, Paris, 1827, and M. Stainslas Julien, the successor of Mr. Rémusat in the professorship, has recently made a new translation under the same title, Paris, 1864.

148. Yuen t'ien t'u shwo.

圜 天 圖 說

The circular heavens, with plates and explanations. A modern Chinese work on astronomy, based in a great degree on European science, but still erroneous. By *Yuen yuen* 阮 元 assisted by *Tsing lai* 青 來 A beautifully printed edition, presented by J. Reeve, Esq., 1825. Three volumes, now bound in one volume, octavo.

149. Bun kiu Bu kan.

文 久 武 鑑

A Japanese genealogical and statistical guide or 'mirror.' It contains the names, position, heraldic devices, forces, etc., of the Japanese princes and daimios. In five volumes, 12mo., now bound in three.

150. Wan pau tsuen shu.

萬 寶 全 書

'Complete Book of Ten Thousand Precious things.'

A small pocket encyclopædia, for the common people, containing a variety of information upon the usual topics—Astronomy, Geography, History, &c. In thirty chapters. In three volumes, now bound in one. By *Ta chwang* 大倉 and others.

151. Wu kien tsi.

舞 劍 集

On Fencing. A small pamphlet.

———o———

ADDENDA:

CHINESE, MANCHU, AND JAPANESE.

152. Chi wan k'i mung

智 環 啟 蒙

Graduated Reading; comprising a circle of knowledge in 200 lessons. A little book in Chinese and English to assist Chinese boys in the acquirement of English. Printed at Hong Kong at the Anglo-Chinese College 1856., 12mo. one vol. Edited by J. L. (i.e. James Legge, D.D. President).

153. Ch'u hio Yue yin tsi yau.

初 學 粵 音 切 要

"The Beginner's Requirements in the Canton sounds." A Chinese Phonetic Vocabulary containing all the most common characters, with their sounds in the Canton Dialect. Hong-Kong. Printed at the London Missionary Society's Press 1855. No meanings are given, but merely the pronunciation by the *fan tsi* method of initials and finals.

154. Yau-li-pa tsung lun.

咬 裏 吧 聰 論

A little work on the Island of Java, its chief city Batavia; its productions, inhabitants &c. By the Rev. W. Medhurst, D.D. late of Batavia and Shanghai.

155. Ching pu kiau.

正 卜 考

A Japanese work on divination. In three volumes, now bound in one. By *Pan Sin-yiu* 伴信友 *Ta jin* 大人.

156. Yu chi kiuen shen yau yen.

御 製 勸 善 要 言

The Imperial work—Important words for admonishing to virtue –In Chinese and Manchu—Dated the 12th. year of *Shun chi* 順治 (A.D. 1656.) The Manchu title runs thus; *Sain-be huwekiyeburen oyonggo.*

157. Lu ying chi li.

綠 營 識 制

Book of the Regulations of the Army. In eight books, 2 vols., all Manchu, with the exception of the above four characters. It is lettered in French: "Ordinnances de l'Empereur actuel." The Manchu title runs thus; *Hesei toktobuha coohai c'uraka i tese simneren bithe.*

158. Abkai edchen-i tachi hiyan-i hashen-i bithe.

Book of the Doctrines of the Lord of Heaven (in Chinese *T'ien-chü* 天主 the word long since adopted by the Roman Catholics for "God" in the usage of Europeans, and now acknowledged by some Protestant Missionaries to be the most suitable.) In two parts—bound in one volume.

MISCELLANEOUS WORKS.

159. Go tei sen-ji-mon.

五 體 千 字 文

The Thousand Character Classic (c. 140). A Japanese edition with five different forms of the characters and Japanese explanations and notes—small 12mo., one volume—No title page—Modern edition.

160. Tsuen ti sin lun.

全 體 新 論

New account of all the members (of the human body). A work on the European systems of Anatomy by Dr. Benjamin Hobson, (late of the *Kumlefow* Hospital, Canton). One volume, 8vo. 1850-52.

161. Kashira gaki zooho kin mo dzu ye.

頭 書 增 補 訓 蒙 圖 會

'Collected Plates for the Instruction of the Ignorant.' An educational encyclopædia with rude wood-cuts and explanations. A new and augmented edition. In twenty one books; bound in one volume. By Nakamura.

162. Nippon san kai mei san dzu ye.

日 本 山 海 名 產 圖 會

'The Noted Products of the Mountains and Seas of Japan.' A very interesting account of a certain limited number of productions. In five volumes—bound in one.

163. Koku shi riyaku.

國 史 畧

Outline of the History of Japan. This is one of the best histories of that country. It was translated in part by Dr. J J. Hoffman of Leiden in Baron Von Siebold's *Archiv Nippon*. Five volumes, bound in one.

164. Miyako bun shoo shoo.

都 文 狀 章

The Imperial Letter-writer. This is one of the numerous books of its class for instructing people in the phraseology suitable for epistolary correspondence.

165. Dai Nippon yei tai sets yoo mu jin zoo.

大 日 本 永 代 節 用 無 盡 藏

'The Inexhaustable Repository of Useful things concerning Japan.' This contains—History, Poetry, Ceremony, Heraldry, Geography, Arithmetic, Botany, Games and Amusements, Cookery, etc., and a very complete dictionary. The Corean Alphabet, Palmestry, and a great variety of information to all whom it may concern is also contained therein. In two vols.

166. Ye do mei sho dzu ye.

江 戶 名 所 圖 會

The Antiquities of the City of Yedo with Plates and Explanations. In twenty volumes. The history of the various

MISCELLANEOUS WORKS.

monasteries and religious houses, and the legends attached to each are contained in these volumes.

167. Kotoba no Tama no O.

詞 乃 玉 乃 緒

A grammatical and exegetical work on the classical language of Japan. In 6 volumes. By Nakashima Hirotaru.

168. So k'wa.

草 花

Japanese Botany. This is a facsimile of a Japanese Book with introductory notes and translations. Lithographed at Philadelphia, and published by J. B. Lippincott & Co. cir. 1855.

169. Kin ko wa ka.

今 古 和 歌

Introduction to Ancient and Modern Japanese Poetry. In four volumes.

170. Musel echen Isus Ghristos-i tutabuha itohe ghese.

A Manchu translation of the New Testament, printed at St. Petersburg at the expense of the Bible Society of London. Commenced in 1821 by Lipoffzoff, but the whole was not finished until 1836. Eight volumes, now bound in two.

Bibliotheca Lindesiana. Catalogue of Chinese Books and Manuscripts

林赛文库中文印本及写本目录

Bibliotheca Lindesiana

CATALOGUE

OF

CHINESE BOOKS AND MANUSCRIPTS

PRIVATELY PRINTED

MDCCCXCV

PREFACE.

I FEEL that I have to confess to a certain amount of self-interest on each occasion that I print a new volume of the *Bibliotheca Lindesiana*. The subjects are those to which I have lately given the greatest attention, and which prove to be getting out of hand when in manuscript; therefore, I print as an invaluable aid to myself, inasmuch as these several works are themselves Keys or Hand Lists to the General Catalogue of the Library, a work that must proceed slowly, though surely, towards finality.

The world of letters is so wide that I have little fear but that each of these Essays may prove of interest to some of my friends and readers—though in the present case I fancy that they will be small in number.

Other volumes are progressing toward the printing stage: Hand Lists of Oriental Manuscripts; a second and third volume of the Catalogue of Royal Proclamations; a Catalogue of English, French, and Italian Broadsides; the latter language comprising some 6,600 items on the Ecclesiastical and Civil History of Rome, mainly of the XVI. and XVII. centuries. All these I intend to print as they become ready, a time I hope not far distant in the case of one or two of them.

Mr. Edmond in his Introduction has dealt with the Chinese works as I could not have done. He has, I think, done justice to a department of the Library to which my father gave great attention, and which he always regarded with feelings of satisfaction and pride.

CRAWFORD.

HAIGH HALL,
May, 1895.

INTRODUCTION.

THE collection of Chinese books in the library at Haigh Hall is of considerable extent, the number of pên or native volumes being about 8000. It was the design of the late Lord Crawford that the Bibliotheca Lindesiana "should include the best and most valuable books, landmarks of thought and progress, in all cultivated languages, Oriental as well as European." With this object in view he formed with great care the Chinese division of the library, and an examination of the catalogue will show how successful he was in procuring many of the finest editions of the best books in the language.

The foundation of the collection was laid by the purchase *en bloc* of the valuable Chinese library belonging to M. Pierre Léopold Van Alstein, which was sold at Ghent in 1863. The books thus acquired were examined, collated and catalogued by the late Mr. John Williams, Secretary of the Royal Astronomical Society, who devoted much time and care to the work. This critical examination revealed a good many imperfections and duplicates, and such defective or superfluous copies were in most cases disposed of, not being considered worthy of a place in the library. To supplement the Van Alstein collection, which roughly speaking forms numbers 1 to 248 in the progressive "Number Key" to be mentioned later on, Lord Crawford purchased works of value from the library of Pauthier, and also from English, French and German booksellers. In addition to these home operations, an agent was employed in Peking to whom lists of *desiderata* were furnished, and several rare works were thus acquired.

The collection is remarkable for the comparatively trifling number of imperfect works as compared with its extent. It is also

b

INTRODUCTION.

worthy of note that nearly all the books are either in good European bindings, or in the neat *tao*, or native envelopes of cloth or of silk. The general condition internally is also exceptionally good, and many works may be cited as very beautiful examples of xylography. The Chinese drawings in the library at Haigh form a separate collection in 57 volumes of various sizes and importance, and are not included in this catalogue.

The present catalogue has been compiled in great measure from that of Mr. Williams referred to above, but much assistance has been derived from Professor Douglas's *Catalogue of Chinese Books in the British Museum.* The orthography adopted by both scholars is unfortunately that employed by Dr. Morrison in his Dictionary; and although it may be the one best suited for English readers, it must in time be displaced by some system in which the vowel sounds are similar in value to those of the continental languages. Acting upon Professor Douglas's advice, the orthography adopted by Sir Thomas Wade for the Peking dialect in his elementary handbook known as the *Tzŭ Érh Chi* has been used in the present catalogue. To ensure uniformity of treatment every character has been looked up in Giles's *Chinese English Dictionary* in which Wade's orthography is given.

A few words are necessary regarding the system of cataloguing. The titles of the works, and the names of authors and editors, form one alphabetical sequence. The chief entry of each work is by its title, which is transliterated, followed by a translation or short explanation of the title or character of the work, the author's or editor's name, the number of volumes, the size in millimetres and the date when known. Where the work is in manuscript, or produced by some process other than xylography, care has been taken to draw attention to the fact. The author's or editor's names with a reference to the title of the book form the majority of the cross entries. A "Number Key" is appended to the catalogue, in which the titles of the works in Chinese characters are printed in progressive order, the numbers in front of the entries in the catalogue corresponding with those in the " Key." Where numbers are missed in the " Key " the Chinese titles are unknown, or the books have no titles in Chinese characters, or, again, the blanks may indicate where books have been rejected from the Van Alstein collection as stated above.

A number of Manchu books and two or three in the Corean language have been included in this catalogue. The titles of those in Manchu are transliterated in Roman letter, being taken for the most part from the sale catalogue of Klaproth's library ; the Corean books happily had explanatory titles in Chinese.

This should be looked upon as a brief hand-list or preparatory study, rather than a catalogue worthy of the importance of the collection. Very little has been attempted in analysing the polygraphs for which Chinese literature is so famous. Then, too, there are points of interest connected with many of the books, such as *provenance*, autograph notes by men of reputation such as Rémusat, Klaproth and Pauthier, or the exceptional value of the work on account of its rarity and condition—all these and many others are worthy of notice in the catalogue, but they would have been out of place in the present essay. The compiler makes no pretension to Chinese scholarship, and it is with diffidence that he offers this hand-list for the criticism and revision of Sinologues. In conclusion he would express his gratitude to Professor Douglas for encouragement and kind assistance in overcoming several difficulties, which but for his aid would have been insurmountable, and for reading the proofs of the " Number Key." Thanks are also due to Messrs. Stephen Austin & Sons, Hertford, for their care in printing the " Number Key " from " copy " supplied by the compiler.

J. P. EDMOND,
Librarian.

前　言

不得不承认，我每次印刷新一册《林赛文库》（*Bibliotheca Lindesiana*）时都有一点私心。这些书的主题都是我近来最关注的，也是事实证明写本形式最容易丢失的；因此，我印刷这些图文其实是给自己提供无价的帮助，因为这几本书本身就是图书馆一般目录的题解或简明参考目录，这项工作必须缓慢而稳妥地进行。

文字的世界如此广阔，我毫不畏惧，只要每篇文章能够得到友人或读者的青睐，尽管目前我认为这样的人并不多。

其他书籍也即将进入印刷阶段：《东方写本简明参考目录》（*Hand Lists of Oriental Manuscripts*）；《王室公告目录》（*Catalogue of Royal Proclamations*）第二、三册；《英、法、意大利文海报目录》（*Catalogue of English, French, and Italian Broadsides*）；意大利文包括大约6600件主要有关十六和十七世纪罗马教会和民间历史的意大利文藏品。准备就绪后，我打算将它们全部进行印刷，希望在不久的将来就能有一两本面世。

埃德蒙德先生（Mr. Edmond）在《引言》中称，他将我未著录的中文书籍进行了编目。我认为，他使得图书馆的这一门类学问得到了公平对待，对此我父亲高度关注，并且始终感到满意和自豪。

克劳福德伯爵（Crawford）

黑格厅（Haigh Hall），

1895年5月

引　言

黑格厅图书馆的这批中文藏书规模非常庞大，写本或来自当地的图书多达8000册。已故的克劳福德伯爵认为《林赛文库》"应该囊括最出色、最有价值的图书，包含标志着思想和进步的书籍，涵盖各种优雅的语言，既包括东方的书籍，也包括欧洲的书籍。"秉持这一目标，克劳福德伯爵高度关注图书馆中文部的设立，而且，通过查看目录就能发现他在购置中文图书最佳版本方面有多么成功。

　　这批藏书的基础是从皮埃尔·利奥波德·范·阿尔斯坦（M. Pierre Léopold Van Alstein）手中整批购得的中文藏书。1863年，克劳福德伯爵在根特（Ghent）买下了这批颇有价值的图书，时任皇家天文学会（Royal Astronomical Society）秘书的约翰·威廉姆斯先生（Mr. John Williams）生前投入大量时间和精力对这批图书进行了审阅、校勘、编目。通过这项重要的整理工作，发现了很多有瑕疵及重复的图书，大部分情况下会丢弃这些有瑕疵或重复的图书，因为认为它们不配在图书馆占有一席之地。范·阿尔斯坦的藏书主要构成不断增加的"数字索引"（Number Key）中的1至248号。除此之外，克劳福德伯爵从颇节（Pauthier）的藏书中购买了一些有价值的图书，从英国、法国和德国书商中购置了部分书籍，作为补充。除了在国内购买中文图书，他还在北京聘请了一位代理人，将一些急需购置的中文书籍清单交给此人，通过这种方式成功买到几本罕见的图书。

　　这批藏书的非凡之处在于，与图书数量相比，其中的瑕疵本相对较少。还有一点值得注意，几乎所有书籍要么采用上乘的欧式装订，要么装在干净的书套中，或装在当地的布套或丝绸套中。另外，书籍内页的品相一般也非常好，很多图书堪称木版印刷的精美典范。黑格厅图书馆里开本和重要性各异的57册中文绘本单独收藏，未收录在本目录中。

　　这份目录主要根据上文提及的威廉姆斯目录编纂而成，不过道格拉斯教授（Professor Douglas）编写的《大英博物馆馆藏中文图书目录》也提供了很多帮助。不巧的是，这两位学者所采用的拼字法都是马礼逊博士（Dr. Morrison）在其字典中采用的方法；尽管这种拼字法可能最适合英文读者，但必须及时将其更换为其他体系，使元音的音值与欧洲大陆语言保持类似。根据道格拉斯教授的建议，本目录采用了威妥玛爵士（Sir Thomas Wade）所著《语言自迩集》（*Tzu Erh Chi*）基础手册中北京方言的拼字法。为确保统一，每个词汇都已在翟理斯《汉英词典》（*Chinese English Dictionary*）中查阅，该词典也采用了威妥玛的拼字法。

　　有必要简单介绍一下编目体系。书名、作者及编者的姓名按字母排序，每部作品的主要条目根据书名分类，书名经过音译，其后附有对书名的翻译或者对书名、作品特点的简短解释、作者或编者的姓名、书籍册数、毫米开本和出版日期。如果某部作品是写本，或以木版印刷之外的工艺制作而成，就需要对此特别留意。作者或编者的姓名和书名构成了主要的交叉检索条目。该目录中添加了一种"数字索引"，将中文形式的书名按照字数逐渐增加的顺序印刷，目录中每个条目前的数字对应"索引"中的数字。如果"索引"中的数字缺失，则代表作品的中文书名未知，或者这些作品本身没有中文书名。这些空白也可能表明，如上文所述，这些来自范·阿尔斯坦藏书中的图书是被图书馆丢弃的。

　　本目录中还著录了若干满文书籍和两三本韩文书籍。满文书籍大部分通过柯恒儒（Klaproth）藏书销售目录购得，书名被音译为罗马字母；而韩文书籍都有恰当的中文题解。

　　本目录应被视作一份简明参考目录或一项预备性研究，而不是重要性能与这批藏书相媲美的目录。中国文献以丛书而闻名，本目录几乎没有尝试对其进行分析。很多图书还有一些引人关注的地方，例如，图书的来源，雷慕沙（Rémusat）、柯恒儒、颇节等名人的亲笔注释，或者某作品因稀缺和品相优良而具有卓越的价值——所有这一切以及其他方面都值得本目录关注，但在目前这篇文章中可能有些格格不入。该目录的编纂者并不会假装自己是汉学专家，正相反，将这份简明参考目录交给汉学家批评修改时会感到缺乏自信。最后，编纂者想感谢道格拉斯教授的鼓励和帮助，如果没有他的帮助，一些困难可能无法克服。感谢道格拉斯教授对"数字索引"进行的校对，还要感谢哈特福德郡的Stephen Austin and Sons公司精心将编纂者提供的"副本"印刷成"数字索引"。

J. P. 埃德蒙德

图书管理员

（管宇译，彭萍校）

CATALOGUE OF CHINESE BOOKS.

426.—ÆSOP. *See* I-shih-pi ch'uan.

427.—AI-HAN-CHÊ. *See* Tung hsi yang k'ao mei yüeh t'ung chi ch'uan.

442.—AI JU-LIO. *See* T'ien chu chiang shêng yen hsing chi hsiang.

30 c.— „ „ „ Wan wu chin yüan.

420.—AÏSIN GOUROUN-I SOUDOURI. History of the kingdom of Aïsin, in Manchu. 9 pên in 1 vol. 320 × 210 mm. [1650?]

442.—ALENI, JULIO. *See* T'ien chu chiang shêng yen hsing chi hsiang.

30 c.— „ „ „ Wan wu chin yüan.

436.—ARTE DE LA LENGUA MANDARINA, cómpuesto par el M. R⁰. P⁰. fr. Francisco Varo. . . . 259 × 170 mm. Canton, 1703.

₊ Printed entirely in Roman and Italic letter from wood blocks in the Chinese fashion. Only three or four copies known.

31.—ARXO, JOSE RAYMONDO DE. *See* K'ang Hsi.

31.—BARROS, ANTONIO DE. „ „ „

A

31.—BEAUVOLLIER, ANTOINE. *See* K‘ang Hsi.

434.—BIBLE.—*New Testament.—Manchu.* *See* Musei echen Isus Ghristos-i tutabuha itche ghese.

33.—BRANCATI, FRANCIS. *See* T‘ien shên hui k‘o.

465.—BUDDHIST DOCUMENT, with a coloured drawing of a pagoda. Roll, 1 m. 27 cm. × 59 cm.

459.—BUDDHIST RITUAL OR PRAYERS. Roll, 6 m. 40 cm. × 26 cm.

38 b.—CH‘A SHIH SU MEI YÜEH T‘UNG CHI CH‘UAN. The Examiner; a monthly periodical. Edited by Po-ai-chê [*i.e.* William Milne, D.D.]. 205 × 125 mm.　　　　　　　　　　　1821.

　　　** Imperfect, only the numbers for the first eight months of 1821.

231.—CHAN KUO TS‘Ê. The Story of the contending states. Arranged by Liu Hsiang. With a commentary. 12 chüan. 5 pên in 1 vol. 246 × 160 mm.

216.—CHAN KUO TS‘Ê CHU. Another edition. With commentaries. 10 chüan. 6 pên in 1 vol. 255 × 162 mm.　　　　　1765.

295.—CH‘AN MÊN JIH SUNG. Buddhist daily liturgies. Compiled by the priest Mo-ch‘ih. 270 × 180 mm.　　　　　　1792.

98.—CHANG CH‘AOU. *See* I yin.

98.— 　　„　　　„　　　„ Ku yin piao.

98.— 　　„　　　„　　　„ Shih pên yin

98.— 　　„　　　„　　　„ T‘ang yün chêng.

98.—CHANG CH'AOU.   *See* Yin hsüeh wu shu.

98—   „   „   „ Yin lun.

147.—CHANG CHU-P'O.   *See* Chin P'ing Mei.

185.—CHANG HUA.   *See* Hsü po wu chih.

185.—   „   „   „ Po wu chih.

304.—CHANG T'ING-YÜ.   *See* Ch'in ting Ch'un Ch'iu ch'uan shuo hui tsuan.

413 xxii.—„   „   „ Ming shih.

206.—   „   „   „ Yü chuan tzǔ chih t'ung chien Ming chi kang mu.

275, 440, 443.—CHANG TSUNG-I.   *See* Ch'ien chih hsin pien.

176, 177.—CHANG T'UAN.   *See* Ta wan pao ch'üan shu.

182.—CHANG YING.   *See* Yüan chien lei han.

290.—CHANG YÜ-SHU.   *See* K'ang-hsi tzǔ tien.

38 c.—CHANG YUAN LIANG YU HSIANG LUN.   Discussions [on Christianity] between the two friends Chang and Yüan. 200 × 120 mm. [1821.]

260.—CH'ANG-AN CHIH.   A Topography of Ch'ang-an, the ancient capital of China, and the modern Hsi-an Fu, in the province of Shen-si. By Sung Min-ch'iu. 20 chüan. 4 pên in 1 vol. 278 × 158 mm. 1787.

293.—CHAO YI-CH'ING.   *See* Shui ching chu shih.

185.—CHAO YEH. *See* Wu Yüeh Ch'un Ch'iu.

413 iv.—CHÊN SHOU. *See* San kuo chih.

292.—CHÊN TÊ-CH'IEN. *See* Ch'in ting kuo ch'ao shih pieh tsai chi.

413 vi.—CHÊN YO. *See* Sung shu.

281.—CH'ÊN LAN-SÊN. *See* T'ai p'ing huan yü chi.

378.—CH'ÊN LUN-CH'IUNG. *See* Hai kou wên chien lu.

458.—CH'ÊN SAN. *See* Lu ching t'u.

331-338.—CH'ÊN SHIH TS'UNG SHU. Miscellaneous collection of works. 48 pên in 8 tao. 250 × 165 mm. [1843?]

413 xi.—CH'ÊN SHU. History of the Ch'ên dynasty. By Yao Ssŭ-lien. 36 chüan. 4 pên in 1 vol. 1578.

250.—CH'ÊN TÊ-HUA. *See* Ta ch'ing i t'ung chih.

290.—CH'ÊN T'ING-CHING. *See* K'ang-hsi tzŭ tien.

374.—CH'ÊN YÜAN SHIH LÜEH. Abridged account of the Imperial Palace. 16 chüan. 8 pên in 1 vol. 177 × 115 mm.

3.—CHÊNG CHIH-CH'IAO. *See* Lu ching t'u.

122.—CHÊNG TZŬ T'UNG. A Chinese dictionary. Compiled by Liao Wên-ying. 24 pên in 6 vols. 257 × 164 mm. 1672.

123.—CHÊNG TZŬ T'UNG. Supplement to the dictionary of that name. 257 × 164 mm.

121.—CHÊNG TZŬ T'UNG. Abridgement of the dictionary of that name. 24 pên in 4 vols. 245 × 157 mm. 1672.

103.—CHÊNG YÜN T'UNG. Dictionary arranged according to the sounds. 5 chüan. 256 × 160 mm. 1634.

10.—CH'ÊNG HAO. *See* Shu ching ta ch'üan.

318.—CH'ÊNG TA-WEI. *See* Suan fa t'ung tsung ta ch'üan.

225, 439.—CH'ÊNG YÜAN-CHANG. *See* Hsi hu chih.

334.—CHI CHIU T'AN CH'I. Short poems for inscribing on tablets, &c. 1 pên. Ch'ên shih ts'ung shu, tao 2.

186.—CHI I CHI. Collection of extraordinary historical narrations. Pi shu nien i chung, pên 8.

268.—CHI KU CHAI CHUNG TING I CH'I. Inscriptions on ancient bells, metal vases, tripods and porcelain vessels with their interpretations. 10 chüan. 4 pên in one vol. 259 × 165 mm. 1804.

185.—CHI MÊNG CHOU SHU. A History of the Chou dynasty for beginners. Edited by Wu Kuan. With notes by K'ung Ch'ao of the Tsin dynasty. 10 chüan. Pi shu nien i chung, pên 1.

58.—CHI YAO. Nomenclature of Buddhist terms in five languages. 2 chüan. 235 × 173 mm.

134.—CHI YÜN P'ING SHÊNG. Tonic dictionary. 10 pên in 1 vol. 257 × 153 mm.

91.—CH'I CH'IAO T'U HO PI. Drawings of puzzles. By "The Guest under the Mulberry Tree." 187 × 123 mm. 1813.

6   CATALOGUE OF CHINESE BOOKS.

430.—CH'I CH'IAO YÜN P'U.   The Figures of the Chinese puzzle.   173 ×
   117 mm.

172.—CH'I HSIU LEI KAO.   Literary encyclopædia.   51 chüan, and supplement 7 chüan.   18 pên in 3 vols.   175 × 110 mm.   1775.

227.—CH'I SHIH-YI.   *See* Hsi yü wên chien lu.

433.—CH'I TAO WÊN TSAN SHÊN SHIH.   Morning prayers and hymns.   By
   Robert Morrison, D.D.   159 × 109 mm.   [1833?]

   ₊ Printed with movable metal types at the Morrison's Albion Press.

191.—CHIA TZŬ HUI CHI.   Complete tables of the cycles.   5 chüan.   257 ×
   170 mm.   1559.

234.—CHIANG HU CH'IH TU.   Manual for travellers and merchants.   8 chüan.
   4 pên in 1 vol.   158 × 115 mm.

163.—CHIANG HU CH'IH TU FÊN YÜN TS'O YAO HO CHI.   A Letter-writer for
   travellers, and a phonetic dictionary.   By Yü Hsüeh-pu and Wên
   Ch'i-shih.   4 chüan.   4 pên in 1 vol.   175 × 118 mm.   1831.

306 a.—CHIANG P'U.   *See* Ch'ien lu.

306.—   „   „   „ Hsi ch'ing ku chien.

304.—CHIANG T'ING-HSI.   *See* Ch'in ting Ch'un Ch'iu ch'uan shuo hui tsuan.

250.—   „   „   „ Ta ch'ing i t'ung chih.

47.—CHIANG YUNG.   *See* Hsiang tang t'u k'ao.

228.—CH'IAO-LIU-PA TSUNG LUN. A Description of Java. By Shang-tê-chê [*i.e.* Walter Henry Medhurst, the elder, D.D.]. 225 × 130 mm.

[1824?]

411.—CHIEH HSIAO SHIH SHIH. The Duties of chastity and filial piety. With illustrations. Printed white, on a black ground. Folded as a screen. 310 × 168 mm. 1830.

406.—CHIEH MÊNG CH'ÜAN SHU. Complete dream book. 210 × 130 mm.

[1850?]

90.—CHIEH TZŬ YÜAN HUA CH'UAN. The Chieh-tzŭ Yüan drawing book. Compiled by Li Li-wêng. In 4 parts. 17 pên in 4 vols. 255 × 160 mm. 1679.

185.—CHIEN CHIEH CH'UAN. Tales of celebrated swordsmen. By Tuan Ch'êng-shih. 4 chüan. Pi shu nien i chung, pên 8.

7.—CHIEN PÊN WU CHING. The Five classical books, with commentaries. 26 chüan. 19 pên in 5 vols. 258 × 160 mm. 1817-18.

*** There is no general title. Each book has a separate title.

400.—CH'IEN CHIH HSIN PIEN. Illustrated treatise on the currency, down to the end of the Ming dynasty, concluding with a section on foreign coins and another on unknown coins. By Chang Tsung-i. 20 chüan. 4 pên in 1 tao. 280 × 176 mm. 1826.

275.—CH'IEN CHIH HSIN PIEN. Another copy. 20 chüan. 4 pen in 1 tao. 280 × 176 mm. 1826.

443.—CH'IEN CHIH HSIN PIEN. Another edition. Revised and published by Fang Chan. Second edition, with a new preface by his son Yi Chan. 20 chüan. 4 pên in 1 tao. 286 × 169 mm. 1854.

366.—CH'IEN CHIN I FANG. A Thousand golden medical receipts. By Sun Ssŭ-mo. 30 chüan. 10 pên in 2 tao. 246 × 160 mm. 1763.

413 ii.—CH'IEN HAN SHU. History of the former Han dynasty. By Pan Ku. 100 chüan. 24 pên in 5 vols. 257 × 168 mm. [1633?]

208.—CH'IEN HAN SHU. Another edition. 70 chüan. 23 pên in 4 vols. 259 × 165 mm.

306 a.—CH'IEN LU. A Record of coins, compiled by a Commission consisting of Liang Shih-chêng, Chiang P'u, Wang Yu-tun, and others. 16 chüan. The last 2 pên of Hsi ch'ing ku chien.

445.—CH'IEN LUNG. *See* Hsü ting ch'ien lu.

287.— „　　„　　„ Yü chih tsêng ting ch'ing wên chien.

152.—CH'IEN TS'AI. *See* Shuo Yo ch'üan ch'uan.

24.—CH'IEN TZU WÊN. The Thousand-character classic. By Chou Hsing-ssŭ. 210 × 120 mm. 1813.

367.—CHIH FAN LIAO CHAI CHIH I. Curious stories from a careless man's study. By P'u Liu-hsien. In Manchu and Chinese. 24 chüan. 24 pên in 3 vols. 246 × 175 mm. 1848.

112.—CHIH KU I WÊN. Dictionary of ancient characters. 2 chüan. 252 × 165 mm. 1592.

173.—CHIH NANG PU. Small literary encyclopædia. 12 chüan. 10 pên in 2 vols. 170 × 113 mm. [1800?]

181.—CHIH PU TSU CHAI TS'UNG SHU. A Collection of works in different branches of literature. 204 treatises in 30 sections. 240 pên in 42 vols. 194 × 115 mm. 1752.

423.—CHIH T'U. Plates of the operations employed in weaving. With short explanations. 307 × 267 mm. 1696.

130.—CHIH TUAN-SHIH. *See* Fên yün ts'o yao.

429.—CH'IH SHAN CHI. Slowly edited collection. 2 pên. 253 × 155 mm.

*** These form part of a collection the extent of which is unknown. One of the volumes contains prose pieces, fu wên ; the other chüan 4-6 of a collection of poems.

141.—CHIN KU CH'I KUAN. A Collection of tales, ancient and modern. 10 pên in 2 vols. 188 × 110 mm.

282.—CHIN K'UEI-CH'IN. *See* Wu li t'ung k'ao.

147.—CHIN P'ING MEI. The Story of Chin, P'ing, and Mei. A novel attributed to Wang Shih-chêng. Edited by Chang Chu-p'o. 100 chapters. 20 pên in 4 vols. 171 × 115 mm. 1695.

369.—CHIN P'ING MEI. The same work, translated into Manchu. 100 chapters. 40 pên in 5 vols. 261 × 168 mm. 1708.

226.—CHIN SHÊNG-T'AN. *See* Hsi yu chên ch'üan.

142.— „ „ „ „ San kuo chih.

413 xx.—CHIN SHIH. History of the Chin dynasty. By T'o-k'o-t'o and others. 135 chüan. 24 pên in 5 vols. 278 × 175 mm. 1739.

185.—CHIN SHIH CH'ÊNG. A Short historical record of the state of Chin. By Wu Yen. Pi shu nien i chung, pên 10.

296.—CHIN SHIH YAO LI. *See* **MU MING CHÜ LI,** pên 2.

70.—CH'IN T'IEN CHIEN TSOU. Ephemerides of the planets for the year (K'ang Hsi 23) 1684, calculated for the meridian of Peking. 325 × 215 mm. 1684.

B

10 CATALOGUE OF CHINESE BOOKS.

339.—CH'IN TING CHIAO P'ING SAN SHÊNG HSIEH FEI FANG LÜEH. Abridged account of military operations in the reign of Chia Ch'ing against certain rebellious provinces. 352 chüan, synopsis 36 chüan, and appendix 12 chüan. 246 pên in 41 tao. 310 × 195 mm.

*** Imperfect, chüan 87-91 are missing.

304.—CH'IN TING CH'UN CH'IU CH'UAN SHUO HUI TSUAN. The Spring and Autumn annals. By K'ung Ch'iu. With a compilation and digest of comments and remarks thereon by Tso Ch'iu-ming, Kung-yang Kao, Tu Yü, and others. Compiled by an Imperial Commission consisting of Wang Yen, Chang T'ing-yü, Chiang T'ing-hsi, and others. With preface by the Emperor K'ang-hsi. 38 chüan. 18 pên in 5 vols. 265 × 180 mm. 1721.

254.—CH'IN TING HUANG YÜ HSI YÜ T'U CHIH. Historical and geographical description of the western countries. 48 chüan. 28 pên in 4 tao. 287 × 182 mm. 1777.

292.—CH'IN TING KUO CH'AO SHIH PIEH TSAI CHI. Separate collection of the poetry of the Ts'ing dynasty. Compiled by Chên Tê-ch'ien. 32 chüan. 16 pên in 4 vols. 144 × 95 mm. 1761.

450.—CH'IN TING MAN-CHOU YÜAN LIU K'AO. Origin and progress of the Manchus : a work prepared by order of the Emperor. MS. 20 chüan. 14 pên in 2 tao. 258 × 170 mm. 1776.

253.—CH'IN TING MAN-CHOU YÜAN LIU K'AO. Printed copy. 8 pên in 1 tao. 275 × 178 mm. 1777.

449.—CH'IN TING MÊNG-KU YÜAN LIU. Origin and progress of the Mongols : a work prepared by order of the Emperor. MS. 8 chüan. 4 pên in 1 tao. 257 × 170 mm. 1776.

358.—CH'IN TING PA CH'I T'UNG CHIH. Complete account of the Eight Banners. Introduction 12 chüan, the work 342 chüan, and supplement 6 chüan. 294 pên in 49 tao. 320 × 200 mm. 1810.

*** Imperfect, wanting chüan 1-6 of the work.

274.—CH'IN TING SSŬ K'U CH'ÜAN SHU. On agricultural field pursuits. 24 pên in 4 vols. 290 × 175 mm. 1843.

169.—CH'IN TING SSŬ K'U CH'ÜAN SHU CHIEN MING MU LU. An Abridgment of the descriptive catalogue of the Imperial Library of the present dynasty. 20 chüan. 4 vols. 196 × 110 mm. 1762.

392.—CH'IN TING SSŬ K'U CH'ÜAN SHU TSUNG MU. Descriptive catalogue of the Imperial Library of the present dynasty, drawn up by an Imperial Commission composed of Princes Yung Yung, Yung Hsüan, Yung Hsing, and others. 200 chüan. In 16 vols. 270 × 176 mm. 1772-90.

59.—CHING CH'AN CHIH YIN TSÊNG PU CH'IEH SHIH. The Correct sounds of characters used in the Buddhist Sûtras and liturgical works. Compiled by the priest Yi-chiu-ling-hsün. Edited by the priest Ch'uan-t'an-yüeh-tu. 238 × 140 mm. 1745.

463.—CHING CH'ÊNG CH'ÜAN T'U. Official map of the capital (Peking). Coloured. Roll, 1 m. 26 cm. × 59 cm.

218.—CHING NI CHI. An Account of the suppression of banditti in Shan-si and other parts. By Lan I, the historian. 6 chüan. 2 pên in one vol. 166 × 118 mm. 1821.

349.—CHING SHIH CHIANG I. Explanation of various passages in the classical books and histories. 30 chüan. 23 pên in 4 tao. 273 × 176 mm. 1755.

2.—CHING TIEN SHIH WÊN. An Explanation of phrases and expressions used in the classics. By Lu Tê-ming, of the T'ang dynasty. Edited by Lu Wên-ch'ao. 30 chüan. 12 pên in 2 vols. 240 × 155 mm. 1791.

265.—CH'ING WÊN HUI SHU. Manchu and Chinese dictionary 12 chüan. 12 pên in 1 vol. 235 × 160 mm.

266.—CH'ING WÊN PU HUI. Chrestomathy in Chinese and Manchu. 8 chüan. 8 pên in 1 vol. 235 × 160 mm. 1786.

387.—CH'ING YUNG CHÜ T'U CHI. Miscellaneous collection of poems and other short essays. By Ch'ing Yung. 50 chüan. 10 pên and supplement in 2 tao. 240 × 150 mm. I chia t'ang ts'ung shu, tao 5, 6. 1840.

64.—CHIU-MO-LO-SHIH. *See* Fo shuo O-mi-to ching.

413 xvii. b.—CHIU WU TAI SHIH. History of the five dynasties. By Hsieh Chü-chêng. 150 chüan. 12 pên in 4 vols. 278 × 178 mm. 1784.

444.—CHIU YU-FÊNG. *See* Lei shu san ts'ai t'u hui.

226.—CH'IU CH'ANG-CH'UN. *See* Hsi yu chên ch'üan.

294.—CH'IU HSÜN. *See* Yu hsüeh ku shih hsün yüan.

206.—CHOU CH'ANG-FA. *See* Yü chuan tzǔ chih t'ung chien Ming chi kang mu.

220.—CHOU CHIH-CH'UNG. *See* Kang chien i chih lu.

220.—CHOU CHIH-TS'AN. *See* Kang chien i chih lu.

24.—CHOU HSING-SSǓ. *See* Ch'ien tzǔ wên.

286.—CHOU I CH'ÜAN SHU. Complete edition of the I ching. 20 chüan. 10 pên in 4 vols. 280 × 170 mm. 1596.

28.—CHOU LI CHU SU. The Chou ritual. With a paraphrase and commentaries. 42 chüan. 14 pên in 3 vols. 229 × 115 mm.

79.—CH'OU HAI T'U PIEN. A Detailed work on the seaboard districts of China, illustrated by an extensive series of maps. By Hu Tsung-hsien. Edited by Mao K'un. 13 chüan. 16 pên in 4 vols. 295 × 183 mm.

422.—CH'OU HAI T'U PIEN. Another edition. 13 chüan. 10 pên in 1 vol. 303 × 182 mm.

167.—CH'OU SHIH CHIN NANG. A Collection of remarkable pieces written in elegant style, with commentaries. 10 pên in 2 vols. 171 × 112 mm. 1771.

259.—CHU HSI. *See* Chu tzǔ ch'üan shu.

10.— „ „ „ Shu ching ta ch'üan.

204, 262.— „ „ T'ung chien kang mu.

63.—CHU HUNG. *See* Mu niu t'u.

38 e.—CHU KUO I SHÊN LUN. A Discourse on idolatry. By Po-ai-chê [*i.e.* William Milne, D.D.]. 204 × 126 mm. [1830?]

193.—CHU SHU CHI NIEN. The Bamboo record. 243 × 160 mm. [1700?]

185.—CHU SHU CHI NIEN. Another edition. Pi shu nien i chung, pên 8.

337.—CHU SHU CHI NIEN CHI CHÊNG. The Bamboo record with a commentary. 22 pên. Ch'ên shih ts'ung shu, tao 5-8.

259.—CHU TZǓ CH'ÜAN SHU. The Complete works of Chu Hsi. 32 pên in 4 vols. 235 × 158 mm. 1713.

40.—CHU TZǓ HUI HAN. Extracts from the writings of all the philosophers from the time of the Chou to that of the Ming dynasty. Compiled by Kuei Yu-kuang. Edited by Wên Chin-mêng. 26 chüan. 27 pên in 4 vols. 241 × 154 mm. 1626.

170.--CH'U HSÜEH CHI. Literary encyclopædia for the use of students. 14 pên in 3 vols. 140 × 95 mm.

171.--CH'U HSUEH HSIAO T'I TÊNG LUNG. Literary encyclopædia for the use of students. 4 pên in 1 vol. 228 × 130 mm. 1806.

180.--CH'U HSÜEH MING CHING. Mirror for beginners. 210 × 112 mm. 1748.

185.--CH'U SHIH T'AO WU. A Collection of memoranda regarding the state of Ch'u. By Wu Yen. Pi shu nien i chung, pên 10.

104.--CHUAN LI HSIN HUA. Dictionary of ancient characters with the corresponding modern ones. 212 × 110 mm. [1600?]

111.--CHUAN TZŬ HUI. Dictionary of the seal characters. 6 pên in 1 vol. 230 × 150 mm. 1691.

59.--CH'UAN-T'AN-YÜEH-TU. *See* Ching ch'an chih yin tsêng pu ch'ieh shih.

52.--CHUANG CHOU. *See* Nan hua ching chien chu.

17.--CH'UN CH'IU CHING CH'UAN CHI CHIEH. The Spring and Autumn annals [by K'ung Ch'iu] and Tso Ch'iu-ming's Narrative. With a collection of comments. 30 chüan. 14 pên in 3 vols. 261 × 158 mm. [1790?]

185.--CHUNG HUA KU CHIN CHU. A Record of historical antiquities. By Ma Kao. Pi shu nien i chung, pên 9.

388.--CHUNG K'O YEN YÜAN CHI. New edition of works collected by Yen Yüan. 6 pên and supplement in 1 tao. 240 × 150 mm. I chia t'ang ts'ung shu, tao 7. 1840.

403.--CHUNG PAI-CHING. *See* Fêng shên yen i.

198.-- „ „ „ Fêng shên yen i ch'üan ch'uan.

38 i.—CHUNG-TÊ-CHÊ. *See* Yeh-su yen hsing tsung lun.

195.—CHUNG TING CH'UN CH'IU TSO CH'UAN CHÜ CHIEH. Traditions of Tso.   By Tso Ch'iu-ming.   6 pên in 1 vol.   230 × 132 mm.

[1700 ?]

203.—CHUNG TING LU SHIH CH'IEN CHI. Complete works of Lo Pi.   24 pên in 3 vols.   244 × 135 mm.

442.—CH'Ü HSI-MAN. *See* T'ien chu chiang shêng yen hsing chi hsiang.

346.—CH'Ü P'U. Collection of songs or short pieces of poetry.   13 pên in 2 vols.   248 × 155 mm.

323.—CH'ÜAN CHIN SHIH TSÊNG. Complete collection of the poets of the Chin dynasty.   32 pên in 4 vols.   247 × 155 mm.   [1711 ?]

299 d.—CH'ÜAN T'I HSIN LUN. A Work on physiology.   By Ho-hsin [*i.e.* Benjamin Hobson].   10 chüan.   261 × 165 mm.   1858.

38 h.—CH'ÜAN TU SHÊNG LU SHU CHIH WÊN. Exhortations to the study of the Bible.   The two first Homilies of the Church of England, translated into Chinese by Dr. Morrison.   238 × 132 mm.   [1820 ?]

194.—CH'ÜEH LI CHIH. Description of Ch'üeh Li.   9 pën in a case.   259 × 168 mm.   [1500 ?]

*** Imperfect, chüan 4-8 wanting.

451.—CH'ÜN FANG P'U. A Herbarium.   By Wang Hsiang-chin.   16 pên in 4 vols.   245 × 158 mm.

236 a.—COLLECTIONS FOR A VOCABULARY OR DICTIONARY. MS.   360 × 235 mm.   About 1800.

236 b.—COLLECTIONS FOR A VOCABULARY OR DICTIONARY. MS. 320 × 200 mm.   About 1800.

38 i.—COLLIE, DAVID. *See* Yeh-su yen hsing tsung lun.

421.—DAI YOUWAN-I BITKHE. Book of the Great Yüan, in Manchu. 15 pên in 2 vols. 320 × 220 mm.

243 b.—DIALOGUES IN CHINESE AND FRENCH; also letters and other memoranda for acquiring a knowledge of Chinese. MS. 200 × 160 mm.   About 1800.

115.—DIAZ, EMMANUEL. *See* Hsieh shêng p'in tzŭ chien.

36.— „   „   „ Shên chên jih k'o.

442.— „   „   „ T'ien chu chiang shêng yen hsing chi hsiang.

135.—DICTIONARY, CHINESE-RUSSIAN. The whole in Chinese characters. MS. 245 × 215 mm.

416.—DICTIONARY. MS. containing only the Chinese vocabulary. 2 vols. 320 × 200 mm.   [1810?]

240 b.—DICTIONNAIRE CHINOIS tiré de Kircher avec les charactères Chinois écrits par le Chinois Arcadius Hwang. MS. 390 × 255 mm.

236 c.—DICTIONNAIRE FRANÇOIS-CHINOIS. MS. 315 × 215 mm.   About 1750.

460.—DIPLOMA RAISING A STUDENT IN THE HAN LIN COLLEGE ONE DEGREE. MS. Manchu and Chinese. On white silk. Roll, 1 m. 83 cm. × 33 cm.   1835.

76.—EPHEMERIDES. The Imperial Calendar for 3rd and 11th years of Yung Chêng [1725 and 1733], and for the 1st, 2nd, 3rd, 4th, and 5th of Ch'ien Lung [1736-1740], and others undated. 335 × 210 mm.   1725-1740.

70.—EPHEMERIDES. *See* Ch'in t'ien chien tsou.

105.—ÊRH YA. Dictionary explaining terms used and things mentioned by ancient writers. Followed by the Hsiao Êrh ya, or Lesser literary expositor, by K'ung Fu. 3 pên in 1 vol. 245 × 160 mm. [1600?]

106.—ÊRH YA CHU SU. The Literary expositor. With a commentary by Kuo P'o, and a paraphrase by the editor, Hsing Ping. 4 pên in 1 vol. 260 × 160 mm. 1803.

418.—ÊRH YA YIN T'U. The Literary expositor, with the sounds of the characters, and with plates. 330 × 245 mm. [1801?]

** Imperfect; chüan 3 only.

94.—EXPLANATION OF THE KEYS OF THE CHINESE CHARACTERS. MS. Attributed to Abel Rémusat. 360 × 225 mm. [1825?]

321.—FA-HSIEN. *See* Fo kuo chi.

102.—FA YÜ HSÜ TZŬ. On Chinese particles or expletives. By Father Gollet. MS. 228 × 130 mm.

302.—FA YÜAN CHU LIN. The Forest of the pearls of the garden of the law. A comprehensive view of the Buddhist system. 100 chüan. 24 pên in 4 tao. 272 × 180 mm. [1700?]

270.—FAN CH'A T'U. A Journey by water throughout the empire, with illustrations. 6 pên in 1 vol. 270 × 185 mm. 1819.

185.—FAN CH'ENG-TA. *See* Kuei hai yü hêng chih.

209, 413 iii. a.—FAN YEH. *See* Hou Han shu.

443.—FANG CHAN. *See* Ch'ien chih hsin pien.

C

73.—FANG HSING T'U CHIEH. Charts of the stars from about 35° N. to 35° S., with explanatory remarks. By Ming Ming-o [*i.e.* Philippe Grimaldi]. Folded as a screen. 295 × 170 mm.　　　　1711.

269.—FANG SHIH MO P'U. Specimens of engravings on cakes of ink as manufactured by Fang Yü-lu. 8 pên in 2 vols. 282 × 180 mm.
　　　　　　　　　　　　　　　　　　　　　　　　　1603.

269.—FANG YÜ-LU. *See* Fang shih mo p'u.

130.—FÊN YÜN TS'O YAO. A Phonetic dictionary. By Wên Ch'i-shan. Edited by Chih Tuan-shih. 4 pên in 1 vol. 181 × 105 mm.

200.—FÊNG CHOU KANG CHIEN. Abridged history of China. By Fêng Chou. 44 pên in 11 vols. 181 × 120 mm.

331.—FÊNG SAO. *See* Li sao ching i.

332.— 　„　　„　　　„　Tu sao lou shih ch'u chi.

403.—FÊNG SHÊN YEN I. The Story of the appointed genii. A tale regarding the adventures of Wu Wang, the founder of the Chou dynasty, in his contest with Chou Hsin, the last of the house of Shang. By Chung Pai-ching. 20 pên. 175 × 115 mm.　　　　1782.

198.—FÊNG SHÊN YEN I CH'ÜAN CH'UAN. Another edition. 20 pên in 3 vols. 170 × 115 mm.　　　　　　　　　　　　　　1813.

185.—FÊNG SU T'UNG. Popular traditions. By Ying Shao. Pi shu nien i chung, pên 10.

321.—FO KUO CHI. An Account of Buddhist countries. A narrative of the travels of Fa-hsien in Central Asia [where he went to obtain information and documents regarding the Buddhist religion]. Edited by Hsü Hsü-kung. 247 × 167 mm.　　　　　　　[1800?]

64.—FO SHUO O-MI-TO CHING. The Amitâtha Sûtra, translated into Chinese by Chiu-mo-lo-shih [*i.e.* Kumâragîva]. 240 × 152 mm. 1765.

62.—FO SHUO YÜ LAN P'ÊN CHING SU. The Sûtra of the Yü-lan p'en festival, delivered by Buddha. Edited, with a commentary, by Tsung-mi. 2 chüan. 230 × 162 mm. [1765?]

322.—FO TSU LI TAI T'UNG TSAI. History of the Buddhist saints or patriarchs. 10 pên in 2 vols. 265 × 170 mm. 1576

58.—FO T'UNG HAO MING; *or,* **CHI YAO**, *q. v.*

345.—FRAGMENTS of Chinese and Manchu books.

99.—FU JU-WEI. *See* Tsêng ting tzŭ hsüeh ching liang.

215.—FU MIAO LU. Memoirs of the subjugation of the Miao. 8 pên in 1 vol. 262 × 168 mm. 1713.

299 b.—FU YING HSIN SHUO. New treatise on midwifery and the diseases of children. By Ho-hsin [*i.e.* Benjamin Hobson]. Edited by Kuan Mou-ts'un. 261 × 165 mm. 1858.

102.—GOLLET, FATHER. *See* Fa yü hsü tzŭ.

441.—GOUVEA, ANTONIO DE. *See* Innocentia Victrix.

95.—GRAMMAR. French treatise on Chinese grammar. MS. 160 × 100 mm. About 1775.

73.—GRIMALDI, PHILIPPE. *See* Fang hsing t'u chieh.

427.—GUETZLAFF, KARL FRIEDRICH AUGUST. *See* Tung hsi yang k'ao mei yüeh t'ung chi ch'uan.

CATALOGUE OF CHINESE BOOKS.

378.—HAI KUO WÊN CHIEN LU. A Geographical treatise, chiefly relating to the islands in the eastern and southern oceans. By Ch'ên Lun-ch'iung. With maps. 2 pên in 1 tao. 182 × 125 mm. [1730?]

128.—HAI P'IEN. Fragment of the dictionary so called. 265 × 160 mm. [1596.]

333.—HAN SHIH T'UNG CHIEN. Short poems for inscribing on tablets, etc. 1 pên. Ch'ên shih ts'ung shu, tao 2.

261.—HAN WEI TS'UNG SHU. Miscellaneous collection of works, written during the Han and Wei dynasties. 60 pên in 12 vols. 245 × 155 mm. 1744.

174.—HAN WÊN K'AO I. Complete works of Han Yin. 12 pên in 2 vols. 254 × 163 mm. 1600.

174.—HAN YIN. *See* Han wên k'ao i.

432.—HAO CH'IU CH'UAN. The Fortunate union. 4 pên. 165 × 105 mm. 1819.

299 d.—HOBSON, BENJAMIN. *See* Ch'üan t'i hsin lun.

299 b.— „ „ „ Fu ying hsin shuo.

299 c.— „ „ „ Hsi i lüeh lun.

299 a.— „ „ „ Nei k'o hsin shuo.

299 e.— „ „ „ Po wu hsin pien.

299 d.—HO-HSIN. *See* Ch'üan t'i hsin lun.

290 b.—HO-HSIN. *See* Fu ying hsin shuo.

290 c.— „ „ „ Hsi i lüeh lun.

290 a.— „ „ „ Nei k'o hsin shuo.

290 e.— „ „ „ Po wu hsin pien.

413 xii.—HOU CHOU SHU. History of the later Chou dynasty. By Ling-hu Tê-fên. 50 chüan. 8 pên in 2 vols. 256 × 164 mm. 1588.

413 iii. a.—HOU HAN SHU. History of the later Han dynasty. By Fan Yeh. 120 chüan. 24 pên in 5 vols. 253 × 170 mm. 1627.

290.—HOU HAN SHU. Another edition. 17 pên in 3 vols. 259 × 165 mm.

393.—HSI CHAO T'U LUEH. Essays on the administration of subject states, by the resident Chinese officials. With maps. 252 × 155 mm. 1798.

308.—HSI CH'ING KU CHIEN. Antiquities [from the Palace?] of Western Purity. Compiled by an Imperial Commission consisting of Liang Shih-chêng, Chiang P'u, Wang Yu-tun, and others. 40 chüan. 26 pên in 4 vols. 400 × 270 mm. Peking, 1749-50.

431.—HSI FAN I YÜ. Tibetan and Chinese vocabulary. 2 pên in 1 tao. 163 × 106 mm.

365.—HSI HSIANG CHIH. *See* Tsêng ting chin p'i hsi hsiang.

430.—HSI HU CHIH. Topography of the western lake in Cheh-kiang. By Li Wei, Ch'êng Yüan-chang, and others. 48 chüan. 20 pên in 4 vols. 272 × 184 mm. 1731.

225.—HSI HU CHIH. Another edition. 48 chüan. 20 pên in 4 vols. 131 × 90 mm.

299 c.—HSI I LÜEH LUN. Short practical work on European surgery. By Ho-hsin [*i.e.* Benjamin Hobson]. Edited by Kuan Mou-ts'un. 3 chüan. 261 × 165 mm.   1858.

437.—HSI JU ÊRH MU TZŬ. Vocabulary arranged by tones, following the order of European words. By Nicolas Trigault. 3 parts in 1 vol. 269 × 175 mm.   1626.

26.—HSI SHIH HSIEN WÊN. Moral maxims of ancient times. 210 × 118 mm.
                                                                          1814.

32.—HSI YANG JÊN. Remonstrances to the Emperor by the missionaries. 260 × 175 mm. Dates: K'ang Hsi 45th [1706] and 50th year [1711]; Ch'ien Lung 1st, 2nd, and 3rd years [1736-38].

226.—HSI YU CHÊN CH'ÜAN. A Complete narrative of travels in the west in search of the sacred books. By Ch'iu Ch'ang-ch'un. Edited by Chin Shêng-t'an. 20 pên in 4 vols. 170 × 115 mm.   1696.

257.—HSI YÜ SHUI TAO CHI. An Account of the water ways of the countries on the western frontier of the empire. Compiled by Hsü Hsing-pai. 5 chüan. 4 pên in 1 tao. 300 × 180 mm.   1823.

227.—HSI YÜ WÊN CHIEN LU. Things heard and seen on the western frontiers. By Ch'i Shih-yi. 168 × 112 mm.   1777.

390.—HSIANG CHIEH CHIU CHANG SUAN FA. Clear explanation of the rules for calculating. 2 pên, and supplement 1 pên. 240 × 150 mm. I chia t'ang ts'ung shu, tao 8.   [1842?]

47.—HSIANG TANG T'U K'AO. An Examination of the tenth book of the Confucian analects. With plates. By Chiang Yung. 10 chüan in 1 vol. 175 × 110 mm.   1776.

185.—HSIAO CH'I. *See* Shih i chi.

223.—HSIAO CHIH-HAN. *See* Li tai ming hsien lieh nü shih hsing p'u.

106.—HSIAO ÊRH YA. The Lesser literary expositor. By K'ung Fu. *See* Êrh ya.

162.—HSIAO HAI HSIN SHÊNG CH'U CHI. A Collection of short tales or anecdotes. 167 × 100 mm.   [1800?]

166.—HSIAO T'UNG. *See* Wên hsüan.

413 viii.—HSIAO TZǓ-HSIEN. *See* Nan Ch'i shu.

413 xvii. b.—HSIEH CHÜ-CHÊNG. *See* Chiu Wu tai shih.

338.—HSIEH LÜ KOU YÜAN. Collection of miscellaneous poems. 2 pên. Ch'ên shih ts'ung shu, tao 4.

114.—HSIEH SHÊNG P'IN TZǓ CHIEN. A Phonetic dictionary. Compiled by Yü Tê-shêng. 3 vols. 255 × 165 mm.   1676.

115.—HSIEH SHÊNG P'IN TZǓ CHIEN. Vol. III.; being the index to the work, with notes by Diaz and Rémusat. 250 × 165 mm.   1676.

116.—HSIEH SHÊNG P'IN TZǓ CHIEN. An Index to facilitate the use of that work. French MS. 245 × 160 mm.

69.—HSIN CHIH I HSIANG T'U. Plates representing various astronomical and other instruments belonging to the observatory of Peking. By Ferdinand Verbiest. 2 pên in 1 case. 375 × 225 mm.   1687.

97.—HSIN LU TZǓ FA. Improved mode of learning the different kinds of writing. 2 pên in 1 vol. 188 × 137 mm.   1812.

CATALOGUE OF CHINESE BOOKS.

38 g.—HSIN TSÊNG YANG HSIN SHEN SHIH. Hymns. A new and enlarged edition. [Compiled by Dr. Milne.] 205 × 130 mm. [1821 ?]

179.—HSIN TSÊNG YU HSÜEH KU SHIH CH'UNG LIN. The Coral forest of ancient learning for the instruction of youth. 2 pên in 1 vol. 245 × 160 mm. [1750?]

148.—HSING HSIN PIEN. A Book to excite the heart to virtue. 4 pên in 1 vol. 163 × 120 mm. 1792.

44.—HSING LI CHÊN CH'ÜAN. Truthful disquisitions on mental philosophy. By Sun Chang. Edited by Sung Chün-jung and others. 4 chüan. 6 pên in 2 vols. 263 × 160 mm. 1753.

53.—HSING MING KUEI CHIH. [A Taouist work on the government of the inner man.] By Yin Shên-jên. 4 pên. 262 × 166 mm. [1669 ?]

₊ Imperfect, pên 2-4 wanting.

106.—HSING PING. *See* Êrh ya chu su.

356.—HSÜ CHI-YÜ. *See* Ying huan chih lüeh.

185.—HSÜ CH'I HSIEH CHI. A Supplementary collection of marvellous tales. By Wu Chün. Pi shu nien i chung, pên 10.

10.—HSÜ CHIU-YI. *See* Shu ching ta ch'üan.

413 iii. b.—HSÜ HOU HAN. History of the reigns of the last two emperors of the Han dynasty. 90 chüan. 24 pên in 5 vols. 245 × 158 mm. 1841.

385.—HSÜ HOU HAN SHU. History of the Hou, or later Han dynasty, with supplement. 7 pên in 1 tao. 240 × 150 mm. I chia t'ang ts'ung shu, tao 1. 1841.

257.—HSÜ HSING-PAI. *See* Hsi yü shui tao chi.

321.—HSÜ HSÜ-KUNG. *See* Fo kuo chi.

185.—HSÜ PO WU CHIH. Continuation of the Po wu chih. By Chang Hua. Pi shu nien i chung, pên 6.

462.—HSÜ SAN KANG HSING SHIH T'U. Supplementary deeds of the three net-ropes (or, the three bonds), with illustrations. 320 × 210 mm.
1514.

₊ A Corean edition, with Corean notes or version at the top of each page.

445.—HSÜ TING CH'IEN LU. Description of coins in the cabinet of Ch'ien Lung. 11 chüan. 4 pên in 1 tao. 275 × 173 mm.

38 f.—HSÜ TSUAN SHÊNG SHÊN SHÊN SHIH. Supplementary collection of protestant hymns. 228 × 130 mm. [1855?]

151.—HSÜ WÊN-CH'ANG. *See* Hung wu ch'üan ch'üan.

348.—HSÜ WÊN HSIEN T'UNG K'AO. Continuation of the Wên hsien t'ung k'ao. By Wang Ch'i. 80 pên in 10 vols. 264 × 167 mm. 1602.

255.—HSÜ WÊN HSIEN T'UNG K'AO YIN. A Synopsis of the continuation of the Wên hsien t'ung k'ao. By Wang Ch'i. 22 chüan. 8 pên in 1 tao. 245 × 155 mm.

41.—HSÜN TZŬ CHIEN SHIH. The Works of the philosopher Hsün Tzŭ with commentary. 20 chüan. 4 pên. 253 × 158 mm. 1804.

117.—HSÜAN CHIN TZŬ HUI. The Dictionary of Mei Tang-hsing arranged according to the keys. 14 pên in 3 vols. 230 × 130 mm. 1786.

D

118.—HSÜAN CHIN TZŬ HUI. Another edition.   14 pên in 1 tao.   230 × 135 mm.   1705.

119.—HSÜAN CHIN TZŬ HUI. Index to the keys of that dictionary.   MS.   320 × 205 mm.

311.—HSÜAN-CHUANG.   *See* Ta T'ang hsi yü chi.

61.—HSÜAN SÊNG T'U SHUO. A Treatise on the election of the Buddhist priests.   170 × 140 mm.   1664.

79, 422.—HU TSUNG-HSIEN.   *See* Ch'ou hai t'u pien.

51.—HUAI NAN HUNG LIEH CHIEH. The Treatise of Liu An, the prince of Huai nan, on the doctrines of Tao, comprehensively explained. Edited by Huang Hsi-hsi.   21 chüan.   6 pên in 1 vol.   239 × 154 mm.   [1750?]

353.—HUANG CHAO LI CH'I T'U SHIH. Drawings of vessels, dresses, &c., used in the imperial court ceremonies.   18 chüan.   16 pên in 4 vols.   295 × 195 mm.   1766.

352.—HUANG CHAO T'UNG TIEN. Complete ritual of the court ceremonies.   48 pên in 6 vols.   290 × 180 mm,   1767.

375.—HUANG CHAO WU KUNG CHI SHÊNG. Account of the military exploits of the present imperial dynasty (Manchu).   4 pên in 1 tao.   245 × 155 mm.   [1792?]

350.—HUANG CHI CHING SHIH SHU. A Philosophical work.   By Shao Yung.   16 pên in 4 tao.   245 × 155 mm.   1757.

1.—HUANG CH'ING CHING CHIEH. The Classics explained by authors of the Ch'ing dynasty.   Compiled by Yen Lieh, under the direction and partly at the expense of Yüan Yüan.   1400 chüan.   360 pên in 74 vols.   254 × 155 mm.   1829.

376.—HUANG CH'ING K'AI KUO FANG LÜEH. Abridged history of the foundation of the present dynasty (Manchu). 32 chüan. 16 pên in 2 tao. 390 × 240 mm. 1786.

185.—HUANG FU-MEI. *See* Kao shih ch'uan.

51.—HUANG HSI-HSI. *See* Huai nan hung lieh chieh.

190.—HUANG HSIAO-FÊNG. *See* T'ai p'ing kuang chi.

285.—HUANG P'EI-LIEH. *See* Shih tzŭ ch'üan shu.

235.—HUANG TI I CHAO. The Will of the Emperor K'ang Hsi. In Chinese with a French translation. MS. 225 × 165 mm.

75.—HUANG YÜ-ÊRH. *See* T'ien wên ta ch'êng.

314.—HUNG CHIEN LU. The Great history of events from the beginning of the T'ang dynasty to the end of the Chin dynasty. By Shao Ching-pang. 254 chüan. 60 pên in 10 tao. 250 × 165 mm. 1688.

*** For the sequel *see* Yüan shih lei pien.

250.—HUNG CHOU. *See* Ta ch'ing i t'ung chih.

412.—HUNG HSÜEH YIN YUEN T'U CHI. Illustrations representing various places in China and the manners and customs of that people. 6 pên in 2 tao. 300 × 175 mm. 1840.

149.—HUNG LOU MÊNG. The Dream of the red chamber. By Ts'ao Hsüeh-ch'in. 20 pên in 4 vols. 168 × 115 mm. 1830.

402.—HUNG LOU MÊNG. Another edition. 24 pên in 4 tao. 195 × 134 mm. 1832.

151.—HUNG WU CH'ÜAN CH'UAN. A Complete narrative of the reign of the Emperor Hung-wu [1368-97]. By Hsü Wên-ch'ang. 10 pên in 1 vol. 170 × 114 mm. [1800?]

415.—HUO YUNG T'U PEI LIU CHUNG SHU. Inscription on stone in six languages at Chiu-Yung-Kuan, on the Great Wall near Peking. 4 pên in 1 tao. 367 × 343 mm. 2 pên folded as fans. 370 × 260 and 305 × 260 mm.

385-391.—I CHIA T'ANG TS'UNG SHU. Works collected by the I Chia Printing Office. 58 pên in 8 tao. 240 × 150 mm. 1840-42.

343.—I CH'IEH CHING YIN I. Explanation of all the foreign technical terms found in the Buddhist works, translated from the Sanscrit, with an examination of the correct sounds. By Yüan Ying. 5 pên. 280 × 168 mm. 1660.

336.—I CHOU SHU PU CHU. Commentaries of I Chou upon various ancient works. 23 chüan. 12 pên. Ch'ên shih ts'ung shu, tao 3, 4.

85.—I FANG K'AO. Medical prescriptions examined. 5th part of the 53rd section. 250 × 158 mm. [1700?]

29.—I LI CHING CH'ÜAN T'UNG CHIEH. The Instructions of the decorum ritual explained. 66 chüan. 24 pên in 5 vols. 262 × 167 mm.

327.—I LI T'U. Book of rites, with illustrations. MS. 12 pên in 2 tao. 284 × 174 mm.

241.—I MING I TZŬ CH'ÊN PING. Lucid interpretation of the letters of the strangers set in order and offered to their superiors. [Petitions addressed to the Emperor by the French merchants in China, with signatures and seals.] MS. 370 × 240 mm. 1759.

344.—I SHIH. History arranged. By Ma Su. Edited by Li Ch'ing. 160 chüan. 48 pên in 6 vols. 275 × 175 mm. 1670.

426.—I-SHIH-PI CH'UAN. Æsop's fables. Translated into Chinese by Lo-pai Tan [*i.e.* Robert Thom]. 4 chüan. 238 × 140 mm. 1838.

*** Imperfect, wants chüan 4.

88.—I TSUNG CHIN CHIEN. The Golden mirror of the medical profession. 40 pên in 6 vols. 240 × 155 mm. 1739.

126.—I WÊN T'UNG LAN. Universal dictionary of classical and ancient characters arranged according to the radicals. 42 pên in 9 vols. 250 × 150 mm. 1806.

98.—I YIN. Sounds of the book of changes. By Ku Yen-wu. Edited by Chang Ch'aou. 3 chüan. 273 × 170 mm. 1643.

441.—INNOCENTIA VICTRIX sive sententia comitiorum Imperii Sinici pro innocentia Christianæ religionis lata juridicè per annum 1669 et jussu R. P. Antonii de Gouvea, S.J. ibidem V. Provincialis Sinico-Latinè exposita. 287 × 180 mm. Quam cheu, 1671.

*** Printed from wood blocks in the Chinese fashion; the Chinese text and transliteration in European letters, as well as the Latin translation of the various documents are given.

45 a.—JÊN HSIANG SHUI CHING CHI CH'ÜAN PIEN. The Bright mirror of human physiognomy complete. 4 chüan. 208 × 118 mm. 1680.

156.—JÊN-KUEI CHÊNG HSI SHUO T'ANG SAN CH'UAN. The Conquests of General Hsieh Jên-kuei in the west of China. By Ju Lien. 10 pên in 1 vol. 158 × 115 mm. 1807.

157.—JÊN-KUEI CHÊNG TUNG SHUO T'ANG HOU CH'UAN. The Conquests of General Hsieh Jên-kuei in the east of China. By Ju Lien. 8 pên in 1 vol. 170 × 115 mm. 1736.

156.—JU LIEN. *See* Jên-kuei chêng hsi shuo t'ang san ch'uan.

157.— „ „ „ Jên-kuei chêng tung shuo t'ang hou ch'uan.

55.—KAN YING P'IEN. The Book of rewards and punishments. By Lao chün. 2 pên in 1 vol. 169 × 115 mm.   1816.

220.—KANG CHIEN I CHIH LU. The Mirror of history made easy. By Wu Shêng-ch'üan, Chou Chih-ch'iung, and Chou Chih-ts'an. 40 pên in 7 vols. 250 × 158 mm.   1711.

248.—KANG CH'ING KO.   Broadsheet.
      MS. 360 × 500 mm. oblong.   1543.

304.—K'ANG HSI. *See* Ch'in ting Ch'un Ch'iu ch'uan shuo hui tsuan.

235.—   „   „   „ Huang ti i chao.

263.—   „   „   „ P'ei wên yün fu.

42.—   „   „   „ Shêng yü kuang hsün.

31.—K'ANG HSI. [An Imperial address in Chinese, Manchu and Latin, concerning the non-appearance of the four Jesuits Antonio de Barros, Antoine Beauvollier, Jose Provana, and Jose Raymondo de Arxo, who had been sent to Europe by that Sovereign.] Broadsheet. 460 mm. × 1 m. 20 mm. oblong.   31st October, 1716.

71.—K'ANG-HSI SHIH NIEN ÊRH YÜEH SHIH WU JIH TING YU YEH WANG YÜEH SHIH T'U. Observations of the eclipse of the moon, on the 15th of the 2nd month of the tenth year of the reign of K'ang Hsi, *i.e.* 1671, taken at the meridian of Peking. By Ferdinand Verbiest. In Chinese and Manchu, with a Latin title-page. Folded as a screen. 285 × 125 mm.   1671.

290.—K'ANG-HSI TZŬ TIEN. K'ang Hsi's dictionary. Compiled by Chang Yü-shu, Ch'ên T'ing-ching, Ling Shao-wên, and others. 12 parts in 9 vols. 225 × 153 mm.   1716.

125.—K'ANG-HSI TZŬ TIEN. Another edition. 32 pên in 8 vols. 170 × 120 mm. 1716.

185.—KAO SHIH CH'UAN. Biographies of eminent scholars. By Huang Fu-mei. Pi shu nien i chung, pên 7.

89.—KAO YO FANG. Medical prescriptions and formularies. 2 pên in 1 vol. 240 × 130 mm. 1829.

249 a.—K'AO KU T'U. Figures of ancient vessels. 10 chüan. 5 pên in 1 vol. 320 × 185 mm. 1752.

185.—KU CHIN CHU. An Examination of historical antiquities. By Ts'ui Pao. Pi shu nien i chung, pên 9.

279.—KU SHÊNG HSIEN HSIANG CH'UAN LÜEH. Short illustrated bio-graphies of ancient sages. By Ku Yüan. 16 chüan. 270 × 170 mm. [1830?]

*** Imperfect ; chüan 9-16 only.

440.—KU TSU-YU. *See* Tu shih fang yü chi yao.

168.—KU WÊN P'ING CHU. Collection of the finest pieces written in the ancient style from the Chou dynasty to the present time. With commentaries. 10 pên in 1 vol. 240 × 135 mm. 1832.

164.—KU WÊN YÜAN CHIEN. Mirror of ancient literature. 28 pên in 6 vols. 288 × 175 mm. [1650?]

98.—KU YEN-WU. *See* I yin.

98.— „ „ „ Ku yin piao.

98.—KU YEN-WU.   *See* Shih pên yin.

98.—   „   „   „   T'ang yün chêng.

98.—   „   „   „   Yin hsüeh wu shu.

98.—   „   „   „   Yin lun.

98.—KU YIN PIAO.   Ancient sounds tabulated.   By Ku Yen-wu.   Edited by Chang Ch'aou.   2 chüan.   273 × 170 mm.   1643.

249 b.—KU YÜ T'U.   Figures of ancient jewels.   2 chüan.   320 × 185 mm.   1752.

∗ Bound with K'ao ku t'u.

279.—KU YÜAN.   *See* Ku shêng hsien hsiang ch'uan lüeh.

299 b.—KUAN MOU-TS'UN.   *See* Fu ying hsin shuo.

299 c.—   „   „   „   Hsi i lüeh lun.

299 a.—   „   „   „   Nei k'o hsin shuo.

82.—KUANG CHÜN FANG P'U.   Botanical encyclopædia.   38 pên in 7 vols. 225 × 140 mm.   1708.

298.—KUANG PO WU CHIH.   An Encyclopædia.   By Tung Ssŭ-chang.   50 chüan.   22 pên in 5 tao.   258 × 169 mm.

464.—KUANG-TUNG YÜ TI TSUNG T'U.   General map of Kuangtung.   Kuangtung shêng ch'êng t'u.   Map of the capital of the province of Kuangtung (Canton).   On one sheet, coloured.   Roll, 1 m. × 36 cm.

229.—KUANG YÜ CHI. A Geography of the empire. Compiled by Lu Ying-yang. Edited by Ts'ai Fang-ping. 10 pên in 2 vols. 248 × 160 mm.

398.—KUEI CHOU CH'ÜAN SHÊNG PA SHIH ÊRH CHUNG MIAO T'U. Drawings illustrative of the complete account of the eighty-two tribes of the Miao of Kuei-chou. MS. 84 paintings. 2 vols. Folded as a screen. 305 × 240 mm. [1750?]

185.—KUEI HAI YÜ HÊNG CHIH. History of the productions of the rivers and mountains of Kuei-lin. By Fan Ch'eng-ta. Pi shu nien i chung, pên 7.

8.—KUEI PI I CHING. The I ching with commentary by Kuei Pi. 4 chüan. 235 × 150 mm.

40.—KUEI YU-KUANG. *See* Chu tzŭ hui han.

64.—KUMÂRAGÎVA. *See* Fo shuo O-mi-to ching.

166.—K'UN HSÜEH CHI WÊN CHI. Criticisms on literature and science. By Wang Ying-lin. With commentaries. 12 pên in 2 vols. 257 × 156 mm. 1815.

10.—KUNG CH'IU. *See* Shu ching ta ch'üan.

304.—KUNG-YANG KAO. *See* Ch'in ting Ch'un Ch'iu ch'uan shuo hui tsuan.

185.—K'UNG CH'AO. *See* Chi mêng Chou shu.

304.—K'UNG CH'IU. *See* Ch'in ting Ch'un Ch'iu ch'uan shuo hui tsuan.

17.— „ „ „ Ch'un Ch'iu ching ch'uan chi chieh.

105.—K'UNG FU. *See* Hsiao Êrh ya.

E

34 CATALOGUE OF CHINESE BOOKS.

39.—K'UNG TZŬ CHIA YŬ. The Family sayings of Confucius. Edited with a commentary by Wang Su. 10 chüan. 4 pên in 1 vol. 234 × 160 mm.

1506.

106.—KUO P'O. *See* Êrh ya chu su.

232.—KUO TS'Ê P'ING LIN. The Story of the contending states. With a commentary. 9 pên in 1 vol. 234 × 152 mm.

1727.

196.—KUO YŬ. The Narratives of the states. By Tso Ch'iu-ming. 4 pên in 1 vol. 246 × 160 mm.

1724.

197.—KUO YŬ. Another edition. 4 pên in 1 vol. 253 × 165 mm. [1700?]

13.—LA CHARME, ALEXANDRE DE. *See* Shih ching.

218.—LAN I. *See* Ching ni chi.

55.—LAO CHÜN. *See* Kan ying p'ien.

50.— „ „ „ Tao Tê ching chieh.

78.—LEI CHING T'U I. On physiology and physics. 11 chüan. 7 pên in 1 vol. 258 × 168 mm.

444.—LEI SHU SAN TS'AI T'U HUI. Collection of all that relates to the three principal agents (heaven, earth, and man), accompanied with plates and explanations. An encyclopædia. By Chiu Yu-fêng and others. Edited by Wang Yuan-han of Yun-Chian. 116 chüan in 14 vols. 260 × 165 mm.

1609.

240 a.—LEXICON LATINO-SINICUM EX BAYERO. CLAVES SINICÆ. MS. 320 × 200 mm.

221.—LI CH'AO KANG CHIEN. History of China to the end of the Yüan dynasty. 50 pên in 3 cases. 270 × 170 mm.

210.—LI CH'AO CHIEN KANG. History of the T'ang, Wu Tai, Sung, and Yüan dynasties. 5 pên in 1 vol. 245 × 143 mm.

*** A portion of a larger work, beginning with chüan 40.

213.—LI CH'AO CHIEN KANG. History of the dynasties of Han, Tsin, Sung, Ch'i, Liang, Ch'ên, and Sui. 6 pên in 1 vol. 242 × 144 mm.

*** A portion of a larger work.

18.—LI CHI P'ANG HSÜN. The Book of rites, with side-notes. 6 chüan. 6 pên in 1 vol. 243 × 147 mm. 1823.

408.—LI CHI T'I CHU. The Book of rites, with commentaries. 4 pên. 267 × 158 mm. 1711.

*** Imperfect; wants the last chapter.

344.—LI CH'ING. *See* I shih.

190.—LI FANG. *See* T'ai p'ing kuang chi.

288.—LI HSÜ. Supplement to the inscriptions of the time of the Han dynasty in the Li characters. Compiled A.D. 1167. 3 pên in 1 vol. 262 × 177 mm. [1550?]

90.—LI LI-WENG. *See* Chieh tzŭ yüan hua ch'uan.

74.—LI MING-CH'È. *See* Yüan t'ien t'u shuo.

413 ix.—LI PAI-LO. *See* Pei Ch'i shu.

138.—LI PEI LIEN CH'ÜAN CHI, *or,* **LI T'AI-PAI WÊN,** *q. v.*

331.—LI SAO CHING I. Poem by Fêng Sao. 3 pên. Ch'ên shih ts'ung shu, tao I.

166.—LI SHAN. *See* Wên hsüan.

81.—LI SHIH-CHÊN. *See* Pên ts'ao kang mu.

219.—LI SHIH KANG CHIEN PU. Abridgement of the annals of China to 1650. 5 vols. 250 × 155 mm.

313.--LI TAI CHI SHIH NIEN PIAO. Chronological tables from Huang Ti. 48 pên in 10 vols. 260 × 160 mm. 1715.

325.— LI TAI HUA SHIH. Brief account of illustrious characters of all times. 24 pên in 4 tao. 190 × 122 mm. 1825.

223.—LI TAI MING HSIEN LIEH NÜ SHIH HSING P'U. A Biographical dictionary of the celebrated men and women of all ages. By Hsiao Chih-han. 110 pên in 26 vols. 242 × 137 mm. 1784.

428.—LI TAI TI WANG NIEN PIAO. Tabulated manual of the reigns of the Emperors of China. From Huang Ti to the end of the Ming dynasty. 4 pên. 269 × 157 mm. 1824.

330.—LI TAI YÜ T'U. Geography of China in all ages. 12 pên. 271 × 168 mm. 1578.

138.—LI T'AI-PAI WÊN. Complete works of Li T'ai-pai. 14 pên in 3 vols. 232 × 153 mm. 1759.

214.—LI T'I CHIN KAO. Great deeds of the reigning dynasty. 7 pên in 2 vols. 170 × 110 mm.

225, 439.—LI WEI. *See* Hsi hu chih.

413 xiii.—LI YEN-SHOU. *See* Nan shih shu.

413 xiv.— „ „ „ Pei shih shu.

289.—LI YÜN. Vocabulary of the Li characters by tones. 6 pên in 1 vol. 262 × 167 mm. 1810.

306 a.—LIANG SHIH-CHÊNG. *See* Ch'ien lu.

306.— „ „ „ Hsi ch'ing ku chien.

413 x.—LIANG SHU. History of the Liang dynasty. By Yao Ssŭ-lien. 56 chüan. 8 pên in 1 tao. 290 × 180 mm. 1739.

453.—LIANG SHU. Another edition. 56 chüan. 8 pên. 257 × 168 mm. 1575.

413 xix.—LIAO SHIH. History of the Liao dynasty. By T'o-k'o-t'o and others. 135 chüan, and 12 supplementary chüan. 18 pên in 3 tao. 275 × 172 mm. 1824.

455.—LIAO SHIH. Another edition. 116 chüan. 8 pên. 260 × 170 mm. 1580.

122, 123, 124.—LIAO WÊN-YING. *See* Chêng tzŭ t'ung.

185.—LIEH HSIEN CH'UAN. Lives of eminent Taouist saints. Pi shu nien i chung, pên 10.

461.—LIN T'AI CHIANG CH'UAN. Biography of General Lin. 27 leaves. 240 × 197 mm.

** Printed entirely in Corean; the Chinese title is written outside the native paper cover.

413 xii.—LING-HU TÊ-FÊN. *See* Hou Chou shu.

129.—LING I-TUNG.   *See* Wu ch'ê yün jui.

290.—LING SHAO-WÊN.   *See* K'ang-hsi tzŭ tien.

341.—LING T'AI I HSIANG CHIH.   Description and regulations of the Imperial Observatory.   14 pên in 2 tao.   255 × 160 mm.   2 pên of plates. 365 × 190 mm.   1712.

424.—LING YEN CHIH LÜEH.   Statistical and topographical account of the mountain Ling Yen.   240 × 150 mm.   1756.

244 a.—LITTÉRATURE CHINOISE (Dialogues in Chinese and French).   Passio J. C. secundum 4ᵒʳ Evangelistas (Chinese and Latin).   Omnium vocum Sinicæ linguæ index generalis (Chinese, Latin and French). Evangelio de las Dominicas de adviento y quaresma (Chinese in Roman letters).   MSS.   In 1 vol.   255 × 190 mm.   About 1775.

51.—LIU AN.   *See* Huai nan hung lieh chieh.

258.—LIU CH'IU KUO CHIH.   History and description of the Lewchew (or Loochoo) Islands.   8 pên in 1 vol.   240 × 165 mm.   1744.

231.—LIU HSIANG.   *See* Chan kuo ts'ê.

362.—LIU SHU KU.   Origin of the six kinds of characters.   An ancient dictionary.   By Tai T'ung.   16 pên in 2 tao.   270 × 175 mm.
1775.

109.—LIU SHU PÊN I.   Dictionary of ancient characters.   253 × 165 mm.
1520.

300.—LIU SHU T'UNG.   Dictionary of ancient characters arranged by the six tones.   5 pên in 1 vol.   243 × 170 mm.   1661.

356.—LIU YÜ-P'O. *See* Ying huan chih lüeh.

278.—LO-FOU SHAN CHIH HUI PIEN. Illustrated topography of the Lo-fou Hills, in the province of Kuang-tung. By Sung Kuang-nieh. 22 chüan. 5 pên in 2 vols. 242 × 152 mm. 1716.

142, 277.—LO KUAN-CHUNG. *See* San kuo chih.

426.—LO-PAI TAN. *See* I-shih-pi ch'uan.

203.—LO PI. *See* Chung ting lu shih ch'ien chi.

281.—LO SHIH. *See* T'ai p'ing huan yü chi.

159.—LO T'UNG SAO PEI CH'IEN HOU CH'UAN. The Exploits of Lo T'ung in the north of China. 3 pên in 1 vol. 160 × 115 mm. [1800?]

35.—LONGOBURDO, NICOLAS. *See* Shêng chiao jih k'o.

458.—LU CHING T'U. Illustrations to accompany the six classics. By Yang Chia. Edited by Mao Pang-han, Ch'ên San and others. 440 × 265 mm. 1615.

3.—LU CHING T'U. Illustrations to the six classics. Compiled by Chêng Chih-ch'iao. 12 chüan. 6 pên in 1 vol. 239 × 155 mm. 1743.

175.—LU LING OU YANG WÊN CHUNG KUNG CH'UAN CHI. The Works of Ou-yang Hsiu. 28 pên in 4 vols. 270 × 190 mm. 1792.

50.—LU SHIH. *See* Tao Tê ching chieh.

2.—LU TÊ-MING. *See* Ching tien shih wên.

2.—LU WÊN-CH'AO. *See* Ching tien shih wên.

229.—LU YING-YANG. *See* Kuang yü chi.

183.—LUNG WEI PI SHU. Collection of forty-six rare works from the archives of the Emperor. 80 pên in 10 vols. 174 × 110 mm.   1675.

340.—LÜ LÜ CHING I. Work on music. By Prince Ts'ai Yü. 19 pên in 4 vols. 350 × 225 mm.

360.—LÜ LÜ CHING I. Another edition. 19 pên in 2 tao. 325 × 225 mm.

50.—LÜ YEN. *See* Tao Tê ching chieh.

185.—MA KAO. *See* Chung hua ku chin chu.

379.—MA SHAO-YÜN. *See* Wei tsang t'u shih.

344.—MA SU. *See* I shih.

187, 188.—MA TUAN-LIN. *See* Wên hsien t'ung k'ao.

43.—MAN HAN HSÜN CHIH SHIH TSÊ. The Ten precepts of Yung-chêng. In Manchu and Chinese. 234 × 155 mm.   1727.

422.—MAO K'UN. *See* Ch'ou hai t'u pien.

458.—MAO PANG-HAN. *See* Lu ching t'u.

142.—MAO SHÊNG-SHAN. See San kuo chih.

14.—MAO SHIH KU HSÜN CH'UAN TING PÊN. Mao's commentary on the book of odes. 30 chüan. 4 pên in 1 vol. 278 × 175 mm. [1800?]

228.—MEDHURST, WALTER HENRY, the Elder, D.D. *See* Ch'iao-liu-pa tsung lun.

456.— „ „ „ Vocabulary of the Chinese, Corean, and Japanese languages.

407.—MEI HUA I SHU. A Work on divination by the Pa Kua, or eight mystical diagrams of Fuh Hsi, according to the principles of the I Ching. 5 pên. 177 × 118 mm.

117, 118.—MEI TANG-HSING. *See* Hsüan chin tzŭ hui.

127.—MEI YING-TZŬ. *See* Yü T'ang tzŭ hui.

21.—MÊNG TZŬ. The Works of Mencius. 1st portion. Chüan 1 and 2. 250 × 160 mm.

237 b.—MÊNG TZŬ WÊN. The works of Mencius. Partly transliterated in Roman letter, and partly translated into Latin. MS. 2 vols. 225 × 185 mm. About 1800.

425.—MIAO FANG PEI LAN. Account of the manners and customs of the Miao-tzŭ. 3 chüan. 275 × 158 mm.

38 b.—MILNE, WILLIAM, D.D. *See* Ch'a shih su mei yüeh t'ung chi ch'uan.

38 e.— „ „ „ Chu kuo i shên lun.

38 g.— „ „ „ Hsin tsêng yang hsin shên shih.

38 a.— „ „ „ San pao jên hui lun.

212.—MING CH'AO CHI. Annals of the Ming dynasty. 20 pên in 4 vols. 240 × 155 mm. 1658.

211.—MING CHI CH'ÜAN TSAI. Annals of the Ming dynasty. 16 chüan. 6 pên in 1 case. 270 × 170 mm.

73.—MING MING-O. *See* Fang hsing t'u chieh.

413 xxii.—MING SHIH. History of the Ming dynasty. By Chang T'ing-yü and others. 310 chüan. 30 pên in 10 vols. 252 × 167 mm. 1697.

295.—MO-CH'IH. *See* Chân mên jih sung.

36.—MONTEYRO, JUAN. *See* Shên chên jih k'o.

433.—MORRISON, ROBERT, D.D. *See* Ch'i tao wên tsan shên shih.

38 h.— ,, ,, ,, Ch'üan tu shêng lu shu chih wên.

296.—MU MING CHÜ LI. Collection of monumental and other inscriptions in metal and stone. 14 chüan. 4 pên in 1 vol. 295 × 185 mm. 1823.

63.—MU NIU T'U. Tending the cow. With illustrations. A Buddhist allegorical work, by P'u Ming. Edited by Chu Hung. 220 × 140 mm. 1619.

335.—MU T'IEN TZŬ CH'UAN CHU PU CHÊNG. Respectful terms for addressing the Emperor and superiors generally. 4 pên. Ch'ên shih ts'ung shu, tao 2.

434.—MUSEI ECHEN ISUS CHRISTOS-I TUTABUHA ITCHE GHESE. Manchu translation of the New Testament. 8 pên in 1 case. 265 × 197 mm. St. Petersburg, 1821-36.

413 viii.—NAN CH'I SHU. History of the southern Ch'i dynasty. By Hsiao Tzŭ-hsien. 59 chüan. 12 pên in 2 vols. 250 × 160 mm. 1589.

52.—NAN HUA CHING CHIEN CHU. The Nan hua classic, by Chuang Chou. With a commentary. 8 chüan. 5 pên in 1 vol. 244 × 160 mm.

1749.

160.—NAN PEI SUNG CHIH CH'UAN. Historical romance relating to the southern and northern Sung. 10 pên in 2 vols. 172 × 115 mm.

[1820 ?]

413 xiii.—NAN SHIH SHU. History of the southern states. By Li Yen-shou. 80 chüan. 20 pên in 4 vols. 254 × 165 mm. 1590.

299 a.—NEI K'O HSIN SHUO. New treatise on the practice of medicine. By Ho-hsin [*i.e.* Benjamin Hobson]. Edited by Kuan Mou-ts'un. 2 chüan. 261 × 165 mm. 1858.

442.—NIEH PO-TO. *See* T'ien chu chiang shêng yen hsing chi hsiang.

413 i.-xxii.—NIEN ÊRH SHIH. The Twenty-two histories. 640 pên in 144 vols. or tao.

448.—NIKAN KHERGEN I OUPALIYAMBOUKHA MANDCHOU GISOUN I BOULEKOU BITKHE. Mirror of the Manchu language interpreted by Chinese. Manchu and Chinese dictionary. 20 chüan in 1 vol. 255 × 170 mm. 1735.

175.—OU-YANG HSIU. *See* Lu ling Ou-yang wên chung kung ch'üan chi.

305, 413 xvi. a, b.— „ „ T'ang shu.

413 xvii. a, 454.— „ „ Wu tai shih.

357.—PA CH'I MAN CHOU SHIH TSU T'UNG P'U. General account of the Eight Banners; being genealogical tables of the most eminent Tartar families or clans. 80 chüan. 24 pên in 4 vols. 275 × 175 mm.

1744.

25.—PAI CHIA HSING.   The Hundred family names.   213 × 130 mm.

185.—PAI HU T'UNG.   The Report of a convocation held in the Pai-hu Kuan. By Pan Ku.   2 chüan.   Pi shu nien i chung, pên 4.

351.—PAI MEI HSIN YUNG T'U CH'UAN.   New collection of sonnets to the hundred beauties.   With illustrated biographies.   By Yen Hsi-yüan. 4 pên in 1 tao.   236 × 145 mm.   1786.

208, 413 ii.—PAN KU.   *See* Ch'ien Han shu.

185.—   „   „   „   Pai hu t'ung.

324.—P'AN SHAN CHIH.   Description of the P'an Mountain.   9 pên in 1 tao. 280 × 175 mm.   1755.

36.—PANTOJA, DIEGO.   *See* Shên chên jih k'o.

413 ix.—PEI CH'I SHU.   History of the northern Ch'i dynasty.   By Li Pai-lo. 58 chüan.   8 pên in 2 vols.   258 × 162 mm.   1588.

413 xiv.—PEI SHIH SHU.   History of the northern states.   By Li Yen-shou. 100 chüan.   30 pên in 6 vols.   256 × 163 mm.   1592.

317.—P'EI WÊN CHAI SHU HUA P'U.   Compilation to enable the student to call to mind the subjects of certain literary productions and pictorial representations.   100 chüan.   64 pên in 8 tao.   220 × 140 mm.

1708.

263.—P'EI WÊN YÜN FU.   A Lexicon arranged according to the usual system of 106 finals distributed among the five tones.   [Compiled under the special superintendence of the Emperor K'ang Hsi.]   127 pên in 51 vols.   193 × 133 mm.   1710.

⁎ For the Supplement *see* Yün fu shih i.

83.—PÊN TS'AO I FANG HO PIEN. A Collection of medical prescriptions from the Pên ts'ao. 6 pên in 2 vols. 174 × 112 mm. 1798.

81.—PÊN TS'AO KANG MU. The Materia medica of Li Shih-chên. Edited by Wu Yü-ch'ang. 52 chüan in 7 vols. 250 × 162 mm. 1655.

456.—PHILO SINENSIS. *See* Vocabulary of the Chinese, Corean, and Japanese languages.

224.—PHILOLOGICAL, HISTORICAL, AND OTHER MEMORANDA, in French, relating to Chinese subjects. MS. 190 × 120 mm. About 1820.

243 a.—PHRASES, of four, five, six, eight, ten and twelve characters ; also extracts from the New Testament in Chinese. MS. 140 × 105 mm. About 1800.

242.—PHRASES, partly translated into French. MS. 305 × 215 mm. About 1790.

246.—PHRASES, without translations. MS. 220 × 180 mm. About 1750.

60.—PI MI LÜ I YAO LÜEH. Abridgement of the precepts to be followed by the Buddhist priests. With commentaries. 227 × 142 mm.

185.—PI SHU NIEN I CHUNG. A Collection of twenty-one reprints. Compiled by Wang Shih-han. 10 pên in 3 vols. 170 × 115 mm. 1805.

356.—P'I HSING-CH'ÜAN. *See* Ying huan chih lüeh.

145.—P'ING SHAN LÊNG YEN. A Celebrated novel of the fourth class. 4 pên in 1 vol. 168 × 114 mm.

88.—P'ING SHIH CHIN NANG. Medical encyclopædia. Printed with notes. 30 pên in 5 vols. 235 × 155 mm. 1702.

372.—P'ING TING CHUN KO ÊRH FANG LÜEH. Abridged history of the destruction of the army of the chief of the Eleuths. 100 pên in 12 vols. 335 × 215 mm. 1771.

308.—P'ING TING LIANG CHIN CH'UAN FANG LÜEH. History of the final conquest of the Miao Tzŭ. 68 pên in 8 tao. 300 × 190 mm. 1755.

345.—P'ING TING SO MO FANG LÜEH. History of the pacification of the Tartar tribes. 24 pên in 4 tao. 330 × 210 mm. 1708.

373.—P'ING TING T'AI WAN CHI LÜEH. Abridged history of the conquest of Formosa. 32 pên in 4 tao. 300 × 195 mm. 1786.

38 b.—PO-AI-CHÊ. *See* Ch'a shih su mei yüeh t'ung chi ch'uan.

38 e.— „ „ „ Chu kuo i shên lun.

38 a.— „ „ „ San pao jên hui lun.

185.—PO I CHI. Collection of extraordinary or wonderful relations. Pi shu nien i chung, pên 7.

267.—PO KU T'U. An Illustrated collection of antiquities. By Wang Fu and others. 16 pên *in* 2 vols. 277 × 170 mm. 1608.

185.—PO WU CHIH. Treatises on diverse matters. By Chang Hua. Pi shu nien i chung, pên 6.

299 e.—PO WU HSIN PIEN. New treatise on the natural sciences. By Ho-hsin [*i.e.* Benjamin Hobson]. 261 × 165 mm. 1858.

438.—POMPELLY, R. *See* Road map from Peking to Kiachta.

31.—PROVANA, JOSE. *See* K'ang Hsi.

110.—PU HSIANG TZŬ I. Dictionary of ancient characters. 251 × 152 mm. [1752 ?]

404.—PU SHIH CHÊNG TSUNG. A Work on divination. By Wang Wei-tê. 4 pên. 171 × 116 mm. 1830.

66.—P'U CH'ÜAN NIEN FO. Exhortations to the study of Buddha. 220 × 140 mm. 1797.

367.—P'U LIU-HSIEN. *See* Chih fan liao chai chih i.

68.—P'U MING. *See* Mu niu t'u.

243 c.—RATIO PROPONENDÆ DIVINÆ LEGIS INFIDELIBUS. Chinese in Roman letter. With other papers on ecclesiastical matters by Roman Catholic missionaries. All in Roman letter. MS. 220 × 165 mm. About 1700.

230.—RECUEIL DE PIÈCES utiles pour apprendre le chinois et les termes civils de cette langue. MS. 350 × 230 mm. About 1750.

94.—RÉMUSAT, ABEL. *See* Explanation of the keys of the Chinese characters.

115.— „ „ „ Hsieh shêng p'in tzŭ chien.

68.— „ „ „ T'ien wên.

438.—ROAD MAP FROM PEKING TO KIACHTA BY THE GREAT CAMEL ROUTE. Geological notes by R. Pompelly. 12 sheets. 625 × 253 mm. Joined in pairs, and folded in 1 tao. Peking, 1864.

30 b.—ROCHA, J. DE. *See* T'ien chu shêng hsiang lüeh shuo.

46.—SAN CHIAO YÜAN LIU SHÊNG TI FO SHIH SOU SHÊN CHI. A History of the founders of the three sects, *i.e.* Confucianism, Buddhism, and Taoism, and of other saints and sages. 4 chüan. 3 pên in 1 vol. 182 × 117 mm.   1819.

185.—SAN FÊN. The Works of the first three mythical Emperors. Edited by Wu Kuan. Pi shu nien i chung, pên 9.

150.—SAN FÊN MÊNG CH'ÜAN CH'UAN. Narration of the dream, in three parts. 4 pên in 1 vol. 167 × 115 mm.   1823.

142.—SAN KUO CHIH. The History of the three kingdoms. By Lo Kuán-chung. Edited by Chin Shêng-t'an. Revised by Mao Shêng-shan. 20 pên in 3 vols. 173 × 112 mm.   1644.

277.—SAN KUO CHIH. Another edition. 20 chüan. 236 × 140 mm. 1684.

413 iv.—SAN KUO CHIH. History of the three kingdoms. By Chên Shou. 65 chüan. 10 pên in 2 vols. 255 × 163 mm.

27.—SAN LI T'U. Illustrations of the vessels, ornaments, &c., referred to in the three rituals. 20 chüan. 2 pên in 1 vol. 275 × 180 mm.

38 a.—SAN PAO JÊN HUI LUN. A Discourse about the three precious benevolent societies, viz.: the Missionary, the Tract, and the Bible Societies. By Po-ai-chê [*i.e.* William Milne, D.D.]. 200 × 130 mm.   [1835 ?]

23.—SAN TZŬ CHING. The Three-character classic. 210 × 122 mm.

293.—SANG CH'IN. *See* Shui ching chu shih.

185.—SHAN HAI CHING. The Hill and river classic. Pi shu nien i chung, pên 5.

49.—SHAN HAI CHING HSIANG CHU. The Hill and river classic. 23 chüan. 4 pên in 1 vol. 169 × 115 mm. 1818.

222.—SHANG-TÊ-CHÊ. *See* Ch'iao-liu-pa tsung lun.

314.—SHAO CH'ING-PANG. *See* Hung chien lu.

350.—SHAO YUNG. *See* Huang chi ching shih shu.

251, 371.—SHAO YÜAN-P'ING. *See* Yüan shih lei pien.

36.—SHÊN CHÊN JIH K'O. Book of prayers, compiled by Juan Monteyro, Diego Pantoja, and Emmanuel Diaz. 5 chüan. 125 × 80 mm.

45.—SHÊN HSIANG CH'ÜAN PIEN. Complete treatise on physiognomy, palmistry, &c. 12 chüan. 6 pên in 1 vol. 243 × 155 mm. 1793.

48.—SHÊN HSIEN T'UNG CHIEN. Complete mirror of gods and genii. 39 chüan. 39 pên in 6 vols. 172 × 117 mm. 1787.

30 a.—SHÊNG CHIAO HSIN CHÊNG. A History of the Jesuit mission to China. 247 × 155 mm. [1680?]

35.—SHÊNG CHIAO JIH K'O. Examination of the most holy doctrine. By Nicolas Longoburdo. Supplement. 172 × 117 mm.

379.—SHÊNG MEI-CH'I. *See* Wei tsang t'u shih.

38 d.—SHÊNG MU WU YÜAN TSUI CHING. Book of prayers. 202 × 128 mm. [1820?]

34.—SHÊNG SHIH CH'U JAO. The Hay or straw which fills the age. By Tin-a Shêng. 4 chüan. 4 pên in 1 tao. 250 × 155 mm.

G

CATALOGUE OF CHINESE BOOKS.

380.—SHÊNG WU CHI. Military annals of the reigning dynasty. By Wei Yüan. 12 pên in 1 tao. 254 × 168 mm. 1842.

42.—SHÊNG YÜ KUANG HSÜN. The Maxims of the Emperor K'ang-hsi amplified by his successor, Yung-chêng. 220 × 135 mm. 1815.

217.—SHIH CH'ÊNG TS'ÊNG I. History of Yung Lê of the Ming dynasty. MS. 245 × 128 mm.

413 i.—SHIH CHI. The Historical record. By Ssŭ-ma Ch'ien. 130 chüan. 40 pên in 6 vols. 238 × 160 mm.

201.—SHIH CHI. Another edition. 5 vols. 244 × 166 mm.

452.—SHIH CHI. Another edition. With a commentary. 120 chüan. 20 pên. 259 × 165 mm. 1596.

13.—SHIH CHING. The Book of odes. Translated into Latin by Alexandre de La Charme. MS. 375 × 240 mm. About 1750.

238.—SHIH CHING. Tracings of portions of the book of odes, with translations into Latin. MS. 305 × 210 mm. About 1795.

16.—SHIH CHING CH'ÜAN CHU. The Book of odes, with complete explanation. 8 chüan. 6 pên in 1 vol. 218 × 120 mm. [1800?]

92.—SHIH CH'ING YA CH'Ü. A Treatise on the game of chess. 5 pên in 1 vol. 213 × 133 mm. 1570.

93.—SHIH CH'ING YA CH'Ü. Instructions for playing a game resembling dominoes. 2 pên in 1 vol. 263 × 169 mm. 1640.

284.—SHIH I CHÊ CHUNG. Commentaries on the book of odes. 10 pên in 2 vols. 273 × 185 mm. 1755.

185.--SHIH I CHI. Lost pages of history. By Wang Chia. Edited by Hsiao Ch'i. Pi shu nien i chung, pên 3.

301.--SHIH LIU CH'IU CHI. Account of an embassy to Loo Choo. 2 pên in 1 vol. 253 × 165 mm. 1798.

207.--SHIH LIU KUO CH'UN CH'IU. The Annals of the sixteen dynasties. By Ts'ui Hung. 18 pên in 4 vols. 287 × 175 mm.

146.--SHIH NAI-AN. *See* Shui hu ch'uan.

98.--SHIH PEN YIN. Original sounds of the book of odes. By Ku Yen-wu. Edited by Chang Ch'aou. 10 chüan. 273 × 170 mm. 1643.

178.--SHIH SHIH T'UNG K'AO. An Encyclopædia. 240 × 130 mm. [1650?]

285.--SHIH TZŬ CH'ÜAN SHU. Complete works of the ten philosophers. Compiled by Huang P'ei-lieh. 26 pên in 5 vols. 300 × 180 mm. 1804.

10.--SHU CHING TA CH'ÜAN. A Complete copy of the book of historical documents. By K'ung Ch'iu. With comments by Ts'ai Shên, Chu Hsi, Ch'êng Hao, and others. Edited by Hsü Chiu-yi. 10 chüan. 12 pên in 2 vols. 258 × 165 mm. [1750?]

364.--SHU P'I P'A CHI. The Story of a lute. A romance or drama. 6 pên in 1 vol. 137 × 100 mm. 1735

389.--SHU SHU CHIU CHANG. A Work on arithmetical computation. 18 chüan in 5 pên, and supplement 4 chüan in 2 pên. I chia t'ang ts'ung shu, tao 8. 240 × 150 mm. [1842?]

293.--SHUI CHING CHU SHIH. The Water classic. By Sang Ch'in. With a commentary by Chao Yi-ch'ing. 40 chüan. 20 pên in 2 tao. 295 × 178 mm. 1786.

146.—SHUI HU CH'UAN. The Story of the river's banks. By Shih Nai-an. 20 pên in 3 vols. 172 × 112 mm.

50.—SHUN-YANG TI CHÜN. *See* Tao Tê ching chieh.

153.—SHUO T'ANG YEN CH'UAN. A History of the T'ang dynasty. By Yüan-hu-yü, or the Fisherman of Lake Yüan. 14 pên in 2 vols. 170 × 112 mm.   [1750?]

108.—SHUO WÊN CHÊN PÊN. Dictionary of the seal characters. Compiled about A.D. 980. 8 pên in 2 vols. 294 × 178 mm.   [1600?]

381.—SHUO WÊN CHIEH TZŬ CHU. Commentary on the explanation of characters in the Shuo wên. By Tuan Yü-ts'ai. 15 chüan. 32 pên in 8 tao. 286 × 177 mm.   1815.

320.—SHUO WÊN TZŬ YÜAN. On the origin of the seal characters. 4 pên in 1 tao. 280 × 175 mm.   1787.

320 a.—SHUO WÊN TZŬ YÜAN. Another edition. Part I. only. 270 × 180 mm.   1350.

152.—SHUO YO CH'ÜAN CH'UAN. The Complete narrative of Yo Fei, a general who served under the Sung dynasty. By Ch'ien Ts'ai. 10 pên in 2 vols. 157 × 103 mm.   1801.

201, 413 i., 452.—SSŬ-MA CH'IEN. *See* Shih chi.

399.—SSŬ SHU. The Four books. With notes and commentaries. 6 pên in 1 vol. 280 × 180 mm.   1797.

19.—SSŬ SHU CHÊNG TI. The Four books. With commentaries. 19 chüan. 6 pên in 1 vol. 200 × 130 mm.

37.—STANISLAUS KOSTKA, ST. *See* Tê hsing p'u.

354.—SU T'IEN-CH'IO. *See* Yüan chao ming ch'ên shi lüeh.

318.—SUAN FA T'UNG TSUNG TA CH'ÜAN. Complete work on the rules of arithmetic, illustrating the principle of the abacus. By Ch'êng Ta-wei. 5 pên in 1 tao. 226 × 133 mm. 1864.

44.—SUN CHANG. *See* Hsing li chên ch'üan.

366.—SUN SSŬ-MO. *See* Ch'ien chin i fang.

44.—SUNG CHÚN-JUNG. *See* Hsing li chên ch'üan.

278.—SUNG KUANG-NIEH. *See* Lo-fou shan chih hui pien.

252.—SUNG, LIAO, CHIN, YÜAN SSŬ SHIH. History of the Sung, Liao, Chin, and Yüan dynasties. 12 pên in 2 vols. 273 × 180 mm. 1744.

413 xxi.—SUNG LIEN. *See* Yüan shih.

260.—SUNG MIN-CH'IU. *See* Ch'ang-an chih.

107.—SUNG PÊN YÜ P'IEN. Dictionary, compiled by the Buddhists. 215 × 165 mm. 1704.

413 xviii.—SUNG SHIH. History of the Sung dynasty. 496 chüan. 100 pên in 22 vols. 257 × 170 mm. 1597.

291.—SUNG SHIH HSIEN CH'ÜAN. Biographies of ten most celebrated philosophers during the Sung dynasty. 280 × 175 mm. 1743.

CATALOGUE OF CHINESE BOOKS.

413 vi.—SUNG SHU. History of the Sung dynasty. By Chên Yo. 100 chüan. 24 pên in 5 vols. 275 × 178 mm. 1739.

413 xv.—SUI SHU. History of the Sui dynasty. By Wei Chêng. 88 chüan. 20 pên in 4 vols. 257 × 162 mm. 1595.

77.—TA CH'ING CHIN SHÊN CH'ÜAN SHU. A Complete official directory of the empire. 4 pên in 1 vol. 155 × 110 mm. 1820.

377.—TA CH'ING CHUNG WAI I T'UNG YÜ T'U. Complete map of the Chinese empire. 32 pên of maps in 2 vols. 290 × 190 mm. 1756.

384.—TA CH'ING CH'ÜAN SHU. Vocabulary, Manchu and Chinese. 15 pên in 2 vols. 284 × 180 mm. 1683.

250.—TA CH'ING I T'UNG CHIH. A Geography of the empire, published under the Ts'ing dynasty. Compiled by an Imperial Commission consisting of Prince Hung Chou, Chiang T'ing-hsi, Ch'ên Tê-hua, and others. 356 chüan. 108 pên in 25 vols. 270 × 175 mm. 1743.

264.—TA CH'ING LÜ LI. The Fundamental laws and subordinate statutes of the Ch'ing dynasty. 40 chüan in 5 vols. 259 × 155 mm. 1821.

237 a.—TA HIO [HSÜEH], sive magna scientia, autore Çem-çu celeberrimo Confucii discipulo. (Chinese in Roman letter, with Latin and French translations.) MS. 230 × 175 mm. About 1800.

80.—TA KUAN PÊN TS'AO. An Enlarged survey of medical botany. Part of the 13th chüan. 2 pên in 1 case. 275 × 170 mm. [1500?]

342.—TA MING SAN TSANG SHÊNG CHIAO. Descriptive catalogue of Buddhist books. Compiled A.D. 1410. 2 pên. 248 × 174 mm.

67.—TA PEI SHÊN CHOU HSIN CHING. Buddhist book (? a ritual). 142 × 52 mm.

311.—TA T'ANG HSI YÜ CHI. An Account of the western frontiers of the empire during the T'ang dynasty. Principally translated from the Sanscrit by the priest Hsüan-chuang. Together with an account of the countries through which he himself passed in his travels. 3 pên in 1 tao. 270 × 178 mm. 1700.

176.—TA WAN PAO CH'UAN SHU. An Encyclopædia. By Chang T'uan. 6 pên in 1 vol. 245 × 138 mm. [1570?]

177.—TA WAN PAO CH'ÜAN SHU. Another edition. 6 pên in 1 vol. 223 × 132 mm. 1758.

362.—TAI T'UNG. *See* Liu shu ku.

281.—T'AI P'ING HUAN YÜ CHI. Geography of the empire, during the reign of T'ai-p'ing-hsing-kuo. By Lo Shih. Edited by Ch'ên Lan-sên. 200 chüan. 47 pên in 6 vols. 247 × 160 mm. 1793.

190.—T'AI P'ING KUANG CHI. Extensive records, compiled during the reign of the Emperor T'ai-tsung. By Li Fang. Edited by Huang Hsiao-fêng. Containing mythological and other tales. 500 chüan. 48 pên in 8 vols. 160 × 103 mm. 1806.

280.—T'AI P'ING YÜ LAN. An Encyclopædia. 1000 chüan. 96 pên in 16 vols. 242 × 155 mm. 1818.

413 v.—T'AI TSUNG. *See* Tsin shu.

101.—TAN SHAN CHI T'IEH. Instruction in Chinese writing. 4 pên in 1 vol. 234 × 140 mm. 1809.

297.—T'AN CHING. The Book of the altar. A Buddhist formulary. 280 × 180 mm.

137.—T'ANG SHIH PI LÜ CHIEN CHU. Selection of poems of. the T'ang dynasty, with notes. 6 pên in 1 vol. 252 × 156 mm.   1784.

413 xvi. a.—T'ANG SHU. History of the T'ang dynasty. By Ou-yang Hsiu. With commentaries. 260 chüan. 73 pên, and supplement 7 pên, in 17 vols. 278 × 175 mm.   1784.

413 xvi. b.—T'ANG SHU. Another edition. 292 chüan. 30 pên in 10 vols. 280 × 183 mm.

305.—T'ANG SHU. Another edition. 225 chüan. 36 pên in 6 vols. 275 × 180 mm.

87.—T'ANG WANG-CHU. *See* Wai t'ai pi yao fang.

98.—T'ANG YÜN CHÊNG. Rectification of the T'ang dynasty finals. By Ku Yen-wu. Edited by Chang Ch'aou. 20 chüan. 273 × 170 mm.   1643.

50.—TAO TÊ CHING CHIEH. The Classic of reason and virtue. By Lao-chün. Explained by Shun-yang Ti chün, *i.e.* Lü Yen. Edited by Lu Shih. 242 × 155 mm.   [1809?]

54.—TAO YEN NEI WAI, *or,* **WU CHUNG PI LU,** *q. v.*

363.—T'AO CHÊNG-AI. *See* T'ien yü hua.

414.—TAÜTSING OLON-OUN TEGRI DJIN TATKOKSAN Ô TERIKON ON. Imperial almanack, in Mongolian, for the 1st year of Ch'ien Lung. 357 × 220 mm.   1736.

37.—TÊ HSING P'U. The Life of St. Stanislaus Kostka. 251 × 180 mm.

426.—THOM, ROBERT. *See* I-shih-pi ch'uan.

401.—TI CHIEN T'U SHUO. Illustrations of the good and bad actions of the Emperors, with descriptions. 6 pên in 1 tao. 305 × 180 mm. 1573.

147.—TI I CH'I SHU, *or*, **CHIN P'ING MEI,** *q. v.*

142.—TI I TS'AI TZŬ SHU, *or*, **SAN KUO CHIH,** *q. v.*

143, 144.—TI SAN TS'AI TZŬ SHU, *or*, **YÜ CHIAO LI,** *q. v.*

145.—TI SSŬ TS'AI TZŬ SHU, *or*, **P'ING SHAN LÊNG YEN,** *q. v.*

146.—TI WU TS'AI SHU, *or*, **SHUI HU CH'UAN,** *q. v.*

442.—T'IEN CHU CHIANG SHÊNG YEN HSING CHI HSIANG. An Illustrated Life of Christ. By Ai Ju-lio [*i.e.* Julio Aleni]. Edited by Ch'ü Hsi-man, Yang-ma-no [*i.e.* Emmanuel Diaz], and Nieh Po-to. 273 × 155 mm. [1630 ?]

30 b.—T'IEN CHU SHÊNG HSIANG LÜEH SHUO. Abridged explanation of the Holy Image of the Lord of Heaven. By J. de Rocha. 247 × 155 mm. 1619.

326.—T'IEN FANG CHÊNG HSÜEH. Introduction to the reading of Arabic. 4 pên in 1 tao. 297 × 192 mm. 1861.

33.—T'IEN SHÊN HUI K'O. Discourse of angels. By Francis Brancati. 253 × 144 mm.

68.—T'IEN WÊN. Chinese uranography. MS. Attributed to Abel Rémusat. 325 × 205 mm. 1807.

75.—T'IEN WÊN TA CH'ÊNG. Complete treatise on astronomy. By Huang Yü-êrh. 80 chüan. 32 pên in 6 vols. 250 × 157 mm. 1652.

H

363.—T'IEN YÜ HUA. The Rain and flowers of heaven. A novel, chiefly in verse. By T'ao Chêng-ai. 32 pên in 4 tao. 180 × 117 mm. 1812.

34.—TIN-A-SHÊNG. *See* Shêng shih ch'u jao.

413 xx.—T'O-K'O-T'O. *See* Chin shih.

413 xix., 455.—„   „   „ Liao shih.

244 b.—TRACTS BY THE MISSIONARIES, and extracts from the Holy Scriptures, in Chinese. MS. 240 × 160 mm.   About 1780.

437.—TRIGAULT, NICOLAS. *See* Hsi ju êrh mu tzŭ.

229.—TS'AI FANG-PING. *See* Kuang yü chi.

10.—TS'AI SHÊN. *See* Shu ching ta ch'üan.

340, 360.—TS'AI YÜ. *See* Lü lü ching i.

154.—TS'AN T'ANG WU TAI CH'ÜAN CH'UAN. History of the five small dynasties that succeeded the T'ang. 6 pên in 1 vol. 158 × 107 mm.   [1750 ?]

149, 402.—TS'AO HSÜEH-CH'IN. *See* Hung lou mêng.

113.—TS'AO TZŬ HUI. Dictionary of the current hand. 270 × 150 mm. 1788.

406.—TSÊNG KUANG HSIEN WÊN. A Short tract on morality. 210 × 130 mm.

20.—TSÊNG PU SSŬ SHU JÊN WU PEI K'AO. The Four books, with commentaries. 12 chüan. 6 pên in 1 vol. 243 × 145 mm.   1727.

365.—TSÊNG TING CHIN P'I HSI HSIANG. Selections from and critical remarks on the Hsi hsiang chih, or "Story of the Western Chamber." 4 pên in 1 tao. 193 × 129 mm.

99.—TSÊNG TING TZŬ HSÜEH CHING LIANG. Bridge for arriving at a knowledge of the characters. By Fu Ju-wei. 258 × 167 mm. 1687.

413 v.—TSIN SHU. History of the Tsin dynasty. By T'ai Tsung. 130 chüan. 32 pên in 4 tao. 289 × 180 mm. 1739.

304.—TSO CH'IU-MING. *See* Ch'in ting Ch'un Ch'iu ch'uan shuo hui tsuan.

17.— „ „ „ Ch'un Ch'iu ching ch'uan chi chieh.

195.— „ „ „ Chung ting ch'un ch'iu Tso ch'uan chü chieh.

196, 197.— „ „ „ Kuo yü.

329.—TSO LIAO SHIH TSÊ. Military regulations of soldiers in garrison. 4 pên in 1 tao. 293 × 155 mm. 1639.

17.—TSO SU, *or,* **CH'UN CH'IU CHING CH'UAN CHI CHIEH,** *q. v.*

65.—TSUAN CHU YÜAN CHIAO CHING. Book relating to the Buddhist saints. 258 × 158 mm. 1692.

368.—TSUI PU TO. In Manchu. 20 pên in 4 tao. 288 × 186 mm.

207.—TS'UI HUNG. *See* Shih liu kuo ch'un ch'iu.

185.—TS'UI PAO. *See* Ku chin chu.

62.—TSUNG-MI.   *See* Fo shuo Yü lan p'ên ching su.

72.—TS'UNG CHÊNG LI SHU.   A Treatise on astronomy, by the Jesuit missionaries.   270 × 165 mm.   Opened out.

> *** Imperfect, chüan 2 only.

139.—TU FU.   *See* Tu shih hsiang chu.

283.—TU LI T'UNG K'AO.   Supplement to the Wu li t'ung k'ao.   12 chüan.
4 vols.   287 × 180 mm.   [1800 ?]

332.—TU SAO LOU SHIH CH'U CHI.   Poems by Fêng Sao.   3 pên.   Ch'ên shih
ts'ung shu, tao 1.

139.—TU SHAO LING CH'ÜAN CHI, *or,* **TU SHIH HSIANG CHU,** *q. v.*

440.—TU SHIH FANG YÜ CHI YAO.   Historical geography of China to assist
in reading the historians.   By Ku Tsu-yu.   134 chüan.   30 pên in
10 vols.   280 × 170 mm.

139.—TU SHIH HSIANG CHU.   Complete works of Tu Fu.   14 pên in 3 vols.
250 × 160 mm.   1693.

304.—TU YÜ.   *See* Ch'in ting Ch'un Ch'iu ch'uan shuo hui tsuan.

312.—T'U HUI PAO CHIEN.   Precious mirror of painting.   Compiled A.D. 1365.
4 pên in 1 tao.   177 × 112 mm.

185.—TUAN CH'ÊNG-SHIH.   *See* Chien chieh ch'uan.

381.—TUAN YÜ-TS'AI.   *See* Shuo wên chieh tzŭ chu.

427.—TUNG HSI YANG K'AO MEI YÜEH T'UNG CHI CH'UAN. Monthly periodical of foreign and domestic news. Edited by Ai-han-chê [*i.e.* Karl Friedrich August Guetzlaff]. 260 × 154 mm. 1837-38.

*** Imperfect, containing only Nos. 1-9, 11, 12 of 1837, and 1-5 of 1838.

222.—TUNG HUA LU. History of the present dynasty to 1735. MS. 16 pên in 4 vols. 173 × 110 mm.

298.—TUNG SSŬ-CHANG. *See* Kuang po wu chih.

204.—T'UNG CHIEN KANG MU. A Condensation of the mirror of history. By Chu Hsi and his disciples. 100 pên in 18 vols. 250 × 157 mm.

262.—T'UNG CHIEN KANG MU. The same work, translated into Manchu. 48 pên in 8 tao. 320 × 205 mm.

323.—T'UNG SU PIEN. Encyclopædia of miscellaneous literature. 10 pên in 2 tao. 245 × 155 mm. 1751.

319.—T'UNG WÊN YÜN T'UNG. Vocabulary in several oriental languages. 4 pên in 1 vol. 278 × 170 mm. 1750.

136.—TZŬ HAI, *or,* **YIN YÜN TZŬ HAI,** *q. v.*

140.—TZŬ I TS'AO. Collection of poems. 262 × 170 mm.

276.—TZŬ YÜAN T'ANG CH'IN P'U. Book of instruction for the Ch'in or seven-stringed lute. 8 pên in 1 vol. 234 × 155 mm. 1802.

436.—VARO, FRANCESCO. *See* Arte de la lengua Mandarina.

69.—VERBIEST, FERDINAND.   *See* Hsin chih i hsian t'u.

71.—   „   „   „ K'ang-hsi shih nien êrh yüeh shih wu jih
ting yu yeh wang yüeh shih t'u.

457.—VIEWS OF BUILDINGS OF THE EMPEROR CH'IEN LUNG, at Nen-ming-
yuen.   Without any descriptive letter-press.   20 copperplate engravings measuring 22 × 36 in. oblong.   [1700 ?]

409.—VIEWS OF REMARKABLE PLACES IN CHINA; chiefly mountains.   Folded
as a screen.   250 × 165 mm.

    ₊ All the places have their names written in Chinese.

417.—VOCABULARY.   MS.   Manchu and Chinese.   310 × 200 mm.   [1840 ?]

**456.—VOCABULARY OF THE CHINESE, COREAN, AND JAPANESE LAN-
GUAGES.**   By Philo Sinensis [*i.e.* Walter Henry Medhurst].   224 ×
139 mm.   Batavia, 1835.

    ₊ Printed as a Chinese book on double leaves.   The last two parts are lithographed
and printed on Chinese paper.

87.—WAI T'AI PI YAO FANG.   An Ancient medical work.   By T'ang Wang-
chu.   24 pên in 4 vols.   242 × 156 mm.

30 c.—WAN WU CHIN YÜAN.   The True origin of all things.   By Ai Ju-lio
[*i.e.* Julio Aleni].   247 × 155 mm.   [1630 ?]

348.—WANG CH'I.   *See* Hsü wên hsien t'ung k'ao.

255.—   „   „   „ Hsü wên hsien t'ung k'ao yin.

185.—WANG CHIA.   *See* Shih i chi.

267.—WANG FU. *See* Po ku t'u.

446.—WANG HAO. *See* Yün fu shih i.

451.—WANG HSIANG-CHIN. *See* Ch'ün fang p'u.

206.—WANG HUI-FÊN. *See* Yü chuan tzŭ chih t'ung chien Ming chi kang mu.

147, 369.—WANG SHIH-CHÊNG. *See* Chin P'ing Mei.

182.— „ „ „ Yüan chien lei han.

38.—WANG SU. *See* K'ung tzŭ chia yü.

256.—WANG TS'UN. *See* Yüan Fêng chiu yü chih.

404.—WANG WEI-TÊ. *See* Pu shih chêng tsung.

304.—WANG YEN. *See* Ch'in ting Ch'un Ch'iu ch'uan shuo hui tsuan.

182.— „ „ „ Yüan chien lei han.

166.—WANG YING-LIN. *See* K'un hsüeh chi wên chi.

306 a.—WANG YU-TUN. *See* Ch'ien lu.

306.— „ „ „ Hsi ch'ing ku chien.

444.—WANG YUAN-HAN. *See* Lei shu san ts'ai t'u hui.

413 xv.—WEI CHÊNG. *See* Sui shu.

413 vii.—WEI SHOU. *See* Wei shu.

413 vii.—WEI SHU. History of the Wei dynasty. By Wei Shou. 104 chüan. 24 pên in 5 vols. 257 × 163 mm.   1596.

572.—WEI TSANG TU SHIH. An Itinerary of Tibet, with an account of the inhabitants, their customs and institutions. With maps and illustrations. By Ma Shao-yün and Shêng Mei-ch'i. 4 chüan. 4 pên in 1 vol. 175 × 110 mm.   1792.

382.—WEI YÜAN. *See* Shêng wu chi.

56.—WÊN CH'ANG TI CHÜN. *See* Yin chih wên tu chu.

132.—WÊN CH'I-SHAN. *See* Fên yün ts'o yao.

133.—WÊN CH'I-SHIH. *See* Chiang hu ch'ih tu fên yün ts'o yao ho chi.

42.—WÊN CHIH-MÊNG. *See* Chu tzŭ hui han.

382.—WÊN FEI CH'ING SHIH. Poems of Wên Fei-ch'ing. 2 pên in 1 tao. 260 × 167 mm.

382.—WÊN FEI CH'ING SHIH CHI. Another edition. 2 pên in 1 tao. 290 × 182 mm.   1697.

187.—WÊN HSIEN TUNG K'AO. A General examination of records and scholars. By Ma Tuan-lin. 100 pên in 12 vols. 244 × 167 mm.   1525.

     ₂ For the continuation *see* Hsü wen hsien tung k'ao.

182.—WÊN HSIEN TUNG K'AO CHÊNG HSÜ HO PIEN. Supplement to Ma Tuan-lin's Wên hsien tung k'ao. 32 pên in 7 vols. 246 × 150 mm.   [1700 ?]

166.—**WÊN HSÜAN.** Elegant extracts from polite literature. Compiled by Prince Hsiao T'ung, of the Liang dynasty. With a commentary by Li Shan. Edited by Yeh Shu-fan. 60 chüan. 12 pên in 2 vols. 296 × 167 mm. 1772.

419.—**WÊN SHOU CH'Ü KO LO SHANG.** Illustrations to a work entitled as above, illustrating the manners and customs of the Chinese on one of their great festivals. 2 rolls. 285 mm. wide.

271.—**WÊN SHOU CH'Ü KO LO SHANG.** Another copy of the illustrations. Folded as a screen. 285 × 350 mm. oblong.

₊ This copy is imperfect, containing only about one half of the pictures found in the two rolls catalogued above.

435.—**WO YÜ LEI CHIEH.** Comparative vocabulary of the Chinese, Corean, and Japanese languages. 2 pên in 1 vol. 285 × 200 mm.

129.—**WU CH'Ê YÜN JUI.** Dictionary according to the tones. By Ling I-tung. 5 vols. 264 × 167 mm.

6.—**WU CHING.** The Five classical books. With commentaries. 58 chüan. 26 pên in 6 vols. 267 × 155 mm. [1750?]

350.—**WU CHING HUAI CHIEH.** Seven treatises on military subjects. 24 pên in 4 tao. 230 × 145 mm. 1705.

54.—**WU CHUNG PI LU.** Five treatises of the Taouist sect. With commentaries. 11 chüan. 4 pên in 1 vol. 245 × 158 mm. 1816-29.

185.—**WU CHÜN.** *See* Hsü ch'i hsieh chi.

161.—**WU HU P'ING NAN HOU CH'UAN.** Pacification of the southern provinces of China. 6 pên in 1 vol. 170 × 115 mm. 1822.

I

185.—WU KUAN. *See* Chi mêng Chou shu.

185.— „ „ „ San fên.

282.—WU LI T'UNG K'AO. Thorough investigation into the five ceremonies. By Chin K'uei-ch'in. 96 pên in 16 vols. 287 × 180 mm. 1753.

* For the Supplement *see* Tu li t'ung k'ao.

220.—WU SHÊNG-CH'ÜAN. *See* Kang chien i chih lu.

413 xvii. a.—WU TAI SHIH. History of the five dynasties. By Ou-yang Hsiu. With commentaries. 74 chüan. 15 pên in 5 vols. 275 × 175 mm.

454.—WU TAI SHIH. Another edition. 74 chüan. 8 pên. 260 × 166 mm. 1576.

185.—WU YEN. *See* Chin shih ch'êng.

185.— „ „ „ Ch'u shih t'ao wu.

81.—WU YÜ-CH'ANG. *See* Pên ts'ao kang mu.

185.—WU YÜEH CH'UN CH'IU. The History of the states of Wu and Yüeh. By Chao Yeh. 6 chüan. Pi shu nien i chung, pên 2.

458.—YANG CHIA. *See* Lu ching t'u.

391.—YANG HUI SUAN FA. Treatise on land surveying, mensuration of heights and distances, &c. 2 pên, and supplement 1 pên. I chia t'ang ts'ung shu, tao 8. 240 × 150 mm. 1842.

442.—YANG-MA-NO. *See* T'ien chu chiang shêng yen hsing chi hsiang.

413 xi.—YAO SSŬ-LIEN. *See* Ch'ên shu.

413 x., 453.—YAO SSŬ-LIEN. *See* Liang shu.

166.—YEH SHU-FAN. *See* Wên hsüan.

38 i.—YEH-SU YEN HSING TSUNG LUN. The Life of Christ. In verse. By Chung-tê-chê [*i.e.* David Collie]. 250 × 140 mm. 1826.

351.—YEN HSI-YÜAN. *See* Pai mei hsin yung t'u ch'uan.

1.—YEN LIEH. *See* Huang Ch'ing ching chieh.

388.—YEN YÜAN. *See* Chung k'o yen yüan chi.

443.—YI CHAN. *See* Ch'ien chih hsin pien.

59.—YI-CHIU-LING-HSÜN. *See* Ching ch'an chih yin tsêng pu ch'ieh shih.

56.—YIN CHIH WÊN T'U CHU. A Treatise on secret rewards and retributions. By Wên-ch'ang ti chün. With illustrations and a commentary. 2 chüan. 4 pên in 1 vol. 258 × 155 mm.

98.—YIN HSÜEH WU SHU. Five works on the science of sounds. By Ku Yen-wu. Edited by Chang Ch'aou. 12 pên in 2 vols. 273 × 170 mm. 1643.

*** The works are: (1) Yin lun. Disquisitions on the sounds. 3 chüan. (2) Shih pên yin. The Original sounds of the book of odes. 10 chüan. (3) I yin. The Sounds of the book of changes. 3 chüan. (4) T'ang yün chêng. A Rectification of the T'ang dynasty finals. 20 chüan. (5) Ku yin piao. Ancient sounds tabulated. 2 chüan.

CATALOGUE OF CHINESE BOOKS.

98.—YIN LUN. Disquisitions on the sounds. By Ku Yen-wu. Edited by Chang Ch'aou. 3 chüan. 273 × 170 mm. 1643.

53.—YIN SHÊN-JÊN. *See* Hsing ming kuei chih.

136.—YIN YÜN TZǔ HAI. The Sea of characters. A tonic dictionary. 235 × 150 mm.

356.—YING HUAN CHIH LÜEH. A Geographical treatise on all within the circuit of the seas. By Hsü Chi-yü. Edited by P'i Hsing-ch'üan and Liu Yü-p'o. 10 chüan. 6 pên in 1 vol. 295 × 205 mm. 1848.

185.—YING SHAO. *See* Fêng su t'ung.

383.—YU CHÊNG-WEI CHAI SHIH CHI. Poems and other writings collected by Yu Chêng-wei. 23 pên in 4 tao. 250 × 160 mm. 1808.

447.—YU HSÜAN T'ANG SHIH. Selection of poems of the T'ang epoch. With commentaries. 33 pên in 6 vols. 255 × 157 mm. 1713.

294.—YU HSÜEH KU SHIH HSÜN YÜAN. A Search into antiquities : a book for beginners. By Ch'iu Hsün. 5 pên in 1 vol. 225 × 130 mm. [1800?]

410.—YU MING T'ANG HUAN HUAN CHI. The Prompter's book of the Pearly Rose Hall. Book of plays, with the parts of the songs, illustrated by the scenes. 2 pên in 1 tao. 298 × 183 mm. 1785.

43.—YUNG-CHÊNG. *See* Man han hsün chih shih tsê.

42.— „ „ „ Shêng yü kuang hsün.

392.—YUNG HSING. *See* Ch'in ting ssŭ k'u ch'üan shu tsung mu.

392.—YUNG HSÜAN. *See* Ch'in ting ssŭ k'u ch'üan shu tsung mu.

392.—YUNG YUNG. *See* Ch'in ting ssŭ k'u ch'üan shu tsung mu.

143.—YÜ CHIAO LI. The Two cousins. 4 pên in 1 vol. 180 × 111 mm.

144.—YÜ CHIAO LI. Another edition. Lithographed by Levasseur. 215 × 140 mm. Paris, 1829.

316.—YÜ CHIH HSÜAN LI TAI SHIH YÜ. Select remains of the poetry of various ages. 32 pên in 4 tao. 248 × 160 mm. 1707.

303.—YÜ CHIH P'ING TING CHIN CH'UAN FANG LÜEH. History of the final conquest of the Miao Tzŭ. 26 chüan. 12 pên in 2 tao. 350 × 210 mm. 1752.

287.—YÜ CHIH TSÊNG TING CH'ING WÊN CHIEN. Mirror of the Manchu language, augmented and revised by the Emperor Ch'ien Lung. 32 chüan, supplement 5 chüan and index 8 chüan. 5 vols. 283 × 190 mm. 1771.

⁎ In Manchu and Chinese.

306.—YÜ CHUAN TZÜ CHIH T'UNG CHIEN MING CHI KANG MU. A Condensed history of the Ming dynasty for the assistance of government. Compiled by an Imperial Commission, consisting of Chang T'ing-yü, Wang Hui-fên, Chou Ch'ang-fa, and others. 20 chüan. 6 pên in 1 vol. 226 × 145 mm. 1746.

186.—YÜ HAI HUI YÜAN WÊN. The Sea of jade, or of jewels. An encyclopædia. 100 pên in 18 vols. 252 × 154 mm. 1738.

CATALOGUE OF CHINESE BOOKS.

163.—YÜ HSÜEH-PU. *See* Chiang hu ch'ih tu fên yün ts'o yao ho chi.

57.—YÜ LI CH'AO CH'UAN CHING SHIH. Exhortations to excite to virtue and to turn from vice. 263 × 145 mm. 1833.

127.—YÜ T'ANG TZŬ HUI. The Jade Hall dictionary. Compiled by Mei Ying-tsu. 173 × 120 mm. 1676.

114, 115.—YÜ TÊ-SHENG. *See* Hsieh shêng p'in tzŭ chien.

386.—YÜ T'I HO CHING HSÜ HOU HAN SHU. History of the Hou, or later Han dynasty. By Yü T'i-ho. 90 chüan. 17 pên, and supplement 3 pên, in 3 tao. I chia t'ang ts'ung shu, tao 2-4. 1841.

192.—YÜ TING WAN NIEN LI. Chronology of ten thousand years. 218 × 125 mm. [1725?]

354.—YÜAN CHAO MING CH'ÊN SHI LÜEH. Biographical notices of forty-six famous ministers under the Yüan dynasty. By Su T'ien-ch'io. 15 chüan. 12 pên in 2 tao. 276 × 174 mm. MS.

182.—YÜAN CHIEN LEI HAN. An Encyclopædia. Arranged according to subjects. Compiled, by Imperial order, by Chang Ying, Wang Shih-chêng, Wang Yen, and others. 450 chüan in 32 vols. 225 × 160 mm. 1701.

303.—YÜAN CH'Ü HSÜAN, *or,* **YÜAN JÊN PAI CHUNG CH'Ü,** *q. v.*

256.—YÜAN FÊNG CHIU YÜ CHIH. A Geography of the nine frontiers during the reign of Yüan Fêng. By Wang Ts'un. 6 pên in 1 case. 248 × 150 mm.

153.—YÜAN-HU-YU. *See* Shuo T'ang yen ch'uan.

308.—YÜAN JÊN PAI CHUNG CH'Ü. The Hundred dramas of the Yüan dynasty. In 8 vols. 250 × 157 mm. [1573-1620.]

413 xxi.—YÜAN SHIH. History of the Yüan dynasty. By Sung Lien and others. 210 chüan. 19 pên in 9 vols. 274 × 178 mm. 1739.

261.—YÜAN SHIH LEI PIEN. History of the Yüan dynasty. By Shao Yüan-p'ing. 18 pên in 3 vols. 275 × 180 mm.

    *** A sequel to the Hung chien lu.

371.—YÜAN SHIH LEI PIEN. Another edition. 42 chüan. 15 pên in 3 tao. 293 × 180 mm.

    *** Printed with metal types.

74.—YÜAN T'IEN T'U SHUO. A Treatise on astronomy. By Li Ming-ch'ê, a Taouist priest. Edited by Yüan Yüan. With illustrations. 3 chüan. 3 pên in 1 vol. 275 × 170 mm. 1819.

343.—YÜAN YING. *See* I ch'ieh ching yin i.

1.—YÜAN YÜAN. *See* Huang Ch'ing ching chieh.

74.— „   „   „ Yüan t'ien t'u shuo.

100 a.—YÜN FA CHIH T'U. Chinese vocabulary. 260 × 165 mm. [1600?]

100 b.—YÜN FA HÊNG T'U. Chinese vocabulary. 260 × 165 mm. [1600?]

131.—YÜN FU CH'ÜN YÜ. Forest of pearls and treasure of rhymes. 10 pên. 260 × 160 mm. 1590.

132.—YÜN FU CH'ÜN YÜ. Another copy.   10 pên in 2 vols.   260 × 160 mm.
1590.

446.—YÜN FU SHIH I. Supplement to the P'ei wên yün fu.   Compiled by an Imperial Commission consisting of Wang Hao and others.   106 chüan.   20 pên in 5 vols.   255 × 160 mm.
1720.

133.—YÜN FU YO PIEN. Dictionary of rhymes.   20 pên in 3 vols.   207 × 119 mm.
1759.

103.—YÜN MU, *or,* **CHÊNG YÜN T'UNG,** *q. v.*

NUMBER KEY.

1.—皇清經解 Huang Ch'ing ching chieh.

2.—經典釋文 Ching tien shih wên.

3.—六經圖 Lu ching t'u.

6.—五經 Wu ching.

7.—監本五經 Chien pên wu ching.

8.—奎壁易經 Kuei pi i ching.

10.—書經大全 Shu ching ta ch'üan.

13.—詩經 Shih ching.

14.—毛詩故訓傳定本 Mao shih ku hsün ch'uan ting pên.

16.—詩經全註 Shih ching ch'üan chu.

17.—春秋經傳集解 Ch'un Ch'iu ching ch'uan chi chieh.

18.—禮記旁訓 Li chi p'ang hsün.

19.—四書正體 Ssŭ shu chêng t'i.

20.—增補四書人物備考 Tsêng pu ssŭ shu jên wu pei k'ao.

21.—孟子 Mêng tzŭ.

23.—三字經 San tzŭ ching.

24.—千字文 Ch'ien tzŭ wên.

25.—百家姓 Pai chia hsing.

26.—昔時賢文 Hsi shih hsien wên.

27.—三禮圖 San li t'u.

28.—周禮註疏 Chou li chu su.

29.—儀禮經傳通解 I li ching ch'uan t'ung chieh.

30*a.*—聖教信證 Shêng chiao hsin chêng.

K

30*b.*—天 主 聖 像 畧 說 T'ien chu shêng hsiang lüeh shuo.

30*c.*—萬 物 眞 原 Wan wu chin yüan.

32.—西 洋 人 Hsi yang jên.

33.—天 神 會 課 T'ien shên hui k'o.

34.—盛 世 芻 蕘 Shêng shih ch'u jao.

35.—聖 敎 日 課 Shêng chiao jih k'o.

36.—神 珍 日 課 Shên chên jih k'o.

37.—德 行 譜 Tê hsing p'u.

38*a.*—三 寳 仁 會 論 San pao jên hui lun.

38*b.*—察 世 俗 每 月 統 記 傳 Ch'a shih su mei yueh t'ung chi ch'uan.

38*c.*—張 遠 兩 友 相 論 Chang Yüan liang yu hsiang lun.

38*d.*—聖 母 無 原 罪 經 Shêng mu wu yüan tsui ching.

38*e.*—諸 國 異 神 論 Chu kuo i shên lun.

38*f.*—積 纂 省 身 神 詩 Hsü tsuan shêng shên shên shih.

38*g.*—新 增 養 心 神 詩 Hsin tsêng yang hsin, shen shih.

38*h.*—勸 讀 聖 錄 熟 知 文 Ch'üan tu shêng lu shu chih wên.

38*i.*—耶 穌 言 行 總 論 Yeh-su yen hsing tsung lun.

39.—孔 子 家 語 K'ung tzǔ chia yü.

40.—諸 子 彙 函 Chu tzǔ hui han.

41.—荀 子 箋 釋 Hsün Tzǔ chien shih.

42.—聖 諭 廣 訓 Shêng yü kuang hsün.

43.—滿 漢 訓 旨 十 則 Man han hsün chih shih tsê.

44.—性 理 眞 詮 Hsing li chên ch'üan.

45.—神 相 全 編 Shên hsiang ch'üan pǐen.

45*a.*—人 相 水 鏡 集 全 編 Jên hsiang shui ching chi ch'üan pien.

46.—三 敎 源 流 聖 帝 佛 師 搜 神 記 San chiao yüan liu Shêng ti
Fo Shih sou shên chi.

47.—郷 黨 圖 考 Hsiang tang t'u k'ao.

48.—神仙通鑑 Shên hsien t'ung chien.

49.—山海經詳註 Shan hai ching hsiang chu.

50.—道德經解 Tao Tê ching chieh.

51.—淮南鴻烈解 Huai nan hung lieh chieh.

52.—南華經箋註 Nan hua ching chien chu.

53.—性命圭旨 Hsing ming kuei chih.

54.—道言內外五種秘錄 Tao yen nei wai wu chung pi lu.

55.—感應篇 Kan ying p'ien.

56.—陰隲文圖註 Yin chih wên t'u chu.

57.—玉歷鈔傳警世 Yü li ch'ao ch'uan ching shih.

58.—佛通號名 Fo t'ung hao ming ; or 集要 Chi yao.

59.—經懺直音增補切釋 Ching ch'an chih yin tsêng pu ch'ieh shih.

60.—泌彌律儀要略 Pi mi lü i yao lüeh.

61.—選僧圖說 Hsüan sêng t'u shuo.

62.—佛說盂蘭盆經疏 Fo shuo Yü lan p'ên ching su.

63.—牧牛圖 Mu niu t'u.

64.—佛說阿彌陀經 Fo shuo O-mi-to ching.

65.—纂註圓覺經 Tsuan chu yüan chiao ching.

66.—普勸念佛 P'u ch'üan nien Fo.

67.—大悲神咒心經 Ta pei shên chou hsin ching.

68.—天文 T'ien wên.

69.—新製儀象圖 Hsin chih i hsiang t'u.

70.—欽天監奏 Ch'in t'ien chien tsou.

71—康熙十年二月十五日丁酉夜望月食圖 K'ang-hsi shih nien êrh yüeh shih wu jih ting yu yeh wang yüeh shih t'u.

72.—崇禎曆書 Ts'ung chêng li shu.

73.—方星圖解 Fang hsing t'u chieh.

74.—圓天圖說 Yüan t'ien t'u shuo.

75.—天文大成 T'ien wên ta ch'êng.

77.—大清搢紳全書 Ta Ch'ing chin shên ch'üan shu.

78.—類經圖翼 Lei ching t'u i.

79.—籌海圖編 Ch'ou hai t'u pien.

80.—大觀本草 Ta kuan Pên ts'ao.

81.—本草綱目 Pên ts'ao kang mu.

82.—廣羣芳譜 Kuang chün fang p'u.

83.—本草醫方合編 Pên ts'ao i fang ho pien.

85.—醫方考 I fang k'ao.

86.—馮氏錦囊 P'ing shih chin nang.

87.—外臺秘要方 Wai t'ai pi yao fang.

88.—醫宗金鑑 I tsung chin chien.

89.—膏藥方 Kao yo fang.

90.—芥子園畫傳 Chieh tzǔ yüan hua ch'uan.

91.—七巧圖合璧 Ch'i ch'iao t'u ho pi.

92.—適情雅趣 Shih ch'ing ya ch'ü.

93.—適情雅趣 Shih ch'ing ya ch'ü.

97.—新錄字法 Hsin lu tzǔ fa.

98.—音學五書 Yin hsüeh wu shu.

　　(1) 音論 Yin lun.

　　(2) 詩本音 Shih pên yin.

　　(3) 易音 I yin.

　　(4) 唐韻正 T'ang yün chêng.

　　(5) 古音表 Ku yin piao.

99.—增訂字學津梁 Tsêng ting tzǔ hsüeh ching liang.

100a.—韻法直圖 Yün fa chih t'u.

100b.—韻法橫圖 Yün fa hêng t'u.

101.—丹山集帖 Tan shan chi t'ieh.

102.—覆 語 虛 字 Fa yü hsü tzŭ.

103.—正 韻 通 Chêng yün t'ung ; or 韻 母 Yün mu.

104.—篆 隸 心 畫 Chuan li hsin hua.

105.—爾 雅 Êrh ya.

106.—爾 雅 註 疏 Êrh ya chu su.

107.—宋 本 玉 篇 Sung pên yü p'ien.

108.—說 文 真 本 Shuo wên chên pên.

109.—六 書 本 義 Liu shu pên i.

110.—補 詳 字 義 Pu hsiang tzŭ i.

111.—篆 字 彙 Chuan tzŭ hui.

112.—搜 古 遺 文 Chih ku i wên.

113.—卿 字 彙 Ts'ao tzŭ hui.

114, 115, 116.—諧 聲 品 字 箋 Hsieh shêng p'in tzŭ chien.

117, 118, 119.—懸 金 字 彙 Hsüan chin tzŭ hui.

121, 122, 123.—正 字 通 Chêng tzŭ t'ung.

125.—康 熙 字 典 K'ang-hsi tzŭ tien.

126.—藝 文 通 覽 I wên t'ung lan.

127.—玉 堂 字 彙 Yü T'ang tzŭ hui.

128.—海 篇 Hai p'ien.

129.—五 車 韻 瑞 Wu ch'ê yün jui.

130.—分 韻 撮 要 Fên yün ts'o yao.

131, 132.—韻 府 群 玉 Yün fu ch'ün yü.

133.—韻 府 約 編 Yün fu yo pien.

134.—集 韻 平 聲 Chi yün p'ing shêng.

136.—字 海 Tzŭ hai ; or 音 韻 字 海 Yin yün tzŭ hai.

137.—唐 詩 比 律 箋 注 T'ang shih pi lü chien chu.

138.—李 青 蓮 全 集 Li pei lien ch'üan chi ; or 李 太 白 文 Li T'ai-pai wên.

CATALOGUE OF CHINESE BOOKS.

139.—杜少陵全集 Tu shao ling ch'üan chi; or 杜詩詳註 Tu shih hsiang chu.

140.—自怡草 Tzŭ i ts'ao.

141.—今古奇觀 Chin ku ch'i kuan.

142.—第一才子書 Ti i ts'ai tzŭ shu; or 三國志 San kuo chih.

143, 144.—第三才子書 Ti san ts'ai tzŭ shu; or 玉嬌梨 Yü chiao li.

145.—第四才子書 Ti ssŭ ts'ai tzŭ shu; or 平山冷燕 P'ing shan lêng yen.

146.—第五才書 Ti wu ts'ai shu; or 水滸傳 Shui hu ch'uan.

147.—第一奇書 Ti i ch'i shu; or 金瓶梅 Chin P'ing Mei.

148.—醒心編 Hsing hsin pien.

149.—紅樓夢 Hung lou mêng.

150.—三分夢全傳 San fên mêng ch'üan ch'uan.

151.—洪武全傳 Hung wu ch'üan ch'uan.

152.—說岳全傳 Shuo Yo ch'üan ch'uan.

153.—說唐演傳 Shuo T'ang yen ch'uan.

154.—殘唐五伐全傳 Ts'an T'ang wu tai ch'üan ch'uan.

157.—仁貴征東說唐後傳 Jên-kuei chêng tung shuo t'ang hou ch'uan.

158.—仁貴征西說唐三傳 Jên-kuei chêng hsi shuo t'ang san ch'uan.

159.—羅通掃比前後傳 Lo T'ung sao pei ch'ien hou ch'uan.

160.—南北宋志傳 Nan pei Sung chih ch'uan.

161.—五虎平南後傳 Wu hu p'ing nan hou ch'uan.

162.—笑海新聲初集 Hsiao hai hsin shêng ch'u chi.

163.—江湖尺牘分韻撮要合集 Chiang hu ch'ih tu fên yün ts'o yao ho chi.

164.—古文淵鑑 Ku wên yüan chien.

165.—困學紀聞集 K'un hsüeh chi wên chi.

166.—文 選 Wên hsüan.

167.—酬 世 錦 囊 Ch'ou shih chin nang.

168.—古 文 評 註 Ku wên p'ing chu.

169.—欽 定 四 庫 全 書 簡 明 目 錄 Ch'in ting ssǔ k'u ch'üan shu chien ming mu lu.

170.—初 學 記 Ch'u hsüeh chi.

171.—初 學 小 題 登 龍 Ch'u hsüeh hsiao t'i têng lung.

172.—七 修 類 稿 Ch'i hsiu lei kao.

173.—智 囊 補 Chih nang pu.

174.—韓 文 考 異 Han wên k'ao i.

175.—盧 陵 歐 陽 文 忠 公 全 集 Lu ling Ou yang wên chung kung ch'üan chi.

176, 177.—大 萬 寶 全 書 Ta wan pao ch'üan shu.

178.—世 事 通 考 Shih shih t'ung k'ao.

179.—新 增 幼 學 故 事 瓊 林 Hsin tsêng yu hsüeh ku shih ch'iung lin.

180.—初 學 明 鏡 Ch'u hsüeh ming ching.

181.—知 不 足 齋 叢 書 Chih pu tsu chai ts'ung shu.

182.—淵 鑑 類 函 Yüan chien lei han.

183.—龍 威 秘 書 Lung wei pi shu.

185.—秘 書 廿 一 種 Pi shu nien i chung.

    (1) 汲 冢 周 書 Chi mêng Chou shu.

    (2) 吳 越 春 秋 Wu Yüeh Ch'un Ch'iu.

    (3) 拾 遺 記 Shih i chi.

    (4) 白 虎 通 Pai hu t'ung.

    (5) 山 海 經 Shan hai ching.

    (6a) 博 物 志 Po wu chih.

    (6b) 續 博 物 志 Hsü po wu chih.

    (7a) 桂 海 虞 衡 志 Kuei hai yü hêng chih.

185.—(7*b*) 博 異 記 Po i chi.

    (7*c*) 高 士 傳 Kao shih ch'uan.

    (8*a*) 劍 俠 傳 Chien chieh ch'uan.

    (8*b*) 集 異 記 Chi i chi.

    (8*c*) 竹 書 紀 年 Chu shu chi nien.

    (9*a*) 中 華 古 今 注 Chung hua ku chin chu.

    (9*b*) 古 今 注 Ku chin chu.

    (9*c*) 三 墳 San fên.

    (10*a*) 風 俗 通 Fêng su t'ung.

    (10*b*) 列 仙 傳 Lieh hsien ch'uan.

    (10*c*) 楚 史 檮 杌 Ch'u shih t'ao wu.

    (10*d*) 晋 史 乘 Chin shih ch'êng.

    (10*e*) 續 齊 諧 記 Hsü ch'i hsieh chi.

186.—玉 海 揮 原 文 Yü hai hui yüan wên.

187.—文 獻 通 考 Wên hsien t'ung k'ao.

188.—文 獻 通 考 正 續 合 編 Wên hsien t'ung k'ao chêng hsü ho pien.

190.—太 平 廣 記 T'ai p'ing kuang chi.

191.—甲 子 會 紀 Chia tzǔ hui chi.

192.—御 定 萬 年 曆 Yü ting wan nien li.

193.—竹 書 紀 年 Chu shu chi nien.

194.—闕 里 誌 Ch'üeh Li chih.

195.—重 訂 春 秋 左 傳 句 解 Chung ting ch'un ch'iu Tso ch'uan chü chieh.

196, 197.—國 語 Kuo yü.

198.—封 神 演 義 全 傳 Fêng shên yen i ch'üan ch'uan.

200.—鳳 洲 綱 鑑 Fêng Chou kang chien.

201.—史 記 Shih chi.

203.—重訂路史前紀 Chung ting lu shih ch'ien chi.

204.—通鑑綱目 T'ung chien kang mu.

206.—御撰資治通鑑明紀綱目 Yü chuan tzǔ chih t'ung chien Ming chi kang mu.

207.—十六國春秋 Shih liu kuo ch'un ch'iu.

208.—前漢書 Ch'ien Han shu.

209.—後漢書 Hou Han shu.

210.—歷朝鑑綱 Li ch'ao chien kang.

211.—明紀全載 Ming chi ch'üan tsai.

212.—明朝紀 Ming ch'ao chi.

213.—歷朝鑑綱 Li ch'ao chien kang.

214.—歷體金膏 Li t'i chin kao.

215.—撫苗錄 Fu Miao lu.

216.—戰國策注 Chan kuo ts'ê chu.

217.—史程曾議 Shih ch'êng ts'êng i.

218.—靖逆記 Ching ni chi.

219.—歷史綱鑑補 Li shih kang chien pu.

220.—綱鑑易知錄 Kang chien i chih lu.

221.—歷朝綱鑑 Li ch'ao kang chien.

222.—東華錄 Tung hua lu.

223.—歷代名賢列女氏姓譜 Li tai ming hsien lieh nü shih hsing p'u.

225.—西湖志 Hsi hu chih.

226.—西遊真詮 Hsi yu chên ch'üan.

227.—西域聞見錄 Hsi yü wên chien lu.

228.—咬唱吧籍論 Ch'iao-liu-pa tsung lun.

229.—廣輿記 Kuang yü chi.

231.—戰國策 Chan kuo ts'ê.

CATALOGUE OF CHINESE BOOKS.

232.—國 策 評 林 Kuo ts'ê p'ing lin.

234.—江 湖 尺 牘 Chiang hu ch'ih tu.

235.—皇 帝 遺 詔 Huang ti i chao.

237a.—大 學 Ta hsüeh.

237b.—孟 子 文 Mêng tzǔ wên.

238.—詩 經 Shih ching.

241.—譯 明 夷 字 陳 裏 I ming i tzǔ ch'ên ping.

248.—耿 清 閣 Kang ch'ing ko.

249a.—考 古 圖 K'ao ku t'u.

249b.—古 玉 圖 Ku yü t'u.

250.—大 清 一 統 志 Ta ch'ing i t'ung chih.

251.—元 史 類 編 Yüan shih lei pien.

252.—宋 遼 金 元 四 史 Sung, Liao, Chin, Yüan ssǔ shih.

253.—欽 定 滿 洲 源 流 考 Ch'in ting Man-chou yüan liu k'ao.

254.—欽 定 皇 輿 西 域 圖 志 Ch'in ting huang yü hsi yü t'u chih.

255.—續 文 獻 通 考 引 Hsü wên hsien t'ung k'ao yin.

256.—元 豐 九 域 志 Yüan Fêng chiu yü chih.

257.—西 域 水 道 記 Hsi yü shui tao chi.

258.—琉 球 國 志 Liu-ch'iu kuo chih.

259.—朱 子 全 書 Chu tzǔ ch'üan shu.

260.—長 安 志 Ch'ang-an chih.

261.—漢 魏 叢 書 Han Wei ts'ung shu.

262.—通 鑑 綱 目 T'ung chien kang mu.

263.—佩 文 韻 府 P'ei wên yün fu.

264.—大 清 律 例 Ta Ch'ing lü li.

265.—清 文 彙 書 Ch'ing wên hui shu.

266.—清 文 補 彙 Ch'ing wên pu hui.

267.—博 古 圖 Po ku t'u.

268.—積 古 齋 鐘 鼎 彝 器 Chi ku chai chung ting i ch'i.

269.—方 氏 墨 譜 Fang shih mo p'u.

270.—泛 槎 圖 Fan ch'a t'u.

271.—文 壽 衢 歌 樂 商 Wên shou ch'ü ko lo shang.

274.—欽 定 四 庫 全 書 Ch'in ting ssǔ k'u ch'üan shu.

275.—錢 志 新 編 Ch'ien chih hsin pien.

276.—自 遺 堂 琴 譜 Tzǔ yüan t'ang ch'in p'u.

277.—三 國 誌 San kuo chih.

278.—羅 浮 山 志 會 編 Lo-fou shan chih hui pien.

279.—古 聖 賢 像 傳 畧 Ku shêng hsien hsiang ch'uan lüeh.

280.—太 平 御 覽 T'ai p'ing yü lan.

281.—太 平 寰 宇 記 T'ai p'ing huan yü chi.

282.—五 禮 通 考 Wu li t'ung k'ao.

283.—讀 禮 通 考 Tu li t'ung k'ao.

284.—詩 義 折 中 Shih i chê chung.

285.—十 子 全 書 Shih tzǔ ch'üan shu.

286.—周 易 全 書 Chou I ch'üan shu.

287.—御 製 增 訂 清 文 鑑 Yü chih tsêng ting ch'ing wên chien.

288.—隸 續 Li hsü.

289.—隸 韻 Li yün.

290.—康 熙 字 典 K'ang-hsi tzǔ tien.

291.—宋 十 賢 傳 Sung shih hsien ch'uan.

292.—欽 定 國 朝 詩 別 裁 集 Ch'in ting kuo ch'ao shih pieh tsai chi.

293.—水 經 注 釋 Shui ching chu shih.

294.—幼 學 故 事 尋 源 Yu hsüeh ku shih hsün yüan.

295.—禪 門 日 誦 Ch'an mên jih sung.

296.—墓 銘 舉 例 Mu ming chü li.

296 (2).—金 石 要 例 Chin shih yao li.

297.—壇 經 T'an ching.

298.—廣 博 物 志 Kuang po wu chih.

299a.—內 科 新 說 Nei k'o hsin shuo.

299b.—婦 嬰 新 說 Fu ying hsin shuo.

299c.—西 醫 略 論 Hsi i lüeh lun.

299d.—全 體 新 論 Ch'üan t'i hsin lun.

299e.—博 物 新 編 Po wu hsin pien.

300.—六 書 通 Liu shu t'ung.

301.—使 琉 球 記 Shih liu ch'iu chi.

302.—法 苑 珠 林 Fa yüan chu lin.

303.—元 曲 選 Yüan ch'ü hsüan ; or 元 人 百 種 曲 Yüan jên pai
chung ch'ü.

304.—欽 定 春 秋 傳 說 彙 纂 Ch'in ting Ch'un Ch'iu ch'uan shuo hui
tsuan.

305.—唐 書 T'ang shu.

306.—西 清 古 鑑 Hsi ch'ing ku chien.

306a.—錢 錄 Ch'ien lu.

308.—平 定 兩 金 川 方 略 P'ing ting liang chin ch'uan fang lüeh.

309.—御 製 平 定 金 川 方 略 Yü chih p'ing ting chin ch'uan fang lüeh.

311.—大 唐 西 域 記 Ta T'ang hsi yü chi.

312.—圖 繪 寶 鑑 T'u hui pao chien.

313.—歷 代 紀 事 年 表 Li tai chi shih nien piao.

314.—弘 簡 錄 Hung chien lu.

316.—御 製 選 歷 代 詩 餘 Yü chih hsüan li tai shih yü.

317.—佩 文 齋 書 畫 譜 P'ei wên chai shu hua p'u.

318.—算 法 統 宗 大 全 Suan fa t'ung tsung ta ch'üan.

319.—同 文 韻 統 T'ung wên yün t'ung.

320, 320a.—說 文 字 原 Shuo wên tzŭ yüan.

321.—佛 國 記 Fo kuo chi.

322.—佛 祖 歷 代 通 載 Fo tsu li tai t'ung tsai.

323.—全 金 詩 增 Ch'üan Chin shih tsêng.

324.—盤 山 志 P'an shan chih.

325.—歷 代 畫 史 Li tai hua shih.

326.—天 方 正 學 T'ien fang chêng hsüeh.

327.—儀 禮 圖 I li t'u.

328.—通 俗 編 T'ung su pien.

329.—佐 遼 實 蹟 Tso liao shih tsê.

330.—歷 代 輿 圖 Li tai yü t'u.

331-338.—陳 氏 叢 書 Ch'en shih ts'ung shu.

331.—離 騷 精 義 Li sao ching i.

332.—讀 騷 樓 詩 初 集 Tu sao lou shih ch'u chi.

333.—漢 詩 統 箋 Han shih t'ung chien.

334.—急 就 探 奇 Chi chiu t'an ch'i.

335.—穆 天 子 傳 注 補 正 Mu t'ien tzŭ ch'uan chu pu chêng.

336.—逸 周 書 補 注 I chou shu pu chu.

337.—竹 書 紀 年 集 匯 Chu shu chi nien chi chêng.

338.—協 律 鈞 元 Hsieh lü kou yüan.

339.—欽 定 剿 平 三 省 邪 匪 方 畧 Ch'in ting chiao p'ing san shêng hsieh fei fang lüeh.

340.—律 呂 精 義 Lü lü ching i.

341.—靈 臺 儀 象 志 Ling t'ai i hsiang chih.

342.—大 明 三 藏 聖 教 Ta ming san tsang shêng chiao.

343.—一 切 經 音 義 I ch'ieh ching yin i.

344.—繹 史 I shih.

345.—平 定 朔 漠 方 畧 P'ing ting so mo fang lüeh.

346.—曲 譜 Ch'ü p'u.

CATALOGUE OF CHINESE BOOKS.

348.—續 文 獻 通 考 Hsü wên hsien t'ung k'ao.

349.—經 史 講 義 Ching shih chiang i.

350.—皇 極 經 世 書 Huang chi ching shih shu.

351.—百 美 新 詠 圖 傳 Pai mei hsin yung t'u ch'uan.

352.—皇 朝 通 典 Huang chao t'ung tien.

353.—皇 朝 禮 器 圖 式 Huang chao li ch'i t'u shih.

354.—元 朝 名 臣 事 略 Yüan chao ming ch'ên shi lüeh.

356.—瀛 環 志 畧 Ying huan chih lüeh.

357.—八 旗 滿 洲 氏 族 通 譜 Pa ch'i man chou shih tsu t'ung p'u.

358.—欽 定 八 旗 通 志 Ch'in ting pa ch'i t'ung chih.

359.—武 經 匯 解 Wu ching huai chieh.

360.—律 呂 精 義 Lü lü ching i.

361.—溫 飛 卿 詩 Wên fei ch'ing shih.

362.—六 書 故 Liu shu ku.

363.—天 雨 花 T'ien yü hua.

364.—書 琵 琶 記 Shu p'i p'a chi.

365.—增 訂 金 批 西 廂 Tsêng ting chin p'i hsi hsiang.

366.—千 金 翼 方 Ch'ien chin i fang.

367.—譯 繒 聊 齋 志 異 Chih fan liao chai chih i.

369.—金 瓶 梅 Chin P'ing Mei.

371.—元 史 類 編 Yüan shih lei pien.

372.—平 定 準 噶 爾 方 畧 P'ing ting chun ko êrh fang lüeh.

373.—平 定 臺 灣 紀 畧 P'ing ting t'ai wan chi lüeh.

374.—宸 垣 識 畧 Ch'ên yüan shih lüeh.

375.—皇 朝 武 功 紀 盛 Huang chao wu kung chi shêng.

376.—皇 清 開 國 方 畧 Huang ch'ing k'ai kuo fang lüeh.

377.—大 清 中 外 壹 統 輿 圖 Ta ch'ing chung wai i t'ung yü t'u.

378.—海 國 聞 見 錄 Hai kuo wên chien lu.

379.—衛 藏 圖 識 Wei tsang t'u shih.

380.—聖 武 記 Shêng wu chi.

381.—說 文 解 字 注 Shuo wên chieh tzǔ chu.

382.—溫 飛 卿 詩 集 Wên fei ch'ing shih chi.

383.—有 正 味 齋 詩 集 Yu Chêng-wei chai shih chi.

384.—大 清 全 書 Ta ch'ing ch'üan shu.

385-391.—宜 稼 堂 叢 書 I Chia t'ang ts'ung shu.

385.—續 後 漢 書 Hsü hou Han shu.

386.—御 題 和 經 續 後 漢 書 Yü t'i ho ching hsü hou Han shu.

387.—清 容 居 士 集 Ch'ing yung chü t'u chi.

388.—重 刻 刲 源 集 Chung k'o yen yüan chi.

389.—數 書 九 章 Shu shu chiu chang.

390.—詳 解 九 章 算 法 Hsiang chieh chiu chang suan fa.

391.—楊 輝 算 法 Yang hui suan fa.

392.—欽 定 四 庫 全 書 總 目 Ch'in ting ssǔ k'u ch'üan shu tsung mu.

393.—西 招 圖 咯 Hsi chao t'u lüeh.

398.—貴 州 全 省 捌 拾 貳 穜 苗 圖 Kuei chou ch'üan shêng pa shih êrh chung miao t'u.

399.—四 書 Ssǔ shu.

400.—錢 志 新 編 Ch'ien chih hsin pien.

401.—帝 鑑 圖 說 Ti chien t'u shuo.

402.—紅 樓 夢 Hung lou mêng.

403.—封 神 演 義 Fêng shên yen i.

404.—卜 筮 正 宗 Pu shih chêng tsung.

405.—解 夢 全 書 Chieh mêng ch'üan shu.

406.—增 廣 賢 文 Tseng kuang hsien wên.

407.—梅 花 易 數 Mei hua i shu.

408.—禮 記 體 註 Li chi t'i chu.

410.—玉茗堂還魂記 Yu ming t'ang huan huan chi.

411.—節孝事實 Chieh hsiao shih shih.

412.—鴻雪因緣圖記 Hung hsüeh yin yuen t'u chi.

413, i.–xxii.—廿二史 Nien êrh shih.

    i. 史記 Shih chi.

    ii. 前漢書 Ch'ien Han shu.

    iii. *a*. 後漢書 Hou Han shu.

    iii. *b*. 續後漢 Hsü Hou Han.

    iv. 三國志 San kuo chih.

    v. 晉書 Tsin shu.

    vi. 宋書 Sung shu.

    vii. 魏書 Wei shu.

    viii. 南齊書 Nan Ch'i shu.

    ix. 北齊書 Pei Ch'i shu.

    x. 梁書 Liang shu.

    xi. 陳書 Ch'en shu.

    xii. 後周書 Hou Chou shu.

    xiii. 南史書 Nan shih shu.

    xiv. 北史書 Pei shih shu.

    xv. 隋書 Sui shu.

    xvi. *a, b*. 唐書 T'ang shu.

    xvii. *a*. 五代史 Wu tai shih.

    xvii. *b*. 舊五代史 Chiu Wu tai shih.

    xviii. 宋史 Sung shih.

    xix. 遼史 Liao shih.

    xx. 金史 Chin shih.

    xxi. 元史 Yüan shih.

    xxii. 明史 Ming shih.

415.—佸庸圖䣓六種書 Huo yung t'u pei liu chung shu.

418.—爾雅音圖 Êrh ya yin t'u.

419.—文壽衢歌樂商 Wên shou ch'ü ko lo shang.

422.—籌海圖編 Ch'ou hai t'u pien.

423.—稶圖 Chih t'u.

424.—靈巖志畧 Ling yen chih lüeh.

425.—苗防備覽 Miao fang pei lan.

426.—意拾秘傳 I-shi-pi ch'uan.

427.—東西洋考每月統記傳 Tung hsi yang k'ao mei yüeh t'ung chi ch'uan.

428.—歷代帝王年表 Li tai Ti Wang nien piao.

429.—遲删集 Ch'ih shan chi.

430.—七巧封譜 Ch'i ch'iao yün p'u.

431.—西番譯語 Hsi fan i yü.

432.—好逑傳 Hao ch'iu ch'uan.

433.—新鐫文壇神詩 Ch'i tao wên tsan shên shih.

435.—倭語類解 Wo yü lei chieh.

437.—西儒耳目資 Hsi ju êrh mu tzǔ.

439.—西湖志 Hsi hu chih.

440.—讀史方輿紀要 Tu shih fang yü chi yao.

442.—天主降生言行紀像 T'ien chu chiang shêng yen hsing chi hsiang.

443.—錢志新編 Ch'ien chih hsin pien.

444.—類書三才圖會 Lei shu san ts'ai t'u hui.

445.—欽定錢錄 Hsü ting ch'ien lu.

446.—韻府拾遺 Yün fu shih i.

447.—御選唐詩 Yu hsüan T'ang shih.

449.—欽定蒙古源流 Ch'in ting Mêng-ku yüan liu.

90   CATALOGUE OF CHINESE BOOKS.

450.—欽 定 滿 洲 源 流 考 Ch'in ting Man-chou yüan liu k'ao.

451.—羣 芳 譜 Ch'ün fang p'u.

452.—史 記 Shih chi.

453.—梁 書 Liang shu.

454.—五 代 史 Wu tai shih.

455.—遼 史 Liao shih.

458.—六 經 圖 Lu ching t'u.

461.—林 大 將 傳 Lin t'ai chiang ch'uan.

462.—續 三 綱 行 實 圖 Hsü san kang hsing shih t'u.

463.—京 城 全 圖 Ching ch'êng ch'üan t'u.

464.—廣 東 輿 地 總 圖 Kuang-tung yü ti tsung t'u. 廣 東 省 城 圖 Kuang-tung shêng ch'êng t'u.

STEPHEN AUSTIN AND SONS, PRINTERS, HERTFORD.

Catalogus Codicum Manuscriptorum Bibliothecae Regiae

Bibliothecae Regiae

皇家图书馆写本目录

CATALOGUS
CODICUM
MANUSCRIPTORUM
BIBLIOTHECÆ REGIÆ.

TOMUS PRIMUS.

PARISIIS,
E TYPOGRAPHIA REGIA.

M. DCCXXXIX.

MONITUM.

CUM ordinis quem sequendum esse duximus, in Librorum editorum Præfatione accuratè sit explicata ratio; pauca nunc restant de quibus Lectorem monitum oporteat. Codicibus Manuscriptis Orientalibus, primo hoc volumine comprehensis, Libri Sinici, Tartarici, & Indici ideo adjuncti sunt, quòd in aliam classem conjici non posse viderentur. Illorum omnium brevis descriptio, Stephani Fourmont, Armenorum autem Guilielmi de Villefroy, Virorum doctissimorum industriæ accepta referenda est, quorum vestigiis, quantùm fieri potuit, insistere conati sumus. In Indicis & Sinicis, non eadem quàm in cæteris Catalogi capitibus partium dispositio reperitur, illudque compluribus de causis, quas enumerare velle nimis longum foret.

说　明

　　在已出版各卷的前言中既已准确说明了我们认为应遵循的排序的理由，现在仍有一些应向读者说明之事。中国、鞑靼及印度的书籍都编入了本目录的第一卷《东方写本》（*Codices Manuscripti Orientales*），因为这些文献无法被归入其他类别。对各书籍的简短描述应归功于傅尔蒙（Étienne Fourmont），亚美尼亚语的则是纪尤姆·德·维尔弗拉（Guillaume de Villefroy）等最博学者的勤勉，而我们尽可能地努力追随他们的脚步。在印度和中国写本部分未使用与目录其他章节相同的编排方式，这是由于诸多因素，一一枚举恐怕过于冗长。

（张天鹄译，李慧校）

amplectuntur. Rex interea gravis annis, egregia de imperio rectè adminiftando habita oratione, regno Sulciman filio natu majori cedit. Is cum vel fapientiffimos principes, Viziri prudentis confiliis fæpenumero egere intelligeret, in Dgiafer magni nominis virum oculos conjicit. Venit in confpectum Sultani, qui ex armillæ motu venenum à Dgiafer occultari cognovit: irafcitur Muflim, re tamen ad examen revocata, cum nihil doli fubeffe conftaret, honorificentiffimè excipitur; variifque ipfum inter & Sultanum ortis fermonibus, narrat Dgiafer fibi vifum in aula regis Tabariftan pifcem argenteum, cujus ope, quicquid vel cafu, vel de induftria in mare fuerat miffum, ad poffefforem redibat. Neque minùs incredibilia produntur de annulo, ea arte fabrefacto, ut ille qui geftaret, pala ad palmam converfa, à nemine videretur.

CODICES SINICI,

Eo ordine difpofiti quo, diverfis temporibus, in Bibliothecam Regiam illati funt.

I.°

Libri Sinici, quos primitus habuit Bibliotheca Regia, à Cupletio ejufque fociis, ut verifimile eft, è Sina allatos.

HISTORICI.

CODEX PRIMUS.

ANnales Sinici infcripti

| cu | adjuvantis |
| chi | gubernationem |

| tum ⎫ | |
| kien ⎭ | fpeculi |

| kam ⎫ | caput ⎫ | |
| mo ⎭ | & oculus ⎭ | feu repræfentatio, |

hoc eft, principia, feu quæ primò difcenda funt, & fpeculi inftar effe poterunt, ad dirigendam reipublicæ feu minifterii publici gubernationem. Hic liber longè ampliffimus eft, & voluminum centum viginti: annales enim funt dynaftiarum particularium plerarumque, & quafi univerfalem imperii Sinenfis hiftoriam exhibent, eam nimirum, quæ à tribunalibus, idque auctoritate publica, confcripta eft, & etiamnum confcribitur. Auctores annalium Sinicorum numero prope infiniti, fi eos numeres à quibus primùm per varia retro fæcula confcripti funt: auctores vero qui annales Sinicos, de quibus nunc, diverfis temporibus collegerunt & ediderunt, quinque funt præfertim:

1.° Su
ma
kum.

2.° Chu
ven
kum.

3.° Kin
gin
xan.

4.° Xam
lu (lo)

5.° Nan
hien.

Primus auctor *Su-ma-kum,* qui hanc, quam nunc exhibent Sinæ collectionem, inchoavit, vixit fub dynaftia Sum, fæculo Chrifti primo; & ab eo auctore eft, quod nomen Cu-chi-tum-kien hodie præ fe ferant hi annales, cum antea ki, id eft, libri memoriales, aut alio generali nomine appellarentur. Cæterùm hi annales incipiunt ab anno primo 的 Guei-lie-vam, qui dynaftiæ 周 Cheu, rex five imperator fuit trigefimus, idque annis ante Chriftum natum 428. Perducti funt autem ufque ad ultimum annum 的 Xi-cum, fecundi & ultimi 周 Heu-cheu imperatoris, id eft, ad annum à Chrifto 951. quod intervallum eft annorum 1379.

Secundus auctor *Chu-ven-kum,* vir ætatis fuæ celeberrimus, annis poftea circiter 300. fub eadem dynaftia 宋 Sum, primùm quidem annalium eorumdem titulo addidit characteres duos kam mo, quod Latinè est, oculus præcipuus, seu de verbo ad verbum, principalitatis oculus; deinde verò, quod hoc additamento innuebat, eosdem annales commentariis, annotationibus quibusdam moralibus, & antiquiorum auctorum testimoniis exornavit.

Tertius auctor *Kin-gin-xan,* vixit initio imperii 元 Yven, familiæ primæ Tartaræ, sæculo Christi XIV. Hic cum tempora vetustiora propter quandam veterum historiarum dispersionem negligi posse animadverteret, annales imperii Sinici antiquissimos, id est, rerum ab anno primo Yao, ante Christum 2353. ad Guei-lie-vam annum primum, unde Su-ma-quam inceperat, gestarum serie continua per annos 1930. repræsentavit.

Auctor quartus *Xam-lu,* vel *lo,* quod idem est, ab anno 12. 宋 Chim-hoa (Christi 963.) ejusdemque imperatoris jussu eosdem annales continuavit per annos 408. usque ad annnm 宋 Xun-ti decimum, ultimumque Ivenidarum. Annus autem ille est post Christum 1371.

Auctor quintus *Nan-hien,* vixit sæculo XVI. medio. Is annales auxit, & ex antiquis auctoribus imperii initia supplevit; neglectisque temporibus fabulosis, historiam orsus est à Fohi, primo gentis non suspecto fundatore, & perduxit ad annum primum 宋 Yao, unde Kin-gin-xan inceperat.

Hi autem, de quibus nunc, annales typis excusi sunt, regnante hac familia Ta-cim, seu Tartara, sub Xun-chi 宋 Kam-hi patre. Liber autem est in 12. involucris, & voluminum 120.

Auctoritas annalium Sinicorum in ipsa Sina est maxima; quippe qui à gravissimis auctoribus creduntur scripti, idque imperatorum jussu, & cura tribunalis ad hoc instituti, ab ipsa imperii Sinensis origine: qui mos scribendorum annalium ab Yao usque repetitus, in tota Sina etiamnum servatur. Neque illi quinque quos nominavi scriptores, annalium Sinicorum auctores habendi sunt, ut jam dixi, sed editores, seu, ut ita dicam, collectores.

I I.

Ku	antiquæ, vel antiquorum
ven	litteraturæ, litteratorum
quen	abyssi
kien	speculum,

hoc est, antiquæ litteraturæ, sive litteratorum antiquorum abyssi speculum.

Litteratorum autem antiquorum nomine, & in hoc libro & ferè apud Sinas, non ii modò qui apud cæteras gentes dicuntur litterati, sed quod lectorem semel monitum volumus, magnates ipsi & imperatores intelliguntur: cum apud Sinas, imperatores, reges, proreges, omnes denique regni administri semper sint esseque debeant docti. Hic autem liber apud Sinas viros politicos, & arti politicæ mirè addictos sit maximi, quippe qui summorum virorum hic facta, illic sententias orationesque stylo antiquo, id est, elegantissimo complectitur. Scriptus est sæculo XVII. regnante 宋 Ta-mim familia, Sinicarum vigesima prima. Auctore *Su-kien-hio,* qui tunc doctor Sinæ fama celeberrimus. Summa vero cura ac singulari quadam characterum pulchritudine editus est anno Christi 1685. 宋 Kam-hi 24. estque vulgo in involucris 4. voluminum 24.

I I I.

Lie
su
kam
kien
pu,

id est, supplementum ad speculum universale, sive annales Sinicos, calendarii modo.

Duo in hocce libro reperias, primùm quidem annalium magnorum compendium, deinde vero facta quædam insigniora virorum, quos virtus bellica, vel pietas, vel regiminis scientia commendavit. Auctor hujus libri *Liao-fan:* & hoc illius supplementum non nisi sub ejusdem sæculi finem impressum est. Libri hujus, mole non ita magni, involucra duo, volumina 34.

Monendus interim lector, præter annales publicos Sinicos, extare monumenta historiæ Sinicæ quam plurima. Porro hoc est annales inter & cæteros libros historicos discrimen, quòd libri historici à quocumque doctore scribi possint, annales autem publici aut imperii ipsius, nonnisi à tribunalibus atque imperatoria auctoritate proficiscantur.

I V.

Tum
kien } 1. 1. 219.
che
kiai,

id est, 宋 Tum-kien expositio litteralis.

Annales primùm Tum-kien appellatos diximus, postea à Chu-ven-kum titulo veteri

veteri additas voces kam mo. Hic liber eorumdem annalium compendium etiam eſt, idque à celebri doctore commentariis illuſtratum, cujus nomen *Cham-kiu-chim*. Fuit autem Cham-kiu-chim, hinc 的 Van-lie unius ex Ta-mim familia, illinc imperii totius adminiſter. At ſæculo XVI. medio, annis poſt circiter 80. *Cham-kia-ha*, cum è litteratis ipſe eſſet, Sinicos eoſdem annales auxit. Quæ igitur ſub eadem Ta-mim familia geſta fuerant per annos ferè 276. ea non ſolùm litteris mandavit, ſed etiam explicatione litterali illuſtravit; continetque hic liber primò annales imperii totius, id eſt, eorum quæ familiam Ta-mim præceſſerunt, & eorum quæ ſub eadem familia facta, enarrationem; deinde, expoſitiones in ea omnia, præſertim in antiquiora, litterales; deſinitque anno Chriſti 1647. Sic quæ per annos circiter 4609. evenere, ea in hoc opere aptè diſpoſita, atque eleganter conſcripta legere eſt. Quod opus, cum non ſemel impreſſum jam eſſet, prodiit denuò regnante Xun-chi, 的 Kam-hi patre. In tribus involucris, voluminbus 16.

V.

Chun
cieu,

id eſt, ver & autumnus.

Atque hic eſt titulus annalium principatus Lu, ab ipſo *Kum-fu-cu*, id eſt, primario Sinarum philoſopho Confucio conſcriptorum. Cujus tituli ratio non in promptu eſt. Porro hic liber pretii apud Sinas ſummi, & inter ſacros tantùm non repoſitus, hiſtoriam exhibet præcipuè regni Lu, aliquando etiam, prout ſe dedit occaſio, imperii ipſius Sinici, idque per annos duntaxat 242. Scilicet in regno Lu natus Confucius è familia honoratiſſima, quæque apud Sinas principatum quemdam etiamnum obtineat, patriæ ſuæ regendæ ac bonis moribus informandæ, per multos annos operam navavit. Tandem abdicato miniſterio jam ſenex, & litteris ac diſcipulis unicè addictus, rerum ante ſe geſtarum hiſtoriam, politicis cogitationibus quàmplurimis ornatam atque diſtinctam, voluit poſteritati relinquere, idque eſt in cæterorum annalium modum executus. Inde verò orta eſt Sinarum reverentia, quòd hic liber prudentiſſimè ac ſententioſè ſcriptus, regum virtutes ac vitia graphicè depingat. Itaque cum apud Sinas libri ſint canonici quinque, vulgo u kim dicti, eodem ferè loco habetur ὁ chun cieu ac ſu xu, ſeu libri illi quatuor, quorum

MSS. Tomus I.

tres à Cupletio editi; ita ut vulgò canonici libri ſex eſſe dicantur. Commentarii in hunc librum ſcripti ſunt à multis philoſophis quàmplurimi, atque etiamnum ſcribuntur: ultimus autem qui famam commentariis ſuis aliquam ſibi pepererit, fuit *Hum-mum-lum*, qui ſub Ta-mim vixit, imperante Tien-ki, ejus dynaſtiæ decimo ſeptimo.

Hic liber involucrorum eſt duorum, voluminum 12.

VI.

Chum

tim

chun

cieu

co

chuen

kieu

kiai,

hoc eſt, expoſitio verborum genuinum 的 chun-cieu ſenſum juſtè determinantium.

Alia eſt editio Confucii annalium, quæ primùm à doctore quodam, *Chu-ſin* appellato, procurata eſt ſæculo X. cum regnaret familia Sum; deinde verò, imperante Xunchi magno, 的 Kam-hi patre, impreſſa eſt. Involucrum eſt unum, volumina 5.

Libri apud Sinas ſacri, aliàs canonici, aliàs claſſici.

Meminerit lector quinque duntaxat libros, ut jam diximus, à Sinis haberi & appellari ſacros, unde u kim nominantur: quibus tamen additur à pleriſque ſextus ὁ chun cieu, liber Confucii, propter reverentiam Confucio ſemper habitam.

Is autem librorum ſacrorum eſt ordo:

1.°	Ye kim.	Combinationum ſeu permutationum liber.
2.°	Xu kim.	Librorum ſeu memorialium liber, ſive liber ex aliis excerptus: eſt autem liber chronicus.
3.°	Xi kim.	Carminum liber.
4.°	Li ki.	Liber rituum ac ceremoniarum.
5.°	Su xu.	Libri quatuor; quibus ſcilicet moralis quædam philoſophia continetur.

Hæc præmoneri ſufficiat, redeamus jam in viam.

A a a

V I I.

Ye y
kim
civen
chi,

id eft, 蔫 ye kim, feu libri combinationum ampla & totalis expofitio.

Hic liber inter canonicos primus eft & antiquiſſimus, quippe qui, ſi credimus Sinis, eo tempore exaratus eft, quo litteræ nondum extarent, ne hieroglyphicæ quidem; & auctorem habet *Fohi* antiquiſſimum monarchiæ Sinicæ fundatorem, annis, ut perhibent, ante Chriftum natum 2961.

Porro hic liber ſtatim à principio combinationes litterarum exhibet 64. de quibus alii alia ſomniavere. Quidam aſſerunt auctorem *Fohi* ea voluiſſe defcribere, quæ ſolent accidere cœlo, terræ & homini; quæ tria à Sinis philofophicis maximè confiderantur. Quidam verò eafdem combinationes ad moralia & reipublicæ adminiftrationem pertinere contendunt. Sed eorum numerus in Sina longè maximus eft, qui combinationes ad magiam nefcio quam, ac prophetandi artem refpicere arbitrentur.

Habuit fuos commentatores hic libellus. Primus eum explicare aggreſſus eft imperator *Ven-vam;* quod cum breviter & perobfcurè feciſſet, filius ejus uberiori commentario eundem libellum illuftravit. Quin & ipfe Confucius fuis notis combinationes adornavit, quas de morali difciplina & arte politica omnino vult intelligi. Extant & recentiores in hunc librum commentatores: hi (maximè verò qui, imperante familia Sum, vixerunt) pleraque de rebus naturalibus interpretantur. Unde liber ifte magno apud Sinas phyficos in pretio. Inter recentiores cenfendus eft celeberrimus doctor *Chu-ven-kum,* qui has combinationes fæculo Chrifti XIII. locupletiori commentario donavit. Hæc editio procurata eft anno 70. regni Cham-hi. Involucrum eft unum, volumina 3.

V I I I.

Ye y
kim
cie cy
chu,

id eft, in ye kim, feu librum combinationum variorum commentarii.

Alia eft editio libri canonici ejufdem; additi autem in hac editione commentarii auctorum duorum, alter fupra, alter infra paginas. Qui fupra, is auctorem habet philofophum *Vam-fu-kuei;* qui infra, eft à philofopho *Chim-moei* compofitus.

Vivebat autem philofophus uterque fæculi XVI. initio & fub finem familiæ Ta-mim; at liber impreſſus anno 1623. imperante Van-lie, ejufdem familiæ ultimo. Involucrum unum, volumina 5.

I X.

Ye
kim
ge
kiam,

id eft, 蔫 ye kim expofitio diurnalis.

Hæc editio exinia characterum forma admirabilis, commentario adornata eft à doctoribus collegii Han-lin, regnante Kam-hi. Voluminum eft 16. fed defunt 8.

X.

Xu
kim
ta
civen,

id eft, magna & totalis 蔫 xu kim collectio.

Liber xu kim de iis tractat potiſſimùm, quæ à temporibus Yao & Xun ufque ad Chim-vam & tutorem ejus Cheu-kum, per legiflatores mandata funt. Legiflatores dico, neque enim eft hiftoria hujus aut illius fæculi, fed tantummodo excerpta ex annalibus tunc temporis, per tribunal hiftoricum, jam inde ab Yao inftitutum, continuatis. Moralis autem liber eft magis quàm hiftoricus. Unde complura ibi occurrunt confilia ac monita de agricultura, de reipublicæ gubernatione, de artibus earumque inventione.

Porro liber xu kim in fex partes, quaſi totidem libellos dividitur. Duobus prioribus libellis, quorum pleraque ad informandos magiftratus fpectant, gefta continentur 蔫 Yao imperatoris ac legiflatoris fapientiſſimi, non fine notis ubique politicis. Acceſſerunt multa de Xun ac præfertim de magno Yu, quem perpetuò in ore ac fcriptis habent geographi Sinæ. Ille Yu diluvii, quod maximum fub Yao contigit, aquis in mare derivatis, agriculturæ in provinciis plurimis intermortuæ loca tandem ficca præftitit; &, in rebus aftronomicis verfatus, imperium ferè immenfum in quindecim provincias divifit. Tertius liber agit de ejectione impii Kie primæ familiæ ultimi;

quæ quidem ejectio annis ante Chriſtum circiter 1766. contigiſſe dicitur. De ſecunda familia Xam, alias Yn-chao dicta: de Co-lao, Chum-hoei, & de ejus præceptis ad Chim-tam & 的 Chim-tam nepotem Tai-kia directis. Tum ſequitur oratio *Puon-kem* ejuſdem familiæ decimæ ſeptimæ, ad po-pulos 的 Hoam-ho fluminis inundationibus vexatos: in qua, pro antiquo illorum tem-porum concionandi more, uniuſcujuſque officia, & magiſtratuum & privatorum refricantur. Acceſſerunt præterea magno-rum virorum Fu-que Co-lai, principis, Vi-cu-ki, atque alius Co-lai-cu-y docu-menta præclariſſima.

Quæ autem tribus libellis poſterioribus continentur, ea ad familiam Cheu, ſeu tertiam, pertinent. omnia. Comparet ergo illic & Un-vam hujus familiæ conditor, qui Sinas ſibi nuper ſubjectos, orationibus nonnullis, ad bene beatèque vivendum adhortatur. Deinde Cheu-kum, princeps ac regulus Ki-cu: alter Un-vam frater, ac tutor 的 Chim-vam, vir propter integrita-tem ac ſapientiam commendatiſſimus; alter ob virtutem Coreæ rex creatus.

Cæterùm in eodem libro xu kim mentio fit quarumdam eclipſεων, antiquis illis tem-poribus obſervatarum.

Commentariis autem illuſtratus eſt li-ber xu kim ab auctoribus plurimis; inter quos celebres ſunt *Kim-ngan-kue,* unus è Confucii nepotibus, iſque duodecimus, imperante apud Sinas Kuam-un-ti ex fa-milia Han; & *Cham-po,* ſeu *pu,* ſæculo XV. dum imperium teneret familia Ta-mim. Hic autem primùm quidem antiquos 的 *Kum-ngan-kue* commentarios denuò edidit, deinde addidit ſuos: atque hinc eſt quod editionem ſuam inſcripſerit ta civen. Duo ſunt involucra, ſed volumina 12.

X I.

Xu
kim
ci
chuen,

id eſt, varii in xu kim commentarii.

Hi commentarii auctorem habuere do-ctorem *Cai-chin.* Vixit autem Cai-chin imperante familia Sum 的 Nim-cum ejuſ-dem familiæ decimæ tertiæ, circa annum Chriſti 1190. impreſſuſque eſt annis poſt ſat multis, nempe ſub finem familiæ vige-ſimæ primæ Ta-mim, idque initio ſæculi XVII. Involucrum unum, volumina 4.

MSS. Tomus I.

X I I.

Xu
kim
chi
kiai,

id eſt, 的 xu kim recta expoſitio.

Editio hæc commentariis duobus illu-ſtrata eſt; quorum prior eſt doctoris inter Sinas notiſſimi & maximi *Kum-ngan-kue;* poſterior à doctore *Chuen-ſun* concinnatus, ita ut in priorem commentarium notas ubique interſerat ſuas, unde exurgit com-mentarius ferè triplex. Impreſſus eſt anno Chriſti 1689. imperatoris Kam-hi anno 24. Involucrum unum, volumina 8.

X I I I.

Xi
xim,

id eſt, odarum, ſeu verſuum liber.

Odæ illæ numero trecentæ ad virtutis laudem ferè ſunt compoſitæ; inſerta tamen ſpuria nonnulla, priſcorum temporum gra-vitate non ſatis digna, & fabulæ genealo-gicæ, quod nimia in reges & principes adulatione factum creditur. Auctores oda-rum illuſtriſſimi plerique imperatores ſcili-cet, reges, reginæ, proreginæ ac miniſtri celebres, quod minimè mirum videatur propter ſolitam virorum principum erudi-tionem. Porro hic liber antiquiſſimus eſt; pertinet enim totus ad regna Xam-chao, aliàs Yn-chao, & ad Cheu-chao, id eſt, ad tertiam & quartam familiam imperatoriam, quas in Sina non præceſſere niſi familia Hia & ſex gentis fundatores. Odæ tamen pleræque ad familiam Cheu referuntur. Liber hic commentarium habet auctoris celeberrimi *Chi-ven-kum,* & denuò im-preſſus eſt imperante 的 Ta-mim familia, ſæculo Chriſti XVI. ineunte. Involucrum eſt unum, volumina 4.

X I V.

Kien
puen
xi
kim,

id eſt, liber xi kim ex typographia imperiali, quæ vocatur kien puen.

Editio eſt libri xi kim in urbe Pe-kim, imperatoris Kam-hi juſſu procurata, anno Chriſti 1685. Kam-hi 24. Involucrum unum, volumina 4.

Aaa ij

X V.

Li
ki
ci cie
xue,

id est, varii discursus in librum rituum, seu officiorum.

Agitur hoc libro li ki, Sinici canonis quarto, non solùm de variis religionibus, sacrificiis, templis, sacerdotibus, funeribus, aulis defunctorum privatis & publicis, quo apparatu imperatores, reges, magistratus in sua quemque urbe, aut sacrificare, aut munera sua obire oporteat; sed etiam de officiis omnibus vitæ humanæ, imò & de re militari, de musica atque innumeris prope artibus. Divisus est hic liber in decem partes quasi totidem libellos, qui ex priscorum Sinarum monumentis collecti sunt. Liber li ki Confucio vulgò tribuitur, sed verius est auctorem ejus præcipuum esse τὸν Chenkum, regni Lu principem, filium regis Ven-vam, fratrem regis Un-vam, patruum ac tutorem regis Chim-vam; eundem verò librum à Confucio postea auctum ac locupletatum. Ex eo tempore omnis vitæ regendæ cura ad philosophos rediit Confucii sectatores, quorum unus, nomine Chim-hao, imperante familia Sum, sæculo Christi XII. librum hunc li ki edidit. Sed impressus idem est denuò anno Christi 1683. sub Kam-hi. Involucrum duplex, volumina 10.

X V I.

Li
ki
ci cie
kiai,

id est, in librum li ki, seu rituum & officiorum commentarius ad manum.

Editio alia τῦ li ki, unà cum notis & commentariis doctoris Vam-ym-kuei. Hic autem florebat imperantibus Ta-mim, ejusque opus impressum est anno Christi 1626. Cim-chim anno 4. Involucrum est unum, volumina 4.

X V I I.

Su
xu,

id est, libri quatuor.

Inde verò libri quatuor, liber ille unus nominatur, sive quòd editus à quatuor Philosophis, qui modò singuli suo ordine appellabuntur, sive quòd quatuor habeat partes. Prima pars quæ Confucium auctorem habet, nuncupatur ta hio, id est, magna, seu magnitudinis scientia. (Alii adultorum, alii magnatum scientiam vertunt) Hujus partis scopus est, ut solâ ratione duce hominem à sensibus & cupiditatibus ad bonam frugem & vitæ humanæ officia convertat. Pars ista parva est, si molem, sed si majestatem quandam operis spectes, longè maxima & admiratione dignissima. Secunda pars vocatur·chum yum, auctorem habet Cem-cu. Auctoris scopus ex ipsa denominatione intelligitur; nam chum significat medium, & yum usum & officium; adeoque liber est de aurea illa mediocritate quam suadet Horatius. Pars tertia, cujus auctor Mem-cu, appellatur lun yn, id est, ratiocinantium colloquia sive sermones. In hac nimirum parte sermocinantur inter se philosophi, de virtutibus & vitiis differentes, sed breviter ac sententiosè, non per argumentationem, sed per exempla & historias, quomodo solent disputare Philosophi Sinici. Veterum philosophorum, Confucii maximè, sermones & dicta, imò & ex eorum operibus excerpta in hunc libellum suum auctor contulit, cujus phrasis nitidior & simplicior est quàm priorum. Quarta pars, cujus idem auctor Mem-cu, elegans itidem & moralis tota est, & mole sua reliquas tres una æquat, scriptaque est annis post Confucium 100. Fuit enim, ut diximus, O-mem-cu discipulus τῦ Cu-cu, nepotis Confucii; unde libelli hujus doctrina eadem est cum doctrina Confucii.

Commendantur autem hi quatuor libri, non ideo solùm, quia quidquid in præcedentibus prudentiæ ac sapientiæ est, graphicè repræsentant, sed etiam quia ad doctoratus Sinici gradum, ac proinde ad magistratum apud Sinas nemo admittitur, nisi ex his quatuor, unum aliquem ad libitum, memoriter teneat. Itaque commentariis longè doctissimis illustrati sunt, hodieque illustrantur. Præcipui tamen commentatores Chu-ven-kum & Cham-kiao-kim. Hic regni administer ac præceptor fuit τῦ Van-lie, ultimi familiæ Ta-mim; quod in hac editione videre est. Eo quippe consilio procurata fuit, ut imperatoris, tum minoris, studia & institutionem adjuvaret. Involucrum duplex, volumina 2.

Atque hi sunt libri quatuor τῦ su xu, quos vulgò Confucii libros appellamus. Qui quidem su xu si addatur libris ye kim, xu kim, xi kim & li ki, de quibus antea, erunt qui vulgò vocantur u kim, id eft, quinque libri, facri fcilicet, canonici & claffici. Quòd autem aliquando appellentur lo kim, five fex libri, inde eft, quòd, ut initio diximus, chun cieu his quinque libris non raro adjungatur.

X V I I I.

Sim

li

ta

civen,

id eft, rationalis naturæ expofitiones à variis Philofophis datæ.

Ita infcribitur liber apud Sinas celeberrimus, qui, ut noftri loquuntur, curfus philofophicus dici poteft. Agit enim de metaphyfica, morali, phyfica & mathefi. Ita tamen ut quidquid Philofophi Sinici, à fæculis triginta & amplius, magna inter fe diffentione commenti funt, in unum hunc librum fit congeftum. Adeoque verè appellabitur hic liber hiftoria variorum fyftematum, quæ circa res philofophicas aliquando in Sina obtinuerunt. Ex operibus quadraginta Philofophorum hæc collectio facta eft, & edita fæculo Chrifti xv. Involucrum duplex, volumina 20.

X I X.

Sim

li

chu,

id eft, commentarius in rationem univerfalem.

Editio eft recens, & imperante Kam-hi, anno Chrifti 1685. procurata. Auctor commentarii Chen-hoai, eodem tempore in vivis fuit. Involucra 2. volumina 12.

X X.

Vu

kim,

id eft, bellorum aut artis militaris liber.

Defcribuntur hoc libro bella quæ Hum-vu, primùm latro, deinde gentis fuæ vindex acerrimus geffit; legefque bellicæ quas idem, imperator declaratus, optimas & ad mentem Sinarum accommodatiffimas promulgavit. Confcriptus eft hic liber anno Chrifti 1367. cui poftea acceffit commentarius, auctore Chim-kiai-hio, imperante Van-lie, familiæ Ta-mim decimo quarto. Jam hæc editio

procurata fub Kam-hi. Involucrum unum, volumina 2.

X X I.

Cem

pu

vu

kim,

id eft, fupplementum ad bellorum, feu rei militaris librum.

Liber idem eft cum præcedente, fed commentariis illuftratus à Lin-fu-hoan, qui multis poft annis, cum notas præcedentium, variafque hominum ætatis fuæ obfervationes fumma cura in unum collegiffet, & fuas addidit. Impreffus hic liber anno Chrifti 1633. imperante Cum-chim, aliàs Hoaicum, ejufdem familiæ Ta-mim decimo feptimo. Involucrum unum, volumina 4.

M A T H E M A T I C I.

X X I I.

Ve

lun

kuam

y,

id eft, lunarum ordinationis lata expofitio.

Is liber non ea folùm continet, quæ ad aftronomiam & aftrologiam Sinicam fpectant, fed etiam res quæ per varia fæcula à regibus & imperatoribus geftæ funt: pro more Sinarum, qui cum obfervationes fiderum ad rempublicam referant, hiftorias varias & imperii mutationes libris aftronomicis inferunt. In eodem libro multa de antiquis mundi fyftematibus reperias. Auctor Lu-pu-guei, adminifter τᷣ Xi-hoam-ti, imperatoris, qui murum illum Sinenfem ædificandum curavit. Commentatores hujus libri plurimi; agmen ducit Chu-ven-kum. Is fæculo Chrifti xiii. librum correxit, edidit & commentariis adornavit. Secutus eft alius commentator Hum-ym-kin, ejufque extant notæ in hunc librum elegantes. Denique fæculo Chrifti xvi. imperante Van-lie, alius commentator Tai-gin, difcipulus ejufdem Hum-ym-kin, expofitionem magiftri fui, animadverfionibus fuis illuftravit (unde noftri libri infcriptio ve lim kuam y) & τᷣ Van-lie imperatori dedicavit. Præfationem imperator ipfe addidit. Impreffus liber anno 1587. τᷣ Van-lie 20. Eftque involucri unius, voluminum 8.

A a a iij

X X I I I.

Cum

chin

lie li

xu,

id eft, 𝜏𝖊 Cum-chim, five imperatoris Cum-chim, kalendarii liber.

Tractatus hic de aftronomia & aliis mathefeos partibus, totus ex Euclide, Clavio & antiquis Mathematicis Græcis & Latinis defumtus eft, & compofitus à doctis Aftronomis è Societate Jefu.

X X I V.

Liber Latinè infcriptus, cœli phœnomena.

Habet autem partes duas, quarum altera agit de lunæ cum cæteris planetis conjunctionibus, & vice verfa; itemque de iis conjunctionibus quæ funt ejufdem lunæ ac cæterorum planetarum cum fixis. Notabis autem id nonnifi ad annum Chrifti 1674. pertinere. In altera funt ephemerides Sinicæ, five motus planetarum feptem, ad annum Chrifti 1679. Prima pars manufcripta eft, altera impreffa. Utraque autem R. P. *Verbieft,* è Societate Jefu.

X X V.

Liber organicus aftronomiæ apud Sinas reftitutæ fub imperatore Sino-Tartarico, Kam-hi appellato; auctore P. *Ferdinando Verbieft,* Flandro-Belga Brugenfi, è Societate Jefu, Academiæ aftronomicæ in regia Pechinenfi præfecto. Anno falutis 1663. opus hoc totum machinis variis, tum ad fphæram, tum ad cæteras mathefeos partes attinentibus, exhibendis delineandifque occupatur. Præmittitur tantùm præfatio, quæ figurarum illic defcriptarum, & modum quo fieri debeant & ufum ad has vel illas artes, ad hæc vel illa opera, idque generatim duntaxat exponit. Multa funt quæ ad geographiam, tabulafque geographicas conficiendas, multa quæ ad luminis refractionem, ad fpecula elaboranda, eorumque fpecies diverfas, imò ad hydraulicam & agriculturam referantur.

X X V I.

Ki

ho

yao

fa,

id eft, geometriæ neceffaria principia, feu primarum geometriæ regularum fundamenta. Auctor hujus libri P. *Aleni,* è Societate Jefu.

M E D I C I.

X X V I I.

Piun

cao

kam

mo,

id eft, medicinalium herbarum ac plantarum repræfentatio, feu principia. *Vide* fupra n.° 1.°

Hic liber quamvis folius botanicæ titulum præ fe ferat, medicinæ tamen Sinicæ artem totam complectitur. Neque enim folùm de herbis, plantis, arboribus, fructibus, feminibus, variis granorum generibus, & omni radicum fpecie in hoc libro differitur, fed etiam de foffilibus, mineralibus & animalibus; quorum omnium defcriptionem ibi reperias accuratam, quæ fingulorum proprietates, & quæ inde medicamenta fieri confueverint. Opus inchoatum à variis Medicis antiquis, à recentioribus, diverfis temporibus, auctum & amplificatum. Horum ultimus fuit *Li-xi-chin,* cujus opera hæc collectio impreffa eft, imperante Xunchi, 𝜏𝖊 Kam-hi patre. Involucra quatuor, volumina 32.

X X V I I I.

Puen

cao

mum

civen,

id eft, inftrumentum quafi pifcatorium, & fagena ad ea excerpenda quæ funt in puen-cao.

Hic liber nonnifi epitome quædam eft amplæ illius collectionis medicæ, de qua fupra. Itaque primo tomo, quafi per catalogum indicantur nomina herbarum omnium, item indices rerum aliarum multiplicium in 𝜏𝜌𝖋 puen-cao contentarum. Tomi cæteri de ipfis plantis, aliifque materiis agunt, fed breviùs. Scriptus eft hic liber & commentariis illuftratus à *Chimkia-mo,* qui auctor fæculi XVI. initio vixit, idque imperante apud Sinas Kia-cin, familiæ vigefimæ primæ Ta-mim. Impreffus verò fub Kam-hi. Volumina 5. fed allata tantum 4.

XXIX.

Fuen
pu
puen
cao,

id eft, tractatus particularis de plantarum proprietate.

In hoc opere plantæ omnes & herbæ ad genus & fpeciem fuam revocantur, & per claffes diftribuuntur; ita ut quamlibet herbam aut plantam ftatim reperias. Auctor *Ku-hum-pe*, qui & *Hoai-cum* appellatur, magni nominis medicus. Vixit imperante Cum-chim, imperatore decimo feptimo, familiæ vigefimæ primæ 大明 Ta-mim. Hic autem liber impreffus eft fæculo Chrifti XVII. fub Xun-chi. Involucrum unum, volumina 3.

XXX.

Lui
kim,

id eft, anatomiæ liber. Quid autem doceat, titulus indicat. 1.° exaratus eft imperantibus Ta-mim. 2.° fub imperatore Tien-ki, ejufdem familiæ decimo quinto. 3.° à doctore *Cham-kiai-pin*, qui ita rem tractavit, ut à principiis 大 Nui-kim, qui primus de anatomia liber Sinicus, non omnino recederet. Hic nofter impreffus eft, imperante eadem familia 大明 Ta-mim. Involucra 3. volumina 15.

XXXI.

Tum ⎞ Tum
gin ⎟ gin
tu ⎬ *aliàs* chin
kim, ⎟ kieu
  ⎠ tu
   kim,

id eft, tum gin bubonum, five puftularum acu aperiendarum, tabulæ & figuræ; feu liber tabularum chirurgicalium.

Liber hic totus figuras varias exhibet, five virorum, five feminarum; idque ea mente ut diverfi hominum à chirurgis pungendorum, in omnibus corporis partibus, fitus cognofcantur, quales apud nos libri chirurgici plerique. Scriptus autem liber fæculo Chrifti XI. cum in Sina imperaret familia Sum, & fub Gin-cum ejufdem

familiæ quarto, cyclo 63. Auctor fuit ejufdem imperatoris medicus. Sed impreffio anni 1442. 大 Chim-tum 4. qui familiæ Ta-mim imperator fextus. Volumina 3.

XXXII.

Tai
fo fu
me
kive,

id eft, 大 *Tai-fu* pulfus motus. A Sinis cognitionem pulfus eximiam expectari poffe, judicare poffunt omnes, cum in hac medicinæ parte experientiam Sinæ medici acquirere fibi cogantur multò majorem, quàm apud cæteras gentes folitum fit. Itaque hîc mira quædam de pulfu, aut potiùs variis variorum corporis membrorum pulfibus: nam pulfum in toto ferè corpore inquirunt, atque ex ea perquifitione fæpe diuturna, morbos mirum in modum perfentifcunt, ut notum eft, & ab omnibus relationum auctoribus dictitatum. Poftquam *Tai-fu* librum hunc feciffet juris publici, commentatorem reperit *Pe-ci-am*, à quo liber me kive commentariis illuftratus eft; idque imperante Van-lie, aliàs Xincum, decimo quarto familiæ vigefimæ primæ, fæculo poft Chriftum natum XVI. Habet idem involucrum cum HH. & eft voluminum 4.

XXXIII.

Y
cum
pie pi
to,

id eft, quod à medicis, tanquam in eorum arte præcipuum, oportet legi; feu medicorum ftudium principale ac neceffarium.

In hoc opere ea inquiruntur, quæ primò, per fe ac præcipuè à medico legantur ac difcantur neceffe eft; quod non folùm ad libros ac ftudia, fed etiam ad dirigendos medici mores, totamque vitæ rationem fpectat. Scripfit autem fummus medicus, cui nomen *Li-chum-cio*, medicus imperatoris Cum-chim, aliàs Hoai-cum, familiæ Ta-mim decimi feptimi, circa annum Chrifti 1626. Impreffumque eodem ferè tempore, & eft voluminum 4.

XXXIV.

Cem

pu

ku

kin

y

kien,

id eft, ad antiquum & novum medicorum fpeculum, fupplementum *Lum-fin*.

Is cum medicus effet & fama apud Sinas celebris, multaque ipfe & ab aliis auditu didiciffet, & in libris tum veterum, tum ætatis fuæ medicorum legiffet, imò & inter plebem, quæ ad ratiocinationem tantummodo & methodum reducenda videbantur, experientiâ factâ, comprobaffet, ea omnia in hunc librum, fed fuo quæque ordine collegit: habet præterea non pauca, quæ arcanorum nomine tradit, tanquam ab aliis medicis aut neglecta, aut ignorata. Fuit autem Lum-fin medicus unius è Ta-mim; ejufque liber impreffus imperante Xun-chi 及 Kam-hi patre. Volumina 4.

GEOGRAPHI.

XXXV.

Kuam

yu

ki,

id eft, lata terræ defcriptio, feu geographia.

Hoc libro continetur provinciarum imperii Sinici quindecim defcriptio ampliffima; itemque regnorum vicinorum omnium, five imperatori Sinæ vectigalia pendant, five libera fint: quod factum, quia olim Sinenfi imperio fubjecta fuere cuncta. Libri hujus auctor *Lo-ym-yam*, qui cum fub Yum-lo, 永 Ta-mim tertio viveret, geographiam & uniufcujufque urbis ac provinciæ ftatum, quomodo tunc fuit, tradit accuratiffimè. Inde eft quòd in tomo fexto, pofteaquam provincias tres Quam-fi, Yunnan & Kuci-cheu commonftravit, multa habeat præcipuè de Tum-kim, Cochinchina, vicinifque aliis regnis, opufque fit eam ob caufam curiofiffimum. Volumina 6.

XXXVI.

Kuam

yu

ki,

id eft, ampla terræ, feu Sinæ totius defcriptio. Eadem eft geographia, fed aucta

& correcta, ac denuò, fed diligentiùs, imperante Kam-hi impreffa. Volumina funt 8. fed ultimum è Sina allatum non eft.

AGRICULTURA.

XXXVII.

Num

chim

civen

xu,

id eft, agriculturæ perficiendæ liber totalis, five abfolutiffimus.

Præter ea quæ ad agriculturam vitamque rufticam, bombycum nutritionem, &c. fpectant, multa in hoc libro reperias de rebus mathematicis, de aftronomia, geometria & hydraulica. Auctor neophitus Chriftianus, *Paulus* nomine, doctrina illuftris, fcientiis Sinicis imprimis eruditus, & aliquando regni adminifter; qui fub finem vitæ ex negotiis publicis rus feceffit, ut uni Deo ferviret. Liber eft figuris ornatus quàmplurimis, & florum atque arborum recenfet nomina pleraque. Involucra 2. volumina 12.

ARTES.

XXXVIII.

Tien

kum

kai

ve,

id eft, rerum à cœlo factarum in artibus patefactio.

Hic liber arcana ferè omnia & naturæ & artium continet, verbi gratia, de porcellanis, de fericis, de tincturis, de atramentis, quomodo & ex quo fiant; item qua ratione gemmæ è mari extrahantur, qui excidantur, aliaque ejufmodi infinita. Auctor *Sum-ymfin* doctor Sinæ, qui artium admodum curiofus, vitam omnem fuam in earum cognitione & rerum artificialium inquifitione confumfit. Debet effe trium voluminum, fed fecundum allatum non eft.

XXXIX.

Xy

fu

tum

kao,

id eft, fæculi negotiorum generale examen, feu cognitio univerfalis.

Tractatus

Tractatus hic per se curiositatis plenus; etenim multa offert omnino singularia, & quæcumque ad imperium Sinicum cognoscendum spectare possunt, quodammodo complectitur. Tractat nimirum de rebus ferè omnibus, de variis Sinicæ gentis populis ac nationibus; de eorumdem populorum enumeratione, moribus, usibus, muneribusque: item quot sint apud Sinas artes, & quænam aut ardentissimè colantur, aut vilissimæ sint: præterea de mutuo inter Sinas commercio, de itinerum susceptione; admiscet quoque nonnulla de medicinæ occultioris remediis, de grammatica, aut potiùs de quibusdam genti Sinicæ propriis phrasibus, ad Sinarum mores, ut inde earum convenientia illustretur, ubique relatis; auctor *Siu-san-sein.* Vivebat autem imperante familia vigesima secunda Tamim. Involucrum habet idem cum PP. estque volumen 1.

X L.

Kiun

xu

pu

kao,

id est, variorum librorum accuratum examen.

Opus illud eximium; nam varia è variis antiquorum libris excerpta repræsentat expenditque; item multas historias in mentem revocat, quæ ab aliis auctoribus omissæ, etiam diligentibus atque illustribus; ita ut aut lumina eorum, indicatis fontibus, suppleat, aut res prorsus novas, nominatis interea scriptoribus referat, addatque, ut plurimùm, judicium de unaquaque re sincerum ac criticum. Auctores autem multi fuere, sed præcipuus *Yiun-hoam.* Cæterùm ejus opus à posteriore quodam philosopho, quem vocant *Yiun-nun,* commentariis illustratum est, & brevibus notis; idque ita ut de ferè omnium librorum priscorum auctoritate philosophicè ac criticè agat. Vixit *Yiun-nun* sæculi XVII. initio & sub Ta-mim. Volumina 4.

X L I.

Xim

yu,

id est, sancta institutio.

Hic liber quem summo in pretio habent Sinæ, brevis est officiorum uniuscujusque conditionis expositio. In decursu operis,

MSS. Tomus I.

de variis religionum Sinicarum dogmatibus disseritur, & in religione Christiana nonnulla reprehenduntur. Auctor *Kam-hi,* imperator maximus, & litteratorum princeps: liber est elegantissimè impressus. Volumen 1.

X L I I.

Siao

hio,

seu titulo ampliori,

hiao

kim

siao

hio

cie ci

sin,

id est, parvulorum institutio, seu liber obedientiæ, in quo quidquid ad puerorum institutionem pertinet, continetur.

Hic autem liber nihil aliud est quàm collectio ex ampliori tractatu, cujus titulus ven kum kiali. Porro hic liber, de quo nunc, auctorem habuit *Chu-u-pie,* sæculo Christi XIII. imperante familia Sum. Impressus autem sub Kam-hi. Volumina 2.

X L I I I.

Ta

cim

Lu,

id est, lex magnæ puritatis, seu ta cim.

Hic liber complectitur varia imperatorum Xun-chi & Kam-hi, edicta, & commentarios ad ea stabilienda necessarios. Auctores habuit Mandarinos, qui tribunali rituum præsunt.

Xim.

kiao

sin

chim,

id est, sanctæ religionis fidele testimonium.

Liber hic nihil aliud est quàm catalogus Patrum Societatis Jesu, qui ab anno 1581. ad annum 1681. id est, per annos 100. in Sina Jesu Christi Domini nostri fidem annuntiarunt propagaruntque; ubi singulorum nomina, patria, prædicatio, mors, sepultura, libri Sinicè editi recensentur. Volumen 1.

Bbb

X L I V.

Cin
ſin
pien
lan,

id eſt, eorum qui ad Mandarinatum pervenerunt & magnum cingulum, commoda
& ad manum inſpectio.

Catalogus eſt omnium omnino Mandarinorum, ſeu imperii Sinici magiſtratuum.
Imprimuntur hujuſmodi quotannis; ſed
cum ſint libri hice è genere almanachico,
ſæpe impreſſio eſt peſſima; & talis eſt quæ
in hoc libro conſpicitur. Cæterùm liber eſt
per ſe curioſus ſatis, cum officia ſingula ac
præterea loca aſſignet; adeoque imperii
totius, quantum ad magiſtratus & functiones
magiſtratuum mentionem faciat.

X L V.

Mum
hio
xi
ce
fa,

id eſt, via ſeu modus quo characteres à
pueris diſci poſſunt.

Rudimentum quoddam eſt, merè Sinicum, abſque ulla methodo, cum illic omnia
uſui dentur, & qui characteres in ta hio,
aut aliis libris antiquis difficiles auctori viſi
ſunt, ii tantummodo adducantur. Porro ad
eorum puerorum inſtitutionem factum eſt,
qui nondum ratione uti poſſunt, ſed ſolis
imaginibus tanguntur. Auctor *Cham-hun;*
atque editio facta ſub Kam-hi. Volumen 1.

X L V I.

Ta
cim
kam
hi
xe
pa
nien,

ephemerides Sinicæ; ſive motus ſeptem
planetarum, anni Chriſti 1679. imperatoris
Sino-Tartari Kam-hi appellati decimi
octavi, calculati ad mediam noctem meri-
diani Pekinenſis. Auctore R. P. *Verbieſt,*
Societatis Jeſu, aſtronomiæ in regia Peki-
nenſi præfecto. Liber eſt imperfectus. Volumen 1.

X L V I I.

Ul
xe
ſu
hiao,

id eſt, 孝 viginti quatuor obedientia.

In hoc libro fit mentio ampliſſima antiquorum quorumdam magni nominis virorum; qui veneratione erga parentes ſumma,
toti imperio admirationi fuerunt. Explicatur
qui officia obedientiæ omnia parentibus
præſtiterint, quæ apud Sinas laus maxima.
Et hujus aut illius occaſione veniunt hiſtoriolæ à magiſtris puero unicuique incul-
candæ, è quibus tanquam exemplis obedire
diſcant. Volumen 1.

DICTIONARIA.

*Monendus hîc lector auctorem præfationis in Ægidii
Menagii etymologias Gallicas, falli, dum à Cupletio
dictionarium Latino-Sinicum in Bibliotheca regia reli-
ctum dicit. Dictionarium quidem Sinico-Latinum ſecum
attulerat Cupletius cum è Sina in Galliam rediret. Sed
idem dictionarium ſecum abſtulit, cum in Germaniam
profectus eſt, & illic in aliquo Societatis ſuæ cænobio
manuſcriptum reliquit.*

X L V I I I.

Cu
luy,

id eſt, collectio characterum.

Dictionarium eſt Sinicum, ſeu potiùs
characterum Sinicorum, non omnino omnium, ſed plerorumque, & eorum qui in
uſu apud Sinas frequentiſſimo. Auctoris
nomen *Muy-yn;* impreſſum eſt imperante
Kam-hi. Volumina 14.

Cum dictionaria Sinica à noſtris multùm
differant, brevem hujus deſcriptionem le-
gentium oculis ſubjiciemus.

Primi tomi is eſt ordo, ea materia. 1.º quidem ſtatim occurrunt tres præfationes,
in quibus multa reperias de characterum
natura, de antiquis litteratis, de variis
characterum accidentibus, pronunciatione
ſcilicet, forma & generibus diverſis. 2.º Dictionarii totius diviſio. 3.º Enumerantur
claves 214. 4.º Explicatur methodus clavium ſcribendarum. 5.º Ordinatur catalogus
characterum qui vulgariter in libris ſcribi
ſolent. 6.º Succedit alius catalogus characterum abrogatorum. 7.º Tertius catalogus characterum antiquis & recentioribus
communium, ſubjunctâ eâ quæ nunc eſt
in uſu figurâ. 8.º Agitur de hac vel illa
clavium figura, duplici, triplici. 9.º denique

disponuntur ordine, & sub sua quisque clavi, characteres, qui propter earum è quibus compositi sunt, clavium multiplicitatem, in hac vel illa clavi quæri possent, & in dictionario ad certam clavem referuntur.

Secundi tomi ea dispositio. 1.° Præfatio nova de arte reperiendorum sonorum & tonorum. 2.° Characteres vocalium, id est, characteres ii quibus vocales apud Sinarum magistros ex condicto solent repræsentari. 3.° Resumit auctor secundum ordinem consonarum, quidquid characterum ad hanc vel illam vocalem pertinet, tabulis ubique ad seriem vocalium suarum conformatis. 4.° denique additur ab auctore catalogus characterum, non eorumdem, sed ferè similium: adducuntur præterea multorum inter se similium exempla, & characteres quidam qui sensim ex una figura vel significatione, in aliam commutati sunt.

Tertio jam tomo & cæteris usque ad decimum quartum & ultimum, characteres omnes sub clavi unusquisque sua comparent unà cum ci e, id est, characteribus duobus, quorum hic usus est, ut è priori, characteris consonam, è posteriori, vocalem elicias. Quæ pronunciatio deinde, alio insuper ejusdem pronunciationis totalis charactere exponitur. Idem denique character, qui majori semper scriptura exaratus est, addita una & alia significatione, eaque principali & notissima, declaratur; remotis interim significationibus multis, aut secundariis, aut metaphoricis, quas vel in chim cu tum, vel in magno dictionario cu goei, reperire est.

XLIX.

Chim
cu
tum,

id est, recta penetratio, seu cognitio characterum, aut potiùs cognitio characterum vulgò appellatorum chim cu; ea enim scriptura ita vocatur.

Aliud dictionarium Sinicum, cujus hæc descriptio. Primo tomo habes primum quidem præfationes quàmplurimas, in quibus de characterum origine, propagatione; de modis characterum efformandorum sex apud antiquos memoratis, de morum & litterarum suscepta ab imperatore Hum-vu reformatione; de antiquis & novis characteribus eorumque alteratione, aliisque plurimis quæ ad litterarum cognitionem faciunt. Sequitur in una quidem ex ultimis editionibus alphabetum quoddam Tartaricum, *MSS. Tomus I.*

ad quasdam voces Sinicas accommodatum; in alia vero, scribendarum clavium methodus; ubi recensentur auctores numero 138. qui de grammatica scripserunt, & ex quibus notas in suum dictionarium auctor transtulit. Tandem huic auctorum catalogo succedunt claves 214. & quæcumque ad clavium duplicium, triplicium figuram pertinent, ea in ipso textu inserta reperies.

Secundo tomo eadem habes quæ in cu goei, aut cu luy; nimirum quos characteres antiquaverit apud Sinas usus, quos retinuerit; item tractatum, juxta clavium seriem, bene longum de characterum ad suas claves reducendorum ambiguitate; item quomodo inter se distinguantur, qui sunt figura similes.

Tandem post tomos illos duos veniunt characteres ipsi omnes, juxta earumdem clavium ordinem, iique amplissima significationum segete conferti. Ibi enim reperias quod in aliis plerisque dictionariis frustra quæras, veterum scilicet & qui in titulis tantùm comparent characterum; quos non raro ex xue ven, characterum antiquissimorum dictionario, de quo infra, sed etiam ex se ac cogitatis suis exponit auctor *Menkiven-hu*, vel *ho*. Liber est voluminum 36. sed inter codices reperta tantum volumina 20.

L.

Hiu
xi } aliàs Hiu xin

xue

ven,

id est, familiæ Hiu orationes.

Dictionarium est characterum & antiquorum & antiquatorum; qui à vulgatis adeo diversi sunt, ut, nisi attendas maximè, alii prorsus videantur. Operi præponitur præfatio longa satis, in qua de characterum numero ac figura, multa lectu digna proferuntur. 1.° verbi gratia, affert auctor exempla tum characterum olim sine ulla tribunalium, id est, clavium nota usurpatorum, tum characterum nunc lineamentis ornatorum, cum antea multò simpliciores essent. Unde statim formatio characterum, formationisque progressus cognoscitur, &c. 2.° Libris ea de re nominatis, è characteribus titulorum seligit quosdam, sed ita ut sub unoquoque apponatur ci e, id est, characteres illi duo ex quibus oritur pronunciatio. 3.° Cum exempla characterum ea sint ex quibus figuræ antiquissimæ primùm

Bbb ij

defignatæ funt, exempla eorum nonnulla allegat, artium videlicet, herbarum, ventorum, infectorum, ferpentium, idque generatim. Tum ad artes reſque arte factas procedit, atque eodem modo ad cætera, ita ut clavium ordinem, partim ſequatur, partim derelinquat. Porro nemo dicitur primam characterum analogiam accuratiùs introfpexiſſe, quàm *Hu-yu-ko* auctor hujus dictionarii, qui ſcripſit ſæculo Chriſti primo; ſed ſæculo decimo idem dictionarium commentariis illuſtratum eſt ab alio doctore, nomine *Su - hi - ven*. Impreſſum autem denuò anno Chriſti 1622. Involucrum unum, volumina 6.

L I.

Hai

pien

chao

cum.

Variè verti hic titulus poſſet, ſed vertendus, maris oræ ſeu latera & aularum imperatoriarum principalia. Comparatur ſcilicet, Sinicæ linguæ cognitio lata & omnimoda, qualis in hoc dictionario traditur, immenſitati marium omnium toti, quæ & piſces omnes & quidquid injectum fuerit, non ſolùm continet, ſed abſorbet. In hoc enim dictionario reperias verba & nomina omnium omnino ſcientiarum, artium, hominum illuſtrium, plantarum, animalium, locorum, mineralium, &c. Idque juxta rei cujuſque ordinem.

Ea autem operis diſpoſitio. Primùm quidem occurrit præfatio, in qua de libris antiquis claſſicis agitur, tum de aliis operibus ex quibus characteres defumtos oportuit, laudata interim diligentia *Hum-vu* in colligendis & characteribus rectiùs efformandis.

Dictionarium verò ipſum incipit à generali quadam naturæ repræſentatione, ut inde lector materiam operis ferè totam mente complectatur. Sequitur totius dictionarii diviſio; deinde diſſertatio de ſex modis quibus accipiuntur aut exponuntur characteres; cui ſubjungitur tractatus de vocalibus earumque numero, de tonis, eorumque varietate ac diſtinctione; de conſonis, earumque per hoc vel illud organum pronunciatione; de geſtibus ad rectam pronunciationem adhibendis; de quibuſdam characterum quorumdam abbreviationibus; de orbis partibus, ventiſque; de conſonarum uſu ad componendos characterum ejuſdem pronunciationis indices. His tandem

omnibus ſuccedit vocabularium, cujus ſectiones undecim, prima de cœlo, ſole, luna, ventis, tonitru, pluvia, igne ac meteoris generatim. Secunda, de tempore, anno, menſe, variis anni & menſium partibus. Tertia, de terra & omnibus quæ ad terram ſpectant; itaque de diverſis locis, de homine, de diverſis hominum ſtatibus, de ſonis, de coloribus. Quarta, de inſtrumentis & utenſilibus, cum ad vitam, tum ad artes neceſſariis. Quinta, de corpore & ſingulis partibus corporis. Sexta, de floribus & arboribus. Septima, de ædificiis, de cibo & potu, de avibus & brutis. Octava, de cyclo, fortibus, litteratura, ac proinde rebus philoſophicis, moralibus, phyſicis, chymicis, de vegetalibus, mineralibus quatenus ad phyſicam ſpectant. Nona, de variis hominum negotiis; qua in re gentis leges, edicta imperatorum, fori & mercaturæ officia, magiſtratuum jura ſubintelligunt. Decima continet numeros & numerandi rationem omnem; ac præterea adjectiva ſeu epitheta, unà cum eorum contrariis ſeu oppoſitis. Undecima, additur quæ ad naturam quidem non pertinet, ſed apud Sinas admodum neceſſaria eſt, enumeratio ſcilicet, characterum quorumdam variorum ac difficiliorum, qui in libris apud Sinas frequentibus reperiuntur. Auctor dictionarii hujus dicitur *Chim-gin*, aliàs *Chim-gin-ſi*, hiſtoricus regius. Is quidquid per omnem vitam ſtudiis aſſiduis colligere potuerat, quod ad linguæ Sinicæ & abundantiam & elegantiam conferret, ſub finem vitæ in hoc dictionarium contribuit. Atque hac in re eos, qui præceſſerant, omnes ſuperavit. Volumina 5.

L I I.

Cu

luy

pu,

hoc eſt, ſupplementum ad Cu-luy.

In hoc ſupplemento tria reperiuntur. 1.° characteres quidam jam diu noti, ſed quibus acceſſit nova & antea incognita ſignificatio. 2.° Characteres aut in aliquo libro, unde nondum eruti fuerant, reperti, aut nuper ab aliquo ſcriptore efformati. 3.° Characteres qui hujus vel illius toni antea fuerant, alio poſtea pronuntiari cœperunt. Auctor ſupplementi hujus *U-gin-chin*, imperante Kam-hi. Involucrum unum, volumina 12.

L I I I.

Sy
ju
ulh
mo
cu,

id eft, quod apud Occidentis litteratos eft aurium & oculorum officium, fupple, in litteratura; feu quod vulgò in litteratura obfervant litterati Europæi, cum litteris dant operam.

Hic liber eò tendit, ut Sinis cognitio tradatur non grammaticæ quidem totius, qualis eft apud Europæos, fed ejus tantùm partis, qua confonarum & vocalium inter fe conjunctio fieri folet in linguis omnibus Europæorum. In principio libri comparent litteræ Latinè fculptæ, juxta pofitis characteribus quibufdam Sinicis, qui Latinis refpondeant. Tum fequuntur nonnulla ad grammaticam fpectantia, fed quæ Sinicè duntaxat exponuntur. Opus parum utile & Sinis & noftris. Auctores R R. Patres Societatis Jefu. Volumina duo, fed unum tantùm allatum eft.

L I V.

Tien
chu
xi   xe
y,

id eft, cœli Domini vera idea, feu expofitio.

Hic liber, quomodo plerique libri à Miffionariis confcripti, agit de Dei natura, de creatione, de hominis origine, de animæ immortalitate, de metempfychofi fectæ Tao, vel Pythagorica, de paradifo poft mortem bonis præparato, &c. Auctor R. P. *Matthæus Ricci;* fed correctus dicitur hic liber à doctore *Paulo Su-kuam-ki,* quantùm ad phrafim, imò & in dialogi formam redactus. Editus autem eft imperante Vanlie, anno Chrifti 1603. adeoque ineunte fæculo XVII. Volumina 2.

L V.

Ce
ke,

id eft, feptem carnis afflictiones, Gallicè *mortifications;* feu tractatus de feptem peccatis capitalibus, & iis, queis devitari poffunt, mediis. Auctores R R. Patres Societatis Jefu.

L V I.

Tien
chu

kiam
fem
yen
him
ki
fiam,

id eft, figuræ Domini, ad nos è cœlo delati, verba & acta denotantes; feu imago vitæ Domini noftri Jefu Chrifti, quoad naturam humanam.

In hoc libro fub unaquaque figura, in qua hæc aut illa Chrifti actio, hoc aut illud miraculum depinguntur, apparet ftatim Sinicæ actionis aut miraculi brevis expofitio. Auctores R R. Patres Societatis Jefu, qui hunc in gratiam neophytorum fuorum ediderunt. 1. volumen.

L V I I.

Xim
kiao
fin
chim,

id eft, fanctæ religionis fidele teftimonium.

Liber hic nihil aliud eft quàm catalogus Patrum Societatis Jefu, qui ab anno 1581. ad annum 1681. id eft, per annos 100. in Sina Jefu Chrifti Domini noftri fidem annuntiarunt propagaruntque. Ibi fingulorum nomina, patria, prædicatio, mors, fepultura, libri Sinicè editi, recenfentur.

L V I I I.

Chin   acu
kieu   puftulas
ce   decerpendi
yao,   velle, vel ars

id eft, ars puftulas acu chirurgica tollendi.

Hic liber non impreffus eft, fed manu fcriptus procul dubio ab Europæis, qui illic chirurgicam exercuere. Pagg. 5. 6. 7. tabulæ funt anatomicæ variorum manus aut brachii fituum, cum eorum locorum indicatione qui pungendi. 1. volumen.

L I X.

Liber imperfectus, infcriptus

xam
pa
cham
tu.

Tabula feu index rerum ad compefcendam vulnerum tyrannidem idoncarum.

Bbb iij

Liber eft chirurgicalis, & non folùm de vulneribus, fed etiam de eorum curatione, & variis ad eam rem neceffariis herbis agit. 1. volumen.

L X.

Liber imperfectus, fine titulo, & laceratus, cujus infcriptio eft

me
kive.

Pulfûs determinatio.

Norunt omnes apud Sinas cognitionem pulfûs femper cultam, idque ita ut medicos orbis terrarum omnes, hac illa pulfûs feu potiùs variorum pulfuum detegendorum dexteritate fuperarint. Hac de re legendi Jefuitæ in epiftolis, & præfertim Cleyerus. Dolendum quod liber ad nos allatus fit mutilus; fed vide fupra & infra, ubi de medicina ac libris medicorum.

L X I.

Liber imperfectus, infcriptus

van
pim,

omnes morbi.

Continet tantummodo quædam libri capita, id eft, volumina, fecundum, quintum; fed præcedunt variæ morborum, ventorum & plantarum enumerationes. 2. volumina.

L X I I.

Liber imperfectus, fine principio & fine, cujus tamen titulus fuit

puen
caó
tum
yue,

id eft, libri, feu tractatûs de plantis, penetratio excitata.

Adeft tamen præfatio triplex, prima, charactere liberiori; fecunda & tertia, iis characteribus, qui vulgares & recti appellantur; ibi autem de libri auctoribus ac fama, itemque de botanicæ utilitate agitur. Sequitur catalogus librorum medicinæ complurium, fermè ad viginti novem, eadem de re ab antiquis medicis editorum. Poftea alius eft etiam index variorum qui de botanica fcripferunt auctorum, & indicantur ferè quadraginta fex. Tum memorantur herbarum prope infinitarum nomina,

quarum deinde proprietates exponuntur, patria uniufcujufque non folùm commonftrata, fed quoad foli naturam indolemque defcripta. 1. volumen.

L X I I I.

Liber imperfectus, infcriptus

puen
cao
kiven
xe
pa,

τᷓ puen cao caput decimum octavum.

Editio eft peffima, & agitur tum de herbis plantifque, tum de animalibus quæ omnia illic depinguntur, fed parum accuratè. Volumina 3. id eft, quartum, duodecimum & decimum tertium.

L X I V.

Mem
cu,

id eft, mem cu, unà cum commentario perpetuo. Liber imperfectus. Volumen 1.

L X V.

Liber clafficus, vulgò dictus mem cu, unà cum antiquorum magiftrorum commentariis, propriè eft τᷓ libri mem cu kiven 7. Commentarius duplex eft & duplici charactere.

L X V I.

Han
lin.

Characterum ejufdem pronunciationis indices à collegio & doctoribus Han - lin redacti.

Pars eft dictionarii, hinc per pronunciationes, feu confonantias ordinati, illinc per tribunalia in eadem pagina oblati; ita ut in fuprema pagina & fonos eofdem, & eos qui iifdem fonis donantur characteres habeas; in infima hanc vel illam clavem, additis linearum numeris. In hoc codice fe fe offerunt claves cannarum & arborum; itaque dictionarium hoc ad τᷓ Hai-pien, fimul & τᷓ Tum-ven, de quo poftea, imitationem factum effe videtur. Volumen 1.

L X V I I.

Liber imperfectus, cujus infcriptio,

Gallicè *dénombrement des éclipses*. Videtur autem inter fchedas Adami Schal, vel Verbiefti, repertus. Non defunt quæ ad hiftoriæ cognitionem faciant, præfertim illorum temporum, cum imperium Ta-mim jam nutaret. Fit etiam mentio ejus anni, quo inventus eft atque è terra effoffus lapis urbis Sigan-fu, de quo Semedo & alii.

LXVIII.

Liber imperfectus, infcriptus

chun

cieu,

id eft, ver & autumnus.

Pars eft libri à Confucio de regno Lu fcripti & fic appellati. Vide fupra E. Eft autem hæc pars commentariis ornata. Volumen 1.

I I.°

Libri Sinici ab Illuftriffimo Abbate BIGNON, Regi dono dati.

GEOGRAPHIA.

CODEX PRIMUS.

Yu

chi

ta

mim

ye

tum

chi,

id eft, regentis magnificè & magna omnia facientis, 天 Ta-mim monarchiæ mens, feu profpectus aut hiftoria geographica.

Hæc eft ampla illa & univerfa Sinæ geographia, quam fumma cura elaboratam atque ab illuftribus collegii Han-lin Præfectis comprobatam, habere voluerunt familiæ Ta-mim imperatores. In lucem verò edita eft imperante Tien-xum, aliàs Ymcum, anno ejus quinto, luna quinta, die decima fexta. Volumina 49. Porro hanc geographiam in epitomen contraxit *Martinius;* quod compendium Thevenotius libri fui inferuit tomo tertio. Hæc fummatim. Non abs re tamen erit hujus geographiæ notionem paulò ampliorem tradere.

Ac primùm quidem operi præmittuntur præfationes, ut fieri folet, multiplices, & pleræque eruditione quadam hiftorica refertæ, in quibus totius operis ratio redditur; id eft, 1.° diligentiæ à multis imperatoribus ad geographiam imperii Sinenfis cognofcendam adhibitæ. 2.° Variarum imperii aut defcriptionum, aut hiftoriarum, è quibus hauriri poterant cognitiones geographicæ. 3.° Quorumdam, qui geographiæ operam dederant, auctorum. 4.° Tabularum quarumdam ab illis auctoribus fculptarum. 5.° Multorum qui de geographia generatim ac terræ menfuris, imò & de Sinæ ipfius in varias partes & regna divifione, confcripti erant tractatuum. Fit deinde tranfitus ad vulgarem quæ, jam à primis temporibus facta eft, imperii divifionem: in provincias fcilicet quindecim, quæ hîc appellantur fingulæ; urbium verò triplex ordo diftinguitur, funt enim primariæ, feu primi ordinis; fecundariæ, feu fecundi ordinis; denique tertii ordinis; mox provinciis fingulis, urbes primi ordinis fubjiciuntur.

Præmiffis præfationibus fequitur liber ipfe, in quo auctor primùm quidem de provincia unaquaque tractat generatim, de fitu fcilicet provinciæ, de primis incolis, de primis & provinciæ & incolarum nominibus, de mutatione unius nominis in aliud, fub hoc vel illo imperatore, ac fæpe de ejufdem mutationis caufa. Nec prætermittit fi quid in hac vel illa provincia eximii & fingularis occurrat, verbi gratia, flumen, lacus, ftagna, templum frequenti populorum concurfu celebratum, mons facer, telluris aut foli proprietas, ædificia, velut murus Sinenfis, quidquid denique ad litteratos vel militares pertinet. Tum ad primariam urbem defcendit, de qua à primis monarchiæ fundatoribus differit; & data occafione enumeratis denuò, quæ antiquitus illic fuerunt, regnis, indicat etiam in quibus provinciæ urbibus, aulæ eorumdem regnorum fuerint, quas deinde, ut Pekimi habitarent, neglexere aut reges, aut imperatores. Cum verò in indice generali, de quo in præfationibus, urbes primi ordinis jam commemorarit, hîc fupereft nihil, nifi ut fub unaquaque provincia urbes ordinum inferiorum defcribat, quod diligenter præftat. Eandem porro methodum auctor perfequitur per 49. volumina: cum hoc tamen levi difcrimine, quòd 48. priora volumina Sinæ ipfi tribuantur, ultimum verò five quadragefimum nonum, gentibus extra, fed prope Sinam pofitis, totum addicatur.

HISTORICI.

I I.

Cu
chi
tum
kien
kam
mo.

Hiftoria Sinica univerfalis, aut Annales Sinici. De verbo ad verbum, adjuvantis gubernationem fpeculi principia; feu, quæ primò ab hominibus rempublicam adminiftrandam fufcepturis difcenda funt, ut ipfis fæculorum priorum exempla infervire poffint.

Liber hic idem qui inter regios numero primo, itaque illic vide. Eft vulgò voluminum 120. fed defunt quædam volumina.

I I I.

Su   fo   v. 1. 170.
cu
chi
tum
kien
kam
mo.

Additio ad fpeculum, feu principia fpeculi, gubernationi atque adminiftrationi rerum dirigendæ neceffarii, quibufdam in locis commentario illuftrati: quod primus tituli character indicat; nihil enim aliud fo, quàm addere aut fupplere. Vide clavem 120. tr. 13. & dictionar. cu guei, tom. 5. pag. 170. Confules quoque codicum regiorum notitias numero primo & fequenti.

I V.

Chun
cicu
ta
civen.

Libri à *Confucio* fcripti & chun cieu, feu veris & autumni titulo editi, magna collectio.

Cum de hoc libro, inter regios numero quinto nominato, jam fusè egerim, nihil hîc addendum, nifi editionem effe pulcherrimam, commentariis ubique litteralibus

illuftratam, & eodem quo fu xu fermone, id eft, facili atque ex aliis Confucii libris defumto; præterea editionem eandem effe, id eft, imperatoris juffu procuratam. Volumina 13.

V.

Xoam
yu
cive
yven,

id eft, 的 xoam yu collectionum fons.

Notæ funt, ac præcipuè de chronologia Sinica difceptationes. Liber peffimè exaratus, & eam ob caufam ferè ubique lectu difficillimus.

V I.

Lun
yn
chi
tien,

id eft, collectio, feu codex ubi fumitur fenfus rotationis (temporum.)

Ita appellant libros almanachicos, feu kalendarios.

V I I.

Tai
xam
fan
yven
fan
pin
fan
kuon
fa
pao,

id eft, trium yven, trium pin, trium kuon vocatorum ordo pretiofus.

Agitur hîc de eo, quem inter fe, & unà cum imperatore egreffi, fervant Mandarini, ordine, & ita pingitur eorum quafi proceffio. Volumen 1. Gallicè *Rouleau,* eft enim folii unius & longiffimi.

ROMANENSES.

V I I I.

Hao
kien
chuen,

id eft, hiftoria fabulofa 的 Hao-kien.

Libellus eft ftylo, feu fermone familiari fcriptus, ex eorum genere, qui apud nos

Romans

第二卷

CODICES MANUSCRIPTI. 385

Romans appellatur, formæ in 8.° Volumina funt 2. 3. & 6. fed effe deberent plura.

Hic autem annotandum, partes eorum, quos fabulas dico, libellorum, quique hiftoriolæ funt, de hoc vel illo aut puero, aut heroe, quem per varia difcrimina huc illuc trahunt; partes, inquam, illas non aliter quam hoci indigitari, ita ut quotiefcumque charaƈterem hoci videris, toties librum ejufmodi vel comœdiam, vel faltem fabulam abfque dubio nuncupare poffis. Voluminum eft nunc duorum, feu duorum hoei, fed effe deberent plura.

I X.

Yo
kiao
li,

id eft, pera τᾶ yo kiao. Aliàs hæc fabula dicitur, fabula 三才子 fan cai cu, feu trium poëtarum. Elegantiæ autem eft apud Sinas laudatæ & maximo in pretio. Volumina 3.

X.

Pim
xan
lem
yen,

aliàs

fu
cai
cu,

id eft, pim, xan, lem, yen, feu quatuor poëtæ fic nominati. Eft etiam fabula ftyli fiao xue. Volumina 4. fed effe deberent plura.

X I.

Ya   142. tr. 4.
mi,   149. tr. 10.

id eft, τᾶ ya mi hiftoria fabulofa. Eft enim ex eorum genere, quæ nos *Romans* dicimus, fed per dialogos & perfonas, quales funt comœdiæ.

X I I.

Xam
xu
kim
ta
civen.

Xu kim, commentariis multorum Philofophorum eximiis illuftratus.
MSS. Tomus I.

Hic liber eft Sinarum canonicus & fecundus, de quo vide ad codices regios. Hæc autem editio pulcherrima & adornata eft ac correƈta à Mandarinis. Volumina 12. quorum primum totum in figuras infumitur earum rerum, quæ à prifcis hominibus Sinis inventæ funt.

X I I I.

Xi
chuen
ta
civen,

id eft, verfuum, & illuftrium in verfus feu odas commentariorum magna colleƈtio.

Egimus fupra ad regios codices num. XIII. & XIV. de illis verfibus, eorumque materia & auƈtoribus. Supereft ut de his commentariis pauca moneamus. Sunt itaque commentarii modo litterales & quafi interlineares; modo fufi adeo, ut per omnem hiftoriam divagentur, quo poëfeos fenfus dilucidior fiat. Porro hæc verfuum, five odarum editio, eft ampliffima & voluminum 16.

LIBRI SACRI ET CANONICI.
X I V.

Li
ki
xue
y,

id eft, fenfus orationum, feu fermonum τᾶ li ki, feu liber cæremonialis, aut, quod idem eft, liber rituum explicatus.

Repetantur hic quæ deli ki diƈta funt in catalogo regiorum codicum num. V. & XV. neceffe non eft. Scito id tu tantummodo editionem hanc aliam effe, anno Kam-hi 14. publicatam, in qua tomus primus, fed feparatus, præfationes de officiis quamplurimas continet; ubi multa de Cheukum & antiquis Sinarum fapientibus. Poft præfationes fequitur index materiarum in li ki contentarum. In cæteris tomis liber ipfe, nec fine commentariis luculentis. Volumina debent effe 15. fed reperiuntur tantùm 1. 2. 3. 4. 5. 6. 7. 8. deeft 9. & habentur 10. 11. 12. 13. 14. 15. Cum ergo 15. effe debeant, funt tantum 14. volumina.

C c c

XV.

Kim
him
xe
kiai,

hoc eft, in libros clafficos expedita & vera expofitio.

' Commentarius eft duplex in Ta-hio, Chum-yum, Lun-yu & Mem-cu; alter eft fuperior, inferior alter. Cæterùm ex ipfius Confucii & Mem-cu verbis conflantur, ut folet, fed tamen minùs accuratè & minùs ad verbum quàm Ge-kiam. Chunyum eft unà cum Ta-hio in primo volumine. Liber vero impreffus anno Kam-hi 22. fed ita ut charaƈteres negligentiùs fculpti, ac peffimè exarati fint; unde mala editio. Volumina 4.

LIBRI CLASSICI.

XVI.

Ge
kiam
fu
xu
kiai
y,

id eft, fenfus explanatorius 㗪 fu xu quatuor librorum ad explicationes quotidianas editus, anno Kam-hi 16. In principio præfationis funt duo charaƈteres Yu chi queis imperatorum felicitas ac magna in regnando virtus indicatur. Id vulgò apponitur, cum imperatorum juffu vel liber vel editio publicatur. Præfatio eft magnifica, de antiquis Philofophis eorumque doƈtrina ac virtutibus, de Ta-hio, Chum-yum, Lun-yu, Mem-cu. Contendit etiam auƈtor, additis ὅις u kim, feu aliis quinque libris canonicis legem ac doƈtrinam Sinarum totam componi. Tum adfunt doƈtorum Pekinenfium & Nainkinenfium approbationes & figna. Poftea in Ta-hio incipit paraphrafis, quæ facilis & quafi fermone familiari. Certè ex aliis eorumdem librorum locis defumtus hic fermo, & methodo omnino commoda, atque à paragrapho ad paragraphum progreditur. Vide codices regios ubi, alius editionis occafione, de libro generatim locuti fumus. Volumina 26.

XVII.

Hiao
kim
yen
y,

id eft, τȣ hiao kim, feu libri de obedientia fenfus ad omnia exundans; hæc enim eft vera vocis yen notio.

Non repetam hoc loco de officiis hîc agi, quæ apud Sinas habentur quinque. Vide regios codices numero 42.

MEDICI.

XVIII.

Vai
ko   kuo
chu
yao.

Extraneorum feu in locis extraneis colligi folitorum remediorum cardo feu methodus.

Dofes funt feu variæ rerum, herbarum fcilicet, mineralium, &c. ad fanandos morbos à Medicis adhibendorum quantitates. Quemadmodum enim apud nos, ita apud Sinas, Medici ad morbos curandos remediis ferè utuntur extraneis. Procedit autem traƈtatus hic, ita ut primò genus morbi apponat, deinde varias remediorum receptiones exponat, qua in re id etiam præftat, ut loca remediorum, id eft, eas, è quibus afferuntur, regiones indicet. Porro hic nonnifi kiven, feu pars libri totius quarta. Vide Cleyerum.

MEDICI BOTANICI.

XIX.

Puen	proprietatis feu
cao	idoneitatis
kam	herbarum
mo,	caput & oculus,

id eft, vera medicinæ herbarum aut plantarum repræfentatio; feu ea principia queis datur fua unicuique plantæ proprietas.

Librum habes eundem in regiis numero 27. ubi leges notitiam. Impreffus autem hic imperante Xun-chi τȣ Kam-hi patre. Statim initio hujus libri occurrunt præfationes complures, in quibus de primis herbarum colleƈtionibus; de Fohi, Hoan-ti,

Xin-num & antiquiffimis Medicis: de herbarum per claffes diftributione; primùm quidem generum, deinde fpecierum; fequitur herbarum ipfarum, deinde variarum plantarum atque etiam animantium repræfentatio. Volumina effe deberent multa, fed funt tantum 26. & præterea tomus trigefimus primus; itaque defunt tomi 27. 28. 29. 30. 32. neque alii è Sina allati. Itaque volumina 27.

MATHEMATICI.
XX.

Tien

muen

lio,

id eft, cœli porta parva, feu parvus de fphæra tractatus. Auctor Jefuita Lufitanus, agit de fphæra, planetis, circulis, &c. Idque juxta antiquorum fyftemata & per figuras. Præfatio triplex eft cum ad libri commendationem, tum ad materiæ per fe difficilis elucidationem. Volumen 1.

ARTES.
XXI.

Tien

kum

kai

ve,

id eft, rerum à cœlo formatarum in artibus patefactio. Vide regios numero 38. Volumen 1.

XXII.

Ejufdem libri, fed ex alia editione male fculpta, pars fecunda. Volumen 1.

MISCELLANEA.
XXIII.

Kio

xi

ya

yen,

id eft, confiderandum effe fæculum, oratio pulchra. Senfus eft, qui fæculum aut res humanas attentè confiderarit, eum optimè facere. Mifcellanea funt hiftorica & geographica peffimè impreffa.

MSS. Tomus I.

RELIGIO.
XXIV.

Chu

kiao

yven

ki.

Cur lex Dei, vel Dei Chriftianorum femper affurgat.

Tractatus eft à Miffionario editus, in quo præcipuæ religionis Chriftianæ partes doctè afferuntur, idque capitibus viginti quatuor: illinc ergo difcere eft, quod apud Sinas auctores noftri philofophicè atque argumentis è rerum natura petitis inculcare coguntur, mundum hunc à fe ipfo fieri aut conftrui non potuiffe; cœlum mundi auctorem dici non poffe; rerum tamen auctorem ab omnibus agnofcendum; auctorem rerum unum tantummodo effe poffe, non duos; eundem fpiritalem effe, nec percipi fenfibus; præterea fine principio fuiffe, fine fine effe ac futurum femper. Capite feptimo primæ partis, agit auctor de Trinitate, & rerum quidem creatorem aftruit unum effe, perfonarum vero trium. Parte fecunda, de angelis differit, tum de morte ejufque caufis atque effectis. Inde ad animam rationalem tranfit, quam contendit à Deo creatam & immortalem effe. Parte tertia, de lege naturæ & gratiæ fermonem habet, earumque legum, Mofaicæ fcilicet ac Chriftianæ fundamenta & differentias expendit. Parte quarta denique, incarnationem, incarnationis neceffitatem, peccati deletionem, ac proinde vitam Chrifti, refurrectionem, in cœlum afcenfionem perfequitur. Auctor *Tam-jo-vam*, id eft, R. P. *Adam Schal*, è Societate Jefu Sacerdos, qui tunc temporis, hoc eft dum Sinam occupabant Tartari, inter tumultus bellicos, Evangelium prædicavit. Impreffus autem anno 15. Cumchim, aliàs Hoai-cum, ultimi imperatoris 𢽾 Ta-mim. Partes libri tantùm quatuor, licet apud Kirkerum memorentur quinque; fed divifio eft in quatuor, neque ulla eft amplius. Volumina 4.

XXV.

Tien

chu

xim

kiao

yo

yen,

id eft, fanctæ Dei legis abbreviata .aut

Ccc ij

congregata verba, feu fumma & confpectus.

Tractatus eft de Dei exiftentia, providentia, legibus, ab uno è Miffionariis Societatis Jefu. Volumen 1.

XXVI.

Tien
chu
kiam
fem
yen
him
ki
lio,

id eft, memoria & notatio Domini, poftquam è cœlo defcendit & natus eft. Aut aliter, Chrifti poft incarnationem inter mortales degentis hiftoria.

Ex multis kiven feu partibus, funt hic tantùm 5. 6. 7. 8. in quibus plurima ex Evangeliis non ϰϱ πόϑας tamen. Liber eft ab eo quem inter regios vidifti numero 56. omnino diverfus. Illic enim nonnifi imagines ac picturæ, hîc orationes ac fermones tantùm. Auctor Miffionarius è Societate Jefu. Volumen 1.

XXVII.

Tien
chu
xim
kiao
ki
mum.

Inftrumentum, id eft, clavis ad aperiendam Dei legem.

Hic liber catechifmus eft, per modum dialogi magiftrum inter & difcipulum, de hominis Chriftiani officiis. Auctor Miffionarius è Societate Jefu. Volumen 1.

XXVIII.

Tien
chu
xim
kiao
hoa
y   nhy
lun,

id eft, cœli Domini fanctæ legis vallis perviæ & dubitationum difceptatio. Verti de verbo ad verbum: fignificatio autem eft,

sermonem five orationem hîc effe de rebus iis quæ fanctam Dei legem non claufam teneant, fed quafi perviam vallem relinquant, aut efficiant; fcilicet, de Xam-ti, de Tai-kie hîc nonnulla proponuntur. Volumen 1.

XXIX.

Tai
y   nhy
pien,

id eft, dubiorum ab aliis fectis propofitorum, aut de aliis fectis nafcentium, difceptatio.

Hic tractatus ex iis eft quos à Miffionariis legendos judicavit auctor, & rectè; namque hîc agitur de fectarum Sinenfium opinionibus; & quæ de diis idololatræ difputant, quæ de inferno aut paradifo, poft varias in varia corpora migrationes acquirendo, ea omnia in fecta Foe, feu Indica, decantata difcutiuntur. Kiven primæ partis funt novem, & fecundæ itidem novem. Præfationes duæ liberiori charactere exaratæ. Volumen 1.

XXX.

Tien
xe xi } 171. tr. 13.
mim
pien,

id eft, de Foe familia ejufque placitis difcurfus, propriè elucidationes, ac diftinctiones.

Agitur de cœlo, inferno prout à Foe fecta intelliguntur, quam pedetentim refutat auctor capitibus viginti octo. Differit ergo de omnibus hujus fectæ dogmatibus, de magna mente, quæ totam hanc molem agitat, de metempfychofi, de tribus generationibus, de triginta cœlis, &c. Vide præfertim capita 2. 9. 13. 14. 15. 16. Volumen 1.

XXXI.

Xim
mu
him
xe,

id eft, fanctæ Matris actionum foliditas, feu Mariæ Virginis vera vita.

Propriè laus eft beatæ Virginis, quæ laus cum per omnes litaniarum partes excurrat, continet quidquid ad Virginem fpectat; imò & quæ in hunc vel illum beneficia, meritis fuis atque interceffione contulit. Auctor

Sacerdos è Societate Jefu. Hîc tantummodo pars tertia. Volumen 1.

XXXII.

Xim

mu

kim

kiai,

hoc eft, fanctæ Matris preces, feu preces ad fanctam Matrem.

Preces funt variæ ad Virginem Mariam directæ, & funt multiplices, aliæ ad aliam diem, aliæ ad aliam diei horam. Nonnullæ ab auctore fcriptæ, nonnullæ ex libris ecclefiafticis defumtæ. Auctor Jefuita Italus. 1. volumen.

XXXIII.

Mi

fa

ci

y,

id eft, miffæ facrificii fenfus aut explicatio. Quid eo libro contineatur titulus declarat. Auctor Miffionarius è Societate Jefu. Impreffus eft 津 Cum-chim ætate. 1. volumen.

XXXIV.

Tie

cui

chim

kuei,

id eft, lavandorum peccatorum recta regula.

Tractatus eft de baptifmo, & præfertim de pœnitentia. Capitum eft fermè triginta octo. Auctor Miffionarius è Societate Jefu. 1. volumen.

XXXV.

Ki

gin

xi

pien.

Decem capita hominis characterem determinantia.

Capita illa funt, de quibus Kirkerus Chinæ illuftratæ pag. 159. à *Matthæo Ricci* concinnata, & apud Sinas Philofophiæ moralis femper curiofos multùm celebrata. Primum de tempore, quàm recte confumendum & quàm fit irreparabile. Secundum, de hujus vitæ neceffitatibus atque ærumnis. Tertium, de morte, effe unicuique debitam, & unicuique accidere. Quartum, quantùm homini profit de morte fæpius cogitare. Quintum, aliquando tacere, aliquando loqui hominem oportere, idque femper opportunè faciendum. Sextum, de tribus pœnitentiæ finibus, & quare omnes jejunare deceat. Septimum, de confcientiæ examine, idque ab unoquoque quotidie fieri debere. Octavum, de paradifo & inferno; & alterum bonis, alterum malis effe deftinatum. Nonum, quantùm peccet qui divinatione, re apud Sinas frequenti, utitur. Decimum, de malis eos in æternum fecuturis, qui avaritiæ dediti, divitias in thefauros congerunt. Editio eft fecunda, & præfatio characteribus eft liberioribus. 2. volumina.

XXXVI.

Tien

chu

kim

kiao

xe

kiai

kiven

lun

xim

cie,

id eft, ad decem præceptorum in fancta Dei lege traditorum obfervationem exhortatoriarum orationum fancti loci, feu puncta prædicationi utilia.

Eæ funt quibus in Chriftianæ religionis exhortationibus oratores aut concionatores uti poffunt materiæ, in certos locos digeftæ; de variis Chriftianorum officiis agitur, idque juxta mandatorum in Pentateucho memoratorum ordinem. Porro loci hîc appellantur, rhetorum more. Auctor Miffionarius è Societate Jefu. 1. volumen.

XXXVII.

Tien

chu

xim

kiao

xe

kiai

chin

civen

hoc eft, cœli Domini (feu Dei) fanctæ legis decem præceptorum vera expofitio, aut eorum quæ à Deo in fancta ejus lege data funt, præceptorum decem vera declaratio. Auctor Sacerdos è Societate Jefu. 1. volumen.

Ccc iij

XXXVIII.

Xim
kiao
kien
yao,

id eft, fanctæ legis placita abbreviata.

Summa eft earum rerum, quas de Deo fciat & credat Chriftianus neceffe eft. Opufculum à Miffionario è Societate Jefu concinnatum atque optimè impreffum. 1. volumen.

XXXIX.

Yum
fo
tien
kiu,

id eft, æternæ felicitatis in cœlo poffidendæ via.

Commentatio eft in fymbolum Apoftolorum à Francifcano edita; in qua quæcumque ad fidem Chriftianam fpectant, enarrantur. Characteres hujus libri elegantiffimi, qui impreffus eft Kam-hi anno 19. 1. volumen.

X L.

Van
ve
chin
yven,

id eft, rerum omnium vera origo.

Sunt in hoc libro Kiven XI. quæ capita argumentis ac tractatulis totidem deftinata. Primum eft res omnes, five hanc rerum univerfitatem incipere debuiffe. Secundum, res humanas per fe exiftere non potuiffe. Tertium, à cœlo & terra hominem creari aut fieri non potuiffe. Quartum, ab yven ki, feu primario acre cœlum & terram, eâ quâ funt formâ, conftrui non potuiffe. Quintum, à li feu ratione illa univerfali, à Sinis litteratis jactata, formari ac conftrui res mundanas nequiviffe. Capitibus vero fequentibus agit auctor de ea, quæ in hoc orbe afpectabili ubique apparet, pulchritudine. Deinde concludit effe qui eum creaverit ac gubernet Dominum; ac demum qui res eas omnes creaverit eum & principio & fine carere oportere. Auctor itidem è Societate Jefu, & idem qui tractatus fan xan fupra memorati. 1. volumen.

X L I.

Tien
chu
xe
y.

Cœli Domini vera intellectio; feu, quid per Deum aut nomine Dei, apud Sinas Tien-chu appellati, intelligendum fit.

Hujus libri hîc nonnifi fecunda pars: fed tractatur de anima rationali, de ejus reminifcentia, de ejus natura à brutarum animantium animabus differenti; de tribus metempfychofeως, juxta Indorum & Bonziorum opiniones, gradibus; de cogitatione, eamque in cæteras, præter hominem, animantes non cadere; de altera poft mortem vita; de mundo futuro, id eft, de paradifo bonis, inferno malis deftinato. Contendit auctor libros Sinarum antiquos de iifdem locis non tacuiffe. Uno verbo, multa illic de Foe fecta, ejufque dogmatibus, de litteratorum xam ti, de Verbi incarnatione apud Occidentales, de Miffionariorum prædicatione. 2. volumina.

X L I I.

San
xan
lun
hio
ki,

id eft, trium montium fcientifica hiftoria; feu potiùs ejus, qui inter montes tres habitus eft, fermonis hiftoria & recordatio. Phrafis hæc montium trium è Sinarum fabulis defumta eft.

Hic liber difputatio eft de religionibus tribus feu litteratorum fectis; difceptantque inter fe doctores quænam cæteris præferenda aut fecta: afferuntur ex hac & illa parte argumenta ad unamquamque religionem tuendam maximè probabilia, & fub finem vincit rationis auctoritate philofophus, feu doctor Chriftianus. Inveniuntur ergo in hoc fermone quamplurima de li, feu ratione illa generali, mundi hujus fecundum litteratos motrice; de tai kie, feu chuo & materia illa prima, quæ, juxta eofdem litteratos, mundi origo; de metempfychofi & aliis Bonziorum dogmatibus illis, quæ ab India Indorumque Brachmanibus orta jamdiu, & à multis retro fæculis inter Bonzios Sinenfes regnant: tum fequitur folida utrorumque refutatio, & religionis tum Mofaicæ tum Chriftianæ laus, earumque demonſtratio. Auctor hujus libri Sacerdos è Societate Jeſu Italus. Volumen 1. Cat. p. 9.

XLIII.

Liber idem, ſed ex alia editione, item præfatione priori & nova ornatus.

XLIV.

Tam-
kim
kiao
pou
gi
xe
chim
civen,

id eſt, in illuſtris atque amœnæ legis lapidis frontem vera explicatio; ſeu quod idem eſt, vera explanatio lapidis illuſtrem & venerabilem legem in fronte inſcriptam repræſentantis.

Lapis ille in urbe Siganfu repertus dicitur, anno 1625. à Mandarinis ipſis effoſſus, nec ſine quadam admiratione à Chriſtianis Sinenſibus ac Miſſionariis conſpectus; jam tum illic ab iiſdem Miſſionariis commentario illuſtratus, à Semedone & aliis memoratus; cujus inſcriptio è Sina allata, edita eſt à *Boymo* atque à *Kirkero* Sinicè & Latinè, minùs quidem accuratè, ut alii volunt.

XLV.

Chao
ſim
hio
yao,

id eſt, de verbo ad verbum, (rerum)

naturam ſuperantium placita: qua quidem phraſi indicatur metaphyſica.

Et re vera metaphyſica eſt liber ille ampliſſima, in qua reperiuntur eæ quæ de Dei natura ejuſque attributis moveri ſolent quæſtiones omnes, non quales apud auctores hujus temporis, ſed quales apud Scholaſticos, & quales etiamnum ab Hiſpanis agitantur ſumma quadam ſubtilitate. Liber 觅 Xun chi ætate compoſitus & nitidiſſimè impreſſus. Auctor Miſſionarius è Societate Jeſu.

XLVI.

Lim
yen
li
cho,

id eſt, ratiocinantium & loquentium medicina.

Norunt omnes hominem apud omnes Orientales dictum animal loquens, dum apud nos vulgò definitur animal rationale. Eundem in ſenſum accipere videtur auctor lim philoſophicè rationalitatem & yen loquelam, ſeu loquendi facultatem, quæ locutio & adjectivè & ſubſtantivè ſumi poteſt, ut è grammaticis diſcitur. Tractatus ergo eſt de anima rationali, quam auctor ubique appellat etiam Sinicè ya-ni-ma. Expendit autem 1.° animæ naturam ejuſque à cæteris ſubſtantiis ſpiritalibus, hoc eſt angelis, differentiam. 2.° Ejus immortalitatem. 3.° Quod titulo occaſionem dedit, animæ peccantis & in varia peccata labentis remedium, ſeu Dei gratiam.

III.°

Libri Sinici, ex Miſſionariorum Extraneorum Bibliotheca in Regiam Bibliothecam illati anno 1720. Cœtu omni volente atque ad voluntatem Regiam ſeſe libenter adjungente.

GEOGRAPHIA.
CODEX PRIMUS.

Leam
kim
xe
ſan
ſim
kiun
ſe.

Aularum duarum Pekimi ſcilicet &

Nankimi, & tredecim provinciarum territorii examinati pictura.

Opus eſt geographicum, in cujus fine comparent varia vicinorum populorum regna. 1. volumen.

II.

Gin
kim
yam
cieu,

id eſt, hominum ſpeculi clarus autumnus,

five pulcher autumnus, in quo rerum humanarum fructus omnes, tanquam in speculo, perspiciuntur.

Hoc opus immensæ cujusdam ac stupendæ lectionis: ea enim quæ ad imperii gubernationem, quæ ad omnes provinciæ uniuscujusque magistratus, quæ ad artes in unâquaque provincia usitatas, quæ ad vectigalia illinc percepta, quæ ad viros & feminas in unaquaque urbe illustres pertinent, uno verbo, historiam Sinarum ferè totam narratiunculis non ita prolixis picturisque more Sinico repræsentat. Præfiguntur operi præfationes quamplurimæ, eæque variis scripturarum, seu characterum generibus. Præfationibus succedunt indices multi, sed præsertim eorum, quibus usus est auctor, librorum index locuples. Ex operibus enim 656. opus à se confarcinatum dicit. Post indices sequuntur summaria rerum in libro contentarum accuratissima. 13. volumina.

III.

Kuam

hoam

yu

kao,

id est, examen libri cujus titulus kuam hoam yu, seu rheda imperatoris.

Opus est geographicum longè utilissimum: sunt enim illic, licet breviùs, quæcumque ad unamquamque provinciam, ad unamquamque hujus vel illius provinciæ urbem cognoscendam pertinent. Additæ sunt locorum distantiæ; & loca ea, quà transeundum, exactissimè indicantur. Præterea urbium fundatores, & si quid illic factum illustrius. Non desunt mappæ urbium saltem primi & secundi ordinis. Volumina 2.

IV.

Fo

cheu

fu

chi,

id est, descriptio urbis Fu, seu Fo; liber imperfectus & pars amplioris decima quarta. Volumen 1.

V.

Ta

mim

hoei

tien,

id est, codices & collectiones de iis omnibus quæ ad Ta-mim pertinent.

Cum familia hæc Sinica, & maxima & illustrissima fuerit, historiam Tamingarum, seu 大明 Ta-mim, nemo est quin admirabilem esse judicet; & revera est. Ea ergo hîc continetur duobus involucris & voluminibus decem. Magistratus præterea omnes, urbium Sinæ totius omnium status, imò varii status repræsentantur. Involucra 2. volumina 10.

HISTORICI.

VI.

Annales Sinici. Sed ibidem reperies & annalium supplementa. Vide quæ nos ad annales, in Regiis & Bignon. Volumina 242. involucra 24.

VII.

Ven

hien

tum

kao,

id est, examen generale (rerum Sinicarum) litteratis oblatum.

Hic liber apud Sinas celeberrimus ea ferè omnia complectitur, quibus Sinæ in studiis suis, ad rerum gubernationem potissimùm spectantibus, dant operam. Hæc est autem totius operis dispositio. Primùm occurrunt præfationes numero viginti quinque, à quindecim auctoribus & litteratis scriptæ, & iis ipsis qui historiarum auctores fuerunt. Illæ autem præfationes sunt totidem dissertationes; quarum quidem prima agit de nova hac editione, aliæ vero de præcipuis historiæ Sinicæ auctoribus. Præfationes sequitur totius operis divisio. Multa igitur habet auctor. 1.° de historia Sinarum ejusque authenticis & per totum imperium celebratis scriptoribus; & cum diversi ii scriptores temporibus extiterint, eorum nomina & exaratarum ab ipsis historiarum aut collectionum titulos indicare non habet satis, sed quæ à posterioribus priorum elaboratæ sunt reprehensiones criticæ, eas etiam addit super, & plerumque, abbreviandi causa, verborum sensum indicat; non rarò etiam verba eorum ipsa affert. Atque ut lectu digna judices, quæ profectò ad justam historiæ Sinicæ cognitionem omnino necessaria, scito hæc per tractatus quinquaginta duos excurrere.

Inde transit ad varia imperii ac præsertim regiæ urbis tribunalia, quæ eo recenset ordine. 1.° quidem tribunal historiæ. 2.° Tribunal subsidiorum. 3.° Tribunal rituum,

rituum, feu cæremoniarum. 4.° Militiæ. 5.° Artium. 6.° Tribunal reparationum; quorum tribunalium nuncupat præfides; primum Xi-lam, &c. Poftea de collegio Han-lin, ejufque officiis ac præfidibus agit. Hinc ad militares afcendit. Mox de imperatore ejufque aula & aulæ officiis differit; & cum religio ubique in honore femper fuerit, de templis eorumque ornatu & miniftris mentionem facit; imò & de iis quæ manè & per diem facere debet imperator. Poftea ad ejus filios & principes tranfit. Ibique de regulis ac regibus tributariis & in aula vivere folitis. Sequitur mufica, cujus harmoniam, tempora & loca defcribit. Tandem militiam, ejufque genera, officia, ordinem & fupplicia depingit. Quo facto ad libros & litteraturam fe accingit: differit fcilicet de ye kim, de xu kim, de xi kim, de li ki, de chun cieu, de lun yu & mem cu; quos libros in varios, ut fieri folet, paragraphos difpertitur. Tum de hiao kim, feu liberorum inftitutione, de hio kim, feu de mufica.

Collectis vero ac commemoratis libris aliis quamplurimis, annotat nonnihil de aftronomia adeoque de folis, lunæ & ftellarum affectionibus, verbi gratia, de eclipfibus, &c. Deinde tractat de aqua, terra, igne, aere, ligno, quinque Philofophorum Sinarum elementis, & variis eorumdem elementorum appendicibus; quales funt, verbi gratia, herbæ, arbores, lapides, metalla, flores, montes, colles, rupes, fluenta, tonitrua, grando, pluviæ, venti, beftiæ, infecta, aves. Et ne quid lectori defit ad legendos auctores Sinicos, de antiqua & nova geographia multa & curiofa congerit. Præterea quæcumque in hiftoriis fabulofis reperiuntur, five de gigantibus, five de feminarum regnis, five de hominibus pygmæis, aut hoc vel alio modo deformatis, five de montibus ac rupibus igneis, uno verbo de gentibus, aut urbibus, aut regnis quæ nunquam extitere; fed à poëtis Sinis verfibus aut poëmatibus commemorantur. Ea omnia auctor fumma cura & labore indefeffo in hoc præftantiffimo opere contribuit. Porro ea utitur methodo, ut quæ facta hic illic legit, tum in annalibus, tum in libris canonicis, clafficis, aut alius generis cujuflibet, ea ad eos, quibus accidere, annos referat, & eum hiftoriæ locum unde haufit, appellet.

MSS. Tomus I.

VIII.

Cu
chi
tum
kien,

hoc eft, fpeculum commune, feu univerfale ad fulciendam gubernationem.

Primi annales funt quales à *Su-ma-kum* fcripti fuerant: iique, ut ad regios codices numero primo diximus, incipiunt ab anno primo 的 Guei-lie-vam, imperatore 朝 Cheu trigefimo, ante Chriftum 428. & continuantur ufque ad annum 的 Xi-cum, qui familiæ 朝 Heu-cheu, fecundus fuit & ultimus; anno poft Chriftum 951. unde intervallum eft 1379. annorum. Volumina 96.

IX.

Cu
chi
tum
kien
kam
mo,

id eft, fpeculi univerfalis ad fulciendam, feu adjuvandam gubernationem ordinatio, feu repræfentatio.

Vide etiam regios codices n. 1.

X.

Cum
yven
tum
kien.

Iidem annales funt, qui hoc tomo titulum hunc præferunt; idque propterea quòd de familia Sum illic agant: quafi diceres, imperatorum è familia Sum annales. Præcedit 1.° nova præfatio. 2.° oratio fatis longa de hiftoriis & hiftoricis tempore prioribus; in qua quidem oratione multa funt lectu digniffima, atque inter cætera effatum illud apud Sinas vulgatiffimum, imperium Sinicum non alio & alio modo, ut alia regna, adminiftratum unquam, fed ab initio iifdem femper ufum legibus. 3.° Denique index eft imperatorum ejufdem familiæ Sum omnium, à Tai-chu-cu fcilicet, ufque ad Ti-pim. Sequuntur autem in eo indice imperatores Ginguiskanidæ, quorum primus non ipfe Ginguiskan, quem Sinæ nondum agnoverant, fed Xi-cu, aliàs

Ddd

Tai-cu, aliàs iterum Ho-pi-lie, apud nos Cublai, ufque ad ultimum, eorumdem Ginguiskanidarum Xun-ti. Sic titulus non-nifi 19. Chao, feu familiam Sum promittit; fed liber ipfe vigefimam quoque familiam 元 Yven, feu Ginguiskani pofteros complectitur. Hæc vero omnia proponuntur chronologicæ, ita ut ad imperatoris uniuf-cujufque nomen apponantur anni, imò ad anni cujufque facta, hic vel ille menfis indicetur. Editio hæc, quæ non omnino nitida, annum tertium præfert 天 Tien-ki, aliàs Hi-cum, familiæ Ta-mim decimi fexti.

X I.

Tum
kien
xe xi
pien
gu,

id eft, quomodo explicent litterati varia in annalibus deficientia.

Hic funt volumina tria, in quibus vel multi annalium defectus fupplentur, vel quædam non fatis explicata traduntur enu-cleatiùs. Si horumce articulorum volumina quæfieris, funt 129.

X I I.

San
kue
chi,

id eft, Gallicè (*les entreprifes des trois Royaumes*) conatus trium regnorum.

Hiftoria eft ejus nimirum temporis quod duravit San-kue, fcilicet inter Han-chao, quod permanferat 425. annis, & Cyn-chao, quod duravit annos 155. Fuit enim regnum illud triplex per annos 45. ab Hien-ti morte, feu anno Chrifti 190. ufque ad mortem Heu-ti, five annum Chrifti 234.

In hoc autem libro hiftoriam regnorum illorum, claritatis caufa, præcedit genealogia principum, feu magnatum de imperio con-tendentium. Volumina 21.

F A B U L Æ.
X I I I.

Pe
gan.

Videtur effe fabula quædam fatis longa, cum hic habeatur kiven 19. Itaque liber eft imperfectus & volumen 1.

X I V.

vel

Yo
kiao
lie,
fan
cai
cu,

id eft, pera 的 yo kiao, vel poëtæ tres. Fabella eft, quam jam habuifti inter codices Bignonianos, numero nono. Volumen 1. & funt hoei 2. defunt cætera.

HISTORIA, feu JUS SINICUM.
X V.

To
fu
hiun
kiai,

id eft, expofitio & explicatio rerum cam-pana (dignarum) Senfus eft, earum rerum, ob quas ad limen regium accedere poffunt Sinæ.

Cum Sinæ imperatorem ipfum adeant non rarò, imperatoris ipfius caufa, hoc eft, ut de vitiis quibufdam aut peccatis repre-hendant, idque etiam cum vitæ fuæ peri-culo; hujufmodi reprehenfionum plenæ funt hiftoriæ ejufdem gentis. Impreffio fub Kam-hi. volumen 1.

LIBRI CANONICI ET CLASSICI.
X V I.

Ye
kim
mum
yn,

id eft, introductio ad res ocultas 的 ye kim.

Explicatio eft rerum arcanarum in variis ye kim lineis contentarum. Volumina 12. Editio charactere currenti, neque admo-dum eleganti.

X V I I.

Yu
chi
ge
kiam
ye
kim
kiai
y,

hoc eft, fenfus 的 ye kim ad explicationem

quotidianam magnificentiſſimè, imperatoris juſſu, datus.

Yu chi, vel de libris ad uſum imperatoris dicitur, vel de libris imperatoris juſſu & auctoritate publicatis. Eſt autem impreſſus hic liber anno Kam-hi 22. continetque commentarios in ye kim ampliſſimos. Volumina 7.

XVIII.

Item alius, impreſſione nitidiſſima, in quo idem ye kim. Duo volumina, quæ ſunt lun yu & mem cu.

XIX.

Ge
kiam
ye
kim
kiai
y,

id eſt, diurnalis expoſitionis ye kim commentarius & ſenſus.

Vide quæ ad regios codices annotavimus numeris 7. 8. de ye kim, ejuſque ſenſu & commentatoribus. Hîc volumina ſunt 9.

XX.

U
kim
pum
hiun,

id eſt, commentarius litteralis u kim, ſeu quinque librorum.

Notæ ſunt marginales ad unumquemque librum canonicum : ſcilicet, ad ye kim, xi kim, li ki, ſu xu & chun cieu, de quibus vide codices regios, numeris 7. 8. 9. 10. 11. 12. 13. 14. 15. 16. 17. & 5. Sunt ergo hîc ad ye kim, volumina 2. ad xi kim, volumina 2. ad xu kim, volumen 1. ad chun cieu, volumina 2. ad li ki, volumina 5. adeoque 12. volumina.

XXI.

Xu kim, li ki, xi kim & chun cieu, itidem pam huin. Unà cum marginali, ſeu potiùs laterali commentario. Sunt autem volumina

xu kim	2.
xi kim	1.
li ki	3.
chun cieu	2.

itaque volumina 8. nam deſunt & ye kim & ſu xu hujus editionis.

MSS. Tomus I.

XXII.

Sin
puon
fuen
cham
fuen
cie
ſu
xu
chim
ven,

id eſt, ſu xu, ſeu quatuor Confucii librorum apta & recta compoſitio; partibus eorum & paragraphis novo quodam judicio collocatis.

Habetur hujuſmodi ta hio tantùm, idque characteribus malè exaratis. Volumen 1.

XXIII.

Cem
pu
ſu
.xu
kiam
y
ye
kien
nem
kiai,

id eſt, additiones & ſupplementa ad librum ſu xu kiam; ita ut uno intuitu intelligi ſenſus poſſit.

Sunt autem libri Confucii ta hio, lun yu, mem cu. Character eſt minutior, ſed nitidus, & commentarius facilis. Deſunt aliquot volumina, ſed ſunt hîc 10.

XXIV.

Mem
cu.

Pars eſt quarta librorum Confucianorum, ſed peſſimè impreſſa. Volumen 1.

Cæterùm idem eſt, qui & alibi commentarius.

XXV.

Ta
hio
chim
ven,

id eſt, ta hio primi libri Confuciani apta compoſitio.

Ddd ij

Apud Sinas inolevit opinio vetus, quæ fabula eſt, libros olim incenſos; idque illi incendio attributum, quod frequenti tranſcriptioni apud nos & verè datur. Itaque reperti ſunt multi, qui paragraphorum Confucianorum ordinem quaſi interverſum repararent; hinc illi tituli. Volumen 1. parvulum & ſat malè exaratum.

X X V I.

Sim
li
ta
civen.

Vide inter regios numero 18. involucra 2. volumina 12.

X X V I I.

Sim
li
ta
civen
xu
cie
yao,

id eſt, directorium ad magnam librorum ſim li collectionem legendam & intelligendam.

Commentarius eſt in eandem philoſophiam Sinicam, variaſque philoſophorum Sinarum opiniones. Vide cod. regios, numeris 18. 19. Voluminum eſt 4. quæ ſunt 1. 3. 5. 7.

X X V I I I.

Sim
li
ta
civen
xu.

Libri ſim li ta civen tomus trigeſimus ſextus imperfectus. 1. volumen.

X X I X.

Idem liber. Involucra 2. volumina 22.

X X X.

Sim
li
ta
civen
cum
yao, .

id eſt, collectio aut concordantia 㳾 ſim li

ta civen, ſive opinionum philoſophicarum in ſim li contentarum.

Vide quæ de hoc libro, ejuſque commentariis diximus ad codices regios, numero 17. Volumina 22.

X X X I.

Ti
u
cai
cu
xu,

id eſt, tractatus ſingularis de quinque elementis.

Elementa apud Sinas habentur quinque aqua, terra, aer, ignis, ut apud philoſophos Græcos, & præterea lignum: qua de re videſis diſſertationem R. P. Longobardi, &c. Auctor nobis incognitus, ſed vixit, aut potiùs opus ejus impreſſum eſt, imperante apud Sinas Cum-chin, id eſt, 㳾 Ta-mim ultimo. Volumina 16.

X X X I I.

Chu
cu
kia
li,

id eſt, 㳾 chu cu, aliàs chu ven kum ritus domus, ſeu quæ ab homine domi obſervanda.

Tractatus eſt moralis de iis omnibus quæ à Sinis domi fiunt, aut fieri debent, ut mores familiæ uniuſcujuſque ad virtutem dirigantur. Agitur de variis hominum in hac vel illa conditione poſitorum officiis, ſed præcipuè de vita domeſtica. Volumina 2.

X X X I I I.

Kum
cu
kia
yu.

Diſcurſus, ſeu diſſertationes in domum, ſeu familiam Confucii.

Per totum hunc librum referuntur dicta factaque philoſophi Confucii, & quidquid ſive domi, ſive inter amicos, etiam dum reipublicæ operam dabat, fecit dixit-ve; ita ut propriè Confucii vita dici poſſit. Volumen 1.

CODICES MANUSCRIPTI. 397

XXXIV.

Vên *aliàs* vên 2. 254.
kum
kia
li,

id eft, 㸃 ven kum, aliàs chu cu ritus, feu modus vivendi domefticus.

Opus apud Sinas magni femper factum: quæcumque enim viro Sinæ agenda, ea per omnem vitæ curfum dirigit, five ad mutua viri & mulieris, parentum & natorum, item propinquorum & amicorum inter fe officia, five ad religionem, aulas majorum, & generatim cultum religiofum. Volumina 4.

RELIGIO.

XXXV.

Xe
guei,

id eft, decem confolationes.

Liber eft omnino moralis de iis quæ homines vera bona & perpetua exiftimant, & tamen amittunt; quorum jactura ne eorum animi frangantur, opponuntur decem confolationes. Auctor Sacerdos è Societate Jefu. Volumen 1.

MEDICI.

XXXVI.

Hoam
ti
nuy
kim
lim
kiu,

id eft, excavatio fpiritalis (inquifitio profunda) in nui kim librum infcriptum, nui kim hoam ti, feu ab hoam ti de medicina compofitum.

Hic liber omnium quos cognofcimus, videtur antiquiffimus. Volumen 1.

PHILOSOPHIA.

XXXVII.

Tai
pim
van
nun
xu,

id eft, 㸃 tai pim liber omnium annorum.

Liber eft mifcellaneus, feu regiftrum; in fine differtatio eft de tai hie, fed non perfecta. Sculpturæ menda etiamnum corrigenda illic indicantur. Volumen 1.

XXXVIII.

Hiao
kim
yen
y,

id eft, hiao kim, feu tractatus de obedientia, apud Sinas commendatiffimus, extenfione debita auctus & ornatus.

Inveftigantur hoc opere officia mortalium omnia, & quæcumque homines ex obedientia exequi neceffe eft, fi officio, ex rationis dictamine, fungi ac proinde ad hujus vitæ tranquillitatem ac felicitatem pervenire voluerint. Porro hic eft ordo totius operis. Occurrit 1.º præfatio triplex & quæ ad virtutis laudem, præfertim ex antiquorum inftitutis tota referatur; nam auctor id ftatuit, quod à Sinis vulgò credi video, gentem fuam totam, à prima antiquitate, femper eandem permanfiffe, nec diverfis unquam ufam effe legibus. Loquitur etiam de libris, quos Sinæ identidem ediderunt de hiao, feu virtute illa, quæ apud eos fumma habetur, obedientia nimirum: judicant enim ex ea oriri bona focietatis humanæ ferè omnia, cum terra nihil homini ad vitam tuendam deneget, rebufque neceffariis nunquam careat, nifi mutua caritate offenfa. Quod, fi terrarum incolæ, fibi invicem divina providentia fubjecti, ea qua debent comitate & bonitate erga fratres & propinquos, erga imperatorem viverent, accidere nullomodo poffet; cum ex mutuo illo nexu cuncta cuncti inter fe concederent. Tandem fuccedit opus ipfum in quo auctor agit primo de juftitia, fide ac cæteris virtutibus atque urbanitate generatim: deinde ad paternitatem feu ea officia defcendit, quorum in patrem ac matrem debitores fumus, idque natura ipfa duce; tum ad fratrum amorem atque concordiam. Inde ad matrimonium marifque & feminæ conjunctionem delapfus, principium quoddam focietatis atque urbanitatis ftatuit; inde cæremoniarum ac rituum ufus, inde harmonia, honor, & contra fuppliciorum quædam ex eadem natura neceffitas. Poftea ad debitam imperatori, magiftris ac magiftratibus obedientiam progreditur. Atque illic campus, rerum infinitus, quem doctè ac fapientiffimè percurrit. Hoc opus in tota

D d d *iij*

Sina nominatiſſimum ab imperatore Kam-hi, anno ejus regni 29. atque typis impe-rialibus impreſſum eſt. Volumina 30.

XXXIX.

Xn
kim
mum
yn
ta
civen.

Magna collectio comprehendens quid-quid ad abſtruſa 的 xu kim explicanda con-ferre poteſt. Editio non eſt nitida, ſed eadem quæ libri præcedentis. Volumina 16.

ARTES.
XL.

Tien
kum
kai
ve,

id eſt, operatio cœli in aperiendis rebus.

Locutio eſt è Sinarum philoſophia de-ſumta, qua artes è cœlo derivatæ dicuntur. Vide inter codices regios numerum 38. Volumina 3.

MATHEMATICI.
XLI.

Ma
tiao
kiai,

id eſt, 的 ma tiao univerſalia.

In hoc opuſculo multa ſunt de arithme-tica, de ponderibus, de menſuris, de muſica & tonis. Sed peſſimè & nimiùm feſtinanter impreſſum eſt, ita ut characteres plerique truncati ſint. Volumen 1.

XLII.

Kia
cu
hoei
ki.

Cyclorum (queis chronologia Sinarum tota nititur) collectio & commemoratio.

In præfatione hujus libri agitur de cyclis, ac præcipuè de cyclo annorum ſexaginta, atque auctore ejus Hoam-ti, annoque ejus 8. Poſtea ſequitur indicatio eorum, in quibus unuſquiſque cyclus incipit, annorum, ab ejuſdem Hoam-ti anno 8. idque per om-nes imperatores ex hiſtoria deſignatos, ab *Hoam-ti,* ad extrema uſque tempora. Ad-duntur etiam diſſertatiunculæ de primis ante Hoam-ti ſæculis, de Fohi ejuſque prædeceſſoribus. Impreſſus eſt Nam-kimi, & eſt voluminum 3.

XLIII.

Vam
chen
pien,

id eſt, de mala uſurpatione diſceptatio.

Expoſtulatio eſt 的 yam kuam ſun à Societatis Jeſu Patribus, ut ipſe dicebat, male ac contra jus omne uſurpato, cum ab imperatore, ob majorem mathemati-corum ſcientiam adſciti ſunt ad matheſeos tribunal. Volumen 1.

XLIV.

Tien
muen,

id eſt, cœli porta.

Tractatus eſt de ſphæra, juxta principia antiquorum. Auctor Sacerdos è Societate Jeſu, idque 的 Van-lie temporibus. Volu-mina 2. exemplaria 2.

XLV.

Tien
muen
lio,

id eſt, cœli porta parva.

Alius de ſphæra tractatus. Volumen 1.

XLVI.

Hoa
ta,

id eſt, reſponſio de pictura.

Cum apud nos picturæ modus à Sina-rum pictura quàm maximè remotus ſit, præſertim quoad figuras, veſtes & linea-menta, ſæpe interrogantur noſtri de vera pingendi & ſculpendi arte; quam naturæ conſentaneam eſſe debere, cum certo cer-tius ſit, mirum eſt, cur Sinæ, alioqui naturæ fautores acerrimi, aliud tamen neſcio quid, quod in rerum natura non eſt, ſectentur. In præfatione, quæ eſt de ſculptoribus & pictoribus generatim, Sinæ veteres repre-henduntur quod figuras 10. 20. brachiorum & ejuſmodi monſtra depinxerint contra omnem naturæ viam. Impreſſio facta ſub

CODICES MANUSCRIPTI.

Cum-chim, & auctor Sacerdos è Societate Jesu. Volumen 1.

XLVII.

Yven
kim
xue,

id est, dissertatio, seu oratio de specillis longè prospicientibus *(des Lunettes d'approche.)*

Præfatio est de specillorum utilitate iis omnibus qui astronomiam rectè tractare volunt, & per totam dissertationem agitur de vitrorum præparatione, ut inde specilla elaborentur. Præterea objectorum elongationem atque appropinquationem, lucis gradus, colorum similitudinem ac dissimilitudinem, pro hac vel illa distantia & linearum ex hac vel illa describendarum rationem expendit auctor. Scripsit autem sub Tien-ki, 太微 Ta-mim, decimo quinto, & anno ejus 6. Europæus fuit, cum Aristotelem ejusque librum ἀκροάσεων appellet. Volumen 1.

XLVIII.

Kaon
yn
lim
kuo.

Documentum quo res prospicere aut prævidere intelligens possit.

Est opusculum quoddam, ex almanachicorum genere, de sortibus, & ad artem divinandi adaptatum. Volumen 1.

XLIX.

Sin
ke
pe
sin
chao
kuan
nan
xui
ce
li,

id est, novæ editionis Pechimi novum registrum ad Nankimi consensum; seu, pacta conventa pro vectigalibus. Sensus est novam editionem factam indicis, seu catalogi hujus, qui est & mercium quæ inter duas urbes, Pekimum & Nankimum, ultro citroque comportantur, & vectigalium pro una-quaque merce solvendorum. Volumen 1.

L.

Lun
yn
chi
tien,

id est, codex dans sensum rotæ annuæ.

Est almanach ecclesiasticum seu christianum, qualia ad usum Christianorum apud Sinas imprimuntur quotannis. Hoc verò pertinet ad Kam-hi annum 44. & sunt exemplaria 20.

LI.

Liber ἀκέφαλος & sine titulo, sed ex genere almanachico, eoque juxta astrologiæ principia. Porro in hoc libro videre est cyclum & quidquid ad anni ac mensium ordinem pertinet, unà cum prædictionibus. Volumen 1.

GRAMMATICI.

LII.

Cu
lui
pu.

Supplementum ad dictionarium cu luy.

Dictionarium est ad ea supplenda quæ in cu luy desunt. Præfatio duplex, prior ad 的 cu luy commendationem, in qua dicit auctor additos à se 4595. characteres. Posterior de characteribus generaliùs; in qua de historicis xe san kim vocatis, de veris kim, de lo xu, de characteribus xim & cie, de characterum dissectione ac lectione, &c. fusè agit. Postea ostendunt se claves omnes, unà cum duplicibus ac triplicibus figuris, quotquot habent. Tum subjicitur numerus eorum qui unicuique clavi additi, aut in unaquaque clavi denuò expositi sunt, characterum. Tandem incipit liber ipse, & ad unamquamque clavim fiunt duo. 1.° supplentur characteres novi. 2.° ad characteres in cu luy expositos adduntur significationes novæ. Editus est anno Kamhi 50. Volumina 5.

Cu
luy, vel *guei*,

aut ampliùs

Yyven
Kin
cu
luy, vel *guei*,

id est, dictionarium vocatum cu luy vel cu

guei, tom. 14. ab *Yven Kin* editum. De hoc dictionario jam diximus ad codices regios num. 48. Sed alia hæc editio, charactere scilicet majori ac nitidiori, unde apud Sinas dictionarium maximi fieri intelligitur. Volumen 14.

L I I I.

Liber manuscriptus & tantùm inceptus, phrasium; solent Sinæ suas phrases dividere juxta numerum characterum. Phrases igitur sunt 2. 3. 4. 5. 6. vocum, seu characterum, & aliæ simplices, elegantiores aliæ. Volumen 1.

L I V.

Ju

yen

cu

cu,

id est, characteres mixti vocum quatuor.

Libellus est sat malè sculptus, in quo phrases multæ, aut potiùs miscellaneæ characterum 4. quales apud Sinas infinitæ. Volumen 1. Sunt autem quorumdam characterum communiorum.

L V.

Cien

cu

ven

chu

kiai.

Litteratorum in characteres mille commentariolus & expositio.

Characteres sunt undecumque extracti, communes tamen, quorum latè ac distinctè Scriptorum datur supernè explicatio brevis, ex re aliqua aut alio charactere notiori, aut etiam è characteris attributo notionem inculcante. Ex præfatione auctor fuisse videtur non Sina, sed Missionarius; quod tamen non affirmamus. Præfatio id ferè insinuat. Volumen 1.

R E L I G I O.
L V I.

Xen

sem

fo

chum

chim

iu,

id est, via recta bonæ vitæ & finis beati.

Tractatus est de vitæ regula, in quo multæ observationes tum quoad corpus, tum quoad animam. Præfatio est de vitæ cursu ac fine, amplissima, ubi de virtutis via. In secunda parte afferuntur multa de beata Virgine, ac de bona morte. Auctor Sacerdos è Societate Jesu. Liber in-4.° magno, & optimè impressus. Volumen 1.

L V I I.

Liber idem de bonæ mortis via, minori forma. 2. exemplaria, sed partis secundæ de beata Virgine. Vol.

L V I I I.

Ti

chim

pien,

id est, sermo in quo justitia exaltatur; seu veræ justitiæ laudes.

Auctor Jesuita, Theologus, doctusque vir, in præfatione agit de peccato originis, atque incarnationis necessitate. In libro ipso & sectionibus quinque, primùm quæcumque ad dogma & Dei attributa, deinde quæ ad virtutis cultum pertinent, breviter attingit. Volumen 1.

L I X.

Tien

xe, xi

mim

pien.

Elucidationes & distinctiones sectæ τʊ̃ Foe oppositæ.

Tractatus hic totus est contra Foe sectam, & eos qui varias per multa sæcula metempsychoses fingunt. Disputat igitur auctor de peccatis, de pœnis, de paradiso, de inferno; itaque religionem christianam astruit, sectam Foe & alias Bonziorum religiones aut opiniones refellit. Volumen 1.

L X.

Ven

miao

li

yo, vel lo

chi

id est, mens (seu scopus & intentio) cæremoniarum & musicæ quæ in templis litteratorum usurpantur.

Auctor Sina est, & multa habet de Sinarum musica, de forma & cæremoniis templorum;

sunt

funt etiam illic tonorum muficorum tabulæ; ac præterea eorum quæ in templis adhibentur, inftrumentorum omnium figuræ. Volumen 1.

L X I.

Tien

chu

xe

y.

Vera Dei notio.

Opus illud nobiliffimum *Matthæi Riccii,* è Societate Jefu Miffionarii illuftriffimi, qui miffionis Jefuitarum fundator, atque omnibus litteratorum honoribus decoratus eft. Vide quæ de hoc libro ad codices Bignonianos diximus n.° 4.° Editio hujus libri multiplex, hæc autem charactere non tam magno, fed nitidiffimo. Volumina 2.

L X I I.

Tien

hio

xe

y.

Cœli fcientiæ folidus fenfus: aut, ex titulo interiori, cœli Domini folidus fenfus. Editio fecunda. Liber eft *Matthæi Riccii,* idem qui fupra. Volumen 1.

L X I I I.

Chin

chu

lim

fim

li

chim.

Demonftratio per rationem, veri Dei naturam effe intellectualem.

Ad hanc demonftrationem partes naturæ omnes, generationem animantium omnium in auxilium advocat auctor, Sacerdos è Societate Jefu. Volumen 1.

L X I V.

Chu

chi

kiun

chim.

Res omnes à Deo fumma cura gubernari ac regi, probatio, feu oratio demonftrans.

Reipfa naturam omnino omnem auctor excutit, & hinc providentiam in Deo

MSS. Tomus I.

fummam effe arguit. Capita libri funt quindecim, partes duæ. Volumen 1.

L X V.

Chu

kiao

yao

chi,

id eft, Dei legis fcopus & mandata; feu, quid fit & quonam confilio data fit lex Dei.

Liber eft capitum decem, quæ de natura & attributis Dei, de rerum origine, de hominis debitis, de bonarum actionum remuneratione, atque inde paradifo & inferno. Volumen 1. exemplaria 2.

L X V I.

Lum

cu

y

civen;

id eft, explicatio fymboli, auctore *Lum-cu.*

Hic liber nihil aliud quam fymboli apoftolici explicatio theologica; cui additus eft tractatus de angelis & anima rationali. Eft igitur duarum partium. Auctor Miffionarius è Societate Jefu, Hifpanus, cujus nomen Sinicum *Lum-cu.* Vide catal. pag. 4. & 5.

L X V I I.

Cie

ke.

Septem victoriæ, feu feptem mortificationes per quas vincere fe ipfe homo poteft.

Liber à *Lum-cu,* feu *Lum-yen-ngo,* Jefuita Hifpano, fic apud Sinas appellato, confcriptus. 1. volumen. Vide catal. Jefuitarum pag. 5. & codices regios n.° 55.

L X V I I I.

Tien

chu

kiam

fem

yn

y.

Introductio ad intelligendam Domini defcenfionem & nativitatem, id eft, incarnationis myfterium.

Tractatus eft de incarnatione, & partes habet duas. Auctor Sacerdos è Societate Jefu. Volumen 1.

Eee

LXIX.

Chim
gin
yao
cie ci.

Articuli in quibus quæritur quomodo Deus homo fieri possit, ac verus hòmo evadere.

Præfatio agit de controversia Bonzios inter ac Missionarios, seu Christianos Sinas, quænam sit homini ad perfectionem via. Itaque hîc de variis spirituum juxta Bonzios incarnationibus agitur, proindeque de incarnatione Christi, ac præcipuè de gratia, quæ hominem perficit & ad bene agendum incitat. Auctor libri, Franciscanus. Vide approbationes. Volumen 1. exemplaria 2.

LXX.

Tien
chu
kiam
sem
yen
him
ki
lo,

Narratio brevis actionum & verborum cœli Domini, (id est hoc loco) Domini nostri, postquam de cœlo descendit & incarnatus est: seu tractatus brevis de Verbi incarnatione. Auctor Sacerdos è Societate Jesu, Italus, ex catalogo pag. 9. Multa hîc loca è scriptura allata. Volumen 1. exemplaria 2.

LXXI.

Tien
chu
xim
kiao
xe
lo,

id est, sanctæ Dei religionis verus color; seu genuina adumbratio.

Tractatus est de præcipuis Christianæ religionis fundamentis; de Deo tanquam òmnium rerum principio; de ejus gubernatione ac providentia; de hominum genere non æterno; de cœli ac terræ creatione; de Adami formatione (cap. 5.) de anima increata, & hominum à bestiis differentia;

de Dei sanctitate, &c. Postea disseritur de natura divina, de præceptis, de baptismo. Auctor Sacerdos è Societate Jesu. Volumen 1.

LXXII.

Xim
kiao
su
kuei,

id est, sanctæ legis regulæ quatuor.

Agitur in hoc libro de mandatis Dei, quæ in partes dividuntur duas; alteram, quæ ad Deum, Deique cultum; alteram, quæ ad homines, hominumque inter se conversationem spectat. Auctor Sacerdos è Societate Jesu. Volumen 1. duplex exemplar.

LXXIII.

Tien
xin
hoei
ko,

id est, methodus cognoscendi & associandi spiritus cœlestes.

Agitur hîc de Deo & angelis. Notum est Christianos à Mahummedanis vocatos esse associatores, Maschriquin, quòd juxta eosdem sectarios, Deo aliquem associent Christiani, nempe Christum; apud Sinas aliter sumitur associatio eadem nimirum, non quòd Deo agnito angelum aut genios associent, sed quòd vel Deum & angelos nullo modo agnoscant, vel agnitorum naturam & attributa ignorent, ac materiales potiùs quàm verè spiritales faciant. Exemplaria 2. volumen 1.

LXXIV.

Tien
xin
hoei
ko.

Modus sese adjungendi spiritibus cœlestibus.

Tractatus est de cognitione Dei, de lege Dei, de angelorum natura, de Maria Virgine, de quatuor hominis finibus, &c. Est autem totus in modum catechismi: à Jesuita compositus dicitur. Volumen 1. sed exemplaria 4.

L X X V.

Chin
fo
chi
chi,

id eft, veræ felicitatis certa & recta demonftratio.

Demonftratur 1.° in terris beatum effe poffe neminem. 2.° Ea quæ in nobis eft ratione, felicitatem detegi poffe. 3.° Eum, qui homines creavit, Deum efficere quoque poffe, ut beatus homo fiat. 4.° Hominem, fi decem mandata obfervet, fieri beatum poffe. 5.° Eundem hominem, fi virtuti operam det, beatitudinis capacem reddi, &c. Agitur poftea de incarnatione Chrifti, de peccatis eorumque remiffione, ac de æterna beatitudine, &c. Auctor Sacerdos è Societate Jefu. Volumen 1. exemplaria 3.

L X X V I.

Tien
chu
xim
kiao
ye
yen,

id eft, fanctæ Dei legis congregata verba; feu fanctæ legis abbreviatio & quafi compendium.

Expofitio eft legis divinæ, philofophica & compendiaria, & impreffionis admirandæ. Volumen 1. exemplaria 2.

L X X V I I.

Vam
chui
kie
hium
pien,

id eft, difputatio, falsè urgeri vel profperitatem, vel infortunia adverfùs religionem: cui, nedum adverfentur, è contrario favent.

Quanquam tractatus non adeo amplus fit, attamen reperiuntur fat multa de felicitate & infelicitate, de fortibus & variis figuris, ad rerum fortuitarum divinationem adhiberi folitis. Volumen 1.

L X X V I I I.

Xim
kiao
yao
li,

id eft, fanctæ Dei legis fcopum effe rationi confentaneum.

Refponfio quædam eft ad refponfiones contra legem Dei propofitas. Auctor è qua fit familia non defignatur. Volumen 1. exemplaria 3.

L X X I X.

Xim
kiao
yao
li,

id eft, fanctæ Dei legis fcopus & ratio.

Parvus eft catechifmus & præcedentis compendium. Volumen 1. exemplaria 2.

L X X X.

Pie
vam
xo
po
ho
ke.

Declaratio vanitatis & rerum fortuitò dictarum refutatio.

Opus adverfus Sinarum fectas, præcipuè 表 Foe difcipulos compofitum. Agitur enim præfertim de animarum revolutionibus & fectæ illius inferno. Auctor *Ho-ke,* è Miffionariis unus. Volumen 1.

L X X X I.

Chim
xi
lio
xue,

id eft, orationem non longam effe, fi quis fæculum & generationes confideret.

Senfus eft ex rerum mundanarum confideratione, Chriftianæ religionis capita comprobari & afferi. Auctor non indicatur; cæterùm hæc omnia tractat philofophicè, & contra Ethnicos agit argumentis validiffimis: oftenditque & hujus mundi originem & generationem hominum unam, & animam immortalem effe, &c. Volumen 1.

LXXXII.

Vam

chen

pien,

id eft, fortes mittere rem omnino vanam effe, difputatio.

Sortes apud Sinas frequentes, ita ut ex ye kim divinent: cui quidem rei multa à Miffionariis oppofita. Videtur autem hic liber contra Vam-kuam-fien compofitus. Volumen 1.

LXXXIII.

Yen

fiam

xin

kum,

id eft, fpirituum igneorum meritum: feu quid cogitandum fit de fpiritibus igneis.

Liber eft à Francifcano compofitus de rebus in China controverfis. Hic propriè ad igneos fpiritus pertinet, eos nempe, quos Sinarum fectæ, five quæ Foe, five quæ Lao-tan eft, folent admittere. Volumen 1.

LXXXIV.

Tien

chu

xim

kiao

mum

yn,

id eft, ad fanctæ Dei legis obfcuritates introductio, iis qui introfpicere volunt.

Tractatus eft revera fublimis de natura, exiftentia atque attributis Dei, de providentia, de perfonis divinis, de præmiis bonorum, de malorum fuppliciis, &c. contra Foiftas. Volumen 1.

LXXXV.

Ta

ke

ven,

id eft, refponfio extraneis interrogantibus.

Non femel, fed fexcenties à Miffionariis quæfierunt Sinæ Bonzii, Foiftæ & Laotaniftæ, cur tandem patriam fuam relinquerent, loca Afiæ tam remota peterent; idque ut gentibus, leges alias tenentibus, legem quandam novam annuntiarent; quæ

an melior, an divinior effet, non cognofceretur. Satis ergo ejufmodi interrogationibus refpondere conatur auctor; & quidquid ad dignitatem Chriftianæ religionis facit, difcutit & fusè tractat. Volumen 1.

LXXXVI.

Tien

chu

xim

kiao

hoa

y ny,

id eft, de fancta Dei lege perplexitates & dubia propofita.

Agitur de tien, de xam ti; & ad controverfias Sinicas pertinet. Volumen 1.

LXXXVII.

Tai

y nhi

pien,

id eft, tractatus de iis dubiis, quæ à litterato Sina adverfus religionem Chriftianam proponi folent ac poffunt.

Auctor Chriftianus, qui doctrinam litteratorum Sinarum ac præterea Fohiftarum apprimè calluit. Quæcumque ergo à litteratis vulgò proponuntur, ea fine fuco & abfque ulla hæfitatione fibi ipfe objicit, ac poftea momentis è ratione defumtis refellit. Tractatus eft ob eam rem curiofus; præfatio litteris fluentibus ac neglectis fculpta; cætera charactere vulgato, eoque nitidiffimo impreffa. Volumen 1.

LXXXVIII.

Kim

kiao

lieu

him

chum

kue

poei

fum

chim

civen,

id eft, de verbo ad verbum, recta explicatio, qua amœnæ legis (quæ Sinæ regnum pervafit) lapideum monumentum cum laude elucidatur; feu, quod idem eft, lapis teftimonii gratia pofitus in laudem magnificæ

CODICES MANUSCRIPTI.

legis, quæ ad Sinæ regnum ufque penetrarat, ibique fufcepta erat, feu diu in honore fuit.

De lapide multi dixerunt. Vide inter Bignonianos n.° 44. & confer, propter quafdam vocum differentias. Volumen 1.

L X X X I X.

Van
ve
chin·
yven,

id eft, rerum omnium vera origo.

Tractatus eft de rerum principio theologicè fumto, quod non eft nifi Deus: & tranfigitur ea res tota capitibus undecim; in queis generatim oftenditur, res omnes à fe non factas, hominem à fe ipfo creatum non effe, hominem neque à cœlo, neque à terra creari potuiffe; per id, quod Sinæ vocant yven ki, nec cœlum, nec terram, ita ut nunc funt, diftribui potuiffe, neque à Li creata hæc effe. His omnibus pofitis, in capitibus fequentibus colligitur, gubernatorem effe aliquem, qui originem ipfe non habuerit. Auctor Sacerdos è Societate Jefu. Volumen 1. exemplaria 2.

X C.

Tien
kiai,

id eft, gradus cœli.

Agitur de variis virtutibus, hominem eum ad cœlum ducturis, quifquis eas coluerit. Volumen 1. exemplaria 2.

X C I.

Yum
can
tim
hem,

id eft, librile ftaterae, æterna à temporibus (fuppliciis) determinans.

Tractatus de igne inferni perpetuo, & fuppliciis purgatorii defituris. Impreffus imperatoris Kam-hi anno 35. Volumen 1.

X C I I.

Xim
kiao
kien
yao,

id eft, fanctæ legis placita abbreviata.

Oratio eft fat brevis de religione, ejufque dogmatibus. Auctor è Societate Jefu. Volumen 1. optimè impreffum.

X C I I I.

Xim
nui
lo
fai
him
xe,

id eft, fanctæ mulieris Lo-fai (appellatæ) vita, feu actiones veræ. Nomen eft mulieris, fed videtur non aliud quàm Rofæ: imò hæc Rofa non Sinenfis fuit, fed Americana, ex urbe Lima. Cæterum liber impreffus eft fub Kam-hi, & charactere quodam pulcherrimo. Volumen 1.

X C I V.

Tien
chu
kiam
fem
yen
him
ki
fiam,

id eft, figuræ queis notantur Domini noftri incarnati verba & actiones.

Jam librum hunc habuimus. Vide inter regios n.° 56. Præfatio eft de incarnatione & incarnationis loco. Tum fequuntur imagines in quibus vita Chrifti tota continetur; additis ad imam paginam figuræ, aut imaginis uniufcujufque explicationibus. Figuræ ab Europæo pictæ. Auctor Sacerdos è Societate Jefu. Volumen 1.

X C V.

Tien
chu
xim
kiao
cum
tu
nuy
kim,

id eft, Dei fanctæ legis preces generales quæ in fcriptura reperiuntur.

Sunt tantùm *Pater, Ave,* &c. Volumen 1.

E e e iij

XCV.

Liber MS. inscriptus

pien

hio.

Tractatus de controversiis Sinicis. Volumen 1.

XCVII.

Tien

chu

xim

kiao

yo

yen,

id est, de sancta Dei lege verba abbreviata.

Doctrinæ Christianæ datur hîc synopsis. Auctor Sacerdos è Societate Jesu. Volumen 1.

XCVIII.

Xim

kim

che

kiai.

Librorum sanctorum expositio vera & solida. Titulus paulò aliter; nempe, Domini nostri, qui de cœlo descendit & natus est, libri sancti vera expositio.

In hoc opere, neque aliud fit per totum librum, varia scripturæ loca exponuntur, prout sese offerunt, juxta ordinem dierum festorum. Accesserunt præfatio in scripturæ commentationem, & indices in festorum notitiam. Sculptus est imperante Cum-chin. Volumina 8.

XCIX.

Xim.

mu

him

xe,

id est, sanctæ Dei matris acta vera.

Auctor Sacerdos è Societate Jesu. Vide inter Bignonianos n.° 31.

C.

Xim

jo

se

him

xe,

id est, veræ divi Josephi actiones & vita: adduntur ejusdem litaniæ.

Auctor unus è Societate Jesu. Volumen 1. exemplaria 2.

CI.

Tien

chu

kiao

yao

chu

lio,

id est, explicatio seu oratio brevis, in qua legis Dei placita exponuntur.

Ut verè dicam, nihil aliud hîc reperitur, quam preces, *Pater noster, Ave Maria, Credo,* mandata decem, unà cum expositione brevissima. Auctor Missionarius Franciscanus. Impressio parum nitida. Volumen 1. exemplaria 2.

CII.

Tien

chu

kim

kiai,

id est, orationis Dominicæ explicatio; seu commentarius in orationem *Pater noster.*

Auctor è Societate Jesu Sacerdos. Volumen 1.

CIII.

O

hoei

ven

ta,

id est, interrogationes & responsiones ad Christianorum initiationem.

Opus est à Franciscano compositum ad erudiendos Catechumenos; in quo, capitibus quatuordecim, quæ ad Christianum informandum pertinent, ea persequitur fusè satis. Volumen 1. exemplaria 2.

CIV.

Kuen

kim

lien

lim

xue,

id est, oratio in qua probatur divites & magnates (vestitu regio decoratos) pauperibus compati, eisque eleemosynam erogare debere.

Hortatio eft qua divites ad eleemofynam erogandam incitantur. Auctor Miffionarius Francifcanus. Volumen 1.

C V.

Tum
yeu
kiao
hio,

id eft, legem effe atque obligationem debiti à Deo, ut pueri ac puellæ alantur atque educentur.

Tractatus eft totus de alitione atque educatione. Quamvis enim Sinæ liberorum in patres amorem atque obedientiam perpetuò prædicent, fæpe tamen & infantes exponunt, & liberos inopia coacti occiderunt. Auctor dicitur PP. Societatis Jefu Congregatio omnis. Res enim momenti fuit maximi & à Chriftianis fortiter tenenda ac defendenda. Eft autem hic tractatus partium duarum, capitum 21. & voluminis 1.

C V I.

Xim
yo
je
him
xe,

id eft, vita & officium fancti Jofephi.

Oratio eft de fancti Jofephi vita & moribus. Sequuntur litaniæ, quales in libris noftris quamplurimis. Volumen 1.

C V I I.

Xim
kiao
je ge
kuo.

Sanctæ Dei legis preces quotidianæ.

Editio hæc majori forma quam aliæ. Volumen 1.

C V I I I.

Tien
chu
xim
kiao
kim
ven.

Sanctæ Dei legis precum compofitio; quales nempe neophytis tradi folent. Volumen 1.

C I X.

Tien
chu
xim
kiao
kim
ven,

id eft, Domini cœli, feu Dei, fanctæ legis preces & catechifmus.

Continet hic liber orationem Dominicam, falutationem angelicam, fymbolum Apoftolorum, confeffionem, præcepta decalogi, catechifmum, &c. qualia fuis profelytis tradunt Miffionarii. Volumen 1.

C X.

Xim
kiao
ge
kao.

De verbo ad verbum, exercitium diurnum fanctæ religionis, id eft, preces horariæ, unoquoque die recitandæ, *Pater nofter, Ave Maria, Credo,* decem præcepta, &c. Exemplaria 3. volumina 3.

C X I.

Xim
mu
him
xe,

id eft, fanctæ matris actiones veræ.

Hujus operis tres fectiones, quarum in prima, ut præfatio exponit, ea funt quæ de Mariæ nativitate ac vita dici folent; in fecunda agitur de ea qua per omne tempus & viri fancti & doctores fuere in Mariam veneratione; tertia eft de cultu Mariæ, ejufque interceffione, atque aliis ejufmodi rebus. Narratur etiam aliquid de Foæ matre, quæ apud Sinas in honore eft. Auctor Jefuita. Exemplaria 2. volumina 2.

C X I I.

Mi
cu
ci
y,

id eft, miffæ facrificii fenfus & expofitio.

Tractatus eft de nomine, origine, excellentia, ordinatione miffæ; adduntur cap. 7. 8. 9. 10. de facrificio, ac facrificii natura multa. Compofuit Sacerdos Italus, è Societate Jefu, doctiffimus, ac librorum quorumdam jam fupra memoratorum auctor, idque Cum-chin, 公 Ta-mim ultimi, temporibus. Circa annum 1628. Volumen 1.

C X I I I.

Mi
cu (fe)
kim
tien,

id eft, miffarum liber & collectio, feu miffale. 3. volumina, ferè in folio, MSS. quorum in uno funt indices, in aliis miffæ.

C X I V.

Su
tu
tien
yao,

id eft, officii ecclefiaftici collectio, feu de officio ecclefiafticorum. Opus manufcriptum, ferè in folio, in quo multa de officiis generatim, de miffa, de præparatione ad miffam, de cæremoniis, aliifque rebus omnibus ad munera ecclefiaftica pertinentibus differuntur.

C X V.

Xim
fu
li
tien,

id eft, liber cæremonialis negotiorum, vel rerum ad Sanctos pertinentium; feu proprium Sanctorum, digeftum per anni dies.

Hîc, multò melius quàm alibi, de Sinica nominum noftrorum fcriptura judicare eft, cum Sanctorum ferè omnium ac feftorum nomina characteribus Sinicis reddita fint. Volumen 1.

C X V I.

Tim
mu
fa
ki
lie,

id eft, audiendi miffam (&) menfæ (fanctæ) ordo.

Libellus eft quem noftri miffæ ordinarium vocant. Auctor Miffionarius Francifcanus. Volumen 1.

C X V I I.

Gai
te
chum
y
li
chi
pien.

Quòd virtus amabilis, refque in medio pofita; idque nonnifi fenfûs acuti ope diftingui poffit.

Difputatio eft philofophica ac theologica de virtutis natura; non folùm per fe & in fe, fed etiam in religione Chriftiana. Refutantur Ariftotelis, Epicuri ac cæterorum Philofophorum opiniones. Auctor Miffionarius Dominicanus. Volumen 1.

C X V I I I.

Y
chu
chi
ki,

id eft, conformandi nos Domino fuprema exaltatio.

Liber in quo modus nofmet erigendi ad fupremam Chrifti conformitatem, traditur. Eft ergo imitationis Jefu Chrifti verfio in linguam Sinicam. Volumina 4.

C X I X.

Tien
chu
xim   } 132. tr. 6.
kiao
lio
xue,

id eft, de fancta Dei lege oratio brevis.

Præfatio eft de hominis perfectione & religionis quæ hominem perficiat, neceffitate. In libro ipfo, quem in varios paragraphos auctor diftribuit, primò cœlum & terram creari nonnifi à Deo potuiffe oftendit; deinde ad varia Chriftiani officia procedit; poftea Foæ & Bonziorum opiniones refert, refellitque; tandem hominis in cætera animantia dominationem ex fcriptura, ejufque inde gratitudinem & varia officia profluere contendit. Auctor Sacerdos è Societate Jefu. Opus editum anno Chrifti 1674. Volumen 1.

CXX.

CODICES MANUSCRIPTI. 409

CXX.

Tien

chu

xim

kiao

pe

ven

tu,

id eft, refponfio ad quæftiones centum de fancta Dei lege.

Catechifmus eft in quo doctrina Chriftiana ferè tota per quæftiones & refponfa. Auctor Sacerdos è Societate Jefu. Volumen 1.

CXXI.

Cin

kiao

lim

fi

cie

lo.

Confenfus Chriftianorum omnium, eos qui in religionem admittuntur, baptizari ftatim oportere.

Tractatus eft de baptifmi neceffitate; & differitur de Trinitate, quatenus inter baptifmi verba adhibentur Pater, Filius & Spiritus fanctus. Auctor Miffionarius Francifcanus. Volumen 1.

CXXII.

Tien

chu

xim

kiao

fiao

yn,

id eft, ad fanctam Dei legem parva introductio.

Præparatio eft ad catechifmum, in qua nimirum, auctor de cœli ac terræ creatore & de interna hominis confcientia differit. Nomen auctoris latet. Exemplaria 2. Volumina 2.

CXXIII.

Kiao

yao

fiu

lun,

id eft, oratio in formam prologi, vel

MSS. Tomus I.

præliminaris de iis quæ ad legem Dei fpectant.

Auctor elegantiffimi hujus & eximiè fculpti operis, Jefuita Sacerdos, qui, ut ad legem Dei veniat, primò creationem, deinde providentiam probat; tum ad hominis peculiarem formationem defcendit, eamque ex fcriptura defcribit. Poftea de peccato originis, atque hominis lapfu multa habet; ac tandem de vita futura loquitur, quam contra Indos & Bonzios æternam ac bonorum remunerationem ftatuit. Volumen 1.

CXXIV.

Tien

chu

xim

fiam

lio

xue.

Oratio parva de fancta Dei imagine.

Imago fumitur hîc metaphoricè: neque enim hîc ulla eft figura, fed de Chrifto ejufque actis ac prædicatione tantummodò agitur. Volumen 1.

CXXV.

Ven

xe

v

yen,

id eft, viginti quinque verba.

Oratio eft parvula, in qua de hominis felicitate, religionum differentia ac difcretione contra Bonzios difputatur. Auctor hujus celebris ille *Riccius*. Liber vero impreffus, imperante Van-lie. Volumen 1.

CXXVI.

U

xe

yen

yu,

id eft, quinquaginta verba nimis.

Scilicet ad verba Riccii referuntur alius Socii Jefuitæ verba, fi viginti quinque non fuerint fatis, quinquaginta dubio procul fuperflua effent. Multa hîc plena pietatis, tum ex Evangelio verfa, tum ex aliis libris defumta. Volumen 1.

F f f

CXXVII.

Pien
hio
y
tu to.

Difputatio fcientifica, & fcriptura teftamenti loco relicta.

Tractatus eft de Deo, & de religione
Chriftiana adversùs fectas Sinarum, ac præcipuè fectam Foe. Volumen 1.

CXXVIII.

Tie
cui
chim
kuei,

id eft, lavandi peccata rectæ leges.

Tractatus eft de baptifmo & pœnitentia,
& hinc de religione Chriftiana generatim,
tum de pœnitentia, qua poft baptifmum ad
conciliandam Dei benevolentiam utimur.
Auctor, qui è Societate Jefu, poftquam
in præfatione de fide egit, diftinctis in varias
fpecies gentis humanæ peccatis, allatifque
tum ex morali difciplina, tum ex religione
Chriftiana auxiliis, quæ ad varia hominum
delicta fpectant, ea fusè perfequitur. Volumen 1.

CXXIX.

Pie
vam,

id eft, falfitas contradictionis, feu aperta
falfitas.

Tractatulus contra infernum Foiftarum,
quem auctor omnibus modis exagitat,
quoad durationem, quoad locum, &c.
Volumen 1.

CXXX.

Ta
ke
ven,

id eft, refponfiones extraneorum quæftio-
nibus, feu Sinis hæc vel illa adversùs religionem Chriftianam objicientibus.

Cum ergo adverfentur non rarò Sinæ
litterati Chriftianis advenis, differentiam
inter fectas Sinicas & religionem Chriftianam non magnam effe contendentes, neque hanc illis fuperiorem videri, propterea
quòd communia habeant multa; refutat
auctor hujufmodi objectiones; illarumque

falfitatem, hujus veritatem confirmat.
Exemplaria 3. volumen 1.

CXXXI.

San
xan
lun
hio
ki,

id eft, recitatio, feu commemoratio trium
montium inter fe difputantium.

Tres montes, proverbium quoddam eft
apud Sinas, idque è Sinarum fabulis ortum,
in quibus nominantur etiam eorumdem
montium reges, & regum tria nomina.
Vide inter Bignonianos n.° 42. Liber à
Jefuita compofitus. Exemplaria 2. volumen 1.

CXXXII.

Liber fculptus apud Sinas (in quo etiam
characteres quidam Sinici & Tartari) infcriptus.

Brevis relatio eorum quæ fpectant ad
declarationem Sinarum imperatoris Kam-hi
circa cœli, Confucii & avorum cultum;
accedunt primatum, doctiffimorumque virorum & antiquiffimæ traditionis teftimo-
nia. Opera PP. Societatis Jefu, Pekimi pro
Evangelii propagatione laborantium.

Librum ipfum fi quis infpexerit, agit
totus de cultu cœli, Confucii, avorum;
de facrificiis in eorum templo fieri folitis,
quæ nonnifi politica effe contendunt auctores, adducuntque ex multis Sinarum &
præfertim antiquorum Sinarum libris tefti-
monia, ex quibus xam ti & tien voces à
Sinis Dei fignificatione acceptas volunt.
Exemplaria 2. volumina 2.

CXXXIII.

Xin
fu
lo,

id eft, diligentis cogitationis affenfus, feu
ingenii acutè & accuratè cogitantis, affenfus.

Liber totus de xam ti & controverfiis
Sinicis. Auctor Miffionarius, eorum fcilicet
ex familia, qui vocantur Hoei-kiao. Vide
ergo quæ affert de xam ti, de tien, aliifque vocibus, olim inter Chriftianos com-
munibus, nunc cautiùs ufurpari folitis; ex
quo fcilicet natæ illæ quæftiones, de queis
differere noftrum non eft, præfertim hoc
loco. Vidimus jam opera in eam rem plurima. Volumen 1.

CXXXIV.

Chim

hio

licu

xe,

id eft, index (Gallicè *Pierre de touche*) rectæ fcientiæ.

Liber eft à Francifcano compofitus de vera religionis Chriftianæ fcientia; & eas præcipuè quæftiones tractat, quæ controverfias in Sina moverunt, an tien chu, feu Deus dici poffit tai kie, an Deus dici poffit xam ti, an him tien, an li 'ki, &c. Capitum eft paucorum, fed ea de re multa habet lectu digna. Volumen 1.

CXXXV.

Yum

fo

tien

kiu,

id eft, æternæ felicitatis (ac) cœli viæ, feu modus, quo ad felicitatem æternam ac cœlum pervenire quis poffit.

Opus de fide Chriftiana variifque ejus articulis, idque juxta ordinem fymboli. Auctor Francifcanus. Volumina 2.

CXXXVI.

Xim

kiao

kien

yao,

id eft, fanctæ legis profpectus & fcopus.

Auctor, qui Miffionariorum extraneorum unus, de iis agit generatim, quæ ad Dei cognitionem, creationem mundi, hominis formationem, animæ immortalis conditionem, fidei fubftantiam, &c. pertinent; refutatque fectarum ac præcipuè fectæ Foeanæ errores. Liber impreffus fub Kamhi, & optimè. Volumen 1.

CXXXVII.

Tien

chu

kiao

yao,

id eft, fcopus religionis Chriftianæ.

Opufculum in quo *Pater, Ave, Credo* & aliæ quædam preces. Volumen 1.

MSS. Tomus I.

CXXXVIII.

Mo

lai

pien

lun.

Oratio in qua probatur diftinctionem nondum veniffe. Senfus eft homines his in terris vivere nunc permixtos, & bonos unà cum malis ita confundi, ut diftingui non poffint; fed eventurum aliquando judicium, quo omnes aut omnia difcernentur. Volumen 1.

CXXXIX.

Tien

chu

xim

kiao

kim

gin, jin

him

xe,

id eft, eorum, qui fanctam Dei legem prædicarunt, virorum opera & actiones, feu vita.

Hîc videre eft, ut in cæteris libris, quantùm Sinæ extrancorum nomina detorqueant; vix ac ne vix quidem cognofci poffunt, qui hîc nuncupantur Apoftoli. Auctor Sacerdos è Societate Jefu. Vol.

Libri Sinici fcriptura Tunquinenfi.

RELIGIO TUNQUIN.

CXL.

Meditationes de Dominicis primæ claffis.

CXLI.

Vita beatæ Virginis; Sinicè, fed fcriptura Tunquinenfi. Volumen 1.

CXLII.

Vita fancti Ignatii; Sinicè, fed fcriptura Tunquinenfi.

CXLIII.

Quæftiones de articulis fidei, fcriptura Tunquinenfi. Tom. 1.

CXLIV.

Tractatus de pietate erga parentes.

CXLV.

Secundus liber confolationum.

F ff ij

C X L V I.

Tien
chu
xim
niu.

Vita fanctarum Domini mulierum, charactere Tunquinenfi. Volumen 1.

C X L V I I.

Meditationes ad tempus Pafchæ; fcriptura Tunquinenfi. Volumen 1.

C X L V I I I.

Examen peccatorum ad examen confcientiæ, eorum præfertim quæ homo contra fe ipfe admittit. Volumen 1.

C X L I X.

De vita Chrifti, liber fecundus.
De vita Chrifti, liber tertius.
Item de vita Chrifti, tom. 4. 7. 8.
Nonus liber de vita Chrifti ex Evangelio.
Decimus liber de vita Chrifti.

C L.

Liber ἀκέφαλος, fed ut ex fequentibus patet, ecclefiafticus, atque etiam officiorum divinorum pars; charactere Tunquinenfi. Fuit olim Tunquinenfis cujufdam, vocati Francifco. Volumen 1.

C L I.

Libri Tunquinenfis pars tertia, qui quidem liber videtur militis cujufdam vita. Volumen 1.

C L I I.

Liber Tunquinenfis, omnino mutilus & ἀκέφαλος, de religione tamen. Volumen 1.

C L I I I.

Vitæ fanctorum variis voluminibus confcriptæ.

1. volumen.	1.	Januarii.
1. volumen.	2.	Februarii.
1. volumen.	3.	Martii.
1. volumen.	4.	Aprilis.
1. volumen.	5.	Maii.
Deeft	6.	Junii.
1. volumen.	7.	Julii.
1. volumen.	8.	Augufti.
1. volumen.	9.	Septembris.
1. volumen.	10.	Octobris.
1. volumen.	11.	Novembris.
1. volumen.	12.	Decembris.

Itaque volumina 11.

I V.°

Libri Sinici à Domino LA BRETECHE Li-tu, apud Cantones Confule, in urbe Nan-kim, Regis nomine empti, & in Galliam miffi anno 1723.

HISTORIA.

CODEX PRIMUS.

Cu
chi
tum
kien,

id eft, fpeculum univerfale, in quo repræfentantur magnorum virorum res geftæ; unde difci poteft ars regnandi. Vide primùm quæ annotavimus ad regios n.° 1. 2. 3. 4. ad Bignonianos n.° 2. 3. & ad Miffionariorum extraneorum codices n.° 7. 8.

Hæc nova librorum Sinicorum collectio, ftatim exhibet his quinque primis articulis hiftoriæ Sinicæ totius monumenta ampliffima, & annales, quales fupra defcripfimus, perfectiffimos: & præterea ferè quæcumque ad eofdem annales illuftrandos pertinent. Porro adeft primùm hiftoria eo quem vides titulo; fed hîc, ut in fuperioribus, tituli funt tres. 1.° Cu chi tum kien. 2.° Cu chi tum kien kam mo, id eft, additio ad principia fpeculi. 3.° Su cu chi tum kien kam mo Hîc de primo tantum agitur. Volumina 128.

I I.

Cien
pien
cu
chi
tum
kien,

id eft, ad partium anteriorum eventus aut res geftas fpeculum; quod eft de rebus antiquitus geftis, & temporibus hiftoriæ tum kien

CODICES MANUSCRIPTI. 413

vocatæ initia antecedentibus, speculum itidem administrationi accommodatum.

Auctor operis, ut alibi diximus, *Kin-gin-xan*, qui Ivenidarum ætate annales per annos 1930. ab Yao nempe ad Guei-lievam, una serie contexuit. Involucrum 1. volumina 10.

I I I.

Cu		Su
chi		cu
tum		chi
kien	&	tum
kam		kien
mo		kam
chim		mo.
pien.		

Partes sunt annalium; altera in qua de ordine eventuum ac chronologia disseritur. Involucra 8. volumina 80. Altera in qua res novæ ac prætermissæ congeruntur. In-lucra 3. volumina 30.

I V.

Tum
kien
ki
su,

渃 tum kien, seu historiæ chronica, quæ eo tantùm tendunt, ut res gestas, ad suum unamquamque tempus revocent. Unde alium quoque titulum præ se ferunt, nempe mim ki, &c. elucidationes. Impressus hic liber regnante Xun-xi, 渃 Kam-hi decessore. Involucra 2. volumina 20.

V.

Sum
yven
tum
kien,

seu historia imperatorum è familiis Sum & Yven, Sum per annos 320. ab anno Christi 960. ad annum 1279. Yven seu Ginguiskanidarum per annos 88. ab anno Christi 1280. ad annum 1367. Porro hic liber pertinet etiam ad annales, eisque vulgò subjungitur. Auctor fuit *Xao-kia-xan*, regnante 渃 Mim familia. Involucra 3. volumina 30.

Nunc corpus quoddam est historiæ Sinicæ, quod dicitur nien ye su, quasi historici 21. Vidisti autem ea historiæ monumenta quæ generalia sunt, & tempora Sinicæ gentis ferè omnia complectuntur, fuimusque hîc breviores ideo, quia de annalibus sigillatim, idque amplissimè ad regios & Bignonianos codices diximus. Præcesserunt igitur opera quinque magna; nunc per ordinem cætera indicabimus, ac primùm quidem de su ki, id est, memoriis historicorum agendum est.

V I.

Su
ki,

id est, memoriæ historicæ.

Atque hæc est historia trium priorum familiarum, nempe 1.° familiæ Hia-chao, quam per annos 441. ab anno scilicet 2207. ante æram vulgarem, ad annum 1767. regnasse didicimus. 2.° Familiæ Xam seu Yn, quæ per annos 644. id est, ab anno 1766. ante Christum, ad annum 1123. viguit. 3.° Denique familiæ Cheu, quæ per annos 874. id est, ab anno ante Christum 1122. ad annum 249. principatum tenuit. Incipit ergo ab Hoam-ti quidem, sed 渃 Yao diluvium atque ejusdem inundationes supponit. Reperias ibi præterea quæcumque ad cycli ab Hoam-ti inventi confirmationem pertinent, eaque sat fusè exposita. Auctor est *Su-ma-cien*, cujus stylum & elegantiam prædicant Sinæ; sed additi postea commentarii à *Su-ma-chim*, qui ad Fohi usque ascendit, ac proinde 渃 Hoam-ti, Xao-hao, Chuen-hio, Ti-ko, Yao & Xim monumenta admittit. Involucra 2. volumina 14.

V I I.

Cien
han
xu,

id est, historia 渃 Cien-han, seu 渃 Han anteriorum; idque propter 渃 Heu-han, quos videbis postea inter U-tai post annum Christi 906.

Tota est hæc historia de familia quinta, seu Han-chao, quæ regnavit annis 425. ab anno scilicet 206. ante æram vulgarem, ad annum ejusdem æræ 219. Auctor *Puon-ku*, qui scripsit familia 渃 Han Orientalium regnante annis post Christum 1000. Porro impressio eadem quæ in historia 渃 Cheu; sed hæc ubique notis illustrata est charactere minutiori. Involucra 3. volumina 22.

F f f iij

VIII.

San

xue

xu,

id eſt, hiſtoria trium regnorum.

Scilicet 𝒞𝑖ς Han prioribus deturbatis, anno poſt Chriſtum 219. imperium in tres partes diviſum eſt. Regna igitur fuerunt tria; ſed eorum maximum ſeptentrionale; quare & ipſe liber in tres quoque partes diſtributus eſt, quarum prima de Goei. Secunda, de U. Tertia, de Gin vel Cho. De Goei ſunt kiven 30. de U vel Gu 20. de Cho vel Gin 15. Auctor appellatur *Chim-xeu;* vixit ſub Cin anterioribus, poſt annum Chriſti 264. Iuvolucrum 1. volumina 10.

IX.

Cin

xu.

Hiſtoria hæc tota eſt de Cin-chao, ſeu eorum imperatorum familia qui ab anno Chriſti 265. ad annum 419. regnaverunt. Nec confundendi ſunt cum cin illis, qui 𝑇𝑢 Cheu ſucceſſores fuerunt; alio enim charactere ſcribuntur: unde priores ab auctoribus Europæis vulgò per I-cin, poſteriores verò per Y-cin ſcribi ſolent. Hujus hiſtoriæ auctor *Tam-tai-cum,* 𝑇𝑢 Tam dynaſtiæ ſecundus fundator, qui vivebat anno Chriſti 627. Involucra 3. volumina 26.

X.

Sum

xu,

id eſt, res geſtæ à Sum imperatoribus.

Sunt autem ii ſeptem, qui è priori familia Sum, ab anno Chriſti 419. & per annos 59. regnaverunt. Differt autem ab alia illa hiſtoria quæ inſcribitur etiam Sum xu, & eſt Sum poſteriorum. Involucra 2. volumina 20.

XI.

Pe

ci

xu,

id eſt, res geſtæ Pekimi.

Ab imperatoribus ſcilicet familiæ Ci ſeptentrionalibus per annos 23. quos duravit Ci-chao, ab anno Chriſti 479. ad annum 502. inter parvum Sum-chao &

Leam-chao. Auctor *So-cu-hien,* vixit regnante familia Tam. Involucrum 1. volumina 8.

XII.

Nan

ci

xu,

id eſt, res geſtæ Nankimi.

Ab imperatoribus ſcilicet familiæ Ci meridionalibus, eodem tempore. Auctor idem. Involucrum 1. volumina 8.

XIII.

Leam

chin

xu,

id eſt, hiſtoria rerum à 𝒞𝑖ς Leam & à 𝒞𝑖ς Chin geſtarum.

Imperatores Leam vocati, quæ eſt familia decima, regnarunt per annos 55. ab anno Chriſti 500. vel 502. ad annum 555. Eos autem ſecuti & comitati ſunt, qui è familia Chin, ita ut horum anni non computentur, & in annis 24. 𝑇𝑢 Ven-ti & 𝒞𝑖ς Leam 2. comprehendantur. Auctor *Tiao-ſu-lien,* qui nonniſi familia Tam regnante ſcripſit. Involucrum 1. volumina 13.

XIV.

Pe

ſu,

id eſt, hiſtoria ſeptentrionalis.

Seu res geſtæ Pekimi, cum imperio diviſo ſederent illic imperatores Nankimenſium adverſarii, quod factum eſt præſertim 𝑇𝑢 Leam & Chin temporibus. Multa præterea ibi reperias, quæ ad peculiarem urbis Pekimi hiſtoriam pertineant. Auctor *Li-yen-xeu,* vixit poſt annum Chriſti 618. & ſcripſit ſub imperatoribus Tam. Involucra 3. volumina 26.

XV.

Nan

ſu,

id eſt, hiſtoria meridionalis. Hîc enim Nan intelligitur & de meridie & de Nankimo, quæ urbs regia meridionalis.

Eſt etiam hæc hiſtoria illorum eorumdem tcmporum quæ à Ci-chao ad Tam-chao effluxerunt, nempe ab anno Chriſti 479 ad annum 618. Volumen primum eſt de Ci, volumen ſecundum de Chin, &c.

CODICES MANUSCRIPTI. 415

Et vocantur Ci-puen-ki, Chin-puen-ki, id eſt, hiſtoria peculiaris 國 Ci, hiſtoria peculiaris 國 Chin: cætera ejuſdem libri volumina alium præ ſe ferunt titulum, nempe Lie-chuen, quaſi dicas, commentarius rerum diſpoſitivus, & diſſertationes ſunt in omnem ætatis illius hiſtoriam; in quibus proinde genealogiæ quamplurimæ & ſumma rerum geſtarum cognitio. Volumen ultimum totum eſt de inſula Hai-nan. Auctor idem *Li-yen-xeu*. Involucra 2. volumina 15.

XVI.

Sui
xu,

id eſt, hiſtoria 國 Sui.

Norunt qui hiſtoriam Sinicam legunt, imperatores Sui 帝 Leam & Chin ſuccefſiſſe annis poſt Chriſtum 581. nec plures quàm tres regnaſſe, Ven-ti ſcilicet, Yam-ti, & Kum-ti. Eorum tamen hiſtoria eſt longa ſatis & ad inſtar præcedentium digeſta, adeo ut hiſtoria 國 Sui præeat, ſequantur commentarius & genealogiæ. Auctor *Gueichim*, vixit ſub 國 Tam dynaſtia. Involucra 2. volumina 16.

XVII.

Tam
xu,

id eſt, hiſtoria 國 Tam.

Dynaſtia hæc ab anno Chriſti 618. ad annum 906. per annos 289. regnavit. In primo volumine imperatorum ejus omnium ſeries genealogica exhibetur; itidem in fine ſui cuique imperatori anni criticè aſſeruntur. Auctor *Ngeu-yam-ſieu*, vixit regnante familia Sum. Involucra 4. volumina 43.

XVIII.

U
tai,

id eſt, magnates quinque.

Per u tai, ſeu magnates quinque, intelliguntur ii, qui poſt familiam 國 Tam imperium rexerunt, idque per annos 53. ab anno Chriſti 906. ad annum 959 Vocantur autem illi quinque Heu-leam, Heu-tam, Heu-cyn, Heu-han, Heu cheu. Hîc autem duo etiam reperiuntur 1.° quidem uniuſcujuſque familiæ monumenta & hiſtoriæ. 2.° verò rerum geſtarum diſpoſitio & quaſi concordia. Initium ducitur à 帝

Leam per capita 5. Sequuntur Heu-tam per capita 2. Poſtea Cyn quorum in Sankue præceſſit Cyn-chao per capita 2. Succedunt Heu-han per caput 1. Denique habentur Heu-cheu per caput 1. Quæ omnia titulum præ ſe ferunt Puen-ki. In commentario eadem reperias ſed multò uberiora, & unà cum genealogiis ampliſſimis. Occurrunt ergo:

1.° Familiæ Leam ſeries, quæ eſt perſonarum 19.

2.° Familia 國 Heu-tam, quæ eſt perſonarum 39.

3.° Familia 國 Cyn, quæ eſt 18.

4.° Familia 國 Heu-han, quæ eſt 5.

5.° Familia 國 Heu-cheu, quæ eſt 19.

Adduntur qui poſtea fuerunt inter vaſſallos ſeu ſubditos, & miſcellanea de iiſdem familiis plurima. Auctor idem *Ngeu-yam-ſieu*. Involucrum 1. volumina 7.

XIX.

Heu
han
xu,

id eſt, hiſtoria 國 Han poſteriorum, cum generali 國 U-tai nomine.

Indicantur dynaſtiæ illæ quinque 國 Heu-han dictæ, quæ nonniſi unum imperatorem vulgò exhibent; ſed plerique ætatis illius turbulentæ imperatores unà ſimul regnarunt, dum ſeries temporum ab hoc aut illo deſumta eſt. Itaque in ordine imperatorum Sinenſium hîc deſignatur tantùm Kao-cu, ſed in hoc de 帝 Heu-han volumine nominantur ſeptem, & quindecim imperatrices quarum facta memorantur. Adduntur præterea res numero propè infinitæ hiſtoricæ ac geographicæ, quas inter de eclipſi lunæ tunc obſervata fit mentio. Duæ ſunt & hujus hiſtoriæ partes, ſicut & præcedentium, quarum prima imperatorum res geſtas & propriè hiſtoriam continet, altera in eandem hiſtoriam commentarios. Auctor *Fan-hoa*, vixit ſub 帝 Sum anterioribus poſt annum Chriſti 420. ſed notæ & ſcholia auctorem habent *Kao-cu*, primum 國 Tam-chao imperatorem. Involucra 2. volumina 18.

XX.

Cheu
xu,

id eſt, hiſtoria 國 Cheu.

Hæc hiſtoria, quæ propriè 後周 Heu-cheu, ad eos imperatores ſpectat, qui ex antiqua 周 priorum Cheu familia anno Chriſti 351. ſolium etiam ipſi recuperarunt. Deſcendebant autem, juxta auctorem, non ſolùm à veteribus Cheu, quorum fundator Vuvam, ſed ab ipſo Xin-num, cujus nomini, inde ab ipſius Fohi temporibus, reverentia ſemper habita eſt. Porro in hoc libro genealogiæ ſunt temporum ferè omnium ampliſſimæ, ſed cum de ætatibus agatur remotiſſimis, rebus obſcuris, unicuique capiti inſeruntur notæ criticæ ac diſſertationes, præter morem, cum in cæteris hiſtoricorum libris conciliatio & concordia ad finem remittatur. Auctor *Lin-kua-te-fuen,* vixit regnantibus τῆς Sum, poſt annum Chriſti 960. Involucrum 1. volumina 8.

XXI.

Hum
kien
lu,

id eſt, rerum hiſtoriæ Sinicæ appenſarum & adjungendarum, ac ſelectarum ſelecta deſcriptio.

Scilicet cum ſub 大明 Ta-mim finem libri hiſtorici quamplurimi ſubito incendio combuſti eſſent, timuerunt imperatores ne hiſtoriæ univerſæ noceret ejuſmodi incendium: itaque ut damnum reſarciretur, nominati ab ipſis quidam viri eruditi è Sinis doctoribus, qui hiſtorias deperditas hinc inde colligerent, atque in compendium redigerent: adeo ut hoc opus dynaſtias novem repræſentet, nimirum τῆς U-tai, τῆς Sum, τῆς Leao, τῆς Kin. Unde hoc hiſtoriæ Sinicæ acceſſit ſupplementum maximum; auctæ enim priores ſex, poſteriores duæ additæ, quæ duæ nonniſi obiter deſcriptæ illuc uſque fuerant. Opus ergo eſt longè maximum & ſummè neceſſarium, cum ea addat de Leao & Kin, id eſt, de Altunchanis, Ginguiskanidis aliiſque ejuſmodi Tartaris, quæ hiſtorici noſtri attigere paululùm, ſed fruſtra alibi requiras, ea qua par eſt abundantia. In primo volumine pro more occurrunt genealogiæ regnorum illorum omnium ampliſſimæ & accuratiſſimæ. Auctor *Chao-kim-pam.* Vide præf. 3. Impreſſio vero procurata anno τῷ Kam-hi 27. Involucra 7. volumina 64.

XXII.

So
hum
kien
lu,

id eſt, additiones ad librum Hum-kien-lu, ſed aliud etiam nomen præ ſe ferunt, ſcilicet Yven ſu luy pien; id eſt, rerum in hiſtoria 元 Yven inæqualium ac difficilium ordinatio.

Notum eſt hodie omnibus poſt Ginguiskami mortem, ei ſucceſſiſſe Cublai Kamum, & ejuſdem Cublai ætate, cum nempe bella unà cum Sinis præſertim Nankinenſibus gereret, ad ea loca acceſſiſſe Marcum Paulum Venetum, adeoque cum ſeditione belliſque, propter Tartorum irruptionem ferverent omnia, eſſentque apud Sinas hinc imperatores Sinenſes, illinc Ginguiskami ſucceſſores & qui τῷ Cublai opitulabantur. Neque verò abs re eſt quod titulum ejuſmodi libro ſuo auctor Sina, cui nomen *Cin-vam,* præfixerit; continet enim tomus primus (videbis etiam penultimum) regum ſeu imperatorum Tartarorum genealogias. Involucra 2. volumina 26.

XXIII.

Hoam
mim
ſu
kai.

Hæc eſt hiſtoria 大明 Ta-mim quaſi compendiaria, quod titulo innuitur, cujus ſenſus eſt hiſtoriam 大明 Ta-mim imperatorum immenſam eſſe, ad hoc tamen compendium poſſe redigi; hîc enim res geſtæ imperatorum hujus familiæ omnium, ab Humvu ad ultimum uſque breviter exhibentur; quorum catalogum voluminis primi pars continet, cætera hiſtoriam complectuntur.

Sed nota eum quem vides titulum nonniſi generalem eſſe, & opus totum idque unum, ex auctoris mente in partes diviſum eſſe quinque, unde exurgunt libri etiam quinque. Primus ergo liber, ſeu prima pars operis inſcribitur hoam mim ſu kai; ſed in primæ partis capite titulus interior eſt, hoam mim ta chim ki, id eſt, 皇明 hoam mim, imperatorum Mim magnarum rerum geſtarum, ſeu rerum regiè ac magnificè geſtarum memoriæ vel hiſtoriæ. In hoc libro rerum militiæ ac domi geſtarum narratio

ſimplex

fimplex ac ferè nuda; attamen liber eft fat ponderofus. Involucrum 1. volumina 12.

XXIV.

Secundus liber, feu fecunda pars operis infcribitur

> hoam
> mim
> ta
> hiun
> ki,

id eft, leges ab imperatoribus dynaftiæ Mim viris latæ: nam vocis hiun hæc fignificatio propria, ut viris non feminis adaptetur.

Eft igitur fecundus ifte liber quafi codex legum per omne 朝 Mim tempus latarum, nec recedit auctor ab eodem regnorum ordine, unde hic novus idemque imperatorum catalogus. Sed quod maximè obfervandum, quæcumque ad libros & litteraturam, fi ita loqui fas eft, pertinent, ea cæteris ubique antepofita videre eft; ita ut ab ipfis etiam imperatoribus, non folùm hi aut illi libri, fed hujus vel illius operis præfationes emanaffe dicantur. Involucrum 1. volumina 7.

XXV.

Tertius liber, feu tertia pars operis infcribitur

> hoam
> mim
> tai
> fu
> ki,

id eft, operum à magnificentiffima 朝 Ta-mim dynaftia factorum aut conftructorum hiftoria.

Hîc reperias breviter collecta ea, quæ per omnes Sinici imperii provincias, regnantibus Ta-mim, facta, conftructa, ftabilita, ræædificata funt: quæ ad canales, ad flumina, ad fluvios, ad fontes, ad lacus, ad hofpitia Mandarinorum, ad præfidia militum, ad urbes bellicas, ad collegia, &c. pertinent.

XXVI.

Liber quartus, feu pars quarta operis infcribitur
MSS. Tomus I.

> hoam
> mim
> kai
> kue
> chin
> chuen,

id eft, commentatio hiftorica, in qua oftenditur quomodo vaffallos & regna extranea aperuerint, id eft, agreffi occuparint dynaftiæ Mim, magni imperatores.

Hîc agitur de bellis à Mim geftis, five internis, ut vaffalli ad obedientiam redigerentur, five externis, ut hoftes debellarentur. Præmittitur ducum ac vaffallorum enumeratio campliffima. Involucrum 1. volumina 6.

XXVII.

Quintus denique liber, feu quinta pars operis infcribitur

> hoam
> mim
> fun
> kue
> chin
> chuen,

id eft, commentatio hiftorica, in qua oftenditur quomodo regna quædam & vaffalli quidam magnificæ 朝 Ta-mim dynaftiæ per fe ipfi, nullo cogente ac libentiffimè obedientiam jurarint ac præftiterint.

Pars hæc eodem involucro includitur, & tomos continet tantùm duos.

Atque hoc eft rerum ab Hum-vu, & fequentibus imperatoribus geftarum compendium. Auctor unus è fummis Mandarinis.

XXVIII.

> Ta
> mim
> hoei
> tien,

quafi dicas, codices quibus ea omnia, quæ ad imperatorum è familia Ta-mim dynaftias pertinent, continentur.

Jam inter codices Miffionariorum Extraneorum n.º 5.º vidifti codicem qui eundem præ fe ferret titulum, & effet volum. 10. fed nihili ifte eft, fi cum eo, de quo nunc agimus libro, contuleris. Hic enim liber opus eft vaftiffimum, in quo habes quidquid à magnis illis imperatoribus geftum

Ggg

eft, leges eorum omnes, quo tempore, quam ob caufam latæ; fi quæ in quindecim provinciis factæ mutationes, fi qua templa ædificata; item tribunalium omnium ordinem, urbium omnium, præfertim Pekimi & Nankimi πολιτείαν quoad magiftratus & fumma tribunalia; quicumque non folùm in iifdem urbibus, fed etiam per omne imperium magiftratum exercuerunt. Præterea quicumque duces exercituum, quicumque militiæ in urbibus & provinciis præfecti; uno verbo, omnes omnino magiftratus omnium omnino urbium primi, fecundi & tertii ordinis: imò & pagorum & arcium fingularum. Itidem enumerationes templorum, collegiorum, Sacerdotum, adeoque earum quæ in Sina regia auctoritate probantur religionum cultus, obfervationes, ipfas etiam ad unumquemque Deum orationes. Denique litteratorum omnium nomina ac lucubrationes. Unde colligas in nulla unquam gente, tantam tamque accuratam rerum ferè omnium defcriptionem factam effe. Involucra 8. volumina magna in folio 60.

XXIX.

Van
fim
tum
pu,

id eft, omnium cognominum epitome, & liber genealogicus.

Ad hiftoriam quoque pertinet hoc opus, quod Sinarum ferè omnium genealogias complectitur; magnorum quidem virorum præcipuè nomina vitafque, quanquam breviufculè, repræfentat, idque in omnibus facultatibus, litteratorum fcilicet, imperatorum, ducum, artificum illuftrium, veluti poëtarum muficorum, architectorum, fabrorum, &c. Sic de Fohi, Niu-va & de San-tai, feu tribus primis familiis, Hia-xam & Cheu, de 漢 Cheu & Cyn profapia, &c. Sed his non contentus auctor, nominum etiam combinationes maximè ufitatas, quolibet tempore & in variis provinciis, per characteres & characterum inter fe conjunctiones, imò fæpe per varios tonos expendit. Ordo idem ferè per omnes libri partes, præter quam in prima, ubi eft virorum celeberrimorum enumeratio. Nam in cæteris nomina per primum faltem characterem, non rarò per duos fimilia exhibentur; ita ut dictionarii hiftorici loco effe poffit. Indicat vero fuo nomine viri uniufcujufque patriam, fæpe

parentes & cognatos, fi fuerint illuftres, opera atque ætatem, id eft, fæculum, ubinam & quonam regnante quifque vixerit. Auctor *Lie-tai-ti-vam.* Liber peffimè impreffus. Involucra 4. volumina 40.

XXX.

Kue
yu
kue
ce,

id eft, fermones de regno; regni libri.

Is eft vulgaris hujus operis titulus, fed in fronte additur:

Pam
yun
fo
puen,

id eft, unà cum expofitione laterali & additionibus fingularibus.

Agunt hi libelli de imperio & optimo imperii adminiftrandi modo, quem exemplis ex hiftoria antiqua petitis confirmant. Antiquiffimi funt, quippe quos fub 漢 Han dynaftia extitiffe, imò & antiquos tunc temporis creditos effe conftat; cum fub iifdem Han à Lieu-hiam revifi ac recogniti fint. Eorum auctores ignorantur. Hæc vero editio Kam-hi regnante procurata eft, anno ejus 24. Involucrum 1. volumina 3.

PHILOSOPHIA.
XXXI.

Chu
cu
civen
xu,

id eft, 書 chu cu librorum collectio.

Atque hic eft horumce librorum titulus generalis, fed opus ipfum veluti triplex, & unumquodque peculiari quodam gaudet titulo.

Primum nempe infcribitur

yven
kim,

quafi dicas, abyffi fpeculum, feu fpeculum quo in abyffum penetrare poffimus, id eft, in cor humanum.

Ita infcripfit fuos in Ta-hio, aut generatim in Su-xu commentarios doctor Chuven-kum; huc verò philofophiæ ferè omnis quafi compendium contulit; namque agit, idque fat fusè, de poëfi, de officiis, de mufica, de naturæ ratione, de ratione per univerfum diffufa; præterea de Lun-yu, de Mem-cu, de Chum-yum per volumina 4. Tum librum Ye-kim affumit volum. 5. 6. 7. Poftea de familia Xam differit; nimirum de Y-yn & Cheu-kum, cujus ultimi extant commentationes in Ye-kim. Imò tractat de auctoribus quibufdam aliis antiquiffimis, aut qui res manifeftò antiquiffimas fcripferunt, ut Lie-tai de quo fupra. Scriptum hoc 㸚 Chu-hi, feu Chu-ven-kum, involucrorum eft 4. voluminum 40.

XXXII.

Secundum opus infcribitur

mo   additiones ad
gan.   Chu-hi.

Hoc fecundum opus continet mifcellanea itidem philofophica; ubi fæpe in utramque partem difputatur liberrimè, pro more Sinarum Philofophorum. Involucra 5. volumina 50.

XXXIII.

Tertium opus infcribitur

tum

pien,

id eft, fimilium & differentium.

Atque illud eft tertium 㸚 Chu-hi opus, illudque latiffimum, in quo fcilicet infinita funt quæ tum ad antiquitatis notitiam, tum ad Philofophorum dogmata fpectant; ita ut propter has lucubrationes 㸚 Chu-hi, vel Chu-ven-kum hominem quafi cœlitus delapfum Sinæ fufpexerint. Hoc ultimum opus eft involucrorum 3. voluminum 26. fed fpifforum.

XXXIV.

Cin

tai

mi

xu,

id eft, 㸚 Mi-xu porta draconis tacta & cuftodita.

Hic titulus ex Sinarum fabulis defumtus eft: fingunt enim locum beatitudinis ac veræ fcientiæ & vitæ undequaque circumfeptum atque ab immenfæ magnitudinis dracone cuftoditum, ne quis impius, five, ut aiunt, non adeptus, ingrediatur; unde qui in arte magna, feu lapide illo philofophico inquirendo operam ponunt, quod & à Sinis

factitatur, illi eidem arti tenebras & caliginem folent offundere. Sed quemadmodum apud Cabaliftas, five noftros, five Hebræos & Mahummedanos, fub arcanorum nomine exponuntur quæftiones philofophicæ, theologicæ & hiftoricæ numero propè infinitæ, ita & hìc apud magnum hunc Cabaliftam, feu potiùs Cabaliftas, nam collectio eft, innumera artis & naturæ miracula reperiuntur. Opus per fe quafi immenfum, cum partium fit quindecim magnarum. Involucra 20. volumina 163.

XXXV.

Vam

yam

mim

ven

cie,

id eft, 㸚 Vam-yam-mim operum collectio.

Mifcellanea funt philofophica, feu hiftorico-philofophica, in articulos breves quidem, fed quingentos circiter divifa; in quibus de antiquis libris & hiftoricis liberè ác criticè differitur. Reperias ibidem ex antiquis monumentis excerpta, & multa de quorumdam regum hiftoria, ac Philofophorum illuftriorum vita & moribus nova; imò de hoc vel illo hiftoriæ articulo, quem vel antiquat Philofophus, vel calculo fuo confirmat. Auctor *Vam-yam-mim,* vixit regnante 㸚 Mim illuftri familia. Involucra 2. volumina 16.

XXXVI.

Han

goei

cum

xu,

id eft, opufculorum 㸚 Han & 㸚 Goei ætatibus editorum collectio, feu coacervatio.

In hanc collectionem contributa opera quædam, non ampla quidem, fed à magnis viris aut elaborata, aut recuperata, è quibus in antiquorum Sinarum doctrinam atque artes redundat non exigua lux. Multa ergo illic de Cheu-kum, de Tai-kia, de Tai-pe, de Y-yn, aliifque quamplurimis aut colais, aut doctoribus; quocirca in voluminis ferè uniufcujufque capite præfatiunculæ funt, quæ de unoquoque opufculo, quodnam fit, & unde venerit, doceant. Auctor collectionis *Tu-lum,* idque 㸚 Mim tempore. Involucra 5. volumina 60.

MSS. Tomus I.

XXXVII.

Yu
chi
fim
li
ta
civen
xu,

id eft, librorum de naturæ ratione philofophicorum magna collectio; eaque impreffionis imperialis. Auctores Mandarini ex
collegio Han-lin. Vide quæ ad regios codices annotavimus n. 18. Invol. 4. vol. 42.

XXXVIII.

Sim
li
ta
civen
hoei
tum,

id eft, collectionis librorum de natura
totius collectio generalis & perfecta; feu
quod idem eft, quæcumque ad intelligen-
dos 㪠 fim li ta civen libros omnes facere
poffunt, unà fimul congregata.

Liber idem editionis alius antiquioris:
eft enim fub dynaftia 㸠 Mim, imperium
tenente Yum-lo procurata. Auctores iidem
Mandarini collegii Han-lin. Vide itidem
codices regios n. 18. Involucra 4. volumina 34.

XXXIX.

Sim
li
hoei
tum,

id eft, 㪠 fim li, feu librorum de natura,
feu phyfica, philofophicorum collectio ge-
neralior. Involucrum 1. volumina 16.

XL.

Sim
li
goei
yao,

id eft, variarum quæ in fim li continentur
opinionum brevis collectio & fcopus.

Auctor *Cheu-hoai*; editio 㸠 Mim temporibus & fub Cum-chim procurata. In-
lucrum 1. volumina 9.

XLI.

Chu
cu
hum
cao,

id eft, 㷌 chu cu vocum magnarum, feu
acutè & fententiosè dictarum, compofitio
& collectio rhetoricè ornata.

Apophthegmata funt veterum, præfertim magnorum imperatorum, litteratorum
ac philofophorum. Liber verè elegans, bre-
vitatifque & fagacitatis laude admirabilis.
Incipit à Ven-vam, & auctor, quifquis
fuerit, videtur 㸠 Lao-fu fectæ favifle. Involucrum 1. volumina 6.

MATHEMATICI.

XLII.

Tien
ven
ta
chim,

id eft, cœli fcientiæ magnum opus; quafi
dicas almageftum.

Agitur enim præcipuè de aftronomia &
aftrologia, quæ fcientiæ apud Orientales
imò apud antiquos omnes ferè conjungun-
tur. Hîc figuras videre eft multas globorum,
aftrorum, planetarum, folis, lunæ, &c. In
primo volumine, poft præfationes, catalogus
eft & enumeratio eorum qui apud Sinas
obfervandis aftris operam dedere omnium,
& funt, ut minimum quid dicam, quingenti.
Tum fequitur rerum aftronomiæ & aftro-
logiæ fubjectarum index propè infinitus.
Auctor *Hoam-lo-gan,* aliàs *Hoam-tim-yo-
ulh,* vulgò *Hoam-tim-yo.* Involucra 2.
volumina 24.

XLIII.

Cem
pu
fuon
fa
tum
cum
civen
xu,

id eft, collectio librorum ad generales numerandi regulas facientium.

Tractatuli funt complures, breves &
mutili, de antiqua Sinarum arithmetica.
Involucrum 1. volumina 4.

CODICES MANUSCRIPTI. 421

MEDICI.

XLIV.

Puen

cao

kam

mo,

id eft, principia neceffaria ad proprietates herbarum cognofcendas.

Vide regios codices n.° 27. & fequentibus. Bignonianos n.° 19. Hîc involucra 4. volumina 40.

LIBRI SACRI ET CANONICI.

Tredecim libri fequentes commentarii funt, vulgò infcripti xe fan kim, vulgò vocati kim, & referuntur inter canonicos, quanquam eorum aliqui non fint canonici. Sunt autem ita compofiti, ut in plerifque commentarius fit & paraphrafis.

XLV.

Primus infcribitur

chcu

ye,

id eft, Ye 書 Cheu, aut à Cheu-kum olim illuftratus.

Hic liber primùm unà cum interpretatione editus à *Vam-pi,* fub 書 Gocy dynaftia, poftea cum paraphrafi à *Kum-yn-ta,* regnantibus Tam. Involucrum 1. volumina 6.

XLVI.

Secundus infcribitur

xam

xu

kim,

id eft, liber xu kim 書 Xam, feu qualis à dynaftia Xam traditus eft; vel libri xu kim editio magnifica.

Hæc eft editio 書 xu kim unà cum paraphrafi, cujus auctor *Kum-xi,* qui vixit fub dynaftia 書 Han; & præterea cum interpretatione ejufdem *Kum-yn-ta,* de quo fuperiùs. Additur in plerifque commentarius alius vocatus chuen. Involucrum 1. volumina 8.

XLVII.

Tertius infcribitur

mao

xi

chu

fu

id eft, xi kim unà cum commentario, cujus auctor *Chim-xi,* & paraphrafi cujus auctor *Kum-yn-ta,* quorum prior fub Han, pofterior fub Tam fcripfit. Involucrum 1. volum. 20.

XLVIII.

Quartus infcribitur

chun

cieu

co

chuen,

id eft, liber chun cieu, feu veris & autumni, cujus auctor *Confucius,* commentariis ad marginem illuftratus.

In hoc autem libro reperitur etiam commentarius cujus auctor *Kum-yn-ta;* & paraphrafis cujus auctor *Hihi-ku,* qui fub Han fcripfit. Involucra 3. volumina 30.

XLIX.

Quintus infcribitur

ku   ku

leam *aliàs* leam

kim   chuen.

Opus aliud etiam in eundem chun cieu, cum commentario & paraphrafi. Commentarii auctor *Fan-yu-chi,* paraphrafis verò *Yam-lu-hum.* Porro hic liber videtur imperfectus. Involucrum 1. volumina 6.

L.

Sextus infcribitur

chun

cieu

kum

yam

chuen.

Commentarius 書 kum yam in chun cieu. Auctor commentarii *Tu-xi,* qui fub Cyn vixit; paraphrafis verò *Kum-yn-ta.* Involucrum 1. volumina 12.

LI.

Septimus infcribitur

cheu

li.

Liber de ritibus Sinarum antiquiffimus, commentario & paraphrafi ornatus. Commentarius auctorem habet *Chim-xi,* qui regnantibus Han vixit; paraphrafis verò *Kum-yen-fm,* qui regnantibus Tam. Impreffus autem liber ifte fub Cum-chin, anno ejus 12. Involucrum 1. volumina 9.

Ggg iij

L I I.

Octavus infcribitur

li

ki.

Liber li ki, de quo vide inter regios codices n.° 15. & 16. unà cum commentario
τȣ Chim-xi, qui fcripfit regnantibus Han, &
paraphrafi τȣ Kum-yn-ta, de quo fuperiùs.
Involucra 3. volumina 28.

L I I I.

Nonus infcribitur

y

li.

Commentarii auctor Chim-xi, de quo
fæpiùs diximus, paraphrafis verò Kia-kum-
yen, qui fub Tam fcripfit. Involucra 2. volumina 14.

L I V.

Decimus infcribitur

ulh

hia,

id eft, ulh hia ad aurium fenfum recta
pronuntiatio.

Dictionarii nefcio quid, fine ullo characterum ordine; ita ut hunc vel illum characterem & querere & reperire fit difficillimum,
cum phrafes potiùs quædam explicatæ,
quàm verum dictionarium aut vocabularium effe videatur : cui præterea nullus
index fit additus. Commentatorem habuit
Kuo pu, fub Cyn, paraphraften verò Na-
pim, fub Sum. Unde colligas librum effe
antiquum. Involucrum 1. volumina 4.

L V.

Undecimus infcribitur

hiao

kim,

de obedientia filiali. Vide inter regios n.°
47. inter Bignonianos n.° 17. inter codices
Miffion. n.° 38. Auctor fuit Na-pim, de
quo fupra, & vixit fub Sum. Involucrum 1.
volumen 1.

L V I.

Duodecimus infcribitur •

lun

yu.

Commentatores Ho-yen, fub dynaftia

Goey, & Na-pim fub Sum. Involucrum
hujus & fequentis idem eft, fed volumina 4.

L V I I.

Decimus tertius

mem

cu,

de quo vide codices regios. Hujus commentatores Chao-xi. fub Han, & Fan-xe
fub Sum. Volumina 8.

Atque hæc funt volumina nuncupata
Xe-fan-kim, libri tredecim, quòd revera
pulcra fint. Character quidem exiguus, fed
nitidiffimus.

L V I I I.

Cheu

ye

che

chum,

id eft, τȣ ye Cheu (ye à Cheu tràditi) media
compenfata, feu fufficientibus commentariis repleta & illuftrata.

Commentarius eft ampliffimus, ultimis
τȣ Kam-hi annis elaboratus, idque à doctoribus collegii Han-lin, & præfide magno
Co-lao, feu primo miniftro Li-kuam-ti.
Textus Ye-kim eminet, ac litteris majoribus impreffus eft. Commentarii minori quidem charactere & littera quafi pendente ac
fufpenfa, fed perfpicua fatis, & quæ lineas
characteris uniufcujufque repræfentet optimè. Commentatio ubique triplex & qua-
dratis nigris, littera alba indicatur. Involucrum 1. volumina 12.

L I X.

Ye

kim

ta

civen,

id eft, τȣ ye kim, feu libri mutationum &
combinationum, itemque commentariorum in eundem librum exaratorum magna
collectio.

De ye kim non dicendum amplius, cum
de eo ad codices regios n.° 6. 7. 8. 9. fatis
egerimus. Editio autem hæc à collegii Han-
lin Mandarinis procurata eft, Kam-hi ju-
bente atque infpectore. Titulus generalis
eft U-kim-ta-civen, 五經 U-kim magna
collectio : & revera in prima præfatione ejufdem mentio fit tanquam fecundæ commentariorum à Chu-cu, aliàs Chu-hi fcriptorum

CODICES MANUSCRIPTI. 423

editionis; sed hoc ideo factum quòd Ye-kim in capite esse soleat. Quòd autem dicatur Cheu-ye, allusio est, ut dixi, ad Ye-kim, vel tanquam ab antiquissima familia Cheu traditum, vel quòd in Yc-kim commentarios ediderit Cheu-kum. Commentatores hujus libri fuerunt sub Sum, *Hu-gan-tim* & *Hu-kim-kum:* sub Mim, *Xu-hum-yo, Yam-xi-kiao, Lieu-yven-van* & *Cham-cu-chum:* sub Cim, seu dynastia hodierna, *Vam-hum-chen,* qui figuras τȣ̃ Ye-kim explicare conatus est; denique Ho kim doctores τȣ̃ Han-lin, inspectore Li-kuam-ti ministro. Involucrum 1. volumina 12.

L X.

Xu

kim

ta

civen,

id est, τȣ̃ xu kim magna collectio, à collegio Han-lin procurata, idque auctoritate regia & sub τοῖς Ta-mim (quod indicatur hîc, ut alibi sæpiùs, charactere Hoam) sed denuò edita sub Kam-hi.

In hac autem collectione magna reperias præfationes complures, in quibus de antiquissimis temporibus agitur, nempe de primis imperii Sinici habitatoribus, de vetustissimis scriptoribus, &c. tum ad Cheu-kim atque illius ætatis doctores descenditur, quos excipiunt alii innumerabiles. Postea disserunt auctores de Philosophis Confucio, Memcio, de viris doctis qui sub Han vixere. Tum multa addunt de Chu-hi, & iis qui sub τοῖς Sum vixerunt scriptoribus. Præfationibus succedit catalogus ferè immensus eorum, qui xu kim commentati sunt, auctorum: additur præterea τȣ̃ Hoam-ti genealogia & tabulæ aliæ quamplurimæ, sive orbis terrarum, qualis tunc fingebatur, sive variorum instrumentorum, à primis illis Sinis inventorum. Sed vide quæ de xu-kim annotavi ad codices regios n.° 10. 11. 12. ad Bignonianos n.° 7. Involucrum 1. volumina 10.

L X I.

Xi

kim

ta

civen,

id est, odarum libri collectio magna, seu quæ commentarios etiam repræsentat.

Præter textum & commentarium, reperiuntur in hac collectione præfationes multorum auctorum, quos inter *Chu-hi;* figuræ rerum, de quibus odæ, mirabilium; catalogi denique cum eorum qui in xi kim scripserunt auctorum, tum eorum, de quibus oda unaquæque intelligitur, imperatorum. Porro textus semper eminet, sed nulla distinctus virgula, sicut & commentarius; quod incommodum non leve. Editio tamen Kam-hi tempore prodiit. Vide ad regios codices n.° 13. 14. Invol. 1. vol. 10.

L X I I.

Li		li
ki		ki
ki	& interius	cie
ta		xue
		ta
civen,		civen,

id est, magna τȣ̃ li ki, seu libri de ritibus collectio, unà cum distinctione orationum.

Auctor hujus editionis vocabatur *Chin-hao.* De li ki vide codices regios n.° 15. & 16. Accesserunt commentatorum, rerum & editionum indices. Invol. 1. vol. 16.

L X I I I.

Chun

cieu

ta

civen,

id est, libri à Confucio editi, & veris atque autumni nomine inscripti, collectio magna, sive unà cum variorum commentariis.

Quid sit chun cieu habes ad codices regios n.° 5. inter libros historicos, quia liber est historicus. Hîc verò eo posuimus ordine, quo à Sinis ponitur. Editus est sub Kam-hi, interprete *Fum-mum-sum.* In primo volumine habes indicem rerum amplissimum, imò ordinationem chronologicam, cum mappa geographica locorum in chun cieu memoratorum. Invol. 2. vol. 8.

L X I V.

Y

li

kim

chuen

tum

kiai,

id est, commentariorum y li explicatio generalis.

Inter xe fan kim n.° 9. habes y li kim, unà cum paraphrafi & commentario fub Han & Tam fcriptis. Hîc commentariorum eorumdem & aliorum poftea fcriptorum enarrationes vides ampliffimas, idque ex traditionibus, quòd indicat vox chuen, hoc loco ufurpata. Accefferunt præfationes plurimæ, in quibus de antiqua Sinarum adminiftratione & variorum, quæ intra Sinam funt, regnorum ritibus differitur. Poft volumen 6. alius occurrit titulus nempe y li cie chuen, id eft, 理 y li fectionum & articulorum partitio, quæ per 7.ᵘᵐ & 8.ᵘᵐ volumina continuatur. Involucrum 1. tituli 2. volumina 8.

L X V.

Y
li
kim
chuen
tum
kiai
fu fo,

id eft, ad expofitiones commentariorum ac traditionum in y li kim additiones ac fupplementa.

In hoc libro declaratio eft rerum ferè omnium & vitæ officiorum, imò & quæ ad religiones ac fuperftitiones Sinicas fpectant. Illic ergo leges quæcumque de xam ti, de fole, luna & ftellis, de variis terræ atque aliarum naturæ partium fpiritibus, de facrificiis ab imperatore cœlo & terræ faciendis, Sinæ & noviffimè & antiquitus cogitarunt. Vide interim quæ de li ki annotavi ad codices regios n.° 15.& 16. ad Bignonianos n.° 14. Involucra 2. volumina 16.

LIBRI CLASSICI.

L X V I.

Su
xu
chu
cu
y
tum
tiao
pien,

id eft, librorum quatuor loca differentia & fimilia à Chu hi notata & conciliata.

Eft ergo editio librorum Confucii à Mem-cu, unà cum concordia *Chu-yen-kum*, feu Chu-hi concinnata, cujus procurator Li-poei-lin, imperante Kam-hi, anno ejus 44. Chu-cu, ut fæpe diximus, vivebat fub 宋 Sum dynaftia. Involucra 2. quorum prius libros ta hio & chum yum continet; pofterius librum Mem-cu folum; deeft lun yu. Volumina 14.

L X V I I.

Cham
ko
lao
che
kiai,

id eft, 四 co lao cham textus librorum quatuor explicatio fincera.

Auctor ergo hujus explicationis *Chamkiu-chim*, qui primus regni adminifter imperantibus Ta-mim. In 1.° volumine eft ta hio; in 2°. chum yum; in 3.° 4. 5. 6. 7. 8. lun yu; in 9.° denique & cæteris Mem-cu. Involucra 2. volumina 16.

L X V I I I.

Kum
xi
kia
yu,

de familia & domo Confucii oratio, feu de Confucio ejufque verbis & apophthegmatibus liber, in quo vita Confucii tota licet breviter; ac præterea ejus fcientia moralis, imò & de elementis ac natura, opiniones. Involucrum 1. volumina 4.

LIBRI SECTARUM TAO.

L X I X.

Lao
cu
cie
kiai,

explicatio articulorum 老 Lao-cu.

Lao kiun, Lao-cu, Lao-tan idem, quem hominem nunquam extitiffe quidam putarunt: fed revera & philofophus & fectæ auctor fuit, qui vitam hanc & 老 Lao-tan articulos fcripfit. Ta-nim-kiu libros ejus omnes ad duo capita revocat, quorum unum tao kim dictum fit, five de norma morum, alterum te kim, five de vera virtute. Sed hi libri breviffimi & per fententias tantummodo propofiti, adeoque antiquitatem quandam

quandam redolent. Alter eorum in primo volumine, alter in fecundo. Invol. 1. vol. 2.

LXX.

Cu
cu
pim
lin,

id eft, το Cu-cu difceptationum fylva.

Auctor hujus libri *Cu-cu,* philofophus antiquiffimus, Scepticus, breviter & magna cum libertate fcripfit, ita ut fenfus ejus non fint cuilibet obvii: quam ob caufam ab interprete *Chu-hi* illuftratus eft & reprehenfus, fub imperatoribus Sum. Unde in unoquoque volumine index primò fefe offert articulorum in volumine expenforum à Cu-cu & à Chu-hi expendendorum. Involucrum 1. volumina 4.

LXXI.

Cie
xe
ulh
kia
pim
chu
cu
cu,

de verbo ad verbum, feptuaginta domus, feu fectas exponere & explicare idem.

Senfus eft, Cu-cu auctorem effe obfcuriffimum, & in eo enucleando jam defudaffe interpretes feptuaginta, quorum nominantur duodecim. Hujus libri editor dicitur *Li-lu-xi,* imperante Kam-hi. Involucrum 1. volumina 4.

LXXII.

Cu
cu
tem,

id eft, lampas το Cu-cu, feu ad illuftrandum το Cu-cu librum.

Interpres *Lin-fi-chum,* qui τοῖς Cyn regnantibus vixiffe dicitur. Invol. 1. vol. 2.

LXXIII.

Choam
cu
nan
hoa
kim,

id eft, το Choam-cu liber dictus flos meridionalis; ea enim Orientali more interpretatio eft.

MSS. Tomus I.

Hic liber nominis apud Sinas maximi à *Choam-cu* fuit compofitus, qui è Tao-kia, feu το Tao-fu fchola. Porro quatuor libros philofophi Sinæ, licet alius alia de caufa, magni femper fecerunt; fcilicet tao te kim & nan hoa kim de homine interiori, & quafi ab hujus mundi vanitate ad virtutem fublimiorem converfo; Li-fao de quo idem dicendum; denique nan hoa kim de quo nunc agitur, quique commentatores habuit plurimos, præfertim verò *Fu-me* & *Lu-fi-fim,* fub dynaftia 明 Mim. Involucrum 1. volumina 4.

LXXIV.

Choam
cu
yn.

Explicatio eft το nan hoa kim; explicaturque imprimis quid fit apud Sinas tien tao & vita interior; tum de virtute & variis virtutis gradibus agitur. Commentator *Lin-fi-chum,* qui Kam-hi regnante fcripfit. Involucrum 1. volumina 4.

LXXV.

Choam
cu
kiai,

id eft, το Choam-cu expofitio.

Interpretes duo funt, *Cie-fan-cieu* & *Kuo-fiam:* differunt præfertim de vita interiori & exteriori. Hic liber impreffus Kam-hi regnante. Involucrum 1. volumina 3.

LIBRI GRAMMATICI.
DICTIONARIA.
LXXVI.

Hiven
kim
cu
luy.

Dictionarium idem quod inter regios codices n.° 48. & Miffion. 52. Vulgatiffimus auctor *Muy-tan* feu *Muy-yn,* qui fub 唐 Tamim dynaftia. Involucra 2. volumina 14.

LXXVII.

Pin
cu
cien,

Habes dictionarium Sinicum maximum,
H h h

ordine facili ac fecundùm fenfus communes & analogiæ characterum Sinicorum leges difpofitum. Porro hujus tres funt partes, in prima quidem parte reperias tractatus qui characterum naturam explicent, claves fimplices ac multiplices doceant, characteres clavium ambiguarum oftendant, &c. In fecunda; omnium omnino characterum catalogum, juxta clavium 214. ordinem; quæ pars eft voluminum duorum magnorum, nec à cu luy chim cu tum illic propriè differt. In tertia denique iidem characteres omnino omnes per fectiones ac tonos difponuntur, fed juxta pronuntiationum ac tonorum fimilitudinem; ita ut fectiones fint totidem quot toni, ac totidem quot monofyllaba hujus vel illius pronunciationis. Unde fit ut characteres fimilis pronunciationis, uno eodemque loco fint; ac præterea quorum partes, lineis clavium exceptis, funt fimiles, eamque ob caufam unà fimul comparere debent, ii characteres unà cum fimilibus repræfententur. Hujus dictionarii à me nunc cu guei, propter primam ejus partem, nunc pin cu cien, quæ vulgaris appellatio eft, nuncupati dotes profecto eximiæ. Cum non folùm ad pronunciationes monofyllaborum Sinicorum omnium, fed etiam ad confonantias in verfificatione reperiendas manifeftò inferviat. Auctor tanti operis *Yu-ven-cu*. Invol. folet effe unum, fed volumina funt 9. quorum duo præfationes & catalogum ex cu guei & chim cu tum ordine, feptem alia eorumdem characterum catalogum ex pronunciationum ac tonorum ordine exhibent. Ordo tamen inter confonantias alius eft in alia editione.

L X X V I I I.

Chim

cu

tum.

Non repetam quæ dixi ad codices regios n.º 49. Addam tantummodò hujus libri auctorem vocari *Leao-pe-cu,* & varias prodiiffe editiones; alias quidem characterum elegantia pulcherrimas, alias verò editorum negligentia viliffimas. Invol. 4. vol. 40.

L X X I X.

Kam

hi

cu

tien.

Atque illud eft doctiffimi imperatoris Kam-hi dictionarium, quod ex omnibus litteraturæ monumentis voluit colligi. Habes itaque in hoc uno opere quidquid ad characterum, five legendorum facilitatem, five intelligendorum regulas conferre poteft. Unde cæteris anteponendum: nam hai pien, de quo inter regios codices n.º 51. quanquam maximum, attamen non tantum characterum numerum, nec tam varias difcendi methodos exhibet; quæcumque enim poftea à doctoribus repertæ, aut breviores, aut faciliores, eæ omnes in hoc eruditiffimi imperatoris dictionarium funt contributæ. Sed de fingulis ejus partibus vide meditationes Sinicas. Involucra 4. volumina 40.

L X X X.

Cu

hio

cin

leam,

id eft, portæ draconis pons ad characterum fcientiam.

Metaphora eft è Sinarum fabulis defumta ad difficultatem rerum indicandam, feu potiùs ut difficultates ab aliquo fuperatæ dicantur. Etenim verò liber eft totus de characteribus laxis, contortis, truncatis ac liberè & fine debito linearum numero fcriptis, qui propterea & fcriptu & lectu difficillimi; quales non rarò in præfationibus, plerumque in fignis, in veteribus monumentis, in cippis quibufdam, in chue ven, item, ut diximus, in chim cu tum reperiuntur. Cæterùm unicuique characteri liberè ac fine veris lineis fcripto ad latus character vulgaris adfcribitur, ut ea comparatione, qui difficilior ac rarior eft, cognofcatur. Auctor hujus operis per fe intricatiffimi *Fu-yn-kuei*. Involucrum 1. volumina 4.

L X X X I.

Ku

y

ven.

Dictionarium aliud characterum antiquorum, in quo & character antiquus, & qui nunc in ufu oftenduntur. Auctor *Chu-men-goei*. Involucrum 1. volumina 2.

L X X X I I.

Chim

yun

tum,

id eft, modus comprehendendorum characterum optimus.

CODICES MANUSCRIPTI. 427

Dictionarium eft, quod etfi ad linguæ cognitionem pertineat, attamen ad verfificationem propriè accommodatum eft. Vide meditationes Sinicas. Involucrum 1. volumina 8.

LXXXIII.

Hiu

xi

xue

ven.

Dictionarium eft characterum antiquorum, auctore *Hiu-xi*. Vide regios codices n.° 50. Involucrum 1. volumina 6.

LXXXIV.

Chuen

cu

lui,

id eft, characterum chuen (vulgò chuen vocatorum) collectio.

Hic etiam de veterum Sinarum contortis quibufdam ac neglectis characteribus agitur. Primò quidem præmittitur præfatio de horumce characterum natura & origine.

Sequuntur claves 214. juxta cæterorum dictionariorum ordinem. Denique per totum dictionarium comparent characteres explicandi aut potiùs monftrandi: in hoc enim auctor incumbit, non ut hujus vel illius characteris fignificationes aperiat, fed ut, qui in cu guei, vel cu luy characteres inveniuntur, eofdem hoc & illo modo ab antiquis fcriptos fuiffe indicet, qui quidem characteres in alio poftea dictionario quærendi funt. Involucrum 1. volumina 6.

LXXXV.

Chuen

cù

cao

xu,

id eft, litteræ cao five herbarum, feu ab herbarum fimilitudine defumtæ.

De litteris & characteribus, quos Sinæ ab herbarum & plantarum imagine & fimilitudine mutuati funt, agitur apud Kirkerum in China illuftrata, libro 5.° Tales autem funt qui in hoc dictionario repræfentantur characteres Sinici. Volumen 1.

V.°

Libri Sinici annis 1728. & fequentibus ad annum ufque 1732. à R. P. Premaro empti, & ad illuftriffimum Abbatem Bignon dono miffi.

HISTORICI.

CODEX PRIMUS.

Yu

chi

pe

kia.

Nomina familiarum Sinicarum ab ipfo imperatore in ordinem digefta. Volumen 1.

II.

Ngheu

yam

fieu

ven

cie,

id eft, collectio fcriptorum 魏 Ngheu-yam-fieu.

MSS. Tomus I.

Hic auctor elegantiffimus, & judicii acerrimi hiftoriam compofuit 唐 Tam & U-tai; data vero occafione de antiquis Kim & multis aliis auctoribus loquitur fæpiffimè. Vixit fub imperatoribus Sum, poft annum Chrifti 960. Involucra 2. ex panno admirabili. Volumina 24.

III.

Ku

ke

niu

chuen,

id eft, feminarum aut mulierum illuftrium vitæ & commemoratio.

Præfationes funt quamplurimæ, eæque omnes de feminis earumque virtutibus; fed pleræque characteres exhibent variarum fcripturarum antiquarum, quas nonnifi in dictionariis difficillimis reperias, quod per oftentationem ab auctore factum judicant

Hhh ij

Sinarum prudentiſſimi. Mulieres autem illuſtres fermè ad 130. memorantur, quarum laudes ita perſequitur, ut ad unamquamque rerum ab ipſa geſtarum imagines appingat. Involucrum 1. volumina 4.

I V.

Lo   lu

chin

chu

ven

ſuen

& brevius

ven

ſuen,

id eſt, numerus ſeu collectio variorum eloquentiæ operum, quæ inter ſex vaſſallos edita 朝 Leam ætate.

Præfationes libri hujus plurimæ, tum à variis editoribus, tum à principe ipſo Chaomim concinnatæ, in quibus de tota collectione ac præcipuè de ſcriptoribus agitur. Sequitur eorumdem ſcriptorum enumeratio accuratiſſima, quos auctor in poëtas, philoſophos, politicos, &c. diſpertitur: atque ut in partes ſuas diſtingueretur oratio unaquæque, aut unumquodque poëmatium, additæ ſunt in pleriſque notæ commatum. Auctor fuit, ſeu potiùs collector *Chao-mim*, qui familiæ Leam hæres regius. Editio facta ſub Van-lie. Involucra 2. volumina 20. eaque magna & ſpiſſa.

LIBRI SACRI.

V.

Cheu

ye,

id eſt, ye 朝 Cheu, ſeu à *Cheu-kum* olim commentario illuſtratus, unà cum notis 孔 *Kum-yn-ta*, &c. Hujus editionis characteres non magni ſed nitidiſſimi, & liber 朝 xeſan-kim primus. Vide ſupra n.° 45. Involucrum 1. volumina 6.

V I.

Yu

chi

cheu

ye

che

chum;

id eſt, Cheu-ye, ſeu Ye-kim 朝 Cheu,

è typographia imperiali, unà cum annotationibus.

Editio hæc longè pulcherrima ac nitidiſſima, & chartæ multò majoris quàm cæteræ; in qua textus characteribus maximis, indicationes verò commentariorum characteribus albis in fundo nigro diſtinguuntur. Hæc tamen editio ad Kuven nondum attingit, cum illic characteres ſint recti, hîc verò proni atque ad ſcripturam accedant propiùs. Involucra 2. ex panno ſerico, floribus ornatiſſima. Volumina 10.

V I I.

Xam

xu,

id eſt, liber xu kim.

Editio magnifica, quod jam obſervavimus ad xe ſan n.° 46. Involucrum 1. volumina 8.

V I I I.

Mao

xi

chu

ſu,

id eſt, xi kim commentarius illuſtratus.

Editio pulcherrima. Idem verò liber habetur ſupra n.° 47. Involucra hujus 2. volumina 20.

I X.

Tu

xi

civen

cie,

id eſt, 詩 xi kim, ſeu libri odarum omnes partes à *Tu*, aliàs *Li,* aliàs *Li-kin* commentariis illuſtratæ.

Editio nova, in qua indices multi cum odarum, tum eorum qui in eaſdem odas ſcripſerunt auctorum; ac præterea rerum ac perſonarum, de quibus in iiſdem facta eſt mentio, additus eſt novus index chronologicus. Involucrum 1. volumina 12.

X.

Cheu

li,

id eſt, li kim 朝 Cheu; cui additi commentarii & paraphraſes auctoribus *Kumyen,* &c. Vide quæ ſupra annotavimus in xe ſan kim n.° 51. Involucra 2. volumina 16.

X I.

Li
ki
chim
y,

id eſt, τᾶ li ki verus ſenſus.

Habet hic liber commentarios τᾶ *Kum-yn-ta;* idemque eſt qui ſupra inter xe ſan. Involucra 2. volumina 24.

X I I.

Y
li,

id eſt, liber y li, in quo ſenſus τᾶ Li-ki aperitur, unà cum novo commentario.

Idem qui impreſſus eſt inter xe ſan n.° 9. Vide ſupra n.° 53. Involucrum 1. volumina 12.

X I I I.

Chun
cieu
co
chuen,

id eſt, ver & autumnus, ſeu opus Confucii ita vocatum, unà cum annotationibus & commentariis à latere ſiniſtro poſitis.

Commentarii ſunt variorum ac præcipuè *Kum-yn-ta.* Involucra 2. volumina 24.

X I V.

Chun
cieu
ku
leam & ulh
chuen ya,

id eſt, liber Chun-cieu, unà cum annotationibus τᾶ *Ku-leam.*

Vide inter xe ſan n.° 49. involucrum 1. volumina 6. ſed quibus ſubjungitur ejuſdem τᾶ xe ſan ultimum opus, quod vocavimus ulh ya, & dictionarium eſt antiquum. Vide ibidem n.° 54. Ejuſdem eſt involucri cum ſuperiori, & voluminum 2.

X V.

Chun
cieu
kum
yam
chuen,

Alius eſt commentarius in Chun-cieu,

de quo etiam ſupra inter xe ſan n.° 50. quem vide. Involucrum 1. volumina 10.

LIBRI CLASSICI.

X V I.

Mem
cu
lun
yu
&
Hiao
kim,

id eſt, liber τᾶ Mem-cu, liber Lun-yu & liber Yao-kim, ejuſdem editionis & unà ſimul compacti. Involucrum 1. volumina verò τᾶ Mem-cu 6. τᾶ Lun-yu 4. τᾶ Hiao-kim 1.

P H I L O S O P H I C I.

X V I I.

Sim
li
hoei
tum,

id eſt, τᾶ ſim li, ſeu eorum qui ſim li, ſeu ſcientiam naturalem aut phyſicam componunt, librorum collectio generalis.

Facta eſt ſub Ta-mim, regnante Yum lo. Idem verò liber qui ſupra n.° 39. Vide & n.ᵘᵐ 38. Item inter regios codices quod diximus de ſim li generatim n.° 18. 19. inter libros Miſſion. n.° 26. 27. 30. Involucrum 1. volumina 14.

X V I I I.

Sim
li
ta
civen
hoei
tum.

Philoſophiæ ſeu potiùs phyſicæ & eorum, quæ ad phyſicam pertinent operum, collectio ampliſſima.

Idem liber eſt qui ſupra n.° 39. in libris è Sina anno *1723.* allatis. Vide & inter regios codices n.° 18. Involucra 2. volumina 40.

Hhh iij

LIBRI SECTARUM.

XIX.

Cu
cu
pim
lin,

id eft; 㦡 Cu-cu difceptationum fylva.

Idem liber eft qui inter codices anno 1723. è Sina allatos n. 70. aliter verò compactus. Auctor *Cu-cu*, de quo jam diximus, philofophus propter obfcuritatem ac libertatem in Sina clariffimus. Involucrum 1. vol.

PHILOLOGICI.

XX.

Kam
hi
cu
tien,

id eft, magna 㦡 Kam-hi, feu imperatoris Kam-hi juffu procurata, characterum collectio.

Liber idem qui fupra n.° 79. Involucra 4. volumina 40.

XXI.

Xan
hai
kim.

Liber eft de maribus & montibus, in quo multa, ut videtur, fabulofa, certè obfcura. Hinc quæ à poëtis in poëmatibus plerumque ufurpantur, omnia ferè defumta. Auctor ipfe antiquus, nunc ignotus. Commentarii in xan hai kim multi; interpretes verò *Ngin-te-chim* & *Kno-pu.* Volumen 1. fat magnum & fpiffum.

PHILOLOGICI COMICI.

XXII.

Yven
gin
ca
ki (kie)
pe
chum,

id eft, hiftoriæ ludicræ aut tragico-comœdiæ centum, quæ fub dynaftia 㦡 Yven actæ.

Divifæ funt in partes quatuor, quarum in prima 22. in fecunda 25. in tertia 26. in quarta denique 27. tragico-comœdiæ continentur. Initio voluminis præmittitur index modorum, five ejus cantus, quo unaquæque tragico-comœdia (cantilenæ fcilicet actibus infertæ) cantillabatur. Tum fequitur pictura multiplex, quali nimirum decorari fcenam unamquamque oporteat. Involucra 4. volumina 40.

XXIII.

Si
fiam
ki
   &
pi
pa
ki,

id eft, comœdiæ Sinicæ, quarum auctores *Si-fiam* & *Pipa*. Si-fiam eft voluminum 3. & Pipa 3. Sed ambo in uno eodemque involucro.

PHILOLOGICI.

XXV.

Chuen
cu
luy
mo,

id eft, characterum antiquorum variæ fpecies ac confpectus.

Dictionarium eft, in quo collecti funt ii omnes modi, quibus unquam fcripti funt characteres Sinici. Obfervatus autem ordo 㦡 pu, id eft, tribunalium aut clavium. Character vulgaris & qui nunc in ufu, quadrato continetur: tum afferuntur fcriptiones variæ olim ufitatæ, quarum in capite apparent eæ quæ in xue ven. Poftea adduntur fcriptiones præfertim characterum currentium, quibus fubjungitur fignificatio. Volumina 12.

XXVI.

Liber Sinicus fine infcriptione, in quo folia funt fcripturarum ferè omnium Sinicarum, quales nempe in variis, quorum mentionem feci, dictionariis reperias. Ac præterea fcripturæ Arabicæ fpecies, non illius antiquiffimæ, quæ Kuphica eft, fed Mauritanicæ, quæ Kuphicæ apud Africanos fucceffit. Volumen 1.

CODICES MANUSCRIPTI. 431

XXVII.

Lo   lu

xu,

id eft, de fex modis, quibus characteres fuos compofuere, aut componere hodie poffunt Sinæ.

Tractatus hic à *Premaro* ipfo fcriptus eft in formam dialogi, in quo characterum Sinicorum analogiam, ex ipfa earum quæ characterem conftituunt linearum confideratione, conatur elicere. Volumen 1.

RELIGIO SINICA.

XXVIII.

Xam

lun,

id eft, imperatoris Yum-chim, feu ultimi, oratio imperialis.

In hac oratione imperator fubditis fuis articulos fedecim accuratè ac diligenter meditandos proponit. Cum autem de variis imperii fectis obiter loquatur, Chriftianam religionem unà cum iis confundit; unde ftatim ejus mentem & in Chrifti cultores odium perceperunt, qui in Sina Miffionarii. Volumen 1.

XXIX.

Xim   fe

yo   chuen.

Divo Jofepho oratio panegyrica, à *Premaro* olim cum Miffionarius & juvenis effet, compofita. Volumen 1.

XXX.

Liber omnino ἀκέφαλος, fed qui tractat de agricultura & chronologia. volumina 2.

XXXI.

Folium quoddam maximum, quod lapidem xen fi, quantus repertus eft, tantum ac totum characteribus magnis exhibet; fed papyrus adeo tenuis, ut in partes quodammodo per fe abeat. Volumen 1.

XXXII.

Opufcula MSS. tria, quorum primum catechifmus eft theologicus; fecundum & tertium controverfiæ funt theologicæ de rebus in Sina difputatis: ubi etiam multa de Tao, de Yn-yam & principiis Sinarum philofophicis. Volumina 3.

XXXIII.

Hoam

ti

nui

kim.

Pars eft .69.ᵃ 的 nui kim libri & commentariorum ejus à *So-ven* editorum. Vide inter Miffion. codices n. 36.

XXXIV.

Su

xu

tum,

id eft, 的 Mem-cu fecunda pars; commentario interlineari illuftrata eft. Volumen 1.

V I.°

Libri Sinici qui Hoamgii fuerunt, & Opera poft ejus mortem reperta.

CODEX PRIMUS.

HOræ Sinicæ MSS. pelle rubra contectæ. 1. volumen in 12.

II.

Preces aliæ feparatæ. Volumina 2.

III.

Catechifmus per quæftiones & refponfa. Volumen 1.

IV.

Libellus in quo characteres aliquot cum hoc titulo *E'clairciffemens,* fed Sinicus totus. Eorum eft temporum cum ad Galliam nuper appulfus Hoamgius Gallicè difceret. Volumen 1.

V.

Volumen quoddam parvulum ac fine titulo, in quo phrafes multæ, merè Sinicæ, cifris notatæ; nimirum ut alicujus Miffionarii operibus, fortè Rofalienfis, infervirent. Volumen 1.

VI.

Libellus qui nihil aliud eft quàm regiftrum diurnale per menfes diftributum ad annum 1709. Volumen 1.

VII.

Codex parvulus, in quo nonnulla de incarnatione, qualia neophitis à Missionariis tradi solent. Volumen 1.

VIII.

Codices in quibus phrases quatuor vel quinque, vel sex, vel septem, vel etiam octo vocum & characterum, ab *Hoamgio* fortè ad usum privatum collectorum. Vol. 1.

IX.

Versio inchoata nec perfecta fabulæ cujusdam ex earum genere, quas vocamus Gallicè *Romans*. Volumen 1.

X.

Volumen quoddam MS. cui titulus *Reflexions sur l'état present de la Chine*. Responsa sunt *Hoamgii* ad quæstiones ipsi ea de re propositas. Volumen 1.

XI.

Fasciculus foliorum Sinicorum tam manuscriptorum quàm impressorum; sed sine titulo & ordine. Volumen 1.

XII.

Initium dictionarii Sinici, juxta clavium ordinem, sed in quo quædam duntaxat claves, & quidam ex illis clavibus characteres selecti. Volumen 1.

XIII.

Schedæ quædam in quibus preces quotidianæ, *Pater, Ave, Credo*. Volumen 1.

XIV.

Dialogi inter Bonzium & Missionarium, inter duos mercatores, alterum extraneum, alterum Sinensem, lingua Sinica, litteris Latinis. Volumen 1.

XV.

Nominum & verborum quorumdam catalogus, seu vocabularium, Sinicum quidem, sed Latinis litteris, quale dictionarium à *Kirkero* in fine Chinæ illustratæ editum est. Volumen 1.

XVI.

Libellus inscriptus kia hiun, &c. de gubernanda domo. Involucrum 1. vol. 6. parvula.

XVII.

Codex chartaceus, duobus constans voluminibus, quibus continetur authographum operis quod inscribitur, Confucius Sinarum Philosophus, sive scientia Sinensis. Ibi nonnulla deprehendas quæ in editis non comparent.

CODICES TARTARICI.

CODEX PRIMUS.

Volumina magna & spissa, quæ à Tartaris de historia & moribus majorum suorum composita, Tartariam ac proinde Sinam ipsam, earumdemque regionum mutationes ac bella fusè repræsentant; si tamen librorum Sinicorum quorumdam interpretationes adjunxeris. Volumina 48.

II.

Centum & tredecim volumina impressione & compactione admirabilia. In iis verò quatuor duntaxat opera continentur, sed ampla & magnifica; quorum alia videntur versiones librorum quorumdam Sinicorum, præsertim eorum qui sacri & canonici appellantur, & cæterorum qui ad vitam dirigendam & mores conformandos pertinent: alia verò sunt historica. Primi operis involucra sex serica, volumina 36. Secundi operis involucra duo serica, volumina 26. Tertii operis involucra duo serica, volumina 20. Quarti denique operis involucra quatuor serica, volumina 31. Quæ omnia volumina, si ea tamen excipias quæ in tertio involucro continentur, floribus sunt in tela ipsa pictis intertexta. Volumina 113.

III.

Dictionarium Tartaro-Sinicum, ea mente compositum, ut à Tartaris vel in Sina morantibus, vel è Tartaria in Sinam venientibus, lingua Sinica faciliùs ediscatur. Vol. 14.

IV.

Dictionarium Tartaro-Sinicum à R. P. Domingio, è Societate Jesu, in Galliam missum; sed cujus duo ferè volumina maris aqua omninò oblitteravit & corrupit mucor. Idem quod superius. Volumina 14.

V.

Catalogus Librorum Bibliothecae Regiae Sinicorum（1）

皇家图书馆藏中国图书目录（1）

PRÆFATIO.

HIC loci, poſt Catalogum Regiæ Bibliothecæ jam impreſſum, quæſtio exurget dubio procul: an non inutilis eſſe nunc debet, Catalogi ejuſdem quaſi repetitio? nequaquam, idque multis de cauſis.

1°. Primum quidem Bibliothecæ Regiæ Catalogus pretio carius quam ut eum poſſideat quivis; idcircone empturus eſt quiſquam, ut illam Librorum Sinicorum cognitionem adipiſcatur?

2°. Deinde verò, inter volumina magnitudine immenſa, qualis futurus eſt ille Librorum tot à ſe invicem & Linguis & rebus toto cælo diverſorum Catalogus, quomodo non deliteſceret particula ejuſmodi, tam neglecta hucuſque, & plærifque ad characteres & Linguam Sinicam non initiatis viſu ipſo horrida?

3°. Poſtea ſi quoad Linguas cæteras, Hebraïcam puta, Syriacam, Arabicam, characteres à manuſcriptorum notitiis abeſſe conqueſti ſunt Litterati plurimi, abſit, putent unquam, aut Orientalium characteribus caruiſſe Galliam, aut quod in Catalogis omnino ſimilibus, eoſdem adhibuerunt Batavi, Angli, Germani, *Noſtrates* id non potuiſſe, à quibus profecta Linguarum Orientalium prima cognitio eſt, quorum ſunt prima Polyglotta, inter quos vixêre Stephani, Vitræuſque, & alii complures. In hoc Regno non uſque huc defuêre Linguarum Orientalium periti, quibus committeretur Catalogi hujus *exemplarium* correctio, abſit, inquam, iſtud exiſtimetur: at, ſi quorum operâ uſus eſſe poterat, ii hoc tempore inutiles facti, ſubita hæc exceptio eſt, fuit tantum Catalogus: atqui ad diſtinguendos Codices, omnino neceſſarius non eſt character Hebraïcus, Syriacus, Arabicus, quia ex adjectis Linguarum illarum verbis, Latino licet charactere tituli uniuſcujuſque ſenſum percipere poſſunt eruditi, atque iſtud in Catalogo ſatis. Sed quî tandem ejuſmodi querelas in Libris Sinicis retundere eſſet? *Abſque characteribus* Tituli omnes ambigui, monoſyllaba omnia & *tono* & *pronunciatione* æquivoca, characteres ipſi etiam vocibus ſæpe 10, ſæpe 20, ſæpe 30, aut 35, aut 40, aut 50 correſpondentes? ita ſe rem habere, nunquis eſt hodie, qui ignoret? Sume ergo Titulum quemlibet, niſi adjunctum *characterem* habueris, non intelliges unquam, quod è noſtris Meditationibus Sinicis, è ſuperiori Grammaticâ, ex omnibus Miſſionariorum Libris, ſatis ſuperque manifeſtum.

Quamobrem, ſuffecerit ad indicandum Libri uniuſcujuſque Hebraïci, Syriaci, Chaldæi, Rabbinici, Copthici, Perſici, Indici, Tartarici titulus, quamquam res aliter magnificentior: at de *Linguâ Sinicâ*, de *Librorum Sinicorum* titulis, cave in animum id induxeris tuum, propter perpetuam illam *vocum* characteribus deſtitutarum *ambiguitatem*: Ratio hæc nequaquam tulerit.

Quæ cum ita ſint, iis, qui abſente me, inſcio me, hujuſce mei

Ssss

Librorum Sinicorum Catalogi manuſcriptum impreſſioni tradide-
runt, Viris doctiſſimis ſane & mei amantiſſimis debentur, fateor,
à me grates, quod mihi, uti ſciunt autumaruntque, graviſſimis ſtudiis occupatiſſimo pepercerint, atque ſummo eo, cui tamen à
pueritiâ aſſuefactus ſum, foliorum emendandorum labore libera-
rint.

4°. Sed quod ante augurabar, & attentè admonueram, hinc effec-
tum, ut ſchedæ omnes, ſummâ diligentiâ primùm à me conſcrip-
tæ, malè dehinc tranſcriptæ, pejus poſt hac impreſſæ, tandem
inemendatæ prodierint.

5°. Tacebo, id quod tamen capitale eſt, abbreviationis prætex-
tu, interpolata quædam, nonnulla etiam in alienum ſenſum detor-
ta, truncata multa, de queis unde quererer, cum bono animo ſint,
ab amicis, atque ut me ſublevarent, perpetratæ; hanc nihilominus
ipſam eandem ob cauſam, & quod characteribus omnino neceſſariis deſtituerentur, & quod mendæ ſubeſſent numero quàm plurimæ; edi à me denuo catalogum hunc oportere Litterati omnes cen-
ſuerunt, atque id etiam præ cæteris magnus ac ſapientiſſimus Regni Adminiſter, bonarum artium, Avis, Ataviſque potens Protec-
tor D. DE MAUREPAS.

6°. Præterea jamjam è multis Dictionariis à me tandiu & tam
impensè elaboratis imprimenda brevi ſunt, ad minimum duo:
Dictionarium id, *quod per tonos* eſt *alterum, alterum quod per claves*
ordinatur. (nam de Latino Sinico, de Gallico Sinico, de Hiſto-
rico, Geographico, aut Latino-Sinico, aut Gallico-Sinico, aliàs
cogitabimus.)

At *ſignificationum* omnium fundus Libri: Librorum cognoſcendi
Authores, Operum cognoſcenda *nomina*, & ad hoc omne, qui ad in-
digitandum Librorum numerum ſolummodo ſatis eſt, quàm inutilis
charactere Europæo Catalogus! aut ipſa Sinica ſtudia nulla erunt, aut
Sinicis characteribus aſſueſcendum. Jam verò non fruſtranei labores noſtri, Regis maximi mandato, juſſuque ſuſcepti. Quænam,
quanta, quàm vaſta ſeſe offerunt rerum ſpatia, apud Gentem ſtu-
dioſiſſimam Hiſtoriæ, Poeſeos, Philoſophiæ, Artiumque uni-
verſarum amatricem, perveſtigatricemque! Sic autem tam multiplici Scriptorum Sinarum eruditione obſtupefactus, atque unà
ſimul tam frequénti eorumdem characterum, earumdem phraſium
uſu fretus & contentus Lector, Dictionariorum Authori laborem
exemptum ſentiet earum, quas appellitant *citationum allegationum*que:
ſed nihilominus ad unumquemque characterem, & in Dictionario
clavium *claves*, & in Dictionario monoſyllaborum tonico *paginas*,
& ſi quis in aliquo Authore *character*, ſi qua in aliquo *Scriptore*
characteris alicujus *ſignificatio* peculiaris, eundem characterem
aut Scriptorem, hæc verò omnia, ut nemo non annotanda perſen-
tiſcet, ſic ſuo quodque loco ſumus, idque diligenter indicaturi.

Quapropter hæc, quam facturus ſum, Librorum Sinenſium commemoratio neceſſariò iterata, utilitatem eſt Reipublicæ Litterariæ
allatura maximam.

1°. *Catalogum* Bibliothecæ Regiæ, eâ, quâ caret, accuratione
donabit, hinc enim, eos qui non adjecti ſunt, *accentus* repono, idque exactè & ad amuſſim, illinc eam, quæ monoſyllaba Sinica nu-

da Latinis ſcripta litteris conſequitur, *ambiguitatem*, additis *cha-*
raĉteribus, tollo omnem.

2°. Qui *Catalogus* in errores de Linguâ Sinicâ non parvos indu-
ceret, ut cum aliquo fruĉtu legi poſſit, id verò efficio hodie, quod
evidens.

3°. Quæ omiſſa ſunt atque abbreviata, ea quidem à mero Catalogo abeſſe poterant, id concedo lubens, ſed adeſſe etiam : *Notitiæ*
longæ nimium : at quot Arabicæ longiores ? Hîc verò, quomodò
exiſtimabuntur αωεισδιονυσοι,? & Grammaticæ Sinicæ poſtponuntur
& præcedunt Diĉtionaria Sinica : illa verò *eruditio*, quæ tam latè
patet, quæ tàm novarum, quæ tantarum rerum parens, tempus
eſt, tandem etiam extollat caput.

Sed perpenſis attentê omnibus, illum ipſum Regiæ Bibliothecæ Catalogi ordinem, hoc non amplius ſervaturi ſumus loco :
Illîc Librorum in Bibliothecam Regiam illatorum tempora, non
unam ob cauſam, & propter *tempora* ipſa, & propter *ſtudiorum*
Sinicorum progreſſum indicavimus, (aliunde in alienas manus inci-
derant ſchedæ noſtræ, & cùm ſeparatæ, ſeparabileſque eſſent, quin
juxta materiarum ordinem ſejungerentur, impedimento fuimus
nulli.) Hîc ſecundùm rerum ſeriem, famæ ſecuri, & explicatis ex-
plicandis, eundem libentiſſimè diſponemus.

Atque ut prioris illinc *per tempora diſpoſitionis* rationem teneas, hoc
tibi ſciendum arbitramur, quamquam jam inde à ſæculis duobus
in Sinam commigraſſent Miſſionarii quamplurimi, nondum tamen
in Europam, ſaltem ad Bibliothecam Regiam allatum ullum Authorum Sinenſium opus fuiſſe.

Ante annum 1647. Libros Sinicos habebat Bibliotheca Regia
tantummodo quatuor, eoſque *Mazarinæos.*

Anno 1697. Maii 27. & Jun. 2. alios numero 49. intulit *Bouve-*
tus, cum è Sinâ reverteretur.

Anno 1720. menſe Oĉtobri, ad Regem Lud. XIV. attulit R.
P. *Fontenayus* volumina magna *duodecim*, Sinicè & Tartaricè ſcripta, aut potius Tartarica ſolummodo, Sinicis perpaucis, ad indi-
candos Librorum converſorum titulos intermixtis.

Ex variis *Cupletii* Societatis Jeſu Socii, *Piĉi* doĉtiſſimi viri in
Collegio Mazarinæo Bibliothecarii, illuſtriſſimi Germanorum in
Litteraturâ Herois *Leibnitii* aliorumque Epiſtolis, vulgatum eſt,
allatos à *Cupletio* è Sinâ, & in Bibliothecam Regiam illatos Libros
complures, ſive Sinicos, ſive Tartaricos, ſed hallucinati Scriptores illi cunĉti ; & fallitur etiam Præfationis in *Ægidii Menagii*
Etymologias Gallicas Author, dum à Cupletio Diĉtionarium Latino-Sinicum in Bibliothecâ Regiâ reliĉtum refert : Diĉtionarium
quidem Sinico-Latinum, cum è Sinâ in Galliam rediret ſecum
attuliſſe *Cupletium*, qui mos eſt Miſſionariorum, res omnino ve-
riſimilis. Sed quid accidit ? édito Pariſiis Confucio, id eſt, Libris
Confucii tribus, Ta hio, Chum yum & Lun yu Latinè tantummodo, Sinicos etiam, quos adjungi volebat, characteres imprimi in
Galliâ non poſſe animadvertit : in Belgium proinde, Germaniam-
que profeĉtus eſt, & illud ipſum Diĉtionarium, alioſque Libros,
quos alioqui Bibliothecæ Regiæ ſeſe conſecraturos non ſemel pro-
miſerat, abſtulit ſecum, & illîc in aliquo Societatis ſuæ cænobio

Ssssij

348 *PRÆFATIO.*

reliquit; quâ de re Lectores, necesse erat, monerentur: ne tantis Authoribus decepti, errasse nos in Bibliothecæ Regiæ Catalogo opinentur.

His ergo ita præmissis, Articulos præcedentis Catalogi, quorum omissa *divisio* est, ita eramus dispertiti, ut essent numero sex, & indicaremus.

1°. Quosnam ad annum 1711. primitus habuerit, sive ex Maza-rinæâ, sive à *Bouveto*, *Fontenayo* ejusque Sociis allatos.

2°. Quosnam ab illustrissimo viro *Paulo Bignonio*, etiam ante-quam Regiæ Bibliothecæ præficeretur, anno 1716. usui nostro consecratos, & postea in Regiis numeratos, acceperit.

3°. Quosnam anno 1720. agente me *Stephano Fourmontio*, Regio Arabicæ Linguæ Professore, Academico & Bibliothecæ Regiæ Interprete, è Bibliothecâ suâ ad Bibliothecam Regiam coornandam, Regi, promptissimis omnes animis, nunquam satis laudandi dede-rint *Externarum Missionum Presbyteri*.

4°. Quosnam novo Catalogo ad Sinas, Regis jussu, & ejusdem summi viri Pauli *Bignonii* curâ, per eundem me *Fourmontium* mis-so, conquisierit anno 1722. & anno 1723. advexerit tunc Socie-tatis Jesu Sacerdos ac Missionarius, nunc Claudiopoleωs Episco-pus ill. D. *Fouquet.*

5°. Quosnam *Premarus* acceptis anno 1727. ab ill. D. *Bignonio* & eodem *Fourmontio* Litteris, Regis jussu emerit, atque ad Bi-bliothecam Regiam destinarit.

6°. Quosnam demum annis sequentibus 1730. 1731. 1732. è suis ipsius Libris, *dono* ad Ill. D. *Bignonium*, & ad eundem me *Four-montium* miserit? hoc ultimum, ex variis ejusdem *Premari* Epistolis constat, in primo Catalogo omissis, at hîc, non unam ob causam insertis, patebit evidenter.

Nunc neglecto illo *temporum*, queis Libri *advenerunt*, ordine, ita juxta materiam unamquamque disponemus:

Ut *Primo*, Grammatici, id est, Dictionaristæ præcedant (quia ab iis incipienda rerum Sinicarum studia) ac Philologici.

Secundo, sequantur Geographici.

Tertio, Historici & Annales illi famosi.

Quarto, appareant Libri Classici & Canonici.

Quinto, exserantur Libri Morales, de Jure, Officiisque.

Sexto, Theologici, Sectarum variarum, ac præcipuè à Christianis compositi.

Septimo, postea accedant Libri Philosophici.

Octavo, Medici.

Nono, Mathematici.

Decimo, Artium cæterarum.

CATALOGUS

前　言

　　皇家图书馆馆藏目录已经印出后，这里无疑会产生这样的问题：当前，重印同一目录是否会无用？完全不是，理由有很多。

　　1. 首先，皇家图书馆馆藏目录的价格太高，无人得以拥有完整一部。所以有谁会为获取关于中国书籍的知识而购买整部？

　　2. 其次，在如此多卷目之中，全世界如此之多不同语言、不同国家各种书籍的目录将会是什么样的？如何不使至今如此受到忽视的部分被埋没，而它对大多数未受习中国文字和语言的人而言只看起来就令人生畏？

　　3. 然后，至于其他语言，如希伯来语、叙利亚语、阿拉伯语，许多学者抱怨对手稿的认识中缺少对文字的认识，他们有时想，或者法国没有东方文字，或者荷兰人、英国人、德国人已经在极为类似的目录中已使用了这些文字，我们法国人却未能使用。而对东方语言的最初认识是由我们完成的，其中有最初的多语学者，如博尔蒙，维特莱乌斯（Vitraeus）以及其他很多人。在这个国家并非至今一直缺少熟知东方语言者，此目录样本之订正便托付与他们，但是却缺少那样一部被推崇备至的作品。如果说之前他们的成果有用，而他们现在变得无用武之地，立刻就有这样一个例外，那只能是这部目录。确实，为辨识各抄本，希伯来、叙利亚、阿拉伯的文字并非完全必要，因为从那些语言的附加说明中，学者们可以利用拉丁字母得知各个标题的含义，这在目录中是够用的。但最后是什么消除了在中国书籍中的这种争议？没有文字，所有标题都模棱两可，单音节、声调和发音都相同，文字本身也会有时而10，时而20，时而30，或35，或40，或50个同音？情况就是这样，今天还有谁不了解？所以你选取任何一个标题，除非有附加的文字，否则你根本不能理解，这在我们的《汉语沉思录》（*Meditationes Sinicae*）、更高级的语法《中国官话》（*Lingua Sinarum Mandarinicae Hieroglyphicae Gr ammatica Duplex*）以及所有传教士的著作中极为充分地表明了。

　　因此，希伯来的、叙利亚的、迦勒底的（Chaldaei）、犹太教经师的（Rabbinici）、埃及的（Copthici）、波斯的、印度的以及鞑靼的书籍标题，自己本身已足以给出明晰意义，尽管用他们的文字会显得更加漂亮；而关于中国语言，关于中国图书的标题，切忌引入此法，因为总有与文字相分离的语音的混乱，人的理性是不能理解这种模棱两可的。

　　情况便是如此，我承认，那些在我不在场、不知情的时候将我中国书籍目录的手稿付印的人，当然是最博学、且对我关爱最多的人，他们应得到我的感激，因为他们在我最繁忙时减轻了我繁重的研究，免除了特别是我自少年时已习惯的、订正书稿的劳苦。

　　4. 但之前我所预料到的，认真告诫的，还是这样发生了，使得最初由我苦心写成的每一页之后糟糕地誊出，甚至未修正地付印，最后出版了。

5. 我不会再说，尽管这是关键。简而言之，有某些篡改的、甚至不少歪曲成别的意思的、许多截断的地方，我抱怨它们，虽然这是朋友们是出于好意，也是为我减轻负担而完成的。正是由于这个原因，加之完全忽视必要的文字，且存在大量错误，学者们都认为应由我重新出版这一目录，尤其是伟大且智慧的国务大臣，不逊先人的艺术的保护者德·莫雷帕先生（D.DE MAUREPAS）。

6. 此外，在诸多由我历时如此之久、用心如此之多编成的词典中，至少有两部不久即将出版，一部按发音排序，另一部按部首排序。（即拉汉、法汉词典，关于历史、地理的，或拉汉，或法汉，其他的我们还会考虑。）

而本作一切意义中最主要的，即认识书籍作者、认识作品名称，对于所有这些，一部使用欧洲文字的、只够指出书籍数量的目录是多么无用！或者汉学研究为空谈，或者就应熟悉中国文字。而如今在伟大国王的命令下，我们的辛苦并非徒劳。因为在对历史、诗歌、哲学、一切技艺渴求着、热爱着、探索着的民族中，这部作品所给予的空间是多么广大！这样，读者将惊奇于如此繁多的中国作家、作品的知识，同时依赖并满足于大量文字、词组的应用，感受到词典编者免去的所谓引用和陈述的工作。不过，对于每一个文字、按部首排列词典中的部首、按音序排列词典中的页，以及如果是在某个作家名字中的字，某个作家中某个字有特殊含义的情况下，对于这个字或作家，每个这样的地方，我们仍然都会仔细指出，使得没有人会感到还有需要附注的地方。

因此，我将有必要地再三提及中国书籍，这会为学界带来莫大益处。

1. 我们的工作让为皇家图书馆馆藏目录更为准确，为此我会精准确切地重新置入未添加的声调，并且，那仅用拉丁字母写出中文单音节字所引起的模棱两可，我以添加文字的方式将它全部消除。

2. 碍于目录关于中国语言不小的错误，为使能有某些益处地供人阅读，今天我所作的贡献显而易见。

3. 一些被省去或缩略的内容，确实在单纯的目录中可以缺少，这我乐意放弃，但仍存有过长的内容（Notitiae）。不过阿拉伯文有多少是更长的？对此，我们又怎能将长的内容看作"不合时宜的"？汉语语法后置，而词典先行。而这一学问涉及甚广，产生如此新颖、如此众多的事物，是时候终于也抬起头来。

但权衡一切之后，我们在此不会继续保留皇家图书馆馆藏目录的顺序。在那里我们指出了书籍加入皇家图书馆的时间，并非由于一个原因，而既因为时间本身，又因为汉学的进展，（我们的书页通过不同的途径落入其他人之手，并且因为它们彼此分离，也可以被分离，况且它们是以材料的顺序相连接，我们没有反对。）而这里，我们将依照事物的序列，对有必要解释之处进行解释，欣然地安排好顺序，对这样安排我们自信会获得良好的口碑。

但为使读者得知先前按时间排列的理由，我们认为应知道这一点：尽管两个世纪以前已有不计其数的传教士前往中国，却不曾有一部中国作者的作品传入欧洲，甚至是皇家图书馆。

1647年之前，皇家图书馆仅有四册中国图书，而且它们是红衣主教马扎冉（Jules Mazarin）的藏书。

1697年5月27日和6月2日，白晋自中国归来时带来另外49册。

1720^①年10月，尊敬的神父洪若翰（Jean de Fontaney）为国王路易十四带来十二卷本，它们以汉文和满文写成，或者更准确地说只有满文字，很少的汉文穿插其中，以提示译作的标题。

从耶稣会成员柏应理（Philippe Couplet）、最博学的马扎冉学院（Collège Mazarin）图书管理员庇库斯（Picus）、德国人中学识最杰出的英才莱布尼茨以及其他人的各种书信中流传得出，由柏应理从中国带来收入皇家图书馆的大量书籍，它们或是汉语的，或是满语的，但都是梦寐以求的作家之作。在引用柏应理留在皇家图书馆的拉汉词典时，吉勒·梅纳（Gilles Ménage）的法语词源学中前言作者也出了错。柏应理如传教士们所习惯的那样，从中国回法国时随身带来的汉拉词典的情况完全类似。究竟发生了什么？孔子著作在巴黎出版时，也就是孔子的三部书，《大学》、《中庸》和《论语》的纯拉丁文本，希望添加中文，但意识到在法国无法印刷，于是启程前往比利时和德国，带着那部词典和其他不止一次保证要敬献给皇家图书馆的书，并放在那里同会的某个修道院。关于此事必须提醒读者，不要被如此之多的作者欺骗，以为我们在皇家图书馆馆藏目录中有误。

在说明了这些情况之后，我们来指出之前未细说的目录的项目分类，共六大类：

1. 直到1711年最初的一批书。它们或是来自马扎冉，或是由白晋、洪若翰及其同僚带来。

2. 从极为著名的比尼昂（Jean-Paul Bignon）获得的，包括1716年，任职于皇家图书馆之前便已经捐献与我们使用的，以及之后列入皇家所有的一批书。

3. 1720年，在我——阿拉伯语钦定教授、皇家学院的学者、皇家图书馆的翻译傅尔蒙的努力下，负责海外传教的神父（或为巴黎外方会神父），大方地把自己的藏书献给国王，为使皇家图书馆增辉。

4. 奉国王之命，在高贵的比尼昂的关照下，通过我傅尔蒙向中国发布新的目录后，1722年和1723年征集得到，由当时的耶稣会神父和传教士，现在作为克劳迪奥波利斯（Claudiopolis）主教的傅圣泽（Jean-François Foucquet）神父运送来的一批书。

5. 马若瑟（Joseph Henri Marie de Prémare）1727年接到比尼昂先生和傅尔蒙的信后，应国王的要求购入，指定送到皇家图书馆的一批书。

6. 最后，1730、1731、1732连续三年从（马若瑟）自己的藏书中赠送与比尼昂先生和我傅尔蒙的一批书。这最后一批从马若瑟的各种信件中汇集而成，在最初的目录中缺失，在此由于多种原因添加进入，后面会清楚说明。

而今忽略书籍到来的时间顺序，我们将如此依次排列各种材料。

第一，语法书，即词典编者（因为应从他们开始汉学研究）和语文学者先行。

第二，地理学书籍紧随其后。

---

① 译者按：疑为"1702年"。

第三，历史学和著名的编年史。

第四，古典和经典书籍。

第五，展示了道德书籍，关于法律和义务。

第六，神学，包含不同派别，主要由基督徒编写。

第七，哲学书籍。

第八，医学。

第九，数学。

第十，其他技艺。

（张天鹄译，李慧校）

CATALOGUS
LIBRORUM
BIBLIOTHECÆ REGIÆ
SINICORUM.
GRAMMATICI. I.

Cat. Bibl. Reg. n. 48. p. 378.

çŭ

lúy,
   id eft, *collectio charaterum.*

字彙

Dictionarium eft characterum Sinicorum non omnino omnium, fed plærorumque, & eorum qui in ufu apud Sinas frequentiffimo. Authori nomen erat

múy

梅

ýn,

誕

& impreffum eft Imperante Kâm hî.
Difpofitio hujus Dictionarii ea eft de

quâ jam in *Meditationibus Sinicis* pag. 123. Primo tomo adfunt 1°. *Præfationes* tres, in queis multa de characterum naturâ, item de antiquis Litteratis, & præterea, id maximè inculcat, quanti fieri debeat characterum fcientia, id quod in primâ *Præfatione* præfertim reperies. In fecundâ, de variis characterum accidentibus differit Author, ac primùm quidem, de *Pronuntiatione*, tum de ipfo characteris uniufcujufque corpore, item de diverfis characterum generibus, alii enim *vulgares*, qui in curfivâ fcripturâ, alii in Libris præcipuè adhibendi, alii itidem hoc vel illo modo exarari poffunt, alii ab antiquis Scriptoribus ufurpati, neque amplius nifi inter Litteratos noti, quæ omnia nifi diftincta à te fuerint, Libros fæpe non intelliges.

2°. Sequitur Dictionarii totius divifio.

3°. Tum apparent claves 214. & fi qua eft, quæ duplici charactere fcribatur, id quoque admonetur Lector.

4°. Poftea, quod apud Sinas magni fit, *clavium fcribendarum* habes methodum, à quo fcilicet lineamento inci-

Tttt

pias, quodnam *secundo*, quodnam *tertio*, & sic deinceps scribendum tibi, quæ nisi accuratè noveris, characteres à te nunquam rectè scribentur, nunquam facilè in Dictionario reperientur. Itaque illic, characterum quamplurium afferuntur tibi exempla, & *lineæ* illæ omnes separatim adducuntur, quâ ex methodo, ea deinde oritur facilitas, ut characteres omnino omnes postea statim dissecare possis, & ad prima sua lineamenta revocare, quod ad evolvenda omnia Dictionaria, ea præsertim, quæ clavium ordinem sequuntur, maximè necessarium.

5°. Venit characterum quorumdam *vulgariter* scriptorum, aut scribi in quibusdam Libris solitorum Catalogus, quomodo enim apud nos verba quædam sunt usus *popularis*, v. g. comici, quæ in stylo sublimiori toleranda non sunt, item quomodo quædam *antiquata* censentur, neque à nobis nunc nisi in Poësi eâque familiari usurpantur, à Tragædiâ autem aut Oratione Rhetoricâ omnino exulant, ita apud Sinas characteres non promiscuè adhibentur.

6°. Succedit characterum omnino *abrogatorum* Catalogus, quos iis, in quibus reperiuntur Libris, relinquunt; eos nimirum explicant in Commentariis sicubi occurrant, sed in suâ ipsi oratione, hac tempestate non admittunt.

7°. Eâ in re, ne peccet Lector, aut Sinicæ Linguæ Studiosus, additur enumeratio quædam characterum apud antiquos simul & recentiores *communium*, subjunctâ nihilominus eâ, quæ in usu nunc est, figurâ.

8°. In hoc nostro Dictionario, quæ pars in aliis, post clavium 214. figuras statim apponitur, scilicet de hâc vel illâ figurâ clavium duplici aut triplici; ea pars, inquam, hîc apparet, quodammodo à Clavibus remotior; sed neque id importunè tamen, propter eum qui sequitur Articulum.

9°. Nam vides ordine, & sub suâ quemque clavi characteres eos, qui propter earum, è quibus compositi sunt, *clavium multiplicitatem*, in hâc vel illâ clavi quæri possent, & tamen in Dictionario ad hanc vel illam clavem, non ad aliam referuntur : res autem hæc, quam necessaria, in Dictionariis ejusmodi amplissimis? nam nisi veram characteris quærendi *clavem* reverâ teneas, dies in quærendo charactere consumeres sæpe non paucos; quapropter cognoscendæ tibi sunt eæ, ad quas rectà ire possis.

Atque hæc tibi offert tomus Dictionarii hujus primus.

Tomo secundo sunt,

1°. Præfatio nova, in quâ de reperiendorum *sonorum*, *tonorum*que arte illâ ipsâ admirabili, quæ tibi à me primò est in *Meditationibus Sinicis* exposita à capite 11. pag. 52. & alibi.

2°. Characteres *Vocalium*, id est, characteres ii, queis *Vocales* apud Sinarum Magistros ex condicto solent repræsentari : scilicet Linguam nullam absque *vocalibus*, absque *consonarum* mentione cognosci atque addisci posse, quidquid animo tibi finxeris, intelligis extemplo. Itaque habent Sinæ, quomodò Gentes aliæ omnes, & *Vocales* & *Consonas*; sed hæc inter cæteras Nationes ac Sinas differentia est, quod præter suos, eosque cunctos *repræsentativos* characteres, in Linguâ suâ agnoscant nihil : si *a*, si *e*, si *i*, si *o*, si *u*, quæras, littera hujusmodi nulla prorsus : si *p*, si *v*, si *f*, si *m*, &c. in omni omnino Litteraturâ Sinicâ, nullam ejusmodi consonam reverà invenies; sed interim loquuntur, docent, discunt, labia habent, dentes, palatum, guttur habent, queis loquantur: loqui nequeunt, quin easdem aut *vocales* aut *consonas* efferant, & quod amplius est, in Gente doctâ & docendi cupidâ, nihil docere, hominem nullum erudire possunt, quin de iisdem *vocalibus*, iisdem *consonis* differant. Nec regerendum, at non habent ullas : falsum est, inquam, & habeant necesse est, quod ni *veras*, certè *fictitias* ac *supposititias* habebunt. Quam id igitur mirum esse debet in Grammaticâ *Premari*, amici mei, viri profectò doctissimi totâ; in Grammaticâ R. P. *Varonis*, in iis quas adhuc vidi omnibus, *Vocalium* & *Consonarum* Sinicarum mentionem fieri nullam, quasi à Sinis, Gente omninò ingeniosâ; & Linguæ suæ, saltem inter suos propagandæ curiosissimâ, nihil in hujusmodi rebus inventum unquam quidquam esset?

Quàm absurdum, eam ipsam rem à quibusdam *Missionariis* supponi, qui à Sinâ ad nos advecti, non ita pridem, id absque ullo rubore audacter asseverabant! Videlicet Scholas ipsas Sinarum non adierant, in quibus quod mihi de iisdem *Vocalibus* aut *Consonis* loquenti statim confessus est Illustrissimus D. D. *de Montigni*, earum rerum Doctrinâ in Sinarum Collegiis esse frequentius nihil, quod cur à *Missionariis* huc usque neglectum esset, nunquam animo concepiſſe ſe, cum *Uſum* tantummodo Linguæ Sinicæ, id eſt, characterum, ſibi aſſumerent Miſſionarii, ſcientiam Sinis omnino reliquerint, è quâ tamen profectus multò major, faciliorque.

Sed redeamus, non ſolum & *vocales* & *conſonas* cognoſcunt, habentque Doctores Sinæ, ex *ſuppoſitione* tamen; & quales character hieroglyphicus poteſt, ſed etiam Dictionarium ſerè nullum eſt, in quo non fiat 1°. *vocalium* & *conſonarum* illarum enumeratio. 2°. Diſtinctio earumdem per *organa*, preciſè atque eodem prorſus modo, quomodo ab *Hebræis*, à *Chaldæis*, ab *Arabibus* facta eſt, quod à me cum in *Meditationibus Sinicis* pag. 55. annotatum ſit, ſuperſedendum hîc mihi; ſed neque id taceri omnino decuit, cum Mûy ỳn, ſeu hujus Dictionarii Author, & alii 10t, doctrinam hanc perpetuò & voluminibus id integris, inculcent.

Hîc nimirum poſtquam tomo hoc ſecundo, mentionem tantum de *conſonarum ſonis*, per Præfationem injeciſſet, datis poſtea characteribus *vocalium*, id eſt, unicuique *vocali* inſervientibus, reſumit *pag.* 4. & ſequentibus, idque omne juxta *conſonarum* ordinem, quidquid characterum ad hanc vel illam *vocalem* pertinet. Sic cum prima *conſona* ſit *k*, ſtatim ſubeſt ſeries vocum per *k*, ſed additâ primâ *vocalium*, unde fit *kum*, & quia ſecunda *conſona* ſit *t*, ſubeſt ſeries vocum per *t*, & additâ eâdem primâ *vocali*, unde fit *tum*, &c. quod uſque ad paginam 39. exequitur, Tabulis ubique ad ſeriem *vocalium* ſuarum conformatis; dico *ſuarum*; nam cum *characteres*, ut annotavimus, huic vel illi vocali efficiendæ idonei, merè ſuppoſititii ſint, ideoque alii ab aliis Grammaticis aſſumi queant: Mûy ỳn, neque eaſdem omnino quas alii *conſonas*, neque eaſdem ferè ubique *vocales* adhibet; ſed quid refert, ut dixi, ſi potentiâ & uſu eaſdem? Si eaſdem, propter unam eandemque Grammaticorum Sinarum de utriſque doctrinam? Cauſa autem cur multiplicentur & *conſonæ* & *vocales*, non alia eſt, quam *variarum ſerierum* inſtruendarum, propter tantam characterum multitudinem, neceſſitas.

4°. Denique, cum per illos *Indices*, characterum nonnullorum emicet ſimilitudo, additur ab Authore Catalogus quidam *characterum non eorumdem, ſed ferè ſimilium*; & cum id non ſolùm ad duos, ſed etiam ad *tres*, ad *quatuor*, ad *ſex* characteres ſpectare poſſit, adducuntur multorum inter ſe *ſimilium* exempla; præterea illic etiam characteres quidam inter ſe, qui ſenſu ac ſine ſenſu *ex unâ figura in aliam*, *ex unâ ſignificatione in aliam* commutati.

Jam tertio tomo & cæteris uſque ad decimum-quartum *characteres* omnes, ſed ſub *clavi* unuſquiſque ſuâ, comparent unâ cum çiĕ, id eſt, characteribus duobus, quorum hîc uſus eſt, ut è *priori conſonam*, *vocalem è poſteriori* elicias, quæ pronunciatio deinde alio itidem ejuſdem pronunciationis totalis, uno tantum charactere exponitur: idem denique character explicandus in hoc Dictionario toto, & *majori* ſemper *ſcripturâ* exaratus eſt, & additâ *unâ & aliâ ſignificatione*, eâque principali & notiſſimâ declaratur; remotis interim ſignificationibus aliis multis aut ſecundariis, aut metaphoricis, quas vel in Chím çû tûm, vel in magno Dictionario Çù goéi reperire eſt, ut poſtea videbis. Cæterum id etiam addendum ſuper, eos, qui à nobis primò ſculpti ſunt, characteres, ex hoc Dictionario ſculpi incepiſſe, & Dictionario per *claves* edendo inſervituros.

Eſt itaque voluminum quatuor-decim.

I I.

Cat. Bibliot. Reg. n. 52. *pag.* 399.

çû

lu\` *vel* guéi.

aut amplius,

yvên	懸
kîn	金
çù	字
lu\` *vel* guéi.	彙

Id eſt, *Dictionarium vocatum* çù luÿ,

Ttttij

vel çū guéi, *tom.* 14. *ab* yuèn kīn *editum.* Idem propriè Dictionarium est, de quo in Catalogo Bibliothecæ Regiæ ad Cod. Regios n. 48. Sed editio alia, voluminum itidem 14. & multo majori & nitidiori charactere; idque ita, ut primi etiam duo, non nisi præparatorii sint, & & in rebus ad Grammaticam pertinentibus toti. Novam inde *notitiam* necessariam non putares, at omnesne Editionem utramque possidebunt? Sed ne tibi tædio sit, *Annotationibus* etiam novis cumulatum dabo. Itaque præmissis eodem modo *Præfationibus*, ubi de generali characterum cognitione, de *xin* seu *tonis*, de characterum investigatione: transitur ad *claves: clavium* duplici aut triplici charactere præditarum characteres, vel *duplices* vel *triplices*, principali characteri supponuntur, & notantur accuratè omnes Dictionarii postea secuturi *Sectiones*: quod fit, ut Sinæ solent, per *Cycli* characteres.

Jam quod repeti sæpius debet, venit earumdem *clavium* scribendarum modus: dispescit Author *clavis* uniuscujusque partes, & postea easdem denuo jungit; ab eâ incipit quæ prior scribenda, ab ea pergit quæ deinde scribenda: Si quis ergo tractatulum hunc rectè calluerit, rectè etiam primò *claves* omnes scribet. Postea characteres Sinici omnes nonnisi *clavium repetitio*: ita clavibus semel rectè scriptis, & per suas omnes partes dissectis, omnem etiam compositionem non solùm earumdem clavium, sed cunctorum characterum percalleamus, necesse est. Hæc Dictionarii pars vocatur

yūn

piě,

運
筆

movere penicillum, seu *penicilli motio*, quomodo movendus sit penicillus ad hunc vel illum characterem scribendum. Sic enim discitur 1°. quomodo *clavium* pars unaquæque, 2°. quomodo *clavium* jam *conjunctarum* partes in unoquoque charactere scribantur; unde exurgit numerus partium in dissectione cognoscendarum, quâ sine frustrà esses. Alius qui sequitur Tractatus, inscribitur

çūm

kú,

從
古

quasi diceres, *characterum originatio*, seu *characterum vulgarium ad suam originem reductio*: positi hîc characteres duo, *prior* characterem exhibet, qualis in Libris rectè exaratis scribi solet ac debet, *alter* seu *posterior* eo modo depingitur quomodo antea negligentius scriptus est, & *scriptura* hæc habetur nunc *vulgatior*, neque in Libris accuratius impressis reperitur; est igitur scriptura non obsoleta prorsus, non antiquata, sed *neglectior*.

Sed ut dignosci queant qui revera antiquati, additur tractatus alius, inscriptus,

çūn

xī,

遵
時

id est, *blandiendi tempus*, seu characteres ii, qui apud antiquos Sinas, in scripturâ faciliori & neglectâ usitati fuere, & in usu non sunt amplius, sed tamen quorum usus ad ostentationem condonatur.

Subjungitur alius tractatus, seu potius Catalogus, kú kīn tūm yúm, id est, eorum characterum, quorum *usus*, licèt *abrogatorum*, permansit, sed ita ut, in alios tamen scriptu faciliores postea inventos mutati sint. Ad unumquemque igitur characterem *antiquum* additur kú *antiquitus*, ad *recentiorem* additur kīn, *nunc* sive *hoc tempore*: & inspecto utroque charactere quid concluditur? priorem ideo *neglectum* quod scriptio ejus longior ac difficilior, posteriorem *ascitum*, quia penicillo alacriori opus fuit.

Sed neque hæc satis, Index habetur novus, illarum, de quibus jam egimus, *clavium* duplicium ac triplicium, & dicitur

kién çū,

kièn

çù

檢字

characteres truncati, his verbis intelliguntur *figuræ clavium* duplices vel triplices : ratio , in compositione crescunt
interdum characteres , tunc figura clavis
vera & simplex , fieret crassior , largior-
que , in ejusdem ergo clavis integræ locum , ad compositionis facilitatem ab-
breviantur truncatione , in alias mu-
tantur clavis primariæ lineamenta : at
omnibusne accidit ? nequaquam : sed
iis tantum, quas in *Meditationibus* nostris
Sinicis multiplici figurâ donatas vides ,
scilicet 9. 18. 26. 43. 47. 58. 60. 64.
65. 71. 78. 85. 86. 93. 94. 95. 122.
130. 140. 146. 161. 163. 168. 170.

Denique in eodem Dictionarii volumine apparent characteres ii &
magno numero ; quid enim fiet , nempe , si clavis ambigua , si inventu per
se difficilis ? hoc loco , quod in ejusmodi
per claves Dictionariis momenti est maximi , scito per totum quidem Dictionarium ex numero *linearum* quæri debere
characteres , sed in Dictionario ipso inter eas *lineas* non numerari *clavem* , seu
clavis ipsius *lineas*, at in hoc tractatu, seu
Catalogo characterum præliminari , nu-
merandas esse *lineas omnes* , id est , tum
lineas clavium , tum cæteras ; causa autem perspicua: in Dictionario ipso statim
eminet *clavis* , clavi inventâ , seu charactere per clavem invento , nihil quæ-
rendum est tibi , character ipse propterea ex *numero linearum* discernendus ,
remotâ *clavi* : in hoc autem Catalogo ,
quinam habentur characteres , nisi characteres , quos ob earum ex quibus com-
ponuntur *clavium multiplicitatem* , ac
proinde *ambiguitatem* , quo in loco Dictionarii existant, nescis? Inde igitur factum, ut in hunc Catalogum conferrentur
characteres , inventu non faciles , &
quorum causâ Lector hærere cogitur.
Inter legendum, hunc vel illum characterem invenisti, propter multas è quibus
componitur claves , ad quamnam refe-
rendus sit , ignoras , ad hunc ipsum indicem recurrendum tibi. Quid tum ? nu-

merandæ characteris *linea cuncta* , ad-
eundum ad characteres linearum totidem ; inter eos , si reipsa difficilis ,
eum illic reperies dubio procul.

Jam verò eæ à te non rectè numerabun-
tur , nisi tractatum de *lineis claves* com-
ponentibus attentè legeris ; si res à te
omissa fuerit , in ambages te est & difficultates æternas projectura ; atque hinc
est, quod è Missionariis, si qui Dictionariis assueti brevioribus , & doctrinâ Sinarum Grammaticâ destituti , labores
tot vulgò experiantur : quod si hoc dicendum de quibusdam post annos triginta illic exactos in Europam reversis ,
de iis , qui illuc pertransierunt tantummodo , idque cursim , quid putas , nisi
eos esse omnino αμιθοδευτας ? quin, *Premarus* ipse amicus meus , hæc , quæ com-
memoro , omnia , aut usu characterum
vulgarium contentus , aut malâ Missio-
nariorum prædecessorûm consuetudine
abreptus omiserat. Cur ? non nisi Dictionaria ab Europæis collecta , & juxta
ordinem Alphabethi , ac proinde malè
digesta, consulere assueverat. Atque hæc
sunt in primo hujus Dictionarii volumine.

In *secundo* alia multa , quæ hactenus
Europæis ignota : scilicet traditur illic
vocalium ac *consonarum* Sinicarum , id
est , characterum , ad hoc *suppositorum*,
atque inservientium , atque ideo in
Scholis Sinicis usitatissimorum cognitio.

1°. Præfatio *eam in rem* non longa ,
sed luculenta , in quâ de *consonis* 36.
postea de *vocalium* naturâ agitur ; illic
etiam , quod res ferebat ac volebat , de
ciê, hoc est, *vocalis* ac *consona* distinctione ac separatione Author disserit.

Tum sese offerunt *vocales* , hoc est ,
characteres vocalibus indicandis desti-
nati : Relege *Meditationes Sinicas*.

Postquam eas omnes enumeravit ,
usum earum commonstrat , adductis per
totum ferè volumen , idque summo ordine , characteribus ex earumdem *vocalium* pronuntiatione legendis. Alium
quoque *Tractatum* aggreditur , de *consonarum* pronuntiatione , & quod mirum , iisdem , juxta organa , cæterorum
Orientalium more, dispositis, *characteres*
subdit innumerabiles , inde iterum co-
gnoscendos.

Et ne qua oriatur characterum confu-
sio , Tractatui illi Grammatico toti ac
quasi coronidem , imponit *Indicem*
quendam longissimum *characterum* Linguæ Sinicæ *similium* , ac distinguendo-

Vuuu

rum tamen, in quo Indice toto, cum characteres sint duo, & ad comparationem inftituendam *linea* fupponantur *duæ*; prior ad *priorem* characterem, pofterior ad *pofteriorem* exponendum, à te referatur necefle eft.

III.

Cat. Bibliot. Reg. n. 52. *p.* 380.

çŭ

luý

pù,

字彙補

hoc eft, *fupplementum ad* çŭ luý : cum characterum Sinicorum numerus infinitus prope fit, mirum elfe debet nemini, quod edita *fupplementa* fuerint, præfertim Dictionarii çŭ luý, *alias* çŭ goéi, in quo characteres quofdam deefle fuprà fignificavimus.

Scriptores funt innumerabiles, neque ab Authoribus Dictionariorum, quantâcumque fuerint diligentiâ, confuli omnes omnino poffunt. Id quoque à nobis animadverfum, *novos* fubinde inventos efle characteres, quos, fi juxta lŏ xŭ, feu *regulas condendorum characterum* ab Antiquis traditas, formatos Sinæ cæteri viderint, adoptant ftatim : eodem ferè modo, quo apud nos, fi qua vox nova, & hactenus inaudita, in ufum nihilominus tranfeat frequentem fatis, illico à nobis accipitur, & in Dictionaria noftra introducitur. Quot in omnibus aut Dictionariis aut vocabulariis funt ejufmodi, non folùm, quæ à Doctis, fed etiam, quæ ab infimâ Plebe nuper ufurpata, inter Academicos invitos licet, tandem *vulgares* fiunt, & fæpe in orationes etiam à populi intellectu remotas, fenfim ac fine fenfu admittuntur ?

Idem ergo fit apud Sinas, unde poftea hæc *fupplementa.*

Reperiuntur hîc tria, *primùm* quidem *characteres* quidam jam diu *noti*, fed quibus acceffit *nova* & antea incognita

fignificatio. 2°. Deinde *characteres* aut in aliquo Libro, unde nondum eruti fuerant, *reperti*, aut *nuper* ab aliquo Scriptore *efformati.* 3°. Aliud quoque eft, idque non rarum, fi quis character, antea hujus vel illius *toni*, deinceps, quæ Linguarum aliarum omnium indoles aboleri nunquam potuit, *alio* quam antea *tono* pronunciari cæperit.

Id verò, fic difcernetur : in aliis, quæ *clavium* ordinem fequuntur, Dictionariis, ea eft pronuntiationis inveniendæ ratio, fi additis infra duobus characteribus per çiĕ, id eft, per *diffectionem, ex altero confonam, ex altero vocalem* defumas; item poft aliam dictionem, fequitur adhuc alius character, ifque fatis notus, cui ineft, ea, quam in charactere explido quæris, pronuntiatio; hoc eodem modo, in *fupplemento* adfunt, vel character

yéu   *amplius,*

又

quod de *novâ* fignificatione additur, vel characteres illi quatuor, aut potius quinque, quorum in primo habes *confonam*, in fecundo *vocalem*, in tertio

çiĕ,

切

id eft, *diffectionis indicium*, in quarto

ўn,

音

id eft, *fonum*, quafi dicas, *fonae ergo* per çiĕ feu diffectionem, &c. 5°. denique characterem ejufdem *pronunciationis.* Omnia hæc etiam exemplo & appofitis characteribus in *Meditationibus Sinicis*, pag. 126. confirmatum invenies, ubi de hoc præcisè *fupplemento* : collectum verò eft à Doctore

gŭ

吳

gĭn

chĭn,

任臣

idque ᴋăm hĭ Imperante 1.
volum. 12.

I V.

Cat. Biblioth. Reg. n. 52. pag. 399.

Liber inſcriptus

çŭ

luý

pù,

字彙補

Supplementum ad Dictionarium çŭ luý,
Dictionarium eſt idem , atque ad ea
ſupplenda , quæ in çŭ luý deſunt , hoc
notitia præcedenti additamentum acci-
pe. *Præfatio* duplex , *prior* ad τὸ çŭ luý
commendationem , in quâ dicit Author
additos à ſe 4595 *characteres*; *poſte-*
rior de characteribus generalius , in quâ
de Hiſtoricis xĕ ſăn kĭm yocatis , de ye-
ris ᴋĭm , de lŏ xŭ , de characterum xĭm
& çĭĕ , de characterum diſſectione ac
lectione , fuſè agit.

Poſtea oſtendunt ſe *claves* omnes unà
cum *duplicibus* ac *triplicibus figuris*,
quotquot habent ; tum ſubjicitur numerus eorum , qui unicuique clavi *additi*
ſunt , aut in unaquaque clavi *denuò ex-*
poſiti ſunt , characterum.

Tum incipit Liber , & ad unamquamque clavem fiunt duo , 1º. ſupplentnr
characteres novi , 2º. *ad characteres* in
çŭ luý expoſitos , adduntur *ſignifica-*
tiones novæ. Editus eſt anno ᴋăm hĭ
quinto , vol. 5.

V.

Cat. Bibliot. Reg. n. 49. pag. 379.

chĭm

çŭ

tŭm,

正字通

id eſt , *recta penetratio* , ſeu *cognitio cha-*
racterum. Dictionarium hoc illud eſt , de
quo in *Meditationibus* , pag. item 123.
hujus expoſitio , ut dixi , ampliſſima,
Authore méu ᴋivĕn hû *vel* hô. Inter eos,
qui apud Regem erant primitus, Libros,
erat imperfectus, tomorum eſt vulgò 36.
aut etiam 40. ſi aliter compingatur , nec
niſi 20. allati fuerant ; ſed poſtea ex
Miſſionariorum Extraneorum Bibliothecâ , in Bibliothecam Regiam illatum eſt
exemplar integrum. ex eo igitur notitia.

Dictionarii hujus apud Sinas vulga-
tiſſimi editiones multæ , & in plæriſque
hæc videbis.

1º. Tomo primo ſunt *Præfationes*
quàmplurimæ , in quibus & de characterum origine ac propagatione , & de
lŏ xŭ , ſeu *characterum efformandorum mo-*
dis ſex , apud antiquos memoratis, & de
animosâ quâdam ab Imperatore hûm yû
ſuſceptâ , & morum , & Litteratorum,
Litterarumque correctione ac reformatione , & de antiquis & novis characteribus , eorumque alteratione agunt Authores , imo de çĭĕ , de ŷn , de yún,
de xĭm , aliiſque *vocabulis* ad Grammaticam pertinentibus , quæ in *Meditatio-*
nibus Sinicis legere potes ; item de *cha-*
racteribus , ſive *ſublimioris* , ſive *infimi*
ſtyli , aliiſque ejuſmodi rebus , quæ res
ad Litteraturam & characterum cognitionem faciunt omnes.

Poſtea ſequitur in *unâ* ex ultimis
editionibus *Alphabethum quoddam Tar-*
taricum , ad quaſdam voces Sinicas ac-
comodatum , ut inde Gentis utriuſque,
& Tartaræ , & Sinicæ , in iiſdem nunc

Vuuuij

tectis ab annis amplius centum degentium, *soni* ac *pronuntiatio* extent quodammodo atque elucefcant; in *aliâ* prima characterum *lineamenta*, unde quis incipere debeat, in quo lineamento definere, feu, quod idem, *clavium fcribendarum methodus*.

Tum verò (quæ res mihi mira) adducuntur *Authores Grammatici*, ii, è quibus *notas* in Dictionarium fuum tranftulit Author, quique unicè de *Linguâ* & *rebus* ad Linguæ Grammaticam attinentibus tractarunt. Sed enim è *titulis* id conftat, & apprimè confiderandum nobis eft. In aliis enim de *xím*, feu *tonis*, in aliis de *çiĕ*, feu *characteris* ad rectam pronuntiationem *diffectione*, in aliis de *ŷn*, feu *fono & vocali*, in aliis de *yún*, feu *confonantiarum* expreffione, in aliis de *ftylo leviori*, feu fiaó xuĕ, in aliis de *ftylo magnifico*, in aliis de *antiquorum*, in aliis de *recentiorum quoad pronuntiationem differentiâ*, in aliis de hujus aut illius *Provinciæ accentu*: uno verbo, numerantur illîc Tractatus de Grammaticâ 138. à diverfis Authoribus elaborati; (malè 188. impreffum in *Meditationibus Sinicis pag. 128. 3.* in 8. commutato.) quæ cuncta repeto hîc, & ideo affero: hinc, ut Gentem Sinicam Linguæ fuæ & Characterum fuorum cultricem effe, in eamque expoliendam, amplificandamque fummopere incubuiffe difcas, illinc, ut infelicitatem noftram deplorem, quorum ad manus opera ejufmodi de tam antiquâ Linguâ & characteribus tam eximiis, nunquam ullius Miffionarii diligentiâ pervenerunt; imo in Sinâ ipfâ, id mihi totum neglexiffe videntur Authores noftri. Nam fi *Premari* amici mei, harum Litterarum curiofiffimi, Grammaticam totam perlegeris, *Eloquentiæ* quidem Sinicæ, ejus præfertim, quæ in antiquis Libris elucet, magnæ, ut vult, & reverà admirandæ, meminit non femel, fed *Grammatici* tantum *unius*, ejufque fortuitò inventi mentionem facit, imo Litteris à me datis, *vifos à fe nullos*, Linguam Sinicam à plærifque ufu tantummodo difci, affeverat, quod quomodo interpretarer, fateor mi Lector, nefciffe me diu, eâque in re contra id quod videbam, ab optimo tamen doctiffimoque viro prolatâ, tortum me nonnihil, ita ut cum fenex effet, atque in exilio, pietatis ac Religionis caufâ, jam dudum tolerato, Libris forfan careret, hæc in verba prolabi potuiffe exiftimarem: aut id demum factum,

quod, quæ in Dictionariis fuis enunciata tam clarè erant, ea non animadvertiffet (neque enim id apud Miffionarios rarum) quia Dictionaria ab antiquis Miffionariis è Sinico verfa legunt, Sinica ipfa non attingunt plærumque: res enimverò per fe non patet? Dictionaria ac Grammaticas Miffionariorum vidimus, & videre apud nos eft, ea ibi omnia prætermittuntur; itidem, cum inter eos, qui ad nos annis fuperioribus è Sinâ redierunt, licèt ab annis viginti aut triginta apud Sinas permanfiffent, reperti fint, qui Linguæ oris, feu loquelæ Mandarinicæ affuefacti, & in eâ etiam exercitati, eadem hæc Dictionariorum Sinicorum à Sinis publicatorum præcepta omnino ignorarent: quid dicendum eft amplius? aut quid cogitandum tibi? Huic illi Authorum Catalogo fuccedunt Claves 214. & quæ ad *Clavium duplicium* ac *triplicium* figuram pertinent, ea in ipfo textu inferta invenies.

2°. Nunc Tomo fecundo eadem habes, quæ in çu luŷ *aut* çu goéi, nimirum quos *charactéres antiquaverit* apud Sinas *ufus*, quos retinuerit. Item *Tractatum*, juxta *Clavium feriem*, valde longum, de *characterum* ad fuas claves reducendorum *ambiguitate*. Item quomodo inter fe diftingui poffint, qui *figurâ fimiles*.

Tandem poft Tomos illos duos veniunt *Charactéres* ipfi omnes, *juxta* earumdem *clavium 214. ordinem*, iique ampliffimâ *fignificationum* ferie conferti.

Sed quod hîc animadvertendum maximè, adeft etiam in chím çu fũm, quod in cæteris plærifque Dictionariis non invenies, *veterum* fcilicet, & eorum qui in *titulis* tantum comparent *Characterum* delineatio, quos non rarò è xuĕ vên, de quo infra, aliquando etiam ex fe, ac cogitatis fuis exponit Author. Liber eft, ut dixi, volum. 36.

V I.

Cat. Bibliot. Reg. n. 51. pag. 380.

haì

海

p̃iĕn ch̃aô çũm,

p̄ĕn

chaŏ

çŭm,

篇朝宗

id eſt, *origo Aulæ*, ſeu *Regia laterum maris*; quod ſi chaŏ ſine clavi lectum, per clavem *aqua* legeretur, vertendum eſſet *origo æſtûs variorum maris laterum*, ſeu potius *maris latera & origo æſtûs*, quod fortè Author in mente habuit: comparatur ſcilicet characterum Sinicæ Linguæ cognitio, lata & omnimoda, qualis in hoc Dictionario traditur, immenſitati marium omnium toti, quæ & piſces omnes, & quidquid injectum fuerit, non ſolùm continet, ſed abſorbet.

Scilicet habentur hîc & *verba* & *nomina* omnium omnino *Scientiarum*, *Artium*, *hominum illuſtrium*, *plantarum*, *animalium*, *locorum*, *mineralium*, &c. idque juxta rei uniuſcujuſque ordinem. Author dicitur chîm gîn, aliàs chîm gîn ſî, qui cùm eſſet inter Doctores vir magni nominis & propter ſummam eruditionem, Sinis omnibus venerandus: præterea apud Imperatores Familiæ iá mîn, non ſolùm in honore eſſet, verùm etiam conſtitutus ab Imperatore Hiſtoricus Regius; per omnem vitam, quidquid longiſſimis & aſſiduis ſtudiis undique colligere potuerat, quod ad Linguæ Sinicæ, & abundantiam & elegantiam conferret, ſub finem vitæ in hoc Dictionarium tandem contribuit, atque hâc in re, eos, qui præceſſerant, omnes ſuperavit.

In Meditationibus Sinicis pag. 124 & 125. eam dedi hujus Dictionarii notitiam, quæ eſſet ſatis, ſed neque ea quæ illîc habes omnino repetenda hic duço, nec nova quædam omittenda, quæ reſcias, utile eſt.

Dictionarium hai p̄ĕn à Miſſionariis in Sinâ viſum, nec ſemel, quis dubitet? at tradita de eo pauciſſima, & à *Semedone*, non niſi nominatum eſt, Mul-

lero, ut dixi, cæteriſque forte nec inſpectum quidem.

Opus eſt eo majus atque in quinque ejus voluminibus eò vaſtius, quod impreſſio compactior ſit, & lineæ conſertiores, item quod characterum potius *Index & Catalogus*, quàm *expoſitio* haberi debeat.

In Præfatione de ú kîm, & antiquis Libris Claſſicis agitur, quæ prima Dictionarii materia, tum de aliis operibus, è quibus *characteres* deſumptos oportuit.

Poſtea ad Húm vù, ejuſque in Libris undique colligendis, & *characteribus* rectius efformandis diligentiam: pauca adduntur de Authore, Dictionarii ac Titul. cauſâ, cujus Tituli verba ſeparatim exponuntur.

Incipit ergo ſtatim *Dictionarium*, non quoad voces aut characteres, nam ſine arte & ſcientiâ, quónam tenderet, qui *characterum* Sinicorum originem, naturam, artificium admirabile, ſignificationes demum vellet ob oculos Lectori ponere?

Itaque Diſſertationem *primò* habes de lŏ xŭ, *ſex* iis *modis*, quibus accipiuntur aut exponuntur *characteres*; Sinæ enim, cur hanc vel illam ſignificationem, non aliam, hic talis & hujus figuræ *character* nobis offerat, cauſas vel rationes invenêre ſex, quæ ſunt, verbi gratiâ, *ſimilitudo rerum* in characteribus unicis ac ſimplicibus: *ſenſus ex duobus* vel *tribus* characteribus conjunctis, neceſſariò, ſed per ratiocinationem exoriens, &c. quæ res cum à nobis alibi delibatæ ſunt, tum verò Dictionariorum noſtrorum initio fuſè explicabuntur. Poſt hæc, quod jam Lector verum eſſe non dubitabit, tractatur de *vocalibus*, earumque numero, *de tonis*, eorumque varietate ac diſtinctione, de *conſonis*, earumque per hoc vel illud *organum* pronuntiatione: ſequuntur variæ characterum ſpecies, quales in xuĕ vên, &c.

Cæterum Tomi primi initio, *diviſio* eſt Dictionarii totius, & Capitum toto Libro ſecuturorum Titulus, idque uſque ad paginam 71. Omnia præcedit *natura* quædam *repræſentatio* generalis, ut inde Lector materiem operis ferè totam mente præcipiat & complectatur.

Poſteaquam igitur è lŏ xŭ, id eſt, *ſex illis* characterum exponendorum *modis*, exempla nonnulla protulit, qualia habes in *Meditationibus Sinicis* pag. 86.

Xxxx

& fequentibus : pofteaquam alia multa addidit de *accentibus*, dè *geftibus* ad rectam pronuntiationem adhibendis, de quibufdam characterum quorumdam abbreviationibus, de *orbis* partibus, *ventisque*, de *confonarum* ufu ad componendos *characterum* ejufdem pronuntiationis *Indices*, vocabularium illud exhibet quod hîc è *Meditationibus Sinicis* tranfcribendum tibi. Quàm rectè autem id Author, qui cum naturam ferè totam, in omnibus Linguæ Sinicæ characteribus expreffam, effet tibi defcripturus, ejus etiam tibi delineationem oftendere primùm voluit!

Sectiones ergo Vocabularii funt omnino undecim.

Prima, de *Cælo, Sole, Lunâ, Ventis, Tonitru, Pluviâ, Igne* ac *Meteoris* generatim.

Secunda, de *tempore, anno, menfe*, variis *anni* & *menfium* partibus.

Tertia, de *Terrâ*, & quidquid ad *terram* fpectat; itaque de *diverfis locis*, de *homine*, de *diverfis hominum ftatibus*, de *fonis*, quod, pro locorum varietate, alii atque alii fint, de *coloribus*, quod rerum è *terrâ*, aut faltem ex *cælo* & *terrâ* fimul prodeuntium ferè fint.

Quarta, de *inftrumentis* & *utenfilibus*, de *armis* igitur, *ponderibus, menfuris, poculis, navibus, curribus, carpentis, plauftrisque, thronis, cathedris, fedilibus* generatim, quot ad unamquamque Artem exercendam inftrumenta neceffaria; ita ut in Gentibus civilibus *Linguam* plærumque *novam*, eamque copiofiffimam efficiant.

Quinta, de *corpore* ejufque membris, *capite, capillis, fronte, oculis, nafo, ore, mento, collo, pectore, ventre*, &c.

Sexta, de *floribus* & *arboribus*, quot hoc loco fpecies tum *florum, fructiferarum, glandiferarum*, &c !

Septima eft de *ædificiis*, de *cibo* & *potu*, de *avibus* & *brutis* quibus vulgo aut defumitur, aut conficitur, aut faltem præparatur.

Octava, Cyclum, fortes, Litteraturam complectitur, ac proinde res Philofophicas, Moralia, Physica, Chymica, & quidquid five in vegetalibus, five in mineralibus ad Physicam fpectat.

Nona agit de variis hominum negotiis, quâ in re, Gentis *Leges, Edicta* Imperatorum, Fori & Mercaturæ *Officia*, Magiftratuum *Jura* fubintelligunt.

Decima continet *veftimenta*, item è quibus confieri foleant, *numeros* &

numerandi rationem omnem, ac præterea *adjectiva* feu *epitheta*, unà cum eorum *contrariis*, feu oppofitis.

Undecima additur, quæ ad naturam quidem non pertinet, fed apud Sinas admodum neceffaria eft, fcilicet *enumeratio characterum* quorumdam *rariorum* ac difficiliorum, qui in Libris apud Sinas frequentibus,

verbi gratiâ,　　　in fú xû
　　　　　　　　in yě kīm
　　　　　　　　in xī kīm
　　　　　　　　in xû kīm
　　　　　　　　in lì kí
　　　　　　　　in chûn cieû
　　　　　　　　in fiaô hiŏ

reperiuntur, ac Lectoribus negotium femper faceffunt.

In hoc magno Dictionario mira ubique Doctrina, unde *notitia characterum* Sinicorum omnium acquiratur, quæ poteft maxima; expendit nimirum varias eorum compofitiones.

1°. Ex *duobus iifdem*, fed quorum unus *fupra* alterum pofitus.

2°. Ex *duobus* quidem *fimilibus*, fed quorum alter *juxta* alterum, & à latere.

3°. è *tribus fimilibus*.

4°. Ex *quatuor fimilibus*.

5°. Qui ex *duobus* aut *quatuor*, quos inter, *alius* infertus deorfum.

6°. Qui ex *quatuor fimilibus*, & *quarto* in medium per latera introducto.

Hæc, ut in *Meditationibus Sinicis*, p. 125. dixi, & curiofa admodum, & fic utilia ad characterum compofitionem cognofcendam, ut nihil fupra: & is apud Sinas omnino barbarus, qui ignoret; inter Sinas etiam litteratos magnus, qui accuratè legerit ac poffideat.

A *pag.* 21. ad 121. numerantur *characterc* 11. qui *variis fonis* prolati, varia fignificant; fed hîc, ut annotavi,

1°. Ordo quidam peculiaris eft, *Characteribus*: ita eos enumerat, ut *feriem* promat, non eandem quam aut *çû guéi*, aut chīm *çû iûm*; quanquam enim per *lineas*, feu *linearum* numerum enumeret, alio tamen ordine opus fuit, quod eos plærumque characterês afferat, quæ ejufdem *clavis* non funt.

2°. Cum ejus *vocabularium ex rerum naturâ* concinnatum fit, Dictionarium cæterorum *feriem* fequi omnino non potuit; repræfentat igitur primo loco characteres è charactere *cæli* compofitos, deinde qui è charactere *Solis*, tum qui è charactere *lunæ*, poftea qui è charactere *venti*, & fic deinceps, tomo fecundos tomo tertio, tomo quarto, ufque ad *pag.* 47.

Poftea quam ea, quæ ad vocabularii ordinem fpectant, expofuit omnia, tum ad characteres Librorum *Canonicorum* & *Claſſicorum* accedit, 1. ta hio. 2. chum yùm. 3. lun yu. 4. mem çu. 5. yĕ kīm. 6. xi kīm. 7. xū kīm. 8. lì kí. 9. chūn cieū. 10. fiaŏ hiŏ.

Tomo quarto characteres profequitur Author eos, qui inter fe *fimiles*: 1°. *generatim* à pag. 42. 2°. *fpeciatim*, ad finem ufque Libri.

Tomo quinto habentur characteres *ejufdem pronuntiationis*, fed alio prorfus ordine, quam in çū guéi.

Cæterum quicumque ea, quæ nos in *Meditationibus Sinicis* præcepta pofuimus, rectè calluerit: is *characteres* in haì piēn, illic expofitos, ex utriufque Libri collatione, illicò eft, idque nullo negotio pronuntiaturus.

Hoc tamen annotavi tibi, atque iterum obfervo, *tonos* in utroque Dictionario, non femper & ubique eofdem; quæ differentia in Dictionariis Sinicis omnibus à me repefta eft; nam cum character idem quoad diverfas fignificationes, diverfos etiam accentus capiat, neque ab eâdem fignificatione femper incipiant variorum Dictionariorum Authores, accidit etiam, licet rarò, ut qui characteres in hoc vel illo Dictionario, *toni* funt, verbi gratiâ, *tertii*, iidem ab alio Authore *fecundi* aut *quarti toni* effe videantur, quod tamen eodem recidit, cum in orationis fuæ decurfu, eos omnes *tonos* juxta *fignificationum* varietatem exponant.

Hoc ergo illud eft, famofum haì piēn *mare immenfum characterum Sinicorum*, non eâdem quidem facilitate quâ cætera *Dictionaria*, fed & multò amplius, & ad fcientiam characterum pleniffimam multò accommodatius: quanquam enim *fignificationes* ubique non apponantur, neque eædem quæ in chím çū tūm, aut çū guéi, nec *tot*, nec plærumque *metaphoricæ* afferantur, tamen & *pronuntiationes* adduntur, quod percommodum, idque ex *Regulis* à me alibi allatis, & *fignificatio* ea, quæ fimplex eft, & è quâ cæteras exfculpere non difficile; at præterea, toties in fcenam revertuntur, tot modis hinc atque hinc fub oculos reducuntur *characteres* Sinici, ut eos, eorumque combinationes omnes difcas vel invitùs.

VII.

Cat. Bibliot. Reg. n. 50. *pag.* 379.

hiŭ

xi

xuĕ

vên.

alias.

hiŭ

xín.

許氏說文許慎

id eft, *Familia* hù *orationes.* Dictionarium eft characterum *antiquorum* feu *antiquatorum.*

Eundem apud Gentem unam fcribendi modum femper viguiffe, id verò nunquam repertum: fic apud Hebræos, Chaldæos, Arabes, alia atque alia fcriptura extitit pro temporibus, & idem apud Romanos, apud Græcos, apud Gallos factitatum, quanto magis fi à Provinciâ ad Provinciam tranfieris: atqui Europam totam æquat Sina. Itaque ab unâ Provinciâ ad aliam varietas in legendo, in fcribendo femper nonnulla, & hinc eft quod, quæ verba in hâc Sinæ Provinciâ hunc vel illum accentum habent, eadem in aliâ atque aliâ, alium itidem atque alium patiantur. Atque idem tibi de variis ætatibus prædicandum. Sed ii, de queis in xuĕ vên agitur *characteres*, non folùm à vulgatis admodum diverfi, verum etiam, nifi attenderes maximè, alii prorfus viderentur, quod de *Japonicis* ac *Tunquin-cis* fere dicendum : at cum ad eruditionem ferviant, & in titulis *Sepulchrorum* aut *Lapidum*, in *figillis*, aliifque ejufmodi *fcripturis* non raro ufurpentur; Xuĕ vên Liber eft pretiofiffimus, ac primûm quidem,fcias neceffe à Philofopho fcriptum effe, nomine hù yú ƙŏ, idque Imperante hŏ tí ʋĕ hán chaŏ, *feu* Familiæ hán, Imperatore 17°. fæculo Chrifti 1°.Sed fæculo 10°. cum regnaret Familia fúm, Commentariis illuftratum effe ab alio Doctore, nempe fù hivên, impreffum autem denuo, Imperante ʃiĕn ƙì, Familiæ tá mîm 15°. anno ejus 7°. Chrifti autem 1622°. Sed cum *characteres vetuftiffimos*, & eos etiam, qui à çám hiĕ, Imperante hoâm tí, inventi fuerant (hoâm tí autem à fŏ hì, fuit decimus, 2704 aut circiter ante natum Chriftum) contineat xuĕ vên:Licet in *Medit. Sin.* identidem à mé fit, prout fe dedit occafio, appellatum, tamen materiem ejufdem defignavi, potius quam declaravi, quod eam ob caufam nunc faciendum.

Itaque præponitur ʋῶ xuĕ vên Præfatio longa fatis, in eâ autem de characterum numero ac figurâ multa lectu digna proferuntur, 1°. verbi gratia, affert Author exempla tum *characterum* olim *fine ullâ tribunalium*, id eft, clavium *notâ* ufurpatorum, tum *characterum* nunc lineamentis *oneratorum*, cum antea multò fimpliciores effent, unde ftatim formatio characterum ejufque progreffus cognofcitur.

2°. Libris eâ de re nominatis, è characteribus *Titulorum* feligit quofdam, fed ita ut fub unoquoque apponatur çiĕ, *characteres* illi *duo*, ex quibus oritur pronuntiatio.

3°. Cum exempla characterum naturalium ea fint, è quibus figuræ àntiquiffimæ primò defignatæ funt; exempla eorum nonnulla allegat, 1°. *Artium*, 2°. *Herbarum*, 3°. *Ventorum*, 4°. *Infectorum*, 5°. *Serpentium*, idque generatim.

4°. Tum ad *artes*, refque arte factas procedit, atque eodem modo ad cætera, ita ut *Clavium* ordinem partim fequatur, partim derelinquat; fed neque id inepte facit, nam juxta Præfationem (quod etiam in *Meditationibus Sinicis*, ad hai ʃiĕn obfervavi, & infra itidem obfervabo) antiquitus *ordo tribunalium*

alius effe potuit ; de alio faltem, eoque tenuiori, atque in particulas minores, ac multò plures diftincto aut diftinguendo cogitatum fuit fæpius ; fed cum, quænam unicuique illarum particulæ attribuenda fignificatio effet, id verò dictu non facile videretur, à *primis illis naturæ & linearum* Sinicarum *notionibus*, ad eum qui nunc eft 214. tribunalium numerum devenêre *Grammatici* ferè omnes. Ex opere *Bayeri*, id fermè conjiciendum relinquitur, nimirum eos, à quibus Dictionariolum habuit, Miffionarios, de *minutioribus* quibufdam *tribunalium partibus*, quafi hoc vel illud fignificarent, cogitaffe ; & cave illud credas ignarorum effe, aut leviter meditantium ; Ex xuĕ vên, characterum Sinicorum inventores maximos viros ac fapientiffimos fuiffe, conftat fatis, & juxta *Premarum* nemo eft, qui primam characterum analogiam Authore noftro accuratius introfpexerit. involucrum eft 1. vol. 6.

VIII.

Cat. Bibliot. Reg. n. 76. pag. 425.

hiuên	懸
kín	金
çú	字
luý.	彙

Dictionarium idem quod inter Regios, n°. 48. & Miffion. n°. 52. (nam vulgatiffimum)Authore muý tǎn, feu muý ýn, qui fub ʋῶ tà mîm Dynaftia in vol. 2. vol. 14.

IX.

IX.

Cat. Bibliot. Reg. n. 78. pag. 426.

chím
çǔ
tǔm.

Non repetam quæ dixi ad *Codices Regios* n°. 49. addam tantùm Authorem vocari

leaó

pĕ

çǔ,

廖百子

& varias hujus Libri editiones factas, alias characterum elegantiâ pulcherrimas, alias negligentiâ viles. vol. 40.

X.

Cat. Biblioth. Reg. n. 77. pag. 425.

pín

çǔ

čiĕn

品字箋

Dictionarium nempe illud maximum, cujus descriptionem habes in *Meditationibus Sinicis*, quod, juxta nos, quamquam ordine nondum optimo, tamen eo est, quem natura quasi commonstrarit, & tam facili ac secundum sensûs communis, atque Analogiæ characterum Sinicorum Leges, ut à quovis homine prudenti ac docto Europæo divinari ac

perspici queat, apud Sinas autem præstantius antea nihil, pars enim hujus Dictionarii triplex est.

Prima ex Tractatibus characterum naturam insinuantibus, *Claves* simplices, ac multiplices docentibus, characteres clavium ambiguarum ostendentibus, &c.

Secunda, ex omnium omnino *characterum*, juxta *clavium* 214. ordinem Catalogo, quæ pars est voluminum duorum magnorum, nec à çǔ luý, *aut* chím çǔ tǔm illic propriè differt.

Tertia, ex iisdem characteribus omnibus per *Sectiones* ac *Tonos* positis, sed juxta *pronuntiationum* ac *tonorum* similitudinem, ita ut *Sectiones* sint totidem quot *Toni*, ac totidem *divisiones* quot *monosyllaba*, hâc vel illâ pronunciatione; unde fit, ut qui *simili pronuntiatione* sunt characteres, ii in uno eodemque loco sint, ac præterea, ut, quorum partes lineis clavium exceptis sunt *similes*, atque eam ob causam unà simul comparere debent, (hinc enim pendet atque aperitur characterum, aut potius characterum inventoris artificium ac sapientia) ii, inquam, characteres, etiam unà cum suis contribulibus ac similibus repræsententur.

Hujus Dictionarii à me nunc çǔ guéi, propter primam ejus partem, nunc pín çǔ čiĕn, quæ vulgaris appellatio est, vocati, dotes profectò eximiæ sunt, cum non solùm ad pronuntiationes monosyllaborum Sinicorum omnium, sed etiam ad consonantias in *Poësi* ac *Versibus* conficiendis reperiendas manifestò inserviat. Author tanti operis nominabatur yú vên çǔ, & involucr. solet esse 1. sed vol. est 9. quorum duo, *Præfationes* & *Catalogum* characterum ex çǔ goéi & chím çǔ tǔm : alii septem, eorumdem catalogum ex *pronuntiationum* ac *tonorum* ordine exhibent. Ordo tamen inter consonantias alius est in aliâ editione. Vide *Med. Sin. p. 50. & seq.*

XI.

Cat. Bibliot. Reg. n. 79. pag. 426.

Kǎm

hị

康熙

çù

字典

tièn,

id eft, magna 字 kăm hī, feu Imperatoris kăm hī juffu, procurata collectio.

Cum Litterarum gloriam ad fummum quemdam gradum non folum affectaffet, fed laboribus doctis ac laboriofis jufte acquifiiffet, quod omnis generis Monumenta, five ejus juffu, five ex ejus ipfius compofitione impreffa conteftantur, Dictionarium quoque, ut eruditionis cujufvis armamentarium quoddam, id extare voluit, ex quo character quivis Sinicus ftatim depromeretur: curavit ergo à Doctoribus & Mandarinis quibufvis, fed præfertim Litterarum famâ illuftriffimis, ex omnibus omnino Litteraturæ monumentis congregarentur quicumque, à quocumque Authore, ad regnum ufque fuum ufurpati characteres effent, quos poftea collectioni huic à fe apparatæ, accuratiffimè inferi juffit.

Continet ergo eos hoc 字 doctiffimi Imperatoris Dictionarium in invol. 4. vol. 40. fed de fingulis ejus partibus vid. *Med. Sinic.* cap. 17. p. 124. Monitum te fufficiat, quæcumque ad characterum five legendorum *facilitatem*, five intelligendorum *regulas* conferre potuit, ea ex omnibus omninò & *Dictionariis* contributa, & *Libris* collecta: unde 'nil majus, nam haì pién, de quo inter Regios nᵒ. 51. quanquam maximum, tamen non tantum characterum numerum, nec tam varias difcendi methodos exhibet, fcilicet, quæ poftea à Doctoribus *reperta*, aut *breviores*, aut etiam unà cum amplitudine ac longitudine *faciliores*, eas omnes in hoc eruditi Imperatoris Dictionario reperies congregatas.

XII.

Cat. Bibliot. Reg. n. 20. pag. 430.

kăm
hī
çù
tièn.

id eft, magno 字 kăm hī, feu Imperatoris kăm hī juffu procurata collectio. idem & quod fupra, totidem voluminum, nempe 40.

XIII.

Cat. Bibliot. Reg. n. 80. pag. 426.

çù

hiŏ

cīn

leâm,

字學津梁

id eft, *Porta Draconis Pons*, *ad characterum fcientiam*; metaphora eft è Sinarum *Fabulis* defumpta ad difficultatem rerum indicandam, feu potius, ut difficultates ab aliquo fuperatæ dicantur: revera Liber eft totus de *characteribus, laxis, contortis, truncatis*, ac generatim liberè ac fine debito linearum numero fcriptis, qui propterea & fcriptu & lectu difficillimi, quales non rarò in *Præfationibus*, quales plærumque in *fignis*, in veteribus *monumentis*, in *cippis* quibufdam, in chuĕ vèn, item, ut diximus, in chīm çù túm, poft characterum vulgarium & rectorum explicationem. Author hujus Operis per fe intricatiffimi, jû jú guéi. Cæterum unâ cum unoquoque charactere neglecto ac libero & fine veris lineis fcripto, ad latus characterem vulgariorem afcribit, ut faltem è vulgatioris vifu, difficilior ac rarior cognofcatur. invol. 1. vol. 4.

XIV.

Cat. Bibl. Reg. n. 25 p. 430.

çhuèn

篆

çŭ

luy

mŏ,

字彙目

id est, *characterum antiquorum varia species ac conspectus.*

Idem Liber est, qui in Catalogo Regio, *pag.* 427. n. 84. & *pag.* 430. n. 25. sed editio non eadem.

Hæc ad me ac pro me, quia in Bibliothecâ Regiâ deesse judicabat *Premarus,* missa est anno 1732.

In hoc Dictionario, collecti sunt ii omnes modi, queis unquam scripti sunt characteres Sinici.

Observatur autem ordo τῶν pú, id est, *Tribunalium* aut *Clavium.*

Character vulgaris, & qui nunc in usu quadrato continetur.

Tum afferuntur scriptiones variæ, olim usitatæ, quarum in capite apparent eæ, quæ in xuĕ vên, postea adduntur scriptiones, præsertim characterum currentium, queis subjungitur significatio. Voluminum est 12.

X V.

Cat. Bibliot. Reg. n. 85. *pag.* 427.

Liber inscriptus

çhuĕn

çŭ

çað

傳字草

xŭ,

書

id est, *Litteræ* çað, sive *Herbarum*, id est, ab herbarum similitudine desumptæ : de litteris seu characteribus ab herbarum & plantarum imagine ac similitudine, mutuò acceptis, agitur apud Kirkerum in Chinâ illustratâ Lib. 5.

Tales sunt qui in hoc Dictionario repræsentantur, *characteres* Sinici omnium fere *antiquissimi.* vol. 1.

X V I.

Cat. Bibliot. Reg. n. 55. p. 400.

çiên

çŭ

vên

chŭ

kiaì,

千字文註解

id est, *Litteratorum in characteres mille Commentariolus & expositio.*

Characteres sunt undecunque extracti, communes tamen, quorum latè ac distinctè scriptorum, datur supernè *explicatio* brevis, ex re aliquâ aut alio charactere notiori, aut etiam è characteris attributo notionem inculcante.

Author, ex Præfatione fuisse videtur, non Sina, sed Missionarius, quod tamen non affirmamus. Præfatio id ferè insinuat. Vol. 1.

XVII.

Cat. Bibliot. Reg. n. 54. p. 400.

sŭ

yên

çă

çŭ,

四言雜字

id est, *characteres mixti vocum quatuor.*

Libellus est sat malè sculptus, in quo phrases multæ, aut potius miscellaneæ, *characterum quatuor*, quales apud Sinas infinitæ. Sunt autem quorumdam characterúm communiorum. vol. 1.

XVIII.

Cat. Bibliot. Reg. n. 83. p. 417.

hiù
xí
xuĕ
vên.

Dictionarium est characterum antiquorum, Authore hiù xí. invol. 1. vol. 6. Sed vide supra n°. 7°.

XIX.

Cat. Bibliot. Reg. n. 53. p. 381.

sī

jŭ

西儒

ùlh

mŏ

çū

耳目資

id est, *quod apud Occidentis Litteratos, aurium & oculorum est officium:* (supple *in Litteraturâ,*) seu *quod vulgò in Litteraturâ observant Litterati Europai, cum Litteris dant operam.*

Hic Liber eò tendit, ut Sinis cognitio tradatur, non *Grammatica* qualis apud Europæos est totius, sed ejus tantum partis, quâ *consonarum* ac *vocalium* inter se conjunctio fieri solet in Linguis omnibus Europæorum, atque etiam Asiaticorum ad Sinæ Occidentem positorum, ut sunt Hebræi, Arabes, Persæ, imo Indi plærique; sed eos nondum noverant hujus Operis Authores, quod cum sit à Societatis Jesu Patribus conscriptum, & iis præcipuè qui Mari Sinam petiverant, Linguarumque Indicarum notitiam adhuc nullam haberent, ad Linguas Europæas tantum respexerunt: Litteræ illic Latinæ, sculptæ in Libri principio comparent, juxtà apponuntur characteres quidam Sinici, quæ iisdem correspondeant: tum sequuntur nonnulla ad Grammaticam spectantia, sed quæ tantummodo Sinicè exponantur. Opus est igitur generatim & Sinis & nostris, eam ob causam, parum utile. volumen est 1.

XX.

Cat. Bibl. Reg. n. 27. p. 431.
Liber Manuscriptus, cui Titulus,

lŭ

xŭ,

六書

id est,

id eft, *De fe modis quibus characteres fuos compofuère, aut componere hodie poffunt Sina.*

Tractatus hic à Premaro ipfo fcriptus eft in formam Dialogi, & illic characterum Sinicorum analogiam ex ipsâ earum, quæ characterem conftituunt, linearum confideratione conatur elicere; quâ de re nihil hîc addemus, nifi, id ab antiquorum Sinarum mente proficifci potuiffe, hactenus mihi vifum non verifimile, Prophetæ non erant. vol. 1.

XXI.

Cat. Bibliot. Reg. n. 66. pag. 382.

hân	han
lîn	lin
chûm	duplex
ǩǎǒ:	examen;
y̆	fenfus
&	&
yûn	confonantiæ
liǔ	leges.

翰林重攷義韻律

id eft, *characterum ejufdem pronuntiationis Indices, à Collegio & Doctoribus* hân lîn *redacti.*

Pars eft Dictionarii, hinc per *pronuntiationes* feu *confonantias* ordinati, illinc per *tribunalia* in eâdem paginâ oblati, ita ut in fupremâ paginâ, & fonos eof-dem, & eos, qui iifdem fonis donantur, characteres habeas: in inferiori hanc vel illam *clavem*, additis linearum numeris; & in hoc codice offerunt fe *claves cannarum & arborum*; ita Dictionarium hoc ad 7̆s̆ haì p̆iên, fimul & ǒ iûm vên, de quo poftea, imitationem factum effe videtur, de haì p̆iên certum eft, ex hoc ipfo codice, tûm vên quid fit, videbis poftea. vol. 1.

XXII.

Cat. Bibl. Reg. n. 45. p. 378.

mûm	
hiǒ	
fǎ,	

蒙學法

id eft, *via feu modus quo characteres à pueris difci poffunt.*

Rudimentum quoddam eft, fed merè Sinicum, præterea abfque ullâ methodo, cum omnia illic ufui dentur, & qui characteres in tá hiǒ, aut aliis Libris antiquis difficiles Authori vifi funt, ii tantummodo adducantur. Qui docendi modus, nonnifi ignaris, atque omnem *characterum Sinicorum* fcientiam refpuentibus, convenire unquam poteft. Author dicitur châm hêm, atque editio facta fub ǩǎm hī. vol. 1.

XXIII.

Cat. Bibl. Reg. n. 84. p. 427.

Liber infcriptus,

chuèn	
çǔ	

篆字

luý.

彙

id eſt, *characterum* chuèn *antiquorum,* vulgò chuèn *vocatorum, collectio.*

Hic etiam de veterum Sinarum *contortis* quibuſdam ac neglectis characteribus agitur, & Author Libri *tum guei fu,* regnante kàm hì. *Primùm* Præfatio eſt de horumce characterum naturâ & origine. *Deinde* juxta cæterorum Dictionariorum ordinem adſunt claves 214. *tertiò,* Per totum poſtea Librum comparent characteres explicandi, aut potius monſtrandi. In hoc enim Author incumbit, non, ut hujus vel illius characteris ſignificationes declaret; ſed ut, qui in çù goéi, vel çù luý, characteres inveniuntur, eoſdem hoc vel illo modo ab antiquis ſcriptos fuiſſe indicet, qui characteres poſtea in alio Dictionario quærendi. invol. 1. vol. 6.

XXIV.

Cat. Bibl. Reg. n. 81. *p.* 426.

chì   *collectio*

撫右遺文

kú   *antiquæ*

&

ŷ   *oblitterata*

vên.   *Litteratura.*

Dictionarium etiam aliud de *antiquis* characteribus, in quo & character antiquus & qui nunc in uſu, vulgò oſtenduntur. Author *chu meu guei.*

XXV.

Cat. Bib. Reg. n. 82. *p.* 426.

Liber inſcriptus,

chím   *recta*

正韻通

yûn   *conſonantiarum*

tûm,   *penetratio.*

id eſt, *modus comprehendorum characterum optimus.*

Dictionarium hoc opus eſt, & de eo ut & de alio ſimili mentionem feci *Med. Sin.* pag. 126. 127. & 141. Sed utrumque, etſi ad Grammaticam & Linguæ cognitionem pertinet, tamen ad verſuum condendorum methodum propriè accommodatum eſt. invol. 1. vol. 8.

XXVI.

Cat. Bibl. Reg. n. 26. *p.* 430.

Liber inſcriptus,

Liber ſine inſcriptione, in quo folia ſunt ſcripturarum fere omnium Sinicarum, quales nempe in variis, quorum mentionem feci, Dictionariis, ac præterea ſcripturæ Arabicæ ſpecies, non antiquiſſimæ, quæ *Kuphica,* ſed Mauritaniæ, quæ *Kuphica* apud Africanos ſucceſſit. Hic Liber itidem ad me è Sinâ miſſus. vol. 1.

FABULÆ ET ROMANENSES.

XXVII.

Cat. Bibl. Reg. n. 21. *p.* 430.

Liber inſcriptus,

xăn   *montium*

山海

haì   *marium*

kīm. *Liber.*

經

Liber est *de maribus & montibus*, in quo multa, ut videntur, fabulosa certè & obscura; hinc, quæ à Poëtis in Poë-matibus plærumque usurpantur, omnia ferè desumpta, Commentarii in xān haì kīm multi, Author ipse antiquus, & nunc ignotus, Interpretes ù gīn tē hīm, & kuò pú, hîc textus unus. vol. 1.

XXVIII.

Cat. Bibl. Reg. n. 8. p. 384.

Liber inscriptus,

haò

好

kiéu

逑

chuén,

傳

id est, *Historia fabulosa* τῷ haò kiéu.

Libellus est stylo siaó xuě, seu sermone familiari scriptus, ex eorum genere, qui apud nos *Romans* appellitantur, formæ *in-8°*.

Hîc autem annotandum tibi, partes eorum, quos *Fabulas* dico, libellorum, quique Historiolæ sunt de hoc, vel illo, aut puero, aut etiam Heroe, quem per varia rerum discrimina huc illuc trahunt, partes, inquam, illas, non aliter quam

hoêi,

回

indigitari, ita ut, quotiescunque characterem hoêi videris, toties Librum ejusmodi, vel *Comœdiam*, vel certè *Fabulam* absque dubio nuncupare possis.

Voluminum est nunc duorum, seu duorum hoêi; sed esse deberent plura.

XXIX.

Cat. Bibl. Reg. n. 9. p. 385.

yǒ

玉

kiaō

嬌

liě lÿ.

梨

id est, *Pera* τῷ yǒ kiaō, Authoris sic vocati; aliàs hæc Fabula dicitur, *Fabula* τῶ sān çaí çù, trium poëtarum: elegantiæ autem est apud Sinas exaltatæ, & maximo in pretio. volum. 6.

XXX.

Cat. Bibl. Reg. n. 14. p. 394.

Opus omnino idem, sed alio etiam Titulo:

sān

三

çaí

才

çù,

子

Poëta tres. vol. hoêi 2.

XXXI.

Cat. Bibl. Reg. n. 10. p. 385.

pīm

平

xān

lém

yèn.

aliàs

sù

çai

çũ ,

山冷燕四才子

id est, pīm, xām, lém, yèn, *seu* quatuor Poëtæ sic nominati : est etiam *Fabella* styli *siaò* xuĕ, volum. 4.

XXXII.

Cat. Bibliot. Reg. n. 11. *pag.* 385.

雅謎

yà,

mî;

id est, tû yà mî *Historia fabulosa.* Est enim ex eorum genere quæ nos *Romans* dicimus. Sed per Dialogos & personas, quomodo sunt Comœdiæ. vol. 1.

XXXIII.

Cat. Bibl. Reg. n. 13. *p.* 394.

Liber fabulosus inscriptus,

拍案

pĕ

gán.

Videtur esse *Fabula* quædam sat longa, cum habeatur kivên 19. itaque est imperfectus, & vol. 1.

XXXIV.

Cat. Bibl. Reg. n. 22. *p.* 430.

Liber inscriptus,

元人雜劇百種

yyên

gîu

çă

kĭ kiĕ

pĕ

chùm ,

id est, *Historia ludicra,* aut *Tragicocomadia centum;* quæ sub *Dynastiâ* τῶν yvên acta. Sunt autem in partes divisæ quatuor, quæ vocantur taò.

Primus taò Fabulas habet 22.
Secundus complectitur 25.
In *tertio* sunt 26.
In *quarto* continentur 27.

Initio

Initio voluminis primi Index eſt modorum, ſeu ejus cantùs, quo unaquaque Tragicocomædia (cantilenæ ſcilicet actibus inſertæ) cantillantur.

Sequitur ibidem pictura multiplex, nimirum quali decorari oportet unamquamque. involucr. ſunt 4. vol. 40.

XXXV.

Cat. Bibliot. Reg. n. 23. pag. 430.

Liber inſcriptus,

sī

fiām

西廂

kī.

&

pî

pă

kī,

記
琵
琶
記

id eſt, *Hiſtoriolæ* τῦ sī fiām, *Hiſtoriolæ*, ſeu *Hiſtoria comica* τῦ pî pă; ſunt Authorum nomina.

SĪ fiām eſt volum. 3. & pî pă 3. etiam, in uno, eodemque involucro.

GEOGRAPHIA.

XXXVI.

Cat. Bibl. Reg. n. 35. p. 376.

ᴋuàm

yû

ᴋî,

廣輿記

id est, *Lata Terræ descriptio*, seu *Geographia.*

Hoc Libro continetur Provinciarum Sinici Imperii 15. descriptio amplissima, itemque Regnorum vicinorum omnium, sive Imperatori Sinæ vectigalia pendant, sive libera sint, quod factum, quia olim Imperio subjecta fuere cuncta. Libri Author lŏ ým yâm, qui cum sub yûm lŏ ᴛàʏ tá mîm tertio viveret, Geographiam & uniuscujusque Urbis ac Provinciæ statum, quomodo tunc fuit, tradidit accuratissimè : inde est quod in tomo sexto, posteaquam Provincias tres

ᴋuàm

sî,

yûn

nân,

廣西雲南

&

kuéi

cheû

commonstravit, multa habeat, præcipuè de

íûm

kîm,

貴州 東京

Cochinchinâ, vicinisque aliis Regnis, opusque sit, eam ob causam, curiosissimum, volum. 6.

XXXVII.

Cat. Bibl. Reg. n. 36. p. 376.

kuàm
yû
ᴋî.

Vide characteres supra nº. 36. & est ampla terræ, hoc est, Sinæ totius *descriptio* : eadem est Geographia, sed aucta & correcta, ac denuo, at negligentius impressa, Imperante ᴋâm hî. Volumina 8. sunt, sed ultimum è Sinâ allatum non est. Itaque volum. 7.

XXXVIII.

Cat. Bibl. Reg. n. 1. p. 391.

yû

御

chí

tá

mîm

yĕ

iûm

chí.

製大朋一統志

Id est, *Regentis magnificè, & magna omnia facientis*, τῶν tá mîm *Monarchiæ mens, seu prospectus, aut Historia Geographica.*

Hæc est ampla illa & universa Sinæ Geographia, qualem summâ curâ elaboratam, atque ab illustribus Collegii hàn lîn Præfectis comprobatam habere voluerunt Familiæ tá mîm Imperatores magnanimi. Scito *characteres hosce* duos yü chì, de Imperatoriâ Majestate & rebus Imperatorum jussu factis vulgo usurpari. In lucem verò edita est, Imperante tïën xùn, anno ejus quinto, Lunâ quintâ, die decimâ sextâ : tïën xún idem, qui alias ŷm çûm, ejusdem Dynastiæ octavus. Vide *Réflexions critiques* lib. 3. pag. 457.

Cæterum hæc eadem ipsa est, quam, ut Sinæ, eorumque Imperium in compendio saltem cognosci possent, abbreviavit *Martinius*, habemusque apud *Thevenotium* tomo 3. sed cognoscenda est accuratius, ideoque cum nos eam in *Dictionario nostro Geographico Historico* totam ferè exscripserimus, idque non solum Latinis Litteris, ut *Martinius*, sed etiam Sinicis characteribus ; idem-

que Liber, & *Geographiam* omnem, & universam fere *Historiam*, tum Regnorum, tum Imperatorum, tum denique virorum, locorumque, atque aliarum rerum infinitarum contineat, quæ ad illustrandam Sinam conferunt maximè, non abs re erit, si operis ejusdem notionem paulò ampliorem tradiderimus, ejusque *methodum*, quam latè pateat, quam exactè tamen progrediatur, attentè consideremus.

At primùm quidem tomo 1º. præcedunt *Præfationes*, ut fieri solet, multiplices, atque in his Geographiæ hujus ratio redditur, id est, 1º. diligentiæ à multis Imperatoribus ad Geographiam Imperii Sinici noscendam adhibitæ. 2º. Variarum Imperii aut descriptionum, aut Historiarum, è quibus hauriri poterant cognitiones Geographicæ. 3º. Quorumdam, qui Geographiæ operam antea dederant, Authorum. 4º. Tabularum quarumdam ab aliis Authoribus exsculptarum. 5º. Multorum, qui de Geographiâ ipsâ, ac Terræ mensuris, Sinæque ipsius in varias partes & Regna divisione, conscripti erant, tractatuum.

Deinde ad vulgarem, quæ jam à primis temporibus facta est, Imperii distributionem transit in Provincias 15. atque eas illic appellat omnes. 1. kuàm tûm. 2. xān tûm. 3. hô nân. 4. xān sī. 5. xén sī. 6. chĕ kiām. 7. kiām sī. 8. hû kuàm. 9. sū chuĕn. 10. fŏ kién. 11. kuàm tûm. 12. kuàm sī. 13. yûn nân. 14. kuéi cheû. 15. adjunges pĕ kïm, seu pĕ chĕ lî, in quâ kïm sù, id est, *Aula Regia* ; unde apud Marcum Paulum Venetum Urbs *Quinsai* ; & cum Terra Sinensium tota trifariam divisa sit, non omissis ibidem τοῖς pám, quæ sunt magnæ Regnorum partes, nec Regnis ipsis, licet in Præfationibus non indicentur : postea distinguit totam in fù, quæ Urbes sunt Provinciarum primariæ, seu *primi ordinis*, in cheû, quæ secundariæ, seu *secundi ordinis*, in hién, quæ *ordinis tertii*, & fù addit esse numero 170.

cheû 234.

hién 1116.

Præterea sunt chīn, id est, Pagi innumerabiles, quorum multi Urbibus etiam maximis, si habitantium multitudinem spectares, facile anteferrentur ; sed inter Urbes non habentur, quod Urbi alicui subjecti semper fuerint, & Magistratibus careant hujus vel illius Dignitatis.

372 CATAL. GEOGRAPHIA.

Poſtquam Author ad Provincias ipſas acceſſit, nomine uniuſcujuſque indicato, omnes fŭ, id eſt, Urbes primi ordinis enumerat:

1. ſub pĕ kīm.
2. ſub nân kīm, *hodie* kiăm nân.
3. ſub xăn ſī.
4. ſub xăn tŭm.
5. ſub hŏ nân.
6. ſub xén ſī.
7. ſub chĕ kiăm.
8. ſub kiăm ſī.
9. ſub hŭ kuăm.
10. ſub ſŭ chuĕn.
11. ſub fŏ kién.
12. ſub kuăm tŭm.
13. ſub kuăm ſī.
14. ſub yûn nân.
15. ſub kueī cheŭ.

Quem tibi ordinem ideo adduco, ut diſcas Sinæ Provincias alias aliis ſemper habitas ſuperiores. Vide hoc loco *Magalhanis* diviſionem pag. 40. quæ eadem cum noſtrā eſt, ubi etiam *Provinciam* leaŏ tŭm, quæ non eſt è 15. Sinicis, ſub xăn tŭm comparere, optimè & juxta Geographum noſtrum annotavit.

Quod ſi *Cupletium* & *Martinium* adieris pag. 105. alium quoque ordinem reperies, quem, unde talem habuerint, neſcimus: habuerunt ſcilicet ab aliquo Geographo recentiori.

Inter yûn nân & kuéi cheŭ multæ inſunt earum Urbium, quæ vocantur *Bellicæ*, item *Arces*.

Poſt eandem Provinciam adducuntur, quæ appellant Sinæ *exteriora & Barbarorum loca*, ut niŭ chĕ, gĕ puĕn kuĕ, ſeu *Regnum Japonicum*, & alia numero 63. quorum nomina Geographis noſtris non admodum cognita.

Hæc, quæ vidiſti, omnia generalia ſunt, & omnibus omnino Provinciis conveniunt, ita ut jam de unâquaque habeas fŭ, ſeu *Urbes* primi ordinis, quo in Catalogo, ne fallaris, animadvertendum id tibi, quaſdam *primi ordinis* vocari cheŭ, nimirum ex frequenti Populorum uſu.

Sequitur nunc Liber ipſe, in quo, quid Author ubique efficiat, audi.

Primò, de Provinciâ unâquaque tractat generaliori quodam ſermone, ubi de ſitu Provinciæ, de primis Incolis, de primis Provinciæ & Incolarum nominibus, de mutatione unius nominis in aliud, ſub hoc vel illo Imperatore, ac ſæpe de ejuſdem mutationis cauſâ, præterea ſi quid in hâc vel illâ Provinciâ eximii & ſingularis, id ſtatim annotat, verbi gratiâ, *Flumen*, *Fluvium*, *Lacum* aut *Stagna*, item, ſi quod *Templum* in Provinciâ, ob Populorum frequentiam, famoſum; ſi qui *Mons*, aut longè ſacer, aut ob *Sepulchra* illuſtris; ſi qua *Telluris*, aut *Soli* proprietas, per totam Provinciam; ſi quid in *Ædificiis* notabile, ut in Provinciâ *Pekimenſi Murus Sinicus*; ſi quid ad *Luteratos*, ſi quid ad *Militares* pertinet.

Tum ad primariam *Urbem* deſcendit, de quâ à primis Monarchiæ Fundatoribus differit; ſic, verbi gratiâ, de Urbe pĕkīm ab hoăm tí ad hûm vù Hiſtoriam pertexit, ejuſque occaſione, enumeratis denuò, quæ antiquitus illic fuerunt, *Regnis*, indicat etiam, in quibus Provinciæ Urbibus, *Aulæ* eorumdem Regnorum fuerint, quas deinde, ut *Pekimi* habitarent, neglexêre aut Reges aut Imperatores. Sed cum in Indice generali Urbes primi ordinis jam commemorarit, hîc ſupereſt nihil, niſi, ut ſub unâquaque *tas* hièn deſignet, quod diligenter facit.

Jam ſi quis Lector hîc, inter illas, quas habemus Geographiæ Tabellas, aut Mappas, verbi gratiâ, *Martinii Atlantis*, *Duhaldii*, aliorumque, & eam, quâ de nunc ago, Geographi Sinæ deſcriptionem, quærat quid interſit; reſciat id à me, neceſſe eſt 1°. apud eos, præter *Urbes* magnas & *montes* quoſdam maximos, nihil indicari tibi: quam obſtupeſcet igitur, cum hîc, ſive in eâdem Provinciâ *Pekimenſi* apud Geographum Sinam, per decem paginas, *montium* 99. vel 100. non ſolùm mentionem ac deſcriptionem brevem factam eſſe, ſed & diſtantias ab hâc vel illâ Urbe indicatas, numeratasque, & ſitum ad *Orientem* vel *Occidentem*, &c. & culturam ac fructus illic naſci idoneos, didicerit? & ita montibus ſuccedere, *rupes* ac *ſcopulos*, & loca omnia prærupta, *valles*, *convalles*, *voragines*, *præcipitia*, *lacus*, *paludes*, *flumina*, *fluvios*, *rivos*, *fontes*, *puteos*, item *ſylvas*, *lucos*, *campos*, *planities*; ſed quod multò magis, adduntur *Ædificia* omnia publica, veſut *Collegia*, quæ in hâc unâ Provinciâ numero 24, item Mandarinorum *Hoſpitia*, quæ numero ultra 40, *Pontes* qui numero 12. *Aulæ* mortuis deſtinatæ, quæ ubique; quid ſi, quæ de *Hiſtoriâ Rerum* per unamquamque dynaſtiam, per prima tempora, per xăm, per cheŭ, per çín, cæteraſque deinceps Imperatorum Familias? ſic habes & *Geographiam* totam,

tam, & de *Hiſtoriâ*, quodcunque ad hanc vel illam Urbem, ad hoc vel illud Templum aut Collegium ſpectat, imo ſi quid ad hominem quempiam famoſum, aut inter Chinas magni nominis, vel ob ſanctitatem, vel ob virtutem bellicam, vel ob Litterarum gloriam, id breviter narratum tibi eſt, imo ſi quis inter Genios notus; *mutatione*ſque ſub hâc vel illâ Dynaſtiâ allatæ, illîc ex ipſo Dynaſtiarum ordine commemorantur omnes, quod Author eodem modo per totum Librum, id eſt, per volumina 49. exequitur. Sunt autem tituli plærique in paginarum capitibus, ſi eos exceperis, qui Dynaſtiarum ſucceſſiones indicant, & ideo ſæpe adducuntur, ut, quod in Provinciâ peculiare, ſub hâc vel illâ Dynaſtiâ fuit, oculis tuis ſubjiciatur illico.

Tomi ergo ita diſtributi, ut *Urbs* & *Provincia* pĕ kīm contineat 4. in tres partes diviſos.

Provincia nân kīm ſequentes ſeptem, id eſt, 4. 5. 6. 7. 8. 9. & 10. complectatur.

Provinciam xān ſī exponant Tomus 11. & 12.

Provinciam xān tûm 13. 14. & 15. ſed in hoc 15. deſcribatur, ut jam dixi, *Regio* leaò tûm.

Provincia hô nân tomos 16. 17. 18. & partem tomi 19. repleat, quod ex malâ compacturâ contigit, numeri enim denuo incipiunt poſt paginam 19. 38. & tunc ſe offert *Provincia* xēn ſī, de quâ etiam tomi 21. 22. ita, ut tom. 19. per dimidium.

Tomum 20. tom. 21. tom. 22. totum occupet una eadem *Provincia* xēn ſī.

Poſtea in tomo 23. 24. 25. 26. reperitur ché kiām, quæ *Provincia* etiam latiſſima.

Provincia kiām ſī, conſecrantur tomi 27. 28. 29. 30. 31.

Provincie hû kuām tomi 32. 33. 34. 35. 36. 37.

Jam *Provincia* ẛù chuèn in tomis 38. 39. 40. 41. per partes, quomodo cæteræ, deſcribitur.

De *Provinciâ* kuàm tûm tractant tomi 44. 45. 46. & 47. ferè ad dimidium.

Superſunt yùn nân & kuęī cheù, quarum altera, id eſt, yùn nân in fine tomi 47. & tomo 48. uſque ad pag. 41. delineatur; altera, nempe kuęī cheù, tomo eodem 48. poſt pag. 41. idque cifris mutatis uſque ad finem ejuſdem tomi 48.

Denique tomus ultimus, ſeu 49. *Gentibus*, *extra*, ſed *prope* Sinam poſitis, addicitur totus, quod aliter fieri non potuit; (nam quædam olim Imperatoribus Sinis ſubjecta, quædam ſponte dedita, quædam armis Sinenſium identidem debellata.) *Præfationes* Authoris plæræque, eruditione quâdam Hiſtoricâ refertæ, & ideo legendæ, quod Imperatores Bellicoſos ferè omnes appellet, eorumque prælia ſaltem indicet.

T. 49. pag. 11. deſcribitur Imperium gĕ puēn, ſive *Japonicum*, & varia ejus Regna.

Pag. 23. de Regno ſī fán, ſeu *Thebetano*, agitur.

Et ſic ibidem breviter exponuntur quæ ad populos, uti Sinæ vocant, Barbaros pertinent, de quibus nonnulla Martinius in Præfatione, atque hoc illud eſt τῶν τὰ μὶν tempore, eorumque juſſu, compoſitum opus Geographico-Hiſtoricum, magnificum profectò, lectu digniſſimum, & ſi totam Sinam, ejuſque *Locos*, *Urbes*, *Regna*, *mutationes*, *magnos Viros*, *Fœminas illuſtres*, *Virgines ſanctas*, &c. cognoſcere in animo habeas, cæteris illis, quas hucuſque vidimus, Geographicis deſcriptionibus longè anteponendum, cum in his Sina, non niſi per partes, eaſque admodum exiles, compareat, ex hoc noſtro Libro pleniſſima & admirabilis Imperii totius cognitio hauriatur. Addendam tamen, judicamus, quam è neotericis Authoribus excerpſit Cupletius, legimuſque nos ipſi ſexcenties enumerationem rerum Sinicarum compendioſam, eam nimirum, quæ ſub finem Editionis Confucianæ, & brevem Sinæ totius imaginem, è Tabulis Geographicis, ad nos miſſis, repræſentat. Hæc eſt autem, in toto Sinarum Imperio, *Flumina* navigabilia & *Lacus* celebriores numerari 1472
Pontes celebriores, 331
Montes præ aliis memorabiles, 2099
Turres & *Arcus triumphales*, aliaque id genus *Ædificia*, Regibus Viriſque illuſtribus erecta, 1159
Bibliotheca item celebres, Libriſque illuſtriſſimæ, 272
Gymnaſia ſapientiæ, ſeu *Academiæ*, Magiſtro Imperii *Confucio* erectæ innumerabiles: totidem enim erectæ, quotquot Urbes ſunt & Civitates, imo in pagis complures invenias, ut Geographiâ hâc noſtrâ liquidum.

Bacchalaureorum numerus (cum *Stu-*

Bbbbb

diosorum sit infinitus) assurgit circiter ad capita, 90000

Avita Templa, seu potius *illustres Aulæ* Majoribus aut Benemeritis, ad perpetuam Familiæ memoriam erectæ, 709

Mausolea Architecturâ suâ apud Posteros commendata, · 688

Viri, seu virtute, seu factis Heroicis illustres, Libris ac Metris celebrati, 3636

Fœminæ virtutibus ob virginitatem constanter servatam, itemque ob fidem maritalem prædicatæ, 208

Palatia Regulorum sunt, 32

Sed quæ singulis ubique Præfectis assignata, pro cujusque gradu & dignitate, idque impensis publicis, 32167

Idolorum Templa præ reliquis, vel ob magnificentiam, vel propter conficta Idolorum miracula, 480

Templa minora ac *Fana* omnino innumerabilia. *Bonzii* in utrisque Templis habitantes, ac Regiis diplomatibus donati, 350000

Bonzii absque diplomate, atque ex mendicitate viventes, multò plures.

Bonzii celebres in solâ Regiâ Pekinensi, 10668

Bonzii uxorati, & diplomate Regio instructi, · 5022

Omnium utriusque Sectæ *Bonziorum*, seu *Sacrificulorum* numerus incredibilis, & passim creditur prope accedere ad 1000000

Mahumetani qui 700 ab hinc annis Sinam ingressi, creduntur *millionem* excedere, 1000000

Pauperes, *Senes*, *Invalidi*, quibus olim sua assignabantur domicilia, & qui ab omni ævo, in singulis *Urbibus* & *Civitatibus*, annonâ Regiâ aluntur, tot sunt, ut nihil dum certi licuerit cognoscere.

Templa Deo vero dicata, præter *Sacella*, ante ultimas persecutiones, aut *Cupletii* tempore, erant circiter 240

Christianorum numerus, anno 1681. jam erat 260000

Quod si *Provincias* 15. & *Metropoles* consideraris, itemque in *Civitatibus Familias*, in *Familiis Viros*, exurgit immensum nescio quid,

Martinii tempore erant:

115 *Metropoles.*

1312 *Civitates* 2 & 3 ordinis, omissis *Pagis.*

10128789 *Familiæ.*

58916783 *Viri.*

Differentia est inter *Martinium* & *Magalhanem* magna, & *Magalhanes* majorem *Urbium* & *Civitatum* ponit quam *Martinius*, quod *Magalhanes* annumerat quasdam particularium Principum Imperatori Sinæ non parentium, & ab eo titulum duntaxat accipientium.

(Ex *Urbes* ac *Civitates* inter Mõntes sitæ in quatuor Provinciis sũ chuẽn, kuéi cheũ, yún nân, kuām sĩ;) item quod annumeret Urbes, & Oppida Regionis leaó tũm, quæ à Sinis, in particularibus tantum Catalogis recensentur, dum *Martinius* eas tantum scripsit, ex quorum districtu Imperatori vectigal penditur.

Itaque juxta *Magalhanem*, Loca partim *civica*, partìm *militaria*, sed muris cincta, 4402

Loca *civica*, 2045

Nimirum *Metropoles*, seu fũ, 175

Civitates 2 ordinis, seu cheũ, 274

Civitates 3 ordinis, seu hién, 1388

Hospitia Regia dicta yĕ, 209

Hospitia inferioris ordinis, seu chín, 103

Hospitia Regia, sed absque muris pro *Præfectis*, *Cursoribus*, aliísque ex *Aulâ* Regio sumptu iter facientibus, yĕ, *vel* chín, *vel* yĕ chín dicta, sunt 1145

Familiæ in toto Imperio recensitæ, 11501872

Virorum numerus, capita, 59788364

Inter loca *Militaria*, *Arces* 1 ordinis kuān dictæ, 627

Arces 2 ordinis, guéi dictæ, 567

Arces 3 ordinis, sõ dictæ, 311

Arces 4 ordinis, chín dictæ, 300

Arces 5 ordinis, paó dictæ, 150

Arces 6 ordinis, pù dictæ, 100

Arces 7 ordinis, chaí dictæ, 300

Murus Sinam ab utrâque Tartariâ separans, complectitur & leaó tũm, & Provincias tres pĕ kīm, xān sĩ, xẽn sĩ, ab ortu ad occasum, leucas Lusitanas circiter 400, juxta *Magalhanem*: juxta *Martinium* per milliaria Germanica 300, quorum in uno gradu 15, quod consideratis flexibus, & montium circuitibus leucarum est 500.

Jam si ad numerum hominum obstupueris, disce eo tanto numero non comprehendi

1. *Parvulos* ante annum ætatis 20.

2. Quicumque è Regio nati sanguine.

3. *Ministros* Regios.

4. Nec *Præfectos*, neque *Ex-Præfectos*.

5. *Milites.*

6. *Baccalaureos.*

7. *Licentiatos.*

8. *Doctores.*

9. *Bonzios* utriufque fectæ.
10. *Mendicos.*
11. Eos omnes, qui in navibus ac fuper flumina habitant, numero infinitos.

Hæc tibi omnia hoc loco exfcribere vifum eft, duabus de caufis; *primùm* quidem, ut lectâ τῶν tá mîm Geographiâ, quales hæ ipfæ eædem res tunc temporis fuerint, cognofcas; dein, ut quantum ab eo tempore progreffum fecerint, quantumque in dies crefcat illud Imperium, omnium profectò, fi non maximum, certè populofiffimum, & eâ majeftate, quam nullibi fere invenire fit. Voluminum eft, ut dixi, 49.

XXXIX.

Cat. Bibl. Reg. n. I. *p.* 391.

Liber Manufcriptus infcriptus,

leàm
kîm
xĕ
sān
sìm
xiûn
sĕ.

兩京十三省郡色

'Aularum duarum (Pekimi fcilicet & Nankimi) & 13 *Provinciarum Terruorii examinata pictura..*

Opus eft Geographicum, in cujus fine comparent varia vicinorum populorum Regna. vol. 1.

LX.

Cat. Biblioth. Reg. n. 2. *pag.* 391.

Liber infcriptus

gîn
kím
yâm
çieŭ,

人鏡陽秋

id eft, *hominum fpeculi clarus Autumnus,* five *pulcher Autumnus,* in quo rerum humanarum fructus omnes, tanquam in fpeculo perfpiciuntur.

Præfationes funt quæ Authorem, propter fummam eruditionem commendent quàm plurimæ, eæque, faltem complures, variis fcripturarum, feu characterum generibus, quod non immeritò factum; nam opus hoc immenfæ cujufdam ac ftupendæ lectionis; fcilicet, quæ ad Imperii *gubernationem,* quæ ad omnes Provinciæ uniufcujufque *Magiftratus,* quæ ad *hanc vel illam artem* in unâquâque Provinciâ ufitatam, quæ ad *vectigalia* illinc percepta, quæ ad *viros* aut *fœminas* in unâquâque Urbe illuftres; illa, inquam, & fimilia omnia, non fufè quidem narrat, fed breviter expendit ac delineat. Author kîn tĕ, vide in fine Præfationis ultimæ.

Poft *Præfationem* ultimam fequuntur *Indices* multi, fed præfertim eorum queis ufus eft Author Librorum & Authorum fat magnus; funt nimirum opera 656, ex quibus opus à fe confarcinatum dicit Scriptor.

Poftea rerum in Libro contentarum fummaria itidem copiofiffima: continet
Bbbbb ij

ergo 1°. narratiunculis non ita prolixis, 2°. figuris ac picturis, Historiam Sinarum ferè totam, & voluminum est 13. kivèn 2 1.

XLI.

Cat. Bibl. Reg. n. 3. p. 39.

Liber inscriptus,

kuàm

hoàm

yû

考,

廣皇輿考

id est, *examen Libri, cujus* titulus kuàm hoàm yû *Rheda Imperatoris lata.*

Opus est Geographicum, longè utillimum. Sunt illic, licet brevius, quæcunque ad unamquamque Provinciam, ad unamquamque hujus & illius Provinciæ Urbem cognoscendam pertinent. additæ suut locorum distantiæ, & loca ea, quâ transeundum ab uno ad alium locum, exactissimè indicantur, præterea Urbium Fundatores, & si quid illic factum illustrius. Non desunt *Mappæ*, Urbium saltem, & secundi ordinis. Sunt tantum volum. 2.

XLII.

Cat. Bibliot. Reg. n. 4. pag. 329.

Liber inscriptus,

fǒ

福

州府志

.cheû

fù

chí,

id est, *descriptio Urbis* fù *seu* fǒ cheû. Liber imperfectus, & pars amplioris decima-quarta. 1. vol.

XLIII.

Cat. Bibl. Reg. n. 5. p. 392.

Liber inscriptus,

tá

mîm

hoèi

tièn,

大明會典

id est, *codices & collectiones de iis omnibus quæ ad* tá mîm *pertinent.*

Cum Familia hæc Sinica & maxima & illustrissima fuerit, Historiam *Tamingarum*, nemo est, quin admirabilem esse judicet, & revera est. Continetur ergo hîc duobus involucris, voluminibus 10. & Magistratus omnes, *Urbium Sinæ* totius omnium statum, imo varios status repræsentat.

HISTORIA.

HISTORIA.

XLIV.

Cat. Bibl. Reg. n. 1. p. 367.

Annales Sinici inscripti,

çù	*adjuvantis*
chí	*gubernationem*
túm	*speculi*
kién	*principia.*
kām	
mǒ.	

資治通鑑綱目

sù
mà
kuām.
chū
vên
kūm,
kīn
gîn

1°.

2°.

3°.

司馬光朱文公金仁山上路

hoc eſt , *principia, ſeu quæ primò diſcenda ſunt , & ſpeculi inſtar eſſe poterunt ad dirigendam Reipublicæ, ſeu Miniſterii publici gubernationem.*

Hic Liber longe ampliſſimus , eſtque voluminum 120. Gentis autem totius, non omnem (Annales enìm ſunt Dynaſtiarum particularium plærarumque) ſed generalem Imperii Sinenſis Hiſtoriam continet, eam nimirum, quæ à Tribunalibus, idque authoritate publicâ, & olim profecta eſt , & hodie etiamnum conſcribitur. Authores Annalium innumerabiles , ſi eos numeres , à quibus per per varia ſæcula collectæ ſunt , ſed Editores, ſeu Authores Annalium hodiernarum ſunt præſertim quinque :

xān.

4°.

xām

lú , ló.

Ccccc

5°.

nàn

hiēn.

南軒

Itaque collectio eſt ab infinitis per varia ſæcula Authoribus orta, & ab illis quinque, in variis etiam ſæculis compilata.

1°. Author primus ſǔ mà kuām, qui hanc, quam nunc exhibent Sinæ, compilationem inchoavit, in vivis fuit ſub Dynaſtiâ ſûm, ſæculo Chriſti 10°. & ab eo eſt, quod nomen nunc præferant çǔ chí tǔm kién, Annales, cum antea, non niſi kí, id eſt, *Memoria*, aut alio quovis nomine inſignirentur : cæterum ab anno 7ǔ guèl liě vām 1°. incipiunt qui Dynaſtiæ 7ǒⱱ cheǔ, Rex ſeu Imperator fuit trigeſimus, idque annis ante Chriſtum natum ſupra vigeſimum octavum quadringentis ; perduxit autem uſque ad annum 7ǔ xí çūm ultimum, id eſt, uſque ad ſecundum & ultimum 7ǒⱱ heǔ cheǔ Imperatorem, annis à Chriſto 951. quod intervallum eſt annorum 1379.

2°. Author ſecundus, chū vên kūm, vir ætatis ſuæ celeberrimus, annis poſtea circiter 300. ſed ſub eâdem etiam 7ǒⱱ ſûm Dynaſtiâ, *primùm* quidem Annalium eorumdem titulo addidit characteres duos kām mǒ, quorum ſignificatio eſt *oculus præcipuus*, ſeu de verbo ad verbum, *principalitatis oculus*. Deinde verò, quod illâ additione indicabat, opus idem & commentariis & annotationibus quibuſdam moralibus & citationibus, ſeu antiquiorum Authorum teſtimoniis exornavit. De kām mǒ, v. Dict.

3°. Tertius Author, kīn gîn xān nomine, vixit initio 7ǔ yuên, Familiæ primæ *Tartaræ*, ſæculo Chriſti 14°. & cum tempora vetuſtiora propter quandam Hiſtoriarum antiquarum diſperſionem negligi poſſe animadverteret, Annales Imperii Sinici antiquiſſimos, id eſt, rerum ab yaô anno 1°. annis ante Chriſtum 2357. ad guéi liě vām annum primum, unde ſǔ mà kuām inceperat, geſtarum, ſerie continuâ, per annos 1930. repræſentavit.

4°. Author quartus xàm lú *vel* ló,

quod idem eſt, ab anno 7ǔ chīm hoá 12°. Chriſti ſcilicet 1465. ejuſdemque Imperatoris juſſu, eoſdem Annales continuavit per annos 408. uſque ad annum 7ǔ xùn ti decimum, ultimumque *Ivenidarum*, quod eſt anni poſt Chriſtum 1368.

5°. Author quintus nân hiên, qui ſæculo 16°. medio vitam degebat, ac proinde ſub iiſdem tá mîm : is Scriptor Annales auxit, ſupplevitque ex antiquis Authoribus ipſa Imperii initia, remotiſque fabuloſis temporibus, à *Fo hi*, primo Gentis non ſuſpecto Fundatore, ad id ætatis, ex quo kīn gîn xān inceperat, nempe annum 7ǔ yaô primum.

Sic Annales Sinici, quales hi, (nam ſemper continuantur) ab anno ante Chriſtum 2951. ad annum Chriſti 1368. perducti ſunt per annos 4313. etſi varii ſint hîc Chronologi. Quoad hanc editionem. Impreſſus Liber eſt, regnante hâc Familiâ tá čim, ſeu Tartarâ ſecundâ, ſub xún chí 7ǔ kām hî patre.

Et ſi eorumdem Scriptorum ſucceſſionem, per omnia ferè ſæcula non interruptam, habere vis, reſumendi tibi ordine retrogrado, qualem dedi in eo Libro, quem gallicè inſcripſi : *Réflexions Critiques ſur les Hiſtoires des anciens Peuples, liv. 3. pag. 428.*

chām kiū hô,
chām kiū chím,
yuên leaò fân,
xám lú,
ſǔ mà kuām,
chù vên kūm,
kīn gîn xān,
hoâm ſū mì,
puôn kú,
ſǔ mà cién,
ſǔ mà ſān.

Item qui inter

ſǔ mà čién, &

ſǔ mà kuām,

ejuſdem Familiæ fuit, ac Librum ſō ýn compoſuit ſǔ mà chín.

Cæterum de *Annalium* Sinicorum authoritate, quidquid cogitarint homines noſtri, certum eſt apud Sinas ſummo in pretio haberi, tanquam Libros *fidei indubitatæ*, à ſummis Authoribus, idque Imperatorum juſſu & Tribunalis ad hoc inſtituti curâ conſcribi ſolitos, qui mos Gentis ab yaô uſque, nec ſine maximo traditionis quaſi æternæ pondere in totâ Sinâ repetitur. Neque verò hi illi, quos vidiſti Scriptores, *Authores* Annalium

Sinicorum, fed tantummodo *Collectores* ducendi & appellandi, cum illud, de quo locutus fum, Tribunal nunquam non extiterit, fimul atque Sinæ in Imperium conceſſerunt, quod certiſſimè annis poſt diluvium non multis factum eſt, ut ii etiam fateri femper coacti, qui hiſtorica cæterarum Gentium monumenta in dubium auſi revocare. Liber eſt in 12. involucris, & volum. 120.

XLV.

Cat. Bibl. Reg. n. 2. p. 368.

Liber inſcriptus,

кù	*antiqua* vel *antiquorum*
vên	*litteraturæ litteratorum*
yuên	*abyſſi*
kién.	*ſpeculum.*

古文淵鑑

Cum apud Sinas, qui imperant, aut Reges funt, aut varias Imperii Provincias gubernant, Imperatores, Reges, Proreges, Miniſtri omnes, femper ſint, eſſeque debeant docti : nec niſi tales, ſtudiiſque ac doctrinâ omnino imbuti, ad regendam Rempublicam admittantur ; quod hîc, ubi de Regum factis, dictiſque ac ſententiis agitur, *Reges* ac *Litterati* eodem modo appellentur, eorumque mores ac cogitationes permiſceantur, mirum eſſe non poteſt cuiquam. Itaque Litteratorum antiquorum nomine & in hoc Libro & ferè ubique veniunt, non ii modò, qui apud cæteras Gentes, *Litterati* dicuntur, ſed quod Lectorem femel monitum volumus, *Magnates* & *Imperatores* ipſi : hîc igitur Liber, qui apud Sinas, viros politicos & Reipublicæ adminiſtrationi mirè addictos ſit maximi, & ſummâ curâ, itaque infinitâ quâdam characterum pulchritu-

dine editus eſt, ita ut *Veſtenios* in Galliâ peregrinantes, & illuſtriſſimum quemque Typographum, in admirationem ac divinum ſtuporem traxerit : ſimile quidquam, ab *Europæis* nunquam impreſſum, aut etiam imprimi poſſe confeſſos, & quod reverâ eſt Virorum maximorum hic facta, illic Sententias Orationeſque ſtylo antiquo, id eſt, elegantiſſimo complectitur.

Scriptus eſt autem ſæculo 17°. regnante τῶν tá mîm Familiâ, Sinicarum 21ª. Authore ſù kiên hiŏ, qui tunc Doctor Sinæ, famâ celeberrimus, & impreſſus anno Chriſti 1685. τῦ kâm hî 24, eſtque vulgo in involucris 4. voluminum 24.

XLVI.

Cat. Bibl. Reg. n. 3. p. 368.

Liber inſcriptus,

lì, liĕ	
sù	
кám	
kién	
pù,	

歷史綱鑑補

id eſt, *Supplementum ad ſpeculum univerſale*, ſeu *Annales Sinicos.*

Kalendarii modo præter *Annales*, ut jam inſinuavi, exiſtunt apud Sinas monumenta Hiſtoriæ Sinicæ quamplurima ; hæc enim eſt *Annal ſ* inter & cæteros Libros hiſtoricos differentia, quod Libri in Hiſtoriam à quocumque Doctore conſcribi poſſint ; (quæ res apud nos, apud Latinos, apud Græcos factitata)

C c c c ij

sed Annales publici, aut Imperii ipsius, non nisi à Tribunalibus, atque Imperatoriâ authoritate proficiscantur. Quam ob causam, apud

leaò

了

fàn,

凡

sic enim appellatur Author, reperies hæc duo : *Primùm* quidem, Annalium Magnorum abbreviationem ac compendium. *Deinde* verò facta quædam præcipua ac singularia, virorum in Imperio, vel rerum gestarum famâ ac virtutibus Bellicis Illustrissimorum, vel pietate ac regiminis scientiâ maximè commendatorum.

Vixit autem Scriptor sæculo 15°. regnante tá mîm familiâ, & appellatur sæpe uên leaò fàn, ejusque supplementum, non nisi sub ejusdem sæculi finem impressum est. Volumina non ita spissa, ita ut involucrorum sit duorum tantummodo, sed continet vol. 36.

XLVII.

Cat. Bibliot. Reg. n, 4. pag. 368.

Liber inscriptus,

iúm

通

kién

鑑

chĕ

直

kiaì,

解

id est, tŭ iûm kién *expositio litteralis.*
Annales primùm iûm kién appellatos

diximus, postea à chŭ vên kŭm titulo veteri additas voces kăm mŏ. Hic Liber, eorumdem Annalium *abbreviatio* etiam est, eaque à celebri Doctore Commentariis illustrata, cujus nomen chām kiŭ chím : fuit autem chām kiŭ chím, hinc tŭ ván liĕ, unius ex tá mîm familiâ, illinc 1mperii totius Administer. At sæculo 1ŏ ferè medio, annis post circiter 80. chām kiă hû, cum è Litteratis ipse esset, Sinicos eosdem Annales auxit. Quæ igitur sub eâdem tá mîm familiâ gesta fuerant per annos fere 276. ea non solùm Litteris mandavit, sed etiam explicatione litterali illustravit : continetque hic Liber 1°. *Annalium* Imperii totius, id est, eorum quæ Familiam tá mîm præcesserunt, *abbreviationem:* deinde, *eorum*, quæ sub eâdem Familiâ facta, *enarrationem:* 3°. *Expositiones* in ea omnia, præsertim in antiquiora, litterales ; desinitque in anno Christi 1647. Sic quæ per annos circiter 4609. evenère, ea in hoc opere aptè disposita, atque eleganter conscripta legere est : quod opus, cum non semel impressum jam esset, prodiit denuò regnante xún chí tŭ kăm hî patre. Est autem in 3. involucris, & voluminum 16.

XLVIII.

Cat. Bibl. Reg. n. 5. p. 369.

Liber inscriptus,

chŭn

春

ciĕu,

秋

id est, *Ver & Autumnus.*

Titulus est Principatûs Lù, *Annalium* ab ipso kŭm fú çù, id est, primario Sinarum Philosopho *Confucio* conscriptorum.

Hic Liber pretii apud Sinas summi, & propter ejusdem Philosophi, à Litteratis in magnâ veneratione habiti authoritatem, inter sacros tantum non repositus, Historiam repræsentat, præcipuè Regni lù, aliquando etiam, pro ut se dedit occasio, Imperii ipsius, idque per

per annos tantum 241. fcilicet in Regno lù natus erat *Confucius*, ibique cum effet è familiâ quâdam honoratiffimâ, quæque apud Sinas etiamnum Principatum quemdam obtinet, Patriæ fuæ regendæ ac bonis moribus informandæ per multos annos operam dedit Vir Philofophus: tandem abdicato minifterio jam fenex, & Litteris ac Difcipulis unicè addictus, rerum ante fe geftarum Hiftoriam, Politicis cogitationibus quamplurimis ornatam atque interfperfam voluit pofteritati relinquere, idque eft in cæterorum Annalium modum executus, ita ut res ad fuum unaquæque tempus referretur. Quod fi nunc tituli rationem à me quæfieris, non alia forte videbitur, quàm hæc, Bella in Sinâ, aliifque Zonarum calidarum locis, Vere præfertim & Autumno fieri, non aliis tempeftatibus, propter æftûs ac frigoris incommoditatem folere.

Jam, ea, in quâ idem hic Liber habetur reverentia, inde orta eft procul dubio, 1°. quod de regendo Imperio Sententias reverà admirabiles complectatur, Regumque, & optimorum virtutes, ac malorum vitia graphicè depingat; ita ut ex hoc Libro, tanquam è fpeculo, quid quifque in fe habeat Princeps aut pulchritudinis aut deformitatis, perfpiciat ftatim, ac proinde difcat, quid faciendum fibi, quid vitandum.

2°. Quod quidquid à *Confucio* fcriptum eft, fummâ id veneratione fufpiciant, & reipfâ nihil unquam quidquam apud cæteras Gentes, fi Veteris ac Novi Teftamenti Moralia exceperis, tantâ prudentiâ exaratum, quantâ id omne quod à Confucio fcriptum legimus. Cæterum cum apud Sinas Libri fint *Canonici* quinque, vulgò ù kìm, eodem ferè loco habetur τò chûn cièu, ac sù xû, feu Libri illi, quorum tres à *Cupletio* editi, ita ut vulgò *Canonici* Libri fex effe dicantur. Commentaria in hunc Librum fcripta funt à multis Philofophis quamplurima, & in hujus Præfatione Hiftoriolam hanc invenies, cum çin chì hoâm Libros omnes comburi juffiffet, exemplar uniufcujufque, & hujufce Libri, & aliorum multorum ab uno è Confucii nepotibus, in vetuftâ quâdam maceriâ abfconditum fuiffe, nec nifi Imperante hán Familiâ, annis ante Chriftum 209. repertum: eum autem hoéi tí, qui tunc præerat, Imperatorem id ftatim præcepiffe, ut editione eorumdem Librorum adornatâ, toti Im-

perio diftribuerentur, atque inde Litteraturam apud Sinas ab çîn chì hoâm tyranni ætate, quafi intermortuam, refufcitatam ac redingratam. Quin per quædam temporum intervalla, & regnantibus quibufdam Regibus atque Imperatoribus, vel otium, vel ædificandi libidinem Studiis ac Philofophiæ, qualis eft hominum natura, anteponentibus; eclipfes quafdam interdum paffa fit Litteratura Sinica, id verò non diffitendum. At *incendia illa* Librorum, ac Studiorum extinctionem, non è rebus effe abfurdis atque omnino impoffibilibus, licet hæc dictitata fint, atque à multis ineptè credantur, quis crediderit nifi qui res humanas, quo fe modo habuerint, oblitus omnino fit? *Gens humana ruit in vetitum*, Libros abolere voluerit quis? quamquam Rex, quanquam Imperator etiam potentiffimus, fatis eft fuperque, ut frequentius exfcribantur, atque attentius conferventur. Philofophos apud Sinas à çîn chì hoâm vexatos, in exilium miffos, tormenta perpeffos, bonis fuis omnibus, ac proinde Libris privatos, accipiam id lubens: imo vetera quædam monumenta, hujufmodi temporibus igni tradita effe, atque exemplaria eorum non pauca periiffe non negandum, cum id non rarò factum fit; fed *Libros omnes*, quod infinuant, Libros eos, quorum jam per Imperium vaftiffimum, jam *Tum kimi*, jam *Cochinchinæ*, jam apud *Japones*, jam denique in Sinæ defertis quibufdam inacceffis, exemplaria longè latèque diftracta fuerant, Libros, inquam, tam multos; apud Gentem Litteraturæ adeo deditam, Litteraturæ adeo amatricem, Majorum fuorum adeo veneratricem, vel extingui, vel etiam exulaffe potuiffe, fac mihi credas, res eft per fe abfurdiffima, & Differtatione ego Academicâ Fabulam effe putidam demonftravi. *Japones* Litteraturam omnem Sinicam amplexi funt, Hiftoriam Sinarum omnem, & à Sinis antiquis habuêre, & in Scholis fuis, non aliter ac Sinæ ipfi, legère, leguntque etiamnum: At fi *Kempferum* legeris, cùm de çîn chì hoâm loquuntur, filentium apud ipfos de Librorum incendio altiffimum.

Hæc autem hoc loco per tranfennam & ex Præfationis minus fanæ occafione dicta fint.

Eorum, qui in chûn cièu Commentarios confcripferunt, Philofophorum, quanquam hodie etiam componantur, ultimus famâ celebris fuit hûm múm lûm, qui fub tá mîm vixit, imperante tiĕn kì, ejufdem Dynaftiæ decimo-fexto. Liber hic involucrorum eft 2. volum. 12.

XLIX.

Cat. Bibl. Reg. n. 6. p. 369.

chúm

tím,

chûn

čieŭ,

çò

重訂春秋左傳句解

chuên,

kiú

kiaì,

hoc eft, *expofitio verborum genuinum* 7ŭ chûn čieŭ *fenfum jufte determinantium.* Alia eft editio eorumdem *Confucii* Annalium, quæ primùm à Doctore quodam chû sīn appellato procurata eft, fæculo 10. cum regnaret Familia súm. Deinde verò, imperante xûn chí, magno 7ŭ kām hī patre denuò impreffa eft. Involucrum eft unum, volumina verò quinque.

L.

Cat. Biblioth. Reg. n. 63. pag. 382.

Liber imperfectus, cujus infcriptio,

chûn

čieŭ,

春秋

Ver & Autumnus. Pars eft Libri à Confucio, de Regno lú fcripti, & fic appellati. Vide fupra. Eft autem Commentariis ornata. 1. vol.

LI.

Cat. Bibliot. Reg. n. 2. pag. 384.

çû
chí
íum
kién
kām
mŏ.

habes fupra characteres n°. 44.

Hiftoria Sinica univerfalis, aut *Annales Sinici,* de verbo ad verbum, *adjuvantis gubernationem fpeculi principia,* feu quæ primò ab hominibus Rempublicam adminiftrandam fufcepturis difcenda funt, ur ipfis fæculorum priorum exempla, fpeculi loco infervire poffint.

Liber hic, idem qui n°.44. Itaque illic vide, volum. eft 120.

LII.

Cat. Bibliot. Reg. n. 3. pag. 384.

sŭ, sŏ

çû

續資

chí,

tûm

xién.

kâm

mŏ.

治通鑑綱目

'Additio ad speculum, seu *principia speculi*, quæ ad gubernationem atque administrationem rerum dirigendam necessaria sunt, comparata : iidem omnino Annales sunt ; sed in quibusdam locis Commentario illustrati, & id, qui initio Tituli est character, indicat satis : nihil enim aliud est, quàm *addere* aut *supplere*. Vide clavem 120. tr. 15. & Dictionar. çú guéi tom. V. x. *pag.* 170. x. volumen.

LIII.

Cat. Bibl. Reg. n. 4 *p.* 384.

Liber inscriptus

chûn

čiêu

tá

春秋大

čivên.

全

Libri à Confucio scripti, & chûn čiêu, seu *Veris* & *Autumni* titulo editi, magna collectio. Cum de hoc Libro inter Regios, jam fusè egerim, nihil hîc addendum mihi existimo, nisi editionem esse pulcherrimam, Commentariis utique munitam litteralibus, & eodem, quo sú xú, sermone, id est, facili ; atque ex aliis Confucii Libris desumpto ; præterea editionem eandem esse, id est, Imperatoris jussu procuratam. Volumina sunt 13. & debuère esse 15. sed desunt primus & secundus.

LIV.

Cat. Bibl. Reg. r. 5 *p.* 384.

Liber inscriptus,

xoâm

yû

civě

yvên,

雙魚聿原

id est, tŏ xoâm yû *collectionum fons*: quis xoâm yû ? nondum deteximus.

Notæ sunt, ac propriè de Chronologiâ Sinicâ Disceptationes.

Liber pessimè exaratus, & eam ob causam, ferè ubique lectu difficillimus. vol. 1.

LV.

Cat. Bibl. Reg. n. 6. *p.* 384.

Liber inscriptus,

Dddddij

384   CAAL. HISTORIA.

lûn

ŷn

chî

tiên,

綸音持典

id est, *Collectio* seu *Codex*, *ubi sumitur sensus rotationis* (*Temporum,*) Ita appellant Libros *Almanachicos*, seu *Kalendaria*. Volum. 1.

LVI.

Cat. Bibliot. Reg. n. 7. p. 384.

Liber folii unius, sed longissimi, inscriptus,

taí

xám

sān

yuên

sān

太上三元三

---

pìn

sān

kuôn

fǎ

pao.

品三官法寶

Magistratuum superiorum, id est, *trium* yuên, *trium* pìn, *trium* kuôn *vocatorum ordo pretiosus.*

Agitur hîc de eo, quem inter se, & unà cum Imperatore egressi, servant Mandarini ordine, & ita pingitur eorum quasi processio. 1. volumen, gallicè *Rouleau.*

L. V I I.

Cat. Bibl. Reg. n. 7. p. 392.

vên

hién

tûm

kao,

文獻通考

id est, *Examen generale (rerum Sinicarum)* Litteratis oblatum.

Hic

Hic Liber apud Sinas nominatiſſimus, & tomorum 100. ea ferè omnia complectitur, quibus Sinæ in Studiis ſuis, ad rerum gubernationem ſemper tendentibus, dant operam.

Primò, Imperatoris juſſu denuò impreſſus eſt, ut in fronte annotatum.

Deinde, Præfationibus eſt ornatus numero 25. à 25. Authoribus & Litteratis, & iis ipſis, qui Hiſtoriarum Authores fuerunt, Scriptoribus: itaque cave *approbationum* eas loco æſtimaris. *Diſſertationes* ſunt, omnes in hanc vel illam materiem, tum in Libris ipſorum, tum in hoc ipſo tractatam, ita ut poſt eam, quæ prima omnium eſt, & de novâ editione agit, in quâ tamen eruditio etiam elucet, quod conſtat variis Confucii & aliorum Authorum citationibus, cæteræ omnes ad hanc vel illam rem elucidandam conſpirent.

in ſecundâ ergo Præfatione, quæ eſt Authoris, ac proinde ad opus propriè pertinet, de Annalium Scriptoribus; loquitur, & appellat ſù mà kūam ejuſque Hiſtoriam ſùm kién, item 17. Hiſtoricos, qui hîc nominantur, & de quibus aliàs à nobis facta mentio: Item varias Hiſtoriarum collectiones, vel tién, vel xù nomine, quarum ætates ac tempora expendit. Poſtquam ergo in 25. illis Diſſertationibus, de præcipuis Hiſtoriæ Sinicæ Authoribus egit, diviſionem Operis hujuſce totius ſubjungit, quæ eſt kivēn 247.

Multa igitur habet, 1°. de Hiſtoriâ Sinarum, ejuſque authenticis, & per totum Imperium celebratis Scriptoribus, & cum diverſis iidem Scriptores temporibus extiterint, eorum nomina, & exaratarum ab ipſis Hiſtoriarum, aut collectionum titulos indicare non habet ſatis, ſed quæ à *poſterioribus*, *priorum* elaboratæ ſunt reprehenſiones *criticæ*, eas etiam addit ſuper, & plærumque abbreviandi cauſâ verborum ſenſum indicat, non rarò etiam verba eorum ipſa affert, atque ut lectu digna judices, quæ profectò ad juſtam Hiſtoriæ Sinicæ cognitionem omnino neceſſaria, ſcito hæc per kivēn, id eſt, Tractatus 52. excurrere.

Inde tranſit ad varia Imperii, ac præſertim Regiæ Urbis Tribunalia, quorum diviſio alibi data eſt in ſex.

1°.	lì	*Officiorum publicorum*
	pú.	*Tribunal.*
2°.	hú	*Subſidiorum*
	pú.	*Tribunal.*
3°.	lì	*Rituum*
	pú.	*Tribunal.*
4°.	pīm	*Militiæ*
	pú.	*Tribunal.*
5°.	hîm	*Scelerum*
	pú.	*Tribunal.*
6°.	kūm	*Artium*
	pú.	*Tribunal.* vid. Dict. in pú.

Sed ordo hîc paulò alius, & ponit Author:

1. Hiſtoriæ Tribunal.
2. Subſidiorum Tribunal.
3. Cæremoniarum, *ſeu* Rituum Tribunal.
4. Militiæ Tribunal.
5. Criminum Tribunal.
6. Artium Tribunal.

Et addit

7. Tribunal ſìm *Reparationum*.

Quorum nuncupat Præſides. *Primùm*, xí lâm, &c.

Poſtea de Collegio hán lîn, ejuſque Officiis ac Præſidibus agit.

Hinc ad *Militares* aſcendit (kivēn 59.)

Kivēn 91. de *Imperatore*, ejuſque *Aulâ* & Aula officiis diſſerit.

Et cum *Religio* ubique in honore ſemper fuerit, (kivēn 91. & ſequentibus) de *Templis*, eorumque ornatu & Miniſtris mentionem habet, imo de iis, quæ & mane & per diem facere debet Imperator.

Poſtea ad ejus Filios ac Principes tranſit. ibique de Regulis ac Regibus tributariis, & in Aulâ vivere ſolitis, loquitur.

Sequitur *Muſica*, cujus harmoniam, tempora ac loca deſcribit, à kivēn 128. uſque ad 131. & inde ad 148.

Tandem (kivēn 149.) *Militiam*, ejuſque & genera, & officia, & ordinem, & ſupplicia depingit.

Quo facto, ad Libros ac Litteraturam ſe accingit. Diſſerit ſcilicet,

De yĕ kīm (kivēn 175. & 176.)

De xù kīm (kivēn 177.)

De xí kīm (kivēn 178. 179.)

De lí kí (kivēn 180. 181.)

De chūn cièu (kivēn 182. 183.)

De lún yú & mêm çù (kivēn 184.

Quos Libros, in varios, ut fieri ſolet, Paragraphos diſpertitur.

Tum de hiaó kīm, *ſeu* de obedientiâ & liberorum inſtitutione. (kivēn 185.)

De yŏ kīm, *ſeu* de Muſicâ (kivēn 186. &c.

Quæ etiam *educationis* pars, cum etiam inter legendum Orientalium, omnium

Eeeee

more cantillent Sinæ, & corpus huc illuc verfent.

Collectis ac commemoratis Libris aliis quamplurimis, annotat nonnihil de *Aftronomia*. Vide kivēn 281. Sic de *Solis*, *Lunæ* & *Stellarum* affectionibus, v. g. *Eclipfibus* tractat (à kivēn 282. ufque ad 295.) & earumdem *Tempora* indicat, fub hoc vel illo Imperatore.

Denique ad *Elementa* delapfus (kivēn 296. ad 301.) non folùm de *aquâ*, *terrâ*, *igne*, *aere*, *ligno*, 5. Philofophorum Sinarum elementis, orationem inftituit; fed & de variis eorumdem elementorum Appendicibus, quales funt v. g. *herbæ*, *arbores*, *lapides*, *metalla*, *flores*, &c. *montes*, *colles*, *rupes*, *fluenta*, *tonitrua*, *grando*, *pluvia*, *venti*, *Beftia*, *Infecta*, *Aves*.

Sed ne quid Lectoribus defit ad legendos Authores Sinicos, de antiquâ & novâ Geographiâ multa & curiofa congerit, ac præterea, quæcumque in Hiftoriis fabulofis reperiuntur, five de *Gigantibus*, five de *Fœminarum* Regnis, five de *Hominibus Pygmæis*, aut hoc vel alio modo deformatis, five de *montibus* ac *rupibus igneis*, uno verbo, de *Gentibus*, aut *Urbibus*, aut *Regnis* quæ nunquam extitêre, fed a Poëtis Sinis, in Verfibus aut Poëmatibus commemorantur, ea omnia Author fummâ curâ & labore indefeffo, in hoc præftantiffimo opere contribuit, atque hinc opus ejus, rerum ad Sinam & Scriptores Sinicos pertinentium, quafi πανσπερμια. Eft autem fic ordinata ejus methodus, ut quæ hic illic legit, tum in Annalibus, tum in Libris Canonicis, Clafficis, aut aliûs generis cujuflibet, ea ed eos, in quibus accidêre, annos referat, v. g. ubi de *igne*, illatifque ab *igne* infortuniis agitur, ubi de *aquâ* & *aqua* inundationibus, illic & varias *aquarum*, *marium*, *fluminum*, *lacuum*, &c. inundationes, & diverfa diverfis temporibus facta incendia, non folùm commemoret, fed eum Hiftoriæ locum, ex quo illud haufit, appellet, annumque hujus aut illius Imperatoris, hujus aut illius Dynaftiæ indigitet, qui ejus ordo ferè ubique eft obfervatus. Eft autem vol. 100.

LVIII.

Cat. Bibl. Reg. n. 1. *p.* 427.

. Liber infcriptus,

---

yû

chî

pĕ

kiã.

御製百家

Nomina Familiarum Sinicarum ab ipfo Imperatore in ordinem digefta. volum. 1. parvulum. pĕ eft 100.

LIX.

Cat. Bibl. Reg. n. 1. *pag.* 432.

Liber infcriptus,

çû

chî

tûm

kién,

資治通鑑

id eft, *Speculum univerfale, in quo repræfentantur magnorum Virorum res geftæ, unde difci poteft ars regnandi*. Vide primùm, quæ annotavimus fupra n°. 44. dici poffet Imperii Sinici Hiftoria generalis. Illa enim eft in quam facta deinceps commentaria.

Cùm hîc Hiſtoriæ Sinicæ totius monumenta ſint ampliora, id eſt, & Annales, quales in ſuperioribus à nobis deſcripti ſunt, perfectiſſimi, & præterea, ferè quæcumque ad eoſdem Annales illuſtrandos facere poſſunt, ex omnibus Authoribus ſummâ curâ collecta, non abs re erit, novam hanc Meſſem ob oculos Lectorum proponere, ut, quàm induſtrios operarios requirat, animo tandem aliquo percipiant, itemque, quantam hinc & factorum & exemplorum cognitionem, ſint in poſterum comparaturi Europæi, ſi quando intellecta, ac penitius cognita hæc eadem monumenta fuerint.

Adeſt ergo omnium prima Hiſtoria generalis, eo quem vides titulo; ſed hîc, ut in ſuperioribus tituli ſunt tres:
1. çû chí tûm kién.
2. çû chí tûm kién kām mŏ chìm piēn, de quo infra n°. 62. eſt.
3. tû vel sŏ çû chí tûm kién kām mŏ.
Sed hic tantum de primo agitur, & eſt volum 128. invol. 13.

LX.

Cat. Bibl. Reg. n. 8. p. 393.

Liber inſcriptus,

çû
chí
tûm
kién.

Habes characteres ſupra n°. 59.

Hoc eſt, *Speculum commune* ſeu *univerſale ad fulçiendam gubernationem.*
Hic çû eſt *inniti*, & chí *gubernatio*, primi Annales ſunt, quales à sû mà kūam ſcriptæ fuerant, atque incipiunt ab anno primo τ͞ʊ guēi liē vâm Imperatore, τῶν cheū 30. ante Chriſtum 428. & continuantur uſque ad annos τ͞ʊ xí çūm, qui familiæ τῶν heú cheū, ſecundus & ultimus, anno poſt Chriſtum 951. unde intervallum eſt annorum 1379. quod in Libri antecedentis Præfationibus accuratè annotatum; ſed releges quæ n°. 44. dicta. De numero voluminum, vide ſupra n°. 59.

XLI.

Cat. Bibl. Reg. n. 9. p. 393.

Liber inſcriptus,

çû
chí
tûm
kién
kām
mŏ.

Habes characteres ſupra n°. 44. p. 377.

id eſt, *Speculi univerſalis ad fulciendam* ſeu *adjuvandam gubernationem ordinatio*, ſeu *repræſentatio.*
De numero voluminum vide n°. 44. ſupra. lin. 15.

LXII.

Cat. Bibl. Reg. n. 3. p. 413.

Liber inſcriptus,

çû

chí

tûm

kién

kām

mŏ

chím

資
治
通
鑑
綱
目
正

piĕn.

編

Liber inſcriptus,

ćiĕn

piĕn

çŭ

chí

ĭûm

前編資治通鑑

Et

sŭ, sŏ
çù
chí
ĭûm
kién
kām
mŏ.

Partes ſunt Annalium , altera in quâ de ordine eventuum , ac Chronologiâ diſſeritur. invol. 1. vol. 8°.
Altera in quâ rei novæ ac prætermiſſæ adducuntur. invol. 3. vol. 30.

LXIII.

Cat. Bibliot. Reg. n. 4. pag. 413.

Liber inſcriptus,

ĭûm

kién

kí

sŭ.

通鑑記事

kién ,

id eſt , *ad partium interiorum eventus , aut res geſtas , ſpeculum.*
Id eſt , de rebus antiquitùs geſtis , & temporibus Hiſtoriæ ĭûm kién vocatæ initia antecedentibus , ſpeculum itidem adminiſtrationi accommodatum.
Author ergo , ut alibi diximus , kĭn gîn xān , Ivenidarum ætate , & Annales per annos 1930. eos nempe qui ab yaô ad guêi lië vâm lapſi erant , unâ ſerie contexit. Invol. 1. volum. 10.

LXV.

Cat. Bibl. Reg. n. 11. p. 394.

Liber inſcriptus,

ĭûm

kién

通鑑

τῶ ĭûm kién , ſeu *Hiſtoriæ Chronica,* quæ eo tantum tendunt , ut res geſtas , ad ſuum unamquamque tempus revocent; unde alium etiam titulum præ ſe ferunt , nempe mîm kí , elucidationes. Impreſſus regnante xún chí τῶ kām hî deceſſore. invol. 2. vol. 20.

LXIV.

Cat. Bib. Reg. n. 2. p. 412.

xĕ, xí

xě, xì

vên

pién

gú,

釋文辯誤

id eſt, *quomodo explicent Litterati varia in Annalibus deficientia.*

Sunt hîc volumina tria, in quibus vel multi Annalium defectus ſupplentur, vel quædam non ſatis explicata, traduntur enucleatius. Si horumce Articulorum 8. 9. 10. 11. volumina quæſieris, ſunt, ut dixi n°. 6. vol. 410.

Nunc corpus quoddam eſt Hiſtoriæ Sinicæ, quod dicitur niên yě ſù, id eſt, Hiſtorici 21.

Vidiſti autem ea Hiſtoriæ monumenta quæ generalia ſunt, & tempora Sinicæ Gentis ferè omnia complectuntur: fuimuſque hîc breviores, ideo quia de Annalibus ſigillatim, idque ampliſſimè ad Regios & Bignonianos Codices diximus.

Præceſſerunt igitur opera quinque magna, nunc per ordinem cætera indicabimus, ac primùm quidem de ſù kì, id eſt, *Memoriis Hiſtoricorum* agendum eſt.

XLVI.

Cat. Bibl. Reg. n. 6. p. 413.

Liber inſcriptus,

ſù

kì,

史記

id eſt, *Memoriæ Hiſtoricæ.*

Hiſtoria hæc de tribus Familiis prioribus tractat, nempe de hiá chaô, de xām *aliàs* ȳn chaô, de cheû chaô.

De Familiâ hiá, quam per annos 441. ab anno ante Æram vulgarem 2207. regnaſſe didicimus.

De Familiâ xām, *ſeu* ȳn, quæ per annos 664. id eſt, ab anno ante Chriſtum 1766. ad annum 1123. duravit.

De Familiâ cheû, quæ per annos 874. id eſt, ab anno ante Chriſtum 1122. ad annum 249. principatum tenuit.

Incipit ergo ab hoâm tí quidem, ſed τῦ yaô *Diluvium* ſupponit, ejuſdemque inundationes deſcribit.

Author eſt ſú má ciên, cujus ſtylum & elegantiam prædicant Sinæ; ſed additi poſtea Commentarii à ſú má chīm, qui ad fǒ hī uſque aſcendit, ac proinde τῶν hoâm tí, xaô haô, chuên kiô, tí kô, yaô & xún monumenta admittit.

Adſunt autem, quæ ad *Cycli* ab hoâm rí inventi confirmationem pertinent, omnia, eaque fuſè expoſita. Involucr. 2, volumina 14.

LXVII.

Cat. Bibliot. Reg. n. 7. p. 413.

Liber inſcriptus,

çhiên

hán

xû

前漢書

Hic Liber tractat de Familiâ quintâ, ſeu hán chaô, quæ regnavit per annos 425. ab anno 206. ante æram vulgarem, ad annum ejuſdem æræ 219. Vocatur autem Hiſtoria τῶν çhiên hán, id eſt, τῶν hán anteriorum, idque propter τῦς heû hán, quos videbis poſtea inter ù taí, poſt annum Chriſti 906.

Impreſſio eadem, quæ in Hiſtoriâ τῶν cheû; ſed hæc ubique notis illuſtrata eſt

F ffff

charactere minutiori.

Author puôn kú, qui fcripfit, Dynaf-tiâ τῶν hán Orientalium regnante, anno poft Chriftum 100. involucr. 3. volu-minum 22.

LXVIII.

Cat. Bibliot. Reg. n. 8. pag. 414.

Liber infcriptus,

sắn

kuě

xŭ.

三國書

Hiftoriâ trium Regnorum, fcilicet τοῖς hán, prioribus extinctis aut detur-batis, poft annum Chrifti 219. Impe-rium in partes divifum eft tres, Regna igitur fuerunt 3. fed quorum maximum *Septentrionale.* Inde eft, quod Liber in tres etiam partes diftributus fit, qua-rum prima eft, de

guĕi,

    fecunda de

vŭ, ú, gú,

    tertia de

gîn *vel* chŏ.

魏吳蜀

De guĕi funt kivĕn 30. de ú *vel* gú 20. de chŏ *vel* gîn 15.

Author appellatur chím xeù, qui vi-xit fub cín anterioribus, poft annum Chrifti 264. involucr. 1. vol. 10.

LXIX.

Cat. Bibl. Reg. n. 9. p. 414.

Liber infcriptus,

cín

chaô.

晉朝

Totus eft de cín chaô, eorum ergo Im-peratorum Familiâ, qui ab anno Chrifti 265. ad annum 419. nec confundendi funt cum cín illis qui τῶν cheū fucceſ-fores fuerant, alio enim charactere fcri-buntur : unde priores ab Authoribus Europæis vulgò per *i* cín, pofterioris per *y* fcribi folent.

Author hujus Hiftoriæ tâm tai çŭm, nimirum quod apud Sinas vulgare, Dy-naftiæ τῶν iâm fecundus Fondator, vixit ergo anno Chrifti.627.

Cæterum Liber eodem titulo gaudet, quo cæteri ferè omnes, & vocatur cín xŭ ; eft autem voluminum plurimo-rum, nempe involucr. 3. volum. 26.

LXX.

Cat. Bibliot. Reg. n. 10. *p.* 414.

Liber infcriptus,

fŭm

xŭ.

宋書

Res gefta à fŭm *Imperatoribus* : funt au-tem ii feptem, qui è Familiâ fŭm priori, nempe ab anno Chrifti 419. & per an-nos 59. regnavêre.

Differt autem ab aliâ illâ Hiftoriâ quæ infcribitur etiam fŭm xŭ, & eft fŭm pofteriorum. Involucra 2. volu-mina 20.

LXXI.

Cat. Bibl. Reg. n. 11. *p.* 414.

Liber inscriptus,

pĕ

çhî, çî

xŭ,

比齊書

id est, *res gestæ Pekimi ab Imperatoribus çî Septentrionalibus*, scilicet per annos 23. quos duravit çî chaô, ab anno Christi 479. ad annum 501. (inter parvum sŭm chaô & leâm chaô anni 502.) Author sŏ çŭ hién, qui vixit regnante Familiâ tâm. Invol. 1. vol. 8.

LXXII.

Cat. Bibliot. Reg. n. 12. *pag.* 414.

Liber inscriptus,

nân

çî

xŭ,

南齊書

id est, *res gestæ Nankimi ab Imperatoribus çî Meridionalibus.* Eodem tempore, Author quoque idem. Invol. 1. vol. 8.

LXXIII.

Cat. Bibliot. Reg. n. 13. *pag.* 414.

Liber inscriptus,

lcâm

chîn

xŭ,

梁陳書

seu *Historia rerum à* τοῖς leâm, *& à* τοῖς chîn *gestarum.*

Imperatores leâm vocati, quæ est Familia decima, regnarunt per annos 55. ab anno Christi 500. aut 502. ad annum 555.

Eos autem secuti & concomitati sunt, qui è Familiâ chîn, ita ut eorum anni non computentur, & in annis 24. τῦ vên tí, è τοῖς leâm secundi, comprehendantur.

Author tiaô sŭ liên, qui nonnisi Familiâ tâm regnante scripsit. Invol. 1. vol. 13.

LXXIV.

Cat. Bibliot. Reg. n. 14. *p.* 414.

Liber inscriptus,

pĕ

sŭ.

比史

Historia Septentrionalis, id est, res gestæ *Pekimi*, cum Imperio diviso federent illic Imperatores *Nankimensium* adversarii, quod factum est præsertim τῶν leâm & chîn temporibus. Multa etiam adducuntur, quæ ad peculiarem Urbis *Pekimi* Historiam pertineant.

Author

lì

李

yên

延寧

xeû,

& fcripfit fub Imperatoribus iâm. in vol. 3. volum. 26.

LXXV.

Cat. Bibliot. Reg. n. 15. pag. 414.

Liber infcriptus

nân

南史

sù.

Hiftoria Meridionalis. nân hîc intelligitur, & de *Meridie*, & de *Nankimo*, quæ Urbs Regia Meridionalis. Eft etiam hæc Hiftoria illorum eorumdem temporum, quæ à cî chaô ad iâm chaô tranfacta funt, nempe ab anno Chrifti 419. ad annum 618. Sic volumen primum eft de cî, volumen fecundum de chîn, & fic de cæteris, & vocantur cî puên kî, chîn puên kî, feu *Hiftoria peculiaris* τῶν chîn; cætera ejufdem Libri volumina titulum præ fe ferunt alium, nempe liě chuén, quafi diceres *Commentarius rerum difpofitus*, & Differtationes funt in omnem ætatis illius Hiftoriam, in quâ proinde Genealogiæ quàmplurimæ, & fumma rerum geftarum cognitio. Volumen ultimum totum eft de Infulâ haì nân.

Author vixit poft annum Chrifti 618. fub Dynaftiâ iâm, & vocabatur lî yên xeû, idem qui fupra. Involucra funt 2. volum. 15.

LXXVI.

Cat. Bibl. Reg. n. 16. p. 415.

Liber infcriptus,

fuî

隋書

xǔ.

Norunt, qui Hiftoriam Sinicam legunt, Imperatores fuî, τοῖς leâm & chîn fucceffiffe, annis poft Chriftum 581, nec plures quam tres regnaffe vên tî, yâm tî, κῦm tî. Hiftoria tamen eft longa fatis, atque eodem modo procedit, quo cæteræ præcedentes, ita ut 1°. Hiftoria τῶν fuî pofita fit, poftea fequatur Commentarius & Genealogiæ.

Author guéi chîm vocatus, & degebat fub τῶν iâm Dynaftiâ. Involucr. 2. volum. 16.

LXXVII.

Cat. Biblioth. Reg. n. 17. pag. 415.

Liber infcriptus,

iâm

唐書

xǔ,

id eft, '*Hiftoria* τῶν iâm.

Dynaftia hæc ab anno Chrifti 618. ad annum 906. per annos 289. regnavit. In primo volumine, quod fieri folet, Imperatorum ejus omnium feries genealogica exhibetur, itidem in fine, eorumdem Imperatorum anni oftenduntur ac conciliantur omnes. Author ngeú yâm fieú, qui vixit regnante Familiâ fúm. Invol. 4. vol. 43.

LXXVIII.

Cat. Bibliot. Reg. n. 18. pag. 415.

Liber infcriptus,

ù taî.

ù

五代

tái.

.Per ù tái, feu *Magnates quinque*, intelliguntur ii, qui poft Familiam τῶν tâm
Imperium rexerunt : funt autem,

     1. heú leâm
     2. heú tâm
     3. heû cýn
     4. heú hán
     5. heú cheû

idque per annos 53, ab anno Chrifti
906. ad annum 959. Unde fentis veteres illas Domos nondum deftructas : hîc
autem fiunt etiam duo, 1°. Adfunt
uniufcujufque Familiæ monumenta &
Hiftoriæ, 2°. adduntur rerum geftarum
difpofitio & quafi concordia.

Initium capitur à τοῖς leâm, per cap.
5. tum fequuntur heú tâm per capita
2. poftea cýn, quorum fán kuě præ-
ceffit cýn chaô per cap. 2. fuccedunt
heú hán per cap. 1. deinde habentur
heú cheû per cap. 1. quæ omnia titulum
præ fe ferunt puèn kī.

In Commentario eadem repetuntur,
fed multò uberiora, & unà cum genealogiis ampliffimis.

Veniunt ergo 1. Familiæ leâm feries,
quæ eft perfonarum 19.

2. Familia τῶν heú tâm, quæ eft perfonarum 39.

3. Familia τῶν cýn, quæ eft 18.

4. Familia τῶν heú hán, quæ eft 5.

5. Familia τῶν heú cheû, quæ eft 19.

Et adduntur qui poftea fuerunt inter
fubditos feu *Vafallos*, & mifcellanea de
iifdem Familiis plurima.

Author hujus Hiftoriæ idem, qui Hiftoriam τῶν tâm concinnavit,

ngeû

歐陽

yâm

fieû,

修

& τῶν fûm Imperatorum temporibus
fcripfit. Invol. 1. vol. 7.

LXXIX.

Cat. Bibliot. Reg. n. 19. p. 415.

heú

後

hán

漢

xû,

書

id eft, *Hiftoria* τῶν hán *pofteriorum*,
cum generali τῶν ú tái *nomine.*

Indicantur Dynaftiæ illæ quinque:
qui heú hán dicti, non nifi unum Imperatorem vulgò exhibent ; fed plærique, illius turbulentæ ætatis Imperatores, unà fimul regnarunt, dum feries temporum ab hoc aut illo defumpta
eft ; itaque in ordine Imperatorum Sinenfium hîc defignatur tantum kaô çû ;
fed in hoc de τοῖς heú hán volumine nominantur feptem, quàm vû tí, çûm
hiaô mîm, &c. poftea cum Domus τῶν
hán magna femper fuiffet, atque inter
nobiles ferè prima, & tunc in Imperio
exifterent fœminæ quædam fortes, quod
præfertim duris in rebus accidere folet :
adducuntur etiam Imperatrices quindecim, quarum memorantur facta : tum
fequuntur res numero infinitæ Hiftoricæ
ac Geographicæ, quas inter de Eclipfi
Lunæ tum obfervatâ, mentio fit.

Author hujus Hiftoriæ fán hòa, &
partes, ficut eæ, quæ præcefferunt, habet duas, 1°. tí kī Imperatorum res
geftas, & propriè Hiftoriam. 2°. liě
chuén, feu in eandem Hiftoriam Commentarios, & rerum inter fe conciliat-
tionem. Vixit autem fán hòa fub τοῖς
fûm anterioribus, poft annum Chrifti
420. Notæ & Scholia ubique inter-

                G gggg

394 CATAL. HISTORIA.

sperſa, Authorem habent kaó çú primum τȣ̃ ſâm chaô Imperatorem. Cæterum involucra ſunt 2. volum. 18.

LXXX.

Cat. Bibl. Reg. n. 20. p. 415.

Liber inſcriptus,

cheŭ

xŭ,

周書

qui propriè τȣ̃ν heŭ cheŭ; ad eos Imperatores ſpectat, qui ex antiquâ τȣ̃ν priorum cheŭ Familiâ, anno Chriſti circiter 351. inter ù taí ſolium etiam ipſi recuperarunt.

Deſcendebant autem, juxta Authorem, non ſolùm à veteribus cheŭ, quorum Fundator vù vâm, ſed ab ipſo xîn nûm, cujus nomen apud Sinas immortale, & ab ipſius fô hî temporibus venerandum. Hîc igitur genealogiæ ſunt temporum ferè omnium ampliſſimæ; ſed cum de ætatibus agatur remotiſſimis, nec ſine quâdam dubitatione hæc à quibuſdam admittantur, in cæteris Hiſtoricorum Libris, conciliatio & concordia ad finem remittitur. Hîc unicuique capiti, eodem tamen titulo liě chuèn inſeruntur Notæ criticæ ac Diſſertationes.

Author hujus Hiſtoriæ vixit, regnantibus τοîs ſúm, poſt annum Chriſti 960. & vocabatur lín kuâ tě fuèn.

Sunt autem invol. 1. vol. 8.

LXXXI.

Cat. Bibl. Reg. n. 21. p. 416.

Liber inſcriptus,

hûm

xièn

弘簡

lŭ.

錄

Rerum Hiſtoriæ Sinicæ appenſarum, & adjungendarum ſelecta deſcriptio.

Scilicet cùm ſub τȣ̃ν tá mîm finem, Libri Hiſtorici quam plurimi, ſubito incendio combuſti eſſent, timuerunt Imperatores, ne quid Hiſtoriæ univerſæ noceret ejuſmodi incendium, & ſtatim, ut damnum reſarciretur, nominati ab ipſis quidam Viri eruditi è Sinis Doctoribus, qui Hiſtorias deperditas hinc inde colligerent, ac compendio quodam traderent, ita ut hoc opus Dynaſtias novem repræſentet, nimirum τȣ̃s ù taí, τȣ̃s ſúm, τȣ̃s leaô, τȣ̃s kîn; unde hoc opere Hiſtoriæ Sinicæ acceſſit ſupplementum maximum: auctæ enim priores ſex, poſteriores duæ additæ, quæ duæ, non niſi obiter deſcriptæ illuc uſque fuerant. Opus ergo eſt, & longè maximum & ſummè neceſſarium, cum ea addat de leaô & kîn, id eſt, de Altunchanis, de Ginguiſchanidis, aliiſque ejuſmodi Tartaris, quæ Hiſtorici noſtri attigêre paulùſum, & tu alibi, eâ, quâ oportet abundantiâ, fruſtra requireres.

In primo volumine, quod ſolet, genealogiæ ſunt Regnorum illorum omnium ampliſſimæ & exactiſſimæ. Author

chaô

kîm

pâm.

邵經邦

Vid. Præf. 5. Impreſſio verò procurata anno τȣ̃ kâm hî 27.

Invol. ſunt 7. volum. 64.

LXXXII.

Cat. Bibl. Reg. n. 22. p. 416.

Liber inſcriptus,

tŏ

hûm

kièn

lŭ,

續弘簡錄

id eft, *Additiones ad Librum* hûm kièn lŭ; fed aliud nomen præ fe ferunt, fcilicet,

yuên

ſŭ

luŷ

piĕn,

元史類編

id eft, *Rerum in Hiftoriâ* τῶν yuên inæqualium ac difficilium ordinatio.

Sciunt nunc omnes poft *Ginguiskani* mortem, ipfi fucceffiffe *Cublaikanum*, eumque à Sinis appellari *ho pi lie*, & ejufdem *ho pi lie*, feu *Kublai* ætate, cum nempe Bella, unà cum Sinis, præfertim *Namkimenfibus* gereret, ad ea loca acceffiffe Marcum Paulum Venetum. Itaque cum feditione tunc bellifque, propter Tartarorum irruptionem ferverent omnia, effentque apud Sinas, hinc Imperatores Sinenfes ipfi, illinc *Ginguiskani* fucceffores, & qui τῷ *Kublai*

opitulabantur, & præterea domûs τῶν kin altas jam radices illic egiffet; non abs te eft, quod titulum ejufmodi Libro fuo præfixerit hujus Hiftoriæ Author Sina, cui nomen,

çín

vâm,

進皇

Continet autem Tomus primus (videbis etiam penultimum) Regum feu Imperatorum Tartarorum Genealogias ac Succeffiones, Invol. 2. vol. 16.

LXXXIII.

Cat. Bibl. Reg. n. 23. p. 416.

Liber infcriptus,

hoâm

mîm

ſú

kaí,

皇朋史概

id eft, *Radius, quo Hiftoriæ* τῶν hoâm mîm *modii menfurantur atque æquantur.* Senfus eft, Hiftoriam Imperatorum taí mîm Familiæ immenfam effe, & ad hanc tamen menfuram breviari & redigi poffe. Uno verbo erit, *Hiftoria* τῶν tá mîm *compendiofè propofita*: reverâ hîc res geftæ Imperatorum hujus Familiæ omnium, ab hûm vù, ad ultimum ufque breviter exhibentur, quorum Catalogus voluminis primi partem continet, cætera Historiam complectuntur. sed nota, eum quem vides titulum, non nisi generalem esse & opus totum, idque unum, ex Authoris mente, in partes divisum esse quinque; unde Libri exurgunt etiam quinque.

Primus ergo inscriptus est, hoâm mîm sû kaî, in primæ partis capite; sed titulus inferior est,

hoâm

mîm

tá

chím

kî;

皇明大政記

Id est, τῶν hoâm mîm, *Imperatorum* mîm *magnarum rerum gestarum*, seu *rerum Regiè ac magnificè gestarum memoriæ*, seu *Historia* in hoc rerum Militiæ ac domi gestarum, narratio simplex ac ferè nuda. Et tamen Liber est sat ponderosus. Invol. 1. sed volum. 12.

LXXXIV.

Cat. Bibliot. Reg. n. 24. *pag.* 417.

Titulum præfert ejusmodi,

hoâm

mîm

皇明

tá

hiún

kî,

大訓記

id est, *Leges ab Imperatoribus, Dynastiæ* mîm *Viris, latæ*; nam vocis hiún hæc significatio propria, ut *viris* non *fœminis* adaptetur. Est igitur quasi Codex Legum per omne τῶν mîm tempus latarum, nec recedit Author ab eodem Regnorum ordine; unde hic novus, idemque *Imperatorum* Catalogus; sed quod maximè observandum, quæ ad Libros ac Litteraturam, si fas ita loqui, pertinent, ea cæteris ubique anteposita videre est, ita ut ab ipsis etiam Imperatoribus, non solùm hi aut illi Libri, sed hujus aut illius Operis Præfationes emanasse dicantur.

Liber est invol. 1. volum. 7.

LXXXV.

Cat. Bibl. Reg. n. 25 *p.* 417.

Libri titulus est,

hoâm

mîm

tá

sú

皇明大事

kî

記

id eft, *Operum à magnificentiſſimâ τῶν tá mîm Dynaſtiâ factorum aut conſtructorum Hiſtoria*. Hîc quæ per omnes Sinici Imperii Provincias, regnantibus tá mîm, facta, conſtructa, ſtabilita, reædificata ſunt, quæ ad *Canales*, ad *flumina*, ad *fluvios*, ad *fontes*, ad *lacus*, ad *Hoſpitia* Mandarinorum, ad *Arces* Militum, ad *Urbes* Bellicas, ad *Collegia*, &c. attinent, ea omnia breviter collecta leges. Adeſt autem rerum Libro contentarum Index in primo volumine, invol. 2. volum. 22.

LXXXVI.

Cat. Bibliot. Reg. n. 26. pag. 417.

Liber inſcriptus,

hoâm

mîm

kaï

kuĕ

chîn

chuén,

皇明開國臣傳

id eft, *Commentatio Hiſtorica, in quâ oſtenditur, quomodo Vaſſallos & Regna extranea eperuerint*, id eſt, aggreſſi occu-

parint *Dynaſtiæ* m'm *magni Imperatores*. Hîc agitur de Bellis à mîm geſtis, ſive internis, ut *Vaſſalli* ad obedientiam redigerentur, ſive externis, ut *Hoſtes* debellarent. Præcedit hîc *Ducum* ac *Vaſſallorum* enumeratio ampliſſima, eſt autem invol. 1. vol. 6.

LXXXVII.

Cat. Bibl. Reg. n. 27. p. 417.

Liber inſcriptus,

hoâm

mîm

ſún

kuĕ

chîn

chuén,

皇明遜國臣傳

id eſt, *Commentatio Hiſtorica, in quâ monſtratur, quomodo Regna quædam & Vaſſalli quidam, magnificæ τῶν mîm Dynaſtiæ, per ſe ipſi, nullo cogente ac libentiſſimè obedientiam jurarint ac præſtiterint.*

Pars hæc eodem involucro contenta eſt, ſed tomos continet tantummodo duos.

Atquè hæc eſt rerum ab *hûm vú* & ſequentibus Imperatoribus geſtarum abbreviatio.

Author unus è ſummis Mandarinis, volum. 2.

Hhhhh

LXXXVIII.

Cat. Bib. Reg. n. 12. p. 394.

Liber infcriptus,

sān

kuĕ

chí,

三國志

id eft, *Conatus trium Regnorum*, gallicè, *Les entreprifes des trois Royaumes.*

Hiftoria ejus temporis, quod duravit fān kuĕ, fcilicet inter hán chaô, quod permanferat 425. annis, & cýn chaô, quod duravit annos 155.

Fuit enim Regnum illud triplex, per annos 45. ab hién tí morte, feu anno Chrifti 190. ufque ad mortem heú tí, feu annum Chrifti 264.

Vide *Reflexions Critiques*, pag. 446. item notam ibidem pag. 423. & 455.

In hoc Libro, Hiftoriam Regnorum illorum, claritatis causâ, præcedit Genealogia Principum, feu Magnatum de Imperio contendentium. Eft autem Liber volum. 21.

LXXXIX.

Cat. Bibl. Reg. n. 10. p. 395.

Liber infcriptus,

fūm

yuĕn

tūm

宋元通

kién.

鑑

Iidem Annales funt, qui hoc tomo titulum hunc præferunt, idque propterea quod de Familiâ fūm illic agant, quafi diceres τῶν Imperatorum è Familiâ fūm. Ante hos tomos adeft 1°. nova Præfatio. 2°. Oratio fatis longa de Hiftoriis & Hiftoricis præcedentibus, in quâ funt plurima lectu digniffima, atque inter cætera, effatum illud apud Sinas vulgatiffimum, Imperium Siniticum, non alio & alio modo, ut alia Regna, adminiftratum unquam, fed ab initio iifdem femper ufum legibus. 3°. Poftea Index eft Imperatorum ejufdem Familiæ fūm omnium, fcilicet à taí chù, ufque ad tí pím.

Sequuntur autem in eodem Indice Imperatores *Ginguiskanida*, quorum primus non ipfe *Ginguiskan*, quem Sinæ nondum agnoverant, fed xí chù, *aliàs* taí chù, *aliàs* iterum hŏ pí liĕ, apud nos *Cublai*, ufque ad ultimum eorumdem *Ginguiskanidarum* xún tiffic titulus, nonnifi decimum-nonum chaô, feu Familiam fūm promittit; fed Liber ipfe vigefimam quoque Familiam τῶν yuen, feu Ginguiskani pofteros complectitur: hæc verò omnia proponuntur chronologicè, ita ut, ad Imperatoris uniufcujufque nomen apponantur anni, imò ad anni uniufcujufque facta, hic vel ille menfis indicetur.

Editio hæc, quæ non omnino nitida, annum præfert τῶ fiēn kì, *aliàs* hí chùm, Familiæ tá mîm decimi-fexti, annum pīm ŷm, id eft, tertium. involucr. 3. vol. 30.

X C.

Cat. Bibl. Reg. n. 5. p. 413.

Liber infcriptus,

fūm
yuĕn
tūm
kién.

Adfunt characteres n°. præcedenti.

Hiftoria Imperatorum è Familiis fūm & yuĕn. fūm per annos 320. ab annô Chrifti 960. ad annum 1279. yuĕn feu

Ginguifchanidarum per annos 88. ab anno Chrifti 1280. ad annum 1367. pertinet etiam ad Annales, eifque vulgò fubjungitur.

Author fuit xaò kiā xān, idque regnante τῶν mîm Familiâ. Involucr. 3. volum. 30.

XCI.

Cat. Bibliot. Reg. n. 28. p. 417.

Liber infcriptus,

tá

mîm

hoeì

tién,

大明會典

quafi diceres, *Codices, queis omnia ad Imperatorum è Familiâ* tá mìm *pertinentia cóntinentur.*

Jam inter Codices Miffionariorum Extraneorum vidifti, qui eundem titulum præ fe ferret, n°. 5. quod erat vol. 10. fed nihili eft, fi cum hoc, de quo nunc agimus Libro, contuleris. Opus enim eft vaftiffimum, in quo habes quidquid à magnis illis Imperatoribus factum & imperatum, Leges eorum omnes quo tempore, quam ob caufam, latæ, fi quæ in 15. Provinciis factæ mutationes, fi qua Templa ædificata, item Tribunalium omnium ordinem, Urbium omnium, præfertim *Pekimi* & *Nankimi*, politiam quoad Magiftratus & fumma Tribunalia, quicunque non folum in iifdem Urbibus, fed etiam per omne Imperium Magiftratum exercuerint, quicumque Militiæ per omnes Urbes ac Provincias Præfecti: uno verbo, omnes omnino Magiftratus, omnium omnino Urbium 1. 2. 3. ordinis, imo & Pagorum & Arcium fingularium, itidem

enumerationes Templorum, Collegiorum, Sacerdotum, & quod fequitur, earum, quæ in Sinâ Regiâ authoritate nituntur, Religionum, cultus, obfervationes, ipfas etiam ad unumquemque Deum Orationes, denique Litteratorum omnium nomina ac lucubrationes; ita ut in nullâ unquam Gente tanta, tamque accurata rerum ferè omnium defcriptio facta fit.

Eft autem involucr. 8. voluminum magnorum atque *in folio* 60.

XCII.

Cat. Bibl. Reg. n. 29. p. 418.

Liber infcriptus,

ván

fìm

tûm

pù;

萬姓統譜

id eft, *Omnium cognominum Epitome & Liber Genealogicus.*

Ad Hiftoriam quoque pertinet hoc opus, quod Sinarum ferè omnium Genealogias complectitur, magnorum quidem Virorum, præcipuè nomen, vitamque, quanquam breviufculè repræfentat, idque in omnibus facultatibus, Litteratorum fcilicet, Imperatorum, Ducum, Artificum illuftrium, ac Poëtarum, Muficorum, Architectorum, Fabrorum, &c. & fic de fò hī, niù và, & de sān íaí, feu tribus primis Familiis hiá xām & cheû, de τῶν cheû & cýn profapiâ; fed his non contentus Author, nominum etiam combinationes maximè ufitatas, idque & temporum omnium, & in variis Provinciis per characteres & characterum inter fe conjunctiones, imo fæpe per varios tonos expendit.

Hh h h h ij

Ordo idem per omnes Libri partes, præterquam in primâ, ubi eſt Virorum celeberrimorum enumeratio ; nam in cæteris, nomina ſaltem per primum charaéterem, non rarò per duos charaéteres ſimilia exhibentur, ita ut Dictionarii Hiſtorici loco eſſe poſſit. Indicat verò ſub nomine viri uniuſcujuſque, Patriam, ſæpe Parentes, aut Cognatos, ſi famoſi fuerint, opera atque ætatem, id eſt, ſæculum, imo in quibus diviſum Imperium fuit temporibus, ubinam, & quonam regnante, vixerit.

Author liĕ taí ví vàm : Liber peſſimè impreſſus. invol. 4. vol. 40.

XCIII.

Cat. Bibliot. Reg. n. 3. pag. 417.

Liber inſcriptus

kŭ

kuă

niŭ

ĉhuĕn,

古刮女傳

id eſt, *Fœminarum aut Mulierum illuſtrium Vitæ & commemoratio.*

Præfationes ſunt quam plurimæ, ac de Fœminis, earumque virtutibus omnes, ſed plæræque *charaéteres* exhibent variarum *ſcripturarum*, illarum dico ve*tuſtarum*, quas nonniſi in Dictionariis difficillimis reperire eſt. Authorem id ad oſtentationem feciſſe nemo non judicabit. Tractat autem de Mulieribus illuſtribus fermè ad 130, quarum laudes ita perſequitur, ut ad unamquamque imagines etiam rerum ab ipſâ faétarum adducat.

Involucr. eſt 1. volum. 4.

XCIV.

Cat. Bibl. Reg. n. 30. p. 418.

Liber inſcriptus,

kŭĕ

yú

kŭĕ

çĕ,

國語國策

id eſt, *Sermones de Regno, Regni Liber.* Ita vulgò hujus Operis titulus concipitur ; ſed in fronte additur,

p̂âm

yún

tö, tŭ

puĕn,

旁訓讀本

id eſt, *unà cum expoſitione laterali & additionibus ſingularibus.*

Libelli ſunt antiquiſſimi, ejuſque Authores ignorantur ; certum eſt ſub τ w hán Dynaſtiâ jam tum extitiſſe, imò *antiquos* tunc temporis creditos, quum ſub iiſdem hán à lieú hiàm reviſi ac recogniti ſint.

Agunt

Agunt hi Libri de Imperio & Imperii recte administrandi modo, quem exemplis ex antiquâ Historiâ desumptis politicè confirmant.

Editio hæc, kām hī regnante, procurata est, anno ejus 24. Involucr. 1. volum. 3.

XCV.

Cat. Bibliot. Reg. n. 14. p. 428.

Liber inscriptus,

lŏ, lŭ 六

chīn 臣

chù 註

vên 文

suèn. 選

Et brevius.

vên 文

suèn; 選

id est, *Numerus*, seu *Collectio variorum Eloquentiæ Operum*, quæ inter sex Vassallos edita, τῶν leâm ætate. Author fuit, aut potius Collector, qui Familiæ leâm, hæres Regius fuit

chaŏ 昭

---

mîm 明

taí 太

çù. 子

Præfationes Libri sunt multæ, in queis de totâ collectione, ac præcipuè de Scriptoribus agitur; sunt verò & Editorum complurium, & Principis, seu τῷ chaŏ mîm ipsius; postea sequitur eorumdem Scriptorum enumeratio exactissima, quos Author in Poëtas, Philosophos, Politicos, &c. dispertitur. Ut in partes suas distingueretur Oratio unaquæque aut unumquodque Poema, additæ sunt in plærisque notæ commatum.

Facta Editio sub ván liě, & invol. 2. sed volum. 20. eorumque & magnorum & spissorum.

XCVI.

Cat. Bibliot. Reg. n. 2. pag. 427.

Liber inscriptus,

ngheū 歐

yâm 陽

sieū 修

vên 文

402 CATAL. HISTORIA.

ciĕ,

集

id est, *Collectio Scriptorum elegantium*, τῶ ngheũ yâm ſieũ; Hiſtoriam compo-

ſuit τῶγ tâm & ũ taí, vivebat autem imperantibus ſûm poſt annum Chriſti 960. Author eſt κριτικώτατ©, de antiquis kĩm, & multis aliis Authoribus loquitur ſæpiſſimè, ac præterea elegantiâ eſt ſummâ. Invol. 2. panni admirabilis, volum. 24.

欧洲藏汉籍目录丛编

Catalogues of Ancient Chinese Classics in Europe

4

张西平　主　编

谢　辉　林发钦　副主编

SPM
南方出版传媒
广东人民出版社
·广州·

文化公所
Hall de Cultura

Catalogue des Livres Chinois, Coréens, Japonais, etc（2）

中韩日文图书目录（2）

CATALOGUE

DES

LIVRES CHINOIS

CORÉENS, JAPONAIS, ETC.

IMP. ORIENTALE A. BURDIN ET Cie, ANGERS

BIBLIOTHÈQUE NATIONALE

DÉPARTEMENT DES MANUSCRITS

CATALOGUE

DES

LIVRES CHINOIS

CORÉENS, JAPONAIS, ETC.

PAR

MAURICE COURANT

Secrétaire interprète du Ministère des Affaires Étrangères
pour les langues chinoise et japonaise,
Professeur près la Chambre de Commerce de Lyon,
Maître de conférences à la Faculté des Lettres de Lyon.

TOME SECOND
Nos 4424-6689

PARIS

ERNEST LEROUX, ÉDITEUR

28, RUE BONAPARTE, VIe

1910

DIVISIONS DU TOME SECOND

——

CHINE

CATALOGUE

DES

LIVRES CHINOIS

Chapitre VIII : LEXICOGRAPHIE

Première Section : DICTIONNAIRES GRAPHIQUES

4424-4425. 說文眞本

Choę oen tchen pęn.

Véritable texte du Choę oen.

D'après l'édition de Siu Hiuen, de Koang-ling (916-991). Ce dictionnaire, titre complet Choę oen kiai tseu, est dû à Hiu Chen, surnom Chou-tchong, de Jou-nan, qui acheva son œuvre en 100 p. C.; les caractères sont rangés sous 540 pou ou clefs. Introduction de Siu Hiuen; à la fin, notices par divers auteurs et pièces datées de 986. Édition du pavillon Ki-kou, d'après un exemplaire des Song.

15 sections formant 30 livres. — Cat. imp., liv. 41, f. 2.

In-4. Papier blanc, titre noir sur blanc. 2 vol., cartonnage.

Nouveau fonds 4562, 4563.

4426. 重刊許氏說文解字五音韻譜

Tchhong khan hiu chi choę oen kiai tseu oou yin yun phou.

Le Choę oen de Hiu Chen, arrangé par tons; réédition.

Arrangement dû à Siu Hiuen, surnom Ting-tchhen. Dédicace à l'Empereur par Siu Hiuen (986). Notice originale datée de 121. Planches conservées à la salle Oou-yun, à Yun-lin (xvie s. ?).

12 livres. — Comparer Cat. imp., liv. 43, f. 6; liv. 41, f. 11 (Choę oen kiai tseu tchoan yun phou, en 5 livres).

Petit in-8. Titre noir sur blanc. 1 vol., reliure au chiffre de Charles X.

Fourmont 7.

1

4427. *Tchhong khan hiu chi choẹ oen kiai tseu oou yin yun phou.*

Même ouvrage; planches un peu plus grandes, mais très analogues, gravées à la maison Tchou-yun, de Mei-chou (XVIe s. ?).

Petit in-8. Titre noir sur blanc. 1 vol., reliure au chiffre de Charles X.
Fourmont 18.

4428-4429. 說文繫傳
Choẹ oen hi tchoan.

Le Choẹ oen annoté.

Par Siu Khiai, surnom Tchhou-kin (920-974), frère de Siu Hiuen. Prononciations données par Tchou Ngao; dissertation par Siu Khiai dans les trois derniers livres; diverses annexes relatives à l'auteur et à l'ouvrage. Édition donnée par Oang Khi-chou, de Chẹ, avec postface du même (1782).

4o livres. — Cat. imp., liv. 41, f. 7.

In-4. Papier blanc, titre noir sur papier teinté. 2 vol., demi-rel., au chiffre de Napoléon III.
Nouveau fonds 1213 et 1214.

4430-4431. 說文長箋
Choẹ oen tchhang tsien.

Le Choẹ oen avec notes.

Par Tchao Hoan-koang, de Oou, et son fils Tchao Kiun, d'après l'ouvrage de Siu Hiuen (n° 4426). Préfaces de Hoan-koang (1606) et de Kiun (1631); préface manuscrite de Tshien Khien-yi (1631). Table générale indiquant la division en tons; à la suite, table pour chaque livre, donnant la liste des caractères traités. — Le livre préliminaire comprend entre autres parties :

1o une notice copieuse par l'auteur (1608);

2o 六書長箋漢義
Lou chou tchhang tsien han yi.

6 livres;

3o 六書合箋
Lou chou ho tsien.

1 livre;

Études sur l'histoire de l'écriture.

Le dictionnaire même abonde en citations, notes et références.

1 livre préliminaire + 100 livres. — Cat. imp., liv. 43, f. 34 (en 104 livres).

Grand in-8. 2 vol., reliure au chiffre de Charles X.
Nouveau fonds 3o4.

4432. — I.
說文字原
Choẹ oen tseu yuen.

Origine des caractères d'après le Choẹ oen.

Par Tcheou Po-khi, surnom Po-oen, de Phoo-yang. Préface de

l'auteur (1349); préface par Yu-oen Kong-liang (1355); préface par Hoang Fang, de Khiong-hai, pour une réédition (1522). Réédition par Hou Tcheng-yen, de Hai-yang (1634). Préface pour l'ouvrage suivant (art. II), par Khong Tcheng-yun, du Kiang-tso (1634).

1 livre. — Cat. imp., liv. 41, f. 40.

— II.

六書正譌
Lou chou tcheng oo.

Dictionnaire critique des six sortes de caractères.

Rangé par ordre de rimes, avec explications et discussions. Par Tcheou Po-khi, publié par Hou Tcheng-yen.

5 livres. — Cat. imp., liv. 41, f. 40.

Grand in-8. 1 vol., demi-reliure. *Nouveau fonds* 256.

4433. 說文字原考略
Choẹ oen tseu yuen khao lio.

Examen abrégé du Choẹ oen tseu yuen.

Études séparées de lexicographie par Oou Tchao, surnom Tchao-nan, de Nan-tchheng, avec préface de l'auteur (1792). Préface par Toan Yu-tshai (1793). Ouvrage gravé à Nan-tchhang à partir de 1790.

6 livres.

In-4. Papier blanc, titre noir sur blanc. 1 vol., demi-rel., au chiffre de Louis-Philippe. *Nouveau fonds* 457.

4434-4436. — I (4434-4436).
說文解字注
Choẹ oen kiai tseu tchou.

Le Choẹ oen kiai tseu avec commentaires.

Commentaires par Toan Yu-tshai, surnoms Jo-ying et Meou-thang, de Kin-than (1735-1815). Préface par Lou Oen-tchhao, de Hang-tong (1786); autres préfaces et postface de 1808, 1814, 1815. Gravé au pavillon King-yun.

30 + 2 livres (la table indique les 2 livres de l'art. II).

Comparer n⁰ˢ 3144-3148.

— II (4436).
六書音均表
Lou chou yin kiun piao.

Traité des sons antiques des caractères.

Avec tableaux, comme au n° 3148, art. LXXXVII. Par Toan Yu-tshai. Préface (1770) par Tshien Ta-hin, de Kia-ting (1727-1804); autres préfaces de 1777.

5 livres.

Grand in-8. Bonne impression, titre noir sur papier teinté. 3 vol., demi-rel., au chiffre de Napoléon III. *Nouveau fonds* 1215 à 1217.

2036

4437. 宋本大廣益會
玉篇

Song pęn ta koang yi hoei yu phien.

Le Yu phien, dictionnaire par ordre de clefs augmenté, d'après un exemplaire des Song.

Composé par Kou Ye-oang (543), augmenté par Soęn Khiang, de Fou-tchhoęn (760), puis par Tchhen Pheng-nien et autres (1013); classé sous 542 clefs. Préface non signée, de l'époque des Song; notice sur les tons et les dialectes par le bonze Chen-kong. Préface pour la présente réédition par Tchou Yi-tsoęn, de Sieou-choei (1704); postface par Tchang Chi-tsiun, de Oou. Édition de la salle Tsę-tshoęn.

3 sections formant 3o livres. — Cat. imp., liv. 4ı, f. ı3 (Tchhong sieou yu phien).

Grand in-8. Titre noir et rouge sur papier blanc. ı vol., demi-rel., au chiffre de Louis-Philippe.
Nouveau fonds 23ı4.

4438. 五經文字
Oou king oen tseu.

Vocabulaire des caractères des Cinq King.

Par Tchang Tshan; préface par l'auteur (776). La première édition a été donnée par Tseu-mou, petit-fils de l'auteur (876). Les caractères sont rangés sous 160 clefs. Gravé au pavillon Tshong-chou.

3 livres. — Cat. imp., liv. 4ı, f. ı7.

In-4.Belle impression sur papier blanc; titre noir sur papier teinté. ı vol., demi-rel., au chiffre de Napoléon III.
Nouveau fonds ı5ı7.

4439. 新校經史海篇
直音

Sin kiao king chi hai phien tchi yin.

Dictionnaire pour les livres canoniques et historiques.

Donnant seulement le son et, très brièvement, le sens des caractères; ceux-ci sont classés sous 429 clefs, et sous chaque clef par nombre de traits; les clefs mêmes sont rangées dans l'ordre phonétique de leurs initiales. En tête de chaque livre, liste des clefs qui y sont traitées; à la fin, liste des caractères difficiles avec renvoi à leur place. Ouvrage antérieur au xvıe siècle (?).

5 livres.

Grand in-8. ı vol., demi-reliure.
Nouveau fonds 65g.

4440-4441. 六書賦
Lou chou fou.

Dictionnaire des six sortes de caractères.

Les caractères sont rangés sous

85 clefs. Auteur : Tchang Chi-pei ; préface de l'auteur (1602) et diverses autres préfaces (1602, 1603, 1605).

20 livres. — Comparer, Cat. imp., liv. 43, f. 21 (Lou chou fou yin yi, 3 livres).

Grand in-8. 2 vol., demi-rel., au chiffre de Louis-Philippe.
Nouveau fonds 251.

———

4442-4443. 字彙
Tseu hoei.

Dictionnaire.

Préface par Mei Ting-tsou, du Kiang-tong (1615) ; autre préface par Han Than, de Tchhang-tcheou (1686). Liste des caractères analogues pour écarter les confusions. Gravé à Oou, au pavillon Pao-han.

— I (4442).

韻法直圖
Yun fa tchi thou.

Première table phonétique.

Par Mei Ying-tsou, surnom Tan-cheng, de Siuen-tchheng.

— II (4442).

韻法橫圖
Yun fa heng thou.

Seconde table phonétique.

Par le même.

— III (4442-4443).

字彙
Tseu hoei.

Dictionnaire.

Par le même. Rangé sous les mêmes clefs que le Khang hi tseu tien (n°s 4522-4619).

1 livre préliminaire et 12 sections.

Grand in-8. Belle impression. 2 vol., demi-rel., au chiffre de Louis-Philippe (provenant des Missions Étrangères).
Fourmont 1.

4444-4445. *Tseu hoei.*

Même ouvrage, édition plus petite.

— I (4444).

運筆。檢字
Yun pi. — Kien tseu.

Mémoire sur l'ordre des traits. Liste comparative des caractères difficiles.

Par Mei Ying-tsou.

— II (4444).
Yun fa tchi thou.

Même table qu'au n° 4442, art. I.

— III (4444).
Yun fa heng thou.

Même table qu'au n° 4442, art. II.

— IV (4444-4445).
Tseu hoei.

Dictionnaire comme aux n°s 4442-

4443, art. III; précédé d'une liste des caractères de forme analogue.

Grand in-8. Couvertures chinoises en soie bleue. 2 vol., reliure au chiffre de Charles X.

Nouveau fonds 3o1.

4446-4447. *Tseu hoei.*

Même ouvrage, planches différentes.

— I (4446).

Yun pi.

Voir n° 4444, art. I.

— II (4446-4447).

Tseu hoei.

Voir nᵒˢ 4442-4443, art. III; manquent les sections 6 et 7.

— III (4447).

Yun fa heng thou

Voir n° 4442, art. II.

— IV (4447).

Yun fa tchi thou.

Voir n° 4442, art. I; suivi de la liste des caractères de forme analogue.

Grand in-8. 2 vol., demi-reliure (provenant de la bibl. de l'Arsenal).

Nouveau fonds 1700, 1701.

4448-4449.   鳳儀字彙

Fong yi tseu hoei.

Même ouvrage.

Planches légèrement différentes, gravées à la salle Thien-tẹ.

Grand in-8. Belle gravure; titre noir et rouge sur papier blanc. 2 vol., reliure, au chiffre de Charles X.

Nouveau fonds 3o3.

4450-4451.   懸金字彙

Hiuen kin tseu hoei.

Même ouvrage.

Planches plus grandes, gravées à la salle Lou-yin, à Oou (1690).

Grand in-8. Titre noir et rouge sur blanc. 2 vol., reliure, au chiffre de Charles X.

Fourmont 8.

4452-4453. *Hiuen kin tseu hoei.*

Même ouvrage.

Planches gravées à la même maison que les précédentes, d'exécution inférieure (1704).

Grand in-8. Titre noir sur blanc. 2 vol., demi-reliure.

Fourmont 2.

4454-4455.   增補字彙

Tseng pou tseu hoei.

Le Tseu hoei augmenté.

Cet ouvrage ne semble pas différer des nᵒˢ 4442-4443; édition beaucoup plus petite et moins nette, revue par Han Yuen-chao, de Tchhang-tcheou; avec préface de Han Than (1696), semblable à celle de 1686. Gravé au Mei-yuen.

Grand in-8. Titre noir sur blanc. 2 vol.,

demi-rel., au chiffre de Louis-Philippe (prov. des Missions Étrangères).
Nouveau fonds 255.

4456. 字彙補

Tseu hoei pou.

Supplément au Tseu hoei.

Par Oou Jen-tchhen Tchi-yi, de Si-ling. Avertissement de l'auteur (1666); préface par Yen Hang (1666). Table des 214 clefs.

12 sections, avec annexe à chaque section.

Grand in-8. Titre noir et rouge sur papier blanc; couvertures en soie bleue. 1 vol., reliure, au chiffre de Charles X.
Fourmont 3.

4457-4458. 增補字彙

Tseng pou tseu hoei.

Le Tseu hoei augmenté.

Préface de Mei Ting-tsou (1615); préface par Khang Min-fou, de Tchong-chan (1675). Gravé au pavillon Chi-khiu, de Mei-chou. Le livre préliminaire comprend :

1° 切韻指掌

Tshie yun tchi tchang.

Manuel phonétique.

2° 運筆。檢字

Yun pi — Kien tseu.

Mémoire sur l'ordre des traits.

Liste comparative des caractères difficiles.

3° 石渠閣新鐫字彙元韻

Chi khiu ko sin tsiuen tseu hoei yuen yun.

Nouvelle table phonétique du pavillon Chi-khiu.

Par Khiao Tchong-hoo Hoan-yi, de Tchong-khieou, et Tshoei Chou-jen Hiuen-tcheou, de Nei-khieou.

4° 辨似

Pien seu.

Liste des caractères de forme analogue.

Ensuite les 12 sections du dictionnaire.

Petit in-8. Titre noir et rouge sur jaune. 2 vol., demi-reliure (prov. de la bibliothèque de la Sorbonne).
Fourmont 4.

4459. 玉堂字彙

Yu thang tseu hoei.

Le Tseu hoei abrégé.

Préface de Tchhen Hao-tseu, de Hang (1676). Gravé à la salle Seu-choei.

4 sections.

In-12. Titre noir sur vert. 1 vol., demi-rel., au chiffre de Louis-Philippe.
Nouveau fonds 771.

4460. *Yu thang tseu hoei.*

Même ouvrage.

Édition plus grande que la précédente, gravée à la salle Tsi-yi.

In-12. Titre noir sur jaune. 1 vol., cartonnage.
Nouveau fonds 4551.

4461-4462. *Yu thang tseu hoei.*

Même ouvrage.

Gravure différente, du pavillon Oou-yun.

In-12. Papier fortement teinté; titre noir sur jaune. 2 vol., cartonnage.
Nouveau fonds 4552, 4553.

4463.   草聖彙辯

Tshao cheng hoei pien.

Dictionnaire des caractères cursifs.

Classés d'après les éléments de la forme cursive; chaque caractère est accompagné de sa lecture et du nom du calligraphe à qui il est dû. Auteurs : Po Fen, surnom Yi-jo, de Ye, et Siao Khi-yuen, surnom Fou-tchhou, du Koan-tong. Préface par Tchhen Hoang (1652). Liste de calligraphes célèbres. L'ouvrage est publié par Tchou Kia-ling, à la salle Oen-ye, à Kia-hoo.

4 livres.

Grand in-8. Belle impression, titre

noir sur papier teinté. 1 vol., reliure, au chiffre de Charles X.
Nouveau fonds 254.

4464-4470.   正字通

Tcheng tseu thong.

Dictionnaire.

Par Liao Oen-ying, surnom Po-tseu, de Lien-yang; toutefois le véritable auteur serait Tchang Tseu-lie (fin des Ming) et Liao, ayant acheté son manuscrit, se serait borné à le publier en le complétant. Préfaces par Tchang Tcheng-cheng, de Koei-chan (1670), par Kong Ting-tseu (1672), et autres. Liste des caractères difficiles, liste des caractères analogues, etc. Dictionnaire rangé suivant les 214 clefs. Gravé par Tchheng Oan-tshai, de Than-yang pour le ministère des Rites.

1 livre préliminaire et 12 sections. — Cat. imp., liv. 43, f. 37.

Grand in-8. Impression très nette, papier blanc, titre bleu et rouge sur blanc; exemplaire incomplet des sections 4, 5 et 6. 7 vol., cartonnage.
Nouveau fonds 4728 à 4734.

4471-4476. *Tcheng tseu thong.*

Même ouvrage.

Édition analogue ne renfermant que les deux préfaces de Tchang et de Kong.

Grand in-8. Papier blanc ; titre noir

sur blanc. 6 vol., reliure au chiffre de Charles X.
Nouveau fonds 340.

4477-4481. *Tcheng tseu thong.*

Même ouvrage.

Format plus petit; renfermant en outre introduction par Liao Loen-ki (1670), table des syllabes mantchoues avec sons correspondants en chinois, liste des ouvrages consultés. Planches du Hong-oen chou-yuen.

P. G. von Möllendorff. Essay on Manchu literature (Journal of the China branch of the Royal Asiatic Society, vol. XXIV, New Series, n° 1, 1889-1890), n° 9.

Grand in-8. Titre noir sur blanc. 5 vol., reliure.
Fourmont 9.

4482-4486. *Tcheng tseu thong.*

Même ouvrage.

Format plus grand que celui du n° précédent, plus petit que celui des n°s 4464-4470; la marge porte en caractères sigillaires l'indication Hong-oen chou-yuen.

Grand in-8. Titre noir sur papier bleu. 5 vol., demi-reliure.
Fourmont 5.

4487. *Tcheng tseu thong.*

Double.

Grand in-8. Fragment de la 9ᵉ section. 1 vol., cartonnage.
Nouveau fonds 3420.

4488-4495. *Tcheng tseu thong.*

Même ouvrage.

Édition analogue aux n°s 4471-4476, plus petite; gravée au pavillon Tai-yue.

Petit in-8. Titre noir sur blanc. 8 vol., demi-reliure (provenant de la bibl. de l'Arsenal).
Nouveau fonds 1692 à 1699.

4496-4501. *Tcheng tseu thong.*

Même ouvrage.

Édition analogue, différences dans la feuille de titre.

Grand in-8. 6 vol., cartonnage.
Nouveau fonds 4735 à 4740.

4502-4506. *Tcheng tseu thong.*

Même ouvrage.

Édition différente, de la salle Tshing-oei. Préface de l'auteur (1670); préface par Oou Yuen-khi, de Sieou-choei (1685).

Grand in-8. Titre noir sur blanc. 5 vol., demi-rel., au chiffre de Louis-Philippe.
Nouveau fonds 305.

4507-4512. *Tcheng tseu thong.*

— I (4507).

Yun fa heng thou.

Table phonétique.

Par Mei Ying-tsou (cf. n° 4442, art. II); avec notice par Li Chi-tse, surnom Kia-chao, de Chang-yuen.

2

— II (4507).

Yun fa tchi thou.

Table phonétique.

Cf. n° 4442, art. I.

— III (4507-4512).

Tcheng tseu thong.

Même ouvrage qu'aux n°ˢ 4464 à 4506. Portant en tête les indications : sons et explications d'après Mei Ying-tsou Tan-cheng; additions par Oang Pin Ooutshao, de Tchhang-tcheou. Préface par ce dernier (1719); double supplément (pei khao, pou yi), tables des caractères analogues, etc.

12 sections.

In-12. 6 vol., cartonnage.
Nouveau fonds 4554 à 4559.

———

4513-4514. 篆字彙

Tchoan tseu hoei.

Dictionnaire des caractères sigillaires.

Rangé suivant les 214 clefs modernes, donnant diverses formes sigillaires de chaque caractère. Par Thong Chi-nan, nom littéraire Oei-fou, de Liao-yang; préface de Liang Pei-lan (1691); gravé en 1700 à la salle To-chan.

12 sections. — Cat. imp., liv. 43, f. 47.

Grand in-8. Papier blanc; titre noir et rouge sur blanc, exemplaire soigné. 2 vol., reliure, au chiffre de Charles X.
Fourmont 23.

4515-4516. *Tchoan tseu hoei.*

Double.

Grand in-8; manque la feuille de titre. 2 vol., cartonnage.
Fourmont 14.

4517. *Tchoan tseu hoei.*

Même ouvrage.

Imitation de l'édition précédente, gravé à la salle Pao-hiu (1700).

Grand in-8. Papier blanc, titre noir sur blanc. 1 vol., reliure, au chiffre de Charles X.
Nouveau fonds 302.

4518-4519. *Tchoan tseu hoei.*

Même ouvrage.

Édition de la salle To-chan, différente de l'ancienne.

Grand in-8. Titre noir sur blanc. 2 vol., reliure, au chiffre de Louis-Philippe.
Nouveau fonds 300 A.

4520-4521. *Tchoan tseu hoei.*

Même ouvrage.

Édition commune.

Grand in-8. Titre noir sur jaune. 2 vol., cartonnage (prov. du chevalier de Paravey).
Nouveau fonds 4560, 4561.

———

4522-4528. 御製康熙字典

Yu tchi khang hi tseu tien.

Dictionnaire de Khang-hi, composé par ordre impérial.

Préface impériale transcrite par Tchhen Pang-yen (1716); décret relatif à l'ouvrage (1710). Liste de la commission de rédaction dirigée par Tchang Yu-chou et Tchhen Thing-king. Avertissement. Table générale indiquant la répartition des 214 clefs en 36 sections.

Kien tseu, liste par nombre de traits des caractères difficiles, y compris les clefs. — Pien seu, liste des caractères qui se ressemblent. — Teng yun, tables phonétiques indiquant la prononciation usitée vers le XVIe et vers le VIIe siècle. — Pei khao, pou yi, double supplément rangé par ordre de clefs et nombre de traits. — Dictionnaire rangé dans le même ordre, en 36 sections; indiquant les formes anciennes, la prononciation, le sens, avec définitions et nombreux exemples dont les sources sont citées :

(4522) préface, listes, tables, suppléments.
(4523) clefs 1 à 38 (sections 1 à 6).
(4524) clefs 39 à 71 (sections 7 à 12).
(4525) clefs 72 à 94 (sections 13 à 18).
(4526) clefs 95 à 139 (sections 19 à 24).
(4527) clefs 140 à 166 (sections 25 à 30).
(4528) clefs 167 à 214 (sections 31 à 36).

Cat. imp., liv. 41, f. 50.

Petit in-8. Belle impression ancienne ; titre sur papier teinté, caractères noirs entourés de dragons rouges. 7 vol., demi-reliure.
Fourmont 12.

4529-4538. *Yu tchi khang hi tseu tien.*

Même ouvrage.

Réédition de 1827 faite par ordre impérial, avec rapport de Yu-lin et Oang Yin-tchi et liste de la commission de publication, comprenant le prince Yi-hoei, Mien-khai, prince de Toen, etc.

Grand in-8. Belle impression, titre noir sur jaune. 10 vol.. demi-rel., au chiffre de Louis-Philippe.
Nouveau fonds 30.

4539-4578. *Yu tchi khang hi tseu tien.*

Même ouvrage sur papier blanc. Planches un peu fatiguées; préface en caractères rouges. Titre rouge sur blanc ; au verso, date (1827) en grands caractères.

Grand in-8. 40 vol. chinois dans 6 enveloppes.
Nouveau fonds 4348 à 4353.

4579-4588. *Yu tchi khang hi tseu tien.*

Même ouvrage.

Format plus petit que celui des

nᵒˢ 4529-4538; édition datée de
1827.

Grand in-8. Titre noir sur jaune.
10 vol., cartonnage.
Nouveau fonds 4531 à 4540.

4589-4594. *Yu tchi khang hi
tseu tien.*

Même ouvrage.

Édition datée de 1827, plus
grande que la précédente; caractères grêles.

Grand in-8. Titre noir sur jaune.
6 vol., reliure, au chiffre de Charles X.
Nouveau fonds 1101.

4595-4601. *Yu tchi khang hi
tseu tien.*

Même ouvrage.

Édition analogue, de 1827, un
peu plus petite; caractères moins
grêles.

Grand in-8. Belle impression. 7 vol.,
reliure, au chiffre de Louis-Philippe.
Nouveau fonds 306.

4602-4609. *Yu tchi khang hi
tseu tien.*

Même ouvrage.

Reproduction de petit format
d'après l'édition de 1827.

In-12. Papier blanc; manquent les
préfaces, listes, tables, etc. 8 vol.,
demi-reliure.
Nouveau fonds 1947 à 1954.

4610-4618. *Yu tchi khang hi
tseu tien.*

Même ouvrage.

Édition un peu plus grande.

In-12. Papier blanc; titre noir et rouge
sur papier teinté; préface en rouge sur
papier teinté. 9 vol., cartonnage.
Nouveau fonds 4549 et 4541 à 4548.

4619. *Yu tchi khang hi tseu tien.*

Édition analogue. Préface, listes, tables, suppléments.

In-12. Papier teinté. 1 vol., cartonnage.
Nouveau fonds 4550.

4620. 康熙字典撮要
Khang hi tseu tien tshoo yao.

Vocabulaire extrait du Khang
hi tseu tien.

Par l'Anglais Tchan Yo-han, John
Chalmers, et par Oang Yang-'an. —
Table générale des phonétiques
rangées par ordre de clefs, avec
numéros de renvoi. Liste des caractères difficiles, tableaux phonétiques. Le vocabulaire indique le
sens d'une manière très brève; les
caractères sont rangés par phonétiques et, sous chaque phonétique,
par clefs. Publié à Canton par la
London Missionary Society (1878).

In-4. Papier blanc; titre noir sur rose.
1 vol., demi-rel., au chiffre de la République française.
Nouveau fonds 4335.

4621. 漢魏音

Han oei yin.

Prononciation de l'époque des Han et des Oei.

Lexique rangé dans l'ordre du Choe oen, par Hong Liang-ki, de Yang-hou. Postface par Soen Sing-yen (1752-1818); autres pièces annexes par Pi Yuen, de Tchen-yang (1729-1797), et Chao Tsin-han, de Yu-yao (1742-1796). Gravé à Si-'an (1785).

4 livres. — Voir plus haut, n° 937, art. III.

Petit in-8. Titre noir sur jaune. 1 vol., demi-rel., au chiffre de Louis-Philippe. *Nouveau fonds* 875.

4622-4629. 埶文備覽。 補詳字義

Tchi oen pei lan — Pou siang tseu yi.

Dictionnaire des caractères avec explication de leurs formes; supplément explicatif.

Donnant les diverses formes antiques, sigillaires, *li* avec indication des sources; rangé suivant les 214 clefs. Par Cha Mou, surnom Tshing-yen, de Kia-hing. Publié par les soins de 'A-khe-tang-'a, surnom Heou-'an, de Tchhang-po (1806). Deux préfaces de l'auteur (1787); diverses autres préfaces (1791, 1799, 1806), plusieurs postfaces.

12 sections de 10 livres chacune et 12 chapitres supplémentaires.

Grand in-8. Titre noir sur blanc, impression soignée. 8 vol., demi-reliure. *Nouveau fonds* 3587 à 3594.

Deuxième Section : **DICTIONNAIRES PHONIQUES**

4630. 大宋重修廣韻

Ta song tchhong sieou koang yun.

Le Koang yun, d'après la réédition des Song.

Dictionnaire par ordre de rimes, donnant le sens des caractères, sans exemples. Liste des rimes en tête de chaque livre, en tout 206. Ouvrage composé par ordre impérial par Tchhen Pheng-nien, Khieou Yong et autres, de 1007 à 1011; d'après le Thang yun, de Soen Mien (751), qui n'est qu'une refonte du Tshie yun composé par

Lou Fa-yen (601), augmenté par Koo Tchi-hiuen. Préface de ce dernier (677); préface de Soẹn Mien (751). Rapports et pièces de 1007 et 1008. L'édition de Tchang Chi-tsiun, de Oou-mẹn, postérieure à 1127, est reproduite par la présente réédition. Postface de Tchang, sans date. Préface par Phan Lei, de Song-ling (1646-1708) pour la présente réédition; préface par Tchou Yi-tsoẹn (1704). Gravé à la salle Tsẹ-tshoẹn.

5 livres. — Cat. imp., liv. 42, f. 3 (Tchhong sieou koang yun).

Grand in-8. Titre noir et rouge sur blanc. 1 vol., demi-rel., au chiffre de Louis-Philippe.
Nouveau fonds 426 A.

4631. 漢隷字源六帙
Han li tseu yuen lou tchi.

Dictionnaire des caractères *li.*

D'après les inscriptions de l'époque des Han, des Oei et des Tsin; les caractères sont rangés par rimes, avec indication des sources pour chaque forme. Notice sur l'écriture à l'époque des Han; liste des inscriptions qui servent de sources. Par Leou Ki, surnom Yen-fa, de Tsoei-li, docteur en 1166; préface de Hong King-lou (1197). Édition non datée du pavillon Ki-kou, salle Cheou-heng, reproduisant une édition des Song.

1 section préliminaire et 5 sections. — Cat. imp., liv. 41, f. 30.

In-4. Papier blanc, titre sur papier teinté; édition soignée. 1 vol., demi-rel., au chiffre de Louis-Philippe.
Nouveau fonds 1096.

4632-4633. 大明萬曆乙亥重刊改併五音類聚四聲篇海集
Ta ming oan li yi hai tchhong khan kai ping ocu yin lei tsiu seu cheng phien hai tsi.

Dictionnaire rangé par initiales et par tons, gravé de nouveau en 1575.

Préface pour la réédition de 1520 par 'An Theng-siao; préface non signée de 1559. Préface (1208) par Han Tao-cheng, de Tchen-ting, qui, avec ses élèves, a édité l'œuvre de son oncle Han Hiao-yen, surnom Yun-tchong. Tables des initiales et des tons : les mots sont rangés par ordre d'initiales, sous chaque initiale par tons; les explications sont très brèves. Annexes et addenda portant les dates de 1229 (?) et de 1471.

15 livres. — Cat. imp., liv. 43, f. 8 (Seu cheng phien hai).

In-folio. Papier blanc, impression ancienne. 2 vol., demi-rel., au chiffre de Louis-Philippe.
Nouveau fonds 286.

4634-4635. — I (4634-4635).

大明萬曆己丑重刊改併五音集韻

Ta ming oan li kitchheou tchhong khan kai ping oou yin tsi yun.

Dictionnaire rangé par rimes et par initiales, gravé de nouveau en 1589.

Publié par Han Tao-cheng (1212); auteurs : Hiao-yen et son fils Tao-tchao, surnom Po-hoei; deux préfaces non signées (1290). Diverses préfaces du Koang yun (n° 4630). Liste des rimes : sous chaque rime, les mots sont rangés par initiales; explications assez développées, peu d'expressions doubles. La liste des rimes est datée à la fin de 1470, époque d'une réédition.

15 livres. — Cat. imp., liv. 42, f. 18 (Oou yin tsi yun).

— II (4635).

經史正音切韻指南

King chi tcheng yin tshie yun tchi nan.

Guide de la prononciation correcte pour les livres canoniques et historiques.

Tableaux phonétiques expliqués pour l'ancienne prononciation, avec notes sur la prononciation moderne, sur les caractères prononcés à deux tons différents, etc. Par Lieou Kien Chi-ming, du Koan-

tchong. Préface de l'auteur (1336). Gravé (1577) par les soins du bonze Jou-tshai, de la bonzerie Yuen-thong, à Tchhong-tę.

1 livre. — Cat. imp., liv. 42, f. 23.

In-folio. Papier blanc, impression ancienne. 2 vol., demi-rel., au chiffre de Louis-Philippe.
Nouveau fonds 287.

4636.   # 漢隸分韻

Han li fen yun.

Caractères *li* de l'époque des Han, rangés par rimes.

Dictionnaire des caractères *li*, sans explications, avec une liste d'inscriptions, de documents justificatifs et diverses notices. L'auteur n'est pas connu; les rimes sont celles de l'époque des Yuen. Gravé pour la première fois par Li Tchou-chi, sans date. Préfaces de Tchang Lien et de Li Tsong-tchhou (1530); préface pour la présente édition (1772) par Chi Yang-hao.

7 livres. — Cat. imp., liv. 41, f. 42.

Grand in-8. 1 vol., demi-rel., au chiffre de Napoléon III.
Nouveau fonds 1555.

4637.   # 再增攄古遺文

Tsai tseng tchi kou yi oen.

Dictionnaire des caractères anciens.

Classé par rimes. Par Li Teng,

surnom Jou-tchen, avec préface de l'auteur (1594). Planches gardées à la salle Oen-oei.

2 livres. — Cat. imp., liv. 43, f. 27 (Tchi kou yi oen).

Petit in-8. 1 vol., cartonnage du XVIIIe siècle, avec le titre *Dictionarium sinicum*.
Fourmont 24.

4638-4643. 五車韻瑞
Oou tchhẹ yun choei.

Dictionnaire par rimes de la littérature.

Donnant la prononciation et le sens des caractères, avec explication des expressions composées; citations avec indication des sources. Table indiquant les caractères traités, rangés dans l'ordre des Rimes de l'époque Hong-oou, Hong oou tcheng yun. Auteur : Ling Tchi-long Yi-tong, de Oou-tchheng, vivant sous les Ming. Préface de l'auteur, non datée. Gravé à la salle Oen-meou.

160 livres. — Cat. imp., liv. 138, f. 28.

Grand in-8. Titre noir sur blanc. 6 vol., demi-rel., au chiffre de Louis-Philippe.
Nouveau fonds 50.

4644. 同文鐸
Thong oen to.

Traités des caractères.

Par Liu Oei-khī Yu-chi, surnom Kiai-jou, de Sin-'an; avec introduction de l'auteur et préface (1633) par son élève Yang Oen-tshong. Gravé à Kin-lin, à la salle Tsikhing.

— I.

音韻日月燈
Yin yun ji yue teng.

Explication des sons.

Traité en 4 sections, renfermant tableaux phonétiques, explications, listes des auteurs consultés, etc.

— II

字學正韻通
Tseu hio tcheng yun thong.

Dictionnaire par ordre de rimes.

Donnant la prononciation et le sens, sans exemples; par Liu Oeikhī et Liu Oei-khí.

30 livres.

Grand in-8. Belle édition, titre noir sur papier teinté. 1 vol., reliure au chiffre de Charles X.
Nouveau fonds 346.

4645. *Tseu hio tcheng yun thong.*

Dictionnaire par ordre de rimes.

Composé par Liu Oei-khī; commenté par Liu Oei-khí Thai-chi, de Sin-'an; les auteurs ont fait leur travail d'après le Hong oou tcheng yun et le Hong oou thong yun. Avertissement signé Kiai-jou ; avertissement par Liu Oei-khī, relié en deux places séparées.

— I.

韻母
Yun mou.

Liste des caractères expliqués.

Rangés par rimes et, sous chaque rime, par initiales.

5 livres.

— II.

韻鑰
Yun yo.

Dictionnaire.

Rangé dans l'ordre du Yun-mou (art. I), analogue au n° 4644, art. II. Préface de Liu Oei-khī (1633) et diverses autres préfaces.

25 livres.

Grand in-8. Belle gravure ; titre noir sur papier teinté. 1 vol., reliure, au chiffre de Charles X.

Fourmont 25.

———

4646-4647. 六書通
Lou chou thong.

Dictionnaire par ordre de finales des caractères antiques et sigillaires.

D'après les inscriptions. Préface de l'auteur, Min Tshi-ki, surnom Yu-oou (1661) ; préface du premier éditeur, Pi Hong-chou (1720) ; préface pour la présente édition par Oou Sing-lan (1795).

10 livres. — Cat. imp., liv. 43, f. 40.

Grand in-8. Titre sur papier teinté. 2 vol., demi-rel., au chiffre de Napoléon III.

Nouveau fonds 1334, 1335.

4648. *Lou chou thong.*

Même ouvrage.

Grand in-8. Titre noir sur papier jaune. 1 vol., demi-rel., au chiffre de Louis-Philippe.

Nouveau fonds 394.

4649. *Lou chou thong.*

Double.

1 vol., cartonnage.

Nouveau fonds 4564.

———

4650-4652. — I (4650-4651).

諧聲品字箋
Hiai-cheng phin tseu tsien.

Dictionnaire par ordre de finales.

Préparé par Yu Hien-hi, surnom Hing-tsong, de Tshien-thang (dynastie actuelle) ; rédigé par son fils Tę-cheng, surnom Oen-tseu, complété par son petit-fils Seu-tsi, surnom Eul-tchheng. Préfaces par Lou Tsong-yuen (1670), par Soęn Tsai-fong (1677), par Khieou Tchhong-mei (1687), etc. — No-

3

tice sur les finales employées, servant de table; dictionnaire explicatif avec exemples et indication des sources.

10 sections. — Cat. imp., liv. 44, f. 37.

— II (4652).

字彙數求聲

Tseu hoei chou khieou cheng.

Table des caractères du dictionnaire, avec renvois.

Rangée sous les 214 clefs et sous chaque clef par nombre de traits. Par Yu Tę-cheng et Mei Ying-tsou. Liste des caractères difficiles, par ce dernier (n° 4444, art. I). Introduction de Yu Tę-cheng (1677).

12 sections.

Petit in-8. Titre noir et rouge sur blanc; impression soignée. 3 vol., reliure, au chiffre de Charles X.
Fourmont 10.

4653-4655. — I (4653).
Tseu hoei chou khieou cheng.
Même ouvrage qu'au n° 4652, art. II.

— II (4654-4655).
Hiai cheng phin tseu tsien.

Même ouvrage qu'aux n°s 4650-4651, art. I. Cet exemplaire est relié tout à fait en désordre, plu-

sieurs feuillets à l'envers; feuilles manuscrites intercalées.

Grand in-8. Titre noir sur blanc. 3 vol., reliure, au chiffre de Charles X.
Nouveau fonds 1106.

4656-4657. *Hiai cheng phin tseu tsien.*

Même ouvrage qu'aux n°s 4650-4651, art. I. Exemplaire relié en désordre, portant la mention : *A Fourmontio in novum ordinem digestum.*

Grand in-8. 2 vol., demi-rel., au chiffre de Louis-Philippe.
Nouveau fonds 257.

4658. 古今韻略
Kou kin yun lio.

Dictionnaire abrégé par ordre de rimes.

Donnant le sens et le son des caractères; peu d'expressions composées. Liste des rimes avec additions explicatives; historique des rimes dans l'introduction. Par Chao Tchhang-heng Tseu-siang, de Phi-ling. Préface (1696) par Song Lo Mou-tchong, surnom Man-thang, de Chang-khieou, éditeur de l'ouvrage.

5 livres.

Grand in-8. Titre noir sur jaune. 1 vol., demi-rel., au chiffre de Louis-Philippe.
Nouveau fonds 364.

4659-4665. 五車韻府

Oou tchhẹ yun fou.

Dictionnaire par rimes de la littérature.

Donnant le son et le sens des mots, avec des exemples. Tables des rimes anciennes. Publié par Tchhen Kai-mou Hien-kho, de Kia-hing. Préface par Phan Ying-pao, du Chan-tso (1708). Gravé à la salle Chen-seu.

10 livres.

Grand in-8. Bonne impression. 7 vol., demi-rel., au chiffre de Louis-Philippe.
Nouveau fonds 443.

4666. 新纂五方元音全書

Sin tsoan oou fang yuen yin tshiuen chou.

Sons originaux des cinq régions, nouveau dictionnaire.

Les mots sont rangés d'après la combinaison de 12 finales et 20 initiales, correspondant à peu près à la prononciation de Nan-king; le sens est donné très brièvement et sans exemples. Auteur : Ling Hiu-fan Theng-fong, de Yao-chan. Préface (1710) par Nien Hi-yao Yun-kong, de Koang-ning, qui a augmenté l'ouvrage. Gravé à la salle Tsiu-sieou (1840).

2 livres, — Cat. imp., liv. 44. f. 48.

Grand in-8. Titre noir sur jaune. 1 vol., demi-rel., au chiffre de Napoléon III.
Nouveau fonds 1345.

4667-4705. 佩文韻府

Pei oen yun fou.

Dictionnaire par rimes de la littérature.

Contenant les expressions complexes, avec exemples et indication des sources ; en tête de chaque livre, liste des caractères traités, disposés par ordre de rimes. Composé par ordre impérial par Tchang Yu-chou, Tchhen Thing-king et autres ; préface impériale (1711) avec sceaux impériaux en rouge.

106 livres. — Cat. imp., liv. 136, f. 22 (Yu ting pei oen yun fou, 444 livres).

Petit in-8. Belle édition sur papier teinté, couvertures en soie bleue. 39 vol., demi-rel., au chiffre de Napoléon III.
Nouveau fonds 1710 à 1747 + 1725 bis.

4706-4713. 韻府拾遺

Yun fou chi yi.

Supplément au Pei oen yun fou.

Par Oang Yen, Oang Hiu-ling et autres ; préface de Oang Yen et Oang Hiu-ling (1720). Ouvrage composé par ordre impérial.

106 livres. — Cat. imp., liv. 136, f. 24 (Yu ting yun fou chi yi, 112 livres).

Petit in-8. Édition analogue à la précédente, un peu moins nette. 8 vol., demi-rel., au chiffre de Louis-Philippe.

Nouveau fonds 65o.

4714-4719. 佩文韻府約編

Pei oen yun fou yo pien.

Abrégé du Pei oen yun fou.

Par Teng Khai-tsi Chan-mei, de Si-chan, avec préface (1795). Table par rimes, incomplète d'un demi-feuillet. Gravé au pavillon Oan-sieou.

24 livres.

Petit in-8. Titre noir sur jaune; impression très médiocre. 6 vol., demirel., au chiffre de Napoléon III.

Nouveau fonds 135o à 1355.

4720-4721. 草韻會編

Tshao yun hoei pien.

Dictionnaire par rimes des caractères cursifs.

Chaque caractère est accompagné de la lecture en caractère régulier et du nom du calligraphe auquel il est dû. Avertissement, liste des calligraphes célèbres. Ouvrage composé dans les années Khang-hi, par Thao Nan-oang, surnom Soen-thing, de Changhai; préface de l'auteur (1750); préfaces par Chen Tẹ-tshien (1754) et par Tchoang Yeou-kong (1755). Gravé à la salle Nan-tshoẹn.

26 li vres. — Cat. imp., liv. 114, f. 23,

Grand in-8. Titre noir sur jaune. 2 vol. demi-rcl., au chiffre de Napoléon III.

Nouveau fonds 1464, 1465.

4722-4723. 新刊韻學會海

Sin khan yun hio hoei hai.

Nouveau dictionnaire d'expressions, par ordre de rimes.

Avec exemples, sources, liste des auteurs consultés, avertissement. Complété par Lou Hong-khi Lie-yuen, de Oou-tong. Préface de Tshi Chao-nan Si-yuen, de Thienthai (1761); préface par Hang Chitsiun Khin-phou, de Jen-hoo (1761). Planches gardées à la maison Lien-tchou.

16 livres.

Grand in-8. Titre noir sur papier teinté. 2 vol., demi-rel., au chiffre de Louis-Philippe.

Nouveau fonds 39o.

4724-4736. 經籍籑 (*sic*) 詁并補遺

King tsi tchoan kou ping pou yi.

Dictionnaire par tons avec suppléments.

Donnant les prononciations et les sens avec indication des sources. Préfaces par Tshien Ta-hin, de Kiating (1799), par Tsang Yong-thang, surnom Tsai-tong, de Oou-tsin (1798), etc. Rapport dédicatoire

(1812) par l'auteur, Yuen Yuen, surnom Po-yuen, de Yi-tcheng (1764-1849). Liste des auteurs consultés; avertissement par l'auteur. Table générale et tables spéciales pour chaque livre. A la fin de chaque livre, supplément par Siu Koen, de Siao-chan. Gravé au pavillon Lang-hiuen-sien.

1 livre préliminaire et 106 livres.

In-12. Papier blanc; titre noir sur rouge. 13 vol., demi-rel., au chiffre de la République française.
Nouveau fonds 543.

4737. 韻字釋同廣義

Yun tseu chi thong koang yi.

Dictionnaire par rimes.

Prononciation et explication des caractères, avec annotations dans le haut des pages; avertissement. Par Tchang Toei-tchhi, de Tan-yai; préface de l'auteur (1806). Gravé au pavillon Pien-hoa.

6 livres.

Petit in-8. Titre noir sur jaune. 1 vol., demi-rel., au chiffre de Louis-Philippe.
Nouveau fonds 427.

4738. 韻字彙錦

Yun tseu hoei kin.

Dictionnaire par rimes.

Contenant les caractères carrés, cursifs, *li*, sigillaires, antiques. Par Kou Loen, surnom Siao-thing, avec préface de l'auteur (1822);

diverses autres préfaces et postfaces. Gravé en 1822, planches à la salle Yu-chan.

5 livres.

Grand in-8. Titre sur papier teinté. 1 vol,, demi-rel., au chiffre de Louis-Philippe.
Nouveau fonds 440.

4739. — I. 詩韻集成

Chi yun tsi tchheng.

Dictionnaire par rimes.

Sans explications; renfermant quelques expressions composées. Avertissement, table des rimes. Par Yu Tchao Tchhoen-thing, de Kiang-tou. Gravé à la salle Fou-oen (1835). Ce dictionnaire est disposé sur le bas des pages; en haut des pages, est imprimé l'ouvrage suivant (art. II).

10 livres.

— II. 詞林典腋

Seu lin tien yi.

Recueil d'expressions poétiques.

Par ordre méthodique.

1 livre.

— III. 廣東事蹟

Koang tong chi tsi.

Souvenirs historiques du Koang-tong.

Ouvrage sans nom d'auteur, placé à la fin du volume.

Petit in-8. Titre noir sur jaune. 1 vol., cartonnage.
Nouveau fonds 4524.

4740. 正韻咀華
Tcheng yin tsiu hoa.
Étude de la prononciation correcte.

Ouvrage destiné à enseigner la langue générale aux Cantonais. Par Cha Yi-tsoẹn Kiu-hiang, de Tchhang-po. Préface non datée par l'auteur; préfaces par Teng Chi-hien, de Nan-hai, et par Khieou Hiao-tchong. Postface de l'auteur. Gravé au pavillon Tchhen-than, à Canton (1853).

Livre 1. Diverses tables comparatives des prononciations, tables de rimes et d'initiales, répertoire de caractères avec la prononciation correcte.

Livre 2. Dialogues en langue générale (parlée).

Livre 3. Répertoire méthodique de caractères et d'expressions.

Supplément. Textes relatifs aux cérémonies, aux visites, en langue générale (parlée).

Grand in-8. Bonne impression; papier blanc, titre noir sur vert. 1 vol., demi-rel., au chiffre de Napoléon III.
Nouveau fonds 1437.

4741. — I.

新鐫增補音郡音義百

家姓
Sin tsiuen tseng pou yin kiun yin yi po kia sing.

Vocabulaire explicatif par ordre phonétique des caractères du Po kia sing, nouvelle édition augmentée.

Gravé par Chi Cheng-fou, de Kin-ling; sans date. Comparer n° 921.

— II.

增補重訂音義千字文
Tseng pou tchhong ting yin yi tshien tseu oen.

Vocabulaire explicatif par ordre phonétique des caractères du Tshien tseu oen, nouvelle édition augmentée.

Gravé par le même. Comparer n° 3290.

In-18. Titre noir sur jaune. 1 vol., cartonnage.
Nouveau fonds 2347.

4742. 分韻撮要字彙
Fẹn yun tshoo yao tseu hoei.
Dictionnaire par rimes, abrégé.

Les rimes sont disposées dans un ordre spécial; le sens est donné très brièvement. Par Oen Yi-fong Khi-chan et Oen Ki-cheng Toan-chi, de Oou-khi. Gravé à la salle Phan-koei.

4 sections.

In-18. Titre noir sur jaune. 1 vol., demi-rel., au chiffre de Napoléon III.
Nouveau fonds 1229.

3ᵉ section : **DICTIONNAIRES ANALOGIQUES, ETC.**

4743-4744. — I (4743-4744).

經典釋文
King tien chi oen.

Même ouvrage qu'aux nᵒˢ 3095-3097, gravé à la salle Pao-king (1791), et revu d'après un exemplaire de l'époque des Song; notice pour cette édition écrite à Tchhang-tcheou (1791); postface par Fong Pan, de Chang-tang (1637).

Titre noir sur blanc.

— II (4744).

經典釋文攷證
King tien chi oen khao tcheng.

Examen critique du King tien chi oen.

Par Lou Oen-tchhao, surnom Tchao-kong, nom littéraire Pao-king, de Yu-yao (1717-1795).

Titre noir sur blanc.

Grand in-8. Belle impression. 2 vol., demi-rel., au chiffre de Napoléon III.
Nouveau fonds 1562, 1563.

4745-4756.   唐宋白孔六帖
Thang song po khong lou thie.

Les six recueils de Po et de Khong.

Dictionnaire d'expressions avec explications et indication des sources, rangé par ordre analogique. Cet ouvrage est formé de la réunion des six recueils (30 livres) de Po Kiu-yi (772-846) et des six recueils (30 livres) de Khong Fou, (époque des Song), qui sont mélangés, mais distingués par l'impression. Préface de Han Kiu, surnom Tseu-tshang, pour les six recueils postérieurs.

100 livres. — Cat. imp., liv. 135, f. 13.

Grand in-8. Gravure du XVIᵉ siècle. 12 vol., demi-rel., au chiffre de la République française.
Nouveau fonds 1095.

4757-4758.   文選類林
Oen siuen lei lin.

Vocabulaire explicatif par ordre analogique des expressions du Oen siuen.

Cf. nᵒˢ 3563-3576. Par Lieou Pan, surnom Kong-fou, de Sin-yu, docteur en 1046; réédition par Oou Seu-hien Oen-fan, de Sin-'an (époque des Ming).

18 livres. — Cat. imp., liv. 137, f. 7.

Grand in-8. Papier blanc. 2 vol., demi-reliure, au chiffre de Napoléon III.
Nouveau fonds 1518, 1519.

4759-4764. 錦繡萬花
谷前集。後集。續集

Kin sieou oan hoa kou tshien tsi — Heou tsi — Siu tsi.

Dictionnaire d'expressions, en trois parties.

Exemples avec citation des sources; table des classes et des sous-classes. Préface de l'auteur, sans signature (1188); préface par Hoa Soei (1494); préface par Kia Yong, de Lin-ying (1535).

40 + 40 + 40 livres.

In-4. Papier blanc. 6 vol., demi-rel., au chiffre de Napoléon III.
Nouveau fonds 1298 à 1303, 1304 (*sic*).

4765-4767. 六書故
Lou chou kou.

Antiquités de l'écriture.

Dictionnaire par ordre analogique avec explication étymologique des formes au moyen du *kou oen*. Par Tai Thong, de Yong-kia, docteur de la période Choen-yeou (1241-1252). Préface non signée contemporaine de l'auteur; préface de Tchao Fong-yi (1320). Préface pour la présente édition (1784) par Me-tchoang chi.

33 sections. — Cat. imp., liv. 41, f. 33.

In-4. Titre sur papier jaune. 3 vol., demi-reliure, au chiffre de Napoléon III.
Nouveau fonds 1331 à 1333.

4768-4770. 韻府羣玉
Yun fou khiun yu.

Le Trésor des rimes.

Dictionnaire d'expressions et de noms historiques, géographiques, littéraires, etc., avec explications et sources; rangé par rimes. Par Yin Chi-fou King-hien, et Yin Tchong-fou Fou-tchhoen, publié par Oang Yuen-tcheng Meng-khi. Préfaces de Yin-Tchou-ye (1307), de Yao Yun (1310), de Yin Tchong-fou (1314). Préface de Tchhen Oen-tchou, pour l'édition de 1590. Réédition de 1758, gravée à la salle Tshing-hoa.

20 livres. — Cat. imp., liv. 135, f. 53.

Grand in-8. Titre sur papier rose; incomplet de quelques pages à la fin. 3 vol., demi-rel., au chiffre de la République française.
Nouveau fonds 260.

4771-4772. 篇海類編
Phien hai lei pien.

Dictionnaire analogique.

Donnant les mots, avec son et sens, répartis en classes et séries. Composé par Song Lien King-lien, de Phou-kiang (1310-1381); complété et publié par Thou Long Tchang-khing, de Yin, docteur en 1577. Préface par Tchhen Ki-jou, de Yun-kien (époque des Ming). Avertissement. Notices sur la phonétique, sur les caractères, etc., par Tchang Kia-hoo Khi-choęn et Kin Ji-cheng Meou-cheng, de Tchhang-tcheou.

20 livres. — Cat. imp., liv. 43, f. 12.

Grand in-8. Bonne impression. 2 vol., demi-reliure.
Nouveau fonds 259.

4773-4782. 天中記
Thien tchong ki.

Mémorial de la montagne Thien-tchong.

Dictionnaire d'expressions avec explication et indication des sources, rangées par ordre analogique. Par Tchhen Yao-oen, nom littéraire Hoei-po, docteur en 1550. Préfaces de Li Koęn (1569), de Tchhen Oen-tchou (1589), de Thou Long-oei (1595); ce dernier a surveillé l'impression .

60 livres. — Cat. imp., liv. 136, f. 10.

Grand in-8. 10 vol., demi-rel., au chiffre de Napoléon III.
Nouveau fonds 1447 à 1456.

4783. 精選黄眉故事
Tsing siuen hoang mei kou chi.

Faits choisis de Hoang-mei.

Dictionnaire par ordre analogique, d'expressions complexes et de faits, avec citation des sources; notes en haut des pages. Par Teng Po-tchoę, de Jao-kiun. Préface par Tong Khi-tchhang Hiuen-tsai, de Yun-kien (1616). Gravé à la salle Thien-tę (1742).

10 livres.

Grand in-8. Titre noir sur jaune. 1 vol., demi-rel., au chiffre de Napoléon III.
Nouveau fonds 1247.

4784. 註釋白眉故事
Tchou chi po mei kou chi.

Faits annotés de Po-mei.

Ouvrage analogue au précédent, par Hiu Yi-tchong Koan-ji; revu par Teng Tchi-mou Ting-so. Introduction non datée par ce dernier. Publication de la salle Tchi-hoo.

10 livres.

Grand in-8. Titre noir sur jaune. 1 vol., demi-rel., au chiffre de Napoléon III.
Nouveau fonds 1349.

4785. 翰林筆削字義韻律京本大板海篇心鏡

4

Han lin pi sio tseu yi yun liu king pẹn ta pan hai phien sin king.

Recueil de textes revus par les Han-lin : dictionnaire.

En bas des pages, dictionnaire par ordre analogique; dans chaque classe, les caractères sont divisés en séries. En haut des pages, caractères difficiles du Chou king dans l'ordre où ils paraissent dans le texte. Son, sens très bref.

Livre 5 seulement du recueil. — Cf. Supplément Bibliographie Coréenne, n° 3241, II.

Grand in-8. 1 vol., reliure du XVIIe siècle.
Nouveau fonds 2158.

4786. 翰林重攷字義大板海篇心鏡

Han lin tchhong khao tseu yi ta pan hai phien sin king.

Recueil de textes, nouvelle révision des Han-lin : dictionnaire.

Double dictionnaire, donnant le son et brièvement le sens, en haut des pages dans l'ordre des rimes, en bas dans l'ordre analogique.

Livres 10 et 12 du recueil. — Voir n° 4785.

Grand in-8. Entre les deux livres, note manuscrite en latin, datée de 1623. 1 vol.,

cartonnage du XVIIIe siècle, avec le titre : *Dictionarium sinicum.*
Fourmont 21 A-B.

4787. 陳明卿太史考古詳訂遵韻海篇朝宗

Tchhen ming khing thai chi khao kou siang ting tsoẹn yun hai phien tchhao tsong.

Recueil lexicographique.

Par Tchhen Jen-si Ming-khing, de Tchhang-tcheou (début du XVIIe siècle) avec préface de l'auteur. Gravé au pavillon Khi-tseu par les soins de Than Yuen-tchhoẹn Yeouhia, de King-ling.

Livre 1. Histoire de l'écriture, composition des caractères; phonétique.
Livres 2 à 10. Dictionnaire par ordre analogique, donnant le son et le sens, sans exemples.
Livre 11. Tables des caractères difficiles et des caractères analogues.
Livre 12. Dictionnaire par ordre phonique.

Grand in-8. Bonne gravure, titre noir et rouge sur blanc. 1 vol., reliure, au chiffre de Charles X.
Fourmont 6.

4788. 增補錦字箋註

Tseng pou kin tseu tsien tchou.

Dictionnaire d'expressions, augmenté.

Avec exemples et indication des sources ; rangé par ordre analogique. Par Hoang Yun Oei-koan, de Tchi-chan. Préface de l'auteur (1689). Publié par lui-même, à la salle Oen-sieou.

4 livres.

Petit in-8. 1 vol., demi-rel., au chiffre de Napoléon III.
Nouveau fonds 1306.

4789. 錦字箋

Kin tseu tsien.

Même ouvrage.

Format plus petit, disposition différente.

Petit in-8. 1 vol., demi-reliure.
Nouveau fonds 201.

4790. *Kin tseu tsien.*

Même ouvrage.

Réédition gravée au pavillon Pou-yue (1830).

In-12. Titre noir sur jaune. 1 vol., demi-rel., au chiffre de Louis-Philippe.
Nouveau fonds 681.

———

4791-4794. 詩學圓機
活法大成

Chi hio yuen ki hoo fa ta tchheng.

Autre titre :

仰止于詳考古今名家
潤色詩林正宗

Yang tchi tseu siang khao kou

kin ming kia joęn sę chi lin tcheng tsong.

Dictionnaire par ordre analogique des expressions poétiques des auteurs célèbres.

Avec indication des sources et explications. Par Yu Siang-teou, surnom Yang-tchi, de San-thai ; préface de l'auteur (1697). Réédition de la salle Yong-'an (1828).

18 livres.

In-12. Titre noir sur jaune. 4 vol., demi-reliure, au chiffre de Napoléon III.
Nouveau fonds 1144 à 1147.

4795-4816. 御定駢字
類編

Yu ting phien tseu lei pien.

Dictionnaire explicatif des expressions doubles par ordre analogique ; publié par ordre impérial.

Ouvrage composé à la suite d'un décret (1719) et revu par une commission comprenant Yun-lou, prince de Tchoang, Yun-li, prince de Koo, Tchang Thing-yu, etc. Préface impériale (1726). Les expressions sont rangées d'après le caractère initial ; nombreuses citations avec indication des sources.

224 + 16 livres. — Cat. imp., liv. 136, f. 19.

Grand in-8. Belle édition ; couvertures originales en papier jaune ; à la garde du premier volume, notice sur papier rouge datée de Péking 1767, sans signature, de la main du P. Amiot. 22 vol., demi-rel., au chiffre de la République française.

Nouveau fonds 3565 à 3586.

4817-4825. 御定子史精華

Yu ting tseu chi tsing hoa.

Choix d'expressions des philosophes et des historiens, fait par ordre impérial.

Ouvrage composé à la suite d'un décret des années Khang-hi. Préface impériale de 1727, liste des membres de la commission de rédaction, prince de Tchoang, etc. Dictionnaire par ordre analogique avec indication des sources et explications.

160 livres. — Cat. imp., liv. 136, f. 21.

In-8. 9 vol., demi-rel., au chiffre de Louis-Philippe.

Nouveau fonds 47.

4826. 重訂詩學含英

Tchhong ting chi hio han ying.

Dictionnaire explicatif des expressions poétiques par ordre analogique.

Par Lieou Oen-oei, surnom Pao-kiun, de Chan-yin. Préface par Tshi Chao-nan, de Thien-thai (1772). Planches à la salle Oei-king.

14 livres.

In-18. Titre noir sur jaune. 1 vol., cartonnage.

Nouveau fonds 5220.

4827. *Tchhong ting chi hio han ying.*

Même ouvrage, édition plus grande, imitée de la précédente. Planches à la salle Lien-mę.

In-12. Titre noir sur jaune. 1 vol., demi-reliure au chiffre de Napoléon III.

Nouveau fonds 1448.

4828. 三刻簡堂訂補直音雜字世事通考

San kho kien thang ting pou tchi yin tsa tseu chi chi thong khao.

Autre titre :

三刻徽郡原板釋義經書雜字士民便用世事通考

San kho hoei kiun yuen pan chi yi king chou tsa tseu chi min pien yong chi chi thong khao.

Répertoire de termes complexes, de caractères difficiles, etc.

En haut des pages, son des caractères difficiles des classiques; renseignements géographiques, administratifs, etc.; formules de prières, d'adresses, etc. En bas des pages, dictionnaire par ordre analogique d'expressions complexes avec explication. Auteur : Siu San-sing Yi-oou, de Hoei-kiun.

3 + 3 livres.

Grand in-8. 1 vol., cartonnage du XVIIIe siècle, avec le titre : *Nomenclator sinicus*.

Fourmont 357.

4829. 四書五經不貳字直音

Seu chou oou king pou eul tseu tchi yin.

Vocabulaire des caractères uniques des Quatre Livres et des Cinq King.

Ce vocabulaire donne seulement la prononciation au moyen d'homophones ; les caractères sont donnés dans l'ordre où ils paraissent dans le texte. Par Long Oan-yu, surnom Sie-thang, de Kin-li ; préface de l'auteur (1808). Planches au pavillon Fou-oen (1808).

Petit in-8. Titre noir sur jaune. 1 vol., demi-rel., au chiffre de Napoléon III.
Nouveau fonds 1812.

4830. 增訂詩賦駢字類珠

Tseng ting chi fou phien tseu lei tchou.

Dictionnaire des expressions complexes de la poésie et de la prose poétique, par ordre analogique, édition augmentée.

Chaque expression est accompagnée d'une phrase où elle se trouve, avec indication de la source ; pas d'explications. Par Siao Hoang, nom littéraire Li-thing, de Tchi-feou. Préface par Oang Chan-pi (1813). Planches à la salle Oen-yuen (1819).

8 livres.

In-12. Titre noir sur jaune. 1 vol., demi-rel., au chiffre de Napoléon III.
Nouveau fonds 1143.

4831. 雙魚尺牘

Choang yu tchhi tou.

Vocabulaire des expressions épistolaires par ordre analogique.

Réédition faite à Canton (1824) par les soins de Tchhen Kin, de Nan-lan-ling, avec préface du même (1813).

4 livres.

In-12. Titre noir sur jaune. 1 vol., demi-rel., au chiffre de Louis-Philippe.
Nouveau fonds 706.

4832. 分類緘腋

Fen lei kien yi.

Répertoire de formules et d'expressions épistolaires, par ordre analogique.

Par Khien Fou-oou, de Sin-oou-thou ; préface de l'auteur (1820).

Planches au pavillon Pien-chan (1827).

4 livres.

In-18. Titre noir sur jaune. 1 vol., demi-rel., au chiffre de Louis-Philippe. *Nouveau fonds* 790.

4833. 詩賦料集腋

Chi fou liao tsi yi.

Dictionnaire par ordre analogique donnant pour chaque mot les expressions poétiques correspondantes.

Par Siuen Tsin-hien, de Lienkiang; planches à la librairie Tshing-te (1828).

5 livres.

In-32. Titre noir sur jaune. 1 vol., demi-rel., au chiffre de Napoléon III. *Nouveau fonds* 1142.

———

4834-4837. 四書字詁

Seu chou tseu kou.

Vocabulaire explicatif des caractères des Quatre Livres.

Par Toan 'O-thing, surnom Jen-'an, de Khien-yang; publié après la mort de l'auteur par Hoang Penki, surnom Hou-tchhi. Préface de l'éditeur (1847); préface par Tchong Yin-hong, de Phing-kou (1851). Le titre est daté de 1849; planches gardées à Tchhang-cha.

Table des caractères par clefs avec renvois. — Table des matières :

dans le vocabulaire, les caractères sont rangés suivant leur ordre d'apparition dans le texte.

78 livres.

Grand in-8. Titre noir sur rose. 4 vol., demi-rel., au chiffre de la République française. *Nouveau fonds* 2214 à 2217.

4838-4840. 羣經字詁

Khiun king tseu kou.

Vocabulaire explicatif des caractères des Livres Canoniques.

Ouvrage du même auteur, publié à Tchhang-cha (1849). Table par clefs; table des matières. Les Canoniques examinés sont les trois King, le Tchhoen-tshieou, les Trois Rituels, les Trois Tchoan du Tchhoen-tshieou, le Hiao-king, le Eul-ya.

72 livres.

Grand in-8. Titre noir sur rose. 3 vol., demi-rel., au chiffre de la République française. *Nouveau fonds* 2218 à 2220.

———

4841. 譽筆堂新刻南北通曉四民便用開蒙雜字大全

Yu pi thang sin kho nan pe thong hiao seu min pien yong khai mong tsa tseu ta tshiuen.

Répertoire par ordre analogique de mots isolés et d'expressions, de la salle Yu-pi.

Ouvrage à l'usage des jeunes gens, donnant quelques prononciations et quelques explications; en bas des pages, texte; en haut, additions. Par Kou Tchi-hien Tsoen-tsio et ses fils, de Oou-fong. Gravé à la salle Fou-oen.

2 livres.

Petit in-8. Titre rouge, titre sur papier teinté. 1 vol., demi-rel., au chiffre de Napoléon III.
Nouveau fonds 1553.

4842. 縹 緗 對 纇

Phiao siang toei lei.

Répertoire de caractères isolés et d'expressions composées.

Classé par ordre analogique, donnant parfois un sens très bref, mais pas de prononciation.

Livre 2 seul.

Grand in-8. 1 vol., cartonnage.
Nouveau fonds 3419.

CHAPITRE IX : SCIENCES ET ARTS

—

Première Section : MATHÉMATIQUES

4843. 孫子算經

Soen tseu soan king.

Le livre du calcul, de Soen-tseu.

Ouvrage mentionné à l'époque des Thang, et peut-être déjà sous les Soei; on n'a aucun renseignement sur l'auteur. Préface de l'auteur. Édition impériale de la salle Oou-ying, d'après le texte des Yong-lo ta tien; préface impériale (1774); notice bibliographique (1776), par Lou Si-hiong, Ki Yun (1724-1805) et Tai Tchen (1722-1777).

3 livres. — Cat. imp., liv. 107, f. 2.

Grand in-8. Bonne impression. 1 vol., demi-rel., au chiffre de Napoléon III.
Nouveau fonds 1390.

4844. 夏侯陽算經

Hia heou yang soan king.

Le livre du calcul, par Hia-heou Yang.

Ouvrage qui paraît dater de l'époque des Soei. Édition impé-riale de la salle Oou-ying, d'après le texte des Yong-lo ta tien; pré-face impériale (1774); notice bi-bliographique par Lou Si-hiong, Ki Yun et Tai Tchen (1776); rap-port final des fonctionnaires qui ont surveillé l'impression.

3 livres. — Cat. imp., liv. 107, f. 8.

In-12. Bonne impression sur papier blanc; titre noir sur blanc. 1 vol., demi-reliure.
Nouveau fonds 3556.

—

4845. 緝古算經

Tshi kou soan king.

Le livre du calcul, d'après l'an-tiquité.

Par Oang Hiao-thong, qui vivait en 626; dédicace de présentation par l'auteur, sans date. Texte an-noté, avec dédicace par Han Tchi et autres (1084). Notice de Mao Yi, du pavillon Ki-kou (1684). Gravé de nouveau en 1780, extrait du Tchi pou tsou tchai tshong chou.

1 livre. — Cat. imp., liv. 107, f. 12.

In-12. Papier blanc, titre noir sur blanc. 1 vol., demi-rel., au chiffre de Napoléon III.

Nouveau fonds 1558.

4846. 緝古算經考注

Tshi kou soan king khao tchou.

Examen annoté du Tshi kou soan king.

Par Li Hoang, de Tchong-siang; préfaces par Li Tchao-lo, de Oou-tsin (début du XIXᵉ siècle) et par Oou Lan-sieou, de Kia-ying.

2 livres.

Grand in-8. Belle impression sur papier blanc; titre noir sur vert. 1 vol., demi-rel., au chiffre de Louis-Philippe.

Nouveau fonds 414.

4847-4850. 測圓海鏡細草

Tchhe yuen hai king si tshao.

Traité d'algèbre et de trigonométrie.

Par Li Ye King-tchai, de Loan-tchheng. Préface de l'auteur (1248); postface par Oang Te-yuen, de Koang-phing (1287). Réédition faite par les soins de Yuen Yuen, avec préface de l'éditeur (1798); postface (1797) par Li Joei, de Yuen-hoo, auteur des notes. Réimprimé en caractères mobiles (1876) au Thong-oen-koan; figures; préface par Li Chan-lan (1876).

12 livres. — Cat. imp., liv. 107, f. 16.

Grand in-8. Bonne gravure; titre noir sur papier teinté. 4 vol. chinois dans 1 enveloppe de toile bleue.

Nouveau fonds 4377.

4851. 新鐫算法統宗大全

Sin tsiuen soan fa thong tsong ta tshiuen.

Traité de mathématiques, nouvelle édition.

Par Tchheng Ta-oei Jou-seu, de Hoei-tcheou (XVIᵉ siècle). Préface par Oou Ki-cheou, de Tsien-kiang (1593); à la fin du volume, date de gravure (1592). Réédition avec figures, gravée au pavillon Cheng-yi (1624 ou 1684).

Livre préliminaire + 17 livres. — Cat. imp., liv. 107, f. 49.

Petit in-8. Titre noir sur blanc; couvertures originales en soie bleue. 1 vol., reliure au chiffre de Charles X.

Nouveau fonds 892.

4852. 新編直指算法統宗

Sin pien tchi tchi soan fa thong tsong.

Traité de mathématiques, nouvelle édition.

Cette édition paraît simplement reproduire la précédente; gravée au pavillon Oou-yun.

Début de l'ouvrage jusqu'à la fin du livre 6.

Petit in-8. Titre noir sur jaune. 1 vol., cartonnage.
Nouveau fonds 2383.

4853. 增補算法統宗全書

Tseng pou soan fa thong tsong tshiuen chou.

Le Soan fa thong tsong augmenté.

Édition refondue du même ouvrage, renfermant la même préface. Gravé à Yun-lin, à la salle Oou-yun.

12 livres.

Petit in-8. Titre noir sur blanc. 1 vol., demi-rel., au chiffre de Louis-Philippe.
Fourmont 350.

4854. *Tseng pou soan fa thong tsong tshiuen chou.*

Double.

Petit in-8. 1 vol., demi-reliure.
Nouveau fonds 3114.

4855-4856. 幾何原本
Ki ho yuen pęn.

Les six premiers livres d'Euclide.

Traduits par le P. Ricci (1552-1610), rédigés par Siu Koang-khi, de Oou-song (1562-1634). Préface de ce dernier; introduction du

P. Ricci (1607). Liste des personnages qui ont surveillé l'impression, etc.

6 livres. — Cat. imp., liv. 107, f. 23. — Cordier, Imprimerie Sino-européenne, 226.

Petit in-8 et grand in-8. Interversion de livres à la reliure. 2 vol., cartonnage (prov. de la Société de Jésus).
Nouveau fonds 2959 et 2356.

4857-4859. *Ki ho yuen pęn.*

Même ouvrage.

Planches plus grandes; incomplet.

6 livres. — Cordier, Imprimerie Sino-européenne, 226.

Grand in-8. 3 vol., cartonnage (prov. de la Société de Jésus).
Nouveau fonds 2960, 2355 et 3530.

4860. *Ki ho yuen pęn.*

Même ouvrage.

Édition plus grande.

Grand in-8. 1 vol., demi-reliure (prov. de la bibl. de l'Arsenal).
Nouveau fonds 1666.

4861-4863. 同文算指
Thong oen soan tchi.

Traité de mathématiques.

Par le P. Ricci et Li Tchi-tsao Tchen-tchi, de Jen-hoo. Préface de ce dernier (1613); préface de Siu Koang-khi (1614).

— I (4861).

前 編

Tshien pien.

Section préliminaire.

Éléments d'arithmétique.

2 livres. — Cat. imp., liv. 107, f. 21.

Grand in-8. 1 vol., cartonnage (prov. de la Société de Jésus).
Nouveau fonds 3305.

— II (4862).

通 編

Thong pien.

Section générale.

Arithmétique et géométrie.

8 livres. — Cat. imp., liv. 107, f. 21. — Cordier, Imprimerie Sino-européenne, 228.

Grand in-8. 1 vol., cartonnage (prov. de la Société de Jésus).
Nouveau fonds 3304.

— III (4863).

別 編

Pie pien.

Section spéciale.

Logarithmes, calculs astronomiques.

Grand in-8. Manuscrit, avec des feuillets blancs au milieu. 1 vol., cartonnage.
Nouveau fonds 3303.

4864. ## 圜 容 較 義

Yuen yong kiao yi.

Abrégé de géométrie plane.

Rédigé par Li Tchi-tsao, d'après les leçons du P. Ricci; préface de Li Tchi-tsao (1614).

1 livre. — Cat. imp., liv. 106, f. 26. — Cordier, Imprimerie Sino-européenne, 232.

Grand in-8. 1 vol., cartonnage (prov. de la Société de Jésus).
Nouveau fonds 2920.

4865. ## 測 量 法 義

Tchhẹ liang fa yi.

Problèmes de géométrie appliquée à l'astronomie.

Introduction par Siu Koang-khi, de Oou-song.

— I.

測 量 異 同

Tchhẹ liang yi thong

Mesure des hauteurs, distances, etc.

Par Siu Koang-khi; texte avec figures.

1 livre. — Cat. imp., liv. 106, f. 23.

— II.

Tchhẹ liang fa yi.

Problèmes de géométrie appliquée.

Par Siu Koang-khi, d'après le

P. Ricci ; texte avec figures .

1 livre. — Cat. imp., liv. 106, f. 23.
— Cordier, Imprimerie Sino-européenne, 240.

Grand in-8. 1 vol., cartonnage.
Nouveau fonds 3310.

4866. 句股義
Keou kou yi.

Questions de trigonométrie.

Par Siu Koang-khi, de Oou-song, avec préface non datée. Texte et figures.

1 livre. — Cat. imp., liv. 106, f. 23.
— Cordier, Imprimerie Sino-européenne, 230.

Grand in-8. 1 vol., cartonnage (prov. de la Société de Jésus).
Nouveau fonds 2947.

4867. 籌算
Tchheou soan.

Calcul népérien.

Par les PP. Giacomo Rho (1590-1638) et Adam Schall (1591-1669?). Préface du P. Rho (1628); publié sous la direction de Siu Koang-khi.

1 livre. — Cordier, Imprimerie Sino-européenne, 222. — Comparer Cat. imp., liv. 106, f. 21 (Sin fa soan chou, 100 livres).

Grand in-8. Titre noir sur papier teinté au verso du feuillet. 1 vol., demi-rel., au chiffre de Napoléon III.
Nouveau fonds 2111.

4868. 比例規解
Pi li koei kiai.

Explication des règles de proportion.

Par les PP. Rho et Schall; préface du P. Rho (1630); publié sous la direction de Siu Koang-khi. Texte et figures.

1 livre. — Cordier, Imprimerie Sino-européenne, 214. — Voir aussi Cat. imp., liv. 106, f. 21 (Sin fa soan chou, 100 livres).

Grand in-8. 1 vol., demi-rel.; au chiffre de Napoléon III.
Nouveau fonds 2112.

4869. 幾何要法
Ki ho yao fa.

Principes de géométrie.

Par le P. Giulio Aleni (1582-1649); rédigé par Khiu Chi-kou, de Hai-yu. Préface par Tcheng Hong-yeou, de Lou-'an (1631). Publié avec autorisation du P. Emmanuel Diaz (1574-1659), à la Mission du Fou-kien.

4 livres. — Cordier, Imprimerie Sino-européenne, 20.

Grand in-8. Belle impression, *titre noir sur papier teinté*. 1 vol., cartonnage du XVIIIe siècle, avec le titre : *Geometriae principia.*
Fourmont 348.

4870. *Ki ho yao fa.*

Double.

Cordier, Imprimerie Sino-euro-péenne, 20.

Grand in-8. Impression médiocre. 1 vol., cartonnage.
Nouveau fonds 2957.

4871. *Ki ho yao fa.*

Double.

Cordier, Imprimerie Sino-euro-péenne, 20.

Grand in-8. Papier blanc. 1 vol., cartonnage.
Nouveau fonds 2958.

4872. 測 量 全 義

Tchhẹ liang tshiuen yi.

Traité de la mesure des lignes, surfaces et volumes.

Par les PP. Giacomo Rho et Adam Schall ; publié sous la direction de Siu Koang-khi. Texte, figures de géométrie, figures d'instruments avec légendes. Édition semblable à celle du n° 4876.

1 livre préliminaire + 10 livres. — Cordier, Imprimerie Sino-euro-péenne, 213. — Comparer Cat. imp., liv. 106, f. 21 (Sin fa soan chou, 100 livres).

Grand in-8. 1 vol., demi-rel., au chiffre de Napoléon III.
Nouveau fonds 2092.

4873. 崇 禎 曆 書 。測 量 全 義

Tchhong tcheng li chou. — Tchhẹ liang tshiuen yi.

Collection relative au calendrier, années Tchhong-tcheng : traité de la mesure des lignes, surfaces et volumes.

Même ouvrage.

Livres 3 et 5. — Comparer Cat. imp., liv. 106, f. 21 (Sin fa soan chou, 100 livres).

Grand in-8. Papier blanc, couverture jaune impérial. 1 vol., cartonnage.
Nouveau fonds 3335.

4874. 崇 禎 曆 書 。割 圓 八 線 表

Tchhong tcheng li chou. — Ko yuen pa sien piao.

Collection relative au calendrier, années Tchhong-tcheng : explication et tables des sinus, etc.

Par le P. Jean Terenz (1576-1630) ; publié par les PP. Rho et Schall, sous la direction de Siu Koang-khi. Édition antérieure à 1644.

1 livre. — Comparer Cat. imp., liv. 106, f. 21 (Sin fa soan chou, 100 livres).

Grand in-8. Papier blanc. 1 vol., cartonnage.
Nouveau fonds 3400.

4875. — I.

西洋新法曆書。割圓 八線表

Si yang sin fa li chou. — Ko yuen pa sien piao.

Collection relative au calendrier, d'après la méthode européenne : explication et tables des sinus, etc.

Même ouvrage, édition postérieure à 1644.

Titre noir sur papier teinté au verso du feuillet.

— II.

Ki ho yao fa.

Même ouvrage qu'au n° 4869, édition différente.

Grand in-8. 1 vol. demi-rel., au chiffre de Napoléon III.
Nouveau fonds 2095.

4876.   大測

Ta tchhẹ.

Trigonométrie.

Par le P. Jean Terenz, publié par le P. Adam Schall, sous la direction de Siu Koang-khi. Texte et figures.

2 livres. — Cordier, Imprimerie Sino-européenne, 306. — Comparer Cat. imp., liv. 106, f. 21 (Sin fa soan **chou**).

Grand in-8. Titre noir sur papier

teinté au verso du feuillet. 1 vol., demi-rel., au chiffre de Napoléon III.
Nouveau fonds 2113.

4877-4878.   御製數理 精蘊

Yu tchi chou li tsing yun.

Traité de mathématiques.

Publié par ordre impérial (1713?); la table indique 8 livres.

Livres 1 à 4 seulement. — Comparer Cat. imp., liv. 107, f. 24 (Yu ting chou li tsing yun en 53 livres).

Grand in-8. Papier blanc, belle impression; couvertures originales en papier jaune. 2 vol., cartonnage.
Nouveau fonds 3404, 3405.

4879.   測算刀圭。三角 法摘要

Tchhẹ soan tao koei. — San kio fa tchẹ yao.

Principes de trigonométrie.

Préface par Nien Hi-yao Yun-kong, de Koang-ning (1718). Texte et figures.

In-12. 1 vol., cartonnage.
Nouveau fonds 3337.

4880-4881.   九數通考

Kieou chou thong khao.

Examen des neuf sections des mathématiques.

Par Khiu Tsheng-fa Sing-yuen,

de Yu-chan, avec préface de l'auteur (1772). Préface par Tai Tchen, de Hieou-ning (1773). Avertissement, texte avec figures. Gravé à la salle Yu-tsan (1772).

1 + 11 + 1 livres.

Grand in-8. Titre noir sur blanc. 2 vol., demi-rel., au chiffre de Louis-Philippe. *Nouveau fonds* 2301.

___

4882.

Table de logarithmes.

Grand in-8. Impression noire et rouge; couvertures originales en soie bleue. En tête du 1er pęn, note manuscrite signée de L. Langlès, 12 septembre 1816. 1 vol., demi-rel., au chiffre de Napoléon III. *Nouveau fonds* 2175.

4883.

Table de logarithmes.

In-12. Impression noire et rouge. 1 vol., cartonnage. *Nouveau fonds* 2732.

4884.

Table de logarithmes.

In-24. Impression noire et rouge. 1 vol., cartonnage. *Nouveau fonds* 3733.

___

4885.   代數學
Tai chou hio.

De Morgan's Algebra.

Traduction chinoise par Alexan- der Wylie (1815-1887), rédigée par Li Chan-lan, de Hai-ning. Préface chinoise par Wylie (1859); préface anglaise, écrite par le même à Chang-hai (octobre 1859), contenant un historique des mathématiques en Chine. Imprimé en caractères mobiles, dans la maison Męhai (1859).

Livre préliminaire + 13 livres.

Petit in-8. Papier blanc; titre chinois noir sur blanc; dédicace : *M. G. Pauthier with A. Wylie's comp^{ts}*. 1 vol., demi-rel., au chiffre de la République Française. *Nouveau fonds* 3557.

4886.   代微積拾級
Tai oei tsi chi ki

Loomis' Analytical Geometry and Differential and Integral Calculus.

Traduction de Wylie, rédigée par Li Chan-lan; préfaces chinoises des deux traducteurs (1859); préface anglaise, écrite à Chang-hai par A. Wylie (juillet 1859). Liste de termes techniques en anglais et en chinois. Gravé à la maison Męhai (1859).

18 livres.

In-4. Papier blanc; titre noir sur blanc; dédicace : *M. G. Pauthier with A. Wylie's comp^{ts}*. 1 vol., demi-rel., au chiffre de la République Française. *Nouveau fonds* 3558.

___

4887-4892. 則古昔齋算學

Tse kou si tchai soan hio.

Traité de mathématiques.

Par Li Chan-lan, de Hai-ning,

avec préface de l'auteur (1867); postface par Lieou Chi-tchong, de Han-yang (1864).

In-4. Belle impression sur papier blanc, titre noir sur blanc. 6 vol. chinois dans 1 enveloppe.
Nouveau fonds 4370.

Deuxième Section : ASTRONOMIE ET COSMOGRAPHIE.

4893. 天文步天歌

Thien oen pou thien ko.

Description versifiée du ciel étoilé.

En vers de sept syllabes; table; figures. Sans nom d'auteur ni date. Attribué à Oang Hi-ming, surnom Tan-yuen-tseu (dynastie des Soei ou des Thang).

Comparer Cat. imp., liv. 107, f. 34 (Pou thien ko en 7 livres).

Grand in-8. 1 vol., cartonnage.
Nouveau fonds 3297.

4894-4896. 古今律曆考

Kou kin liu li khao.

Examen historique des tubes musicaux et du calendrier.

Par Hing Yun-lou Chi-teng, de

Chang-kou, docteur en 1580; publié par les soins de Oei Oen-khoei, de Man-tchheng. Préface de l'auteur; préfaces par Oang Pang-tsiun (1600) et par Tchou Tchi-fan; postfaces.

72 livres. — Cat. imp., liv. 106, f. 14.

Grand in-8. Papier blanc; quelques feuillets manuscrits; manquent les livres 5 et 6. 3 vol., cartonnage.
Nouveau fonds 2990 à 2992.

4897. 乾坤體義

Khien khoen thi yi.

Principes du système du monde.

Par le P. Ricci (1552-1610). Texte relatif à la cosmographie et à la géographie, avec figures.

3 livres. — Cat. imp., liv. 106,

f. 16 (en 2 livres). — Cordier, Imprimerie Sino-européenne, 236.

Petit in-8. 1 vol., cartonnage.
Nouveau fonds 2953.

4898. *Khien khoẹn thi yi.*

Double.

Cordier, Imprimerie Sino-européenne, 236.

Petit in-8. 1 vol., cartonnage (prov. de la Société de Jésus).
Nouveau fonds 2954.

4899. 渾蓋通憲圖說

Hoẹn kai thong hien thou choẹ.

Explication de la sphère céleste, avec figures.

Par Li Tchi-tsao Tchen-tchi, de Jen-hoo, avec préface de l'auteur (1607). Postface de la même date par Fan Liang-tchhou Tchi-hiu, de Yu-tchang. Ouvrage publié par les soins de Tcheng Hoai-khoei Lou-seu, de Tchang-nan; attribué au P. Ricci.

Livre préliminaire + 2 livres. — Cat. imp., liv. 106, f. 24 (en 2 livres). — Cordier, Imprimerie Sino-européenne, 242.

Grand in-8. 1 vol., cartonnage (prov. de la Société de Jésus).
Nouveau fonds 1691.

4900. *Hoẹn kai thong hien thou choẹ.*

Même ouvrage; édition plus petite.

Petit in-8. 1 vol., cartonnage.
Nouveau fonds 3415.

4901. 簡平儀說

Kien phing yi choẹ.

Traité sur un instrument de projection orthographique.

Par le P. Sabatthinus de Ursis (1575-1620). Préface de Siu Koang-khi (1611).

1 livre. — Cat. imp., liv. 106, f. 19. — Cordier, Imprimerie Sino-européenne, 316.

Grand in-8. 1 vol., cartonnage (prov. de la Société de Jésus).
Nouveau fonds 2974.

4902. *Kien phing yi choẹ.*

Même ouvrage, copie manuscrite.

Petit in-8. 1 vol., cartonnage.
Nouveau fonds 2975.

4903. 表度說

Piao tou choẹ.

Traité de gnomonique.

Par le P. Sabatthinus de Ursis; rédigé par Tcheou Tseu-yu, de Tsheu-choei, et par Tcho Eul-khang, de Oou-lin. Préfaces par Li Tchi-tsao, de Jen-hoo, et par

Tcheou Tseu-yu (1614). Texte avec figures.

1 livre. — Cat. imp., liv. 106, f. 17. — Cordier, Imprimerie Sino-européenne, 315.

Grand in-8. 1 vol., cartonnage (prov. de la Société de Jésus).
Nouveau fonds 3053.

4904. 天問略

Thien oen lio.

Abrégé d'astronomie.

D'après le système de Ptolémée. Par le P. Emmanuel Diaz (1574-1659); préface de l'auteur (1615). Autre préface par Khong Tchengchi Tchong-fou (1615). Introduction (1615). Texte et figures.

1 livre. — Cat. imp., liv. 106, f. 20. — Cordier, Imprimerie Sino-européenne, 99.

Grand in-8. 1 vol., cartonnage.
Nouveau fonds 3299.

4905. *Thien oen lio.*

Même ouvrage; édition plus petite comprenant en plus une introduction non datée.

Cordier, Imprimerie Sino-européenne, 99.

Petit in-8. 1 vol., cartonnage.
Nouveau fonds 3296.

4906. *Thien oen lio.*

Double.

Petit in-8. Papier teinté. 1 vol., cartonnage du XVIIIe siècle, avec le titre *Tractatus de sphaera.*

Fourmont 338.

4907. *Thien oen lio.*

Double, moins l'introduction non datée.

Petit in-8. 1 vol., cartonnage.
Nouveau fonds 3298.

4908. *Thien oen lio.*

Double.

Cordier, Imprimerie Sino-européenne, 99.

Petit in-8. Papier teinté. 1 vol., cartonnage du XVIIIe siècle, avec le titre *Tractatus de sphaera.*

Fourmont 339.

4909. *Thien oen lio.*

Double.

1 vol., cartonnage du XVIIIe siècle, même titre que ci-dessus (prov. des Missions Étrangères).

Fourmont 340.

4910. *Thien oen lio.*

Même ouvrage, composé comme le n° 4905 ; édition plus petite.

Grand in-8. Papier blanc. 1 vol., cartonnage (prov. des Missions Étrangères).

Fourmont 390.

4911. 測天約說

Tchhe̦ thien yo choe̦.

Traité abrégé de cosmographie.

Par les P. P. Jean Terenz (1576-1630) et Adam Schall (1591-1669?). Publié sous la direction de Siu Koang-khi.

2 livres. — Cordier, Imprimerie Sino-européenne, 303. — Voir aussi Cat. imp., liv. 106, f. 21 (Sin fa soan chou, 100 livres).

Grand in-8. Titre noir sur papier teinté au verso du feuillet. 1 vol., demi-rel., au chiffre de Napoléon III.

Nouveau fonds 2093.

4912. 赤道南北兩總星全圖

Tchhi tao nan pe̦ liang tsong sing tshiuen thou.

Carte des deux hémisphères célestes au sud et au nord de l'équateur.

Autour de la carte sont des figures d'instruments et diverses légendes; notices non datées par Siu Koang-khi et par le P. Adam Schall. Planches au Nei-ko.

Comparer Cordier, Imprimerie Sino-européenne, 278.

9 feuilles papier blanc de 0,65 sur 1,85.
Nouveau fonds 2211 A.

4913. 赤道南北兩總星圖說

Tchhi tao nan pe̦ liang tsong sing thou choe̦.

Carte des deux hémisphères célestes au sud et au nord de l'équateur, avec légendes.

Par le P. Schall, sans date.

1 feuille papier blanc; de 0,40 sur 1 m.
Nouveau fonds 2211 B.

4914. 恒星經緯圖說

Heng sing king oei thou choe̦.

Carte des latitudes et longitudes des étoiles fixes; avec légende. Cartes des deux hémisphères comme la précédente (n° 4913), plus grande.

1 feuillet grand format, replié + 3 feuillets doubles, format grand in-8; papier blanc.

Nouveau fonds 2211 C.

4915. 渾天儀說

Hoe̦n thien yi choe̦.

Usage et explication des sphères célestes.

Par les P. P. Adam Schall et Giacomo Rho (1590-1638); publié sous la direction de Li Thien-king; préface de ce dernier (1636). Texte et figures.

5 livres. — Cordier, Imprimerie Sino-européenne, 274. — Voir aussi Cat. imp., liv. 106, f. 21 (Sin fa soan chou, 100 livres).

Grand in-8. 1 vol., demi-rel., au chiffre de Napoléon III.

Nouveau fonds 2110.

4916. 空際格致

Khong tsi ko tchi.

Traité de cosmographie et de météorologie.

Avec la théorie des cinq éléments. Par le P. Alfonso Vagnoni (1566-1640).

2 livres. — Cat. imp., liv. 125, f. 34. — Cordier, Imprimerie Sino-européenne, 333.

Grand in-8. 1 vol., cartonnage (prov de la Société de Jésus).

Nouveau fonds 2955.

—————

4917. — I.

Compendium latinum proponens XII posteriores figuras Libri obseruationum necnon priores VII figuras Libri Organici.

Texte latin, en écriture latine cursive. Gravé en Chine, sans date.

Comparer n° 4918. — Cordier, Imprimerie Sino-européenne, 340.

9 feuillets doubles.

— II.

Astronomia Europæa sub Imperatore Tartaro-Sinico Cām-Hȳ appellato ex vmbra in lucem reuocata A. P. Ferdinando Verbiest Flandro-Belga Brugensi E Societate Jesu Academiæ Astronomicæ In Regia Pekinensi Præfecto Anno Salutis MDCLXVIII.

Titre d'une gravure analogue, suivi de figures.

Cordier, Imprimerie Sino-européenne, 339.

12 feuillets doubles.

— III.

Double partiel du n° 4918 (titre latin et début).

In-folio. Papier blanc, gravure soignée. 1 vol., cartonnage.

Nouveau fonds 4928'.

4918. 新製儀象圖

Sin tchi yi siang thou.

Liber organicus Astronomiæ Europææ apud Sinas Restitutæ sub Imperatore Sino-Tartarico Cām-Hȳ appellato Auctore P. Ferdinando Verbiest Flandro-Belga Brugensi E Societate Jesu Academiæ Astronomicæ In Regia Pekinensi Præfecto Anno Salutis MDCLXVIII.

Après le titre chinois et le titre latin, notice en chinois du P. Verbiest (1623-1688), datée de 1674;

puis figures de l'Observatoire et des instruments.

Cordier, Imprimerie Sino-européenne, 340.

In-folio. Papier blanc ; gravure et disposition analogues au nº précédent. 1 vol., cartonnage.
Nouveau fonds 4926.

4919. *Sin tchi yi siang thou.*

Double, sans titre européen.

In-folio. Papier plus fort que le précédent. 1 vol., cartonnage.
Nouveau fonds 4927.

4920.

Liber organicus Astronomiæ Europææ, etc.

Double : titre latin, notice, quelques figures.

1 vol., cartonnage.
Nouveau fonds 4928².

4921. 測食畧

Tchhę chi lio.

Théorie abrégée des éclipses.

Par le P. Adam Schall ; publié par Tcheou Tseu-yu, de Tsheu-choei, et Tcho Eul-khang, de Ooulin. Texte et figures.

2 livres. — Cordier, Imprimerie Sino-européenne, 286.

Grand in-8, 1 vol., demi-rel., au chiffre de Napoléon III.
Nouveau fonds 2117.

4922.   坤輿格致略說

Khoęn yu ko tchi lio choę.

Traité abrégé de cosmographie, géographie, sciences naturelles.

Par le P. Verbiest. Préface par Siu Eul-kio (1676). Titre sur papier teinté daté de 1674.

Grand in-8. 1 vol., cartonnage (provenant de la Société de Jésus).
Nouveau fonds 2993.

4923-4925.   新製靈臺
儀象志

Sin tchi ling thai yi siang tchi.

Description du nouvel observatoire.

Par le P. Ferdinand Verbiest ; préface de l'auteur (1674) ; rapport dédicatoire du même.

16 livres. — Cordier, Imprimerie Sino-européenne, 351 et 352. — Comparer Cat. Imp., liv. 106, f. 33, à la fin de la notice Yu ting yi siang khao tchheng. — Cf. plus haut, nᵒˢ 1329-1331.

Grand in-8, titre sur papier blanc (incomplet des livres 15 et 16).

(4923). 1 vol., demi-rel., au chiffre de Napoléon III.
Nouveau fonds 2108.

(4924-4925). 2 vol., cartonnage.
Nouveau fonds 3008, 2927.

4926.   康熙十三年歲

次甲寅月五星凌犯
時憲曆

*Khang hi chi san nien soei tsheu
kia yin yue oou sing ling fan
chi hien li.*

Liber conjunctionum lunæ
cum planetis et planetarum inter
se, necnon conjunctionis lunæ
et planetarum cum stellis fixis
toto anno Christi 1674, Imperatoris Cām-Hy 13[io] Auctore P. Ferdinando Verbiest Soc[tis] Jesu
[Academiæ] Astronomicæ in
Regia Pekinensi Præfecto.

In-folio. Manuscrit en noir et rouge;
couverture en soie bleue. 1 vol., cartonnage.
Fourmont 347.

4927. 天元曆理三書
Thien yuen li li san chou.

Trois traités sur le calendrier
et l'astronomie.

Par Siu Fa Phou-tchhen, de Kia-
hing; préface par Fong Phou, de
Phien (1682). Avertissement par
l'auteur; table des matières.

Livre préliminaire + 12 livres.

— I.

述畧總序
Chou lio tsong siu.

Exposé général et historique.
Par Siu Fa.

Livre préliminaire.

— II.

原理
Yuen li.

Cosmographie et astronomie.

Par le même; publié par Tchheng
Yu-koęn, de Pę-hai. Texte annoté
et tableaux. Table des matières.

6 livres (1 à 6).

— III.

考古
Khao kou.

Étude historique.

Par Siu Fa, publié par Tchheng
Yu-koęn. Texte annoté, figures,
tableaux chronologiques et autres.
Table des matières.

4 livres (7 à 10).

— IV.

定法
Ting fa.

Tableaux pour la marche des
astres.

Par les mêmes. Texte annoté;
table des matières.

4 livres (11 et 12).

Petit in-8. Titre noir sur blanc. 1 vol.,
reliure au chiffre de Charles X.
Nouveau fonds 340 A

4928. 方星圖解

Fang sing thou kiai.

Planisphère céleste avec légendes.

Donnant les astérismes chinois. Notice (1711) par le P. Grimaldi (1639-1712); à la fin une autre notice non signée.

9 planches de 0,18 sur 0,30; papier blanc. Au début, note manuscrite : *Planisphère du P. Grimaldi en 1711*. 1 vol., cartonnage recouvert de papier chinois. Département des Estampes, Oc 167.

4929. 方星圖

Fang sing thou.

Même ouvrage.

In-folio. 1 vol., en paravent, couvert en soie.
Section des Cartes Inventaire général 1725 C 17315.

4930. 黃道總星圖

Hoang tao tsong sing thou.

Carte des constellations chinoises de l'écliptique et des deux hémisphères.

Avec figures de la lune, des planètes, etc. Gravée par Li Po-ming, d'après le P. Kögler (1680-1746); légende datée de 1723.

1 feuille de 0,65 × 0,40, montée en Chine.
Section des Cartes Inventaire général 1601 B 1734 *quater*.

4931. 雍正十三年三月十五日乙酉望月食圖

Yong tcheng chi san nien san yue chi san ji yi yeou oang yue chi thou.

Khūwaliyasun tob i ǰuwan ilaci aniya ilan biya tofokhon de niokhon čoko inenkgi biya ǰetere nirugan.

Figures de l'éclipse de lune du 7 avril 1735. Textes mantchou et chinois; figures de l'éclipse pour diverses provinces.

Comparer Cordier, Imprimerie Sino-européenne, 341.

Grand in-8. 1 vol., cartonnage.
Nouveau fonds 5232.

4932-4934. 欽定儀象考成

Khin ting yi siang khao tchheng.

Examen des instruments astronomiques et de la voûte céleste, ouvrage imprimé par ordre impérial.

Rapport des auteurs, le P. Kögler et autres, daté de 1744; rapport de Yun-lou, prince de Tchoang, et autres rapports portant diverses dates de 1745 à 1754. Préface impériale, avec les sceaux impériaux en rouge (1756). Liste des personnages qui ont surveillé l'impression. Texte avec figures et cartes.

2 livres préliminaires + 30 livres. — Cat. imp., liv. 106, f. 31. — Cordier, Imprimerie Sino-européenne, 140.

Grand in-8. Belle impression; couvertures originales en soie jaune. 3 vol., demi-rel., au chiffre de Louis-Philippe. *Nouveau fonds* 592.

4935. — I.

太平萬年書

Thai phing oan nien chou.

Traités sur le système du monde.

Présentés à l'Empereur par Koo Thing-chang; rapport de celui-ci et rescrits impériaux, sans date.

9 traités (manquent les 4 derniers). — Ouvrage imprimé.

— II.

南京羅主教神道碑記

Nan king lo tchou kiao chen tao pei ki.

Épitaphe du R. P. Alexandre Ciceri, évêque de Nanking.

Rédigée ou copiée par Koo Pao-lou Thing-chang. Alexandre Ciceri, de Come, nom chinois Lo Li-chan, surnom Teng-yong, consacré évêque en 1696, mort en 1704.

Copie manuscrite.

Petit in-8 . 1 vol. , cartonnage du

XVIIIe siècle, avec le titre : *Tractatus chronologicus* (prov. des Missions Étrangères).
Fourmont 307.

———————

4936. 全圖會意

Tshiuen thou hoei yi.

Traité de cosmographie.

Inspiré des idées chrétiennes et chinoises.

In-12. Manuscrit. 1 vol., cartonnage. *Nouveau fonds* 3318.

4937. 輿圖彙言

Yu thou hoei yen.

Même ouvrage, avec une table.

Petit in-8. Manuscrit. 1 vol., cartonnage.
Nouveau fonds 3390.

———————

4938. — I.

天文問答

Thien oen oen ta.

Dialogue sur l'astronomie.

En langue parlée.

2 cahiers manuscrits.

— II.

地理圖

Ti li thou.

[Légende d'une] carte de géographie.

1 cahier manuscrit d'une écriture différente.

— III.

五諫賢夫

Oou kien hien fou.

Recueil de prédictions (?).

2 cahiers manuscrits d'une autre écriture.

Petit in-8. 1 vol., cartonnage.
Nouveau fonds 5057.

4939.

22 cartes célestes de formats divers ; sans texte ; pliées.

Grand in-8. 1 vol., cartonnage.
Nouveau fonds 2735.

4940. 赤道南北兩總星圖

Tchhi tao nan pẹ liang tsong sing thou.

Carte des deux hémisphères célestes au nord et au sud de l'équateur.

Constellations chinoises. Légende sans lieu ni date ni nom d'auteur.

1 feuille de 65 centim. × 1,75, collée sur toile.
Section des Cartes Inventaire général 1602 C 8940.

4941. 高厚蒙求

Kao heou mong khieou.

Collection de traités scientifiques.

Par Siu Tchhao-tsiun, de Yun-kien. Préface de l'auteur (1807). Gravé la même année chez l'auteur.

— I.

天學入門

Thien hio jou mẹn.

Éléments de cosmographie.

— II.

海域大觀

Hai yu ta koan.

Éléments de géographie.

Préface de l'auteur, sans date. Gravé en 1807.

Titre noir sur blanc.

— III.

天地圖儀

Thien ti thou yi.

Des cartes célestes et terrestres.

Préface par Tchou Tẹ-lin, de Hai-ning (1797).

3 parties.

Titre noir sur blanc.

— IV.

日晷圖法

Ji koei thou fa.

Figure et explication du cadran solaire et d'autres instruments.

Préface de l'auteur (1808).

Titre noir sur blanc.

6

— V.

自鳴鐘表圖法

Tseu ming tchong piao thou fa.

Figure et explication des horloges européennes.

Préface de l'auteur (1809).

Titre noir sur blanc.

Grand in-8. Papier blanc; titre général noir sur jaune. 1 vol., demi-rel., au chiffre de Louis-Philippe.
Nouveau fonds 907.

———

4942-4944. ## 園天圖說

Yuen thien thou choẹ.

Traité de cosmographie et de géographie, texte et cartes.

Par Li Ming-tchhẹ Tshing-lai. Préface de l'auteur (1819); préface par Yuen Yuen (1819). Postface par Hoang Yi-koei Si-phing, de Khien-nan. Gravé au pavillon Song-mei (1819).

3 livres.

In-4. Belle impression sur papier blanc; titre noir sur vert. 3 volumes chinois dans 1 enveloppe demi-reliure européenne.
Nouveau fonds 418.

4945. — I.

園天圖說續編

Yuen thien thou choẹ siu pien.

Suite au Yuen thien thou choẹ.

Cartes célestes; traité de cosmo-

graphie et d'astronomie. Par le même auteur; imprimé au pavillon Song-mei (1821) par les soins de Yuen Yuen. Préfaces par Tchhen Hong-tchang, sans date, et par Yue-yo chan-jen (1833).

Livre préliminaire + 2 livres.

Belle édition sur papier blanc, titre noir sur rose.

— II.

Yuen thien thou choẹ.

Double des n°ˢ 4942-4944.

Grand in-8. 1 vol., cartonnage.
Nouveau fonds 4596.

———

4946-4947. ## 新釋地理 備考

Sin chi ti li pei khao.

Nouveau traité de cosmographie et géographie.

Avec des notions de météorologie, séismologie, etc. Par un auteur portugais, dont le nom est transcrit Ma-ki-chi. Préface de l'auteur (1847). Texte et figures. Édité (1847) à la librairie Hai-chan sien-koan.

10 livres.

In-12. Papier blanc, titre noir sur jaune. 2 vol., demi-rel., au chiffre de Napoléon III.
Nouveau fonds 1445, 1446.

———

4948. 譚天

Than thien.

Herschell's Outlines of Astronomy.

Traduction d'Alexander Wylie (1815-1887), rédigée par Li Chanlan. Préface anglaise de Wylie, écrite à Chang-hai (décembre 1859), suivie d'une note relative à la publication des n⁰ˢ 4885 et 4886. Vocabulaire de termes techniques. Préface chinoise de Wylie (1859). Texte et figures ; les planches hors texte sont tirées sur papier euro-péen. Imprimé en caractères mobiles, dans la maison Mẹ-hai.

18 livres.

Grand in-8. Belle édition ; exemplaire sur papier teinté. 1 vol. cartonnage.
Nouveau fonds 4601.

4949. *Than thien.*

Même ouvrage.

In-4. Papier blanc ; dédicace : *Monsieur G. Pauthier with A. Wylie's comptˢ* 1 vol., demi-rel., au chiffre de la République Française.
Nouveau fonds 3559.

Troisième Section : CALENDRIER.

4950. 治曆緣起

Tchi li yuen khi.

Pièces diverses relatives à la réforme du calendrier.

Collection d'apparence factice, comprenant :

— I.

勅諭

Tchhi yu.

Décrets impériaux de 1629.

— II.

閣題

Ko thi.

Pièces émanant du Grand Secrétariat (1629).

— III.

題疏

Thi sou.

Rapports du Ministère des Rites.

— IV.

曆書總目

Li chou tsong mou.

Liste de livres relatifs au calendrier.

— V.

奏疏

Tseou sou.

Rapports présentés par Siu Koang-khi.

— VI.

題 疏
Thi sou.

Autre série de rapports, du même.

— VII.

奏 疏 · 題 疏
Tseou sou; thi sou.

Rapports divers du Ministère des Rites et de Siu Koang-khi (1632).

— VIII.

奏 疏 · 題 疏
Tseou sou; thi sou.

Rapports divers avec figures.

Présentés par le P. Schall (1659), par Li Keng-sien (1634, 1636, etc.), par Li Thien-king (1644, etc.).

Grand in-8. 1 vol., demi-rel., au chiffre de Napoléon III.
Nouveau fonds 2118.

4951. ### 學 曆 小 辯
Hio li siao pien.

Courte explication du calendrier.

Avec une lettre (1631) pour présenter l'ouvrage au Ministère des Rites ; sans nom d'auteur. L'auteur est le P. Adam Schall.

Cordier, Imprimerie Sino-européenne, 285.

Grand in-8. 1 vol., demi-rel., au chiffre de Napoléon III.
Nouveau fonds 2120.

4952. ### 新 法 表 異
Sin fa piao yi.

Différence des anciens calendriers et du nouveau calendrier.

Par le P. Schall. Exposé du système des divers calendriers usités depuis 104 a. C. jusqu'aux Ming ; exposé scientifique du système nouveau.

2 livres. — Cordier, Imprimerie Sino-européenne, 293.

Grand in-8. 1 vol., demi-rel., au chiffre de Napoléon III.
Nouveau fonds 2098.

4953. ### 新 法 曆 引
Sin fa li yin.

Introduction au nouveau calendrier.

Par le P. Schall.

1 livre. — Cordier, Imprimerie Sino-européenne, 291.

Grand in-8. 1 vol., demi-rel., au chiffre de Napoléon III.
Nouveau fonds 2090.

4954. ### 曆 法 西 傳
Li fa si tchoan.

Connaissances occidentales sur le calendrier.

Introduction et plan d'un ouvrage sur la cosmographie et le calendrier, par le P. Schall.

1 livre. — Cordier, Imprimerie Sino-européenne, 292.

Grand in-8. 1 vol., demi-rel., au chiffre de Napoléon III.

Nouveau fonds 2091.

4955. 黄赤道距度表

Hoang tchhi tao kiu tou piao.

Table des degrés de distance entre l'écliptique et l'équateur.

Publiée par ordre impérial avant 1644, par Siu Koang-khi et le P. Terenz (1576-1630).

Cordier, Imprimerie Sino-européenne, 304. — Comparer aussi, Cat. imp., liv. 106, f. 21 (Sin fa soan chou, 100 livres).

Grand in-8. Papier blanc, couverture en soie jaune impérial. 1 vol., cartonnage.

Nouveau fonds 2337.

4956. 黄赤道距度表

Hoang tchhi tao kiu tou piao.

Même ouvrage, réédition postérieure à 1644, portant les noms de Siu Koang-khi et des PP. Jean Terenz et Nicolao Longobardi (1566-1654).

Grand in-8. 1 vol., demi-rel., au chiffre de Napoléon III.

Nouveau fonds 2109.

4957. 崇禎曆書。日躔曆指

Tchhong tcheng li chou. — Ji tchhan li tchi.

Collection relative au calendrier, années Tchhong-tcheng : théorie du mouvement du soleil.

Par les PP. Giacomo Rho (1590-1638), Nicolao Longobardi et Adam Schall; publié sous la direction de Siu Koang-khi. Édition antérieure à 1644. Texte et figures.

9 sections. — Cordier, Imprimerie Sino-européenne, 219. — Comparer aussi Cat. imp., liv. 106, f. 21 (Sin fa soan chou, 100 livres).

Grand in-8. Papier blanc; couvertures en soie jaune impérial. 1 vol., cartonnage.

Nouveau fonds 2932.

4958. 西洋新法曆書。日躔曆指

Si yang sin fa li chou. — Ji tchhan li tchi.

Collection relative au calendrier d'après la méthode européenne : théorie du mouvement du soleil.

Même ouvrage; édition postérieure à 1644.

Grand in-8. Titre noir sur papier teinté, au verso du feuillet. 1 vol., demi-rel., au chiffre de Napoléon III.

Nouveau fonds 2096.

4959. 崇禎曆書。日躔表

·*Tchhong tcheng li chou. — Ji tchhan piao.*

Collection relative au calendrier, années Tchhong-tcheng : tables du mouvement du soleil.

Par les PP. Rho et Schall; publié sous la direction de Siu Koang-khi. Édition antérieure à 1644.

2 livres. — Cordier, Imprimerie Sino-européenne, 220. — Voir aussi Cat. imp., liv. 106, f. 21 (Sin fa soan chou, 100 livres).

Grand in-8. Papier blanc, couverture en soie jaune impérial. 1 vol., cartonnage.
Nouveau fonds 2933.

4960. *Ji tchhan piao.*

Même ouvrage; édition postérieure à 1644.

Grand in-8. Titre noir sur papier teinté, au verso du feuillet. 1 vol., demi-rel., au chiffre de Napoléon III.
Nouveau fonds 2097.

———

4961. 月離曆指
Yue li li tchi.

Théorie du mouvement de la lune.

Par les PP. Rho et Schall; publié sous la direction de Siu Khoang-khi. Texte et figures. Édition postérieure à 1644.

4 livres, 30 sections. — Cordier, Imprimerie Sino-européenne, 217. — Voir aussi Cat. imp., liv. 106, f. 21 (Sin fa soan chou, 100 livres).

Grand in-8. 1 vol., demi-rel., au chiffre de Napoléon III.
Nouveau fonds 2102.

———

4962. 月離表
Yue li piao.

Tables du mouvement de la lune.

Par les PP. Rho et Schall; publié sous la direction de Siu Koang-khi. Édition postérieure à 1644.

4 livres. — Cordier, Imprimerie Sino-européenne, 218. — Voir aussi Cat. imp., liv. 106, f. 21 (Sin fa soan chou, 100 livres).

Grand in-8. 1 vol., demi-rel., au chiffre de Napoléon III.
Nouveau fonds 2103.

———

4963. — I. 交食曆指
Kiao chi li tchi.

Théorie des éclipses.

Par les PP. Schall et Rho; publié par Siu Koang-khi. Texte et figures.

7 livres. — Cordier, Imprimerie Sino-européenne, 279. — Voir aussi Cat. imp., liv. 106, f. 21 (Sin fa soan chou, 100 livres).

— II.

古今交食考

Kou kin kiao chi khao.

Examen des éclipses anciennes et modernes.

Notant les éclipses depuis l'époque du Chou-king jusqu'en 1627.
Par les PP. Schall et Rho ; publié
sous la direction de Li Thien-king.

1 livre. — Cordier, Imprimerie Sino-
européenne, 276. — Comparer Cat.
imp., liv. 106, f. 21 (Sin fa soan chou,
100 livres).

Grand in-8. 1 vol., demi-rel., au chiffre
de Louis-Philippe.
Nouveau fonds 104.

4964-4965.　交食表

Kiao chi piao.

Tables des éclipses.

Texte, tables et figures ; par les
PP. Schall et Rho ; publié sous la
direction de Siu Koang-khi.

7 livres + tables finales sans indication de livres. — Cordier, Imprimerie Sino-européenne, 280. — Voir
Cat. imp., liv. 106, f. 21 (Sin fa soan
chou, 100 livres).

Grand in-8. 2 vol., demi-rel., au chiffre
de Napoléon III.
Nouveau fonds 2107, 2106.

4966.　崇禎曆書

Tchhong tcheng li chou.

Collection relative au calendrier, années Tchhong-tcheng.

Publiée, sous la direction de Siu
Koang-khi, par le P. Schall ;
gravée à la salle Oou-ying avant
1644. Texte et figures.

Comparer Cat. imp., liv. 106, f. 21
(Sin fa soan chou, 100 livres).

— I.

恒星曆指

Heng sing li tchi.

Théorie des étoiles fixes.

Texte et tables.

Livres 2 et 3 seulement. — Cordier,
Imprimerie Sino-européenne, 281.

— II.

恒星經緯表

Heng sing king oei piao.

Tables des latitudes et longitudes des étoiles fixes.

Livres 5 et 6 (formant la suite de
l'art. I). — Comparer Cordier, Imprimerie Sino-européenne, 282 (Heng
sing piao en 5 livres).

Grand in-8. Papier blanc ; couvertures
en soie jaune impérial. 1 vol., cartonnage.
Nouveau fonds 2906.

4967.

Heng sing king oei piao.

Double du n° précédent, art. II.

Grand in-8. Papier blanc ; couverture
en soie jaune impérial. 1 vol., cartonnage.
Nouveau fonds 3401.

4968. — I.

Heng sing li tchi.

Théorie des étoiles fixes.

Texte différent du nᵉ 4966, art. I. Par les PP. Schall et Rho; publié sous la direction de Siu Koang-khi. Édition postérieure à 1644. Tables et figures.

3 livres.

— II.

恒星經緯圖說

Heng sing king oei thou choe.

Carte des latitudes et longitudes des étoiles fixes, avec légendes.

Comparer n° 4914.

Grand in-8. 1 vol., demi-rel., au chiffre de Napoléon III.
Nouveau fonds 2114.

4969.

Heng sing li tchi.

Théorie des étoiles fixes.

Feuillets détachés.

Nouveau fonds 4976.

4970.

Heng sing king oei piao.

Tables des longitudes et latitudes des étoiles fixes.

Différentes du n° 4966, art. II. Par les PP. Schall et Rho; publié sous la direction de Siu Koang-khi. Édition postérieure à 1644.

Livres 6 et 5.

Grand in-8. 1 vol., demi-rel., au chiffre de Napoléon III.
Nouveau fonds 2116.

―――――――

4971.　五緯曆指

Oou oei li tchi.

Théorie des cinq planètes.

Texte, figures et tableaux, par les PP. Rho et Schall; publié sous la direction de Siu Koang-khi et Li Thien-king.

9 livres. — Cordier, Imprimerie Sino-européenne, 216. — Voir Cat. imp., liv. 106, f. 21 (Sin fa soan chou, 100 livres).

Grand in-8. 1 vol., demi-rel., au chiffre de Napoléon III.
Nouveau fonds 2100.

―――――――

4972.　西洋新法曆書。五緯表

Si yang sin fa li chou. — Oou oei piao.

Collection relative au calendrier d'après la méthode européenne : tables des cinq planètes.

Texte et figures, par les PP. Rho et Schall; publié sous la direction de Siu Koang-khi et Li Thien-king.

Livre préliminaire + 10 livres. — Cordier, Imprimerie Sino-européenne, 215. — Voir Cat. imp., liv. 106, f. 21 (Sin fa soan chou, 100 livres).

Grand in-8. 1 vol., demi-rel., au chiffre de Napoléon III.
Nouveau fonds 2101.

4973. 恒星出沒表

Heng sing tchhou mou piao.

Tables du lever et du coucher des étoiles fixes.

Par les PP. Schall et Rho, sous la direction de Li Thien-king.

2 livres. — Cordier, Imprimerie Sino-européenne, 284. — Cat. imp., liv. 106, f. 21 (Sin fa soan chou, 100 livres).

Grand in-8. 1 vol., demi-rel., au chiffre de Napoléon III.
Nouveau fonds 2115.

4974. 順治壬辰

Choen tchi jen tchhen.

Calendrier officiel pour 1652.

Petit in-8. Gravure grossière, incomplet. 1 vol., reliure du XVIIᵉ siècle.
Nouveau fonds 2123.

4975. 大清康熙五十年歲次辛卯時憲曆

Ta tshing khang hi oou chi nien soei tsheu sin mao chi hien li.

Calendrier officiel pour 1711.

Grand in-8. 1 vol., cartonnage du XVIIIᵉ siècle, avec le titre : *Ephemerides sinicae.*
Fourmont 342.

4976. 大清康熙五十四年歲次乙未時憲曆

Ta tshing khang hi oou chi seu nien soei tsheu yi oei chi hien li.

Calendrier officiel pour 1715.

Grand in-8. Titre en bleu sur blanc; couverture en soie jaune. 1 vol. chinois.
Nouveau fonds 4915.

4977. 大清乾隆五年歲次庚申時憲書

Ta tshing khien long oou nien soei tsheu keng chen chi hien chou.

Calendrier officiel pour 1740.

Grand in-8. Papier blanc; couverture jaune. 1 vol., cartonnage.
Nouveau fonds 2728.

4978. 大清乾隆十年歲次乙丑時憲書

Ta tshing khien long chi nien soei tsheu yi tchheou chi hien chou.

Calendrier officiel pour 1745.

In-4. Titre rouge et bleu sur blanc; couverture jaune. 1 vol., demi-rel., au chiffre de Napoléon III (prov. de la bibl. de l'Arsenal).
Nouveau fonds 1684.

4979.

Calendrier officiel pour 1753.

In-4. Papier blanc; incomplet du début. 1 vol., cartonnage.
Nouveau fonds 2393.

6*

4980.   大清乾隆三十
三年歲次戊子時憲書

*Ta tshing khien long san chi san
nien soei tsheu oou tseu chi
hien chou.*

Calendrier officiel pour 1768.

Grand in-8. Papier blanc, couverture
jaune; en partie interfolié, notes en latin. 1 vol., demi-reliure.
Nouveau fonds 3560.

4981.   大清乾隆四十
二年歲次丁酉時憲書

*Ta tshing khien long seu chi eul
nien soei tsheu ting yeou chi
hien chou.*

Calendrier officiel pour 1777.

Grand in-8. Papier blanc. 1 vol., cartonnage.
Nouveau fonds 2712.

———

4982.   民曆鋪註解惑

Min li phou tchou kiai hoe.

Réponse à des doutes exposés
à propos des éphémérides.

Distinction établie entre la partie astronomique du calendrier et
les superstitions qui s'y rattachent.
Par le P. Schall; publié par les
soins du P. Verbiest (1623-1688).
Introduction de l'auteur (1662).
Préface par Hou Chi-'an, surnom
Sieou-yen lao-chi. Liste des fonctionnaires qui ont surveillé l'im-

pression. A la fin, décret impérial
(1679) intitulé Hi tchhao ting 'an
(cf. n°ˢ 1329-1331).

Cordier,   Imprimerie   Sino-européenne, 269.

Grand in-8. 1 vol., cartonnage.
Nouveau fonds 3026.

4983.

Min li phou tchou kiai hoe.

Même ouvrage; planches différentes, plus petites.

Cordier,   Imprimerie   Sino-européenne, 269.

Grand in-8. 1 vol., cartonnage.
Nouveau fonds 3027.

———

4984. — I.

不得已辯
Pou te yi pien.

Réfutation d'un libelle contre
le christianisme, de l'astronome
musulman Yang Koang-sien.

Par le P. Luigi Buglio (1606-
1682). Même ouvrage qu'au n° 1883,
art. II, édition différente. Illustration au feuillet 31.

Cordier,   Imprimerie   Sino-européenne, 56.

— II.

附中國初人辯
Fou tchong koe tchhou jen pien.

Autre réfutation, relative aux
anciens Chinois.

Sans nom d'auteur.

3 feuillets, dont la pagination fait suite à celle de l'art. I.

Petit in-8. 1 vol., cartonnage.

Nouveau fonds 3066.

4985. — I.

Pou tẹ yi pien.

— II.

Fou tchong koẹ tchhou jen pien.

Double.

Cordier, Imprimerie Sino-européenne, 56.

Grand in-8. 1 vol., cartonnage.
Nouveau fonds 3067.

4986. — I.

Pou tẹ yi pien.

— II.

Fou tchong koẹ tchhou jen pien.

Même ouvrage, planches plus petites.

Cordier, Imprimerie Sino-européenne, 56.

Grand in-8. 1 vol., cartonnage.
Nouveau fonds 3070.

4987. — I.

Pou tẹ yi pien.

Même ouvrage qu'au n° 4984, art. I; édition plus grande.

Cordier, Imprimerie Sino-européenne, 56.

— II.

天主正教約徵

Thien tchou tcheng kiao yo tcheng.

Preuves de la religion catholique.

Par le P. Luigi Buglio. Même ouvrage qu'au n° 1885, art. II, édition différente. La pagination ne fait pas suite à celle de l'art. I.

Cordier, Imprimerie Sino-européenne, 50.

Grand in-8. 1 vol., cartonnage.
Nouveau fonds 3068.

4988. — I.

Pou tẹ yi pien.

— II.

Thien tchou tcheng kiao yo tcheng.

Double.

Cordier, Imprimerie Sino-européenne, 56 et 50.

Grand in-8. 1 vol., cartonnage.
Nouveau fonds 3072.

———

4989. # 不得已辯

Pou tẹ yi pien.

Réfutation d'un libelle contre le christianisme, de l'astronome musulman Yang Koang-sien.

Par le P. Verbiest. Préface de l'auteur, non datée. Table des matières. Texte et figures.

2 livres. — Cordier, Imprimerie Sino-européenne, 350.

Grand in-8. Incomplet à la fin. 1 vol.,
cartonnage (prov. de la Société de Jésus).
Nouveau fonds 3069.

4990.

Pou tę yi pien.

Double.

1ᵉʳ livre seul. — Cordier, Imprimerie Sino-européenne, 350.

Grand in-8. 1 vol., cartonnage.
Nouveau fonds 3071.

4991.

Pou tę yi pien.

Double.

1ᵉʳ livre seul.

Grand in-8. 1 vol., demi-rel. au chiffre de Napoléon III.
Nouveau fonds 2121.

———

4992. 欽定新曆測驗紀略

Khin ting sin li tchhę yen ki lio.

Abrégé d'observations relatives au nouveau calendrier, imprimé par ordre impérial.

Recueil de rapports et pièces diverses (1668 et 1669), émanant du P. Verbiest et d'autres fonctionnaires : texte et figures.

1 livre. — Cordier, Imprimerie Sino-européenne, 354.

Grand in-8. Incomplet de plusieurs feuillets. 1 vol., cartonnage.
Nouveau fonds 3336.

———

4993. 妄擇辯

Oang tsę pien.

Discussion du choix des jours fastes.

Par le P. Verbiest (1669), contre Yang Koang-sien. Notes dans la marge supérieure.

Grand in-8. 1 vol., cartonnage.
Nouveau fonds 3365.

4994.

Oang tsę pien.

Double.

Grand in-8. 1 vol., cartonnage.
Nouveau fonds 3366.

———

4995. 妄推吉凶辯

Oang tchoei ki hiong pien.

Réfutation de Yang Koang-sien et des devins.

Par le P. Verbiest (1669); texte avec annotations dans la marge supérieure. Gravé de nouveau à Canton, à la salle Ta-yuen.

17 sections. — Cordier, Imprimerie Sino-européenne, 342.

Grand in-8. 1 vol., cartonnage (prov. des Missions Étrangères).
Fourmont 257.

4996.

Oang tchoei ki hiong pien.

Double.

Cordier, Imprimerie Sino-européenne, 342.

Grand in-8. 1 vol., cartonnage.
Nouveau fonds 3363.

4997.

Oang tchoei ki hiong pien.

Double.

Grand in-8. 1 vol., cartonnage (prov. de la Société de Jésus).
Nouveau fonds 3364.

4998. 妄占辯

Oang tchan pien.

Discussion contre les sorts.

Dirigée contre Yang Koang-sien et les devins, par le P. Verbiest (1669). Gravé de nouveau à Canton, à la salle Ta-yuen.

A la table, 17 sections; manquent les sections 3 à 17; toutefois le volume paraît complet. — Cordier, Imprimerie Sino-européenne, 358.

Grand in-8. Papier blanc. 1 vol., cartonnage (prov. de la Société de Jésus).
Fourmont 256.

4999.

Oang tchan pien.

Double.

Petit in-8. 1 vol., cartonnage.
Nouveau fonds 3360.

5000.

Oang tchan pien.

Double.

Petit in-8. 1 vol., cartonnage du XVIIIe siècle, avec le titre : *Yam Kuam Sien expostulatio.*
Fourmont 333.

5001.

Oang tchan pien.

Même ouvrage. Gravé de nouveau à la Mission de Tsi-ning.

Petit in-8. 1 vol., cartonnage (prov. des Missions Étrangères).
Nouveau fonds 3361.

5002. 崇正必辯

Tchhong tcheng pi pien.

Discussion en faveur de la vérité.

Ouvrage relatif à l'affaire du calendrier, par Ho Chi-tcheng Kong-kiai, de Yu. Préface de l'auteur (1672); préface (1672) du P. Buglio, suivie du sceau de la Mission. Avertissement montrant les rapports entre le culte catholique et le culte de Chang-ti. Annexes : rapport du prince de Khang, contre Yang Koang-sien; autres documents relatifs à la même affaire. Table générale, table détaillée.

2 sections (4 + 3 livres). — Manque la 1re section.

Petit in-8. 1 vol., cartonnage.
Nouveau fonds 3343.

5003-5006. 康熙永年
曆法

Khang hi yong nien li fa.

Calendrier astronomique pour les années Khang-hi.

Par les PP. Verbiest et Gri-maldi (1639-1712); publié sous la direction de Yi-tha-la.

— I.

月離
Yue li.

Mouvement de la lune.
4 livres.

— II.

交食
Kiao chi.

Éclipses.
4 livres.

— III.

土星
Thou sing.

La planète Saturne.
4 livres.

— IV.

木星
Mou sing.

La planète Jupiter.
4 livres.

— V.

火星
Hoo sing.

La planète Mars.
4 livres.

— VI.

金星
Kin sing.

La planète Vénus.
4 livres.

— VII.

水星
Choei sing.

La planète Mercure.
4 livres.

— VIII.

日躔
Ji tchhan.

Mouvement du soleil.

Livres 2, 3 et 4.

Cordier, Imprimerie Sino-euro-péenne, 353.

Grand in-8. Titre noir sur papier teinté; tous les livres 1 sont reliés à la suite les uns des autres; de même pour les livres 2, 3 et 4.

(5oo3-5oo5). 3 vol., demi-rel., au chif-fre de Napoléon III.
Nouveau fonds 2119, 2104, 2105.
(5oo6). 1 vol., cartonnage.
Nouveau fonds 2949.

―――――――

5007. ## 交食表
Kiao chi piao.

Tables des éclipses.

Théorie des éclipses, sans tables, par le P. Grimaldi; avec rapport officiel du même (1703). Texte et figures.

Grand in-8. Titre noir sur papier teinté, au verso du feuillet. 1 vol., demi-rel., au chiffre de Napoléon III.
Nouveau fonds 2099.

―――――――

5008. 大清雍正十三年歲次乙卯七政經緯宿度五星伏見目錄

Ta tshing yong tcheng chi san nien soei tsheu yi mao tshi tcheng king oei sou tou oou sing fou hien mou lou.

Tables de la position et des levers et couchers des sept astres pour 1735.

In-4. Papier blanc; pages reliées à l'envers. 1 vol., cartonnage.
Nouveau fonds 2731.

5009. 大清乾隆四年歲次己未七政經緯宿度五星伏見目錄

Ta tshing khien long seu nien soei tsheu ki oei tshi tcheng king oei sou tou oou sing fou hien mou lou.

Tables de la position et des levers et couchers des sept astres pour 1739.

In-4. Papier blanc; couverture jaune. 1 vol., cartonnage.
Nouveau fonds 2727.

5010. 大清乾隆五年歲次庚申七政經緯宿度五星伏見目錄

Ta tshing khien long oou nien

soei tsheu keng chen tshi tcheng king oei sou tou oou sing fou hien mou lou.

Tables de la position et des levers et couchers des sept astres pour 1740.

Grand in-8. Papier blanc; couverture jaune. 1 vol., cartonnage.
Nouveau fonds 2730.

5011. 大清乾隆四十二年歲次丁酉七政經緯宿度五星伏見目錄

Ta tshing khien long seu chi eul nien soei tsheu ting yeou tshi tcheng king oei sou tou oou sing fou hien mou lou.

Tables de la position et des levers et couchers des sept astres pour 1777.

In-4. Papier blanc; couverture jaune. A la fin du volume, note manuscrite : *Éphémérides astronomiques. Reçues en août* 1779 *M. Amiot.* 1 vol., cartonnage.
Nouveau fonds 2729.

5012. 大清嘉慶玖年歲次甲子選集日用必需

Ta tshing kia khing kieou nien soei tsheu kia tseu siuen tsi ji yong pi siu.

Calendrier populaire pour 1804.

Un feuillet noir sur jaune représentant une éclipse de lune ; titre en noir sur rouge vif avec figures astrologiques et légendes.

In-12. Impression grossière. 1 vol. cartonnage.
Nouveau fonds 2335.

5013. 道光二十四年正百篇大全

Tao koang eul chi seu nien tcheng po phien ta tshiuen.

Calendrier populaire pour 1844.
Avec illustrations.

Petit in-8. Titre noir sur rouge ; impression en noir et rouge sur papier teinté ; exécution grossière. 1 vol., cartonnage.
Nouveau fonds 2389.

———

5014. 中西合厤
Tchong si ho li.

Calendrier concordant chinois et européen.

Concordance jour par jour ; levers et couchers du soleil. Préface (1877) par Tseng Ki-tse, de Siang-hiang (1837-1890). Avertissement. Imprimé en caractères mobiles au Thong-oen-koan.

Grand in-8. Impression soignée sur papier blanc. 1 vol., demi-rel., au chiffre de la République Française.
Nouveau fonds 4338.

———

5015. 日食分秒時刻并起復方位

Ji chi fen miao chi kho ping khi fou fang oei.

Formules par secondes à remplir pour noter les observations d'une éclipse de soleil.

Grand in-8. Feuilles imprimées en rouge. 1 vol., cartonnage.
Nouveau fonds 2348.

Quatrième Section : DIVINATION

5016. 地理辨正
Ti li pien tcheng.

Recueil de géoscopie complété et corrigé.

Préface par Tsiang Phing-kiai Ta-hong, de Yun-kien, sans date. Les compléments et discussions sont par Tsiang-Phing-kiai et par son élève, Kiang Yao Jou-kao, de Koai-ki. Gravé à la salle Yun-king (1797).

5 livres. — Comparer Cat. imp., liv. 111, f. 7 (à la fin de l'art. Yu tchhi king).

— I, livre 1.

青囊經補注

Tshing nang king pou tchou.

Le Tshing nang king (Livre sacré du Sac vert) avec compléments et notes.

Ouvrage remis par Hoang-chi-kong (fin des Tshin, début des Han) à Tchhi-song-tseu.

— II, livre 2.

青囊序

Tshing nang siu.

Préface pour le Tshing nang king.

Attribuée à Tseng Khieou-yi Kong-'an, de Kan-choei, ou à Tseng Oen-tchhan, fils du précédent et élève de Yang Yun-song (ixᵉ siècle). Édité par Tsiang Phing-kiai, Yu Hong-yi, de Lin-'an, et Kiang Yao.

Cat. imp., liv. 109, f. 5.

— III, livre 2.

青囊奧語

Tshing nang 'ao yu.

Mystères du Tshing nang king.

Par Yang Yi Yun-song, surnom Khieou-phin, de Teou-tcheou (seconde moitié du ixᵉ siècle).

Cat. imp., liv. 109, f. 5,

— IV, livre 3.

天玉經

Thien yu king.

Le Thien yu king (Livre sacré du Jade céleste).

Attribué à Yang Yi. Édité par Tsiang Phing-kiai, Kiang Yao et Hou Kong-tcheng, de Oou-ling.

Section interne (3 livres). — Comparer Cat. imp., liv. 109, f. 6. — Voir plus bas n° 5019, art. I.

— V, livre 4.

都天寶照經

Tou thien pao tchao king.

Le Livre sacré des précieuses lumières du Ciel resplendissant.

Attribué à Yang Yi.

3 sections.

— VI, livre 5.

平砂玉尺辨僞

Phing cha yu tchhi pien oei.

Discussion du Phing cha yu tchhi king.

Par Tsiang Phing kiai et Kiang Yao.

Voir plus bas n° 5024, art. I.

Petit in-8. Titre noir sur jaune. 1 vol., demi-rel., au chiffre de Louis-Philippe. *Nouveau fonds* 861.

7

5017. 新刻增補萬法歸宗

Sin kho tseng pou oan fa koei tsong.

Nouveau traité augmenté de divination et de sorcellerie.

Par Li Choen-fong (début du vii° siècle) ; complété par Yuen Thien-kang, de Tchheng-tou († 627).

5 livres + supplément.

Petit in-8. Titre noir sur jaune. 1 vol., demi-rel., au chiffre de Louis-Philippe. *Nouveau fonds* 880.

5018. 三世演禽骨書

San chi yen khin kou chou.

Livre expliqué de divination.

D'après divers procédés (astrologie, chiromancie, géoscopie, etc.) Par Yuen Thien-kang. Texte et figures. Édition de la salle Fou-oen (1820).

Petit in-8. Titre noir sur jaune ; format très large. 1 vol., demi-rel., au chiffre de Louis-Philippe. *Nouveau fonds* 826.

5019. — I.

天玉經註

Thien yu king tchou.

Le Thien yu king annoté.

Même ouvrage qu'au n° 5016, art. IV ; avec introduction géné-rale et préface (1721), par l'anno-tateur Hoang Yue Tsi-fei, de Chang-yuen. Gravé à la salle Koang-tsi.

Section interne (3 livres) et section externe (1 livre). — Cat. imp., liv. 109, f. 6 et liv. 111, f. 4.

Titre noir sur jaune.

— II.

吳公克誠教子景鸞書

Oou kong khe tchheng kiao tseu king loan chou.

Autre titre :

四十八局

Seu chi pa kiu.

Les instructions de Oou Khe-tchheng à son fils King-loan.

L'auteur était originaire de Te-hing ; King-loan vivait dans les années 1041-1048. Annotations de Hoang Yue.

3 livres. — Cat. imp., liv. 111, f. 4 (Seu chi pa kiu thou, en 1 livre).

— III.

穴法分受

Hiue fa fen cheou.

Traité des excavations.

Par Hoang Yue Thoei-seu ; avec notes et préface de l'auteur (1721). Texte avec figures. Gravé à la salle Koang-tsi.

2 livres. — Comparer Cat. imp., liv. 111, f. 5 (Kieou sing hiue fa,

4 livres) et f. 12 (Tshoẹn kiu hiue fa, 2 livres).

Titre noir sur blanc.

— IV.

天玉經說

Thien yu king choẹ.

Explication du Thien yu king.

Traité d'astrologie par Hoang Yue. Préface et postface par l'auteur (1721). Texte et figures. Gravé à la salle Koang-tsi.

7 livres.

Titre noir sur blanc.

Grand in-8. 1 vol., demi-rel., au chiffre de Louis-Philippe.

Nouveau fonds 459.

5020.   家傳太素脈秘訣

Kia tchhoan thai sou mẹ pi kiue.

Prescriptions mystérieuses pour la divination par le pouls.

Par Tchang Thai-sou, surnom Tshing-tchheng chan-jen (époque des Song?); notes par Lieou Po-siang, de Thing-tcheou. Préface par Kong Thing-hien Yun-lin, de Yu-tchang. Texte avec figures. Gravé à la salle Tchi-hoo.

2 livres. — Comparer Cat. imp., liv. 111, f. 51 (Thai sou mẹ fa, 1 livre).

Grand in-8. Titre noir sur jaune. 1 vol., demi-reliure.

Nouveau fonds 359.

5021.   新刻太素脈訣

Sin kho thai sou mẹ kiue.

Autre titre :

鍥太上天寶太素張神仙脉訣玄微綱領宗統

Khie thai chang thien pao thai sou tchang chen sien mẹ kiue hiuen oei kang ling tsong thong.

Nouvelle édition du Thai sou mẹ kiue.

Texte avec figures et notes; édition développée de la salle 'An-tcheng (1599); ces indications se trouvent à la fin du volume dans un cartouche orné. Préface (1599), par Oei Chi-heng Fong-thai, surnom Kiao-thing, de 'An-fou. Gravé par Lieou Tchi-tshien, de Than-yang.

7 livres.

Petit in-8. 1 vol., cartonnage du XVIIIe siècle, portant le titre : *Liber de pulsus motu.*

Fourmont 323.

5022-5023.   神相全編

Chen siang tshiuen pien.

Traité de métoposcopie.

Enseignements de Tchhen Thoan Hi-yi originaire de Po-tcheou († vers 989), publiés par Yuen Tchong-tchhẹ Lieou-tchoang, des Ming. Préface non datée par Yi Yo, de Tshien-thang. Texte avec figures. Édition de la salle Hoei-oen (1820).

Livre préliminaire + 12 livres.

In-18. Titre noir sur jaune. 2 vol., demi-rel., au chiffre de Louis-Philippe. *Nouveau fonds* 705.

5024. — I.

新刻石函平砂玉尺經全書眞機

Sin kho chi han phing cha yu tchhi king tshiuen chou tchen ki.

Le Yu tchhi king (Livre sacré du Pied en jade), nouvelle édition.

Par Lieou Ping-tchong Tchong-hoei, premier postnom Khan, nom posthume Oen-tcheng, de Choei-tcheou († 1274). Expliqué par Lieou Ki Po-oen, nom posthume Oen-tchheng, de Tshing-thien (1311-1375). Préface non signée (1606). Texte et figures.

6 livres. — Cat. imp., liv. 111 f. 5 (Yu tchhi king en 4 livres).

— II.

新刊地理五經四書解義郭朴塟經

Sin khan ti li oou king seu chou kiai yi koo pho tsang king.

Le Tsang king (Livre sacré des Sépultures), nouvelle édition expliquée.

Ouvrage attribué à Koo Pho, de Oen-hi (276-324) ; annoté par Tcheng Chi Hiuen-mẹ, de Kin-hoa. Édition corrigée par Oou Tcheng, nom posthume Oen-tcheng, nom littéraire Tshao-liu sien-cheng.

1 livre. — Comparer Cat. imp., liv. 109, f. 1 (Tsang chou).

— III.

秘訣仙機

Pi kiue sien ki.

Signes magiques expliqués.

Figure et texte ; manque le début.

— IV.

新刻法師選擇紀全

Sin kho fa chi siuẹn tsẹ ki tshiuen.

Traité complet du choix des jours fastes, nouvelle édition.

Ouvrage sans nom d'auteur, rapportant au début un fait de l'an 627. Revu et corrigé par Hou Oen Hoantẹ, de Tshien-thang (époque des Ming).

— V.

魯班經
Lou pan king.

Autre titre :

新鐫京板工師雕斲正式魯班經匠家鏡

Sin tsiuen king pan kong chi tiao tcho tcheng chi lou pan king tsiang kia king.

Le Livre sacré de Lou Pan, nouvelle édition.

Traité sur la divination appliquée à la construction des édifices; attribué à Kong-chou Pan, surnom Yi-tchi, contemporain et compatriote de Confucius; rédigé par Oou-yong et Tchang Yen.

3 livres.

Petit in-8. Titre noir sur jaune. 1 vol., reliure au chiffre de Charles X.
Nouveau fonds 884.

———

5025. 魯班經
Lou pan king.

Le Livre sacré de Lou Pan.

Édition de 1824, comprenant :

— I.

靈驅解法洞明眞言秘書

Ling khiu kiai fa tong ming tchen yen pi chou.

Autre titre :

Pi kiue sien ki.

Même ouvrage qu'au n° précédent, art. III.
Édition avec figures.

— II.

新鐫工師雕斲正式魯班木經匠家鏡

Sin tsiuen kong chi tiao tcho tcheng chi lou pan mou king tsiang kia king.

Le livre sacré de Lou Pan.

Même ouvrage qu'au n° précédent, art. V; illustré.

3 livres.

Grand in-8. Titre noir sur rouge. 1 vol., demi-reliure.
Nouveau fonds 1934.

5026. 法師選擇記
Fa chi siuen tsẹ ki.

Même ouvrage qu'au n° 5024, art. IV. Au début du volume tableau astrologique, avec quelques extraits d'ouvrages de même nature.

Grand in-8. Manuscrit. 1 vol., cartonnage du XVIIIᵉ siècle, intitulé : *Explicatio rerum*.

Fourmont 344.

5027. 新編評註通玄先生張果星宗大全

Sin pien phing tchou thong hiuen sien cheng tchang koo sing tsong ta tshiuen.

Traité d'astrologie de Tchang Koo Thong-hiuen ; nouvelle édition annotée.

Édition donnée (1797), à la salle Chou-ye, de Kin-tchhang, par Lou Oei Teou-nan, de Lan-khi ; reproduisant une ancienne préface sans nom d'auteur (1593). L'auteur, auquel est attribué l'ouvrage, est un immortel, qui aurait vécu au VIIᵉ siècle. Texte, figures, tableaux ; notes dans la marge supérieure.

10 livres.

Grand in-8. Titre noir sur jaune. 1 vol. demi-rel. au chiffre de Louis-Philippe. *Nouveau fonds* 391.

5028. 三元百中經。考正未來曆

San yuen po tchong king : khao tcheng oei lai li.

Autre titre :

司天曆正星平秘覽七政未來曆

Seu thien li tcheng sing phing pi lan tshi tcheng oei lai li.

Calendrier astrologique pour la divination.

Préface sans nom d'auteur (1605). Gravé par Tchhen Khi-tshiuen.

Comparer Cat. imp., liv. 111, f. 34 (Po tchong king).

Grand in-8. Exemplaire en mauvais état, coupé comme un livre européen ; au début, note manuscrite : *Livre chinois qui m'a été donné par Monsieur de Basseville*, 1649. *Menard*. 1 vol., couverture parchemin.

Nouveau fonds 2718.

5029. 新參後續百中經

Sin tshan heou siu po tchong king.

Autre titre :

新鋟謹遵依時憲未來曆百中經訂正四餘七政經緯通微

Sin tshin kin tsoen yi chi hien oei lai li po tchong king ting tcheng seu yu tshi tcheng king oei thong oei.

Suite au Po tchong king, nouvellement gravée.

Par Hoang Tsong-cheng, de Nan-hai. Figures et tableaux.

In-12. Titre noir sur jaune. 1 vol., demi-reliure.
Nouveau fonds 766.

5030. — I.

金丹眞傳

Kin tan tchen tchoan.

Traité du Kin tan.

Par Soen Jou-tchong Yi-tcheng, de Tchhang-tchi ; annoté par Tchang Tchhong-lie Heng-lou, de Ying-tchheng. Préface par Jou-tchong et Jou-hiao (1615). Gravé par Tchheng Tchi-lou, de Koang-ling.

9 sections + annexes.

— II.

規中指南

Koei tchong tchi nan.

Guide des adeptes.

Préface non datée par Li Kien-yi, surnom Yu-khi-tseu. Texte et figures.

Manque le premier feuillet du texte.

— III.

悟眞篇外集

Oou tchen phien oai tsi.

Recueil de formules et d'éloges poétiques.

Grand in-8. 1 vol., demi-reliure.
Nouveau fonds 367.

5031. — I.

新刻羅經解

Sin kho lo king kiai.

Le Lo king (Livre sacré de la Boussole), expliqué, nouvelle édition.

Par Tsong Yen-hiong Jou-yu, surnom Than san-jen. Préface de l'auteur (1618) ; préface (1618) de l'éditeur, Oou Thien-hong Oang-kang, de Sin-'an. Édition de la salle Tchen-hien. Texte, tableaux et figures.

3 livres. — Comparer Cat. imp., liv. 111, f. 10 (Lo king ting men tchen, 2 livres), et f. 11 (Lo king siao na tcheng tsong, 2 livres).

— II.

新刻賴太素天星催官解

Sin kho lai thai sou thien sing tshoei koan kiai.

Traité d'astrologie de Lai Thai-sou, avec explications ; nouvelle édition.

Lai Thai-sou, postnom Oen-tsiun, surnom Pou-yi-tseu, originaire de Tchhou-tcheou, vivait à la fin de la dynastie des Song. Texte, avec notes, par Oou Thien-hong et Tchou Fou. Préface par ce dernier, surnommé Liu-chi chan-jen.

2 livres. — Comparer Cat. imp., liv. 109, f. 9 (Tshoei koan phien, 2 livres).

— III.

破 愚 論

Pho yu loen.

Introduction à la géoscopie.

Par Tchou Fou. Préface sans date placée à la fin.

Forme le livre 3 de l'oúvrage précédent.

Petit in-8. Titre noir sur jaune. 1 vol., demi-rel., au chiffre de Louis-Philippe.
Nouveau fonds 863.

5032-5036. 天文大成 管窺輯要

Thien oen ta tchheng koan khoei tsi yao.

Traité complet d'astrologie.

Par Hoang Ting Yu-eul, de Lou-'an. Préface de l'auteur (1652); préface (1653) par l'éditeur de l'ouvrage, Fan Oen-tchheng Hien-teou. Postface (1695) par Hoang Kieou-si, neveu de l'auteur. Aver-tissement; note bibliographique; texte avec figures.

80 livres. — Cat. imp., liv. 110, f. 35.

Grand in-8. Titre noir sur blanc. 5 vol., demi-rel., au chiffre de Louis-Philippe.
Fourmont 337.

5037. 新增廣玉匣記

Sin tseng koang yu hia ki.

Autre titre :

新鐫許眞君玉匣記增補諸家選擇日用通書

Sin tsiuen hiu tchen kiun yu hia ki tseng pou tchou kia siuen tse ji yong thong chou.

Le Yu hia ki, de Hiu Tchen-kiun, pour le choix des jours fastes, avec additions de divers auteurs; nouvelle édition.

Hiu tchen-kiun, à qui l'ouvrage est attribué, avait pour postnom Soen, surnom King-tchi; il est né à Jou-ning en 239. Préface (1684) par Oang Siang Tsin-cheng, de Kia-phing. Édition de la salle Ho-'an (1827). Texte avec tableaux et figures.

6 livres.

In-12. Titre noir sur jaune. 1 vol., demi-rel., au chiffre de Louis-Philippe.
Nouveau fonds 758.

5038. 地理天機一貫秘書

Ti li thien ki yi koan pi chou.

Traité de géoscopie, d'astro-logie, etc.

Par Li San-sou, de Sin-tchhang, avec préfaces de l'auteur datées de 1669 et de 1786. Préface par Oan Jen (1693). Texte avec quelques figures.

6 livres.

In-12. Titre noir sur vermillon. 1 vol., demi-rel., au chiffre de Louis-Philippe.
Nouveau fonds 842.

5039. 三才發祕
San tshai fa pi.

Manifestations mystérieuses des trois pouvoirs.

Traité de divination par Tchhen Oen Keng-chan, de Sin-'an. Préface de l'auteur, manquant du feuillet final; préface par Tsin Si Tsheu-seu, de Yen-ling (1695). Diverses introductions. Texte et figures.

2 + 3 + 4 livres.

Grand in-8. Titre noir sur jaune. 1 vol., demi-rel., au chiffre de Louis-Philippe.
Nouveau fonds 278.

5040-5041. 秘藏大六壬全善本.
Pi tshang ta lou jen tshiuen chan pen.

Traité complet de sorcellerie.

Avec préface (1704) de l'auteur Koo Tsai-lai Yu-tshing, de Po. Planches gardées à la maison Yang, à Hoai-khing.

3 sections formant 13 livres. — Cat. imp., liv. 109, f. 18 (Lou jen ta tshiuen, 12 livres).

Grand in-8. Titre noir sur vert. 2 vol.,

demi-rel., au chiffre de Louis-Philippe.
Nouveau fonds 686.

5042. 六圖沈新周先生地學
Lou phou chen sin tcheou sien cheng ti hio.

Traité de géoscopie par Chen Sin-tcheou, surnom Lou-phou.

Préface de l'auteur (1712); introduction. Texte avec figures. Édition de 1821.

2 livres.

Grand in-8 très large. Titre noir sur jaune. 1 vol., demi-rel., au chiffre de Louis-Philippe.
Nouveau fonds 698.

5043. 易冒
Yi mao.

Traité de sorcellerie.

Édition de Tchheng Liang-yu, surnom Kou-mou, de Sin-'an : applications du Yi-king à la construction des maisons, à la conclusion des mariages, à la guérison des maladies, etc.

Livres 6 et 7 seulement. — Cat. imp., liv. 111, f. 28 (en 10 livres).

Petit in-8. 1 vol., reliure parchemin, portant à la garde *ex dono S. M. N. Gaillande Doctoris ac Socii Sorbonici* (prov. de la bibl. de la Sorbonne).
Nouveau fonds 2345.

第四卷

5044. 先天易數

Sien thien yi chou.

Traité de chiromancie et de divination.

Préfaces de Kiang Yi-kin (1782) et de Oang Tcheng-fang (1782) ; chez ce dernier sont gardées les planches d'impression. Tables des koa et texte.

4 livres.

In-24. Titre noir sur jaune. 1 vol., demi-rel., au chiffre de Louis-Philippe.

Nouveau fonds 858.

5045. 富桂堂吉祥如意通書

Fou koei thang ki siang jou yi thong chou.

Traité de divination, médecine, etc.

Publié à la salle Fou-koei, à Canton (1844). Texte avec figures et tableaux, en noir, en rouge, en rouge et noir.

Petit in-8. Titre noir sur rouge. 1 vol., cartonnage.

Nouveau fonds 4568.

5046. 三元堂諏吉通書

San yuen thang tsiu ki thong chou.

Petit traité pour le choix des jours favorables.

Avec diverses figures, des légendes, une carte de l'empire, des renseignements usuels.

Petit in-8. Titre en caractères d'or sur papier rouge ; texte imprimé en différentes couleurs sur papier teinté. 1 vol., cartonnage.

Nouveau fonds 5105.

5047. 太上聖祖金液紫粉大丹秘訣

Thai chang cheng tsou kin yi tseu fen ta tan pi kiue.

Préceptes mystérieux de l'alchimie, dus à Thai-chang.

Texte manuscrit sans date ni signature, avec un dessin représentant le fourneau de l'alchimiste ; dessin et caractères d'or sur papier bleu foncé.

Paravent de format in-32 et de 3 m. 10 de longueur ; renfermé dans une boîte. 1 vol. (provenant de la collection Billequin).

Nouveau fonds 5087.

5048. 滿堂吉慶

Man thang ki khing.

Traité d'astrologie et de sciences occultes appliquées.

Texte avec figures nombreuses et tableaux ; publié à la capitale provinciale (?), à la salle Tsai-king (1882).

Grand in-8. Impression en rouge et noir sur papier teinté ; titre noir sur rouge. 1 vol., demi-rel., au chiffre de la République Française.

Nouveau fonds 4591.

5049. 新刻天如張先生石渠精選萬寶全書

Sin kho thien jou tchang sien cheng chi khiu tsing siuen oan pao tshiuen chou.

Livres des trésors de Tchang Thien-jou, nouvelle édition.

Géoscopie, onirocritie, métoposcopie ; liste d'hommes célèbres, degrés du mandarinat, etc. Les pages sont divisées en moitiés supérieure et inférieure, le texte se continuant d'une moitié supérieure à la moitié supérieure suivante. Figures.

Petit in-8. Impression grossière. 1 vol., cartonnage.

Nouveau fonds 3351.

Cinquième Section : ART MILITAIRE

5050-5051. 新鐫武經七書陽明先生批武經

Sin tsiuen oou king tshi chou : yang ming sien cheng phi oou king.

Les Sept Livres canoniques militaires, annotés par Yang-ming, nouvelle édition.

Yang-ming, nom et postnom Oang Cheou-jen, de Yu-yao (1472-1528). Préface par Siu Koang-khi (1621) ; préface (1543) par Hou Tsong-hien, surnom Mei-lin chan-jen, de Sin-'an ; les deux préfaces sont suivies de sceaux imprimés en rouge. Introduction par Mao Tchen-tong Cheng-cheng. Liste des personnes qui ont surveillé l'impression. Notes dans la marge supérieure et à la fin des chapitres.

— I, livre 1 (5050).

孫武子

Soen oou tseu.

Le Soen tseu.

Traité par Soen Oou, du royaume de Tshi (vie siècle a. C.).

13 sections. — Cat. imp., liv. 99, f. 4.

— II, livre 2 (5050).

吳子

Oou tseu.

Le Oou tseu.

Traité par Oou Khi, du royaume de Oei († 381 a. C.).

6 sections. — Cat. imp., liv. 99, f. 5.

— III, livre 3 (5050).

司馬法

Seu ma fa.

Règles du Seu-ma.

Par le Seu-ma Jang-tsiu, de la famille Thien, de Tshi (vie s. a. C.).

5 sections. — Cat imp., liv. 99, f. 6.

— IV, livre 4 (5050).

李衛公問對

Li oei kong oen toei.

Dialogues de Li, duc de Oei.

Entretiens avec Thai-tsong de Li Tsing, duc de Oei, nom posthume King-oou (571-649), recueillis par un anonyme ; ouvrage d'une authenticité contestée, attribué par d'autres personnes à Yuen Yi.

3 livres. — Cat. imp., liv. 99, f. 12.

— V, livre 5 (5051).

尉繚子

Oei liao tseu.

Le Oei liao tseu.

Traité par Oei Liao, du royaume de Oei, ou du royaume de Tshi (ive s. a. C.).

24 sections. — Cat. imp., liv. 99, f. 7.

— VI, livre 6 (5051).

三略

San lio.

Les Trois Abrégés.

Ouvrage apocryphe, attribué à Hoang - chi - kong (époque des Tshin).

3 sections. — Cat. imp., liv. 99, f. 8 (Hoang chi kong san lio).

— VII, livre 7 (5051).

六韜

Lou thao.

Les Six Enveloppes.

Ouvrage apocryphe attribué à Kiang Liu Chang, surnoms Tseu-ya et Thai-kong-oang (xiie s. a. C.).

Sections 1 à 12 (l'enveloppe littéraire, Oen thao).

— 13 à 17 (l'enveloppe militaire, Oou thao).

— 18 à 30 (l'enveloppe du Dragon, Long thao).

— 31 à 42 (l'enveloppe du Tigre, Hou thao).

— 43 à 50 (l'enveloppe du Léopard, Pao thao).

— 51 à 60 (l'enveloppe du Chien, Khiuen thao).

Cat. imp., liv. 99, f. 3.

Grand in-8. Très belle édition sur papier blanc ; ponctuation et notes en rouge ; encadrements rouges autour des pages. 2 vol., demi-rel., au chiffre de Louis-Philippe.

Nouveau fonds 474.

5052. 新鑴增補標題武經七書

Sin tsiuen tseng pou piao thi oou king tshi chou.

Les Sept Livres canoniques militaires, nouvelle édition annotée.

Édition avec notes intercalées dans le texte et notes dans la marge supérieure; publiée par Tchhen Kieou-hio, surnom Yun-tseu kiu-chi, de Yu-yue, au pavillon Chi-tchheng, de Kin-tchhang. Préface par Tchhen Kieou-hio (1614). Les Sept Livres sont disposés dans le même ordre qu'aux n°s 5050-5051.

Grand in-8. Titre noir et rouge sur blanc. 1 vol., demi-rel., au chiffre de Louis-Philippe.

Fourmont 353.

5053. 武經纂序說約大全集註

Oou king tsoan siu choẹ yo ta tshiuen tsi tchou.

Les Livres canoniques militaires, édition commentée.

D'après les lettrés Pheng et Tsiang. Préface par Pheng Ki-yao

Jou-hi, de Kin-ling. Préfaces (1671) par les éditeurs Lin Tseu-hai Seu-hoan, de Tsin-kiang, et Tshien Thai-koan Teng-fong, de Tsieou-chan. Les Sept Livres sont dans le même ordre qu'aux n°s 5050-5051; en bas des pages, texte et notes; en haut des pages, commentaire intitulé :

還讀齋秘擬鄉會兩闈標題主意

Hoan tou tchai pi yi hiang hoei liang oei piao thi tchou yi.

Commentaire pour les examens de licence et de doctorat, du pavillon Hoan-tou.

Illustrations. Édition du pavillon Hoan-tou.

1 livre préliminaire + 7 livres.

Petit in-8. Titre bleu sur blanc. 1 vol., demi-rel., au chiffre de Louis-Philippe.

Fourmont 354.

5054. 武經標題正說

Oou king piao thi tcheng choẹ.

Les Livres canoniques militaires, avec notes.

Par Tchang Li-tchhi Han-fou, de Lin-'an. Préface par Tchang Li-tchhi (1693); préfaces (1696) par Tcheng Koang et par Tsiang Pin, de Yu-hang. En bas des pages, texte des Canoniques, dans le même ordre qu'aux n°s 5050-5051;

en haut des pages, commentaires. Édition de la salle Kin-seu, à Yu-hang (1697).

7 livres.

Petit in-8. Titre noir et rouge sur blanc, couvertures originales en soie bleue. 1 vol., demi-rel., au chiffre de Louis-Philippe.

Nouveau fonds 886.

5055. 增補武經體註標題詳解

Tseng pou oou king thi tchou piao thi siang kiai.

Les Livres canoniques militaires, avec commentaire, édition augmentée.

Publiée à la salle Chou-lin-oen-yuen, sous la direction de Oang Oou-tshao, par Fan Tseu-teng. Préface (1711) par Khieou Tchao-'ao. Avertissement avec sept figures. Ensuite texte double, disposé en haut et en bas des pages.

— I.

武經體註說約大全彙解合參

Oou king thi tchou choe yo ta tshiuen hoei kiai ho tshan.

Commentaire sur les Livres canoniques militaires.

Par Thang Kang Tsę-san, de Hou-khi; Hia Tchen-yi Toęn-'an,

de Yu-hou; Hou Ping-tchong Ming-kao, de Kin-khi. Augmenté par Chen Chi-heng Siang-khi, de Hang-tcheou.

3 livres. — Comparer Cat. imp., liv. 100, f. 6 (Oou king thi tchou ta tshiuen hoei kiai, 7 livres).

Ce texte occupe le haut des pages, les textes suivants étant tous placés en bas.

— II.

孫子

Sǫn tseu.

Le Sǫn tseu.

Texte et notes.

1 livre. — Voir n° 5050, art. I.

— III.

吳子

Oou tseu.

Le Oou tseu.

Texte et notes.

1 livre. — Voir n° 5050, art. II.

— IV.

司馬法

Seu ma fa.

Règles du Seu-ma.

Texte et notes.

1 livre. — Voir n° 5050, art. III.

Grand in-8. Titre noir sur blanc. 1 vol.,

demi-reliure (prov. de la bibl. de l'Arsenal).

Nouveau fonds 1688.

5056. 素書註

Sou chou tchou.

Le Sou chou commenté.

Traité d'art militaire attribué à Hoang-chi-kong; commentaire par Tchang Chang-ying, surnoms Ootsin kiu-chi et Thien-kio, de Sintsin († 1121). Préface de Tchang Chang-ying. Édition sans date, de Hai-tchhoang.

6 sections. — Cat. imp., liv. 99, f. 10.

Grand in-8. Papier blanc. 1 vol. demi-reliure.

Nouveau fonds 101.

5057. 虎鈐經

Hou khien king.

Le Hou khien king.

Traité d'art militaire et de sciences occultes par Hiu Tong, surnom Yuen-fou, de Oou-hing, docteur en 1000. Préface et rapport dédicatoire de l'auteur. Notice extraite du Catalogue Impérial. Texte et figures.

20 livres. — Cat. imp., liv. 99, f. 15.

Grand in-8. Papier blanc, titre noir sur jaune. 1 vol., demi-rel., au chiffre de Louis-Philippe.

Nouveau fonds 818.

5058-5059. 武經備纂要

Oou king pei tsoan yao.

Principes des Livres canoniques militaires.

Publiés par Li Ting Tchang-khing, surnom Sin-tchai, de Yu-tchang.

— I (5058).

武經總要百戰奇法前集

Oou king tsong yao po tchan khi fa tshien tsi.

Principes des Livres canoniques militaires : traité des combats, premier recueil.

Préface (1504) par Li Tsan, de Si-phing. Table des 10 sections.

Sections 1 à 5 seulement.

— II (5058).

武經總要行軍須知

Oou king tsong yao hing kiun siu tchi.

Principes des livres canoniques militaires : commandement d'une armée.

Préface (1439) par Li Tsin Ping-tchong, de Yun-tchong.

2 livres.

— III (5058).

武經總要前集

Oou king tsong yao tshien tsi.

Principes des Livres canoniques militaires : premier recueil.

Publié par Li Ting ; revu par Thang Fou-tchhoen Toei–khi, de Kin–ling. Commandement, troupes, armes, géographie militaire : texte et illustrations.

22 livres.

— IV (5059).

武經總要後集

Oou king tsong yao heou tsi.

Principes des Livres canoniques militaires : second recueil.

Par les mêmes. Postface (1599) par Tcheng Oei-thing. La table indique 21 livres, servant de complément au premier recueil.

Manque le texte.

— V (5059).

武經總要百戰奇法後集

Oou king tsong yao po tchan khi fa heou tsi.

Principes des Livres canoniques militaires : traité des combats, second recueil. Suite de l'art. I.

Sections 6 à 10.

— VI (5059).

Oou king tsong yao heou tsi.

Texte de l'art. IV.

21 livres.

Grand in-8. Titre noir sur blanc. 2 vol., demi-reliure.
Nouveau fonds 425.

———

5060-5065. 武編

Oou pien.

Recueils militaires.

Par Thang King-tchhoan, postnom Choen-tchi, de Oou-tsin. Préfaces non datées par Oou Yong-sien, surnom Feou-tou kiu-chi ; par Koo Yi-'o Jou-tsien, de Liu-ling ; par Yao Oen-oei, de Tshien-thang.

— I (5060-5063).

前編

Tshien pien.

Premier recueil.

Traitant des officiers et soldats, des combats, de l'ordre de bataille, des armes ; discussion d'anciens textes. Revu par Tsiao Hong, de Lang-ye (1541-1620). Table des matières.

6 livres. — En tête du tome IV (n° 5063) sont reliées la moitié du livre 5 et la totalité du livre 6 de l'article suivant.

— II (5063-5065).

武後編

Oou heou pien.

Second recueil militaire.

Table des matières.

6 livres (voir pour les livres 5 et 6 à l'article précédent). — Comparer Cat. imp., liv. 99, f. 19 (10 livres).

Grand in-8. Titre noir sur rouge. 6 vol., demi-rel., au chiffre de Louis-Philippe.

Nouveau fonds 464.

5066. 五緯陣圖解

Oou oei tchen thou kiai.

Sur la disposition des corps de troupes.

Par Tshang-lang tiao-seou. Texte et figures.

Grand in-8. Bonne impression. 10 feuillets ; 1 vol. cartonnage.
Nouveau fonds 4977.

5067.

Peintures sur papier de riz représentant les exercices des soldats.

1 vol., couverture chinoise en soie brochée ; contenant 12 feuillets de 34 centim. sur 25.

Département des Estampes, Oe 61.

Sixième Section : **MÉDECINE GÉNÉRALE**

5068. 重廣補注黃帝
內經素問

Tchhong koang pou tchou hoang ti nei king sou oen.

Le Sou oen (Questions de médecine interne) de Hoang-ti, édition augmentée et commentée.

Édition de Lin Yi, Soen Khi et Kao Pao-heng (époque des Song), commentée par Khi Hiuen-tseu. Ouvrage mentionné sous les Han.

Livre 20, incomplet. — Cat. imp., liv. 103, f. 1. — Comparer Bibl. coréenne, 2519.

Grand in-8. 1 vol., reliure parchemin.
Fourmont 314.

5069. *Tchhong koang pou tchou hoang ti nei king sou oen.*

Même ouvrage, même commentaire ; édition plus petite.

Livres 15 et 16, début du livre 17.

Grand in-8. 1 vol., reliure parchemin.
Nouveau fonds 2338.

5070 — I.

Tchhong koang pou tchou hoang ti nei king sou oen.

Double du précédent.

Fin du livre 15; livre 16; livre 17 incomplet.

— II.

新刊古今醫鑑

Sin khan kou kin yi kien.

Miroir de la médecine antique et moderne.

Même ouvrage qu'au n° 5101; édition plus récente et plus nette.

Livre 4 incomplet.

Grand in-8. 1 vol., reliure (prov. de la bibl. de l'Arsenal et auparavant de la bibliothèque des Minimes de Paris).
Nouveau fonds 2339.

5071. *Tchhong koang pou tchou hoang ti nei king sou oen.*

Double du n° 5069.

Livres 15, 16, début du livre 17.

Grand in-8.
Nouveau fonds 5230.

5072-5075. 黃帝內經素問靈樞合編

Hoang ti nei king sou oen ling tchhou ho pien.

Le Sou oen et le Ling tchhou king, de Hoang-ti; édition collective.

— I (5072-5074).

黃帝內經素問註證發微

Hoang ti nei king sou oen tchou tcheng fa oei.

Examen et commentaire du Sou oen.

Par Ma Chi Tchong-hoa, sur-nom Hiuen-thai-tseu, de Koai-ki (dynastie des Ming). Préface (1805) pour la réédition des deux ouvrages, par Pao Seou-fang Si-fen, de Hi. Texte avec figures. Gravé à la salle Yun-cheng.

9 livres (81 sections). — Cat. imp., liv. 105, f. 2.

— II (5074-5075).

黃帝內經靈樞註證發微

Hoang ti nei king ling tchhou tchou tcheng fa oei.

Examen et commentaire du Ling tchhou king (Livre du Pivot merveilleux).

Même auteur; texte avec figures. Gravé à la salle Yun-cheng.

9 livres (81 sections) + 1 livre supplémentaire. — Comparer Cat. imp., liv. 103, f. 3.

Grand in-8. Titre noir sur rouge et titre noir sur blanc. 4 vol., demi-rel., au chiffre de Louis-Philippe.
Nouveau fonds 809.

5076-5079. 黃帝素問靈樞經合註

Hoang ti sou oen ling tchhou king ho tchou.

Le Sou oen et le Ling tchhou king, de Hoang-ti ; édition collective commentée.

D'après l'ouvrage de Ma Yuen-thai ; additions et commentaires, par Tchang Tchi-tshong Yin-'an, de Oou-ling ; publié par Tchang Oen-khi Khai-tchi.

— I (5076-5077).

黃帝內經素問

Hoang ti nei king sou oen.

Le Sou oen.

Préface pour la présente édition commentée , par Tchang Tchi-tshong (1670). Préfaces de Kao Pao-heng et Lin Yi.

9 livres. — Interversions de reliure dans le 2ᵉ volume.

Petit in-8. Titre noir et rouge sur blanc. 2 vol., reliure au chiffre de Charles X.
Nouveau fonds 339.

— II (5078-5079).

靈樞經

Ling tchhou king.

Le Ling tchhou king.

Traité médical, commenté. Préface de Tchang Yin-'an (1672).

9 livres.

Petit in-8. 2 vol., cartonnage.
Nouveau fonds 3006, 3007.

5080. 新刊黃帝內經靈樞經

Sin khan hoang ti nei king ling tchhou king.

Le Ling tchhou king, nouvelle édition.

Fragment de la table, livre 1, début du livre 2.

Grand in-8. 1 vol. cartonnage du XVIIIᵉ siècle, avec le titre : *Imperatoris Hoamti liber medicus.*
Fourmont 315.

5081. 素問靈樞類纂約註

Sou oen ling tchhou lei tsoan yo tchou.

Le Sou oen et le Ling tchhou king mis en ordre méthodique ; avec commentaires.

Par Oang 'Ang Jen-'an, de Hieou-ning. Préface de l'auteur (1689). Édition de la salle Hong-tę (1817).

3 livres.

Grand in-8. Titre noir sur jaune. 1 vol., demi-rel., au chiffre de Louis-Philippe.
Nouveau fonds 409.

5082-5083. 巢氏諸病源侯總論

Tchhao chi tchou ping yuen heou tsong loęn.

Traité et description des maladies.

Par Tchhao Yuen-fang (années Ta-ye, 605-616) et autres. Préface (1027) par Song Cheou. Édition préparée par Hou Yi-khien, de Oou-hing, et gravée au pavillon King-yi (1809). Table générale et tables détaillées.

5o livres. — Cat. imp., liv. 1o3, f. 13.

Grand in-8. Titre noir sur blanc. 2 vol., demi-rel., au chiffre de Louis-Philippe.

Nouveau fonds 419.

5084-5085. 重鐫丹溪 心法附餘

Tchhong tsiuen tan khi sin fa fou yu.

Traité méthodique de médecine par Tan-khi; réédition.

Auteur: Tchou Tchen-heng Yen-sieou, pseudonyme Tan-khi sien-cheng, de Kin-hoa (dynastie des Yuen). L'ouvrage a été disposé méthodiquement par Fang Koang Yo-tchi, de Hieou-ning. Préface (1536) par Kia Yong, de Lin-ying. Table des sections, table détaillée des matières. A la fin, en appendice, notice sur l'auteur par Tchou Lien. Gravé à la salle Ta-oen.

Livre préliminaire + 24 livres. — Cat. imp., liv. 1o5, f. 24.

Petit in-8. Titre noir sur jaune. 2 vol., demi-rel., au chiffre de Louis-Philippe.
Nouveau fonds 583.

5086. 丹溪心法附餘

Tan khi sin fa fou yu.

Même ouvrage; revu par Oou Koe-loen, de Oou-yang; édition plus petite que la précédente.

Livre 24.

In-4. Les feuillets sont déployés et reliés par le bas. 1 vol., reliure XVII° siècle.
Nouveau fonds 3141.

5087-5095. 古今醫統

Kou kin yi thong.

Traité général de médecine, avec un historique.

Par Siu Tchhoen-fou, de Sin-'an; préface de l'auteur (1556); préface par Oang Kia-ping (1570); autres préfaces sans date. Table générale; table en tête de chaque livre. Cet ouvrage a été gravé aux frais de divers grands personnages.

1oo livres.

In-4. Papier blanc; titre sur papier doré; couvertures originales en soie bleue. 9 vol., demi-rel., au chiffre de la République Française.
Nouveau fonds 313.

5096-5098. 編註醫學入門

Pien tchou yi hio jou men.

Introduction à l'étude de la médecine, avec commentaires.

Par Li Thing, de Nan-fong, avec introduction de l'auteur (1575). Texte avec figures. Gravé au pavillon Oou-yun, de Koang-tchheng (1814).

1 + 7 livres.

Grand in-8. Titre noir sur blanc. 3 vol., demi-rel., au chiffre de Louis-Philippe.
Nouveau fonds 553.

5099. *Pien tchou yi hio jou men.*

Même ouvrage ; édition plus nette et plus grande.

Livre 7 incomplet.

Grand in-8. Note manuscrite datée de Rouen, 16 septembre 1633 ; ex-libris armoiries. 1 vol., reliure parchemin.
Nouveau fonds 3437.

5100. *Pien tchou yi hio jou men.*

Même ouvrage ; édition différente.

Livre 2 incomplet.

Grand in-8. 1 vol., reliure en forme de portefeuille, parchemin armorié.
Nouveau fonds 3438.

5101. 十刻龔雲林先生增補古今醫鑑

Chi kho kong yun lin sien cheng tseng pou kou kin yi kien.

Miroir de la médecine antique et moderne, de Kong Yun-lin ; dixième édition augmentée.

Par Kong Sin, de Kin-khi ; complété par son fils Thing-hien, surnom Tseu-tshai. Ancienne édition gravée à Kin-ling, non datée. Quelques figures.

8 livres.

Petit in-8. Titre noir sur blanc. 1 vol., demi-rel., au chiffre de Louis-Philippe.
Fourmont 316.

5102-5103. 新刊萬病回春

Sin khan oan ping hoei tchhoen.

Traité des maladies.

Par Kong Yun-lin ; complété et publié par son fils Kong Tseu-tshai.

Livres 2, 3 et 5, incomplets à la fin.

Grand in-8. 2 vol., cartonnage du XVIIIᵉ siècle avec le titre : *Tractatus de morbis.*
Fourmont 319, 319 A.

5104-5105. 六刻增補萬病回春

Lou kho tseng pou oan ping hoei tchhoen.

Traité des maladies, sixième édition augmentée.

Préface par Mao Khoẹn , de Koei-'an (1589). Les additions sont de Yu Yi-koan. Édition de la salle Tchong-tcheng, à Canton (1801).

8 livres.

Grand in-8. Titre noir sur jaune. 2 vol., demi-rel., au chiffre de Louis-Philippe. *Nouveau fonds* 3gɪ.

5106. 太醫院龔先生
雲林神彀

*Thai yi yuen kong sien cheng
yun lin chen keou.*

Autre titre :

新鐫雲林醫彀

Sin tsiuen yun lin yi keou.

Traité médical de Kong Yun-lin.

Préface par Mao Khoẹn, de Koei-'an (1591).

4 livres.

Petit in-8. Titre noir sur jaune. ɪ vol., demi-rel., au chiffre de Louis-Philippe. *Nouveau fonds* 8ȹ9.

5107-5108. 新刊醫林
狀元壽世保元

*Sin khan yi lin tchoang yuen
cheou chi pao yuen.*

Traité général de médecine.

Par Kong Sin Yun-lin ; revu par

Tcheou Liang-teng Yuen-long. Préface non datée par Tchang Oei, de Hong-yang ; à la fin de la préface, date d'une réédition : 1718. Édition de la salle Fou-oen.

ɪo livres.

In-8. Titre noir sur jaune. ȷ vol., demi-rel., au chiffre de Louis-Philippe. *Nouveau fonds* 4ȹ9.

5109-5113 — I (5109-5112).

赤水玄朱

Tchhi choei hiuen tchou.

Traité de médecine.

Par Soẹn Yi-khoei Oen-yuen, surnom Tong-sou, pseudonyme Cheng-cheng-tseu, de Sin-'an. Préface (1596) par Tchou Chi-lou, de Yu-tchang ; autres préfaces non datées. Portrait de l'auteur.

3o livres. — Cat. imp., liv. ɪo4, f. 29.

— II (5112-5113).

醫旨緒餘

Yi tchi siu yu.

Supplément aux principes de la médecine.

Par le même auteur.

2 livres. — Cat. imp., liv. ɪo4, f. 3o.

— III (5113).

醫案

Yi 'an.

Archives médicales, comprenant :

三吳治驗

San oou tchi yen.

Observations des trois Oou.

新都治驗

Sin tou tchi yen.

Observations de Sin-tou.

宜興治驗

Yi hing tchi yen.

Observations de Yi-hing.

Recueil posthume avec une préface incomplète et une préface (1573) par Soen Tchi-'an, de Oou-kiang.

5 livres.

Grand in-8. Titre noir sur rouge. 5 vol., demi-rel., au chiffre de Louis-Philippe.
Nouveau fonds 904.

———

5114-5117. 類經

Lei king.

Traité méthodique de médecine.

Par Tchang Kiai-pin King-yo, surnom Thong-yi-tseu, de Koai-ki, avec préface de l'auteur (1624); autre préface (1624) par Ye Ping-king. Édition gravée à Kin-tchhang. Texte avec commentaires.

32 livres. — Cat. imp., liv. 104, f. 37.

Grand in-8. Titre noir et rouge sur blanc. 4 vol., demi-rel., au chiffre de Louis-Philippe.
Fourmont 320.

5118. 類經圖翼

Lei king thou yi.

Figures et supplément pour le Lei king.

Par le même auteur.

Livres 3 à 5.

Grand in-8. 1 vol., cartonnage.
Nouveau fonds 2368.

———

5119-5126. 景岳全書

King yo tshiuen chou.

Œuvres de Tchang King-yo.

Même auteur; autre surnom Hoei-khing. Traité général de médecine, publié par Yun Tchi-kao Tsai-tshing, de Khiong-nan. Préface par Fan Chi-tchhong, de Chen-yang. Gravé au pavillon Yi-fang (1670).

64 livres (24 sections). — Cat. imp., liv. 104, f. 38.

In-18. Titre noir sur jaune. 8 vol., demi-rel., au chiffre de Louis-Philippe.
Nouveau fonds 492.

———

5127. 醫宗必讀

Yi tsong pi tou.

Lectures médicales.

Par Li Tchong-tseu Chi-tshai, de Yun-kien; revu et publié par ses élèves Oou Tchao-koang Yo-cheng, de Sin-'an, et autres. Préface de l'auteur (1637); préfaces par Oou Tchao-koang et par Tchhen Ki-jou. Texte avec quelques figures.

10 livres (manquent les livres 5 et 6).

Petit in-8. 1 vol., demi-rel., au chiffre de Louis-Philippe.
Fourmont 317.

5128.　增補醫宗必讀

Tseng pou yi tsong pi tou.

Lectures médicales, édition augmentée.

Édition de 1801; le titre porte les indications : 1815, à la salle Tchhoan-king.

5 livres.

In-18. Titre noir sur jaune. 1 vol., demi-rel.; au chiffre de Louis-Philippe.
Nouveau fonds 791.

5129.　删補頤生微論

Chan pou yi cheng oei loen.

Traité de médecine, corrigé et augmenté.

Par Li Tchong-tseu Chi-tshai, surnom Nien-'o, publié par son élève, Chen Thing Lang-tchong, de Oou-tshiu. Texte avec figures.

Livre 2 seul. — Cat. imp., liv. 105, f. 27 (en 4 livres).

Petit in-8. 1 vol., cartonnage.
Nouveau fonds 3332.

5130.　泰西人身說槩

Thai si jen chen choe kai.

Traité abrégé du corps humain, d'après la science occidentale.

Par le P. Jean Terenz (1576-1630); publié avec préface par Pi Kong-tchhen, surnom Tchhan-thi kiu-chi, de Tong-lai. Texte avec figures.

2 livres. — Cordier, Imprimerie Sino-européenne, 302.

Petit in-8. Manuscrit. 1 vol., cartonnage.
Nouveau fonds 2934.

5131. *Thai si jen chen choe kai.*

Même ouvrage; manuscrit d'une écriture plus soignée; manquent les figures et la table.

Petit in-8. 1 vol., cartonnage.
Nouveau fonds 2935.

5132. *Thai si jen chen choe kai.*

Même ouvrage, sans figures ni table.

Cordier, Imprimerie Sino-européenne, 302.

Petit in-8. Manuscrit. 1 vol., cartonnage.
Nouveau fonds 2936.

5133-5135 — I (5133-5134).

醫門法律
Yi men fa liu.

Principes de la médecine.

Par Yu Tchhang Kia-yen, de Si-tchhang. Préface par Feou-yuen tchou-jen. Table en tête de chaque livre.

6 livres. — Cat. imp., liv. 104, f. 47.

Titre noir sur jaune.

— II (5134).

尚論篇
Chang loen phien.

Dissertations critiques.

A propos de divers traités médicaux de Tchang Ki Tchong-king (période Kien-'an, 196-219), par Yu Tchhang, avec préface de l'auteur (1648) et note finale du même (1650).

1 + 2 livres. — Comparer Cat. imp., liv. 104, f. 45.

Titre noir sur blanc.

— III (5135).

尚論篇後四卷
Chang loen phien heou seu kiuen.

Dissertations critiques, suite.

Par le même. Préface (1740) par Oang Toan Tseu-tchoang, de Li. Gravé en 1785 au pavillon Pou-yue.

4 livres.

Titre noir sur blanc.

— IV (5135).

寓意草
Yu yi tshao.

Notes médicales.

Par le même. Préface de l'auteur (1643). Édition donnée par Hou Yeou-tchhen, de Leou-tong.

1 livre. — Cat. imp., liv. 104, f. 47.
Titre noir sur blanc.

Petit in-8. 3 vol., demi-rel., au chiffre de Louis-Philippe.
Nouveau fonds 604.

5136-5137. 醫宗秘傳蒼生保元
Yi tsong pi tchhoan tshang cheng pao yuen.

Autre titre :

蒼生司命
Tshang cheng seu ming.

Conservation de la santé.

Traité médical par Yu Thoan Thien-min, de Hoa-khi. Préfaces par Tchhen Oei-khoen Tseu-heou, de Thien-tou (1667) et par Li Kin, de Ta-liang (1677). Introduction par Tsai 'An-khoen (1667). Gravé à la salle Hoan-te.

1 + 8 livres.

Petit in-8. Titre noir sur jaune. 2 vol., demi-rel., au chiffre de Louis-Philippe. *Nouveau fonds* 589.

5138-5142 — I (5138-5141).

馮氏錦囊秘錄雜症大小合參

Fong chi kin nang pi lou tsa tcheng ta siao ho tshan.

Traité de médecine générale.

Par Fong Tchao-tchang Tchhou-tchan, de Hai-yen; publié par ses élèves Oang Tchhong-tchi Chen-tchhou et autres. Préface de l'auteur (1694); préface par Tchang Chi-tchen, de Lou-ho (1686). Texte avec notes. Réédition de la salle Hoei-tchheng (1813).

20 livres.

— II (5141-5142).

馮氏錦囊秘錄痘疹全集

Fong chi kin nang pi lou teou tchen tshiuen tsi.

Traité des éruptions cutanées.

Par le même. Préface de l'auteur (1702).

15 livres.

— III (5142).

馮氏錦囊秘錄雜症痘疹藥性主治合參

Fong chi kin nang pi lou tsa

tcheng teou tchen yo sing tchou tchi ho tshan.

Traité de la nature des médicaments convenant aux diverses maladies et aux éruptions cutanées.

Par le même auteur.

Livre préliminaire $+$ 12 livres.

Grand in-8. Titre noir sur jaune. 5 vol., demi-rel., au chiffre de Louis-Philippe.

Nouveau fonds 595.

5143-5149 — I (5143-5146).

張氏醫通

Tchang chi yi thong.

Traité de médecine générale.

Par Tchang Lou Lou-yu, pseudonyme Chi-oan, de Tchhang-tcheou. Préface de l'auteur (1695); préface de Koo Sieou (1689); préface par Tchou Yi-tsoen, de Sieou-choei (1709). Préliminaires, liste des auteurs consultés, liste des personnages qui ont surveillé l'édition. Texte. Gravé au pavillon Pao-han.

16 livres. — Cat. imp., liv. 105, f. 33.

Titre noir sur jaune.

— II (5146-5147).

本經逢原

Pen king fong yuen.

Traité des médicaments rangés par classes naturelles.

Par Tchang Lou; introduction de l'auteur (1695. Gravé à Kin-tchhang, à la salle Chou-ye.

4 livres (incomplet à la fin). — Cat. imp., liv. 105, f. 35.

Titre noir sur jaune.

— III (5147).

石頑老人診宗三昧

Chi oan lao jen tchen tsong san mei.

Sur les difficultés de l'examen du pouls, par Chi-oan.

Questions et réponses rassemblées par son fils Tchang Teng Tan-sien.

1 livre. — Cat. imp., liv. 105, f. 35.

— IV (5148).

傷寒大全

Chang han ta tshiuen.

Autre titre :

傷寒纘論

Chang han tsoan loen.

Traité de la fièvre typhoïde.

Par Tchang Lou; préface de l'auteur (1667); préface par Hou Tcheou-tseu, de Leou-tong (1665). Postface du fils de l'auteur, Tchang Tcho Fei-tchheou. Gravé à la salle Chou-ye, à Kin-tchhang.

2 livres. — Cat. imp., liv. 105, f. 34.

— V (5148-5149).

傷寒緒論

Chang han siu loen.

Suite au traité de la fièvre typhoïde.

Par le même auteur. Préface de Li Kin.

2 livres. — Cat. imp., liv. 105, f. 34.

— VI (5149).

傷寒兼證析義

Chang han kien tcheng si yi.

Sur la fièvre typhoïde.

Par Tchang Tcho.

1 livre. — Cat. imp., liv. 104, f. 49.

— VII (5149).

傷寒舌鑑

Chang han chẹ kien.

Examen de la langue dans la fièvre typhoïde.

Par Tchang Teng. Texte, figures et légendes. Préface de l'auteur (1668).

1 livre. — Cat. imp., liv. 104, f. 48.

Petit in-8. Titre noir sur jaune. 7 vol., demi-rel., au chiffre de Louis-Philippe. *Nouveau fonds* 488.

5150. 嵩厓尊生書

Song yai tsoẹn cheng chou.

Traité de médecine, de Song-yai.

Par King Ji-tchen Tong-yang (ou Tong-yi), surnom Yo-cheng-thang, de Song-yai. Préface de l'auteur (1696) ; préface par Oou Lien (1714).

15 livres.

Grand in-8. Titre noir sur jaune. 1 vol., demi-rel., au chiffre de Louis-Philippe. *Nouveau fonds* 467.

5151-5152. 醫書十二種

Yi chou chi eul tchong.

Douze traités médicaux.

Autre titre :

醫林指月

Yi lin tchi yue.

Recueil dû à Oang Khi Tcho-yai, surnom Siu-chan lao-jen, de Tshien-kiang ; gravé au pavillon Pao-hou. Préface de Oang Khi (1767). Préfaces pour le Yi hio tchen tchhoan (voir ci-dessous, art. I) par Oang Kia-seu Tseu-kia, de Tshien-thang (1699), et par Yao Yuen Cheng-kong, de Tshien-thang (1710). Table du Yi hio tchen tchhoan. Table générale du Yi lin tchi yue.

— I (5151).

高士宗先生手授醫學眞傳

Kao chi tsong sien cheng cheou cheou yi hio tchen tchhoan.

Leçons de médecine de Kao Chi-tsong.

Ces leçons ont été faites par Kao Chi-chi Chi-tsong, à partir de 1696 pendant plus de quatre ans, et ont été recueillies par ses élèves Oang Kia-seu et autres. Postface (1766) par Oang Khi.

1 livre.

— II (5151).

質疑錄

Tchi yi lou.

Examen de points douteux.

D'après les œuvres de Tchang Kiai-pin King-yo , pseudonyme Thong-yi-tseu, de Chan-yin (époque des Ming). Préface (1687) par Chi Kiai, de Tong-hai. Vie de Tchang Kiai-pin par Hoang Tsong-hi Thai-tchhong, de Yao-kiang. Postface de Oang Khi (1764).

1 livre.

— III (5151).

四明高鼓峯先生心法

Seu ming kao kou fong sien cheng sin fa.

Préceptes de Kao Kou-fong, de Seu-ming.

D'après Kao Kou-fong, du Tchę-tchong; publié par Hou Kio Nien-'an, de Tshien-thang. Préface par ce dernier (1725). Texte avec figures.

1 livre.

— IV (5151).

易氏醫按
Yi chi yi'an.

Archives médicales.

Recueil d'observations, par Yi Ta-ken Seu-lan, de Fou-tcheou. Postface par Oang Khi (1765).

1 livre.

— V (5151).

芷園臆草存案
Tchi yuen yi tshao tshoęn 'an.

Archives médicales de Tchi-yuen.

Par Lou Feou Pou-yuen, de Tshien-thang (époque des Ming). Postface de Oang Khi (1765).

1 livre.

— VI (5151).

敖氏傷寒金鏡錄
'Ao chi chang han kin king lou.

Traité de la langue dans la fièvre typhoïde.

Ouvrage transmis depuis Tchang Ki Tchong-king (période Kien-'an), augmenté et publié par Tou Tshing-

pi. Préface par ce dernier (1341); préfaces par Sie Yi, de Tchhang-tcheou (1529 et 1556); préface par Lou Feou, de Tshien-thang (1617). Postface de Oang Khi (1764). Texte et figures.

1 livre. — Comparer Cat. imp., liv. 103, f. 9 (Chang han loęn tchou); voir plus bas, n° 5173, art. VIII.

— VII (5151).

芷園素社痎瘧論疏
Tchi yuen sou chę kiai yo loęn sou.

Traité commenté de la fièvre intermittente, de Tchi-yuen.

Commentaire par Lou Tchi-yi Tseu-yeou, de Tshien-thang (dynasties des Ming et des Tshing).

1 livre. — Cat. imp., liv. 104, f. 41.

— VIII (5151).

芷園素社痎瘧疏方
Tchi yuen sou chę kiai yo sou fang.

Formules pour la fièvre intermittente, de Tchi-yuen; avec commentaire.

Commentaire par Lou Tchi-yi. Postface de Oang Khi (1764).

1 livre.

— IX (5151).

達生編
Ta cheng pien.

Traité sur la gestation et l'ac-couchement.

Par Khi-tchai kiu-chi (dynastie actuelle). Préface par Tou Fei Tchao-thang, de Yen-chan (1727); introduction de l'auteur (1715).

2 sections.

— X (5151).

扁鵲心書

Pien tshio sin chou.

Le Livre de Pien-tshio.

Traité attribué à cet ancien mé-decin (v° s. a. C.); compilé de nou-veau par Teou Tshai; réédition an-notée par Hou Kio Nien-'an. Pré-face de Teou Tshai (1146).

1 + 3 livres.

— XI (5151).

扁鵲心書神方

Pien tshio sin chou chen fang.

Formules merveilleuses du Livre de Pien-tshio.

Publiées par les mêmes. Post-face de Oang Khi (1765).

1 livre.

— XII (5152).

本草崇原

Pẹn tshao tchhong yuen.

Traité sur le Pẹn tshao de Chen-nong.

Par Kao Chi-chi Chi-tsong; notes de Tchang Tchi-tshong Yin-'an. Texte et notes. Pour le Chen nong pẹn tshao, voir plus bas n°ˢ 5315-5316. Postface de Oang Khi (1767).

3 livres.

— XIII (5152).

侶山堂類辯

Liu chan thang lei pien.

Traité méthodique des affec-tions et des remèdes, de Liu-chan-thang.

Par Tchang Tchi-tshong Yin-'an, de Si-ling. Préface de l'au-teur (1670). Postface de Oang Khi (1769).

2 livres.

— XIV (5152).

學古診則

Hio kou tchen tsẹ.

Règles de l'examen des ma-lades.

Par Lou Tchi-yi Tseu-yeou (dy-nastie actuelle). Postface de Oang Khi (1770). Texte et notes.

4 sections.

Grand in-8. Titre noir sur jaune. 2 vol., demi-rel., au chiffre de Louis-Philippe.

Nouveau fonds 585.

5153.   增補醫宗說約

Tseng pou yi tsong choẹ yo.

Traité de médecine, augmenté.

Par Pao Jou-hoo, de Oou-yi; complété par Oang Nien-hi, de Tong-koan; publié par Tsiang Tchong-fang, à la salle Li-pẹn. Dédicace à l'Empereur (1713), par Oang Nien-hi.

1 + 6 livres.

Petit in-8. Titre noir sur jaune. 1 vol., demi-rel., au chiffre de Louis-Philippe. *Nouveau fonds* 898.

5154-5155 — I (5154-5155).

醫學心悟

Yi hio sin oou.

Traité de médecine.

Par Tchheng Koẹ-pang Tchong-ling, surnom Phou-ming-tseu, de Thien-tou; d'après l'original de Tchheng Chan-ling, de Hi. Préface par Tchheng Koẹ-pang (1732). Préface par Oang Yi Chao-tchai, de Hieou-ning (1748). Réédition de la salle Yong-lien, avec préface de Oang Oen-tchi (1791).

5 livres.

— II (5155).

外科十法。症治方藥

Oai khoo chi fa. Tcheng tchi fang yo.

Médecine externe. Formules de remèdes.

Par Tchheng Koẹ-pang, avec préface de l'auteur (1733).

1 livre.

In-12. Titre noir sur jaune. 2 vol., demi-rel., au chiffre de Louis-Philippe. *Nouveau fonds* 523.

5156-5157.   醫學纂要

Yi hio tsoan yao.

Principes de la médecine.

Par Lieou Yuen Cheng-tshiuen, de Hoei-yang, du Ling-nan. Édition donnée au pavillon Oou-yun (1822). Préface par Oang Chou, du Si-chou (1739).

— I (5156).

心法靈機

Sin fa ling ki.

Actions merveilleuses.

1 livre.

— II (5156-5157).

靈機條辯

Ling ki thiao pien.

Actions merveilleuses discutées par articles.

Postface par Siu Hoei, de Chang-yuen (1737).

4 livres.

— III (5157).

湯方活法

Thang fang hoo fa.

Formules.

1 livre.

Petit in-8. Titre noir sur jaune. 2 vol., demi-rel., au chiffre de Louis-Philippe. *Nouveau fonds* 602.

5158-5160 — I (5158-5160).

臨証指南醫案

Lin tcheng tchi nan yi'an.

Guide du diagnostic et archives médicales.

D'après Ye Koei Thien-chi, de Oou; par ses élèves Hoa Nan-thien Sieou-yun, de Si-chan, et Li Ta-tchan Han-phou, de Hou-koan. Préface par Li Tchi-yun, de Oou-kiang (1764); préface par Li Koe-hoa Ta-tchan (1766). Préface et avertissement de Hoa Sieou-yun (1766). Édition de la salle Tsiu-sieou.

10 livres. — Cat. imp., liv. 105, f. 41.

Titre noir sur rouge.

— II (5160).

續刻臨証指南温熱論

Siu kho lin tcheng tchi nan oen je loen.

Guide du diagnostic et traités sur le tiède et le chaud.

Autre titre :

種福堂精選良方兼刻古吳名醫精論

Tchong fou thang tsing siuen liang fang kien kho kou oou ming yi tsing loen.

Formules choisies de la salle Tchong-fou et traités essentiels de médecins célèbres de Oou.

Compilation par Ye Koei, publiée par Hoa Nan-thien. Préface par Tou Yu-lin (1775). Édition de la salle San-hoai, à Kin-tchhang.

4 livres.

Titre noir sur jaune.

In-12. 3 vol., demi-rel., au chiffre de Louis-Philippe. *Nouveau fonds* 540.

_____

5161. ## 吳醫彙講

Oou yi hoei kiang.

Collection de traités des médecins de Oou.

Préparée par Thang Ta-lie Li-san, de Tchhang-tcheou; publiée par Oang Thao Oen-hai et Chen Oen-sie Yu-thiao. Préface (1792) et postface de Thang Ta-lie; préfaces par Mieou Tsoen-yi, de Oou-tshiu (1792) et Tsiang Phien, de Koei-lin (1793). Postface par Thang Khing-khi, petit-fils du compilateur (1814). Table des matières en tête de chaque livre.

— I, livre 1.

禱告藥王誓疏

Tao kao yo oang chi sou.

Prière au dieu de la médecine.

Composée (1692) par Oang Kia-tsan Yun-lin, nom littéraire Kien-tchai, de Siu-tcheou (1645-1710).

— II, livre 1.

温 證 論 治
Oen tcheng loẹn tchi.

Du traitement en cas de diagnostic par le tiède.

Par Ye Koei Thien-chi, nom littéraire Hiang-yen (XVIIIe siècle).

20 règles.

— III, livre 1.

人 身 一 小 天 地 論
Jen chen yi siao thien ti loẹn.

Traité des analogies entre le corps humain (microcosme) et l'univers.

Par Tchhen Hien-tchoan Kia-tchhen, nom littéraire Kien-tchai.

— IV, livre 1.

書 方 宜 人 共 識 說
Chou fang yi jen kong chi choẹ.

Traité sur l'exécution des ordonnances.

Par Kou Yu-thien Oen-hiuen, nom littéraire Si-tchheou.

— V, livre 2.

日 講 雜 記
Ji kiang tsa ki.

Notes sur des leçons quotidiennes.

De Sie Cheng-po Siue, nom littéraire Yi-phiao, de Tong-lai (époque de Ye Thien-chi). Ce médecin n'a pas écrit; les notes sont dues à son descendant Sie Khi-tshien Ying-mei.

— VI, livre 2.

金 匱 上 工 治 未 病 一 節 辯
Kin koei chang kong tchi oei ping yi tsie pien.

Discussion d'un point du Kin koei yao lio loẹn.

Le Kin koei yao lio loẹn est dû à Tchang Ki Tchong-king, de Nan-yang (époque des Han). Discussion par Thang Ta-lie, autre nom littéraire Lin-teng. Suivent 18 autres traités très courts du même auteur.

Comparer Cat. imp., liv. 103, f. 8 (Kin koei yao lio loẹn tchou).

— VII, livre 3.

石 芝 醫 話
Chi tchi yi hoa.

Notes médicales de Chi-tchi.

Par Soẹn Khing-tseng Tshong-thien, nom littéraire Chi-tchi (1692-1767).

— VIII, livre 3.

管 見 芻 言
Koan kien tchhou yen.

Vues étroites et paroles humbles.

Par Fou Hio-yuen Tshoẹn-jen, nom littéraire Yo-yuen.

— IX, livre 3.

核骨踝脛腨辨

Ho kou hoa hing chạn pien.

Discussion relative à la cheville, au tibia, au mollet.

Par Kiang Tchhao - tsong Tchheng-li.

— X, livre 3.

爛喉丹痧論

Lan heou tan cha (?) loẹn.

Traité des inflammations et ulcérations de la gorge.

Par Thang Ying-tchhoan Hio-ki, nom littéraire Tsai-tchang. La maladie nommée cha (?) n'est pas décrite dans les anciens auteurs ; le caractère ne se trouve pas dans les dictionnaires. A la suite, six autres traités du même auteur :

臟腑受盛辨

Tsang fou cheou cheng pien.

Discussion du contenu des organes internes.

辨紫茸之僞

Pien tseu jong tchi oei.

Pour distinguer le faux tseu-jong, etc.

— XI, livre 3.

大豆黃卷辯

Ta teou hoang kiuen pien.

Discussion au sujet du médicament ta-teou-hoang-kiuen.

Par Tcheou Seu-tchẹ Koei, nom littéraire Hiang-lin. Du même auteur :

瘟疫贅言

Òen yi tchoei yen.

Notes sur les maladies épidémiques.

— XII, livre 3.

合論丹溪景岳相火大意

Ho loẹn tan khi king yo siang hoo ta yi.

Sur le sens de l'expression siang hoo, d'après Tan-khi et King-yo.

Tchou Tan-khi (époque des Yuen) et Tchang King-yo ont expliqué différemment cette expression. Traité par Tsiang Sing-tchhi Thing-sieou, nom littéraire Tshin-jou. Ensuite trois autres traités du même auteur.

— XIII, livre 4.

人身一小天地亦有南北兩極論

Jen chen yi siao thien ti yi yeou nan pẹ liang ki loẹn.

Le corps humain, étant un microcosme, a un pôle nord et un pôle sud.

Traité par Chen Cheou-yi Khien nom littéraire Mou-'an (1669-1732). Ensuite, du même auteur :

命 門 脈 診 辯

Ming men me tchen pien.

De l'examen de la veine du rein droit.

— XIV, livre 4.

治 肝 補 脾 論

Tchi kan pou phi loen.

Traitement du foie et de la rate.

A propos d'une prescription du Kin koei yao lio loen (voir plus haut, art. VI). Par Chen Yue-thing Tcho-chi, nom littéraire Yue-thing (1701-1752), fils de Chen Cheou-yi.

— XV, livre 4.

四 維 相 代 陽 氣 乃 竭 解

Seu oei siang tai yang khi nai kie kiai.

Explication de la phrase : par la succession des quatre oei, le souffle mâle s'épuise.

L'expression, les quatre oei, est expliquée différemment; elle désigne les quatre membres, ou le sang, la chair, les tendons, les os,
ou le sang, les veines, les tendons, les os, etc. Traité par Chen Chi-fou Koo-tchi, nom littéraire Kiu-yuen (1739-1785), petit-fils de Chen Cheou-yi. A la suite trois autres traités du même auteur.

— XVI, livre 4.

辯 素 問 濁 氣 歸 心 之 訛

Pien sou oen tcho khi koei sin tchi oo.

Discussion de l'assertion erronée du Sou oen que le souffle trouble revient au cœur.

Pour le Sou oen, voir n°s 5068 à 5081. Par Chen Seu-khiu Kia-yuen, nom littéraire Siao-oei, arrière-petit-fils de Chen Cheou-yi.

— XVII, livre 4.

祖 氣 論

Tsou khi loen.

Sur l'influence productrice du ciel et de la terre.

Par Tcheou Yun-chi Pang-yen, autre surnom Pho-yuen. A la suite, dix pièces de vers du même auteur.

— XVIII, livre 5.

痘 毒 藏 脾 經 說

Teou tou tshang phi king choe.

Le virus de la petite vérole est contenu dans la rate.

Traité par Sie Ho-chan Kingfou, nom littéraire Song-tchoang. Du même auteur, cinq autres traités :

痘 出 同 時 論

Teou tchhou thong chi loẹn.

Sur l'apparition simultanée de la petite vérole.

痘 由 太 陰 轉 屬 陽 明 論

Teou yeou thai yin tchoan chou yang ming loẹn.

La petite vérole, du principe femelle, évolue vers le principe mâle.

— XIX, livre 5.

擬 張 令 韶 傷 寒 直 解 辨 證 歌

Yi tchang ling chao chang han tchi kiai pien tcheng ko.

Sur le diagnostic de la fièvre typhoïde.

Par Sie Kong-oang Tchheng-ki, nom littéraire Sing-thien, fils de Sie Ho-chan.

22 articles.

— XX, livre 6.

三 皇 藥 王 考

San hoang yo oang khao.

Sur la divinité de la médecine.

Oei Sin-tao, nom littéraire Tsheu-tsang, issu d'une famille de médecins, vivait sous les Thang; il fut considéré comme dieu de la médecine. Traité par Khang Tso-lin Chi-hing, nom littéraire Tchou-lin, de Song-kiang (1705-1772).

— XXI, livre 6.

脈 訣 正 訛

Mẹ kiue tcheng oo.

Correction au Mẹ kiue.
Comparer n° 5170, art. I. Par Kou Tsou-keng Pheng-nien, nom littéraire Yen-thing. Suivent deux autres traités du même auteur.

— XXII, livre 6.

趨 庭 雜 記

Tshiu thing tsa ki.

Notes d'après Tshiu-thing.

Par Ho Koei-yen Koẹ-tong, nom littéraire Liao-tchai; d'après les leçons de son père (1726-1780).

— XXIII, livre 6.

辨 醫 書 音 義

Pien yi chou yin yi.

Discussion sur le son et le sens de termes employés dans les livres de médecine.

Par Lieou Kieou-tchheou Thien-si, nom littéraire Kiong-tshiuen. Du même auteur :

夏月忌枳說

Hia yue ki tchi choe.

Traité sur l'oranger épineux qui doit être évité pendant l'été.

— XXIV, livre 6.

喜傷心恐勝喜解

Hi chang sin khong cheng hi kiai.

Traité sur les maladies provenant de l'excès ou du défaut du souffle vital.

Par Oong Cheou-tchheng Kiai-cheou, nom littéraire Nan-hien. A la suite, quatre autres traités du même auteur.

— XXV, livre 6.

百合病贅言

Po ho ping tchoei yen.

Notes sur la maladie appelée po-ho.

Par Thao Heou-thang Tsong-hiuen, nom littéraire Tchi-thing.

— XXVI, livre 7.

辨脾胃升降

Pien phi oei cheng kiang.

Discussion sur un traitement de la rate et de l'estomac.

Par Oang Ming-kang Fong-oou, nom littéraire Tchhoang-chan.

— XXVII, livre 7.

氣有餘便是火解

Khi yeou yu pien chi hoo kiai.

Explication de la phrase : s'il y a excès d'esprit, c'est l'influence du feu.

Par Koan Siang-hoang Ting, nom littéraire Ying-tchai, de Sou-tchheng. Suivi de trois autres traités du même auteur, dont l'un est intitulé :

東垣景岳論相火辯

Tong yuen king yo loen siang hoo pien.

Discussion des opinions de Tchang King-yo et de Li Kao sur l'examen du principe feu.

Comparer nos 5114-5117, 5119-5126 et 5170-5171.

— XXVIII, livre 7.

幼科似驚非驚辨

Yeou khoo seu king fei king pien.

Discussion sur une affection qui ressemble à la maladie dite king (trouble, effroi).

Par Yao Te-phei Pen-heou, nom littéraire Fen-khi. A la suite, un autre traité du même auteur.

— XXIX, livre 7.

司天運氣贅言

Seu thien yun khi tchoei yen.

Notes sur les influences exercées par les principes célestes.

Par Thang Li-san. Suivi d'un autre traité du même auteur :

週身經絡總訣

Tcheou chen king lo tsong kiue.

Traité du système des vaisseaux.

5 sections.

— XXX, livre 8.

木鬱達之論

Mou yu ta tchi loęn.

Traité relatif à une phrase du Nei king.

Cf. nᵒˢ 5068, etc. Par Tchou Ying-kiai Cheng-heng, nom littéraire Yu-thien. Avec deux autres traités du même auteur.

— XXXI, livre 8.

保護元陽說

Pao hou yuen yang choę.

Traité sur la protection du principe mâle.

Par Yang Tshoęn-keng Thai-ki, nom littéraire Kin-tchhen ; autre nom littéraire Mien-tchai (né en 1747, docteur en 1766), de l'école de Ye Thien-chi. A la suite, un autre traité du même auteur.

— XXXII, livre 8.

讀傷寒論附記

Tou chang han loęn fou ki.

Notes à propos du traité de la fièvre typhoïde.

Par Yang Li-fang Yue-heng. Le traité de la fièvre typhoïde est de Tchang Ki, des Han.

Comparer Cat. imp., liv. 103, f. 9 (Chang han loęn tchou) en 10 livres.

— XXXIII, livre 8.

論白㾦

Loęn po phei.

Dissertation sur la maladie appelée phei blanche (ulcères laissant des croûtes ou cicatrices blanches).

Par Thou Yi-tsoęn Siuen, nom littéraire Sou-tshoęn, originaire du Tchę-kiang.

— XXXIV, livre 8.

爛喉痧論

Lan heou cha (?) *loęn.*

Traité des inflammations et ulcérations de la gorge.

Par Li Choęn-sieou Ki-tę, nom littéraire Yun-phou.

Comparer plus haut, art. X.

— XXXV, livre 8.

爛喉丹痧治宜論

Lan heou tan cha (?) *tchi yi loęn.*

Sur le traitement des inflammations et ulcérations de la gorge.

Par Tsou Hong-fan Chi-tchhen, nom littéraire Siao-fan.

Comparer art. X et art. XXXIV.

— XXXVI, livre 8.

痧疹今昔不同治法亦異說

Cha (?) tchen kin si pou thong tchi fa yi yi choẹ.

La maladie appelée cha (?) n'étant pas la même aujourd'hui qu'autrefois, le traitement aussi doit différer.

Traité par Tchhen Yuen-yi Tchhang-ling, nom littéraire Pan-fan. Avec un autre traité du même auteur.

— XXXVII, livre 8.

攝生雜話

Chẹ cheng tsa hoa.

Notes pour régler la vie.

Par Thang Li-san.

— XXXVIII, livre 9.

四大家辯

Seu ta kia pien.

Discussion à propos de quatre personnages célèbres.

Par Siu Hie-hiun Yong, nom littéraire Yu-thai, originaire de Song-kiang. Suivent deux autres traités du même auteur.

— XXXIX, livre 9.

攷正古方權量說

Khao tcheng kou fang khiuen liang choẹ.

Traité sur la correction des poids des anciennes formules.

Par Oang Cheng-lin Ping, nom littéraire Pho-tchoang, de Oou.

— XL, livre 9.

生氣通天論病因章句辯

Cheng khi thong thien loẹn ping yin tchang kiu pien.

Discussion de quatre paragraphes de l'ouvrage de Tan-khi intitulé : Ko tchi yu loẹn.

Cet ouvrage est dû à Tchou Tchen-heng. Auteur du traité : Thang Li-san. A la suite, un autre traité du même auteur.

Comparer plus bas, n° 5170, art. IV.

— XLI, livre 10.

虛勞論

Hiu lao loẹn.

Traité de la maladie appelée hiu-lao (consomption?).

Par Oang Tsoan-kong Koang-tsio, nom littéraire Hio-tcheou (1663-1718).

— XLII, livre 10.

讀先祖保陰煎謹記

Tou sien tsou pao yin tsien kin ki.

Notes sur la formule Pao yin tsien, composée par son aïeul.

Oang Koang-tsio traitait à l'aide de ce médicament la maladie hiu-lao. Les Notes sont par Oang Tcheng-hi Yuen-chi, nom littéraire Kou-hiang, petit-fils de Koang-tsio.

— XLIII, livre 10.

六味地黃九方解

Lou oei ti hoang hoan fang kiai.

Explication de la formule des pilules dites à six ingrédients et à base jaune.

Par Chen Hiang-yen Kia-hiong, nom littéraire Oei-siang, descendant de Cheou-yi. Suivi d'un traité du même auteur.

— XLIV, livre 10.

司天運氣徵驗

Seu thien yun khi tcheng yen.

Preuves des influences exercées par les principes célestes.

Par Thang Li-san.

Comparer plus haut, art. XXIX.

— XLV, livre 11.

三焦說

San tsiao choe.

Traité des trois tsiao.

Les trois tsiao sont l'œsophage, l'estomac, l'intestin ; d'après d'autres auteurs, les trois tsiao sont des principes non figurés ; ils sont mis en rapport avec le brouillard, les bulles sur l'eau et les cours d'eau. Auteur du traité : Tcheou Sing-oou Tseu-pi. Suivent quatre autres traités du même.

Petit in-8. 1 vol., demi-rel., au chiffre de Louis-Philippe.
Nouveau fonds 397.

5162. 太史醫案初編

Thai chi yi'an tchhou pien.

Archives médicales, premier recueil.

Par Hoang Kong-sieou Kin-fang, de Yi-hoang (vers 1750). Préface (1799) écrite à Canton par Ho Tchi-phei Thoei-seu, de Sin-tchheng.

— I.

誡子八則

Kiai tseu pa tse.

Huit règles pour ses fils.

Datées de 1799.

— II.

錦芳醫案
Kin fang yi'an.

Archives médicales par Kin-fang.

Préface par l'auteur, non datée ; postface sans auteur ni date.

5 livres (10 sections).

Petit in-8. Titre noir sur jaune. 1 vol., demi-rel., au chiffre de Louis-Philippe. *Nouveau fonds 426.*

5163-5165. 醫書匯參輯成

Yi chou hoei tshan tsi tchheng.

Traité de médecine.

Par Tshai Tsong-yu Siang-tcheng, de Long-tshiuen. Publié par Oang Cheng-yuen Ming-khiu, de Long-tshiuen. Préface de l'auteur (1807); préface par Tshai Chang-siang (1802). Texte avec figures. Édition de 1807.

24 livres.

Petit in-8. Titre noir sur jaune. 3 vol., demi-rel., au chiffre de Louis-Philippe. *Nouveau fonds 882.*

5166. 仙拈集
Sien nien tsi.

Recueil de médecine générale.

Formé par Li Oen-ping Hoan-

tchang, de Mien-chang. Préface et liste des personnes qui ont aidé à la gravure de l'ouvrage. Édition de la salle Tsiu-oen, à Kou-sou (1810).

4 livres.

Grand in-8. Titre noir sur jaune. 1 vol., demi-rel., au chiffre de Louis-Philippe. *Nouveau fonds 370.*

—————

5167. 全體新論
Tshiuen thi sin loen.

Anatomie et physiologie de l'homme et des animaux.

Par un médecin anglais Ho Sin (Benj. Hobson?), avec la collaboration de Tchhen Sieou-thang, de Nan-hai. Préface de l'auteur (1851). Texte avec figures. Édition de la salle Hoei-'ai, à Canton (1851). A la fin, date et lieu de gravure ; puis six grandes planches repliées.

39 sections.

Grand in-8. Titre noir sur vert. 1 vol., demi-rel., au chiffre de Napoléon III. *Nouveau fonds 2012.*

5168-5169 — I (5168).

西醫略論
Si yi lio loen.

Traité abrégé de médecine européenne.

Par Ho Sin (Hobson?) et Koan Meou-tshai, de Kiang-ning. Pré-

9*

face par Ho Sin (1857); avertissement. Gravé au pavillon Jen, à Chang-hai (1857). Texte avec figures.

3 livres.

Titre noir sur blanc.

— II (5168).

婦嬰新說
Fou ying sin choe.

Traité de médecine relatif aux femmes et aux enfants.

Par les mêmes. Texte et figures. Préface de Ho Sin (1858). Gravé au pavillon Jen, à Chang-hai (1858).

1 livre.

Titre noir sur blanc.

— III (5169).

內科新說
Nei khoo sin choe.

Nouveau traité de médecine interne.

Par les mêmes. Préface de Ho Sin (1858). Même lieu et même date de gravure.

2 livres.

Titre noir sur blanc.

— IV (5169).

全體新論
Tshiuen thi sin loen.

Anatomie et physiologie de l'homme et des animaux.

Même ouvrage qu'au n° 5167. Éloge (1853) par Ye Soei-oong. Pas de grandes planches. Gravé à Chang-hai, au pavillon Me-hai.

Titre noir sur blanc, daté de 1851.

Grand in-8. Papier blanc. 2 vol., cartonnage.

Nouveau fonds 4599 et 4600.

Septième Section : **TRAITÉS MÉDICAUX SPÉCIAUX**

5170-5171. 東垣十書
Tong yuen chi chou.

Ouvrages de Tong-yuen.

Recueil sans nom d'auteur, comprenant, avec des œuvres de Tong-yuen (1181-1251) et de son école, des œuvres de source différente. Préface sans nom d'auteur ni date.

Édition de la salle Tsoei-hoa, publiée par Oang Yu-thai, de Kin-than.

Comparer Cat. imp., liv. 105, f. 11.

— I, livre 1 (5170).

脉訣
Me kiue.

Traité des vaisseaux.

Par Tshoei tchen-jen Tseu-hiu; publié par Oou Mien-hio Siao-yu, de Hi (époque des Ming). L'ouvrage a été annoté par Li Kao, surnom Tong-yuen lao-jen. Texte en phrases de quatre caractères. Sur le Mẹ king, par Oang Chou-hoo, de Kao-phing (époque des Tsin occidentaux) et sur le Mẹ kiue par Kao-yang Cheng, voir Cat. imp., liv. 104, f. 18, Mẹ kiue khan oou, par Tai Khi-tsong Thong-fou, de Kin-ling (époque des Yuen).

1 livre. — Cat. imp., liv. 105, f. 10 (Tshoei tchen jen mẹ kiue).

— II, livre 1 (5170).

局方發揮
Kiu fang fa hoei.

Discussion annexe au Hoo tsi kiu fang.

Le Thai phing hoei min hoo tsi kiu fang, traité de pharmacopée en 10 livres, a été composé par ordre impérial à l'époque des Song par Tchhen Chi-oen et autres. Discussion composée par Tchou Tchen-heng Yen-sieou, de Kin-hoa (époque des Yuen), élève de Lo Tchi-ti et de Lieou Cheou-tchen. Édité par Oou Tchong-heng, de Sin-'an (époque des Ming).

1 livre. — Cat. imp., liv. 104, f. 14. — Comparer Cat. imp., liv. 103, f. 40

(Thai phing hoei min hoo tsi kiu fang, en 10 livres).

— III, livres 2 à 4 (5170).

脾胃論
Phi oei loẹn.

Traité de la rate et de l'estomac.

Par Li Kao Ming-tchi, de Tchen-ting (1181-1251); publié par Oou Tchong-heng et Oou Mien hio.

3 livres. — Cat. imp., liv. 104, f. 6.

— IV, livre 5 (5170).

格致餘論
Ko tchi yu loẹn.

Recueil de traités médicaux et de formules.

Par Tchou Tchen-heng; publié par Oou Tchong-heng. Préface non datée.

1 livre. — Cat. imp., liv. 104, f. 13.

— V, livres 6 à 8 (5170).

蘭室秘藏
Lan chi pi tsang.

Trésors du Sou oen.

Par Li Kao. Une édition renferme une préface de Lo Thien-yi (1276), qui n'est pas contenue ici. Édition de Oou Mien-hio.

3 livres. — Cat. imp., liv. 104, f. 7.

— VI, livres 9 à 11 (5170).

內 外 傷 辯 惑 論

Nei oai chang pien hoe loen.

Discussion des maladies internes et externes.

Par Li Kao ; publié par Oou Mien-hio . Préface de l'auteur (1247).

3 livres. — Cat. imp., liv. 104, f. 5.

— VII, livres 12 et 13 (5171).

此 事 難 知

Tsheu chi nan tchi.

Notes sur la médecine.

D'après les leçons de Li Kao, par Oang Hao-kou Tsin-tchi, sur-nom Hai-tsang, de Tchao-tcheou. Préface de l'auteur (1308) ; postface par King-nan yi-jen (1484). Texte avec quelques figures.

2 livres + supplément. — Cat. imp., liv. 104, f. 9.

— VIII, livres 14 à 16 (5171).

湯 液 本 草

Thang yi pen tshao.

Traité de matière médicale et de pharmacopée.

D'après Li Kao ; par Oang Hao-kou. Publié par Oou Tchong-heng.

3 livres. — Cat. imp., liv. 104, f. 10.

— IX, livre 17 (5171).

醫 經 溯 洄 集

Yi king sou hoei tsi.

Traité sur les fièvres et autres affections.

Par Oang Li 'An-tao, de Koen-chan, élève de Tchou Tchen-heng. Édition de Oou Mien-hio.

1 livre. — Cat. imp., liv. 104, f. 18.

— X, livres 18 et 19 (5171).

外 科 精 義

Oai khoo tsing yi.

Principes de la médecine externe.

Par Tshi Te-tchi (époque des Yuen) ; édition de Oou Mien-hio.

2 livres. — Cat. imp., liv. 104, f. 16.

— XI, livre 20 (5171).

醫 壘 元 戎

Yi lei yuen jong.

Table des formules thérapeutiques.

De Oang Hao-kou ; édition de Oou Tchong-heng.

1 livre. — Comparer Cat. imp., liv. 104, f. 8 (Yi lei yuen jong, en 12 livres).

— XII, livre 21 (5171).

海 藏 癍 證 萃 英

Hai tsang pan (?) tcheng tsoei ying.

Traité de Hai-tsang sur les symptômes de la maladie appelée pan.

Par Oang Hao-kou; édition de Oou Mien-hio.

ı livre.

Petit in-8. Titre noir sur jaune. 2 vol., demi-rel., au chiffre de Louis-Philippe. *Nouveau fonds* 6o3.

5172-5179. 薛院判醫
案二十四種

Sie yuen phan yi'an eul chi seu tchong.

Archives médicales du médecin impérial Sie.

Préface pour l'édition collective de ces diverses œuvres, par Oou Koan, de Sin-'an : table générale de l'ouvrage par Oou Soo, de Sin-'an, revue par Tchou Thing-tchhou, de Po-hia. Édition de la salle Koang-hoa. Cette collection, qui comprenait d'abord dix-sept ouvrages, a été formée et publiée pour la première fois par Sie Yi Li-tchai, de Oou (époque des Ming).

Cat. imp., liv. 1o4, f. 24 (Sie chi yi 'an, en 78 livres).

內科
Nei khoo.
Médecine interne.

— I (5172).

十四經絡發揮
Chi seu king lo fa hoei.

Examen des quatorze vaisseaux.

Par Hoa Cheou, surnom Po-jen, de Hiu-tchhang (fin des Yuen); édition de Sie Khai Liang-oou, (période Hong-tchi), père de Sie Yi; revue par Oou Hiuen-yeou, de Sin-'an. Préface par Cheng Ying-yang, de Si-tchhang (1528). Texte avec figures.

3 livres.

— II (5172).

難經本義
Nan king pẹn yi.

Sens du Nan king.

Le Nan king a été écrit pour élucider le Sou oen et le Ling tchhou king (nᵒˢ 5068-5081); il est attribué à Tshin Yue-jen Pien-tshio, du pays de Lou (vᵉ s. a. C.). Commentaire par Hoa Cheou. Liste des ouvrages cités; figures avec légendes; texte revu par Sie Yi; publié par Oou Hiuen-yeou. Préfaces par Kie Hong (1366), par Tchang Tchou (1364?), par Lieou Jen-pẹn, de Thien-thai (1361).

2 livres. — Cat. imp., liv. 1o3, f. 4.

— III (5172).

本草發揮

Pen tshao fa hoei.

Traité de matière médicale.

Par Siu Yen-choen, de Koai-ki ; revu par Sie Khai et publié par Oou Hiuen-yeou. Préface non datée par Kou Mong-koei, de Oou.

4 livres.

— IV (5172).

平治會萃

Phing tchi hoei tsoei.

Traité sur diverses maladies.

Par Tchou Tchen-heng ; revu par Sie Yi ; publié par Oou Hiuen-yeou.

3 livres.

— V (5173).

家居醫錄內科摘要

Kia kiu yi lou nei khoo tche yao.

Éléments de médecine interne.

Par Sie Yi ; revu par Oou Hiuen-yeou.

2 livres. — Voir Cat. imp., liv. 104, f. 24 (Sie chi yi 'an), mentionnant le présent ouvrage.

— VI (5173).

明醫雜著

Ming yi tsa tchou.

Traités divers de médecins célèbres.

Recueillis par Oang Loen Tsie-tchai, de Yin ; annotés par Sie Yi. Préface par Tshien Oei, de Hai-yen (1549).

6 livres. — Voir Cat. imp., liv. 104, f. 24 (Sie chi yi 'an) : l'ouvrage est mentionné dans le texte.

— VII (5173).

傷寒鈐法

Chang han khien fa.

Étude du traité de la fièvre typhoïde.

Traité de Tchang Ki, des Han, annoté et publié par de nombreux médecins ; le présent ouvrage est revu par Oou Tchong-heng, de Sin-tou (époque des Ming).

1 livre. — Voir Cat. imp., liv. 103, f. 9 (Chang han loen tchou).

— VIII (5173).

敖氏外傷金鏡錄圖

'Ao chi oai chang kin king lou thou.

Traité de la langue dans la fièvre typhoïde.

Préfaces par Tou Tshing-pi (1341) et par Sie Yi (1556). Texte avec figures.

1 livre. — Voir plus haut n° 5151, art. VI ; Cat. imp., liv. 104, f. 24 (Sie chi yi 'an) : l'ouvrage est mentionné

sous le titre de Tou pẹn chang han kin king lou.

— IX (5173-5174).

原機啓微

Yuen ki khi oei.

Traité sur les maladies et les médicaments.

Par Yi Oei-tẹ, surnom Tchhi-chan lao-jen (époque des Yuen); revu sous les Ming par Sie Yi, puis par Oou Hiuen-yeou. Préface par Oang Thing, de Tchhang-tcheou (1532).

2 + 1 livres. — Comparer Cat. imp., liv. 104, f. 24 (Sie chi yi 'an), mentionnant cet ouvrage comme étant de Sie Yi.

幼科

Yeou khoo.

Médecine infantile.

— X (5174-5175).

保嬰撮要

Pao ying tshoo yao.

Traité général de médecine infantile.

Par Sie Khai, revu par son fils Sie Yi; édition donnée par Oei Yi-yuen, de Kiang, et Oou Tchong-heng. Préface par Lin Meou-kiu, de Min (1556).

20 livres. — Voir Cat. imp., liv. 104,

f. 24 (Sie chi yi 'an) : l'ouvrage est mentionné en 20 livres. Au Cat. imp., liv. 105, f. 17, même titre pour un ouvrage du même auteur en 8 livres.

— XI (5176).

錢氏小兒直(眞)訣

Tshien chi siao eul tchi (tchen) kiue.

Traité de médecine infantile.

Par Tshien Tchong-yang Yi, de Tshien-thang (fin du xiᵉ siècle); revu et publié par Yen Hiao-tchong; annoté par Sie Yi; édition de Oei Yi-yuen.

4 livres (la table n'en indique que 3). — Voir Cat. imp., liv. 104, f. 24 (Sie chi yi 'an), mentionnant l'ouvrage sous le titre de Siao eul tchen kiue, 4 livres.

— XII (5176).

陳氏小兒痘疹方論

Tchhen chi siao eul teou tchen fang loẹn.

Formules et traité pour la petite vérole chez les enfants.

Par Tchhen Oen-tchong, avec notes de Sie Yi; édition de Oei Yi-yuen.

1 livre (2 livres à la table). — Voir Cat. imp., liv. 104, f. 24 (Sie chi yi 'an) : l'ouvrage est indiqué sous le titre de Siao eul teou tchen fang.

— XIII (5176).

保嬰金鏡錄

Pao ying kin king lou.

Traité de médecine infantile.

Texte avec figures et légendes, annoté par Sie Yi; édition de Oei Yi-yuen.

1 livre (2 livres à la table). — Voir Cat. imp., liv. 104 f. 24 (Sie chi yi 'an), mentionnant l'ouvrage comme étant de Sie Yi.

女科

Niu khoo.

Gynécologie.

— XIV (5176-5177).

婦人良方

Fou jen liang fang.

Formules pour les maladies des femmes.

Texte avec figures par Tchhen Tseu-ming Liang-fou, de Lin-tchhoan (époque des Song); annoté par Sie Yi; édition préparée par Min Tao-tcheng, de Sin-tou, et par Oou Tchong-heng. Préface par Chen Mi, de Sieou-choei (1547).

24 livres. — Cat. imp., liv. 103, f. 47 (Fou jen ta tshiuen liang fang); liv. 104, f. 24 (Sie chi yi 'an), mentionnant l'ouvrage sous le titre de Fou jen liang fang.

— XV (5178).

女科撮要

Niu khoo tshoo yao.

Principes de gynécologie.

Par Sie Yi; édition de Min Tao-tcheng. Préface par Fan Khing, de Kien-kiang (1548).

2 livres. — Cat. imp., liv. 104, f. 24 (Sie chi yi 'an), mentionnant l'ouvrage.

外科

Oai khoo.

Médecine externe.

— XVI (5178).

立齋外科發揮

Li tchai oai khoo fa hoei.

Examen de la médecine externe.

Par Sie Yi; édition de Oou Hiuen-yeou. Préface incomplète.

8 livres.

— XVII (5178).

外科心法

Oai khoo sin fa.

Préceptes de médecine externe.

Par Sie Yi; édition de Oou Hiuen-yeou.

7 livres.

— XVIII (5179).

外科樞要

Oai khoo tchhou yao.

Principes de médecine externe.

Par Sie Yi; édition de Oou Hiuen-yeou. Préface par Chen Khi-yuen Tao-khing, de Tsoei-li (1571).

4 livres. — Voir Cat. imp., liv. 104, f. 24 (Sie chi yi 'an), mentionnant l'ouvrage.

— XIX (5179).

外科精要

Oai khoo tsing yao.

Éléments de médecine externe.

Par Tchhen Tseu-ming; annoté par Sie Yi; édition de Oou Hiuen-yeou. Préface par Oang Siun, de Tchheng-tou (1548).

3 livres + supplément. — Voir Cat. imp., liv. 104, f. 24 (Sie chi yi 'an), mentionnant l'ouvrage.

— XX (5179).

癰疽神秘驗方

Yong tsiu chen pi yen fang.

Formules pour les furoncles.

Par Thao Hoa, de Yu-hang; revu par Sie Yi, publié par Oou Hiuen-yeou.

1 livre.

— XXI (5179).

外科經驗方

Oai khoo king yen fang.

Formules éprouvées de médecine externe.

Par Sie Yi; publié par Oou Hiuen-yeou.

1 livre.

— XXII (5179).

正體類要

Tcheng thi lei yao.

Exposé méthodique du corps humain.

Par Sie Yi; publié par Oou Hiuen-yeou. Préface sans date, de Lou Chi-tao.

1 livre. — Voir Cat. imp., liv. 104, f. 24 (Sie chi yi 'an), mentionnant l'ouvrage.

— XXIII (5179).

口齒類要

Kheou tchhi lei yao.

Exposé méthodique de la bouche et des dents.

Par Sie Yi; édition de Oou Hiuen-yeou.

1 livre. — Cat. imp., liv. 104, f. 24 (Sie chi yi 'an), mentionnant l'ouvrage.

— XXIV (5179).

癘瘍機要

Li yang ki yao.

Traité des ulcères.

Par Sie Yi; édition de Oou Hiuen-yeou. Préface par Chen Khi-yuen (1554).

3 livres. — Cat. imp., liv. 104, f. 24 (Sie chi yi 'an), mentionnant l'ouvrage.

Grand in-8. Titre noir sur rouge. 8 vol., demi-rel., au chiffre de Louis-Philippe.

Nouveau fonds 798.

5180. 新刻陶節菴家藏秘授傷寒六書

Sin kho thao tsie 'an kia tshang pi cheou chang han lou chou.

Traité sur la fièvre typhoïde, transmis dans la famille de Thao Tsie-'an, nouvelle édition.

Par Thao Hoa Tsie-'an, de Yu-hang (xvᵉ siècle). Préface par Li Tshoen-yu (1832). Table des matières; liste de caractères difficiles avec leur prononciation.

— I, livres 1 et 2.

傷寒六書

Chang han lou chou.

Six traités sur la fièvre typhoïde.

— II, livre 3.

傷寒瑣言

Chang han soo yen.

Notes sur la fièvre typhoïde.

Avec préface de l'auteur (1445).

Titre sur papier teinté.

— III, livre 4.

明理續論

Ming li siu loen.

Suite au Ming li loen.

Le Ming li loen, en 3 livres, est dû à Tchheng Oou-yi, de Liao-che, (né vers 1060, encore vivant en 1156) et est noté avec le Chang han loen tchou. Le présent ouvrage est dû à Thao Hoa, qui a écrit la préface.

Cat. imp., liv. 103, f. 9 (Chang han loen tchou, Ming li loen).

Titre sur papier teinté.

In-12. Titre noir sur jaune. 1 vol., demi-rel., au chiffre de Louis-Philippe.

Nouveau fonds 729.

5181-5182. 增補李士材三書

Tseng pou li chi tshai san chou.

Trois traités de Li Chi-tshai, édition augmentée.

Par Li Tchong-tseu Chi-tshai, de Yun-kien; édition publiée au pavillon Tsoei-king par Yeou Cheng Cheng-tcheou, de Oou-men. Préfaces par Yeou Thong (1667) et Yeou Cheng (1667).

— I, livres 1 et 2 (5181).

診家正眼

Tchen kia tcheng yen.

Principes du diagnostic.

Texte annoté datant environ de 1637. Préfaces par Yeou Cheng et par Tong Yi Tsin-tchhen.

2 livres.

— II, livres 3 et 4 (5181).

本草通元

Pẹn tshao thong yuen.

Traité de matière médicale.
Voir n° 5320.

2 livres.

Titre noir sur papier teinté.

— III, livres 5 et 6 (5182).

病機沙篆

Ping ki cha tchoan.

Sur les maladies.

2 livres.

— IV, livre 7 (5182).

壽世青編

Cheou chi tshing piẹn.

Recueil de formules.

1 livre.

In-18. Titre noir sur jaune. 2 vol., demi-rel., au chiffre de Louis-Philippe. *Nouveau fonds* 665.

5183. ## 明吳又可先生温疫論

Ming oou yeou kho sien cheng oen yi loẹn.

Traité des maladies épidémiques, de Oou Yeou-kho.

Par Oou Yeou-sing Yeou-kho, de Tong-thing. Préface de l'auteur (1642). Planches gardées à la salle Ying-tẹ. Le volume comprend :

— I.

疫病篇

Yi ping phien.

Sur les maladies contagieuses.
Par Yu Kia-yen.

— II.

林起龍論疫

Lin khi long loẹn yi.

Sur les maladies contagieuses.
Par Lin Khi-long.

— III.

Ming oou yeou kho sien cheng oen yi loẹn.

Traité des maladies épidémiques, de Oou Yeou-kho.

Publié par Yang Ta-jen Tchạn-yi, de Li-choei, et par Tchhen Yuen Tsie-'an.

2 livres. — Cat. imp., liv. 104, f. 40 (Oen yi loẹn).

In-12. Titre noir sur jaune. 1 vol., demi-rel., au chiffre de Louis-Philippe.
Nouveau fonds 764.

5184. 醫門普度

Yi men phou tou.

Recueil médical.

Publié (1786) à la salle Kien-yi. Préfaces par Tchhen Yuen Tsie-'an (1772); par Yang Fen; par Yang Ta-jen. Préface de Oou Yeou-kho pour le Oen yi loen (1642).

— I.

Ming oou yeou kho sien cheng oen yi loen.

Même ouvrage qu'au n° 5183, art. III; édition de Yang et de Tchhen.

2 livres.

— II.

痢病論

Li ping loen.

Traité de la dyssenterie.

Par Khong Yu-li Yi-li, de Li-choei; édition revue par Tchhen Yuen. Préface de l'auteur (1751); préface de Yang Ta-jen (1772).

4 livres.

Grand in-8. Titre noir sur jaune. 1 vol., demi-rel., au chiffre de Louis-Philippe.
Nouveau fonds 822.

5185. 瘟疫彙編

Oen yi hoei pien.

Collection relative aux maladies contagieuses.

D'après Oou Yeou-sing Yeou-kho, de Yen-ling; augmenté par Tai Thien-tchang Lin-kiao, de Chang-yuen; publié par Oang Khi-lien Mei-hien, de Tsing-yang, et par Lieou Khoei Song-fong, de Tchou-tchheng. Préfaces par Oang Khi-lien (1828) et par Ti Khoei-koang, de King-tchhoan (1828). Planches conservées chez la famille Oang, dans la salle Phei-tchi.

16 livres.

Grand in-8. Titre noir sur jaune. 1 vol., demi-rel., au chiffre de Louis-Philippe.
Nouveau fonds 412.

———

5186. 脉訣

Me kiue.

Traité des vaisseaux et du pouls.

Comparer n° 5170, art. I.

Livre 3, incomplet au début.

Grand in-8. 1 vol., cartonnage du XVIIIᵉ siècle avec le titre : *Tractatus de pulsus motu.*
Fourmont 324.

5187. 刻馬玄臺先生註證脉訣正義

Kho ma hiuen thai sien cheng tchou tcheng mẹ kiue tcheng yi.

Le Mẹ kiue, édition de Ma Hiuen-thai.

Même ouvrage, même édition, de Ma Chi (époque des Ming).

Livre 2, incomplet à la fin.

Grand in-8. 1 vol., cartonnage. *Nouveau fonds* 4961.

5188. 沈微垣先生規正圖註王叔和難經脉訣大全

Chen oei yuen sien cheng koei tcheng thou tchou oang chou hoo nan king mẹ kiue ta tshiuen.

Le Mẹ kiue et le Nan king, édition collective.

Publiée à la salle Fou-oen; par Tchang Chi-hien Thien-tchheng, nom littéraire Tsing-tchai, de Seu-ming (période Tcheng-tẹ). Liste des médecins célèbres.

— I.

删註脈訣規正

Chan tchou mẹ kiue koei tcheng.

Le Mẹ kiue corrigé.

Édition de Tchang Chi-hien; texte; figures dont l'origine est attribuée à Oang Chou-hoo. Préface sans nom d'auteur (1693), à la fin de laquelle on trouve la date de gravure de la présente édition (1800).

2 livres. — Voir plus haut, n° 5170, art. I; Cat. imp., liv. 105, f. 8 (Thou tchou mẹ kiue fou fang, 4 + 1 livres).

— II.

圖註八十一難經

Thou tchou pa chi yi nan king.

Le Nan king illustré, en 81 sections.

Par Tchang Chi-hien. Historique de l'ouvrage. Texte et figures.

2 livres. — Comparer n° 5172, art. II; Cat. imp., liv. 105, f. 4 (Thou tchou nan king, 8 livres)

In-18. Titre noir sur jaune. 1 vol., demi-rel., au chiffre de Louis-Philippe. *Nouveau fonds* 756.

5189. 醫方經絡湯頭歌訣俗要

Yi fang king lo thang theou ko kiue pei yao.

Traité des vaisseaux et traité des formules.

Par Oang 'Ang Jen-'an, de Hieou-ning; publié par son fils Oang Toan Khi-liang, son frère Oang Hoan Tien-oou, son neveu Oang Oei Tchhong-tseu. Préface de l'auteur (1694). Édition de la salle Fou-oen, à Fo-chan.

— I.

經絡歌訣

King lo ko kiue.

Traité des vaisseaux.

Texte et notes.

— II.

湯頭歌訣

Thang theou ko kiue.

Traité des formules.

Recueil de formules et ordonnances avec notes. Avertissement; préface de l'auteur (1694).

5 livres.

Petit in-8. Titre noir sur papier teinté. 1 vol., cartonnage.
Nouveau fonds 2358.

————————

5190-5191. — I (5190-5191).

傷寒辨證錄

Chang han pien tcheng lou.

Traité des fièvres typhoïdes.

Par Tchhen Chi-to King-tchi, nom littéraire Yuen-kong, de Chan-yin (dynastie actuelle). Préface de l'auteur; préface par Nien Hi-yao, de Yu-ning (1725). Édition de la salle Yu-yi (1748).

14 livres.

— II (5191).

鬼眞君脉訣

Koei tchen kiun mẹ kiue.

Autre titre :

洞垣全書脉訣闡微

Tong yuen tshiuen chou mẹ kiue tchhạn oei.

Explication du Mẹ kiue, de Koei Tong-yuen.

Par Tchhen Chi-to, avec préface de l'auteur. Postface par Leou Khing-tchhang, de Yin.

Grand in-8. Titre noir sur jaune. 2 vol., demi-rel., au chiffre de Louis-Philippe.
Nouveau fonds 551.

5192. — I.

傷寒來蘇集

Chang han lai sou tsi.

Traité de la fièvre typhoïde.

Notes et commentaires rassemblés par Ko Khin Yun-po, de Tsheu-khi, pour le traité de Tchang Ki Tchong-king. Préface de Tchang Ki, non datée; préface par Ko Khin (1729); préface par Ma Tchong-hoa (1755). Édition de Ye Thien-chi, de Oou. Gravé à Kin-tchhang, à la salle King-yi.

4 livres. — Voir Cat. imp., liv. 103, f. 9 (Chang han loẹn tchou); voir plus haut n° 5151, art. VI.

— II.

傷寒附翼

Chang han fou yi.

Supplément au Traité de la fièvre typhoïde.

Par Ko Khin. Préface de l'auteur (1734).

2 livres.

Grand in-8. Titre noir sur rouge. 1 vol., demi-rel., au chiffre de Louis-Philippe.

Nouveau fonds 366.

5193. 丹溪朱氏脈因証治

Tan khi tchou chi mẹ yin tcheng tchi.

Traité des vaisseaux.

Attribué à Tchou Tchen-heng Tan-khi; publié par Thang Oang-kieou Lai-sou. Préface par ce dernier (1775); autre préface par Mieou Tsoẹn-yi, de Oou-tsiu (1775). Édition de la maison Sao-ye.

2 livres. — Comparer Cat. imp., liv. 105, f. 44 (Mẹ yin tcheng tchi, en 8 livres).

Grand in-8. Titre noir sur jaune. 1 vol., demi-rel., au chiffre de Louis-Philippe.

Nouveau fonds 374.

5194. 瘟疫扼要鄭氏遺書

Oen yi 'o yao tcheng chi yi chou.

Traité des maladies épidémiques.

Par Tcheng Yi Tien-yi; avec préface de l'auteur, non datée; postface non datée; l'ouvrage est postérieur à celui de Oang Yeou-kho. Notice datée de 1822 par Kao Yin Yang-khiao. Gravé en 1822 à la salle Ying-hoa. Le dernier livre renferme des formules.

4 + 1 livres.

In-18. Titre noir sur rouge. 1 vol., demi-rel., au chiffre de Louis-Philippe.

Nouveau fonds 783.

5195. — I.

證治圖註喉科秘集

Tcheng tchi thou tchou heou khoo pi tsi.

Traité illustré des maladies de la gorge.

Sans lieu, ni date, ni nom d'auteur.

25 feuillets.

— II.

張氏咽喉總論

Tchang chi yin heou tsong loẹn.

Traité général de la gorge, par Tchang.

Texte et figures.

Édition très commune de la salle Oen-king (1822).

In-18. Titre noir sur jaune. 1 vol., demi-rel., au chiffre de Louis-Philippe.

Nouveau fonds 772.

5196. 銀海精微

Yin hai tsing oei.

Traité d'ophthalmologie.

Par Soen Seu-miao, de Hoa-yuen (581?-689); revu et publié par Tcheou Liang-tsie Cheng-tchi (dynastie régnante). Introduction non datée par Tshi Yi-king, de Pe-hai. Texte avec figures. Édition gravée à la salle Lao-hoei-hien.

2 livres. — Cat. imp., liv. 103, f. 17.

Petit in-8. 1 vol., demi-rel., au chiffre de Louis-Philippe.

Nouveau fonds 280.

5197-5198. 竇太師全書

Teou thai chi tshiuen chou.

Autre titre :

瘡瘍經驗全書

Tchhoang yang king yen tshiuen chou.

Traité des ulcères.

Par Teou Han-khing, de Yen-chan (époque des Song); publié par Hong Tchan-yen, de Thien-tou, et par Tchhen Yeou-kong, de Thong-tchhoan. Préface par Tchhen Thing-tchou, de Thong-tchhoan (1717). Édition du pavillon Hao-jan, d'après un exemplaire des Song.

13 livres. — Cat. imp., liv. 105, f. 9.

Grand in-8. Titre noir sur jaune.

2 vol., demi-rel., au chiffre de Louis-Philippe.

Nouveau fonds 552.

5199. 秘傳眼科龍木醫書總論

Pi tchhoan yen khoo long mou yi chou tsong loen.

Traité d'ophthalmologie.

Sans nom d'auteur, d'après les leçons de Pao-koang tao-jen. Préface par Oang Oen (1575). Édition de la salle Chou-ye.

1 + 10 livres.

Grand in-8. Titre noir sur jaune. 1 vol., demi-rel., au chiffre de Louis-Philippe.

Nouveau fonds 406.

5200. 外科樞要

Oai khoo tchhou yao.

Principes de médecine externe.

Même ouvrage qu'au n° 5179, art. XVIII; avec la préface du Oai khoo tsing yao (n° 5179, art. XIX). A la fin, date de gravure et localité : 1582, à Kin-ling.

Livre 4 seulement.

Grand in-8. 1 vol., cartonnage.
Nouveau fonds 2719.

5201. 增補外科正宗大成

Tseng pou oai khoo tcheng tsong ta tchheng.

Traité augmenté de médecine externe.

Par Khi Koang-cheng. Préface par Oang Siang-tsin, de Tsi-nan (1631). Texte avec figures. Édition de la salle Fou-oen, au Koang-tong (1830).

1 + 4 livres.

In-18. Titre noir sur jaune. 1 vol., demi-rel., au chiffre de Louis-Philippe. *Nouveau fonds* 777.

5202-5203.   傅氏眼科審視瑤函

Fou chi yen khoo chen chi yao han.

Traité d'ophthalmologie de la famille Fou.

Par Fou Jen-yu Yun-khoo et son fils, Oei-fan Koe-tong, de Leng-ling; complété par Lin Tchhang-cheng Cheng-tchen, de Koang-ling. Préface de Fou Koe-tong, sans date. Préfaces par Tchhen Meng et Lou Pin (1644). Avertissement; notes sur les anciens médecins célèbres. Édition de la salle Fou-oen (1831).

1 + 6 livres.

In-18. Titre noir sur jaune. 2 vol., demi-rel., au chiffre de Louis-Philippe. *Nouveau fonds* 529.

5204.   攝生堂痘疹正宗

Che cheng thang teou tchen tcheng tsong.

Traités de la salle Che-cheng, relatifs à la petite vérole.

Par Song Lin-siang Tchong-yo. Introduction par l'auteur (1695). Préface de Li Koan-oo (1695); diverses préfaces, entre autres une de Ho Yong-fou (1783). Édition du pavillon Pao-han (1825).

Grand in-8. Titre noir sur jaune. 1 vol., demi-rel., au chiffre de Louis-Philippe. *Nouveau fonds* 619.

5205.   洞天奧旨。外科秘錄

Tong thien 'ao tchi. Oai khoo pi lou.

Traité de médecine externe.

Par Tchhen Yuen-kong, autre surnom Ta-ya-thang, de Chan-yin. Édition donnée par Thao Chi-yu Chang-po, de Koai-ki. Préface de Thao Chi-yu (1698); postface par Thao Fong-hoei Yu-yi, arrière-petit-fils du précédent (1790). Texte avec figures.

16 livres.

Petit in-8. Titre noir sur vert. 1 vol., demi-rel., au chiffre de Louis-Philippe. *Nouveau fonds* 823.

5206.   痘疹定論

Teou tchen ting loen.

Traité de la petite vérole.

Par Tchou Choen-kia Yu-thang, de Yu-tchang. Préface de l'auteur

(1713); préface pour une réédition par Oang Ming-cheng Si-tchoang (1767). Planches gardées chez la famille Yao, au jardin Hou.

4 livres.

Grand in-8. Titre noir sur rouge. 1 vol., demi-rel., au chiffre de Louis-Philippe.
Nouveau fonds 482.

5207. 重訂外科症治全生集

Tchhong ting oai khoo tcheng tchi tshiuen cheng tsi.

Recueils relatifs à la médecine externe, réédition.

Par Oang Oei-tẹ Hong-siu, de Oou. Préface de l'auteur (1740). Réédition de 1817.

2 recueils comprenant chacun 3 livres.

In-18. Titre noir sur jaune, 1 vol., demi-rel., au chiffre de Louis-Philippe.
Nouveau fonds 778.

5208-5209. 種痘新書

Tchong teou sin chou.

Traité sur l'inoculation de la petite vérole.

Par Tchang Yen Soẹn-yu, de Thing. Préface de l'auteur (1741); préface non datée par Oou Chi-yu Tcho-tchang. Réédition de la salle Hoei-oen (1795). Texte avec quelques figures.

12 livres.

In-12. Titre noir sur jaune. 2 vol., demi-rel., au chiffre de Louis-Philippe.
Nouveau fonds 510.

5210. 痘科辨症分類遂日察色捷要全書

Teou khoo pien tcheng fen lei soei ji tchha chẹ tsie yao tshiuen chou.

Recueil relatif à la petite vérole.

Préface primitive par Tchong Ling Kie-jen (1766); autres préfaces par Fou Siuen-tsẹ Chen-yu (1798) et par Li Han Hio-phou (1800). Édition de 1814. Texte avec figures, comprenant :

— I.

痘科利用二集十八朝

Teou khoo li yong eul tsi chi pa tchhao.

Textes divers relatifs à la petite vérole.

2 livres.

— II.

痘科利用二集要畧衍義

Teou khoo li yong eul tsi yao lio yen yi.

Résumé et explication du recueil.

Préface de Fou Siuen-tsẹ.

3 livres.

— III.

利用二集十八朝

Li yong eul tsi chi pa tchhao.

Suite de l'art. I.

Livres 4 à 7.

Petit in-8. Titre noir sur blanc. 1 vol., demi-rel., au chiffre de Louis-Philippe. *Nouveau fonds* 827.

5211-5221.   瘍醫大全

Yang yi ta tshiuen.

Traité de la médication des ulcères et abcès.

Par Kou Chi-tchheng Lien-kiang, de Oou-hou. Préface par Oang Li-tẹ Kien-thang, de Sin-'an (1773). Texte avec figures. Édition de la salle Yi-kou.

40 livres.

In-12. Papier blanc; titre noir sur rouge. 11 vol., demi-rel., au chiffre de Louis-Philippe. *Nouveau fonds* 494.

5222.   天花精言

Thien hoa tsing yen.

Notes sur diverses éruptions.

Publié par Choang-oou tchou-jen; préface par Tchang Tao Yuen-hien, de Feou-chan (1786). Texte avec figures. Publication de la salle Tẹ-king.

6 livres.

Petit in-8. Titre noir sur jaune. 1 vol., demi-rel., au chiffre de Louis-Philippe. *Nouveau fonds* 881.

5223.

Peintures très soignées représentant des éruptions infantiles, qui semblent avoir été observées et notées; chaque peinture porte le nom de l'affection représentée.

61 feuillets de taffetas, de 0m,13 × 0m,30, montés et reliés; formant 1 vol. recouvert de soie.

Département des Estampes, Oe 168.

5224.

Peintures un peu moins fines, un peu plus grandes, copies des précédentes soit exactes, soit disposées symétriquement.

61 feuillets, montés et reliés. Petit in-8. 1 vol., reliure. *Nouveau fonds* 2155.

5225.   痘疹扼要新書

Tcou tchen 'o yao sin chou.

Autre titre :

痘科扼要

Tcou khoo 'o yao.

Nouveau traité de la petite vérole.

Par Tchhen. Préface par Kin Oen-choẹn, originaire de Tshien-thang (1798). Édition de la salle Tchhoan-king; le titre est daté de 1797.

1 livre.

In-18. Titre noir sur jaune. 1 vol., demi-rel., au chiffre de Louis-Philippe.
Nouveau fonds 720.

5226. 唉咭唎國新出種痘奇書

Ying ki li koe sin tchhou tchong teou khi chou.

Traité de la vaccination, nouvellement inventée en Angleterre.

Publié et gravé (1805) pour la Compagnie des Indes Orientales, par un employé de la Compagnie, To-lin-oen ; traduit par Tcheng Tchhong-khien, qui avait été interprète de la mission anglaise de 1793.

Voir Cordier, Bibl. Sinica, 693.

Petit in-8. Papier blanc; couverture jaune, portant une note manuscrite du 6 juillet 1818; la note est signée de L. Langlès qui a reçu ce volume de Staunton, fils du secrétaire de Lord Macartney. 1 vol., cartonnage.
Nouveau fonds 1105.

5227. *Ying ki li koe sin tchhou tchong teou khi chou.*

Double.

Petit in-8. Papier teinté. 1 vol., cartonnage.
Nouveau fonds 4719.

5228. 異授眼科

Yi cheou yen khoo.

Petit traité d'ophthalmologie.

D'après l'ouvrage de Oang, trésorier provincial. Édition grossière, non datée, de la salle Cheng-te.

Petit in-8. Titre noir sur rouge. 1 vol., demi-rel., au chiffre de Napoléon III.
Nouveau fonds 1253.

5229. — I.

錢氏小兒藥症直訣

Tshien chi siao eul yo tcheng tchi kiue.

Traité de médecine infantile.

Par Tshien Yi. Vie de l'auteur par Lieou Khi, de Ho-kien. L'ouvrage a été publié par Yen Hiao-tchong qui a ajouté 1 livre de formules. Réédition de la salle Khi-sieou, conforme à un exemplaire de l'époque des Song. Préface pour la réédition (1719?, 1779?) par Jou Tsie.

3 + 1 livres. — Comparer n° 5176, art. XI.

— II.

董氏小兒斑疹備急方論

Tong chi siao eul pan tchen pei ki fang loen.

Formules contre les éruptions appelées pan chez les enfants.

Par Tong Ki Ki-tchi, de Tong-phing (fin du xı⁰ siècle). Postface par Tshien Yi (1093); préface non datée par Soẹn Tchoẹn Phing-fou, nom littéraire Chi-lieou kiu-chi, de Tong-phing.

1 livre. — Comparer Cat. imp., liv. 103, f. 27 (Kio khi tchi fa tsong yao) menticnnant cet ouvrage.

In-4. Papier blanc; titre noir sur jaune. 1 vol., demi-rel., au chiffre de Louis-Philippe.

Nouveau fonds 626.

5230. 增補儒醫婦人良方

Tseng pou jou yi fou jen liang fang.

Formules pour les maladies des femmes, édition augmentée.

Même ouvrage qu'aux nᵒˢ 5176-5177, art. XIV; édition de Min Tao-tcheng; préface de Chen Mi. Gravé au pavillon Oou-yun.

24 livres. — Cat. imp., liv. 103, f. 47 (Fou jen ta tshiuen liang fang).

Grand in-8. Titre noir sur jaune. 1 vol., demi-rel., au chiffre de Louis-Philippe.

Nouveau fonds 475.

5231. 重訂嬰童百問

Tchhong ting ying thong po oen.

Questions médicales sur les enfants au-dessous de quinze ans, réédition.

Ouvrage présenté à l'empereur (1539) avec dédicace de Hiu Tsan. Édition de Oang Yu-thai, gravée à la salle Tsiu-kin.

10 livres (10 questions par livre).

Grand in-8. Impression grossière; titre noir sur jaune. 1 vol., demi-rel., au chiffre de Louis-Philippe.

Nouveau fonds 365.

5232. 萬氏婦人科

Oan chi fou jen khoo.

Traité de gynécologie, de Oan.

Préface pour la réédition (1714) par le nouvel éditeur Khieou Lang Yu-cheng, de Si-tchhang. Impression du pavillon Oou-yun.

4 livres (la table n'en marque que 3).

Grand in-8. Titre noir sur jaune. 1 vol., demi-rel., au chiffre de Louis-Philippe.

Nouveau fonds 620.

5233. 著石堂新刻幼科直言

Tchou chi thang sin kho yeou khoo tchi yen.

Autre titre :

幼幼指掌集成

Yeou yeou tchi tchang tsi tchheng.

Manuel de la santé des enfants, de la salle Tchou-chi.

Par Meng Ho Kiai-chi et son fils Tchoang Yao-oen, de Kiang-ning. Préface par Soẹn Kia-kan, de Ho-ho (1726). Édition datée de 1798.

6 livres.

Grand in-8. Titre noir sur jaune. 1 vol., demi-rel., au chiffre de Louis-Philippe. *Nouveau fonds* 483.

5234. — I.

濟陰綱目
Tsi yin kang mou.

Principes de traitement des maladies des femmes.

Par Oou Tchi-oang Chou-khing, du Koan-tchong; annoté par Oang Khi Tchạn-yi, autre surnom Yeou-tseu, de Si-ling. Préface par ce dernier (1728). Texte avec notes dans la marge supérieure. Édition du Si-yuen (1739).

14 livres. — Cat. imp., liv. 105, f. 37.

— II.

保生碎事
Pao cheng soei chi.

Premiers soins à donner aux enfants.

Par Oang Khi.

1 livre. — Cat. imp., liv. 105, f. 37.

Petit in-8. Titre noir sur jaune. 1 vol.,

demi-rel., au chiffre de Louis Philippe. *Nouveau fonds* 821.

5235·5236. 鼎鍥增訂 幼幼集成
Ting khie tseng ting yeou yeou tsi tchheng.

Médecine des enfants, édition augmentée.

Par Tchhen Fou-tcheng Fei-hia, de Lo-feou. Introduction de l'auteur (1750). Deux préfaces non datées, par Khieou Yue-sieou, de Si-tchhang, et par Liang Yu, de Long-tshiuen. Édition de la salle Hoei-oen.

6 livres.

In-18. Titre noir sur jaune. 2 vol., demi-rel., au chiffre de Louis-Philippe. *Nouveau fonds* 532.

5237. 增訂達生篇
Tseng ting ta cheng phien.

Traité augmenté sur la gestation et l'accouchement.

Préface par Kiang Tẹ-hoei Lou-fong, de Jou-kao (1810). Réédition (1847) de la salle Ting-oen, à Canton.

2 livres. — Comparer n° 5151, art. IX.

Petit in-8. Titre noir sur jaune. 1 vol., demi-reliure. *Nouveau fonds* 3533.

5238. 靜觀堂校正幼科指南家傳秘方

Tsing koan thang kiao tcheng yeou khoo tchinan kia tchhoan pi fang.

Formules et guide de médecine infantile, de la salle Tsingkoan.

Par Oan Tshiuen Mi-tchai, de Lo-thien, revu par Tcheng Tchou Hong-kiu, de Long-yen. Édition de la salle Fou-oen, au Koangtong (1829).

4 livres (le livre 2 est relié à la fin).

In-18. Titre noir sur jaune. 1 vol., demi-rel., au chiffre de Louis-Philippe. *Nouveau fonds* 747.

5239. 保嬰秘旨

Pao ying pi tchi.

Médecine de l'enfance.

Texte avec figures, incomplet au début et à la fin. Impression de la salle Ning-yuen.

1 livre.

Petit in-8. 1 vol., cartonnage. *Nouveau fonds* 2375.

Huitième Section : MATIÈRE MÉDICALE, PHARMACOPEE

5240. 重修正和經史證類備用本草

Tchhong sieou tcheng hoo king chi tcheng lei pei yong pen tshao.

Traité des simples d'après les livres classiques et historiques, datant de la période Tchenghoo, nouvelle édition.

Par Thang Chen-oei Chen-yuen, de Hoa-yang (période Yuen-yeou, 1086-1093); édition de Tshao Hiao-tchong (1116) reproduite au xvᵉ siècle. Texte avec figures.

Livres 4, 15, 16, 17, 18, 19. — Cat. imp., liv. 103, f. 36 (dans l'article

Tcheng lei pen tshao, 30 livres). — Bibl. coréenne, 2494, 2495.

Grand in-8. 1 vol., cartonnage du XVIIIᵉ siècle avec le titre : *Tractatus de plantis et animalibus.*
Fourmont 328.

5241. 本草發明蒙筌

Pen tshao fa ming mong tshiuen.

Traité explicatif des simples.

Par Tchhen Kia-mou Yue-pheng, de Sin-'an, et Oang Khen-thang Yu-thai, de Kin-than. Préface par Tchhen Kia-mou (1529); préface par Hiu Koe, de Sin-'an. Texte avec figures. Édition du pavillon Pao-pien.

Dissertation générale $+$ 12 livres (manquent les livres 5 à 8).

Grand in-8. Bonne gravure; titre noir et rouge sur blanc. 1 vol., cartonnage du XVIIIᵉ siècle, avec le titre : *Tractatus d plantis*.

Fourmont 33o.

5242-5249. — I (5242-5249).

吳氏重訂本草綱目

Oou chi tchhong ting pen tshao kang mou.

Traité des simples, réédition de Oou Yu-tchhang.

Par Li Chi-tchen Tong-pi, de Khi-tcheou. Dédicace de présentation à l'empereur par Li Kien-yuen (1596); préfaces par Tchang Ting-seu, de Tchhang-tcheou (1603) et par Oang Chi-tcheng, de Fong-tcheou (1590). Préfaces pour la présente réédition par Oou Pen-thai Lin-si (1655) et par Oou Yu-tchhang Yu-han, nom littéraire Tan-ning-tseu, de Tshien-thang (1655). Table générale des 52 livres; table détaillée pour chaque livre. Figures (1ᵉʳ livre seul, au lieu de 3 livres). Gravé à la salle Thai-hoo.

(5242), préfaces, tables, avertissement, etc., livres 1 et 2.

(5243), correspondance des médicaments et des maladies, livres 3 et 4.

(5244), eaux, livre 5.

(5244), feux, livre 6.

(5244), terres, livre 7.

(5244), métaux, livre 8.

(5244), pierres, livres 8 à 11.

(5245-5246), herbes, livres 12 à 21.

(5247), grains comestibles (kou), livres 22 à 25.

(5247), légumes, livres 26 à 28.

(5247), fruits, livres 29 à 33.

(5248), arbres, livres 34 à 37.

(5248), vêtements et ustensiles (effet et emploi), livre 38.

(5248), reptiles, insectes, mollusques (tchhong), livres 39 à 42.

(5249), animaux écailleux (lin), livres 43 et 44.

(5249), animaux à carapace (kiai), livres 45 et 46.

(5249), volatiles, livres 47 à 49.

(5249), quadrupèdes, livres 50 et 51.

(5249), hommes, livre 52.

Cat. imp., liv. 104, f. 32.

— II (5249).

奇經八脈考

Khi king pa me khao.

Examen des huit vaisseaux dits khi king (impairs).

Par Li Chi-tchen, surnom Pin-hou. Introduction par Kou Oen Ji-yen, de Khi-tcheou (1577). Préface pour une réédition (1603) par Tchang Ting-seu.

1 livre. — Cat imp., liv. 104, f. 33.

— III (5249).

瀕湖脈學

Pin hou me hio.

Traité des vaisseaux, de Pin-hou.

Même auteur. Texte et notes.

1 livre. — Cat. imp., liv. 104, f. 33. — Comparer plus haut nᵒˢ 5170, art. I ; 5188, art. I.

— IV (5249).

脉訣考證

Mẹ kiue khao tcheng.

Examen du Mẹ kiue.

Par le même auteur.

Comparer nᵒˢ 5186 à 5188.

Grand in-8. Titre noir sur blanc. 8 vol., demi-reliure (prov. de la bibl. de l'Arsenal).
Nouveau fonds 1702 à 1709.

5250-5257.   本草綱目

Pẹn tshao kang mou.

Traité des simples.

Réédition (1684) conforme à l'édition précédente ; publiée dans les salles Lou-yin et Oen-ya, à Kin-tchhang ; comprenant :

— I (5250).

Pin hou mẹ hio.

Traité des vaisseaux, de Pin-hou.

Même ouvrage qu'au nᵒ 5249, art. III.

— II (5250).

Mẹ kiue khao tcheng.

Examen du Mẹ kiue.

Même ouvrage qu'au nᵒ 5249, art. IV.

— III (5250).

Khi king pa mẹ khao.

Examen des huit vaisseaux impairs.

Même ouvrage qu'au nᵒ 5249, art. II.

— IV (5250-5257).

Pẹn tshao kang mou.

Traité des simples.

Même ouvrage qu'aux nᵒˢ 5242-5249, art. I. Figures, 2 livres au lieu de 3.

Grand in-8. Belle édition, couvertures originales en soie jaune. 8 vol., reliure au chiffre de Charles X.
Fourmont 325.

5258-5263. *Pẹn tshao kang mou.*

Double des nᵒˢ 5250-5257, art. IV. Manquent les figures ; planches un peu usées.

Grand in-8. 6 vol., demi-rel. au chiffre de Louis-Philippe.
Nouveau fonds 336.

———

5264-5271. — I (5264-5271).

本立堂重訂本草綱目

Pẹn li thang tchhong ting pẹn tshao kang mou.

Traité des simples, réédition de la salle Pẹn-li.

Préface par Tchang Tchhao-lin, de San-han (1657); préface par Li Yuen-ting (1658); préface par Li Ming-joei (1658); préfaces par Li Yuen-khoan, Hiong Oen-kiu, de Nan-tcheou, etc. Préfaces anciennes de Tchang Ting-seu, Oang Chi-tcheng; dédicace de présentation de Li Kien-yuen. Petite introduction non datée; table générale. Figures : 3 livres. Texte. Réédition de 1717.

Voir n°s 5242-5249, art. I.

— II (5271).

Khi king pa mẹ khao.

Examen des huit vaisseaux impairs.

Même ouvrage qu'au n° 5249, art. II; titre et début seulement.

— III (5271).

Pin hou mẹ hio.

Traité des vaisseaux, de Pin-hou.

Même ouvrage qu'au n° 5249, art. III.

— IV (5271).

Mẹ kiue khao tcheng.

Examen du Mẹ kiue.

Même ouvrage qu'au n° 5249, art. IV.

— V (5271).

Texte de l'ouvrage noté à l'art. II.

Grand in-8. Titre noir et rouge sur blanc. 8 vol., demi-rel., au chiffre de Louis-Philippe.
Fourmont 327.

5272-5278. — I (5272-5278).

Pẹn li thang tchhong ting pẹn tshao kang mou.

Même ouvrage qu'aux n°s 5264-5271, art. I; réédition plus récente.

Figures : 1 seul livre.
Texte : livres 1 à 44 et 50 à 52.

— II (5278).

Khi king pa mẹ khao.

Même ouvrage qu'au n° 5271, art. II.

— III (5278).

Pin hou mẹ hio.

Même ouvrage qu'au n° 5271, art. III.

— IV (5278).

Mẹ kiue khao tcheng.

Même ouvrage qu'au n° 5271, art. IV.

Grand in-8. Titre noir et rouge sur blanc. 7 vol., cartonnage.
Nouveau fonds 4748 à 4754.

5279. 本草綱目

Pẹn tshao kang mou.

Double des nᵒˢ 5272-5278, art. I.
Livres 48 et 49.

Grand in-8. 1 vol., cartonnage.
Nouveau fonds 3418.

———

5280. 三樂齋重訂本
草綱目

San yo tchai tchhong ting pẹn tshao kang mou.

Traité des simples, réédition de la salle San-yo.

Édition de 1735, imitée de celle de 1717 (nᵒˢ 5264-5271, art. I). Préfaces, table, avertissement, dédicace, introduction.

3 livres de figures (manque le texte).

Grand in-8. Titre noir sur blanc. 1 vol., Reliure du XVIIᵉ ou du XVIIIᵉ siècle. *Nouveau fonds* 2148.

———

5281-5291. 芥子園重
訂本草綱目

Kiai tseu yuen tchhong ting pẹn tshao kang mou.

Traité des simples, réédition du jardin Kiai-tseu.

Préfaces de Tchang Tchhao-lin, de Oou Yu-tchhang. Préface de l'éditeur de la présente édition, Tshai Lie-sien Tchheng-heou, de Tchong-chan, en Yue : cette pré-

face non datée est postérieure à l'année ting-hai, 1767 (?). Dédicace de Li Kien-yuen. Table générale.

— I (5281).

本草藥品總目

Pẹn tshao yo phin tsong mou.

Table générale des médicaments du Pẹn tshao.

Avec renvois aux livres de l'ouvrage. Par Tshai Lie-sien Kientchai, de Chan-yin.

— II (5281).

本草萬方鍼線

Pẹn tshao oan fang tchen sien.

Index méthodique des formules du Pẹn tshao.

Renvoyant aux livres et feuillets. Par le même.

8 livres.

— III (5282-5291).

本草綱目

Pẹn tshao kang mou.

Le Pẹn tshao kang mou.

3 livres de figures + 52 livres de texte.

— IV (5291).

脈學奇經八脈攷

Mẹ hio khi king pa mẹ khao.

Même ouvrage qu'au n° 5249, art. II; liste des ouvrages cités et préfaces.

— V (5291).

Pin hou me hio.

Même ouvrage qu'au n° 5249, art. III.

— VI (5291).

Texte de l'ouvrage noté à l'art. IV.

— VII (5291).

Me kiue khao tcheng.

Même ouvrage qu'au n° 5249, art. IV.

In-12; papier blanc; titre noir sur jaune. Toutefois l'art. IV est de format in-18, papier teinté, titre sur papier teinté. 11 vol., cartonnage.
Nouveau fonds 4495 à 4505.

5292-5302. *Kiai tseu yuen tchhong ting pen tshao kang mou.*

Double des n°s 5281-5291.

— I (5292).

Pen tshao yo phin tsong mou.
Voir n° 5281, art. I.

— II (5292).

本草綱目圖

Pen tshao kang mou thou.

Figures du Pen tshao kang mou.

3 livres. — Voir n°s 5282-5291, art. III.

— III (5293).

Pen tshao oan fang tchen sien.
Voir n° 5281, art. II.

— IV (5294-5302).

Pen tshao kang mou.

Voir n°s 5282-5291, art. III; pour les figures, voir plus haut, art. II.

— V (5302).

Me kiue khao tcheng.
Voir n° 5291, art. VII.

— VI (5302).

Me hio khi king pa me khao.
Voir n° 5291, art. IV.

— VII (5302).

Pin hou me hio.
Voir n° 5291, art. V.

— VIII (5302).

Texte de l'ouvrage noté à l'art. VI.

In-18. 11 vol., cartonnage.
Nouveau fonds 4506 à 4516.

5303-5314. *Kiai tseu yuen tchhong ting pen tshao kang mou.*

Double des n°s 5281-5291.

In-18. Bonne édition sur papier teinté.

12 vol., demi-rel., au chiffre de la République Française.

Nouveau fonds 128.

5315-5316. 神農本草經疏

Chen nong peṇ tshao king sou.

Traité des simples de Chennong, avec commentaire.

Par Mieou Hi-yong Tchong-choeṇ, de Tong-oou (XVIᵉ, XVIIᵉ siècles); revu et publié par son élève Li Tchi, à la salle Ya-yen, à Kin-tchhang. Préface de l'auteur; préface par Yao Ying-tchi, de Oou-hing, sans date.

3o livres (1o sections). — Cat. imp., liv. 1o4, f. 36.

Grand in-8. Titre noir et rouge sur blanc. 2 vol., reliure au chiffre de Charles X.

Nouveau fonds 337.

5317-5318. 本草彙言

Peṇ tshao hoei yen.

Traité des simples.

Par Yi Tchou-mou Choeṇ-yu, de Tshien-thang; publié par Chen Koan Si-yu, de Tshien-thang. Préface par Yuen-lou, oncle de l'auteur (1624); préface de l'auteur (1624). Réédition faite chez l'auteur (1645). Texte annoté avec figures; table générale et tables détaillées.

20 livres.

Grand in-8. Titre noir sur blanc; exemplaire dont les coins sont rongés. 2 vol., reliure au chiffre de Charles X.

Nouveau fonds 337 A.

5319. 分部本草

Feṇ pou peṇ tshao.

Étude des médicaments rangés suivant leur emploi.

Par Kou Fong-po Kiun-cheng, de Oou. Préface de l'auteur (1630); autre préface par Ling Khang-tsi (1630).

1o livres.

Grand in-8. 1 vol., demi-rel., au chiffre de Louis-Philippe.

Fourmont 331.

5320. 本草通玄

Peṇ tshao thong hiuen.

Traité de matière médicale.

Par Li Tchong-tseu Chi-tshai, de Yun-kien (vers 1637); revu par son élève Tai Tseu-lai Oen-chou, de Sin-'an, et par Tchheng Tcheng Yi-tchong. Préfaces non datées par Song Khi et par Tai Tseu-lai, la première incomplète du début. Avertissement. Liste de personnages qui ont surveillé l'impression.

2 livres. — Voir n° 5181, art. II.

Grand in-8. Bonne impression. 1 vol., demi-rel., au chiffre de Louis-Philippe.

Fourmont 329.

5321. 吸毒石原由用法

Hi tou chi yuen yeou yong fa.

Origine et usage de la pierre qui absorbe le venin.

Par le P. Verbiest (1623-1688) avec introduction du même.

Grand in-8. 1 vol., chinois.
Nouveau fonds 4935'.

5322. *Hi tou chi yuen yeou yong fa.*

Double.

Grand in-8. 1 vol., chinois.
Nouveau fonds 4935².

5323. — I.

重鐫食物本草會纂

Tchhong tsiuen chi oou pẹn tshao hoei tsoan.

Traité des aliments, réédition.

Préface (1691) par Chen Li-long Yun-tsiang, de Si-hou. Réédition de la salle Tchi-hoo, à Kin-ling. Texte avec figures.

8 livres. Le livre 8 forme un traité séparé, savoir :

— II.

脈訣秘傳

Mẹ kiue pi tchoan.

Traité relatif au Mẹ kiue.

Comparer nᵒˢ 5170, art. I; 5188, art. I.

Grand in-8. Titre noir sur jaune. 1 vol., demi-rel., au chiffre de Louis-Philippe.
Nouveau fonds 239.

5324. — I.

增訂圖註本草備要

Tseng ting thou tchou pẹn tshao pei yao.

Le Pẹn tshao mis en ordre d'après la nature des simples, édition illustrée augmentée, avec commentaires.

Par Oang 'Ang Jen-'an, de Hieou-ning; publié par son fils Toan Khi-liang, son frère Hoan Tien-oou, son neveu Oei Tchhong-tseu. Préface de l'auteur. Édition du jardin Kiai-tseu. Figures réunies avant le texte.

4 livres.

— II.

醫方湯頭歌括

Yi fang thang theou ko koo.

Traité des formules.

Même ouvrage qu'au nᵒ 5189, art. II, sans division en livres.

— III.

經絡歌訣

King lo ko kiue.

Traité des vaisseaux.

Même ouvrage qu'au nº 5189, art. I, sans division en livres.

In-18. Titre noir sur jaune. 1 vol., demi-rel., au chiffre de Louis-Philippe. *Nouveau fonds* 732.

5325. *Tseng ting thou tchou pẹn tshao pei yao.*

Même ouvrage qu'à l'art. I précédent. Deux préfaces de l'auteur, l'une non datée, l'autre de 1694; préface par Tchhen Fong. Édition donnée par Tcheng Tsheng-khing Tsan-hoan, à la salle Fou-oen, à Fo-chan. Les figures sont mêlées au texte.

4 livres.

Petit in-8. Titre noir sur jaune. 1 vol., cartonnage. *Nouveau fonds* 2378.

5326-5327. 新鐫本草醫方合編

Sin tsiuen pẹn tshao yi fang ho pien.

Nouvelle édition collective du Pẹn tshao et d'autres traités.

Publiée de nouveau à la salle Tsiu-kin par Hou Hio-fong, de Sieou-kou. Deux préfaces incomplètes. Les ouvrages suivants (art. I à IV) occupent la moitié supérieure des pages; la moitié inférieure est remplie par l'art. V.

— I (5326-5327).

本草俺要

Pẹn tshao pei yao.

Même ouvrage qu'au nº 5324, art. I.

— II (5327).

醫方湯頭歌訣

Yi fang thang theou ko kiue.

Même ouvrage qu'au nº 5324, art. II.

— III (5327).

經絡歌括

King lo ko koo.

Même ouvrage qu'au nº 5324, art. III.

— IV (5327).

續增日食菜物

Siu tseng yue chi tshai oou.

Traité des divers aliments, édition augmentée.

Sans nom d'auteur.

— V (5326-5327).

醫方集解

Yi fang tsi kiai.

Recueil de formules.

Par Oang 'Ang et sa famille. Avertissement, table des matières.

3 livres.

Grand in-8. Titre noir sur jaune. 2 vol., demi-rel., au chiffre de Napoléon III.

Nouveau fonds 1915, 1916.

5328-5329. 圖註本艸醫方合編

Thou tchou pẹn tshao yi fang ho pien.

Le Pẹn tshao, suivi d'autres traités, édition illustrée.

Réédition d'après la précédente (nᵒˢ 5326-5327), de plus petit format et d'exécution peu soignée; faite à la salle Fou-oen (1826). Même disposition sur le haut et le bas des pages.

— I (5328-5329).

增訂本草備要

Tseng ting pẹn tshao pei yao.

Le Pẹn tshao pei yao, édition augmentée.

Même ouvrage qu'au nᵒ 5324, art. I.

5 livres.

— II (5329).

醫方湯頭歌括

Yi fang thang theou ko koo.

Même ouvrage qu'au nᵒ 5324, art. II.

— IIL (5329).

經絡歌訣

King lo ko kiue.

Même ouvrage qu'au nᵒ 5324, art. III.

— IV (5329).

續增日食物

Siu tseng yue chi ôou.

Même ouvrage qu'au nᵒ 5327, art. IV.

— V (5328-5329).

Yi fang tsi kiai.

Même ouvrage qu'aux nᵒˢ 5326-5327, art. V. Avec table et figures.

In-18. Papier teinté; titre noir sur jaune. 2 vol., demi-rel., au chiffre de Louis-Philippe.

Nouveau fonds 511.

5330-5331. *Thou tchou pẹn tshao yi fang ho pien.*

Même ouvrage qu'aux nᵒˢ 5328-5329, même disposition; gravure plus grande et plus soignée. Édition des salles Fou-oen et Cheng-tẹ (1839), conforme à une édition de 1817.

— I (5330-5331).

Tseng ting pẹn tshao pei yao.

Voir nᵒˢ 5328-5329, art. I.

— II (5331).

Yi fang ihang theou ko koo.

Voir n° 5329, art. II.

— III (5331).

King lo ko kiue.

Voir n° 5329, art. III.

— IV (5331).

Siu tseng yue chi oou.

Voir n° 5329, art. IV.

— V (5330-5331).

Yi fang tsi kiai.

Voir n°ˢ 5328-5329, art. V.

In-12. Papier blanc; titre noir sur jaune. 2 vol., cartonnage.
Nouveau fonds 4517, 4518.

5332. 本草補

Pęn tshao pou.

Supplément au Pęn tshao.

Par Chi To-lou Tchen-to, occidental; l'auteur est vraisemblablement un Franciscain, mais son nom européen est ignoré. Préface (1697) par Lieou Ying, de Nan-fong.

Voir Catalogus librorum, n° 61.

Petit in-8. 1 vol., demi-reliure.
Nouveau fonds 1943.

5333. 吳氏醫學述第三種。增訂本草從新

Oou chi yihio chou ti san tchong.

Tseng ting pęn tshao tshong sin.

Le troisième ouvrage de l'étude de la médecine, par Oou : le nouveau Pęn tshao.

Par Oou Yi-lo Tsoęn-tchheng, de Kan-choei (Oou-yuen). Préface de l'auteur (1757). Texte et notes. Postface de l'auteur (1757). Réédition de la salle Yu-ni (1809).

6 livres (3 sections par livre).

Grand in-8. Titre noir sur blanc. 1 vol., demi-rel., au chiffre de Louis-Philippe.
Nouveau fonds 471.

5334. 本草原始

Pęn tshao yuen chi.

Traité des simples.

Par Li Tchong-li Tcheng-yu, de Yong-khieou; revu et publié de nouveau par Tcheou Liang-teng Yuen-long, de Kin-khi. Préface par Ma Ying-long Po-koang, de Pou-hai. Texte avec figures. Édition de la salle Oen-hoei.

12 livres.

Grand in-8. Titre noir sur jaune. 1 vol., demi-rel., au chiffre de Louis-Philippe.
Nouveau fonds 436.

5335-5340. 孫眞人千金方衍義

Soęn tchen jen tshien kin fang yen yi.

12

Développement des Formules de Soęn tchen-jen.

Les Formules, Tshien kin fang, sont dues à Soęn Seu-miao, de Hoa-yuen (581?-689). Vie de cet auteur; préface non datée. Dédicace d'une réédition par Kao Paoheng, Soęn Khi, etc. (époque des Song). Préface par Ma Li Sanyuen, surnom Khi-thien kiu-chi (1544). Dans le présent ouvrage, les formules ont été commentées et rangées méthodiquement selon les maladies auxquelles elles correspondent. Auteur : Tchang Lou ; éditeur Si Chi-tchhen , surnom Ying-kho, de Nan-cha. Préface de l'auteur (1698); notice par l'éditeur (1800). Édition de la maison Sao-yue (1801).

3o livres. — Comparer Cat. imp., liv. 1o3, f. 15 (Tshien kin yao fang, 93 livres).

Grand in-8. Titre noir sur rose. 6 vol., demi-rel., au chiffre de Louis-Philippe.
Nouveau fonds 23o3 à 23o8.

5341.   銅人腧穴鍼灸圖經

Thong jen chou hiue tchen kieou thou king.

Traité illustré de l'acuponcture et du moxa, indiquant les places correspondant aux organes.

Peut-être dú à Oang Oei-tę (début du xiᵉ siècle), qui présenta à l'empereur (1027?) un modèle en cuivre du corps humain. Le titre porte l'indication : ouvrage composé dans la période Thien-cheng (1023-1031), gravé de nouveau en 1443. Préface de 1443. Texte, figures, tableaux.

3 livres. — Comparer Cat. imp., liv. 1o3, f. 21 (Thong jen tchen kieou king, 7 livres).

Grand in-8. Titre noir sur blanc. 1 vol., demi-rel., au chiffre de Louis-Philippe.
Fourmont 332.

5342. — I.

增補珍珠囊藥性賦

Tseng pou tchen tchou nang yo sing fou.

Traités sur la nature des médicaments, édition augmentée.

Plusieurs de ces dissertations sont versifiées. L'ouvrage primitif est attribué, à tort, semble-t-il, à Li Kao. Édition augmentée due à Tchang Koang-teou Oei-yuen, de Choęn-yi; gravée par les soins de Tchhen Koę-oang Yu-oo, à la salle Thong-tę.

2 livres, le 1ᵉʳ en 3 sections. — Cat. imp., liv. 1o5, f. 11 (Tchen tchou nang tchi tchang pou yi yo sing fou, 4 livres).

— II.

新增雷公炮製

Sin tseng lei kong phao tchi.

Nouveau recueil d'ordonnances de Lei kong.

Réunies par Hiuen-hou tao-jen, de Min.

In-12. Titre noir sur jaune. 1 vol., demi-rel., au chiffre de Louis-Philippe. *Nouveau fonds* 111.

5343. 增補藥性雷公 炮製

Tseng pou yo sing lei kong phao tchi.

Recueil d'ordonnances et traité sur les médicaments, d'après Lei kong.

Par Tchang Koang-teou; gravé par les soins de Tchhen Koe-oang. Préface de l'auteur, sans date. Édition de la salle Thong-te (1818).

8 livres.

In-12. Titre noir sur jaune. 1 vol., demi-rel., au chiffre de Louis-Philippe. *Nouveau fonds* 762.

5344-5346. 重刊鍼灸 大成

Tchhong khan tchen kieou ta tchheng.

Traité de l'acuponcture et du moxa, réédition.

Par Yang Ki-tcheou, de Phing-yang (?), à l'époque Oan-li. Préface par Li Yue-koei, de Chen, pour une réédition (1680). Texte avec figures ; une grande planche repliée

représentant le corps humain. Édition commune de la salle Tchi-te (1801).

10 livres. — Cat. imp., liv. 105, f. 26 (Tchen kieou ta tshiuen).

In-12. Papier blanc, titre noir sur jaune. 3 vol., demi-rel., au chiffre de Louis-Philippe. *Nouveau fonds* 677.

5347. — I.

攝生總要

Che cheng tsong yao.

Autre titre :

石渠閣精訂攝生秘剖

Chi khiu ko tsing ting che cheng pi pheou.

Formules importantes de médecine usuelle.

Attribuées à Liu tsou ; publiées par Hong Ki Kieou-yeou, de Sin-'an. Diverses préfaces non datées. A la fin de la table, on lit la date de 1638.

4 livres.

— II.

種子金編

Tchong tseu kin pien.

Autre titre :

精訂種子攝生秘剖

Tsing ting tchong tseu che cheng pi pheou.

Traité de gymnastique et d'hygiène taoïstes.

Par Song-mei lao-jen. Texte et figures; exercices pour obtenir des fils.

2 livres.

— III.

繼嗣珍寶。種子方

Ki seu tchen pao : tchong tseu fang.

Trésor des recettes pour avoir des fils.

— IV.

房術奇書月

Fang chou khi chou yue.

Autre titre :

陳希夷房術玄機中萃纂要

Tchhen hi yi fang chou hiuen ki tchong tsoei tsoan yao.

Traité taoïste de Tchhen Hi-yi.

Ce personnage taoïste a vécu au x° siècle (postnom Thoan, surnom Thou-nan; de Po-tcheou, † 989). Préface par Jen Kong-tchhen, surnom Khan-kong tao-jen (1550), de Tong-ming.

In-24. Titre noir sur jaune. 1 vol., demi-rel., au chiffre de Napoléon III. *Nouveau fonds* 1138.

5348. 採艾編

Tshai 'ai pien.

Traité sur les médicaments et sur la médecine.

Par Ye Koang-tsou, de Tchha-chan. Préface par Phan Yu-heng, de Tha-chan (1668). Édition de la salle Choei-oen.

1 + 3 livres.

Grand in-8. Titre noir sur jaune. 1 vol., demi-rel., au chiffre de Louis-Philippe.
Nouveau fonds 216.

5349. 古今名醫方論

Kou kin ming yi fang loen.

Formules dues à des médecins célèbres anciens et modernes.

Recueillies et publiées par Lo Mei Tong-yi, de Sin-'an; revues par Ko Yun-po, de Tsheu-choei. Préface de l'auteur (1675). Édition du pavillon Pou-yue, de Kin-tchhang.

4 livres.

Grand in-8. Titre noir sur jaune. 1 vol., demi-rel., au chiffre de Louis-Philippe.
Nouveau fonds 465.

5350-5351. 醫方集解

Yi fang tsi kiai.

Recueil de formules.

Par Oang 'Ang Jen-'an , avec

préface de l'auteur (1682). Texte et notes. Édition du jardin Kiai-tseu.

3 livres. — Voir plus haut n⁰ˢ 5326-5327, art. V.

In-18. Titre noir sur jaune. 2 vol., demi-rel., au chiffre de Louis-Philippe. *Nouveau fonds* 512.

5352. 法製醫方藥性石室秘籙

Fa tchi yi fang yo sing chi chi pi lou.

Formules et prescriptions médicales.

Ouvrage d'inspiration taoïste, par Tchhen Chi-to Yuen-kong, de Chan-yin. Texte et notes, dont l'auteur attribue l'origine à Khi po, Tchang Ki, Hoa Tho († 220 p. C.), Lei kong, etc. Préfaces par Khi po (1687), par Liu tao-jen, par Kin Yi-meou Hiao-khi, de Yi-oou (1689).

6 livres. — Cat. imp., liv. 105, f. 36 (Chi chi pi lou).

Petit in-8. Titre noir sur rouge. 1 vol., demi-rel., au chiffre de Louis-Philippe. *Nouveau fonds* 878.

5353. 類編活人書括指掌續方

Lei pien hoo jen chou koo tchi tchang siu fang.

Autre titre :

傷寒指掌圖

Chang han tchi tchang thou.

Recueils de formules.

Par Hiong Tsong-li Tao-hien, de 'Ao-fong. Vieille édition.

Livres 8 à 10.

Grand in-8. 1 vol., cartonnage du XVIIIᵉ siècle, avec le titre : *Liber chirurgicalis.*

Fourmont 321.

5354. 丹方彙編

Tan fang hoei pien.

Recueil de formules.

Préfaces par Siu Chi-yong Yunpai (1707) et par Tshien Siun Tshing-loen, de Thiao-tchheng (1707); introduction par ce dernier (1707). Réédition par Chen Hoaiyu, de Oou, publiée à la salle Fonglien. Après divers préliminaires traitant des remèdes et des maladies, on trouve les traités suivants :

— I.

諸症歌訣

Tchou tcheng ko kiue.

Petit traité sur les maladies. Rédigé en vers.

— II.

單方摘要

Tan fang tche yao.

Recueil de formules simples.

— III.

幼科良方

Yeou khoo liang fang.

Formules pour les enfants.

2 sections.

— IV.

經驗單方彙編

King yen tan fang hoei pien.

Recueil de formules.

Rassemblées par Tshien Siun; revues par Siu Chi-yong Yun-pai et par Chen Ping-kiun Yu-phing.

— V.

保產良方

Pao tchhan liang fang.

Formules pour l'accouchement.

Un feuillet est déplacé et relié à la fin du volume.

— VI.

濟陰纂要方

Tsi yin tsoan yao fang.

Formules pour les maladies des femmes.

Par Tshien Siun.

Grand in-8. Titre noir sur jaune. 1 vol., demi-reliure.
Nouveau fonds 372.

5355-5356. 新增集驗良方

Sin tseng tsi yen liang fang.

Recueil de traités et de formules, édition augmentée.

Première préface par Liang Oen-khoo Ying-heou, de Cheou-tchhoęn (1710). Préface écrite à Oou-yang (1724) par un second éditeur, Nien Hi-yao, de Koang-ning. Préface (1822) par un troisième éditeur Tchheng Han-tchang, de Yue-tchhoan, au Tien-si. Le titre porte la date de 1820. Texte avec quelques figures; table générale; table détaillée pour chaque livre.

8 livres.

Petit in-8. Titre noir sur jaune. 2 vol., demi-rel., au chiffre de Louis-Philippe.
Nouveau fonds 533.

5357-5359. 本草綱目類方

Pęn tshao kang mou lei fang.

Formules du Pęn tshao kang mou, classées dans l'ordre des maladies.

Par Nien Hi-yao, surnom 'Eou-tchai tchou-jen, de Koang-ning; avec préface de l'auteur (1735). Publié par les soins de Hoang Hiao-fong, de Thien-tou. Édition de la salle Chou-ye, à Tsin-khi

(1805). La place d'une table des matières est tenue par

諸 症 歌 訣

Tchou tcheng ko kiue.

Petit traité sur les maladies. En vers.

10 sections. — Comparer n° 5354, art. I.

In-12. Titre noir sur rose. 3 vol., demi-rel., au chiffre de Louis-Philippe. *Nouveau fonds* 666.

———

5360. 增 補 醫 方 一 盤 珠 全 集

Tseng pou yi fang yi phan tchou tshiuen tsi.

Petit traité de médecine usuelle : collection de formules.

Par Hong Kin-ting Tchi-yeou, de Kin-tchhoan. Préface de l'auteur (1749). Édition de la salle Kin-cheng.

10 livres.

In-18. Titre noir sur jaune. 1 vol., demi-rel., au chiffre de Louis-Philippe. *Nouveau fonds* 741.

5361-5362. 靜 耘 齋 集 驗 方

Tsing yun tchai tsi yen fang.

Médecine usuelle : collection de formules.

Par Hoang Yuen-ki Tan-yuen, de Koei-ling. Préface de l'auteur (1763); préface par Fan Tchheng (1763). Édition de la salle Hoei-oen (1799).

8 livres.

Petit in-8. Titre noir sur jaune. 2 vol., demi-rel., au chiffre de Louis-Philippe. *Nouveau fonds* 556.

———

5363. 新 編 壽 世 傳 眞

Sin pien cheou chi tchhoan tchen.

Nouveau traité d'hygiène.

Inspiré des idées taoïstes. Par Siu Oen-pi Tsin-chan, de Ming-fong, à Fong-tchheng. Publié par Oang Chi-fang, surnom Hiang-chan lao-jen; préface du même (1771). Édition de la salle Tchi-cheng. Texte avec figures.

In-12. Titre noir sur jaune. 1 vol., demi-rel. *Nouveau fonds* 773.

5364. — I.

仙 傳 各 種 經 驗 奇 方

Sien tchhoan ko tchong king yen khi fang.

Recueil de formules dues aux immortels.

Rangées dans l'ordre méthodique des maladies. Édition du palais Hao-thien et de la salle Koang-king (1789).

4 livres.

— II.

續刻經驗奇方

Siu kho king yen khi fang.

Recueil de formules, suite.

Petit in-8. Titre noir sur jaune. 1 vol., demi-rel., au chiffre de Louis-Philippe. *Nouveau fonds* 866.

5365. 醫貫

Yi koan.

Recueil de traités et de formules.

Par Yi Oou-liu-tseu. Édition de la salle Yong-cheng (1813).

6 livres. — Comparer Cat. imp., liv. 105, f. 40 (Yi koan pien, 2 livres).

Petit in-8. Titre noir sur jaune. 1 vol., demi-rel., au chiffre de Louis-Philippe. *Nouveau fonds* 395.

5366. 針灸摘要

Tchen kieou tche yao.

Principes de l'acuponcture et du moxa.

Manuscrit, sans nom d'auteur ni date.

Petit in-8. 1 vol., cartonnage du XVIIIᵉ siècle, avec le titre : *Tabulae anatomicae.*
Fourmont 322.

Neuvième Section : ART VÉTÉRINAIRE

5367. 馬經

Ma king.

Autre titre :

元亨療馬集

Yuen heng liao ma tsi.

Des soins à donner au cheval.

Traité vétérinaire par Yu Jen Pen-yuen et Yu Kie Pen-heng, de

Lou-'an. Préface par Ting Pin Kai-thing, de Kia-chan (1608). Édition de la salle Oan-siuen. Texte et figures.

4 livres + supplément. — Cat. imp., liv. 105, f. 46 (Liao ma tsi ; fou lou).

Petit in-8. Titre noir sur blanc. 1 vol., demi-rel., au chiffre de Louis-Philippe. *Nouveau fonds* 817.

Dixième Section : AGRICULTURE, SÉRICICULTURE, ÉLEVAGE

5368. 重刊東魯王氏農書

Tchhong khan tong lou oang chi nong chou.

Le livre du labourage par Oang, de Tong lou.

Par Oang Tcheng Po-chan, de Tong-phing (époque des Yuen). Illustrations avec légendes, représentant les divinités et les actes de l'agriculture (10 planches); rose des vents pour les influences astrologiques et géoscopiques. Texte. Préface par Yen Hong Li-tsi, de Lin-tshing (1530); préface par Fou Hi-tchi (1574).

6 livres (16 sections). — Cat. imp., liv. 102, f. 6 (Nong chou, en 22 livres).

Grand in-8. Papier blanc, gravure un peu usée. 1 vol., demi-rel., au chiffre de Napoléon III.

Nouveau fonds 1805.

5369-5371. 農政全書

Nong tcheng tshiuen chou.

Traité général d'agriculture.

Par Siu Koang-khi (1562-1634); publié après la mort de l'auteur par Tchang Koe-oei. Préface par ce dernier (1639); préface par Oang Ta-hien, de Liu-ling (1639); préface non datée par Tchang Phou Si-ming, de Leou-tong. Texte avec nombreuses figures. Édition de la salle Phing-lou.

60 livres. — Cat. imp., liv. 102, f. 8.

Grand in-8. 3 vol., demi-rel., au chiffre de Louis-Philippe.

Fourmont 352.

5372-5376. *Nong tcheng tshiuen chou.*

Même ouvrage, réédition de 1843 faite au pavillon Chou-hai. Préface par Phan Tsheng-yi, de

Oou (1843); notice du Catalogue Impérial; biographie de Siu Koang-khi.

60 livres.

Grand in-8. Belle impression sur papier teinté; titre noir sur blanc. 5 vol., demi-rel., au chiffre de Napoléon III.

Nouveau fonds 1961 à 1965.

5377-5392. *Nong tcheng tshiuen chou.*

Double.

Petit in-8. Papier commun, titre noir sur rouge. 16 vol. chinois, dans 2 enveloppes.

Nouveau fonds 4373, 4374.

5393. 重訂增補致富奇書

Tchhong ting tseng pou tchi fou khi chou.

Traité sur l'agriculture et l'élevage, édition augmentée.

Par Thao Tchou-kong; la présente édition est due à Chi-yen yi-seou, de Tchong-chan. Préface de ce dernier (1678). Planches à la salle Pao-king.

4 livres.

In-12. Titre noir sur jaune. 1 vol., demi-rel., au chiffre de Napoléon III.

Nouveau fonds 1433.

5394.

Culture et Récolte du Riz.

12

Éducation des Vers à Soie. Gravés en 42 planches en Chine.

御製耕織圖

Yu tchi keng tchi thou.

Dessins faits par ordre impérial, représentant les travaux agricoles et séricicoles ; une brève légende en haut de chaque planche, texte relatif à chaque planche. Préface impériale avec sceaux impériaux (1696).

23 + 23 planches. — Comparer Cat. imp., liv. 102, f. 13 (Keng tchi thou chi).

Format 0,29 × 0,36 ; les dessins sont montés sur papier fort et reliés par le côté plié ; ils sont disposés de droite à gauche. Edition soignée, tirée sur des planches en bon état. 1 vol., cartonnage chinois.

Département des Estampes, Oe 90.

5395.

Double ; 41 planches reliées en désordre, la préface est reliée à l'envers. Notices manuscrites en français à la fin du volume.

Format 0,25 × 0,32. 1 vol., cartonnage européen.

Département des Estampes, Oe 89.

5396. *Yu tchi keng tchi thou.*

Même ouvrage, sans légendes en haut des planches ; la préface est presque illisible.

23 + 23 planches.

In-4. 1 vol., demi-reliure.
Nouveau fonds 1837.

5397. 農家耕田圖

Nong kia keng thien thou.

Les travaux agricoles.

Peintures d'exécution fine, imitées de la série agricole de l'ouvrage précédent.

23 peintures sur papier.

Format 0,30 × 0,38. 1 vol., couverture soie (prov. de la bibl. de l'Arsenal).
Département des Estampes, Oe 71.

5398.

Culture du riz.

Planches imitées des précédentes, avec légendes chinoises manuscrites ; les scènes sont peintes sur taffetas ; les vêtements sont en fragments d'étoffes de soie, les visages en ivoire peint, le tout collé sur le fond.

24 planches.

Format 0,28 × 0,30. 1 vol., couverture soie.
Département des Estampes, Oe 75.

———

5399-5402. 欽定授時通考

Khin ting cheou chi thong khao.

Traité général d'agriculture composé par ordre impérial.

Préface impériale suivie des sceaux rouges (1742) ; décret (1737) ordonnant de composer l'ouvrage. Table, avertissement Liste de la commission de rédaction, comprenant le prince de Hoo, 'O-eul-thai, Tchang Thing-yu, etc. Texte et planches.

78 livres (8 sections). — Cat. imp., liv. 102, f. 11.

Grand in-8. Belle édition. 4 vol., reliure au chiffre de Charles X.

Nouveau fonds 338.

5403.

Scènes des travaux agricoles; dessins avec titres chinois, collés sur papier européen, pliés par le milieu et montés à l'européenne.

11 feuillets.

Format 0,32 × 0,50. 1 vol., cartonnage à l'européenne.

Département des Estampes, Oe 73.

5404.

Riz.

Peintures sur papier de riz, représentant la série des opérations agricoles; avec titres en chinois et table manuscrite en français.

12 feuillets.

Format 0,24 × 0,31. 1 vol., cartonnage chinois.

Département des Estampes, Oe 76.

La présente section (10e) et les 11e, 13e, 15e, 16e renferment un grand nombre de dessins chinois et de peintures chinoises, qui ne portent en général ni date ni signature. Les séries les plus récentes (dessins à l'encre de Chine et peintures sur papier de riz) paraissent dater de la première moitié du XIXe siècle et provenir des ateliers cantonais; on trouve sur quelques cartonnages les noms de Yoeequa, Sunqua, Tingqua, peintres; un grand nombre des albums sur papier de riz sont d'un fini remarquable. Les peintures sur papier et sur taffetas paraissent plus anciennes d'un demi-siècle environ : une partie provient de Péking.

5405.

Riz; Culture; Récolte; Mouture.

Dessins à l'encre de Chine; titres en chinois; table manuscrite en français.

12 dessins sur 6 feuillets doubles. — Comparer n° 5437.

Format 0,21 × 0,29. 1 vol., cartonnage chinois.

Département des Estampes, Oe 77.

5406.

Blé.

Peintures sur papier de riz représentant la série des opérations de la culture du blé; titres en chinois, table manuscrite en français.

12 feuillets.

Format 0,23 × 0,30. 1 vol., cartonnage chinois.

Département des Estampes, Oe 72.

5407.

Mûriers, Vers à soie, Soie.

Dessins à l'encre de Chine; titres

en chinois, table manuscrite en français.

36 dessins. — Comparer n° 5437.

Format 0,22 × 0,30. 1 vol., cartonnage chinois.

Département des Estampes, Oe 88.

5408.

Soie.

Dessins à l'encre de Chine ; titres en chinois.

120 dessins sur 60 feuillets doubles.

Format 0,29 × 0,30. 1 vol., couverture soie.

Département des Estampes, Oe 103.

5409-5412.

Soie. Fabrication, tissage et exploitation.

Dessins à l'encre de Chine, avec légendes chinoises et titres en français.

144 dessins.

Format 0,38 × 0,38. 4 vol., couverture soie.

Département des Estampes, Oe 100, 100 a, 100 b, 100 c.

5413.

Dessins à l'encre de Chine représentant la culture et la préparation de la soie, du chanvre, du coton, du thé, de l'opium ; scènes de la vie quotidienne. Table manuscrite en anglais.

120 dessins.

Format 0,29 × 0,30. 1 vol., couverture soie.

Département des Estampes, Oe 131.

5414. 蠶桑合編
Tshan sang ho pien.

Traité de sériciculture.

Par Cha Chi-'an, Lou Yi-mei, Oei Me-chen. Préface (1843) par Cha Chi-'an ; préface (1844) par Oen Koei, de Choei-tchhang. Réédition (1845) faite à Tan-thou. Figures avec légendes.

Grand in-8. Bonne impression, titre noir sur papier teinté. 1 vol., demi-rel., au chiffre de la République Française. *Nouveau fonds* 3561.

5415. 棉花圖
Mien hoa thou.

Dessins sur l'industrie du coton.

Estampes gravées et coloriées à la main, chaque planche est accompagnée d'explications imprimées en blanc sur noir et dues probablement à Fang Koan-tchheng, qui a signé la dédicace à l'Empereur (1765) et la postface ; poésie de l'Empereur Cheng-tsou.

1 vol. paravent 0,33 × 0,31 ; couverture chinoise en soie.

Département des Estampes, Oe 99.

5416.

Coton (culture et exploitation du).

Peintures sur papier de riz; titres en chinois, table manuscrite en français.

18 feuillets.

Format 0,24 × 0,32. 1 vol., couverture soie.

Département des Estampes, Oe 97.

5417.

Coton (industrie du).

Peintures sur papier de riz; titres chinois, table manuscrite en français.

12 feuillets.

Format 0,24 × 0,31. 1 vol., cartonnage chinois.

Département des Estampes, Oe 96.

5418.

Coton.

Dessins à l'encre de Chine; titres chinois avec traduction française.

12 dessins sur 6 feuillets doubles.

Format 0,23 × 0,29. 1 vol., cartonnage chinois.

Département des Estampes, Oe 98.

5419-5421.

Ma ou chanvre.

Peintures sur papier de riz; titres chinois; table manuscrite en

français au début de chaque volume.

35 feuillets.

Format 0,25 × 0,37. 3 vol., couvertures soie.

Département des Estampes, Oe 93, 93 a, 93 b.

5422-5424.

Culture et préparation de la plante textile *ma*.

Peintures sur papier de riz; titres chinois, table manuscrite en français au début de chaque volume.

36 feuillets.

Format 0,25 × 0,36. 3 vol., couvertures soie, dans 1 étui en papier chinois.

Département des Estampes, Oe 91.

5425.

Ma, ou Chanvre de *Tchou-ma,* Urtica nivea.

Peintures sur papier de riz; titres chinois, table manuscrite en français.

15 feuillets.

Format 0,23 × 0,32. 1 vol., couverture soie.

Département des Estampes, Oe 95.

5426.

Exploitation du *Ma* ou Chanvre de la Chine.

Peintures sur papier de riz; titres chinois, table manuscrite en français.

12 feuillets.

Format 0,24 × 0,31. 1 vol., cartonnage chinois.

Département des Estampes, Oe 94.

5427.

Ma, ou Chanvre d'Urtica nivea.

Dessins à l'encre de Chine; titres chinois, table manuscrite en français.

12 dessins sur 6 feuillets doubles. — Comparer n° 5437.

Format 0,23 × 0,29. 1 vol., cartonnage chinois.

Département des Estampes, Oe 92.

5428. — I.

茶 經

Tchha king.

Traité du thé.

Par Lou Yu Hong-tsien, autres postnom et surnom Tsi Ki-tsheu, nom littéraire Sang-tchou-oong, de King-ling (VIII° siècle); traitant des points suivants : origine, récolte, préparation des feuilles, vases pour l'infusion, infusion, manière de boire, notes historiques, lieux de production, sommaire, notes relatives aux figures. Préface par Phi Ji-hieou (IX° s.).

3 livres. — Cat. imp., liv. 115, f. 31.

— II.

十六湯品

Chi lou thang phin.

Seize notices sur la manière de faire bouillir l'eau.

Ébullition parfaite; comment verser l'eau bouillante; vases et combustible à employer. Par Sou Yi (époque des Thang).

— III.

煎茶水記

Tsien tchha choei ki.

Notice sur les eaux pour l'infusion du thé.

Par Tchang Yeou-sin Khong-tchao, de Chen-tcheou, docteur en 814.

1 livre. — Cat. imp., liv. 115, f. 37.

— IV.

食譜

Chi phou.

Le livre des mets.

Par Oei Kiu-yuen.

In-18. 1 vol., demi-rel., au chiffre de Napoléon III.
Nouveau fonds 1430.

5429. — I.

元本茶經

Yuen pen tchha king.

Le Tchha king, d'après un

exemplaire de l'époque des Yuen.

Même ouvrage (n° 5428, art. I), texte et notes. Préface non datée par Tchhen Chi-tao (époque des Song). Vie de Lou Yu. En tête, figures avec notice, par Lou Thing-tshan (xviiie siècle).

3 livres. — Cat. imp., liv. 115, f. 31.

— II.

續茶經

Siu tchha king.

Suite au Tchha king.

Par Lou Thing-tshan Man-thing, surnom Tchi-tchao, de Kia-ting. Texte; figures avec éloges.

3 livres. — Cat. imp., liv. 115, f. 36.

— III.

附錄。茶法

Fou lou. Tchha fa.

Supplément. Sur le thé.

Par Lou Thing-tshan.

Cat. imp., liv. 115, f. 36.

Grand in-8. Bonne édition. 1 vol., demi-rel., au chiffre de Napoléon III.
Nouveau fonds 1374.

5430. 茶譜

Tchha phou.

Le livre du thé.

Recueil de passages d'auteurs;

texte annoté, sans nom d'auteur ni date.

3 livres.

Petit in-8. Manuscrit. 1 vol., cartonnage.
Nouveau fonds 1111 A.

—————

5431.

Peintures sur taffetas représentant les diverses opérations relatives au thé, depuis le moment où il est récolté jusqu'à celui où, apporté à Canton, il est embarqué sur un vaisseau européen.

50 feuillets.

Format 0,33 × 0,39. 1 vol., couverture soie.
Département des Estampes, Oe 78.

5432.

Recueil analogue de peintures sur papier.

30 feuillets.

Format 0,32 × 0,39. 1 vol., couverture soie.
Département des Estampes, Oe 79.

5433.

Thé.

Peintures sur papier de riz; titres chinois et table manuscrite en français.

12 feuillets.

Format 0,31 × 0,24. 1 vol., couverture soie.
Département des Estampes, Oe 82.

5434.

Thé. Vers à soie. Riz.

Peintures sur papier de riz (paysages); table manuscrite en français.

9 feuillets.

Format 0,30 × 0,24. 1 vol., couverture soie.

Département des Estampes, Oe 83.

5435.

Dessins à l'encre de Chine; deux séries : 1° culture et préparation du thé; 2° vases; la première série a des titres en chinois et en français.

12 + 12 dessins.

Format 0,29 × 0,22. 1 vol., cartonnage chinois.

Département des Estampes, Oe 80.

5436.

Thé. Culture et préparation.

Dessins à l'encre de Chine; titres chinois et table manuscrite en français.

12 dessins (6 feuillets doubles). — Comparer n° 5437.

Format 0,29 × 0,21. 1 vol., cartonnage chinois.

Département des Estampes, Oe 81.

5437.

Dessins à l'encre de Chine avec titres chinois et tables manus-

crites en français; rangés par séries relatives à divers métiers et analogues à d'autres séries formant des albums séparés.

Thé	12 dessins, comp. n°	5436
Charbon de terre	12	—	—	5583
Papier	12	—	—	5577
Ma	12	—	—	5427
Encre	12	—	—	5579
Opium et occupations des femmes	22	—	—	5604
Culture du riz	12	—	—	5405
Fer	12	—	—	5587
Plantes textiles et diverses sortes de mûriers	24	—	—	5407
Verre	12	—	—	5573
Porcelaine	12	—	—	5571

In-4. 1 vol., demi-rel., au chiffre de Napoléon III.

Nouveau fonds 1845.

5438. 秘傳花鏡

Pi tchhoan hoa king.

Traité d'horticulture.

Par Tchhen Hao-tseu, surnoms Si-hou hoa-yin oong et Fou-yao, de Hang-tcheou. Préface de l'auteur (1688). Édition de la salle Chou-ye, à Kin-tchhang. Texte et planches; le dernier livre traite de l'élevage de divers animaux.

6 livres.

Grand in-8. Titre noir sur jaune. 1 vol., demi-reliure.

Nouveau fonds 1933.

5439. *Pi tchhoan hoa king.*

Même ouvrage ; à la fin de la préface, on lit la date de 1783. Réédition de la salle Seu-yeou.

In-12. Titre noir sur jaune. 1 vol., demi-rel., au chiffre de Louis-Philippe. *Nouveau fonds* 545.

5440. 花信詩
Hoa sin chi.

Odes sur les fleurs de chaque saison.

Recueil de vingt-quatre pièces, avec une préface non signée (1704). Postface par Lin Ki (1717). A la suite, on lit la date de 1741.

Grand in-8. Manuscrit relié de gauche à droite, dans l'ordre européen. 1 vol., cartonnage. *Nouveau fonds* 3463.

5441. — I.

六畜相法
Lou tchhou siang fa.

Sur les six animaux domestiques.

Cheval, chien, chat, porc ; manquent le bœuf, le mouton, la poule. Une figure de chaque sorte d'animal ; une chanson rappelant les qualités, les variétés de chaque espèce, les soins qu'elle exige, etc. Gravé à la salle Oen-te (1860).

— II.

增補文狀元雜字
Tseng pou oen tchoang yuen tsa tseu.

Autre titre :

增補天下雜字大全
Tseng pou thien hia tsa tseu ta tshiuen.

Manuel encyclopédique augmenté.

Cosmologie, mœurs, histoire, arbres, plantes, calcul, etc. ; rédigé en phrases de quatre caractères, par Oen Tchen-meng, de Tchhang-tcheou. Gravé à la salle Oen-te (1860).

Petit in-8. Titre noir sur jaune. 1 vol., cartonnage. *Nouveau fonds* 4567.

Onzième Section : SCIENCES NATURELLES

5442. 地震解
Ti tchen kiai.
Explication des tremblements de terre.

Par le P. Nicolao Longobardi (1566-1654) ; conversation avec Li Song-yu, de l'année 1626. Réédition de 1679.

Cordier, Imprimerie Sino-européenne, 155.

Grand in-8. 1 vol., cartonnage. *Nouveau fonds* 4932³.

5443. 博物新編
Po oou sin pien.

Traité de sciences naturelles.

Texte et figures; relatif à la physique et à la cosmographie, à l'histoire naturelle. Par Ho Sin (Hobson?), médecin anglais. Édition de la librairie Me-hai, à Changhai (1855).

3 parties.

Grand in-8. Papier blanc; titre noir sur papier blanc; semble incomplet à la fin. 1 vol., cartonnage. *Nouveau fonds* 4598.

5444. 獅子說
Chi tseu choe.

Du lion.

Avec une figure. Par le P. Luigi Buglio (1606-1682), à propos d'un lion offert à la cour de Chine (1678). Préface de l'auteur.

Cordier, Imprimerie Sino-européenne, 53.

Grand in-8. 1 vol., cartonnage. *Nouveau fonds* 3130.

5445.

Animaux de la Chine.

Peintures sur papier, avec le nom chinois de chaque animal. Au début du volume, note manuscrite: 17 *octobre* 1787. *Reçu de M. Bourgeois missionnaire français à Peking.*

159 feuillets.

Format 0,36 × 0,50. 1 vol., demi-rel., au chiffre de Napoléon III.

Département des Estampes, Oe 152.

5446.

Peintures sur papier de riz, représentant des oiseaux.

25 feuillets.

Format 0,29 × 0,39. 1 vol., couverture soie.

Département des Estampes, Oe 157.

5447.

Oiseaux.

Peintures sur papier de riz, avec quelques noms en chinois.

6 feuillets.

Format 0,31 × 0,24. 1 vol., couverture soie.

Département des Estampes, Oe 155

5448.

Oiseaux.

Peintures sur papier de riz, avec noms en chinois.

10 feuillets.

Format 0,31 × 0,24. 1 vol., cartonnage chinois.

Département des Estampes, Oe 153.

5449.

Oiseaux.

Peintures sur papier de riz.

9 feuillets.

Format 0,31 × 0,25. 1 vol., cartonnage chinois.

Département des Estampes, Oe 154.

5450.

Oiseaux de la Chine.

Oiseaux et plantes; peintures sur papier, avec noms en chinois.

68 feuillets.

Format 0,62 × 0,47. 1 vol., cartonnage européen.

Département des Estampes, Oe 156.

———

5451.

Papillons et Insectes.

Peintures sur papier de riz.

9 feuillets.

Format 0,31 × 0,24. 1 vol., couverture soie.

Département des Estampes, Oe 160 b.

5452.

Papillons.

Peintures sur papier de riz.

9 feuillets.

Format 0,31 × 0,24. 1 vol., cartonnage chinois.

Département des Estampes, Oe 160.

5453.

Papillons.

Peintures sur papier de riz.

11 feuillets.

Format 0,32 × 0,25. 1 vol., cartonnage chinois.

Département des Estampes, Oe 160 a.

5454.

Insectes.

Peintures sur papier de riz.

11 feuillets.

Format 0,31 × 0,25. 1 vol., cartonnage chinois.

Département des Estampes, Oe 159.

5455.

Insectes.

Peintures sur papier de riz.

10 feuillets.

Format 0,31 × 0,25. 1 vol., cartonnage chinois.

Département des Estampes, Oe 159 a.

———

5456.

Peintures sur papier de riz.

Poissons	12 feuillets.
Insectes et divers	12 —

Format 0,29 × 0,39. 1 vol., couverture soie.

Département des Estampes, Oe 162.

5457.

Poissons.

Peintures sur papier de riz.

10 feuillets.

Format 0,32 × 0,24. 1 vol., couverture soie.

Département des Estampes, Oe 163.

5458.

Poissons.

Peintures sur papier de riz, avec noms en chinois.

11 feuillets.

Format 0,32 × 0,24. 1 vol., cartonnage chinois.

Département des Estampes, Oe 163 a.

5459.

Poissons.

Peintures sur papier de riz, avec noms en chinois.

12 feuillets.

Format 0,32 × 0,24. 1 vol., cartonnage chinois.

Département des Estampes, Oe 163 b.

5460.

Poissons.

Peintures sur papier de riz, avec noms en chinois.

12 feuillets.

Format 0,32 × 0,24. 1 vol., cartonnage chinois.

Département des Estampes, Oe 163 c.

5461.

Poissons.

Peintures sur papier de riz, avec noms en chinois.

12 feuillets.

Format 0,32 × 0,24. 1 vol., cartonnage chinois.

Département des Estampes, Oe 163 d.

5462.

Poissons.

Peintures sur papier de riz, avec noms en chinois.

12 feuillets.

Format 0,32 × 0,24. 1 vol., cartonnage chinois.

Département des Estampes, Oe 163 e.

5463.

Poissons.

Peintures sur papier de riz, avec noms en chinois.

10 feuillets.

Format 0,32 × 0,24. 1 vol., cartonnage chinois.

Département des Estampes, Oe 163 f.

5464.

Poissons.

Peintures sur papier de riz, avec noms en chinois.

12 feuillets.

Format 0,32 × 0,24. 1 vol., cartonnage chinois.

Département des Estampes, Oe 163 g.

5465.

Poissons.

Peintures sur papier de riz, avec noms en chinois.

12 feuillets.

Format 0,32 × 0,24. 1 vol., cartonnage chinois.

Département des Estampes, Oe 163 h.

5466.

Poissons.

Peintures sur papier de riz, avec noms en chinois.

12 feuillets.

Format 0,32 × 0,24. 1 vol., cartonnage chinois.

Département des Estampes, Oe 163 i.

5467.

Poissons.

Peintures sur papier de riz, avec noms en chinois.

12 feuillets.

Format 0,32 × 0,24. 1 vol., cartonnage chinois.

Département des Estampes, Oe 163 j.

5468.

Coquilles.

Peintures sur papier de riz, avec noms en chinois.

9 feuillets.

Format 0,32 × 0,24. 1 vol., cartonnage chinois.

Département des Estampes, Oe 164.

5469.

Coquilles.

Peintures sur papier de riz, avec noms en chinois.

12 feuillets.

Format 0,32 × 0,24. 1 vol., cartonnage chinois.

Département des Estampes, Oe 164 a.

5470.

Coquilles.

Peintures sur papier de riz, avec noms en chinois.

12 feuillets.

Format 0,32 × 0,24. 1 vol., cartonnage chinois.

Département des Estampes, Oe 164 b.

5471.

Coquilles.

Peintures sur papier de riz, avec noms en chinois.

11 feuillets.

Format 0,32 × 0,24. 1 vol., cartonnage chinois.

Département des Estampes, Oe 164 c.

5472.

Coquilles.

Peintures sur papier de riz, avec noms en chinois.

12 feuillets.

Format 0,32 × 0,24. 1 vol., cartonnage chinois.

Département des Estampes, Oe 164 d.

5473.

Coquilles.

Peintures sur papier de riz, avec noms en chinois.

12 feuillets.

Format 0,32 × 0,24. 1 vol., cartonnage chinois.

Département des Estampes, Oe 164 e.

5474.

Coquilles.

Peintures sur papier de riz, avec noms en chinois.

12 feuillets.

Format 0,32 × 0,24. 1 vol., cartonnage chinois.

Département des Estampes, Oe 164 f.

5475.

Coquilles.

Peintures sur papier de riz, avec noms en chinois.

12 feuillets.

Format 0,32 × 0,24. 1 vol., cartonnage chinois.

Département des Estampes, Oe 164 g.

5476.

Coquilles.

Peintures sur papier de riz, avec noms en chinois.

12 feuillets.

Format 0,32 × 0,24. 1 vol., cartonnage chinois.

Département des Estampes, Oe 164 h.

5477.

Coquilles.

Peintures sur papier de riz.

12 feuillets.

Format 0,32 × 0,24. 1 vol., couverture soie.

Département des Estampes, Oe 164 i.

5478.

Coquilles.

Peintures sur papier de riz, avec noms en chinois.

12 feuillets.

Format 0,32 × 0,24. 1 vol., cartonnage chinois.

Département des Estampes, Oe 164 j.

5479.

Dessins à l'encre de Chine, quelques-uns avec titres en chinois ; table manuscrite en français. Sur la garde, on lit le nom de Tingqua, qui est celui du dessinateur.

Coquilles et poissons	24 dessins
Soldats et civils	12 —
Oiseaux	12 —
Fruits	12 —
Insectes, plantes	12 —
Industrie de la soie	10 —
Soldats	12 —
Divinités	24 —

118 dessins (59 feuillets doubles).

Format 0,29 × 0,29. 1 vol., cartonnage chinois.

Département des Estampes, Oe 170.

5480-5483. 重鐫二如亭群芳譜

Tchhong tsiuen eul jou thing khiun fang phou.

Recueil relatif aux plantes, nouvelle édition.

Texte principal avec notes; nombreuses citations dont les sources sont indiquées. Par Oang Siang-tsin Tsin-tchhen, surnom Hao-cheng kiu-chi, de Sin-tchheng, docteur en 1604. Préface de l'auteur; préface par Mao Fong-pao, de Hai-yu. Édition du pavillon Ki-kou (XIXᵉ siècle).

4 sections comprenant :

Du ciel	3	livres
De l'année	4	—
Grains comestibles	1	—
Légumes	2	—
Fruits	4	—
Thé et bambous	3	—
Mûrier, chanvre, pueraria phaseoloïdes (ko), urtica nivea (tchou).	1	—
Plantes médicinales	3	—
Arbres	3	—
Fleurs	3	—
Plantes herbacées (hoei)	2	—
Grues et poissons	1	—

Cat. imp., liv. 116, f. 38.

Grand in-8. Titre noir sur jaune. 4 vol., demi-rel., au chiffre de Louis-Philippe. *Nouveau fonds* 41.

5484-5492. 佩文齋廣羣芳譜

Pei oen tchai koang khiun fang phou.

Développement du Khiun fang phou.

Composé par ordre de l'Empereur; préface impériale (1708); dédicace (1708) par Lieou Hao; avertissement. Table formant 2 livres.

(5484), saisons, livres 1 à 6.
(5484), grains comestibles, livres 7 à 10.
(5485), mûrier et chanvre, livres 11 et 12.
(5485), légumes, livres 13 à 17.
(5485), thé, livres 18 à 21.
(5486-5488), fleurs, livres 22 à 53.
(5488-5489), fruits, livres 54 à 67.
(5490-5491), arbres, livres 68 à 81.
(5491), bambous, livres 82 à 86.
(5491-5492), plantes herbacées (hoei), livres 87 à 92.
(5492), plantes médicinales, livres 93 à 100.

Cat. imp., liv. 115, f. 56 (Yu ting koang khiun fang phou).

Petit in-8. 9 vol., demi-rel., au chiffre de Louis-Philippe. *Nouveau fonds* 48.

5493-5496. 植物名實圖攷

Chi oou ming chi thou khao.

Traité des végétaux.

Par Oou Khi-siun, de Kou-chi; publié par Lou Ying-kou, de Mongtseu. Préface par ce dernier (1848). Texte et figures.

38 livres.

In-4. Papier blanc, bonne gravure; couvertures en papier jaune. 4 vol., demi-rel., au chiffre de Napoléon III.
Nouveau fonds 2086 à 2089.

5497-5500. *Chi oou ming chi thou khao.*

Supplément au traité des végétaux.

Texte seul, par le même auteur; publié par Lou Ying-kou.

22 livres.

In-4. Papier blanc, bonne gravure; couvertures en papier jaune. 4 vol., demi-rel., au chiffre de Napoléon III.
Nouveau fonds 2082 à 2085.

5501.

Plantes de la Chine dessinées et peintes par des missionnaires.

Peintures sur papier, avec noms en chinois et quelques explications en français; portant l'indication : tome Ier.

Feuillets cotés de 3 à 132.

Format 0,25 × 0,37. 1 vol., reliure. Département des Estampes, Oe 137.

5502-5503.

Collection de Plantes Vénéneuses de la Chine. Gravées et imprimées en couleur par les Missionnaires Jésuites.

Peintures sur papier comme celles de l'ouvrage précédent.

Tome II : feuillets cotés de 1 à 95.

Tome III : feuillets cotés de 1 à 87; plus, terminant le volume, 13 dessins à la plume, représentant des plantes, avec les noms en latin.

Format 0,25 × 0,37. 2 vol., reliure. Département des Estampes, Oe 137 a, 137 b.

5504.

Recueil de Plantes, Animaux, Travaux et Habillements de la Chine.

Recueil factice comprenant :

Plantes avec légendes	2 estampes européennes, en couleur.
Plantes avec légendes en chinois et en français.	11 peintures chinoises.
Animaux avec légendes en chinois et en français.	4 peintures chinoises.
Plantes, légendes chinoises et françaises	2 peintures chinoises.
Travaux et métiers, légendes en chinois et en français	6 peintures chinoises.
Sujets divers	4 peintures et 1 dessin.

Format 0,32 × 0,37. Sur le premier feuillet, on lit la date de 1779. 1 vol., cartonnage européen.

Département des Estampes, Oe 150.

5505.

Mil et Millet de Chine.

Feuille portant en caractères imitant les caractères d'imprimerie le titre manuscrit :

Kou-Tsée et Kao-Leang ou Mil et Millet.

Peintures sur papier, représentant les feuilles et épis de grandeur naturelle, avec noms chinois et traduction. — A la suite, peinture représentant un vase de fleurs.

3 + 1 planches.

Format 0,63 × 0,71. 1 vol., cartonnage européen.

Département des Estampes, Oe 74.

5506.

Plantes de la Chine.

Titre frontispice en rouge :

Collection précieuse et enluminée des Fleurs les plus belles et les plus curieuses, qui se cultivent tant dans les jardins de la Chine, que dans ceux de l'Europe, dirigée par les soins et sous la conduitte de Mr Buchoz. — Partie Ire Plantes de la Chine peintes dans le Pays. — à Paris, chez Lacombe Libraire rue Christine Et chez l'Auteur rue Hautefeuille.

Cet ouvrage a été fait d'après des peintures chinoises ; pour quelques plantes, le nom chinois a été ajouté à la main ; colorié à la main (1776).

Planches cotées de 1 à 100. — Cordier, Bibl. Sinica, 190.

Format 0,28 × 0,44. 1 vol., reliure
Département des Estampes, Oe 135.

5507-5508.

Plantes de la Chine et du Japon.

Peintures sur papier ; un certain nombre portent les noms en chinois, avec transcription (dialecte cantonais) et traduction française. Ces peintures, montées sur carton, ne sont pas reliées.

53 + 55 planches.

Format 0,42 × 0,50. 2 portefeuilles demi-reliure.

Département des Estampes, Oe 136, 136 a.

5509.

Arbres.

Peintures sur papier de riz. A la garde de l'album, on lit le nom de l'artiste : Sunqua.

12 feuillets.

Format 0,36 × 0,25. 1 vol., couverture soie.

Département des Estampes, Oe 84.

5510.

Arbres divers.

Peintures sur papier de riz, avec noms en chinois et table manuscrite en français.

13

12 feuillets.

Format 0,28 × 0,39. 1 vol., couverture soie.

Département des Estampes, Oe 85.

5511.

Fruits.

Peintures sur papier de riz, avec noms en chinois.

12 feuillets.

Format 0,31 × 0,24. 1 vol., couverture soie.

Département des Estampes, Oe 145.

5512.

Mûriers; Plantes textiles.

Peintures sur papier de riz, avec noms en chinois et table manuscrite en français.

12 feuillets.

Format 0,24 × 0,32. 1 vol., cartonnage chinois.

Département des Estampes, Oe 86.

5513.

Plantes textiles, Mùriers; Arbre à thé; Plante indigofère; Cotonnier.

Peintures sur papier de riz, avec noms en chinois et table manuscrite en français.

12 feuillets.

Format 0,25 × 0,32. 1 vol., cartonnage chinois.

Département des Estampes, Oe 87.

5514.

Fleurs.

Peintures sur papier de riz, avec noms en chinois et table manuscrite en français.

11 feuillets.

Format 0,31 × 0,24. 1 vol., cartonnage chinois.

Département des Estampes, Oe 142.

5515.

Fruits.

Peintures sur papier de riz, avec noms en chinois et table manuscrite en français.

11 feuillets.

Format 0,31 × 0,24. 1 vol., cartonnage chinois.

Département des Estampes, Oe 144.

5516.

Fruits et légumes.

Peintures sur papier de riz, avec noms en chinois et table manuscrite en français.

8 feuillets.

Format 0,31 × 0,24. 1 vol., cartonnage chinois.

Département des Estampes, Oe 143.

5517.

Plantes textiles et diverses espèces de Mûriers.

Dessins à l'encre de Chine avec noms en chinois.

12 dessins (6 feuillets doubles).

Format 0,22 × 0,29. 1 vol., cartonnage chinois.

Département des Estampes, Oe 138.

5518.

Fleurs et Insectes.

Peintures sur taffetas, très soignées.

5o feuillets.

Format o,33 × o,4o. 1 vol., couverture soie.

Département des Estampes, Oe 151 a.

5519.

Fleurs et Oiseaux.

Peintures sur taffetas, très soignées.

5o feuillets.

Format o,33 × o,4o. 1 vol., couverture soie.

Département des Estampes, Oe 151.

5520.

Fleurs, fruits.

Peintures sur papier de riz (fleurs, fruits, insectes).

44 feuillets.

Format o,3o × o,39. 1 vol., couverture soie.

Département des Estampes, Oe 14o.

5521.

Fleurs sur soie.

Peintures sur taffetas.

12 feuillets, montés en paravent.

Format o,25 × o,28. 1 vol., couverture soie.

Département des Estampes, Oe 141.

5522. 李元間先生花卉

Li yuen kien sien cheng hoa hoei.

Fleurs, herbes et oiseaux, par Li Yuen-kien.

Peintures sur taffetas avec titres.

12 feuillets.

Format o,33 × o,4o. 1 vol., couverture soie.

Département des Estampes, Oe 158.

5523.

Peintures sur taffetas (fruits, fleurs, insectes), par Cheou-phing; exécutées à 'Eou-hiang-tsiao, en l'année yi-tchheou (1745 ou 1805?).

12 feuillets montés en paravent.

Format o,19 × o,23. 1 vol., entre deux planchettes.

Département des Estampes, Oe 149.

5524.

Estampes coloriées à la main (plantes, oiseaux, insectes); quelques lignes ou quelques caractères sur chaque feuillet; sans lieu ni date.

Grand in-8, large. Bon nombre de feuillets sont reliés à l'envers. 1 vol., cartonnage.

Nouveau fonds 4914.

Douzième Section : DESSIN ET CALLIGRAPHIE

5525.

Fleurs et fruits.

— I.

十竹齋墨華

Chi tchou tchai me hoa.

Premier recueil du pavillon Chi-tchou.

Estampes imprimées en plusieurs couleurs, d'après divers peintres connus, avec des légendes calligraphiées ; 1ʳᵉ série, écrans. Avertissement écrit au pavillon Oen-yue. Sur la marge extérieure, on lit la date de 1627.

— II.

十竹齋書畫

Chi tchou tchai chou hoa.

Second recueil du pavillon Chi-tchou.

Recueil analogue, peintures diverses avec légendes calligraphiées.

— III.

十竹齋蘭譜

Chi tchou tchai lan phou.

Troisième recueil du pavillon Chi-tchou : fleurs de lan.

Préface écrite par Kiuen-chi chan-jen, à Kin-ling. Règles et modèles pour dessiner les lan, d'après divers auteurs ; quelques modèles sont coloriés.

— IV.

十竹齋翎毛譜

Chi tchou tchai ling mao phou.

Quatrième recueil du pavillon Chi-tchou : animaux.

Préface par Yang Oen-tshong (1627). Modèles, les uns en noir, les autres en couleurs, d'après divers artistes ; légende calligraphiée pour chaque planche.

— V.

十竹齋梅譜

Chi tchou tchai mei phou.

Cinquième recueil du pavillon Chi-tchou : fleurs de prunier.

Par Hou Tcheng-yen Yue-ti, de Hai-yang. Préface par Yu-chan Tong, reliée au milieu du recueil. Modèles, avec légendes calligraphiées, les uns en noir, les autres en couleurs ; d'après divers peintres.

— VI.

十竹齋竹譜

Chi tchou tchai tchou phou.

Sixième recueil du pavillon Chi-tchou : bambous.

Par Hou Tcheng-yen. Conseils et procédés, modèles d'après divers artistes, avec légendes calligraphiées ; partie en noir, partie en couleurs.

— VII.

十竹齋石譜

Chi tchou tchai chi phou.

Septième recueil du pavillon Chi-tchou : rochers.

Modèles, les uns en noir, les autres en couleurs, avec légendes calligraphiées.

— VIII.

十竹齋果譜

Chi tchou tchai koo phou.

Huitième recueil du pavillon Chi-tchou : fruits.

Modèles en couleurs avec légendes calligraphiées. Préface écrite à Kin-ling. Introduction pour la collection des recueils par Lan-hi kiu-chi (1643?)

Format 0,29 × 0,26 ; les feuillets du volume sont dépliés et reliés par la marge extérieure. 1 vol., couverture soie.

Département des Estampes, Oe 139.

5526. # 芥子園畫傳

Kiai tseu yuen hoa tchoan.

Recueil de dessins du jardin Kiai-tseu.

Règles et procédés, modèles ; le dernier livre est en couleurs. Par Oang 'An-tsie, de Sieou-choei ; publié par Li Li-oong, postnom Yu, de Hou-chang. Préface par ce dernier (1679). Notice finale par Tchhen Fou-yao, postnom Hao-tseu, de Oou-lin. Table en tête de chaque livre..

5 livres.

Grand in-8. Titre noir sur jaune. 1 vol., demi-rel., au chiffre ~~de Louis-Philippe~~.
Nouveau fonds 421.

5527. *Kiai tseu yuen hoa tchoan.*

Même ouvrage, planches plus petites ; les cinq tables sont réunies en tête.

Grand in-8. 1 vol., demi-reliure.
Nouveau fonds 1920.

5528. — I.

Kiai tseu yuen hoa tchoan.

Même ouvrage, disposition différente.

Livres 2, 3 et 5.

— II.

二妙。竹譜

Eul miao. Tchou phou.

Recueil de bambous.

Dessins avec de brèves légendes; préface sans nom d'auteur ni date.

Voir plus bas, n° 5590, art. III.

Titre noir sur blanc.

— III.

青在堂花卉翎毛譜

Tshing tsai thang hoa hoei ling mao phou.

Autre titre :

翎毛華卉譜

Ling mao hoa hoei phou.

Recueil d'animaux et de plantes de la salle Tshing-tsai.

Fleurs et oiseaux, modèles et préceptes. Préface par Oang Chi, de Sieou-choei (1701).

Table et texte du livre 1er seul. Grand in-8. Exemplaire cousu par la pliure, à l'européenne. 1 vol., demi-rel., au chiffre de Napoléon III. *Nouveau fonds* 1922.

5529. ## 畫傳二集
Hoa tchoan eul tsi.

Second recueil de dessins du jardin Kiai-tseu.

Ouvrage dû à Oang 'An-tsie, Oang Mi-tshao, Oang Seu-tchi, de Sieou-choei. Préface de 1701. Avertissement par Chen Sin-yeou Yin-po, de Si-ling, pour la pré-

sente réédition faite à Kin-ling, au jardin Kiai-tseu (1800). Table générale.

— I.

青在堂蘭譜

Tshing tsai thang lan phou.

Recueil de lan, de la salle Tshing-tsai.

Modèles et règles; postface par Oang Mei, de Sieou-choei.

2 livres.

Titre noir sur blanc.

— II.

青在堂梅譜

Tshing tsai thang mei phou.

Recueil de fleurs de prunier, de la salle Tshing-tsai.

Règles et modèles, quelques-uns coloriés. Préface (1701) par Yu Tchhoen, de Hiong-tcheou. A la fin, notice par Oang Tchi, de Tong-hai.

2 livres.

Titre noir sur blanc.

— III.

青在堂菊譜

Tshing tsai thang kiu phou.

Autre titre :

鞠 (sic) 譜
Kiu phou.

Recueil de chrysanthèmes, de la salle Tshing-tsai.

Règles et modèles.

2 livres, le 1er en noir, le 2e colorié.

Titre noir sur blanc.

Grand in-8. Titre général noir sur jaune. 1 vol., demi-reliure.
Nouveau fonds 1921.

5530. 畫傳三集

Hoa tchoan san tsi.

Troisième recueil de dessins du jardin Kiai-tseu.

Par Oang 'An-tsie, Oang Mi-tshao et Oang Seu-tchi. Préface (1701), transcrite par Oou Chi-yu, de Sin-'an; le nom de l'auteur est arraché en partie. Table générale. Réédition de Kin-ling.

— I.

草蟲華卉譜

Tshao tchhong hoa hoei phou.

Recueil de fleurs, herbes et insectes.

Règles et modèles. Préface (1701) par Oang Chi, de Sieou-choei. Tables des livres 1 et 2.

Livre 1er seul.

Titre noir sur blanc.

— II.

翎毛華卉譜

Ling mao hoa hoei phou.

Recueil d'animaux et de plantes.

Même ouvrage qu'au n° 5528, art. III.

Table et texte du 1er livre; table du 2e livre.

Titre noir sur blanc.

— III.

畫傳三集卷末

Hoa tchoan san tsi kiuen mo.

Dernier livre du troisième recueil.

Sur la préparation des couleurs; table et texte. A la fin, notice par Chen Sin-yeou Yin-po, de Si-ling.

Grand in-8. Titre général noir sur jaune. 1 vol., cartonnage.
Nouveau fonds 4913.

5531. *Hoa tchoan san tsi.*

Troisième recueil de dessins du jardin Kiai-tseu.

Par Oang 'An-tsie, Oang Mi-tshao et Oang Seu-tchi; réédition de Kin-ling.

— I.

艸虫華卉譜

Tshao tchhong hoa hoei phou.

Recueil de fleurs, herbes et insectes, de la salle Tshing-tsai.

Autre titre :

青在堂花卉草蟲譜

Tshing tsai thang hoa hoei tshao tchhong phou.

Table générale du troisième recueil; table de la section I.

Préfaces (1701) par Oang Tsẹ-hong, de Tchou-tchheng, et par Oang Chi, de Sieou-choei. Modèles et règles.

2 livres.

Titre général noir sur jaune; titre spécial noir sur blanc.

— II.

Hoa tchoan san tsi. Tshao tchhong hoa hoei phou.

Double de l'article précédent.

Titre général noir sur vert, titre spécial noir sur blanc.

— III.

青在堂花卉翎毛譜

Tshing tsai thang hoa hoei ling mao phou.

Autre titre :

翎毛華卉譜

Ling mao hoa hoei phou.

Même ouvrage qu'au n° 5528, art. III. Les modèles du 2ᵉ livre sont coloriés.

2 livres.

Titre noir sur blanc.

Grand in-8. 1 vol., cartonnage.
Nouveau fonds 2336.

5532. ## 芥子園畫傳四集

Kiai tseu yuen hoa tchoan seu tsi.

Quatrième recueil de dessins du jardin Kiai-tseu.

Publication du pavillon Pao-tshing, à Kin-ling. Préface par Yi Mou, surnom Ta-lei kiu-chi (1818). Introduction par Ting Seu-ming Sin-jou.

— I.

寫眞秘訣

Sie tchen pi kiue.

Recueil pour les visages et les personnages.

Conseils et modèles par Ting Kao Ho-tcheou, de Tan-yang. Revu par Keng Oei Yong-tchai et par Yu Tchen Yi-tchhoan, de Tan-yang. Préface non datée par l'auteur.

— II.

仙佛圖。賢俊圖。美人圖

Sien fo thou. Hien tsiun thou. Mei jen thou.

Portraits de divinités. Portraits de héros. Portraits de jolies femmes.

Dessins avec biographie de chaque personnage.

3 livres.

— III.

芥子園圖章會纂

Kiai tseu yuen thou tchang hoei tsoan.

Recueil des sceaux et marques. Par Li Li-oong.

Grand in-8. Titre général noir sur rouge. 1 vol., cartonnage.
Nouveau fonds 3416.

5533.

Leçons de Perspective Imprimées en Chine.

Figures gravées et imprimées en Chine, montées et reliées en Europe. Les planches sont en désordre et semblent appartenir à deux sériès : 1° perspective et géométrie descriptive, figures avec légendes ; 2° dessins d'architecture, sans légendes. Je n'ai trouvé ni titre chinois, ni lieu, ni date.

Format 0,31 × 0,37. Planches reliées par la marge du haut. 1 vol., reliure.
Département des Estampes, Oe 29.

5534.

Harmonie des couleurs.

Nuances dégradées de gris, violet, rouge, jaune, vert ; sans un caractère ni un mot.

1 bande de papier, de 0,19 de hauteur, roulée sur un bâton ; dans 1 étui cartonnage.
Département des Estampes, Oe 169.

5535. 蘇州時樣花譜

Sou tcheou chi yang hoa phou.

Recueil de personnages et de fleurs, de Sou-tcheou.

Sans texte ; publié à la salle Kin-oen.

In-18. Titre noir sur rouge. 1 vol., cartonnage.
Nouveau fonds 2382.

5536. 文圖菁華

Oen phou tsing hoa.

Collection de peintures et de textes.

Trois peintures et trois textes, l'un noir sur bleu, le second blanc sur noir, le troisième noir sur or. Sans date.

6 feuilles taffetas montées sur carton.

Grand in-8. 1 vol. en paravent, dont une partie forme une boîte, couverture soie ; dans 1 étui.
Nouveau fonds 2396.

5537. 筆陣圖

Pi tchen thou.

Enseignement de la calligraphie.

Préceptes et modèles d'après Oang Hi-tchi (321-379). Portrait de ce dernier avec notice au verso.

Petit in-8. Titre noir sur papier teinté,

1 vol., demi-rel., au chiffre de Napoléon III.

Nouveau fonds 1346.

5538. 歷代字法心傳

Li tai tseu fa sin tchoan.

Modèles et préceptes d'après les calligraphes célèbres.

Ouvrage analogue au précédent, d'après Oang Hi-tchi et Oang Yeou Toen-lin, de Song-tshiuen.

Petit in-8. Papier blanc. 1 vol., demi-rel., au chiffre de Napoléon III.

Nouveau fonds 1208.

5539. 清照齋四體書法

Tshing tchao tchai seu thi chou fa.

Modèles d'écriture en caractères de quatre styles, du pavillon Tshing-tchao.

Préface de 1818; autre préface de 1800 par Kien-tshiao; autre préface sans date. Publication du pavillon Tshing-tchao.

— I.

羣仙高會賦

Khiun sien kao hoei fou.

Pièce poétique sur l'assemblée des divinités.

Par Liu Tong-pin. Portant la date de 1807.

— II.

Modèles par séries de quatre caractères, en caractères li et en caractères kiai (carrés modernes). Préparés par Yang Pin-tsi, au pavillon Tshing-tchao.

— III.

雙字類例

Choang tseu lei li.

Liste de caractères doubles.

Caractères li différents, mais ayant des formes analogues.

— IV.

書法摘要善本

Chou fa tche yao chan pen.

Préceptes de l'art d'écrire.

Par Yi Tchen-lien Ta-yeou, de Sin-yu. Exemples et préceptes; citations de divers auteurs.

2 livres.

— V.

王羲之草訣歌

Oang hi tchi tshao kiue ko.

Chanson des caractères tshao (cursifs), de Oang Hi-tchi.

Texte en vers pentasyllabes; formes kiai à côté des formes tshao. Écrit et gravé par Yang Pin-tsi (1814).

— VI.

篆法偏旁諺歌

Tchoan fa phien phang oo ko.

Chanson des caractères tchoan (sigillaires).

Avec la lecture en caractères kiai. Par Li Teng, surnom Jou-tchen lao-jen, de Chang-yuen.

Petit in-8. Papier blanc, titre sur papier rouge. 1 vol., demi-rel., au chiffre de Napoléon III.

Nouveau fonds 1389.

Treizième Section : **ARCHITECTURE**

5540. 唐岱沈源合畫。圓明園四十景

Thang tai chen yuen ho hoa. Yuen ming yuen seu chi king.

Peintures de Thang Tai et Chen Yuen : quarante vues du Yuen-ming yuen (Palais d'été).

Peintures sur taffetas ; légendes descriptives calligraphiées sur taffetas, en regard de chaque peinture. Le premier et le dernier feuillet de chaque livre portent le sceau du Yuen-ming yuen. Sur le dernier feuillet de chaque livre, on lit : peint par ordre impérial par Thang Tai et Chen Yuen à la 9e lune en 1744. La dernière notice du 1er livre est signée par le calligraphe, Oang Yeou-toęn, président du ministère des Travaux ; la dernière notice du 2e livre, composée par l'empereur, est datée de 1744.

2 livres, compris sous la couverture du livre 1er ; les feuillets de chaque livre sont cotés en chinois de 2 à 21.

Format 0,73 × 0,81. Les peintures et notices sont montées sur des cartons recouverts de soie ; disposition en paravent. Couvert de planches en bois dur avec incrustations.

Département des Estampes, Réserve.

5541.

Recueil de paysages et monuments, avec noms en chinois ; formé à l'occasion d'un voyage de l'empereur dans les provinces centrales. Note manuscrite du P. Amiot, datée : à Pe-king, ce 15me septembre 1765.

46 gravures chinoises sur feuillets doubles.

Format 0,18 × 0,27. Semble incomplet. 1 vol. en paravent, couverture soie.

Département des Estampes, Oe 12.

5542.

6 planches de serres chinoises reçues en 1777.

Peintures très fines sur papier ;

feuillets doubles reliés par la pliure.

Format 0,40 × 0,48. 1 vol., cartonnage chinois.

Département des Estampes, Oe 3o.

5543.

Première Partie de l'Essai sur l'Architecture Chinoise.

Titre et notice en français; lettres dessinées à l'imitation des caractères d'imprimerie. Peintures représentant les outils et instruments de l'industrie du bâtiment; divers appareils de construction en pierre; bâtiments. Renvois aux notices placées en regard.

135 peintures sur papier montées et reliées.

Format 0,26 × 0,35. 1 vol., reliure aux armes de Bertin.

Département des Estampes, Oe 13.

5544.

Seconde Partie de l'Essai sur l'Architecture Chinoise.

Suite de l'ouvrage précédent, disposition et exécution semblables. Avertissement, notices, observations finales. Peintures représentant des bâtiments, plans et perspectives.

53 peintures sur papier, montées et reliées.

Format 0,44 × 0,34. 1 vol., reliure aux armes de Bertin.

Département des Estampes, Oe 13 a.

5545.

Plans relatifs à l'Essai sur l'Architecture Chinoise.

3 plans coloriés avec légendes (voir nᵒˢ 5543, 5444).

2 peintures représentant des vases de fleurs.

5 feuillets.

Format 0,52 × 0,63. 1 vol., cartonnage bleu.

Département des Estampes, Oe 15.

5546.

Recueil relatif à l'Architecture Chinoise. Plafonds chinois.

Analogue aux trois albums précédents. Notice en lettres d'imprimerie dessinées; peintures représentant des plafonds et des pavillons.

1 + 2 + 2 feuillets.

Format 0,63 × 0,96. 1 vol., cartonnage bleu.

Département des Estampes, Oe 25.

5547.

Recueil de Tombeaux chinois.

Avertissement; peintures avec titres en chinois; notices explicatives en face de chaque peinture. Le texte français est écrit en lettres dessinées, imitant les caractères d'imprimerie.

2 feuillets et 22 peintures.

Format 0,47 × 0,60. 1 vol., reliure aux armes de Berlin.

Département des Estampes, Oe 27.

5548.

Suite des Tombeaux chinois. Dessins du Tombeau de la Cong Tchou ou Fille de l'Empereur Régnant.

Album analogue ; 2 peintures avec légende.

Format 0,51 × 0,74. 1 vol., cartonnage bleu.

Département des Estampes, Oe 28.

5549.

Haitien. Maison de Plaisance, de l'Empereur de la Chine.

Peintures sur papier, avec noms en chinois : vues et bâtiments du Palais d'été.

40 peintures.

Format 0,38 × 0,32. 1 vol., cartonnage bleu.

Département des Estampes, Oe 21.

5550.

Palais d'Été de l'Empereur de la Chine. Photographies.

Photographies de peintures chinoises sur taffetas. Sans date.

40 photographies.

Format 0,51 × 0,42. 1 vol., cartonnage.

Département des Estampes, Oe 21 a.

5551.

Vue de l'une des maisons de Plaisance de l'Empereur de la Chine, à Yuen-ming-yuen, construites dans le goût Européen.

Note manuscrite : « Ces dessins ont été copiés par des peintres Chinois sur les Peintures originales exécutées par les Missionnaires eux-mêmes à la demande et aux frais de M. Van-Braam Houckgeest, Chef de la Factorerie Hollandaise à Canton en 1794. » — Ces maisons ont été construites par le P. Benoit vers 1750.

19 peintures avec titres chinois et titres français en regard au verso.

Format 0,49 × 0,36. 1 vol., cartonnage chinois.

Département des Estampes, Oe 18.

5552.

Paysages chinois. Tirés des Jardins de l'Empereur, et autres.

4 peintures montées sur toile et réunies en album ; sans aucun texte.

Format 0,63 × 0,67. 1 vol., cartonnage bleu.

Département des Estampes, Oe 26.

5553.

Recueil de Plans, de différents Miao, ou Temples d'Idoles, avec les monastères des Bonzes. Miao et Temples de Bonzes.

5 peintures sur taffetas, avec noms en chinois.

Format 0,64 × 0,53. 1 vol., cartonnage bleu.

Département des Estampes, Oe 17.

5554.

Édifices chinois.

4 peintures collées sur toile ; formant
de grandes feuilles doubles pliées par
le milieu ; reliées du côté de la pliure,
à l'européenne.

Format 0,69 × 0,60. 1 vol., couverture
soie.

Département des Estampes, Oe 23.

5555.

Constructions Chinoises.

4 peintures sur papier, collées sur
toile, montées en album et repliées ;
titres en français.

Format 0,72 × 0,80. 1 vol., couverture soie.

Département des Estampes, Oe 16.

5556.

Arcs de triomphe chinois

11 peintures sur papier, avec titres
en chinois et en français.

Format 0,75 × 0,64. 1 vol., cartonnage bleu.

Département des Estampes, Oe 24.

5557.

Pierres employées pour Orne-
mens, dans les Jardins Chinois.

Peintures très fines sur papier
chinois, montées sur papier euro-

péen avec nom chinois de chaque
objet ; d'une bonne exécution.

42 feuillets.

Format 0,33 × 0,40. 1 vol., cartonnage européen.

Département des Estampes, Oe 44.

5558.

Paysages peints sur papier de
riz, l'un est une vue des factoreries
de Canton avec les pavillons de
chaque nation, France (pavillon
tricolore), États-Unis, Angleterre,
Pays-Bas.

16 peintures.

Format 0,29 × 0,39. 1 vol., couverture chinoise.

Département des Estampes, Oe 33.

5559.

Villes de Chine.

Peintures sur papier de riz avec
noms : vues de Macao, Canton,
Bogue, Wampoa, Hongkong.

5 peintures.

Format 0,34 × 0,26. 1 vol., couverture
soie.

Département des Estampes, Oe 32.

5560.

Sujets divers.

Dessins à l'encre de Chine avec
noms en chinois ; table manuscrite
en français.

Bâtiments de bonzerie (quelques-uns sont de Hai-tchhoang-seu). 14 dessins

Divinités. 2 —

Industries de la porcelaine et du laque. 14 —

Divinités. 10 —

Culture des céréales. 10 —

Divinités. 4 —

Culture et porte monumentale. 2 —

Divinités. 8 —

Lanternes de procession. 12 —

Poissons, coquilles. 24 —

Procession du dragon. 12 dessins

Industrie du coton. 8 —

60 feuillets doubles.

Format 0,29 × 0,30. 1 vol., cartonnage chinois.

Département des Estampes, Oe 171.

5561.

Paysages chinois.

3 peintures sur papier.

Format 0,29 × 0,28. 1 cahier.
Département des Estampes, Oe 31.

Quatorzième Section : MUSIQUE

5562. — I.

琴 譜 大 全

Khin phou ta tshiuen.

Recueil de mélodies pour le khin.

Par Tchheng Yun-ki Yu-chan, de Sin-'an ; publié par son frère Yun-phei King-chan, à la salle Tsiu-kin. Préface de l'auteur (1705). Préface par Hou Siun-long Yuen-chan, de Hoa-thing. Mélodies notées.

6 livres.

— II.

誠 一 堂 琴 談

Tchheng yi thang khin than.

Traité de khin, de la salle Tchheng-yi.

Par les mêmes. Théorie musicale, historique, lecture des caractères, conseils pour l'exécution.

2 livres. — Cat. imp., liv. 114, f. 30.

Grand in-8. Titre noir sur jaune. 1 vol., demi-rel., au chiffre de la République Française.
Nouveau fonds 266.

Quinzième Section : MÉTIERS

5563. # 天 工 開 物

Thien kong khai oou.

Traités des industries diverses.

Par Song Ying-sing, de Fong-sin ; préface de l'auteur (1637). Texte avec figures nombreuses : nourriture, vêtement, condiments, terre cuite, fer, voitures et bateaux, métaux, armes, pierres précieuses, etc.

18 livres en 3 sections.

Grand in-8. 1 vol., demi-rel., au chiffre de Louis-Philippe (prov. des Missions Étrangères).

Fourmont 359.

5564. 宋先生著天工開物

Song sien cheng tchou thien kong khai oou.

Traité des industries diverses, de Song Ying-sing.

Même ouvrage; la préface est reproduite mais sans date. Texte avec figures.

3 sections.

Petit in-8. Titre noir sur blanc; édition commune. 1 vol., demi-rel., au chiffre de Louis-Philippe.

Fourmont 360.

————————

5565·5567.

Professions diverses.

Dessins à l'encre de Chine portant des titres en chinois.

360 dessins (180 feuillets doubles).

Format 0,30 × 0,30. 3 vol., couvertures soie.

Département des Estampes, Oe 128, 129, 130.

————————

5568. 景德鎮陶錄

King te tchen thao lou.

Traité de la porcelaine de King-te-tchen.

Historique et procédés; nombreuses illustrations. Par Lan Phou Pin-nan, de Tchhang-nan; complété par Tcheng Thing-koei Oen-kou. Préface (1815) par Lieou Ping, de Koang-te. Édition de la salle Yi-king.

10 livres.

Grand in-8. Bonne impression sur papier blanc; titre noir sur jaune. 1 vol., demi-rel., au chiffre de Louis-Philippe.

Nouveau fonds 910.

————————

5569.

Porcelaine.

Peintures sur papier de riz avec une table manuscrite en français : fabrication de la porcelaine.

12 feuillets.

Format 0,24 × 0,31. 1 vol., couverture soie.

Département des Estampes, Oe 106.

5570.

Peintures sur papier de riz représentant la fabrication de la porcelaine ; table manuscrite en français.

11 feuillets.

In-4. 1 vol., demi-reliure.

Nouveau fonds 1846.

5571.

Porcelaine.

Dessins à l'encre de Chine, avec titres chinois ; table manuscrite en français.

12 dessins (6 feuillets doubles). — Comparer n° 5437.

Format 0,22 × 0,28. 1 vol., cartonnage chinois.

Département des Estampes, Oe 107.

5572.

Verre.

Peintures sur papier de riz, avec titres en chinois ; table manuscrite en français : fabrication du verre.

12 feuillets.

Format 0,24 × 0,31. 1 vol., cartonnage chinois.

Département des Estampes, Oe 108.

5573.

Verre.

Dessins à l'encre de Chine, avec titres en chinois et table manuscrite en français.

12 dessins (6 feuillets doubles). — Comparer n° 5437.

Format 0,22 × 0,28. 1 vol., cartonnage chinois.

Département des Estampes, Oe 109.

5574.

Art de faire le papier à la Chine.

Peintures avec titres chinois et européens ; l'album porte la note suivante : Les explications ont été envoyées en 1775 à M. de la Tour, par le P. Benoist, missionnaire Jésuite mort à Pékin.

27 feuillets.

Format 0,35 × 0,52. 1 vol., couverture soie.

Département des Estampes, Oe 110.

5575.

Fabrication du Papier.

Peintures sur papier, avec texte chinois manuscrit en regard de chacune ; chaque notice est signée d'un nom différent.

24 peintures.

Format 0,37 × 0,35. 1 vol., couverture soie.

Département des Estampes, Oe 111.

5576.

Papier.

Peintures sur papier de riz, avec titres chinois et table manuscrite en français.

12 feuillets.

Format 0,24 × 0,31. 1 vol., cartonnage chinois.

Département des Estampes, Oe 112.

5577.

Papier.

Dessins à l'encre de Chine, avec titres chinois et table manuscrite en français.

14

12 dessins (6 feuillets doubles). — Comparer n° 5437.

Format 0,23 × 0,29. 1 vol., cartonnage chinois.

Département des Estampes, Oe 113.

5578.

Encre de Chine. Fabrication.

Peintures sur papier de riz, avec titres chinois et table manuscrite en français.

12 feuillets.

Format 0,24 × 0,31. 1 vol., cartonnage chinois.

Département des Estampes, Oe 122.

5579.

Encre de Chine.

Dessins à l'encre de Chine, avec titres chinois traduits en anglais ; table manuscrite en français.

12 dessins (6 feuillets doubles). — Comparer n° 5437.

Format 0,22 × 0,28. 1 vol., cartonnage chinois.

Département des Estampes, Oe 123.

5580.

Vernis.

Peintures sur papier, avec légendes en français.

15 feuillets.

Format 0,34 × 0,43. 1 vol., couverture soie.

Département des Estampes, Oe 121.

5581.

Céruse et vermillon.

Dessins à l'encre de Chine, titres chinois avec traduction française manuscrite.

12 dessins (6 feuillets doubles).

Format 0,23 × 0,29. 1 vol., cartonnage chinois.

Département des Estampes, Oe 120.

5582.

Charbon de terre ou houille.

Peintures sur papier de riz, avec titres chinois et table manuscrite en français.

12 feuillets.

Format 0,24 × 0,32. 1 vol., cartonnage chinois.

Département des Estampes, Oe 116.

5583.

Charbon de terre.

Dessins à l'encre de Chine, avec titres chinois et européens.

12 dessins (6 feuillets doubles). — Comparer n° 5437.

Format 0,22 × 0,29. 1 vol., cartonnage chinois.

Département des Estampes, Oe 115.

5584. 炭稿
Than kao.

Houille.

Dessins à l'encre de Chine, avec

titres et légendes en chinois; traduction française.

24 dessins.

Format 0,30 × 0,30. 1 vol., cartonnage chinois.

Département des Estampes, Oe 117.

5585.

Fer.

Peintures sur papier de riz; titres en chinois, table manuscrite en français.

12 feuillets.

Format 0,33 × 0,24. 1 vol., couverture soie.

Département des Estampes, Oe 119.

5586.

Fer.

Peintures sur papier de riz; titres en chinois, table manuscrite en français.

12 feuillets.

Format 0,25 × 0,32. 1 vol., cartonnage chinois.

Département des Estampes, Oe 118.

5587.

Fer.

Dessins à l'encre de Chine, avec titres en chinois et table manuscrite en français.

12 dessins (6 feuillets doubles). — Comparer n° 5437.

Format 0,22 × 0,29. 1 vol., cartonnage chinois.

Département des Estampes, Oe 114.

5588. — I.

銀經發秘

Yin king fa pi.

Traité des alliages et falsification de l'argent.

Par Liang Seu-tsẹ 'En-ta, de Choẹn-tẹ. Préface de l'auteur (1844). Texte et figures nombreuses.

2 livres.

— II.

紫府太微仙君功過格

Tseu fou thai oei sien kiun kong koo ko.

Traité des mérites et des fautes.

Extrait d'un ouvrage taoïste. Planches à la salle Chi-hoo, à Fochan.

Voir plus bas, n°s 5677, art. XXI, et autres.

In-18. Titre noir sur jaune. 1 vol., demi-rel., au chiffre de Napoléon III. *Nouveau fonds* 2003.

Seizième Section : COUTUMES, COSTUME, MOBILIER, ETC.

5589. — I.

無雙譜

Oou choang phou.

Recueil sans égal.

Portraits de quarante personnages célèbres, des Han aux Song; quarante autres dessins accompagnés de poésies. Par maître Kin, de Nan-ling. Préface sans auteur ni date.

Papier blanc ; titre noir sur blanc.

— II.

官子譜

Koan tseu phou.

Traité du jeu de dames (oei khi).

Planches représentant des parties, sans texte. Préface non signée ni datée.

Papier blanc, titre noir sur blanc.

III.

東坡遺意

Tong pho yi yi.

Pensées de Tong-pho.

Reproduction d'autographes de Liang Khi et de Kou Tcheou, de la fin des Ming. Postface de 1660, non signée.

Papier blanc, titre noir sur blanc. Grand in-8. 1 vol., demi-reliure. *Nouveau fonds* 1925.

5590. 賞奇軒四種合編

Chang khi hien seu tchong ho pien.

Quatre ouvrages de la maison Chang-khi.

— I.

Oou choang phou.

Même ouvrage qu'au n° 5589, art. I, édition plus grande ; sans préface.

Titre noir sur blanc.

— II.

Tong pho yi yi.

Comme au n° 5589, art. III ; planches plus petites. En outre une préface non signée ni datée, qui appartient à l'article suivant.

Titre noir sur blanc.

— III.

二妙

Eul miao.

Sous-titre :

竹譜

Tchou phou.

Recueil de bambous.

Même recueil qu'au n° 5528, art. II ; planches différentes, sans préface. Accompagné de la préface de l'art. I ci-dessus.

Papier blanc, titre noir sur blanc.

— IV.

Koan tseu phou.

Même ouvrage qu'au n° 5589, art. II. Planches plus petites.

Titre noir sur blanc.

In-4. Titre noir sur rose, 1 vol. demi-rel., au chiffre de Louis-Philippe.

Nouveau fonds 2315.

5591-5592.

Les Rues de Pékin.

Peintures chinoises montées sur papier européen ; pour chaque planche, titre chinois et titre français, celui-ci en lettres d'imprimerie dessinées. Quelques planches portant des notes manuscrites extraites des Costumes de la Chine, in-4, Londres, 1800 (the Costume of China, illustrated by Sixty Engravings : with Explanations in English and French. By George Henry Mason... Voir Cordier, Bibl. Sinica, 850, 851).

193 + 193 planches.

Format 0,31 × 0,29. Reliure aux armes de Bertin ; tranches dorées. 2 vol.

Département des Estampes, Oe 55, 55 a.

5593.

Vie d'un Chinois.

Dessins à l'encre de Chine représentant les principales scènes de la vie, depuis la naissance jusqu'à la mise en bière ; avec titres chinois et français.

12 dessins (6 feuillets doubles).

Format 0,36 × 0,28. 1 vol., cartonnage chinois.

Département des Estampes, Oe 66.

5594.

Personnages de distinction et Habitants des Provinces.

Dessins à l'encre de Chine, avec titres en chinois et table manuscrite en français.

24 feuillets simples.

Format 0,21 × 0,29. 1 vol., cartonnage chinois.

Département des Estampes, Oe 64.

5595.

Peintures sur papier de riz représentant des personnages.

24 feuillets.

Format 0,29 × 0,39. 1 vol., cartonnage chinois.

Département des Estampes, Oe 50.

5596.

Peintures représentant des personnages, non reliées.

48 feuillets.

Format 0,51 × 0,41. 1 vol., couverture soie.

Département des Estampes, Oe 54.

5597.

Peintures sur papier de riz, représentant des soldats et des femmes.

12 + 12 feuillets.

Format 0,29 × 0,39. 1 vol., couverture soie.

Département des Estampes, Oe 126.

5598.

Femmes chinoises.

Peintures sur papier de riz, avec titres chinois et table manuscrite en français ; très finement exécutées.

12 feuillets.

Format 0,23 × 0,33. 1 vol., couverture soie.

Département des Estampes, Oe 124.

5599.

Musique chinoise.

Autre titre :

Instruments de musique employés en Chine.

Peintures sur papier de riz, représentant des musiciens et des musiciennes ; titres en chinois, table manuscrite en français.

9 feuillets.

Format 0,31 × 0,23. 1 vol., couverture soie.

Département des Estampes, Oe 125.

5600.

Peintures sur papier de riz.

Personnages	13 feuillets.
Oiseaux	2 feuillets.
Bateaux	3 feuillets.

Format 0,22 × 0,28. 1 vol., couverture soie.

Département des Estampes, Oe 52.

5601.

Personnages de distinction. Dames nobles. Musiciennes.

Dessins à l'encre de Chine, titres en chinois et table manuscrite en français.

24 dessins (12 feuillets doubles).

Format 0,21 × 0,29. 1 vol., cartonnage chinois.

Département des Estampes, Oe 63.

5602.

Personnages de distinction. Dames nobles et Musiciennes.

Dessins à l'encre de Chine, avec titres en chinois et table manuscrite en français.

24 dessins (12 feuillets doubles).

Format 0,21 × 0,29. 1 vol., cartonnage chinois.

Département des Estampes, Oe 65.

5603.

Professions diverses. Musiciennes.

Dessins à l'encre de Chine, avec

titres en chinois et table manuscrite en français.

36 dessins (18 feuillets doubles).

Format 0,23 × 0,30. 1 vol., cartonnage chinois.

Département des Estampes, Oe 133.

5604.

Opium et occupations des dames chinoises.

Dessins à l'encre de Chine, avec titres en chinois et table manuscrite en français.

24 feuillets simples. — Comparer n° 5437.

Format 0,36 × 0,28. 1 vol., cartonnage chinois.

Département des Estampes, Oe 67.

5605.

Femmes chinoises (Jeux, amusements et occupations).

Dessins à l'encre de Chine, avec titres en chinois et table manuscrite en français.

24 feuillets simples.

Format 0,21 × 0,29. 1 vol., cartonnage chinois.

Département des Estampes, Oe 62.

5606.

Professions et amusements.

Dessins à l'encre de Chine, avec titres en chinois et table manuscrite en français; recueil paraissant relatif à la province du Foukien.

24 dessins (12 feuillets doubles).

Format 0,22 × 0,29. 1 vol., cartonnage chinois.

Département des Estampes, Oe 134.

5607.

Professions et jeux.

Dessins à l'encre de Chine, avec titres en chinois et table manuscrite en français.

24 feuillets.

Format 0,30 × 0,23. 1 vol., cartonnage chinois.

Département des Estampes, Oe 132.

5608.

Costumes Chinois. Marchans. Gens du Peuple et quelques autres. Instruments, Vases et Meubles.

Peintures sur papier.

Personnages	46 feuillets
Instruments divers	23 —

Format 0,29 × 0,41. 1 vol., couverture soie.

Département des Estampes, Oe 53.

5609.

Peintre chinois. Boutiques de Pékin.

Peintures sur papier représentant des scènes diverses.

36 feuillets.

Format 0,39 × 0,39. 1 vol., recouvert en soie européenne.

Département des Estampes, Oe 22.

5610.

Dessins à l'encre de Chine représentant des boutiques et diverses scènes, avec titres en français.

12 feuillets.

Format 0,35 × 0,27. 1 vol., cartonnage chinois.

Département des Estampes, Oe 127.

5611.

Peintures sur taffetas représentant des paysages avec personnages; quelques scènes dans des comptoirs européens.

50 feuillets.

Format 0,34 × 0,38. 1 vol., couverture soie.

Département des Estampes, Oe 104.

5612.

Peintures sur papier, représentant des paysages et des scènes populaires.

26 feuillets.

Format 0,32 × 0,39. 1 vol., couverture soie.

Département des Estampes, Oe 105.

———

5613.

Bateaux.

Peintures sur papier de riz, avec titres chinois.

9 feuillets.

Format 0,31 × 0,24. 1 vol., cartonnage chinois.

Département des Estampes, Oe 38 a.

5614.

Bateaux.

Peintures sur papier de riz, avec titres chinois.

13 feuillets.

Format 0,31 × 0,24. 1 vol., couverture soie.

Département des Estampes, Oe 38.

5615.

Bateaux et poissons.

Dessins à l'encre de Chine, avec table manuscrite en français.

Bateaux, avec noms en
　chinois,　　　　　　　12 feuillets
Poissons,　　　　　　　12　—

24 feuillets simples.

Format 0,30 × 0,23. 1 vol., cartonnage chinois.

Département des Estampes, Oe 161.

———

5616.

Instruments, meubles, armes.

Dessins à l'encre de Chine avec noms chinois et numérotage en chiffres arabes, correspondant à une table manuscrite en français. Album provenant de Canton.

598 dessins sur 72 feuillets doubles.

Format 0,30 × 0,22. 1 vol., couverture soie.

Département des Estampes, Oe 36.

5617.

Album analogue paraissant être un calque du premier ; les feuillets sont dans un ordre différent et débutent à gauche, à l'européenne.

5g8 dessins sur 72 feuillets doubles.

Petit in-8 large. 1 vol., demi-reliure. *Nouveau fonds* 2014.

5618.

Vêtements, chars, instruments de musique ; dessins, avec nom en français écrit de la main du P. Amiot auprès de chaque objet.

4 feuillets à encadrement.

In-folio large. 1 vol., cartonnage. *Nouveau fonds* 5037.

5619.

Agraffes de Ceinture et boucles pour les Bourses, etc.

Peintures très fines sur papier.

20 feuillets.

Format 0,30 × 0,32. 1 vol., reliure aux armes de Bertin.
Département des Estampes, Oe 45.

5620.

Peintures sur papier de riz.

Objets d'ameublement,		
bibelots	12	feuillets
Bateaux	12	—

Format 0,29 × 0,3g. 1 vol., couverture soie.
Département des Estampes, Oe 37.

5621.

Ameublement.

11 peintures sur papier de riz.

Format 0,31 × 0,23. 1 vol., couverture soie.
Département des Estampes, Oe 35.

5622.

Vases anciens, et diverses porcelaines de Chine.

Peintures très fines sur papier chinois, montées sur papier européen. Au début du volume (à gauche, à l'européenne), notice manuscrite en français sans signature ni date. En haut du feuillet 1, on lit : Collection de vases anciens, au nombre de 53 ; reçue en 1777. Sur chaque feuillet, nom chinois de l'objet.

Vases	53	feuillets
Jades	11	—
Vases de porcelaine	7	—

Format 0,37 × 0,36. 1 vol., cartonnage européen.
Département des Estampes, Oe 42.

5623.

Théières et Vases à boire, usités chez les Chinois.

Peintures analogues et montées de même ; en grandes feuilles doubles reliées par la pliure.

6 feuillets.

Format 0,34 × 0,33. 1 vol., cartonnage européen.
Département des Estampes, Oe 43.

5624.

Vases usités en Chine pour faire chauffer les aliments.

Peintures analogues et montées de même.

33 feuillets.

Format 0,32 × 0,34. 1 vol., cartonnage européen.

Département des Estampes, Oe 41.

5625.

Fourneaux chinois.

Peintures analogues, avec le nom de chaque modèle.

32 feuillets.

Format 0,36 × 0,39. 1 vol., cartonnage européen.

Département des Estampes, Oe 41 a.

5626.

Pots à Fleurs, et Vases Chinois.

Peintures analogues.

Vases vides	60 feuillets
Vases avec des plantes; à côté de chacun, on lit le nom du vase et de la disposition des plantes	13 —

Une dernière série de 21 feuillets est formée d'estampes imprimées en couleurs ou coloriées à la main, dont quelques-unes portent des légendes; elles représentent des vases avec des fleurs.

Format 0,29 × 0,45. 1 vol., cartonnage chinois.

Département des Estampes, Oe 40.

5627.

Bouquets.

24 peintures sur papier de riz.

Format 0,29 × 0,39. 1 vol., couverture soie.

Département des Estampes, Oe 146.

5628-5631.

Chine. Costumes et Mœurs. Corée. Thibet.

Recueil factice de pièces collées, montées et reliées, renfermant des gravures de toutes provenances, anciennes et modernes, des estampes en couleurs, des photographies, des peintures sur papier de riz et sur taffetas, des fragments d'imprimés, etc.; les pièces les plus récentes datent de la guerre sino-japonaise. A noter, dans le vol. Oe 47 b :

— I.

大清嘉慶二十五年四
季春牛圖

Ta tshing kia khing eul chi oou nien seu ki tchhoen nieou thou.

Calendrier des quatre saisons et figure du bœuf du printemps pour 1820.

1 feuille coloriée.

— II.

大清嘉慶二十五年新春得意圖

Ta tshing kia khing eul chi oou nien sin tchhoẹn tẹ yi thou.

Figure du printemps nouveau pour 1820.

1 feuille coloriée.

Format 0,53 × 0,63. 4 vol., demi-rel., au chiffre de Napoléon III.

Département des Estampes, Oe 47, 47 a, 47 b, 47 c.

5632.

Chine. Costumes et Mœurs. Ornements, etc.

Recueil factice de peintures, estampes coloriées, etc.

Personnages	14 feuillets
Scènes diverses (entre autres fragments du n° 5394)	21 —
Oiseaux, fleurs	20 —

1 pou-tseu civil en soie brodée (plastron et dos) 1 feuillet

Format 0,53 × 0,63. 1 vol., demi-rel., au chiffre de Napoléon III.

Département des Estampes, Oe 46.

5633.

Livre de desseins chinois, tirés d'après des originaux de Perse, des Indes, de la Chine et du Japon, dessinés et gravés en taille-douce par le Sr Fraisse, Peintre de S. A. S. Monseigneur le Duc..... Paris 1735.

Dédicace de Fraisse. Privilège. 53 planches sans titres ni légendes.

Format 0,38 × 0,49. 1 vol., reliure aux armes de France.

Département des Estampes, Oe 147.

5634.

4 peintures sur papier de riz.

Format 0,24 × 0,31. 1 vol., couverture soie.

Département des Estampes, Oe 101.

Dix-septième Section : JEUX, ETC.

5635. 進呈鷹論

Tsin tchheng ying loẹn.

Opuscule sur les faucons offerts à l'Empereur.

Petit traité de fauconnerie, par le P. Luigi Buglio (1606-1682).

Cordier, Imprimerie Sino-européenne, 74.

Grand in-8. Papier blanc. 1 vol., cartonnage.

Nouveau fonds 3412.

5636. *Tsin tchheng ying loẹn.*

Double.

Grand in-8. Papier teinté. 1 vol., cartonnage (prov. de la Société de Jésus).
Nouveau fonds 3411.

5637. *Tsin tchheng ying loẹn.*

Double.

Grand in-8. 1 vol., cartonnage (prov.
de la Société de Jésus).
Nouveau fonds 4901.

5638. 適情雅趣
Tchi tshing ya tshiu.

Autre titre :

陳搏百局
Tchhen thoan po kiu.

Cent parties d'échec, par
Tchhen Thoan.

Auteur : surnom Hi-yi († 989).
Règles du jeu ; figure et explication
de coups célèbres, chacun ayant
une dénomination particulière.
Édition de la salle Yong-hien.

8 livres.

In-18. Titre noir sur jaune. 1 vol.,
demi-rel., au chiffre de Louis-Philippe.
Nouveau fonds 1089.

5639. — I.

馬吊譜
Ma tiao phou.

Règles d'un jeu.

Par Si-hou yi-seou.

Titre noir sur papier teinté ; bonne
impression.

— II.

精選名家十番清曲譜
*Tsing siuen ming kia chi fan
tshing khiu phou.*

Recueil de chansons.

Poésies et musique notée pour
flûte.

Petit in-8. 1 vol., cartonnage du
XVIIIe siècle, intitulé : *Tractatus de
ludo* (prov. des Missions Étrangères).
Fourmont 351.

5640. 雄拳折法
Hiong khiuen tchẹ fa.

Autre titre :

雄拳演法
Hiong khiuen yen fa.

Exercices de boxe, haltères,
etc.

Traité par Kao Hing-fang ; texte
très court et figures. Impression
grossière de la salle Han-king, à
Canton.

2 sections.

Petit in-8. Titre noir sur rouge et titre
noir sur papier teinté. 1 vol., cartonnage.
Nouveau fonds 2333.

5641. 新雄拳拆法
Sin hiong khiuen tchẹ fa.

Même ouvrage, réédition plus grossière, de la salle Kin-oen.

Petit in-8. Titre noir sur rouge. 1 vol., cartonnage.
Nouveau fonds 2334.

5642. 七巧圖解
Tshi khiao thou kiai.

Livre des sept fragments merveilleux.

Sorte de jeu de casse-tête; figures indiquant la disposition des sept fragments; figures correspondantes avec leurs noms. Publié au pavillon Thing-yu (1816).

2 sections.

In-18. Papier blanc; titre noir sur blanc et titre noir sur jaune. 1 vol., demi-rel., au chiffre de la République Française.
Nouveau fonds 3627.

5643. 七巧新譜
Tshi khiao sin phou.

Nouveau livre des sept fragments merveilleux.

Planche initiale représentant les sept fragments et donnant leurs noms; figures combinées avec noms; figures indiquant la disposition des fragments. Préface (1813) par Sang hia kho. Réédition de la salle Fou-oen et du pavillon Tchhoen-yu (1823).

2 sections.

In-18. Titre noir sur jaune et titre noir sur papier teinté. 1 vol., cartonnage.
Nouveau fonds 3402.

5644. *Tshi khiao sin phou.*

Double.

In-18. 1 vol., demi-reliure.
Nouveau fonds 1969.

5645. *Tshi khiao sin phou.*

Double.

In-18. 1 vol., cartonnage.
Nouveau fonds 3403.

5646. *Tshi khiao sin phou.*

Double.

In-18. 1 vol., cartonnage.
Nouveau fonds 4900^1.

5647. *Tshi khiao sin phou.*

Double.

In-18. 1 vol., cartonnage.
Nouveau fonds 4900^2.

5648. *Tshi khiao sin phou.*

Double.

In-18. 1 vol., cartonnage.
Nouveau fonds 4900^3.

5649.

Même ouvrage, sans titre; figures sans un seul caractère.

2 sections.

In-18. 1 vol., cartonnage.
Nouveau fonds 2400.

5650.

Double, seconde section seule (morceaux disposés en figures).

In-18. 1 vol., cartonnage.
Nouveau fonds 4569.

5651. — I.

古今秘苑

Kou kin pi yuen.

Jardin des recettes.

Recettes usuelles pour la calligraphie, le dessin, l'élevage des poissons rouges, la capture des serpents, la préparation de l'eau-de-vie, la cuisine, la lessive, la confection des antidotes, etc. Recueillies par Mẹ-mo tchou-jen ; éditées (1846?) à la salle Hoan-oen.

15 livres.

— II.

古今秘苑續錄

Kou kin pi yuen siu lou.

Suite au Jardin des recettes.

13 livres.

In-18. Titre noir sur jaune. 1 vol., demi-rel., au chiffre de Louis-Philippe.
Nouveau fonds 780.

5652. 新鍥全補(*sic*)天下四民利用便觀五車拔錦

Sin khie tshiuen pou thien hia seu min li yong pien koan oou tchhẹ pa kin.

Encyclopédie de la vie pratique.

Ouvrage rangé par ordre méthodique ; divisé en deux séries de textes qui occupent l'une la moitié supérieure, l'autre la moitié inférieure des pages ; modèles de suppliques, calcul, lutte, tir à l'arc, cuisine, médecine : texte avec figures.

Livres 24 et 20.

Grand in-8, large. Les feuillets sont dépliés et reliés par la marge extérieure. 1 vol., reliure en parchemin armorié.
Nouveau fonds 2741.

5653. 衛濟餘編

Oei tsi yu pien.

Encyclopédie de la vie pratique.

Médecine, cuisine, jeux, etc.

Livres 6 à 18.

In-18. 1 vol., demi-reliure.
Nouveau fonds 1967.

Dix-huitième Section : SCIENCES EUROPÉENNES, APPLICATIONS.

5654. 泰西水法

Thai si choei fa.

Sur les machines hydrauliques.

Par le P. Sabatthinus de Ursis (1575-1620), avec la collaboration de Siu Koang-khi ; publié par les soins de Li Tchi-tsao, de Oou-lin. Préfaces par Tshao Yu-phien, de

Ho-tong (1592); par Pheng Oei-tchheng, de Liu-ling (1592); par Siu Koang-khi, de Oou-song (1592); par Tcheng Yi-oei, de Chang-jao. Note sur l'hydraulique par l'auteur (1592). Liste des personnes qui ont surveillé l'impression. Cet ouvrage a été aussi inséré dans le Nong tcheng tshiuen chou (n°ˢ 5369-5371).

5 livres $+$ 1 livre de figures. — Cat. imp., liv. 102, f. 9. — Cordier, Imprimerie Sino-européenne, 314.

Grand in-8. 1 vol., cartonnage (prov. de la Société de Jésus).
Nouveau fonds 3209.

5655. *Thai si choei fa.*

Double.

Petit in-8. 1 vol., cartonnage.
Nouveau fonds 3210.

5656. 記法

Ki fa.

Traité de mnémotechnie.

Publié par les PP. Alfonso Vagnoni (1566-1640) et Francesco Sambiaso (1582-1649), avec l'autorisation du P. Emmanuel Diaz (1574-1659). Préface par Tchou Yu-hoan, de Tong-yong, à l'église catholique dite King-kiao-thang. Auteur : le P. Matteo Ricci (1552-1610).

Grand in-8. Gravure grossière, 1 vol.,

cartonnage (prov. de la Société de Jésus).
Nouveau fonds 3089.

5657. 遠鏡說

Yuen king choe.

Des lunettes d'approche.

Texte avec nombreuses figures. Par le P. Adam Schall (1591-1666), désigné par le nom chinois de Thang Jo-oang. Préface de l'auteur (1626).

Cordier, Imprimerie Sino-européenne, 272.

Grand in-8. Papier blanc. 1 vol., demi-rel., au chiffre de Napoléon III.
Nouveau fonds 2122.

5658. *Yuen king choe.*

Double sur papier teinté.

Cordier, Imprimerie Sino-européenne, 272.

Grand in-8. 1 vol., cartonnage.
Nouveau fonds 3383.

5659. *Yuen king choe.*

Même ouvrage. A la fin de la préface, le nom chinois du P. Schall est Thang Jou-oang, au lieu de Thang Jo-oang.

Cordier, Imprimerie Sino-européenne, 272.

Grand in-8. Exemplaire incomplet, relié en désordre. 1 vol., cartonnage du XVIIIᵉ siècle, portant le titre : *Tractatio de specillis longe prospicientibus.*
Fourmont 349.

5660. *Yuen king choe.*

Même ouvrage, édition plus grande, sans préface ; l'auteur est nommé Thang Jou-oang.

Cordier, Imprimerie Sino-européenne, 272.

Grand in-8. 1 vol., cartonnage (prov. de la Société de Jésus).
Nouveau fonds 3382.

5661. 遠 西 奇 器 圖 說
Yuen si khi khi thou choe.

Mémoire sur les instruments (mécaniques) des Européens.

Texte et figures. Par le P. Jean Terenz (1576-1630) ; rédigé par Oang Tcheng, du Koan-si. Préface (1627) par Oang Tcheng, surnom Liao-yi tao-jen, de King. Autre préface par Oang Ying-khoei, de Sin-'an. Postface (1628) par Oou Oei-tchong.

3 livres. — Cordier, Imprimerie Sino-européenne, 301.

Grand in-8. Incomplet à la fin du 3ᵉ livre. 1 vol., cartonnage.
Nouveau fonds 3384.

5662. 驗 氣 圖 說
Yen khi thou choe.

Figure et traité du baromètre.

Par le P. Ferdinand Verbiest (1623-1688) ; revu par Tchou Chi,

de Lan-khi, Fong Oen-tchhang, de Tshien-thang, Tcheou Tchi, de Tchhang-tcheou. A la fin du texte, on lit la date de 1671.

Cordier, Imprimerie Sino-européenne, 344.

Grand in-8. Titre noir sur papier teinté ; au verso figure du baromètre. 1 vol., cartonnage.
Nouveau fonds 3039.

5663. *Yen khi thou choe.*

Même ouvrage, édition un peu plus grande, ne portant pas les noms de Tchou, Fong et Tcheou.

Cordier, Imprimerie Sino-européenne, 344.

Grand in-8. Pas de feuille de titre ; la figure est au verso du feuillet 5. 1 vol., cartonnage.
Nouveau fonds 3040.

5664. 電 報 新 書
Thien pao sin chou.

Code télégraphique chinois.

Par Septime A. Viguier. Introduction de l'auteur (1871) ; préface du même. Imprimé en 1872 à Chang-hai, American Presbyterian Mission Press.

Cordier, Bibl. Sinica, 802, 804.

Petit in-8. Papier blanc ; titre noir sur rouge. 1 vol., demi-reliure (prov. du Ministère de l'Intérieur, Bureau de la Protection Littéraire).
Nouveau fonds 3628.

5665. *Tien pao sin chou.*

Double, avec dédicace de l'auteur.

Petit in-8. 1 cahier chinois (prov. de la collection Schefer).

Département des Imprimés, 8° π 220.

———

5666-5667. — I (5666-5667).

化學指南

Hoa hio tchi nan.

Guide de la chimie.

Texte avec figures; table des métalloïdes avec noms chinois et européens, équivalents chimiques. Table des matières pour chaque livre. Errata à la fin du 8ᵉ livre. Avertissement. Préface par Tong Siun, de Yang-tcheou. Impression en caractères mobiles, du Thong-oen koan, à Péking (1873). Traduction par Billequin d'un ouvrage de Würtz.

8 livres.

Titre noir sur papier teinté.

— II (5667).

Hoa hio tchi nan.

Guide de la chimie.

Table des principaux corps simples et composés, formant 2 livres qui portent les nᵒˢ 9 et 10. Impression en caractères mobiles (1873).

Titre noir sur papier teinté.

In-4. 2 vol., demi-rel., au chiffre de Louis-Philippe.

Nouveau fonds 4336, 4337.

———

Chapitre X : TAOÏSME

—

Première Section : TRAITÉS DOGMATIQUES, MORAUX, ETC.

5668. 道言內外五種秘錄

Tao yen nei oai oou tchong pi lou.

Collection de cinq œuvres taoïstes.

Éditée par Khieou Tshang-tchou, de Yong-chang (1800); planches conservées à la salle Ying-king.

— I.

周易參同契脉望

Tcheou yi tshan thong khi mo oang.

Traité sur le Tshan thong khi.

Par Thao Sou-seu, surnom Tshoen-tshoen-tseu, avec notice préliminaire de ce commentateur (1700). Texte et planches. Le Tshan thong khi est un traité relatif à l'immortalité, basé sur le Yi king; il est dû à Oei Po-yang Oei-koei, surnoms Yun-ya-tseu et Koai-ki tchen-jen (IIᵉ siècle p. C.).

3 livres (manquent les préfaces annoncées par la table). — Cf. Cat. imp., liv. 146, f. 33 (Tcheou yi tshan thong khi thong tchen yi), etc.; liv. 147, f. 14 (Tcheou yi tshan thong khi tchou kiai), etc.

— II.

悟眞篇約註

Oou tchen phien yo tchou.

Traité de l'éveil à la vérité, avec commentaires.

Auteur : Tchang Po-toan Phing-chou, autre postnom Yong-tchheng, surnom Tseu-yang tchen-jen, de Thien-thai. Commentaires de Thao Sou-seu; notice du même (1711).

4 livres. — Comparer Cat. imp., liv. 146, f. 52 (Oou tchen phien tchou sou fou tchi tchi siang choe); liv. 147, f. 43 (Oou tchen phien tchou kiai).

— III.

承志錄

Tchheng tchi lou.

Traité sur la communication de la volonté.

Par Pheng Choen-yi Tchengfou, de Thai-hoa-chan, avec préface de l'auteur (1583). Édition avec postface de Thao Sou-seu (1707); annexes.

3 livres.

— IV.

金丹就正篇

Kin tan tsieou tcheng phien.

Traité sur le perfectionnement taoïste.

Par Lou Si-sing Tchhang-keng, surnom Tshien-hiu-tseu, de Hoai-hai. Préface sans nom d'auteur ni date; postface par Tshien-hiu-tseu.

3 sections.

— V.

玄慮論

Hiuen liu loen.

Collection de traités taoïstes.

20 petits traités.

— VI.

金丹大要

Kin tan ta yao.

Principes du taoïsme.

Avec préface (1718) par Thao Sou-seu, surnom Thong-oei tao-jen.

— VII.

上藥三品說

Chang yo san phin choe.

Traité sur le taoïsme.

— VIII.

金丹妙用章

Kin tan miao yong tchang.

Merveilleux usages du kin tan.

9 articles.

— IX.

運火行符須知

Yun hoo hing fou siu tchi.

Connaissances élémentaires sur le taoïsme.

8 articles.

— X.

丹法參同十八訣

Tan fa tshan thong chi pa kiue.

Conseils de conduite.

18 articles.

Grand in-8. Titre noir sur jaune. 1 vol., demi-rel., au chiffre de Louis-Philippe.

Nouveau fonds 472.

———

5669. ## 化書新聲

Hoa chou sin cheng.

Le livre de la transformation, nouveau commentaire.

Par Than King-cheng, postnom Tshiao, autre surnom Tseu-siao tchen-jen (xe siècle). Commentaire

par Oang Yi-tshing Sieou-yun, surnom Thi-oou-tseu, avec préface du
même (1594). Préface par Oou
Tchi-pheng Yi-yun (1597).

6 livres. — Cat. imp., 117, f. 26
(Hoa chou) ; liv. 124, f. 3 (Hoa chou
sin cheng).

Grand in-8. 1 vol., demi-rel., au chiffre de Louis-Philippe.
Nouveau fonds 652.

5670.　悟眞篇三註。參
同契

*Oou tchen phien san tchou. Tshan
thong khi.*

Traité de l'éveil à la vérité
avec trois commentaires. Le
Tshan thong khi.

Édition de la salle Tsiu-kin
(1809).

— I.

Oou tchen phien san tchou.

Traité de l'éveil à la vérité,
avec trois commentaires.

Pour l'auteur, voir n° 5668, art. II.
Commentaires par Sie Tao-koang
Tao-yuen, surnom Tseu-hien tchen-
jen ; par Lou Ye, surnom Tseu-
ye tchen-jen ; par Tchhen Tchi-
hiu, surnoms Chang-yang tseu et
Koan-oou (dynastie des Yuen).
Préface (1075) et postface (1078),
par l'auteur. Préfaces par Lou Ye
et Tchhen Tchi-hiu ; notice relative
au commentaire.

3 livres. — Comparer Cat. imp.,
liv. 146, f. 52, Oou tchen phien tchou
sou fou tchi tchi siang choę.

— II.

參同契分節解

Tshan thong khi fẹn tsie kiai.

Le Tshan thong khi avec commentaire.

Pour l'auteur, voir n° 5668,
art. I. Commentaire par Tchhen
Tchi-hiu, de Liu-ling (époque des
Yuen) ; édition donnée par Yao
Jou-siun, de Ta-ming (époque des
Ming), avec préface par Yang
Tchen, de Tchheng-tou (1546).

3 livres. — Cat. imp., liv. 146, f. 38,
Tcheou yi tshan thong khi fẹn tchang
tchou.

Paraît incomplet.

— III.

參同契箋註分節解

*Tshan thong khi tsien tchou fẹn
tsie kiai.*

Le Tshan thong khi avec commentaire.

Texte différent par Siu King-
hieou (dynastie des Han orientaux). Commentaire de Tchhen
Tchi-hiu, publié par Yao Jou-
siun.

3 livres. — Le 3e livre forme un
ouvrage distinct, voir art. IV.

— IV.

參同契三相類

Tshan thong khi san siang lei.

Par Choen-yu Chou-thong, de Koai-ki (dynastie des Han orientaux). Commentaire de Tchhen Tchi-hiu, publié par Yao Jou-siun.

Grand in-8. Titre noir sur jaune. 1 vol., demi-rel., au chiffre de Louis-Philippe.

Nouveau fonds 217.

5671-5672. — I (5671-5672).

勸善要言。太上感應篇疏衍增删

Khiuen chan yao yen. Thai chang kan ying phien sou yen tseng chan.

Le livre des récompenses et des peines (Thai chang kan ying phien) avec commentaire et développement, édition corrigée.

Ouvrage d'un auteur inconnu, de l'époque des Song; avec des exemples moraux dus à divers auteurs dits les sages de Choei-yun. Préface impériale (1655) pour une édition publiée par ordre de l'empereur; réédition de la salle Yen-seu, préparée par Ling-pi tseu, de 'O-mei, Ho-khong tseu, de Seu-ming, Oo-yun tseu, de la montagne Heng; préfaces par Ling-pi tseu et Ho-khong tseu (1667).

12 livres. — Comp. Bibl. coréenne, nᵒˢ 2590, 2591, etc.

— II (5672).

太上感應篇緒論

Thai chang kan yin phien siu loen.

Dissertations sur le Thai chang kan ying phien.

Par les sages de Choei-yun. Postface par Khou-hing tseu Yu-chan.

Grand in-8. Belle édition, titre noir et rouge sur blanc. 2 vol., demi-reliure (prov. de la bibl. de l'Arsenal).

Nouveau fonds 1647, 1648.

5673-5674. 丹桂籍

Tan koei tsi.

Collection de traités taoïstes.

Publiée à la salle Sieou-oen du Hai-kong-thing, à Tshiuen-tcheou, et à la salle San-yi, à Fou-tcheou; par les soins de Tchao Song Yi-sien, de Leou-tong. Commentaires par Yen Thing-piao, de Yun-kien. Préface (1711) par Tchoang Tchao-tchong Tsheu-yeou, de Song-ling.

Liste des personnes qui ont contribué à la gravure de l'ouvrage.

— I (5673).

太上感應篇

Thai chang kan ying phien.

Le Thai chang kan ying phien.

Texte seul; voir n°ˢ 5671-5672, art. I.

— II (5673).

文昌帝君陰騭文

Oen tchhang ti kiun yin tchi oen.

Traité de la fixation mysté-rieuse, par le dieu de la Littéra-ture.

Texte seul, gravé par les soins de Tshong-yu hien, de Oen-ling.

Comparer Bibl. coréenne, n° 2601, p. 160, 1°.

— III (5673).

關夫子覺世真經

Koan fou tseu kio chi tchen king.

Le livre sacré de l'éveil du monde, de Koan fou-tseu.

Par Koan Yu, dieu de la Guerre. Texte et récit de miracles. Gravé par Oou Thing-yun, de Tsin-choei.

Comparer Bibl. coréenne, n° 2607, p. 193, 3°.

— IV (5673).

關聖帝君降筆真經

Koan cheng ti kiun kiang pi tchen king.

Livre sacré écrit par le dieu de la Guerre.

Texte en vers de six syllabes; imprimé en gros caractères.

Comparer Bibl. coréenne, n° 2618, p. 206, 18°.

— V (5673).

關聖帝君顯應戒士文

Koan cheng ti kiun hien ying kiai chi oen.

Conseils aux lettrés, traité par le dieu de la Guerre.

— VI (5673).

東嶽聖帝垂訓

Tong yo cheng ti tchhoei hiun.

Instructions du dieu du Tong yo.

Gravées par Lieou Fong-hoei.

— VII (5673).

呂純陽祖師勸世戒食牛犬

Liu choen yang tsou chi khiuen chi kiai chi nieou khiuen.

Défense de manger le bœuf et le chien, traité par Liu Choen-yang.

Gravé par les soins de Li Hiang-kao et Lin Tsai-tshai.

Comparer Bibl. coréenne, n° 2618, 41°.

— VIII (5673).

文昌孝經

Oen tchhang hiao king.

Livre sacré de la piété filiale, par Oen-tchhang.

Six articles en prose mêlée de vers ; table des matières. Postface par Oang Ngao (1492).

Comparer Bibl. coréenne, n° 2601, p. 156, 1°.

— IX (5673).

蕉窓十則

Tsiao tchhoang chi tse.

Les dix commandements de Tsiao-tchhoang.

Texte et notes.

Comparer Bibl. coréenne, n° 2601, p. 167, 6ᵉ livre, 1ʳᵉ partie, 1°.

— X (5673).

功過格纂要

Kong koo ko tsoan yao.

Éléments des règles du mérite et du péché.

Comparer Bibl. coréenne, n° 2619, 16°.

— XI (5673).

桂香殿功過格

Koei hiang tien kong koo ko.

Règles du mérite et du péché, de la salle Koei-hiang.

— XII (5673).

靈驗記

Ling yen ki.
Exemples miraculeux.

— XIII (5673).

文昌帝君降乩惜字功罪例

Oen tchhang ti kiun kiang ki si tseu kong tsoei li.

Règlement du mérite et du péché, relativement au respect des caractères d'écriture ; donné par le dieu de la Littérature.

Comparer Bibl. coréenne, n° 2618, 11°.

— XIV, livre préliminaire (5673).

募刊疏引

Mou khan sou yin.

Rapport et introduction sur la gravure de l'ouvrage.

Par Thang Soen-hoa Ki-jen (1690).

— XV, livre préliminaire (5673).

婁東善書目錄

Leou tong chan chou mou lou.

Liste d'ouvrages recommandés, dressée à Leou-tong.

Indiquant les titres, noms d'auteurs, lieux d'édition.

— XVI, livre préliminaire (5673).

文昌帝君丹桂籍靈驗記。續記

Oen tchhang ti kiun tan koei tsi ling yen ki. Siu ki.

Notice des miracles dus au Tan koei tsi du dieu de la Littérature, partie principale et suite.

Gravé aux frais de divers; la suite est par Yen Tchang-king Cheng-yu.

— XVII, livre préliminaire (5673).

顏廷表先生傳

Yen thing piao sien cheng tchoan.

Vie de Yen Thing-piao.

Yen, postnom Tcheng, surnom Yi-phing, nom littéraire Nai-'an, licencié en 1453, mort à 55 ans après 1466, descendant à la neuvième génération du ministre Po-yen. Auteur : Oou Khi, de Hoa-thing.

— XVIII, livre préliminaire (5673).

顏雲麓先生傳

Yen yun lou sien cheng tchoan.

Vie de Yen Yun-lou.

Yen, postnom Oen-choei, surnom Po-tcheng. Auteur : Oang Sieou-yu, de Oou-lin (1684).

— XIX, livre préliminaire (5673).

丹桂籍奉行心法

Tan koei tsi fong hing sin fa.

Préceptes pour pratiquer les règles du Tan koei tsi.

— XX, livre préliminaire (5673).

文昌帝君降筆記

Oen tchhang ti kiun kiang pi ki.

Notice dictée par le dieu de la Littérature.

— XXI, livre préliminaire (5673).

玉皇寶號

Yu hoang pao hao.

Les noms précieux de Yu-hoang.

— XXII, livres 1 à 4 (5673-5674).

九天開化主宰元皇司錄宏仁文昌帝君陰隲文註案

Kieou thien khai hoa tchou tsai yuen hoang seu lou hong jen oen tchhang ti kiun yin tchi oen tchou'an.

Traité de la fixation mystérieuse, par le dieu de la Littérature ; avec commentaires et exemples.

Les commentaires sont de Yen Tcheng Thing-piao; les exemples sont de son descendant à la cinquième génération, Yen Oen-choei Yun-lou; publié par Yen Tchang-king Cheng-yu, descendant de Yen Tcheng à la sixième génération. Gravé de nouveau à la salle Sieou-oen.

Voir plus haut, n° 5673, art. II.

— XXIII, livre final (5674).

文昌帝君救劫寶章

Oen tchhang ti kiun kieou kie pao tchang.

Précieux articles du dieu de la Littérature pour le salut du monde.

Voir n° 5677, art. VIII. — Comparer Bibl. coréenne, n° 2618, 8°.

— XXIV, livre final (5674).

梓潼帝君降筆戒士子文

Tseu thong ti kiun kiang pi kiai chi tseu oen.

Conseils aux lettrés, deux traités par le dieu de la Littérature.

— XXV, livre final (5674).

文昌帝君勸孝文

Oen tchhang ti kiun khiuen hiao oen.

Traité pour conseiller la piété filiale, par le dieu de la Littérature.

Comparer Bibl. coréenne, n° 2601, p. 161, 3°.

— XXVI, livre final (5674).

玉中書勸孝歌

Yu tchong chou khiuen hiao ko.

Chanson pour conseiller la piété filiale.

Avec introduction et conclusion en prose.

— XXVII, livre final (5674).

圓明斗母天尊勸世文

Yuen ming teou mou thien tsoen khiuen chi oen.

Conseils au monde, traité de la déesse Yuen ming teou mou.

Traité révélé en l'année kia yin.

Comparer Bibl. coréenne, n° 2618, 14°.

— XXVIII, livre final (5674).

俞淨意先生遇竈神記

Yu tsing yi sien cheng yu tsao chen ki.

Entrevue de Yu Tsing-yi avec l'esprit du Foyer.

Voir plus bas n° 5677, art. XX. — Comparer Bibl. coréenne, n° 2618, 27°. — Cordier, Bibl. sinica, col. 305.

— XXIX, livre final (5674).

袁了凡先生四訓。立命之學

Yuen liao fan sien cheng seu hiun. Li ming tchi hio.

Quatre exhortations de Yuen Liao-fan. Première section : Science de la direction de la vie.

Autobiographie donnée comme exemple; l'auteur, élève de Yu Tsing-yi, vivait sous la dynastie des Ming.

Comparer Bibl. coréenne, nᵒ 2618, 26ᵒ.

— XXX, livre final (5674).

積善之方
Tsi chan tchi fang.

Deuxième section : Recette pour accumuler les bonnes actions.

Par le même.

— XXXI, livre final (5674).

改過之法
Kai koo tchi fa.

Troisième section : Moyen de corriger les fautes.

Par le même.

— XXXII, livre final (5674).

謙德之效
Khien te tchi hiao.

Quatrième section : Manifestation d'humilité.

-- XXXIII, livre final (5674).

佛母準提神咒
Fo mou tchoen thi chen tcheou.

Invocation de la mère du Bouddha.

Rédigée en chinois; texte de gravure différente, formant un feuillet ajouté (nᵒ 46 *bis*, yeou seu chi lou).

— XXXIV, livre final (5674).

袁了凡先生勸喪文
Yuen liao fan sien cheng khiuen sang oen.

Traité de Yuen Liao-fan sur les funérailles.

— XXXV, livre final (5674).

遏淫說
'O yin choe.

Traité contre l'impureté.

Comparer Bibl. coréenne, nᵒ 2618, 31ᵒ.

-- XXXVI, livre final (5674).

行不費錢功德例
Hing pou fei tshien kong te li.

Manière d'obtenir des mérites sans dépenser d'argent.

Règlement méthodique s'appliquant aux diverses classes de la société.

Comparer Bibl. coréenne, nᵒ 2619, 14ᵒ.

In-18. Titre noir sur jaune. 2 vol., demi-rel., au chiffre de Louis-Philippe. *Nouveau fonds* 230.

———

5675-5676. 太上感應篇圖說
Thai chang kan ying phien thou choe.

Le Thai chang kan ying phien illustré.

Texte ; une gravure pour chaque anecdote morale. Édition donnée par Tchang Yi Tsong-mei, de Koan-tchong, Yi-la-tshi King-cheng, de San-han, et Teng Tchao Yuen-thing, de Hiu-kiang. Préface par ce dernier (1745). Préfaces de deux rééditions, par Thong Hing (1798) et par Li Oen-tchao (1850).

7 livres (paraît incomplet d'un livre).

Petit in-8. 2 vol. cartonnage. *Nouveau fonds* 4392.

5677. 增訂敬信錄

Tseng ting king sin lou.

Le livre du respect et de la foi, édition augmentée.

Collection gravée à Canton, à la salle Tsiu-ying. La gravure est médiocre et varie suivant les traités, la table ne correspond pas à la totalité de l'ouvrage. Préface par Yin Ki-chan (1769), préface de la première édition par Hiu Yun-pheng Te-tchhoei (1749) ; une préface non datée pour une réédition ; préface par Hiu Pao-chan (1769) ; préface par Lieou Kao-kang (1797). Table des divers traités ; un feuillet double de conseils moraux.

Comparer Bibl. coréenne, nº 2618.

— I.

太上感應篇

Thai chang kan ying phien.

Le Thai chang kan ying phien.

Texte avec un appendice spécial attribué au dieu de la Littérature.

— II.

感應篇讀法纂要

Kan ying phien tou fa tsoan yao.

Principes pour la lecture du Kan ying phien.

5 articles.

— III.

太上洞玄靈寶梓潼本願眞經

Thai chang tong hiuen ling pao tseu thong pen yuen tchen king.

Autre titre :

文昌帝君本願眞經

Oen tchhang ti kiun pen yuen tchen king.

Le vrai livre sacré des vœux du dieu de la Littérature.

Texte seul.

Comparer Bibl. coréenne, nº 2601, p. 157, 4º.

— IV.

文昌帝君陰騭文

Oen tchhang ti kiun yin tchi oen.

Même ouvrage qu'au nº 5673, art. II.

— V.

文昌帝君勸孝文

Oen tchhang ti kiun khiuen hiao oen.

Traité pour conseiller la piété filiale, par le dieu de la Littérature.

Comparer n° 5674, art. XXV.

— VI.

南無大慈大悲觀世音菩薩救苦經

Na mo ta tsheu ta pei koan chi yin phou sa kieou khou king.

Sūtra de Koan-yin miséricordieuse qui sauve du malheur.

Texte bouddhique.

— VII.

南無大慈大悲觀世音菩薩感應保生經

Na mo ta tsheu ta pei koan chi yin phou sa kan ying pao cheng king.

Sūtra de Koan-yin miséricordieuse qui répond aux prières et préserve les êtres vivants.

Texte bouddhique.

— VIII.

文昌帝君救劫寶章

Oen tchhang ti kiun kieou kie pao tchang.

Précieux articles du dieu de la Littérature pour le salut du monde.

Introduction, six préceptes avec développement, exemples. Texte différent du n° 5674, art. XXIII, mais analogue au n° 5680, art. XV.

— IX.

文昌帝君聖訓。蕉窻十則

Oen tchhang ti kiun cheng hiun. Tsiao tchhoang chi tse.

Même texte qu'au n° 5673, art. IX.

— X.

文昌帝君勸敬字紙文

Oen tchhang ti kiun khiuen king tseu tchi oen.

Autre titre :

勸敬惜字文

Khiuen king si tseu oen.

Traité pour conseiller le respect des caractères d'écriture.

Comparer Bibl. coréenne, n° 2601, p. 161, 6°.

— XI.

文昌聖願十戒

Oen tchhang cheng yuen chi kiai.

Les dix défenses du dieu de la Littérature.

Texte avec introduction.

Comparer Bibl. coréenne, nº 2601, p. 167, 4º.

— XII.

東嶽大帝回生寶訓

Tong yo ta ti hoei cheng pao hiun.

Précieuses instructions du dieu du Tong-yo sur la transmigration.

Comparer Bibl. coréenne, nº 2618, 13º. Le début est le même qu'au nº 5673, art. VI, mais la suite diffère.

— XIII.

圓明斗帝勸世文

Yuen ming teou ti khiuen chi oen.

Autre titre :

斗姥勸世文

Teou mou kiuen chi oen.

Conseils au monde, traité de la déesse Yuen ming teou mou.

Voir plus haut nº 5674, art. XXVII.

— XIV.

玄天上帝金科玉律

Hiuen thien chang ti kin khoo yu liu.

Lois de l'Empereur céleste.

Comparer Bibl. coréenne, nº 2618, 15º. Ce texte est suivi de :

勸世格言

Khiuen chi ko yen.

Conseils au monde, par l'Empereur céleste.

— XV.

關聖帝君眞經

Koan cheng ti kiun tchen king.

Autre titre :

關聖帝君寶訓

Koan cheng ti kiun pao hiun.

Le vrai livre sacré du réveil du monde, par le dieu de la Guerre.

Comparer nº 5673, art. III.

— XVI.

魏元君勸世文

Oei yuen kiun khiuen chi oen.

Conseils au monde de Oei Yuen-kiun.

Comparer Bibl. coréenne, nº 2618, 24º.

— XVII.

蓮池大師放生文

Lien tchhi ta chi fang cheng oen.

Traité conseillant de mettre en liberté les êtres qui ont vie, par Lien-tchhi.

Comparer Bibl. coréenne, nᵒ 2618, 25ᵒ.

— XVIII.

純陽祖師延壽育子歌

Choẹn yang tsou chị yen cheou yu tseu ko.

Chant sur la longévité et l'obtention de fils, par le dieu Fou-yeou.

— XIX.

袁了凡先生立命篇

Yuen liao fan sien cheng li ming phien.

Même traité qu'au nᵒ 5674, art. XXIX, texte différent.

— XX.

俞淨意公遇竈神記

Yu tsing yi kong yu tsao chen ki.

Même texte qu'au nᵒ 5674, art. XXVIII, attribué ici à Lo Tcheng. Yu Tou Liang-tchhen, du Kiang-nan, vivait à l'époque Kia-tsing (1522-1566).

— XXI.

文昌帝君功過格

Oen tchhang ti kiun kong koo ko.

Autre titre :

太微仙君功過格

Thai oei sien kiun kong koo ko.

Échelle des mérites et des péchés, par le dieu de la Littérature.

Texte incomplet. — Comparer Bibl. coréenne, nᵒ 2618, 29ᵒ.

— XXII.

呂叔簡先生居官戒刑八章

Liu chou kien sien cheng kiu koan kiai hing pa tchang.

Huit conseils aux fonctionnaires, relativement aux châtiments.

Par Liu Chou-kien, postnom Khoẹn, nom littéraire Sin-oou, de Ning-ling (1536-1618).

Comparer Bibl. coréenne, nᵒ 2618, 30ᵒ.

— XXIII.

過淫說

'O yin choẹ.

Même traité qu'au nᵒ 5674, art. XXXV.

— XXIV.

戒賭十條

Kiai tou chi thiao.

Dix articles contre le jeu.

Comparer Bibl. coréenne, nᵒ 2618, 32ᵒ.

— XXV.

勸戒溺女言

Khiuen kiai ni niu yen.

Paroles pour interdire l'infanticide des filles.

Comparer Bibl. coréenne, n° 2618, 33°.

— XXVI.

感應篇致福靈驗

Kan ying phien tchi fou ling yen.

Exemples miraculeux de bonheur produit par le Kan ying phien.

Traité en neuf articles.

Comparer Bibl. coréenne, n° 2618, 34°.

— XXVII.

文昌帝君陰騭文靈驗

Oen tchhang ti kiun yin tchi oen ling yen.

Miracles du Yin tchi oen.

Comparer Bibl. coréenne, n° 2618, 35°.

— XXVIII.

損子墮胎異報

Soen tseu too thai yi pao.

Châtiment extraordinaire de l'infanticide et de l'avortement.

Comparer Bibl. coréenne, n° 2618, 36°.

— XXIX.

救急五絕良方

Kieou ki oou tsiue liang fang.

Recettes contre cinq genres de mort.

Suicide par strangulation, mort par la chute d'une muraille, par submersion, par l'action des mauvais esprits, par congélation.

Comparer Bibl. coréenne, n° 2618, 37°.

— XXX.

安胎催生藥方

'An thai tshoei cheng yo fang.

Remèdes pour faciliter l'accouchement.

Formules conservées dans la famille de Li Tshoen-jen.

Comparer Bibl. coréenne, n° 2618, 38°.

— XXXI.

異傳不出天花經驗奇方

Yi tchhoan pou tchhou thien hoa king yen khi fang.

Recettes merveilleuses pour éviter la petite vérole.

— XXXII.

經驗瘧疾方

King yen yo tsi fang.

Recette contre la fièvre intermittente.

— XXXIII.

經驗救急艮方

King yen kieou ki liang fang.

Formules pour les cas urgents, avec suppléments.

Gravé par Lieou Kao-kang, de Thie-tchheng.

— XXXIV.

勸世艮言

Khiuen chi liang yen.

Conseils au monde.

— XXXV.

百忍說

Po jen choẹ.

Traité des cent résignations.

Par Tcheou Tchhou-phing, surnom Tan-han tao-jen, de Kia-hing. Gravé à la salle Liang Lo-chạn.

— XXXVI.

百忍歌

Po jen ko.

Chant des cent résignations.

Gravé par Liang Po-kang, de Si-khi.

— XXXVII.

文昌帝君救世文

Oen tchhang ti kiun kieou chi oen.

Traité pour sauver le monde, par le dieu de la Littérature.

Comparer Bibl. coréenne, n° 2601, p. 161, 4°.

— XXXVIII.

道德天尊像

Tao tẹ thien tsoẹn siang.

Portrait de Lao-tseu.

Avec légende au verso; gravé à Canton, à la salle Tsiu-ying.

— XXXIX.

靈通萬應丸

Ling thong oan ying hoan.

Pilules de la pénétration spirituelle et des 10.000 effets.

Recette due au grand secrétaire Song; gravée par Lin Song-hien, de Koei-tcheou.

— XL.

敬信陰騭文獲報

King sin yin tchi oen hoo pao.

Effets miraculeux du Yin tchi oen.

Par Tcheou Chi-thai (1805).

— XLI.

牙頤神方

Ya yi chen fang.

Formules merveilleuses contre le mal de dents et la fluxion.

— XLII.

功過格分類彙編

Kong koo ko fẹn lei hoei pien.

Liste méthodique des mérites et des péchés.

Deux sections relatives à la morale envers autrui et à la morale envers soi-même. Incomplet à la fin. A la suite, liste des personnes qui ont contribué à la gravure (1829).

Grand in-8. 1 vol., demi-rel., au chiffre de Louis-Philippe.

Nouveau fonds 215.

5678.   ## 全人矩矱

Tshiuen jen kiu hoo.

La règle de tout l'homme.

Recueil d'une bonne impression, gravé pour la première fois au Koang-tong (1800), planches conservées au pavillon de Kong-pẹ (Lappa). Préface par Tchou Koei, de Ta-hing (1792); préface par Lou Oen-tchhao, de Hang-tong (1792); préface par Soẹn Nien-kiu Kie-tchai (1790). Avertissement de la première édition. Table des 1+4 +1 livres.

— I, livre préliminaire.

太上感應篇纂註

Thai chang kan ying phien tsoan tchou.

Le Thai chang kan ying phien, avec commentaires.

Texte mêlé de commentaires, notes en haut des pages. Préface (1795) par Soẹn Nien-kiu Chou-fou; avertissement par le même (1796). Gravé par les soins de Li Pei-cheng, de Choẹn-tẹ.

— II, livre préliminaire.

文昌帝君陰騭文纂註

Oen tchhang ti kiun yin tchi oen tsoan tchou.

Le Yin tchi oen, du dieu de la Littérature, avec commentaires.

Voir nᵒ 5673, art. II; même disposition qu'à l'art. I ci-dessus.

— III, livre préliminaire.

文昌帝君覺世文纂註

Oen tchhang ti kiun kio chi oen tsoan tchou.

Traité pour éveiller le monde, par le dieu de la Littérature.

Comparer Bibl. coréenne, nᵒ 2601, p. 157, 7ᵒ. Même disposition qu'à l'art. I ci-dessus.

— IV, livre préliminaire.

關聖帝君覺世經。釋略幷諭

Koan cheng ti kiun kio chi king. Chi lio ping yu.

Le vrai livre sacré du réveil

16

du monde, par le dieu de la Guerre.

Même **texte** qu'au nº 5677, art. XV; disposé comme à l'art. I ci-dessus. En plus, texte d'un décret du dieu.

— V, livre préliminaire.

純陽祖師警士文

Choen yang tsou chi king chi oen.

Avertissement aux lettrés, traité du dieu Fou-yeou.

Texte avec peu de notes.

— VI, livre préliminaire.

魏元君勸世文

Oei yuen kiun khiuen chi oen.

Même traité qu'au nº 5677, art. XVI; texte avec quelques notes.

— VII, livre 1.

勸孝集說

Khiuen hiao tsi choe.

Recueil de **textes** recommandant la piété filiale.

Formé par Soen Nien-kiu Chou-fou Sien-min. Les textes sont classés en instructions des divinités, propos de religieux défunts, règles pour servir les parents.

— VIII, livre 2.

戒淫集說

Kiai yin tsi choe.

Recueil de textes contre l'impureté.

Formé par le même auteur, avec très peu de notes. Comprenant des extraits rangés sous divers chefs et, auparavant, les quatre traités suivants (art. IX à XII).

— IX, livre 2.

文昌帝君戒淫文

Oen tchhang ti kiun kiai yin oen.

Traité contre l'impureté, par le dieu de la Littérature.

Comparer Bibl. coréenne, nº 2605, p. 188, 5ᵉ partie, 4º et 5º.

— X, livre 2.

文昌帝君天戒錄

Oen tchhang ti kiun thien kiai lou.

Défenses célestes, notées par le dieu de la Littérature.

Comparer Bibl. coréenne, nº 2601, p. 167, 8º.

— XI, livre 2.

三丰張眞人戒淫說

San fong tchang tchen jen kiai yin choe.

Traité contre l'impureté, par l'homme vrai Tchang, de San-fong.

— XII, livre 2.

文昌帝君慾海廻狂寶訓

Oen tchhang ti kiun yu hai hoei khoang pao hiun.

Instructions pour tirer l'insensé de la mer de la concupiscence, par le dieu de la Littérature.

Voir Bibl. coréenne, n° 2601, p. 167, 2°.

— XIII, livre 3.

勸戒彙抄

Khiuen kiai hoei tchhao.

Recueil de conseils et de défenses.

Comprenant les traités suivants :

文帝勸忠

Oen ti khiuen tchong.

Traité pour conseiller la fidélité, par le dieu de la Littérature.

— XIV, livre 3.

文帝戒士子文

Oen ti kiai chi tseu oen.

Conseils aux lettrés, par le dieu de la Littérature.

Comparer n° 5674, art. XXIV. — Bibl. coréenne, n° 2601, p. 162, 12°.

— XV, livre 3.

文帝鱣壇勸世文

Oen ti tchan than khiuen chi oen.

Conseils donnés au monde par le dieu de la Littérature, à l'autel Tchan.

2 pièces.

Comparer Bibl. coréenne, n° 2601, p. 161, 8°.

— XVI, livre 3.

文帝鱣壇語錄

Oen ti tchan than yu lou.

Entretiens du dieu de la Littérature à l'autel Tchan.

2 pièces.

Comparer Bibl. coréenne, n° 2601, p. 166, 1°.

— XVII, livre 3.

蕉窻十則并序

Tsiao tchhoang chi tsę ping siu.

Les dix commandements de Tsiao-tchhoang, avec préface.

Voir n° 5673, art. IX.

— XVIII, livre 3.

文帝三教論。七願、十戒

Oen ti san kiao loęn. Tshi yuen. Chi kiai.

Dissertation sur les trois religions ; les sept vœux ; les dix commandements : du dieu de la Littérature.

— XIX, livre 3.

呂 祖 師 訓 世 文

Liu tsou chi hiun chi oen.

Instructions au monde par le dieu Fou-yeou.

Huit conseils et huit défenses, avec préface révélée par le dieu auteur (1694).

Comparer Bibl. coréenne, n° 2605, p. 187, 4ᵉ partie, 1°.

— XX, livre 3.

勸 敬 惜 字 紙 文

Khiuen king si tseu tchi oen.

Traité pour conseiller le respect des caractères d'écriture.

Par Chan-chan ta-chi.

Voir n° 5677, art. X.

— XXI, livre 3.

敬 字 說

King tseu choe̩.

Traité sur le respect des caractères d'écriture.

— XXII, livre 3.

惜 字 說

Si tseu choe̩.

Traité sur le ménagement des caractères d'écriture.

— XXIII, livre 3

勸 敬 惜 五 穀 文

Khiuen king si oou kou oen.

Traité du respect des cinq sortes de grains.

Par Tsiang Sing-'an, de Yu-chan.

Comparer Bibl. coréenne, n° 2601, p. 163, 25°.

— XXIV, livre 3.

戒 殺 生 說

Kiai cha cheng choe̩.

Traité pour défendre de tuer les êtres ayant vie.

Par le même auteur.

— XXV, livre 3.

戒 溺 女 說

Kiai ni niu choe̩.

Traité pour défendre de noyer les petites filles.

Comparer n° 5677, art. XXV.

— XXVI, livre 3.

戒 賭 文

Kiai tou oen.

Traité contre le jeu.

Par Tsiang Sing-'an.

Comparer n° 5677, art. XXIV.

— XXVII, livre 3.

戒嗜酒

Kiai chi tsieou.

Défense d'aimer le vin.

Par Soẹn Nien-kiu.

— XXVIII, livre 3.

戒貪財

Kiai than tshai.

Défense de convoiter les richesses.

Par le même.

— XXIX, livre 3.

戒聽讒

Kiai thing tchhan.

Défense d'écouter la calomnie.

— XXX, livre 3.

戒口過文

Kiai kheou koo oen.

Traité pour interdire les péchés de langue.

— XXXI, livre 3.

戒損人利己說

Kiai soẹn jen li ki choẹ.

Traité pour interdire de chercher des avantages personnels au détriment d'autrui.

Par Soẹn Nien-kiu.

— XXXII, livre 3.

不自棄文

Pou tseu khi oen.

Traité recommandant de ne pas s'abandonner au vice.

Par Tchou Hi.

Bibl. coréenne, n° 3o1.

— XXXIII, livre 3.

戒慢葬

Kiai man tsang.

Traité pour défendre d'user de négligence dans les funérailles.

Par Soẹn Nien-kiu.

— XXXIV, livre 3.

戒不修治墳墓

Kiai pou sieou tchi fẹn mou.

Traité recommandant d'entretenir les tombes.

— XXXV, livre 3.

勸塾師培植子弟

Khiuen chou chi phei tchi tseu ti.

Traité recommandant aux maîtres de prendre soin de leurs élèves.

Par Tsiang Sing-'an.

— XXXVI, livre 3.

勸尊重師傅

Khiuen tsoẹn tchong chi fou.

Traité recommandant aux élèves d'honorer leur maître.

Par Soen Nien-kiu.

— XXXVII, livre 3.

勸幕賓

Khiuen mo pin.

Conseils aux secrétaires privés des mandarins.

— XXXVIII, livre 3.

勸公門修行

Khiuen kong men sieou hing.

Dans les affaires publiques, il faut régler sa conduite.

— XXXIX, livre 3.

勸擇術愼業

Khiuen tse chou chen ye.

Il faut choisir un métier et s'y appliquer.

Traité par Soen Nien-kiu.

— XL, livre 3.

勸化惡助善

Khiuen hoa 'o tsou chan.

Il faut corriger le mal et contribuer au bien.

Traité par le même.

— XLI, livre 3.

勸排難解紛

Khiuen phai nan kiai fen.

Il faut écarter les obstacles et dissiper les difficultés.

Traité par le même.

— XLII, livre 3.

勸謙和雍睦

Khiuen khien hoo yong mou.

Traité pour conseiller l'esprit de conciliation et de concorde.

Par le même.

— XLIII, livre 3.

勸救濟

Khiuen kieou tsi.

Il faut aider (ceux qui ont besoin d'aide).

Par le même.

— XLIV, livre 3.

賑饑十二善

Tchen ki chi eul chan.

Il faut nourrir les affamés.

— XLV, livre 3.

勸敬說

Khiuen king choe.

Traité sur le respect.

Par Soen Nien-kiu.

— XLVI, livre 3.

勸畏說

Khiuen oei choẹ.

Traité sur la crainte respec-
tueuse.

Par le même.

— XLVII, livre 3.

改過之法

Kai koo tchi fa.

Moyen de corriger les fautes.
Par Yuen Liao-fan.
Voir nᵒ 5674, art. XXXI.

— XLVIII, livre 3.

勸惜福

Khiuen si fou.

Il faut ménager sa part de
bonheur.

Traité par Soẹn Nien-kiu, avec
une postface.

— XLIX, livre 3.

耕心說

Keng sin choẹ.

Autre titre :

勸耕治心地

Khiuen keng tchi sin ti.

Il faut cultiver son cœur.

— L, livre 3.

廣立命說

Koang li ming choẹ.

Développement du traité sur
la direction de la vie.

Comparer nᵒ 5674, art. XXIX.

— LI, livre 3.

爲學當從事性道

Oei hio tang tshong chi sing tao.

Pour étudier, il faut s'appliquer à la voie naturelle.

Traité par Soẹn Nien-kiu.

— LII, livre 3.

性道集說

Sing tao tsi choẹ.

Recueil de textes sur la voie
naturelle.

— LIII, livre 3.

夢覺圖說

Mong kio thou choẹ.

Traité et figure sur l'illusion
universelle.

— LIV, livre 4.

功過格彙編

Kong koo ko hoei pien.

Liste des mérites et des péchés.

Préface; postface par Hou Tchen-
'an Tchou-kong.

Comparer nᵒ 5677, art. XLII.

— LV, livre 4.

行功過格說

Hing kong koo ko choe.

Traité sur l'usage de l'échelle des mérites et des péchés.

— LVI, livre 4.

功過格例

Kong koo ko li.

Règles annexes à l'échelle des mérites et des péchés.

— LVII, livre 4.

功過格分類彙編

Kong koo ko fen lei hoei pien.

Liste méthodique des mérites et des péchés.

Le début de ce texte est analogue au nᵒ 5680, art. IV. Texte semblable au nᵒ 5677, art. XXI, mais complet et formant 8 parties ; différent des autres textes de titre analogue.

— LVIII, livre 4.

不費錢功德例

Pou fei tshien kong te li.

Manière d'obtenir des mérites sans dépenser d'argent.

Texte différent du nᵒ 5674, art. XXXVI ; division analogue.

— LIX, livre final.

勸世詩歌

Khiuen chi chi ko.

Recueil de poésies morales.

Par divers auteurs. Précédé d'une note sur la gravure de la partie complémentaire du volume (1796 ?). Précédé et suivi de listes de souscripteurs, donateurs, bienfaiteurs.

Grand in-8. Titre noir sur jaune. 1 vol., demi-rel., au chiffre de Napoléon III.

Nouveau fonds 1480.

———————

5679. — I.

太上感應篇註證

Thai chang kan ying phien tchou tcheng.

Autre titre :

感應篇註解

Kan ying phien tchou kiai.

Le Thai chang kan ying phien avec notes et exemples moraux.

Préface (1804) par Tchhen Hoei-hoai et Tchhen Hoei-khai, de Sieou-choei. Réédition de Canton, à la salle Kin-chou (1821).

2 livres.

— II.

文昌帝君救世文

Oen tchhang ti kiun kieou chi oen.

Traité pour sauver le monde, par le dieu de la Littérature.

Voir nº 5677, art. XXXVII.

— III.

文昌帝君蕉窗十則聖訓

Oen tchhang ti kiun tsiao tchhoang chi tse cheng hiun.

Les dix commandements de Tsiao-tchhoang.

Voir nº 5673, art. IX.

— IV.

太微仙君功過格

Thai oei sien kiun kong koo ko.

Échelle des mérites et des péchés, par Thai-oei sien kiun.

Le texte diffère du nº 5677, art. XXI. Préface d'inspiration divine, datée de 1724. A la fin, on trouve comme annexe le traité suivant.

— V.

遏淫說

'O yin choe.

Traité contre l'impureté.

Voir nº 5674, XXXV.

— VI.

戒賭十條

Kiai tou chi thiao.

Dix articles contre le jeu.

Voir nº 5677, art. XXIV.

— VII.

救五絶艮方

Kieou oou tsiue liang fang.

Recettes contre cinq genres de mort.

Voir nº 5677, art. XXIX.

— VIII.

安胎催生藥方

'An thai tshoei cheng yo fang.

Remèdes pour faciliter l'accouchement.

Formules conservées dans la famille de Li Yeou-jen.

Voir nº 5677, art. XXX.

— IX.

經驗瘧疾方

King yen yo tsi fang.

Recette contre la fièvre intermittente.

Voir nº 5677, art. XXXII.

— X.

敬刻延生保身立命遏淫避戾

King kho yen cheng pao chen li ming 'o yin pi tou.

Conseils moraux.

Suivis de la liste des personnes qui ont souscrit pour la gravure de l'ouvrage.

Petit in-8. Titre noir sur jaune. 1 vol., demi-reliure.

Nouveau fonds 264.

5680. 聖經彙纂

Cheng king hoei tsoan.

Collection des livres sacrés.

Édition d'une bonne gravure, caractères de genre semi-cursif; donnée à Canton en 1806. Préfaces (1806) par Pheng Kieou-sieou, de Mei-tchhoan, et par Lou Khiao-mou, de Yu. Table générale; avertissement; liste des bienfaiteurs et souscripteurs. Portrait de Lao-tseu, avec légende au verso.

— I, livre 1.

太上感應經

Thai chang kan ying king.

Le Thai chang kan ying phien. Texte seul.

— II, livre 1.

感應經解

Kan ying king kiai.

Le Thai chang kan ying phien, texte et commentaires.

A la fin, diverses pièces de poésie construites sur les mêmes rimes.

— III, livre 1.

玄天上帝金科玉律

Hiuen thien chang ti kin khoo yu liu.

Lois de l'Empereur céleste.

Voir n° 5677, art. XIV.

— IV, livre 1.

明袁了凡先生力行功過格

Ming yuen liao fan sien cheng li hing kong koo ko.

Échelle des mérites et des péchés, de Yuen Liao-fan, de la dynastie des Ming.

Reçue de Yun-kou chang-jen par Yuen Liao-fan. Texte différent du n° 5677, art. XXI, et du n° 5679, art. IV. Préface (1744) par Han Hiao-ki, surnom Tong-li lao-jen.

— V, livre 1.

明袁了凡先生四訓。立命之學

Ming yuen liao fan sien cheng

seu hiun. Li ming tchi hio.

Même texte qu'au n° 5674, art. XXIX.

— VI, livre 1.

積善之方
Tsi chạn tchi fang.

Même texte qu'au n° 5674, art. XXX.

— VII, livre 1.

改過之法
Kai koo tchi fa.

Même texte qu'au n° 5674, art. XXXI.

— VIII, livre 1.

謙德之效
Khien tẹ tchi hiao.

Même texte qu'au n° 5674, art. XXXII.

— IX, livre 1.

準提王菩薩神咒
Tchoẹn thi oang phou sa chen tcheou.

Invocation du bodhisattva roi Caṇḍī.

Texte différent du n° 5674, art. XXXIII ; avec préface par Oan Oen-yu, de King-chan. A la fin, dates des dix abstinences annuelles.

— X, livre 1.

千手千眼觀世音菩薩 廣大圓滿無礙大悲 神咒
Tshien cheou tshien yen koan chi yin phou sa koang ta yuen man oou'ai ta pei chen tcheou.

Sahasrabāhu saharākṣa avalokiteçvara bodhisattva mahāpūrṇāpratihata mahākāruṇikahṛdaya dhāraṇī sūtra.

Dhāraṇī de la grande miséricorde de Koan-yin.

Texte chinois et transcription du sanscrit.

Bunyiu Nanjio, 320.

— XI, livre 1.

拔一切業障根本得生 淨土陀羅尼
Pa yi tshie ye tchang ken pẹn tẹ cheng tsing thou tho lo ni.

Autre titre :

往生咒
Oang cheng tcheou.

Dhāraṇī de la renaissance en Sukhāvatī.

Transcription du sanscrit.

Bunyiu Nanjio, 201.

— XII, livre 1.

摩訶般若波羅蜜多心
經

Mo ho pan jo po lo mi to sìn king.

Mahāprajñāpāramitā hṛdaya sūtra.

Texte chinois et transcription du sanscrit. A la fin, notice par Oan Oen-yu.

Comparer Bunyiu Nanjio, 3 et 20.

— XIII, livre 2.

文昌孝經

Oen tchhang hiao king.

Livre sacré de la piété filiale, par le dieu de la Littérature.

Même texte qu'au n° 5687, art. I ; plus complet qu'au n° 5673, art. VIII. Préface sans date par Pheng Kieou-sieou King-tchai ; autre préface (1492) par Khieou Siun. Portrait et éloge de Oen-tchhang ; pièce de vers de genre bouddhique (gāthā). Préface sans signature ni date pour les trois livres sacrés (art. XIII, XIV, XV).

6 articles.

Titre noir sur blanc.

— XIV, livre 2.

太上消劫梓潼本願眞
經

Thai chang siao kie tseu thong pęn yuen tchen king.

Le vrai livre sacré des vœux du dieu de la Littérature.

Texte différent du n° 5677, art. III ; pièce de vers de genre bouddhique. Préface (1734) par Ki Yun-fei, ministre de gauche du dieu de la Littérature.

— XV, livre 2.

救劫寶經

Kieou kie pao king.

Texte voisin du n° 5677, art. VIII.

— XVI, livre 2.

文昌應化張仙大眞人
說注生延嗣妙應眞
經

Oen tchhang ying hoa tchang sien ta tchen jen choę tchou cheng yen seu miao ying tchen king.

Le vrai livre sacré de l'obtention, par grâce divine, de la longévité et de la postérité.

Pièce de vers ; texte ; décalogue d'inspiration bouddhique.

Comparer Bibl. coréenne, n° 2601, p. 157, 5°.

— XVII, livre 2.

文昌帝君陰騭文

Oen tchhang ti kiun yin tchi oen.

Texte seul ; comme au nº 5673, art. II.

— XVIII, livre 3.

關聖帝君降筆忠義眞經

Koan cheng ti kiun kiang pi tchong yi tchen king

Autre titre :

關聖帝君感應忠義神武眞經

Koan cheng ti kiun kan ying tchong yi chen oou tchen king.

Livre sacré de la fidélité, révélé par le dieu de la Guerre.

Préface par Pheng Kieou-sieou ; préface primitive par Yang Po, de Phou-tcheou ; autre préface (1750) écrite à la salle Si-yin, à Tchheng-kiang. Table générale du 3ᵉ livre de la présente collection. Portrait, noms honorifiques, éloge du dieu de la Guerre. Texte en 18 articles.

Comparer Bibl. coréenne, nº 2607, p. 193, 1º.

Titre noir sur blanc.

— XIX, livre 3.

關聖覺世經

Koan cheng kio chi king.

Même ouvrage qu'au nº 5677, art. XV.

— XX, livre 3.

謨訓

Mou hiun.

Instructions.

— XXI, livre 3.

降鸞寶訓

Kiang loan pao hiun.

Précieuses instructions révélées.

Datées de 1760.

— XXII, livre 3.

關夫子筆帖九則

Koan fou tseu pi thie kieou tse.

Neuf règles dictées par le dieu de la Guerre.

Avec notes finales par Hoang Ming, de Tsin-kiang, et par Ho Tchen-yu, de Si-ling.

— XXIII, livre 3.

關聖帝君封號

Koan cheng ti kiun fong hao.

Titres du dieu de la Guerre.

Liste des titres décernés à cette divinité depuis 582 ; dressée par Hoang Ming en 1711.

- XXIV, livre 3.

關聖譜敘。再敘。世系宗圖

Koan cheng phou siu. Tsai siu. Chi hi tsong thou.

Table généalogique du dieu de la Guerre, avec deux préfaces.

La première préface (1711) est de Hoang Ming. La table généalogique est publiée d'après Oang Soẹn, de Hang-tcheou.

— XXV, livre 3.

關聖帝君世家

Koan cheng ti kiun chi kia.

Annales de la famille du dieu de la Guerre.

Par Oang Soẹn, de Oou-lin.

— XXVI, livre 3.

關聖帝君實錄

Koan cheng ti kiun chi lou.

Vie du dieu de la Guerre.

— XXVII, livre 3.

關聖帝君感應神武傳

Koan cheng ti kiun kan ying chen oou tchoan.

Histoire des miracles du dieu de la Guerre.

Avec postface par Hoang Ming (1709).

— XXVIII, livre 4.

玉歷鈔傳警世

Yu li tchhao tchhoan king chi.

Sous-titre :

玉帝慈恩纂載通行世間男婦改悔前非准贖罪惡玉歷

Yu ti tsheu 'en tsoan tsai thong hing chi kien nan fou kai hoei tshien fei tchoẹn chou tsoei 'o yu li.

Exemples de châtiment et de rachat des châtiments par le repentir.

Préfaces par Pheng Kieou-sieou et par Lou Khiao-mou. Figures représentant les châtiments et les récompenses (4 feuillets doubles). Auteur : Oou-mi tao-jen.

Titre noir sur blanc.

— XXIX, livre 4.

謹集增勸敬信懺悔

Kin tsi tseng khiuen king sin tchhan hoei.

Conseils de repentir.

Tirés de divers auteurs par le bonze de Thien-thai, Song-jan.

— XXX, livre 4.

鈔傳玉歷超度亡母夢驗

Tchhao tchhoan yu li tchhao tou oang mou mong yen.

Songe au sujet d'une mère défunte.

Rapporté par Ki Liang.

— XXXI, livre 4.

玉歷鈔傳敬信福報求
已堂李氏謹集

Yu li tchhao tchhoan king sin fou pao khieou yi thang li chi kin tsi.

Exemples de rétribution rapportés par Li, de la salle Khieou-yi.

Postface par Li Tsong-min, de Ming-chan (1794) ; notice par Tchou Yong, de Tshien-thang (1794).

— XXXII, livre 5.

廣生延壽錄

Koang cheng yen cheou lou.

Recueil relatif à la vie et à la longévité.

Collection de textes. Préface par Lou Khiao-mou. Préface primitive (1665) par Tchou Ying-cheng, surnom Ho-hien tao-jen, de Tshin-hoai. Préface de la réédition de 1797 par Chao Yuen-yin, de Chang-yu. Postface (1792 ?) par Si-yin.

Titre noir sur blanc.

— XXXIII, livre 5.

遵訓自敘

Tsoen hiun tseu siu.

Préface de l'auteur pour l'Observation des instructions.

Postérieure à 1785 ; non suivie d'un texte.

— XXXIV, livre 5.

禮佛日期

Li fo ji khi.

Dates des fêtes du Bouddha.

— XXXV, livre 5.

聖神寶誕日期

Cheng chen pao tan ji khi.

Dates des fêtes anniversaires de naissance des divinités taoïstes.

— XXXVI, livre 5.

救苦感應膏。丹方

Kieou khou kan ying kao.
Tan fang.

Formules de remèdes.

Grand in-8. Papier blanc ; titre noir sur blanc. 1 vol., demi-rel., au chiffre de Napoléon III.

Nouveau fonds 1207.

5681. — I.

太上感應篇

Thai chang kan ying phien.

Le Thai chang kan ying phien.

Préface (1813) et notice finale par Tcheou Khi-fen, surnom Koei-chan, de Choen-te. Préface par le dieu de la Littérature. Texte.

Édition en rouge sur papier teinté, par Liang Chou-thang (1829).

— II.

朱伯廬先生治家格言

Tchou po liu sien cheng tchi kia ko yen.

Instructions domestiques de Tchou Po-liu.

Même ouvrage qu'au n° 3440.

Impression en rouge sur papier teinté.

— III.

觀世音菩薩感應保生經

Koan chi yin phou sa kan ying pao cheng king.

Sūtra de Koan-yin qui répond aux prières et protège les êtres vivants.

Texte différent du n° 5677, art. VII.

Impression en rouge sur papier teinté.

— IV.

觀世音菩薩救苦經

Koan chi yin phou sa kieou khou king.

Sūtra de Koan-yin qui sauve du malheur.

Voir n° 5677, art. VI.

Impression en rouge sur papier teinté.

— V.

佛說高王觀世音經

Fo choe kao oang koan chi yin king.

Sūtra du souverain élevé Koan-yin (?)

Texte bouddhique.

Impression en rouge sur papier teinté.

— VI.

文昌帝君陰騭文

Oen tchhang ti kiun yin tchi oen.

Voir n° 5673, art. II.

Impression en rouge sur papier teinté.

— VII.

關聖帝君覺世眞經

Koan cheng ti kiun kio chi tchen king.

Le livre sacré de l'éveil du monde, par le dieu de la Guerre.

Comparer n° 5673, art. III.

Impression en rouge sur papier teinté.

— VIII.

經驗良方

King yen liang fang.

Formules éprouvées.

Préface en caractères rouges par Koei-chan; autre préface en caractères rouges (1829) écrite par Liang Yu-tchheng, à la salle Chou, à Choen-yi. Texte d'ordonnances pour pilules, décoctions, etc., imprimé en noir. Liste de bienfaiteurs.

Grand in-8. Titre noir sur jaune. 1 vol., demi-rel., au chiffre de Louis-Philippe.
Nouveau fonds 219.

5682. 同善錄。感應篇註證

Thong chan lou. Kan ying phien tchou tcheng.

Le Kan ying phien commenté.
Comparer n° 5679, art. I. Édition de la salle Thien-tsio.

Grand in-8. Exemplaire incomplet. 1 vol., cartonnage.
Nouveau fonds 5047.

5683. 帝君書鈔。陰騭文

Ti kiun chou tchhao. Yin tchi oen.

Traité de la fixation mystérieuse, par le dieu de la Littérature.

Texte et commentaire d'après Tchou Koei Chi-kiun, de Ta-hing. Réédition par Koo Tshing, de Min.

Préfaces par Tchou Koei (1768) et par Koo Tshing (1809).

Comparer n° 5673, art. II.

In-12. Papier blanc, titre noir sur rouge. 1 vol., demi-rel., au chiffre de Napoléon III.
Nouveau fonds 1444.

5684. 文昌帝君繪像寶訓

Oen tchhang ti kiun hoei siang pao hiun.

Précieuses instructions du dieu de la Littérature, avec illustrations.

Édition de la salle Tsiu-hien, à Canton (1833).

— I.

陰騭文圖註
Yin tchi oen thou tchou.

Le Yin tchi oen, illustré et commenté.

Texte seul; texte avec commentaire; exemples moraux avec illustrations. Préface par Pheng Lo-fong (1777); autre préface sans nom d'auteur, écrite à Canton (1833). Au début de l'ouvrage, préceptes moraux en grands caractères. Commentaire par Yen Tcheng Thing-piao, de Yun-kien; exemples moraux par Hoang Tcheng-yuen Thai-yi, de Min.

2 livres. Voir n° 5683.

— II

百善孝爲先

Po chan hiao oei sien.

De toutes les vertus, la piété filiale est la première.

Traité sans nom d'auteur ni date.

— III.

萬惡淫爲首

Oan 'o yin oei cheou.

De tous les vices, la luxure est le premier.

Sans nom d'auteur ni date.

— IV.

戒賭歌

Kiai tou ko.

Chanson contre le jeu.

— V.

續附應驗良方

Siu fou ying yen liang fang.

Annexes : recettes médicales diverses.

Petit in-8. Titre noir sur jaune. 1 vol., demi-rel., au chiffre de Napoléon III.
Nouveau fonds 1503.

———

5685. 新輯陰騭靈驗記

Sin tsi yin tchi ling yen ki.

Miracles du Yin tchi oen.

Texte du traité avec commentaires et exemples nombreux. Ouvrage composé à la salle Tchi-chan (1783); gravé à Canton (1796). A la fin, liste de bienfaiteurs.

Voir n° 5683.

Grand in-8. Titre noir sur jaune. 1 vol., demi-rel., au chiffre de Napoléon III.
Nouveau fonds 1373.

5686. 陰騭文詩箋

Yin tchi oen chi tsien.

Le Yin tchi oen avec paraphrases, rapprochements, commentaires.

Par Tchheng Koe-jen. Gravé de nouveau à la salle Lo-chan à Canton (1814).

Voir n° 5683.

Petit in-8. Titre noir sur jaune. 1 vol., demi-rel., au chiffre de Napoléon III.
Nouveau fonds 1257.

———

5687. 文帝全書內函

Oen ti tshiuen chou nei han.

Livres du dieu de la Littérature, première partie.

— I, livres 5 et 6.

文昌孝經新註

Oen tchhang hiao king sin tchou.

Livre sacré de la piété filiale, par Oen-tchhang.

Reproduction annamite (1847), de gravure très inégale, d'un ouvrage chinois gravé de nouveau (1845) à la salle Hoai-tę, à Tchhang-cha. Première préface sans auteur ni date. Préface (1492) par Khieou Khiong-chan, postnom Siun, surnom Tchong-chen, de Hai-nan; préface (1492) par Oang 'Ao Cheou-khi. Préface de 1706 par Pheng Ting-khieou, de Tchhang-tcheou; préfaces de 1693 et de 1735. Préface (1722) par l'auteur du commentaire, Thang Oan-hoang. Le texte a été compilé par Lieou Thi-chou Oou-oo-tseu, de Yi-ling; gravé de nouveau par Oang Tsi-tchai, de Tchang-chan. Pièce de vers de genre bouddhique; diverses annexes.

6 articles. Voir n° 5680, art. XIII.

— II, livres 7 à 9.

大洞經示讀註釋

Ta tong king chi tou tchou chi.

Le livre sacré de Ta-tong avec instructions pour la lecture et commentaires.

Publié par Lieou Thi-chou et Oang Tsi-tchai. Préface sans auteur ni date; préface par Oen-tchhang, datée de 1728, année de la révélation du livre; préface (1736) pour les instructions relatives à la lecture, par Ma-thien-kiun, divinité de la constellation Khoei.

Texte et commentaire suivis de 25 poésies.

3 livres (24 articles). — Comparer Bibl. coréenne, n° 2601, p. 168, 6° et 7°.

In-12. Titre noir sur rouge. 1 vol., cartonnage.
Nouveau fonds 4712.

5688. # 文始經釋辭

Oen chi king chi seu.

Le livre sacré de l'homme vrai Oen-chi, avec commentaire.

Préface (1597) au commentaire par Oou Tchi-pheng Yi-yun; préface par Oang Yi-tshing Sieou-yun, éditeur de divers ouvrages taoïstes, auteur du commentaire du présent ouvrage et d'une introduction de 1597. Vie de Oen-chi tchen-jen, auteur supposé de l'ouvrage, nom, postnom et surnom Yin Hi Kong-oen, vivant au XIᵉ siècle avant l'ère chrétienne et encore à l'époque de Lao-tseu. A la fin du volume, son et explication des caractères difficiles.

9 livres (9 sections). — Comparer Cat. imp., liv. 146. f. 16, Koan yin tseu (voir dans l'article, au f. 17, r°).

Grand in-8. 1 vol., demi-rel., au chiffre de Napoléon III.
Nouveau fonds 656.

5689. 性命圭旨

Sing ming koei tchi.

Autre titre :

性命雙修萬神圭旨

Sing ming choang sieou oan chen koei tchi.

Recueil de traités taoïstes.

Ouvrage révélé par Yin tchen-jen Kao-ti à l'un de ses élèves et conservé dans la famille Thang, de Sin-'an; gravé par les soins de Oou Seu-ming avec une notice (1615) par Yu Yong-ning Tchhang-ki, surnom Tchen-tchhou-tseu, de Sin-'an. Autre notice de la même date par Tcheou Yuen-piao. Préface (1669) par Yeou Thong; préface (1670) par Li Pho Tseu-tchong. Table pour les quatre sections; au verso, figure représentant les trois saints. Planches à la maison Yi-chan.

4 sections (les sections 3 et 4 sont interverties).

— I, section 1.

大道說

Ta tao choe.

Traité de la grande voie.

— II, section 1.

性命說

Sing ming choe.

Traité de la nature donnée par le ciel.

— III, section 1.

死生說

Seu cheng choe.

Traité de la vie et de la mort.

— IV, section 1.

邪正說

Sie tcheng choe.

Traité du pervers et du correct.

— V, section 1.

普照反照時照內照四圖

Phou tchao fan tchao chi tchao nei tchao seu thou.

Figures taoïstes de l'homme.

Quatre figures avec légendes.

— VI, section 1.

太極圖

Thai ki thou.

Figure du Thai-ki.

Avec légende.

— VII, section 1.

太極發揮

Thai ki fa hoei.

Guide du Thai-ki.

Texte.

— VIII, section 1.

中心圖

Tchong sin thou.

Figure du cœur.

Avec légende et texte.

— IX, section 1.

火龍水虎圖說

Hoo long choei hou thou choę.

Figures, avec légende, du dragon igné et du tigre aquatique.

— X, section 1.

日烏月兔圖說

Ji oou yue thou thou choę.

Figures, avec légende, du corbeau solaire et du lièvre lunaire.

— XI, section 1.

大小鼎爐圖說

Ta siao ting lou thou choę.

Figures, avec légende, des trépieds et fourneaux grands et petits.

— XII, section 1.

內外二藥圖說

Nei oai eul yo thou choę.

Figures, avec légende, des deux médications interne et externe.

— XIII, section 1.

順逆三關圖說

Choęn yi san koan thou choę.

Figures, avec légende, des trois communications.

Par la première, l'essence, tsing, se transmue en souffle, khi; par la seconde, le khi devient esprit, chen; par la troisième, le chen arrive au vide, hiu.

— XIV, section 1.

盡性了命圖說

Tsin sing liao ming thou choę.

Figures, avec légende, de l'achèvement de la nature et du mandat céleste.

— XV, section 1.

心安眞土圖。眞土根心說

Sin 'an tchen thou thou. Tchen thou ken sin choę.

Figures, et légende, sur les rapports du cœur et de la vraie terre.

— XVI, section 1.

魂魄圖說

Hoęn po thou'choę.

Figures, avec légende, de l'âme supérieure et de l'âme inférieure.

— XVII, section 1.

蟾光圖說

Chan koang thou choe.

Figures, avec légende, de la lune.

— XVIII, section 1.

降龍圖說

Hiang long thou choe.

Figures, avec légende, du dragon soumis.

— XIX, section 1.

伏虎圖說

Fou hou thou choe.

Figures, avec légende, du tigre soumis.

— XX, section 1.

三家相見圖說

San kia siang hien thou choe.

Figures, avec légende, sur les rapports du corps, de l'intelligence et du désir à leur apparition dans l'être humain.

— XXI, section 1.

和合四象圖說

Hoo ho seu siang thou choe.

Figures, avec légende, sur l'accord du dragon, du tigre, de l'oiseau et du guerrier.

— XXII, section 1.

取坎填離圖說

Tshiu khan thien li thou choe.

Figures, avec légende, relatives aux koa khan et li.

— XXIII, section 1.

念觀音咒圖說

Nien koan yin tcheou thou choe.

Figures, avec légende, relatives à la lecture des dhāraṇī de Koan-yin.

— XXIV, section 1.

九鼎煉心丹圖說

Kieou ting lien sin tan thou choe.

Figures, avec légende, sur la purification du cœur.

— XXV, section 1.

八識歸元圖說

Pa tchi koei yuen thou choe.

Figures, avec légende, relatives à la source des huit vijñāna.

— XXVI, section 1.

五氣朝元圖說

Oou khi tchhao yuen thou choe.

Figures, avec légende, relatives à la source des cinq influences.

— XXVII, section 1.

待詔圖說

Tai tchao thou choẹ.

Figures, avec légende, relatives à l'attente des ordres célestes.

— XXVIII, section 1.

飛昇圖說

Fei cheng thou choẹ.

Figures, avec légende, relatives à l'ascension du taoïste.

— XXIX, sections 2 à 4.

性命雙修萬神圭旨

Sing ming choang sieou oan chen koei tchi.

Préceptes de purification.

Texte avec figures; formant 9 articles.

Grand in-8. Bonne impression sur papier blanc; titre noir sur papier teinté. 1 vol., cartonnage.
Nouveau fonds 4593.

5690. 性命圭旨
Sing ming koei tchi.

Même ouvrage qu'au n° précédent, mêmes parties composantes et même disposition; gravure différente.

Grand in-8. Titre noir sur rose. Manquent la légende de l'art. XXIII et la planche de figures de l'art. XXIV. 1 vol., demi-rel., au chiffre de Louis-Philippe.
Nouveau fonds 433.

5691. — I.

呂祖醒心眞經

Liu tsou sing sin tchen king.

Livre sacré pour éveiller le cœur, par le dieu Fou-yeou.

Poésies de genre bouddhique; texte imité des sūtra, poésie, développement. Gravé à Canton (1707) à la salle Tchong Pao-koang; planches conservées au pavillon Chang-kou.

Comparer Bibl. coréenne, n° 2605, p. 179, 2e livre, 2°.

— II.

呂祖親示奉行規條果報

Liu tsou tshin chi fong hing koei thiao koo pao.

Rétribution pour l'observance des règles du Livre sacré.

Préceptes promulgués par le dieu Fou-yeou en personne. A la fin, notice.

Grand in-8. Bonne impression. 1 vol., demi-reliure.
Nouveau fonds 368.

5692. 唱道眞言

Tchhang tao tchen yen.

Véritables paroles pour étendre la religion.

Traité attribué à Tshing-hoa chang-ti. Diverses préfaces non datées; préface (1723) par Oan Tshing-hoo Koei-yi, de Ki-choei. Note spéciale sur la transmission des livres sacrés, par Tshing-hoa chang-ti. Préface par le même, sans date. Préface (1807) pour une réédition, par Hoang-yo chan-jen. Planches conservées à la salle Toęn-chan, à Han-tchen.

5 livres.

Grand in-8. Papier blanc; titre noir sur rouge. 1 vol., demi-rel., au chiffre de Louis-Philippe.

Nouveau fonds 437.

5693. 太微仙君純陽
祖師功過格

Thai oei sien kiun choęn yang tsou chi kong koo ko.

Echelle des mérites et des péchés par le dieu Fou-yeou.

Planches conservées au Collège provincial, à Canton. Table des matières.

— I.

功過格受持法

Kong koo ko cheou tchhi fa.

Echelle détaillée des mérites et des péchés.

Avec introduction et avertissement. Texte différent des nᵒˢ 5679, art. IV, et 5680, art. IV.

— II.

增訂居官功過格

Tseng ting kiu koan kong koo ko.

Echelle des mérites et des péchés de ceux qui sont dans les fonctions publiques.

Avec modèle de registre tenu par jour.

— III.

太上感應篇靈經

Thai chang kan ying phien ling king.

La Thai chang kan ying phien.

Texte seul, avec un avertissement.

Voir nᵒˢ 5671-5672, art. I.

— IV.

文昌帝君陰騭文

Oen ichhang ti kiun yin tchi oen.

Le Yin tchi oen.

Texte seul.

Voir nᵒ 5683.

— V.

孚佑帝君純陽呂祖師垂訓

Fou yeou ti kiun choẹn yang liu tsou chi tchhoei hiun.

Instructions du dieu Fou-yeou.

— VI.

袁了凡先生立命之學

Yuen liao fan sien cheng li ming tchi hio.

Science de la direction de la vie, par Yuen Liao-fan.

Le texte diffère du n° 5674, art. XXIX.

— VII.

佛母準提神咒

Fo mou tchoẹn thi chen tcheou.

Invocation de Caṇḍī, mère du Bouddha.

Voir n°ˢ 5674, art. XXXIII, et 5680, art. IX.

— VIII.

南無觀世音菩薩救苦神咒

Na mo koan chi yin phou sa kieou khou chen tcheou.

Invocation de Koan-yin qui sauve du malheur.

Texte en chinois et en transcription du sanscrit.

Comparer n° 5677, art. VI.

— IX.

俞淨意公遇竈神記

Yu tsing yi kong yu tsao chen ki.

Entrevue de Yu Tsing-yi avec l'esprit du Foyer.

Texte différent du n° 5677, art. XX.

— X.

感應篇靈驗記

Kan ying phien ling yen ki.

Miracles du Kan ying phien.

— XI.

陰騭文靈驗記

Yin tchi oen ling yen ki.

Miracles du Yin tchi oen.

Petit in-8. Papier blanc, bonne impression; titre noir sur jaune, 1 vol., demi-reliure.

Nouveau fonds 399.

5694. 大洞眞經

Ta tong tchen king.

Le vrai livre sacré de Ta-tong.

Même ouvrage qu'au n° 5687, art. II; n'ayant pas la préface sans date et ne portant pas le nom des éditeurs. A la fin de la table, on lit la date de 1819. En outre, postface par Tshing-hoa tao-tsou. Gravé à Canton (?) à la salle Pi-chou (1825).

Grand in-8. Bonne impression; titre noir sur jaune. 1 vol., demi-reliure.
Nouveau fonds 361.

5695-5696. 呂祖全書
Liu tsou tshiuen chou.

Œuvres de Liu tsou.

Attribuées à Liu Tong-pin, post-nom Yen, surnom Choẹn-yang-tseu, nom divin Fou-yeou. Gravées par les soins de Yu Tsieou-fong, de Oou-lin; planches conservées au jardin Khi. Préface (1744) par Tchhen Tẹ-yong Mi-chan, de Oou-hing; préface (1742) par Lieou Tshiao Ko-tchhen, de Oou-ling; préface sans date par Hoang Chao-cheng, surnom Yi-hing-tseu, de Cha-yi. Table générale, avertissement. Le recueil a été préparé par Lieou Tshiao.

— I, livre 1 (5695).

呂祖本傳
Liu tsou pẹn tchoan.

Vie de Liu tsou.

Par Lieou Tshiao, d'après divers ouvrages taoïstes. Préface, table; portrait et éloge du dieu; texte et annexes. Gravé par les soins de

Yu Oen-yao Pho-tshoẹn, de Oou-lin.

— II, livre 2 (5695).

靈應事蹟
Ling ying chi tsi.

Miracles du dieu.

Ouvrage préparé et édité par les mêmes. Préface sans auteur ni date.

— III, livre 3 à 5 (5695).

文集
Oen tsi.

Recueil d'œuvres en prose et en vers, du dieu Fou-yeou.

Avec diverses préfaces; l'une est signée de Tchhen Tẹ-yi Kou-chen-tseu; une autre (1422) est par Tchang Cheou-tshing Si-pi-oong, descendant de Tchang Tao-ling à la quarante-quatrième génération.

3 livres.

— IV, livre 6 (5695).

指玄三燦篇
Tchi hiuen san tshan phien.

Traité du triple éclat pour indiquer le mystère.

Par le dieu Fou-yeou, avec préface de l'auteur. Préface par Koo Tchhou-yang, surnom Khi-kou-tseu, de Tseu-yang; commentaire par Po Tseu-tshing.

— V, livres 7 et 8 (5695).

忠孝誥

Tchong hiao kao.

Prescriptions relatives à la fidélité et à la piété filiale.

Avec une préface sans auteur ni date, et une préface signée Chi Ta-tchheng.

— VI, livres 9 et 10 (5695).

前八品仙經

Tshien pa phin sien king.

Le premier livre sacré des génies, en huit sections.

Par le même dieu Fou-yeou, avec présace de l'auteur. Préface (1614) par Tchao Sing-soei, surnom Hoan-yang tao-jen; autre préface (1589) par Li Ying-yang, de Koang-ling. Figures relatives à la cosmogonie. Vers de genre bouddhique.

2 livres.

— VII, livre 11 (5695).

後八品經

Heou pa phin king.

Le second livre sacré, en huit sections.

Préfaces, dont une par l'auteur; texte suivi de formules d'exorcisme, de charmes, etc. Postface sans nom d'auteur (1675).

— VIII, livre 12 (5695).

五品仙經

Oou phin sien king.

Le livre sacré des génies, en cinq sections.

Préface sans nom d'auteur ni date. Autre préface non datée par Hoang Tchheng-chou Yi-hing-tseu, de Cha-yi. Figures; éloges. Vie du lettré Fou.

— IX, livres 13 à 15 (5695-5696).

清微三品經

Tshing oei san phin king.

Le livre sacré en trois sections, du palais Tshing-oei.

Deux préfaces non datées, l'une est due à Hoang Tchheng-chou; préface par l'auteur. Vers de genre bouddhique, éloge, notice finale.

3 livres. — Comparer Bibl. coréenne, n° 2605, p. 177, 1°.

— X, livres 16 à 18 (5696).

參同經

Tshan thong king.

Le Tshan thong king.

3 livres. — Comparer n° 5668, art. I.

— XI, livre 19 (5696).

聖德諸品經

Cheng te tchou phin king.

Le livre sacré de la sainteté.

Préface sans nom d'auteur ni date.

Comparer Bibl. coréenne, n° 2605, p. 179, 5°.

— XII, livre 19 (5696).

賢德經

Hien te king.

Le livre sacré de la sagesse.

Bibl. coréenne, n° 2605, p. 180, 6°.

— XIII, livre 19 (5696).

修養經

Sieou yang king.

Le livre sacré du perfectionnement moral.

Bibl. coréenne, n° 2605, p. 180, 7°.

— XIV, livre 19 (5696).

養氣存神經

Yang khi tshoen chen king.

Le livre sacré de l'entretien du souffle et de la conservation de l'esprit.

Bibl. coréenne, n° 2605, p. 180, 8°.

— XV, livre 19 (5696).

定證經

Ting tcheng king.

Le livre sacré des témoignages certains.

Bibl. coréenne, n° 2605, p. 180, 9°.

— XVI, livre 19 (5696).

夜氣妙經

Ye khi miao king.

Le merveilleux livre sacré du souffle pendant la nuit.

Bibl. coréenne, n° 2605, p. 180, 10°.

— XVII, livre 19 (5696).

無有執著經

Oou yeou tchi tcho king

Le livre sacré de l'intangible.

Bibl. coréenne, n° 2605, p. 180, 11°.

— XVIII, livre 19 (5696).

湛寧經

Tchan ning king.

Le livre sacré de la sérénité.

Bibl. coréenne, n° 2605, p. 180, 12°.

— XIX, livre 19 (5696).

玄宗大乘經

Hiuen tsong ta cheng king.

Le livre sacré du grand véhicule du chef mystérieux.

Bibl. coréenne, n° 2605, p. 180, 13°.

— XX, livre 19 (5696).

無上大乘經

Oou chang ta cheng king.

Le livre sacré du grand véhicule suprême.

Bibl. coréenne, n° 2605, p. 180, 14°.

— XXI, livre 19 (5696).

證修經

Tcheng sieou king.

Le livre sacré du perfectionnement.

Comparer Bibl. coréenne, n° 2605, p. 180, 15° (Tcheng oou king).

— XXII, livre 20 (5696).

金丹直指經

Kin tan tchi tchi king.

Le livre sacré de l'élixir d'immortalité.

Bibl. coréenne, n° 2605, p. 180, 16°.

— XXIII, livre 20 (5696).

明道歸眞經

Ming tao koei tchen king.

Le livre sacré du chemin pour revenir à la vérité.

Bibl. coréenne, n° 2605, p. 180, 17°.

— XXIV, livre 20 (5696).

寂淡宗一經

Tsi tan tsong yi king.

Le livre sacré de l'unité originelle dans le silence.

Bibl. coréenne, n° 2605, p. 180, 18°.

— XXV, livre 20 (5696).

萬化歸一經

Oan hoa koei yi king.

Le livre sacré des dix mille transformations aboutissant à l'unité.

Bibl. coréenne, n° 2605, p. 181, 19°.

— XXVI, livre 20 (5696).

辟幻眞經

Pi hoan tchen king.

Le vrai livre sacré dissipant le faux.

Bibl. coréenne, n° 2605, p. 181, 20°.

— XXVII, livre 20 (5696).

尊生妙經

Tsoen cheng miao king.

Le merveilleux livre sacré du respect de la vie.

Bibl. coréenne, n° 2605, p. 181, 21°.

— XXVIII, livre 20 (5696).

克己妙經

Khe ki miao king.

Le merveilleux livre sacré de la victoire sur soi-même.

Bibl. coréenne, n° 2605, p. 181, 22°.

— XXIX, livre 20 (5696).

斷障歸一經

Toan tchang koei yi king.

Le livre sacré pour dompter et unifier.

Bibl. coréenne, n° 2605, p. 181, 23°.

— XXX, livre 20 (5696).

制 發 妙 經

Tchi fa miao king.

Le merveilleux livre sacré réglant les manifestations.

Bibl. coréenne, n° 2605, p. 181, 24°.

— XXXI, livre 20 (5696).

止 了 妙 經

Tchi liao miao king.

Le merveilleux livre sacré de la fin.

Bibl. coréenne, n° 2605, p. 181, 25°.

— XXXII, livre 20 (5696).

真 密 經

Tchen mi king.

Le livre sacré du secret véritable.

Bibl. coréenne, n° 2605, p. 181, 26°.

— XXXIII, livre 20 (5696).

眞 默 經

Tchen me king.

Le livre sacré du silence véritable.

Bibl. coréenne, n° 2605, p. 181, 27°.

— XXXIV, livre 20 (5696).

烏 有 說

Oou yeou choe.

Dialogue avec un voyageur.

Bibl. cor., n° 2605, p. 188, 4e partie, 4°.

— XXXV, livre 20 (5696).

湖 濱 宵 話

Hou pin siao hoa.

Paroles prononcées la nuit au bord du lac.

Bibl. coréenne, n° 2605, p. 188, 4e partie, 5°.

— XXXVI, livre 20 (5696).

湖 濱 再 說

Hou pin tsai choe.

Nouvelles paroles prononcées au bord du lac.

Bibl. coréenne, n° 2605, p. 188, 4e partie, 6°.

— XXXVII, livre 20 (5696).

清 靜 元 君 坤 元 經

Tshing tsing yuen kiun khoen yuen king.

Le livre sacré du mystère terrestre.

A la différence des ouvrages précédents, celui-ci n'est pas du dieu Fou-yeou, mais du génie Soen Tshing-tsing.

— XXXVIII, livre 21 (5696).

醒 心 眞 經

Sing sin tchen king.

Le vrai livre sacré pour éveiller le cœur, par le dieu Fou-yeou.

Préface (1707) par Kou Tcheou-keng, de Thai-tshang. Texte et poésies analogues au n° 5691, art. I.

— XXXIX, livre 21 (5696).

呂 祖 親 示 奉 行 規 條 果 報

Liu tsou tshin chi fong hing koei thiao koo pao.

Rétribution pour l'observance des règles du Livre sacré précédent.

Voir n° 5691, art. II.

— XL, livre 22 (5696).

太 上 說 呂 祖 斗 光 度 厄 護 命 大 神 咒 經

Thai chang choẹ liu tsou teou koang tou 'o hou ming ta chen tcheou king.

Le livre sacré de l'invocation pour traverser l'infortune et protéger la vie, donné au dieu Fou-yeou.

Préface sans nom d'auteur ni date. Texte, suivi d'une invocation en quatre articles.

— XLI, livre 22 (5696).

救 苦 難 神 咒

Kieou khou nan chen tcheou.

Invocation pour sauver des calamités.

— XLII, livre 22 (5696).

滌 氛 神 咒

Ti fen chen tcheou.

Invocation contre les mauvaises influences.

— XLIII, livre 23 (5696).

棲 眞 宣 演 拔 濟 苦 海 雪 過 修 眞 仙 懺

Si tchen siuen yen pa tsi khou hai siue koo sieou tchen sien tchhan.

Invocation pour tirer des calamités, effacer les péchés, progresser dans la vérité.

Avec préface. Texte et formule d'invocation.

Comparer Bibl. coréenne, n° 2605, p. 178, 2°.

— XLIV, livre 23 (5696).

呂 祖 讚. 呂 祖 九 陽 齋 期

Liu tsou tsan. Liu tsou kieou yang tchai khi.

Prières et fêtes en l'honneur du dieu Fou-yeou.

— XLV, livre 24 (5696).

玉樞寶經 讚

Yu tchhou pao king; tsan.

Le livre sacré du Pivot de jade.

Préface, texte du livre sacré, éloge.

Bibl. coréenne, n° 2594.

— XLVI, livre 24 (5696).

一行子玉樞或問

Yi hing tseu yu tchhou hoẹ oen.

Questions sur le Yu tchhou king, par Yi-hing-tseu.

— XLVII, livres 25 et 26 (5696).

葫頭集

Hou theou tsi.

Collection de Hou theou.

Œuvres du dieu Fou-yeou. Préface sans nom d'auteur ni date; préfaces par Tchong tsou et par Tchhen sien-cheng; préface de l'auteur. Postface de 1661.

2 livres. — Comparer Bibl. coréenne, n° 2605, p. 185, 22°.

— XLVIII, livre 27 (5696).

涵三雜詠

Han san tsa yong.

Chants de Han-san.

Le Han-san kong est un temple

du dieu Fou-yeou, situé à 'O-tchheng. Préface sans nom d'auteur ni date, rapportant divers miracles depuis 1702.

— XLIX, livre 28 (5696).

涵三語錄

Han san yu lou.

Entretiens de Han-san.

Avec préface.

— L, livre 28 (5696).

涵三語錄續輯

Han san yu lou siu tsi.

Entretiens de Han-san, suite.

— LI, livre 28 (5696).

涵三語錄後記

Han san yu lou heou ki.

Autre titre :

峨眉王仙師後記

'O mei oang sien chi heou ki.

Dernière notice des entretiens de Han-san.

Texte incomplet; voir art. LIX.

— LII, livre 29 et 30 (5696).

修真傳道論

Sieou tchen tchhoan tao loẹn.

Dissertation sur le développement de la vérité et la diffusion du tao.

Texte communiqué au dieu Fou-yeou par Tcheng-yang tsou-chi. Préface sans nom d'auteur ni date.

2 livres (18 sections).

— LIII, livre 31 (5696).

無瑕子敲爻歌註

Oou hia tseu khiao hiao ko tchou.

Le chant de l'action réciproque des deux principes, avec commentaire.

Par Tshien Tao-hoa, surnom Oou-hia-tseu, de Kou-sou. Préface de 1443.

— LIV, livre 31 (5696).

沁園春註

Tshin yuen tchhoen tchou.

Le printemps du jardin de Tshin, avec commentaire.

Texte sur les transformations du kin tan. Commentaire par Siao Thing-tchi Yuen-choei, surnom Tseu-hiu liao-tchen tseu.

— LV, livre 31 (5696).

沁園春註

Tshin yuen tchhoen tchou.

Le printemps du jardin de Tshin, avec commentaire.

Même texte; commentaire par Yu Yen, surnoms Tshiuen-yang tseu et Lin-oou chan-jen.

— LVI, livre 32 (5696).

呂祖誥

Liu tsou kao.

Pièces diverses relatives à Liu tsou.

9 pièces.

— LVII, livre 32 (5696).

柳眞君誥

Lieou tchen kiun kao.

Pièces relatives à Lieou tchen-kiun.

Lieou Khi, surnom Tshing-tshing tseu, est un dignitaire de la cour céleste taoïste.

— LVIII, livre 32 (5696).

葛天君誥

Ko thien kiun kao.

Pièces relatives à Ko thien-kiun.

Ko Ming-yang est un dignitaire de la cour céleste.

— LIX, livre 32 (5696).

王仙師誥

Oang sien chi kao.

Pièces relatives à Oang sien-chi.

Oang 'Tchen Thong-ki, surnom 'O-mei-tseu, est un élève du dieu Fou-yeou. Postfaces pour le re-

20

cueil total, par Yi-hing-tseu et Oou-oo-tseu.

Grand in-8. Titre noir sur jaune. 2 vol., demi-rel., au chiffre de Louis-Philippe.

Nouveau fonds 590.

5697. 帝君降乩遏慾訓註証

Ti kiun kiang ki'o yu hiun tchou tcheng.

Instructions divines contre les convoitises.

Rassemblées et commentées par Oang Tao-tshiuen, de Tang-khiu; l'ouvrage provient originairement de Khien-yang. Préface pour la présente réédition par Pheng Thien Hoei-'an, de Tan-ling. Gravé en 1802; planches conservées au Collège provincial de Canton. A la fin, liste des donateurs. Le texte est accompagné d'explications disposées par colonnes alternant avec celles du texte.

Grand in-8. Bonne impression sur papier blanc; titre noir sur jaune. 1 vol., demi-reliure.

Nouveau fonds 360.

5698. 新刻暗室燈註。敬信錄解

Sin kho'an chi teng tchou. King sin lou kiai.

La lampe de la salle obscure, avec commentaire. Le livre du respect et de la foi expliqué.

Réimpression de Canton (1831), nette, mais d'aspect vulgaire, avec préface (1831) par Tcheng Joenthing. Préface (1816) par Liao Khang-khing Koei-thien, de Heng, pour une autre réédition; cette préface rappelle une édition précédente donnée en 1807 par Chenchan kiu-chi. Table des matières, coïncidant mal avec l'ouvrage.

2 livres. — Bibl. coréenne, nᵒˢ 2618, 2619. — Actes du Congrès international des Orientalistes, Paris 1897, 2ᵉ tome, p. 37 (2ᵉ tome, grand in-8, Paris 1898). Voir plus haut, nᵒ 5677.

— I, livre 1.

文昌帝君曉世文敘

Oen tchhang ti kiun hiao chi oen siu.

Traité pour éclairer le monde, par le dieu de la Littérature : préface.

— II, livre 1.

關聖帝君新降惺言勸世文

Koan cheng ti kiun sin kiang sing yen khiuen chi oen.

Conseils au monde, par le dieu de la Guerre.

Révélés en 1810, sur le bord du ruisseau du roc de Pi-lou.

— III, livre 1.

關聖帝君寶訓

Koan cheng ti kiun pao hiun.

Précieuses instructions du dieu de la Guerre.

Données à Pi-lou-chi (1811).

— IV, livre 1.

暗室燈前議

'An chi teng tshien yi.

La lampe de la salle obscure : explication préliminaire.

— V, livre 1.

曉世文

Hiao chi oen.

Traité pour éclairer le monde.

Révélé par le dieu de la Littérature, à Pao-tou (1803). Texte et commentaire.

— VI, livre 1.

一清道人積福歌

Yi tshing tao jen tsi fou ko.

Chants de Yi-tshing tao-jen sur le bonheur.

Trois chants en vers de cinq et de sept syllabes.

— VII, livre 1.

文昌帝君警世文

Oen tchhang ti kiun king chi oen.

Avertissements au monde par le dieu de la Littérature.

Révélés en 1800 à un homme du Kiang-nan. Texte sans commentaire.

— VIII, livre 1.

關聖帝君靈驗記

Koan cheng ti kiun ling yen ki.

Miracles du dieu de la Guerre.

Texte avec annexes.

— IX, livre 1.

原釋道正論

Yuen chi tao tcheng loen.

Dissertation sur le tao et la rectitude.

Texte en 9 articles, avec exemples annexes.

— X, livre 1.

重刻感應篇

Tchhong kho kan ying phien.

Le Kan ying phien.

Texte; avertissement; préface moderne.

Voir n°s 5671-5672, art. I.

— XI, livre 1.

感應篇靈驗記

Kan ying phien ling yen ki.

Miracles du Kan ying phien.

Comparer nº 5693, art. X.

— XII, livre 1.

文昌帝君重申陰騭文訓

Oen tchhang ti kiun tchhong chen yin tchi oen hiun.

Instructions sur la fixation mystérieuse, données de nouveau par le dieu de la Littérature.

Ouvrage différent du nº 5673, art. II; avec récit de miracles et dissertation en annexe.

— XIII, livre 1.

重刻戒溺女文

Tchhong kho kiai ni niu oen.

Traité pour interdire l'infanticide des filles.

Préface, texte et annexes.

Comparer nº 5677, art. XXV.

— XIV, livre 2.

集鑑

Tsi kien.

Collection de miroirs.

Préceptes et exemples relatifs à dix-neuf séries d'actes bons et mauvais; avec une dissertation générale et quelques poésies.

— XV, livre 2.

袁了凡立命篇

Yuen liao fan li ming phien.

Science de la direction de la vie, par Yuen Liao-fan.

Texte analogue au nº 5674, art. XXIX.

Gravure beaucoup plus élégante qu'aux articles précédents.

— XVI, livre 2.

準提咒

Tchoẹn thi tcheou.

Invocation de Caṇḍī.

Voir nº 5693, art. VII.

— XVII, livre 2.

文昌帝君功過格

Oen tchhang ti kiun kong koo ko.

Autre titre :

太微仙君功過格

Thai oei sien kiun kong koo ko.

Echelle des mérites et des péchés par le dieu de la Littérature.

Même préface et même texte qu'au nº 5679, art. IV.

— XVIII, livre 2.

文昌帝君戒條

Oen tchhang ti kiun kiai thiao.

Défenses du dieu de la Littérature.

Différentes du n° 5679, art. VI.

Petit in-8. Titre noir sur jaune. 1 vol., demi-rel.
Nouveau fonds 423.

5699. 呂祖三世因果說

Liu tsou san chi yin koo choe.

Traité de la rétribution s'étendant à trois générations, par le dieu Fou-yeou.

En vers de sept syllabes; avec explications et commentaires en prose. Préface (1819) dictée par le dieu; portrait du dieu, avec éloge. Postface sans nom d'auteur ni date. Gravé par Tchou Jen-loen, fidèle taoïste, de Liang-chan (1822).

Grand in-8. Papier blanc; bonne impression; titre noir sur jaune. 1 vol., demi-reliure.
Nouveau fonds 369.

5700. 平旦鐘聲
Phing tan tchong cheng.

Recueil d'exhortations et d'exemples.

Compilé au pavillon Hao-te; gravé de nouveau par Lo-chan chan-jen; planches conservées au pavillon Fou-oen, à Canton (?)

2 livres.

Petit in-8. Titre noir sur jaune. 1 vol., demi-rel., au chiffre de Napoléon III.
Nouveau fonds 1356.

5701. *Phing tan tchong cheng·*

Même ouvrage; réédition de la salle Lien-chan.

In-12. Papier blanc. 1 vol., demi-rel., au chiffre de Louis-Philippe.
Nouveau fonds 93.

5702. 高上玉皇本行集經
Kao chang yu hoang pen hing tsi king.

Le Livre sacré des actions de Kao-chang yu hoang.

Au début, tablette portant des vœux pour l'empereur et cinq gravures représentant diverses scènes. Préface par Phou-hoa thien-ti. Éloges, formules d'invocation; rites à accomplir, etc. Texte rédigé à l'imitation des sūtra, avec commentaire. A la fin gravé : en 1818 par Lieou-thong, de Hai-tchhoang; figure de dieu guerrier.

2 + 3 livres. — Voir Bibl. coréenne, n° 2601, p. 167, 6ᵉ livre, 2ᵉ partie, 1°.

Petit in-8. Bonne impression sur papier blanc. 1 vol., demi-rel., au chiffre de Louis-Philippe.
Nouveau fonds 89.

5703. 靈應泰山娘娘寶卷

Ling ying thai chan niang niang pao kiuen.

Le livre précieux des déesses du Thai-chan.

Sorte d'office de ces divinités, en langue parlée. Gravures représentant des divinités et tablettes portant des vœux (4 feuillets doubles).

1er livre seul.

Format 0,38 × 0,12 en paravent. Belle impression; couverture en soie, titre en lettres d'or. 1 vol. Renfermé dans 1 étui demi-reliure.

Nouveau fonds 2319.

Deuxième Section : BIOGRAPHIES ET LÉGENDES

5704-5707. 夷堅志

Yi kien tchi.

Collection de légendes et de faits miraculeux.

Par Hong Mai King-lou, surnom Yong-tchai, de Pho-yang (1124-1203). Préfaces (1778) par Chen Pi-tchan, de Jen-hoo, et par Ho Khi.

20 sections. — Comparer Cat. imp., liv. 142, f. 38 (Yi kien tchi tchi, en 50 livres).

In-12. Titre noir sur jaune. 4 vol., demi-rel., au chiffre de Louis-Philippe.
Nouveau fonds 668.

5708. — I.

在茲堂新鐫繡像列仙傳

Tsai tseu thang sin tsiuen sieou siang lie sien tchoan.

Vies des génies, avec portraits, édition de la salle Tsai-tseu.

Recueillies par Hoan-tchhou tao-jen, nom littéraire Tseu-tchheng. Introduction par Yuen Hoang Liao-fan (époque des Ming). Le titre est daté de 1833.

3 livres. — Différent du Cat. imp., liv. 146, f. 32 (Lie sien tchoan, en 2 livres).

— II.

長生詮

Tchhang cheng tshiuen.

Dissertations sur l'immortalité.

Extraits de traités taoïstes, rassemblés par le même auteur; forme le 4e livre de l'ouvrage.

1 livre.

Grand in-8. Titre sur papier rouge.

1 vol., demi-rel., au chiffre de Louis-Philippe.

Nouveau fonds 451.

5709. 刻出像增補搜神記大全

Kho tchhou siang tseng pou seou chen ki ta tshiuen.

Nouvelles recherches sur les divinités.

Ouvrage illustré, traitant de toutes les divinités, y compris Confucius, les divinités bouddhiques, les génies taoïstes, etc. Introduction par Lo Meou-teng, qui a lu en 1593 le Seou chen ki de Yu Pao. Gravé par Thang Fou-tchhoen, à Kin-ling.

6 livres. — Comparer Cat. imp., liv. 142, f. 14 (Seou chen ki, en 20 livres).

Petit in-8. Titre sur papier teinté. 1 vol., demi-rel., au chiffre de Louis-Philippe.

Nouveau fonds 883.

5710. 三教源流聖帝佛帥搜神大全

San kiao yuen lieou cheng ti fo choai seou chen ta tshiuen.

Histoire des divinités des trois religions.

Ouvrage analogue au précédent; sans préface ni nom d'auteur. Illustrations.

7 livres.

Petit in-8. Impression grossière; titre noir sur jaune. 1 vol., cartonnage (prov. de la collection Mohl).

Nouveau fonds 4383.

5711. 關聖帝君聖蹟圖誌全集

Koan cheng ti kiun cheng tsi thou tchi tshiuen tsi.

Histoire et images du dieu de la Guerre.

Collection de documents archéologiques, historiques, littéraires et autres, relatifs à cette divinité; avec des gravures. Table en tête de chaque livre. Par Lou Tchan Siun-chen, de Thao-yuen. Préface (1693) par Yu Tchheng-long Tchen-kia, de San-han; préface (1692) par Oang Oei-tchen Mei-kou, de San-han; autres préfaces. Table générale des matières; liste des ouvrages cités; liste des bienfaiteurs. A la fin, postface (1729) par Khang Hong-mou, de King-yang.

5 livres. — Bibl. coréenne, n° 3709.

Grand in-8. Belle impression sur papier blanc. 1 vol., demi-rel., au chiffre de Louis-Philippe.

Nouveau fonds 455.

5712-5715. 歷代神仙通鑑

Li tai chen sien thong kien.

Histoire des divinités sous les dynasties successives.

Biographies et légendes taoïstes, publiées à la salle Tchi-hoo, par les soins de Tchang ta tchen-jen, postnom Ki-tsong, de Long-hou-chan, et de Hoang Tchang-loen, de Pao-chan. Auteur : Siu Tao, surnom Ming-yang siuen-chi, de Kiang-hia. Préface (1700) par Tchang Ki-tsong; autre préface sans nom d'auteur, de 1712; préface de l'auteur, avec une notice de la période Khang-hi. Illustrations.

22 livres. — Wylie, Notes on Chinese literature (1 vol. in-4, Shanghae, 1867), p. 179.

Grand in-8. Titre noir sur jaune. 4 vol., demi-rel., au chiffre de Louis-Philippe.
Nouveau fonds 377.

5716-5720. *Li tai chen sien thong kien.*

Double.

5 vol., cartonnage.
Nouveau fonds 4406 à 4410.

5721. 天后聖母聖蹟圖誌全集

Thien heou cheng mou cheng tsi thou tchi tshiuen tsi.

Histoire et images de l'Impératrice céleste.

Divinité des marins, née au ix⁰ ou au x⁰ siècle. Généalogie; notes sur divers temples et sur le culte qui y est célébré, la dernière est de 1810. Portrait de la déesse, gravures représentant des scènes de sa vie, avec légendes : depuis la naissance (960) jusqu'à 1826. Formules d'invocation, notes rituelles.

Comparer Wylie, Notes on Chinese literature, p. 180.

Grand in-8. Bonne impression sur papier blanc. 1 vol., demi-rel., au chiffre de Louis-Philippe.
Nouveau fonds 460.

———

5722. 集說詮眞

Tsi choe tshiuen tchen.

Veritas collectis textibus demonstrata.

Notes méthodiques au sujet des divinités, donnant, avec les textes des auteurs, des commentaires et discussions. Par le P. Hoang Paul, surnom Fei-me, de la mission du Kiang-nan. Imprimé à la salle Jen-tsheu (orphelinat de Zi-ka-wei) près de Chang-hai, avec l'autorisation de Mgr. Garnier; première édition de 1879, nouvelle édition de 1885. Préface de l'auteur (1878); préface par Tsiang Tchhao-fan Hing-tsou, prêtre. Liste des références; avertissement; table des matières avec renvoi aux pages. Postface (1878) par Kiu Jean, surnom Oan-chi cheng.

Catalogus librorum, n° 18.

Grand in-8. Bonne impression sur papier blanc; titre noir sur blanc, avec la date au verso. 1 vol., cartonnage.
Nouveau fonds 5130.

Troisième Section : **CULTE, EXORCISMES, ETC.**

5723.

Cong = Fou ou Postures de Bonzes Tao = sée.

20 peintures grossières.

Petit in-8. 1 cahier.
Département des Estampes, Oc 59.

5724. — 1.

秘傳祝由科
Pi tchhoan tchou yeou khoo.

Autre titre :

祝由科秘旨救世靈書
Tchou yeou khoo pi tchi kieou chi ling chou.

Recueil de talismans contre les maladies.

Figures magiques avec explications. D'après l'ouvrage original de Hien-yuen Hoang ti.

Titre noir sur jaune.

— II.

秘傳文筆籙
Pi tchhoan oen pi lou.

Recueil magique.

D'après Hoang ti.

Titre noir sur papier teinté.
Petit in-8. 1 vol., demi-rel., au chiffre de Louis-Philippe.

Nouveau fonds 386.

5725. # 新刻京板觀音靈課
Sin kho king pan koan yin ling khoo.

Divination à l'aide des koa et en invoquant Koan-yin, édition de la Capitale.

Ouvrage revu au pavillon Tshoen-khien, gravé par Tchang Kong-kao.

21

Petit in-8. Gravure médiocre; titre noir sur papier teinté. 1 vol., cartonnage (prov. des Missions Étrangères).
Fourmont 345.

5726. 太上三元賜福赦罪解厄消灾延生保命妙經

Thai chang san yuen seu fou chę tsoei kiai'o siao tsai yen cheng pao ming miao king.

Le livre sacré des trois dieux suprêmes.

Recueil de formules d'invocation, éloges, pièces rituelles en l'honneur de Tseu-oei ta ti, Tshing-hiu ta ti et Tong-yin ta ti, qui président respectivement au ciel, à la terre, à l'eau. Au début, deux feuillets doubles de gravures; à la fin une tablette d'invocation aux trois dieux.

Petit in-8. Bonne impression sur papier blanc. 1 vol., en paravent dans 1 étui demi-rel., au chiffre de Napoléon III.
Nouveau fonds 1945.

Chapitre XI : BOUDDHISME[1] (MAHĀYĀNA SŪTRA)

Première Section : PRAJÑĀPĀRAMITĀ SŪTRA

5727. 放光般若波羅
蜜經

Fang koang pan jẹ po lo mi king.

Pañcaviṃçati sāhasrikā pra-jñāpāramitā sūtra.

Traduit par Oou-lo-tchha (Mok-ṣala [Nanjio], ou plutôt Gorakṣa), de Khoten, et Tchou Chou-lan, d'origine hindoue (291). Lecture des signes difficiles. Édition de 1610.

3o livres (manquent les 5 derniers). — Bunyiu Nanjio 2.

Grand in-8. Frontispice (1 feuillet double); bonne gravure. 1 vol. demi-rel., au chiffre de la République.
Nouveau fonds 3694.

5728. — I.

金剛般若波羅蜜經

Kin kang pan jẹ po lo mi king.

Vajracchedikā prajñāpāramitā sūtra.

Traduction de Kumārajīva, religieux d'origine hindoue, traducteur en 402-412. Frontispice, deux feuillets doubles et un feuillet simple; éloge, dhāraṇī, etc., puis texte. A la fin, figure d'une divinité. Édition de la bonzerie de Hai-tchhoang (1771).

Bunyiu Nanjio 10.

—II.

補闕眞言

Pou khiue tchen yen.

Dhāraṇī.

---

1. Pour ce chapitre et les suivants relatifs au bouddhisme, M. Sylvain Lévi, professeur au Collège de France, a bien voulu m'aider de sa grande compétence. — M. C.

In-4. Papier blanc; 1 vol. en paravent à couvertures rouges; dans 1 étui demi-rel. au chiffre de Louis-Philippe.
Nouveau fonds 150.

5729. — I.

Kin kang pan je po lo mi king.

Même ouvrage avec prière au début.

— II.

般 若 無 盡 藏 眞 言。補 闕 眞 言

Pan je oou tsin tsang tchen yen. Pou khiue tchen yen.

Deux dhāraṇī.

Suivies d'un éloge. Édition de Hai-tchhoang (1807).

In-12. Papier blanc. 1 vol. en paravent couverture rouge; dans 1 étui demi-reliure.
Nouveau fonds 137.

5730. 金 剛 般 若 經 六 譯 本

Kin kang pan je king lou yi pen.

Six traductions du Vajracchedikā prajñā sūtra.

Édition de 1831. Table générale.

— I.

金 剛 般 若 波 羅 蜜 經

Kin kang pan je po lo mi king.

Vajracchedikā prajñāpāramitā sūtra.

Traduction de Kumārajīva.

14 feuillets. — Nº 5728, art. I.

— II.

Kin kang pan je po lo mi king.

Traduction de Bodhiruci, Hindou, traducteur en 508-535.

17 feuillets. — Bunyiu Nanjio 11.

— III.

Kin kang pan je po lo mi king.

Traduction de Paramārtha, Hindou (562).

17 feuillets. — Bunyiu Nanjio 12.

— IV.

金 剛 能 斷 般 若 波 羅 蜜 經

Kin kang neng toan pan je po lo mi king.

Traduction de Dharmagupta, Hindou, traducteur en 616.

19 feuillets. — Bunyiu Nanjio 15.

— V.

能 斷 金 剛 般 若 波 羅 蜜 多 經

Neng toan kin kang pan je po lo mi to king.

Traduction de Hiuen-tsang, Chinois de Lo-yang de la famille Tchhen, traducteur entre 645 et 664.

21 feuillets — Bunyiu Nanjio 13.

— VI.

能斷金剛般若波羅蜜經

Neng toan kin kang pan jẹ po lo mi king.

Traduction de Yi-tsing, de la famille Tchang, de Tshi-tcheou, traducteur en 695-713.

14 feuillets — Bunyiu Nanjio 14.

Postface par Tsou-ting (1832).

Grand in-8. Bonne impression. 1 vol. demi-rel., au chiffre de Napoléon III.

Nouveau fonds 1297.

5731. — I.

Kin kang pan jẹ po lo mi king.

Traduction de Kumārajīva, précédée et suivie de formules d'invocation en chinois et en transcription. Frontispice, deux feuillets doubles et un feuillet simple, représentant des divinités autour du Bouddha ; à la fin formules de souhaits pour l'empereur, figure d'une divinité. Édition de Hai-tchhoang seu.

Nº 5728, art. I.

— II.

般若無盡藏眞言．金剛心眞言．補闕眞言．普回向眞言

Pan jẹ oou tsin tsang tchen yen. Kin kang sin tchen yen. Pou khiue tchen yen. Phou hoei hiang tchen yen.

Quatre dhāraṇī.

In-4. Papier blanc. 1 vol. en paravent à couvertures de bois ; dans 1 étui in-4, demi-rel., au chiffre de Louis-Philippe. *Nouveau fonds* 140.

5732.

Kin kang pan jẹ po lo mi king.

Double du précédent y compris les dhāraṇī.

1 vol. en paravent, couvertures rouges ; dans 1 étui demi-rel. au chiffre de Louis-Philippe. *Nouveau fonds* 151.

5733-5734. 大乘三寶尊經全部

Ta cheng san pao tsoẹn king tshiuen pou.

Collection de sūtra du Mahāyāna.

— I (5733).

金剛般若波羅蜜經

Kin kang pan jẹ po lo mi king.

Vajracchedikā prajñāpāramitā sūtra.

Traduction de Kumārajīva précédée et suivie de formules de purification, prières, dhāraṇī. Au début, frontispice (3 feuillets simples).

Nº 5728, art. I.

— II (5733).

般若波羅蜜多心經

Pan je po lo mi to sin king.

Prajñāpāramitā hṛdaya sūtra.

Texte, suivi d'éloges. A la fin, figure de divinité. Traduction de Hiuen-tsang.

Bunyiu Nanjio 20; cf. nº 5680, art. XII.

— III (5734).

佛說阿彌陀經

Fo choe 'o mi tho king.

Sukhāvatyamitavyūha sūtra.

Version de Kumārajīva, précédée et suivie d'éloges, gāthā, dhāraṇī, rituel. Frontispice comme à l'autre tome (art. I).

Bunyiu Nanjio 200.

— IV (5734).

拔一切業障根本得生淨土陀羅尼

Pa yi tshie ye tchang ken pen te cheng tsing thou tho lo ni.

Dhāraṇī pour renaître en Terre Pure (Sukhāvatī).

Version de Guṇabhadra, Hindou (453).

Bunyiu Nanjio 201; cf. nº 5680, art. XI.

— V (5734).

鴻名寶懺儀式

Hong ming pao tchhan yi chi.

Rituel.

— VI (5734).

佛說盂蘭盆經

Fo choe yu lan phen king.

Ullambana sūtra.

Version de Tchou Fa-hou (Dharmarakṣa), Yue-tchi (266-313 ou 317), suivie d'éloge. Note en petit texte.

Bunyiu Nanjio 303.

— VII (5734).

妙法蓮華經觀世音菩薩普門品

Miao fa lien hoa king koan chi yin phou sa phou men phin.

Avalokiteçvara bodhisattva samantamukha parivarta, chapitre (XXIV du texte sanscrit) du Saddharma puṇḍarīka sūtra.

Texte précédé et suivi de prières. A la fin, figure de guerrier. Traduc-

tion par Kumārajīva et par Jñānagupta, Hindou (561-578).

Bunyiu Nanjio 137.

Petit in-8. 2 vol. en forme de paravent,
impression grossière sur papier blanc,
couvertures en bois rouge semé d'or;
dans 1 enveloppe papier bleu.

Nouveau fonds 4689, 4690.

5735 — I.

金 剛 般 若 經 疏

Kin kang pan je king sou.

Commentaire du Vajracche-
dikā prajñāpāramitā sūtra.

Par Tchi-tche ta-chi, *alias* Tchi-
yi, de l'école Thien-thai († 597).
Liste des caractères rares. Édition
de Hoa-tchheng seu (1627).

1 livre. — Bunyiu Nanjio 1550;
cf. plus haut, n° 5728, art. I.

Bonne gravure.

— II.

天 台 四 教 儀

Thien thai seu kiao yi.

Les quatre divisions de l'enseignement, de l'école Thien-
thai.

Par Tyei-koan (Ti-koan) religieux coréen (960). Texte commenté. Édition de Leng-yen seu
(1666).

1 livre. —Bunyiu Nanjio 1551.

Bonne gravure.

— III.

觀 音 玄 義

Koan yin hiuen yi.

Sens mystérieux de l'Avalokiteçvara sūtra.

Par Tchi-yi, rédigé par son disciple Koan-ting († 632). Lecture
des mots difficiles. Même lieu d'é-
dition (1663).

2 livres. — Bunyiu Nanjio 1555; voir
plus haut, n° 5734, art. VII.

Bonne gravure.

— IV.

重 刻 三 時 繫 念

Tchhong kho san chi ki nien.

Méditations religieuses en
trois offices, nouvelle édition.

Après une préface sans signature, sorte de sūtra intitulé :

念 佛 正 因 說

Nien fo tcheng yin choe.

Traité sur les causes de la méditation religieuse.

1 + 2 feuillets.

Gravure de genre cursif, peu soignée.

— V.

中峯三時擊念儀範.
第一時佛事

Tchong fong san chi ki nien yi fan. Ti yi chi fo chi.

Prières et rituels, premier office.

13 feuillets.

Gravure comme à l'art. précédent.

— VI.

齋佛儀式

Tchai fo yi chi.

Rituel de l'uposadha.

4 feuillets. — Cf. n° 6407, art. LXXIX.

Même genre de gravure.

— VII.

第二時佛事

Ti eul chi fo chi.

Rituel, second office.

6 feuillets.

Gravure comme à l'art. IV.

— VIII.

彌陀懺儀

Mi tho tchhan yi.

Confession en l'honneur d'A-mitabuddha.

9 feuillets.

Même gravure.

— IX.

西方讚

Si fang tsan.

Éloge du paradis occidental.

1 feuillet.

Gravure de genre identique.

— X.

第三時佛事

Ti san chi fo chi.

Rituel, troisième office.

6 feuillets.

Même gravure.

— XI.

勸人念佛

Khiuen jen nien fo.

Exhortation à la méditation

3 feuillets.

A la suite, liste des donateurs, date (1591).

Même gravure que pour les articles IV à X.

— XII.

佛說阿彌陀經句解

Fo choę 'o mi tho king kiu kiai.

Explication du Sukhāvatyami-tavyūha sūtra.

Par Sing-tchheng, bonze de Yue-khi. Texte précédé d'un tableau récapitulatif.

5o feuillets. — Cf. plus haut, n° 5734, art. III.

Gravé en caractères cursifs, exécution plus soignée; frontispice (1 feuillet double).

— XIII.

拔一切業障根本得生淨土神咒

Pa yi tshie ye tchang ken pęn tę cheng tsing thou chen tcheou.

Dhāraṇī pour renaître en Terre Pure.

Lecture des caractères rares.

2 feuillets. — Cf. plus haut n° 5734, art. IV.

A la suite, postface de Sing-tchheng (1341).

Même gravure qu'à l'art. précédent.

Grand in-8. 1 vol. demi-rel., au chiffre de la République.
Nouveau fonds 3984.

5736. 金剛般若波羅蜜經解義

Kin kang pan ję po lo mi king kiai yi.

Explication du Vajracchedikā prajñāpāramitā sūtra.

Par le sixième patriarche, Hoei-neng, de la famille Lou, de Sin-tcheou (637–712). Texte de Kumārajīva et explication. Préface pour une réédition sans nom d'auteur ni date; postface. Édition de la bonzerie de Hai-tchhoang. Frontispice (1 feuillet double).

Livre 1ᵉʳ seul. — Cf. n° 5728, art. I.

Grand in-8. Papier blanc. 1 vol. demi-rel. au chiffre de Louis-Philippe.
Nouveau fonds 72.

5737-5738. — I (5737).

金剛經纂要疏分三

Kin kang king tsoan yao sou fęn san.

Tableaux explicatifs du commentaire du Vajra sūtra.

Par Tseu-siuen, de l'école Avataṃsaka (vers 1020).

— II (5737).

金剛般若經疏論纂要

Kin kang pan ję king sou loęn tsoan yao.

Extrait d'un commentaire sur le Vajracchedikā sūtra çāstra.

Par Tsong-mi, de l'école Avataṃsaka (†840 ou 841); revu par Tseu-siuen. Préface. Édition de Leng-yen seu (1636, 1637).

22

2 livres. — Bunyiu Nanjio 1630 ; 1167, 1168, 1231. — Voir plus haut n° 5728, art. I.

— III (5737-5738).

金剛經纂要刊定記
Kin kang king tsoan yao khan ting ki.

Commentaire de l'ouvrage précédent.

Par Tseu-siuen (1024). Édition de 1636, 1637.

7 livres. — Bunyiu Nanjio 1631.

Grand in-8. Bonne gravure.

1 vol. demi-rel., au chiffre de la République.
Nouveau fonds 3705.

1 vol. cartonnage.
Nouveau fonds 4602.

5739. 天目中峯和尚廣錄卷第十五
Thien mou tchong fong hoo chang koang lou kiuen ti chi oou.

Discours du bonze Tchong-fong, de Thien-mou. Livre 15.

Livre 15 réédité seul portant comme sous-titre :

金剛般若略義
Kin kang pan je lio yi.

Sens abrégé du Vajracchedikā prajñāpāramitā sūtra.

Explication, sans texte suivi du sūtra ; préface non datée par Eul-yen tchou-jen pour la présente réédition. Le compilateur de l'ouvrage, Tsheu-tsi, vivait en 1321-1323. Gravé à la bonzerie de Hai-tchhoang.

Bunyiu Nanjio 1533. — Cf. plus haut n° 5728, art. I.

Petit in-8. Papier blanc. 1 vol. demi-reliure.
Nouveau fonds 67.

5740. 金剛決疑解
Kin kang kiue yi kiai.

Explication des doutes sur le Vajracchedikā, etc.

Préface (1612) par Ṭe-tshing (1546-1622), de Han-chan, auteur de l'ouvrage. Introduction, éloge, poésies, etc. Texte. Postface pour la réédition de Hai-tchhoang (1733) par Li Kia Meou-sing.

Cf. plus haut, n° 5728, art. I ; voir aussi pour l'auteur n° 3764.

Petit in-8. Papier blanc. 1 vol. demi-reliure.
Nouveau fonds 635.

5741. — I.
金剛般若波羅蜜經筆記
Kin kang pan je po lo mi king pi ki.

Vajracchedikā prajñāpāramitā sūtra, avec commentaire.

Traduction de Kumārajīva; commentaire du bonze Jou-koan, de Tchhong-fou 'an, à Oou-yuen. Préface par le commentateur (1637); préface par Than Tcheng-mẹ (1637). Notice à la fin.

1 livre. — Cf. plus haut, n° 5728, art. I.

— II.

金剛大意書
Kin kang ta yi chou.

Sens général du Vajra sūtra.

Par Oang Khi-long Tchi-'an, de Sieou-choei; postface de l'auteur (1655). Introduction de Than Tcheng-mẹ. Impression de Leng-yen seu.

Cf. plus haut, n° 5728, art. I.

— III.

心經大意附撮㮣
Sin king ta yi fou tshoo kai.

Notes annexes et sens général du Hṛdaya sūtra.

Par le même, avec postface (1655). Édition de Leng-yen seu.

Voir plus haut, n° 5733, art. II.

Grand in-8. Feuillets retournés dans les art. I et III. 1 vol. demi-rel. au chiffre de la République Française. *Nouveau fonds* 3701.

5742. — I.

金剛經正法眼
Kin kang king tcheng fa yen.

Le Vajracchedikā prajñāpāramitā sūtra avec commentaire.

Traduction de Kumārajīva; commentaire par Han-chi (1608-1688). Préface par Khong-yin tao-jen (1645, année Hong-koang); préface par Siang-tchong de Hai-tchhoang pour la présente édition (1826).

33 feuillets. — Voir plus haut, n° 5728, art. I.

— II.

金剛正法眼十明論
Kin kang tcheng fa yen chi ming loẹn.

Dix éclaircissements pour l'ouvrage précédent.

Par Han-chi.

6 feuillets.

Petit in-8. Papier blanc, caractères genre cursif; titre noir sur blanc. 1 vol. demi-reliure. *Nouveau fonds* 76.

5743. 金剛經如是解
Kin kang king jou chi kiai.

Le Vajra sûtra expliqué par le bonze Jou-chi.

L'auteur a pour autre désignation Oou-chi tao-jen, de Chi-king chan. Préface de l'auteur ; préface de Than Tcheng-mę Tao-yi kiu-chi (1657) ; préface par Ling-yin tao-jen Hong-li. Deux postfaces.

1 livre. — Cf. plus haut, n° 5728, art. I.

Grand in-8. Bonne gravure. 1 vol. demi-rel. au chiffre de la République Française.

Nouveau fonds 3703.

5744. 金剛般若波羅蜜經註釋
Kin kang pan ję po lo mi king tchou chi.

Vajracchedikā prajñāpāramitā sūtra, avec commentaire.

Traduction de Kumārajīva ; commentaire par Lei-fong ta-chi. Préface du même (1661) ; préface de Kou-kheou Tseu-tchen (1661) ; postface de Tchao-yuen-tchai (1664).

Cf. plus haut, n° 5728, art. I.

Grand in-8. 1 vol. demi-rel. au chiffre la République Française.

Nouveau fonds 3700.

5745. 重訂金剛經石註 (注)
Tchhong ting kin kang king chi tchou.

Le Vajracchedikā sûtra, commenté par Chi, réédition.

Préface (1784) par Oong Fang-kang, de Pei-phing ; préface primitive (1702) par Chi Tchheng-kin Liang-kio kiu-chi.

— I.

金剛經總旨
Kin kang king tsong tchi.

Sens général du sūtra.

— II.

金剛經辨異
Kin kang king pien yi.

Divergences relatives au sūtra.

Suivi de l'avertissement.

— III.

金剛經讀法
Kin kang king tou fa.

Conseils pour la lecture du sūtra.

— IV.

誦經祛妄
Song king khiu oang.

Règles pour la récitation du sūtra.

— V.

般若波羅蜜多心經

Pan je po lo mi to sin king.

Prajñāpāramitā hṛdaya sūtra.

Texte, commentaire attribué à Choen-yang tao-tsou Fou-yeou ti. Postfaces.

4 feuillets. — Cf. n° 5733, art. II.

— VI.

金剛經石註

Kin kang king chi tchou.

Commentaire.

Par Chi Thien-ki Tchheng-kin, de Yang-tcheou, revu par Khing Ling Hiao-fong, de Ye-ho.

68 feuillets. — Cf. n° 5728, art. I.

— VII.

金剛經呪補缺眞言

Kin kang king tcheou pou khiue tchen yen.

Dhāraṇī.

Formules transcrites; vœux, éloges en chinois. Cette partie et les suivantes ont été ajoutées pour l'édition de la salle Koan Meou-lan.

— VIII.

金剛經受持靈驗記

Kin kang king cheou tchhi ling yen ki.

Mémorial des miracles du Vajracchedikā sūtra.

Postface par Koan Sieou-tsang, de Canton (1820).

6 feuillets.

— IX.

金剛經啓請

Kin kang king khi tshing.

Dhāraṇī et vœux.

Transcription du sanscrit et texte chinois.

2 feuillets.

Grand in-8. Titre noir sur jaune, daté de 1821. 1 vol. demi-rel. au chiffre de Napoléon III.
Nouveau fonds 1442.

5746. 金剛般若波羅蜜經直說

Kin kang pan je po lo mi king tchi choe.

Explication du Vajracchedikā prajñāpāramitā sūtra.

Par Tsi-chan-tsieou, du mont Tong-tshiao, avec préface de l'auteur; le commentaire suit la traduction de Kumārajīva. Avertissement. Réédition (1772) donnée par Tchhoan-sieou, de la bonzerie de Khai-yuen, et Sin-tan, de la bonzerie de Hai-tchhoang, province de Canton.

Cf. n. 5728, art. I.

Petit in-8. Papier blanc. 1 vol. demi-reliure.
Nouveau fonds 98.

5747. — I.

金剛般若波羅蜜經如義

Kin kang pan je po lo mi king jou yi.

Le Vajracchedikā prajñāpāramitā sūtra avec explications.

Traduction de Kumārajīva ; explications du bonze Yuen-hai, de Sa-yun. Préface par le bonze Khihoo, de Hai-tchhoang (1787). Ce texte, en gros caractères, est disposé dans le bas des pages.

Cf. plus haut, n. 5728, art. I.

— II.

上層彙集諸註精義

Chang tsheng hoei tsi tchou tchou tsing yi.

Extraits choisis des commentaires.

Ensuite liste des signes difficiles. Ce texte, en petits carac-

tères, est dans le haut des pages. Édition de Hai-tchhoang (1787).

73 feuillets.

Grand in-8. Papier blanc. 1 vol. demi-rel. au chiffre de Louis-Philippe.
Nouveau fonds 2278.

5748. 金剛般若波羅蜜經宗通

Kin kang pan je po lo mi king tsong thong.

Résumé des commentaires sur le Vajracchedikā sūtra.

Par Tseng Fong-yi Choentcheng, avec préface de l'auteur. D'après la traduction de Kumārajīva, le commentaire de Tseu-siuen et le çāstra du bodhisattva Guṇada. Gravé à la bonzerie de Haitchhoang, à Canton (1810) avec une postface de Tseng Feou-tchi, surnom Chi-sin kiu-chi ; liste de donateurs.

2 livres. — Cf. Bunyiu Nanjio 10, 1192, 1630, 1631. — Voir plus haut, n° 5728, art. I.

In-8. Papier blanc. 1 vol., demi-rel. au chiffre de Louis-Philippe.
Nouveau fonds 102.

5749. 金剛般若波羅蜜經部旨

Kin kang pan je po lo mi king pou tchi.

Le Vajracchedikā prajñāpāramitā sūtra expliqué par sections.

Texte, explications. Par le bonze Ling-yao, de Thien-thai ; tableau explicatif au début.

2 livres. — Cf. plus haut, nº 5728, art. I.

Grand in-8. 1 vol. demi-rel. au chiffre, de la République Française.
Nouveau fonds 3702.

5750. 仁王護國般若經疏

Jen oang hou koe pan je king sou.

Commentaire du Kāruṇikarāja deçapāla prajñāpāramitā sūtra.

Par le bonze Koan-ting, la traduction du sūtra est de Kumārajīva. Préface de Tchao Yue-tchi (1112). Lecture des caractères difficiles. Édition du Hoa-yen ko (1642).

5 livres. — Bunyiu Nanjio 1566, 17.

Grand in-8. 1 vol. demi-rel., au chiffre de la République Française.
Nouveau fonds 3697.

5751. — I.

佛說仁王護國般若波羅蜜經疏神寶記

Fo choe jen oang hou koe pan je po lo mi king sou chen pao ki.

Commentaire du précédent.

Par le bonze Po-thing Chan-yue, de Seu-ming (1230). Lecture des signes difficiles. Édition du Hoa-yen ko (1642).

4 livres. — Bunyiu Nanjio 1567.

— II.

天台八教大意

Thien thai pa kiao ta yi.

Sens général des huit sections de l'enseignement, de l'école Thien-thai.

Par le bonze Koan-ting. Liste des caractères difficiles. Édition de Leng-yen seu à Kia-hing (1661).

1 livre. — Bunyiu Nanjio 1568 ; cf. aussi nº 5735, art. II.

Grand in-8. Belle gravure. 1 vol. demi-rel., au chiffre de la République Française.
Nouveau fonds 3696.

5752-5777. — I (5752).

三藏聖教序。三藏聖教記

San tsang cheng kiao siu. San tsang cheng kiao ki.

Préface et historique des saints enseignements du Tripiṭaka.

Par les empereurs Thai-tsong et Kao-tsong des Thang.

Cf. Bunyiu Nanjio 1.

— II (5752-5777).

大般若波羅蜜多經
Ta pan je po lo mi to king.

Mahāprajñāpāramitā sūtra.

Traduction de Hiuen-tsang (659), avec lecture des signes difficiles pour chaque livre. Édition de Tsi-tchao 'an, gravée de 1608 à 1624.

Livres 1 à 515 (manquent les 85 derniers). — Bunyiu Nanjio 1.

Comprenant : *a* livres 1-400 (5752-5771).

初會
Tchhou hoei.

Première section.

Préface de Hiuen-tse, de Si-ming seu ; sūtra prononcé au Gṛdhrakūṭa.

79 chapitres (plusieurs sont subdivisés).

— *b* livres 401-478 (5772-5775).

二會
Eul hoei.

Seconde section.

Préface de Hiuen-tse ; sūtra prononcé au Gṛdhrakūṭa.

85 chapitres (plusieurs sont subdivisés).

— *c* livres 479-515 (5775-5777).

三會
San hoei.

Troisième section.

Préface de Hiuen-tse ; sūtra prononcé au Gṛdhrakūṭa.

Chapitres 1 à 21, 1ʳᵉ partie (le sūtra a 31 chap.)

Grand in-8. Bonne gravure : frontispice (1 feuillet double). 26 vol. demi-rel., au chiffre de la République Française.
Nouveau fonds 3668 à 3693.

5778-5787. — I (5778).

三藏聖教序。三藏聖教記
San tsang cheng kiao siu. San tsang cheng kiao ki.

Préface et historique des

saints enseignements du Tripiṭaka.

Par les empereurs Thai-tsong et Kao-tsong des Thang.

4 + 7 feuillets doubles. — Cf. n° 5752, art. I.

— II (5778-5787).

大般若波羅蜜多經
Ta pan jẹ po lo mi to king.

Mahāprajñāpāramitā sūtra.

Première section, avec préface de Hiuen-tsẹ.

— Livres 1 à 10 (chap. 1 à 6). — Nᵒˢ 5752-5771, art. II, *a*.

In-folio. Frontispice (1 feuillet double); à la fin figure de guerrier (1 feuillet simple). 10 **vol.** en paravent sans couvertures; dans 1 étui cartonnage.
Nouveau fonds 2317.

5788. 佛母出生三法藏般若波羅蜜多經
Fo mou tchhou cheng san fa tsang pan jẹ po lo mi to king.

Daçasāhasrikā prajñāpāramitā sūtra.

Traduction par Chi-hou (Dānapāla), Hindou (980-1000). Liste

des caractères difficiles. Édition de Tsie-tai seu (1624).

25 livres. — Bunyiu Nanjio 927. — Voir plus haut nᵒˢ 5752-5787.

Grand in-8. Bonne gravure. 1 vol. demi-rel., au chiffre de la République Française.
Nouveau fonds 3706.

5789-5793 大智度論
Ta tchi tou loẹn.

Mahāprajñāpāramitā sūtra çāstra.

Commentaire sur Bunyiu Nanjio 1. Par le bodhisattva Nāgārjuna; traduit par Kumārajīva (402-405). Préface par le bonze Seng-joei de Tchhang-'an. Liste des signes difficiles. Édition de Miaotẹ 'an (1591, 1592); pages suppléées en 1681.

100 livres (manquent les livres 16 à 20). — Bunyiu Nanjio 1169. — Voir plus haut nᵒˢ 5752-5787.

Grand in-8. Frontispice (1 feuillet double). Bonne gravure. 5 vol. demi-rel. au chiffre de la République Française.
Nouveau fonds 3707 à 3711.

5794-5797.
Ta tchi tou loẹn.

Double.

23

Livres 31 à 100.

4 vol. cartonnage.
Nouveau fonds 4648 à 4651.

5798. 金剛持驗紀
Kin kang tchhi yen ki.

Récit des miracles du Vajra-cchedikā, etc.

Préface par Tchhong-chang pour la réédition du Tchhi yen ki (art. V); autre préface du même ouvrage. Introduction par Khẹ-fou Thong-chạn tao-jen. Table des matières.

— I.

念經儀式
Nien king yi chi.

Règles rituelles de la lecture des sūtras.

2 feuillets.

— II.

般若波羅蜜多心經
Pan jẹ po lo mi to sin king.

Prajñāpāramitā hṛdaya sūtra.

1 feuillet. — No 5733, art. II.

— III.

金剛般若波羅蜜經
Kin kang pan jẹ po lo mi king.

Vajracchedikā prajñāpāramitā sūtra.

23 feuillets. — No 5728, art. I.

— IV.

補闕眞言
Pou khiue tchen yen.

Dhāraṇī.

No 5728, art. II.

— V.

歷朝金剛持驗紀
Li tchhao kin kang tchhi yen ki.

Récit des miracles opérés par le Vajracchedikā, etc., sous les dynasties successives.

Par Tcheou Khẹ-fou Tchhong-lang de King-khi. Édition de la bonzerie de Hai-tchhoang (1799), avec une note finale ajoutée lors de la nouvelle gravure.

2 livres.

In-4. Papier blanc. 1 vol. demi-rel., au chiffre de Louis-Philippe.
Nouveau fonds 621 A.

5799. — I.

Nien king yi chi.

— II.

Kin kang pan jẹ po lo mi king.

— III.

Pou khiue tchen yen.

— IV.

Li tchhao kin kang tchhi yen ki.

Mêmes ouvrages qu'aux art. I, III, IV, V du n° précédent, édition plus grande, faite à Leng-yen-seu, sans date.

Grand in-8. 1 vol., demi-rel., au chiffre de la République.
Nouveau fonds 3699.

5800. — I.

般 若 波 羅 蜜 多 心 經

Pan jẹ po lo mi to sin king.

Prajñāpāramitā hṛdaya sūtra.
2 feuillets. — N° 5733, art. II.

— II.

般 若 波 羅 蜜 多 心 經
要 論

Pan jẹ po lo mi to sin king yao loẹn.

Traité sur le Hṛdaya sūtra.

Par le bonze Seng-kho.

10 feuillets.

Le catalogue de Fujii indique à tort le II comme un autre titre du III.

— III.

般 若 波 羅 蜜 多 心 經
直 談

Pan jẹ poʼlo mi to sin king tchi than.

Explication du Hṛdaya sūtra.

Par le bonze Tchen-kho.

4 feuillets.

— IV.

奉 法 要

Fong fa yao.

Principes de l'acceptation de la loi.

Par Khi Tchhao, de l'époque des Tsin.

18 feuillets.

— V.

心 經 說

Sin king choẹ.

Explication du Hṛdaya sūtra,

Par le bonze Siue-lang Hong-'en.

2 feuillets.

— VI.

心經開度說

Sin king khai tou choẹ.

Introduction au Hṛdaya sūtra.

Transcrite par Too-tao-jen de Lo-fong, à Sin-'an.

2 feuillets.

— VII.

修慧篇。修慧偈

Sieou hoei phien. Sieou hoei ki.

Traité et poésie sur la prudence.

Ecrits en 1661 par Kou-kheou Tseu-tchen.

2 feuillets.

— VIII.

心經開度

Sin king khai tou.

Explication du Hṛdaya sūtra.

Par le bonze Hong-li de Lo-fong, à Sin-'an.

18 feuillets.

Grand in-8. Les art. I à V sont en caractères de genre cursif, VI à VIII en caractères carrés. 1 vol., demi-rel., au chiffre de la République.

Nouveau fonds 3912.

5801 — I.

般若波羅蜜多心經添足

Pan jẹ po lo mi to sin king thien tsou.

Le Prajñāpāramitā hṛdaya sūtra avec commentaires.

Préface (1642) par Ting-hou chan Tsai-san tao-jen; tableau résumé. Texte d'après la traduction de Hiuen-tsang; commentaire par Hong-tsan Tsai-san, de Ting-hou chan. Liste des caractères difficiles.

37 feuillets. — Cf. plus haut, n° 5733, art. II.

— II.

持誦準提眞言法要

Tchhi song tchoẹn thi tchen yen fa yao; alias :

受持準提眞言法要

Cheou tchhi tchoẹn thi tchen yen fa yao.

Sur la récitation de la Cundī devī dhāraṇī.

Par Hong-tsan Tsai-san. Texte et notes.

9 feuillets. — Cf. plus bas, n° 5987, art. V.

— III.

眞言梵書

Tchen yen fan chou.

Texte sanscrit de la dhāraṇī,

Avec notes et transcription chinoise.

2 feuillets.

— IV.

八關齋法

Pa koan tchai fa.

Sur les huit abstinences.

Par le même. Liste des signes difficiles. Édition de Oang Liang (1674).

12 feuillets. — Cf. Bunyiu Nanjio 701.

Grand in-8, 1 vol. demi-rel., au chiffre de la République.
Nouveau fonds 3948.

5802 — I.

摩訶般若波羅蜜多心經註疏

Mo ho pan je po lo mi to sin king tchou sou.

Mahāprajñāpāramitā hṛdaya sūtra, avec commentaire.

Commentaire par Tchong Tchiping Chou-jo, de Kia-hing (dynastie des Tshing). Préface par le bonze Pen-yue, de Tsoei-li (1673).

Cf. plus haut, n° 5733, art. II.

— II.

金剛經註正訛

Kin kang king tchou tcheng wo.

Vajracchedikā sūtra, avec commentaire et discussions.

Commentaire par Tchong Tchiping Chi-chi, de Tchhang-choei. Préface incomplète; seconde préface par Siu Lai-pin Kieou-yi (1676); ces deux préfaces sont en tête du volume, avant l'art. I.

Cf. n° 5728, art. I.

Grand in-8, 1 vol. demi-rel., au chiffre de la République.
Nouveau fonds 3698.

Deuxième section : RATNAKŪṬA SŪTRA

5803. — I.

佛說大乘入諸佛境界智光明莊嚴經

Fo choe ta cheng jou tchou fo king kiai tchi koang ming tchoang yen king.

Sarvabuddhaviṣayāvatāra jñā-nālokālaṅkāra sūtra.

Version par Fa-hou (Dharma-rakṣa), Hindou (1004-1058) du même texte que Bunyiu Nanjio 56 (traduction de Saṅghapāla, Cambodgien, 506-520) et que Bunyiu Nanjio 245 (traduction de Dharmaruci, Hindou. 501-507). Lecture des caractères rares. Édition de Hoa-tchheng seu (1627).

5 livres — Bunyiu Nanjio 1013.

— II.

佛說大乘智印經

Fo choe ta cheng tchi yin king.

Tathāgata jñāna mudrā sūtra.

Version par Tchi-ki-siang (Jñā-naçrī), Hindou (1053) du même texte que Bunyiu Nanjio 255, 256. Liste des mots difficiles. Même localité (1629).

5 livres. — Bunyiu Nanjio 1014. — Voir plus bas, n° 6079, art. VIII; n° 6078, art. I.

— III.

佛說法乘義決定經

Fo choe fa cheng yi kiue ting king.

Arthaviniçcaya dharmapa-ryāya sūtra.

Version de Kin-tsong-tchhi (Suvarṇadhāraṇī) étranger (1113). Édition du Hoa-yen ko.

3 livres. — Bunyiu Nanjio 1015.

— IV.

佛說大白傘蓋總持陀羅尼經

Fo choe ta po san kai tsong tchhi tho lo ni king.

Sitātapatra dhāraṇī sūtra.

Version de Tsi-na-ming-te-li-lien-te-lo-mo-ning, Hindou, et Tchen-tchi, Chinois (dynastie des Yuen).

1 livre — Bunyiu Nanjio 1016.

— V.

大白傘蓋佛母總讚歎禱祝偈

Ta po san kai fo mou tsong tsan than tao tchou ki.

Gāthās en l'honneur de la mère des Bouddhas.

A la suite liste des caractères difficiles. Édition de 1643.

Feuillets 12 à 14. — Cf. Bunyiu Nanjio 1016.

Grand in-8. Bonne gravure. 1 vol.

demi-rel., au chiffre de la République. *Nouveau fonds* 3960.

5804-5806. 大寶積經
Ta pao tsi king.

Mahāratnakūṭa sūtra.

Collection formée par Bodhiruci, Hindou (713). Lecture des caractères rares Édition de Hing-cheng oan-cheou chan-seu (1595, 1596).

120 livres (manquent les livres 1-75 comprenant les sūtra I à XV et début du XVI). — Bunyiu Nanjio 23.

— XVI, livre 76 (5804).

菩薩見實會
Phou sa kien chi hoei.

Pitā putra samāgama.

Version de Narendrayaças, Hindou (557-568).

Livre 16ᵉ et dernier.

— XVII, livres 77 à 79 (5804).

富樓那會
Fou leou na hoei.

Pūrṇa paripṛcchā.

Version de Kumārajīva.

3 livres.

— XVIII, livres 80 et 81 (5804-5805).

護國菩薩會
Hou koe phou sa hoei.

Rāṣṭrapāla paripṛcchā.

Version de Jñānagupta (585-592).

2 livres.

— XIX, livre 82 (5805).

郁伽長者會
Yu kia tchang tche hoei.

Ugra paripṛcchā.

Version de Khang Seng-khai (Saṅghavarman), Tibétain (252).

1 livre.

— XX, livres 83 et 84 (5805).

無盡伏藏會
Oou tsin fou tsang hoei.

Le titre sanscrit manque.

Version de Bodhiruci (693-713).

2 livres.

— XXI, livre 85 (5805).

授幻師跋陀羅記會
Cheou hoan chi po tho lo ki hoei.

Bhadra māyākāra pariprcchā (*alias* vyākaraṇa).

Du même.

1 livre.

— XXII, livres 86 et 87 (5805).

大神變會
Ta chen pien hoei.

Mahāpratihāryopadeça,

Du même.

2 livres.

— XXIII, livres 88 et 89 (5805).

摩訶迦葉會
Mo ho kia chę hoei.

Mahākāçyapi ; *alias* : Mahākāçya saṅgīti ; *alias* : Maitreya mahāsiṃhanādana.

Version d'Upaçūnya, Hindou (538-541).

2 livres.

— XXIV, livre 90 (5805).

優波離會
Yeou po li hoei.

Vinayaviniçcaya Upāli pariprcchā.

Version de Bodhiruci (voir art. XX).

1 livre.

— XXV, livres 91 et 92 (5805).

發勝志樂會
Fa cheng tchi yo hoei.

Adhyāçaya saṃcodana.

Du même.

2 livres.

— XXVI, livres 93 et 94 (5805).

善臂菩薩會
Chạn phi phou sa hoei.

Subāhu pariprcchā.

Version de Kumārajīva.

2 livres.

— XXVII, livre 95 (5805).

善順菩薩會
Chạn choẹn phou sa hoei.

Surata pariprcchā.

Version de Bodhiruci (voir art. XX).

1 livre.

— XXVIII, livre 96 (5805).

勤授長者會
Khin cheou tchang tchę hoei.

Vīradatta paripṛcchā.

Du même.

1 livre.

— XXIX, livre 97 (5805).

優陀延王會

Yeou tho yen oang hoei.

Udayana vatsarāja paripṛcchā.

Du même.

1 livre.

— XXX, livre 98 (5805).

妙慧童女會

Miao hoei thong niu hoei.

Sumati dārikā paripṛcchā.

Du même.

1 livre.

— XXXI, livre 98 (5805).

恒河上優婆夷會

Heng ho chang yeou pho yi hoei.

Gaṅgottaropāsikā paripṛcchā.

Du même.

1 livre.

— XXXII, livre 99 (5805.)

無畏德菩薩會

Oou oei tẹ phou sa hoei.

Açokadattā vyākaraṇa.

Version de Buddhaçānta, Hindou (524-538).

1 livre.

— XXXIII, livre 100 (5805).

無姤施菩薩應辯會

Oou keou chi phou sa ying pien hoei

Vimaladattā paripṛcchā.

Version de Nie Tao-tchen, Chinois (vers 312).

1 livre.

— XXXIV, livre 101 (5806).

功德寶華敷菩薩會

Kong tẹ pao hoa fou phou sa hoei.

Guṇaratnasaṃkusumita paripṛcchā.

Version de Bodhiruci (voir art. XX).

Feuillets 1 à 6.

— XXXV, livre 101 (5806).

善德天子會

Chạn tẹ thien tseu hoei.

Acintyabuddhaviṣaya nirdeça.

Du même.

Feuillets 6 à 24.

— XXXVI, livres 102 à 105 (5806).

善住意天子會

Chan tchou yi thien tseu hoei.

Susṭhitamati paripṛcchā.

Version de Dharmagupta.

4 livres.

— XXXVII, livre 106 (5806).

阿闍世王子會

'O chẹ chi oang tseu hoei (sic).

Siṃha paripṛcchā; *alias* : Su-bāhu paripṛcchā.

Version de Bodhiruci (voir art. XX).

Feuillets 1 à 7.

— XXXVIII, livres 106, feuillet 7, à 108 (5806).

大乘方便會

Ta cheng fang pien hoei.

Jñānottara bodhisattva paripṛcchā.

Version de Nandi, Occidental (419).

3 livres.

— XXXIX, livres 109 et 110 (5806).

賢護長者會

Hien hou tchang tchẹ hoei.

Bhadrapāla çreṣṭhi paripṛcchā.

Version de Jñānagupta (voir art. XVIII).

2 livres.

— XL, livre 111 (5806).

淨信童女會

Tsing sin thong niu hoei.

Çuddhaçraddhā dārikā pari-pṛcchā.

Version de Bodhiruci (voir art. XX).

Feuillets 1 à 14.

— XLI, livre 111 (5806).

彌勒菩薩問八法會

Mi lẹ phou sa oen pa fa hoei.

Maitreya paripṛcchā dhar-māṣṭa.

Version de Bodhiruci (508-535).

Feuillets 14 à 18.

— XLII, livre 111 (5806).

彌勒菩薩所問會

Mi lẹ phou sa so oen hoei.

Maitreya paripṛcchā.

Version de Bodhiruci (voir art. XX).

Feuillets 18 à 30.

— XLIII, livre 112 (5806).

普 明 菩 薩 會
Phou ming phou sa hoei.

Kāçyapa parivarta.

Version de l'époque des Tshin (350-431).

1 livre.

— XLIV, livres 113 et 114 (5806).

寶 梁 聚 會
Pao liang tsiu hoei.

Ratnarāçi; *alias* : Ratnaparāçi.

Version de Tao-kong, Chinois (402-412).

2 livres.

— XLV, livre 115 (5806).

無 盡 慧 菩 薩 會
Oou tsin hoei phou sa hoei.

Akṣayamati paripṛcchā.

Version de Bodhiruci (voir art. XX).

Feuillets 1 à 9.

— XLVI, livres 115, feuillet 9, et 116 (5806).

文 殊 說 般 若 會
Oen chou choe pan je hoei.

Maṅjuçrī buddhakṣetragunavyūha; *alias* : Saptaçatikā prajñāpāramitā.

Version par Mandra (Mandrarṣi), Cambodgien (503) du même texte que Bunyiu Nanjio 21.

2 livres.

— XLVII, livres 117 et 118 (5806).

寶 髻 菩 薩 會
Pao ki phou sa hoei.

Ratnacūḍa paripṛcchā.

Version de Tchou Fa-hou.

2 livres.

— XLVIII, livre 119 (5806).

勝 鬘 夫 人 會
Cheng man fou jen hoei.

Vyūha paripṛcchā; *alias* : Çrīmālā devī siṃhanāda.

Version de Bodhiruci (voir art. XX).

1 livre.

— XLIX, livre 120 (5806).

廣博仙人會

Koang po sien jen hoei.

Vyāsa paripṛcchā.

Du même.

1 livre.

Grand in-8. Bonne gravure. 3 vol., cartonnage.

Nouveau fonds 4636 à 4638.

5807. 佛說大乘菩薩藏正法經

Fo choe ta cheng phou sa tsang tcheng fa king.

Bodhisattva piṭaka sūtra.

Version par Fa-hou (1004-1058) du même texte que Bunyiu Nanjio 23 (12) (version de Hiuen-tsang, 645). Lecture des caractères rares. Édition de Tsie-tai-seu, à Oou-kiang (1624, 1625).

40 livres. — Bunyiu Nanjio 1005.

Grand in-8. Bonne gravure. 1 vol. demi-rel., au chiffre de la République Française.

Nouveau fonds 3868.

5808. — I.

佛說護國尊者所問大乘經

Fo choe hou koe tsoen tche so oen ta cheng king.

Rāṣṭrapāla paripṛcchā sūtra.

Version par Chi-hou du même texte que nᵒˢ 5804-5805, art. XVIII. Liste des caractères rares.

4 livres. — Bunyiu Nanjio 873.

— II.

佛說四無所畏經

Fo choe seu oou so oei king.

Caturvaiçāradya sūtra.

Par le même. Sūtra du Hīnayāna.

2 feuillets. — Bunyiu Nanjio 874.

— III.

增慧陀羅尼經

Tseng hoei tho lo ni king.

Jñānavṛddhikara dhāraṇī sūtra.

Par le même.

1 feuillet. — Bunyiu Nanjio 875.

— IV.

聖六字增壽大明陀羅尼經

Cheng lou tseu tseng cheou ta ming tho lo ni king.

Ārya ṣaḍakṣarāyurvṛddhikara mahāvidyā dhāraṇī sūtra.

Du même. Lecture des caractères difficiles.

2 feuillets. — Bunyiu Nanjio 876.

— V.

佛說大乘戒經

Fo choẹ ta cheng kiai king.

Mahāyāna çīla sūtra.

Du même.

2 feuillets. — Bunyiu Nanjio 877.

— VI.

佛說聖最勝陀羅尼經

Fo choẹ cheng tsoei cheng tho lo ni king.

Āryānuttaravijaya dhāraṇī sūtra.

Par le même. Liste des caractères rares.

5 feuillets. — Bunyiu Nanjio 878; cf. id. 831.

— VII.

佛說五十頌聖般若波羅蜜經

Fo choẹ oou chi song cheng pan jẹ po lo mi king.

Prajñāpāramitā ardhaçatikā sūtra.

Par le même; version du même

texte que Bunyiu Nanjio 18 (version de Bodhiruci).

2 feuillets. — Bunyiu Nanjio 879.

— VIII.

大乘八大曼拏羅經

Ta cheng pa ta man na lo king.

Aṣṭamaṇḍalaka sūtra.

Version de Fa-hien, Hindou (982-1001).

2 feuillets. — Bunyiu Nanjio 880.

— IX.

佛說較量一切佛剎功德經

Fo choẹ kiao liang yi tshie fo tchha kong tẹ king.

Sarvabuddhakṣetraguṇopamānasaṅkhyāna sūtra.

Par le même; version du même texte que Bunyiu Nanjio 95 (version de Hiuen-tsang; cf. aussi Buddhāvataṃsaka mahāvaipulya sūtra).

2 feuillets. — Bunyiu Nanjio 881.

— X.

囉嚩拏說救療小兒疾病經

Lo fo na choẹ kieou liao siao eul tsi ping king.

Rāvaṇabhāṣita kumāraka sūtra.

Du même. Lecture des mots
rares.

11 feuillets. — Bunyiu Nanjio 882.

— XI.

迦葉仙人說醫女人經

*Kia chę sien jen choę yi niu jen
king.*

Kāçyaparṣi bhāṣita strĭbhi-
ṣajyā sūtra.

Du même. Liste des caractères
difficiles.

4 feuillets. — Bunyiu Nanjio 883.

Grand in-8. Bonne gravure. 1 vol.
demi-rel., au chiffre de la République
Française.
Nouveau fonds 3921.

5809. — I.

佛說三十五佛名禮懺文

*Fo choę san chi oou fo ming li
tchhan oen.*

Pañcatriṃçadbuddhanāmapū-
jā svīkāra lekha.

Extrait du Oou po li so oen
king. Version par Amoghavajra,
Hindou (746-771), du même texte
que n° 5805, art. XXIV.

3 feuillets. — Bunyiu Nanjio 979.

— II.

觀自在菩薩說普賢陀羅尼經

*Koan tseu tsai phou sa choę
phou hien tho lo ni king.*

Avalokiteçvara bodhisattva
bhāṣita samantabhadra dhāraṇī
sūtra.

Version du même.

5 feuillets. — Bunyiu Nanjio 980.

— III.

佛說八大菩薩曼茶羅經

*Fo choę pa ta phou sa man
tchha lo king.*

Aṣṭamaṇḍalaka sūtra.

Du même; traduction du même
texte que n° 5808, art. VIII.

5 feuillets. — Bunyiu Nanjio 981.

— IV.

佛說能淨一切眼疾病陀羅尼經

*Fo choę neng tsing yi tshie yen
tsi ping tho lo ni king.*

2311

Cakṣuviçodhana vidyā dhāraṇī sūtra.

Du même; traduction du même texte retraduit par Fa-hien (982-1001); autre traduction antérieure par Than-oou-lan (381-395).

3 feuillets. — Bunyiu Nanjio 982; cf. id. 483, 905.

— V.

佛說除一切疾病陀羅尼經

Fo choe tchhou yi tshie tsi ping tho lo ni king.

Sarvarogapraçamanī dhāraṇī sūtra.

Du même. Lecture des caractères difficiles.

1 feuillet. — Bunyiu Nanjio 983.

— VI.

佛說救拔焰口餓鬼陀羅尼經

Fo choe kieou pa yen kheou 'o koei tho lo ni king.

Jvalapraçamanī dhāraṇī sūtra.

Du même; même texte traduit déjà par Çikṣānanda (695-700). Lecture des mots rares. Édition de Leng-yen seu (1664).

5 feuillets. — Bunyiu Nanjio 984; cf. id. 539.

— VII.

瑜伽集要救阿難陀羅尼焰口儀軌經

Yu kia tsi yao kieou 'o nan tho lo ni yen kheou yi koei king.

Yogasaṅgrahamahārthānandaparitrāṇa dhāraṇī jvala vaktra preta kalpa sūtra.

Du même. Lecture des termes rares. Édition du Hoa yen ko (1643).

1 livre. — Bunyiu Nanjio 985.

— VIII.

佛說蟻喻經

Fo choe yi yu king.

Pipīlikopamāna sūtra.

Version de Chi-hou (Dānapāla), Hindou (980-1000). Sūtra du Hīnayāna. Lecture des caractères difficiles.

3 feuillets. — Bunyiu Nanjio 986.

— IX.

聖觀自在菩薩不空王秘密心陀羅尼經

Cheng koan tseu tsai phou sa pou khong oang pi mi sin tho lo ni king.

Amoghapāça dhāraṇī sūtra.

Traduction par Chi-hou, de fragments divers, nᵒˢ 6056, art. V ; 6062, art. III et IV ; 6063-6064. Lecture des mots difficiles. Édition de Hoa-tchheng seu (1613).

12 feuillets. — Bunyiu Nanjio 987.

— X.

佛說勝軍王所問經

Fo choe cheng kiun oang so oen king.

Rājāvavādaka sūtra.

Du même.

8 feuillets. — Bunyiu Nanjio 988. — Voir nᵒ 6079, art. I, II et III.

— XI.

佛說輪王七寶經

Fo choe loen oang tshi pao king.

Cakravartirāja saptaratna sutra.

Du même. Sūtra du Hīnayāna, même texte que Bunyiu Nanjio 542 (58), Madhyamāgama.

5 feuillets. — Bunyiu Nanjio 989.

— XII.

佛說園生樹經

Fo choe yuen cheng chou king.

Ārāmajāta druma sūtra.

Du même. Sūtra du Hīnayāna, même texte que Bunyiu Nanjio 542 (2), Madhyamāgama.

2 feuillets. — Bunyiu Nanjio 990.

— XIII.

佛說了義般若波羅蜜多經

Fo choe liao yi pan je po lo mi to king.

Prasannārtha prajñāpāramitā sūtra.

Du même ; extrait du Prajñā-pāramitā.

3 feuillets. — Bunyiu Nanjio 991.

— XIV.

佛說大方廣未曾有經善巧方便品

Fo choe ta fang koang oei tsheng yeou king chan khiao fang pien phin.

Mahāvaipulyādbhuta sūtra upāyakauçalyādhyāya.

Du même. Édition de Hoa-tchheng seu (1615).

5 feuillets. — Bunyiu Nanjio 992.

— XV.

佛說大堅固婆羅門緣起經

Fo choę ta kien kou pho lo męn yuen khi king.

Mahāsthira brāhmaṇa nidāna sūtra.

Du même. Sūtra du Hīnayāna, même texte que n₀ 6153, art. III. Liste des caractères rares. Édition de Hoa-tchheng seu (1631).

2 livres. — Bunyiu Nanjio 993.

Grand in-8. Bonne gravure. 1 vol. demi-rel., au chiffre de la République Française.
Nouveau fonds 3931.

5810. — I.

佛說無畏授所問大乘經

Fo choę oou oei cheou so oen ta cheng king.

Vīradatta paripṛcchā mahāyāna sūtra.

Version par Chi-hou du même texte que nᵒˢ 5805, art. XXVIII;

6112, art. IV. Édition du Hoa-yen ko (1643).

3 livres (17 feuillets). — Bunyiu Nanjio 947.

— II.

佛說月喻經

Fo choę yue yu king.

Candropamāna sūtra.

Du même; sūtra du Hīnayāna. Mêmes lieu et date d'édition.

3 feuillets. — Bunyiu Nanjio 948.

— III.

佛說醫喻經

Fo choę yi yu king.

Bhiṣagupamāna sūtra.

Du même; sūtra du Hīnayāna. Mêmes lieu et date.

2 feuillets. — Bunyiu Nanjio 949.

— IV.

佛說灌頂王喻經

Fo choę koan ting oang yu king.

Mūrddhābhiṣiktopamāna sūtra.

Du même; sūtra du Hīnayāna. Lecture des caractères difficiles. Mêmes lieu et date d'édition.

2 feuillets. — Bunyiu Nanjio 950.

— V.

佛說尼拘陀梵志經

Fo choȩ ni kiu tho fan tchi king.

Nyagrodha brahmacāri sūtra.

Du même; sūtra du Hīnayāna; même texte que le n° 6153, art. VIII. Lecture des caractères difficiles.

2 livres (16 feuillets). — Bunyiu Nanjio 951.

— VI.

佛說白衣金幢二婆羅門緣起經

Fo choȩ po yi kin tchhoang eul pho lo mȩn yuen khi king.

Çuklavastra suvarṇadhvaja dvibrāhmaṇa nidāna sūtra.

Du même; sūtra du Hīnayāna; même texte que le n° 6153, art. V. Liste des mots rares. Édition de Hoa-tchheng seu (1612).

3 livres (21 feuillets). — Bunyiu Nanjio 952.

— VII.

佛說福力太子因緣經

Fo choȩ fou li thai tseu yin yuen king.

Puṇyabalāvadāna sūtra.

Du même; sūtra du Hīnayāna. Liste des caractères difficiles. Édition du Hoa-yen ko (1643).

3 livres (24 feuillets). — Bunyiu Nanjio 953.

— VIII.

佛說身毛喜豎經

Fo choȩ chen mao hi chou king.

Saṃharṣitaromakūpajāta sūtra.

Version de Oei-tsing, Chinois (1009-1050); sūtra du Hīnayāna. Liste des caractères rares. Mêmes lieu et date.

3 livres. — Bunyiu Nanjio 954.

Grand in-8. Bonne gravure. 1 vol. demi-rel., au chiffre de la République Française.

Nouveau fonds 4038.

———————

5811. — I.

彌勒菩薩所問經論

Mi lȩ phou sa so oen king loȩn.

Maitreya bodhisattva paripṛcchā sūtra çāstra.

Version par Bodhiruci (508-535) du commentaire du n° 5806, art. XLI. Liste des caractères rares.

7 livres. — Bunyiu Nanjio 1203 ; voir aussi 54.

— II.

無量壽經優波提舍

Oou liang cheou king yeou po thi che.

Aparimitāyus sūtra çāstra.

Traité du bodhisattva Vasubandhu sur les textes indiqués Bunyiu Nanjio 23 (5), 25, 26, 27, 863. Version de Bodhiruci (529). Édition du Hoa-yen ko (1632).

9 feuillets. — Bunyiu Nanjio 1204. — Voir plus bas n° 5813, art. I.

— III.

轉法輪經優波提舍

Tchoan fa loen king yeou po thi che.

Dharmacakrapravartana sūtropadeça.

Traité du bodhisattva Vasubandhu traduit par Vimokṣasena (prajña ?), Hindou. Notice sur la traduction qui date de 541. Lecture des caractères rares.

12 feuillets. — Bunyiu Nanjio 1205.

— IV.

大般涅槃經論

Ta pan nie phan king loen.

Nirvāṇa çāstra.

Traité du bodhisattva Vasubandhu sur les textes n°ˢ 5956-5958, art. I ; 5961-5963 ; 5955, art. I ; version de Dharmabodhi, Hindou (dynastie des Oei orientaux, 534-550). Édition du Hoa-yen ko (1642).

12 feuillets. — Bunyiu Nanjio 1206.

— V.

涅槃經本有今無偈論

Nie phan king pen yeou kin oou kie loen.

Nirvāṇa sūtra çāstra, sur la gāthā de l'existence et de la non-existence.

Traité de Vasubandhu, traduit par Paramārtha (550). Même lieu d'édition (1643).

7 feuillets. — Bunyiu Nanjio 1207. — N°ˢ 5956-5958, art. I.

— VI.

能斷金剛般若波羅蜜多經論頌

Neng toan kin kang pan je po lo mi to king loen song.

Vajracchedikā sūtra çāstra gāthā.

Poésie du bodhisattva Asaṅga, traduite par Yi-tsing. Lecture des mots rares.

6 feuillets. — Bunyiu Nanjio 1208.

— VII.

遺教經論
Yi kiao king loẹn.

Çāstra sur le sūtra des dernières instructions du Bouddha.

Par Vasubandhu ; traduction de Paramārtha. Liste des caractères difficiles.

1 livre. — Bunyiu Nanjio 1209. — N° 5955, art. III.

Grand in-8. Bonne gravure. 1 vol. demi-rel. au chiffre de la République Française.

Nouveau fonds 3939.

5812.

Mi lẹ phou sa so oẹn king loẹn.

Même ouvrage qu'au n° précédent, art. I ; avec des feuillets portant la mention : gravé de nouveau, 1678.

Livres 1 à 5.

Grand in-8. Bonne gravure. 1 vol. demi-rel., au chiffre de la République Française.

Nouveau fonds 4640.

Troisième section : SUKHĀVATĪ SŪTRA

5813. 重刊淨土三經
Tchhong khan tsing thou san king.

Les trois sūtra de la Terre Pure, réédition.

Préface par l'éditeur Pheng Tsi-tshing (1792).

— I.

佛說無量壽經
Fo choẹ oou liang cheou king.

Aparimitāyus sūtra ; *alias* Amitāyuṣa vyūha sūtra ; *alias* Sukhāvatīvyūha sūtra.

Traduction par Khang Seng-khai (252) du même texte que Bunyiu Nanjio 23 (5). Postface par l'éditeur. Lecture des signes difficiles.

2 livres. — Bunyiu Nanjio 27.

— II.

佛說觀無量壽佛經

Fo choẹ koan oou liang cheou fo king.

Amitāyurdhyāna sūtra.

Traduction par Kālayaças, Occidental (424). Postface de l'éditeur. Lecture des signes difficiles.

1 livre. — Bunyiu Nanjio 198.

— III.

佛 說 阿 彌 陀 經

Fo choẹ 'o mi tho king.

Sukhāvatīvyūha sūtra; *alias* Sukhāvatyamita vyūha sūtra.

Postface de l'éditeur. Lecture des signes difficiles.

Nᵒ 5734, art. III.

Gravé à la bonzerie de Hai-tchhoang (1823).

Grand in-8. Papier blanc. 1 vol. demi-rel. au chiffre de Louis-Philippe. *Nouveau fonds* 80.

5814. — I.

Fo choẹ 'o mi tho king.

Même ouvrage qu'au nᵒ précédent, art. III.

5 feuillets.

— II.

佛 說 阿 彌 陀 經 疏 鈔

Fo choẹ 'o mi tho king sou tchhao.

Commentaire du sūtra précédent.

Par le bonze Tchou-hong, de la bonzerie de Yun-tshi à Hang-tcheou; texte et commentaire en caractères cursifs.

4 livres.

— III.

彌 陀 經 疏 鈔 事 義

Mi tho king sou tchhao chi yi.

Explication du commentaire précédent.

Texte en caractères carrés d'une gravure différente.

37 feuillets.

Édition de la bonzerie de Hai-tchhoang (1765), gravure médiocre, caractères genre cursif pour I et II; frontispice de 9 feuillets doubles représentant des scènes bouddhiques.

Petit in-8. Papier blanc. 1 vol. demi-rel., au chiffre de Louis-Philippe. *Nouveau fonds* 59.

5815. — I.

Fo choẹ 'o mi tho king.

Même sūtra qu'au nº 5813, art. III. Au début, frontispice, un feuillet double; prière.

— II.

拔一切業障根本得生淨土陀羅尼

Pa yi tshie ye tchang ken pẹn tẹ cheng tsing thou tho lo ni; alias:

往生淨土神咒

Oang cheng tsing thou chen tcheou.

Dhāraṇī pour renaître en Terre Pure.

Nº 5734, art. IV.

— III.

阿彌陀經不思議神力傳

'O mi tho king pou seu yi chen li tchoan.

Miracle du sūtra précédent.

Texte en petits caractères, récit de l'époque des Tcheou postérieurs.

Voir nº 5817, art. VI.

Édition de Hai-tchhoang seu (1766).

In-4. Papier blanc. 1 vol. en paravent,

couverture rouge; dans 1 étui in-4, demi-rel., au chiffre de Louis-Philippe. *Nouveau fonds* 136.

5816. 無量壽佛經

Oou liang cheou fo king.

Sukhāvatīvyūha sūtra.

Même texte qu'au nº 5813, art. III.

Texte copié par Yuen Yuen; 9 feuillets doubles et 2 feuillets simples en caractères li; copie à l'encre noire sur papier doré; gardes en papier jaune orné de dragons; plats en bois dur incrusté de jade et d'argent; dos en soie de couleurs variées.

1 vol. dans un carton in-folio. *Nouveau fonds* 3539.

———

5817. — I.

御製無量壽佛贊

Yu tchi oou liang cheou fo tsan.

Éloge de l'Amitāyurdhyāna sūtra, composé par l'Empereur.

Soixante vers.

2 feuillets. — Bunyiu Nanjio 198.

— II.

佛說觀無量壽佛經

Fo choę koan oou liang cheou fo king.

Amitāyurdhyāna sūtra.

Liste des caractères rares. Édition de Miao-tę chạn-yuen (1591); feuillets gravés de nouveau en 1669, 1670.

1 livre. — No 5813, art. II.

— III.

稱讚淨土佛攝受經

Tchheng tsan tsing thou fo chę cheou king.

Sukhāvatīvyūha sūtra.

Version de Hiueṅ-tsang (650). Liste des caractères difficiles. Feuillets gravés de nouveau en 1669, 1681, 1691.

11 feuillets. — Bunyiu Nanjio 199.

— IV.

Fo choę 'o mi tho king.

Lecture des caractères rares.

5 feuillets. — No 5813, art. III.

— V.

Pa yi tshie ye tchang ken pęn tę cheng tsing thou chen tcheou.

Dhāraṇī pour renaître en Terre Pure.

Texte extrait du Siao oou liang cheou king, Petit Amitāyus sūtra.

1/2 feuillet. — No 5734, art. IV.

— VI.

阿彌陀經不思議神力傳

'O mi tho king pou seu yi chen li tchoan.

Miracle du sūtra précédent.

Ouvrage d'un auteur inconnu (époque des Soei). Liste des caractères difficiles.

2 feuillets. — No 5815, art. III.

— VII.

後出阿彌陀佛偈經

Heou tchhou 'o mi tho fo kie king.

Sūtra en vers sur Amitāyurbuddha.

Version de la dynastie des Han postérieurs (25-220). Lecture des mots rares. Édition de Miao-tę chạn-yuen (1591). Feuillets gravés de nouveau en 1682.

2 feuillets. — Bunyiu Nanjio 202.

— VIII.

佛說大阿彌陀經

Fo choę ta 'o mi tho king.

Le grand Amitāyus sūtra.

Texte préparé par Long-chou Oang Ji-hieou, avec préface du même (1162). Table des matières; texte. Postface par Fa-khi (1249). Édition de Miao-tẹ chạn-yuen (1591); feuillets gravés de nouveau à Tsi- tchao 'an (1659).

2 livres. — Bunyiu Nanjio 2o3.

— IX.

禮祝儀式
Li tchou yi chi.

Rituel relatif au sūtra précédent.

Texte en transcription chinoise; prescriptions; intercalé après la table des matières de l'art. VIII.

2 feuillets.

Grand in-8. Bonne gravure. 1 vol. demi-rel., au chiffre de la République Française.
Nouveau fonds 3981.

5818. 佛說觀無量壽佛經
Fo choẹ koan oou liang cheou fo king.

Buddhabhāṣitāmitāyurbuddha dhyāna sūtra.

Préfaces (1655) par Pao Oong

Hing-cheng, de Nan-hou, et par Tchang Oen-kia Tchong-kia, de Oou-lin. Notice en petit texte sur l'histoire de l'œuvre.

— 1.

觀無量壽佛經圖頌
Koan oou liang cheou fo king thou song.

Illustrations et éloges pour l'Amitāyurdhyāna sūtra.

Par Oou-tsin Tchhoan -teng, de Thien-thai.

34 illustrations.

— II.

Fo choẹ koan oou liang cheou fo king.

Lecture des caractères difficiles.

No 5813, art. II.

— III.

大阿彌陁佛經
Ta 'o mi tho fo king.

Le grand Amitāyus sūtra.

Par Oang Ji-hieou, avec préface de l'auteur (1162). Lecture des caractères difficiles. Notice finale (1249) par Khong-chang Fa-khi.

2 livres. — No 5817, art. VIII.

— IV.

禮祝儀式

Li tchou yi chi.

Rituel.

Contenant des passages en transcription du sanscrit; placé avant le texte principal du précédent.

Même texte qu'au n° 5817, art. IX.

Grand in-8. Belle gravure. 1 vol. demirel., au chiffre de la République Française.

Nouveau fonds 579.

5819.

Fo choẹ ta 'o mi tho king.

Préface de l'auteur (1162). Édition de la bonzerie de Hai-tchhoang (1792).

2 livres. — N° 5817, art. VIII.

Petit in-8. Papier blanc. 1 vol. demirel. au chiffre de Louis-Philippe.

Nouveau fonds 63.

5820-5821.

— I (5820).

佛說觀無量壽佛經疏

Fo choẹ koan oou liang cheou fo king sou.

Commentaire de l'Amitāyur-dhyāna sūtra.

Par Tchi-tchẹ ta-chi. Lecture des termes difficiles. Édition de Leng-yen seu (1662).

1 livre. — Bunyiu Nanjio 1559. — Voir n° 5813, art. II.

— II (5820-5821).

觀無量壽佛經疏妙宗鈔

Koan oou liang cheou fo king sou miao tsong tchhao.

Commentaire de l'ouvrage précédent.

Par Tchi-li; avec préface de l'auteur (1021). Liste des caractères rares. Mêmes lieu et date d'édition.

6 livres. — Bunyiu Nanjio 1560.

— III (5821).

天台智者大師禪門口訣

Thien thai tchi tchẹ ta chi chạn men kheou kiue.

Transmission orale de la doctrine du dhyāna, par Tchi-tchẹ ta-chi.

Édition de Leng-yen seu (1667).

13 feuillets. — Bunyiu Nanjio 1561.

Grand in-8. Bonne gravure.

26

1 vol. demi-rel., au chiffre de la République Française.

Nouveau fonds 3980.

1 vol. cartonnage.

Nouveau fonds 4670.

5822. — I.

佛說阿彌陁經[句解]

Fo choe 'o mi tho king [kiu kiai].

Sukhāvatīvyūha sūtra, expliqué.

Traduction de Kumārajīva, explications par Sing-tchheng, bonze de Yue-khi. Tableau résumé.

Cf. n° 5813, art. III.

— II.

拔一切業障根本得生淨土神咒

Pa yi tshie ye tchang ken pen te cheng tsing thou chen tcheou.

Dhāraṇī pour renaître en Terre Pure.

Lecture des caractères difficiles.

N° 5734, art. IV.

Postface de Sing-tchheng (1341).

Grand in-8. Frontispice (1 feuillet double). 1 vol. demi-reliure.

Nouveau fonds 803.

5823. 佛說阿彌陀經 要解

Fo choe 'o mi tho king yao kiai.

Le Sukhāvatīvyūha sūtra annoté.

Traduction de Kumārajīva; notes par 'Eou-yi Tchi-hiu (vers 1630-1650), avec postface par le même. Préface non datée pour la gravure, par Tcheng-tchi.

1 livre. — N° 5813, art. III.

Grand in-8. Bonne gravure. 1 vol. demi-rel., au chiffre de la République Française.

Nouveau fonds 694.

5824. — I.

Fo choe 'o mi tho king yao kiai.

Double du n° 5823.

— II.

佛說齋經科註

Fo choe tchai king khoo tchou.

Upavasatha sūtra, avec commentaire.

Traduction de Tchi Khien, Yue-tchi (223-253); commentaire par Tchi-hiu.

1 livre. — Cf. Bunyiu Nanjio 577.

— III.

百癡禪師語錄

Po tchhi chan chi yu lou.

Entretiens et œuvres diverses du bonze Po-tchhi.

Recueillis par ses élèves Tchhao-siuen et autres (fin des Ming). Préfaces par Siu Tchhang-tchi Kin-tcheou, surnom Oou-yi tao-jen (1661); par Yen Ta-tshan, surnom To-li tao-jen (1659); par Hong-chang Tan-siun (1660). Table : 30 livres. Bonne gravure.

Livres 1 à 5 seulement.

— IV.

圓覺句釋正白

Yuen kio kiu chi tcheng po.

Explication de l'intelligence parfaite (des pratyeka buddha).

Par le bonze Lo-fong Hong-li, revu par Tsai-san Hong-tsan. Texte et tableaux.

Livre 1er seul.

Grand in-8. 1 vol. demi-rel. au chiffre la République Française.
Nouveau fonds 3983.

5825. 靈峯蕅益大師選定淨土十要

Ling fong 'eou yi ta chi siuen ting tsing thou chi yao.

Dix œuvres relatives à la Terre Pure, réunies par 'Eou-yi ta-chi, de Ling-fong.

Nouvelle édition ponctuée par Tchheng Chi, de Che; préface du même (1788?). Table générale des 10 livres comprenant treize ouvrages.

I, livre 1 (seul).

佛說阿彌陀經要解

Fo chœ 'o mi tho king yao kiai.

Le Sukhāvatīvyūha sūtra annoté.

Commentaire par Tchi-hiu. Préface de Tchheng Chi (1788?). Impression de la bonzerie de Hai-tchhoang (1799).

1 livre. — N° 5823.

Grand in-8. Papier blanc, belle gravure. 1 vol. demi-reliure.
Nouveau fonds 79.

5826.

Ling fong 'eou yi ta chi siuen ting tsing thou chi yao.

Double (livre 1 seul).

1 vol. demi-reliure.
Nouveau fonds 70.

Quatrième section : AVALOKITEÇVARA SŪTRA

5827. 妙法蓮華經

Miao fa lien hoa king.

Saddharmapuṇḍarīka sūtra.

Version de Kumārajīva. Préface impériale (1420). Postface du bonze Seng-joei (406).

— I.

妙法蓮華經弘傳序

Miao fa lien hoa king hong tchhoan siu.

Préface sur la diffusion du Saddharmapuṇḍarīka sūtra.

Par Tao-siuen, bonze de Tchong-nan chan (✝ 667).

— II.

Miao fa lien hoa king.

Texte chinois. Lecture des caractères difficiles. Édition de Tsi-tchao 'an et de Hing-cheng oan-cheou chan-seu (1600).

7 livres. — Bunyiu Nanjio 134.

Grand in-8. Bonne gravure. 1 vol. demi-rel., au chiffre de la République Française.
Nouveau fonds 3819.

5828-5834.

大乘玅法蓮華經

Ta cheng miao fa lien hoa king.

Mahāyāna saddharmapuṇḍarīka sūtra.

— I (5828).

Miao fa lien hoa king hong tchhoan siu.

Voir nº 5827, art. I.

— II (5828-5834).

Miao fa lien hoa king.

Traduction, avec invocation finale pour chaque livre ; à la fin du 1ᵉʳ livre : édition de Hai-tchhoang (1670).

7 livres. — Nº 5827, art. II.

In-4. Bonne impression sur papier blanc ; 7 vol. en paravent, couvertures rouges ; dans 3 étuis demi-rel., au chiffre de Louis-Philippe.
Nouveau fonds 158.

5835.

Miao fa lien hoa king.

Copie par Tchhen Yuen-long, de la traduction de Kumārajīva.

1ᵉʳ feuillet : dragons or sur papier jaune, souhaits de longévité ; 2ᵉ et 3ᵉ feuillets : Bouddha avec saints, dessin très fin ; ensuite texte du livre 7, d'une écriture médiocre ; à la fin tablette votive, figure d'un guerrier.

Nᵒ 5827, art. II.

Grand in-8. Manuscrit; couverture soie, titre noir sur or. 1 vol. paravent.
Nouveau fonds 5240.

5836-5837. 妙法蓮華經文句會本

Miao fa lien hoa king oen kiu hoei pẹn.

Explication du Saddharmapuṇḍarīka sūtra.

Par Tchi-tchẹ ta-chi Tchi-yi. Gravure ancienne.

10 livres en 2 sections chacun. — Bunyiu Nanjio 1536; cf. nᵒ 5827, art. II.

Grand in-8. 2 vol. demi-rel., au chiffre de Louis-Philippe.
Nouveau fonds 463.

5838. 法華文句記
Fa hoa oen kiu ki.

Commentaire du précédent.

Par le bonze Tchan-jạn, de l'école Thien-thai († 782). Lecture des caractères rares. Édition de Leng-yen seu (1665).

Livres 1 à 3 et 1ʳᵉ section du livre 4. — Bunyiu Nanjio 1537.

Grand in-8. Bonne gravure. 1 vol. cartonnage.
Nouveau fonds 4632.

5839-5840.

— I (5839).

法華經弘傳序科文. 妙法蓮華經解科文

Fa hoa king hong tchhoan siu khoo oen. Miao fa lien hoa king kiai khoo oen.

Tableaux résumés pour le Hong tchhoan siu et pour le commentaire du Saddharmapuṇḍarīka sūtra.

23 feuillets. — Cf. nᵒ 5827.

— II (5839).

妙法蓮華經解
Miao fa lien hoa king kiai.

Commentaire du Saddharmapuṇḍarīka sūtra.

弘傳序
Hong tchhoan siu.

Préface sur la diffusion du sūtra.

Commentaire par Siang-mai, surnom Jou-yi ye-lao, de Tao-tche chan (vers 1291). Préface par le bonze Ki-nan, de Fou-tcheou (1127).

N° 5827, art. I.

— III (5839-5840).

Miao fa lien hoa king kiai.

Ce commentaire est dû à Kiai-hoan, bonze à Oen-ling (xiiiᵉ siècle). Lecture des caractères difficiles. Édition de Miao-te 'an, au Tshing-liang chan (1690, 1691).

7 livres. — Bunyiu Nanjio 1623. — Voir n° 5827, art. II.

Grand in-8. Bonne gravure; frontispice (1 feuillet double). 2 vol. demi-rel., au chiffre de la République Française.
Nouveau fonds 3820, 3821.

5841-5843. 妙法蓮華經科註

Miao fa lien hoa king khoo tchou.

Le Saddharmapuṇḍarīka sūtra avec tableaux et commentaires.

Frontispice (1 feuillet double). Préface pour les tableaux par Chao Tai-tshe, de Yong-kia. Préfaces pour la réédition de 1696 par Thang Kien-tchang, pour celle de 1627 par le bonze Tchhoan-teng. Préface de 1418 par Yao Koang-hiao.

— I (5841).

妙法蓮華經弘傳序

Miao fa lien hoa king hong tchhoan siu.

N° 5827, art. I.

— II (5841).

玅法蓮華經註科

Miao fa lien hoa king tchou khoo.

Tableaux explicatifs du sūtra.

Par le bonze Tcheng-lou, de Siu.

— III (5841-5843).

Miao fa lien hoa king khoo tchou.

Texte et commentaires.

Le commentaire est du bonze Yi-jou, Chinois (époque des Ming). A la fin de chaque livre, liste des donateurs; lecture des caractères difficiles. Réédition de 1699, incomplète à la fin.

7 livres. — Cf. n° 5827, art. II.

Grand in-8. 3 vol. demi-rel., au chiffre de Louis-Philippe.
Nouveau fonds 345.

5844. 妙法蓮華經通義
Miao fa lien hoa king thong yi.

Le Saddharmapuṇḍarīka sūtra, texte et commentaire.

Explications par Tę-tshing de Han-chan. Édition de Kia-hing, sans date.

2 livres. — Voir nº 5827, art. II.

Grand in-8. 1 vol. demi-rel., au chiffre de la République Française.
Nouveau fonds 3822.

5845-5846. 妙法蓮華經台宗會義

Miao fa lien hoa king thai tsong hoei yi.

Explication du Saddharma-puṇḍarīka sūtra, de l'école Thien-thai.

Par 'Eou-yi Tchi-hiu. Préface de 1649; postface de 1680.

16 livres. — Cf. nº 5827, art. II.

In-4. 2 vol. demi-rel., au chiffre de Napoléon III.
Nouveau fonds 1221, 1222.

5847. 歷朝法華持驗紀

Li tchhao fa hoa tchhi yen ki.

Miracles du Saddharmapuṇḍarīka sūtra sous les dynasties successives.

Par Tcheou Khę-fou, avec préface du même. Historique depuis les Tsin jusqu'aux Ming. Édition de Leng-yen seu.

2 sections.

Grand in-8. 1 vol. demi-rel., au chiffre de la République Française.
Nouveau fonds 4034.

5848. — I.

妙法蓮華經觀世音菩薩普門品[經]

Miao fa lien hoa king koan chi yin phou sa phou męn phin [king].

Avalokiteçvara bodhisattva samantamukha parivarta, chapitre du Saddharmapuṇḍarīka sūtra.

Version de Kumārajīva, d'un chapitre du nº 5827, art. II.

8 feuillets. — Bunyiu Nanjio 137; cf. nº 5983, art. V.

— II.

觀世音大悲心陀羅尼

Koan chi yin ta pei sin tho lo ni.

Avalokiteçvara mahākāruṇi-kahṛdaya dhāraṇī.

Version d'Amoghavajra.

8 feuillets. — Cf. Bunyiu Nanjio 1444 et 320. — Voir plus bas nº 5860, art. III et IV.

— III.

白衣大悲五印心陀羅尼經

Po yi ta pei oou yin sin tho lo ni king.

Sūtra de la dhāraṇī du cœur aux cinq sceaux de la miséricordieuse en vêtements blancs.

ı feuillet.

— IV.

般若波羅蜜多心經

Pan jẹ po lo mi to sin king.

Prajñāpāramitā hṛdaya sūtra.

ı feuillet. — Nᵒ 5733, art. II.

— V.

禮觀音文

Li koan yin oen.

Prière à Koan-yin.

ı feuillet.

— VI.

觀世音持驗紀

Koan chi yin tchhi yen ki.

Miracles de Koan-yin.

Préface par Tcheou Khẹ-fou, de King-khi (1659). Introduction du même, surnom Thong-chạn tao-jen. Table des matières indiquant les articles précédents I à V. Texte. Édition de Leng-yen seu.

5ı feuillets.

Grand in-8. Frontispice représentant Koan-yin (ı feuillet double); les articles I à V sont en caractères grêles. l'art. VI est d'une bonne calligraphie. ı vol. demi-rel., au chiffre de la République Française.

Nouveau fonds 3987.

5849. — I.

Miao fa lien hoa king koan chi yin phou sa phou mẹn phin king.

Frontispice (5 feuillets simples). Texte de Kumārajīva. A la fin, invocation, figure de guerrier. Publié à la bonzerie de Hai-tchhoang (1795).

Nᵒ 5848, art. I.

— II.

眞言。讚

Tchen yen. Tsan.

Dhāraṇī. Éloge.

In-4. Papier blanc. ı vol. en paravent, couverture rouge; dans ı étui demirel., au chiffre de Louis-Philippe.

Nouveau fonds 232.

5850. — I.

Miao fa lien hoa king koan chi yin phou sa phou mẹn phin king.

— II.

Tchen yen. Tsan.

Double.

1 vol. en paravent, couvertures de bois, dans 1 étui demi-rel., au chiffre de Louis-Philippe.

Nouveau fonds 141.

5851.

Miao fa lien hoa king koan chi yin phou sa phou men phin.

Version de Kumārajīva copiée par Hoang Yen-lan, de Phan-yu; gravée à Canton (1828). Illustrations (4 feuillets doubles). Texte (15 feuillets).

Nᵒ 5848, art. I.

Grand in-8. Papier blanc, couverture jaune. 1 vol. demi-rel. au chiffre de Napoléon III.

Nouveau fonds 1326.

5852. — I.

Miao fa lien hoa king koan chi yin phou sa phou men phin.

Même ouvrage; sans date.

Nᵒ 5848, art. I.

— II.

眞言．讚
Tchen yen. Tsan.

Dhāraṇī. Éloge.

Cf. nᵒ 5849, art. II.

In-12. Papier blanc. 1 vol. en paravent, couverture rouge; renfermé dans 1 étui, demi-reliure.

Nouveau fonds 231.

_____

5853. — I.

觀音義疏
Koan yin yi sou.

Commentaire de l'Avalokite-çvara sūtra.

Par Tchi-tche ta-chi, rédigé par son disciple Koan-ting. Lecture des caractères rares. Édition de Leng-yen seu (1664).

2 livres. — Bunyiu Nanjio 1557.

Exemplaire en mauvais état.

— II.

蘇州竹菴衍禪師語錄
Sou tcheou tchou 'an yen chan chi yu lou.

Entretiens et œuvres du bonze Tchou-'an Yen, de Sou-tcheou.

Auteur: Tchen-yen (1621-1677), surnom 'Eou-'an, de l'école de Lin-tsi.

Vie de l'auteur par Tseng Thong-ki (1675). Préfaces par Hoang Yu-kien Jen-'an (1673); par Hoang

Yong 'Ai-'an; par Lo Tchen-sing (1673). Les œuvres ont été recueillies par les disciples Ki-jou et Ki-yong.

2 livres. — Cf. n° 6623, art. I, composé différemment.

— III.

大准提菩薩焚修悉地懺悔玄文

Ta tchoen thi phou sa fen sieou si ti tchhan hoei hiuen oen; alias :

佛母准提修懺儀

Fo mou tchoen thi sieou tchhan yi; alias :

佛母准提焚修悉地懺悔玄文

Fo mou tchoen thi fen sieou si ti tchhan hoei hiuen oen.

Rituel et prières en l'honneur de Mahācundī.

Texte chinois et dhāraṇī; 17 figures de divinités avec légendes au verso; texte chinois à la suite. Préfaces par Hiang Khien Hong-tsheu (1652); par Than Tcheng-mẹ Tao·yi kiu-chi, de Fou-tcheng (1657), etc. Publication de Hiang Kien (1652).

Cf. n° 5987 et suivants.

Cet article et les précédents sont d'une bonne gravure.

— IV.

教觀綱宗釋義

Kiao koan kang tsong chi yi.

Explication du Kiao koan kang tsong.

Par le bonze Tchi-hiu.

28 feuillets.

Édition en caractères plus grêles que les art. précédents.

— V.

教觀綱宗

Kiao koan kang tsong; alias :

一代時教權實綱要圖

Yi tai chi kiao khiuen chi kang yao thou.

Principes des enseignements et des méditations.

Par le même. Texte, figures et notes. Édition de Leng-yen seu.

24 feuillets.

Caractères comme à l'art. IV.

— VI.

傳授三壇弘戒法儀

Tchhoan cheou san than hong kiai fa yi.

Rituel annoté des initiations.

Compilé par Fa-tsang, bonze en 1621-1627 ; revu et publié par Tchhao-yuen, bonze du Tchong-nan chan. Édition de Leng-yen seu (1688).

Livre 1, 1ʳᵉ section, initiation des çramaṇera.

Livre 2, 2ᵉ section, initiation des bhikṣu.

Livre 3, 3ᵉ section, initiation des bodhisattva.

Bonne gravure, usée.

— VII.

終南山天龍會集緇門世譜

Tchong nan chan thien long hoei tsi tchi men chi phou.

Liste de patriarches, chefs d'écoles et chefs de branches.

Depuis Bodhidharma. Préface par Sin-lei Ming-hi chan-chi, disciple de Tchhao-yuen (1703).

3 + 8 feuillets.

Grand in-8. 1 vol. demi-rel., au chiffre de la République Française.
Nouveau fonds 3992.

5854. 觀音義疏記
Koan yin yi sou ki.

Commentaire du Koan yin yi sou.

Par Tchi-li, de Seu-ming (vers 1020). Texte et lecture des caractères difficiles. Édition de la bonzerie de Leng-yen à Kia-hing (1666, 1670).

4 livres. — Bunyiu Nanjio 1558 ; voir nº 5853, art. I.

Grand in-8. Bonne gravure. 1 vol. demi-rel., au chiffre de la République Française.
Nouveau fonds 270.

5855.

Koan yin yi sou ki.

Même ouvrage.

Incomplet d'un feuillet à la fin du 4ᵉ livre.

Grand in-8. Bonne gravure. 1 vol. demi-rel., au chiffre de la République Française.
Nouveau fonds 3986.

5856. 觀音玄義記
Koan yin hiuen yi ki.

Commentaire du Koan yin hiuen yi.

Par le bonze Tchi-li. Édition de Leng-yen seu (1663).

4 livres. — Bunyiu Nanjio 1556 ; cf. id. 1555.

Grand in-8. Bonne gravure. 1 vol. demi-reliure.

Nouveau fonds 1053.

5857.

Koan yin hiuen yi ki.

Double.

1 vol. demi-rel., au chiffre de la République Française.

Nouveau fonds 3985.

5858. — I.

觀世音菩薩普門品
膚說

Koan chi yin phou sa phou men phin fou choe.

Exposé du Avalokiteçvara bodhisattva samantamukha parivarta.

Par Ling-yao, bonze de l'école Thien-thai, à Kia-hoo. Préface par l'auteur (année oou oou). Résumé en tableau par le même.

25 feuillets. — Cf. n° 5848, art. I.

— II.

孟蘭盆經折中疏

Yu lan phen king tche tchongsou.

Explication de l'Ullambana sūtra.

Par le même. Préface et résumé du même.

32 feuillets. — Cf. n° 5734, art. VI.

— III.

見聞錄

Kien oen lou.

Mémoires et notes.

Par le bonze Tchi-hiu; rédigés après 1620.

23 feuillets.

Gravure en caractères plus grands et plus élégants.

— IV.

鍾振之居士寄初徵
與際明禪師柬

Tchong tchen tchi kiu chi ki tchhou tcheng yu tsi ming chan chi kien.

Lettres de Tchong Tchen-tchi et du bonze Tsi-ming.

Quatre lettres non datées.

2 feuillets.

Gravés en caractères cursifs peu soignés.

— V.

闢邪集。天學初徵°再
徵

Phi sie˙ tsi. Thien hio tchhou tcheng. Tsai tcheng.

Traité contre les mauvaises doctrines.

Dirigé spécialement contre la religion chrétienne. Par Tchong Chi-cheng Tchen-tchi, de Kin-tchhang; ponctué par Tchheng Tchi-yong Yong-kieou, de Sin-'an. Préface de 1643 par Kao-'an de Yue-khi. Postface par Tchheng Tchi-yong.

2 sections (6 + 17 feuillets).

Même gravure qu'à l'art. IV.

Grand in-8. 1 vol. demi-rel., au chiffre de la République Française.

Nouveau fonds 3989.

5859. — I.

觀世音菩薩得大勢菩薩受記經

Koan chi yin phou sa te ta chi phou sa cheou ki king.

Avalokiteçvara bodhisattva mahāsthāmaprāpta bodhisattva vyākaraṇa sūtra.

Version par Than-oou-kie (Dharmaçūra), Chinois de la famille Li, de Yeou-tcheou (453). Liste des mots rares. Édition de Hoa-tchheng seu (1627).

17 feuillets. — Bunyiu Nanjio 395.

— II.

不思議光菩薩所說經

Pou seu˙ yi koang phou sa so choe king.

Acintyaprabhāsa nirdeça sūtra.

Version par Kumārajīva. Liste des caractères rares. Même lieu d'édition (1631).

17 feuillets. — Bunyiu Nanjio 396.

— III.

超日明三昧經

Tchhao ji ming san mei king.

Sūrya jihmīkaraṇa prabhā samādhi sūtra.

Version de Nie Tchheng-yuen, Chinois (290-306). Lecture des caractères rares.

2 livres. — Bunyiu Nanjio 397.

— IV.

除恐災患經

Tchhou khong tsai hoan king.

Çrīkaṇṭha sūtra.

Version de Cheng-kien, Chinois (388-407). Liste des caractères difficiles. Édition de Hoa-tchheng seu (1629).

20 feuillets. — Bunyiu Nanjio 398.

Grand in-8. Bonne gravure. 1 vol. demi-rel., au chiffre de la République Française.

Nouveau fonds 4039.

5860. — I.

千眼千臂觀世音菩薩陀羅尼神咒經

Tshien yen tshien phi koan chi yin phou sa tho lo ni chen tcheou king.

Nīlakaṇṭha sūtra.

Version de Tchi-thong, de la famille Tchao, Chinois (627-649). Préface du bonze Po-loen, datant de 697 ou postérieure à cette époque. Lecture des mots rares. Édition de 1610.

2 livres. — Bunyiu Nanjio 318.

— II.

千手千眼觀世音菩薩姥陀羅尼身經

Tshien cheou tshien yen koan chi yin phou sa mou tho lo ni chen king.

Nīlakaṇṭha sūtra.

Version du même texte par Bodhiruci, Hindou (709). Liste des caractères rares.

1 livre. -- Bunyiu Nanjio 319.

— III.

千手千眼觀世音菩薩廣大圓滿無礙大悲心陀羅尼經

Tshien cheou tshien yen koan chi yin phou sa koang ta yuen man oou 'ai ta pei sin tho lo ni king.

Sahasrabāhu sahasrākṣāvalokiteçvara bodhisattva mahāpūrṇāpratihata mahākāruṇikahṛdaya dhāraṇī sūtra.

Version de Kia-fan-ta-mo (Bhagavaddharma?), Hindou (dynastie des Thang). Préface impériale (1411).

1 livre. — Bunyiu Nanjio 320 ; cf. n° 5680, art. X.

— IV.

番大悲神咒

Fan ta pei chen tcheou.

Mahākāruṇika dhāraṇī.

Lecture des caractères difficiles pour les articles III et IV.

4 feuillets. — Cf. Bunyiu Nanjio 320.

— V.

觀世音菩薩祕密藏神咒經

Koan chi yin phou sa pi mi tsang chen tcheou king.

Padmacintāmaṇi dhāraṇī sūtra.

Version de Çikṣānanda, de Khoten (695-700).

10 feuillets. — Bunyiu Nanjio 321.

— VI.

觀世音菩薩如意摩尼陀羅尼經

Koan chi yin phou sa jou yi mo ni tho lo ni king.

Padmacintāmaṇi dhāraṇī sūtra.

Version du même texte par Ratnacinta, Hindou (693-706).

8 feuillets. — Bunyiu Nanjio 322.

— VII.

觀自在菩薩如意心陀羅尼經

Koan tseu tsai phou sa jou yi sin tho lo ni king.

Padmacintāmaṇi dhāraṇī sūtra.

Version du même texte par Yitsing (710). Liste des mots rares.

4 feuillets. — Bunyiu Nanjio 323.

— VIII.

如意輪陀羅尼經

Jou yi loen tho lo ni king.

Padmacintāmaṇi dhāraṇī sūtra.

Version du même texte par Bodhiruci (709); extrait du Ta lien hoa kin kang san mei ye kia tchhi pi mi oou tchang 'ai king. Lecture des termes rares. Gravé de nouveau à Hoa-tchheng seu (1662).

1 livre. — Bunyiu Nanjio 324.

Grand in-8. Bonne gravure. 1 vol. demi-rel., au chiffre de la République Française.

Nouveau fonds 3990.

5861. — I.

觀自在菩薩怛嚩多唎隨心陀羅尼經

Koan tseu tsai phou sa ta fo to li soei sin tho lo ni king.

Avalokiteçvara bodhisattva samantabhadrānuhṛdaya dhāraṇī sūtra.

Version de Tchi-thong (653). Lecture des mots difficiles.

1 livre. — Bunyiu Nanjio 325.

— II.

請觀世音菩薩消伏毒害陀羅尼咒經

Tshing koan chi yin phou sa siao fou tou hai tho lo ni tcheou king.

Dhāraṇī pour prier Avalokiteçvara bodhisattva de détruire l'effet du poison.

Version de Nandi (420). Édition de Tsi-tchao 'an (1606).

14 feuillets. — Bunyiu Nanjio 326.

— III.

佛說十一面觀世音神咒經

Fo choẹ chi yi mien koan chi yin chen tcheou king.

Avalokiteçvaraikadaçamukha dhāraṇī sūtra.

Version de Yaçogupta, étranger (561-578); extrait du Dhāraṇī saṅgraha sūtra. Liste des mots rares.

12 feuillets. — Bunyiu Nanjio 327; voir n° 6209.

— IV.

十一面神咒心經

Chi yi mien chen tcheou sin king.

Avalokiteçvaraikadaçamukha dhāraṇī sūtra.

Version du même texte par Hiuen-tsang (656).

11 feuillets. — Bunyiu Nanjio 328.

— V.

千轉陀羅尼觀世音菩薩咒經

Tshien tchoan tho lo ni koan chi yin phou sa tcheou king.

Sahasrapravartana dhāraṇyavalokiteçvara bodhisattva mantra sūtra.

Version par Tchi-thong (653) d'un texte qui se trouve dans le Dhāraṇī saṅgraha sūtra et dans le Nānā saṃyukta mantra sūtra.

4 feuillets. — Bunyiu Nanjio 329; cf. aussi n°s 6209 et 5987, art. VI.

— VI.

咒五首經

Tcheou oou cheou king.

Pañcamantra sūtra.

Version de Hiuen-tsang (664); comprenant cinq dhāraṇī.

2 feuillets. — Bunyiu Nanjio 330.

1. 能滅眾罪千轉陀羅尼

Neng mie tchong tsoei tshien tchoan tho lo ni.

Même texte de la dhāraṇī qu'à l'art. V ci-dessus.

2. 六字咒
Lou tseu tcheou.

Même texte de la dhāraṇī qu'à l'art. VII ci-dessous.

3. 七俱胝佛咒
Tshi kiu tchi fo tcheou.

Même texte de la dhāraṇī que Bunyiu Nanjio 344 (n° 5987, art. III).

4. 一切如來隨心咒
Yi tshie jou lai soei sin tcheou.

Sarvatathāgatānuhṛdaya dhāraṇī.

5. 觀自在菩薩隨心咒
Koan tseu tsai phou sa soei sin tcheou.

Même texte de la dhāraṇī qu'à l'art. I ci-dessus.

— VII.
六字神咒經
Lou tseu chen tcheou king.

Ṣaḍakṣaravidyāmantra sūtra.

Version de Bodhiruci, Hindou (693); extrait du Dhāraṇī saṅgraha sūtra et du Nānā saṃyukta mantra sūtra.

3 feuillets. — Bunyiu Nanjio 331. Voir n°s 6209 et 5987, art. VI.

— VIII.
咒三首經
Tcheou san cheou king.

Trimantra sūtra.

Version de Divākara, Hindou (676-688); comprenant trois dhāraṇī. Lecture des mots difficiles.

1 feuillet. — Bunyiu Nanjio 332.

1. 大輪金剛陀羅尼
Ta loen kin kang tho lo ni.

Mahācakravajra dhāraṇī.

Cf. n° 6209.

2. 日光菩薩咒
Ji koang phou sa tcheou.

Sūryaprabha bodhisattva dhāraṇī.

3. 摩利支天咒
Mo li tchi thien tcheou.

Mārīcī devī dhāraṇī.

Cf. n° 6209.

— IX.
大方廣菩薩藏經中文殊師利根本一字陀羅尼法

28

Ta fang koang phou sa tsang king tchong oen chou chi li ken peṇ yi tseu tho lo ni fa.

Ekākṣara dhāraṇī dharma, tiré du Mahāvaipulya bodhisattva piṭaka sūtra.

Version de Ratnacinta, Hindou (702).

4 feuillets. — Bunyiu Nanjio 333.

— X.

曼殊室利菩薩咒藏中一字咒王經

Man chou chi li phou sa tcheou tsang tchong yi tseu tcheou oang king.

Ekākṣara mantrarāja sūtra, tiré du Mañjuçrī bodhisattva mantra piṭaka.

Version du même texte, par Yitsing (703).

4 feuillets. — Bunyiu Nanjio 334.

— XI.

十二佛名神咒校量功德除障滅罪經

Chi eul fo ming chen tcheou kiao liang kong tẹ tchhou tchang mie tsoei king.

Dvādaçabuddhaka sūtra.

Version de Jñānagupta (587).

7 feuillets. — Bunyiu Nanjio 335.

— XII.

佛說稱讚如來功德神咒經

Fo choẹ tchheng tsan jou lai kong tẹ chen tcheou king.

Dvādaçabuddhaka sūtra.

Version du même texte par Yitsing (711). Liste des caractères difficiles. Édition de Tsi-tchao 'an (1611).

4 feuillets. — Bunyiu Nanjio 336.

— XIII.

華積陀羅尼神咒經

Hoa tsi tho lo ni chen tcheou king.

Puṣpakūṭa sūtra.

Version de Tchi Khien. Liste des caractères rares. Édition de 1656.

3 feuillets. — Bunyiu Nanjio 337.

— XIV.

師子奮迅菩薩所問經

Chi tseu fẹn sin phou sa so oen king.

Puṣpakūṭa sūtra.

Version de l'époque des Tsin orientaux (317-420); même texte qu'à l'art. XIII. Liste des caractères difficiles. Édition de 1656.

3 feuillets. — Bunyiu Nanjio 338.

— XV.

佛說華聚陀羅尼咒經

Fo choę hoa tsiu tho lo ni tcheou king.

Puṣpakūṭa sūtra.

Autre version du même texte, même époque qu'à l'art. précédent.

3 feuillets. — Bunyiu Nanjio 339.

— XVI.

六字咒王經

Lou tseu tcheou oang king.

Ṣaḍakṣara vidyāmantra sūtra.

Version de la même époque qu'à l'art. XIV; même texte qu'à l'art. VII ci-dessus. Édition de même date.

6 feuillets. — Bunyiu Nanjio 340.

— XVII.

六字神咒王經

Lou tseu chen tcheou oang king.

Ṣaḍakṣara vidyāmantra sūtra.

Version de la dynastie des Liang (502-557), même texte que ci-dessus. Liste des caractères rares. Édition de 1656.

8 feuillets. — Bunyiu Nanjio 341.

Grand in-8. Bonne gravure. 1 vol. demi-rel., au chiffre de la République Française.

Nouveau fonds 3991.

5862. — I.

請觀世音菩薩消伏毒害陀羅尼咒經

Tshing koan chi yin phou sa siao fou tou hai tho lo ni tcheou king.

Lecture des caractères difficiles. Texte incomplet à la fin.

Nᵒ 5861, art. II.

— II.

文殊師利問菩提經

Oen chou chi li oen phou thi king.

Gayāçīrṣa sūtra.

Traduction de Kumārajīva.

Bunyiu Nanjio 238.

— III.

佛說觀普賢菩薩行法經

Fo choe koan phou hien phou sa hing fa king ; alias :

觀普賢觀經

Koan phou hien koan king ; alias :

二山深功德經

Eul chan chen kong te king.

Samantabhadra bodhisattva dhyāna caryā dharma sūtra.

Traduction de Dharmamitra, de Ki-pin (en Chine 424-442). Lecture des caractères difficiles. A la fin, indication du lieu d'édition : Kin-ling, le reste illisible.

Bunyiu Nanjio 394.

Grand in-8. Bonne gravure, frontispice (1 feuillet double). 1 vol. demi-reliure.
Nouveau fonds 695.

5863. — I.

請觀音經疏

Tshing koan yin king sou.

Commentaire de l'Avalokite-çvara yācana sūtra.

Explications de Tchi-tche ta-chi, rédigées par son disciple Koan-ting. Liste des caractères rares.

1 livre. — Bunyiu Nanjio 1562 ;
cf. aussi n° 5861, art. II.

— II.

請觀音經疏闡義鈔

Tshing koan yin king sou tchhan yi tchhao.

Commentaire de l'ouvrage précédent.

Par Tchi-yuen, de l'école Thien-thai (998-1022). Préface de 999. Lecture des mots rares. Édition de Leng-yen seu (1664).

4 livres. — Bunyiu Nanjio 1563.

Grand in-8. Bonne gravure. 1 vol. demi-rel. au chiffre de la République Française.
Nouveau fonds 3988.

5864. — I.

文殊師利般涅槃經

Oen chou chi li pan nie phan king.

Mañjuçrī parinirvāṇa sūtra.

Traduction de Nie Tao-tchen (après 313). Édition de 1604.

Feuillets 4 et 5 en mauvais état. — Bunyiu Nanjio 508.

— II.

異出菩薩本起經

Yi tchhou phou sa pen khi king.

Abhiniṣkramaṇa sūtra.

Du même. Sūtra du Hīnayāna. Édition de Tsi-tchao 'an (1604). Lecture des caractères difficiles.

Feuillets 9 à 12 en mauvais état. — Bunyiu Nanjio 509 ; cf. id. 664 à 666.

— III.

佛說賢首經

Fo choe hien cheou king.

Bhadraçrī sūtra.

Version de Cheng-kien. Mêmes lieu et date.

3 feuillets. — Bunyiu Nanjio 510.

— IV.

八大人覺經

Pa ta jen kio king.

Sūtra sur les huit connaissances des hommes supérieurs.

Version de 'An Chi-kao, Perse (148-170). Édition de Tsi-tchao 'an (1602).

2 feuillets. — Bunyiu Nanjio 512.

— V.

千佛因緣經

Tshien fo yin yuen king.

Sahasrabuddha nidāna sūtra.

Version de Kumārajīva. Édition de Tsi-tchao 'an (1604).

23 feuillets. — Bunyiu Nanjio 511.

— VI.

佛說月明菩薩經

Fo choe yue ming phou sa king.

Buddhabhāṣita candraprabha bodhisattva sūtra.

Version de Tchi Khien. Lecture des caractères rares. Édition de King-chan seu (1604).

4 feuillets. — Bunyiu Nanjio 513.

— VII.

佛說心明經

Fo choe sin ming king.

Cittaprabhā sūtra.

Version de Tchou Fa-hou. Liste des signes rares. Mêmes lieu et date que ci-dessus.

4 feuillets. — Bunyiu Nanjio 514.

— VIII.

佛說滅十方冥經

Fo choe mie chi fang ming king.

Daçadig andhakāra vidhvaṃsana sūtra.

Du même (306). Lecture des signes difficiles. Mêmes lieu et date ; feuillets gravés de nouveau en 1670.

8 feuillets. — Bunyiu Nanjio 5ı5.

— IX.

佛說鹿母經

Fo choę lou mou king.

Mṛgamātṛ sūtra.

Du même. Liste des caractères rares. Édition de Tsi-tchao 'an (1604).

9 feuillets. — Bunyiu Nanjio 5ı6.

— X.

佛說魔逆經

Fo choę mo yi king.

Sūtra sur l'opposition de Māra.

Du même (289). Liste des signes rares. Mêmes lieu et date.

1 livre. — Bunyiu Nanjio 5ı7.

— XI.

佛說賴吒和羅所問德 光太子經

Fo choę lai tchha hoo lo so oen te koang thai tseu king.

Buddhabhāṣita rāṣṭrapāla paripṛcchā guṇaprabha kumāra sūtra.

Du même (276). Liste des caractères difficiles. Mêmes lieu et date.

1 livre. — Bunyiu Nanjio 5ı8.

Grand in-8. Bonne gravure. 1 vol. demi-rel., au chiffre de la République Française.

Nouveau fonds 3908.

———

5865. — I.

佛說高王觀世音經

Fo choę kao oang koan chi yin king.

Sūtra du souverain élevé Koan-yin.

Frontispice (2 feuillets simples). Note sur l'origine du sūtra; invocations transcrites du sanscrit, poésie. Texte.

Voir n° 5681, art. V.

— II.

觀音夢授經

Koan yin mong cheou king.

Sūtra donné par Koan-yin en songe.

Texte seul.

— III.

觀音救苦經

Koan yin kieou khou king.

Sūtra de Koan-yin qui sauve du malheur.

Texte semblable au n° 5681,

art. IV, différent du n° 5677, art. VI.

— IV.

白衣大悲五印心陀羅尼

Po yi ta pei oou yin sin tho lo ni.

Dhāraṇī du cœur aux cinq sceaux de la miséricordieuse en vêtements blancs.

N° 5848, art. III.

A la fin postface par Oang Chi-tsiun (1727); figure de divinité. Réédition de Hai-tchhoang (1835).

In-4. Papier blanc. 1 vol. en paravent, couvertures rouges; dans 1 étui demi-rel., au chiffre de Louis-Philippe.
Nouveau fonds 143.

5866. — I.

佛說高王觀世音經

Fo choe kao oang koan chi yin king.

Avant le texte, figure de Koan-yin; avertissement, prières et dhāraṇī.

Cf. n° 5865, art. I.

— II.

觀音救苦經

Koan yin kieou khou king.

Cf. n° 5865, art. III.

— III.

觀音救生經

Koan yin kieou cheng king.

Sūtra de Koan-yin qui sauve les êtres vivants.

Cf. n° 5681, art. III.

— IV.

齋戒日期

Tchai kiai ji khi.

Calendrier des cérémonies.

Suivi du récit de divers miracles. Édition de Canton (?) semi-officielle.

Cf. n° 5867, art. VII.

In-18. Titre noir sur jaune. 1 vol. cartonnage.
Nouveau fonds 5242.

5867. — I.

高王觀世音菩薩眞經

Kao oang koan chi yin phou sa tchen king.

Sūtra du souverain élevé Avalokiteçvara.

Calendrier des cérémonies; préface; formules de purification. Texte. Frontispice (1 feuillet simple) représentant Koan-yin.

7 feuillets. — Voir n° 5865, art. I.

— II.

觀世音咒
Koan chi yin tcheou.

Dhāraṇī de Koan-yin.

Formule en chinois et en transcription du sanscrit; note en petit texte.

1 feuillet. — Cf. n° 5694, art. VIII.

— III.

消萬病眞言
Siao oan ping tchen yen.

Dhāraṇī contre les maladies.

Formule en transcription, avec note en petit texte.

1/2 feuillet.

— IV.

觀世音前印後印降魔印
Koan chi yin tshien yin heou yin kiang mo yin.

Formules de Koan-yin : formule antérieure, formule postérieure, formule pour soumettre les démons.

Chinois et transcription.

1 feuillet.

— V.

補闕眞言
Pou khiue tchen yen.

Dhāraṇī.

Transcription.

1/2 feuillet. — N° 5728, art. II.

— VI.

般若波羅蜜多心經
Pan je po lo mi to sin king.

Prajñāpāramitā hṛdaya sūtra.

2 1/2 feuillets. — N° 5733, art. II.

— VII.

觀世音菩薩聖誕齋戒日期
Koan chi yin phou sa cheng tan tchai kiai ji khi.

Calendrier de l'anniversaire de naissance et des fêtes du bodhisattva Avalokiteçvara.

2 feuillets en petit texte : illustration finale (divinité). Cf. n° 5866, art. IV.

Petit in-8. Papier blanc. 1 vol. demi-reliure.

Nouveau fonds 3550.

5868. 正信除疑無修證自在寶經

Tcheng sin tchhou yi oou sieou tcheng tseu tsai pao king.

Sūtra relatif à la foi droite qui dissipe les doutes.

25 chapitres.

In-folio. Frontispice (4 feuillets doubles); à la fin, figure de guerrier. Grande impression ancienne sur papier blanc. 1 vol. en paravent, plats en bois; le plat de tête est recouvert de soie brochée, titre en lettres d'or.

Nouveau fonds 2318, 2316.

Cinquième Section : **MAHĀSANNIPĀTA SŪTRA**

5869-5870. — I (5869).

般舟三昧經

Pan tcheou san mei king; alias :

十方現在佛悉在前立定經

Chi fang hien tsai fo si tsai tshien li ting king.

Pratyutpanna buddhasammu-khāvasthita samādhi sūtra.

Version de Tchi Leou-kia-tchhan (Lokarakṣa?), Yue-tchi (147 ou 164-186). Liste des termes rares.

3 livres. — Bunyiu Nanjio 73.

— II (5869-5870).

阿差末菩薩經

'O tchha mo phou sa king.

Akṣayamati nirdeça sūtra.

Version de Tchou Fa-hou.

7 livres. — Bunyiu Nanjio 74.

Grand in-8. Bonne gravure. 1 vol. demi-rel., au chiffre de la République Française.

Nouveau fonds 4007.

1 vol. cartonnage.

Nouveau fonds 4639.

5871. 無盡意菩薩經

Oou tsin yi phou sa king.

Akṣayamati nirdeça sūtra.

Version de Tchi-yen et de Pao-yun, tous deux Chinois de Liang-tcheou (427). Liste des signes rares. Édition de Leng-yen seu (1657).

4 livres. — Bunyiu Nanjio 77; voir ci-dessus, art. II.

Grand in-8. Bonne gravure. 1 vol. demi-rel., au chiffre de la République Française.

Nouveau fonds 3875.

5872. — I.

大哀經

Ta 'ai king.

Tathāgata mahākāruṇika nirdeça sūtra.

Version par Tchou Fa-hou du
même texte qu'une partie du
Mahāvaipulya mahāsannipāta sūtra (traducteur Dharmarakṣa, Hindou 414-421). Liste des caractères
rares.

8 livres. — Bunyiu Nanjio 79; cf.
id. 61.

— II.

大集譬喻王經
Ta tsi phi yu oang king.

Mahāsannipātāvadānarāja sūtra.

Traduction de Jñānagupta (585-
592). Liste des caractères rares.

2 livres. — Bunyiu Nanjio 78.

Grand in-8. Bonne gravure; frontispice (1 feuillet double). 1 vol. demi-rel.,
au chiffre de la République Française.
Nouveau fonds 3841.

5873. 寶女所問經
Pao niu so oen king.

Ratnastrī paripṛcchā sūtra.

Version par Tchou Fa-hou d'une
partie du même texte que le Mahāvaipulya mahāsannipāta sūtra.Lec-
ture des mots rares.

4 livres. — Bunyiu Nanjio 80; cf.
id. 61.

Grand in-8. Bonne gravure. 1 vol.
demi-rel., au chiffre de la République
Française.
Nouveau fonds 3945.

5874. — I.

無言童子經
Oou yen thong tseu king.

Mūka kumāra sūtra.

Version par Tchou Fa-hou du
même texte qu'une partie du Mahāvaipulya mahāsannipāta sūtra.
Liste des mots rares.

2 livres. — Bunyiu Nanjio 81; cf.
id. 61.

— II.

自在王菩薩經
Tseu tsai oang phou sa king.

Īçvararāja bodhisattva sūtra.

Version par Kumārajīva, d'une
partie du Mahāvaipulya mahāsannipāta sūtra. Lecture des mots
difficiles.

2 livres. — Bunyiu Nanjio 82; cf.
id. 61.

— III.

奮迅王問經
Fẹn sin oang oen king.

Īçvararāja paripṛcchā sūtra.

Version par Gautama Prajñā-ruci, Hindou (538-543), du même texte qu'à l'art. II. Note indiquant pour la traduction la date de 542. Liste des caractères rares.

2 livres. — Bunyiu Nanjio 83 ; cf. id. 61.

Grand in-8. Bonne gravure. 1 vol. demi-rel., au chiffre de la République Française.

Nouveau fonds 3935.

5875. 守護國界主陀羅尼經

Cheou hou koę kiai tchou tho lo ni king.

Deçāntapālapati dhāraṇī sūtra.

Version de Prājña, de Ki-pin (785-810) ; même texte qu'une partie du Mahāvaipulya mahāsannipāta sūtra. Liste des caractères difficiles. Édition du Hoa-yen ko (1642).

10 livres. — Bunyiu Nanjio 978 ; cf. id. 61.

Grand in-8. Bonne gravure. 1 vol. demi-rel., au chiffre de la République Française.

Nouveau fonds 4015.

5876. — I.

海意菩薩所問淨印法門經

Hai yi phou sa so oen tsing yin fa mẹn king.

Sāgaramati pariprcchā sūtra.

Traduction d'une partie du Mahāvaipulya mahāsannipāta sū-tra, par Oei-tsing et Fa-hou (vers 1009). Lecture des caractères rares. Édition de Hoa-tchheng 'an, au Han-chan.

9 livres. — Bunyiu Nanjio 976 ; cf. id. 61.

— II.

佛說如幻三摩地無量印法門經

Fo choę jou hoan san mo ti oou liang yin fa mẹn king.

Māyopamasamādhyamitamu-drādharmaparyāya sūtra.

Version de Chi-hou ; même texte que Bunyiu Nanjio 395. Lecture des mots rares.

3 livres. — Bunyiu Nanjio 977.

Grand in-8. Bonne gravure. 1 vol. demi-rel., au chiffre de la République Française.

Nouveau fonds 3937.

5877. — I.

寶星陀羅尼經

Pao sing tho lo ni king.

Ratnatārā dhāraṇī sūtra.

Version par Prabhāmitra, Hindou (628-630) d'une partie du Mahāvaipulya mahāsannipāta sūtra. Préface de Fa-lin († 640). Lecture des mots rares. Édition de 1657, 1658.

8 livres. — Bunyiu Nanjio 84; cf. id. 61.

— II.

度諸佛境界智光嚴經

Tou tchou fo king kiai tchi koang yen king.

Sarvatathāgataviṣayāvatāra sūtra.

Version de l'époque des dynasties Tshin (350-431). Liste des mots rares.

1 livre. — Bunyiu Nanjio 85; cf. n° 5951, art. I.

— III.

大乘金剛髻珠菩薩修行分經

Ta cheng kin kang ki tchou phou sa sieou hing fen king.

Mahāyāna vajracūḍāmaṇi bodhisattvacaryā varga sūtra.

Version de Bodhiruci (693-713). Lecture des termes difficiles.

1 livre. — Bunyiu Nanjio 86.

Grand in-8. Bonne gravure. 1 vol. demi-rel., au chiffre de la République Française.
Nouveau fonds 4016.

5878. ## 佛說菩薩念佛三昧經

Fo choę phou sa nien fo san mei king.

Bodhisattva buddhānusmṛti samādhi sūtra.

Version de Kong-tę-tchi (Guṇaçīla?), Occidental (462), et Hiuentchhang. Liste des caractères difficiles. Édition du Miao-tę chanyuen, du Tshing-liang chan (1591); gravé de nouveau (1670).

6 livres. — Bunyiu Nanjio 71.

Grand in-8. Bonne gravure. 1 vol. demi-rel., au chiffre de la République Française.
Nouveau fonds 4004.

5879. ## 佛說大方等大集菩薩念佛三昧經

Fo choę ta fang teng ta tsi phou sa nien fo san mei king.

Mahāvaipulya mahāsannipāta bodhisattva buddhānusmṛti samādhi sūtra.

Version de Dharmagupta, Hindou (590-616) ; du même texte que ci-dessus. Lecture des mots rares.

10 livres. — Bunyiu Nanjio 72 ; cf. n° 5878.

Grand in-8. Bonne gravure ; 1 feuillet déplacé dans le livre 6. 1 vol. demi-rel., au chiffre de la République Française. *Nouveau fonds* 4008.

5880. — I.

大方等大集賢護經

Ta fang teng ta tsi hien hou king.

Mahāvaipulya mahāsannipāta bhadrapāla sūtra.

Version de Jñānagupta, Dharmagupta, et autres (589-592). Traduction du même texte que le Pratyutpanna mahāsannipāta bodhisattva buddhānusmṛti samādhi sūtra. Liste des caractères rares. Édition du bonze Tchhe-oei Yin-khai (1660).

5 livres. — Bunyiu Nanjio 75 ; cf. id. 73.

— II.

拔陂菩薩經

Pa pho phou sa king ; alias :

拔陁經

Pa tho king ; alias :

安公古典經

'An kong kou tien king.

Bhadrapāla sūtra.

Version par Tchi Leou-kia-tchhan du même texte qu'à l'art. I. Lecture des caractères difficiles. Mêmes lieu et date d'édition.

1 livre. — Bunyiu Nanjio 76.

Grand in-8. Bonne gravure. 1 vol. demi-rel., au chiffre de la République Française. *Nouveau fonds* 3890.

Sixième Section : AVATAMSAKA SŪTRA

5881. — I.

諸菩薩求佛本業經

Tchou phou sa khieou fo pen ye king.

Sūtra sur les actions des bodhisattva qui recherchent l'état de bouddha.

Version de Nie Tao-tchen ; même texte que Bunyiu Nanjio 100 (version de Tchi Khien) et que des parties de Bunyiu Nanjio 87 et 88. Liste des signes rares.

12 feuillets. — Bunyiu Nanjio 107 ; cf. n°⁵ 5884 à 5887 et 5888 à 5891.

— II.

菩薩十住行道品經

Phou sa chi tchou hing tao phin king.

Bodhisattvadaçasthānacaryā-dhyāya sūtra.

Version de Tchou Fa-hou. Lecture des caractères rares.

9 feuillets. — Bunyiu Nanjio 108 ; cf. id. 87, 88.

— III.

佛說菩薩十住經

Fo choę phou sa chi tchou king.

Bodhisattva daçasthāna sūtra.

Version par Gītamitra, Occidental (époque des Tsin orientaux, 317-420), du même texte qu'à l'art. II. Édition de Tsi-tchao 'an (1608) ; feuillets gravés de nouveau en 1691.

5 feuillets. — Bunyiu Nanjio 109 ; cf. id. 87, 88.

— IV.

等目菩薩所問三昧經

Teng mou phou sa so oen san mei king.

Samacakṣurbodhisattva pari-pṛcchā samādhi sūtra.

Version de Tchou Fa-hou. Liste des mots difficiles. Édition de Tsi-tchao 'an (1607).

3 livres. — Bunyiu Nanjio 111 ; cf. id. 87, 88.

— V.

文殊師利問菩薩署經

Oen chou chi li oen phou sa chou king.

Sūtra sur le devoir du bodhisattva en réponse à Mañjuçrī.

Version de Tchi Leou-kia-tchhan. Liste des signes difficiles. Même lieu et même date qu'à l'art. IV.

1 livre. — Bunyiu Nanjio 112.

Grand in-8. Bonne gravure. 1 vol. demi-rel., au chiffre de la République Française.

Nouveau fonds 3901.

5882. 度世品經

Tou chi phin king.

Sūtra sur la traversée du monde.

Traduit par Tchou Fa-hou. Même texte que le chapitre Li chi kien du Hoa-yen king. Lecture des signes rares. Édition de Tsi-tchao 'an (1598).

6 livres. — Bunyiu Nanjio 104 ; cf. nᵒˢ 5884-5887, 5888-5891.

Grand in-8. Bonne gravure. 1 vol. demi-rel., au chiffre de la République Française.

Nouveau fonds 3794.

5883. 佛說羅摩伽經
Fo choe lo mo kia king.

Rāmaka sūtra.

Version de Cheng-kien ; traduction partielle de Bunyiu Nanjio 87, 88. Liste des mots rares. Édition de Tsi-tchao 'an (1608, 1610); feuillets gravés de nouveau en 1704.

4 livres. — Bunyiu Nanjio 106; cf. nᵒˢ 5884-5887, 5888-5891.

Grand in-8. Bonne gravure. 1 vol. demi-rel., au chiffre de la République Française.

Nouveau fonds 3970.

5884-5887. 大方廣佛華嚴經
Ta fang koang fo hoa yen king.

Buddhāvataṃsaka mahāvaipulya sūtra.

Traduction de Buddhabhadra, Hindou (420). Notice finale relative à ce travail. Lecture des caractères rares. Édition de Tsi-tchao 'an (1608-1610).

60 livres. — Bunyiu Nanjio 87.

Grand in-8. Bonne gravure ; frontispice (1 feuillet double). 4 vol. demi-rel., au chiffre de la République Française.

Nouveau fonds 3760 à 3763.

5888-5891.
Ta fang koang fo hoa yen king.

Buddhāvataṃsaka mahāvaipulya sūtra.

Préface impériale (1412); préface de l'impératrice Oou (699). Traduction par Çikṣānanda (695-699). Lecture des caractères difficiles. Edition de Tsi-tchao 'an (1601, 1602); gravée de nouveau par Ling-hoei.

80 livres (manquent la fin du livre 77 et les livres suivants). — Bunyiu Nanjio 88.

Grand in-8. Bonne gravure ; frontispice (1 feuillet double). 4 vol. demi-rel., au chiffre de la République Française.

Nouveau fonds 3764 à 3767.

5892-5899. — I (5892-5899).
大方廣佛華嚴經
Ta fang koang fo hoa yen king.

Buddhāvataṃsaka mahāvaipulya sūtra.

Préface impériale (1412); préface de l'impératrice Oou (699). Traduction de Çikṣānanda ; lecture des caractères difficiles.

-- II (5899).

補闕眞言

Pou khiue tchen yen.

Dhāraṇī.

Nº 5728, art. II.

— III (5899).

大方廣佛華嚴經普賢行願品

Ta fang koang fo hoa yen king phou hien hing yuen phin.

Buddhāvataṃsaka mahāvaipulya sūtra samantabhadra praṇidhānādhyāya.

Traduction de Prājña. A la fin liste des donateurs.

17 feuillets du livre 40. — Bunyiu Nanjio 89; voir nᵒˢ 5900-5901.

— IV (5899).

復菴和尚華嚴經論貫

Fou 'an hoo chang hoa yen king loen koan.

Traité du bonze Fou-'an sur le Buddhāvataṃsaka, etc.

10 feuillets.

Édition de Hai-tchhoang seu (1769).

Grand in-8. Papier blanc. 8 vol. demi-rel., au chiffre de Louis-Philippe.
Nouveau fonds 620 A.

5900-5901. 大方廣佛華嚴經

Ta fang koang fo hoa yen king.

Buddhāvataṃsaka mahāvaipulya sūtra.

Traduction par Prājña (796-798). A la fin de l'ouvrage, notice sur la traduction et la présentation (795-798). Lecture des signes rares. Édition de Miao-tę 'an, de la montagne Tshing-liang (1590, 1591); gravée de nouveau par Ling-hoei.

40 livres. — Bunyiu Nanjio 89.

Grand in-8. Bonne gravure; frontispice (1 feuillet double). 2 vol. demi-rel., au chiffre de la République Française.
Nouveau fonds 3758, 3759.

5902. 大方廣總持寶光明經

Ta fang koang tsong tchhi pao koang ming king.

Mahāvaipulya dhāraṇī ratnaprabhāsa sūtra.

Version par Fa-thien (Dharmadeva, Fa-hien), Hindou (973-981);

d'une section du Bunyiu Nanjio 88. Lecture des mots rares. Édition de Hoa-tchheng seu (1632).

5 livres. — Bunyiu Nanjio 785; nᵒˢ 5888-5891.

Grand in-8. Bonne gravure. 1 vol. demi-rel., au chiffre de la République Française.

Nouveau fonds 4048.

5903. 漸備一切智德經
Tsien pei yi tshie tchi te king.

Daçabhūmika sūtra.

Version par Tchou Fa-hou de sections du Buddhāvataṃsaka mahāvaipulya sūtra. Lecture des mots difficiles. Édition de Tsi-tchao 'an (1608).

5 livres. — Bunyiu Nanjio 110; cf. nᵒˢ 5884-5887 et 5888-5891.

Grand in-8. Bonne gravure. 1 vol. demi-rel., au chiffre de la République Française.

Nouveau fonds 4047.

5904. 十住經
Chi tchou king.

Daçabhūmika sūtra.

Version du même texte par Kumārajīva et Buddhayaças, de Kipin (403-413). Édition de Tsi-tchao 'an (1607).

6 livres. — Bunyiu Nanjio 105; cf. nᵒ 5903.

Grand in-8. Bonne gravure. 1 vol. demi-rel., au chiffre de la République Française.

Nouveau fonds 3923.

5905. 十住毘婆沙論
Chi tchou phi pho cha loen.

Daçabhūmi vibhāṣā çāstra.

Commentaire du Daçabhūmika sūtra et autres textes semblables par le bodhisattva Nāgārjuna. Version de Kumārajīva (vers 405). Lecture des caractères rares. Édition de l'association Hong-fa, de Song-kiang (1643).

10 livres (24 chapitres seulement). — Bunyiu Nanjio 1180; cf. nᵒ 5903.

Grand in-8. Caractères grêles; manquent les feuillets 1, 2, 3 du 1ᵉʳ livre. 1 vol. demi-rel., au chiffre de la République Française.

Nouveau fonds 4111.

5906. 十地經論
Chi ti king loen.

Daçabhūmika sūtra çāstra.

Commentaire des mêmes textes par le bodhisattva Vasubandhu. Version de Bodhiruci (508-535). Préface par Tshoei Koang (508). Lecture des termes difficiles. Édi-

30

tion de la société Hong-fa, à Song-kiang (1644).

12 livres. — Bunyiu Nanjio 1194; cf. n° 5903.

Grand in-8. Bonne gravure; frontis-pice (1 feuillet double). 1 vol. demi-rel., au chiffre de la République Française.
Nouveau fonds 3924.

5907-5910. 大方廣佛華 嚴經疏

Ta fang koang fo hoa yen king sou.

Commentaire du Buddhāvataṃsaka vaipulya sūtra.

Par le bonze Tchheng-koan, de l'école Avataṃsaka (740?-810?). Lecture des caractères difficiles. Édition de Hoa-tchheng seu (1629-1632).

Livres 1 à 30 et 41 à 60. — Bunyiu Nanjio 1589; cf. n°s 5888-5891.

Grand in-8. Bonne gravure; frontis-pice (1 feuillet double). 4 vol. carton-nage.
Nouveau fonds 4605 à 4608.

5911-5916. 大方廣佛華 嚴經隨疏演義鈔

Ta fang koang fo hoa yen king soei sou yen yi tchhao.

Commentaire de l'ouvrage précédent.

Par le même, avec préface de l'auteur. Lecture des caractères difficiles. Édition de Hoa-tchheng seu (1629-1632).

90 livres. — Bunyiu Nanjio 1590; cf. n°s 5907-5910.

Grand in-8. Bonne gravure; frontis-pice (1 feuillet double). 6 vol demi-rel., au chiffre de la République Française.
Nouveau fonds 3774 à 3779.

5917-5925. 大方廣佛華 嚴經疏鈔

Ta fang koang fo hoa yen king sou tchhao.

Commentaire du Ta fang koang fo hoa yen king sou.

Par le même auteur.

Livres 1 à 34, 63 à 72. — Cf. Bunyiu Nanjio 1590; voir aussi n°s 5907-5910.

Grand in-8. Gravure médiocre. 9 vol. cartonnage.
Nouveau fonds 4609 à 4617.

5926.

Ta fang koang fo hoa yen king sou tchhao.

Double.

Livres 67 à 69.

1 vol. cartonnage.
Nouveau fonds 4618.

5927-5928. 大方廣佛華嚴經疏演義鈔

Ta fang koang fo hoa yen king sou yen yi tchhao.

Ouvrage du même auteur; sans date ni lieu d'édition.

Livres 4 à 8. — Cf. nᵒˢ 5907-5910, 5911-5916, 5917-5925.

Grand in-8. 2 vol. cartonnage. *Nouveau fonds* 4619, 4620.

5929-5930.

— I (5929).

大方廣佛華嚴經疏鈔科文

Ta fang koang fo hoa yen king sou tchhao khoo oen.

Tableaux résumant le commentaire du Buddhāvatamsaka mahāvaipulya sūtra.

Préparés par Tchheng-koan. Édition de Hoa-tchheng seu (1616).

32 feuillets.

— II (5929-5930).

大方廣佛華嚴經疏演義鈔

Ta fang koang fo hoa yen king sou yen yi tchhao.

Commentaire du Buddhāvatamsaka, etc.

Extrait par le même des commentaires précédents. Préface de l'auteur. Édition donnée à Tsi-tchao 'an, Hoa-tchheng seu, etc. (1610-1616).

29 livres. — Bunyiu Nanjio 1639; cf. nᵒˢ 5907-5910, 5911-5916.

Grand in-8. Bonne gravure; frontispice (1 feuillet double). 2 vol. demi-rel., au chiffre de la République Française. *Nouveau fonds* 3768, 3769.

5931. — I.

大方廣佛華嚴經普賢行願品疏科文

Ta fang koang fo hoa yen king phou hien hing yuen phin sou khoo oen.

Tableaux résumant le commentaire du chapitre sur la pratique et les vœux du bodhisattva Samantabhadra, dans le Buddhāvatamsaka, etc.

Préface générale par Tao-khoei pour la présente réédition sans date. Le tableau est de Tsong-mi.

21 feuillets.

— II.

大方廣佛華嚴經普賢行願品別行疏鈔

*Ta fang koang fo hoa yen king
phou hien hing yuen phin pie
hing sou tchhao.*

Commentaire du Buddhāva-
taṃsaka, etc., chapitre de la
prière et des vœux de Samantabhadra.

Résumé par Tsong-mi, du commentaire plus étendu dû à Tchheng-
koan. Édition de 1642.

6 livres. — Cf. n⁰ˢ 5929-5930, art.
II; 5900-5901.

— III.

華嚴宗七祖

Hoa yen tsong tshi tsou; alias :

大方廣佛華嚴經七祖行蹟

*Ta fang koang fo hoa yen king
tshi tsou hing tsi.*

Vies des sept chefs de l'école
Avataṃsaka.

Extrait du Fo tsou thong tsai
(n⁰ˢ 345-347) avec un tableau final.

15 feuillets.

Grand in-8. 1 vol. demi-rel., au chiffre
de la République Française.
Nouveau fonds 3773.

5932-5936. 大方廣佛新華嚴經合論

*Ta fang koang fo sin hoa yen
king ho loen.*

Traités sur le Buddhāvataṃsaka vaipulya sūtra.

D'après la version de Çikṣānanda; composés par Li Thong-
hiuen (époque des Thang); réunis
par un bonze de Khai-yuen seu, à
Fou-tcheou, Tchi-ning Li-king
(même dynastie). Lecture des mots
difficiles. Édition de Miao-te-'an
au Oou-thai-chan (1590, 1591).

Livres 21 à 55 et 71 à 115. — N⁰ˢ
5888-5891.

Grand in-8. Bonne gravure. 5 vol.
cartonnage.
Nouveau fonds 4622 à 4626.

5937. 大方廣佛華嚴經要解

*Ta fang koang fo hoa yen king
yao kiai.*

Explication du Buddhāvataṃsaka sūtra.

Par Kiai-hoan, de la bonzerie
de Po-lien à Oen-ling, avec préface de 1128.

60 feuillets. — N⁰ˢ 5884, etc.

In-4. Belle impression sur papier
blanc. 1 vol. demi-rel., au chiffre de la
République Française.
Nouveau fonds 318.

5938-5940. 華嚴懸談會玄記

Hoa yen hiuen than hoei hiuen ki.

Explication du sens caché du commentaire sur le Buddhāvataṃsaka, etc.

Par Phou-choei de Tshang-chan (époque des Yuen). Texte avec tableaux. Liste des signes difficiles. Édition de Hoa-tchheng seu (1628-1631).

40 livres. — Bunyiu Nanjio 1622; nᵒˢ 5907-5910.

Grand in-8. Bonne gravure; frontispice (1 feuillet double). Manquent les feuillets 1-8 du livre 11 et le dernier feuillet du livre 40. 3 vol. demi-rel. au chiffre de Louis-Philippe.

Nouveau fonds 3770 à 3772.

5941. — I. 大方廣佛華嚴經普賢行願品疏

Ta fang koang fo hoa yen king phou hien hing yuen phin sou; alias :

大方廣佛華嚴經入不思議解脫境界普賢行願品

Ta fang koang fo hoa yen king jou pou seu yi kiai thoo king kiai phou hien hing yuen phin.

Commentaire du Buddhāvataṃsaka, etc., chapitre de la pratique et des vœux de Samantabhadra.

D'après la traduction de Prājña et les commentaires de Tchhengkoan; par Ming-te, bonze de Tongchan seu à Sieou-choei, de la dynastie des Ming.

1 livre. — Nᵒ 5931, art. II. — Cf. Bunyiu Nanjio 89, 1589, 1590, 1639.

— II. 大方廣佛華嚴經疏鈔釐合凡例

Ta fang koang fo hoa yen king sou tchhao li ho fan li.

Notice historique et avertissement pour le commentaire, etc.

Cette notice datée de 1625 et signée Ye Khi-yin, indique que l'ouvrage était depuis l'ère Kiatsing (1522-1566), conservé à la bonzerie de Tchao-khing à Ooulin. L'avertissement est signé Li Yu-fang. Liste des donateurs.

13 feuillets.

— III. 大方廣佛華嚴經疏鈔音釋

Ta fang koang fo hoa yen king sou tchhao yin chi; alias :

華嚴入經疏鈔音釋

Hoa yen jou king sou tchhao yin chi.

Lecture des caractères diffi-ciles pour le commentaire, etc.

Table disposée en suivant les livres de l'ouvrage; complément et liste des donateurs.

3o feuillets.

— IV.

鐫清涼國師華嚴疏鈔後序

Tsiuen tshing liang koę chi hoa yen sou tchhao heou siu

Postface du commentaire de Tshing-liang koę-chi sur le Bud-dhāvataṃsaka, etc.

Postface de Ye Khi-yin de Tchhang-choei (1627) pour la réé-dition en 78 volumes, gravée en 1626, de l'œuvre de Tchheng-koan.

8 feuillets.

Grand in-8. Bonne gravure. I vol. demi-rel., au chiffre de la République Française.

Nouveau fonds 3793.

5942-5947. 大方廣佛華嚴經綱要

Ta fang koang fo hoa yen king kang yao.

Principes du Buddhāvataṃ-saka, etc.

D'après la traduction de Çikṣā-nanda et les commentaires de Tchheng-koan, par Tę-tshing de Han-chan. Préface de Koan-heng, disciple de l'auteur (1637). Intro-duction pour la gravure de l'ou-vrage. Édition de Tshing-tsing chạn-lin à Hai-yang (1626-1631).

8o livres (feuillets déchirés, manque la fin du dernier livre). — Nᵒˢ 5929-5930, 5907-5910, etc.

Grand in-8. Bonne gravure. 6 vol. demi-rel., au chiffre de la République Française.

Nouveau fonds 3787 à 3792.

5948. 華嚴寶鏡

Hoa yen pao king.

Miroir précieux de l'Avataṃ-saka.

Par le bonze Tao-tou de Lo-feou; préface de l'auteur (1656); postface par Kin-tchong. Édition de la bonzerie de Hai-tchhoang; réimprimée en 1826.

Petit in-8. Papier blanc, titre noir sur vert. I vol. demi-rel. au chiffre de Louis-Philippe.

Nouveau fonds 6I.

5949-5950. 閱經十二種
Yue king chi eul tchang.

Douze traités relatifs à des sūtra.

Par Tsing-thing, autres noms Liang-thing, King-hou tchhoan-kho, de l'école Tshao-tong, bonze à Yun-khi ou Yun-men. Préfaces par Khi Tsiun-kia Tsing-tchhao; par Yang Yong-kien (1670); par Li Yuen-khoan Po-'an tao-jen, de Yu-tchang. Table des douze traités. Liste des donateurs.

— I (5949).

華嚴經頌
Hoa yen king song.

Éloge de l'Avataṃsaka sūtra.

Par Tsing-thing, publié sous la direction de Tshao Yong Tshieou-yo kiu-chi et de Tchou Meou-chi Koei-chi tao-jen.

10 feuillets. — Nᵒˢ 5884-5887, etc.

— II (5949).

梵網戒光
Fan oang kiai koang.

Explication du Brahmajāla sūtra.

Par Tsing-thing; publié par Yang Yong-kien Tsing-song et Siu Hiu-ling Tsing-yo. Préface de l'auteur; postface par Chi Po Yo-'an tao-jen.

9 feuillets. — Cf. nᵒ 6238.

— III (5949).

楞伽心印
Leng kia sin yin.

Sceau du cœur du Laṅkāvatāra sūtra.

Par le même. Publié sous la direction de Tshien Kiang de Thiao-khi, et de Tchhen Tchi de Yun-tchhoan.

13 feuillets. — Cf. nᵒ 6041.

— IV (5949).

維摩饒舌
Oei mo jao che.

Traité sur le Vimalakīrtti nir-deça sūtra.

Par Tsing-thing; revu et publié par Oou Tchou Tchhai-oan lao-jen et par Chen Thing-mai Tchhi-kien theou-tho. Préface par ce dernier.

7 feuillets. — Cf. nᵒ 5975.

— V (5949).

圓覺連珠
Yuen kio lien tchou.

Perles du Pūrṇabuddha sūtra.

Par le même, publié par Tchou Cheng Tsing-Tchhou et Oou Po-pheng Tsing-yuen. Préface par Yen Tsheng-kiu Tchi-ting.

12 feuillets. — Cf. n° 6065.

— VI (5949).

楞嚴荅問
Leng yen ta oen.

Questions sur le Çūraṅgama sūtra.

Par le même; publié par Ho Yuen-ying Joei-yin et Tseng Oang-soen Tao-fou de Tchhang-choei. Préface de Tseng Oang-soen.

29 feuillets. — Cf. n° 5991.

— VII (5950).

藥師燈燄
Yo chi teng yen.

Éclaircissement du Bhaiṣajya-guru sūtra.

Par Tsing-thing. Revu par Siu-Chi-yu et Tchhen Tsou-tchhang.

5 feuillets. — Cf. n° 6103.

— VIII (5950).

彌陀舌相
Mi tho chẹ siang.

Explication des Amitābha sūtra.

Par le même; revu et publié par Oou Chan-thao et Tai Pan-li.

4 feuillets. — Cf. n° 5813, etc.

— IX (5950).

雲溪佷亭挺和尚金剛隨說
Yun khi liang thing thing hoo chang kin kang soei choẹ.

Notes sur le Vajra sūtra, par Tsing-thing.

Publiées par les soins de Yen Hang Hao-thing kiu-chi. Préface par le même (1667); préface pour l'art. XII par Oang Thing (1669). Introduction pour le présent article par Ta-tcheou.

9 feuillets. — Cf. n° 5728, art. I.

— X (5950).

雲溪佷亭挺和尚金剛別傳
Yun khi liang thing thing hoo chang kin kang pie tchoan.

Anecdotes relatives au Vajra sūtra, par Tsing-thing.

Publiées par Yen Hang.

16 feuillets. — Cf. n° 5728, art. I.

— XI (5950).

雲溪倀亭挻和尙㧽金剛經五十三則

Yun khi liang thing thing hoo chang nyen kin kang king oou chi san tsẹ.

Cinquante-trois règles du bonze Tsing-thing pour la lecture du Vajra sūtra.

Recueillies par Yang Chi-yi Khou-tsẹ kiu–chi.

8 feuillets. — Cf. n° 5728, art. I.

— XII (5950).

心經句義

Sin king kiu yi.

Explication du Hṛdaya sūtra.

Par Tsing-thing; publiée par Oang Thing Yen-yuen et Tchhen Tchi-tsoẹn Tsing-'an.

11 feuillets. — Cf. n° 5733, art. II.

— XIII (5950).

法華懸譚

Fa hoa hiuen than.

Entretiens sur le Saddharma puṇḍarīka sūtra.

Par Tsing-thing; revus par Oang Yi-pheng Ho-chan tao-jẹn, de Hao-thing, et par Kou Pao-oen Tshie-'an, de Chi-ning.

12 feuillets. -- Cf. n° 5827.

— XIV (5950).

湼槃末後句

Nie phan mo heou kiu.

Sur le Parinirvāṇa sūtra.

Par le même; revu par Tchang Thien-tchou et Tchang Thien-tchi, de Tsoei-li. Préface par Tchao Yun de Oou-kiang.

16 feuillets. — Cf. n° 5954.

Grand in-8. 2 vol. demi-rel., au chiffre de la République Française.
Nouveau fonds 4026, 4042.

───────────

5951. — I.

佛華嚴入如來德智不思議境界經

Fo hoa yen jou jou lai tẹ tchi pou seu yi king kiai king.

Tathāgataguṇajñānācintyaviṣayāvatāra nirdeça sūtra.

Traduction par Jñānagupta (589-592) du même texte que le Sarvatathāgataviṣayāvatāra sūtra. Lecture des signes difficiles.

1 livre. — Bunyiu Nanjio 91 ; cf. n° 5877, art. II.

— II.

佛說如來興顯經

Fo choe jou lai hing hien king.

Sūtra au sujet de l'aspect du Tathāgata.

Version par Tchou Fa-hou, de sections du Buddhāvataṃsaka sūtra. Liste des caractères difficiles. Édition de Miao-te 'an du Tshing-liang chan (1591).

4 livres. — Bunyiu Nanjio 92; cf. nᵒˢ 5884, etc.

Grand in-8. Bonne gravure. 1 vol. demi-rel., au chiffre de la République Française.

Nouveau fonds 3797.

5952. — I.

大方廣入如來智德不思議經

Ta fang koang jou jou lai tchi te pou seu yi king.

Tathāgataguṇajñānācintyaviṣayāvatāra nirdeça sūtra.

Version par Çikṣānanda (695-700) du même texte que ci-dessus, art. I. Lecture des termes difficiles. Édition de Tsi-tchao 'an (1598).

1 livre. — Bunyiu Nanjio 93.

— II.

大方廣佛華嚴經修慈分

Ta fang koang fo hoa yen king sieou tsheu fen.

Mahāvaipulya buddhāvataṃsaka sūtra, section sur la compassion.

Version de Devaprajña, de Khoten (689-691). Mêmes lieu et date.

8 feuillets. — Bunyiu Nanjio 94; cf. nᵒˢ 5884, etc.

— III.

顯無邊佛土功德經

Hien oou pien fo thou kong te king.

Anantabuddhakṣetraguṇa nirdeça sūtra.

Version par Hiuen-tsang (645-664), du chapitre Cheou liang, de l'Avataṃsaka sūtra. Mêmes lieu et date.

2 feuillets. — Bunyiu Nanjio 95; cf. nᵒˢ 5884, etc.

— IV.

大方廣佛華嚴經不思議佛境界分

Ta fang koang fo hoa yen king pou seu yi fo king kiai fen.

Mahāvaipulya buddhāvataṃsaka sūtra, section Acintyaviṣaya.

Traduction par Devaprajña. Liste des mots rares. Édition de Tsi-tchao 'an, même date.

1 livre. — Bunyiu Nanjio 96; voir nᵒˢ 5884, etc.

— V.

大方廣如來不思議境界經

Ta fang koang jou lai pou seu yi king kiai king.

Mahāvaipulya tathāgatācintyaviṣaya sūtra.

Version par Çikṣānanda du même texte qu'à l'art. précédent. Lecture des caractères rares. Mêmes lieu et date.

1 livre. — Bunyiu Nanjio 97.

— VI.

大方廣普賢所說經

Ta fang koang phou hien so choę king.

Mahāvaipulya samantabhadra nirdeça sūtra.

Version par Çikṣānanda. Liste des mots difficiles. Mêmes lieu et date.

5 feuillets. — Bunyiu Nanjio 98.

— VII.

莊嚴菩提心經

Tchoang yen phou thi sin king.

Bodhihṛdaya vyūha sūtra.

Version de Kumārajīva. Lecture des caractères difficiles. Mêmes lieu et date.

8 feuillets. — Bunyiu Nanjio 99.

— VIII.

佛說菩薩本業經

Fo choę phou sa pęn ye king.

Sūtra sur les actes des bodhisattva.

Version par Tchi Khien, du chapitre Tsing hing de l'Avataṃsaka sūtra. Liste des caractères rares. Mêmes lieu et date.

1 livre. — Bunyiu Nanjio 100; voir nᵒˢ 5884, etc.

— IX.

大方廣佛華嚴經續入法界品

Ta fang koang fo hoa yen king siu jou fa kiai phin.

Mahāvaipulya buddhāvataṃsaka sūtra, chapitre sur l'entrée dans le dharmadhātu, suite.

Version de Divākara (676-688). Lecture des caractères rares. Mêmes lieu et date.

10 feuillets. — Bunyiu Nanjio 101; voir nᵒˢ 5884, etc.

— X.

佛說兜沙經
Fo choę teou cha king.

Tathāgata viçeṣaṇa sūtra.

Version par Tchi Leou-kia-tchhan d'un chapitre de l'Avataṃsaka. Lecture des mots rares. Mêmes lieu et date.

6 feuillets. — Bunyiu Nanjio 102; voir nᵒˢ 5884, etc.

— XI.

大方廣菩薩十地經
Ta fang koang phou sa chi ti king.

Mahāvaipulya bodhisattva daçabhūmi sūtra.

Version par Ki-kia-ye (Kiṅkara), Occidental (472) et Than-yao (462), du même texte qu'à l'art. VII. Liste des mots rares. Mêmes lieu et date; feuillets gravés de nouveau en 1682.

8 feuillets. — Bunyiu Nanjio 103.

Grand in-8. Bonne gravure. 1 vol. demi-rel., au chiffre de la République Française.

Nouveau fonds 3926.

———

5953. 信力入印法門經
Sin li jou yin fa męn king.

Çraddhābaladhānāvatāramudrā sūtra.

Version de Dharmaruci, Hindou (501-507). Liste des signes difficiles. Édition de Miao-tę'an (1591).

6 livres. — Bunyiu Nanjio 90.

Grand in-8. Bonne gravure; frontispice (1 feuillet double). 1 vol. demi-rel., au chiffre de la République Française.

Nouveau fonds 3880.

Septième Section : NIRVĀṆA SŪTRA

5954. — I.

大般涅槃經
Ta pan nie phan king.

Mahāparinirvāṇa sūtra.

Version de Fa-hien, Chinois de la famille Kong de Oou-yang, traducteur en 414-420. Liste des signes difficiles. Édition de Tsi-tchao 'an (1605).

3 livres. — Bunyiu Nanjio 118; cf. n° 6153, art. II; cf. Bunyiu Nanjio 552.

— II.

佛說方等泥洹經

Fo choe̤ fang teng ni yuen king.

Mahāparinirvāṇa sūtra.

Version du même texte, de l'époque des Tsin orientaux (317-420). Lecture des caractères rares. Édition de Tsi-tchao 'an (1606).

2 livres. — Bunyiu Nanjio 119.

Grand in-8. Bonne gravure. 1 vol. demi-rel. au chiffre de la République Française.
Nouveau fonds 3810.

5955. — I.

大般泥洹經

Ta pan ni yuen king.

Mahāparinirvāṇa sūtra.

Version par Fa-hien et Buddha-bhadra. Lecture des caractères rares. Édition de Hoa-tchheng seu (1612).

6 livres. — Bunyiu Nanjio 120.

— II.

四童子三昧經

Seu thong tseu san mei king.

Caturdāraka samādhi sūtra.

Version du même texte que Bunyiu Nanjio 116, par Jñāna-gupta (585-592). Liste des mots difficiles. Même lieu d'édition (1617, 1618).

3 livres. — Bunyiu Nanjio 121; n° 5960, art. II.

— III.

佛垂般涅槃略說教誡經

Fo tchhoei pan nie phan lio choe̤ kiao kiai king; alias :

佛遺教經

Fo yi kiao king.

Sūtra des dernières instructions du Bouddha.

Version de Kumārajīva.

7 feuillets. — Bunyiu Nanjio 122; cf. n° 3695, art. III.

— IV.

佛臨涅槃記法住經

Fo lin nie phan ki fa tchou king.

Mahāparinirvāṇa sūtra.

Version de Hiuen-tsang.

6 feuillets. — Bunyiu Nanjio 123.

— V.

佛滅度後棺歛葬送經

Fo mie tou heou koan lien tsang song king.

Sūtra sur les funérailles du Bouddha.

Version des Tsin occidentaux (265-316).

4 feuillets. — Bunyiu Nanjio 124.

— VI.

般泥洹後灌臘經

Pan ni yuen heou koan la king.

Sūtra sur les fêtes postérieures au parinirvāṇa.

Version de Tchou Fa-hou. Lecture des mots rares. Édition de Hoa tchheng seu (1627).

3 feuillets. — Bunyiu Nanjio 125.

Grand in-8. Bonne gravure. 1 vol. demi-rel., au chiffre de la République Française.

Nouveau fonds 4025.

5956-5958.

— I (5956-5958).

大般涅槃經

Ta pan nie phan king.

Mahāparinirvāṇa sūtra.

Version complète par Dharmarakṣa (423), du même texte que Bunyiu Nanjio 120. Préface par le bonze Tao-lang, contemporain. Lecture des signes difficiles. Édition de Tsi-tchao 'an (1604, 1605).

40 livres. — Bunyiu Nanjio 113; n° 5955, art. I.

— II (5958).

大般涅槃經後分

Ta pan nie phan king heou fen.

Dernière partie du Mahāparinirvāṇa sūtra.

Traduction de Jñānabhadra, Méridional, et de Hoei-ning, Chinois (664-665). Liste des signes rares.

2 livres. — Bunyiu Nanjio 115.

Grand in-8. Bonne gravure. Frontispice (1 feuillet double). 3 vol. demi-rel., au chiffre de la République Française.

Nouveau fonds 3803 à 3805.

5959.

Ta pan nie phan king.

Mahāparinirvāṇa sūtra.

Même ouvrage qu'au n° précédent, art. I; frontispice différent. Édition de Tsi-tchao-'an (1603).

Préface, table, livres 1 à 5.

Grand in-8. Bonne gravure. 1 vol.
cartonnage.

Nouveau fonds 4628.

5960. — I.

Ta pan nie phan king heou fẹn.

Même ouvrage qu'au n° 5958,
art. II. Lecture des signes difficiles. Édition de Tsie-tai seu à
Oou-kiang (1624).

— II.

佛説方等般泥洹經

*Fo chọẹ fang teng pan ni yuen
king.*

Caturdāraka samādhi sūtra.

Version de Tchou Fa-hou. Lecture des caractères rares. Édition
de Tsi-tchao 'an (1607).

2 livres. — Bunyiu Nanjio 116.

Grand in-8. Bonne gravure. 1 vol.
demi-rel., au chiffre de la République
Française.

Nouveau fonds 3809.

5961-5963. # 南本大般湼
槃經

Nan pẹn ta pan nie phan king.

Mahāparinirvāṇa sūtra, texte
méridional.

Traduction de Dharmarakṣa,
revue par Hoei-yen et Hoei-koan

avec Sie Ling-yun (424-453). Lecture des signes difficiles. Édition
de Hoa-tchheng seu (1612, 1613,
1615, 1617).

36 livres. — Bunyiu Nanjio 114;
cf. n° 5956, art. I.

Grand in-8. Bonne gravure, frontispice (1 feuillet double). 3 vol. demi-rel.,
au chiffre de la République Française.

Nouveau fonds 3806 à 3808.

5964-5965.

Nan pẹn ta pan nie phan king.

Même ouvrage, extrait d'une
collection intitulée : Fo tsang tsi
yao.

Grand in-8. 2 vol. demi-rel., au chiffre
de Napoléon III.

Nouveau fonds 1392, 1393.

———

5966. — I.

大般湼槃經立義

Ta pan nie phan king hiuen yi.

Sens mystérieux du Mahāparinirvāṇa sūtra.

Par Koan-ting. Liste des signes
difficiles. Édition de l'association
Tshing-lien, à Kin-cha (1638).

2 livres. — Bunyiu Nanjio 1544.

— II.

法華經安樂行義

Fa hoa king 'an lo hing yi.

Explication du Saddharma-puṇḍarīka sūtra, chapitre Sukhavihāra.

Par Hoei-seu de l'école Thien-thai (✝ 577). Édition de Kou Long-chan, de Kin-cha (1641).

1 livre. — Bunyiu Nanjio 1547; cf. n° 5827, art. II.

Grand in-8. Bonne gravure. 1 vol. demi-rel., au chiffre de la République Française.

Nouveau fonds 3812.

5967-5969. 大般湼槃經疏

Ta pan nie phan king sou.

Commentaire du Mahāpari-nirvāṇa sūtra.

— I (5967).

科南本湼槃經序

Khoo nan pen nie phan king siu.

Tableaux résumés et préface pour le Mahāparinirvāṇa sūtra, texte méridional.

Par Chi-tcheng, bonze de Thien-thai (1282).

Cf. n°ˢ 5956-5958, art. I.

— II (5967-5969).

Ta pan nie phan king sou.

Commentaire par Koan-ting; annoté par Tchan-jan. Lecture des termes difficiles. Édition de l'association Tong-chan tshing-lien à Kin-cha (1638 1641).

33 livres. — Bunyiu Nanjio 1545.

Grand in-8. Bonne gravure; frontispice (1 feuillet double).

1 vol. demi-rel., au chiffre de la République Française.

Nouveau fonds 3811.

2 vol. cartonnage.
Nouveau fonds 4629, 4630.

———

5970. 湼槃玄義發源機要

Nie phan hiuen yi fa yuen ki yao.

Commentaire du Ta pan nie phan king hiuen yi.

Par Tchi-yuen, surnom Oou-oai, bonze de Tshien-thang (1014). Préface de l'auteur. Lecture des signes difficiles. Édition de Kou Long-chan, de Kin-cha (1641).

4 livres. — Bunyiu Nanjio 1546; cf. n° 5966, art. I.

Grand in-8. Bonne gravure. 1 vol. demi-rel., au chiffre de la République Française.

Nouveau fonds 3813.

Huitième Section : KARUṆĀPUṆḌARĪKA SŪTRA, ETC.

5971.   悲華經
Pei hoa king.

Karuṇāpuṇḍarīka sūtra.

Traduction de Dharmarakṣa. Lecture des caractères difficiles. Édition de Tsi-tchao 'an et Hoa-tchheng seu (1608 1614).

10 livres. — Bunyiu Nanjio 142.

Grand in-8. Bonne gravure. 1 vol. demi-rel., au chiffre de la République Française.
Nouveau fonds 3839.

5972-5973.

— I (5972-5973).

大乘大悲分陀利經
Ta cheng ta pei fen tho li king.

Mahākaruṇāpuṇḍarīka sūtra.

Traduction de l'époque des Tshin (350-431). Liste des caractères rares. Édition de Tsie-tai seu à Oou-kiang (1625, 1626).

8 livres. — Bunyiu Nanjio 180.

— II (5973).

善思童子經
Chan seu thong tseu king.

Vimalakīrti nirdeça sūtra.

Version par Jñānagupta (591) du même texte que n° 5975. Lecture des signes difficiles. Édition de 1611.

2 livres. — Bunyiu Nanjio 181.

Grand in-8. Bonne gravure.
1 vol. demi-rel., au chiffre de la République Française.
Nouveau fonds 3838.
1 vol. cartonnage.
Nouveau fonds 4633.

5974.   大悲經
Ta pei king.

Mahākaruṇāpuṇḍarīka sūtra.

Version de Narendrayaças et de Fa-tchi (Gautama Dharmaprajña, Than Fa-tchi) Hindou, traducteur (557-568). Liste des caractères difficiles. Édition de Tsie-tai seu (1624).

5 livres. — Bunyiu Nanjio 117 ; cf. n° 5971.

Grand in-8. Bonne gravure ; frontispice (1 feuillet double). 1 vol. demi-rel., au chiffre de la République Française.
Nouveau fonds 3840.

Neuvième Section : VIMALAKĪRTI SŪTRA, ETC.

5975. 維摩詰經

Oei mo khie king; alias :

不可思議法門

Pou kho seu yi fa men.

Vimalakīrti nirdeça sūtra.

Version de Tchi Khien. Lecture des caractères rares. Édition de Leng-yen seu (1662).

3 livres. — Bunyiu Nanjio 147; cf. n° 5973, art. II.

Grand in-8. Bonne gravure. 1 vol. demi-rel., au chiffre de la République Française.

Nouveau fonds 3946.

5976. 維摩詰所說經

Oei mo khie so choe king; alias :

不可思議解脫經

Pou kho seu yi kiai thoo king.

Vimalakīrti nirdeça sūtra.

Version du même texte par Kumārajīva. Liste des mots difficiles. Édition donnée par Tchhe-oei (1661).

3 livres. — Bunyiu Nanjio 146.

Grand in-8. Bonne gravure. 1 vol. demi-rel., au chiffre de la République Française.

Nouveau fonds 3947.

5977. 維摩詰所說經註

Oei mo khie so choe king tchou.

Le Vimalakīrti nirdeça sūtra, avec commentaires.

Texte de Kumārajīva; commentaire de Seng-tchao, de Tchhang-'an, disciple de l'auteur (début du v° siècle). Préface de Seng-tchao. Lecture des caractères difficiles. Édition de Tsi-tchao 'an (1599, 1601).

10 livres. — Bunyiu Nanjio 1632; cf. n° 5976.

Grand in-8. Bonne gravure. 1 vol. demi-rel., au chiffre de la République Française.

Nouveau fonds 3951.

5978.

Oei mo khie so choe king tchou.

Double.

Livres 6 à 10.

1 vol. cartonnage.
Nouveau fonds 4641.

5979.

Oei mo khie so choę king tchou.

Même ouvrage. Préface du commentateur. Lecture des caractères difficiles.

Grand in-8. Belle édition sur papier blanc. 1 vol. demi-rel., au chiffre de Louis-Philippe.
Nouveau fonds 624 A.

5980. — I.

大乘頂王經
Ta cheng ting oang king.

Vimalakīrti nirdeça sūtra.

Version du même texte par Upaçūnya (545). Édition de Hoa-tchheng seu (1627).

1 livre. — Bunyiu Nanjio 144.

— II.

大方等頂王經
Ta fang teng ting oang king;
alias :

維摩詰子問經
Oei mo khie tseu oen king.

Vimalakīrti nirdeça sūtra.

Version par Tchou Fa-hou du même texte. Lecture des signes rares. Même lieu d'édition (1628).

1 livre. — Bunyiu Nanjio 145.

— III.

法幢禪師語錄
Fa tchhoang chạn chi yu lou.

Entretiens et œuvres de Fa-tchhoang chạn-chi.

Préface par Hong-yuen, de Han-thang (1695). Les œuvres ont été recueillies par les disciples de l'auteur, Thong-hoei et autres. Édition de Leng-yen seu.

1 livre.

— IV.

純備禪師語錄
Choęn pei chạn chi yu lou.

Entretiens et œuvres de Choęn-pei chạn-chi.

Préface par Tao-long Po-ta (1670). Les œuvres ont été recueillies par les disciples Tchi-yuen et autres. Édition de Leng-yen seu.

2 livres.

— V.

松巘善權位禪師語錄
Song khoei chạn khiuen oei chạn chi yu lou.

Entretiens et œuvres de Chạn-khiuen chạn-chi.

Auteur : Kiu (1618-1684), nom religieux Ta-oei, du Hou-pei ; les œuvres ont été recueillies par ses disciples Ta-tchhan et autres. Préface de Oou Tchi-oei (1688).

2 livres.

— VI.

天一悅禪師語錄

Thien yi yue chạn chi yu lou.

Entretiens et œuvres de Thien-yi Yue chạn-chi.

Recueillis par son disciple Hio-yu. Édition de Leng-yen seu (1707).

15 feuillets.

— VII.

禪燈大方禪師語錄

Chạn teng ta fang chạn chi yu lou.

Entretiens et œuvres de Ta-fang chạn-chi, de Chạn-teng.

Recueillis par son disciple Tchhao-ming. Préfaces par Tshien Koang-kiu et par Oou Oei-ye, de Leou-tong. L'auteur était bonze en 1669.

6 livres (manquent les livres 4, 5, 6).

— VIII.

大比丘三千威儀

Ta pi khieou san tshien oei yi.

Mahābhikṣu trisahasra karma.

Version de 'An Chi-kao. Lecture des mots difficiles. Édition de Hoa-tchheng seu (1633, 1636).

2 livres. — Bunyiu Nanjio 1126.

Grand in-8. Bonne gravure. 1 vol. demi-rel., au chiffre de la République Française.

Nouveau fonds 3953.

5981. 說無垢稱經

Choẹ oou keou tchheng king.

Vimalakīrti nirdeça sūtra.

Traduction par Hiuen-tsang du même texte que plus haut. Lecture des mots rares. Édition de Tsi-tchao 'an (1611).

6 livres. — Bunyiu Nanjio 149; cf. n° 5980, art. II.

Grand in-8. Bonne gravure. 1 vol. demi-rel., au chiffre de la République Française.

Nouveau fonds 3952.

Dixième Section : **APARIVARTYA SŪTRA, ETC.**

5982. 阿惟越致遮經

'O oei yue tchi tchę king.

Avaivartya sūtra; alias : Aparivarttya sūtra.

Version de Tchou Fa-hou. Liste des caractères rares. Édition de Tsi-tchao 'an (1611).

4 livres. — Bunyiu Nanjio 150.

Grand in-8. Bonne gravure. 1 vol. demi-rel., au chiffre de la République Française.

Nouveau fonds 3861.

5983. — I.

廣博嚴淨不退轉法輪經

Koang po yen tsing pou thoei tchoan fa loen king.

Aparivartya sūtra.

Traduction du même texte par Tchi-yen, de Liang-tcheou, et Paoyun, de Liang-tcheou (427). Liste des caractères difficiles. Édition de Tsi-tchao 'an (1610).

4 livres. — Bunyiu Nanjio 158; voir n° 5982.

— II.

無量義經

Oou liang yi king.

Amitārtha sūtra.

Version de Dharmagatayaças, Hindou (vers 481). Préface par Lieou Khieou, de la même époque. Lecture des termes difficiles. Édition de Tsi-tchao 'an (1598).

1 livre. — Bunyiu Nanjio 133.

— III.

法華三昧經

Fa hoa san mei king.

Saddharma samādhi sūtra.

Version de Tchi-yen. Lecture des mots rares. Mêmes lieu et date qu'à l'art. II.

1 livre. — Bunyiu Nanjio 135.

— IV.

薩曇芬陀利經

Sa than fęn tho li king.

Saddharma puṇḍarīka sūtra.

Traduction partielle du même

texte que nº 5827 art. II, datant des Tsin occidentaux (265-316). Édition de King-chan seu (1598), feuillets gravés de nouveau en 1670.

4 feuillets. — Bunyiu Nanjio 136.

— V.

妙法蓮華經觀世音菩薩普門品經

Miao fa lien hoa king koan chi yin phou sa phou men phin king.

Saddharma puṇḍarīka sūtrāvalokiteçvara bodhisattva samantamukha parivarta.

Version de Kumārajīva; les gāthā ont été traduites de nouveau par Jñānagupta (561-578). Préface impériale (1411). Lecture des caractères difficiles.

6 feuillets. — Nº 5848, art. I.

Grand in-8. Bonne gravure. 1 vol. demi-rel., au chiffre de la République Française.
Nouveau fonds 3928.

5984. — I.

不退轉法輪經

Pou thoei tchoan fa loen king.

Aparivartya sūtra.

Version de l'époque des Liang septentrionaux (397-439). Liste des expressions rares. Édition de 1611.

4 livres. — Bunyiu Nanjio 157; voir nº 5982.

— II.

相續解脫地波羅蜜了義經

Siang siu kiai thoo ti po lo mi liao yi king.

Sandhinirmocana sūtra.

Version par Guṇabhadra (435-443).

13 feuillets. — Bunyiu Nanjio 154.

— III.

相續解脫如來所作隨順處了義經

Siang siu kiai thoo jou lai so tso soei choen tchhou liao yi king.

Sandhinirmocana sūtra.

Traduction par le même d'une autre partie du même texte. Lecture des caractères difficiles. Édition de Hoa-tchheng seu (1629).

9 feuillets. — Bunyiu Nanjio 155.

— IV.

佛說解節經

Fo choe kiai tsie king.

Sandhinirmocana sūtra.

Version par Paramārtha d'une autre partie du même texte. Lecture des caractères rares.

1 livre (12 feuillets). — Bunyiu Nanjio 156; voir aussi n° 5986.

Grand in-8. Bonne gravure; frontispice (1 feuillet double). 1 vol. demi-rel., au chiffre de la République Française.
Nouveau fonds 3929

5985. 深密解脱經
Chen mi kiai thoo king.

Sandhinirmocana sūtra.

Version par Bodhiruci (533) du texte complet de ce sūtra; préface par le bonze Hoei-koang Thanning. Lecture des mots difficiles.

Édition de Tsi-tchao 'an (1600, 1601).

5 livres. — Bunyiu Nanjio 246; cf. n° 5984, art. II à IV.

Grand in-8. Bonne gravure. 1 vol. demi-rel., au chiffre de la République Française.
Nouveau fonds 4024.

5986. 解深密經
Kiai chen mi king.

Sandhinirmocana sūtra.

Version du même texte par Hiuen-tsang (645). Liste des caractères rares. Édition de Tsi-tchao 'an (1604).

5 livres. — Bunyiu Nanjio 247.

Grand in-8. Bonne gravure. 1 vol. demi-rel., au chiffre de la République Française.
Nouveau fonds 3958.

Onzième Section : CUNDĪ DEVĪ SŪTRA, ETC.

5987. — I.
梵女首意經
Fan niu cheou yi king.

Çrīmatī brāhmaṇī paripṛcchā sūtra.

Version par Tchou Fa-hou. Liste des caractères difficiles. Édition de King-chan Oan-cheou chan-seu (1593); réédition partielle de 1670.

6 feuillets. — Bunyiu Nanjio 342.

— II.
有德女所問大乘經
Yeou tę niu so oen ta cheng king.

Çrīmatī brāhmaṇī paripṛcchā sūtra.

Version du même texte par Bodhiruci (693). Liste des mots rares. Mêmes lieu et date d'édition.

5 feuillets. — Bunyiu Nanjio 343.

— III.

佛說七俱胝佛母心大准 (sic) 提陀羅尼經

Fo choę tshi kiu tchi fo mou sin ta tchoęn thi tho lo ni king.

Cundī devī dhāraṇī sūtra.

Version de Divākara (685). Lecture des mots difficiles. Mêmes lieu et date.

5 feuillets. — Bunyiu Nanjio 344; cf. nᵒˢ 5674, art. XXXIII; 5680, art. IX; 5693, art. VII; 5698, art. XVI.

— IV.

佛說七俱胝佛母准 (sic) 提大明陀羅尼經。觀 行法附

Fo choę tshi kiu tchi fo mou tchoęn thi ta ming tho lo ni king. Koan hing fa fou.

Cundī devī dhāraṇī. En annexe, pratique du dhyāna.

Traduction du même texte par

Vajrabodhi, Hindou (723). Liste des mots rares. Édition de Leng yen seu (1641).

20 feuillets. — Bunyiu Nanjio 345.

— V.

七俱胝佛母所說准 (sic) 提陀羅尼經

Tshi kiu tchi fo mou so choę tchoęn thi tho lo ni king.

Cundī devī dhāraṇī.

Même texte traduit par Amoghavajra. Lecture des caractères difficiles. Édition de Hoa-tchheng-seu (1617).

24 feuillets. — Bunyiu Nanjio 346.

— VI.

種種雜咒經

Tchong tchong tsa tcheou king.

Nānā saṃyuktamantra sūtra.

Version de Jñānagupta (561-578), transcrite par le bonze Yuen-ming. Collection de dhāraṇī en transcription. Lecture des mots rares.

10 feuillets. — Bunyiu Nanjio 347.

1. 妙法蓮華經內咒六 首

Miao fa lien hoa king nei tcheou lou cheou.

Six dhāraṇī tirées du Saddharma puṇḍarīka sūtra.

Cf. n° 5827, art. II.

2. 旋塔滅罪陀羅尼
Siuen tha mie tsoei tho lo ni.

Dhāraṇī pour anéantir le péché en honorant les stūpa.

3. 禮拜滅罪命終諸佛來迎咒
Li pai mie tsoei ming tchong tchou fo lai ying tcheou.

Dhāraṇī pour saluer les Bouddhas qui anéantissent le péché et la mort.

4. 供養三寶咒
Kong yang san pao tcheou.

Dhāraṇī pour offrir la nourriture au Triratna.

5. 觀世音懺悔咒
Koan chi yin tchhan hoei tcheou.

Dhāraṇī du repentir, d'Avalokiteçvara.

6. 金剛咒蛇咒
Kin kang tcheou chẹ tcheou.

Dhāraṇī du vajra, dhāraṇī du serpent.

7. 坐禪安隱咒
Tsoo chạn 'an yin tcheou.

Dhāraṇī de la paix cachée dans le dhyāna.

8. 咒腫咒
Tcheou tchong tcheou.

Dhāraṇī pour conjurer les enflures.

9. 金剛咒治惡鬼病
Kin kang tcheou tchi 'o kwei ping.

Dhāraṇī du vajra pour guérir les maladies causées par les démons.

10. 千轉陀羅尼
Tshien tchoan tho lo ni.

Sahasrapravartana dhāraṇī.

Cf. n°ˢ 5861, art. V; 6218, art. III.

11. 觀世音隨心咒四首
Koan chi yin soei sin tcheou seu cheou.

Avalokiteçvarānuhṛdaya dhāraṇī, quatre pièces.

Cf. n° 5861, art. I.

12. 七俱胝佛神咒

Tshi kiu tchi fo chen tcheou.

Cundī devī dhāraṇī,

Cf. plus haut, art. III à V.

13. 隨一切如來意神咒

Soei yi tshie jou lai yi chen tcheou.

Dhāraṇī conforme à l'esprit de tous les Bouddhas.

14. 六字陀羅尼咒

Lou tseu tho lo ni tcheou.

Ṣaḍakṣara dhāraṇī mantra.

Cf. Bunyiu Nanjio 876; voir aussi nᵒˢ 5861, art. VII et XVI; 6204, art. V; 6218, art. II.

15. 歸依三寶咒

Koei yi san pao tcheou.

Dhāraṇī du recours au Tri-ratna.

— VII.

佛頂尊勝陀羅尼經

Fo ting tsoeṇ cheng tho lo ni king.

Sarvadurgatipariçodhanoṣṇī-ṣa vijaya dhāraṇī sūtra.

Version de Buddhapāla, de Ki-pin (687). Préface impériale (1411); préface par le bonze Tchi-tsing (689). Lecture des caractères rares. Édition de King-chan seu (1597).

8 feuillets. — Bunyiu Nanjio 348.

— VIII.

佛頂尊勝陀羅尼經

Fo ting tsoeṇ cheng tho lo ni king.

Sarvadurgatipariçodhanoṣṇī-ṣa vijaya dhāraṇī sūtra.

Version du même texte par Tou Hing-yi (679). Mêmes lieu et date d'édition.

9 feuillets. — Bunyiu Nanjio 349.

— IX.

佛說佛頂尊勝陀羅尼經

Fo choẹ fo ting tsoeṇ cheng tho lo ni king.

Sarvadurgatipariçodhanoṣṇī-ṣa vijaya dhāraṇī sūtra.

Version du même texte par Yi-tsing (710). Lecture des mots rares. Mêmes lieu et date d'édition.

8 feuillets. — Bunyiu Nanjio 350.

— X.

佛頂最勝陀羅尼經

Fo ting tsoei cheng tho lo ni king.

Sarvadurgatipariçodhanoṣṇī-ṣa vijaya dhāraṇī sūtra.

Version du même texte par Divākara (682) avec préface du bonze Yen-tshong (682). Lecture des caractères rares. Mêmes lieu et date.

8 feuillets. — Bunyiu Nanjio 352.

— XI.

最勝佛頂陀羅尼淨除業障經

Tsoei cheng fo ting tho lo ni tsing tchhou ye tchang king.

Sarvadurgatipariçodhanoṣṇī-ṣa vijaya dhāraṇī sūtra.

Seconde version du même texte par Divākara. Liste des caractères difficiles. Mêmes lieu et date.

15 feuillets. — Bunyiu Nanjio 351.

Grand in-8. Bonne gravure; frontispice (1 feuillet double). 1 vol. demi-rel., au chiffre de la République Française. *Nouveau fonds* 4018.

5988. # 准提淨業
Tchoẹn thi tsing ye.

Culte de Cundī devī.

Préface pour la présente réédition par Sie Yu-kiao Tshing-lien kiu-chi, de Khien (1623). Introduction du même.

— I (livre 1).

佛說七俱胝佛母心大准提陀羅尼經

Fo choẹ tshi kiu tchi fo mou sin ta tchoẹn thi tho lo ni king.

Cundī devī dhāraṇī sūtra.

5 feuillets. — N° 5987, art. III.

— II (livre 1).

佛說七俱胝佛母准提大明陀羅尼經。咒文節略

Fo choẹ tshi kiu tchi fo mou tchoẹn thi ta ming tho lo ni king. Tcheou oen tsie lio.

Cundī devī dhāraṇī sūtra : abrégé des formules finales.

2 feuillets. — Cf. n° 5987, art. IV.

— III (livre 1).

心月梵字觀門。陀羅尼布字法竟

Sin yue fan tseu koan mẹn. Tho lo ni pou tseu fa king.

Modèle de talisman.

Caractères hindous et explication.

2 feuillets.

— IV (livre 1).

准提眞言持誦便覽
Tchoẹn thi tchen yen tchhi song pien lan.

Rituel de Cundī devī.

1 feuillet.

— V (livre 1).

持誦儀軌
Tchhi song yi koei.

Rituel.

Dhāraṇī et texte annoté.
6 feuillets.

— VI (livre 1).

般若波羅密 (sic) 多心經
Pan jẹ po lo mi to sin king.

Prajñāpāramitā hṛdaya sūtra.

2 feuillets. — N° 5733, art. II.

— VII (livre 1).

觀無量壽佛經上品上生章

Koan oou liang cheou fo king chang phin chang cheng tchǎng.

Amitāyurbuddha dhyāna sūtra, chapitre premier, section de la naissance supérieure.

1 feuillet. — Cf. n° 5813, art. II.

— VIII (livre 1).

拔一切業障根本往生淨土神咒
Pa yi tshie ye tchang ken pẹn oang cheng tsing thou chen tcheou.

Dhāraṇī pour renaître en Terre Pure.

2 feuillets. — N° 5734, art. IV.

— IX (livre 1).

囘向西方願文
Hoei hiang si fang yuen oen.

Vœu relatif au Paradis occidental.

3 feuillets.

— X (livre 1).

十念法門
Chi nien fa mẹn.

Introduction aux dix méditations.

2 feuillets.

— XI (livre 2).

觀 行 儀 軌

Koan hing yi koei.

Rites de l'exercice de la médi-tation (dhyāna).

16 feuillets.

— XII (livre 3).

顯 密 雙 修 觀 行 說

Hien mi choang sieou koan hing choẹ.

Traité sur les pratiques exo-tériques et ésotériques de la méditation (dhyāna).

25 feuillets.

— XIII (livre 3).

淨 業 圓 修 說

Tsing ye yuen sieou choẹ.

Sur la pratique parfaite rela-tive à la Terre Pure.

10 feuillets.

— XIV (livre 3).

供 佛 利 生 儀

Kong fo li cheng yi.

Rituel de l'offrande aux Boud-dha et de la pitié pour les créa-tures.

Dhāraṇī, texte et notes.

4 feuillets.

Grand in-8. Frontispice (1 feuillet double) représentant le Bouddha dans un jardin, la mère du Bouddha Cundī devī. 1 vol. demi-rel., au chiffre de la République Française.

Nouveau fonds 4032.

5989. — I.

佛 說 七 俱 胝 佛 母 心 大 准 提 陀 羅 尼 經

Fo choẹ tshi kiu tchi fo mou sin ta tchoẹn thi tho lo ni king.

Buddhabhāṣita saptakoṭibu-ddhamātṛka hṛdaya mahācundī dhāraṇī sūtra ; alias : Cundī devī dhāraṇī.

Explication du caractère 唵, après les figures du début ; puis traduction du sūtra.

4 feuillets. — Nᵒ 5987, art. III.

— II.

准 提 菩 薩 一 十 八 臂 頌

Tchoẹn thi phou sa yi chi pa pi song.

Poésie des dix-huit bras de Cundī bodhisattva.

3 feuillets.

— III.

持准提陀羅尼

Tchhi tchoen thi tho lo ni.

Dhāraṇī de Cundī.

Par le lettré Hien-oen.

6 feuillets.

Édition de la bonzerie de Hai-tchhoang (1812).

Petit in-8. Frontispice (1 feuillet double et 1 feuillet simple) avec légendes. Papier blanc. 1 vol. demi-reliure.
Nouveau fonds 73.

———

5990. — I.

七俱胝佛母所說準提 陀羅尼經會釋

Tshi kiu tchi fo mou so choe tchoen thi tho lo ni king hoei chi.

Explication du Cundī devī dhāraṇī sūtra.

D'après la traduction d'Amo-ghavajra, par Hong-tsan, de Ting-hou chan, au Koang-tong. Réédition du Long-kiang (1671).

3 livres. — Cf. n° 5987, art. V.

— II.

五悔儀

Oou hoei yi.

Rituel des cinq confessions.

Texte et notes.

6 feuillets.

— III.

持誦法要

Tchhi song fa yao.

Recueil de formules à réciter.

En transcription et en traduc-tion, texte et notes.

12 feuillets.

— IV.

初修敬田

Tchhou sieou king thien.

D'abord il faut cultiver le res-pect.

Règles de conduite, avec dhā-raṇī en transcription seulement.

3 feuillets.

— V.

次修悲田

Tsheu sieou pei thien.

Ensuite il faut cultiver la pitié.

Texte analogue avec une longue note.

4 feuillets.

— VI.

智炬如來心破地獄眞言

Tchi kiu jou lai sin pho ti yu tchen yen.

Dhāraṇī du tathāgata Jñānolka qui brise l'enfer.

En sanscrit et en transcription.

1 feuillet. — Cf. n° 6210, art. II.

— VII.

毘盧遮那佛大灌頂光眞言

Phi lou tchẹ na fo ta koan ting koang tchen yen.

Dhāraṇī du Bouddha Vairocana.

Texte analogue, avec une longue note.

2 feuillets. — Cf. Bunyiu Nanjio 530.

— VIII.

觀自在菩薩甘露眞言

Koan tseu tsai phou sa kan lou tchen yen.

Avalokiteçvara bodhisattvāmṛta dhāraṇī.

Texte analogue avec note.

2 feuillets. — Cf. Bunyiu Nanjio 540.

— IX.

六字大明眞言

Lou tseu ta ming tchen yen.

Ṣaḍakṣara mantra dhāraṇī.

Formule en sanscrit et en transcription, suivie d'un texte chinois.

3 feuillets. — Cf. n° 5987, art. VI.

— X.

文殊菩薩五字心咒

Oen chou phou sa oou tseu sin tcheou.

Mañjuçrī bodhisattva pañcākṣara hṛdaya dhāraṇī.

Texte analogue au précédent.

2 feuillets. — Cf. Bunyiu Nanjio 537.

— XI.

大寶廣博樓閣善住秘密陀羅尼

Ta pao koang po leou ko chạn tchou pi mi tho lo ni.

Mahāmaṇi vipula vimāna viçva supratiṣṭhitaguhya parama rahasya kalparāja dhāraṇī.

Transcription, sanscrit, longue note.

3 feuillets. — Cf. Bunyiu Nanjio 1028.

— XII.

功德寶山陀羅尼

Kong te̞ pao chan tho lo ni.

Dhāraṇī de la montagne des mérites.

Transcription et texte chinois.

1 feuillet.

— XIII.

三字總持眞言

San tseu tsong tchhi tchen yen.

Dhāraṇī en trois syllabes.

Sanscrit, transcription, texte chinois annoté.

4 feuillets.

— XIV.

數珠功德法

Chou tchou kong te̞ fa.

Traité du chapelet.

Texte avec notes. Lecture des signes difficiles.

2 feuillets. — Cf. Bunyiu Nanjio 295, 1036; n° 6110, art. VIII et IX.

Grand in-8. Bonne gravure. 1 vol. demi-rel., au chiffre de la République Française.

Nouveau fonds 4022.

Douzième Section : ÇŪRAṄGAMA SŪTRA, ETC.

5991. — I.

佛說首楞嚴三昧經

Fo cho̞e cheou leng yen san mei king.

Çūraṅgama samādhi sūtra.

Version de Kumārajīva. Liste des signes rares. Édition de Yun-tshi seu (1610).

3 livres. — Bunyiu Nanjio 399.

— II.

未曾有因緣經

Oei tsheng yeou yin yuen king.

Adbhutadharmaparyāya sūtra.

Traduction de Than-king (479-502). Lecture des caractères rares. Édition de Hoa-tchheng seu (1612).

2 livres. — Bunyiu Nanjio 400.

Grand in-8. Bonne gravure; frontispice (1 feuillet double). 1 vol. demi-rel., au chiffre de la République Française.

Nouveau fonds 3852.

5992. 大佛頂如來密因修證了義諸菩薩萬行首楞嚴經

Ta fo ting jou lai mi yin sieou tcheng liao yi tchou phou sa oan hing cheou leng yen king.

Mahābuddhoṣṇīṣa tathāgata guhyahetu sākṣātkṛta prasannārtha sarvabodhisattvacaryā çūraṅgama sūtra.

Traduction par Pramiti et Meghaçikha, Hindous (705), écrite par Faṅg Yoṅg, de Tshing-ho. A la fin lecture des caractères difficiles. Impression de la bonzeric de Tsi-tchao à King-chan (1603).

10 livres. — Bunyiu Nanjio 446.

Grand in-8. Bonne gravure. 1 vol. demi-rel., au chiffre de la République Française.

Nouveau fonds 3843.

5993.

Ta fo ting jou lai mi yin sieou tcheng liao yi tchou phou sa oan hing cheou leng yen king.

Même ouvrage.

A la fin, lecture des caractères difficiles. Impression de la bonzerie de Hai-tchhoang (1739?) en caractères de genre cursif.

10 livres. — Bunyiu Nanjio 446.

Petit in-8. Papier blanc. 1 vol. demi-rel., au chiffre de Louis-Philippe.

Nouveau fonds 56.

5994. 大佛頂如來密因修證了義諸菩薩萬行首楞嚴經要解

Ta fo ting jou lai mi yin sieou tcheng liao yi tchou phou sa oan hing cheou leng yen king yao kiai

Commentaire du Mahābuddhoṣṇīṣa çūraṅgama sūtra.

Par Kiai-hoan; préface par Ki-uan (1127). Postface du bonze Hing-yi (1129). Lecture des signes difficiles. Édition de Hing-cheng oan-cheou chạn-seu (1593, 1594).

20 livres. — Cf. n° 5992.

Grand in-8. Bonne gravure. 1 vol. demi-rel., au chiffre de la République Française.

Nouveau fonds 3845.

5995-5996. 首楞嚴經義海

Cheou leng yen king yi hai.

Commentaire du Çūraṅgama sūtra.

Par Hien-hoei; d'après des commentaires antérieurs intitulés Tcheng yi, par Hoai-ti (vers 705), Yi sou par Tseu-siuen, Piao tchi yao yi par Hiao-yue, Tsi kiai par Jen-yo. Préface générale par Tseng Hoai (1172); préfaces du Yi sou par Oang Soei (1030), du Piao tchi yao yi par Fan Siun (1073), du Tsi kiai par Hou Sou (1059); préface et historique de Hien-hoei (1165). Liste des signes difficiles. Édition de Hoa-tchheng seu (1632).

3o livres. — Bunyiu Nanjio 1588.

Grand in-8. Bonne gravure; frontispice (1 feuillet double). 2 vol. demi-rel., au chiffre de la République Française.

Nouveau fonds 3847, 3848.

5997. 大佛頂首楞嚴經會解

Ta fo ting cheou leng yen king hoei kiai.

Explications rassemblées du Mahābuddhoṣṇīṣa çūraṅgama sū-tra.

Par le bonze Oei-tsẹ, de Chi-tseu lin, à Liu-ling (1342). Préface par le bonze Khẹ-li. Table des ouvrages consultés. Liste des signes rares. Édition de Leng-yen seu (1633).

20 livres. — Bunyiu Nanjio 1624.

Grand in-8. Bonne gravure. 1 vol. demi-rel., au chiffre de la République Française.

Nouveau fonds 3844.

5998. 大佛頂如來密因脩證了義諸菩薩萬行首楞嚴經集註

Ta fo ting jou lai mi yin sieou tcheng liao yi tchou phou sa oan hing cheou leng yen king tsi tchou.

Mahābuddhoṣṇīṣa tathāgata guhyahetu sākṣātkṛta prasannārtha sarvabodhisattvacaryā çūraṅgama sūtra, avec commentaires et notes.

Commentaire par Oei-tsẹ, de Liu-ling (1342); édition et notes par Tchhoan-cheng, bonze de Lei-fong. Préface de Oei-tsẹ; préface de Tchhoan-cheng (1734). Liste des ouvrages consultés.

10 livres. — Cf. n° 5997.

Grand in-8. Belle gravure sur papier blanc. 1 vol. demi-rel., au chiffre de Louis-Philippe.

Nouveau fonds 648.

5999-6000. 楞嚴正脉疏

Leng yen tcheng mẹ sou.

Principes commentés du Çū-raṅgama sūtra.

Préface par Kiao-koang Tchen-kien, bonze de Si-hou à la capitale. Notice sur cet ouvrage par Tchou Tsiun-thing, autres noms Oou-yi tao-jen et Koang-fong (1613).

— I (5999).

楞嚴正脉科略

Leng yen tcheng me̞ khoo lio.

Tableau explicatif.

Par Yun-tsi ta-chi.

9 feuillets.

— II (5999).

楞嚴正脉懸示

Leng yen tcheng me̞ hiuen chi.

Instructions relatives aux principes commentés, etc.

Par Kiao-koang Tchen-kien, avec postface de l'auteur (1600).

45 feuillets en petit texte.

— III (5999-6000).

楞嚴正脉

Leng yen tcheng me̞.

Principes du Çūraṅgama sū-tra.

Par Kiao-koang Tchen-kien; édition donnée par Miao-fong Fou-teng, bonze de Pou tcheou, revue par Hong-fang Ho Hao-tchen et par Hong-oou Tchang Eul-koo, de Pao-'an. Postfaces par Tchang Eul-koo (1633), par Tchou Tsiun-thing (1600). Texte et commentaire.

10 livres. — Cf. n° 5992.

In-4. Papier blanc. 2 vol. demi-rel., au chiffre de Louis-Philippe. *Nouveau fonds 647.*

6001. — 1.

大佛頂首楞嚴經正脉疏懸示

Ta fo ting cheou leng yen king tcheng me̞ sou hiuen chi.

Instructions relatives à l'ouvrage précédent.

Même ouvrage qu'au n° précédent, art. II, avec la préface de Kiao-koang Tchen-kien; sans postface. Édition revue par Lou Ki-tchong Si-yuen kiu-chi, de Phing-hou.

90 feuillets.

— II.

皈敬三寶請求加被偈

Koei king san pao tshing khieou kia pei kie.

Poésie pour chercher refuge près des Trois Joyaux.

1 feuillet.

Grand in-8. Bonne gravure. 1 vol. demi-rel., au chiffre de la République Française.

Nouveau fonds 3851.

6002. 大佛頂首楞嚴經正脉疏

Ta fo ting cheou leng yen king tcheng mę sou.

Même ouvrage qu'aux n°ˢ 5999-6000, art. III. Postfaces de l'auteur (1600) et de Tchou Tsiun-thing Thi-hiuen-tseu (1600). Édition revue par Yo Hoo-cheng Ta-sin kiu-chi, de Tchhang-choei.

Livres 9 et 10.

Grand in-8. Bonne gravure. 1 vol. cartonnage.

Nouveau fonds 4627.

6003-6005. 大佛頂如來密因修證了義諸菩薩萬行首楞嚴經

Ta fo ting jou lai mi yin sieou tcheng liao yi tchou phou sa oan hing cheou leng yen king.

Mahābuddhoṣṇīṣa tathāgata guhyahetu sākṣātkṛta prasa-

nnārtha sarvabodhisattvacaryā çūraṅgama sūtra.

Superbe édition avec commentaires et annotations imprimés en plusieurs couleurs. Liste de traducteurs, annotateurs, etc. Une planche avec légende au verso. Historique pour la gravure de l'ouvrage (1620), par Ling Hong-hien Cheng-seou, surnom Thien-tchhi kiu-chi, de Oou-hing. Préface (1606) par Yu Oang-yen Kao-jou, de Sin-'an. Introduction (1602) par Tchou-hong, de Yun-tshi seu. Postface par Yo Thoęn Seu-po, de Min. Texte de Pramiti et Meghaçikha. Lecture des caractères difficiles.

10 livres. — Cf. n° 5992.

Grand in-8. Papier blanc. 3 vol. demi-rel., au chiffre de Louis-Philippe.

Nouveau fonds 902.

6006. 大佛頂如來密因修證了義諸菩薩萬行首楞嚴經玄義

Ta fo ting jou lai mi yin sieou tcheng liao yi tchou phou sa oan hing cheou leng yen king hiuen yi.

Explication du Mahābuddhoṣṇīṣa çūraṅgama sūtra.

Par 'Eou-yi Tchi-hiu, avec préface du même (1644).

2 livres. — Cf. nº 5992.

Grand in-8. 1 vol. demi-rel., au chiffre de Louis-Philippe.

Nouveau fonds 691.

6007. 大佛頂如來密因修證了義諸菩薩萬行首楞嚴經文句

Ta fo ting jou lai mi yin sieou tcheng liao yi tchou phou sa oan hing cheou leng yen king oen kiu ; alias :

佛頂文句

Fo ting oen kiu.

Texte et explication du Mahābuddhoṣṇīṣa ēuraṅgama sūtra.

Traduction avec commentaires de Tchi-hiu.

4 livres.

Grand in-8. Manque le 1er feuillet du livre 3. 1 vol. demi-rel., au chiffre de Louis-Philippe.

Nouveau fonds 689.

6008-6011.

— I (6008-6010).

大佛頂首楞嚴經疏解蒙鈔

Ta fo ting cheou leng yen king sou kiai mong tchhao.

Mahābuddhoṣṇīṣa ēuraṅgama sūtra avec commentaires.

Edition préparée et publiée par Tshien Khien-yi, de Hai-yin. Table des matières. Trois notices de Tshien Khien-yi, datées de 1654, 1657, 1660. Liste d'éditions et de commentaires : entre beaucoup d'autres, on y trouve ceux qui portent les nᵒˢ 1489, 1588, 1624 du catalogue de Bunyiu Nanjio. Texte et notes abondantes. Édition de Yu-chan (1658).

1 + 10 + 1 livres. — Cf. nᵒˢ 5992, 5995-5996, 5997.

— II (6011).

佛頂五錄

Fo ting oou lou.

Cinq suppléments au Commentaire précédent.

Par Tshien Khien-yi ; comprenant :

Livre 1 (6011).

佛頂圖錄

Fo ting thou lou.

Tableaux explicatifs et planches.

Avec légendes.

Livre 2 (6011).

佛頂序錄

Fo ting siu lou.

Préfaces et postfaces du Mahābuddhoṣṇīṣa, etc.

Textes et notes; la dernière pièce reproduite est de 1594 et signée par Kiu Jou-tsi.

Livre 3 (6011).

佛頂枝錄

Fo ting tchi lou.

Recueil de notes explicatives.

Préface et 7 sections.

Livre 4 (6011).

佛頂通錄

Fo ting thong lou.

Recueil d'extraits annexes.

Préface et 2 sections.

Livres 5 à 8 (6011).

佛頂宗錄

Fo ting tsong lou.

Notes sur les religieux.

Préface et 4 sections.

In-4. Bonne gravure ancienne. 4 vol. demi-rel., au chiffre de Louis-Philippe.
Nouveau fonds 2288 à 2291.

6012-6014.

— I (6012-6013).

Ta fo ting cheou leng yen king sou kiai mong tchhao.

Même ouvrage qu'aux nᵒˢ 6008-6010, art. I.

Frontispice, scènes bouddhiques (1 feuillet double). Table des matières et notes. Texte.

Livre initial et livres 1 à 4; la suite manque.

— II (6014).

Fo ting oou lou.

Même ouvrage qu'au nᵒ 6011, art. II, comprenant seulement : Thou lou, Siu lou, Tchi lou.

Livres 1 à 3; la suite manque.

Grand in-8. Bonne gravure, édition plus petite que l'autre.
1 vol. cartonnage.
Nouveau fonds 4631.
1 vol. demi-rel., au chiffre de la République Française.
Nouveau fonds 3846.
1 vol. cartonnage.
Nouveau fonds 4674.

6015-6016.

— I (6015-6016).

大佛頂如來密因修證了義諸菩薩萬行首楞嚴經直指

Ta fo ting jou lai mi yin sieou tcheng liao yi tchou phou sa oan hing cheou leng yen king tchi tchi.

Mahābuddhoṣṇīṣa tathāgata guhyahetu sākṣātkṛta prasannārtha sarvabodhisattvacaryā çūraṅgama sūtra, texte et commentaire.

Commentaire par Han-chi Thien-jan (1608-1688), bonze de Tan-hia. Préface par Kin-chi, élève du précédent; historique par Kin-pien, autre disciple du même. Notice générale. Lecture des caractères difficiles. Édition donnée aux frais de Fou Hong-lie, gouverneur du Koang-si.

10 livres. — Cf. n° 5992.

— II (6016).

首楞嚴經直指科文

Cheou leng yen king tchi tchi khoo oen.

Résumé en tableaux du commentaire du Çūraṅgama sūtra.

Grand in-8. Caractères un peu grêles. 2 vol. demi-rel., au chiffre de la République Française.

Nouveau fonds 3849, 3850.

6017-6018.

— I (6017).

楞嚴講錄

Leng yen kiang lou.

Explication du Çūraṅgama sūtra.

Par Cheng-chi, de Tchhai-tseu chan. Préface de l'auteur (1622).

7 feuillets.

— II (6017).

科文

Khoo oen.

Même résumé qu'au n° 6016, art. II; paginé 8 à 46, devrait se trouver à la fin de l'ouvrage.

— III (6017-6018).

Ta fo ting jou lai mi yin sieou tcheng liao yi tchou phou sa oan hing cheou leng yen king tchi tchi.

Même ouvrage qu'aux n°s 6015-6016, art. I, sans les préfaces et notices; le livre 1er manque également. Édition plus petite.

Grand in-8. 2 vol. demi-rel., au chiffre de Louis-Philippe.

Nouveau fonds 2312, 2313.

Treizième Section : SUVARṆAPRABHĀSA SŪTRA, ETC.

6019. 金光明經

Kin koang ming king.

Suvarṇaprabhāsa sūtra.

Version de Dharmarakṣa (414-421). Préface par Tsong-yi Tsheu-kio ta-chi (1081). Lecture des caractères difficiles. Édition de Tsi-tchao 'an (1608).

4 livres. — Bunyiu Nanjio 127.

Grand in-8. Bonne gravure. 1 vol. demi-rel., au chiffre de la République Française.

Nouveau fonds 3832.

6020-6023.

Kin koang ming king.

Même ouvrage. Préface sans nom d'auteur ni date; à la fin du 1er livre, date de la gravure (1710); à la fin de chaque livre, lecture des caractères rares. Invocation finale.

4 livres.

In-4. Papier blanc, 4 vol. en paravent, couvertures rouges; dans 2 étuis demi-rel., au chiffre de Louis-Philippe.

Nouveau fonds 146.

———

6024-6025.
— I (6024).

金光明經玄義

Kin koang ming king hiuen yi.

Sens caché du Suvarṇaprabhāsa sūtra.

Par Tchi-tche ta-chi, rédigé par son disciple Koan-ting. Liste des signes rares. Édition de Leng-yen seu (1663).

2 livres. — Bunyiu Nanjio 1548.

— II (6024-6025).

金光明經玄義拾遺記

Kin koang ming king hiuen yi chi yi ki.

Commentaire de l'ouvrage précédent.

Par Tchi-li, préface de 1023. Lecture des signes dificiles. Édition comme ci-dessus.

6 livres. — Bunyiu Nanjio 1549.

Grand in-8. Bonne gravure; frontispice (1 feuillet double).

1 vol. demi-rel., au chiffre de la République Française.

Nouveau fonds 3837.

1 vol. cartonnage.

Nouveau fonds 4635.

6026. 金光明經文句

Kin koang ming king oen kiu.

Explication du Suvarṇaprabhāsa sūtra.

Par Tchi-tchẹ ta-chi, rédigée
par son disciple Koan-ting. Lecture des signes difficiles. Édition
de Leng-yen seu (1663).

6 livres. — Bunyiu Nanjio 1552.

Grand in-8. Bonne gravure. 1 vol.
demi-rel., au chiffre de la République
Française.
Nouveau fonds 3834.

6027. 金光明經文句記

Kin koang ming king oen kiu ki.

Commentaire de l'ouvrage
précédent.

Par le bonze Tchi-li (1027).
Lecture des signes rares. Édition
de Leng-yen seu (1663).

6 livres (12 sections). — Bunyiu
Nanjio 1553.

Grand in-8. Bonne gravure. 1 vol.
demi-rel., au chiffre de la République
Française.
Nouveau fonds 3835.

6028.

Kin koang ming king oen kiu ki.

Double.

Livres 1, 2, 3 seulement.

1 vol. demi-rel., au chiffre de la
République Française.
Nouveau fonds 3836.

6029. — I.

合部金光明經

Ho pou kin koang ming king.

Collection de trois versions
du Suvarṇaprabhāsa sūtra.

Ouvrage de Pao-koei, Chinois,
et de Jñānagupta (Tchi-tẹ) (597).
Préface par Yen-tsong (597). Liste
des signes rares. Édition de Tsi-
tchao 'an (1611).

8 livres. — Bunyiu Nanjio 130.

— II.

入定不定印經

Jou ting pou ting yin king.

Niyatāniyatagati mudrāvatāra
sūtra.

Traduction de Yi-tsing (700)
avec préface de l'impératrice Oou.
Lecture des signes difficiles. Édition de Hoa-tchheng yuen (1612).

1 livre. — Bunyiu Nanjio 131.

— III.

不必定入定入印經

Pou pi ting jou ting jou yin king.

Niyatāniyatagati mudrāvatāra sūtra.

Traduction de Gautama Prajñāruci (542). Liste des caractères rares. Édition de Hoa-tchheng seu (1612).

1 livre. — Bunyiu Nanjio 132.

Grand in-8. Bonne gravure; frontispice (1 feuillet double). 1 vol. demi-rel., au chiffre de la République Française.
Nouveau fonds 3833.

6030. 金光明最勝王經
Kin koang ming tsoei cheng oang king.

Suvarṇaprabhāsottamarāja sūtra.

Traduit par Yi-tsing (700-712). Liste des mots rares. Édition de Miao-tę 'an (1591, 1592).

10 livres. — Bunyiu Nanjio 126; voir nᵒˢ 6019, 6029.

Grand in-8. Bonne gravure. 1 vol. demi-rel., au chiffre de la République Française.
Nouveau fonds 3831.

6031-6040.
Kin koang ming tsoei cheng oang king.

Même ouvrage avec lecture des caractères douteux à la fin de chaque livre. Édition en grands caractères; notice finale sur la gravure, sans date.

10 livres. — Bunyiu Nanjio 126.

In-4. Papier blanc; 10 vol. en paravent, couvertures rouges; dans 4 étuis demi-rel., au chiffre de Louis-Philippe.
Nouveau fonds 155.

Quatorzième Section : LAṄKĀVATĀRA SŪTRA, ETC.

6041. 楞伽阿跋多羅寶經會譯
Leng kia 'o po to lo pao king hoei yi.

Textes juxtaposés du Laṅkāvatāra ratna sūtra.

Versions de Guṇabhadra (443), de Bodhiruci (513), de Çikṣānanda (700-704). Édition préparée par le bonze Yuen-kho. Préface par Fong Mong-tcheng (1580).

4 livres (8 sections). — Bunyiu Nanjio 175, 176, 177.

Grand in-8. Texte en caractères de genre cursif. 1 vol. demi-rel., au chiffre de la République Française.
Nouveau fonds 3830.

6042. 楞伽阿跋多羅寶經

Leng kia 'o po to lo pao king.

Laṅkāvatāra ratna sūtra.

Traduction de Guṇabhadra (443). Préfaces de Tsiang Tchi-khi et de Sou Chi (1085). Lecture des caractères difficiles. Édition de Tsi-tchao 'an (1603).

4 livres. — Bunyiu Nanjio 175; n° 6041.

Grand in-8. Bonne gravure. 1 vol. demi-rel., au chiffre de la République Française.

Nouveau fonds 3826.

6043.

Leng kia 'o po to lo pao king.

Même ouvrage; édition imitée de la précédente, sensiblement plus grande.

In-4. Belle gravure. 1 vol. demi-rel., au chiffre de Napoléon III.

Nouveau fonds 1560.

6044-6045. 楞伽阿跋多羅寶經註解

Leng kia 'o po to lo pao king tchou kiai.

Commentaire du Laṅkāvatāra sūtra.

Par Tsong-lẹ et Jou-khi; préface pour présenter à l'Empereur; décret impérial (1378). Édition de Leng-yen seu (1632).

4 livres (8 sections). — Bunyiu Nanjio 1613; cf. n° 6042.

Grand in-8.
1 vol. demi-rel., au chiffre de la République Française.

Nouveau fonds 3827.

1 vol. cartonnage.
Nouveau fonds 4634.

6046-6047. 觀楞伽阿跋多羅寶經記

Koan leng kia 'o po to lo pao king ki.

Le Laṅkāvatāra sūtra avec notes.

Préfaces du sūtra par Tsiang Tchi-khi et par Sou Chi (1085).

— I (6046).

觀楞伽寶經閣筆記

Koan leng kia pao king ko pi ki.

Notice du Laṅkāvatāra sūtra.

Par Tẹ-tshing, de Kien-ye, datée de 1599.

— II (6046).

略科

Lio khoo.

Tableaux résumés.

Par le même, datés de 1598.

— III (6046-6047).

Koan leng kia 'o po to lo pao king ki.

Traduction de Guṇabhadra. Notes de Tę-tshing. A la fin note (1724) sur la gravure de l'ouvrage par Kin-tan, surnom Lo-feou hoa-jen.

4 livres, chacun en 2 sections. — Cf. n° 6042.

In-4. Belle impression sur papier blanc. 2 vol. demi-rel., au chiffre de Louis-Philippe.

Nouveau fonds 237.

6048. — I.

楞伽阿跋多羅寶經玄義

Leng kia 'o po to lo pao king hiuen yi.

Sens mystérieux du Laṅkāvatāra sūtra.

Par le bonze Tchi-hiu.

1 livre (34 feuillets).

— II.

楞伽阿跋多羅寶經義疏

Leng kia 'o po to lo pao king yi sou.

Commentaire du Laṅkāvatāra sūtra.

D'après la version de Guṇabhadra; par Tchi-hiu. Lecture des termes rares.

3 livres (7 sections). — Cf. n° 6042.

Grand in-8. Bonne gravure. 1 vol. demi-rel., au chiffre de la République Française.

Nouveau fonds 3829.

———————

6049. — I.

楞伽阿跋多羅寶經心印科文

Leng kia 'o po to lo pao king sin yin khoo oen.

Tableaux résumés du commentaire du Laṅkāvatāra sūtra.

9 feuillets.

— II.

楞伽阿跋多羅寶經心印

Leng kiao 'o po to lo pao king sin yin.

Commentaire du Laṅkāvatāra sūtra.

Par Han-chi, bonze de Lei-fong. Notice sur l'ouvrage par Kin-oou (1664); le commentaire a été écrit dans les années 1662 et 1663. Liste des termes difficiles.

4 livres (8 sections). — Cf. n° 6042.

Grand in-8. Bonne gravure. 1 vol. demi-rel., au chiffre de la République Française.

Nouveau fonds 3828.

6050. 楞伽阿跋多羅寶經心印

Leng kiao 'o po to lo pao king sin yin.

Texte et commentaire du Laṅkāvatāra sūtra.

— I.

楞伽心印緣起

Leng kia sin yin yuen khi.

Historique de l'ouvrage.

Par Kin-oou (1664).

— II.

科文

Khoo oen.

Résumé en tableaux.

9 feuillets.

— III.

Leng kia 'o po to lo pao king sin yin.

Même ouvrage qu'au n° précédent, art. II. Lecture des caractères difficiles. Notice finale de Han-kin (1723).

4 livres de 2 sections chacun.

In-4. Bonne gravure sur papier blanc. 1 vol. demi-rel., au chiffre de Louis-Philippe.

Nouveau fonds 649.

6051. 入楞伽經

Jou leng kia king.

Laṅkāvatāra sūtra.

Traduction (513) de Bodhiruci. Lecture des caractères difficiles. Édition de la bonzerie de Tsi-tchao à King-chan (1607).

10 livres. — Bunyiu Nanjio 176; n° 6041.

Grand in-8. Belle impression; frontispice (1 feuillet simple, manque le recto); manque une partie du dernier feuillet du volume. 1 vol. demi-rel., au chiffre de la République Française.

Nouveau fonds 316.

6052.

Jou leng kia king.

Même ouvrage. Lecture des caractères difficiles. Édition de Tsi-tchao 'an (1607).

10 livres. — Bunyiu Nanjio 176.

Grand in-8. Bonne gravure. 1 vol. demi-rel., au chiffre de la République Française.

Nouveau fonds 3823.

6053-6054.

— I (6053-6054).

大乘入楞伽經

Ta cheng jou leng kia king.

Laṅkāvatāra sūtra.

Traduit par Çikṣānanda (700-704). Préface par l'impératrice Oou. Lecture des termes rares. Édition de 1645 ?

7 livres. — Bunyiu Nanjio 177 ; n° 6041.

— II (6053).

菩薩行方便境界神通變化經

Phou sa hing fang pien king kiai chen thong pien hoa king.

Bodhisattvagocaropāyaviṣaya-vikurvaṇa nirdeça sūtra.

Version de Guṇabhadra (435-468). Lecture des caractères difficiles. Édition de Tsi-tchao 'an (1608) ; feuillets gravés de nouveau en 1677 ou 1617.

3 livres. — Bunyiu Nanjio 178.

Grand in-8. Bonne gravure. 2 vol. demi-rel., au chiffre de la République Française.

Nouveau fonds 3824, 3825.

6055. 大薩遮尼乾子受記經

Ta sa tchę ni khien tseu cheou ki king.

Mahāsatya nirgranthaputra vyākaraṇa sūtra.

Version de Bodhiruci (519). Liste des caractères rares. Édition de Hoa-tchheng seu (1628).

10 livres. — Bunyiu Nanjio 179.

Grand in-8. Bonne gravure. 1 vol. demi-rel., au chiffre de la République Française.

Nouveau fonds 3968.

Quinzième Section : MAHĀMAYŪRĪ SŪTRA, ETC.

6056. — I.

佛說孔雀王咒經

Fo choe khong tsio oang tcheou king.

Mahāmayūrī vidyārājñī sūtra.

Version par Saṅghapāla, Cambodgien (506-520). Liste des caractères rares. Édition de Hoa-tchheng seu (1632), réédition partielle en 1680.

2 livres. — Bunyiu Nanjio 3o8.

— II.

佛說大孔雀王神咒經

Fo choe ta khong tsio oang chen tcheou king.

Mahāmayūrī vidyārājñī sūtra.

Version du même texte par Po Çrīmitra, Occidental (317-322).

6 feuillets. — Bunyiu Nanjio 3o9.

— III.

佛說大孔雀王雜神咒經

Fo choe ta khong tsio oang tsa chen tcheou king.

Mahāmayūrī vidyārājñī sūtra.

Même texte, version du même. Lecture des caractères difficiles. Édition de Hoa-tchheng seu (1632).

12 feuillets. — Bunyiu Nanjio 3io.

— IV.

大金色孔雀王咒經

Ta kin se khong tsio oang tcheou king.

Mahāmayūrī vidyārājñī sūtra.

Même texte, version de Kumārajīva. Édition de Kia-hing (1655).

12 feuillets. — Bunyiu Nanjio 3ii.

— V.

佛說不空羂索咒經

Fo choe pou khong kiuen so tcheou king.

Amoghapāça dhāraṇī sūtra.

Version de Jñānagupta (587). Liste des mots rares. Édition de Kia-hing (1656).

13 feuillets. — Bunyiu Nanjio 3i2 cf. n° 58o9, art. IX.

Grand in-8. Bonne gravure. 1 vol. demi-rel., au chiffre de la République Française.

Nouveau fonds 4041.

6057. — I.

佛說大孔雀咒王經

Fo choe ta khong tsio tcheou oang king.

Mahāmayūrī vidyārājñī sūtra.

Version par Yi-tsing (705), du même texte qu'au n° 6056, art. I. Liste des caractères difficiles. Édition de Hing-cheng oan-cheou chan-seu (1597).

3 livres. — Bunyiu Nanjio 306.

— II.

讀誦佛母大孔雀明王經前啓請法

Tou song fo mou ta khong tsio ming oang king tshien khi tshing fa.

Préliminaires à la récitation du sūtra suivant.

Prières diverses et notice; préface par Amoghavajra.

3 feuillets.

— III.

佛母大孔雀明王經

Fo mou ta khong tsio ming oang king.

Mahāmayūrī vidyārājñī sūtra.

Même texte, traduction d'Amoghavajra. Lecture des caractères rares. Mêmes lieu et date d'édition qu'à l'art. I.

3 livres. — Bunyiu Nanjio 307.

Grand in-8. Bonne gravure. 1 vol. demi-rel., au chiffre de la République Française.

Nouveau fonds 4044.

6058.

Fo mou ta khong tsio ming oang king.

Même ouvrage qu'au n° précédent, art. III.

Livre 1er seul, précédé de prières, dhāraṇī, etc.

In-folio. Impression en grands caractères sur papier blanc; illustrations (9 feuillets simples). 1 vol. en paravent couverture toile bleue, dans 1 étui cartonnage.

Nouveau fonds 5106.

6059-6061.

Fo mou ta khong tsio ming oang tcheou king.

Frontispice (2 feuillets doubles).

— I (6059).

香讚.消災吉祥神咒

Hiang tsan. Siao tsai ki siang chen tcheou.

Cérémonies préliminaires et éloge. Dhāraṇī pour chasser les calamités.

Texte, suivi de lecture des caractères difficiles.

— II (6059).

佛母大孔雀明王經

Fo mou ta khong tsio ming oang king.

Même ouvrage qu'au n° 6057, art. III. Lecture des caractères difficiles.

1ᵉʳ livre.

— III (6059).

諸佛菩薩寶誯 (sic) 成道

Tchou fo phou sa pao tan (?) tchheng tao.

Recueil de prières pour divers objets.

Dix-neuf invocations en chinois imprimées en texte plus fin.

— IV (6060-6061).

Fo mou ta khong tsio ming oang king.

Suite de l'art. II, avec lecture des signes difficiles.

Livres 2 et 3.

— V (6061).

次明壇場畫像法式

Tsheu ming than tchhang hoa siang fa chi.

Règles pour le dessin des images de l'aire et de l'autel.

Traduction par Yi-tsing, avec notes et lecture des caractères difficiles. Texte plus fin.

In-4. Papier blanc. 3 vol. en paravent couvertures rouges ; dans 1 étui demi-rel., au chiffre de Louis-Philippe.

Nouveau fonds 149.

6062. — I.

不空羂索心咒王經

Pou khong kiuen so sin tcheou oang king.

Amoghapāça hṛdaya mantra-rāja sūtra.

Version par Ratnacinta (693), du même texte que n° 6056, art. V. Lecture des mots rares. Édition de 1655.

3 livres. — Bunyiu Nanjio 313.

— II.

不空羂索陀羅尼經

Pou khong kiuen so tho lo ni king.

Amoghapāça dhāraṇī sūtra.

Traduction du même texte qu'à l'art. précédent, achevée en 700. Les chapitres 1 à 16 ont été traduits par un Hindou, Li Oou-thao, et rédigés par Po-loen; le chapitre 17 est dû à Hoei-ji, Chinois, et à Çrīmat, Hindou; Saṅghamitra et Bodhiruci sont aussi mentionnés à propos de ce travail. Préface par Po-loen. Notice finale relative à la traduction. Liste des caractères difficiles. Édition de 1655.

2 livres. — Bunyiu Nanjio 314.

— III.

不空羂索咒心經

Pou khong kiuen so tcheou sin king.

Amoghapāça hṛdaya sūtra.

Version du même texte qu'au n° 6056, art. V, et que le 1er chapitre du n° 6063-6064, par Bodhiruci (693-713). Liste des caractères rares. Édition de Hoatchheng seu (1612).

12 feuillets. — Bunyiu Nanjio 315.

— IV.

不空羂索神咒心經

Pou khong kiuen so chen tcheou sin king.

Amoghapāça hṛdaya sūtra.

Version du même texte par Hiuen-tsang (659). Lecture des signes difficiles. Mêmes lieu et date.

1 livre. — Bunyiu Nanjio 316.

Grand in-8. Bonne gravure. 1 vol. demi-rel., au chiffre de la République Française.

Nouveau fonds 4000.

6063-6064. 不空羂索神變真言經

Pou khong kiuen so chen pien tchen yen king.

Amoghapāça kalparāja sūtra.

Version de Bodhiruci (707-709). Préface pour la présente édition, donnée à Hoa-tchheng 'an, de Han chan, par Tchang Tshiuen (1612); feuillets gravés de nouveau (1618 ou 1678). Lecture des caractères difficiles.

30 livres. — Bunyiu Nanjio 317; cf. n° 6062, art. III et IV, n° 6056, art. V.

Grand in-8. Bonne gravure; frontispice (1 feuillet double). 2 vol. demi-rel., au chiffre de la République Française.

Nouveau fonds 3998, 3999.

Seizième Section : PŪRNABUDDHA SŪTRA, ETC.

6065. — I.

大方廣圓覺修多羅了義經

Ta fang koang yuen kio sieou to lo liao yi king.

Mahāvaipulya pūrṇabuddha sūtra prasannārtha sūtra.

Traduction de Buddhatrāta, de Ki-pin (viie siècle). Préfaces de Tsong-mi et de Phei Hieou, homme d'état (†870), pour le commentaire. Texte du sūtra; liste des signes rares. Édition de Hing-cheng oan-cheou chan-seu (1598).

2 livres. — Bunyiu Nanjio 427.

— II.

佛說施燈功德經

Fo choe chi teng kong te king.

Pradīpadānīya sūtra.

Version de Narendrayaças (558). Liste des signes rares. Édition de Tsi-tchao 'an (1598).

1 livre. — Bunyiu Nanjio 428.

— III.

金剛三昧經

Kin kang san mei king.

Vajrasamādhi sūtra.

Traduction de l'époque des Liang (397-439). Lecture des signes difficiles. Même date, même localité qu'à l'art. II.

2 livres. — Bunyiu Nanjio 429.

Grand in-8. Bonne gravure. 1 vol. demi-rel., au chiffre de la République Française.

Nouveau fonds 3866.

———

6066. 大方廣圓覺經疏

Ta fang koang yuen kio king sou.

Commentaire du Mahāvaipulya pūrṇabuddha sūtra.

Par Tsong-mi. Préface par Phei Hieou ; préface de l'auteur. Table des matières. Édition de Tsi-tchao 'an (1607).

Livre préliminaire + 3 livres (12 sections) + livre final. — Cf. Bunyiu Nanjio 1629; n° 6065.

Grand in-8. Bonne gravure; manque le livre final, l'exemplaire est relié en désordre. 1 vol. cartonnage.

Nouveau fonds 4667.

6067. — I.

大方廣圓覺經畧疏科

Ta fang koang yuen kio king lio sou khoo.

Tableau résumé du commentaire du Mahāvaipulya pūrṇabuddha sūtra.

Avec avertissement initial.

24 feuillets.

— II.

大方廣圓覺脩多羅了義經畧疏註 (alias 注)

Ta fang koang yuen kio sieou to lo liao yi king lio sou tchou.

Commentaire abrégé du Mahāvaipulya, etc.

Par Tsong-mi. Préfaces de Phei Hieou et de Tsong-mi.

2 livres, chacun en 2 sections. — Cf. n° 6066.

— III.

圭峯定慧禪師遙稟清涼國師書

Koei fong ting hoei chan chi yao pin tshing liang koę chi chou.

Lettre de Tsong-mi à Tshing-liang koę-chi.

Datée de 811, 9ᵉ lune, 13ᵉ jour.

4 feuillets.

— IV.

清涼國師誨答

Tshing liang koę chi hoei ta.

Réponse de Tchheng-koan.

Même année, 10ᵉ lune.

1 feuillet.

— V.

Réplique de Tsong-mi.

Même année, même lune.

2 feuillets.

Grand in-8. Bonne gravure; frontispice (1 feuillet double). 1 vol. demi-rel., au chiffre de la République Française. *Nouveau fonds* 3865.

6068. — I.

大方廣圓覺了義經畧疏

Ta fang koang yuen kio liao yi king lio sou.

Commentaire abrégé du Mahāvaipulya pūrṇabuddha sūtra.

Préfaces par Phei Hieou et par Tsong-mi. Le texte du commentaire est absent.

Comparer n° 6067, art. II.

— II.

大方廣圓覺修多羅了義經

Ta fang koang yuen kio sieou to lo liao yi king.

Mahāvaipulya pūrṇabuddha sūtra prasannārtha sūtra.

Même ouvrage qu'au n° 6065, art. I.

— III.

眞歇了禪師頌圓覺經

Tchen hie liao chan chi song yuen kio king.

Éloge du Pūrṇabuddha sūtra par le bonze Tchen-hie Liao.

Texte en vers formant 12 sections.

6 feuillets.

Édition de la bonzerie de Hai-tchhoang (1680).

Petit in-8. Bonne impression sur papier blanc. 1 vol. demi-reliure.

Nouveau fonds 185.

6069. 圓覺經略疏之鈔

Yuen kio king lio sou tchi tchhao; alias :

大方廣圓覺經略鈔

Ta fang koang yuen kio king lio tchhao.

Extrait d'un commentaire du Mahāvaipulya, etc.

Par Tsong-mi. Préface par Ming-yi ta-chi Seu-tshi (1041).

25 livres. — Bunyiu Nanjio 1629.

Grand in-8. Bonne gravure. 1 vol. demi-rel., au chiffre de la République Française.

Nouveau fonds 3867.

6070. 大方廣圓覺修多羅了義經句釋正白

Ta fang koang yuen kio sieou to lo liao yi king kiu chi tcheng po.

Mahāvaipulya pūrṇabuddha sūtra, avec commentaire détaillé.

D'après la version de Buddha-trāta. Par le bonze Hong-li Lo-fong; revu par Hong tsan Tsai-san. Préface de Oang Ying-hoa, contemporain de Hong-li (1597). Post-face par Thong-ho Kiang Khi-long.

2 livres (6 sections).

Grand in-8. Bonne gravure; figures. 1 vol. demi-rel., au chiffre de la République Française.

Nouveau fonds 3864.

6071. 大方廣圓覺修多羅了義經要解

Ta fang koang yuen kio sieou to lo liao yi king yao kiai.

Le Mahāvaipulya pūrṇabuddha sūtra prasannārtha sūtra, avec commentaire.

Commentaire par Khin-si Tsi-tcheng, bonze de Oou-lin; préface (1617) et postface par le même.

1 livre.

Grand in-8. Gravé en caractères de genre cursif. 1 vol. demi-rel., au chiffre de la République Française.
Nouveau fonds 3863.

6072. 大方廣圓覺脩多羅了義經直解

Ta fang koang yuen kio sieou to lo liao yi king tchi kiai.

Commentaire du Mahāvaipulya pūrṇabuddha sūtra prasannārtha sūtra.

Par Tẹ-tshing, de Han-chan. Préface de Tsong-mi; postfaces par Tchheng Mong-yang (1622) et par Tẹ-tshing (1622).

2 livres.

Grand in-8. 1 vol. demi-rel., au chiffre de la République Française.
Nouveau fonds 3862.

6073.

Ta fang koang yuen kio sieou to lo liao yi king tchi kiai.

Même ouvrage, même préface et mêmes postfaces; en outre, préface de Phei Hieou; édition de Hai-tchhoang, plus petite, imitée de la précédente.

Grand in-8. Bonne impression sur papier blanc. 1 vol. demi-rel., au chiffre de Louis-Philippe.
Nouveau fonds 644.

Dix-septième Section : SŪTRA MÉLANGÉS

6074. — I.

佛眞陀羅所問寶如來三昧經

Toẹn tchen tho lo so oen pao jou lai san mei king.

Mahādruma kinnararāja pari-pṛcchā sūtra.

Version de Tchi Leou-kia-tchhan. Lecture des caractères difficiles.

3 livres. — Bunyiu Nanjio 161.

— II.

諸法本無經

Tchou fa peṇ ooa king.

Sarvadharma pravṛtti nirdeça sūtra.

Version de Jñānagupta (595). Liste des mots rares.

3 livres. — Bunyiu Nanjio 163.

Grand in-8. Bonne gravure; frontispice (1 feuillet double). 1 vol. demi-rel., au chiffre de la République Française.
Nouveau fonds 4011.

6075. 大樹緊那羅王所問經

Ta chou kin na lo oang so oen king.

Mahādruma kinnararāja pari-pṛcchā sūtra.

Version par Kumārajīva, du même texte qu'au nº précédent, art. I. Liste des caractères rares.

4 livres. — Bunyiu Nanjio 162.

Grand in-8. Bonne gravure. 1 vol. demi-rel., au chiffre de la République Française.
Nouveau fonds 3943.

6076. — I.

諸法無行經

Tchou fa oou hing king.

Sarvadharma pravṛtti nirdeça sūtra.

Version par Kumārajīva du même texte qu'au nº 6074, art. II. Liste des signes rares. Édition de Tsi-tchao 'an (1636).

2 livres. — Bunyiu Nanjio 164.

— II.

持人菩薩所問經

Tchhi jen phou sa so oen king.

Vasudhara bodhisattva pari-pṛcchā sūtra.

Traduction de Tchou Fa-hou. Lecture des caractères difficiles. Édition de Tsi-tchao 'an (1637).

4 livres. — Bunyiu Nanjio 165.

Grand in-8. Bonne gravure. 1 vol. demi-rel., au chiffre de la République Française.
Nouveau fonds 3860.

6077. 持世經

Tchhi chi king; alias :

佛說法印品經

Fo choẹ fa yin phin king.

Vasudhara sūtra (Dharmamu-drā sūtra).

Version par Kumārajīva du même texte qu'au nº précédent, art. II.

Liste des mots rares. Édition de Tsi-tchao 'an (1637).

4 livres. — Bunyiu Nanjio 166.

Grand in-8. Bonne gravure. 1 vol. demi-rel., au chiffre de la République Française.

Nouveau fonds 3954.

6078. — I.

佛說慧印三昧經

Fo choę hoei yin san mei king.

Tathāgata jñānamudrā samādhi sūtra.

Version par Tchi Khien. Liste des caractères difficiles. Édition de Tsi-tchao 'an (1604).

1 livre. — Bunyiu Nanjio 256.

— II.

佛說無極寶三昧經

Fo choę oou ki pao san mei king.

Anantaratna samādhi sūtra.

Version de Tchou Fa-hou (307). Lecture des mots difficiles. Mêmes lieu et date.

2 livres. — Bunyiu Nanjio 257.

— III.

寶如來三昧經

Pao jou lai san mei king.

Ratnatathāgata samādhi sūtra.

Version du même texte par Gī-tamitra. Lecture des caractères difficiles. Mêmes lieu et date.

2 livres. — Bunyiu Nanjio 258.

Grand in-8. Bonne gravure. 1 vol. demi-rel., au chiffre de la République Française.

Nouveau fonds 4002.

———

6079. — I.

佛說諫王經

Fo choę kien oang king.

Rājāvavādaka sūtra.

Version de Tsiu-khiu King-cheng, Chinois (455). Lecture des caractères difficiles. Édition de King-chan seu (1604).

5 feuillets. — Bunyiu Nanjio 248.

— II.

如來示教勝軍王經

Jou lai chi kiao cheng kiun oang king.

Rājāvavādaka sūtra.

Version du même texte par Hiuen-tsang (649). Liste des caractères rares. Mêmes lieu et date d'édition.

8 feuillets. — Bunyiu Nanjio 249.

— III.

佛爲勝光天子說王法經

Fo oei cheng koang thien tseu choẹ oang fa king.

Rājāvavādaka sūtra.

Même texte traduit par Yi-tsing (710). Lecture des caractères rares. Mêmes lieu et date.

7 feuillets. — Bunyiu Nanjio 250.

— IV.

寶積三昧文殊師利菩薩問法身經

Pao tsi san mei oen chou chi li phou sa oen fa chen king.

Ratnakūṭa sūtra.

Version par 'An Chi-kao, du même texte que Bunyiu Nanjio 51. Mêmes lieu et date d'édition.

7 feuillets. — Bunyiu Nanjio 251.

— V.

佛說濟諸方等學經

Fo choẹ tsi tchou fang teng hio king.

Sarvavaipulyavidyāsiddha sūtra.

Version par Tchou Fa-hou. Liste des caractères difficiles. Édition de Tsi-tchao-'an (1604).

17 feuillets. — Bunyiu Nanjio 252.

— VI.

大乘方廣總持經

Ta cheng fang koang tsong tchhi king.

Mahāyānavaipulya dhāraṇī sūtra.

Version du même texte par Vinītaruci, Hindou (582). Lecture des mots rares. Mêmes lieu et date d'édition, réédition partielle de 1620.

16 feuillets. — Bunyiu Nanjio 253.

— VII.

太子須大挐經

Thai tseu siu ta na king.

Sudāna kumāra sūtra.

Version par Cheng-kien (388-407). Lecture des caractères difficiles. Mêmes lieu et date d'édition.

20 feuillets. — Bunyiu Nanjio 254.

— VIII.

佛說如來智印經

Fo choẹ jou lai tchi yin king ;
           alias :

諸佛法身經

Tchou fo fa chen king.

Tathāgatajñānamudrā samādhi sūtra.

Version de la dynastie des Song (420-479). Liste des caractères difficiles.

25 feuillets. — Bunyiu Nanjio 255; cf. n° 6078, art. I.

Grand in-8. Bonne gravure. 1 vol. demi-rel., au chiffre de la République Française.

Nouveau fonds 4037.

6080. 持心梵天所問經

Tchhi sin fan thien so oen king; alias :

莊嚴佛法經

Tchoang yen fo fa king; alias :

等御諸法經

Teng yu tchou fa king.

Viçeṣacinta brahma paripṛcchā sūtra.

Traduction par Tchou Fa-hou (286). Lecture des caractères difficiles.

4 livres. — Bunyiu Nanjio 197.

Grand in-8. Bonne gravure. 1 vol. demi-rel., au chiffre de la République Française.

Nouveau fonds 3944.

6081. 思益梵天所問經

Seu yi fan thien so oen king.

Viçeṣacinta brahma paripṛcchā sūtra.

Version par Kumārajīva (402), du même texte qu'au n° 6080. Lecture des caractères difficiles.

4 livres. — Bunyiu Nanjio 190.

Grand in-8. Bonne gravure. 1 vol. demi-rel., au chiffre de la République Française.

Nouveau fonds 3940.

6082. 勝思惟梵天所問經

Cheng seu oei fan thien so oen king.

Viçeṣacinta brahma paripṛcchā sūtra.

Version par Bodhiruci (517), du même texte qu'au n° précédent. Liste des mots rares.

6 livres. — Bunyiu Nanjio 189.

Grand in-8. Bonne gravure. 1 vol. demi-rel., au chiffre de la République Française.

Nouveau fonds 3942.

6083. — I.

佛說文殊師利現寶藏經

Fo choẹ oen chou chi li hien pao tsang king.

Ratnakāraṇḍakavyūha sūtra.

Version de Tchou Fa-hou (270)·
Liste des mots difficiles. Édition
de Tsi-tchao 'an (1609).

2 livres. — Bunyiu Nanjio 168.

— II.

大方廣寶篋經

Ta fang koang pao khie king.

Ratnakāraṇḍakavyūha sūtra.

Version du même texte par
Guṇabhadra (435-443). Lecture
des caractères difficiles. Même
lieu d'édition (1608).

2 livres. — Bunyiu Nanjio 169.

Grand in-8. Bonne gravure. 1 vol.
demi-rel., au chiffre de la République
Française.

Nouveau fonds 3969.

6084. — I.

等集眾德三昧經

Teng tsi tchong tẹ san mei king.

Sarvapuṇyasamuccaya samā-
dhi sūtra.

Version de Tchou Fa-hou. Liste
des caractères difficiles. Édition
portant les indications : Hoa-
tchheng seu (1616, 1617), Tsie-
tai seu (1626).

3 livres. — Bunyiu Nanjio 128.

— II.

集一切福德三昧經

Tsi yi tshie fou tẹ san mei king.

Sarvapuṇyasamuccaya samā-
dhi sūtra.

Autre traduction du même texte,
par Kumārajīva. Lecture des caractères rares. Édition de Hieou-
ning ta seu (1629).

3 livres. — Bunyiu Nanjio 129.

Grand in-8. Bonne gravure. 1 vol.
demi-rel., au chiffre de la République
Française.

Nouveau fonds 4006.

6085. 道神足無極變化
經

*Tao chen tsou oou ki pien hoa
king.*

Trayastriṃçatparivarta sūtra.

Version de 'An Fa-khin, Perse
(281-306). Liste des mots rares.
Édition donnée par Tchhẹ-oei
(1660).

4 livres. — Bunyiu Nanjio 148.

Grand in-8. Bonne gravure. 1 vol.
demi-rel. au chiffre de la République
Française.

Nouveau fonds 3964.

6086. — I.

佛說寶雲經

Fo choẹ pao yun king.

Ratnamegha sūtra.

Version de Mandra, Cambod-gien, et Saṅghapāla, de même origine (503). Liste des signes rares. Édition de Tsie-tai seu (1625).

7 livres. — Bunyiu Nanjio 152.

— II.

佛昇忉利天爲母說法經

Fo cheng tao li thien oei mou choẹ fa king.

Trayastriṃçatparivarta sūtra.

Version par Tchou Fa-hou, du même texte qu'au n° 6085. Lecture des signes difficiles. Édition de Tsi-tchao 'an (1608).

3 livres. — Bunyiu Nanjio 153.

Grand in-8. Bonne gravure. 1 vol. demi-rel., au chiffre de la République Française.
Nouveau fonds 3876.

6087. 佛說寶雨經

Fo choẹ pao yu king; alias :

顯授不退轉菩薩記經

Hien cheou pou thoei tchoan phou sa ki king.

Ratnamegha sūtra.

Traduction par Dharmaruci (693), du même texte qu'au n° 6086, art. I. Lecture des caractères difficiles.

10 livres. — Bunyiu Nanjio 151.

Grand in-8. Bonne gravure. 1 vol. demi-rel., au chiffre de la République Française.
Nouveau fonds 3858.

6088.

     Fo choẹ pao yu king.

Double.

Manquent les premiers feuillets du 1er livre et les 4 premiers du 6e.

1 vol. demi-rel., au chiffre de Napo-léon III.
Nouveau fonds 1231.

6089-6090.

— I (6089-6090).

佛說除蓋障菩薩所問經

Fo choẹ tchhou kai tchang phou sa so oen king.

Ratnamegha sūtra.

Autre version du n° 6087, par Fa-hou, Oei-tsing et autres (vers

1000). Lecture des mots rares. Édition de Tsi-tchao 'an (1608).

20 livres. — Bunyiu Nanjio 964.

— II (6090).

仁王護國般若波羅蜜多經

Jen oang hou koẹ pan jẹ po lo mi to king.

Rāṣṭrapāla prajñāpāramitā sūtra.

Version par Amoghavajra, du texte de Bunyiu Nanjio 17. Préface par l'empereur Tai tsong, des Thang (762-779). Liste des caractères rares. Édition de Leng-yen seu (1634).

2 livres. — Bunyiu Nanjio 965; cf. nᵒˢ 5750, 5751.

Grand in-8. Bonne gravure. 2 vol. demi-rel., au chiffre de la République Française.

Nouveau fonds 4028, 3938.

6091. — I.

文殊師利菩薩問菩提經論

Oen chou chi li phou sa oen phou thi king loẹn; alias :

伽耶山頂經論

Kia ye chan ting king loẹn.

Gayāçīrṣa sūtra ṭīkā.

Commentaire du Gayāçīrṣa sūtra (Bunyiu Nanjio 238 à 241) par le bodhisattva Vasubandhu; version de Bodhiruci (535). Édition du Hong-fa-hoei de Song-kiang (1644).

2 livres. — Bunyiu Nanjio 1191.

— II.

金剛般若波羅蜜經破取著不壞假名論

Kin kang pan jẹ po lo mi king pho tshiu tchou pou hoai kia ming loẹn.

Vajracchedikā prajñāpāramitā sūtra çāstra, contre l'attachement à un faux nom.

Œuvre du Bodhisattva Guṇada; traduit par Divākara (683). Lecture des caractères difficiles. Édition du bonze Tchhẹ-oei (1661).

2 livres. — Bunyiu Nanjio 1192; cf. nᵒ 5730.

— III.

勝思惟梵天所問經論

Cheng seu oei fan thien so oen king loẹn.

Viçeṣacinta brahma pariprcchā sūtra ṭīkā.

Commentaire du Viçeṣacinta brahma pariprcchā sūtra (nᵒˢ 6080 à 6082), traduit par Bodhiruci (531). Lecture des caractères difficiles. Édition de Leng-yen seu (1646).

3 livres. — Bunyiu Nanjio 1193.

Grand in-8. Bonne gravure. 1 vol. demi-rel., au chiffre de la République Française.

Nouveau fonds 4150.

6092. 菩薩本行經
Phou sa pẹn hing king.

Bodhisattva pūrvacaryā sūtra.

Traduction des Tsin orientaux (317-420). Liste des signes rares. Édition de Hing-cheng oan-cheou chan-seu (1596).

3 livres. — Bunyiu Nanjio 432; **cf.** nᵒ 6112, art. IV.

Grand in-8. Bonne gravure. 1 vol. demi-rel., au chiffre de la République Française.

Nouveau fonds 3872.

6093. 大乘修行菩薩行門諸經要集
Ta cheng sieou hing phou sa hing mẹn tchou king yao tsi.

Mahāyāna caraṇa bodhisattva caryādvāra sarvasūtra mahārtha saṅgraha.

Collection sur la conduite d'un bodhisattva.

Frontispice (1 feuillet double). Traduction (721) par Tchi-yen, (Yu-tchhi Lo) de Khoten. Lecture des signes difficiles. Édition de la bonzerie de Tsi-tchao (1607).

3 livres. — Bunyiu Nanjio 1380.

Grand in-8. Belle impression. 1 vol. demi-rel., au chiffre de la République Française.

Nouveau fonds 273.

6094. — I.
大法鼓經
Ta fa kou king.

Mahābherī hāraka parivarta sūtra.

Traduction de Guṇabhadra. Lecture des signes difficiles.

2 livres. — Bunyiu Nanjio 440.

— II.
大方廣如來祕密藏經
Ta fang koang jou lai pi mi tsang king.

Tathāgata garbha sūtra.

Traduction de l'époque des Tshin (350-431). Liste des signes difficiles.

2 livres. — Bunyiu Nanjio 443.

— III.

如意輪陀羅尼經
Jou yi loen tho lo ni king.

Padmacintāmaṇi dhāraṇī sūtra.

Même ouvrage qu'au nº 5860, art. VIII. Lecture des caractères difficiles. Édition de Hoa-tchheng (1722).

1 livre. — Bunyiu Nanjio 324.

Grand in-8. Bonne gravure; frontispice (1 feuillet double). 1 vol. demi-rel., au chiffre de Napoléon III.

Nouveau fonds 1391.

6095. — I.

大方廣如來祕密藏經
Ta fang koang jou lai pi mi tsang king.

Tathāgata garbha sūtra.

Même ouvrage qu'au nº 6094, art. II.

— II.

唐三藏聖教序
Thang san tsang cheng kiao siu.

Préface pour le Tripiṭaka des Thang.

Par l'empereur Tchong-tsong (après 685).

2 feuillets.

— III.

大乘密嚴經
Ta cheng mi yen king.

Ghanavyūha sūtra.

Version de Divākara, Hindou (676-688). Liste des caractères difficiles.

3 livres. — Bunyiu Nanjio 444.

— IV.

南嶽思大禪師立誓願文
Nan yo seu ta chan chi li chi yuen oen.

Prière de Hoei-seu, du Nan-yo.

Auteur : Hoei-seu (✝ 577). Lecture des mots difficiles. Édition de Leng-yen seu; vérifié et gravé par Kiu-tchhe Tsi-sien (1676).

1 livre. — Bunyiu Nanjio 1576.

— V.

隋天台智者大師別傳
Soei thien thai tchi tche ta chi pie tchoan.

Vie de Tchi-tchẹ ta chi.

Nom bouddhique Tchi-yi, surnom Tẹ-'an, de la famille Tchhen, de Ying-tchhoan (†597). Vie écrite par son disciple Koan-ting. Liste des caractères difficiles. Mêmes lieu et date que l'art. précédent.

1 livre. — Bunyiu Nanjio 1577.

— VI.

止觀大意
Tchi koan ta yi.

Résumé du Mo ho tchi koan.

Par Tchan-jạn; tableaux et texte.

21 feuillets. — Bunyiu Nanjio 1578; cf. nᵒˢ 6485-6486.

— VII.

始終心要
Chi tchong sin yao.

Début et fin de l'importance du cœur.

Par le même, tableau et texte. Mêmes lieu et date que plus haut, art. V.

2 feuillets. — Bunyiu Nanjio 1579; cf. nᵒ 6499, art. II.

— VIII.

修懺要旨
Sieou tchhan yao tchi.

Par Tchi-li. Tableau et texte. Liste des caractères rares. Mêmes lieu et date.

17 feuillets. — Bunyiu Nanjio 1580.

— IX.

十不二門
Chi pou eul mẹn.

Sur les dix sujets inséparables.

Par Tchan-jan, de King-khi, extrait du Fa hoa hiuen yi chi tshien. Texte et tableaux. Mêmes lieu et date.

14 feuillets. — Bunyiu Nanjio 1581; cf. id. 1535.

Grand in-8. 1 vol. demi-rel., au chiffre de la République Française.
Nouveau fonds 3978.

6096. 大乘密嚴經
Ta cheng mi yen king.

Ghanavyūha sūtra.

Version par Amoghavajra, du même texte qu'au nᵒ 6095, art. III. Préface de l'empereur Tai-tsong (762-779). Lecture des signes rares. Édition de Hoa-tchheng 'an, au Han-chan.

3 livres. — Bunyiu Nanjio 971.

Grand in-8. Bonne gravure. 1 vol. demi-rel., au chiffre de la République Française.
Nouveau fonds 3859.

6097. — I.

佛說觀彌勒菩薩上生兜率陀天經

Fo choẹ koan mi lẹ phou sa chang cheng tcou ̓choai tho thien king.

Sūtra sur Maitreya bodhisattva qui va renaître au ciel Tuṣita.

Version par Tsiu-khiu King-cheng (455). Lecture des caractères rares. Édition de King-chan-seu (1597).

10 feuillets. — Bunyiu Nanjio 204.

— II.

佛說彌勒下生經

Fo choẹ mi lẹ hia cheng king; alias :

彌勒當來成佛

Mi lẹ tang lai tchheng fo.

Maitreya vyākaraṇa sūtra.

Version de Kumārajīva. Liste des mots difficiles. Mêmes lieu et date.

8 feuillets. — Bunyiu Nanjio 205.

— III.

佛說彌勒來時經

Fo choẹ mi lẹ lai chi king.

Maitreya vyākaraṇa sūtra.

Version du même texte (317-420). Lecture des mots rares. Mêmes lieu et date.

3 feuillets. — Bunyiu Nanjio 206.

— IV.

佛說彌勒下生成佛經

Fo choẹ mi lẹ hia cheng tchheng fo king.

Maitreya vyākaraṇa sūtra.

Version du même texte par Yi-tsing (701). Lecture des caractères difficiles. Édition des mêmes lieu et date.

8 feuillets. — Bunyiu Nanjio 207.

— V.

佛說觀彌勒菩薩下生經

Fo choẹ koan mi lẹ phou sa hia cheng king.

Sūtra sur la naissance de Maitreya.

Version par Tchou Fa-hou. Liste des termes rares. Mêmes lieu et date.

9 feuillets. — Bunyiu Nanjio 208.

— VI.

佛說彌勒成佛經

Fo choẹ mi lẹ tchheng fo king.

Maitreya prasthāna sūtra.

Version de Kumārajīva (402). Lecture des caractères rares. Édition de Hing-cheng oan-cheou chan-seu (1597).

21 feuillets. — Bunyiu Nanjio 209.

— VII.

佛說第一義法勝經

Fo choe ti yi yi fa cheng king.

Paramārthadharmavijaya sūtra.

Version de Gautama Prajñāruci (542) avec la collaboration de Than-lin; notice sur la traduction. Lecture des caractères difficiles. Mêmes lieu et date qu'à l'art. précédent.

16 feuillets. — Bunyiu Nanjio 210.

— VIII.

佛說大威燈光仙人問疑經

Fo choe ta oei teng koang sien jen oen yi king.

Paramārthadharmavijaya sūtra.

Version du même texte par Jñā-nagupta (586). Lecture des mots difficiles. Mêmes lieu et date.

18 feuillets. — Bunyiu Nanjio 211.

— IX.

一切法高王經

Yi tshie fa kao oang king.

Sarvadharmoccarāja sūtra.

Version de Gautama Prajñāruci (542). Liste des mots rares. Mêmes lieu et date; réédition partielle en 1670, 1681.

23 feuillets. — Bunyiu Nanjio 212.

Grand in-8. Bonne gravure. 1 vol. demi-rel., au chiffre de la République Française.

Nouveau fonds 4040.

6098. — I.

佛說諸法勇王經

Fo choe tchou fa yong oang king.

Sarvadharma nirbhayarāja sūtra.

Version par Dharmamitra (424-441), du même texte que Bunyiu Nanjio 212. Liste des caractères rares. Édition de Hing-cheng oan-cheou chan-seu (1593); feuillets gravés de nouveau en 1669 et 1691.

1 livre. — Bunyiu Nanjio 213; cf. n° 6097, art. IX.

— II.

順權方便經

Choen khiuen fang pien king.

Strīvivarta vyākaraṇa sūtra.

Version de Tchou Fa-hou. Lecture des mots difficiles. Édition de King chan seu (1593); feuillets gravés de nouveau en 1670 et 1682.

2 livres. — Bunyiu Nanjio 214.

— III.

佛說樂瓔珞莊嚴方便經

Fo choe lo ying lo tchoang yen fang pien king; alias :

轉女身菩薩問荅經

Tchoan niu chen phou sa oen ta king.

Strīvivarta vyākaraṇa sūtra.

Version du même texte par Dharmayaças, de Ki-pin (407-415). Liste des termes difficiles. Édition de Hing-cheng oan-cheou chan-seu (1593).

2 livres. — Bunyiu Nanjio 215.

— IV.

菩薩睒子經

Phou sa chan tseu king.

Sāmaputra bodhisattva sūtra.

Version sans nom d'auteur, de la dynastie des Tsin occidentaux

(265-316); le même texte se retrouve dans le n° 6179. Liste des caractères rares. Mêmes lieu et date.

7 feuillets. — Bunyiu Nanjio 216.

— V.

佛說睒子經

Fo choe chan tseu king.

Sāmaputra sūtra.

Version du même texte par Cheng-kien (388-407). Lecture des mots rares. Mêmes lieu d'édition (1597); gravé de nouveau en 1691.

7 feuillets. — Bunyiu Nanjio 217.

— VI.

佛說九色鹿經

Fo choe kieou se lou king.

Navavarṇamṛga sūtra.

Version par Tchi Khien. Édition de King-chan seu (1593).

3 feuillets. — Bunyiu Nanjio 218; cf. aussi n° 6179.

— VII.

佛說太子沐魄經

Fo choe thai tseu mou pho king.

Mūka kumāra sūtra.

Version par Tchou Fa-hou. Mêmes lieu et date.

4 feuillets. — Bunyiu Nanjio 219: cf. aussi n° 6179, art. VI.

— VIII.

太子慕魄經
Thai tseu mou pho king.

Mūka kumāra sūtra.

Version du même texte par 'An Chi-kao. Mêmes lieu et date.

6 feuillets. — Bunyiu Nanjio 220.

Grand in-8. Bonne gravure. 1 vol. demi-rel., au chiffre de la République Française.

Nouveau fonds 3975.

6099. — I.

月燈三昧經
Yue teng san mei king.

Candradīpa samādhi sūtra.

Version de Chi Sien-kong, Chinois (?), de la dynastie des Song (420-479), partie du même texte qu'au n° 6100.

1 livre. — Bunyiu Nanjio 192.

— II.

佛說象腋經
Fo choe siang yi king.

Hastikakṣyā sūtra.

Version de Dharmamitra (424-441). Liste des caractères rares.

1 livre. — Bunyiu Nanjio 193.

— III.

佛說無所希望經
Fo choe oou so hi oang king; alias :

象步經
Siang pou king.

Hastikakṣyā sūtra.

Version par Tchou Fa-hou, du même texte qu'à l'art. II. Liste des caractères rares. Édition de Leng-yen seu (1664).

1 livre. — Bunyiu Nanjio 194.

— IV.

佛說大乘同性經
Fo choe ta cheng thong sing king.

Mahāyānābhisamaya sūtra.

Version de Jñānayaças, Hindou, et Seng-'an (570). Liste des caractères rares.

2 livres. — Bunyiu Nanjio 195.

— V.

佛說證契大乘經
Fo choe tcheng khi ta cheng king.

Mahāyānābhisamaya sūtra.

Traduction du même texte qu'à l'art. IV par Divākara (680). Préface de l'impératrice Oou. Liste des signes rares.

2 livres. — Bunyiu Nanjio 196.

Grand in-8. Bonne gravure; frontispice (1 feuillet double). 1 vol. demi-rel., au chiffre de la République Française. *Nouveau fonds* 3891.

6100. 月燈三昧經
Yue teng san mei king.

Candradīpa samādhi sūtra.

Version par Narendrayaças (557-568), du texte complet du n° 6099, art. I. Lecture des caractères rares. Édition de 1645 (?).

11 livres. — Bunyiu Nanjio 191.

Grand in-8. Bonne gravure. 1 vol. demi-rel , au chiffre de la République Française. *Nouveau fonds* 4001.

6101. — I.
無字寶篋經
Oou tseu pao khie king.

Anakṣara granthaka rocana-garbha sūtra.

Version de Bodhiruci (508-535). Liste des mots rares. Édition de

Hing-cheng oan-cheou chạn-seu (1593).

7 feuillets. — Bunyiu Nanjio 221,

— II.
大乘離文字普光明藏 經
Ta cheng li oen tseu phou koang ming tsang king.

Anakṣara granthaka rocana-garbha sūtra.

Version du même texte par Divākara (683). Lecture des caractères rares. Édition des mêmes lieu et date.

5 feuillets. — Bunyiu Nanjio 222.

— III.
大乘徧照光明藏無字 法門經
Ta cheng pien tchao koang ming tsang oou tseu fa mẹn king.

Anakṣara granthaka rocana-garbha sūtra.

Autre version du même texte par Divākara. Lecture des signes difficiles. Édition des mêmes lieu et date.

7 feuillets. — Bunyiu Nanjio 223.

— IV.

佛說老女人經

Fo choẹ lao niu jen king.

Vṛddhastrī sūtra.

Version de Tchi Khien. Lecture des caractères difficiles. Mêmes lieu et date.

2 feuillets. — Bunyiu Nanjio 224.

— V.

佛說老母經

Fo choẹ lao mou king.

Vṛddhamātṛ sūtra.

Même texte, traduit à l'époque des Song (420-479). Liste des caractères rares. Mêmes lieu et date.

3 feuillets. — Bunyiu Nanjio 225.

— VI.

佛說老母女六英經

Fo choẹ lao mou niu lou ying king.

Ṣaṭpuṣpā vṛddhamātṛ sūtra.

Version du même texte par Guṇabhadra (435-443). Liste des caractères difficiles. Mêmes lieu et date.

1 feuillet. — Bunyiu Nanjio 226.

— VII.

佛說長者子制經

Fo choẹ tchang tchẹ tseu tchi king.

Jeta çreṣṭhi putra sūtra.

Version de 'An Chi-kao (148-170). Liste des mots difficiles. Mêmes lieu et date.

5 feuillets. — Bunyiu Nanjio 227.

— VIII.

佛說菩薩逝經

Fo choe phou sa chi king.

Jeta bodhisattva sūtra.

Version du même texte par Po Fa-tsou (Oan Yuen), Chinois de Ho-nei, traducteur en 290-306. Mêmes lieu et date.

4 feuillets. — Bunyiu Nanjio 228.

— IX.

佛說逝童子經

Fo choe chi thong tseu king.

Jeta kumāra sūtra.

Version du même texte par Tchi Fa-tou, d'origine inconnue (301). Liste des caractères difficiles. Mêmes lieu et date.

4 feuillets. — Bunyiu Nanjio 229.

— X.

佛說月光童子經

Fo choe yue koang thong tseu king; alias :

申日經

Chen ji king.

Candraprabha kumāra sūtra.

Version de Tchou Fa-hou. Lecture des mots rares. Mémes lieu et date.

10 feuillets. — Bunyiu Nanjio 230.

— XI.

佛說申日兒本經

Fo choe chen ji eul pęn king.

Candraprabha kumāra sūtra.

Autre version par Guṇabhadra. Mêmes lieu et date.

3 feuillets. — Bunyiu Nanjio 231.

— XII.

佛說德護長者經

Fo choe tę hou tchang tchę king.

Çrīgupta sūtra.

Version du même texte par Narendrayaças (583). Mêmes lieu et date.

2 livres. — Bunyiu Nanjio 232.

— XIII.

佛說犢子經

Fo choe tou tseu king.

Vatsa sūtra.

Version de Tchi Khien. Liste des mots rares. Mêmes lieu et date.

2 feuillets. — Bunyiu Nanjio 233.

— XIV.

佛說乳光佛經

Fo choe jou koang fo king.

Vatsa sūtra.

Traduction du même texte par Tchou Fa-hou. Lecture des mots difficiles. Mêmes lieu et date.

7 feuillets. — Bunyiu Nanjio 234.

— XV.

佛說無垢賢女經

Fo choe oou keou hien niu king.

Strīvivarta vyākaraṇa sūtra.

Version par Tchou Fa-hou, du même texte qu'au n° 6098, art. II et III. Liste des signes rares. Mêmes lieu et date.

4 feuillets. — Bunyiu Nanjio 235.

— XVI.

佛說腹中女聽經

Fo choę fou tchong niu thing king.

Strīvivarta vyākaraṇa sūtra.

Version du même texte par Dharmarakṣa (414-421). Lecture des caractères difficiles. Mêmes lieu et date.

3 feuillets. — Bunyiu Nanjio 236.

Grand in-8. Bonne gravure. 1 vol. demi-rel., au chiffre de la République Française.

Nouveau fonds 3915.

6102. — 1.

佛說銀色女經

Fo choę yin sę niu king.

Rūpyavarṇastrī sūtra.

Version par Buddhaçānta (539), du même texte que Bunyiu Nanjio 270. Lecture des mots rares.

8 feuillets. — Bunyiu Nanjio 271.

— II.

佛說阿闍世王受決經

Fo choę 'o chę chi oang cheou kiue king.

Buddhabhāṣitājātaçatru rāja vyākaraṇa sūtra.

Version par Fa-kiu, d'origine inconnue (290-306). Liste des caractères rares.

5 feuillets. — Bunyiu Nanjio 272.

— III.

探華達王上佛授 (sic) 決經

Tshai hoa oei oang chang fo cheou kiue king.

Sūtra sur une prophétie reçue du Bouddha.

Version par Tchou Than-ooulan (Dharmarakṣa), Occidental (381-395), du même texte qu'à l'art. précédent. Lecture des mots rares. Édition de Tsi-tchao 'au (1610).

3 feuillets. — Bunyiu Nanjio 273.

— IV.

佛說正恭敬經

Fo choę tcheng kong king king.

Supūjā sūtra.

Version par Buddhaçānta (539). Lecture des caractères difficiles. Édition de Tsi-tchao 'an (1610).

6 feuillets. — Bunyiu Nanjio 274.

— V.

佛說善恭敬經

Fo choẹ chạn kong king king.

Supūjā sūtra.

Version du même texte par Jñānagupta (585-592). Lecture des caractères rares.

8 feuillets. — Bunyiu Nanjio 275.

— VI.

稱讚大乘功德經

Tchheng tsan ta cheng kong tẹ king.

Mahāyānaguṇastuti sūtra.

Version de Hiuen-tsang (654). Lecture des mots rares.

5 feuillets. — Bunyiu Nanjio 276.

— VII.

妙法決定業障經

Miao fa kiue ting ye tchang king.

Sūtra sur la bonne loi.

Traduction du même texte par Tchi-yen, de Khoten (721). Édition de Tsi-tchao 'an (1607).

4 feuillets. — Bunyiu Nanjio 277.

— VIII.

佛說貝多樹下思惟十二因緣經

Fo choẹ pei to chou hia seu oei chi eul yin yuen king; alias :

聞城十二因緣經

Oen tchheng chi eul yin yuen king.

Pratītyasamutpāda sūtra.

Version de Tchi Khien. Liste des caractères rares.

5 feuillets. — Bunyiu Nanjio 278.

— IX.

佛說緣起聖道經

Fo choẹ yuen khi cheng tao king.

Pratītyasamutpāda sūtra.

Version du même texte par Hiuen-tsang (649). Lecture des mots difficiles.

5 feuillets. — Bunyiu Nanjio 279.

— X.

佛說稻稈經

Fo choẹ tao kan king.

Çālisambhava sūtra.

Version de l'époque des Tsin orientaux (317-420). Liste des caractères difficiles. Édition de Tsi-tchao 'an (1610).

8 feuillets. — Bunyiu Nanjio 280; cf. n° 6140, art. IV, n° 6170, art. XIII.

— XI.

佛 說 了 本 生 死 經

Fo choę liao pęn cheng seu king.

Çālisambhava sūtra.

Version du même texte, par Tchi Khien. Lecture des caractères difficiles.

6 feuillets. — Bunyiu Nanjio 281.

— XII.

佛 說 自 誓 三 昧 經

Fo choę tseu chi san mei king.

Sūtra sur le samādhi appelé vœu.

Version de 'An Chi-kao. Liste des caractères rares.

9 feuillets. — Bunyiu Nanjio 282.

— XIII.

如 來 獨 證 自 誓 三 昧 經

Jou lai tou tcheng tseu chi san mei king.

Sūtra sur le samādhi appelé vœu.

Version du même texte par Tchou Fa-hou. Liste des mots rares. Édition de Hoa-tchheng seu (1612).

8 feuillets. — Bunyiu Nanjio 283.

— XIV.

佛 說 轉 有 經

Fo choę tchoan yeou king.

Bhavasaṅkrāmita sūtra.

Version de Buddhaçānta.

2 feuillets. — Bunyiu Nanjio 284.

— XV.

大 方 等 修 多 羅 王 經

Ta fang teng sieou to lo oang king.

Bhavasaṅkrāmita sūtra.

Version du même texte par Bodhiruci (508-535).

3 feuillets. — Bunyiu Nanjio 285.

— XVI.

佛 說 文 殊 師 利 巡 行 經

Fo choę oen chou chi li siun hing king.

Mañjuçrī vihāra sūtra.

Version de Bodhiruci (508-535).

7 feuillets. — Bunyiu Nanjio 286.

— XVII.

佛說文殊尸利行經

Fo choẹ oen chou chi li hing king.

Mañjuçrī vihāra sūtra.

Traduction du même texte par Jñānagupta (586). Lecture des caractères difficiles. Édition de Tsi-tchao 'an (1610).

9 feuillets. — Bunyiu Nanjio 287.

Graud in-8. Bonne gravure. 1 vol. demi-rel., au chiffre de la République Française.

Nouveau fonds 3930.

6103. — I.

佛說藥師如來本願經

Fo choẹ yo chi jou lai pẹn yuen king.

Bheṣajyaguru pūrvapraṇidhāna sūtra.

Version de Dharmagupta (615). Préface. Lecture des caractères rares. Édition de Leng-yen seu (1664).

1 livre. — Bunyiu Nanjio 170; cf. nº 6203, art. XII.

— II.

藥師瑠璃光如來本願功德經

Yo chi lieou li koang jou lai pẹn yuen kong tẹ king.

Bheṣajyaguru vaiḍūryapra-bhāsa pūrvapraṇidhāna sūtra.

Version du même texte par Hiuen-tsang (650). Liste des signes rares. Édition de 1611.

1 livre. — Bunyiu Nanjio 171.

— III.

藥師瑠璃光七佛本願功德經

Yo chi lieou li koang tshi fo pẹn yuen kong tẹ king.

Saptatathāgata pūrvapraṇi-dhāna viçeṣa vistara sūtra.

Version du même texte par Yi-tsing (707). Liste des signes rares. Édition de Tsï-tchao 'an (1608).

2 livres. — Bunyiu Nanjio 172.

— IV.

佛說阿闍世王經

Fo choẹ 'o chẹ chi oang king.

Ajātaçatru kaukṛtya vinodana sūtra.

Version de Tchi Leou-kia-tchhan (186). Liste des caractères rares. Édition de Hoa-tchheng seu (1631).

2 livres. — Bunyiu Nanjio 174.

Grand in-8. Bonne gravure. 1 vol. demi-rel., au chiffre de la République Française.

Nouveau fonds 3892.

6104. 御筆藥師瑠璃光 如來本願功德經

Yu pi yo chi lieou li koang jou lai pęn yuen kong tę king.

Bheṣajyaguru vaiḍūryaprabhāsa pūrvapraṇidhāna sūtra, texte transcrit par l'Empereur.

Traduction de Hiuen-tsang (650). Illustrations très fines : 1 grande planche (2 feuillets simples) au début, 1 planche à la fin, 43 planches, scènes diverses, répandues dans le texte. Transcrit au Yuenming yuen (1758).

Nº 6103, art. II.

In-4. Belle impression. 1 vol. paravent, couverture soie, dans un étui cartonnage.

Nouveau fonds 2398.

6105.

Yo chi lieou li koang jou lai pęn yuen kong tę king.

Même ouvrage. Frontispice, deux feuillets doubles, représentant des saints autour du Bouddha, une tablette votive. A la fin du texte, formules de prières. Gravé à la bonzerie de Hai-tchhoang (1805).

Nº 6103, art. II.

In-4. Papier blanc. 1 vol. en paravent, couverture rouge ; renfermé dans un étui demi-rel., au chiffre de Louis-Philippe.

Nouveau fonds 132.

6106. — I.

普超三昧經

Phou tchhao san mei king.

Ajātaçatru kaukṛtya vinodana sutra.

Version de Tchou Fa-hou (286). Liste des termes rares.

4 livres. — Bunyiu Nanjio 182 ; voir nº 6103, art. IV.

— II.

佛說放鉢經

Fo choę fang po king.

Ajātaçatru kaukṛtya vinodana sūtra.

Version d'une partie du texte précédent, de la dynastie des Tsin occidentaux (265-316). Lecture des mots difficiles.

1 livre. — Bunyiu Nanjio 183.

— III

佛說大淨法門品經

Fo choę ta tsing fa męn phin king.

Mañjuçrī vikrīḍita sūtra.

Version de Tchou Fa-hou (313).
Liste des caractères difficiles. Edition de Hoa-tchheng seu (1631).

1 livre. — Bunyiu Nanjio 184.

Grand in-8. Bonne gravure; frontispice (1 feuillet double). 1 vol. demi-rel.,
au chiffre de la République Française.
Nouveau fonds 4003.

6107. — I.

大莊嚴法門經

Ta tchoang yen fa meṇ king.

Mañjuçrī vikrīḍita sūtra.

Traduction de Narendrayaças
(583). Liste des caractères rares.
Édition de Tsi-tchao 'an (1609).

2 livres. — Bunyiu Nanjio 185;
n° 6106, art. III.

— II.

佛說大方等大雲請雨經

*Fo choṇ ta fang teng ta yun
tshing yu king.*

Mahāmegha sūtra.

Version de Jñānagupta (585-
592). Lecture des signes rares.
Édition du bonze Tchhe-oei Yin-
khai (1661).

1 livre. — Bunyiu Nanjio 186; cf.
n° 6109.

— III.

大雲請雨經

Ta yun tshing yu king.

Mahāmegha sūtra.

Version par Jñānayaças (564-
572), du même texte que ci-dessus.
Liste des caractères difficiles.

1 livre. — Bunyiu Nanjio 187.

— IV.

大雲輪請雨經

Ta yun loeṇ tshing yu king.

Mahāmegha sūtra.

Version par Narendrayaças (585)
du même texte que plus haut.
Liste des signes rares. Édition de
Tsi-tchao 'an (1661).

2 livres. — Bunyiu Nanjio 188.

Grand in-8. Bonne gravure. 1 vol.
demi-rel., au chiffre de la République
Française.
Nouveau fonds 3877.

6108. — I.

佛說未曾有正法經

*Fo choṇ oei tsheng yeou tcheng
fa king.*

Adbhuta saddharma sūtra.

Version du même texte qu'au n° 6106, art. I, par Fa-thien. Liste des caractères rares. Édition de Hoa-tchheng seu (1613).

6 livres. — Bunyiu Nanjio 925.

— II.

佛說大方廣善巧方便經

Fo choẹ ta fang koang chạn khiao fang pien king.

Jñānottara bodhisattva paripr̥cchā sūtra.

Version par Chi-hou, du texte de Bunyiu Nanjio 23 (38) et 52. Lecture des mots difficiles. Mêmes lieu et date.

4 livres. — Bunyiu Nanjio 926; cf. n° 5806, art. XXXVIII.

Grand in-8. Bonne gravure. 1 vol. demi-rel., au chiffre de la République Française.
Nouveau fonds 4027.

6109. 大方等大雲經
Ta fang teng ta yun king.

Mahāmegha sūtra.

Version par Dharmarakṣa (414-421), du même texte qu'au n° 6107, art. II. Liste des signes rares. Édition de Tsi-tchao 'an (1599).

4 livres. — Bunyiu Nanjio 244.

Grand in-8. Bonne gravure. 1 vol. demi-rel., au chiffre de la République Française.
Nouveau fonds 3878.

6110. — I.

大乘造像功德經
Ta cheng tsao siang kong tẹ king.

Tathāgata pratibimba pratiṣṭhānuçaṃsā sūtra.

Version de Devaprajña (691). Lecture des caractères rares. Édition de Hing-cheng oan-cheou chạn-seu (1593).

2 livres. — Bunyiu Nanjio 288.

— II.

佛說作佛形像經
Fo choẹ tso fo hing siang king.

Tathāgata pratibimba pratiṣṭhānuçaṃsā sūtra.

Version du même texte, de l'époque des Han orientaux (25-220). Liste des signes difficiles. Édition de King-chan seu (1597).

3 feuillets. — Bunyiu Nanjio 289.

— III.

佛說造立形像福報經
Fo choẹ tsao li hing siang fou pao king.

Tathāgata pratibimba pratiṣṭhānuçaṃsā sūtra.

Version du même texte que ci-dessus, des Tsin orientaux (317-420). Lecture des mots rares. Même lieu, même date.

5 feuillets. — Bunyiu Nanjio 290.

— IV.

佛說灌佛經

Fo choẹ koan fo king; alias :

灌洗佛形像經

Koan si fo hing siang king.

Sūtra relatif au lavage des images du Bouddha.

Traduction de Fa-kiu. Lecture des mots difficiles. Mêmes lieu et date d'édition.

2 feuillets. — Bunyiu Nanjio 291.

— V.

佛說灌洗佛經

Fo choẹ koan si fo king; alias :

摩訶刹頭經

Mo ho tchha theou king.

Buddhābhiṣeka sūtra.

Version du même texte par Cheng-kien (388-407). Liste des caractères rares. Mêmes lieu et date.

4 feuillets. — Bunyiu Nanjio 292.

— VI.

佛說浴像功德經

Fo choẹ yu siang kong tẹ king.

Pratibimbābhiṣekaguṇa sūtra.

Version de Ratnacinta (705). Lecture des signes difficiles. Mêmes lieu et date.

4 feuillets. — Bunyiu Nanjio 293.

— VII.

浴像功德經

Yu siang kong tẹ king.

Pratibimbābhiṣekaguṇa sūtra.

Version du même texte par Yi-tsing (710). Liste des caractères rares. Mêmes lieu et date ; feuillets gravés de nouveau en 1669.

5 feuillets. — Bunyiu Nanjio 294.

— VIII.

佛說校量數珠功德經

Fo choẹ kiao liang chou tchou kong tẹ king.

Sūtra sur le mérite du rosaire.

Version de Ratnacinta (705). Liste des signes rares. Mêmes lieu et date.

2 feuillets. — Bunyiu Nanjio 295.

— IX.

曼殊室利咒藏中校量數珠功德經

Man chou chi li tcheou tsang tchong kiao liang chou tchou kong tẹ king.

Sūtra sur le mérite du rosaire.

Version du même texte par Yitsing (703). Mêmes lieu et date.

2 feuillets. — Bunyiu Nanjio 296.

— X.

佛說龍施女經

Fo choẹ long chi niu king.

Nāgadattā dārikā sūtra.

Version de Tchi Khien. Mêmes lieu et date.

3 feuillets. — Bunyiu Nanjio 297.

— XI.

佛說龍施菩薩本起經

Fo choẹ long chi phou sa pẹn khi king.

Nāgadattā bodhisattva nidāna sūtra.

Version du même texte par Tchou Fa-hou. Lecture des caractères rares. Mêmes lieu et date.

5 feuillets. — Bunyiu Nanjio 298.

— XII.

佛說八吉祥神咒經

Fo choẹ pa ki siang chen tcheou king.

Aṣṭabuddhaka sūtra.

Version de Tchi Khien. Liste des mots rares. Mêmes lieu et date.

4 feuillets. — Bunyiu Nanjio 299.

— XIII.

佛說八陽神咒經

Fo choẹ pa yang chen tcheou king.

Aṣṭabuddhaka sūtra.

Version du même texte par Tchou Fa-hou. Lecture des caractères difficiles. Mêmes lieu et date.

3 feuillets. — Bunyiu Nanjio 300.

— XIV.

佛說八吉祥經

Fo choẹ pa ki siang king.

Aṣṭabuddhaka sūtra.

Version du même texte par Saṅghapāla (506-520). Mêmes lieu et date.

3 feuillets. — Bunyiu Nanjio 301.

— XV.

佛說八佛名號經

Fo choẹ pa fo ming hao king.

Aṣṭabuddhaka sūtra.

Version du même texte par Jñānagupta (586). Lecture des caractères rares. Mêmes lieu et date.

5 feuillets. — Bunyiu Nanjio 302.

— XVI.

佛說盂蘭盆經

Fo choẹ yu lan phẹn king.

Ullambana sūtra.

Même texte qu'au n° 5734, art. VI. Liste des mots difficiles. Mêmes lieu et date.

2 feuillets.

— XVII.

佛說報恩奉盆經

Fo choẹ pao 'en fong phẹn king; alias:

報像功德經

Pao siang kong tẹ king.

Ullambanapātra sūtra.

Version du même texte, de l'époque des Tsin orientaux (317-420). Mêmes lieu et date.

1 feuillet. — Bunyiu Nanjio 304.

— XVIII.

佛說觀藥王藥上二菩薩經

Fo choẹ koan yo oang yo chang eul phou sa king

Bhaiṣajyarāja bhaiṣajyasamudgati sūtra.

Version de Kālayaças (424). Liste des caractères rares. Mêmes lieu et date.

1 livre. — Bunyiu Nanjio 305.

Grand in-8. Bonne gravure. 1 vol. demi-rel., au chiffre de la République Française.
Nouveau fonds 3910.

6111. 佛說盂蘭盆經疏

Fo choẹ yu lan phẹn king sou.

Commentaire sur l'Ullambana sūtra.

Par Tsong-mi. Impression de la bonzerie de Pao-'en, datée de l'année yi-yeou.

26

2 livres. — Bunyiu Nanjio 1601 ; **cf. n° 6110, art. XVI.**

Petit in-8. Papier blanc ; frontispice (1 feuillet double). 1 vol. demi-reliure. *Nouveau fonds* 69.

6112. — I.

佛說內藏百寶經

Fo choę nei tsang po pao king.

Lokānusamānāvatāra sūtra.

Version de Tchi Leou-kia-tchhan.

8 feuillets. — Bunyiu Nanjio 386.

— II.

佛說溫室洗浴衆僧經

Fo choę oen chi si yu tchong seng king.

Sūtra sur l'invitation au bain adressée aux religieux.

Version par 'An Chi-kao.

4 feuillets. — Bunyiu Nanjio 387.

— III.

佛說菩薩行五十緣身經

Fo choę phou sa hing oou chi yuen chen king.

Sūtra sur les marques caractéristiques du Bouddha.

Version de Tchou Fa-hou.

7 feuillets. — Bunyiu Nanjio 388.

— IV.

佛說菩薩修行經

Fo choę phou sa sieou hing king.

Sūtra sur la pratique de la condition de bodhisattva.

Version de Po Fa-tsou. Lecture des caractères rares. Édition de Hoa-tchheng seu (1628).

11 feuillets. — Bunyiu Nanjio 389.

— V.

佛說金色王經

Fo choę kin sę oang king.

Kanakavarṇa pūrvayoga sūtra.

Version de Gautama Prajñāruci (542), transcrite par Than-lin.

11 feuillets. — Bunyiu Nanjio 390.

— VI.

佛語法門經

Fo yu fa męn king.

Dharmaparyāya sūtra.

Version de Bodhiruci (508-535). Lecture des mots difficiles.

5 feuillets. — Bunyiu Nanjio 391.

— VII.

佛 說 四 不 可 得 經

Fo choe seu pou kho te king.

Caturdurlabha sūtra.

Version de Tchou Fa-hou. Édition de Leng-yen seu (1666).

6 feuillets. — Bunyiu Nanjio 392.

— VIII.

須 眞 天 子 經

Siu tchen thien tseu king.

Suvikrānta devaputra sūtra.

Du même. Lecture des caractères rares.

2 livres. — Bunyiu Nanjio 393.

— IX.

佛 說 觀 普 賢 菩 薩 行 法 經

Fo choe koan phou hien phou sa hing fa king; alias :

觀 普 賢 觀 經

Koan phou hien koan king; alias :

出 深 功 德 經

Tchhou chen kong te king.

Samantabhadra bodhisattva dhyāna caryādharma sūtra.

Version de Dharmamitra (424-441). Lecture des mots difficiles.

18 feuillets. — Bunyiu Nanjio 394.

Grand in-8. Bonne gravure. 1 vol. demi-rel., au chiffre de la République Française.

Nouveau fonds 4035.

6113. — I.

成 具 光 明 定 意 經

Tchheng kiu koang ming ting yi king.

Pūrṇaprabhāsa samādhimati sūtra.

Version de Tchi Yao, Yue-tchi (185). Lecture des signes difficiles. Édition de Hoa-tchheng seu (1627).

1 livre. — Bunyiu Nanjio 381.

— II.

摩 訶 摩 耶 經

Mo ho mo ye king ; alias :

佛 昇 忉 利 天 爲 母 說 法 經

Fo cheng tao li thien oei mou choe fa king.

Mahāmāyā sūtra.

Version de Than-kiug, d'origine douteuse (dynastie des Tshi 479-502). Lecture des signes rares.

Édition de l'association Hong-fa, à Song-kiang (1643).

2 livres. — Bunyiu Nanjio 382; cf. n° 6086, art. II.

— III.

諸德福田經

Tchou tę fou thien king.

Sarvaguṇa puṇyakṣetra sūtra.

Version de Fa-li et Fa-kiu, d'origine inconnue (290-306).

7 feuillets. — Bunyiu Nanjio 383.

— IV.

大方等如來藏經

Ta fang teng jou lai tsang king.

Tathāgatagarbha sūtra.

Version de Buddhabhadra. Liste des signes rares. Édition de Hoa-tchheng seu (1629).

13 feuillets. — Bunyiu Nanjio 384.

— V.

佛說寶網經

Fo choę pao oang king.

Ratnajāli paripṛcchā sūtra.

Version de Tchou Fa-hou. Lecture des caractères rares.

1 livre. — Bunyiu Nanjio 385.

Grand in-8. Bonne gravure. 1 vol. demi-rel., au chiffre de la République Française.

Nouveau fonds 3899.

6114. 大方便佛報恩經

Ta fang pien fo pao 'en king.

Sūtra de la reconnaissance du Bouddha pour les bienfaits.

Version de l'époque des Han postérieurs (25-220). Lecture des caractères difficiles. Édition de Tsi-tchao 'an (1598).

7 livres. — Bunyiu Nanjio 431.

Grand in-8. 1 vol. demi-rel., au chiffre de la République Française.

Nouveau fonds 3967.

6115. — I.

菩薩道樹經

Phou sa tao chou king; alias :

私呵昧經

Seu ho mei king; alias :

私呵三昧經

Seu ho san mei king; alias :

道樹三昧經

Tao chou san mei king.

Bodhisattva bodhivṛkṣa sūtra.

Version de Tchi Khien. Liste des signes rares.

1 livre. — Bunyiu Nanjio 377.

— II.

菩薩生地經

Phou sa cheng ti king.

Kṣāmākāra bodhisattva sūtra.

Du même. Liste des signes rares.

4 feuillets. — Bunyiu Nanjio 378.

— III.

佛說字經

Fo choę po king ; alias :

字經抄

Po king tchhao.

Sūtra relatif à Puṣya (?).

Du même. Liste des signes rares. Édition de Leng-yen seu (1637).

1 livre. — Bunyiu Nanjio 379.

— IV.

無垢淨光大陀羅尼經

Oou keou tsing koang ta tho lo ni king.

Vimalaçuddhaprabhāsa mahā-dhāraṇī sūtra.

Version de Mi-tho-chan (Mitra-çānta), du Tokharestan (705). Lecture des caractères rares. Édition de Leng-yen seu (1663).

1 livre. — Bunyiu Nanjio 380.

Grand in-8. Bonne gravure. 1 vol. demi-rel., au chiffre de la République Française.

Nouveau fonds 3898.

6116. — I.

佛說海龍王經

Fo choę hai long oang king.

Sāgara nāgarāja paripṛcchā sūtra.

Version de Tchou Fa-hou. Liste des caractères rares. Édition du Hoa-yen ko (1642).

4 livres. — Bunyiu Nanjio 456.

— II.

佛爲海龍王說法印經

Fo oei hai long oang choę fa yin king.

Sāgara nāgarāja paripṛcchā sūtra.

Version de Yi-tsing (711). Mêmes lieu et date.

1 feuillet. — Bunyiu Nanjio 457.

— III.

右遶 (sic) 佛塔功德經

Yeou jao fo tha kong tẹ king.

Caitya pradakṣiṇa gāthā sūtra.

Version de Çikṣānanda. Mêmes lieu et date.

4 feuillets. — Bunyiu Nanjio 458.

— IV.

佛說妙色王因緣經

Fo choẹ miao sẹ oang yin yuen king.

Buddhabhāṣita suvarṇa rāja nidāna sūtra.

Version de Yi-tsing (701). Mêmes lieu et date.

4 feuillets. — Bunyiu Nanjio 459.

— V.

師子素馱娑王斷肉經

Chi tseu sou tho so oang toan jeou king.

Sūtra sur le roi Saudāsa, fils d'une lionne, coupant sa chair.

Version de Tchi-yen, de Khoten (721). Même lieu, même date.

5 feuillets. — Bunyiu Nanjio 460.

— VI.

差摩婆帝受記經

Tchha mo po ti cheou ki king.

Kṣamāvatī vyākaraṇa sūtra.

Version de Bodhiruci (519-524). Mêmes lieu et date.

5 feuillets. — Bunyiu Nanjio 461.

— VII.

師子莊嚴王菩薩請問 經

Chi tseu tchoang yen oang phou sa tshing oen king.

Siṃhavyūharāja bodhisattva paripṛcchā sūtra.

Version de Na-thi (Nadi), Hindou (663). Préface par Tao-siuen. Lecture des caractères rares. Mêmes lieu et date.

4 feuillets. — Bunyiu Nanjio 462.

Grand in-8. Bonne gravure. 1 vol. demi-rel., au chiffre de la République Française.

Nouveau fonds 3903.

6117. — I.

三昧弘道廣顯定意經

San mei hong tao koang hien ting yi king; alias :

入金剛問定意經

Jou kin kang oen ting yi king.

Anavatapta nāgarāja paripṛcchā sūtra.

Version de Tchou Fa-hou (308). Liste des caractères rares.

4 livres. — Bunyiu Nanjio 437.

— II.

佛說明度五十校計經

Fo choṣ ming tou oou chi kiao ki king.

Daçadigbodhisattva sūtra.

Version de 'An Chi-kao (151). Lecture des mots rares.

2 livres. — Bunyiu Nanjio 438.

Grand in-8. Bonne gravure. 1 vol. demi-rel., au chiffre de la République Française.
Nouveau fonds 4005.

6118. — I.

佛說寶網經

Fo choṣ pao oang king.

Ratnajāli paripṛcchā sūtra.

Même ouvrage qu'au n° 6113, art. V.

30 feuillets (incomplet).

— II.

菩薩道樹經

Phou sa tao chou king.

Bodhisattva bodhivṛkṣa sūtra.

Même ouvrage qu'au n° 6115, art. I.

1 livre (débute au feuillet 8).

— III.

菩薩生地經

Phou sa cheng ti king.

Kṣāmākāra bodhisattva sūtra.

Même ouvrage qu'au n° 6115, art. II.

— IV.

摩訶摩耶經

Mo ho mo ye king.

Mahāmāyā sūtra.

Même ouvrage qu'au n° 6113, art. II.

2 livres (le 2ᵉ incomplet à la fin).

— V.

三具足經優波提舍

Trisaṃbhāva sūtropadeça.

Composé par le bodhisattva Vasubandhu; traduit par Vimokṣa-prajñarṣi, Hindou, en 541.

1 livre (incomplet à la fin). — Bunyiu Nanjio 1196.

— VI.

佛說了本生死經

Fo choę liao pęn cheng seu king.

Çālisambhava sūtra.

Même ouvrage qu'au n° 6102, art. XI.

— VII.

佛說自誓三昧經

Fo choę tseu chi san mei king.

Sūtra sur le samādhi appelé vœu.

Même ouvrage qu'au n° 6102, art. XII.

— VIII.

如來獨證自誓三昧經

Jou lai tou tcheng tseu chi san mei king.

Même ouvrage qu'au n° 6102, art. XIII.

— IX.

不空羂索神咒心經

Pou khong kiuen so chen tcheou sin king.

Amoghapāça hṛdaya sūtra.

Même ouvrage qu'au n° 6062, art. IV.

Grand in-8. Bonne impression, 1 vol. demi-rel., au chiffre de Napoléon III. *Nouveau fonds* 1230.

6119. 菩薩瓔珞經

Phou sa ying lo king; alias :

現在報經

Hien tsai pao king.

Bodhisattvamālā sūtra.

Version de Tchou Fo-nien, Chinois de Liang-tcheou (376). Lecture des caractères rares. Édition de 1645, 1646.

10 livres. — Bunyiu Nanjio 445.

Grand in-8. Bonne gravure; frontispice (1 feuillet double); manque le feuillet final du livre 1. 1 vol. demi-rel., au chiffre de la République Française. *Nouveau fonds* 3873.

6120. — I.

中陰經

Tchong yin king.

Antarā bhava sūtra.

Traduction de Tchou Fo-nien (374-394). Édition de Hoa-tchheng seu (1627, 1628).

2 livres. — Bunyiu Nanjio 463.

— II.

占察善惡業報經

Tchan tchha chan 'o ye pao king.

Sūtra sur la recherche par la divination des résultats du bien et du mal.

Version de Phou-thi-teng (Bodhidīpa), étranger (époque des Soei): le texte est extrait du Lou ken tsiu king. Édition de Hoa-tchheng seu (1632); feuillets gravés de nouveau en 1691.

2 livres. — Bunyiu Nanjio 464.

— III.

佛說蓮華面經

Fo choe lien hoa mien king.

Padmamukha sūtra.

Version de Narendrayaças. Liste des mots rares. Édition de Hoa-tchheng seu (1628).

2 livres. — Bunyiu Nanjio 465.

— IV.

佛說三品弟子經

Fo choe san phin ti tseu king; alias :

弟子學有三輩

Ti tseu hio yeou san pei.

Trivargaçisya sūtra.

Version de Tchi Khien. Édition du Hoa-yen ko (1642).

3 feuillets. — Bunyiu Nanjio 466.

— V.

佛說四輩經

Fo choe seu pei king; alias :

四輩學經

Seu pei hio king.

Caturvarga çisya sūtra.

Version de Tchou Fa-hou. Mêmes lieu et date.

4 feuillets. — Bunyiu Nanjio 467.

— VI.

佛說當來變經

Fo choe tang lai pien king.

Anāgatavikriyā sūtra.

Du même.

3 feuillets. — Bunyiu Nanjio 468.

— VII.

過去佛分衛經

Koo khiu fo fẹn oei king.

Atīta buddha paiṇḍapātika sū-tra.

Du même. Lecture des carac-tères rares.

2 feuillets. — Bunyiu Nanjio 469.

— VIII.

佛說法滅盡經

Fo choẹ fa mie tsin king.

Dharmavināça sūtra.

Version de la dynastie des Song (420-479). Mêmes lieu et date qu'à l'art. IV.

3 feuillets. — Bunyiu Nanjio 470.

— IX.

佛說甚深大迴向經

Fo choẹ chen chen ta hoei hiang king.

Avaropita kuçalamūla sūtra.

Version de la même époque; mêmes lieu et date.

5 feuillets. — Bunyiu Nanjio 471.

— X.

天王太子辟羅經

Thien oang thai tseu phi lo king.

Devarāja kumāra sūtra.

Version des dynasties Tshin (350-431). Mêmes lieu et date.

2 feuillets. — Bunyiu Nanjio 472.

Grand in-8. Bonne gravure. 1 vol. demi-rel., au chiffre de la République Française.

Nouveau fonds 3949.

6121. 占察善惡業報經疏

Tchạn tchha chạn 'o ye pao king sou.

Le sūtra sur la recherche, etc.

Commentaire de Tchi-hiu (xviie siècle).

2 livres. — Cf. n° 6120, art. II.

Grand in-8. 1 vol. demi-rel., au chiffre de la République Française.

Nouveau fonds 3882.

6122. 占察善惡業報經玄義

Tchạn tchha chạn 'o ye pao king hiuen yi.

Sens caché du sūtra sur la recherche, etc.

Par Tchi-hiu.

61 feuillets. — Cf. n° 6120, art. II.

Grand in-8. 1 vol. demi-rel., au chiffre de la République Française.
Nouveau fonds 4043.

6123. 佛說華手經

Fo choę hoa cheou king; alias :

攝諸善根經

Chę tchou chạn ken king.

Kuçalamūla samparigraha sūtra; alias :

Kuçalamūla paridhara sūtra.

Version de Kumārajīva. Lecture des caractères rares.

10 livres. — Bunyiu Nanjio 425.

Grand in-8. Bonne gravure. 1 vol. demi-rel., au chiffre de la République Française.
Nouveau fonds 3881.

6124. 觀佛三昧海經

Koan fo san mei hai king.

Buddhadhyāna samādhisāgara sūtra.

Version de Buddhabhadra. Lecture des mots rares.

Livres 6 à 10. — Bunyiu Nanjio 430.

Grand in-8. Bonne gravure. 1 vol. cartonnage.
Nouveau fonds 4673.

6125. — I.

佛說長者法志妻經

Fo choę tchang tchę fa tchi tshi king.

Çreṣṭhi dharmacāri bhāryā sūtra.

Traduction de la dynastie des Liang septentrionaux (302-439).

4 feuillets. — Bunyiu Nanjio 416.

— II.

佛說薩羅國經

Fo choę sa lo koę king.

Kosala deça sūtra.

Traduction de l'époque des Tsin orientaux (317-420). Gravé de nouveau en 1681.

4 feuillets. — Bunyiu Nanjio 417.

— III.

佛說十吉祥經

Fo choę chi ki siang king.

Daçaçrī sūtra.

Traduction des dynasties Tshin (350-431).

2 feuillets. — Bunyiu Nanjio 418.

— IV.

佛說長者女菴提遮師子吼了義經

Fo choe tchang tche niu 'an thi tche chi tseu heou liao yi king.

Çreṣṭhi duhitṛ siṃhanāda sūtra.

Traduction de la dynastie des Liang (502-557), ou peut-être de Kumārajīva. Gravé de nouveau en 1681.

8 feuillets. — Bunyiu Nanjio 419.

— V.

佛說一切智光明仙人慈心因緣不食肉經

Fo choe yi tshie tchi koang ming sien jen tsheu sin yin yuen pou chi jeou king.

Sūtra sur l'abstinence de viande.

Traduction d'époque douteuse. Liste des caractères rares.

5 feuillets. — Bunyiu Nanjio 420.

— VI.

大方等陀羅尼經
Ta fang teng tho lo ni king.

Pratyutpanna buddha sammukhāvasthita samādhi sūtra.

Version de Fa-tchong, Chinois de Tourfan (402-412). Lecture des mots rares. Édition de 1655, réédition partielle de 1691.

4 livres. — Bunyiu Nanjio 421.

Grand in-8. Bonne gravure. 1 vol. demi-rel., au chiffre de la République Française.

Nouveau fonds 3936.

———

6126.　　法集經
Fa tsi king.

Dharmasaṅgīti sūtra.

Version de Bodhiruci (515). Lecture des caractères rares. Édition de Tsi-tchao 'an (1598).

6 livres. — Bunyiu Nanjio 426.

Grand in-8. Bonne gravure; frontispice (1 feuillet double). 1 vol. demi-rel., au chiffre de la République Française.

Nouveau fonds 3956.

6127.

Fa tsi king.

Même ouvrage.

3 livres (incomplet des livres 4 à 6).

Grand in-8. Belle gravure. 1 vol. demi-reliure.

Nouveau fonds 269.

6128. 無所有菩薩經

Oou so yeou phou sa king.

Akiñcana bodhisattva sūtra.

Version de Jñānagupta (585-592). Liste des caractères rares.

4 livres. — Bunyiu Nanjio 439.

Grand in-8. Bonne gravure. 1 vol. demi-rel., au chiffre de la République Française.

Nouveau fonds 3874.

6129. — I.

商主天子所問經

Chang tchou thien tseu so oen king.

Banikpati devaputra sūtra.

Version de Jñānagupta (585-592). Édition de Tsi-tchao 'an (1604).

1 livre. — Bunyiu Nanjio 519.

— II.

離垢慧菩薩所問禮佛法經

Li keou hoei phou sa so oen li fo fa king.

Vimalajñāna bodhisattva pari-prcchā sūtra.

Version de Na-thi (662). Préface par Tao-siuen. Lecture des mots rares. Édition de King-chan seu (1604).

6 feuillets. — Bunyiu Nanjio 521.

— III.

大乘四法經

Ta cheng seu fa king.

Catuṣka nirhāra sūtra.

Version de Çikṣānanda (695-700). Liste des caractères rares. Édition de Tsi-tchao 'an (1602).

10 feuillets. — Bunyiu Nanjio 520.

— IV.

寂照神變三摩地經

Tsi tchao chen pien san mo ti king.

Praçāntaviniçcaya pratihārya samādhi sūtra.

Version de Hiuen-tsang (663). Lecture des mots difficiles. Édition de Tsi-tchao 'an (1604).

1 livre. — Bunyiu Nanjio 522.

— V.

佛說造塔功德經

Fo choẹ tsao tha kong tẹ king.

Caityakaraṇaguṇa sūtra.

Version de Divākara (680). Préface du bonze Yuen-tshę (même époque). Liste des mots difficiles. Édition de King-chan seu (1604).

2 feuillets. — Bunyiu Nanjio 5₂3.

— VI.

佛 說 不 增 不 減 經

Fo choę pou tseng pou kien king.

Sūtra sur l'absence d'augmentation et de diminution.

Version de Bodhiruci (519-524). Mêmes lieu et date.

7 feuillets. — Bunyiu Nanjio 5₂4.

— VII.

佛 說 堅 固 女 經

Fo choę kien kou niu king.

Sthiradhī sūtra.

Version de Narendrayaças (582). Mêmes lieu et date.

7 feuillets. — Bunyiu Nanjio 5₂5.

— VIII.

佛 說 大 乘 流 轉 諸 有 經

Fo choę ta cheng lieou tchoan tchou yęou king.

Bhavasaṅkrānti sūtra.

Version de Yi-tsing (701). Mêmes lieu et date.

3 feuillets. — Bunyiu Nanjio 5₂6.

— IX.

佛 說 大 意 經

Fo choę ta yi king; alias :

大 意 抒 海 經

Ta yi chou hai king.

Mahāmati sūtra.

Version de Guṇabhadra (435-443). Lecture des caractères difficiles. Mêmes lieu et date.

6 feuillets. — Bunyiu Nanjio 5₂7.

— X.

受 持 七 佛 名 號 所 生 功 德 經

Cheou tchhi tshi fo ming hao so cheng kong tę king.

Sapta buddhaka sūtra.

Version de Hiuen-tsang (651). Mêmes lieu et date.

5 feuillets. — Bunyiu Nanjio 5₂8.

— XI.

金 剛 光 焰 止 風 雨 陀 羅 尼 經

Kin kang koang yen tchi fong yu tho lo ni king.

Vajraprabhāsa dhāraṇī sūtra.

Version de Bodhiruci (710).
Liste des caractères rares. Mêmes
lieu et date.

1 livre. — Bunyiu Nanjio 529.

Grand in-8. Bonne gravure. 1 vol.
demi-rel. au chiffre de la République
Française.
Nouveau fonds 3950.

6130. 觀察諸法行經
Koan tchha tchou fa hing king.

Sarvadharmacaryā dhyāna sūtra.

Version de Jñānagupta (595).
Lecture des caractères rares. Édition donnée par Kou Long-chan
(1625).

4 livres. — Bunyiu Nanjio 424.

Grand in-8. Bonne gravure. 1 vol.
demi-rel., au chiffre de la République
Française.
Nouveau fonds 3959.

6131. 地藏菩薩本願經
Ti tsang phou sa pen yuen king.

Kṣitigarbha bodhisattva pūrvapraṇidhāna sūtra.

Version par Çikṣānanda (695-
700). Lecture des caractères diffi-

ciles. Édition de Tsi-tchao-'an
(1598).

2 livres. — Bunyiu Nanjio 1003.

Grand in-8. Bonne gravure. 1 vol.
cartonnage.
Nouveau fonds 4684.

6132-6133.
Ti tsang phou sa pen yuen king.

Même ouvrage.
Frontispice (2 feuillets simples);
invocation. Éloge. Lecture des
mots difficiles. Notice finale par
Tchou-hong. Réédition de Hai-
tchhoang (1800).

2 livres. — Bunyiu Nanjio 1003.

In-4. Papier blanc. 2 vol. en paravent, couvertures rouges; dans 1 étui
demi-rel., au chiffre de Louis-Philippe.
Nouveau fonds 152.

6134. 一字佛頂輪王經
Yi tseu fo ting loen oang king;
alias :

五佛頂經
Oou fo ting king.

Ekākṣara buddhoṣṇīṣarāja sūtra.

Version de Bodhiruci (709). Lecture des caractères difficiles.

6 livres. — Bunyiu Nanjio 532.

Grand in-8. Bonne gravure. 1 vol. demi-rel., au chiffre de la République Française.

Nouveau fonds 3971.

6135. — I.

大毗盧遮那成佛神變加持經

Ta phi lou tchẹ na tchheng fo chen pien kia tchhi king; alias :

大日經
Ta ji king.

Mahāvairocanābhisambodhi sūtra.

Version de Çubhakara, Hindou, traducteur en 716-724 et de Yi-hing, Chinois (Tchang Soei, 672-717). Liste des signes rares. Édition de Tsi-tchao 'an (1608).

7 livres. — Bunyiu Nanjio 530.
Le livre 7 forme une section à part, savoir :

— II.

供養念誦三昧耶法門
Kong yang nien song san mei ye fa mẹn.

Principes de l'offrande des mets et de la récitation des prières.

5 chapitres. — Bunyiu Nanjio 530.

— III.

蘇婆呼童子經
Sou phọ hou thong tseu king.

Subāhu kumāra sūtra.

Traduction des mêmes. Liste des caractères rares. Édition de 1611.

3 livres. — Bunyiu Nanjio 531.

Grand in-8. Bonne gravure. 1 vol. demi-rel., au chiffre de la République Française.

Nouveau fonds 3887.

6136. — I.

佛爲優填王說王法政論經
Fo oei yeou thien oang choẹ oang fa tcheng loẹn king.

Rājādeça sūtra, prononcé par le Bouddha pour le roi Udayana.

Traduction d'Amoghavajra (746-771). Liste des caractères rares. Édition de Tsi-tchao 'an (1601).

9 feuillets. — Bunyiu Nanjio 1006.

— II.

佛說五大施經
Fo choẹ oou ta chi king.

Buddhabhāṣita pañcamahā-pradāna sūtra.

Version de Chi-hou. Mêmes lieu et date.

1 feuillet. — Bunyiu Nanjio 1007.

— III.

佛說無畏陀羅尾經

Fo choę oou oei tho lo ni king.

Buddhabhāṣitābhaya dhāraṇī sūtra.

Version de Fa-hien, Hindou (982-1001). Mêmes lieu et date d'édition.

3 feuillets. — Bunyiu Nanjio 1008.

— IV.

佛說大威德金輪佛頂熾盛光如來消除一切灾難陀羅尾經

Fo choę ta oei tę kin loęn fo ting tchhi cheng koang jou lai siao tchhou yi tshie tsai nan tho lo ni king.

Buddhabhāṣita mahābalaguṇa suvarṇacakra buddhoṣṇīṣa teja-prabhā tathāgata sarvāpadvināça dhāraṇī sūtra.

Traduction de l'époque des Thang (618-907).

3 feuillets. — Bunyiu Nanjio 1009.

— V.

九曜眞言

Kieou yao tchen yen.

Nava graha dhāraṇī.

Mêmes lieu et date d'édition qu'à l'art. I.

1 feuillet.

— VI.

佛說熾盛光大威德消灾吉祥陀羅尾經

Fo choę tchhi cheng koang ta oei tę siao tsai ki siang tho lo ni king.

Buddhabhāṣita tejaprabhā ma-hābalaguṇāpadvināça çrī dhāra-ṇī sūtra.

Version par Amoghavajra du même texte qu'à l'art. IV. Préface du bonze Sing-tchheng (1322). Édition de Hing cheng oan-cheou chạn-seu (1601).

2 feuillets. — Bunyiu Nanjio 1010.

— VII.

佛說頂生王因緣經

Fo choę ting cheng oang yin yuen king.

Buddhabhāṣita mūrdhajāta rā-jāvadāna sūtra.

Version de Chi-hou. Liste des caractères rares. Édition du Hoa-yen ko (1643).

6 livres. — Bunyiu Nanjio 1011.

— VIII.

佛說大乘隨轉宣說諸法經

Fo choę ta cheng soei tchoan siuen choę tchou fa king.

Sarvadharma pravṛtti nirdeça sūtra.

Version de Chao-tę, d'origine inconnue (dynastie des Song). Liste des signes rares. Édition de mêmes lieu et date. Traduction du même texte que nᵒˢ 6074, art. II et 6076, art. I.

3 livres. — Bunyiu Nanjio 1012.

Grand in-8. Bonne gravure; frontis-pice (1 feuillet double). 1 vol. demi-rel., au chiffre de la République Française.
Nouveau fonds 3895.

6137. 大乘理趣六波羅蜜多經

Ta cheng li tshiu lou po lo mi to king.

Mahāyānabuddhi ṣaṭpāramitā sūtra.

Version de Prājña (788). Liste des caractères rares. Édition de Miao-tę 'an (1591).

10 livres. — Bunyiu Nanjio 1004.

Grand in-8. Bonne gravure; frontis-pice (1 feuillet double). 1 vol. demi-rel., au chiffre de la République Française.
Nouveau fonds 3884.

6138. 大乘本生心地觀經

Ta cheng pęn cheng sin ti koan king.

Mahāyāna mūlajāta hṛdaya-bhūmi dhyāna sūtra.

Version du même (785-810). Préface par l'empereur Hien-tsong (821). Liste des mots rares. Édi-tion de Hing-cheng oan-cheou chan-seu, au King-chan (1598); gravé de nouveau en 1704.

8 livres. — Bunyiu Nanjio 955.

Grand in-8. Bonne gravure. 1 vol. demi-rel., au chiffre de la République Française.
Nouveau fonds 3974.

6139. — I.

妙臂菩薩所問經

Miao phi phou sa so oen king.

Subāhu pariprcchā sūtra.

Version par Fa-thien (973-981) du même texte qu'au n° 6135, art. III. Liste des caractères difficiles.

4 livres. — Bunyiu Nanjio 822.

— II.

佛說苾芻五法經

Fo choę pi tchhou oou fa king.

Bhikṣu pañcadharma sūtra.

Du même; sūtra du hīnayāna.

6 feuillets. — Bunyiu Nanjio 823.

— III.

佛說苾芻迦尸迦十法經

Fo choę pi tchhou kia chi kia chi fa king.

Bhikṣuka çikṣāpada daçadharma sūtra.

Du même; sūtra du hīnayāna. Édition du Hoa-yen ko (1642).

3 feuillets. — Bunyiu Nanjio 824.

— IV.

諸佛心印陀羅尼經

Tchou fo sin yin tho lo ni king.

Buddhahṛdaya dhāraṇī sūtra.

Du même; autre traduction de Bunyiu Nanjio 489.

2 feuillets. — Bunyiu Nanjio 825; cf. n° 6204, art. XVII.

— V.

大乘寶月童子問法經

Ta cheng pao yue thong tseu oen fa king.

Mahāyāna ratnacandra kumāra paripṛcchā sūtra.

Version de Chi-hou. Mêmes lieu et date qu'à l'art. III.

5 feuillets. — Bunyiu Nanjio 826.

— VI.

佛說蓮華眼陀羅尼經

Fo choę lien hoa yen tho lo ni king.

Puṇḍarīkākṣa dhāraṇī sūtra.

Par le même. Mêmes lieu et date.

1 feuillet. -- Bunyiu Nanjio 827.

— VII.

佛說觀想佛母般若波羅蜜多菩薩經

Fo choę koan siang fo mou pan ję po lo mi to phou sa king.

Dhyāna sañjñana buddhamātṛka prajñāpāramitā sūtra.

Version de Thien-si-tsai, Hindou 980-1001). Mêmes lieu et date.

3 feuillets. — Bunyiu Nanjio 828.

— VIII.

佛說如意摩尼陀羅尼經

Fo choę jou yi mo ni tho lo ni king.

Padmacintāmaṇi dhāraṇī sūtra.

Traduction du même texte qu'au n° 5860, art. V à VIII, par Chi-hou. Lecture des mots rares. Mêmes lieu et date.

4 feuillets. — Bunyiu Nanjio 829.

— IX.

佛說聖大總持王經

Fo choę cheng ta tsong tchhi oang king.

Āryamahādhāraṇīrāja sūtra.

Du même traducteur.

5 feuillets. — Bunyiu Nanjio 830.

— X.

佛說最上意陀羅尼經

Fo choę tsoei chang yi tho lo ni king.

Anuttaramati dhāraṇī sūtra.

Du même.

7 feuillets. — Bunyiu Nanjio 831.

— XI.

佛說持明藏八大總持王經

Fo choę tchhi ming tsang pa ta tsong tchhi oang king.

Prabhāsadharagarbhāṣṭama- hādhāraṇīrāja sūtra.

Du même.

7 feuillets. — Bunyiu Nanjio 832.

— XII.

聖無能勝金剛火陀羅尼經

Cheng oou neng cheng kin kang hoo tho lo ni king.

Ārya durjaya vajrāgni dhāraṇī sūtra.

Version de Fa-thien.

5 feuillets. — Bunyiu Nanjio 833.

— XIII.

佛說尊勝大明王經

Fo choę tsoęn cheng ta ming oang king.

Āryottama mahāvidyārāja sūtra.

Version de Chi-hou.

5 feuillets. — Bunyiu Nanjio 834.

— XIV.

佛說智光滅一切業障陀羅尼經

*Fo choǫ tchi koang mie yi tshie
ye tchang tho lo ni king.*

Jñānolkā dhāraṇī sarvadu-
rgati pariçodhanī sūtra.

Du même; traduction du même
texte qu'au n° 6210, art. II.

4 feuillets. — Bunyiu Nanjio 835.

— XV.

佛說如意寶總持王經

*Fo choǫ jou yi pao tsong tchhi
oang king.*

Cintāmaṇi dhāraṇī sūtra.

Du même. Lecture des caractères rares. Édition de Hoa-tchheng
seu (1627).

3 feuillets. — Bunyiu Nanjio 836.

Grand in-8. Bonne gravure. 1 vol.
demi-rel., au chiffre de la République
Française.

Nouveau fonds 3934.

6140. — I.

佛母寶德藏般若波羅蜜經

*Fo mou pao tǫ tsang pan jǫ po
lo mi king.*

Prajñāpāramitā sañcayagāthā
sūtra.

Version de Fa-hien (982-1001).
Liste des caractères rares.

3 livres. — Bunyiu Nanjio 864.

— II.

佛說帝釋般若波羅蜜多心經

*Fo choǫ ti chi pan jǫ po lo mi to
sin king.*

Kauçika prajñāpāramitā sūtra.

Version de Chi-hou. Liste des
caractères rares.

5 feuillets. — Bunyiu Nanjio 865.

— III.

佛說諸佛經
Fo choǫ tchou fo king.

Sarvabuddha sūtra.

Du même, traduction partielle
d'un sūtra du hīnayāna (n°° 6184-
6185. Lecture des mots difficiles

4 feuillets. — Bunyiu Nanjio 866.

— IV.

大乘舍黎娑擔摩經

Ta cheng chẹ li so tan mo king.

Çālisambhava sūtra.

Du même, autre version du n° 6102, art. X et XI. Liste des caractères rares. Édition de Tsi-tchao 'an (1609), gravée de nouveau en 1677 (?).

8 feuillets. — Bunyiu Nanjio 867.

— V.

佛說大金剛香陀羅尼經

Fo chọ ta kin kang hiang tho lo ni king.

Mahāvajragandha dhāraṇī sū-tra.

Du même.

4 feuillets. — Bunyiu Nanjio 868.

— VI.

最上大乘金剛大教寶王經

Tsoei chang ta cheng kin kang ta kiao pao oang king.

Vajragarbha ratnarāja tantra sūtra.

Version de Fa-thien (Fa-hien)

(973-981). Liste des caractères rares.

2 livres. — Bunyiu Nanjio 869.

— VII.

佛說薩鉢多酥哩踰捺野經

Fo chọ sa po to sou li yu na ye king.

Saptasūryanaya sūtra.

Du même (982-1001). Sūtra du hīnayāna, traduction partielle de Bunyiu Nanjio 542(8).

4 feuillets. — Bunyiu Nanjio 870.

— VIII.

佛說一切如來烏瑟膩沙最勝總持經

Fo chọ yi tshie jou lai oou sẹ ni cha tsoei cheng tsong tchhi king.

Sarvadurgati pariçodhanoṣṇī-ṣa vijaya dhāraṇī sūtra.

Du même (973-981); traduction du même texte qu'aux n° 5987, art. VII à IX; n° 6217, art. VII.

9 feuillets. — Bunyiu Nanjio 871.

— IX.

菩提心觀釋

Phou thi sin koan chi.

Bodhihṛdaya dhyāna vyākhyā.

Du même. Édition de King-chan seu (1609).

3 feuillets. — Bunyiu Nanjio 872.

Grand in-8. Bonne gravure. 1 vol. demi-rel., au chiffre de la République Française.

Nouveau fonds 3913.

6141. — I.

佛說大自在天子因地經

Fo choç ta tseu tsai thien tseu yin ti king.

Maheçvara devaputra hetu-bhūmi sūtra.

Version de Chi-hou.

9 feuillets. — Bunyiu Nanjio 837.

— II.

佛說寶生陀羅尼經

Fo choç pao cheng tho lo ni king.

Ratnajāta dhāraṇī sūtra.

Du même.

2 feuillets. — Bunyiu Nanjio 838.

— III.

佛說十號經

Fo choç chi hao king.

Daçanāma sūtra.

Version de Thien-si-tsai (980-1001).

3 feuillets. — Bunyiu Nanjio 839.

— IV.

佛爲娑伽羅龍王所說大乘法經

Fo oei so kia lo long oang so choç ta cheng fa king.

Sāgara nāgarāja paripṛcchā sūtra.

Version de Chi-hou. Lecture des mots rares. Édition de Hoa-tchheng seu (1630).

10 feuillets. — Bunyiu Nanjio 840.

— V.

佛說普賢菩薩陀羅尼經

Fo choç phou hien phou sa tho lo ni king.

Samantabhadra bodhisattva dhāraṇī sūtra.

Version de Fa-thien (973-981). Réédition de 1677.

4 feuillets. — Bunyiu Nanjio 841.

— VI.

大金剛妙高山樓閣陀羅尼

Ta kin kang miao kao chan leou ko tho lo ni.

Mahāvajrameru çekhara kūṭā-gāra dhāraṇī.

Version de Chi-hou.

11 feuillets. — Bunyiu Nanjio 842.

— VII.

廣大蓮華莊嚴曼拏羅滅一切罪陀羅尼經

Koang ta lien hoa tchoang yen man na lo mie yi tshie tsoei tho lo ni king.

Mahāpuṇḍarīkavyūhasarvapā-pavināça maṇḍala dhāraṇī sūtra.

Du même. Lecture des caractères rares.

12 feuillets. — Bunyiu Nanjio 843.

— VIII.

宋譯三藏聖教序

Song yi san tsang cheng kiao siu.

Préface pour la traduction du Tripiṭaka faite sous les Song.

Par l'empereur Thai-tsong (975-997), pour les traductions de Thien-si-tsai et autres.

2 feuillets.

— IX.

佛說大摩里支菩薩經

Fo choę ta mo li tchi phou sa king.

Mahāmarīcī bodhisattva sūtra.

Version de Thien-si-tsai. Liste des termes difficiles. Édition du Hoa-yen ko (1642).

7 livres. — Bunyiu Nanjio 844; cf. n° 6209, art. LXXI; 6142, art. I, etc.

Grand in-8. Bonne gravure; frontispice très dégradé (1 feuillet double). 1 vol. demi-rel., au chiffre de la République Française.

Nouveau fonds 3976.

6142. — I.

佛說末利支提婆華鬘經

Fo choę mo li tchi thi pho hoa man king.

Marīcī devī puṣpamālā sūtra.

Version d'Amoghavajra (746-771).

14 feuillets. — Bunyiu Nanjio 845; cf. n° 6141, art. IX.

— II.

佛說摩利支天經

Fo choę mo li tchi thien king.

Marīcī devī sūtra.

Du même. Liste des caractères rares. Édition de Hoa-tchheng seu (1630).

5 feuillets. — Bunyiu Nanjio 846; cf. n° 6141, art. IX.

— III.

佛說摩利支天陀羅尾咒經

Fo choę mo li tchi thien tho lo ni tcheou king.

Marīcī devī dhāraṇī sūtra.

Version de la dynastie des Liang (502-557). Édition du Hoa-yen ko (1642).

2 feuillets. — Bunyiu Nanjio 847; cf. n° 6141, art. IX.

— IV.

佛說長者施報經

Fo choę tchang tchę chi pao king.

Çreṣṭhi dānaphala sūtra.

Version de Fa-thien; sūtra du hīnayāna. Mêmes lieu et date.

8 feuillets. — Bunyiu Nanjio 848; cf. Bunyiu Nanjio 542 (155).

— V.

佛說毗沙門天王經

Fo choę phi cha męn thien oang king.

Vaiçramaṇa devarāja sūtra.

Du même. Mêmes lieu et date.

9 feuillets. — Bunyiu Nanjio 849.

— VI.

毗婆尸佛經

Phi pho chi fo king.

Vipaçyi buddha sūtra.

Du même (hīnayāna); version d'une partie du n° 6153, art. I. Mêmes lieu et date.

2 livres. — Bunyiu Nanjio 850.

— VII.

佛說大三摩惹經

Fo choę ta san mo ję king.

Mahāsamaya sūtra.

Du même; traduction du même texte (hīnayāna) que n° 6154, art. XIX.

6 feuillets. — Bunyiu Nanjio 851.

— VIII.

佛說月光菩薩經

Fo choẹ yue koang phou sa king.

Candraprabha bodhisattvāvadāna sūtra.

Du même ; sūtra du hīnayāna.

6 feuillets. — Bunyiu Nanjio 852.

— IX.

佛說普賢曼拏羅經

Fo choẹ phou hien man na lo king.

Samantabhadra maṇḍala sūtra.

Version de Chi-hou. Lecture des caractères difficiles. Édition de Hoa-tchheng seu (1633).

10 feuillets. — Bunyiu Nanjio 853.

Grand in-8. Bonne gravure. 1 vol. demi-rel., au chiffre de la République Française.

Nouveau fonds 3977.

6143. # 佛說摩利支天陀羅尼經

Fo choẹ mo li tchi thien tho lo ni king.

Marīcī devī dhāraṇī sūtra ; alias :

Maricīye dhāraṇī sūtra.

Traduction attribuée à Oouneng-cheng, Hindou, peut-être de l'époque des Thang. Formules de prières au début et à la fin. Gravé à la bonzerie de Haï-tchhoang.

1 livre. — Comparer Bunyiu Nanjio 847 ; ci-dessus, n° 6142, art. I.

Petit in-8. Papier blanc. 1 vol. en paravent, couverture rouge ; dans 1 étui demi-rel., au chiffre de Louis-Philippe. *Nouveau fonds* 133.

6144. — I.

佛說守護大千國土經

Fo choẹ cheou hou ta tshien koẹ thou king.

Mahāsahasrapramardana sūtra ; alias :

Mahāsahasramaṇḍala sūtra.

Version de Chi-hou. Lecture des mots rares. Édition de Hoatchheng seu (1631, 1632).

3 livres. — Bunyiu Nanjio 784.

— II.

佛說大乘聖無量壽決定光明王如來陀羅尼經

Fo choẹ ta cheng cheng oou liang cheou kiue ting koang ming oang jou lai tho lo ni king.

Mahāyānāryāmitāyurniçcita-
prabhāsarāja tathāgata dhāraṇī
sūtra.

Version de Fa-thien (973-981).

7 feuillets. — Bunyiu Nanjio 786.

— III.

佛說大乘聖吉祥持世陀羅尼經

*Fo choẹ ta cheng c'eng ki siang
tchhi chi tho lo ni king.*

Vasudhara dhāraṇī sūtra.

Du même ; autre traduction du
n° 6204, art. XX et de Bunyiu
Nanjio 962. Liste des caractères
rares. Édition de Hoa-tchheng seu
(1633).

9 feuillets. — Bunyiu Nanjio 787 ;
cf. n°⁵ 6089-6090, art. I.

— IV.

佛說大乘日子王所問經

*Fo choẹ ta cheng ji tseu oang so
oen king.*

Udayana vatsarāja paripṛcchā
sūtra.

Version de Fa-thien ; même texte
qu'au n° 5805, art. XXIX. Édition
de 1611.

13 feuillets. — Bunyiu Nanjio 788 ;
cf. id. 38.

— V.

佛說金耀童子經

Fo choẹ kin yao thong tseu king.

Suvarṇaraçmi kumāra sūtra.

Version de Thien-si-tsai. Liste
des caractères difficiles. Même date
d'édition.

9 feuillets. — Bunyiu Nanjio 789.

Grand in-8. Bonne gravure. 1 vol.
demi-rel., au chiffre de la République
Française.
Nouveau fonds 3996.

6145. — I.

讚法界頌
Tsan fa kiai song.

Dharmadhātu stotra.

Par le bodhisattva Nāgārjuna ;
version de Chi-hou. Édition du
Hoa-yen ko (1644).

9 feuillets. — Bunyiu Nanjio 1070.

— II.

八大靈塔梵讚
Pa ta ling tha fan tsan.

Aṣṭa mahāçrīcaitya saṃskṛta
stotra.

Par le roi Çīlāditya; version de Fa-hien, Hindou (982-1001). Mêmes lieu et date.

2 feuillets. — Bunyiu Nanjio 1071.

— III.

三身梵讚

San chen fan tsan.

Trikāya saṃskṛta stotra.

Version du même; mêmes lieu et date.

2 feuillets. — Bunyiu Nanjio 1072.

— IV.

大明太宗文皇帝御製文殊讚

Ta ming thai tsong oen hoang ti yu tchi oen chou tsan.

Éloge de Mañjuçrī par l'empereur Thai-tsong des Ming.

Édition du Hoa-yen ko (1644).

2 feuillets. — Bunyiu Nanjio 1073.

— V.

佛說文殊師利一百八名梵讚

Fo choç oen chou chi li yi po pa ming fan tsan.

Mañjuçrī nāmāṣṭaçataka saṃskṛta stotra.

Version de Fa-thien. Mêmes lieu et date.

5 feuillets. — Bunyiu Nanjio 1073.

— VI.

曼殊室利菩薩吉祥伽陀

Man chou chi li phou sa ki siang kia tho.

Mañjuçrī bodhisattva çrī gāthā.

Transcription par Fa-hien (982-1001). Mêmes lieu et date.

2 feuillets. — Bunyiu Nanjio 1074.

— VII.

聖金剛手菩薩一百八名梵讚

Cheng kin kang cheou phou sa yi po pa ming fan tsan.

Ārya vajrapāṇi bodhisattva nāmāṣṭaçataka saṃskṛta stotra.

Du même. Lecture des caractères rares. Mêmes lieu et date.

5 feuillets. — Bunyiu Nanjio 1075.

— VIII.

大明太宗文皇帝御製觀音讚

Ta ming thai tsong oen hoang ti yu tchi koan yin tsan.

Éloge d'Avalokiteçvara par l'empereur Thai-tsong des Ming.

2 feuillets. — Bunyiu Nanjio 1076.

— IX.

大明太宗文皇帝御製大悲觀世音菩薩讚

Ta ming thai tsong oen hoang ti yu tchi ta pei koan chi yin phou sa tsan.

Éloge de Koan-yin miséricordieuse par l'empereur Thai-tsong des Ming.

Daté de 1411.

1 feuillet. — Bunyiu Nanjio 1076.

— X.

聖觀自在菩薩功德讚

Cheng koan tseu tsai phou sa kong te tsan.

Āryāvalokiteçvara bodhisattva guṇa stotra.

Version de Chi-hou.

5 feuillets. — Bunyiu Nanjio 1076.

— XI.

讚觀世音菩薩頌

Tsan koan chi yin phou sa song.

Avalokiteçvara bodhisattva stotra.

Version (692) de Hoei-tchi, Hindou d'origine, né en Chine.

5 feuillets. — Bunyiu Nanjio 1077.

-- XII.

佛說聖觀自在菩薩梵讚

Fo choç cheng koan tseu tsai phou sa fan tsan.

Āryāvalokiteçvara bodhisattva saṃskṛta stotra.

Version de Fa-thien.

3 feuillets. — Bunyiu Nanjio 1078.

— XIII.

聖多羅菩薩梵讚

Cheng to lo phou sa fan tsan.

Āryatārā bodhisattva saṃskṛta stotra.

Version de Chi-hou.

8 feuillets. — Bunyiu Nanjio 1079.

— XIV.

事師法五十頌

Chi chi fa oou chi song.

Guru sevā dharma pañcāçadgāthā.

Par le bodhisattva Açvaghoṣa;
version de Ji-tchheng, Hindou
(1004-1058).

4 feuillets. — Bunyiu Nanjio 1080.

— XV.

犍 椎 梵 讚

Kien tchhoei fan tsan.

Ghaṇṭi sūtra.

Version de Fa-thien. Lecture
des caractères rares. Édition de
Tsi-tchao 'an (1608).

10 feuillets. — Bunyiu Nanjio 1081.

— XVI.

佛 說 菩 薩 內 戒 經

Fo choẹ phou sa nei kiai king.

Sūtra sur le çīla des bodhisattva.

Version de Guṇabhadra, Hindou
(435-443) (vinaya). Liste des caractères rares. Édition de Hoa-tchheng
seu (1627).

1 livre. — Bunyiu Nanjio 1082.

— XVII.

菩 薩 優 婆 塞 五 戒 威 儀 經

*Phou sa yeou pho sẹ oou kiai
oei yi king.*

Sūtra sur les commandements
des bodhisattva et upāsaka.

Du même (vinaya). Lecture des
mots difficiles. Mêmes lieu d'édition (1629).

1 livre. — Bunyiu Nanjio 1083.

— XVIII.

佛 說 文 殊 師 利 淨 律 經

*Fo choẹ oen chou chi li tsing liu
king.*

Paramārthasaṃvṛtisatyanirdeçanāma mahāyāna sūtra.

Version de Tchou Fa-hou (289)
(vinaya). Lecture des mots rares.
Mêmes lieu et date.

1 livre. — Bunyiu Nanjio 1084.

Grand in-8. Bonne gravure. 1 vol.
demi-rel., au chiffre de la République
Française.

Nouveau fonds 3997.

6146. — I.

佛 說 巨 力 長 者 所 聞 大 乘 經

*Fo choẹ kiu li tchang tchẹ so oen
ta cheng king.*

Buddhabhāṣita mahābala çre-
ṣṭhipariprcchā mahāyāna sūtra.

Version de Tchi-ki-siang (Jñā-
naçrī), Hindou (1053). Édition de
Hoa-tchheng seu (1613).

3 livres. — Bunyiu Nanjio 994.

— II.

佛說妙吉祥菩薩所問大乘法螺經

Fo choę miao ki siang phou sa so oen ta cheng fa loo king.

Buddhabhāṣita mañjuçrī bodhisattva paripṛcchā mahāyāna dharmaçaṅkha sūtra.

Version par Fa-hien, Hindou (982-1001) du même texte que Bunyiu Nanjio 264, 265.

7 feuillets. — Bunyiu Nanjio 995.

— III.

佛說四品法門經

Fo choę seu phin fa męn king.

Buddhabhāṣita caturvarga dharmaparyāya sūtra.

Du même.

6 feuillets. — Bunyiu Nanjio 996.

— IV.

佛說八大菩薩經

Fo choę pa ta phou sa king.

Buddhabhāṣita aṣṭamahābodhisattva sūtra.

Du même.

— V.

佛說施一切無畏陀羅尼經

Fo choę chi yi tshie oou oei tho lo ni king.

Sarvābhaya pradāna dhāraṇī sūtra.

Version de Chi-hou.

3 feuillets. — Bunyiu Nanjio 998.

— VI.

聖八千頌般若波羅蜜多一百八名眞寶圓義陀羅尼經

Cheng pa tshien song pan ję po lo mi to yi po pa ming tchen chi yuen yi tho lo ni king.

Āryāṣṭasahasragāthā prajñāpāramitā nāmāṣṭaçata satyapūrṇārtha dhāraṇī sūtra.

Du même. Édition de Hoatchheng seu (1613).

3 feuillets. — Bunyiu Nanjio 999.

— VII.

佛說一髻尊陀羅尼經

Fo choę yi ki tsoęn tho lo ni king.

Buddhabhāṣitaikacūḍārya dhāraṇī sūtra.

Version d'Amoghavajra. Édition de 1657.

16 feuillets. — Bunyiu Nanjio 1000.

— VIII.

金剛摧碎陀羅尼

Kin kang tshoei soei tho lo ni.

Vajra bhañjana dhāraṇī.

Version de Tsheu-hien (Maitreyabhadra), Hindou (entre 960 et 1066). Édition du Hoa-yen ko, à Yu-chan (1643).

3 feuillets. — Bunyiu Nanjio 1001.

— IX.

不空胃 (sic) 索毘盧遮那佛大灌頂光眞言經

Pou khong kiuen so phi lou tche na fo ta koan ting koang tchen yen king.

Amoghapāça vairocana buddha mahābhiṣikta prabhāsa mantra sūtra.

Version d'Amoghavajra. Lecture des caractères difficiles.

2 feuillets. — Bunyiu Nanjio 1002; cf. n° 6056, art. V.

Grand in-8 Bonne gravure. 1 vol. demi-rel., au chiffre de la République Française.

Nouveau fonds 3920.

Chapitre XII : BOUDDHISME (HĪNAYĀNA SŪTRA)

Première Section : SŪTRA DES 42 ARTICLES, ETC.

6147. — 1.

佛說四十二章經

Fo choe seu chi eul tchang king.

Le sūtra des quarante-deux articles.

Traduit (67 p. C.) par Kāçyapa Mātaṅga et Tchou Fa-lan (Dharmarakṣa), Hindous. Texte, avec une postface (1129) par Cheou-soei de Kiao-fong-chan.

11 feuillets. — Bunyiu Nanjio 678; cf. nº 3695, art. IV.

— II.

大唐太宗文武聖皇帝 施行遺教經勅

Ta thang thai tsong oen oou cheng hoang ti chi hing yi kiao king tchhi.

Décret de l'empereur Thai-tsong des Thang, relatif à la diffusion du sūtra des dernières instructions du Bouddha.

— III.

佛遺教經

Fo yi kiao king.

Sūtra des dernières instructions du Bouddha.

Même ouvrage qu'au nº 5955, art. III. Le texte, en écriture de genre cursif, a été transcrit par Tcheng Chi-pao. A la fin, date (1667) et lieu de publication (bonzerie de Hai-tchhoang).

9 feuillets (le 1er feuillet est en double).

Petit in-8. Papier blanc. 1 vol. demi-reliure.

Nouveau fonds 99.

6148. — I.

薩沙王五願經

Phing cha oang oou yuen king.

Bimbisāra rāja pañca praṇidhāna sūtra.

Version de Tchi Khien.

8 feuillets. — Bunyiu Nanjio 670.

— II.

瑠璃王經

Lieou li oang king.

Vaiḍūrya rāja sūtra.

Version de Tchou Fa-hou.

8 feuillets. — Bunyiu Nanjio 671.

— III.

佛說海八德經

Fo choẹ hai pa tẹ king.

Sūtra sur les huit vertus de la mer.

Version de Kumārajīva.

3 feuillets. — Bunyiu Nanjio 672.

— IV.

佛說法海經

Fo choẹ fa hai king.

Dharmasamudra sūtra.

Version de Fa-kiu. Traduction du même texte qu'à l'art. III. Liste des signes rares. Édition de Leng-yen seu (1661).

4 feuillets. — Bunyiu Nanjio 673.

— V.

佛說義足經

Fo choẹ yi tsou king.

Sūtra sur la vérité suffisante.

Version de Tchi Khien. Liste des caractères rares. Édition de Tsi-tchao 'an (1611).

2 livres. — Bunyiu Nanjio 674.

— VI.

鬼問目連經

Koei oen mou lien king.

Sūtra des questions posées par les preta à Maudgalyāyana.

Version de 'An Chi-kao.

4 feuillets. — Bunyiu Nanjio 675.

— VII.

雜藏經

Tsa tsang king.

Saṃyukta piṭaka sūtra.

Version de Fa-hien. Chinois (après 414). Traduction du même texte qu'à l'art. précédent.

11 feuillets. — Bunyiu Nanjio 676.

— VIII.

餓鬼報應經

'O koei pao ying king.

Preta phala sūtra.

Autre traduction du même texte, de la dynastie des Tsin orientaux (317-420). Liste des caractères rares. Édition de même localité et même date (art. V).

7 feuillets. — Bunyiu Nanjio 677.

— IX.

佛教西來玄化應運略錄

Fo kiao si lai hiuen hoa ying yun lio lou.

Histoire du Bouddha et de la religion.

Par Tchheng Hoei, de la dynastie des Song.

2 feuillets.

— X.

佛說四十二章經

Fo choę seu chi eul tchang king.

Sūtra des quarante-deux articles.

Même ouvrage qu'au nº 6147, art. I ; commentaire par l'empereur Tchen-tsong des Song et préface du même pour le commentaire. Préface du bonze Phou-koang (1312).

1 livre. — Bunyiu Nanjio 678.

— XI.

題焚經臺詩

Thi fęn king thai chi.

Poésie pour la terrasse Fęn-king, à Lo-yang.

Huit vers heptasyllabes par l'empereur Thai-tsong des Thang avec une longue note. Liste des caractères difficiles. Édition de Leng-yen seu (1664).

Grand in-8. Bonne gravure. 1 vol. demi-rel., au chiffre de la République Française.

Nouveau fonds 3905.

6149. — I.

佛說四十二章經解

Fo choę seu chi eul tchang king kiai.

Commentaire du sūtra en quarante-deux articles.

Par le bonze 'Eou-yi Tchi-hiu (XVIIᵉ siècle).

Cf. nº 6147, art. I.

— II.

佛遺教經解

Fo yi kiao king kiai.

Commentaire du sūtra des dernières instructions du Bouddha.

Par le même. Postface par un contemporain (1644). Édition de Leng-yen seu (1648).

Cf. n° 6147, art. III; n° 3695, art. III.

— III.

八大人覺經畧解

Pa ta jen kio king lio kiai.

Commentaire du sūtra sur les huit connaissances des hommes supérieurs.

Par le même. D'après la traduction de 'An Chi-kao; l'ouvrage est attribué à Cheng-hien, Occidental.

Cf. n° 6407, art. XIII.

Grand in-8. 1 vol. demi-rel., au chiffre de la République Française.
Nouveau fonds 3906.

Deuxième Section : ĀGAMA SŪTRA, ETC.

6150. — I.

佛說大安般守意經

Fo choe ta 'an pan cheou yi king.

Mahānāpāna dhyāna sūtra.

Version de 'An Chi-kao. Préface par Khang Seng-hoei, Hindou (241-280). Liste des caractères difficiles. Édition de Hoa-tchheng seu (1631).

2 livres. — Bunyiu Nanjio 681.

— II.

佛說罵意經

Fo choe ma yi king.

Sūtra sur la pensée d'injurier.

Du même.

1 livre. — Bunyiu Nanjio 682.

— III.

禪行法想經

Chan hing fa siang king.

Dhyānacaryā dharmasañjñāna sūtra.

Du même. Lecture des caractères difficiles. Même lieu d'édition (1632).

1 feuillet. — Bunyiu Nanjio 683.

— IV.

佛說處處經

Fo choẹ tchhou tchhou king.

Sūtra relatif à diverses localités.

Du même. Liste des caractères rares. Édition de Tsi-tchao 'an (1611).

1 livre. — Bunyiu Nanjio 684.

— V.

佛說分別善惡所起經

Fo choẹ fẹn piẹ chạn 'o so khi king.

Sūtra sur l'origine du bien et du mal.

Karmavibhāga dharmagrantha sūtra.

Du même. Lecture des mots difficiles. Mêmes lieu d'édition (1637).

1 livre. — Bunyiu Nanjio 685.

— VI.

佛說出家緣經

Fo choẹ tchhou kia yuen king.

Nandapravrajyā sūtra.

Du même.

3 feuillets. — Bunyiu Nanjio 686.

— VII.

佛說阿含正行經

Fo choẹ 'o han tcheng hing king.

Āgamasamyakcaryā sūtra.

Du même.

5 feuillets. — Bunyiu Nanjio 687.

— VIII.

佛說十八泥犁經

Fo choẹ chi pa ni li king.

Aṣṭādaçanaraka sūtra.

Du même.

7 feuillets. — Bunyiu Nanjio 688.

— IX.

佛說法受塵經

Fo choẹ fa cheou tchhen king.

Dharmasañjñānarajas sūtra.

Du même.

2 feuillets. — Bunyiu Nanjio 689.

— X.

佛說進學經

Fo choẹ tsin hio king.

Sūtra sur l'avancement dans l'étude.

Version de Tsiu-khiu King-cheng (455).

2 feuillets. — Bunyiu Nanjio 690.

— XI.

佛說得道梯隥錫杖經

Fo choẹ tẹ tao thi teng si tchang king.

Sūtra sur le khakkhara comme moyen d'atteindre la bodhi.

Traduction de la dynastie des Tsin orientaux (317-420).

4 feuillets. — Bunyiu Nanjio 691.

— XII.

持錫杖法

Tchhi si tchang fa.

Règles de l'usage du khakkhara.

4 feuillets. — Bunyiu Nanjio 691.

— XIII.

佛說貧窮老公經

Fo choẹ phin khiong lao kong king.

Sūtra à un pauvre homme.

Version de Hoei-kien, religieux d'origine inconnue (457). Liste des caractères rares. Édition de Tsi-tchao 'an (1637).

3 feuillets. — Bunyiu Nanjio 692.

Grand in-8. Bonne gravure; frontispice (1 feuillet double). 1 vol. demi-rel., au chiffre de la République Française.
Nouveau fonds 3911.

6151. — I.

分別功德論

Fẹn pie kong tẹ loẹn.

Guṇanirdeça çāstra.

Version de l'époque des Han orientaux (25-220). Commentaire de deux chapitres de l'Ekottarāgama sūtra. Liste des caractères difficiles. Édition de Tsie-tai seu (1639).

3 livres. — Bunyiu Nanjio 1290; cf. id. 543.

— II.

入阿毗達磨論

Jou 'o phi ta mo loẹn.

Abhidharmāvatāra çāstra.

Oeuvre de l'arhat Skandila, traduite par Hiuen-tsang (658). Lecture des mots rares. Mêmes lieu et date.

2 livres. — Bunyiu Nanjio 1291.

Grand in-8. Bonne gravure. 1 vol. demi-rel., au chiffre de la République Française.
Nouveau fonds 4138.

6152. — I.

大正句王經

Ta tcheng kiu oang king.

Mahāsatpāda rāja sūtra.

Version de Fa-hien, Hindou (982-1001). Liste des signes rares. Édition du Hoa-yen ko (1642).

2 livres. — Bunyiu Nanjio 904; cf. id. 542 (71).

— II.

佛說善樂長者經

Fo choẹ chạn yo tchang tchẹ king.

Svāçaya çreṣṭhi sūtra.

Du même. Liste des caractères rares.

4 feuillets. — Bunyiu Nanjio 905; cf. id. 982.

— III.

佛說聖多羅菩薩經

Fo choẹ cheng to lo phou sa king.

Āryatārā bodhisattva sūtra.

Du même. Liste des caractères rares.

7 feuillets. — Bunyiu Nanjio 906.

— IV.

佛說大吉祥陀羅尼經

Fo choẹ ta ki siang tho lo ni king.

Mahāçrī dhāraṇī sūtra.

Du même.

2 feuillets. — Bunyiu Nanjio 907.

— V.

佛說寶賢陀羅尼經

Fo choẹ pao hien tho lo ni king.

Maṇibhadra dhāraṇī sūtra.

Du même.

2 feuillets. — Bunyiu Nanjio 908.

— VI.

佛說秘密八名陀羅尼經

Fo choẹ pi mi pa ming tho lo ni king.

Guhyāṣṭanāma dhāraṇī sūtra.

Du même. Lecture des caractères difficiles.

2 feuillets. — Bunyiu Nanjio 909; cf. n° 6204, art. XIX.

— VII.

觀自在菩薩母陀羅尼經

Koan tseu tsai phou sa mou tho lo ni king.

Avalokiteçvara mātṛkā dhāraṇī sūtra.

Du même. Liste des caractères rares.

3 feuillets. — Bunyiu Nanjio 910.

— VIII.

佛說戒香經

Fo choẹ kiai hiang king.

Çīlagandha sūtra.

Du même. Liste des caractères difficiles. Édition de Hoa-tchheng seu (1631).

2 feuillets. — Bunyiu Nanjio 911; cf. id. 588.

— IX.

佛說妙吉祥菩薩陀羅尼

Fo choẹ miao ki siang phou sa tho lo ni.

Mañjuçrī bodhisattva dhāraṇī.

Du même.

4 feuillets. — Bunyiu Nanjio 912.

— X.

佛說無量壽大智陀羅尼

Fo choẹ oou liang cheou ta tchi tho lo ni.

Amitāyur mahājñāna dhāraṇī.

Du même.

1/2 feuillet. — Bunyiu Nanjio 913.

— XI.

佛說宿命智陀羅尼

Fo choẹ sou ming tchi tho lo ni.

Pūrvanivāsajñāna dhāraṇī.

Du même.

1/2 feuillet. — Bunyiu Nanjio 914.

— XII.

佛說慈氏菩薩陀羅尼

Fo choẹ tsheu chi phou sa tho lo ni.

Maitreya bodhisattva dhāraṇī.

Du même.

1/2 feuillet. — Bunyiu Nanjio 915.

— XIII.

佛說虛空藏菩薩陀羅尼

Fo choẹ hiu khong tsang phou sa tho lo ni.

Ākāçagarbha bodhisattva dhāraṇī.

Du même.

1/2 feuillet. — Bunyiu Nanjio 916.

— XIV.

寶授菩薩菩提行經

Pao cheou phou sa phou thi hing king.

Ratnadatta bodhisattva bodhi-caryā sūtra.

Du même. Liste des signes rares.

14 feuillets. — Bunyiu Nanjio 917.

— XV.

佛說延壽妙門陀羅尼經

Fo choẹ yen cheou miao mẹn tho lo ni king.

Āyurvardhanī sumukha dhāranī sūtra.

Du même. Édition du Hoa-yen ko (1642).

8 feuillets. — Bunyiu Nanjio 918; cf. n° 6202, art. VI à VIII.

— XVI.

一切如來名號陀羅尼經

Yi tshie jou lai ming hao tho lo ni king.

Sarvatathāgatanāma dhāranī sūtra.

Du même.

3 feuillets. — Bunyiu Nanjio 919.

— XVII.

佛說息除賊難陀羅尼經

Fo choẹ si tchhou tsẹ nan tho lo ni king.

Caura vidhvaṃsana dhāranī sūtra.

Du même. Édition du Hoa-yen-ko (1642).

2 feuillets. — Bunyiu Nanjio 920.

— XVIII.

佛說法身經

Fo choẹ fa chen king.

Dharmaçarīra sūtra.

Du même.

5 feuillets. — Bunyiu Nanjio 921.

— XIX.

信佛功德經

Sin fo kong tẹ king.

Buddhaçraddhāguṇa sūtra.

Du même. Liste des mots difficiles.

10 feuillets. — Bunyiu Nanjio 922; cf. id. 545 (18) (?).

— XX.

佛說解夏經

Fo choę kiai hia king.

Grīṣma nidarçana sūtra.

Du même. Lecture des signes difficiles.

4 feuillets. — Bunyiu Nanjio 923.

— XXI.

佛說帝釋所問經

Fo chóę ti chi so oen king.

Indra pariprchhā sūtra.

Du même.

15 feuillets. — Bunyiu Nanjio 924; **cf. n° 6153, art. XIV.**

Grand in-8. Bonne gravure; frontispice (1 feuillet double). 1 vol. demi-rel., au chiffre de la République Française. *Nouveau fonds* 3914.

6153-6154. 佛說長阿含經

Fo choę tchhang 'o han king.

Dīrghāgama sūtra.

Traduction par Buddhayaças et Tchou Fo-nien (410-413). Préface par le bonze Seng-tchao, contemporain des traducteurs. Édition de Tsi-tchao 'an (1606); feuillets gravés de nouveau en 1680, 1681, 1706.

Livre préliminaire + 22 livres. — Bunyiu Nanjio 545.

— I, livre 1 (6153).

初大本緣經

Tchhou ta pęn yuen king.

Mahā pradhāna sūtra.

Liste des signes difficiles.

1 livre.

— II, livre 2 à 4 (6153).

遊行經

Yeou hing king.

Mahā parinirvāṇa sūtra (?).

Liste des signes difficiles.

3 livres. — Cf. n° 5954, art. I, II.

— III, livre 5 (6153).

典尊經

Tien tsoęn king.

Sūtra relatif au ministre Tientsoęn.

Feuillets 1-15.

— IV, livre 5 (6153).

闍尼沙經

Chę ni cha king.

Janarṣabha sūtra.

Liste des caractères difficiles.

Feuillets 15-22.

— V, livre 6 (6153).

四 姓 經
Seu sing king.

Caturvarṇa sūtra.

Feuillets 1-10.
Cf. n° 5810, art. VI.

— VI, livre 6 (6153).

轉 輪 聖 王 修 行 經
Tchoan loen cheng oang sieou hing king.

Cakravarti rāja sūtra.

Lecture des caractères difficiles.

Feuillets 10-22.

— VII, livre 7 (6153).

弊 宿 經
Pi sou king.

Pāyāsi sūtra.

Liste des caractères difficiles.

1 livre.

— VIII, livre 8 (6153).

散 陀 那 經
San tho na king.

Sandhāna gṛhapati sūtra.

Feuillets 1-9.
Cf. n° 5810, art. V.

— IX, livre 8 (6153).

衆 集 經
Tchong tsi king.

Saṅgīti sūtra.

Liste des signes difficiles.

Feuillets 9-20.

— X, livre 9 (6153).

十 上 經
Chi chang king.

Daçottaradharma sūtra.

1 livre.

— XI, livre 10 (6153).

增 一 經
Tseng yi king.

Ekottaradharma sūtra.

Feuillets 1-7.

— XII, livre 10 (6153).

三 聚 經
San tsiu king.

Trirāçidharma sūtra.

Feuillets 7-10.

— XIII, livre 10 (6153).

大緣方便經
Ta yuen fang pien king.

Mahānidānopāya sūtra.

Feuillets 10-18.

— XIV, livre 10 (6153).

釋提桓因問經
Chi thi hoan yin oen king.

Çakra devendra paripṛcchā sūtra.

Liste des caractères difficiles.

Feuillets 18-29.
Cf. n° 6152, art. XXI.

— XV, livre 11 (6154).

阿㝹夷經
'O neou yi king.

Sūtra sur la cité de 'O-neou-yi.

Feuillets 1-15.

— XVI, livre 11 (6154).

善生經
Chan cheng king.

Sujāta sūtra.

Lecture des caractères difficiles·

Feuillets 15-23.
Cf. Bunyiu Nanjio 542 (135).

— XVII, livre 12 (6154).

清淨經
Tshing tsing king.

Sūtra sur la pureté.

Feuillets 1-14.

— XVIII, livre 12 (6154).

自歡喜經
Tseu hoan hi king.

Sūtra sur la joie.

Feuillets 14-23.

— XIX, livre 12 (6154).

大會經
Ta hoei king.

Mahāsamaya sūtra.

Lecture des signes difficiles.

Feuillets 24-31.
Cf. n° 6142, art. VII.

— XX, livre 13 (6154).

阿摩晝經
'O mo tcheou king.

Ambaṣṭha sūtra.

Liste des signes difficiles.

1 livre.

— XXI, livre 14 (6154).

梵動經
Fan tong king.

Brahmajāla sūtra.

Liste des signes difficiles.

1 livre.
Cf. n° 6214, art. X.

— XXII, livre 15 (6154).

種德經
Tchong tę king.

Sūtra sur le brahmane Tchong-tę.

Feuillets 1-10.

XXIII, livre 15 (6154).

究羅檀頭經
Kieou lo than theou king.

Kuladaṇḍa sūtra.

Lecture des signes difficiles.

Feuillets 10-26.

— XXIV, livre 16 (6154).

堅固經
Kien kou king.

Sthira sūtra.

Feuillets 1-6.

— XXV, livre 16 (6154).

倮形梵志經
Loo hing fan tchi king.

Acelabrahmacāri sūtra.

Feuillets 6-12.

— XXVI, livre 16 (6154).

三明經
San ming king.

Traividya sūtra.

Lecture des signes difficiles.

Feuillets 12-21.

— XXVII, livre 17 (6154).

沙門果經
Cha męn koo king.

Çrāmaṇyaphala sūtra.

Feuillets 1-10.

— XXVIII, livre 17 (6154).

布咤婆樓經
Pou tchha pho leou king.

Proṣṭhapāda sūtra.

Feuillets 10-20.

— XXIX, livre 17 (6154).

露遮経

Lou tchẹ king.

Ruci sūtra.

Liste des signes difficiles.

Feuillets 21-26.

— XXX, livres 18 à 22 (6154).

世記經

Chi ki king.

Sūtra sur l'univers.

Lecture des signes difficiles.

5 livres (12 sections); dans le livre 20, 1 feuillet à l'envers.

Grand in-8. Bonne gravure; frontispice (1 feuillet double). 2 vol. demi-rel., au chiffre de la République Française. *Nouveau fonds* 3752, 3753.

6155. — I.

別譯雜阿含經

Pie yi tsa 'o han king.

Saktavargāgama sūtra.

Traduction de l'époque des Tshin (350-431), les 5 premiers livres portent le titre de Pie yi tsa 'o han king tchhou song, 初誦; traduction partielle des n°ˢ 6156-

6158. Lecture des signes difficiles. Édition de Hoa-tchheng seu (1618).

20 livres. — Bunyiu Nanjio 546.

— II.

雜阿含經

Tsa 'o han king.

Saṃyuktāgama sūtra.

Collection de vingt-cinq petits sūtra sans titre. Traduction des dynasties des Oei et des Oou (220-280). Même texte qu'une partie des n°ˢ 6156-6158. Liste des caractères difficiles.

1 livre. — Bunyiu Nanjio 547.

— III.

長阿含十報法經

Tchhang 'o han chi pao fa king.

Sūtra sur la loi des dix récompenses dans le Dīrghāgama.

Traduction par 'An Chi-kao, du même texte qu'au n° 6153, art. X. Lecture des caractères difficiles. Mêmes date et localité d'édition.

2 livres. — Bunyiu Nanjio 548.

Grand in-8. Bonne gravure; frontispice (1 feuillet double). 1 vol. demi-rel., au chiffre de la République Française. *Nouveau fonds* 3754.

6156-6158. 雜阿含經

Tsa 'o han king.

Saṃyuktāgama sūtra.

Traduction par Guṇabhadra; texte partiellement semblable à Bunyiu Nanjio 542, 543. Lecture des signes difficiles. Édition de Tsi-tchao 'an (1609, 1610).

50 livres. — Bunyiu Nanjio 544.

Grand in-8. Bonne gravure; frontispice (1 feuillet double). 3 vol. demi-rel., au chiffre de la République Française.
Nouveau fonds 3755 à 3757.

6159.

Tsa 'o han king.

Double.

Livres 31 à 40.

1 vol. cartonnage.
Nouveau fonds 4604.

Troisième Section : SŪTRA MÉLANGÉS

6160. — I.

阿難問事佛吉凶經

'O nan oen chi fo ki hiong king.

Sūtra sur la condition heureuse ou malheureuse des serviteurs du Bouddha.

Version de 'An Chi-kao. Édition du Hoa-yen ko (1642).

7 feuillets. — Bunyiu Nanjio 635.

— II.

慢法經

Man fa king.

Sūtra sur le mépris de la loi.

Version du même texte par Fa-kiu. Même localité (1643).

2 feuillets. — Bunyiu Nanjio 636.

— III.

阿難分別經

'O nan fẹn pie king.

Sūtra sur les idées d'Ānanda.

Version du même texte par Cheng-kien, Chinois (388-407). Mêmes lieu et date qu'à l'art. II.

7 feuillets. — Bunyiu Nanjio 637.

— IV.

五母子經

Oou mou tseu king.

Sūtra sur le fils de cinq mères.

Version de Tchi Khien. Liste des caractères difficiles.

2 feuillets. — Bunyiu Nanjio 638.

— V.

沙彌羅經
Cha mi lo king.

Çrāmaṇera sūtra.

Version du même texte, des dynasties des Tshin (350-431). Édition du Hoa-yen ko (1642).

2 feuillets. — Bunyiu Nanjio 639.

— VI.

玉耶經
Yu ye king.

Sūtra sur Yu-ye (belle-fille d'Anāthapiṇḍika).

Version de Tchou Than-oou-lan. Mêmes lieu et date.

5 feuillets. — Bunyiu Nanjio 640.

— VII.

玉耶女經
Yu ye niu king.

Sūtra sur Yu-ye.

Version du même texte, de l'époque des Tsin occidentaux (265-316). Mêmes lieu et date.

4 feuillets. — Bunyiu Nanjio 641.

— VIII.

阿漱達經
'O sou ta king.

Asutā sūtra.

Version du même texte par Guṇabhadra (435-443). Mêmes lieu et date.

2 feuillets. — Bunyiu Nanjio 642.

— IX.

摩鄧女經
Mo teng niu king.

Mātaṅgī sūtra.

Version de 'An Chi-kao. Mêmes lieu et date.

3 feuillets. — Bunyiu Nanjio 643.

— X.

摩登 (sic) 女解形中六事經
Mo teng niu kiai hing tchong lou chi king.

Mātaṅgī sūtra.

Traduction du même texte, datant des Tsin occidentaux (265-316). Lecture des caractères rares.

3 feuillets. — Bunyiu Nanjio 644.

— XI.

摩登伽經

Mo teng kia king.

Mātaṅgī sūtra.

Même texte plus complet, traduit par Tchi Khien. Liste des mots difficiles.

2 livres. — Bunyiu Nanjio 645.

Grand in-8. Bonne gravure ; frontispice (1 feuillet double). 1 vol. demi-rel., au chiffre de la République Française. *Nouveau fonds* 3933.

6161. — I.

舍頭諫經

Chẹ theou kien king.

Mātaṅgī sūtra.

Version de Tchou Fa-hou, même texte qu'au n° 6160, art. IX à XI. Liste des mots rares. Édition du Hoa-yen ko (1642) ; réédition partielle (1677).

33 feuillets. — Bunyiu Nanjio 646.

— II.

治禪病秘要經

Tchi chạn ping pi yao king.

Sūtra pour la guérison des maladies du dhyāna (?).

Version de Tsiu-khiu King-cheng (455). Lecture des caractères rares. Édition du Hoa-tchheng seu (1630).

2 livres. — Bunyiu Nanjio 647 ; cf. n°ˢ 6156-6158.

— III.

佛說七處三觀經

Fo chọ tshi tchhou san koan king.

Saptāyatana tridhyāna sūtra.

Version par 'An Chi-kao (151). Lecture des mots rares.

2 livres. — Bunyiu Nanjio 648 ; cf. n°ˢ 6156-6158.

— IV.

阿那邠邸化七子經

'O na pin ti hoa tshi tseu king.

Sūtra sur la conversion des sept fils d'Anāthapiṇḍada,

Version par le même, du texte de Bunyiu Nanjio 543 (51).

5 feuillets. — Bunyiu Nanjio 649.

— V.

佛說大愛道般涅槃經

Fo chọ ta 'ai tao pan nie phan king.

Mahāprajāpatī parinirvāṇa sūtra.

Version de Po Fa-tsou (290-306). Édition du Hoa-yen ko (1643).

9 feuillets. — Bunyiu Nanjio 650; **cf.** id. 543 (52).

— VI.

佛母般泥洹經

Fo mou pan ni yuen king.

Buddhamātṛ parinirvāṇa sūtra.

Version de Hoei-kien (457).

5 feuillets. — Bunyiu Nanjio 651; **cf.** id. 543 (52).

— VII.

佛般泥洹後變記

Fo pan ni yuen heou pien ki.

Appendice au sūtra précédent.

Mêmes lieu et date d'édition qu'à l'art. V.

1 feuillet. — Bunyiu Nanjio 651; **cf.** n° 5955, art. IV.

— VIII.

佛說聖法印經

Fo choe cheng fa yin king.

Āryadharmamudrā sūtra.

Version de Tchou Fa-hou. Lecture des caractères rares. Mêmes lieu et date.

2 feuillets. — Bunyiu Nanjio 652; cf. n⁰ˢ 6156-6158.

— IX.

五陰譬喩經

Oou yin phi yu king.

Pañcaskandhāvadāna sūtra.

Version par 'An Chi-kao.

3 feuillets. — Bunyiu Nanjio 653; cf. n⁰ˢ 6156-6158.

— X.

佛說水沬所漂經

Fo choe choei mo so phiao king.

Sūtra sur les bulles de l'eau.

Version par Tchou Than-oou-lan (381-395).

4 feuillets. — Bunyiu Nanjio 654; cf. n⁰ˢ 6156-6158.

— XI.

佛說不自守意經

Fo choe pou tseu cheou yi king.

Sūtra sur le fait de ne pas garder ses pensées.

Version par Tchi Khien.

2 feuillets. — Bunyiu Nanjio 655; cf. n° 6156-6158.

— XII.

佛說滿願子經

Fo choç man yuen tseu king.

Pūrṇamaitrāyaṇīputra sūtra.

Version des Tsin orientaux (317-420).

3 feuillets. — Bunyin Nanjio 656; cf. nᵒˢ 6156-6158.

— XIII.

轉法輪經

Tchoan fa loçn king.

Dharmacakra pravartana sūtra.

Version par 'An Chi-kao.

3 feuillets. — Bunyiu Nanjio 657; cf. nᵒˢ 6156-6158.

— XIV.

佛說三轉法輪經

Fo choç san tchoan fa loçn king.

Dharmacakra pravartana sūtra.

Version par Yi-tsing (710), **du** même texte.

3 feuillets. — Bunyiu Nanjio 658; cf. nᵒˢ 6156-6158.

— XV.

佛說八正道經

Fo choç pa tcheng tao king.

Aṣṭāṅga samyaṅ mārga sūtra.

Version par 'An Chi-kao.

3 feuillets. — Bunyiu Nanjio 659; cf. nᵒˢ 6156-6158.

— XVI.

難提釋經

Nan thi chi king.

Nandi pravrajyā sūtra.

Version par Fa-kiu (290-306).

5 feuillets. — Bunyiu Nanjio 660; cf. nᵒˢ 6156-6158.

— XVII.

佛說馬有三相經

Fo choç ma yeou san siang king.

Sūtra sur les trois marques d'un cheval.

Version par Tchi Yao (185).

2 feuillets. — Bunyiu Nanjio 661; cf. nᵒˢ 6156-6158.

— XVIII.

佛說馬有八態譬人經

Fo choç ma yeou pa thai phi jen king.

Sūtra sur les huit caractères distinctifs d'un cheval comparés à ceux d'un homme.

Du même.

2 feuillets. — Bunyiu Nanjio 662 ; cf. 6156-6158.

— XIX.

佛說相應相可經

Fo choę siang ying siang kho king.

Sūtra sur ce qui est convenable.

Version par Fa-kiu. Liste des caractères rares. Édition de Hoatchheng-seu (1627).

3 feuillets. — Bunyiu Nanjio 663 ; cf. n° 6155, art. II.

Grand in-8. Bonne gravure. 1 vol. demi-rel., au chiffre de la République Française.
Nouveau fonds 4033.

6162. — I.

禪祕要法經

Chạn pi yao fa king.

Sūtra sur les principes importants et secrets du dhyāna.

Version de Kumārajīva. Lecture des mots rares. Édition du Hoayen ko (1642).

3 livres. — Bunyiu Nanjio 779.

— II.

陰持入經

Yin tchhi jou king.

Skandha dhātvāyatana sūtra.

Version de 'An Chi-kao. Lecture des caractères rares. Mêmes lieu et date.

2 livres. — Bunyiu Nanjio 780.

Grand in-8. Bonne gravure ; frontispice (1 feuillet double) 1 vol. demi-rel., au chiffre de la République Française.
Nouveau fonds 4046.

6163. — I.

佛說因緣僧護經

Fo choę yin yuen seng hou king.

Saṅgharakṣitāvadāna sūtra.

Version de la dynastie des Tsin orientaux (317-420). Liste des caractères rares. Édition du Hoayen ko (1642).

1 livre. — Bunyiu Nanjio 781.

— II.

佛說大乘莊嚴寶王經

Fo choę ta cheng tchoang yen pao oang king.

Karaṇḍavyūha sūtra ; alias : Ghanavyūha sūtra.

Version de Thien-si-tsai. Lecture des signes difficiles.

4 livres. — Bunyiu Nanjio 782 ; cf. n° 6083 ; n° 6095, art. III ; n° 6096.

— III.

分別善惡報應經

Fen pie chan 'o pao ying king.

Sukṛta duḥkṛta phalaviçeṣa sūtra.

Du même. Liste des caractères rares. Mêmes lieu et date qu'à l'art. I.

2 livres. — Bunyiu Nanjio 783 ; cf. id. 610, 611.

Grand in-8. Bonne gravure. 1 vol. demi-rel., au chiffre de la République Française.

Nouveau fonds 3904.

6164. — I.

佛說四天王經

Fo choç seu thien oang hing.

Caturdevarāja sūtra.

Traduction par Tchi-yen et Pao-yun (427).

4 feuillets. — Bunyiu Nanjio 722.

— II.

佛說八師經

Fo choç pa chi king.

Aṣṭaguru sūtra.

Traduction par Tchi Khien.

6 feuillets. — Bunyiu Nanjio 710.

Édition de la bonzerie de Hai-tchhoang (1797).

Petit in-8. Papier blanc. 1 vol. demi-reliure.

Nouveau fonds 74.

6165-6167.   正法念處經

Tcheng fa nien tchhou king.

Saddharmasmṛtyupasthāna sūtra.

Version de Gautama Prajñāruci (539). Lecture des caractères difficiles. Édition de 1613.

Livres 6 à 25 et 56 à 70. — Bunyiu Nanjio 679.

Grand in-8. Bonne gravure. 3 vol. cartonnage.

Nouveau fonds 4652 à 4654.

6168. — I.

妙法聖念處經

Miao fa cheng nien tchhou king.

Saddharmārya smṛtyupasthāna sūtra.

Version par Dharmadeva, d'un texte analogue aux n°ˢ 6165-6167. Lecture des signes rares.

8 livres. — Bunyiu Nanjio 804.

— II.

佛說大迦葉問大寶積 正法經

Fo choę ta kia chę oen ta pao tsi tcheng fa king.

Kāçyapa parivarta sūtra.

Version par Dānapāla, du même texte qu'au n° 5806, art. XLIII. Lecture des caractères difficiles.

5 livres. — Bunyiu Nanjio 805.

Grand in-8. Bonne gravure. 1 vol. demi-rel., au chiffre de la République Française.

Nouveau fonds 3886.

6169. — I.

佛說業報差別經

Fo choę ye pao tchha pie king.

Sūtra sur la différence des résultats du karman.

Traduction de Gautama Dharmaprajña (582). Lecture des signes difficiles.

15 feuillets. — Bunyiu Nanjio 739.

— II.

佛說輪轉五道罪福報 應經

Fo choę loęn tchoan oou tao tsoei fou pao ying king.

Sūtra sur la transmigration comme rétribution du bien et du mal.

Traduction de Guṇabhadra.

5 feuillets. — Bunyiu Nanjio 741.

— III.

大阿羅漢難提蜜多羅 所說法住記

Ta 'o lo han nan thi mi to lo so choę fa tchou ki.

Mémoire sur la durée de la loi prononcée par l'Arhat Nandimitra.

Traduction par Hiuen-tsang (654). Lecture des signes difficiles.

8 feuillets. — Bunyiu Nanjio 1466.

Édition de la bonzerie de Haitchhoang (1811).

Petit in-8. Papier blanc. 1 vol. demireliure.

Nouveau fonds 91.

6170. — I.

嗟韈曩法天子受三 歸依獲免惡道經

Tsie wa nang fa thien tseu cheou san koei yi hoo mien 'o tao king.

Sukārikāvadāna.

Version de Fa-thien ; sūtra du hīnayāna. Édition du Hoa-yen ko (1642).

4 feuillets. — Bunyiu Nanjio 806.

— II.

佛說較量壽命經

Fo choę kiao liang cheou ming king.

Upamitāyus sūtra.

Version de Tien-si-tsai ; sūtra du hīnayāna. Liste des caractères difficiles. Mêmes lieu et date.

11 feuillets. — Bunyiu Nanjio 807.

— III.

佛說沙彌十戒儀則經

Fo choę cha mi chi kiai yi tsę king.

Çrāmaṇera çikṣāpadaniyama sūtra.

Traduction de Chi-hou ; vinaya du hīnayāna.

6 feuillets. — Bunyiu Nanjio 808.

— IV.

佛說聖持世陀羅尼經

Fo choę cheng tchhi chi tho lo ni king.

Vasudhara dhāraṇī sūtra.

Du même.

Bunyiu Nanjio 809. Cf. id. 962. N° 6144, art. III, n° 6204, art. XX.

— V.

佛說布施經

Fo choę pou chi king.

Dāna sūtra.

Version de Fa-thien ; sūtra du hīnayāna.

3 feuillets. — Bunyiu Nanjio 810.

— VI.

佛說聖曜母陀羅尼經

Fo choę cheng yao mou tho lo ni king.

Grahamātṛkā dhāraṇī sūtra.

Du même. Lecture des signes rares. Édition de Hoa-tchheng seu (1629).

5 feuillets. — Bunyiu Nanjio 811.

— VII.

法集名數經

Fa tsi ming chou king.

Dharmasaṅgraha nāmasaṅkhyā sūtra.

Version de Chi-hou.

7 feuillets. — Bunyiu Nanjio 812.

— VIII.

聖多羅菩薩一百八名陀羅尼經

Cheng to lo phou sa yi po pa ming tho lo ni king.

Āryatārā bodhisattva nāmāṣṭaçataka dhāraṇī sūtra.

Version de Fa-thien. Lecture des caractères difficiles.

8 feuillets. — Bunyiu Nanjio 813.

— IX.

十二緣生祥瑞經

Chi eul yuen cheng siang choei king.

Dvādaçanidāna jātamaṅgala sūtra.

Version de Chi-hou; sūtra du hīnayāna. Lecture des caractères rares.

2 livres. — Bunyiu Nanjio 814.

— X.

讚揚聖德多羅菩薩一百八名經

Ts'an yang cheng tẹ to lo phou sa yi po pa ming king.

Tārābhadra nāmāṣṭaçataka sūtra.

Version de Thien-si-tsai.

6 feuillets. — Bunyiu Nanjio 815.

— XI.

聖觀自在菩薩一百八名經

Cheng koan tseu tsai phou sa yi po pa ming king.

Avalokiteçvara nāmāṣṭaçataka sūtra.

Du même. Édition de 1643.

6 feuillets. — Bunyiu Nanjio 816.

— XII.

佛說目連所問經

Fo choẹ mou lien so oen king.

Maudgalyāyana paripṛcchā sūtra.

Version de Fa-thien; vinaya du hīnayāna.

2 feuillets. — Bunyiu Nanjio 817.

— XIII.

外道問聖大乘法無我義經

Oai tao oen cheng ta cheng fa oou oo yi king

Çālisambhava sūtra.

Du même.

4 feuillets. — Bunyiu Nanjio 818 ; cf. n° 6102, art. X et XI.

— XIV.

毗俱胝菩薩一百八名經

Phi kiu tchi phou sa yi po pa ming king.

Vikukṣi bodhisattva nāmāṣṭaçataka sūtra.

Du même. Liste des caractères rares.

5 feuillets. — Bunyiu Nanjio 819.

— XV.

勝軍化世百喻伽他 (sic) 經

Cheng kiun hoa chi po yu kia tho king.

Jayasena lokādhyāpanāvadānaçataka gāthā sūtra.

Version de Thien-si-tsai.

10 feuillets. — Bunyiu Nanjio 820.

— XVI.

六道伽陀經

Lou tao kia tho king.

Ṣaḍgatigāthā sūtra.

Version de Fa-thien. Lecture des mots rares. Édition gravée de nouveau en 1691.

8 feuillets. — Bunyiu Nanjio 821.

Grand in-8. Bonne gravure. 1 vol. demi-rel., au chiffre de la République Française.

Nouveau fonds 3917.

6171. — I.

佛說決定義經

Fo choç kiue ting yi king.

Vinirṇītārtha sūtra.

Version de Fa-hien, Hindou (982-1001) ; sūtra du hīnayāna.

12 feuillets. — Bunyiu Nanjio 928.

— II.

佛說護國經

Fo choç hou koç king.

Rāṣṭrapāla sūtra.

Du même ; sūtra du hīnayāna.

10 feuillets. — Bunyiu Nanjio 929 ; cf. id. 542 (132).

— III.

佛說分別布施經

Fo choç fen pie pou chi king.

Dānacintana sūtra.

Version de Chi-hou; sūtra du hīnayāna. Édition du Hoa-yen ko (1642).

4 feuillets. — Bunyiu Nanjio 930.

— IV.

佛說分別緣生經

Fo choẹ fẹn pie yuen cheng king.

Nidāna sūtra.

Version de Fa-thien; sūtra du hīnayāna. Mêmes lieu et date.

3 feuillets. — Bunyiu Nanjio 931.

— V.

佛說法印經
Fo choẹ fa yin king.

Dharmamudrā sūtra.

Version de Chi-hou; sūtra du hīnayāna. Mêmes lieu et date.

2 feuillets. — Bunyiu Nanjio 932; cf. nᵒˢ 6156 6158.

— VI.

佛說大生義經
Fo choẹ ta cheng yi king.

Mahājātārtha sūtra.

Du même; sūtra du hīnayāna.

9 feuillets. — Bunyiu Nanjio 933; cf. id. 542 (97).

— VII.

佛說發菩提心破諸魔經

Fo choẹ fa phou thi sin pho tchou mo king.

Bodhihṛdaya jāta sarvamāra-vināça sūtra.

Du même.

1 livre (18 feuillets). — Bunyiu Nanjio 934; cf. nᵒ 6213, art. III.

— VIII.

佛說聖佛母般若波羅蜜多經
Fo choẹ cheng fo mou pan jẹ po lo mi to king.

Prajñāpāramitā hṛdaya sūtra.

Du même; traduction du même texte que Bunyiu Nanjio 19 et 20. Lecture des caractères rares. Mêmes lieu et date que plus haut.

2 feuillets. — Bunyiu Nanjio 935; cf. nᵒ 5733, art. II.

— IX.

佛說大乘不思議神通境界經
Fo choẹ ta cheng pou seu yi chen thong king kiai king.

Mahāyānācintyarddhi viṣaya sūtra.

Du même. Lecture des termes rares. Edition de Leng-yen seu (1664).

3 livres. — Bunyiu Nanjio 936.

— X.

佛說給孤長者女得度因緣經

Fo choę ki kou tchang tchę niu tę tou yin yuen king.

Anāthapiṇḍada çreṣṭhi duhitṛparitrāṇaprāpta nidāna sūtra.

Du même; sūtra du hīnayāna. Liste des mots rares. Édition de Hoa-tchheng seu (1616).

3 livres. — Bunyiu Nanjio 937; cf. id. 543.

— XI.

佛說大集法門經

Fo choę ta tsi fa męn king.

Mahāsaṅgīti dharmaparyāya sūtra.

Du même; traduction du même texte que n° 6153, art. IX; sūtra du hīnayāna. Lecture des mots difficiles. Édition de Hoa-tchheng 'an, du Han-chan (1607).

1 livre (25 feuillets). — Bunyiu Nanjio 938.

Grand in-8. Bonne gravure. 1 vol. demi-rel., au chiffre de la République Française.
Nouveau fonds 3927.

6172. — I.

佛說光明童子因緣經

Fo choę koang ming thong tseu yin yuen king.

Prabhāsa kumāra nidāna sūtra.

Version de Chi-hou; sūtra du hīnayāna. Lecture des caractères difficiles. Édition de Hoa-tchheng seu (1612).

4 livres. — Bunyiu Nanjio 939.

— II.

佛說寶帶陀羅尼經

Fo choę pao tai tho lo ni king.

Mekhalā dhāraṇī sūtra.

Du même; traduction du même texte que n° 6218, art. I.

10 feuillets. — Bunyiu Nanjio 940.

— III.

佛說金身陀羅尼經

Fo choę kin chen tho lo ni king.

Suvarṇakāya dhāraṇī sūtra.

Du même.

3 feuillets. — Bunyiu Nanjio 941.

— IV.

佛說入無分別法門經

Fo choę jou oou fęn pie fa męn king.

Avikalpapraveça dharmaparyāya sūtra.

Du même.

6 feuillets. — Bunyiu Nanjio 942.

— V.

佛說淨意優婆塞所問經

Fo choę tsing yı yeou pho sę so oen king.

Çuddhamatyupāsaka paripṛcchā sūtra.

Du même; sūtra du hīnayāna. Lecture des caractères difficiles. Édition de Hoa-tchheng seu (1630).

6 feuillets. — Bunyiu Nanjio 943.

— VI.

佛說金剛場莊嚴般若波羅蜜多教中一分

Fo choę kin kang tchhang tchoang yen pan ję po lo mi to kiao tchong yi fęn.

Une partie de la doctrine du Vajramaṇḍālaṅkāra prajñā pāramitā.

Du même. Liste des caractères difficiles. Édition du Hoa-yen ko (1643).

11 feuillets. — Bunyiu Nanjio 944.

— VII.

佛說息諍因緣經

Fo choę si tcheng yin yuen king.

Vivādavināça nidāna sūtra.

Du même; sūtra du hīnayāna. Lecture des mots rares. Mêmes lieu et date.

9 feuillets. — Bunyiu Nanjio 945; cf. id. 542 (196).

— VIII.

佛說初分說經

Fo choę tchhou fęn choę king.

Prathama vargavacana sūtra.

Du même; sūtra du hīnayāna. Lecture des caractères rares. Mêmes lieu et date.

2 livres. — Bunyiu Nanjio 946.

Grand in-8. Bonne gravure; frontispice (1 feuillet double). 1 vol. demi-rel., au chiffre de la République Française. *Nouveau fonds* 3909.

CHAPITRE XIII : BOUDDHISME
(SŪTRA, SÉRIES DIVERSES)

Première Section : AVADĀNA SŪTRA

6173. — I.

僧伽斯那所撰菩薩本緣經

Seng kia seu na so tchoan phou sa pẹn yuen king.

Bodhisattva pūrvāvadāna sū-tra, composé par Sanghasena.

Version de Tchi Khien. Liste des mots difficiles.

4 livres. — Bunyiu Nanjio 1357.

— II.

那先比丘經

Na sien pi khieou king.

Nāgasena bhikṣu sūtra.

Version des Tsin orientaux (317-420). Lecture des caractères rares.

3 livres. — Bunyiu Nanjio 1358.

Grand in-8. Bonne gravure ; frontis-pice (1 feuillet double). 1 vol. demi-rel., au chiffre de la République Française.
Nouveau fonds 4057.

6174-6175. 撰集百緣經

Tchoan tsi po yuen king.

Pūrṇamukhāvadānaçataka sū-tra.

Version de Tchi Khien. Édition de Hoa-tchheng seu (1630, 1631).

10 livres. — Bunyiu Nanjio 1324.

Grand in-8. Bonne gravure.
1 vol. demi-rel., au chiffre de la République Française.
Nouveau fonds 3955.

1 vol. cartonnage.
Nouveau fonds 4686.

6176. 出曜經

Tchhou yao king.

Avadāna sūtra.

Œuvre de Dharmatrāta ; traduite par Saṅghabhūti, de Ki-pin, et Tchou Fo-nien (398). Préface de Seng-joei (399). Lecture des mots difficiles.

Livres 1 à 8 (manquent livres 9 à 20). — Bunyiu Nanjio 132.

Grand in-8. Bonne gravure; frontispice (1 feuillet double). 1 vol. demi-rel., au chiffre de la République Française.
Nouveau fonds 3979.

6177. — I.

阿育王譬喩經

'O yu oang phi yu king.

Açoka rājāvadāna sūtra.

Version des Tsin orientaux (317-420).

8 feuillets. — Bunyiu Nanjio 1344; cf. id. 1343, 1366.

— II.

三慧經

San hoei king.

Trijñāna sūtra.

Version des Liang septentrionaux (397-439).

14 feuillets. — Bunyiu Nanjio 1345.

— III.

阿毗曇五法行經

'O phi than oou fa hing king.

Abhidharma pañcadharmacaryā sūtra.

Version de 'An Chi-kao; sūtra du hīnayāna. Liste des caractères difficiles.

12 feuillets. — Bunyiu Nanjio 1346.

— IV.

賓頭盧突羅闍爲優陀延王說法緣經

Pin theou lou tou lo chẹ oei yeou tho yen oang chọ fa yuen king.

Dharmanidāna sūtra prononcé pour le roi Udayana.

Version de Guṇabhadra (435-443); sūtra du hīnayāna.

10 feuillets. — Bunyiu Nanjio 1347.

— V.

請賓頭盧經

Tshing pin theou lou king.

Sūtra sur l'invitation à Piṇḍola bharadvāja.

Version de Hoei-kien (457).

3 feuillets. — Bunyiu Nanjio 1348.

— VI.

大勇菩薩分別業報略經

Ta yong phou sa fẹn pie ye paọ lio king.

Mahāçūra bodhisattva nirdeça karmaphala saṅkṣipta sūtra.

Version de Saṅghavarman, Hindou (434). Liste des caractères difficiles. Édition de Hoa-tchheng seu (1632).

13 feuillets. — Bunyiu Nanjio 1349.

— VII.

坐禪三昧法門經

Tsoo chan san mei fa men king.

Sūtra sur le dhyāna samādhi.

Œuvre de Saṅgharakṣa, traduite par Kumārajīva (402 et 407). Liste des mots rares. Mêmes lieu et date d'édition.

2 livres. — Bunyiu Nanjio 1350.

Grand in-8. Bonne gravure. 1 vol. demi-rel., au chiffre de la République Française.
Nouveau fonds 4036.

6178. 雜寶藏經

Tsa pao tsang king.

Saṃyuktaratnapiṭaka sūtra.

Version de Ki-kia-ye (Kiṅkara), Occidental (472) et Than-yao, religieux d'origine inconnue, sūtra du hīnayāna. Liste des caractères rares. Édition de Hoa-tchheng seu (1630).

5 livres (récits 1 à 78); manquent les livres 6 à 8. — Bunyiu Nanjio 1329.

Grand in-8. Bonne gravure. 1 vol. demi-rel., au chiffre de la République Française.
Nouveau fonds 4058.

Deuxième Section : **JĀTAKA SŪTRA**

6179. 六度集經

Lou tou tsi king.

Ṣaṭpāramitā sannipāta (alias : saṅgraha) sūtra.

Version de Khang Seng-hoei, Hindou (241-280). Préface (1590) par Tchhen Oen-tchou Yu-chou, de Mien-yang ; introduction par Hia Ji-khoei (1588).

8 livres (livres 1 à 4 seulement). — Bunyiu Nanjio 143.

Livre 1, sans divisions.

— I, livre 2.

波耶王經

Po ye oang king.

Sūtra du roi Po-ye.

Feuillets 1 et 2.

— II, livre 2.

波羅奈國王經

Po lo nai koę oang king.

Sūtra du roi de Po-lo-nai.

Feuillets 2 à 4.

— III, livre 2.

薩和檀王經

Sa hoo than oang king.

Sūtra du roi Sarvadāna.

Feuillets 4 à 6.

— IV, livre 2.

須大拏經

Siu ta na king.

Sudāna sūtra.

Lecture des signes difficiles.

Feuillets 6 à 17.
Cf. nº 6079, art. VII.

— V, livre 3, une partie de ce livre n'offre pas de divisions, on trouve toutefois :

佛說四姓經

Fo choę seu sing king.

Caturvarṇa sūtra.

Feuillets 2 à 5.
Cf. nº 6153, art. V.

— VI, livre 4, sans divisions, sauf les suivantes :

太子慕魄經

Thai tseu mou phę king.

Mūka kumāra sūtra.

Feuillets 13 à 15.
Cf. nº 6098, art. VII et VIII.

— VII, livre 4.

彌蘭經

Mi lan king.

Sūtra du marchand Mi-lan.

Feuillets 15 à 17.

— VIII, livre 4.

頂生聖王經

Ting cheng cheng oang king.

Sūtra du saint roi Ting-cheng.

Feuillets 18 à 20.

— IX, livre IV.

普明王經

Phou ming oang king.

Sūtra du roi Phou-ming.

Feuillets 20 à 25.

Grand in-8. Bonne gravure. 1 vol. demi-rel., au chiffre de la République Française.

Nouveau fonds 3883.

6180. 佛說生經

Fo choe cheng king.

Jātaka nidāna sūtra.

Version de Tchou Fa-hou (285). Collection de sūtra; lecture des caractères difficiles après chaque livre. Édition donnée par Tchhe-oei (1661).

Bunyiu Nanjio 669.

— I, livre 1.

佛說那賴經

Fo choe na lai king.

Nārada sūtra.

Feuillets 1 à 3.

— II, livre 1.

佛說分衛比丘經

Fo choe fen oei pi khieou king.

Piṇḍapātika bhikṣu sūtra.

Feuillets 3 à 6.

— III, livre 1.

佛說和難經

Fo choe hoo nan king.

Upananda sūtra.

Feuillets 6 à 10.

— IV, livre 1.

佛說邪業自活經

Fo choe sie ye tseu hoo king.

Duṣkṛtapunarjanma sūtra.

Feuillets 10 à 12.

— V, livre 1.

佛說是我所經

Fo choe chi oo so king.

Sūtra [de l'oiseau] Mahyaka.

Feuillets 12 à 14.

— VI, livre 1.

佛說野雞經

Fo choe ye ki king.

Kukkuṭa sūtra.

Feuillets 14 à 18.

— VII, livre 1.

佛說前世諍女經

Fo choe tshien chi tcheng niu king.

Pūrva janmastrī nindā sūtra.

Feuillets 18 et 19.

— VIII, livre 1.

佛說墮珠著海中經

Fo choe too tchou tchou hai tchong king.

Sāgara ratnapāta sūtra.

Feuillets 19 à 21.

— IX, livre 1.

佛說栴闍摩暴志謗佛
經

Fo choȩ tchạn tchȩ mo pao tchi pang fo king,

Cañcā māṇavikā sūtra.

Feuillets 21 à 23. — Cf. Bunyiu Nanjio 243.

— X, livre 1.

佛說鱉獼猴經

Fo choȩ pie eul heou king.

Kacchapa kapi sūtra.

Feuillets 23 et 24.

— XI, livre 1.

佛說五仙人經

Fo choȩ oou sien jen king.

Pañca ṛṣi sūtra.

Feuillets 25 à 29.

— XII, livre 1.

佛說舅甥經

Fo choȩ kieou cheng king.

Pitṛvya bhrātṛvya sūtra.

Feuillets 29 à 32.

— XIII, livre 2.

佛說閑居經

Fo choȩ hien kiu king.

Kausīdya sūtra.

Feuillets 1 à 3.

— XIV, livre 2.

佛說舍利弗般泥洹經

Fo choȩ chȩ li fou pan ni yuen king.

Çāriputraparinirvāṇa sūtra.

Feuillets 3 à 6. — Cf. Bunyiu Nanjio 650, 651.

— XV, livre 2.

佛說于命過經

Fo choȩ tseu ming koo king.

Putra maraṇa sūtra.

Feuillet 6. — Cf. Bunyiu Nanjio 582.

— XVI, livre 2.

佛說比丘各言志經

Fo choȩ pi khieou ko yen tchi king.

Sva sva citta bhikṣu vāda sūtra.

Feuillets 6 à 12.

— XVII, livre 2.

佛說迦旃延說無常經

Fo choȩ kia tchạn yen choȩ oou chang king.

Kātyāyana proktānityatā sūtra.

Feuillets 13 à 15. — Cf. Bunyiu Nanjio 727.

— XVIII, livre 2.

佛說和利長者問事經

Fo choę hoo li tchang tchę oen chi king.

Pāli (?) gṛhapati vastu paripṛcchā sūtra.

Feuillets 15 à 17.

— XIX, livre 2.

佛說心總持經

Fo choę sin tsong tchhi king.

Hṛdaya dhāraṇī sūtra.

Feuillets 17 à 20.

— XX, livre 2.

佛說護諸比丘咒經

Fo choę hou tchou pi khieou tcheou king.

Bhikṣu paritrāṇa dhāraṇī sūtra.

Feuillets 20 et 21.

— XXI, livre 2.

佛說吉祥咒經

Fo choę ki siang tcheou king.

Çrī dhāraṇī sūtra.

Feuillets 21 à 24.

— XXII, livre 2.

佛說總持經

Fo choę tsong tchhi king.

Dhāraṇī sūtra.

Feuillets 24 à 26.

— XXIII, livre 3.

佛說所欣釋經

Fo choę so hin chi king.

Nanda çākyaputra sūtra.

Feuillets 1 à 3.

— XXIV, livre 3.

佛說國王五人經

Fo choę koę oang oou jen king.

Pañca rājaputra sūtra.

Feuillets 3 à 9. — Cf. Bunyiu Nanjio 775.

— XXV, livre 3.

佛說蠱狐烏經

Fo choę kou hou oou king.

Kokālika sūtra.

Feuillets 9 à 11.

— XXVI, livre 3.

佛說比丘疾病經

Fo choę pi khieou tsi ping king.

Bhikṣu vyādhi sūtra.

Feuillets 11 à 13.

— XXVII, livre 3.

佛說審裸形子經

Fo choę chen loo hing tseu king.

Sūtra sur les gymnosophistes (?).

Feuillets 13 à 18.

— XXVIII, livre 3.

佛說腹使經

Fo choę fou chi king.

Feuillets 18 à 22.

— XXIX, livre 3.

佛說弟子過命經

Fo choę ti tseu koo ming king.

Atikrānta çiṣya sūtra.

Feuillets 22 à 25.

— XXX, livre 4.

佛說水牛經

Fo choę choei nieou king.

Mahiṣa sūtra.

Feuillets 1 et 2. — Cf. Bunyiu Nanjio 233, 627 et 764.

— XXXI, livre 4.

佛說兔王經

Fo choę thou oang king.

Çaça rāja sūtra.

Feuillets 3 et 4.

— XXXII, livre 4.

佛說無懼經

Fo choę oou kiu king.

Abhaya sūtra.

Feuillets 4 et 5.

— XXXIII, livre 4.

佛說五百幼童經

Fo choę oou po yeou thong king.

Pañca çata māṇavaka sūtra.

Feuillets 6 et 7. — Cf. Bunyiu Nanjio 729.

— XXXIV, livre 4.

佛說毒草經

Fo choę tou tshao king.

Viṣauṣadhi sūtra.

Feuillets 7 et 8.

— XXXV, livre 4.

佛說鼈喻經

Fo choe pie yu king.

Kacchapopamā sūtra.

Feuillets 8 et 9.

— XXXVI, livre 4.

佛說菩薩曾爲鼈王經

Fo choe phou sa tsheng oei pie oang king.

Kacchapa rāja bodhisattva sū-tra.

Feuillets 9 et 10.

— XXXVII, livre 4.

佛說毒喻經

Fo choe tou yu king.

Viṣopamā sūtra.

Feuillets 10 à 12.

— XXXVIII, livre 4.

佛說誨子經

Fo choe hoei tseu king.

Kumārāvavāda.

Feuillets 12 à 15.

— XXXIX, livre 4.

佛說貞爲牛者經

Fo choe fou oei nieou tche king.

Gobhāra hāra sūtra.

Feuillets 15 à 18.

— XL, livre 4.

佛說光華梵志經

Fo choe koang hoa fan tchi king.

Prabhā puṣpa brahmacāri sū-tra.

Feuillets 18 et 19.

— XLI, livre 4.

佛說變悔喻經

Fo choe pien hoei yu king.

Kaukṛtya parivartopamā sū-tra.

Feuillets 19 à 21.

— XLII, livre 4.

佛說馬喻經

Fo choe ma yu king.

Açvopamā sūtra.

Feuillets 21 et 22. — Cf. Bunyiu Nanjio 661, 662.

— XLIII, livre 4.

佛說比丘尼現變經

Fo choę pi khieou ni hien pien king.

Bhikṣuṇī parivarta sūtra.

Feuillets 22 et 23.

— XLIV, livre 4.

佛說孤獨經

Fo choę kou tou king.

Kaivalya sūtra.

Feuillets 23 et 24.

— XLV, livre 5.

佛說梵志經

Fo choę fan tchi king.

Brahmacāri sūtra.

Feuillets 1 à 3.

— XLVI, livre 5.

佛說君臣經

Fo choę kiun tchhen king.

Bhṛtya bhaṭṭāraka sūtra.

Feuillets 3 à 5.

— XLVII, livre 5.

佛說拘薩國烏王經

Fo choę kiu sa koę oou oang king.

Kosala rāja sūtra

Feuillets 5 à 8. — Cf. Bunyiu Nanjio 417.

— XLVIII, livre 5.

佛說蜜具經

Fo choę mi kiu king.

Guhya pāda (?) sūtra.

Feuillets 8 à 10.

— XLIX, livre 5.

佛說雜讚經

Fo choę tsa tsan king.

Saṃyuktānucaṃsā sūtra.

Feuillets 10 à 12.

— L, livre 5.

佛說草驢馳經

Fo choę tshao liu tchhi king.

Gardabhī sūtra.

Feuillets 12 à 14.

— Ll, livre 5.

佛說孔雀經

Fo choę khong tsio king.

Mayūra sūtra.

Feuillets 14 à 16. — Cf. nº 6056, art. I à IV.

— LII, livre 5.

佛說仙人撥劫經

Fo choę sien jen po kie king.

Pauṣkara ṛṣi sūtra.

Feuillets 16 à 18.

— LIII, livre 5.

佛說清信士阿夷扇持父子經

Fo choę tshing sin chi'o yi chạn tchhi fou tseu king.

Sūtra sur les fidèles 'O-yi-chạn-tchhi, père et fils.

Feuillets 18 à 20.

–- LIV, livre 5.

佛說夫婦經

Fo choę fou fou king.

Dampati sūtra.

Feuillets 20 à 23.

— LV, livre 5.

佛說譬喻經

Fo choę phi yu king.

Upamā sūtra.

Feuillets 23 à 28. — Cf. Bunyiu Nanjio 1353, 1359, 1364, 1366, 1368, 1372.

Grand in-8. Bonne gravure. 1 vol. demi-rel., au chiffre de la République Française.

Nouveau fonds 3962.

6181.   # 普曜經

Phou yao king.

Lalitavistara sūtra.

Traduction de Tchou Fa-hou. Liste des caractères rares. Édition de Tsi-tchao 'an (1609).

8 livres. — Bunyiu Nanjio 160.

Grand in-8. Bonne gravure. 1 vol. demi-rel., au chiffre de la République Française.

Nouveau fonds 3816.

6182.   # 方廣大莊嚴經

Fang koang ta tchoang yen king;
alias :

神通遊戲

Chen thong yeou hi.

Lalitavistara sūtra.

Version du même texte par Dī-vākara (685). Préface par l'impé-ratrice Oou. Lecture des signes difficiles. Édition de Hoa-tchheng seu (1631).

12 livres. — Bunyiu Nanjio 159.

Grand in-8. Bonne gravure. 1 vol. demi-rel., au chiffre de la République Française.

Nouveau fonds 3814.

6183. 過去現在因果經
Koo khiu hien tsai yin koo king.

Atītapratyutpanna hetuphala sūtra.

Version par Guṇabhadra, du même texte que Bunyiu Nanjio 664 et 665. Lecture des mots rares. Édition de Hoa-tchheng seu (1632).

4 livres. — Bunyiu Nanjio 666.

Grand in-8. Bonne gravure. 1 vol. demi-rel., au chiffre de la République Française.

Nouveau fonds 3966.

6184-6185. 佛本行集經
Fo pẹn hing tsi king.

Buddhacaritra sūtra; alias : Abhiniṣkramaṇa sūtra.

Version de Jñānagupta (587). Lecture des signes difficiles. Édition donnée par Kou Long chan, de Kin-cha (1640-1642).

30 livres seulement (1 à 30, manquent 31 à 60). — Bunyiu Nanjio 680.

Grand in-8. Bonne gravure; frontispice (1 feuillet double). 2 vol. demi-rel., au chiffre de la République Française.

Nouveau fonds 3817, 3818.

6186. 佛說眾許摩訶帝經
Fo choẹ tchong hiu mo ho ti king.

Mahā saṃmatarāja sūtra.

Version de Fa-hien, Hindou (982-1001). Liste des caractères rares. Édition de Hoa-tchheng seu (1636).

13 livres. — Bunyiu Nanjio 859.

Grand in-8. Bonne gravure. 1 vol. demi-rel., au chiffre de la République Française.

Nouveau fonds 3972.

Troisième Section : SARVABUDDHA SŪTRA

6187. — I.
諸佛要集經
Tchou fo yao tsi king.

Buddhasaṅgīti sūtra.

Version de Tchou Fa-hou. Liste des caractères rares. Édition de Hoa-tchheng seu (1633).

2 livres. — Bunyiu Nanjio 401.

— II.

稱揚諸佛功德經

Tchheng yang tchou fo kong tẹ king; alias :

集諸佛華

Tsi tchou fo hoa.

Kusumasañcaya sūtra.

Version par Ki-kia-ye et Than-yao (462-472). Liste des mots difficiles. Édition de Tsi-tchao 'an (1608).

3 livres. — Bunyiu Nanjio 402.

Grand in-8. Bonne gravure. 1 vol. demi-rel., au chiffre de la République Française.

Nouveau fonds 3922.

6188. 賢劫經

Hien kie king; alias :

颰陀劫三昧經

Po tho kie san mei king; alias :

賢劫定意經

Hien kie ting yi king.

Bhadrakalpika sūtra.

Version de Tchou Fa-hou (300). Liste des caractères difficiles. Édition de Hoa-tchheng seu (1637, 1638).

10 livres. — Bunyiu Nanjio 403.

Grand in-8. Bonne gravure. 1 vol. demi-rel., au chiffre de la République Française.

Nouveau fonds 3854.

6189. 佛說佛名經

Fo chọẹ fo ming king.

Buddhanāma sūtra.

Version de Bodhiruci, Hindou (508-535). Lecture des caractères rares. Édition de Kou Long-chan, de Kin-cha (1641).

12 livres. — Bunyiu Nanjio 404.

Grand in-8. Bonne gravure. 1 vol. demi-rel., au chiffre de la République Française.

Nouveau fonds 3853.

6190-6192.
— I (6190).

Fo chọẹ fo ming king.

Même ouvrage qu'au n° précédent.

— II (6190).

三劫三千佛緣起

San kie san tshien fo yuen khi.

Trikalpa trisahasra buddha nidāna.

Traduction de Kālayaças ; extrait du Tẹ tseu han koan yo oang yo chang king (Bunyiu Nanjio 305).

第四卷

Bunyiu Nanjio 4o5.

— III (6190).

過去莊嚴劫千佛名經

*Koo khiu tchoang yen kie tshien
fo ming king*; alias :

集 諸 佛 大 功 德 山

Tsi tchou fo ta kong te chan.

Atīta vyūhakalpa sahasrabu-
ddhanāma sūtra.

Traduction de la dynastie des
Liang (502-557).

Bunyiu Nanjio 4o5.

— IV (6191).

現 在 賢 劫 千 佛 名 經

*Hien tsai hien kie tshien fo ming
king*; alias :

集 諸 佛 大 功 德 山

Tsi tchou fo ta kong te chan.

Pratyutpanna bhadrakalpa sa-
hasrabuddhanāma sūtra.

Traduction de la dynastie des
Liang (502-557).

Bunyiu Nanjio 4o6.

— V (6192).

未 來 星 宿 劫 千 佛 名 經

*Oei lai sing sou kie tshien fo
ming king*; alias :

集 諸 佛 大 功 德 山

Tsi tchou fo ta kong te chan.

Anāgata nakṣatratārākalpa sa-
hasrabuddhanāma sūtra.

Traduction de la dynastie des
Liang (502-557).

Bunyiu Nanjio 4o7.

In-4. Bonne impression sur papier
blanc; 3 vol. en paravent, couvertures
rouges; dans 1 étui demi-rel., au chiffre
de Louis-Philippe.

Nouveau fonds 279.

6193. — I.

San kie san tshien fo yuen khi.

Même ouvrage qu'au n° 6190,
art. II.

— II.

*Koo khiu tchoang yen kie tshien
fo ming king.*

Même ouvrage qu'au n° 6190,
art. III. Liste des caractères rares.
Édition de Hoa-tchheng seu (1631).

— III.

*Hien tsai hien kie tshien fo ming
king.*

Même ouvrage qu'au n° 6191,
art. IV. Lecture des caractères
difficiles. Édition de Hoa-tchheng
seu (1628).

— IV.

Oei lai sing sou kie tshien fo ming king.

Même ouvrage qu'au n° 6192, art. V. Liste des signes difficiles. Édition de Tsi-tchao 'an (1611).

Grand in-8. Bonne gravure. 1 vol. demi-rel., au chiffre de la République Française.

Nouveau fonds 3855.

6194. — I.

力莊嚴三昧經

Li tchoang yen san mei king.

Balavyūha samādhi sūtra.

Traduction de Narendrayaças (585). Lecture des caractères difficiles.

3 livres. — Bunyiu Nanjio 409.

— II.

佛說八部佛名經

Fo choẹ pa pou fo ming king.

Aṣṭabuddhaka sūtra.

Traduit par Gautama Prajñāruci (542).

Bunyiu Nanjio 410.

— III.

百佛名經

Po fo ming king.

Çatabuddhanāma sūtra.

Traduit par Narendrayaças (582). Lecture des signes difficiles. Édition de Tsi-tchao 'an à King-chan.

Bunyiu Nanjio 411.

Grand in-8. Bonne gravure ; au début, frontispice (1 feuillet double). 1 vol. demi-rel., au chiffre de Napoléon III.

Nouveau fonds 1322.

6195. — I.

Li tchoang yen san mei king.

Même ouvrage qu'au n° 6194, art. I ; frontispice différent, édition plus petite faite par les soins de Ling-hoei.

— II.

Fo choẹ pa pou fo ming king.

Même ouvrage qu'au n° 6194, art. II ; même édition qu'à l'art. I ci-dessus.

3 feuillets.

— III.

Po fo ming king.

Même ouvrage qu'au n° 6194, art. III ; même édition qu'aux art. I et II ci-dessus.

8 feuillets.

— IV.

佛 說 不 思 議 功 德 諸 佛 所 護 念 經

Fo choę pou seu yi kong tę tchou fo so hou nien king.

Acintyaguṇa sarvabuddha parigrāha sūtra.

Traduction de Jñānagupta (585-592). Extrait du Tchong king. Liste des signes difficiles. Édition de Hoa-tchheng seu à King-chan (1631).

2 livres. — Bunyiu Nanjio 412.

— V.

金 剛 三 昧 本 性 清 淨 不 壞 不 滅 經

Kin kang san mei pęn sing tshing tsing pou hoai pou mie king;
alias :

金 剛 清 淨 經

Kin kang tshing tsing king.

Vajrasamādhi sūtra.

Traduction de l'époque des Tshin (350-431).

8 feuillets. — Bunyiu Nanjio 413.

— VI.

佛 說 師 子 月 佛 本 生 經

Fo choę chi tseu yue fo pęn cheng king.

Siṃhacandra buddha jātaka sūtra.

Traduction de l'époque des Tshin.

9 feuillets. — Bunyiu Nanjio 414.

— VII.

演 道 俗 業 經

Yen tao sou ye king.

Sūtra relatif à la conduite des religieux et des laïques.

Traduit par Cheng-kien. Lecture des signes difficiles.

12 feuillets. — Bunyiu Nanjio 415.

Grand in-8. Bonne gravure. 1 vol. demi-rel., au chiffre de la République Française.

Nouveau fonds 3941.

6196-6197. 諸 佛 世 尊 如 來 菩 薩 尊 者 神 僧 名 經

Tchou fo chi tsoęn jou lai phou sa tsoęn tchę chen seng ming king.

Sūtra des noms des Buddha, bodhisattva, ārya, etc.

Ouvrage chinois sans nom d'auteur ; préface de 1417, postface de la même date. Édition de diverses bonzeries (1635 à 1640).

4o livres. — Bunyiu Nanjio 1617.

Grand in-8. Bonne gravure ; frontispice (1 feuillet double). 2 vol. demi-rel., au chiffre de la République Française.
Nouveau fonds 3856, 3857.

6198-6200.
— I (6198-6200).

諸佛世尊如來菩薩尊者名稱歌曲

Tchou fo chi tsoẹn jou lai phou sa tsoẹn tchẹ ming tchheng ko khiu.

Poésies sur les noms des Buddhabhagavattathāgata, des bodhisattva, des ārya.

Postface (1417) ; postface impériale (1420). Édition de Kou-mei 'an (1666).

Livres 11 à 48 (manquent les livres 1 à 11 ; le livre 48 termine l'ouvrage).
— Bunyiu Nanjio 1618.

— II (6200).

諸佛世尊如來菩薩尊者名稱歌曲感應

Tchou fo chi tsoẹn jou lai phou sa tsoẹn tchẹ ming tchheng ko khiu kan ying.

Poésies sur l'influence des Buddha, bodhisattva, ārya.

Forment les livres 48 à 51 de l'ouvrage précédent. Préface pour chaque livre (1419). Édition portant la double indication : Kou-mei 'an (1666), Leng-yen seu (1634).

3 livres. — Bunyiu Nanjio 1619.

Grand in-8. Bonne gravure ; manque le feuillet 11 du livre 48, remplacé par un feuillet 11 du livre 47. 3 vol. cartonnage.
Nouveau fonds 4645 à 4647.

Quatrième Section : DHĀRAṆĪ SŪTRA

6201. 佛說安宅神咒經
Fo chọẹ 'an tsẹ chen tcheou king.

Sūtra du mantra pour mettre la maison en paix.

Invocations au début et à la fin. Traduction sans nom d'auteur, de la dynastie des Han orientaux (25-220). Lecture des signes difficiles. A la fin, figure de divinité Édition de Hai-tchhoang seu (1834).

Bunyiu Nanjio 478.

In-12. Papier blanc; frontispice (1 feuillet double). 1 vol. en paravent couvertures rouges: dans 1 étui demi-rel., au chiffre de Louis-Philippe.

Nouveau fonds 153.

6202. — I.

佛 說 持 句 神 咒 經

Fo choe tchhi kiu chen tcheou king; alias :

陀 羅 尼 句 經

Tho lo ni kiu king.

Padadhararddhimantra sūtra.

Version de Tchi Khien. Édition de 1655.

3 feuillets. — Bunyiu Nanjio 364.

— II.

佛 說 陀 鄰 尼 鉢 經

Fo choe tho lin ni po king.

Dhāraṇī pātra sūtra.

Version par Tchou Than-oou-lan (381-395) du même texte qu'à l'art. I. Lecture des caractères rares.

3 feuillets. — Bunyiu Nanjio 365.

— III.

東 方 最 勝 燈 王 如 來 助 護 持 世 間 神 咒 經

Tong fang tsoei cheng teng oang jou lai tsou hou tchhi chi kien chen tcheou king.

Lokapāla dhāraṇī sūtra.

Version du même texte, par Jñānagupta (585-592). Lecture des caractères difficiles. Édition de 1655.

15 feuillets. — Bunyiu Nanjio 366.

— IV.

如 來 方 便 善 巧 咒 經

Jou lai fang pien chan khiao tcheou king.

Saptabuddhaka sūtra.

Version de Jñānagupta (587). Liste des caractères rares. Édition de 1655.

11 feuillets. — Bunyiu Nanjio 367.

— V.

虛 空 藏 菩 薩 問 七 佛 陀 羅 尼 咒 經

Hiu khong tsang phou sa oen tshi fo tho lo ni tcheou king.

Saptabuddhaka sūtra.

Version du même texte, de la dynastie des Liang (502-557). Liste des caractères rares. Édition de 1656.

13 feuillets. — Bunyiu Nanjio 368.

— VI.

善法方便陀羅尼咒經

Chan fa fang pien tho lo ni tcheou king.

Saddharmopāya dhāraṇī mantra sūtra.

Version de l'époque des Tsin orientaux (317-420).

6 feuillets. — Bunyiu Nanjio 369.

— VII.

金剛祕密善門陀羅尼經

Kin kang pi mi chan men tho lo ni king.

Vajraguhya saddharma paryāya dhāraṇī sūtra.

Version de l'époque des Tsin orientaux, du même texte.

6 feuillets. — Bunyiu Nanjio 370.

— VIII.

護命法門神咒經

Hou ming fa men chen tcheou king.

Āyuṣpāla dharmaparyāyarddhimantra sūtra.

Version du même texte par Bodhiruci, Hindou (693). Liste des mots rares. Édition de Tsi-tchao 'an (1611).

13 feuillets. — Bunyiu Nanjio 371.

Grand in-8. Bonne gravure. 1 vol. demi-rel., au chiffre de la République Française.
Nouveau fonds 3916.

6203. 佛說大灌頂神咒經

Fo choe ta koan ting chen tcheou king.

Mahābhiṣekarddhidhāraṇī sūtra.

Version de Po Çrīmitra : collection de dhāraṇī.

Bunyiu Nanjio 167.

— I, livre 1.

灌頂三歸五戒帶佩護身咒經

Koan ting san koei oou kiai tai pei hou chen tcheou king.

Dhāraṇī protectrice de la personne, du triçaraṇa et du pañcaçīla.

Cf. Bunyiu Nanjio 605.

— II, livre 2.

灌頂七萬二千神王護比丘咒經

Koan ting tshi oan eul tshien chen oang hou pi khieou tcheou king.

Dhāraṇī de la protection des religieux, des soixante-douze mille devarāja.

Lecture des caractères difficiles

— III, livre 3.

灌頂十二萬神王護比丘尼咒經

Koan ting chi eul oan chen oang hou pi khieou ni tcheou king.

Dhāraṇī protectrice des religieuses, des cent vingt mille devarāja.

— IV, livre 4.

灌頂百結神王護身咒經

Koan ting po kie chen oang hou chen tcheou king.

Dhāraṇī protectrice de la personne, du devarāja Po-kie.

Lecture des caractères rares. Édition de 1610.

— V, livre 5.

灌頂宮宅神王守鎮左右咒經

Koan ting kong tsẹ chen oang cheou tchen tso yeou tcheou king.

Dhāraṇī du devarāja des palais et maisons.

Cf. Bunyiu Nanjio 478 (nº 6201).

— VI, livre 6.

灌頂塚墓因緣四方神咒經

Koan ting tchong mou yin yuen seu fang chen tcheou king.

Dhāraṇī des deva des quatre points cardinaux, du nidāna des tombeaux.

Liste des caractères rares. Édition de 1610, gravée de nouveau en 1681.

— VII, livre 7.

灌頂伏魔封印大神咒經

Koan ting fou mo fong yin ta chen tcheou king.

Dhāraṇī de Mahādeva, de la mudrā qui soumet Māra.

Cf. Bunyiu Nanjio 934.

— VIII, livre 8.

灌頂摩尼羅亶大神咒經

Koan ting mo ni lo tan ta chen tcheou king.

Abhiṣeka maṇirata mahādeva dhāraṇī sūtra.

Liste des mots difficiles. Édition de 1610.

Cf. n° 6204, art. XIV.

— IX, livre 9.

灌頂召五方龍王攝疫毒神咒經

Koan ting tchao oou fang long oang chẹ yi tou chen tcheou king.

Dhāraṇī appelant à l'aide, contre les contagions, les nāgarāja des cinq régions.

Cf. Bunyiu Nanjio 326 et 481.

— X, livre 10.

灌頂梵天神策經

Koan ting fan thien chen tshẹ king.

Dhāraṇī des plans merveilleux de Brahmadeva.

Liste des caractères difficiles. Édition de 1610.

Cf. n° 6577, art. IX.

— XI, livre 11.

灌頂隨願往生十方淨土經

Koan ting soei yuen oang cheng chi fang tsing thou king; alias :

普廣所問品

Phou koang so oen phin.

Sūtra des vœux pour renaître dans les terres pures des dix régions.

Cf. n° 5734, art. IV.

— XII, livre 12.

灌頂章句拔除過罪生死得度經

Koan ting tchang kiu pa tchhou koo tsoei cheng seu tẹ tou king.

Sūtra de l'anéantissement du péché et du salut obtenu dans la vie et dans la mort.

Lecture des caractères rares. Édition de 1610.

Grand in-8. Bonne gravure. 1 vol. demi-rel., au chiffre de la République Française.

Nouveau fonds 3965.

6204. — I.

大吉義神咒經

Ta ki yi chen tcheou king.

Mahāçryartharddhimantra sūtra.

Version de Than-yao (462). Liste des caractères rares. Édition de Hoa-tchheng seu (1612).

2 livres. — Bunyiu Nanjio 473.

— II.

阿吒婆拘鬼神大將上佛陀羅尼經

'O tchha pho kiu koei chen ta tsiang chang fo tho lo ni king.

Āṭavikāsurasena dhāraṇī sū-tra.

Version de l'époque des Liang (502-557). Lecture des mots diffi-ciles.

6 feuillets. — Bunyiu Nanjio 474.

— III.

佛說大普賢陀羅尼經

Fo choe ta phou hien tho lo ni king.

Samantabhadra dhāraṇī sūtra.

Version de la même époque. Liste des mots rares. Gravé de nouveau en 1692.

3 feuillets. — Bunyiu Nanjio 475; cf. n° 6141, art. V.

— IV.

佛說大七寶陀羅尼經

Fo choe ta tshi pao tho lo ni king.

Mahāsaptaratna dhāraṇī sūtra.

Traduction de la même époque. Gravé de nouveau en 1692.

1 feuillet. — Bunyiu Nanjio 476.

— V.

六字大陀羅尼咒經

Lou tseu ta tho lo ni tcheou king.

Ṣaḍakṣara mahādhāraṇī ma-ntra sūtra.

Version de la même époque.

2 feuillets. — Bunyiu Nanjio 477; cf. n°s 5987, art. VI, et 5990, art. IX.

— VI.

Fo choe 'an tse chen tcheou king.

Même sūtra qu'au n° 6201.

5 feuillets.

— VII.

幻師颰陀神咒經

Hoan chi po tho chen tcheou king; alias :

玄師颰陀所說神咒經

Hiuen chi po tho so choe chen tcheou king.

Māyākāra bhadrarddhi mantra sūtra.

Version de Tchou Than-oou-lan. Lecture des caractères difficiles.

2 feuillets. — Bunyiu Nanjio 479.

— VIII.

佛說辟除賊害咒經

Fo choẹ pi tchhou tsẹ hai tcheou king.

Sūtra pour éviter le dommage des voleurs.

Version de la dynastie des Tsin orientaux.

1 feuillet. — Bunyiu Nanjio 480.

— IX.

佛說咒時氣病經

Fo choẹ tcheou chi khi ping king.

Sūtra pour soulager une épidémie.

Version de Tchou Than-oou-lan.

1 feuillet. — Bunyiu Nanjio 481.

— X.

佛說咒齒經

Fo choẹ tcheou tchhi king.

Sūtra pour soulager les dents.

Du même.

1 feuillet. — Bunyiu Nanjio 482.

— XI.

佛說咒目經

Fo choẹ tcheou mou king.

Sūtra pour soulager les yeux.

Du même.

1 feuillet. — Bunyiu Nanjio 483.

— XII.

佛說咒小兒經

Fo choẹ tcheou siao eul king.

Sūtra pour soulager un enfant.

Du même.

1 feuillet. — Bunyiu Nanjio 484.

— XIII.

阿彌陀鼓音聲王陀羅尼經

'O mi tho kou yin cheng oang tho lo ni king.

Amitadundubhisvararāja dhāraṇī sūtra.

Traduction de la dynastie des Liang (502-557).

4 feuillets. — Bunyiu Nanjio 485.

— XIV.

佛說摩尼羅亶經

Fo choẹ mo ni lo tan king.

Maṇirata sūtra.

Version de Tchou Than-oou-lan. Édition de Tsi-tchao-'an (1607).

3 feuillets. — Bunyiu Nanjio 486; cf. 6203, art. VIII.

— XV.

佛 說 檀 持 羅 麻 油 述 經

Fo choę than tchhi lo ma yeou chou king.

Mahādaṇḍa dhāraṇī sūtra.

Du même.

2 feuillets. — Bunyiu Nanjio 487; cf. n° 6217, art. XI.

— XVI.

佛 說 護 諸 童 子 陀 羅 尼 咒 經

Fo choę hou tchou thong tseu tho lo ni tcheou king.

Sarvabālapāla dhāraṇī sūtra.

Version de Bodhiruci, Hindou (508-535).

4 feuillets. — Bunyiu Nanjio 488.

— XVII.

諸 佛 心 陀 羅 尼 經

Tchou fo sin tho lo ni king.

Buddha hṛdaya dhāraṇī sūtra.

Version de Hiuen-tsang (650). Lecture des caractères difficiles.

3 feuillets. — Bunyiu Nanjio 489; voir n° 6139, art. IV.

— XVIII.

拔 濟 苦 難 陀 羅 尼 經

Pa tsi khou nan tho lo ni king; alias :

勝 福 往 生 淨 土 經

Cheng fou oang cheng tsing thou king.

Duḥkhonmūlana dhāraṇī sū-tra.

Version de Hiuen-tsang (654). Liste des mots rares.

2 feuillets. — Bunyiu Nanjio 490.

— XIX.

八 名 普 密 陀 羅 尼 經

Pa ming phou mi tho lo ni king.

Aṣṭanāma samantaguhya dhā-raṇī sūtra.

Version du même (654).

2 feuillets. — Bunyiu Nanjio 491; cf. n° 6152, art. VI.

— XX.

佛 說 持 世 陀 羅 尼 經

Fo choę tchhi chi tho lo ni king.

Vasudharā dhāraṇī sūtra.

Version de Hiuen-tsang (654). Lecture des mots rares.

4 feuillets. — Bunyiu Nanjio 492; cf. id. 962; n°⁵ 6144, art. III; 6170, art. IV.

— XXI.

佛說六門陀羅尼經

Fo choe lou men tho lo ni king.

Ṣaṇmukhī dhāraṇī sūtra.

Du même (645).

1 feuillet. — Bunyiu Nanjio 493.

— XXII.

清淨觀世音菩薩普賢陀羅尼經

Tshing tsing koan chi yin phou sa phou hien tho lo ni king.

Samantabhadra dhāraṇī sūtra.

Version de Tchi-thong (653). Lecture des caractères rares. Édition de Hoa-tchheng seu (1612).

7 feuillets. — Bunyiu Nanjio 494.

Grand in-8. Bonne gravure. 1 vol. demi-rel., au chiffre de la République Française.

Nouveau fonds 3995.

6205. — I.

舍利弗陀羅尼經

Che li fou tho lo ni king.

Anantamukha sādhaka dhāraṇī sūtra.

Version de Saṅghapāla. Lecture des caractères rares. Édition de 1655; gravé de nouveau en 1681.

11 feuillets. — Bunyiu Nanjio 353.

— II.

佛說無量門破魔陀羅尼經

Fo choe oou liang men pho mo tho lo ni king.

Anantamukha sādhaka dhāraṇī sūtra.

Version du même texte par Kong-te-tchi, et Yin-yang (462). Lecture des mots difficiles.

13 feuillets. — Bunyiu Nanjio 354.

— III.

佛說無量門微密持經

Fo choe oou liang men oei mi tchhi king.

Anantamukha sādhaka dhāraṇī sūtra.

Même texte; version de Tchi

Khien. Liste des caractères rares. Édition de 1655.

7 feuillets. — Bunyiu Nanjio 355.

— IV.

佛說出生無量門持經

Fo choę tchhou cheng oou liang men tchhi king.

Anantamukha sādhaka dhāraṇī sūtra.

Même texte; version de Buddhabhadra. Édition de 1655.

10 feuillets. — Bunyiu Nanjio 356.

— V.

阿難陀目佉尼訶離陀鄰尼經

'O nan tho mou khiu ni ho li tho lin ni king.

Anantamukha sādhaka dhāraṇī sūtra.

Même texte; version de Buddhaçānta. Lecture des caractères rares. Édition de 1656.

13 feuillets. — Bunyiu Nanjio 357.

— VI.

阿難陀目佉尼訶離陀經

'O nan tho mou khiu ni ho li tho king.

Anantamukha sādhaka dhāraṇī sūtra.

Même texte; version de Guṇabhadra. Liste des mots difficiles.

12 feuillets. — Bunyiu Nanjio 358.

— VII.

佛說一向出生菩薩經

Fo choę yi hiang tchhou cheng phou sa king.

Anantamukha sādhaka dhāraṇī sūtra.

Même texte; version de Jñānagupta. Lecture des caractères rares. Édition de Hoa-tchheng seu (1613).

1 livre. — Bunyiu Nanjio 359.

— VIII.

出生無邊門陀羅尼經

Tchhou cheng oou pien men tho lo ni king.

Anantamukha sādhaka dhāraṇī sūtra.

Même texte; version de Tchi-yen, de Khotan (721). Lecture des mots difficiles.

1 livre. — Bunyiu Nanjio 360.

— IX.

勝幢臂印陀羅尼經

Cheng tchhoang phi yin tho lo ni king.

Sudhvaja bāhu mudrā dhāraṇī sūtra.

Version de Hiuen-tsang (654).

3 feuillets. — Bunyiu Nanjio 361.

— X.

妙臂印幢陀羅尼經

Miao phi yin tchhoang tho lo ni king.

Subāhu mudrā dhvaja dhāraṇī sūtra.

Version du même texte par Çikṣānanda. Édition de Hoa-tchheng seu (1616).

2 feuillets. — Bunyiu Nanjio 362.

Grand in-8. Bonne gravure. 1 vol. demi-rel., au chiffre de la République Française.

Nouveau fonds 3918.

6206. — I.

金剛場陀羅尼經

Kin kang tchhang tho lo ni king.

Vajramantra dhāraṇī sūtra.

Version de Jñānagupta (587). Édition de Tsi-tchao 'an (1611).

16 feuillets. — Bunyiu Nanjio 372.

— II.

金剛上味陀羅尼經

Kin kang chang oei tho lo ni king.

Vajramantra dhāraṇī sūtra.

Version du même texte par Buddhaçānta (524). Liste des caractères rares. Édition de Hoa-tchheng seu (1627).

16 feuillets. — Bunyiu Nanjio 373.

— III.

佛說無崖(sic)際總持法門經

Fo choç oou yai tsi tsong tchhi fa mẹn king.

Ananta dhāraṇī dharmaparyāya sūtra.

Version de Cheng-kien. Lecture des caractères rares. Mêmes lieu et date.

18 feuillets. — Bunyiu Nanjio 374.

— IV.

尊勝菩薩所問一切諸法入無量法門陀羅尼經

Tsoẹn cheng phou sa so oen yi

tshie tchou fa jou oou liang fa men tho lo ni king.

Āryajina bodhisattvaparipṛcchā sarvadharmāvatārāmitadharmaparyāya dhāraṇī sūtra.

Version du même texte par Oan Thien-yi, dynastie des Tshi septentrionaux (562-563). Lecture des caractères rares. Édition de Hoatchheng seu (1629).

21 feuillets. — Bunyiu Nanjio 375.

Grand in-8. Bonne gravure. 1 vol. demi-rel., au chiffre de la République Française.

Nouveau fonds 4021.

6207. 大法炬陀羅尼經
Ta fa kiu tho lo ni king.

Mahādharmolkā dhāraṇī sūtra.

Version de Jñānagupta (592). Liste des caractères rares. Édition de Kou Long-chan (1625).

20 livres. — Bunyiu Nanjio 422.

Grand in-8. Bonne gravure. 1 vol. demi-rel., au chiffre de la République Française.

Nouveau fonds 4013.

6208. 大威德陀羅尼經
Ta oei te tho lo ni king.

Mahābaladhārmika dhāraṇī sūtra.

Version de Jñānagupta (595). Lecture des caractères difficiles. Édition donnée par Kou Long-chan, de Kin-cha (1625).

20 livres. — Bunyiu Nanjio 423.

Grand in-8. Bonne gravure; frontispice (1 feuillet double). 1 vol. demi-rel., au chiffre de la République Française.

Nouveau fonds 4012.

6209. 佛說陀羅尼集經
Fo choe tho lo ni tsi king.

Dhāraṇī saṅgraha sūtra.

Version par Ta-te 'o-ti-khiu-to (Atigupta ?), Hindou (653-654). Lecture des caractères rares. Édition de 1656.

13 livres. — Bunyiu Nanjio 363.

Livre 1, section du Buddha.

— I, livre 1.

釋迦佛頂身印咒
Chi kia fo ting chen yin tcheou.

Çākya buddhoṣṇīṣakāya dhāraṇī.

Feuillet 4.

— II, livre 1.

佛頂破魔結界降伏印咒

Fo ting pho mo kie kiai kiang fou yin tcheou.

Māra pramardana buddhoṣṇīṣa dhāraṇī.

Feuillet 9.

— III, livre 1.

奉請印咒

Fong tshing yin tcheou.

Pūjā dhāraṇī

Feuillet 11.

— IV, livre 1.

蓮華捧足印咒

Lien hoa fong tsou yin tcheou; alias :

華光印

Hoa koang yin.

Padma prabha dhāraṇī.

Feuillet 11.

— V, livre 1.

坐印

Tsoo yin.

Āsana mudrā.

Feuillet 11.

— VI, livre 1.

金剛藏菩薩印咒

Kin kang tsang phou sa yin tcheou.

Vajra piṭaka bodhisattva dhāraṇī.

Feuillet 12.

— VII, livre 1.

十一面觀世音菩薩印咒

Chi yi mien koan chi yin phou sa yin tcheou.

Avalokiteçvaraikadaçamukha dhāraṇī.

Feuillet 12. — Cf. nº 5861, art. III.

— VIII, livre 1.

大三昧勑語結界印咒

Ta san mei tchhi yu kie kiai yin tcheou.

Mahāsamādhi dhāraṇī.

Feuillet 13.

— IX, livre 1.

那謨悉羯囉印咒

Na mou si kie lo yin tcheou; alias :

禮拜下有讚歡咒

Li pai hia yeou tsan hoan tcheou.

Sastotra namaskāra dhāraṇī.

Feuillet 15.

— X, livre 1.

數珠印咒

Chou tchou yin tcheou.

Japa mālā dhāraṇī.

Feuillet 16. — Cf. n° 5990, art. XIV.

— XI, livre 1.

佛頂頭印

Fo ting theou yin.

Buddhoṣṇīṣa mudrā.

Feuillet 17.

— XII, livre 1.

佛頂轉法輪印咒

Fo ting tchoan fa loen yin tcheou.

Buddhoṣṇīṣa dharmacakra pravartana dhāraṇī.

Feuillet 17. — Cf. n° 6161, art. XIII.

— XIII, livre 1.

帝殊囉施金輪印咒

Ti chou lo chi kin loen yin tcheou.

Tejorāçi suvarṇacakra dhāraṇī.

Feuillet 18.

— XIV, livre 1.

又帝殊囉施金輪佛頂
心法印咒

Yeou ti chou lo chi kin loen fo ting sin fa yin tcheou.

Tejorāçi suvarṇacakra buddhoṣṇīṣa hṛdaya dharma dhāraṇī, autre dhāraṇī.

Feuillet 18.

— XV, livre 1.

放白光明佛頂印

Fang po koang ming fo ting yin;
alias :

放十方光印

Fang chi fang koang yin.

Daça dik prabhāsa [buddhoṣṇīṣa] mudrā.

Feuillet 20.

— XVI, livre 1.

又有白光明佛頂印

Yeou yeou po koang ming fo ting yin.

Çukla prabhāsa buddhoṣṇīṣa mudrā, autre mudrā.

Feuillet 21.

— XVII, livre 1.

若那斫迦囉印咒

Jẹ na tcho kia lo yin tcheou;
alias :

智輪

Tchi loẹn.

Jñānacakra dhāraṇī.

Feuillet 22. — Cf. Bunyiu Nanjio 1014.

— XVIII, livre 1.

若奴瑟你（二合）沙印咒

Jẹ nou sẹ ni (eul ho) cha yin tcheou; alias :

智頂

Tchi ting.

Jñānoṣṇīṣa dhāraṇī.

Feuillet 23.

— XIX, livre 1.

迦黎沙舍尼印咒

Kia li cha chẹ ni yin tcheou;
alias :

滅罪

Mie tsoei.

Kaliçāsanī dhāraṇī.

Feuillet 23.

— XX, livre 1.

阿跋囉質多印咒

'O po lo tchi to yin tcheou; alias :

無能勝

Oou neng cheng.

Aparājita dhāraṇī.

Feuillet 24. — Cf. Bunyiu Nanjio 1377, 1378.

— XXI, livre 1.

釋迦牟尼佛懺悔法印咒

Chi kia meou ni fo tchhan hoei fa yin tcheou.

Çākyamuni buddha pratideçanā dharma dhāraṇī.

Feuillet 24.

— XXII, livre 1.

佛頂刀印咒

Fo ting tao yin tcheou.

Dhāraṇī du couteau du buddhoṣṇīṣa.

Feuillet 24.

— XXIII, livre 1.

佛頂索印咒

Fo ting so yin tcheou.

Buddhoṣṇīṣa bandha dhāraṇī.

Feuillet 26.

— XXIV, livre 1.

佛頂縛鬼印咒

Fo ting fo koei yin tcheou.

Mārabandhana buddhoṣṇīṣa dhāraṇī.

Feuillet 26.

— XXV, livre 1.

釋迦佛眼印咒

Chi kia fo yen yin tcheou.

Çākyamuni cakṣur dhāraṇī.

Feuillet 27.

— XXVI, livre 1.

釋迦佛印

Chi kia fo yin.

Çākya buddha mudrā.

Trois mudrā sans mantra.

Feuillet 27.

— XXVII, livre 1.

斫迦羅跋羅（上聲）底印咒

Tcho kia lo po lo (chang cheng) ti yin tcheou; alias :

輪轉

Loen tchoan.

Cakravartti mudrā dhāraṇī.

Feuillet 28.

— XXVIII, livre 1.

佛斫迦羅法印

Fo tcho kia lo fa yin.

Buddhacakra dharma mudrā.

Feuillet 28.

— XXIX, livre 1.

如來施衆生無畏法印咒

Jou lai chi tchong cheng oou oei fa yin tcheou.

Tathāgatadatta sarvasattvā-bhaya dharma dhāraṇī.

Feuillet 28. — Cf. n° 6136, art. III.

— XXX, livre 1.

一字佛頂法印咒

Yi tseu fo ting fa yin tcheou.

Ekākṣara buddhoṣṇīṣa dhā-raṇī.

Feuillet 29. — Cf. n° 6134.

Livre 2, section du Buddha, fin ; sous-titre :

畫一切佛頂像法

Hoa yi tshie fo ting siang fa.

Sarva buddhoṣṇīṣa pratimā dharma.

Ce livre renferme des dhāraṇī et autres morceaux distincts encadrés dans un texte.

— XXXI, livre 2,

薩婆菩陀烏瑟膩沙印咒

Sa pho phou tho oou sẹ ni cha yin tcheou ; alias :

一切佛頂

Yi tshie fo ting.

Sarvabuddhoṣṇīṣa dhāraṇī.

Feuillet 4. — Cf. n° 6140, art. VIII.

— XXXII, livre 2.

釋迦佛心印咒

Chi kia fo sin yin tcheou.

Çākyabuddha hṛdaya dhāraṇī.

Quatre mudrā et mantra.

Feuillet 4.

— XXXIII, livre 2.

一切佛心印咒

Yi tshie fo sin yin tcheou.

Sarvabudhha hṛdaya dhāraṇī.

Feuillet 7. — Cf. n° 6204, art. XVII.

— XXXIV, livre 2.

又一切佛心印咒

Yeou yi tshie fo sin yin tcheou ; alias :

大心印咒

Ta sin yin tcheou.

Mahāhṛdaya dhāraṇī.

Feuillet 8.

— XXXV, livre 2.

一切佛小心印

Yi tshie fo siao sin yin.

Sarvabuddha kṣudra hṛdaya mudrā.

Feuillet 9.

— XXXVI, livre 2.

一切佛眼印咒

Yi tshie fo yen yin tcheou ; alias :

佛母印

Fo mou yin.

Sarvabuddha cakṣur dhāraṇī.

Feuillet 10.

— XXXVII, livre 2.

佛眉間白毫相印咒

Fo mei kien po hao siang yin tcheou.

Buddhorṇā dhāraṇī.

Feuillet 10.

— XXXVIII, livre 2.

佛牙印咒

Fo ya yin tcheou.

Buddha danta dhāraṇī.

Feuillet 11.

— XXXIX, livre 2.

又一切佛眼印咒

Yeou yi tshie fo yen yin tcheou.

Sarva buddha cakṣur dhāraṇī.

Feuillet 11.

— XL, livre 2.

佛跋折羅止一切毒蠱印咒

Fo po tchę lo tchi yi tshie tou tchhong yin tcheou

Sarva viṣa damana buddha-vajra dhāraṇī.

Trois mudrā et mantra.

Feuillet 11.

— XLI, livre 2.

一切佛棒印咒

Yi tshie fo pang yin tcheou.

Sarvabuddha gadā dhāraṇī.

Feuillet 13.

— XLII, livre 2.

一切佛刀刺一切鬼印咒

Yi tshie fo tao la yi tshie koei yin tcheou.

Sarva māra pramardana sarva-buddha dhāraṇī.

Feuillet 13.

— XLIII, livre 2.

淨王佛頂印咒

Tsing oang fo ting yin tcheou;
alias :

阿閦佛頂印

'O tchhou fo ting yin.

Akṣobhya buddhoṣṇīṣa mudrā.

Feuillet 14. — Cf. Bunyiu Nanjio 28.

— XLIV, livre 2.

鉢頭摩婆旛娑佛頂印咒

Po theou mo pho pho so fo ting yin tcheou.

Padma prabhāsa buddhoṣṇīṣa dhāraṇī.

Feuillet 14.

— XLV, livre 2.

毗摩羅婆旛娑佛印咒

Phi mo lo pho pho so fo yin tcheou; alias :

無憂德佛

Oou yeou tẹ fo.

Vimala prabhāsa buddha dhāraṇī.

Feuillet 14.

— XLVI, livre 2.

尸緊雞佛印咒

Chi kin ki fo yin tcheou; alias :

旃檀德佛

Tchạn than tẹ fo.

Çikhi buddha dhāraṇī.

Feuillet 15.

— XLVII, livre 2.

毗婆尸佛印咒

Phi pho chi fo yin tcheou.

Vipaçyi buddha dhāraṇī.

Feuillet 15. — Cf. Bunyiu Nanjio 850.

— XLVIII, livre 2.

因陀囉達婆闍佛印咒

Yin tho lo ta pho chẹ fo yin tcheou; alias :

相德佛

Siang tẹ fo.

Indra dhvaja buddha dhāraṇī.

Feuillet 15.

— XLIX, livre 2.

北方相德佛頂印咒

Pẹ fang siang tẹ fo ting yin tcheou.

Uttara dhvaja buddhoṣṇīṣa dhāraṇī.

Feuillet 16.

— L, livre 2.

藥師瑠璃光佛印咒

Yo chi lieou li koang fo yin tcheou.

Bhe̦sajyaguru   vaiḍūryaprabhāsa buddha dhāraṇī.

Feuillet 16. — Cf. n° 6103, art. II.

— LI, livre 2.

續驗灌頂印咒

Siu yen koan ting yin tcheou.

Abhiṣekānvīkṣā dhāraṇī.

Feuillet 18.

— LII, livre 2.

阿彌陀佛大思惟經說 序分

*'O mi tho fo ta seu oei king choe̦
siu fe̦n.*

Amitabuddha mahācitta sūtro-
ktānukramaṇī.

Texte et nombreuses dhāraṇī.

Feuillet 19.

— LIII, livre 2.

佛說作數珠法相品

*Fo choe̦ tso chou tchou fa siang
phin.*

Japamālā dharma lakṣaṇa.

Feuillet 29. — Cf. n° 5990, art. XIV.

— LIV, livre 2.

大輪金剛陀羅尼

Ta loe̦n kin kang tho lo ni.

Mahācakra vajra dhāraṇī.

Feuillet 31.

— LV, livre 2.

佛說跋折囉功能法相 品

*Fo choe̦ po tche̦ lo kong neng fa
siang phin*; alias :

金剛杵

Kin kang tchhou.

Vajra musala.

Feuillet 32.

— LVI, livre 3.

般若波羅蜜多大心經

Pan je̦ po lo mi to ta sin king.

Prajñāpāramitā   mahāhṛdaya
sūtra.

Texte, suivi de 20 dhāraṇī.

Feuillet 1. — Cf. n° 5733, art. II.

— LVII, livre 3.

十六神王咒

Chi lou chen oang tcheou.

Seize dhāraṇī des devarāja.

Feuillet 16.

Livres 4 et 5, section d'Avalokite-çvara.

— LVIII, livres 4 et 5.

十一面觀世音神咒經

Avalokiteçvaraikaḍaçamukha dhāraṇī sūtra.

Texte suivi de 52 dhāraṇī.

Feuillet 1. — Cf. n° 5861, art. III.

Livre 6, section d'Avalokiteçvara, suite.

— LIX, livre 6.

千轉觀世音菩薩印咒

Tshien tchoan koan chi yin phou sa yin tcheou.

Sahasrapravartanāvalokite-çvara bodhisattva dhāraṇī.

A la suite, 12 autres dhāraṇī.

Feuillet 1. — Cf. n° 5861, art. V.

— LX, livre 6.

畫觀世音菩薩像法

Hoa koan chi yin phou sa siang fa.

Sur les images d'Avalokite-çvara bodhisattva.

Feuillet 9.

— LXI, livre 6.

觀世音毗俱知菩薩三昧法印咒品

Koan chi yin phi kiu tchi phou sa san mei fa yin tcheou phin.

Avalokiteçvara vikukṣi bodhi-sattva samādhi dharma dhāraṇī.

Texte suivi de 31 dhāraṇī.

Feuillet 12. — Cf. n° 6170, art. XIV.

— LXII, livre 6.

毗俱知菩薩使者法印品

Phi kiu tchi phou sa chi tchę fa yin phin.

Mudrā de l'envoyé de Vikukṣi bodhisattva.

Texte suivi de 12 dhāraṇī.

Feuillet 23.

— LXIII. livre 6.

毗俱知救病法壇品

Phi kiu tchi kieou ping fa than phin.

Rituel de Vikukṣi qui secourt les malades.

Feuillet 26.

Livre 7, section d'Avalokiteçvara et autres bodhisattva.

— LXIV, livre 7.

阿耶揭唎婆觀世音菩薩法印咒品

'O ye kie li pho koan chi yin phou sa fa yin tcheou phin; alias :

馬頭
Ma theou.

Hayagrīvāvalokiteçvara bodhisattva dharma dhāraṇī.

Texte et 13 dhāraṇī.

Feuillet 1.

— LXV, livre 7.

諸大菩薩法會印咒品

Tchou ta phou sa fa hoei yin tcheou phin.

Sarvamahābodhisattva dharma sabhā dhāraṇī.

Texte et 13 dhāraṇī.

Feuillet 18.

Livre 8, section du vajra.

— LXVI, livre 8.

佛說金剛藏大威神力三昧法印咒品

Fo choẹ kin kang tsang ta oei chen li san mei fa yin tcheou phin.

Vajragarbha mahāgaurava bala samādhi dharma dhāraṇī.

Texte et 57 dhāraṇī.

Feuillet 1.

Livre 9, section du vajra, suite.

— LXVII, livre 9.

金剛阿蜜哩多軍茶利菩薩自在神力咒印品

Kin kang 'o mi li to kiun tchha li phou sa tseu tsai chen li tcheou yin phin.

Vajrāmṛtakuṇḍali bodhisattveçvara devabala dhāraṇī.

Texte et 27 dhāraṇī.

Feuillet 1. — Cf. Bunyiu Nanjio 1413.

— LXVIII, livre 9.

跋折囉吒訶娑身印咒

Po tchẹ lo tchha ho so chen yin tcheou; alias :

大笑金剛
Ta siao kin kang.

Vajrāṭṭahāsa kāya dhāraṇī.

Texte et 5 dhāraṇī.

Feuillet 27.

Livre 10, section du vajra, fin.

— LXIX, livre 10.

金剛烏樞沙摩法印咒品

Kin kang oou tchhou cha mo fa yin tcheou phin; alias :

不淨潔金剛印

Pou tsing kie kin kang yin.

Vajrocchuṣma dharma dhāraṇī.

Texte et 42 dhāraṇī.

Feuillet 1.

— LXX, livre 10.

大清面金剛咒法

Ta tshing mien kin kang tcheou fa.

Mahāçuddha mukha vajra dhāraṇī.

Texte et 16 dhāraṇī.

Feuillet 25.

Livre 11, section des deva.

— LXXI, livre 11.

佛說摩利支天經

Fo choe mo li tchi thien king.

Marīcī devī sūtra.

Texte et dhāraṇī.

Feuillet 1. — Cf. n° 6142, art. II.

— LXXII, livre 11.

功德天法

Kong te thien fa.

Guṇa deva dharma.

Version de trois religieux, 'O-nan (Ānanda ?), Kia-che (Kāçyapa ?) et Kiu-to (Gupta ?). Texte et dhāraṇī.

Feuillet 21.

— LXXIII, livre 12.

諸天等獻佛助成三昧法印咒品

Tchou thien teng hien fo tsou tchheng san mei fa yin tcheou phin.

Sarvadeva buddhānuvṛtti sādhana samādhi dharma dhāraṇī.

Texte avec 53 dhāraṇī.

Feuillet 1.

— LXXIV, livre 13.

佛說諸佛大陀羅尼都會道塲印咒品

Fo choe tchou fo ta tho lo ni tou hoei tao tchhang yin tcheou phin.

Dhāraṇī des grandes assemblées des dhāraṇī de tous les Bouddha.

Texte, rituel.

Feuillet 1.

— LXXV, livre 13.

普集會壇下方莊嚴十六時圖

Phou tsi hoei than hia fang tchoang yen chi lou chi thou.

Figure de l'autel des assemblées générales.

Description de l'autel.

Feuillet 35.

Grand in-8. Bonne gravure. 1 vol. demi-rel., au chiffre de la République Française.

Nouveau fonds 4014.

————

6210. — I.

諸佛集會陀羅尼經

Tchou fo tsi hoei tho lo ni king.

Sarvabuddhāṅgavatī dhāraṇī sūtra.

Traduction par Devaprajña (691), du même texte que le Si tchhou tchong thien king (traducteur Chi-hou). Lecture des termes rares.

4 feuillets. — Bunyiu Nanjio 495.

— II.

佛說智炬陀羅尼經

Fo choę tchi kiu tho lo ni king.

Jñānolka dhāraṇī sarvadurgati pariçodhanī sūtra.

Version par le même traducteur (691), du même texte qu'au n° 6139, art. XIV.

4 feuillets. — Bunyiu Nanjio 496.

— III.

佛說隨求即得大自在陀羅尼神咒經

Fo choę soei khieou tsi tę ta tseu tsai tho lo ni chen tcheou king.

Sūtra sur la liberté aussitôt obtenue que cherchée.

Version de Ratnacinta. Lecture des caractères rares. Édition de Hoa-tchheng seu (1612).

1 livre. — Bunyiu Nanjio 497.

— IV.

佛說一切法功德莊嚴王經

Fo choę yi tshie fa kong tę tchoang yen oang king.

Sarvadharmaguṇavyūharāja sūtra.

Version de Yi-tsing (705). Notice finale sur la traduction. Liste des termes rares.

1 livre. — Bunyiu Nanjio 498.

— V.

佛說拔除罪障咒王經

Fo choṣ pa tchhou tsoei tchang tcheou oang king.

Sūtra sur le mantrarāja qui supprime le péché.

Version du même traducteur (710). Lecture des mots difficiles.

3 feuillets. — Bunyiu Nanjio 499.

— VI.

佛說善夜經

Fo choṣ chạn ye king.

Bhadrakā rātrī sūtra.

Du même (701). Liste des caractères rares.

4 feuillets. — Bunyiu Nanjio 500.

— VII.

佛說虛空藏菩薩能滿諸願最勝心陀羅尼求聞持法

Fo choṣ hiu khong tsang phou sa neng man tchou yuen tsoei cheng sin tho lo ni khieou oen tchhi fa.

Règles pour retenir la dhāraṇī d'Ākāçagarbha bodhisattva.

Version de Subhakara (717); texte extrait du Kin kang ting king. Lecture des mots difficiles. Édition de Hoa-tchheng seu (1612).

5 feuillets. — Bunyiu Nanjio 501.

— VIII.

佛說佛地經

Fo choṣ fo ti king.

Buddhabhūmi sūtra.

Version par Hiuen-tsang (645).

10 feuillets. — Bunyiu Nanjio 502.

— IX.

百千印陀羅尼經

Po tshien yin tho lo ni king.

Çatasahasramudrā dhāraṇī sūtra.

Version de Çikṣānanda.

2 feuillets. — Bunyiu Nanjio 503.

— X.

莊嚴王陀羅尼咒經

Tchoang yen oang tho lo ni tcheou king.

Sarvatathāgatādhiṣṭhāna sattvāvalokana buddhakṣetrasandarçana vyūharāja sūtra.

Version de Yi-tsing (701).

4 feuillets. — Bunyiu Nanjio 5o4.

— XI.

香王菩薩陀羅尼咒經
Hiang oang phou sa tho lo ni tcheou king.

Gandharāja bodhisattva dhāraṇī sūtra.

Du même (705). Édition de Tsi-tchao 'an (1601).

3 feuillets. — Bunyiu Nanjio 5o5.

— XII.

優婆夷淨行法門經
Yeou pho yi tsing hing fa men king.

Upāsikā brahmacaryā dharmaparyāya sūtra.

Version de la dynastie des Liang septentrionaux (397-439). Lecture des mots difficiles. Édition de Hoa-tchheng seu (1612).

2 livres. — Bunyiu Nanjio 5o6.

— XIII.

諸法最上王經
Tchou fa tsoei chang oang king.

Sarvadharmānuttararāja sūtra.

Version de Jñānagupta (595). Mêmes lieu et date.

1 livre. — Bunyiu Nanjio 5o7.

Grand in-8. Bonne gravure. 1 vol. demi-rel., au chiffre de la République Française.
Nouveau fonds 3957.

6211-6212. 佛地經論
Fo ti king loen.

Buddhabhūmi sūtra çāstra.

Par le bodhisattva Bandhuprabha. Version de Hiuen-tsang (649). Lecture des termes difficiles. Édition de Song-kiang (1643).

7 livres. — Bunyiu Nanjio 1195; cf. n° 6210, art. VIII.

Grand in-8. Bonne gravure. 1 vol. demi-rel., au chiffre de la République Française.
Nouveau fonds 3925.

1 vol. cartonnage.
Nouveau fonds 4675.

―――――

6213. — I.
文殊師利寶藏陀羅尼經
Oen chou chi li pao tsang tho lo ni king ; alias :

文殊師利菩薩八字三昧法
Oen chou chi li phou sa pa tseu san mei fa.

Mañjuçrī ratnagarbha dhāraṇī sūtra.

Version de Bodhiruci (710). Liste des signes rares. Édition de Hoa-tchheng seu (1632).

1 livre. — Bunyiu Nanjio 448.

— II.

僧伽吒經
Seng kia tchha king.

Saṅghāṭī sūtra dharmaparyāya.

Version d'Upaçūnya (538). Liste des signes rares. Édition du Hoa-yen ko (1642).

4 livres. — Bunyiu Nanjio 449.

— III.

出生菩提心經
Tchhou cheng phou thi sin king.

Utpādita bodhicitta sūtra.

Version de Jñānagupta (595); autre traduction du n° 6171, art. VII.

1 livre. — Bunyiu Nanjio 450.

— IV.

佛說佛印三昧經
Fo choę fo yin san mei king.

Buddhamudrā samādhi sūtra.

Version de 'An Chi-kao. Liste des caractères rares. Édition de Tsi-tchao 'an (1608).

4 feuillets. — Bunyiu Nanjio 451.

— V.

佛說十二頭陀經
Fo choę chi eul theou tho king; alias :

沙門頭陀經
Cha męn theou tho king.

Dvādaçadhūta sūtra.

Version de Guṇabhadra.

6 feuillets. — Bunyiu Nanjio 452.

— VI.

佛說樹提伽經
Fo choę chou thi kia king.

Jyotiṣka sūtra.

Du même,

3 feuillets. — Bunyiu Nanjio 453

— VII.

佛說法常住經
Fo choę fa chang tchou king.

Dharmanityasthāna sūtra.

Traduction des Tsin occidentaux (265-316).

3 feuillets. — Bunyiu Nanjio 454.

— VIII.

佛 說 長 壽 王 經

*Fo choę tchhang cheou oang
king.*

Dīrghāyūrāja sūtra.

Traduction de la même dynastie.
Édition de Tsi-tchao 'an (1609).

6 feuillets. — Bunyiu Nanjio 455.

Grand in-8. Bonne gravure. 1 vol.
demi-rel., au chiffre de la République
Française.

Nouveau fonds 3889.

6214. — I.

穢 跡 金 剛 說 神 通 大 滿 陀 羅 尼 法 術 靈 要 門 經

*Oei tsi kin kang choę chen thong
ta man tho lo ni fa chou ling
yao męn king.*

Malapādavajra nirdeçarddhi-
mahāpūrṇa dhāraṇī dharmaçrī-
mahārthamukha sūtra.

Traduction de Oou-neng-cheng.

4 feuillets. — Bunyiu Nanjio 966.

— II.

穢 跡 金 剛 法 禁 百 變 法 門 經

*Oei tsi kin kang fa kin po pien
fa męn king.*

Malapādavajra dharmaçatavi-
kriyā dharma paryāya sūtra.

Version de 'O-tchi-ta-sien, Hindou (époque des Thang).

8 feuillets. — Bunyiu Nanjio 967.

— III.

佛 說 大 乘 大 方 廣 佛 冠 經

*Fo choę ta cheng ta fang koang
fo koan king.*

Mahāyāna mahāvaipulya bu-
ddhamukuṭa sūtra.

Version de Fa-hou (1004-1058).

2 livres. — Bunyiu Nanjio 968.

— IV.

佛 說 八 種 長 養 功 德 經

*Fo choę pa tchong tchhang yang
kong tę king.*

Aṣṭavargavardhamānaguṇa
sūtra.

Du même; sūtra du hīnayāna.
Liste des caractères rares. Édition
de Tsi-tchao 'an (1608).

2 feuillets. — Bunyiu Nanjio 969.

— V.

大雲輪請雨經

Ta yun loẹn tshing yu king.

Mahāmegha sūtra.

Traduction du même texte qu'au n° 6107, art. II à IV, par Amogha-vajra. Lecture des caractères rares. Édition de Hoa-tchheng 'an, de Hoei-tcheou.

2 livres. — Bunyiu Nanjio 970.

— VI.

佛說大集會正法經

Fo choẹ ta tsi hoei tcheng fa king.

Mahāsaṅgīti saddharma sūtra.

Version par Chi-hou, du texte du n° 6213, art. II. Liste des caractères rares.

5 livres. — Bunyiu Nanjio 972.

— VII.

葉衣觀自在菩薩經

Ye yi koan tseu tsai phou sa king.

Parṇaçavarī dhāraṇī sūtra.

Version d'Amoghavajra. Édition du Hoa-yen ko (1643).

10 feuillets. — Bunyiu Nanjio 973.

— VIII.

毘沙門天王經

Phi cha mẹn thiẹn oang king.

Vaiçramaṇa divyarāja sūtra.

Du même. Traduction partielle du texte du n° 6030. Mêmes lieu et date d'édition.

6 feuillets. — Bunyiu Nanjio 974.

— IX.

文殊問經字母品

Oen chou oen king tseu mou phin.

Mañjuçrī paripṛcchā sūtra a-kṣara mātṛkādhyāya.

Du même. Lecture des signes rares.

3 feuillets. — Bunyiu Nanjio 975.

— X.

佛說梵網經

Fo choẹ fan oang king.

Brahmajāla sūtra.

Version de Kumārajīva (406) (vinaya). Préface de Seng-tchao. Lecture des signes rares. Édition de Miao-tẹ 'an, du Oou-thai chan (1590).

2 livres. — Bunyiu Nanjio 1087.

Grand in-8. Bonne gravure; frontispice (1 feuillet double). 1 vol. demi-rel., au chiffre de la République Française. *Nouveau fonds* 3893.

6215. 佛說大乘聖無量壽決定光明王如來陀羅尼經

Fo choę ta cheng cheng oou liang cheou kiue ting koang ming oang jou lai tho lo ni king.

Mahāyānāryāmitāyurniçcitaprabhāsarājatathāgata dhāraṇī sūtra.

Même ouvrage qu'au nº 6144, art. II. A la fin invocation. Note finale pour la réédition à Haitchhoang seu (1719).

In-4. Papier blanc. 1 vol. en paravent, couvertures rouges; dans 1 étui demi-rel., au chiffre de Louis-Philippe. *Nouveau fonds* 156.

6216. — I.

佛說俱枳羅陀羅尼經

Fo choę kiu tchi lo tho lo ni king.

Kokila dhāraṇī sūtra.

Version de Fa-hien, Hindou (982-1001). Édition du Hoa-yen ko (1643).

2 feuillets. — Bunyiu Nanjio 884.

— II.

佛說消除一切災障寶髻陀羅尼經

Fo choę siao tchhou yi tshie tsai tchang pao ki tho lo ni king.

Sarvāpadvināçaratnoṣṇīṣa dhāraṇī sūtra.

Du même; mêmes lieu et date.

5 feuillets. — Bunyiu Nanjio 885.

— III.

佛說妙色陀羅尼經

Fo choę miao sę tho lo ni king.

Suvarṇa dhāraṇī sūtra.

Du même; mêmes lieu et date.

1 feuillet. — Bunyiu Nanjio 886.

— IV.

佛說栴檀香身陀羅尼經

Fo choę tchan than hiang chen tho lo ni king.

Candanagandhakāya dhāraṇī sūtra.

Du même; mêmes lieu et date.

2 feuillets. — Bunyiu Nanjio 887.

— V.

佛說鉢蘭那賒嚩哩大陀羅尼經

Fo choę po lan na chę fo li ta tho lo ni king.

Parṇaçavarī mahādhāraṇī sū-tra.

Du même; mêmes lieu et date.

3 feuillets. — Bunyiu Nanjio 888.

— VI.

佛說宿命智陀羅尼經

Fo choę sou ming tchi tho lo ni king.

Pūrvanivāsānusmṛtijñāna dhā-raṇī sūtra.

Du même; mêmes lieu et date.

1 feuillet. — Bunyiu Nanjio 889.

— VII.

佛說慈氏菩薩誓願陀羅尼經

Fo choę tsheu chi phou sa chi yuen tho lo ni king.

Maitrī pratijñā dhāraṇī sūtra.

Du même; mêmes lieu et date.

1 feuillet. — Bunyiu Nanjio 890.

— VIII.

佛說滅除五逆罪大陀羅尼經

Fo choę mie tchhou oou yi tsoei ta tho lo ni king.

Pañcānantaryakarmavināça dhāraṇī sūtra.

Du même; mêmes lieu et date.

1 feuillet. — Bunyiu Nanjio 891.

— IX.

佛說無量功德陀羅尼經

Fo choę oou liang kong tę tho lo ni king.

Amitaguṇa dhāraṇī sūtra.

Du même; mêmes lieu et date.

1 feuillet. — Bunyiu Nanjio 892.

— X.

佛說十八臂陀羅尼經

Fo choę chi pa phi tho lo ni king.

Aṣṭādaçabāhu dhāraṇī sūtra.

Du même; mêmes lieu et date.

2 feuillets. — Bunyiu Nanjio 893.

— XI.

佛說洛叉陀羅尼經

Fo choę lo tchha tho lo ni king.

Lakṣa dhāraṇī sūtra.

Du même; mêmes lieu et date.

2 feuillets. — Bunyiu Nanjio 894.

— XII.

佛 說 辟 除 諸 惡 陀 羅 尼 經

Fo choę phi tchhou tchou 'o tho lo ni king.

Sarvapāpavināça dhāraṇī sūtra.

Du même. Lecture des mots difficiles. Mêmes lieu et date.

2 feuillets. — Bunyiu Nanjio 895.

— XIII.

佛 說 大 愛 陀 羅 尼 經

Fo choę ta 'ai tho lo ni king.

Mahāpriyā dhāraṇī sūtra.

Du même.

2 feuillets. — Bunyiu Nanjio 896.

— XIV.

佛 說 阿 羅 漢 具 德 經

Fo choę 'o lo han kiu tę king.

Arhat pūrṇaguṇa sūtra.

Du même; sūtra du hīnayāna. Lecture des mots rares. Feuillets gravés de nouveau en 1678.

10 feuillets. — Bunyiu Nanjio 897; cf. id. 543.

— XV.

佛 說 八 大 靈 塔 名 號 經

Fo choę pa ta ling tha ming hao king.

Aṣṭamahāçrīcaityanāma sūtra.

Du même; sūtra du hīnayāna.

2 feuillets. — Bunyiu Nanjio 898.

— XVI.

佛 說 尊 那 經

Fo choę tsoęn na king.

Cunda sūtra.

Du même. Édition de Tsi-tchao 'an (1609).

6 feuillets. — Bunyiu Nanjio 899.

— XVII.

佛 說 頻 婆 娑 羅 王 經

Fo choę phin pho so lo oang king.

Bimbisārarāja sūtra.

Du même; sūtra du hīnayāna. Édition du Hoa-yen ko (1642).

7 feuillets. — Bunyiu Nanjio 900; cf. id. 542 (62).

— XVIII.

佛說人仙經

Fo choẹ jen sien king.

Nararṣi sūtra.

Du même; sūtra du hīnayāna. Mêmes lieu et date d'édition qu'à l'art. XVII.

9 feuillets. — Bunyiu Nanjio 901; voir n° 6153, art. IV.

— XIX.

佛說舊城喻經

Fo choẹ kieou tchheng yu king.

Purāṇanagaropamāna sūtra.

Du même; autre traduction du n° 6102, art. VIII et IX. Mêmes lieu et date.

6 feuillets. — Bunyiu Nanjio 902.

— XX.

佛說信解智力經

Fo choẹ sin kiai tchi li king.

Adhimuktijñānabala sūtra.

Du même; sūtra du hīnayāna. Liste des caractères rares. Mêmes lieu et date.

7 feuillets. — Bunyiu Nanjio 903.

Grand in-8. Bonne gravure. 1 vol. demi-rel., au chiffre de la République Française.
Nouveau fonds 3932.

6217. — I.

佛頂放無垢光明入普門觀察一切如來心陀羅尼經

Fo ting fang oou keou koang ming jou phou mẹn koan tchha yi tshie jou lai sin tho lo ni king.

Samantamukha praveça raçmivimaloṣṇīṣa prabhā sarvatathāgatahṛdaya samavirocana dhāraṇī sūtra.

Version de Chi-hou. Lecture des caractères difficiles.

2 livres. — Bunyiu Nanjio 790.

— II.

佛說樓閣正法甘露鼓經

Fo choẹ leou ko tcheng fa kan lou kou king.

Vimāna saddharmāmṛta dundubhi sūtra.

Version de Thien-si-tsai.

5 feuillets. — Bunyiu Nanjio 791.

— III.

佛說大乘善見變化文殊師利問法經

Fo choẹ ta cheng chạn kien pien hoa oen chou chi li oen fa king.

Bodhivakṣo mañjuçrī nirdeça sūtra.

Du même.

7 feuillets. — Bunyiu Nanjio 792.

— IV.

聖虛空藏菩薩陀羅尼經

Cheng hiu khong tsang phou sa tho lo ni king.

Saptabuddhaka sūtra.

Version par Fa-thien, du même texte qu'au nº 6202, art. IV et V.

9 feuillets. — Bunyiu Nanjio 793.

— V.

佛說大護明大陀羅尼經

Fo choȩ ta hou ming ta tho lo ni king.

Mahāprabhāpāla mahādhāraṇī sūtra.

Du même. Liste des mots rares.

8 feuillets. — Bunyiu Nanjio 794.

— VI.

佛說無能勝旛王如來莊嚴陀羅尼經

Fo choȩ oou neng cheng fan oang jou lai tchoang yen tho lo ni king.

Dhvajāgrakeyūra dhāraṇī sūtra.

Version de Chi-hou.

5 feuillets. — Bunyiu Nanjio 795.

— VII.

最勝佛頂陀羅尼經

Tsoei cheng fo ting tho lo ni king.

Sarvadurgati pariçodhanoṣṇī-ṣa vijaya dhāraṇī sūtra.

Version par Fa-thien, du même texte qu'au nº 6140, art. VIII.

4 feuillets. — Bunyiu Nanjio 796.

— VIII.

聖佛母小字般若波羅蜜多經

Cheng fo mou siao tseu pan jȩ po lo mi to king.

Alpākṣara prajñāpāramitā sū-tra.

Version de Thien-si-tsai.

5 feuillets. — Bunyiu Nanjio 797.

– IX.

消除一切閃電障難隨求如意陀羅尼經

Siao tchhou yi tshie chȧn lien tchang nan soei khieou jou yi tho lo ni king.

Sūtra de la dhāraṇī conforme aux demandes et aux pensées, qui anéantit la foudre et défend du malheur.

Version de Chi-hou.

5 feuillets. — Bunyiu Nanjio 798.

— X.

聖最上燈明如來陀羅尼經

Cheng tsoei chang teng ming jou lai tho lo ni king.

Āryānuttaradīpa tathāgata dhāraṇī sūtra.

Du même. Lecture des caractères difficiles.

8 feuillets. — Bunyiu Nanjio 799.

— XI.

大寒林聖難拏陀羅尼經

Ta han lin cheng nan na tho lo ni king.

Mahādaṇḍa dhāraṇī sūtra.

Version de Fa-thien. Édition du Hoa-yen-ko de Yu-chan (1643).

6 feuillets. — Bunyiu Nanjio 800 ; cf. nº 6204, art. XV.

— XII.

佛說諸行有爲經

Fo choẹ tchou hing yeou oei king.

Sarvasaṃskāra saṃskṛta sūtra.

Du même. Mêmes lieu et date.

2 feuillets. — Bunyiu Nanjio 801.

— XIII.

息除中夭陀羅尼經

Si tchhou tchong yao tho lo ni king.

Cintāmaṇināma sarvaghāta-mṛtyu vāraṇī dhāraṇī sūtra.

Version de Chi-hou. Mêmes lieu et date de gravure.

3 feuillets. — Bunyiu Nanjio 802.

— XIV.

一切如來正法祕密篋印心陀羅尼經

Yi tshie jou lai tcheng fa pi mi khie yin sin tho lo ni king.

Sarvatathāgata saddharma guhyakaraṇḍa mudrā hṛdaya dhāraṇī sūtra.

Du même. Lecture des caractères difficiles.

10 feuillets. — Bunyiu Nanjio 803.

Grand in-8. Bonne gravure. 1 vol. demi-rel., au chiffre de la République Française.

Nouveau fonds 4019.

6218. — I.

佛說聖莊嚴陀羅尼經

Fo choę cheng tchoang yen tho lo ni king.

Āryavyūha dhāraṇī sūtra.

Version de Chi-hou.

2 livres. — Bunyiu Nanjio 854; cf. n° 6172, art. II.

— II.

佛說聖六字大明王陀羅尼經

Fo choę cheng lou tseu ta ming oang tho lo ni king.

Ārya ṣaḍakṣarī mahāvidyā rā-jñī dhāraṇī sūtra.

Du même.

2 feuillets. — Bunyiu Nanjio 855.

— III.

千轉大明陀羅尼經

Tshien tchoan ta ming tho lo ni king.

Sahasra pravartana mahāvidyā dhāraṇī sūtra.

Du même.

4 feuillets. — Bunyiu Nanjio 856.

— IV.

佛說華積樓閣陀羅尼經

Fo choę hoa tsi leou ko tho lo ni king.

Puṣpakūṭa dhāraṇī sūtra.

Version par Chi-hou du même texte qu'au n° 5861, art. XIII à XV.

4 feuillets. — Bunyiu Nanjio 857.

— V.

佛說勝旛瓔珞陀羅尼經

Fo choę cheng fan ying lo tho lo ni king.

Jayadhvajamālā dhāraṇī sūtra.

Du même. Lecture des caractères rares. Édition de Hoa-tchheng seu (1637).

3 feuillets. — Bunyiu Nanjio 858.

— VI.

佛說七佛經

Fo choę tshi fo king.

Sapta buddhaka sūtra.

Version de Fa-thien; sūtra du hīnayāna.

15 feuillets. — Bunyiu Nanjio 860; cf. n° 6153, art. I.

— VII.

佛說解憂經

Fo choę kiai yeou king.

Çokavināça sūtra.

Du même; sūtra du hīnayāna.

4 feuillets. — Bunyiu Nanjio 861.

— VIII.

佛說徧照般若波羅蜜經

Fo choę pien tchao pan ję po lo mi king.

Samantaprakāçamāna prajñā-pāramitā sūtra.

Version de Chi-hou. Liste des mots rares. Édition de Hoa-tchheng seu (1636).

9 feuillets. — Bunyiu Nanjio 862.

— IX.

佛說大乘無量壽莊嚴經

Fo choę ta cheng oou liang cheou tchoang yen king.

Amitāyuṣa (Sukhāvatī) vyūha sūtra.

Version par Fa-hien, Hindou (982-1001) du même texte que Bunyiu Nanjio 23, 25, 26, 27. Lecture des caractères rares. Édition de Hoa-tchheng seu (1636).

3 livres. — Bunyiu Nanjio 863; cf. n° 5813, art. I.

Grand in-8. Bonne gravure. 1 vol. demi-rel., au chiffre de la République Française.

Nouveau fonds 4020.

Cinquième Section : TANTRA SŪTRA, ETC.

6219. 蘇悉地羯羅經
Sou si ti kie lo king.

Susiddhikāra mahātantra sādhanopāyika paṭala sūtra.

Version de Çubhakara (724). Lecture des signes rares.

4 livres. — Bunyiu Nanjio 533.

Grand in-8. Bonne gravure. 1 vol. demi-rel., au chiffre de la République Française.

Nouveau fonds 3888.

6220. — I.

蘇悉地羯羅供養法

Sou si ti kie lo kong yang fa.

Susiddhikāra pūjā kalpa.

Traduction de Çubhakara (717-724). Lecture des caractères rares.

3 livres. — Bunyiu Nanjio 1425; cf. n° 6219.

— II.

不動使者陀羅尼祕密法

Pou tong chi tchę tho lo ni pi mi fa.

Acala dūta dhāraṇī guhya kalpa.

Version de Vajrabodhi (723-730).

15 feuillets. — Bunyiu Nanjio 1426.

— III.

金剛頂經瑜伽修習毗盧遮那三摩地法

Kin kang ting king yu kia sieou si phi lou tchę na san mo ti fa.

Vajraçekhara yoga caryā vairocana samādhi kalpa.

Du même. Liste des signes rares.

17 feuillets. — Bunyiu Nanjio 1427.

— IV.

金剛頂瑜伽經文殊師利菩薩儀軌供養法

Kin kang ting yu kia king oen chou chi li phou sa yi koei kong yang fa.

Vajraçekhara yoga sūtra mañjuçrī bodhisattva kalpa pūjā dharma.

Version d'Amoghavajra.

14 feuillets. — Bunyiu Nanjio 1428.

— V.

瑜伽蓮華部念誦法

Yu kia lien hoa pou nien song fa.

Yoga puṇḍarīka vargādhyāya kalpa.

Du même. Lecture des signes difficiles.

9 feuillets. — Bunyiu Nanjio 1429.

— VI.

金剛頂經瑜伽觀自在王如來修行法

Kin kang ting king yu kia koan tseu tsai oang jou lai sieou hing fa.

Vajraçekhara sūtra yogāvalokiteçvara rāja tathāgata caryā kalpa.

Version de Vajrabodhi. Liste des signes rares.

1 livre. — Bunyiu Nanjio 1430.

Grand in-8. Bonne gravure. 1 vol. demi-rel., au chiffre de la République Française.

Nouveau fonds 3896.

6221. — I.

金剛頂瑜伽中略出念誦經

Kin kang ting yu kia tchong lio tchhou nien song king.

Sūtra extrait du Vajraçekharayoga.

Traduction de Vajrabodhi (723). Liste des signes rares. Édition du Hoa-yen ko (1643).

4 livres. — Bunyiu Nanjio 534.

— II.

金剛頂經曼殊室利菩薩五字心陀羅尼品

Kin kang ting king man chou chi li phou sa oou tseu sin tho lo ni phin.

Vajraçekhara sūtra mañjuçrī bodhisattva pañcākṣara hṛdaya dhāraṇī varga.

Du même (730).

13 feuillets. — Bunyiu Nanjio 537.

— III.

觀自在如意輪菩薩瑜伽法要

Koan tseu tsai jou yi loen phou sa yu kia fa yao.

Avalokiteçvara cintāmaṇī bodhisattva yogadharma mahārtha.

Du même (730). extrait du Vajra çekhara sūtra. Liste des caractères rares. Même édition et même date qu'à l'art. I.

15 feuillets. — Bunyiu Nanjio 538.

— IV.

佛說救面然餓鬼陀羅尼神咒經

Fo choç kieou mien jan 'o koei tho lo ni chen tcheou king.

Jvālāmukha preta paritrāṇa dhārāṇyṛddhi mantra sūtra.

Version de Çikṣānanda. Édition du Hoa-yen ko (1643).

3 feuillets. — Bunyiu Nanjio 539.

— V.

佛說甘露經陀羅尼

Fo choç kan lou king tho lo ni.

Amṛta sūtra dhāraṇī.

Du même. Mêmes lieu et date.

1 feuillet. — Bunyiu Nanjio 540.

Grand in-8. Bonne gravure. 1 vol. demi-rel., au chiffre de la République Française.

Nouveau fonds 3897.

6222. 大乘瑜伽金剛性海曼殊室利千臂千鉢大教王經

Ta cheng yu kia kin kang sing hai man chou chi li tshien pi tshien po ta kiao oang king.

Mahāyāna yoga vajra prakṛti-sāgara mañjuçrī sahasrabāhu sahasrapātra mahātantrarāja sū-tra.

Traduction d'Amoghavajra (740). Préface; lecture des caractères difficiles. Édition de Tsi-tchao 'an, au King-chan (1610).

10 livres. — Bunyiu Nanjio 1044.

Grand in-8. Bonne gravure. 1 vol. demi-rel., au chiffre de la République Française.

Nouveau fonds 3704.

6223. 修設瑜伽集要燄口施食壇儀軌

Sieou chẹ yu kia tsi yao yen kheou chi chi than yi koei.

Yogamahārthasaṅgraha jvālā-mukhānnadāna kalpa.

Cérémonial pour les offrandes de mets aux Preta.

Traduction d'Amoghavajra avec notes; figures de mudrā avec légendes; caractères hindous accompagnés de leur lecture. Réédition donnée par Tchou-hong, de la bonzerie de Yun-tshi à Hang-tcheou. Préface (1606). Gravé à la bonzerie de Hai-tchhoang.

1 livre. — Bunyiu Nanjio 1467; cf. nᵒˢ 6140, art. VIII, 6217, art. VII.

Petit in-8. Papier blanc. 1 vol. demi-reliure.

Nouveau fonds 60.

6224. 瑜伽集要施食儀軌

Yu kia tsi yao chi chi yi koei.

Rituel des offrandes de nourriture d'après le Yoga mahārthasaṅgraha.

Frontispice (1 feuillet double). Préface de Tchou-hong (1606).

— I.

佛說救拔燄口餓鬼陀羅尼經

Fo chọ kieou pa yen kheou 'o koei tho lo ni king.

Jvalapraçamani dhāraṇī sūtra.

Traduction d'Amoghavajra.

6 feuillets. — Bunyiu Nanjio 984.

— II.

脩設瑜伽集要施食壇儀

Sieou chẹ yu kia tsi yao chi chi than yi.

Rituel des offrandes de nourriture d'après le Yoga mahārthasaṅgraha.

Même ouvrage qu'au n° précédent, revu par Tchou-hong et autres. Texte ; nombreuses figures de mudrā ; invocations en caractères hindous avec lecture ; notes annexes. Notice finale de Tchou-hong, datée de Oan-li sin oei, date impossible. Édition de Hai-tchhoang seu (1737).

In-4. Papier blanc. 1 vol. demi-rel., au chiffre de Louis-Philippe.
Nouveau fonds 638.

6225. — I.
瑜 伽 燄 口 儀 軌
Yu kia yen kheou yi koei.

Rites pour les preta.

Note générale publiée par Tseu-jo Tsing-koan, de Thiao-choei, et Nei-heng Tchi-tshiuen, de Tchheng-chan. Préface (1675) ; l'auteur de la note (1675) signe Tsi-sien Kiu-tchhe.

13 feuillets.

— II.
瑜 伽 燄 口 註 集 纂 要 儀 軌
Yu kia yen kheou tchou tsi tsoan yao yi koei ; alias :

瑜 伽 燄 口
Yu kia yen kheou.

Yogamahārthasaṅgraha jvālā-mukhānnadāna kalpa.

Même ouvrage qu'au n° 6223 ; édition annotée par Tsi-sien Kiu-tchhe, revue par Tseu-jo Tsing-koan et Nei-heng Tchi-tshiuen. Outre le texte, on trouve les mudrā avec caractères hindous et les formules magiques. Édition de Leng-yen seu (1675).

2 livres.

— III.
附 增 津 濟 疏
Fou tseng tsin tsi sou.

Modèle d'adresse en faveur des preta.

Postface de Tsi-sien (1676).

Grand in-8. Texte de genre cursif, frontispice (1 feuillet double). 1 vol. demi-rel., au chiffre de la République Française.
Nouveau fonds 4157.

6226. 俻 習 瑜 伽 集 要 施 食 壇 儀
Sieou si yu kia tsi yao chi chi than yi ; alias :

瑜 伽 燄 口
Yu kia yen kheou.

Yogamahārthasaṅgraha jvālā-
mukhānnadāna kalpa.

Ouvrage analogue au n° 6223.
Frontispice (1 feuillet simple) ; au
verso légende ; ensuite préliminaires de la cérémonie. Texte avec
quelques notes. Figures diverses ;
mudrā avec caractères hindous.
Édition de Tchao-khing seu (1712).

2 livres. — Bunyiu Nanjio 1467.

Grand in-8. 1 vol. demi-rel., au chiffre
de Napoléon III.

Nouveau fonds 1511.

6227. — I.

佛 說 聖 寶 藏 神 儀 軌 經

*Fo choe cheng pao tsang chen yi
koei king.*

Jambhala jalendra yathāla-
bdha kalpa sūtra.

Version de Fa-thien. Liste des
caractères difficiles. Édition de
1664.

2 livres. — Bunyiu Nanjio 1045.

— II.

佛 說 寶 藏 神 大 明 曼 拏 羅 儀 軌 經

*Fo choe pao tsang chen ta ming
man na lo yi koei king.*

Ratnagarbharddhi mahāvidyā
maṇḍala kalpa sūtra.

Du même. Lecture des mots
rares. Même date d'édition.

2 livres. — Bunyiu Nanjio 1046.

— III.

金 剛 恐 怖 集 會 方 廣 軌 儀 觀 自 在 菩 薩 三 世 最 勝 心 明 王 經

*Kin kang khong pou tsi hoei fang
koang koei yi koan tseu tsai
phou sa san chi tsoei cheng
sin ming oang king.*

Vajrabhaya sannipāta vaipu-
lyakalpāvalokiteçvara bodhisattva tribhāvānuttarahṛdaya vidyārāja sūtra.

Version d'Amoghavajra. Lecture des mots difficiles. Édition
du Hoa-yen ko (1643).

1 livre. — Bunyiu Nanjio 1047.

— IV.

金 剛 恐 怖 集 會 方 廣 軌 儀 觀 自 在 菩 薩 三 世 最 勝 心 明 王 大 威 力 烏 樞 瑟 摩 明 王 經

*Kin kang khong pou tsi hoei
fang koang koei yi koan tseu
tsai phou sa san chi tsoei
cheng sin ming oang ta oei li
oou tchhou se mo ming oang
king.*

Mahābalavajrakrodha sūtra.

Version de 'O-tchi-ta-sien. Lecture des caractères difficiles. Édition de 1664.

3 livres. — Bunyiu Nanjio 1048.

Grand in-8. Bonne gravure. 1 vol. demi-rel., au chiffre de la République Française.

Nouveau fonds 3963.

6228. — I.

三藏聖教序
San tsang cheng kiao siu.

Préface pour le Tripiṭaka.

Par l'empereur Tchen-tsong des Song (997-1022).

Bunyiu Nanjio 1037.

— II.

佛說最上根本大樂金剛不空三昧大教王經

Fo choe tsoei chang ken pen ta lo kin kang pou khong san mei ta kiao oang king.

Anuttaramūla mahāsaṅkhya vajrāmogha samaya mahātantrarāja sūtra.

Version de Fa-hien, Hindou (982-1001). Liste des caractères difficiles. Édition du Hoa-yen ko (1642).

7 livres. — Bunyiu Nanjio 1037.

Grand in-8. Bonne gravure. 1 vol. demi-rel., au chiffre de la République Française.

Nouveau fonds 4009.

6229. — I.

佛說大乘觀想曼拏羅淨諸惡趣經

Fo choe ta cheng koan siang man na lo tsing tchou 'o tshiu king.

Mahāyāna dhyānasañjñāna-maṇḍala sarvadurbhāva prasādaka sūtra.

Version de Fa-hien, Hindou (982-1001). Liste des mots rares.

2 livres. — Bunyiu Nanjio 1049.

— II.

佛說大方廣曼殊室利經觀自在多羅菩薩儀軌經

Fo choe ta fang koang man chou chi li king koan tseu tsai to lo phou sa yi koei king.

Mahāvaipulya mañjuçrī sūtrāvalokiteçvara tārā bodhisattva kalpa sūtra.

Version d'Amoghavajra.

15 feuillets. — Bunyiu Nanjio 1050.

— III.

佛說一切佛攝相應大教王經聖觀自在菩薩念誦儀軌經

Fo choę yi tshie fo chę siang ying ta kiao oang king cheng koan tseu tsai phou sa nien song yi koei king.

Sarvabuddha saṅgraha yukta mahātantrarāja sutrāvalokite-çvara bodhisattvādhyāya kalpa sūtra.

Version de Fa-hien, Hindou (982-1001). Lecture des caractères rares.

12 feuillets. — Bunyiu Nanjio 1051.

— IV.

瑜伽金剛頂經釋字母品

Yu kia kin kang ting king chi tseu mou phin.

Yoga vajraçekhara sūtrākṣa-ramātṛkā vyākhyā varga.

Version d'Amoghavajra.

3 feuillets. — Bunyiu Nanjio 1052.

— V.

佛說一切如來安像三昧儀軌經

Fo choę yi tshie jou lai 'an siang san mei yi koei king.

Sarvatathāgata pratibimba-pratiṣṭhā samaya kalpa sūtra.

Version de Chi-hou.

9 feuillets. — Bunyiu Nanjio 1053.

— VI.

文殊師利菩薩根本大教王金翅鳥王品

Oen chou chi li phou sa ken pęn ta kiao oang kin tchhi niao oang phin.

Garuḍagarbharāja varga, alias :

Garuḍagarbhatantra varga.

Extrait du Mañjuçrī mūla tantra (nᵒˢ 6235-6236); version d'Amoghavajra. Liste des mots rares.

14 feuillets — Bunyiu Nanjio 1054.

— VII.

十一面觀自在菩薩心密言念誦儀軌經

Chi yi mien koan tseu tsai phou sa sin mi yen nien song yi koei king.

Ekādaçamukhāvalokiteçvara bodhisattva hṛdaya mantrādhyā-ya kalpa sūtra.

Version par le même. Lecture des caractères rares. Édition de Leng-yen seu (1660).

3 livres. — Bunyiu Nanjio 1055.

Grand in-8. Bonne gravure. 1 vol. demi-rel., au chiffre de la République Française.

Nouveau fonds 3993.

6230. — I.

佛 說 持 明 藏 瑜 伽 大 教 尊 那 菩 薩 大 明 成 就 儀 軌 經

Fo choę tchhi ming tsang yu kia ta kiao tsoęn na phou sa ta ming tchheng tsieou yi koei king.

Tejodhara piṭaka yogamahātantra cuṇḍa bodhisattva mahāvidyāsiddhikalpa sūtra.

Version de Fa-hien, Hindou (982-1001); le texte, extrait du Tchhi ming tsang, est attribué à Nāgārjuna bodhisattva. Lecture des caractères rares. Edition du Hoa-yen ko (1643).

4 livres. — Bunyiu Nanjio 1057.

— II.

佛 說 金 剛 香 菩 薩 大 明 成 就 儀 軌 經

Fo choę kin kang hiang phou sa ta ming tchheng tsieou yi koei king.

Vajragandha bodhisattva mahāvidyāsiddhikalpa sūtra.

Version de Chi-hou. Lecture des mots difficiles. Mêmes lieu et date.

3 livres. — Bunyiu Nanjio 1058.

Grand in-8. Bonne gravure. 1 vol. demi-rel., au chiffre de la République Française.

Nouveau fonds 3961.

6231. — I.

金 剛 薩 埵 說 頻 那 夜 迦 天 成 就 儀 軌 經

Kin kang sa too choę phin na ye kia thien tchheng tsieou yi koei king.

Vajrasattva bhāṣita vināyaka deva siddhi kalpa sūtra.

Version de Fa-hien. Liste des caractères rares. Edition du Hoa-yen ko (1643).

4 livres. — Bunyiu Nanjio 1059.

— II.

佛 說 大 悲 空 智 金 剛 大 教 王 儀 軌 經

Fo choę ta pei khong tchi kin kang ta kiao oang yi koei king.

He vajra tantra sūtra.

Version de Fa-hou (1004-1058). Liste des signes rares. Édition du Hoa-yen ko (1644).

5 livres. — Bunyiu Nanjio 1060.

— III.

佛說幻化網大瑜伽教十忿怒明王大明觀想儀軌經

Fo choe hoan hoa oang ta yu kia kiao chi fen nou ming oang ta ming koan siang yi koei king.

Māyājāla mahāyoga tantra daçakrodha vidyārāja mahāvidyā dhyānasañjñāna kalpa sūtra.

Version de Fa-hien (982-1001). Lecture des signes difficiles. Édition du Hoa-yen ko (1643).

1 livre. — Bunyiu Nanjio 1061.

Grand in-8. Bonne gravure. 1 vol. demi-rel., au chiffre de la République Française.

Nouveau fonds 3894.

6232. — I.

佛說妙吉祥瑜伽大教金剛陪囉嚩輪觀想成就儀軌經

Fo choe miao ki siang yu kia ta kiao kin kang phei lo fo loen koan siang tchheng tsieou yi koei king.

Vajra bhairava tantra krodha tattvarāja sūtra.

Version de Fa-hien, Hindou (982-1001). Lecture des caractères rares. Édition de Hoa-tchheng seu (1627).

1 livre. — Bunyiu Nanjio 1062.

— II.

底哩三昧耶不動尊威怒王使者念誦法

Ti li san mei ye pou tong tsoen oei nou oang chi tche nien song fa.

Trisamayācalārya krodharāja dūtādhyāya dharma.

Version par Amoghavajra. Liste des mots difficiles. Édition du Hoa-yen ko (1644).

1 livre. — Bunyiu Nanjio 1063.

— III.

聖迦柅忿怒金剛童子菩薩成就儀軌經

Cheng kia ni fen nou kin kang thong tseu phou sa tchheng tsieou yi koei king.

Vajra kumāra tantra sūtra.

Par le même; extrait du Susiddhikāra mahātantra sādhanopāyika paṭala sūtra (nº 6219). Liste des caractères rares. Mêmes lieu et date qu'à l'art. II.

3 livres. — Bunyiu Nanjio 1064.

— IV.

七佛讚唄伽陀

Tshi fo tsan pai kia tho.

Saptabuddha stotragāthā.

Version de Fa-thien. Mêmes lieu et date.

3 feuillets. — Bunyiu Nanjio 1065.

— V.

佛三身讚

Fo san chen tsan.

Buddha trikāya stotra.

Version de Fa-hien, Hindou (982-1001). Mêmes lieu et date.

2 feuillets. — Bunyiu Nanjio 1066.

— VI.

御製釋迦牟尼佛讚

Yu tchi chi kia meou ni fo tsan.

Éloge de Çākyamuni Buddha, composition impériale.

Stances sans date. Mêmes lieu et date de gravure qu'aux articles précédents.

2 feuillets.

— VII.

佛一百八名讚經

Fo yi po pa ming tsan king.

Buddha nāmāṣṭaçataka stotra sūtra.

Version de Fa-thien. Mêmes lieu et date.

3 feuillets. — Bunyiu Nanjio 1067.

— VIII.

御製救度佛母讚

Yu tchi kieou tou fo mou tsan.

Éloge de la mère du Bouddha, composition impériale.

Stances sans date. Lieu et date de composition comme aux articles précédents.

2 feuillets.

— IX.

聖救度佛母二十一種 禮讚經

Cheng kieou tou fo mou eul chi yi tchong li tsan king.

Ārya trāta buddhamātṛkā vimçati pūjā stotra sūtra.

Version de 'An Tsang, Chinois (époque des Yuen). Texte suivi de deux mantra en caractères hindous avec transcription. Mêmes lieu et date.

4 feuillets. — Bunyiu Nanjio 1068.

— X.

佛說一切如來頂輪王一百八名讚

Fo choę yi tshie jou lai ting loęn oang yi po pa ming tsan.

Sarvatathāgatoṣṇīṣacakra nāmāṣṭaçataka stotra.

Version de Chi-hou. Mêmes lieu et date.

2 feuillets. — Bunyiu Nanjio 1069.

Grand in-8. Bonne gravure. 1 vol. demi-rel., au chiffre de la République Française.

Nouveau fonds 3919.

6233. — I.

佛說一切如來眞實攝大乘現證三昧大教王經

Fo choę yi tshie jou lai tchen chi chę ta cheng hien tcheng san mei ta kiao oang king.

Sarvatathāgata satya saṅgraha mahāyāna pratyutpannābhisa-

mbuddha samādhi mahātantra-rāja sūtra.

Version de Chi-hou. Lecture des termes difficiles. Édition de Tsi-tchao-'an (1637, 1638).

30 livres. — Bunyiu Nanjio 1017.

— II.

一切如來大祕密王未曾有最上微妙大曼拏羅經

Yi tshie jou lai ta pi mi oang oei tsheng yeou tsoei chang oei miao ta man na lo king.

Sarvatathāgata mahāguhyarā-jādbhutānuttara praçasta mahā-maṇḍala sūtra.

Version de Thien-si-tsai. Liste des caractères rares. Édition de 1638.

5 livres. — Bunyiu Nanjio 1018.

Grand in-8. Bonne gravure. 1 vol. cartonnage.

Nouveau fonds 4655.

6234.

Fo choę yi tshie jou lai tchen chi chę ta cheng hien tcheng san mei ta kiao oang king.

Double du n° 6233, art. I.

Livres 20 à 28.

Grand in-8. 1 vol. cartonnage.
Nouveau fonds 4656.

6235-6236. 大方廣菩薩
藏文殊師利根本儀
軌經

*Ta fang koang phou sa tsang
oen chou chi li ken pęn yi koei
king.*

Bodhisattvapiṭakāvataṃsaka

mañjuçrī mūlagarbha tantra sūtra; alias :

Mañjuçrī mūla tantra sūtra.

Version de Thien-si-tsai. Lecture des caractères difficiles.

20 livres. — Bunyiu Nanjio 1056.

Grand in-8. Bonne gravure; frontispice (1 feuillet double). 1 vol. demi-rel.
au chiffre de la République Française.
Nouveau fonds 3994.

1 vol. cartonnage.
Nouveau fonds 4676.

CHAPITRE XIV : BOUDDHISME (VINAYA)

Première Section : MAHĀYĀNA VINAYA

6237. — I.

菩薩瓔珞本業經

Phou sa ying lo pen ye king.

Bodhisattvamālā mūlakarma sūtra.

Version de Tchou Fo-nien. Liste des mots rares. Édition de Hoa-tchheng seu (1629).

2 livres. — Bunyiu Nanjio 1092.

— II.

佛說受十善戒經

Fo choe cheou chi chan kiai king.

Daçaçīla samādāna sūtra.

Version des Han postérieurs (25-220). Lecture des caractères rares. Même lieu d'édition (1631).

21 feuillets. — Bunyiu Nanjio 1093.

— III.

佛說淨業障經

Fo choe tsing ye tchang king.

Karmāvaraṇa viçuddhi mahā-yāna sūtra.

Version des dynasties Tshin (350-431). Même lieu d'édition (1631).

18 feuillets. — Bunyiu Nanjio 1094.

Grand in-8. Bonne gravure. 1 vol. demi-rel., au chiffre de la République Française.

Nouveau fonds 4023.

6238. 梵網菩薩戒經

Fan oang phou sa kiai king;
alias :

梵網經菩薩戒

Fan oang king phou sa kiai;
alias :

梵網戒經

Fan oang kiai king.

Brahmajāla sūtra.

Même ouvrage qu'au n° 6214, art. X : traduction, suivie d'une invocation. Ensuite note signée Yun-tchhao (1641). Gravé à la bonzerie de Long-hing (1651).

1 livre. — Bunyiu Nanjio 1087.

In-4. Papier blanc; 1 vol. en paravent couvertures rouges; dans 1 étui demi-rel., au chiffre de Louis-Philippe.

Nouveau fonds 142.

6239. — I.

佛說梵網經菩薩心地品下略疏

Fo choẹ fan oang king phou sa sin ti phin hia lio sou.

Commentaire abrégé du Brahmajāla sūtra, chap. Phou sa sin ti.

Par Hong-tsan de Pao-siang lin, à Koang-tcheou. Préface par un contemporain, Soẹn Thing-to (1679). Résumé en tableau. Liste des caractères rares.

8 livres. — Cf. n° 6238.

— II.

附半月誦菩薩戒儀式註

Fou pan yue song phou sa kiai yi chi tchou.

Service de quinzaine des bodhisattva, avec commentaire.

Sans nom d'auteur, se rattache au Pratimokṣa sūtra (n° 6241, art. II) et date probablement du x° siècle. Commentaire par Hong-tsan. Liste des mots rares. Liste des donateurs. Édition de 1675.

Forme le livre 8 de l'art. I, feuillets 20 à 34

Grand in-8. 1 vol. demi-rel., au chiffre de la République Française.

Nouveau fonds 3842.

6240. 梵網經心地品菩薩戒疏義

Fan oang king sin ti phin phou sa kiai sou yi.

Commentaire du Brahmajāla sūtra, chap. Sin ti.

Par le bonze Tchhoan-cheng, de Lei-fong. Texte, commentaire, notes; lecture des caractères difficiles. Édition de Hai-tchhoang (1737).

2 livres. — Cf. n° 6238.

Grand in-8. Papier blanc. 1 vol. demi-rel., au chiffre de Louis-Philippe.

Nouveau fonds 626 A.

6241. — I.

佛藏經

Fo tsang king.

Buddhapiṭaka nigrahanāma mahāyāna sūtra.

Version de Kumārajīva (405). Liste des signes rares. Édition de Tsi-tchao 'an (1606).

4 livres. — Bunyiu Nanjio 1095.

— II.

菩薩戒本經

Phou sa kiai pẹn king.

Bodhisattva pratimokṣa sūtra.

Prononcé par Maitreya; traduit par Dharmarakṣa. Extrait du Ti tchhi kiai phin.

12 feuillets. — Bunyiu Nanjio 1096.

— III.

菩薩戒羯磨文

Phou sa kiai kie mo oen.

Bodhisattva karma.

Prononcé par Maitreya; traduit par Hiuen-tsang (649); extrait des nᵒˢ 6247-6251. Liste des signes rares. Édition de Hoa-tchheng seu (1631).

8 feuillets. — Bunyiu Nanjio 1097.

— IV.

菩薩戒本

Phou sa kiai pẹn.

Bodhisattva pratimokṣa.

Par Maitreya et Hiuen-tsang (649), extrait des nᵒˢ 6247-6251. Préface du bonze Tsing-mai. Liste des caractères rares. Édition de Hoa-tchheng seu (1632).

1 livre. — Bunyiu Nanjio 1098; cf. id. 1083. Cf. ci-dessus, art. II et nᵒˢ 6247-6251.

Grand in-8. Bonne gravure. 1 vol. demi-rel., au chiffre de la République Française.

Nouveau fonds 3900.

6242. # 菩薩戒義疏

Phou sa kiai yi sou.

Commentaire du Bodhisattva pratimokṣa sūtra.

Par Tchi-tchẹ ta-chi; écrit par son disciple Koan-ting. Lecture des signes difficiles. Édition de Leng-yen seu (1664).

2 livres. — Bunyiu Nanjio 1554; cf. nᵒ 6241, art. II.

Grand in-8. Bonne gravure. 1 vol. demi-rel., au chiffre de la République Française.

Nouveau fonds 3871.

6243. — I.

菩薩戒本經箋要

Phou sa kiai pẹn king tsien yao.

Explication du Bodhisattva pratimokṣa sūtra.

Par 'Eou-yi Tchi-hiu, avec post-face de l'auteur (1651).

36 feuillets. — Cf. n° 6241, art. II.

— II.

優婆塞戒經受戒品

Yeou pho sẹ kiai king cheou kiai phin.

Chapitre Cheou kiai, Accep-tation des commandements, du Upāsaka çīla sūtra.

Postface par le bonze Ta-hien; édition de Leng-yen seu (1632).

14 feuillets. — Cf. n°ˢ 6244-6245.

Bonne gravure.

— III.

沙彌十戒威儀錄要

Cha mi chi kiai oei yi lou yao.

Principaux points du Çrāma-ṇera daçaçīla karmavācā.

Par Tchi-hiu.

29 feuillets. — Cf. Bunyiu Nanjio 1145, 1164.

— IV.

四分律藏大小持戒犍度畧釋

Seu fẹn liu tsang ta siao tchhi kiai kien tou lio chi.

Dharmagupta vinaya : expli-cation abrégée du Ta siao tchhi kiai kien tou.

Par Tchi-hiu Tsi-ming.

44 feuillets. — Cf. n°ˢ 6265-6266.

Grand in-8. 1 vol. demi-rel., au chiffre de la République Française.

Nouveau fonds 4094.

6244-6245.

— I (6244-6245).

優婆塞戒經

Yeou pho sẹ kiai king.

Upāsaka çīla sūtra.

Version de Dharmarakṣa (428). Liste des mots rares. Notices fina-les.

7 livres. — Bunyiu Nanjio 1088.

— II (6245).

寂調音所問經

Tsi thiao yin so oen king; alias :

如來所說清淨調伏經

Jou lai so choẹ tshing tsing thiao fou king.

45

Paramārthasaṃvṛtisatyanirdeçanāma mahāyāna sūtra.

Version par Fa-hai, Chinois (?) de la dynastie des Song (420-479) du même texte que Bunyiu Nanjio 1084. Édition de Hoa-tchheng seu (1629).

1 livre. — Bunyiu Nanjio 1089.

— III (6245).

大乘三聚懺悔經

Ta cheng san tsiu tchhan hoei king.

Karmāvaraṇa pratiçaraṇa sūtra (Triskandhaka sūtra).

Version par Jñānagupta et Dharmagupta (590). Édition de mêmes lieu et date.

15 feuillets. — Bunyiu Nanjio 1090.

— IV (6245).

佛說文殊悔過經

Fo choe oen chou hoei koo king.

Mañjuçrī kṣamā sūtra.

Version de Tchou Fa-hou. Liste des caractères rares. Édition de Hoa-tchheng seu (1612).

24 feuillets. — Bunyiu Nanjio 1091.

Grand in-8. Bonne gravure; frontispice (1 feuillet double), 2 vol. demi-rel., au chiffre de la République Française. *Nouveau fonds* 4080, 4081.

6246. 菩薩善戒經

Phou sa chan kiai king; alias:

菩薩地經

Phou sa ti king.

Bodhisattvacaryā nirdeça sūtra.

Version par Guṇavarman, de Ki-pin (431). Lecture des signes difficiles. Édition de Kou Long-chan (1643, 1644).

10 livres. — Bunyiu Nanjio 1085.

Grand in-8. Bonne gravure; frontispice (1 feuillet double). 1 vol. demi-rel., au chiffre de la République Française. *Nouveau fonds* 3870.

6247-6251. 瑜伽師地論

Yu kia chi ti loen.

Yogācāryabhūmi çāstra; alias: Saptadaçabhūmi çāstra yogācāry bhūmi.

Commentaire de l'ouvrage précédent.

Par le bodhisattva Maitreya; version de Hiuen-tsang (647, 648). Préface par Hiu King-tsong, surnom Thing-tsou (592-672). Liste des caractères difficiles. Édition de Tsi-tchao 'an (1599-1601).

100 livres. — Bunyiu Nanjio 1170; cf. n° 6246.

Grand in-8. Bonne gravure; frontispice (1 feuillet double). 5 vol. demi-rel., au chiffre de la République Française.

Nouveau fonds 4126 à 4130.

6252. 菩薩地持經
Phou sa ti tchhi king.

Bodhisattvacaryā nirdeça sūtra.

Ouvrage semblable au n° 6246, version de Dharmaraksa. Liste des caractères rares. Édition de Kou Long-chan (1643).

8 livres. — Bunyiu Nanjio 1086.

Grand in-8. Bonne gravure. 1 vol. demi-rel., au chiffre de la République Française.

Nouveau fonds 3869.

Deuxième Section : HĪNAYĀNA VINAYA

6253. 戒因緣經
Kiai yin yuen king.

Vinayanidāna sūtra.

Version de Tchou Fo-nien (378). Préface par Tao-'an. Lecture des termes difficiles. Édition de Hoa-tchheng seu (1632).

10 livres. — Bunyiu Nanjio 1130.

Grand in-8. Bonne gravure. 1 vol. demi-rel., au chiffre de la République Française.

Nouveau fonds 4029.

6254-6257. 十誦律
Chi song liu.

Sarvāstivāda vinaya.

Version par Puṇyatara, de Ki-pin, et Kumārajīva (404). Lecture

des caractères difficiles. Édition de Hoa-tchheng seu (1633-1636).

65 livres. — Bunyiu Nanjio 1115.

Grand in-8. Bonne gravure; frontispice (1 feuillet). 4 vol. demi-rel., au chiffre de la République Française.

Nouveau fonds 4063 à 4066.

6258. — I.

薩婆多毘尼毘婆沙
Sa pho to phi ni phi pho cha.

Sarvāstivāda vinaya vibhāṣā.

Traduction de l'époque des Tshin (350-431).

8 livres. — Bunyiu Nanjio 1135.

— II.

續薩婆多毘尼毘婆沙
Siu sa pho to phi ni phi pho cha.

Suite à l'ouvrage précédent.

Traduction de l'époque des Tshin. Préface par Tchi-cheou, de Si-king (vers 606) Lecture des caractères difficiles.

1 livre, formant le livre 9 du recueil total. — Bunyiu Nanjio 1136.

— III.

根本說一切有部出家授近圓羯磨儀範

Ken pẹn choẹ yi tshie yeou pou tchhou kia cheou kin yuen kie mo yi fan; alias :

出家授, *etc.*

Tchhou kia cheou, etc.

Mūlasarvāstivāda nikāya pravrajyā upasampadā karmavācā.

Œuvre de Bachpa, Tibétain; préface de 1270.

1 livre. — Bunyiu Nanjio 1137.

— IV.

根本說一切有部苾芻習學畧法

Ken pẹn choẹ yi tshie yeou pou pi tchhou si hio lio fa.

Règles abrégées d'étude pour les bhikṣu.

Par le même Notice finale (1271). Liste des caractères difficiles.

12 feuillets. — Bunyiu Nanjio 1137.

Grand in-8. Belle gravure ; frontispice (1 feuillet double). 1 vol. demi-rel., au chiffre de Napoléon III.

Nouveau fonds 1360.

6259. 薩婆多部毘尼摩得勒伽

Sa pho to pou phi ni mo tẹ lẹ kia.

Sarvāstivāda nikāya vinaya mātṛkā.

Version de Saṅghavarman, Hindou (445). Liste des mots rares. Édition du Hoa-yen ko (1644).

Livres 6 à 10. — Bunyiu Nanjio 1132.

Grand in-8. Bonne gravure. 1 vol. cartonnage.

Nouveau fonds 4669.

6260. 根本薩婆多部律攝

Ken pẹn sà pho to pou liu chẹ.

Mūlasarvāstivāda vinaya saṅgraha.

Compilation de Jinamitra, Hindou (630?), traduite par Yi-tsing (700). Lecture des mots difficiles. Édition du Hoa-yen ko (1644).

14 livres. — Bunyiu Nanjio 1127.

Grand in-8. Bonne gravure; frontispice spécial (1 feuillet double). 1 vol. demi-rel., au chiffre de la République Française.

Nouveau fonds 4067.

6261-6262. 根本說一切有部毗奈耶雜事

Ken pęn chǫ yi tshie yeou pou phi nai ye tsa chi.

Mūlasarvāstivāda nikāya vinaya kṣudrakavastu.

Version par Yi-tsing (710). Liste des mots rares. Édition donnée par Kou Long-chan, de Kin-cha (1633).

35 livres (livres 1 à 25 et 31 à 40). — Bunyiu Nanjio 1121.

Grand in-8. Bonne gravure; frontispice (1 feuillet double). 1 vol. demi-rel., au chiffre de la République Française.

Nouveau fonds 4068.

1 vol. cartonnage.

Nouveau fonds 4657.

6263. 根本說一切有部毗奈耶破僧事

Ken pęn chǫ yi tshie yeou pou phi nai ye pho seng chi.

Saṅghabhedakavastu.

Version de Yi-tsing (710). Lecture des mots difficiles. Édition de Kou Long-chan, de Kin-cha (1636).

20 livres. — Bunyiu Nanjio 1123.

Grand in-8. Bonne gravure; frontispice (1 feuillet double). 1 vol. cartonnage.

Nouveau fonds 4658.

6264. — I. 三藏聖教序

San tsang cheng kiao siu.

Préface générale du Tripiṭaka.

Par l'empereur Tchong-tsong (684 et 705-709).

4 feuillets.

— II. 根本說一切有部苾芻尼毗奈耶

Ken pęn chǫ yi tshie yeou pou pi tchhou ni phi nai ye.

Mūlasarvāstivāda nikāya bhikṣuṇī vinaya.

Version de Yi-tsing (710). Lecture des caractères rares. Édition de Kou Long-chan (1637); réédition de 1691.

Livres 1 à 5 et 11 à 20. — Bunyiu Nanjio 1124.

Grand in-8. Bonne gravure. 1 vol. cartonnage.

Nouveau fonds 4659.

6265-6266. 四分律藏

Seu fẹn liu tsang.

Dharmagupta vinaya.

Version par Buddhayaças et par Tchou Fo-nien (405). Lecture des mots rares. Édition de Hoa-tchheng seu (1635-1637).

Livres 21 à 60. — Bunyiu Nanjio 1117.

Grand in-8. Bonne gravure. 2 vol. cartonnage.

Nouveau fonds 4663, 4664.

6267. 比丘戒本疏義

Pi khieou kiai pẹn sou yi.

Règles des bhikṣu, avec explications.

Gravé en 1725.

— I.

律制緣起

Liu tchi yuen khi.

Origine des règles de discipline.

Par le bonze Tchhoan-yen, de Hai-tchhoang (1735).

— II.

四分戒本

Seu fẹn kiai pẹn.

Caturvarga pratimokṣa.

Par Hoai-sou (629-682), disciple de Hiuen-tsang. Texte et notes; extrait du n° précédent.

11 feuillets. — Bunyiu Nanjio 1154; cf. n°ˢ 6265-6266.

— III.

比丘戒本疏義

Pi khieou kiai pẹn sou yi.

Commentaire du précédent.

Par Tchhoan-yen.

2 livres + appendice.

Petit in-8. Papier blanc. 1 vol. demi-rel., au chiffre de Louis-Philippe.

Nouveau fonds 100.

6268.

Seu fẹn kiai pẹn.

Même ouvrage qu'au n° précédent, art. II. Texte d'après un exemplaire de l'époque des Thang; quelques notes. A la fin, lecture des caractères difficiles. Impression de la bonzerie de Hai-tchhoang.

41 feuillets.

Petit in-8. Papier blanc. 1 vol. demi-reliure.

Nouveau fonds 54.

6269. 四分比丘尼戒本

Seu fẹn pi khieou ni kiai pẹn.

Caturvarga bhikṣuṇī prati-mokṣa.

Texte avec quelques notes, par Hoai-sou. Extrait du n° 6265-6266. Édition de la bonzerie de Hai-tchhoang (1678).

Pas de division en livres, 46 feuillets. — Bunyiu Nanjio 1156.

Petit in-8. Papier blanc. 1 vol. demi-reliure.

Nouveau fonds 77.

6270. — I.

四分僧羯磨

Seu fẹn seng kie mo.

Dharmagupta bhikṣu karman.

Extrait du Dharmagupta vinaya par Hoai-sou. Préface de Hoai-sou. Texte et notes. Lecture des mots rares. Édition du Hoa-yen ko (1643).

5 livres. — Bunyiu Nanjio 1128; cf. n°ˢ 6265-6266.

— II.

四分比丘尼羯磨法

Seu fẹn pi khieou ni kie mo fa.

Dharmagupta bhikṣuṇī karman.

Extrait du Dharmagupta vinaya, traduit par Guṇavarman (431).

Liste des caractères difficiles. Édition de Hoa-tchheng seu (1631).

25 feuillets. — Bunyiu Nanjio 1129; cf. n°ˢ 6265-6266.

Grand in-8. Bonne gravure. 1 vol. demi-rel., au chiffre de la République Française.

Nouveau fonds 4086.

6271. 曇無德部四分律刪補隨機羯磨

Than oou tẹ pou seu fẹn liu chan pou soei ki kie mo.

Dharmagupta nikāya caturvarga, extrait.

Composé par le religieux Tao-siuen (660), d'après le Dharmagupta vinaya. Liste des mots rares. Texte et notes. Édition de Kou Long-chan, de Kin-cha (1634).

4 livres (10 sections). — Bunyiu Nanjio 1120; cf. n°ˢ 6265-6266.

Grand in-8. Bonne gravure. 1 vol. demi-rel., au chiffre de la République Française.

Nouveau fonds 4073.

6272. — I.

比丘尼僧祇律波羅提木叉戒經

Pi khieou ni seng khi liu po lo thi mou tchha kiai king.

Mahāsāṅghika bhikṣuṇī vinaya.

Version par Fa-hien, de Phing-yang, et Buddhabhadra, Hindou (414). Liste des caractères difficiles. Édition de Tsi-tchao 'an (1637).

1 livre. — Bunyiu Nanjio 1150.

— II.

沙彌尼戒經

Cha mi ni kiai king.

Çrāmaṇerikā çīla sūtra.

Version des Han orientaux (25-220).

5 feuillets. — Bunyiu Nanjio 1151.

— III.

舍利弗問經

Chę li fou oen king.

Çāriputra paripṛcchā sūtra.

Version de la dynastie des Tsin orientaux (317-420). Liste des caractères rares.

12 feuillets. — Bunyiu Nanjio 1152.

— IV.

彌沙塞羯磨本

Mi cha sę kie mo pęn.

Mahīçāsaka karman.

Extrait du Mahīçāsaka vinaya (nᵒˢ 6276-6277) par 'Ai-thong, Chinois (700). Texte et notes. Liste des caractères difficiles. Édition de Tsi-tchao-'an (1637).

2 livres. — Bunyiu Nanjio 1153.

Grand in-8. Bonne gravure. 1 vol. demi-rel., au chiffre de la République Française.

Nouveau fonds 4079.

6273-6275. 摩訶僧祇律

Mo ho seng khi liu.

Mahāsāṅghika vinaya.

Version (416) par Buddhabhadra et Fa-hien, de Phing-yang. Lecture des mots difficiles. Édition donnée par Kou Long-chan, de Kin-cha (1634).

40 livres. — Bunyiu Nanjio 1119.

Grand in-8. Bonne gravure. 3 vol. demi-rel., au chiffre de la République Française.

Nouveau fonds 4074 à 4076.

6276-6277. 彌沙塞部和醯五分律

Mi cha sę pou hwo hi oou fęn liu.

Mahīçāsaka vinaya.

Version par Buddhajīva de Ki-pin (423), et Tchou Tao-cheng. Lecture des mots difficiles. Édition de Leng-yen seu (1635).

30 livres. — Bunyiu Nanjio 1122.

Grand in-8. Bonne gravure. 2 vol. demi-rel., au chiffre de la République Française.

Nouveau fonds 4077, 4078.

6278. — I.

佛説大愛道比丘尼經

Fo choę ta 'ai tao pi khieou ni king.

Mahāprajāpatī bhikṣuṇī sūtra.

Version de la dynastie des Liang septentrionaux (397-439). Lecture des mots difficiles. Édition de Tsi-tchao 'an (1637).

2 livres. — Bunyiu Nanjio 1147.

— II.

佛説目連問戒律中五百輕重事經

Fo choę mou lien oen kiai liu tchong oou po khing tchong chi king.

Sūtra des cinq cents questions de Maudgalyāyana au sujet du vinaya.

Version des Tsin orientaux (317-420). Lecture des caractères rares. Édition de Miao-tę 'an (1591); réédition de 1682.

2 livres. — Bunyiu Nanjio 1148.

— III.

根本説一切有部苾芻尼戒經

Ken pęn choę yi tshie yeou pou pi tchhou ni kiai king.

Mūlasarvāstivāda bhikṣuṇī vinaya sūtra.

Version par Yi-tsing (710). Liste des caractères rares. Édition de Tsi-tchao 'an (1636).

2 livres. — Bunyiu Nanjio 1149.

Grand in-8. Bonne gravure: frontispice (1 feuillet double). 1 vol. demi-rel., au chiffre de la République Française.

Nouveau fonds 4069.

6279. ## 善見毘婆沙律

Chęn kien phi pho cha liu.

Vibhāṣā vinaya.

Version de Saṅghabhadra, Occidental (489). Lecture des caractères rares. Édition de Kou Long-chau, de Kin-cha (1639).

18 livres. — Bunyiu Nanjio 1125; cf. id. 1109.

Grand in-8. Bonne gravure; frontispice (1 feuillet). 1 vol. demi-rel., au chiffre de la République Française.

Nouveau fonds 4118.

CHAPITRE XV : BOUDDHISME (ABHIDHARMA)

Première Section : MAHĀYĀNA ABHIDHARMA

6280. 大莊嚴經論

Ta tchoang yen king loẹn.

Sūtrālaṅkāra çāstra.

Par le bodhisattva Açvaghoṣa ; traduit par Kumārajīva (405). Lecture des caractères difficiles. Édition de Tẹ-tsang seu à Kia-hing (1656, 1657).

15 livres. — Bunyiu Nanjio 1182.

Grand in-8. Bonne gravure. 1 vol. demi-rel., au chiffre de Napoléon III.

Nouveau fonds 1395.

6281.

Ta tchoang yen king loẹn.

Double.

1 vol. demi-rel., au chiffre de la République Française.
Nouveau fonds 3815.

6282. — I.

十二門論

Chi eul mẹn loẹn.

Dvādaçanikāya çāstra.

Par le bodhisattva Nāgārjuna ; version de Kumārajīva (408). Préface par Seng-joei ; table des 12 sections. Lecture des caractères rares. Édition du Hoa-yen ko (1686).

32 feuillets. — Bunyiu Nanjio 1186.

— II.

十八空論

Chi pa khong loẹn.

Aṣṭādaçākāça çāstra ; alias Aṣṭādaçaçūnyatā çāstra.

Par le même bodhisattva ; traduction de Paramārtha. Liste des mots difficiles. Édition du Hoa-yen ko (1643).

23 feuillets. — Bunyiu Nanjio 1187.

— III.

百 論
Po loẹn.

Çata çāstra.

Œuvre du bodhisattva Deva, expliquée par le bodhisattva Vasubandhu; traduite par Kumārajīva (404). Préface par Seng-tchao, disciple du traducteur. Liste des caractères rares. Édition du Hoa-yen ko (1686).

2 livres. — Bunyiu Nanjio 1188.

— IV.

廣 百 論 本
Koang po loẹn pẹn.

Çata çāstra vaipulya.

Par le bodhisattva Deva; traduction de Hiuen-tsang (650). Lecture des caractères difficiles. Mèmes lieu et date.

15 feuillets. — Bunyiu Nanjio 1189.

Grand in-8. Bonne gravure. 1 vol. demi-rel., au chiffre de la République Française.

Nouveau fonds 4144.

6283. 廣 百 論 釋 論
Koang po loẹn chi loẹn.

Vaipulya çata çāstra vyākhyā çāstra.

Œuvre de Dharmapāla commentant le n° précédent, art. IV; traduction par Hiuen-tsang (650). Lecture des caractères difficiles.

10 livres. — Bunyiu Nanjio 1198.

Grand in-8. Frontispice (1 feuillet double), bonne gravure un peu grêle. 1 vol. demi-rel., au chiffre de la République Française.

Nouveau fonds 4030.

6284. 中 論
Tchong loẹn.

Prāmāṇyamūla çāstra ṭīkā.

Par Nāgārjuna bodhisattva; traduit par Kumārajīva (409). Préface par le bonze Seng-joei (des Tshin postérieurs, 384-417). Lecture des caractères difficiles. Édition de Miao-tẹ 'an, du Oou-thai chan (1590).

6 livres. — Bunyiu Nanjio 1179.

Grand in-8. Bonne gravure. 1 vol. demi-rel., au chiffre de la République Française.

Nouveau fonds 4141.

6285.

Tchong loẹn.

Même ouvrage, édition non datée, un peu plus petite.

Grand in-8. Bonne gravure. 1 vol. demi-rel., au chiffre de Napoléon III.

Nouveau fonds 1441.

6286-6287.

— I (6286).

大乘中觀釋論

Ta cheng tchong koan chi loen.

Madhyamaka vṛtti.

Œuvre du bodhisattva Sthita-mati, commentant le Prāmāṇya-mūla çastra (n° 6284); version de Oei-tsing. Liste des caractères rares. Édition de Miao-tẹ 'an (1591); réédition de 1662.

4 livres (paraît complet). — Bunyiu Nanjio 1316.

— II (6286-6287).

施設論

Chi chẹ loen.

Prajñapatipāda çastra.

Œuvre de Mahāmaudgalyāyana, traduite par Fa-hou (1004-1058). Liste des caractères difficiles. Édition de King-chan (1661).

7 livres (autre division en 3 livres). — Bunyiu Nanjio 1317.

— III (6287).

大乘法界無差別論

Ta cheng fa kiai oou tchha pie loen.

Mahāyāna dharmadhātvaviçẹsatā çastra.

Par le bodhisattva Sthiramati; version par Devaprajña (691) du même texte que Bunyiu Nanjio 1258.

8 feuillets. — Bunyiu Nanjio 1318.

— IV (6287).

金剛頂瑜伽中發阿耨多羅三藐三菩提心論

Kin kang ting yu kia tchong fa 'o neou to lo san miao san phou thi sin loen; alias :

瑜伽總持教門說菩提心觀行修持義

Yu kia tsong tchhi kiao mẹn choẹ phou thi sin koan hing sieou tchhi yi.

Vajraçekharayogānuttarasamyaksambodhicittotpāda çastra.

Version d'Amoghavajra. Lecture des caractères rares. Édition de Hoa-tchheng seu (1631).

8 feuillets. — Bunyiu Nanjio 1319.

— V (6287).

彰所知論

Tchang so tchi loen.

Çāstra expliquant des objets connus.

Par le Tibétain Bachpa († 1280); traduit par son disciple Cha-lo-pa († 1314). Lecture des caractères difficiles. Édition de Hoa-tchheng seu (1631).

2 livres. — Bunyiu Nanjio 1320.

Grand in-8. Bonne gravure. 1 vol. cartonnage.

Nouveau fonds 4678.

1 vol. demi-rel., au chiffre de la République Française.

Nouveau fonds 4148.

6288. 般若燈論
Pan je teng loen.

Prajñāpradīpa çāstra kārikā.

Par les bodhisattva Nāgārjuna et Bhāvaviveka. Traduit par Prabhākaramitra, Hindou (630-632). Préface. Lecture des signes difficiles. Édition de 1644.

15 livres. — Bunyiu Nanjio 1185; cf. n° 6284.

Grand in-8. Frontispice (1 feuillet double); bonne gravure. 1 vol. demi-rel., au chiffre de la République Française.

Nouveau fonds 3695.

6289. — I.

攝大乘論
Che ta cheng loen.

Mahāyānasamparigraha çāstra.

Par le bodhisattva Asaṅga; version de Paramārtha (563). Préface du bonze Hoei-khai. Lecture des caractères rares.

3 livres. — Bunyiu Nanjio 1183.

— II.

Che ta cheng loen.

Mahāyānasamparigraha çāstra.

Même texte traduit par Buddhaçānta (531). Liste des mots difficiles.

2 livres. — Bunyiu Nanjio 1184.

Grand in-8. Bonne gravure. 1 vol. demi-rel., au chiffre de la République Française.

Nouveau fonds 4115.

6290-6292.
— I (6290-6292).

攝大乘論釋
Che ta cheng loen chi.

Mahāyānasamparigraha çāstra vyākhyā.

Collection de quatre commentaires sur le Mahāyāna samparigraha çāstra; cf. n° 6289, art. I et II et Bunyiu Nanjio 1247; comprenant :

1. (6290).

Commentaire du bodhisattva Oou-sing (Asvabhāva), traduit par Hiuen-tsang (647-649). Lecture des termes difficiles. Édition de Leng-yen seu (1640).

Livres 1 à 10.

2. (6290-6291).

Commentaire du bodhisattva Vasubandhu, traduit par Paramārtha (563). Préface du bonze Hoei-khai, en tête du livre 11.

Livres 11 à 20.

3. (6291).

Même commentaire, traduit par Dharmagupta (590-616).

Livres 21 à 30.

4. (6291-6292).

Même commentaire, traduction de Hiuen-tsang. Liste des mots rares. Édition de Leng-yen seu (1641-1643).

Livres 31 à 40.

5. (6292).

Addition au n° 2 (6290-6291), traduite par Paramārtha. Lecture des caractères difficiles. Édition de Leng-yen seu (1642-1644).

Livres 41 à 48.

Bunyiu Nanjio 1171.

— II (6292).

無相思塵論

Oou siang seu tchhen loẹn.

Anākāracintāyatana çāstra.

Par le bodhisattva Jina ; traduction de Paramārtha.

Feuillets 1 à 4. — Bunyiu Nanjio 1172.

— III (6292).

觀所緣緣論

Koan so yuen yuen loẹn.

Ālambanapratyayadhyāna çāstra.

Par le bodhisattva Jina ; version de Hiuen-tsang (657).

Feuillets 4 à 7. — Bunyiu Nanjio 1173.

— IV (6292).

觀所緣緣論釋

Koan so yuen yuen loẹn chi.

Ālambanapratyayadhyāna çāstra vyākhyā.

Commentaire de l'art. III par le bodhisattva Dharmapāla ; version de Yi-tsing (710). Lecture des mots difficiles. Édition de Leng-yen seu (1642).

Feuillets 8 à 18. — Bunyiu Nanjio 1174.

— V (6292).

大乘廣五蘊論
Ta cheng koang oou yun loẹn.

Pañcaskandhavaipulya çāstra.

Commentaire de l'art. VI par le bodhisattva Sthitamati; version de Divākara (685).

Feuillets 1 à 17. — Bunyiu Nanjio 1175.

— VI (6292).

大乘五蘊論
Ta cheng oou yun loẹn.

Pañcaskhandaka çāstra.

Par le bodhisattva Vasubandhu; version de Hiuen-tsang (647). Liste des mots difficiles. Édition de Leng-yen seu (1644).

Feuillets 17 à 26. — Bunyiu Nanjio 1176.

Grand in-8. Bonne gravure. 3 vol. demi-rel., au chiffre de la République Française.

Nouveau fonds 4112 à 4114.

6293. — I.

中邊分別論
Tchong pien fẹn pie loẹn.

Madhyāntavibhāga çāstra.

Par le bodhisattva Vasubandhu; traduction de Paramārtha. Lecture des signes difficiles. Édition du Hoa-yen ko (1643).

2 livres. — Bunyiu Nanjio 1248; cf. id. 1244.

— II.

大乘起信論
Ta cheng khi sin loẹn.

Mahāyāna çraddhotpāda çāstra.

Par le bodhisattva Açvaghoṣa; traduction de Çikṣānanda. Liste des caractères difficiles.

Livres 1 et 2. — Bunyiu Nanjio 1249 (1 livre).

— III.

Ta cheng khi sin loẹn.

Par le bodhisattva Açvaghoṣa; traduction de Paramārtha (553). Liste des caractères difficiles. Préface par le bonze Tchi-khai, de Yang-tcheou. Édition de Miao-te 'an, du Tshing-liang chan (1590); feuillets gravés de nouveau en 1678 et 1691.

Livre 3 (ouvrage semblant complet). — Bunyiu Nanjio 1250 (2 livres).

Grand in-8. Bonne gravure. 1 vol. demi-rel., au chiffre de la République Française.

Nouveau fonds 3750.

6294. 起信論疏筆削記

Khi sin loẹn sou pi sio ki.

Commentaire revu du Khi sin loẹn sou.

Par Tseu-siuen (1020). Lecture des caractères difficiles. Édition de Miao-tẹ 'an (1591).

20 livres. — Bunyiu Nanjio 1626; cf. id. 1625. Voir n° précédent, art II et III.

Grand in-8. Bonne gravure. 1 vol. demi-rel., au chiffre de la République Française.

Nouveau fonds 4124.

6295. 大乘起信論裂網疏

Ta cheng khi sin loẹn lie oang sou.

Explication du Mahāyāna çraddhotpāda çāstra.

Texte et notes par Tchi-hiu, de Ling-fong.

6 livres. — Cf. n° 6293, art. II et III.

Grand in-8. 1 vol. demi-rel., au chiffre de la République Française.

Nouveau fonds 4143.

_____

6296. 菩提資糧論
Phou thi tseu liang loẹn.

Çāstra sur l'obtention de la bodhi.

Composé par le bodhisattva Nāgārjuna et expliqué par le bhikṣu Īçvara ; traduction de Dharmagupta. Lecture des caractères difficiles. Édition de l'association Hong-fa, à Song-kiang (1643), reproduite en 1669.

6 livres. — Bunyiu Nanjio 1181.

Grand in-8. Bonne impression. 1 vol. demi-rel., au chiffre de la République Française.

Nouveau fonds 4136.

6297.

Phou thi tseu liang loẹn.

Double.

Grand in-8. Bonne impression. 1 vol. demi-rel., au chiffre de la République Française.

Nouveau fonds 276.

6298. 大乘阿毗達磨雜集論

Ta cheng 'o phi ta mo tsa tsi loẹn.

Mahāyānābhidharma saṃyuktasaṅgīti çāstra.

Par le bodhisattva Sthitamati ; traduction de Hiuen-tsang (646). Liste des signes difficiles. Édition de Leng-yen seu (1662).

16 livres. — Bunyiu Nanjio 1178; cf. id. 1199.

Grand in-8. Bonne gravure. 1 vol. demi-rel., au chiffre de la République Française.

Nouveau fonds 3713.

6299. 相宗八要
Siang tsong pa yao.

Huit ouvrages fondamentaux de l'École du (Dharma-) lakṣaṇa.

Table des huit traités.

— I.
因明入正理論
Yin ming jou tcheng li loẹn.

Hetuvidyā nyāyapraveça çāstra ; alias : Nyāyapraveçatāraka çāstra.

Par le bodhisattva Çaṅkarasvāmin ; traduction de Hiuen-tsang (647). En tête, introduction par Fong Mong-tcheng Tchen-chi kiuchi, de Sieou-choei. Postface.

11 feuillets. — Bunyiu Nanjio 1216 ; cf. n° 6303, art. I.

— II.
規矩頌
Koei kiu song.

Éloge des règles de la connaissance.

2 feuillets. — Cf. Bunyiu Nanjio 1646 ; n° 6303, art. VII.

— III.
大乘百法明門論
Ta cheng po fa ming mẹn loẹn.

Mahāyāna çatadharma vidyādvāra çāstra.

Par le bodhisattva Vasubandhu ; version de Hiuen-tsang (648).

3 feuillets. — Bunyiu Nanjio 1213 ; cf. nᵒˢ 6247-6251 ; n° 6303, art. II.

— IV.
唯識三十論
Oei chi san chi loẹn.

Vidyāmātrasiddhi tridaça çāstra kārikā.

Par le même ; traduction de Hiuen-tsang (648).

7 feuillets. — Bunyiu Nanjio 1215 ; cf. n° 6303, art. III.

— V.
觀所緣緣論
Koan so yuen yuen loẹn.

Même ouvrage qu'au n° 6292, art. III.

6 feuillets. — Cf. n° 6303, art. IV.

— VI.
唐奘師眞唯識量
Thang tsang chi tchen oei chi liang.

Traité de Hiuen-tsang sur la Vidyāmātrasiddhi.

18 feuillets. — Voir n° 6303, art. VI; n° 6305.

— VII.

六 離 合 釋 法 式

Lou li ho chi fa chi.

Règles des six relations d'éloignement et de rapprochement.

3 feuillets. — Voir n° 6303, art. VIII.

— VIII.

觀 所 綠 [緣] 論 釋

Koan so yuen yuen loęn chi.

Même ouvrage qu'au n° 6292, art. IV.

19 feuillets. — Cf. n° 6303, art. V.

— IX.

八 識 規 矩 頌 略 說

Pa chi koei kiu song lio choę.

Explication du Pa chi koei kiu song.

Traité relatif à des vers de Hiuen-tsang, par Tcheng-hoei; préface du même (1589); postface (1593) par Sin-yi kiu-chi, de Tsoei-li.

32 feuillets. — Cf. Bunyiu Nanjio 1646; voir plus haut, art. II; n° 6303, art. VII.

Grand in-8. Caractères grêles, semi-cursifs. 1 vol. demi-rel., au chiffre de la République Française.

Nouveau fonds 4180.

6300. — 1.

因 明 入 正 理 論

Yin ming jou tcheng li loęn.

Même ouvrage qu'au n° précédent, art. I. Postface (647).

1 livre.

— II.

顯 識 論

Hien chi loęn.

Vidyānirdeça çāstra.

Extrait du Oou siang loęn; traduction de Paramārtha. Liste des signes difficiles. Édition du Hoa-yen ko (1644).

1 livre. — Bunyiu Nanjio 1217.

— III.

發 菩 提 心 論

Fa phou thi sin loęn.

Bodhicittotpādana çāstra.

Par le bodhisattva Vasubandhu; traduction de Kumārajīva (405). Lecture des signes difficiles. Mêmes localité et date que ci-dessus.

2 livres. — Bunyiu Nanjio 1218.

— IV.

三 無 性 (*alias* 相) 論
San oou sing (siang) loẹn.

Tryalakṣaṇa çāstra.

Traduction de Paramārtha. Liste des signes difficiles. Mêmes localité et date.

2 livres. — Bunyiu Nanjio 1219.

Grand in-8. Bonne gravure ; manquent les feuillets 1 à 5 avant l'art. I. 1 vol. demi-rel., au chiffre de la République Française.

Nouveau fonds 3749.

6301-6302. 相 宗 八 要 解
Siang tsong pa yao kiai.

Huit ouvrages fondamentaux de l'École du (Dharma-) lakṣaṇa avec explications.

Préface par Kao-yuen ta-chi, du Seu-tchhoan occidental ; préface par Cheng-hing de Phou-thi-'an, à Yu-khi (1612).

— I (6301).

大 乘 百 法 明 門 論 贅 言
Ta cheng po fa ming mẹn loẹn tchoei yen.

Mahāyāna çatadharma vidyādvāra çāstra, avec commentaire.

Explications de Khoei-ki ; commentaire par Ming-yu, du Seu-tchhoan occidental.

44 feuillets. — Cf. n° 6299, art. III.

— II (6301).

唯 識 三 十 論 約 意
Oei chi san chi loẹn yo yi.

Sens de la Vidyāmātrasiddhi tridaça çāstra kārikā.

Par Ming-yu.

29 feuillets. — Cf. n° 6299, art. IV.

— III (6301).

觀 所 緣 緣 論 會 釋
Koan so yuen yuen loẹn hoei chi.

Explication de l'Ālambanapratyayadhyāna çāstra.

Par le même.

13 feuillets. — Cf. n° 6299, art. V.

— IV (6301).

六 離 合 釋 法 式 通 關
Lou li ho chi fa chi thong koan.

Explication des Règles des six relations d'éloignement et de rapprochement.

Par le même.

6 feuillets. — Voir n° 6299, art. VII.

— V (6301).

觀所緣緣論釋記

Koan so yuen yuen loẹn chi ki.

Commentaire de l'Ālambana pratyaya dhyāna çāstra vyākhyā.

Par le même. Préface par Oang Ye-tsao. Introduction de Ming-yu (1609). Résumé sous forme de tableaux. Gravé à Oou-yi, de Li-choei.

59 feuillets. — Cf. n° 6299, art. VIII.

— VI (6301).

觀所緣緣論釋記問荅釋疑

Koan so yuen yuen loẹn chi ki oen ta chi yi.

Réponses et doutes résolus relatifs à l'ouvrage précédent.

2 feuillets.

— VII (6302).

因明入正理論直疏

Yin ming jou tcheng li loẹn tchi sou.

Commentaire pour le Hetu-vidyā nyāyapraveça çāstra.

Par Ming-yu; préface du bonze Ta-chan, de Oou-lin (1612); post-face.

32 feuillets. — Cf. n° 6299, art. I.

— VIII (6302).

三支比量義鈔

San tchi pi liang yi tchhao.

Explication du San tchi pi liang.

Traité de Yen-cheou († 975) sur un thème de Hiuen-tsang; explication par Ming-yu.

25 feuillets. — Voir n° 6299, art. VI.

— IX (6302).

八識規矩補註證義

Pa chi koei kiu pou tchou tcheng yi.

Commentaire et explications du Pa chi koei kiu.

Par Ming-yu; commentaire du traité dû à Phou-thai (1511) et développant une poésie de Hiuen-tsang.

47 feuillets. — Cf. nos 6299, art. II et IX; 6438, art. I; 6462, art. II.

Grand in-8. 2 vol. demi-rel., au chiffre de la République Française.

Nouveau fonds 4151, 4142.

6303. 八要

Pa yao.

Les huit ouvrages fondamentaux.

— I.

因明入正理論直解

Yin ming jou tcheng li loẹn tchi kiai.

Explication du Hetuvidyā nyāyapraveça çāstra.

Par 'Eou-yi Tchi-hiu (1647).

35 feuillets. — Cf. n° 6299, art. I.

— II.

大乘百法明門論直解

Ta cheng po fa ming mẹn loẹn tchi kiai.

Explication du Mahāyāna çatadharma vidyādvāra çāstra.

Par le même.

18 feuillets. — Cf. n° 6299, art. III.

— III.

唯識三十論直解

Oei chi san chi loẹn tchi kiai.

Explication de la Vidyāmātrasiddhi tridaça çāstra kārikā.

Par le même.

19 feuillets. — Cf. n° 6299, art. IV.

— IV.

觀所緣緣論直解

Koan so yuen yuen loẹn tchi kiai.

Explication de l'Ālambanapratyayadhyāna çāstra.

Par le même.

15 feuillets. — Cf. n° 6299, art. V.

— V.

觀所緣緣論釋直解

Koan so yuen yuen loẹn chi tchi kiai.

Explication de l'Ālambanapratyayadhyāna çāstra vyākhyā.

Par le même.

41 feuillets. — Cf. n° 6299, art. VIII.

— VI.

唐奘師眞唯識量畧解

Thang tsang chi tchen oei chi liang lio kiai.

Explication abrégée du traité sur la Vidyāmātrasiddhi.

Extrait du Tsong king lou; explication par Tchi-hiu.

18 feuillets. — Cf. n° 6299, art. VI.

— VII.

八識規矩直解

Pa chi koei kiu tchi kiai.

Explication du Pa chi koei kiu.

Par Tchi-hiu.

12 feuillets. — Cf. n° 6299, art. II et IX.

— VIII.

六離合釋法式畧解

Lou li ho chi fa chi lio kiai.

Explication abrégée des Règles des six relations d'éloignement et de rapprochement.

Par le même. Édition de Kinling (1647).

5 feuillets. — Voir n° 6299, art. VII.

Grand in-8. 1 vol. demi-rel., au chiffre de la République Française.
Nouveau fonds 4133.

———

6304. — I.

大乘阿毗達磨集論

Ta cheng 'o phi ta mo tsi loen.

Mahāyānābidharma saṅgīti çāstra.

Par le bodhisattva Asaṅga; traduction par Hiuen-tsang (652). Lecture des caractères difficiles. Édition du Hoa-yen ko au Yu-chan (1644).

7 livres. — Bunyiu Nanjio 1199; cf. n° 6298.

— II.

王法正理論

Oang fa tcheng li loen.

Rājadharma nyāya çāstra.

Par le bodhisattva Maitreya; traduction par Hiuen-tsang (649). Liste des signes difficiles. Édition du Hoa-yen ko (1644).

1 livre. — Bunyiu Nanjio 1200.

— III.

瑜伽師地論釋

Yu kia chi ti loen chi.

Yogācāryabhūmi çāstra kārikā.

Par le bodhisattva Jinaputra; traduction de Hiuen-tsang (654). Liste des signes difficiles. Même édition, même date que ci-dessus.

1 livre. — Bunyiu Nanjio 1201; cf. n°ˢ 6247 à 6251.

— IV.

顯揚聖教論頌

Hien yang cheng kiao loen song.

Prakaraṇāryavākā çāstra kārikā.

Par le bodhisattva Asaṅga ; traduction de Hiuen-tsang (645). Liste des lectures difficiles. Même édition, même date.

1 livre. — Bunyiu Nanjio 1202.

Grand in-8. Bonne gravure. 1 vol. demi-rel., au chiffre de la République Française.

Nouveau fonds 3712.

6305. 成 唯 識 論

Tchheng oei chi loen.

Vidyāmātrasiddhi çāstra.

Commentaire de la Vidyāmātrasiddhi tridaça çāstra kārikā (nº 6299, art. IV), par les bodhisattva Dharmapāla et autres ; version de Hiuen-tsang (659). Lecture des mots rares. Édition de Ooukiang.

10 livres. — Bunyiu Nanjio 1197.

Grand in-8. Gravure grêle ; frontispice (1 feuillet simple) au 1er et au 6e livre. 1 vol. demi-rel., au chiffre de la République Française.

Nouveau fonds 4121.

6306.

Tchheng oei chi loen.

Double.

Livres 6 à 10.

1 vol. cartonnage.
Nouveau fonds 4681.

6307. 成 唯 識 論 俗 詮

Tchheng oei chi loen sou tshiuen.

Commentaire du Vidyāmātrasiddhi çāstra.

Par Ming-yu (époque des Ming). Postface par le bonze Tchhoanjou ; autre postface (1611).

Livres 7 à 10. — Cf. nº 6305.

Grand in-8. 1 vol. cartonnage.
Nouveau fonds 4665.

6308-6309. 成 唯 識 論 觀 心 法 要

Tchheng oei chi loen koan sin fa yao.

Commentaire du Vidyāmātrasiddhi çāstra.

Par Tchi-hiu, de Yeou-si seu (1647) ; postface de la même date, par l'auteur.

10 livres. — Cf. nº 6305.

Grand in-8. Caractères grêles. 2 vol. demi-rel., au chiffre de la République Française.

Nouveau fonds 4122, 4123.

6310. — I.

成 唯 識 寶 生 論

Tchheng oei chi pao cheng loen;
alias :

二十唯識順釋論

Eul chi oei chi choęn chi loęn.

Vidyāmātrasiddhi ratnajāti çāstra.

Commentaire de l'ouvrage Bunyiu Nanjio 1238, 1239, 1240 par le bodhisattva Dharmapāla; version de Yi-tsing (710). Liste des caractères rares.

5 livres. — Bunyiu Nanjio 1210.

— II.

十二因緣論

Chi eul yin yuen loęn.

Pratītyasamutpāda çāstra.

Par le bodhisattva Çuddhamati; version de Bodhiruci, Hindou (508-535). Édition du Hoa-yen ko (1644).

4 feuillets. — Bunyiu Nanjio 1211.

— III.

壹輸盧迦論

Yi chou lou kia loęn.

Ekaçloka çāstra.

Œuvre du bodhisattva Nāgārjuna, traduite par Gautama Prajñāruci. Mêmes lieu et date d'édition.

4 feuillets. — Bunyiu Nanjio 1212.

— IV.

大乘百法明門論

Ta cheng po fa ming męn loęn.

Même ouvrage qu'au n° 6299, art. III. Mêmes lieu et date que ci-dessus.

2 feuillets. — Bunyiu Nanjio 1213.

— V.

轉識論

Tchoan chi loęn.

Vidyāpravartana çāstra.

Version de Paramārtha. Liste des caractères difficiles. Mêmes lieu et date d'édition.

8 feuillets. — Bunyiu Nanjio 1214.

— VI.

唯識三十論

Oei chi san chi loęn.

Vidyāmātrasiddhi tridaça çāstra kārikā.

Même ouvrage qu'au n° 6299, art. IV. Liste des caractères difficiles. Mêmes lieu et date que ci-dessus.

5 feuillets. — Bunyiu Nanjio 1215.

Grand in-8. Bonne gravure. 1 vol. demi-rel., au chiffre de la République Française.

Nouveau fonds 4147.

Deuxième Section : HĪNAYĀNA ABHIDHARMA

6311. — I.

鞞婆沙論
Pi pho cha loęn.

Vibhāṣā çāstra.

Œuvre de Kātyāyanīputra, traduite par Saṅghabhūti (383). Liste des caractères difficiles. Édition de Tsie-tai seu à Oou-kiang (1638).

14 livres (42 chapitres). — Bunyiu Nanjio 1279.

— II.

隨相論
Soei siang loęn.

Lakṣaṇānusāra çāstra.

Œuvre de Guṇamati, traduite par Paramārtha.

2 livres. — Bunyiu Nanjio 1280.

Grand in-8. Bonne gravure. 1 vol. demi-rel., au chiffre de la République Française.

Nouveau fonds 4110.

6312. 阿毗曇八犍度論
'O phi than pa kien tou loęn.

Abhidharma jñānaprasthāna çāstra.

Œuvre de Kātyāyanīputra, traduite par Gautama Saṅghadeva, de Ki-pin, et Tchou Fo-nien (383). Liste des caractères difficiles. Édition de Tsie-tai seu (1641).

Livres 7 à 24. — Bunyiu Nanjio 1273.

Grand in-8. Bonne gravure. 1 vol. cartonnage.

Nouveau fonds 4603.

6313-6316. 阿毗曇毗婆沙論
'O phi than phi pho cha loęn.

Abhidharma vibhāṣā çāstra.

Œuvre du vénérable Kātyāyanīputra en rapport avec le n° précédent ; traduction par Buddhavarman, Occidental, et Tao-thai, Chinois (437-439). Préface par le bonze Tao-thing. Lecture des caractères difficiles. Édition de Kou Long-chan (1625 à 1628).

82 livres. — Bunyiu Nanjio 1264.

Grand in 8. Bonne gravure ; frontispice (1 feuillet double). 4 vol. demi-rel., au chiffre de la République Française.

Nouveau fonds 3733 à 3736.

6317.

'O phi than phi pho cha loęn.

Même ouvrage; frontispice différent (1 feuillet double); édition un peu plus grande.

Préface et livres 1 à 5.

Grand in-8. Bonne gravure. 1 vol. demi-rel., au chiffre de la République Française.

Nouveau fonds 3737.

6318-6327. 阿毗達磨大毗婆沙論

'O phi ta mo ta phi pho cha loẹn.

Abhidharma mahāvibhāṣā çāstra.

Compilation des cinq cents arhat analogue aux nᵒˢ 6313-6316; traduite par Hiuen-tsang (656-659). Liste des caractères difficiles. Édition de Hoa-tchheng seu au King-chan (1612-1616). Gravure nouvelle en 1678 (?).

200 livres (manquent les livres 81 à 85). — Bunyiu Nanjio 1263.

Grand in-8. Bonne gravure; frontispice (1 feuillet double). 10 vol. demi-rel., au chiffre de la République Française.

Nouveau fonds 3738 à 3747.

6328. 尊婆須蜜菩薩所集論

Tsoẹn pho siu mi phou sa so tsi loẹn.

Ārya vasumitra bodhisattva saṅgīti çāstra.

Version (384) par Saṅghabhūti, Nanda, inconnu d'autre part, et Deva (Gautama Saṅghadeva?). Lecture des caractères rares. Édition de Tsie-tai seu (1639).

15 livres. — Bunyiu Nanjio 1289.

Grand in-8. Bonne gravure; frontispice (1 feuillet double). 1 vol. demi-rel., au chiffre de la République Française.

Nouveau fonds 4125.

6329. 阿毗曇心論

'O phi than sin loẹn.

Abhidharma hṛdaya çāstra.

Par le vénérable Dharmajina. Traduit par Gautama Saṅghadeva et Hoei-yuen (391). Liste des caractères difficiles. Édition de Tsie-tai seu à Oou-kiang (1639).

4 livres. — Bunyiu Nanjio 1288.

Grand in-8. Bonne gravure. 1 vol. demi-rel., au chiffre de la République Française.

Nouveau fonds 3717.

6330. 雜阿毗曇心論

Tsa 'o phi than sin loẹn.

Saṃyuktābhidharma hṛdaya çāstra.

Commentaire du précédent par le vénérable Dharmatrāta; traduction de Sanghavarman, Hindou (434) Lecture des caractères difficiles. Édition de Tsie-tai seu à Oou-kiang (1638).

11 livres. — Bunyiu Nanjio 1287; cf. n° 6329.

Grand in-8. Frontispice (1 feuillet double); bonne gravure. 1 vol. demi-rel., au chiffre de la République Française.

Nouveau fonds 3719.

6331. — I.

法勝阿毗曇心論

Fa cheng 'o phi than sin loen.

Dharmajinābhidharma hṛdaya çāstra.

Commentaire du n° 6329 par le vénérable Upaçānta; traduit par Narendrayaças (563). Préface. Liste des signes difficiles. Édition de Tsie-tai seu à Oou-kiang (1640).

6 livres. — Bunyiu Nanjio 1294.

— II.

勝宗十句義論

Cheng tsong chi kiu yi loen.

Vaiçeṣikanikāya daçapadārtha çāstra.

Par le vaiçeṣika Jñānacandra; ouvrage non bouddhique traduit par Hiuen-tsang (648). Lecture des signes difficiles. Même édition, même date.

1 livre. — Bunyiu Nanjio 1295.

Grand in-8. Bonne gravure. 1 vol. demi-rel., au chiffre de la République Française.

Nouveau fonds 3718.

6332. 成實論

Tchheng chi loen.

Satyasiddhi çāstra.

Par Harivarman; version de Kumārajīva (407-408). Liste des caractères rares. Édition de Hoa-tchheng seu (1614-1615).

20 livres. — Bunyiu Nanjio 1274.

Grand in-8. Bonne gravure; frontispice (1 feuillet double). 1 vol. demi-rel., au chiffre de la République Française.

Nouveau fonds 4119.

6333. 眾事分阿毗曇論

Tchong chi fen 'o phi than loen.

Abhidharma prakaraṇapāda çāstra.

Par le vénérable Vasumitra; traduction par Guṇabhadra, Hindou, et Bodhiyaças (435-443). Texte du Sarvāstivāda nikāya. Lecture des signes difficiles. Édition de Tsie-tai seu (1639).

12 livres. — Bunyiu Nanjio 1292.

Grand in-8. Bonne gravure ; frontispice (1 feuillet double). 1 vol. demi-rel., au chiffre de la République Française. *Nouveau fonds* 3748.

6334. 阿毗達磨品類足論

'O phi ta mo phin lei tsou loen.

Abhidharma prakaraṇapāda çāstra.

Traduction du même texte qu'au nº précédent, par Hiuen-tsang (659). Liste des signes difficiles. Édition de Tshing-lien chę (1638).

18 livres. — Bunyiu Nanjio 1277.

Grand in-8. Bonne gravure ; frontispice (1 feuillet double), 1 vol. demi-rel., au chiffre de la République Française. *Nouveau fonds* 3723.

6335. 阿毗達磨識身足論

'O phi ta mo chi chen tsou loen.

Abhidharma vijñānakāyapāda çāstra.

Texte du Sarvāstivāda nikāya par l'arhat Devaçarman ; traduction de Hiuen-tsang (649). Liste des caractères difficiles. Édition de Tsie-tai seu (1638).

16 livres. — Bunyiu Nanjio 1281.

Grand in-8. Frontispice (1 feuillet double) ; bonne gravure. 1 vol. demi-rel., au chiffre de la République Française. *Nouveau fonds* 3722.

6336. — I. 阿毗達磨界身足論

'O phi ta mo kiai chen tsou loen.

Abhidharma dhātukāyapāda çāstra.

Texte du Sarvāstivāda nikāya par le vénérable Vasumitra ; traduction de Hiuen-tsang (663). Lecture des signes difficiles. Édition de Tsie-tai seu à Oou-kiang (1638).

2 livr s. — Bunyiu Nanjio 1282.

— II. 五事毗婆沙論

Oou chi phi pho cha loen.

Pañcavastu vibhāṣā çāstra.

Par le vénérable Dharmatrāta ; traduction de Hiuen-tsang (663). Lecture des signes difficiles. Mêmes lieu et date d'édition.

2 livres. — Bunyiu Nanjio 1283.

— III. 十八部論

Chi pa pou loen.

Aṣṭādaçanikāya çāstra.

L'ouvrage ne porte pas de nom d'auteur ni de traducteur.

9 feuillets. — Bunyiu Nanjio 1284.

— IV.

部執異論
Pou tchi yi loẹn.

Çāstra relatif aux divergences des écoles.

Même texte qu'à l'article précédent par le bodhisattva Vasumitra ; traduction de Paramārtha.

11 feuillets. — Bunyiu Nanjio 1285.

— V.

異部宗輪論
Yi pou tsong loẹn loẹn.

Çāstra relatif à la roue de la loi dans les diverses écoles.

Même texte qu'aux deux articles précédents, par Vasumitra ; traduction de Hiuen-tsang (662). Lecture des signes difficiles. Même localité, même date.

10 feuillets. — Bunyiu Nanjio 1286.

Grand in-8. Bonne gravure. 1 vol. demi-rel., au chiffre de la République Française.
Nouveau fonds 3721.

6337. 阿毗達磨法蘊足論
'O phi ta mo fa yun tsou loẹn.

Abhidharma dharma skandha-pāda çāstra.

Texte du Sarvāstivāda nikāya par le vénérable Mahāmaudgalyāyana ; traduction de Hiuen-tsang (659). Liste des signes difficiles. Édition de Tsie-tai seu à Oou-kiang (1640).

10 livres. — Bunyiu Nanjio 1296.

Grand in-8. Bonne gravure ; frontispice (1 feuillet double). 1 vol. demi-rel., au chiffre de la République Française.
Nouveau fonds 3720.

6338. 解脫道論
Kiai thoo tao loẹn.

Vimokṣamārga çāstra.

Par l'arhat Upatiṣya ; version de Saṅghapāla (505). Liste des caractères difficiles. Édition de Tsie-tai-seu (1639, 1640).

12 livres. — Bunyiu Nanjio 1293.

Grand in-8. Bonne gravure. 1 vol. demi-rel., au chiffre de la République Française.
Nouveau fonds 4120.

6339-6340. 阿毗達磨俱舍釋論

'O phi ta mo kiu chẹ chi loẹn.

Abhidharma koça vyākhyā çāstra.

Par le vénérable Vasubandhu; traduction de Paramārtha (564-567). Préface du bonze Hoei-khai. Lecture des signes difficiles. Édition de Tsie-tai seu à Oou-kiang (1641).

22 livres. — Bunyiu Nanjio 1269.

Grand in-8. Frontispice (1 feuillet double). 2 vol. demi-rel., au chiffre de la République Française.
Nouveau fonds 3715, 3716.

6341-6342. 阿毗達磨俱舍論

'O phi ta mo kiu chẹ loẹn.

Abhidharma koça çāstra.

Version du même texte qu'aux nᵒˢ 6339-6340, par Hiuen-tsang (651-654). Liste des signes difficiles. Édition de Tsi-tchao 'an, au King-chan.

30 livres. — Bunyiu Nanjio 1267.

Grand in-8. Bonne gravure; frontispice (1 feuillet double). 2 vol. demi-rel., au chiffre de la République Française.
Nouveau fonds 3726, 3727.

6343. — I. 阿毗達磨俱舍論本頌

'O phi ta mo kiu chẹ loẹn pẹn song.

Abhidharma koça kārikā.

Par le vénérable Vasubandhu; texte expliqué dans les deux ouvrages précédents (nᵒˢ 6339 à 6342); traduction de Hiuen-tsang (651). Lecture des signes difficiles. Édition de Tsie-tai seu à Oou-kiang (1641).

2 livres. — Bunyiu Nanjio 1270.

— II. 三法度論

San fa tou loẹn.

Tridharmaka çāstra.

Par le vénérable Giribhadra; traduction par Gautama Saṅghadeva et Hoei-yuen (391). Liste des signes difficiles. Édition de Tsie tai seu (1641).

3 livres. — Bunyiu Nanjio 1271.

— III. 三彌底部論

San mi ti pou loẹn.

Sammitīya nikāya çāstra.

Traduction des Tshin (350-431). Liste des signes difficiles. Édition de Tsie-tai seu (1641).

3 livres. — Bunyiu Nanjio 1272.

Grand in 8. 1 vol. demi-rel., au chiffre de la République Française.

Nouveau fonds 3714.

6344-6348. 阿毗達磨順正理論

'O phi ta mo choen tcheng li loen.

Nyāyānusāra çāstra.

Réfutation des nᵒˢ 6339 à 6342 par le vénérable Saṅghabhadra ; traduction de Hiuen-tsang (653-654). Lecture des signes difficiles. Édition de Kou Long-chan (1632, 1633).

80 livres. — Bunyiu Nanjio 1265.

Grand in-8. Bonne gravure ; frontispice (1 feuillet double). 5 vol. demi-rel., au chiffre de la République Française.

Nouveau fonds 3728 à 3732.

6349-6350. 阿毗達磨藏顯宗論

'O phi ta mo tsang hien tsong loen.

Abhidharma piṭaka prakaraṇaçāsana çāstra.

Extrait de l'ouvrage précédent par le vénérable Saṅghabhadra ; traduit par Hiuen-tsang (651-652). Lecture des signes difficiles. Édi-

tion de Kou Long-chan, du Kin-cha (1632).

40 livres. — Bunyiu Nanjio 1266.

Grand in-8. Bonne gravure ; frontispice (1 feuillet double). 2 vol. demi-rel., au chiffre de la République Française.

Nouveau fonds 3724, 3725.

6351. — I.

四諦論

Seu ti loen.

Catuḥsatya çāstra.

Composé par Vasuvarman ; traduit par Paramārtha. Liste des mots difficiles. Èdition donnée par Tchhę-oei (1661).

4 livres. — Bunyiu Nanjio 1261.

— II.

辟支佛因緣論

Phi tchi fo yin yuen loen.

Pratyeka buddha nidāna çāstra.

Traduction des dynasties Tshin (350-431). Lecture des caractères difficiles. Mêmes lieu et date.

1 livre. — Bunyiu Nanjio 1262.

Grand in-8. Bonne gravure. 1 vol. demi-rel., au chiffre de la République Française.

Nouveau fonds 3973.

Troisième Section : ŒUVRES DIVERSES

6352. — I.

金七十論

Kin tshi chi loẹn.

Saptati çāstra; alias Sāṅkhya-kārikā bhāṣya çāstra.

Ouvrage de l'hérétique Kapila, traduit par Paramārtha. Liste des caractères rares. Édition de Leng-yen seu (1661).

3 livres. — Bunyiu Nanjio 1300.

— II.

廣 釋 菩 提 心 論

Koang chi phou thi sin loẹn.

Bodhihṛdaya vaipulya vyākhyā çāstra.

Œuvre du bodhisattva Padma-çīla, traduite par Chi-hou. Lecture des mots difficiles. Édition de Hoa-tchheng seu (1631).

4 livres. — Bunyiu Nanjio 1301.

Grand in-8. Bonne gravure. 1 vol. demi-rel., au chiffre de la République Française.

Nouveau fonds 4321.

6353. — I.

集 諸 法 寶 最 上 義 論

Tsi tchou fa pao tsoei chang yi loẹn.

Sarvadharmaratnottarārtha saṅgīti çāstra.

Par le bodhisattva Sumuni; traduction de Chi-hou. Lecture des caractères difficiles. Édition du Hoa-yen ko (1643).

2 livres. — Bunyiu Nanjio 1302.

— II.

金 剛 針 論

Kin kang tchen loẹn.

Vajrasūci çāstra.

Par le bodhisattva Dharmakīrti; traduction de Fa-thien. Édition de même localité et même date.

9 feuillets. — Bunyiu Nanjio 1303.

— III.

菩 提 心 離 相 論

Phou thi sin li siang loẹn.

Lakṣaṇavimukta bodhihṛdaya çāstra.

Par le bodhisattva Nāgārjuna; traduction de Chi-hou. Mêmes localité et date d'édition.

9 feuillets. — Bunyiu Nanjio 1304.

— IV.

大乘破有論

Ta cheng pho yeou loen.

Mahāyāna bhavabheda çāstra.

Par le bodhisattva Nāgārjuna; traduction de Chi-hou. Liste des signes difficiles.

2 feuillets. — Bunyiu Nanjio 1305.

— V.

集大乘相論

Tsi ta cheng siang loen.

Mahāyāna lakṣaṇasaṅgīti çāstra.

Par le bodhisattva Buddhaçrījñāna; traduction de Chi-hou.

2 livres. — Bunyiu Nanjio 1306.

— VI.

六十頌如理論

Lou chi song jou li loen.

Gāthāṣaṣṭi yathārtha çāstra.

Par le bodhisattva Nāgārjuna; traduction de Chi-hou.

6 feuillets. — Bunyiu Nanjio 1307.

— VII.

大乘二十頌論

Ta cheng eul chi song loen.

Mahāyāna gāthāviṃçati çāstra.

Par le bodhisattva Nāgārjuna; traduction de Chi-hou.

3 feuillets. — Bunyiu Nanjio 1308.

— VIII.

佛毋般若波羅蜜多圓集要義論

Fo mou pan ję po lo mi to yuen tsi yao yi loen.

Buddhamātṛkā prajñāpāramitā mahārtha saṅgīti çāstra.

Par le bodhisattva Diṅnāga (Ta-yu-long); traduction de Chi-hou. Édition de Hoa-tchheng seu (1631).

5 feuillets. — Bunyiu Nanjio 1309; cf. id. 1223, 1224.

— IX.

佛毋般若波羅蜜多圓集要義釋論

Fo mou pan ję po lo mi to yuen tsi yao yi chi loen.

Commentaire du çāstra précédent.

Par le bodhisattva Triratnadāsa ; traduction de Chi-hou. Lecture des signes difficiles. Édition de Leng-yen seu (1661).

4 livres. — Bunyiu Nanjio 1310.

Grand in-8. Bonne gravure. 1 vol. demi-rel., au chiffre de la République Française.

Nouveau fonds 3751.

6354. — I.

大乘集菩薩學論

Ta cheng tsi phou sa hio loẹn.

Mahāyāna saṅgītibodhisattva-vidyā çāstra.

Par le bodhisattva Dharmakīrti ; version de Fa-hou (1004-1058). Lecture des caractères difficiles. Édition du Hoa-yen ko (1643).

25 livres. — Bunyiu Nanjio 1298.

— II.

大宗地玄文本論

Ta tsong ti hiuen oen pẹn loẹn.

Mahāyānabhūmiguhyavācā-mūla çāstra.

Par le bodhisattva Açvaghoṣa ; version de Paramārtha. Liste des mots rares. Mêmes lieu et date.

8 livres. — Bunyiu Nanjio 1299.

Grand in-8. Bonne gravure. 1 vol. demi-rel., au chiffre de la République Française.

Nouveau fonds 4117.

6355. 大乘寶要義論

Ta cheng pao yao yi loẹn.

Mahāyāna ratnamahārtha çāstra.

Version de Fa-hou (1004-1058). Liste des caractères difficiles. Édition du bonze Tchhẹ-oei, de King-chan (1661).

10 livres. — Bunyiu Nanjio 1311.

Grand in-8. Bonne gravure. 1 vol. demi-rel., au chiffre de la République Française.

Nouveau fonds 4131.

6356. — I.

菩薩本生鬘論

Phou sa pẹn cheng man loẹn.

Jātakamālā çāstra.

Ouvrage du bodhisattva Ārya-çūra ; traduit par Chao-tẹ, Hoei-siun et autres religieux de l'époque des Song (960-1127). Lecture des mots rares.

16 livres. — Bunyiu Nanjio 1312.

— II.

聖佛母般若波羅蜜多 九頌精義論

Cheng fo mou pan jẹ po lo mi to kieou song tsing yi loẹn.

Āryabuddhamātṛkā prajñāpāramitā navagāthā mahārtha çāstra.

Œuvre du bodhisattva Çrīguṇaraktāmbara, traduite par Fahou (1004-1058).

2 livres (5 + 5 feuillets). — Bunyiu Nanjio 1313.

— III.

大 乘 緣 生 論

Ta cheng yuen cheng loen.

Mahāyāna nidāna çāstra.

Œuvre de l'arhat Ullaṅgha, traduite par Amoghavajra; traduction ultérieure de Bunyiu Nanjio 1227.

15 feuillets. — Bunyiu Nanjio 1314.

— IV.

諸 教 決 定 名 義 論

Tchou kiao kiue ting ming yi loen.

Sarvaçikṣā sthita nāmārtha çāstra.

Œuvre du bodhisattva Maitreya, traduite par Chi-hou. Lecture des termes difficiles. Édition du Hoa-tchheng seu (1631).

6 feuillets. — Bunyiu Nanjio 1315.

Grand in-8. Bonne gravure; frontispice (1 feuillet double). 1 vol. demi-rel., au chiffre de la République Française. *Nouveau fonds* 4145.

CHAPITRE XVI : BOUDDHISME (ŒUVRES CHINOISES)

Première Section : DHĀRAṆĪ

6357. 陀羅尼雜集

Tho lo ni tsa tsi.

Collection de dhāraṇī.

Compilée à l'époque des Liang (502-557). Table en tête de chaque livre ; lecture des termes difficiles. Édition de Heng-choei seu à King-chan.

— I, livre 1.

七佛所說大陀尼神咒
并八菩薩所說神咒

Tshi fo so choẹ ta tho ni chen tcheou ping pa phou sa so choẹ chen tcheou.

Dhāraṇī prononcées par les sept Bouddha et les huit bodhisattva.

Quinze pièces, en partie transcrites, en partie traduites.

Cf. Bunyiu Nanjio 447 ; nᵒˢ 5809, art. III ; 6146, art. IV.

— II, livre 2.

釋摩男咒

Chi mo nan tcheou.

Çākya Mahānāma dhāraṇī.

Transcrites ou traduites.

Cf. Bunyiu Nanjio 580.

— III, livre 2.

阿難比丘所說神咒

'O nan pi khieou so choẹ chen tcheou.

Ānanda bhikṣu bhāṣita dhāraṇī.

Surtout en traduction.

— IV, livre 2.

普賢菩薩所說大神咒

Phou hien phou sa so choẹ ta chen tcheou.

Samantabhadra bodhisattva bhāṣita mahādhāraṇī.

Parties transcrites et parties traduites.

Cf. n⁰ˢ 6141, art. V ; 6204, art. III.

— V, livre 2.

文殊師利神咒

Oen chou chi li chen tcheou.

Mañjuçrī dhāraṇī.

Parties en transcription, parties en traduction.

Cf. n° 6213, art. I.

— VI, livre 2.

定自在王菩薩咒

Ting tseu tsai oang phou sa tcheou.

Samādhīçvararāja bodhisattva dhāraṇī.

Transcription et traduction.

— VII, livre 2.

妙眼菩薩咒

Miao yen phou sa tcheou.

Sadakṣa bodhisattva dhāraṇī.

Transcription et traduction.

— VIII, livre 2.

功德相嚴菩薩咒

Kong tę siang yen phou sa tcheou.

Guṇalakṣaṇālaṃkāra bodhi-sattva dhāraṇī.

Transcription et traduction.

— IX, livre 2.

善名稱菩薩咒

Chạn ming tchheng phou sa tcheou.

Sukīrti bodhisattva dhāraṇī.

Transcription et traduction.

— X, livre 2.

寶月光明菩薩神咒

Pao yue koang ming phou sa chen tcheou.

Ratnacandraprabha bodhisa-ttva dhāraṇī.

Transcription et traduction.

— XI, livre 2.

北辰菩薩神咒

Pę tchhen phou sa chen tcheou.

Dhruva bodhisattva dhāraṇī.

Transcription et traduction.

— XII, livre 2.

太白仙人神咒

Thai po sien jen chen tcheou.

Dhāraṇī de la planète Vénus.

Transcription et traduction.

— XIII, livre 2.

熒惑仙人神咒

Yong hoẹ sien jen chen tcheou.

Dhāraṇī de la planète Mars.

Transcription et traduction.

— XIV, livre 2.

大梵天王大陀羅尼

Ta fan thien oang ta tho lo ni.

Mahābrahmadevarāja mahā-dhāraṇī.

Transcription et traduction.

— XV, livre 2.

大自在天王神咒

Ta tseu tsai thien oang chen tcheou.

Māheçvara devarāja dhāraṇī.

Transcription et traduction.

— XVI, livre 2.

化樂天王大陀羅尼

Hoa lo thien oang ta tho lo ni.

Nirmāṇarati devarāja mahā-dhāraṇī.

Transcription et traduction.

— XVII, livre 2.

兜率陀天王大陀羅尼

Teou choai tho thien oang ta tho lo ni.

Tuṣita devarāja mahādhāraṇī.

Transcription et traduction.

— XVIII, livre 2.

燄摩天王大神咒

Yen mo thien oang ta chen tcheou.

Yama devarāja dhāraṇī.

Transcription et traduction.

— XIX, livre 2.

忉利天王大神咒

Tao li thien oang ta chen tcheou.

Trayastriṃça devarāja mahā-dhāraṇī.

Transcription et traduction.

Cf. n° 6086, art. II.

— XX, livre 3.

摩醯首羅天王咒

Mo hi cheou lo thien oang tcheou.

Maheçvara devarāja dhāraṇī.

Transcription et traduction.

— XXI, livre 3.

八臂那羅延天神咒

Pa pi na lo yen thien chen tcheou.

Aṣṭabāhu nārāyaṇa deva dhāraṇī.

Transcription et traduction.

— XXII, livre 3.

大功德天王神咒

Ta kong tẹ thien oang chen tcheou.

Mahāguṇa devarāja dhāraṇī.

Transcription et traduction.

— XXIII, livre 3.

八龍王陀羅尼并諸菩薩天王龍王發願說偈

Pa long oang tho lo ni ping tchou phou sa thien oang long oang fa yuen choẹ kie.

Dhāraṇī des huit nāgarāja et gāthā de tous les bodhisattva, devarāja, nāgarāja.

Huit dhāraṇī suivies d'autres pièces.

— XXIV, livre 4.

阿彌陀鼓音聲王陀羅尼經

'O mi tho kou yin cheng oang tho lo ni king.

Amitadundubhisvararāja dhāraṇī sūtra.

Transcription et traduction.

Nᵒ 6204, art. XIII.

— XXV, livre 4.

發菩提心陀羅尼

Fa phou thi sin tho lo ni.

Bodhihṛdaya janaka dhāraṇī.

Transcription et traduction.

Cf. nᵒˢ 6171, art. VII.

— XXVI, livre 4.

日藏菩薩陀羅尼

Ji tsang phou sa tho lo ni.

Sūryagarbhabodhisattva dhāraṇī.

Transcription et traduction.

Cf. Bunyiu Nanjio 62.

— XXVII, livre 4.

佛說護諸童子陀羅尼咒經

Fo choẹ hou tchou thong tseu tho lo ni tcheou king.

Kumārapāla dhāraṇī sūtra.

Version de Bodhiruci.

N° 6204, art. XVI.

— XXVIII, livre 4.

金剛祕密善門陀羅尼

Kin kang pi mi chạn mẹn tho lo ni.

Vajraguhya saddharma paryā-ya dhāraṇī.

Traduction et transcription.

N° 6202, art. VII.

— XXIX, livre 4.

華聚陀羅尼

Hoa tsiu tho lo ni.

Puṣpakūṭa dhāraṇī.

Traduction et transcription.

N° 5861, art. XV.

— XXX, livre 4.

佛說最勝燈王如來所遣陀羅尼句

Fo choẹ tsoei cheng teng oang jou lai so khien tho lo ni kiu.

Anuttaradīpa rāja tathāgata dhāraṇī ou Lokapāla dhāraṇī.

Traduction et transcription.

Cf. n° 6202, art. III.

— XXXI, livre 4.

阿逸多王菩薩說饒益善利色力名譽陀羅尼

'O yi to oang phou sa choẹ jao yi chạn li sẹ li ming yu tho lo ni.

Ajitarāja bodhisattva bhāṣita svarthavarṇabalanāmastutiva-rdhanī dhāraṇī.

Traduction et transcription.

Feuillet 21.

— XXXII, livre 4.

文殊師利菩薩說饒益善利色力名譽陀羅尼

Oen chou chi li phou sa choẹ jao yi chạn li sẹ li ming yu tho lo ni.

Mañjuçrī bodhisattva bhāṣita svarthavarṇabalanāmastutiva-rdhanī dhāraṇī

Traduction et transcription.

Feuillet 21.

— XXXIII, livre 4.

釋迦牟尼佛說大饒益陀羅尼

Chi kia meou ni fo choẹ ta jao yi tho lo ni.

Çākyamuni buddha bhāṣita mahāvṛddhi dhāraṇi.

Traduction et transcription.

Feuillet 22.

— XXXIV, livre 4.

四天王說護持前咒者陀羅尼

Seu thien oang choę hou tchhi tshien tcheou tchę tho lo ni.

Dhāraṇī des quatre devarāja.

Traduction et transcription.

Feuillet 24.

— XXXV, livre 4.

佛說救阿難伏魔陀羅尼句

Fo choę kieou 'o nan fou mo tho lo ni kiu.

Dhāraṇī pour aider Ānanda à abattre les démons.

Traduction et transcription; extrait du Ta nie phan king.

Cf. nᵒˢ 5956-5958, art. I.

— XXXVI, livre 4.

正語梵天所說陀羅尼

Tcheng yu fan thien so choę tho lo ni.

Brahmadeva bhāṣita dhāraṇī.

Transcription et traduction.

— XXXVII, livre 4.

摩尼跋陀天王陀羅尼句

Mo ni po tho thien oang tho lo ni kiu.

Maṇibhadra devarāja dhāraṇī.

Transcription et traduction.

— XXXVIII, livre 4.

婆視羅仙人大神咒

Pho chi lo sien jen ta chen tcheou.

Vajirarṣi mahādhāraṇī.

Transcription et traduction.

— XXXIX, livre 5.

除一切恐畏毒害伏惡魔陀羅尼

Tchhou yi tshie khong oei tou hai fou 'o mo tho lo ni.

Dhāraṇī pour écarter la crainte et le poison, pour abattre les méchants démons.

Transcription et traduction.

Cf. n⁰ˢ 5861, art. II; 6136, art. III; 6146, art. V.

— XL, livre 5.

佛說止女人患血至困陀羅尼

Fo choe tchi niu jen hoan hiue tchi khoen tho lo ni.

Dhāraṇī contre les pertes de sang chez les femmes.

Transcription et traduction.

— XLI, livre 5.

佛說婦人產難陀羅尼

Fo choe fou jen tchhan nan tho lo ni; alias :

除產難陀羅尼

Tchhou tchhan nan tho lo ni.

Dhāraṇī pour faciliter l'accouchement.

Transcription et traduction.

— XLII, livre 5.

佛說除灾患諸惱毒神咒

Fo choe tchhou tsai hoan tchou nao tou chen tcheou.

Dhāraṇī contre les calamités et autres afflictions.

Transcription et traduction.

Cf. n⁰ˢ 5859, art. IV; 6136, art. IV.

— XLIII, livre 5.

佛說多聞陀羅尼

Fo choe to oen tho lo ni.

Bahuçruta dhāraṇī.

Transcription et traduction.

— XLIV, livre 5.

佛說治瘧病陀羅尼

Fo choe tchi yo ping tho lo ni.

Dhāraṇī contre la fièvre intermittente.

Transcription.

— XLV, livre 5.

觀世音菩薩說消除熱病諸邪所不能忤大神咒

Koan chi yin phou sa choe siao tchhou je ping tchou sie so pou neng oou ta chen tcheou.

Grande dhāraṇī irrésistible d'Avalokiteçvara contre le typhus.

Transcription.

— XLVI, livre 5.

四天王說咒葛莆舍之令他人歡喜陀羅尼

Seu thien oang choȩ tcheou ko phou han tchi ling tho jen hoan hi tho lo ni.

Dhāraṇī des quatre devarāja; dhāraṇī de Ko-phou-han ordonnant aux autres hommes de se réjouir.

Transcription et traduction.

— XLVII, livre 5.

觀世音菩薩心陀羅尼句

Koan chi yin phou sa sin tho lo ni kiu.

Avalokiteçvara bodhisattva hṛdaya dhāraṇī.

Transcription et traduction.

Cf. n° 5860, art. VII.

— XLVIII, livre 5.

請觀世音菩薩陀羅尼句

Tshing koan chi yin phou sa tho lo ni kiu.

Dhāraṇī pour prier Avalokiteçvara.

Transcription et traduction.

Cf. n° 5861, art. II.

— XLIX, livre 5.

觀世音菩薩行道救願陀羅尼句

Koan chi yin phou sa hing tao kieou yuen tho lo ni kiu.

Dhāraṇī d'Avalokiteçvara qui voyage et exauce les prières.

Transcription et traduction.

— L, livre 5.

佛說乞雨咒

Fo choȩ khi yu tcheou.

Dhāraṇī pour demander la pluie.

Transcription et traduction.

Cf. Bunyiu Nanjio 962; n°ˢ 6087, 6214, art. V.

— LI, livre 5.

那羅延天王除滅瘧病神咒

Na lo yen thien oang tchhou mie yo ping chen tcheou.

Dhāraṇī de Nārāyaṇa devarāja contre la fièvre intermittente.

Transcription.

— LII, livre 5.

佛說滅除十惡神咒

Fo choȩ mie tchhou chi 'o chen tcheou.

Dhāraṇī pour éteindre les dix maux.

Transcription et traduction.

— LIII, livre 5.

觀世音說治五舌塞喉陀羅尼

Koan chi yin choȩ tchi oou chȩ sȩ heou tho lo ni.

Dhāraṇī de Koan-yin pour guérir les cinq obstructions du gosier par la langue.

Transcription et traduction.

— LIV, livre 5.

佛說小兒中人惡眼者咒經

Fo choȩ siao eul tchong jen 'o yen tchȩ tcheou king.

Sūtra et dhāraṇī pour les enfants et les hommes qui ont de mauvais yeux.

Transcription.

Cf. nº 6204, art. XI et XII.

— LV, livre 5.

滅罪得入初地陀羅尼

Mie tsȩei tȩ jou tchhou ti tho lo ni.

Dhāraṇī pour anéantir le péché et entrer dans la première bhūmi.

Transcription et traduction.

— LVI, livre 5.

佛說若欲讀誦一切經典先誦此陀羅尼

Fo choȩ jo yu tou song yi tshie king tien sien song tsheu tho lo ni.

Dhāraṇī à réciter avant la lecture de tout sūtra.

Transcription et traduction.

— LVII, livre 5.

結帶禁兵賊陀羅尼
Kie tai kin ping tsȩ tho lo ni.

Dhāraṇī contre les voleurs armés.

Transcription et traduction.

Cf. nº 6152, art. XVII; nº 6204, art. VIII.

— LVIII, livre 5.

咒齒痛陀羅尼
Tcheou tchhi thong tho lo ni;
alias :

咒牙齒痛陀羅尼
Tcheou ya tchhi thong tho lo ni.

Dhāraṇī contre le mal de dents.

Transcription et traduction.

Cf. n° 6204, art. X.

— LIX, livre 5.

降雨陀羅尼
Kiang yu tho lo ni.

Dhāraṇī pour faire tomber la pluie.

Transcription et traduction; texte extrait du Mahāmegha sūtra.

Cf. nᵒˢ 6107, art. III et IV; 6109.

— LX, livre 5.

繫龍王陀羅尼
Hi long oang tho lo ni.

Dhāraṇī pour lier le nāgarāja.

Transcription et traduction; texte extrait du Mahāmegha sūtra.

Cf. nᵒˢ 6107, art. III et IV; 6109.

— LXI, livre 5.

觀世音菩薩所說諸根具足陀羅尼
Koan chi yin phou sa so choę tcheou ken kiu tsou tho lo ni; alias :

觀世音說諸根不具咒草摩之陀羅尼
Koan chi yin choę tchou ken pou kiu tcheou tshao mo tchi tho lo ni.

Avalokiteçvara bhāṣita vikalendriya praçamanī dhāraṇī.

Transcription et traduction.

— LXII, livre 5.

尼乾天所說產生難陀羅尼咒
Ni khien thien so choę tchhan cheng nan tho lo ni tcheou.

Dhāraṇī pour les accouchements difficiles, prononcée par Nirgrantha deva.

Transcription et traduction.

— LXIII, livre 5.

咒穀 (sic) 子種之令無灾蝗陀羅尼
Tcheou kou tseu tchong tchi ling oou tsai hoang tho lo ni.

Dhāraṇī contre les sauterelles.

Transcription et traduction.

— LXIV, livre 5.

咒蝎中毒陀羅尼
Tcheou hie tchong tou tho lo ni.

Dhāraṇī contre le venin du scorpion.

Transcription et traduction.

— LXV, livre 5.

咒卒得重病悶絶者陀羅尼

Tcheou tsou tẹ tchong ping mẹn tsiue tchẹ tho lo ni.

Dhāraṇī contre les maladies soudaines et les pertes de connaissance.

Traduction et transcription.

— LXVI, livre 6.

除腫患陀羅尼

Tchhou tchong hoan tho lo ni.

Dhāraṇī contre les enflures.

Traduction et transcription.

— LXVII, livre 6.

治熱病陀羅尼

Tchi jẹ ping tho lo ni.

Dhāraṇī contre le typhus.

Traduction et transcription.

— LXVIII, livre 6.

治百病諸毒陀羅尼

Tchi po ping tchou tou tho lo ni.

Dhāraṇī contre toutes les maladies et tous les venins.

Transcription et traduction.

Cf. nº 5809, art. V.

— LXIX, livre 6.

佛說咒僧伽梨文。欲縫咒文。受法衣文

Fo choẹ tcheou seng kia li oen. Yu fong tcheou oen. Chcou fa yi oen.

Dhāraṇī relative à la saṅghāṭi, à la couture, à la réception du vêtement religieux.

Texte chinois.

— LXX, livre 6.

佛說咒應器文。咒錫杖文。咒獨坐文

Fo choẹ tcheou ying khi oen. Tcheou si tchang oen. Tcheou tou tsoo oen.

Dhāraṇī relative au pātra, au khakkhara, au siège.

Texte chinois.

— LXXI, livre 6.

五戒神名

Oou kiai chen ming.

Liste des divinités qui président aux cinq commandements (pañcaçīla).

— LXXII, livre 6.

三歸神名

San koei chen ming.

Liste des divinités qui président au triçaraṇa.

— LXXIII, livre 6.

護僧伽藍神

Hou seng kia lan chen.

Liste des divinités qui protègent le saṅghārāma.

— LXXIV, livre 6.

觀世音菩薩說燒華應現得願陀羅尼

Koan chi yin phou sa choẹ chao hoa ying hien tẹ yuen tho lo ni.

Dhāraṇī de Koan-yin, relative aux vœux exaucés en brûlant des fleurs.

Transcription et traduction.

— LXXV, livre 6.

觀世音說散華供養應沒陀羅尼

Koan chi yin choẹ san hoa kong yang ying mou tho lo ni.

Dhāraṇī de Koan-yin, relative aux offrandes de fleurs et de nourriture.

Transcription et traduction.

— LXXVI, livre 6.

觀世音說滅罪得願陀羅尼

Koan chi yin choẹ mie tsoei tẹ yuen tho lo ni.

Dhāraṇī de Koan-yin pour l'extinction du péché et la réalisation des prières.

Transcription et traduction.

— LXXVII, livre 6.

觀世音說除一切眼痛陀羅尼

Koan chi yin choẹ tchhou yi tshie yen thong tho lo ni.

Cakṣurviçodhana vidyā dhāraṇī.

Transcription et traduction.

Cf. nᵒ 5809, art. IV.

— LXXVIII, livre 6.

觀世音說能令諸根不具足者具足陀羅尼

Koan chi yin choẹ neng ling tchou ken pou kiu tsou tchẹ kiu tsou tho lo ni.

Avalokiteçvara bhāṣita vika-lendriya sakalīkaraṇī dhāraṇī.

Transcription et texte chinois.

— LXXIX, livre 6.

觀世音說治熱病陀羅尼

Koan chi yin choẹ tchi jẹ ping tho lo ni.

Dhāraṇī d'Avalokiteçvara contre le typhus.

Transcription et texte chinois.

— LXXX, livre 6.

觀世音說除一切顛狂魍魎鬼神陀羅尼

Koan chi yin choẹ tchhou yi tshie tien khoang oang liang koei chen tho lo ni.

Dhāraṇī d'Avalokiteçvara contre tous les génies furieux des rivières.

Transcription et traduction.

— LXXXI, livre 6.

觀世音說除種種怖畏陀羅尼

oan chi yin choẹ tchhou tchong tchong pou oei tho lo ni.

Dhāraṇī d'Avalokiteçvara pour écarter toutes les frayeurs.

Transcription et traduction.

Cf. n°ˢ 6136, art. III ; 6146, art. V.

— LXXXII, livre 6.

觀世音說除一切腫陀羅尼

Koan chi yin choẹ tchhou yi tshie tchong tho lo ni.

Dhāraṇī d'Avalokiteçvara contre toutes les enflures.

Transcription et traduction.

— LXXXIII, livre 6.

觀世音說除身體諸痛陀羅尼

Koan chi yin choẹ tchhou chen thi tchou thong tho lo ni.

Dhāraṇī d'Avalokiteçvara contre toutes les douleurs corporelles.

Transcription et traduction.

— LXXXIV, livre 6.

觀世音說除卒腹痛陀羅尼

Koan chi yin choẹ tchhou tsou fou thong tho lo ni.

Dhāraṇī d'Avalokiteçvara contre les douleurs soudaines du ventre.

Transcription et traduction.

— LXXXV, livre 6.

觀世音說除中毒乃至已死陀羅尼

Koan chi yin choẹ tchhou tchong tou nai tchi yi seu tho lo ni.

Dhāraṇī d'Avalokiteçvara contre les effets de l'absorption du poison, y compris la mort.

Transcription et traduction.

— LXXXVI, livre 6.

觀世音說除卒病悶絕不覺者陀羅尼

Koan chi yin choẹ tchhou tsou ping mẹn tsiue pou kio tchẹ tho lo ni.

Dhāraṇī d'Avalokiteçvara contre les maladies soudaines et pertes de connaissance.

Transcription et traduction.

— LXXXVII, livre 6.

觀世音說除五舌若喉塞若舌縮陀羅尼

Koan chi yin choẹ tchhou oou chẹ jo heou sẹ jo chẹ chou tho lo ni.

Dhāraṇī d'Avalokiteçvara contre les cinq obstructions du gosier et de la langue, et les contractions de la langue.

Transcription et traduction.

— LXXXVIII, livre 6.

觀世音說除種種癩病乃至傷破咒土陀羅尼

Koan chi yin choẹ tchhou tchong tchong lai ping nai tchi chang pho tcheou thou tho lo ni.

Dhāraṇī d'Avalokiteçvara contre toutes les lésions de la peau y compris les blessures.

Transcription et traduction.

— LXXXIX, livre 6.

觀世音說咒裀底土吹之令毒氣不行陀羅尼

Koan chi yin choẹ tcheou kien ti thou tchhoei tchi ling tou khi pou hing tho lo ni.

Dhāraṇī d'Avalokiteçvara contre les vapeurs miasmatiques.

Transcription et traduction.

— XC, livre 6.

觀世音說咒藥服得一聞持陀羅尼

Koan chi yin choę tcheou yo fou tę yi oen tchhi tho lo ni.

Dhāraṇī d'Avalokiteçvara, relative aux médicaments.

Transcription et traduction.

— XCl, livre 6.

觀世音說咒五種色菖蒲服得聞持不忘陀羅尼

Koan chi yin choę tcheou oou tchong sę tchhang phou fou tę oen tchhi pou oang tho lo ni.

Dhāraṇī d'Avalokiteçvara sur l'acorus de cinq couleurs qui affermit la mémoire et empêche d'oublier.

Transcription et traduction.

— XCII, livre 6.

觀世音說除病肌生陀羅尼

Koan chi yin choę tchhou ping ki cheng tho lo ni.

Dhāraṇī d'Avalokiteçvara pour chasser la maladie et procurer l'embonpoint.

Transcription et traduction.

— XCIII, livre 6.

觀世音說咒吐 (*alias* 土) 冶赤白下痢陀羅尼

Koan chi yin choę tcheou thou tchi tchhi po hia li tho lo ni.

Dhāraṇī d'Avalokiteçvara contre les vomissements et la dyssenterie.

Traduction et transcription.

— XCIV, livre 6.

觀世音說咒草拭一切痛處即除愈陀羅尼

Koan chi yin choę tcheou tshao chi yi tshie thong tchhou tsi tchhou yu tho lo ni.

Dhāraṇī d'Avalokiteçvara pour faire disparaître immédiatement toutes les douleurs.

Transcription et texte chinois.

— XCV, livre 6.

觀世音說隨心所願陀羅尼

Koan chi yin choę soei sin so yuen tho lo ni.

Dhāraṇī d'Avalokiteçvara pour satisfaire les désirs du cœur.

Transcription et texte chinois.

— XCVI, livre 7.

觀世音說滅一切罪過得一切所願陀羅尼

Koan chi yin choę mie yi tshie tsoei koo tę yi tshie so yuen tho lo ni.

Dhāraṇī d'Avalokiteçvara pour éteindre tout péché, exaucer toute prière.

Transcription et traduction.

— XCVII, livre 7.

除障滅病至獲道果陀羅尼

Tchhou tchang mie ping tchi ho tao koo tho lo ni.

Dhāraṇī pour écarter les maladies, pour obtenir les fruits de la sagesse.

Transcription et traduction.

— XCVIII, livre 7.

獲諸禪三昧一切佛法門陀羅尼

Ho tchou chạn san mei yi tshie fo fa mẹn tho lo ni.

Dhāraṇī sur les moyens d'obtenir le dhyāna et le samādhi.

Transcription et traduction.

— XCIX, livre 7.

見一切諸佛從心所願陀羅尼

Kien yi tshie tchou fo tshong sin so yuen tho lo ni.

Dhāraṇī pour obtenir des Bouddhas satisfaction des vœux.

Transcription et traduction.

— C, livre 7.

修念佛三昧陀羅尼

Sieou nien fo san mei tho lo ni.

Buddhānusmṛti samādhi dhāraṇī.

Transcription et traduction.

Cf. n° 5878.

— CI, livre 7.

無盡意菩薩說幢蓋願陀羅尼

Oou tsin yi phou sa choę tchhoang kai yuen tho lo ni.

Dhāraṇī d'Akṣayamati bodhisattva.

Transcription et traduction.

Cf. n° 5871.

— CII, livre 7.

勝敵安退并治毒嚙及腫陀羅尼

Cheng ti 'an thoei ping tchi tou yao ki tchong tho lo ni.

Dhāraṇī contre les ennemis, contre le poison et contre l'enflure.

Transcription et traduction.

— CIII, livre 7.

吉祥神咒

Ki siang chen tcheou.

Çrī dhāraṇī.

Texte chinois.

Cf. n° 6152, art. IV.

— CIV, livre 7.

佛說旋塔陀羅尾

Fo choę siuen tha tho lo ni

Stūpa pradakṣiṇa dhāraṇī.

Transcription seule.

— CV, livre 7.

辟賊陀羅尾

Pi tsę tho lo ni.

Dhāraṇī contre les voleurs.

Transcription seule.

Cf. n° 6204, art. VIII.

— CVI, livre 7.

聞持陀羅尾

Oen tchhi tho lo ni.

Dhāraṇī pour écouter et garder les instructions.

Transcription seule.

— CVII, livre 7.

佛說大七寶陀羅尾

Fo choę ta tshi pao tho lo ni.

Mahāsaptaratna dhāraṇī.

Transcription et traduction.

N° 6204, art. IV.

— CVIII, livre 7.

佛說大普賢陀羅尾

Fo choę ta phou hien tho lo ni.

Samantabhadra dhāraṇī.

Traduction et transcription.

N° 6204, art. III.

— CIX, livre 7.

四天王所說大神咒

Seu thien oang so choę ta chen tcheou.

Caturdevarāja bhāṣita mahādhāraṇī.

Transcription et traduction, 66 pièces.

Cf. n° 6164, art. I.

— CX, livre 8.

佛說六字大陀羅尼咒經

Fo choe lou tseu ta tho lo ni tcheou king.

Ṣaḍakṣara mahādhāraṇī mantra sūtra.

Nᵒ 6204, art. V.

— CXI, livre 8.

佛說檀持羅麻油述神咒經

Fo choe than tchhi lo ma yeou chou chen tcheou king.

Mahādaṇḍa dhāraṇī sūtra.

Nᵒ 6204, art. XV.

— CXII, livre 8.

阿夷颭咒病經

'O yi tcheou tcheou ping king.

Sūtra de 'O-yi-tcheou contre les maladies.

— CXIII, livre 8.

佛說咒六字神王經

Fo choe tcheou lou tseu chen oang king.

Ṣaḍakṣara vidyāmantra sūtra.

Cf. nᵒˢ 5861, art. XVI et XVII; 6218, art. II.

— CXIV, livre 8.

尼乾陀天所說產 (*alias* 生) 難咒

Ni khien tho thien so choe tchhan (alias cheng) nan tcheou.

Dhāraṇī prononcée par Nirgrantha deva pour les accouchements difficiles.

Transcription et texte chinois.

Cf. plus haut, art. LXII.

— CXV, livre 8.

大自在天王所說名摩醯首羅天咒

Ta tseu tsai thien oang so choe ming mo hi cheou lo thien tcheou.

Maheçvara devarāja bhāṣita maheçvara deva mantra.

Texte chinois, transcription.

— CXVI, livre 8.

大自在天及其眷屬所說咒

Ta tseu tsai thien ki khi kiuen chou so choe tcheou.

Dhāraṇī prononcée par Maheçvara et son entourage.

Transcription.

— CXVII, livre 8.

大神仙所說咒

Ta chen sien so choe tcheou.

Maharṣi bhāṣita mantra.

Transcription et traduction.

— CXVIII, livre 8.

阿修羅天神斷注不得還著病人咒

'O sieou lo thien chen toan tchou pou te hoan tcho ping jen tcheou.

Dhāraṇī pour empêcher que les hommes soient affligés de maladies par les asura, les deva et les esprits.

Transcription et traduction.

— CXIX, livre 8.

大神仙赤眼咒牙齒齲（*alias* 蹬）經

Ta chen sien tchhi yen tcheou ya tchhi khiu (alias teng?) king.

Sūtra contre le mal de dents, du maharṣi Tchhi-yen.

Traduction et transcription.

— CXX, livre 8.

梵天咒句文

Fan thien tcheou kiu oen.

Brahmadeva dhāraṇī.

Transcription seule.

— CXXI, livre 8.

一大梵天女尙衢梨所說咒

Yi ta fan thien niu chang khiu li so choe tcheou.

Dhāraṇī de la devī Jāṅgulī.

Transcription et traduction.

— CXXII, livre 8.

甘露天說一切毒咒

Kan lou thien choe yi tshie tou tcheou.

Dhāraṇī d'Amṛtadeva contre tous les poisons.

Transcription.

Cf. nº 6221, art. V.

— CXXIII, livre 8.

大梵天說甘露咒甘露能使毒氣入地咒

Ta fan thien choe kan lou tcheou; kan lou neng chi tou khi jou ti tcheou.

Mahābrahma deva bhāṣitāmṛta dhāraṇī; dhāraṇī pour que l'amṛta fasse rentrer en terre les influences vénéneuses.

Transcription.

Cf. n° 6221, art. V.

— CXXIV, livre 8.

甘露梵天女阿婆耆說 一切毒咒

Kan lou fan thien niu 'o pho khi choẹ yi tshie tou tcheou.

Dhāraṇī contre tous les poisons, prononcée par l'amṛtabrahmadevī 'O-pho-khi.

Transcription et texte chinois.

Cf. n° 6221, art. V.

— CXXV, livre 8.

觀世音菩薩說陀羅尼

Koan chi yin phou sa choẹ tho lo ni.

Avalokiteçvara bodhisattva bhāṣita dhāraṇī.

Transcription et texte chinois.

— CXXVI, livre 8.

咒疫病文

Tcheou yi ping oen.

Dhāraṇī contre les maladies épidémiques.

Transcription et traduction.

— CXXVII, livre 8.

咒癰腫文

Tcheou yong tchong oen.

Dhāraṇī contre les furoncles et les enflures.

Traduction seule.

— CXXVIII, livre 8.

佛說摩尼羅亶咒經

Fo choẹ mo ni lo tan tcheou king.

Maṇirāta sūtra.

Texte chinois et transcription.

N° 6204, art. XIV.

— CXXIX, livre 8.

佛說神水咒經

Fo choẹ chen choei tcheou king.

Sūtra de l'eau spirituelle.

Transcription et traduction.

— CXXX, livre 8.

梵天王釋提桓因神咒

Fan thien oang chi thi hoan yin chen tcheou.

Dhāraṇī de Brahmadevarāja et Çakra Devendra.

Texte chinois et transcription.

— CXXXI, livre 8.

四天王神咒

Seu thien oang chen tcheou.

Caturdevarāja dhāraṇī.

Texte et transcription.

Cf. n° 6164. art. I.

— CXXXII, livre 8.

淨陀羅尼神咒

Tsing tho lo ni chen tcheou.

Dhāraṇī pure.

Transcription.

— CXXXIII, ltvre 9.

阿吒婆拘鬼神大將上佛陀羅尼

'O tcha pho kiu koei chen ta tsiang chang fo tho lo ni.

Āṭavikāsurasena dhāraṇī

Texte chinois et transcription.

N° 6204, art. II.

— CXXXIV, livre 9.

佛說陀鄰尼鉢經

Fo choę tho lin ni po king.

Dhāraṇī pātra sūtra.

Texte chinois et transcription.

N° 6202, art. II.

— CXXXV, livre 9.

佛說集法悅捨苦陀羅尼經

Fo choę tsi fa yue chę khou tho lo ni king.

Sūtra et dhāraṇī pour rassembler la joie de la loi et rejeter l'amertume.

Transcription et traduction.

— CXXXVI, livre 9.

觀世音說隨願陀羅尼

Koan chi yin choę soei yuen tho lo ni.

Dhāraṇī d'Avalokiteçvara pour exaucer les vœux.

Transcription et traduction.

— CXXXVII, livre 9.

乞夢卽知吉凶陀羅尼

Khi mong tsi tchi ki hiong tho lo ni.

Dhāraṇī pour demander de prévoir en songe le bonheur et le malheur.

Transcription et traduction.

— CXXXVIII, livre 9.

除一切顛狂病陀羅尼

Tchhou yi tshie tien khoang ping tho lo ni.

Dhāraṇī pour écarter toutes les maladies soudaines.

Transcription et traduction.

— CXXXIX, livre 9.

除怖畏陀羅尼

Tchhou pou oei tho lo ni.

Dhāraṇī pour écarter la frayeur.

Transcription et traduction.
Cf. nº 6136, art. III.

— CXL, livre 9.

結藥界陀羅尼

Kie yo kiai tho lo ni.

Dhāraṇī du dhātu des remèdes liés.

Transcription et traduction.

— CXLI, livre 9.

復有求夢陀羅尼

Feou yeou khieou mong tho lo ni.

Autre dhāraṇī pour demander des songes.

Transcription et traduction.
Voir plus haut, art. CXXXVII.

— CXLII, livre 9.

佛說咒時氣病經

Fo choẹ tcheou chi khi ping king.

Sūtra et dhāraṇī contre les épidémies.

Transcription et traduction.
Nº 6204, art. IX.

— CXLIII, livre 9.

行住隨方面歸依稱十方佛名號

Hing tchou soei fang mien koei yi tchheng chi fang fo ming hao.

Noms des Bouddhas des dix régions invoqués en faisant profession de foi.

Texte chinois.

— CXLIV, livre 9.

佛說偈令人誦得長壽

Fo choẹ kie ling jen song tẹ tchhang cheou.

Gāthā pour obtenir la longévité.

Texte chinois.

— CXLV, livre 9.

佛說一切大吉祥滅一切惡陀羅尼

Fo choẹ yi tshie ta ki siang mie yi tshie 'o tho lo ni.

Dhāraṇī de toutes les félicités et contre tous les maux.

Transcription seule.

— CXLVI, livre 9.

佛說觀佛三昧觀四威儀品

Fo choẹ koan fo san mei koan seu oei yi phin; alias :

佛說大小乘觀

Fo choẹ ta siao cheng koan.

Buddhabhāṣita mahāhīnayāna dhyāna.

Texte chinois, extrait du Koan fo san mei king, Buddhadhyāna samādhi sūtra.

Cf. nº 6124.

— CXLVII, livre 10.

定志慧見陀羅尼

Ting tchi hoei kien tho lo ni.

Dhāraṇī de la volonté fixée et de la connaissance.

Transcription et texte chinois.

— CXLVIII, livre 10.

八兄弟陀羅尼

Pa hiong ti tho lo ni.

Dhāraṇī des huit frères.

Transcription et texte chinois.

— CXLIX, livre 10.

觀世音說應現與願陀羅尼

Koan chi yin choẹ ying hien yu yuen tho lo ni.

Dhāraṇī de Koan-yin qui répond et exauce.

Transcription et traduction.

— CL, livre 10.

日藏經中除罪見佛陀羅尼

Ji tsang king tchong tchhou tsoei kien fo tho lo ni.

Dhāraṇī pour écarter le péché et voir le Bouddha, tirée du Sūryagarbha sūtra.

Transcription et traduction.
Cf. Bunyiu Nanjio 62.

— CLI, livre 10.

獲果利神增善陀羅尼

Ho koo li chen tseng chạn tho lo ni.

Dhāraṇī pour obtenir les fruits de la connaissance, etc.

Transcription et traduction.

— CLII, livre 10.

善護除病陀羅尼

Chan hou tchhou ping tho lo ni.

Dhāraṇī qui protège et qui écarte les maladies.

Transcription et traduction.

— CLIII, livre 10.

進果獲證修業陀羅尼

Tsin koo ho tcheng sieou ye tho lo ni.

Dhāraṇī pour avancer dans la voie, etc.

Transcription et texte chinois.

— CLIV, livre 10.

結縷除睡蒙護陀羅尼

Kie liu tchhou choei mong hou tho lo ni.

Dhāraṇī pour écarter le sommeil et recevoir protection.

Transcription et texte chinois.

— CLV, livre 10.

咒酥除睡不饞益乳陀羅尼

Tcheou sou tchhou choei pou ki yi jou tho lo ni.

Dhāraṇī pour écarter le sommeil, pour ne pas avoir faim, pour augmenter le lait.

Transcription et texte chinois.

— CLVI, livre 10.

見佛隨願陀羅尼

Kien fo soei yuen tho lo ni.

Dhāraṇī pour voir le Bouddha et exaucer les vœux.

Transcription et traduction.

— CLVII, livre 10.

觀世音現身施種種願除一切病陀羅尼

Koan chi yin hien chen chi tchong tchong yuen tchhou yi tshie ping tho lo ni.

Dhāraṇī d'Avalokiteçvara qui réalise tous les vœux et écarte toutes les maladies.

Transcription et texte chinois.

— CLVIII, livre 10.

散華觀世音足下陀羅尼

San hoa koan chi yin tsou hia tho lo ni.

Dhāraṇī de Koan-yin qui répand des fleurs.

Transcription et traduction.

— CLIX, livre 10.

念觀世音求願陀羅尼

Nien koan chi yin khieou yuen tho lo ni.

Dhāraṇī de la méditation de Koan-yin et des prières.

Transcription et traduction.

— CLX, livre 10.

誦咒手摩眼除一切痛陀羅尼

Song tcheou cheou mo yen tchhou yi tshie thong tho lo ni.

Dhāraṇī écartant toutes les douleurs.

Transcription et traduction.

— CLXI, livre 10.

除腹痛陀羅尼

Tchhou fou thong tho lo ni; alias :

咒鹽水飲腹痛者陀羅尼

Tcheou yen choei yin fou thong tchę tho lo ni.

Dhāraṇī contre les douleurs de ventre.

Transcription et texte chinois.

— CLXII, livre 10.

除卒中毒病欲死者陀羅尼

Tchhou tsou tchong tou ping yu seu tchę tho lo ni.

Dhāraṇī contre les maladies soudaines et contre le désir de la mort.

Transcription et texte chinois.

— CLXIII, livre 10.

除瞋恚陀羅尼

Tchhou tchhen hoei tho lo ni.

Dhāraṇī pour écarter le mécontentement et la réprimande.

Transcription et texte chinois; extrait du Sūryagarbha sūtra.

Cf. Bunyiu Nanjio 62.

— CLXIV, livre 10.

觀世音除業障陀羅尼

Koan chi yin tchhou ye tchang tho lo ni.

Dhāraṇī de Koan-yin qui écarte les obstacles du karman.

Transcription et traduction.

Cf. n° 5987, art. XI.

— CLXV, livre 10.

佛說咒泥陀羅尼

Fo chọe tcheou ni tho lo ni; alias :

佛說咒泥塗身塗幢塗
藥塗毒塗腫陀羅尼

Fo choe tcheou ni thou chen thou tchhoang thou yo thou tou thou tchong tho lo ni.

Dhāraṇī de la boue.

Traduction chinoise et transcription.

— CLXVI, livre 10.

樂虛空藏菩薩陀羅尼
咒

Lo hiu khong tsang phou sa tho lo ni tcheou.

Dhāraṇī d'Ākāçagarbha bodhisattva.

Transcription et traduction.

Cf. Bunyiu Nanjio 68; nᵒˢ 6152, art. XIII; 6210, art. VII; 6217, art. IV.

— CLXVII, livre 10.

觀世音菩薩陀羅尼

Koan chi yin phou sa tho lo ni.

Avalokiteçvara bodhisattva dhāraṇī.

Transcription et traduction.

— CLXVIII, livre 10.

懺悔擲華陀羅尼

Tchhan hoei tchi hoa tho lo ni.

Dhāraṇī du repentir.

Transcription et traduction.

— CLXIX, livre 10.

除殃病滅毒陀羅尼.
咒腫陀羅尼

Tchhou yang ping mie tou tho lo ni. Tcheou tchong tho lo ni.

Dhāraṇī pour écarter les maladies envoyées par le ciel et pour anéantir le poison. Dhāraṇī contre les enflures.

Transcription et texte chinois.

— CLXX, livre 10.

咒癰瘡中惡陀羅尼

Tcheou yong tchhoang tchong 'o tho lo ni.

Dhāraṇī contre les furoncles et ulcères.

Transcription et texte chinois.

— CLXXI, livre 10.

日藏中護眼陀羅尼

Ji tsang tchong hou yen tho lo ni.

Dhāraṇī pour protéger les yeux, tirée du Sūryagarbha sūtra.

Transcription et texte chinois.

Cf. Bunyiu Nanjio 62.

— CLXXII, livre 10.

四天王咒經

Seu thien oang tcheou king.

Caturdevarāja dhāraṇī sūtra.

Transcription et texte chinois.

Cf. n° 6164, art. I.

Grand in-8. Bonne gravure; frontispice (1 feuillet double). 1 vol. demi-rel., au chiffre de la République Française.
Nouveau fonds 4017.

Deuxième Section : RITUELS

6358-6367. 慈悲道場懺法

Tsheu pei tao tchhang tchhan fa.

Règles pour la confession dans le temple du Bouddha.

Frontispice (5 feuillets simples) représentant des divinités. Historique de l'ouvrage qui a été compilé par l'empereur Oou (502-549) des Liang. Invocations au début et à la fin du texte. Lecture des caractères difficiles. A la fin du 1er livre, figure de divinité. Édition de Hai-tchhoang (1679).

10 livres. — Bunyiu Nanjio 1509.

In-4. Papier blanc. 10 vol. en paravent couvertures rouges; dans 3 étuis demi-rel., au chiffre de Louis-Philippe.
Nouveau fonds 154.

6368.

Tsheu pei tao tchhang tchhan fa.

Même ouvrage. Frontispice (1 feuillet double); après l'historique, cérémonial, invocations, etc.; puis le texte; lecture des signes difficiles. Édition de Hai-tchhoang non datée.

10 livres.

Grand in-8. Papier blanc. 1 vol demi-rel., au chiffre de Louis-Philippe.
Nouveau fonds 160.

6369-6375.
— I (6369).

華嚴海印道場九會請佛儀

Hoa yen hai yin tao tchhang kieou hoei tshing fo yi.

Rites pour inviter le Bouddha pour la cérémonie de la confession, etc.

Préfaces pour l'art. II par Tshien Khien-yi de Yu-chan (1641) et par Mao Fong-pao de Yu-chan (1641). Texte.

19 feuillets.

— II (6369-6375).

大方廣佛華嚴經海印 道場十種行願常徧 禮懺儀

Ta fang koang fo hoa yen king hai yin tao tchhang chi tchong hing yuen chang pien li tchhan yi; alias :

華嚴經海印道場懺儀

Hoa yen king hai yin tao tchhang tchhan yi; alias :

華嚴懺法

Hoa yen tchhan fa.

Règles de la confession de l'Avataṃsaka.

Par le bonze Yi-hing Hoei-kio de Lan-chan (672-717); supplément et commentaire par Phou-joei de Tshang-chan (dynastie des Song); revu et publié par Mou-Tseng, Tou-tchhe, Tcheng-tchi

fidèle et bonzes sous la dynastie des Ming. Notice relative à la gravure faite au Ki-kou ko (1640-1641), placée à la fin du 1er livre. Notices finales; l'une d'elles indique que l'ouvrage a été retrouvé au Tchhong-cheng seu, de Ye-yu.

42 livres.

Grand in-8. Bonne gravure; frontispice (1 feuillet double). 7 vol. demi-rel., au chiffre de la République Française. *Nouveau fonds* 3780 à 3786.

6376. — 1.

大方廣佛華嚴經寶懺

Ta fang koang fo hoa yen king pao tchhan.

La précieuse confession du Buddhāvataṃsaka mahāvaipulya sūtra.

Texte publié à Hai-tchhoang seu.

Comparer nos 5884, etc.

— II.

大方廣佛華嚴經普賢 行願品

Ta fang koang fo hoa yen king phou hien hing yuen phin.

Buddhāvataṃsaka mahāvaipulya sūtra samantabhadra praṇidhānādhyāya.

Texte suivi de dhāraṇī et d'une note finale en chinois.

A la fin formules sanscrites et prière, figure de divinité. Frontispice, 2 feuillets doubles.

Cf. n⁰ˢ 5899, art. III.

In-4. Papier blanc. 1 vol. en paravent couverture rouge : dans 1 étui demi-rel., au chiffre de Louis-Philippe.

Nouveau fonds 138.

6377. 選僧圖說
Siuen seng thou choe.

Planches et légendes pour la divination.

Choix des élèves, divination, chiromancie ; un avertissement (1664) par Pan-pien tao-jen attribue l'ouvrage au bonze Yi-hing.

1 feuillet double de figures, 27 feuillets de texte.

In-18 large. Papier blanc. 1 vol. demi-reliure.

Nouveau fonds 78.

6378. 慈悲道塲水懺
Tsheu pei tao tchhang choei tchhan.

Règles pour la confession de l'eau de compassion.

Texte précédé de prescriptions sur les cérémonies, formules de prières, éloges, etc., d'après le bonze Oou-ta Tchi-hiuen († 881).

Préface sans nom d'auteur ; préface de . l'empereur Tchheng-tsou (1416). A la fin, lecture des signes difficiles.

3 livres. — Bunyiu Nanjio 1523.

Petit in-8. Papier blanc. 1 vol. demi-rel., au chiffre de Louis-Philippe.

Nouveau fonds 64.

6379-6381. 慈悲三昧水懺法
Tsheu pei san mei choei tchhan fa.

Règles pour la confession de l'eau de compassion.

Même ouvrage.

Préface de 1633 semblable à la préface non signée du n⁰ précédent ; prescriptions rituelles, éloges, etc. Texte ; lecture des signes difficiles ; invocation finale. Frontispice (2 feuillets doubles).

3 livres.

In-4. Papier blanc, gravure médiocre. 3 vol. en paravent couvertures rouges ; dans 1 étui demi-rel., au chiffre de Louis-Philippe.

Nouveau fonds 147.

6382. — I.
千手千眼大悲心咒行法
Tshien cheou tshien yen ta pei sin tcheou hing fa; alias :

大悲懺法
Ta pei tchhan fa.

Règles pour la dhāraṇī du cœur miséricordieux de Koan-yin.

Traité composé primitivement par Tchi-li Seu-ming tsoen-tchẹ (vers 1020); corrigé et revu par Tou-thi, du Hoa-chan; illustré et gravé par le bonze Tsi-sien, de Kia-hoo. Après le texte, notice sur l'œuvre qui a été gravée en 1675 et 1699. Autres notices, texte de vœux. Édition de Leng-yen seu (1675). En tête, frontispice (1 feuillet double), Koan-yin, une tablette de souhaits.

23 feuillets. — Cf. Bunyiu Nanjio 1517; n° 5860, art. III.

— II.

藥師瑠璃光如來本願功德經直觧
Yo chi lieou li koang jou lai pẹn yuen kong tẹ king tchi kiai.

Commentaire du Bheṣajyaguru vaiḍūryaprabhāsa pūrva praṇidhāna sūtra.

Par le bonze Ling-yao, de Thien-thai. Préface de l'auteur (année ki-yeou). Résumé sous forme de tableau (3 feuillets).

56 feuillets. — N° 6103, art. II.

Texte en caractères fins.

— III.

歷朝華嚴經持驗紀
Li tchhao hoa yen king tchhi yen ki.

Miracles de l'Avataṃsaka sū-tra sous les dynasties successives.

Par Tcheou Khẹ-fou Tchhong-lang, de King-khi; revu par Tchhen Tsi-cheng Hoang-chi, de Oou-kiun. Édition de Leng-yen seu.

23 feuillets.

— IV.

鶴峰悟禪師語錄
Ho fong oou chạn chi yu lou;
alias :

龍潭鶴峰和尙語錄
Long than ho fong hoo chang yu lou.

Œuvres et propos de Ho-fong Oou chạn-chi.

Réunis par ses disciples Chang-tchen et autres. Préfaces par Tsi-ji, de 'An-chan (1692), par Siu Sing (1692), par Tchong Hong-tao (1692), par Hoei-lou (1695).

4)

2 livres.

Bonne gravure.

— V.

行 狀

Hing tchoang.

Vie de Ho-fong chạn-chi.

Par Hoei-lou. Ho-fong, de l'école de Lin-tsi, nom religieux Tsi-oou, de la famille Fei de Oou-mẹn (1626-1687).

2 feuillets.

— VI.

鶴 峯 悟 禪 師 塔 誌 銘

Ho fong oou chạn chi tha tchi ming.

Inscription du stūpa de Ho-fong Oou chạn-chi.

Par Tchong Hong-tao, de Thong-khi.

2 feuillets.

Suivis d'une postface (1742) par Neng-yin.

— VII.

三 峯 藏 和 尚 年 譜

San fong tsang hoo chang nien phou.

Biographie en forme d'annales de San-fong Tsang hoo-chang.

Par Hong-tchhou, de Yun-yen seu, à la montagne Hou-khieou. San-fong hoo-chang, né en 1573, mort en 1635, de la famille Sou, de Oou-si, nom religieux Fa-tsang.

39 feuillets.

— VIII.

與 毘 陵 人 華 禪 師 書. 與 靈 隱 禮 和 尚 書

Yu phi ling jen hoa chạn chi chou. Yu ling yin li hoo chang chou.

Lettres de San-fong à deux bonzes.

Feuillets 39 à 44.

Suivis d'une postface par Nan-tsien, de Yao-fong (1661) et d'une autre par Hiao-tshing.

Grand in-8. 1 vol. demi-rel., au chiffre de la République Française.

Nouveau fonds 4184.

6383. — I.

千 手 千 眼 大 悲 心 咒 懺 法

Tshien cheou tshien yen ta pei sin tcheou tchhan fa.

Ouvrage analogue au n° précédent, art. I. Préface impériale (1411); trois feuillets doubles d'illustrations, figures de divinités; texte comprenant rites et formules ; illustrations (53 feuillets simples) représentant des divinités et des scènes diverses. A la fin figure de divinité.

— II.

禮拜觀想偈畧釋

Li pai koan siang kie lio chi.

Explication abrégée des vers sur les cérémonies de la méditation.

Vers par Tchan-jan ; explication par Khieou-tsi Tchi-hiu.

— III.

大悲心咒行法方便議

Ta pei sin tcheou hing fa fang pien yi.

Des avantages attachés à la récitation de la dhāraṇī de Koan-yin.

— IV.

受八關戒齋法

Cheou pa koan kiai tchai fa.

Règles pour recevoir les huit commandements.

Une note finale attribue les Règles (art. I) à un bonze de Seu-ming de l'époque des Song ; cette note est signée de Ming-tchou-chi Kio-lo (1682). Liste de bienfaiteurs. Édition de Hai-tchhoang (1803).

In-4. Papier blanc. 1 vol. en paravent, couvertures rouges ; dans 1 étui demi-rel., au chiffre de Louis-Philippe. *Nouveau fonds* 144.

6384. 大悲懺法

Ta pei tchhan fa.

Règles pour la confession de la grande compassion.

Préface impériale (1411). Édition de Hai-tchhoang.

— I.

大悲懺法規則

Ta pei tchhan fa koei tsę.

Règles pour la confession, etc.

Par Chen Hi-cheng Mę-sing, de Lien-tcheou.

2 feuillets.

— II.

大悲懺法啓請

Ta pei tchhan fa khi tshing.

Invocation au début de la confession, etc.

5 feuillets.

— III.

大悲懺法便誦

Ta pei tchhan fa pien song.

Prières à dire pour la confession, etc.

13 feuillets.

— IV.

禮經式
Li king chi.

Règles rituelles.

5 feuillets.

Petit in-8. Papier blanc. 1 vol. demi-reliure.

Nouveau fonds 633.

6385. — I.

得遇龍華修證懺儀
Tẹ yu long hoa sieou tcheng tchhan yi.

Traité de la vie religieuse.

Par le bonze Jou-sing, de Tsheu-yun seu au Thien-thai chan. Préface par un contemporain Koan Tchi-tao, de Leou-kiang (1607). Postface par Jou-kien, de Leng-yen seu à Tsoei-li (1610).

4 livres.

— II.

大阿羅漢難提蜜多羅 所說法住記
Ta 'o lo han nan thi mi to lo so chọ fa tchou ki.

Sur la durée de la Loi, par l'arhat Nandimitra.

Version de Hiuen-tsang (654). Lecture des mots rares. Note finale du bonze Jou-kien (1608).

9 feuillets. — Bunyiu Nanjio 1466.

— III.

布袋和尚傳
Pou tai hoo chang tchoan.

Vie du bonze au sac.

Ce bonze, qui se donnait le nom de Khi, vivait à Ming-tcheou; il disparut en 916 ou 917.

2 feuillets.

Grand in-8. Bonne gravure. 1 vol. demi-rel., au chiffre de la République Française.

Nouveau fonds 4167.

6386. ## 化生儀軌
Hoa cheng yi koei.

Cérémonial pour la transformation et la naissance.

Par Tẹ-tshing, de Han-chan. Impression de la bonzerie de Hai-tchhoang.

32 feuillets.

Petit in-8. Papier blanc. 1 vol demi-reliure.

Nouveau fonds 66.

6387. 修八十八佛洪名
寶懺

Sieou pa chi pa fo hong ming pao tchhan.

La précieuse confession des noms des quatre-vingt-huit Bouddhas.

Introduction et historique (1663) par Tao-phei.

— I.

修洪名懺儀式

Sieou hong ming tchhan yi chi.

Cérémonial de la confession des noms.

— II.

禮五十三佛懺悔法

Li oou chi san fo tchhan hoei fa.

Confession en l'honneur des cinquante-trois Bouddhas.

Par le bonze Tao-phei, de Kou-chan.

— III.

禮三十五佛懺悔法

Li san chi oou fo tchhan hoei fa.

Confession en l'honneur des trente-cinq Bouddhas.

Par le même auteur.

Postface du bonze Kou-yun. Gravé à la bonzerie de Hai-tchhoang.

Comparer n° 5809, art. I.

In-4. Papier blanc. 1 vol. en paravent, couverture rouge; dans 1 étui demi-rel., au chiffre de Louis-Philippe.

Nouveau fonds 134.

6388. — I.

准提三昧行法

Tchoen thi san mei hing fa.

Pratique du samādhi de Cun-dī.

Par le bonze Cheou-teng, de Thien-khi. Préfaces par Fan Siang (1669) et par le bonze Ming-yuen (1665).

25 feuillets.

— II.

本咒同譯

Pen tcheou thong yi; alias:

准提三昧行法附咒

Tchoen thi san mei hing fa fou tcheou.

Dhāraṇī en annexe à l'art. I.

Formules en chinois et en transcription. Édition de Thien-khi Ta-kio 'an (1669).

2 feuillets. — Cf. n°ˢ 5987 et suivants.

— III.

正覺潤光澤禪師澡雪集

Tcheng kio joẹn koang tsẹ chạn chi tsao siue tsi.

Œuvres et entretiens du bonze Joẹn-koang Tsẹ, de Tcheng-kio.

La table porte l'indication : édition de Leng-yen seu (1700). Préface par Tchhen Oen-tao (1685). Œuvres recueillies par Hiang-yen Tchao-choei.

1 livre.

Vie du bonze Joẹn-koang par lui-même. Rédaction de Tchao-choei, indiquant que Joẹn-koang est mort en 1682.

— IV.

般若波羅蜜多心經註解

Pan jẹ po lo mi to sin king tchou kiai.

Le Prajñāpāramitā hṛdaya sūtra, avec commentaire.

Commentaire de Tsong-lẹ et Jou-khi (1378). Préface impériale pour le Hṛdaya sūtra.

4 feuillets. — Bunyiu Nanjio 1614; cf. n° 5733, art. II.

— V.

金剛般若波羅蜜經註解

Kin kang pan jẹ po lo mi king tchou kiai.

Le Vajracchedikā prajñāpāramitā sūtra, avec commentaire.

Commentaire de Tsong-lẹ et Jou-khi (1378). Notice finale sur la publication faite par ordre impérial (1378). Édition de Leng-yen seu (1632).

28 feuillets. — Bunyiu Nanjio 1615; cf. n° 5728, art. I.

— VI.

大明太宗文皇帝御製序讚文

Ta ming thai tsong oen hoang ti yu tchi siu tsan oen.

Préfaces et éloges composés par l'Empereur Thai-tsong Oen, des Ming.

1.　　御製藏經讚

Yu tchi tsang king tsan.

Éloge des Piṭaka sūtra.

Daté de 1410, 3ᵉ lune.

Feuillets 1 à 3.

2. 御製如來正宗大覺妙經序

Yu tchi jou lai tcheng tsong ta kio miao king siu.

Préface des sūtra merveilleux de la grande science.

Datée de 1412, 9ᵉ lune.

Feuillets 3, 4.

3. 御製四部經序

Yu tchi seu pou king siu.

Préface pour les sūtra des quatre sections.

Datée de 1412, 8ᵉ lune.

Feuillets 4, 5.

4. 御製聖妙吉祥眞實名經序并讚

Yu tchi cheng miao ki siang tchen chi ming king siu ping tsan.

Préface et éloges des sūtra bienheureux et vrais du nom.

Datés de 1411, 4ᵉ lune.

Feuillets 5 à 7.

5. 御製喜金剛本續序

Yu tchi hi kin kang pęn siu siu.

Préface des traités du Vajra.

Datée de 1415, 4ᵉ lune.

Feuillets 7, 8.

6. 御製般若論中道論對論律論比量論序

Yu tchi pan ję loęn tchong tao loęn toei loęn liu loęn pi liang loęn siu.

Préface pour les çāstra relatifs à prajñā, tchong tao, toei, vinaya, pi-liang.

Datée de 1415, 6ᵉ lune.

Feuillets 8, 9.

7. 御製經牌讚

Yu tchi king phai tsan.

Éloge des sūtra.

Daté de 1411, 5ᵉ lune.

Feuillets 9, 10.

8. 御製釋迦如來金像讚

Yu tchi chi kia jou lai kin siang tsan.

Éloge des images de Çākya tathāgata.

Sans date.

Feuillet 10.

9. 御製尊勝佛母讚

Yu tchi tsoęn cheng fo mou tsan.

Éloge de la mère du Bouddha.

Sans date.

Feuillets 10 à 12.

10. 御製藏經跋尾

Yu tchi tsang king po oei.

Postface pour les piṭaka sūtra.

Datée de 1411, 12ᵉ lune inter-calaire.

Bunyiu Nanjio 1616.

Édition de Leng-yen seu (1662).

Grand in-8. 1 vol. demi-rel., au chiffre de la République Française.
Nouveau fonds 4149.

6389. 請諸天科儀

Tshing tchou thien khoo yi.

Rituel de l'invocation à tous les deva.

Édition de Hai-tchhoang (1710).

Cf. n° 6401, art. V.

In-4. Papier blanc. 1 vol. en paravent couvertures rouges ; dans 1 étui demi-rel., au chiffre de Louis-Philippe.
Nouveau fonds 157.

6390-6392. 消災延壽藥師懺法

Siao tsai yen cheou yo chi tchhan fa.

Règles de la confession en l'honneur de Bheṣajyaguru qui écarte les calamités et prolonge la longévité.

Frontispice (2 feuillets doubles). Texte comprenant :

— I (6390).

熏俻藥師懺儀

Hiun sieou yo chi tchhan yi.

Préliminaires de l'office et purification.

10 plis.

-- II (6390-6392).

Siao tsai yen cheou yo chi tchhan fa.

Texte par Tchheng-tsieou, de la bonzerie de Pao-koang à Ta-thong. Édition de 1746.

3 livres + appendice.

In-4. Papier blanc. 3 vol. en paravent couvertures rouges ; dans 1 étui demi-rel., au chiffre de Louis-Philippe.
Nouveau fonds 145.

6393. 讚本

Tsan pęn.

Liturgie.

Préface de 1815 par le bonze Siang-tchou ; gravé à la bonzerie de Hai-tchhoang. Comprenant :

— I.

開壇演淨發奏式

Khai than yen tsing fa tseou chi.

Cérémonial et formulaire des rites pour les preta.

27 sections.

— II.

祝聖儀

Tchou cheng yi.

Cérémonial des prières aux saints.

Avec des compositions d'éloge et des poésies.

43 feuillets.

— III.

受生圖。藏經圖式

Cheou cheng thou. Tsang king thou chi.

Tableau de donations. Tableau pour la récitation des formules sacrées.

3 feuillets.

— IV.

爲亡僧尼求課誦儀式

Oei oang seng ni khieou khoo song yi chi.

Cérémonial pour les prières en l'honneur des religieux et religieuses défunts.

4 feuillets.

Grand in-8. Papier blanc. 1 vol. demi-rel., initiales au chiffre de Louis-Philippe.

Nouveau fonds 68.

6394. — I.

依楞嚴究竟事懺

Yi leng yen kieou king chi tchhan ; alias :

修次依楞嚴了義究竟事懺

Sieou tsheu yi leng yen liao yi kieou king chi tchhan.

Rituel conforme au Çūraṅgama prasannārtha.

Sans nom d'auteur ; postface. Lecture des caractères rares.

2 livres. — Cf. n° 5992.

Bonne gravure.

— II.

擬寒山詩

Yi han chan chi.

Poésies inspirées de celles de Han-chan.

Par Tchang Cheou-yo Mei-tshoen kiu-chi ; publiées par Lou Koang-tsou Oou-thai kiu-chi. Préface de l'auteur ; préfaces par Thang Cheou-li et par Tshai Chan-ki.

57 feuillets. — Cf. n° 3694.

Caractères grêles.

— III.

雲峯體宗寧禪師語錄

Yun fong thi tsong ning chạn chi yu loù.

Œuvres et entretiens de Thi-tsong Ning chạn-chi.

Réunis par ses disciples Siu-tshing et autres. Préfaces par Tchhẹ-cheng (1695) et par Tẹ-yu (1685). Le bonze Thi-tsong vivait à l'époque Choẹn-tchi.

28 feuillets.

Bonne gravure.

Grand in-8. 1 vol. demi-rel., au chiffre de la République Française.

Nouveau fonds 4186.

6395-6397. 慈悲冥府十王妙懺法

Tsheu pei ming fou chi oang miao tchhan fa.

Règles pour la confession en l'honneur des dix rois infernaux miséricordieux.

Frontispice (1 feuillet double); introduction, éloges, litanies; texte de l'office. Prière finale. Édition de Hai-tchhoang seu.

3 livres.

In-4. Papier blanc; 3 vol. en paravent couvertures rouges; dans 1 étui demi-rel., au chiffre de Louis-Philippe.

Nouveau fonds 148.

6398. 釋門疏式雅俗通用

Chi mẹn sou chi; ya sou thong yong.

Modèles de prières, adresses, etc. à l'usage des bonzes.

Rassemblés par le bonze Ping-siue Jou-tẹ; revus par Oei-lin Tao-phei. Préface et introduction par l'auteur.

10 livres.

Grand in-8. Titre noir sur papier jaune. 1 vol. demi-rel., au chiffre de Louis-Philippe.

Nouveau fonds 899.

6399. 重刊京板攷正佛門定制

Tchhong khan king pan khao tcheng fo mẹn ting tchi.

Règles fixées des bonzes, réédition revue.

Modèles de prières, suppliques, adresses aux divinités, réunies par Tchạn Tchheng-kao, de Min-kien.

7 livres + 1 livre (supplément).

Petit in-8. Titre noir sur jaune. 1 vol. demi-rel., au chiffre de Louis-Philippe.

Nouveau fonds 819.

Troisième Section : DISCIPLINE

6400. 沙彌律儀要略
Cha mi liu yi yao lio.

Abrégé des règles et du rituel pour les çrāmaṇera.

Par Tchou-hong de la bonzerie de Yun-tshi (début du XVIIᵉ siècle). Texte et notes.

2 sections. — Cf. nᵒˢ 6243, art. III ; 6272, art. II ; pour l'auteur, voir nᵒ 3763.

Petit in-8. Papier blanc. 1 vol. demi-reliure.
Nouveau fonds 82.

6401. — I.

沙彌律儀要略增註
Cha mi liu yi yao lio tseng tchou.

Principales règles des çrāmaṇera, avec adjonctions et commentaires.

Par Tchou-hong; commentaire de Hong-tsan Tsai-san (milieu du XVIIᵉ siècle). Lecture des termes difficiles.

2 livres. — Cf. nᵒ 6400.

— II.

沙彌學戒儀軌頌
Cha mi hio kiai yi koei song.

Règles des çrāmaṇera, en pentasyllabes.

Par Hong-tsan Tsai-san.

9 feuillets. — Voir nᵒ 6403, art. I.

— III.

式叉摩那尼戒本
Chi tchha mo na ni kiai pen.

Règles des çikṣamāṇa bhikṣuṇī.

Extraites du Dharmagupta ; rassemblées par Hong-tsan avec préface par le même (1650). Lecture des termes difficiles. Édition de 1671.

24 feuillets. — Cf. nᵒˢ 6265 6266 et suivants.

— IV.

比丘尼受戒錄
Pi khieou ni cheou kiai lou.

Sur les devoirs des bhikṣuṇī.

Par le même.

9 feuillets. — Voir n⁰ˢ 6408, art. II ; 6269 ; 6270, art. II.

— V.

供諸天科儀

Kong tchou thien khoo yi.

Rituel de l'office en l'honneur des deva.

Par le même.

21 feuillets. — Cf. n° 6389.

— VI.

禮舍利塔儀式

Li chę li tha yi chi.

Rituel en l'honneur des çarīra.

Par le même; avec explication détaillée des termes difficiles. Daté de 1670.

19 feuillets.

— VII.

供齋讚

Kong tchai tsan.

Éloge à propos des offrandes des fêtes.

1 feuillet. — Cf. n° 6383, art. IV.

Grand in 8 1 vol. demi-rel., au chiffre de la République Française.
Nouveau fonds 4192.

6402. — I.

四分戒本如釋

Seu fęn kiai pęn jou chi.

Explication du Caturvarga pratimokṣa.

Par Hong-tsan Tsai-san, avec préface de l'auteur (1643). Introduction; tableaux récapitulatifs, table des matières. Texte annoté, lecture des termes difficiles.

12 livres. — Cf. n° 6267, art. II.

— II.

攝頌戒相圖

Chę song kiai siang thou.

Commandements et règles en pentasyllabes.

3 feuillets.

— III.

戒相篇聚圖

Kiai siang phien tsiu thou.

Tableaux et légendes pour les commandements.

2 feuillets (incomplet).

Grand in-8. 1 vol. demi-rel., au chiffre de la République Française.
Nouveau fonds 4072.

6403. — I.

沙彌學戒儀軌頌註

Cha mi hio kiai yi koei song tchou.

Commentaire des Règles des çrāmaṇera.

Par Hong-tsan Tsai-san ; avec lecture des caractères rares Daté de 1666.

32 feuillets. — Voir n° 6401, art. II.

— II.

禮佛儀式
Li fo yi chi.

Rituel en l'honneur du Bouddha.

Prières à dire soit six fois, soit trois fois, soit deux fois par jour. Texte et notes de Hong-tsan. Lecture des caractères difficiles. Daté de 1670.

10 feuillets.

— III.

何一自禪師語錄
Ho yi tseu chạn chi yu lou ; alias :

何一和尙語錄
Ho yi hoo chang yu lou.

Œuvres et entretiens du bonze Ho-yi.

L'auteur, de la famille Oang, de Khai-fong, était chef d'une bonzerie en 1681. Œuvres rassemblées par ses disciples Ming-sieou, Ming-hoei, Ming-tchi. Préfaces de Tchang Khai-tsong (1697), de Oang Tsẹ-hong (1697), de Jạn Kin-tsou (1693).

2 livres.

Grand in-8. Bonne gravure. 1 vol. demi-rel., au chiffre de la République Française.
Nouveau fonds 4083.

Quatrième Section : EXERCICES QUOTIDIENS

6404-6405. 雲棲法彙
Yun tshi fa hoei.

Collection bouddhique de Yun-tshi.

Publiée à Yun-tshi seu. Frontispice (1 feuillet double).

— I (6404).

梵網經心地品菩薩戒義疏發隱
Fan oang king sin ti phin phou sa kiai yi sou fa yin.

Commentaire du Brahmajāla sūtra et du Bodhisattva pratimokṣa sūtra, avec explications.

Le commentaire est de Tchi-tche; les explications sont dues à Tchou-hong, de Yun-tshi. Préface de ce dernier (1587); avertissement. Notice finale sur la gravure (1642).

5 livres. — Cf. nᵒˢ 6238, 6242.

— II (6404).

戒疏發隱事義

Kiai sou fa yin chi yi.

Notes pour l'ouvrage précédent.

42 feuillets.

— III (6404).

菩薩戒疏間辯

Phou sa kiai sou oen pien; alias :

戒疏間辯

Kiai sou oen pien.

Questions et discussions sur le Commentaire, etc.

27 feuillets.

— IV (6405).

佛說阿彌陀經

Fo choę 'o mi tho king.

Sukhāvatyamṛtavyūha sūtra.

Même ouvrage qu'au nᵒ 5734, art. III. Illustrations (8 feuillets doubles, déchirés en haut); au verso de la dernière planche, notice (1642). Texte seul.

5 feuillets.

— V (6405).

拔一切業障根本得生 淨土陀羅尼

Pa yi tshie ye tchang ken pęn tę cheng tsing thou tho lo ni.

Même ouvrage qu'au nᵒ 5734, art. IV.

1 feuillet.

— VI (6405).

佛說阿彌陀經疏鈔

Fo choę 'o mi tho king sou tchhao.

Commentaire du Sukhāvatī sūtra.

Par Tchou-hong. A la fin, date (1642).

4 livres.

— VII (6405).

彌陀經疏鈔事義

Mi tho king sou tchhao chi yi.

Notes pour le commentaire précédent.

37 feuillets.

— VIII (6405).

佛說阿彌陀經疏鈔問辯

Fo choę 'o mi tho king sou tchhao oen pien.

Questions et discussions sur le Commentaire, etc.

21 feuillets.

— IX (6405).

疏鈔續問荅

Sou tchhao siu oen ta.

Suite aux questions et réponses.

6 feuillets.

— X (6405).

疏鈔荅問

Sou tchhao ta oen.

Réponses aux questions.

3 feuillets.

— XI (6405).

荅四十八問

Ta seu chi pa oen.

Réponse à quarante-huit questions.

Préface de Tchou-hong (1584); texte; postface par Li Yang-

tchhoęn, surnom Tchou-fang kiu-chi.

28 feuillets.

— XII (6405).

淨土疑辯

Tsing thou yi pien.

Doutes et discussions au sujet de la Terre Pure.

3 feuillets.

— XIII (6405).

佛遺敎經施行勅

Fo yi kiao king chi hing tchhi.

Édit pour l'observation du Fo yi kiao king.

De l'empereur Thai-tsong des Thang.

Voir art. suivant.

— XIV (6405).

佛遺敎經論疏節要

Fo yi kiao king loęn sou tsie yao.

Commentaire sur le çāstra du sūtra des dernières instructions du Bouddha.

Le commentaire, de Tjyeng-ouen, bonze coréen (entre 960 et 1127), est annoté par Tchou-hong. Édition de Kia-hing (1642).

62 feuillets. — Cf. Bunyiu Nanjio 1597. 1209; n° 5955, art. III.

Grand in-8. Bonne impression. 2 vol. demi-rel., au chiffre de Napoléon III. *Nouveau fonds* 1515, 1516.

6406. 淨土晨鐘
Tsing thou tchhen tchong.

Cloche de la Terre Pure.

Préface (1659) de l'auteur Tcheou Khẹ-fou Tchhong-lang, surnom Thong-chạn tao-jen, de King-khi. Introduction du même. Table des 2 sections préliminaires et des 10 sections principales.

1re section préliminaire, tchhen khoo, office du matin, comprenant des invocations, formules, etc., et en outre :

— I.

佛 說 觀 無 量 壽 佛 經
Fo choẹ koan oou liang cheou fo king.

Feuillets 1 et 2. — N° 5813, art. II.

— II.

般 若 波 羅 蜜 多 心 經
Pan jẹ po lo mi to sin king.

Feuillet 2. — N° 5733, art. II.

— III.

楞 嚴 大 勢 至 菩 薩 念 佛 章

Leng yen ta chi tchi phou sa nien fo tchang.

Çūraṅgama sūtra, section de la méditation du bodhisattva.

Feuillets 2, 3 — N• 5992.

2e section préliminaire, si khoo, office du soir, comprenant des invocations, formules, etc., et de plus :

— IV.

佛 說 阿 彌 陀 經
Fo choẹ 'o mi tho king.

Feuillets 4 à 8. — N° 5734, art. III.

— V.

拔 一 切 業 障 根 本 得 生 淨 土 陀 羅 尼
Pa yi tshie ye tchang ken pẹn tẹ cheng tsing thou tho lo ni.

Feuillets 8, 9. — N° 5734, art. IV.

— VI.

慈 雲 懺 主 願 文
Tsheu yun tchhan tchou yuen oen.

Vœu du tchhan-tchou Tsheu-yun.

Feuillet 11.

— VII.

善 導 和 尙 臨 睡 入 觀 文
Chạn tao hoo chang lin choei jou koan oen.

Méditation avant le sommeil, par le bonze Chạn-tao.

Feuillets 11, 12.

— VIII, 1ʳᵉ à 10ᵉ sections principales.

Tsing thou tchhen tchong.

Croyances, pratiques, mérites, miracles relatifs à la Terre Pure par Tcheou Khẹ-ſou; publié par son fils Tcheou Chi Kou-tchheng. Édition du Leng-yen seu.

Grand in-8. 1 vol. demi-rel., au chiffre de la République Française.
Nouveau fonds 4153.

———

6407. 諸 經 日 誦 集 要
Tchou king ji song tsi yao.

Les sūtra les plus importants à réciter chaque jour.

Édition de Kia-hing (1662). Table des 3 livres, le dernier feuillet est relié à l'envers. Texte en caractères assez fins, grandes marges.

— I (livre 1).

看 經 警 文。啓 經 儀 式。 開 經 偈

Khan king king oen. Khi king yi chi. Khai king kie.

Règles et avertissement pour la lecture des sūtra.

Feuillet 1.

— II (livre 1).

般 若 波 羅 蜜 多 心 經
Pan jẹ po lo mi to sin king.

Feuillets 2 et 3. — Nᵒ 5733, art. II.

— III (livre 1).

金 剛 般 若 波 羅 蜜 經
Kin kang pan jẹ po lo mi king.

32 sections. — Nᵒ 5728, art. I.

Feuillets 4 à 26 ; à la suite, en manuscrit :

補 闕 眞 言。讚
Pou khiue tchen yen. Tsan.

Dhāraṇī; éloge.

Cf. nᵒ 5728, art. II.

— IV (livre 1).

妙 法 蓮 華 經 觀 世 音 菩 薩 普 門 品
Miao fa lien hoa king koan chi yin phou sa phou mẹn phin; alias :

觀 世 音 菩 薩 普 門 品
Koan chi yin phou sa phou mẹn phin.

Feuillets 27 à 35. — Nᵒ 5734, art. VII.

— V (livre 1).

藥師瑠璃光如來本願功德經

Yo chi lieou li koang jou lai pẹn yuen kong tẹ king; alias :

藥師經

Yo chi king.

Feuillets 35 à 56. — Nᵒ 6103, art. II.

— VI (livre 1).

佛說消災吉祥陀羅尼經

Fo choẹ siao tsai ki siang tho lo ni king; alias :

消災經

Siao tsai king.

Feuillets 56 à 59. — Cf. nᵒ 6136, art. VI.

— VII (livre 1).

生天十戒陀羅尼經

Cheng thien chi kiai tho lo ni king; alias :

生天經

Cheng thien king.

Svargopapatti daçaçīla dhāraṇī sūtra.

Feuillets 59 et 60.

— VIII (livre 1).

佛說解百生冤結陀羅尼經

Fo choẹ kiai po cheng yuen kie tho lo ni king; alias :

解冤經

Kiai yuen king.

Sūtra et dhāraṇī pour délivrer les êtres.

Feuillets 60 et 61.

— IX (livre 1).

佛說盂蘭盆經

Fo choẹ yu lan phẹn king.

Feuillets 61 à 64. — Nᵒ 5734, art. VI.

— X (livre 1).

金光明經空品

Kin koang ming king khong phin.

Suvarṇaprabhāsa sūtra, chapitre sur le vide.

Feuillets 64 à 67. — Nᵒ 6019.

— XI (livre 2).

佛說四十二章經

Fo choẹ seu chi eul tchang king.

Feuillets 1 à 12. — Nᵒ 6147, art. I.

— XII (livre 2).

佛遺敎經

Fo yi kiao king.

Feuillets 1 à 9. — N° 5955, art. III.

— XIII (livre 2).

八大人覺經

Pa ta jen kio king.

Sūtra des huit connaissances des hommes supérieurs.

Version de 'An-Chi-kao.

Feuillets 1 et 2 ; cf. n° 6149, art. III. — Bunyiu Nanjio 512.

— XIV (livre 2).

大方廣佛華嚴經淨行品

Ta fang koang fo hoa yen king tsing hing phin.

Buddhāvataṃsaka mahāvaipulya sūtra, chapitre de l'action pure.

Feuillets 1 à 15. — Cf. n°ˢ 5884 à 5891 et 5900-5901.

— XV (livre 2).

大方廣佛華嚴經梵行品

Ta fang koang fo hoa yen king fan hing phin.

Buddhāvataṃsaka mahāvaipulya sūtra, chapitre du brahmacarya.

Feuillets 1 à 4. — Cf. article précédent.

— XVI (livre 2).

大方廣佛華嚴經入不思議解脫境界普賢行願品

Ta fang koang fo hoa yen king jou pou seu yi kiai thoo king kiai phou hien hing yuen phin.

Buddhāvataṃsaka mahāvaipulya sūtra, section Acintyaviṣaya, chapitre des actes et des vœux de Samantabhadra.

Feuillets 1 à 22. — Cf. n°ˢ 5900-5901 et 5952, art. IV.

— XVII (livre 2).

大彌陀經四十八願

Ta mi tho king seu chi pa yuen.

Les quarante-huit vœux de l'Amitāyus sūtra.

Précédés de deux colonnes de dhāraṇī.

Feuillets 1 à 11. — Cf. n° 5817, art. VIII.

咒類

Tcheou lei.

Section des dhāraṇī.

— XVIII (livre 2)

受戒搭衣偈咒

Cheou kiai ta yi kie tcheou.

Dhāraṇī de la réception des commandements et de la prise du vêtement.

3 formules.

— XIX (livre 2).

展尼師壇偈咒

Tchan ni chi than kie tcheou.

Dhāraṇī pour étendre la natte (niṣīdana).

— XX (livre 2).

登殿塔咒

Teng tien tha tcheou.

Dhāraṇī en montant à la salle et au stūpa.

— XXI (livre 2).

登道場咒

Teng tao tchhang tcheou.

Dhāraṇī en se rendant à une place consacrée.

— XXII (livre 2).

延壽咒

Yen cheou tcheou.

Dhāraṇī pour prolonger la vie.

Cf. n° 6152, art. XV.

— XXIII (livre 2).

求智慧咒

Khieou tchi hoei tcheou.

Dhāraṇī pour demander la sagesse.

— XXIV (livre 2).

消萬病咒

Siao oan ping tcheou.

Dhāraṇī pour écarter les maladies.

— XXV (livre 2).

七佛滅罪咒

Tshi fo mie tsoei tcheou.

Dhāraṇī des sept Bouddhas qui détruisent le péché.

Cf. Bunyiu Nanjio 447 ; n° 6218, art. VI.

— XXVI (livre 2).

滅罪真言

Mie tsoei tchen yen.

Dhāraṇī pour détruire le péché.

— XXVII (livre 2).

護身咒

Hou chen tcheou.

Dhāraṇī pour protéger la personne.

— XXVIII (livre 2).

救苦咒

Kieou khou tcheou.

Dhāraṇī pour sauver du malheur.

— XXIX (livre 2).

斷瘟咒

Toan oen tcheou.

Dhāraṇī pour couper les épidémies.

— XXX (livre 2).

入厠咒

Jou tsheu tcheou.

Dhāraṇī pour entrer aux latrines.

— XXXI (livre 2).

洗淨咒

Si tsing tcheou.

Dhāraṇī à prononcer en se lavant.

— XXXII (livre 2).

去穢咒

Khiu oei tcheou.

Dhāraṇī contre les souillures.

— XXXIII (livre 2).

洗手咒

Si cheou tcheou.

Dhāraṇī à dire en se lavant les mains.

— XXXIV (livre 2).

淨身咒

Tsing chen tcheou.

Dhāraṇī pour purifier le corps.

— XXXV (livre 2).

下床咒

Hia tchhoang tcheou.

Dhāraṇī à prononcer en descendant du lit.

— XXXVI (livre 2).

行步不傷蟲咒

Hing pou pou chang tchhong tcheou.

Dhāraṇī à dire pour ne pas blesser en marchant les animaux rampants.

— XXXVII (livre 2).

摩利支天神咒

Mo li tchi thien chen tcheou.

Mārīcī devī dhāraṇī.

Cf. n° 6142, art. III.

— XXXVIII (livre 2).

佛頂尊勝陀羅尼

Fo ting tsoęn cheng tho lo ni.

Sarvadurgatipariçodhanoṣṇī-ṣa vijaya dhāraṇī.

Feuillets 3 et 4. — Cf. n° 5987, art. VII.

— XXXIX (livre 2).

尊勝佛母大陀羅尼

Tsoęn cheng fo mou ta tho lo ni.

Dhāraṇī de la mère du Bouddha.

Extrait du Mong kan king.

Feuillets 4 à 7.

— XL (livre 2).

功德天咒

Kong tę thien tcheou.

Guṇa deva dhāraṇī.

— XLI (livre 2).

十二因緣咒

Chi eul yin yuen tcheou.

Dvādaça nidāna dhāraṇī.

— XLII (livre 2).

華嚴補闕咒

Hoa yen pou khiue tcheou.

Dhāraṇī pour suppléer aux omissions relativement à l'Avataṃsaka.

— XLIII (livre 2).

穢跡金剛神咒

Oei tsi kin kang chen tcheou.

Malapāda vajra dhāraṇī.

Cf. n° 6214, art. I et II.

— XLIV (livre 2).

毘盧灌頂神咒

Phi lou koan ting chen tcheou.

Vairocanābhiṣeka dhāraṇī.

Cf. n° 6146, art. IX.

— XLV (livre 2).

祈雨咒

Khi yu tcheou.

Dhāraṇī pour demander la pluie.

Cf. n° 6357, art. L.

— XLVI (livre 2).

雨寶陀羅尼心真言

Yu pao tho lo ni sin tchen yen.

Formule sanscrite de la Ratnamegha dhāraṇī.

Cf. Bunyiu Nanjio 962.

— XLVII (livre 2).

（執金剛菩薩）延命陀羅尼

(Tchi kin kang phou sa) yen ming tho lo ni.

Vajradharabodhisattva dīrghāyur dhāraṇī.

— XLVIII (livre 2).

（觀世音菩薩破惡業陀）消伏毒害陀羅尼

(Koan chi yin phou sa pho 'o ye tho) siao fou tou hai tho lo ni.

Dhāraṇī d'Avalokiteçvara contre le poison.

Cf. n° 5861, art. II.

— XLIX (livre 2).

普庵祖師神咒

Phou 'an tsou chi chen tcheou.

Dhāraṇī de Phou-'an tsou chi.

Feuillets 10 à 12. — N° 6409, art. XL.

— L (livre 2).

二佛神咒

Eul fo chen tcheou.

Dhāraṇī des deux Bouddhas.

Feuillets 12 à 15. — N° 6409, art. XLI.

— LI (livre 2).

佛說小涅槃經

Fo choe siao nie phan king.

Petit Nirvāṇa sūtra.

Feuillets 1 à 3. — Cf. n°ˢ 5954 et suivants.

— LII (livre 2).

（佛說大藏正教）血盆經

(Fo choe ta tsang tcheng kiao) hiue phen king.

Sūtra du vase de sang.

Feuillets 3 à 5. — Cf. n° 6459.

— LIII (livre 2).

佛說壽生經

Fo choe cheou cheng king.

Sūtra de la longévité.

Feuillets 5 à 8.

— LIV (livre 2).

六十甲子十二生相

Lou chi kia tseu chi eul cheng siang.

Les soixante années du cycle et les douze qualités de la vie.

Texte et tableau; article non marqué à la table.

Feuillets 8 à 11.

— LV (livre 2).

奉填還謹專獻上

Fong thien hoan kin tchoan hien chang.

Prières à divers esprits.

Article non marqué à la table.

Feuillet 12.

朝 課

Tchao khoo.

Office du matin.

— LVI (livre 3).

大佛頂首楞嚴咒

Ta fo ting cheou leng yen tcheou; alias :

楞嚴神咒

Leng yen chen tcheou.

Mahābuddhoṣṇīṣa çūraṅgama dhāraṇī.

Feuillets 1 à 18. — Cf. nᵒˢ 5992; 6409, art. I.

— LVII (livre 3).

千手千眼無礙大悲陀羅尼

Tshien cheou tshien yen oou 'ai ta pei tho lo ni; alias :

大悲心咒

Ta pei sin tcheou.

Sahasrabāhu sahasrākṣapratihata mahākāruṇikahṛdaya dhāraṇī.

Feuillets 18 à 20. — Cf. nᵒˢ 5860, art. III; 6409, art. II.

— LVIII (livre 3).

如意寶輪王陀羅尼 (alias 神咒)

Jou yi pao loen oang tho lo ni (alias chen tcheou).

Padmacintāmaṇi rāja dhāraṇī.

Feuillet 20. — Cf. nᵒˢ 5860, art. VIII; 6409, art. III.

— LIX (livre 3).

消災吉祥神咒

Siao tsai ki siang chen tcheou.

Āpadvināça çrī dhāraṇī.

Cf. nᵒˢ 6136, art. VI; 6409, art. IV.

— LX (livre 3).

功德寶山神咒

Kong tę pao chan chen tcheou.

Guṇa ratnagiri dhāraṇī.

Cf. n° 6409, art. V.

— LXI (livre 3).

佛母準提神咒

Fo mou tchoęn thi chen tcheou.

Buddhamātṛkā cundī devī dhāraṇī.

Cf. n°ˢ 5987, art. V; 6409, art. VI.

— LXII (livre 3).

聖無量壽決定光明王陀羅尼

Cheng oou liang cheou kiue ting koang ming oang tho lo ni;
alias :

聖無量壽眞言

Cheng oou liang cheou tchen yen.

Āryāmitāyurniçcitaprabhāsarāja dhāraṇī.

Cf. n°ˢ 6144, art. II; 6409, art. VII.

— LXIII (livre 3).

藥師灌頂眞言

Yo chi koan ting tchen yen.

Bheṣajyagurvabhiṣeka dhāraṇī.

Cf. n°ˢ 6103, etc.; 6409, art. VIII.

— LXIV (livre 3).

觀音感應眞言

Koan yin kan ying tchen yen;
alias :

觀音靈感眞言

Koan yin ling kan tchen yen.

Avalokiteçvara anubhava mantra.

Cf. n° 6409, art. IX.

— LXV (livre 3).

七佛滅罪眞言

Tshi fo mie tsoei tchen yen.

Saptabuddhapāpa dhvaṃsana mantra.

Cf. Bunyiu Nanjio 447, 528; n°ˢ 6218, art. VI; 6409, art. X.

— LXVI (livre 3).

往生淨土神咒

Oang cheng tsing thou chen tcheou.

Dhāraṇī pour renaître en Terre Pure.

Cf. nᵒˢ 5734, art. IV; 6409, art. XI.

— LXVII (livre 3).

善天女咒
Chạn thien niu tcheou.

Sudevī mantra.

Cf. nᵒ 6409, art. XII.

Suivi de quelques autres formules.

— LXVIII (livre 3).

清晨普願偈
Tshing tchhen phou yuen kie.

Prière à l'aube.

暮時課誦
Mou chi khoo song.

Office du soir.

— LXIX (livre 3).

佛說阿彌陀經
Fo chọẹ 'o mi tho king.

Sukhāvatyamitavyūha sūtra.

Feuillets 26 à 33. — Nᵒ 5734, art. III.

— LXX (livre 3).

拔一切業障根本得生淨土陀羅尼
Pa yi tshie ye tchang ken pẹn tẹ cheng tsing thou tho lo ni; alias :

往生咒
Oang cheng tcheou.

Feuillet 33. — Nᵒ 5734, art. IV.

— LXXI (livre 3).

三十五佛五十三佛名懺悔經
San chi oou fo oou chi san fo ming tchhan hoei king; alias :

八十八佛名經
Pa chi pa fo ming king;

La confession des quatre-vingt-huit Bouddhas.

Texte partie en gros caractères, partie en caractères fins.

Feuillets 33 à 41. — Cf. nᵒ 6387; Bunyiu Nanjio 979.

— LXXII (livre 3).

蒙山施食文
Mong chan chi chi oen.

Office pour donner de la nourriture aux esprits, par Mong-chan.

Feuillets 41 à 45. — Nᵒ 6409, art. XX.

— LXXIII (livre 3).

念 佛 緣 起
Nien fo yuen khi.

Sur la méditation du Bouddha.

Feuillets 45 et 46.

— LXXIV (livre 3).

淨 土 文
Tsing thou oen.

Traité sur la Terre Pure.

Suivi de diverses prières.

Feuillets 46 à 49. — Cf. n° 6409, art. XLIII.

雜 集
Tsa tsi.

Section mélangée.

— LXXV (livre 3).

祝 延 萬 壽 儀 文
Tchou yen oan cheou yi oen.

Traité et rituel de la longévité.

Feuillets 50 et 51.

— LXXVI (livre 3).

祈 禱 諸 司 儀
Khi tao tchou seu yi.

Rituel pour implorer les préposés (?).

Feuillets 51 à 56.

— LXXVII (livre 3).

嚴 淨 儀
Yen tsing yi.

Rituel pour l'empereur.

Feuillets 56 et 57. — N° 6409, art. XXXI.

— LXXVIII (livre 3).

禮 懺 起 止 儀
Li tchhan khi tchi yi.

Rites pour le début et la fin des services de confession.

Feuillets 57 à 61.

— LXXIX (livre 3).

齋 佛 儀
Tchai fo yi.

Rituel de l'uposadha.

Cf. n°s 5735, art. VI; 6409, art. XXXVI.
Feuillet 62.

— LXXX (livre 3).

二 時 臨 齋 儀
Eul chi lin tchai yi.

Rituel des deux temps proches de l'uposadha.

Feuillet 63. — Cf. n° 6409, art. XXXVIII.

— LXXXI (livre 3).

誦 經 囘 向 。 偈
Song king hoei hiang. Kie.

Vœux pour la récitation des sūtra. Gāthā.

3 sections.

Feuillets 64 et 65.

— LXXXII (livre 3).

華 嚴 道 塲 字 毋
Hoa yen tao tchhang tseu mou;
alias :

諷 華 嚴 經 儀 式 字 毋
Fong hoa yen king yi chi tseu mou.

Tableau phonétique pour l'avataṃsaka.

Avec un texte préliminaire.

Feuillets 65 à 72. — Cf. nᵒˢ 6214, art. IX ; 6229, art. IV.

— LXXXIII (livre 3).

禮 華 嚴 文
Li hoa yen oen.

Traité en l'honneur de l'avataṃsaka.

Par Soei chan-chi, de Ta-hong chan, à Soei-tcheou.

Feuillets 72 et 73. — N° 6409, art. XXX.

— LXXXIV (livre 3).

小 淨 土 文
Siao tsing thou oen.

Application des mérites à toutes les créatures.

Par Tsheu-yun tchhan-tchou.

Feuillet 74. — Cf. n° 6409, art. XXI.

— LXXXV (livre 3).

新 定 西 方 願 文
Sin ting si fang yuen oen.

Vœux à propos du Paradis occidental, nouveau texte.

Par Tchou-hong, de Yun-tshi seu.

Feuillets 74 à 77.

— LXXXVI (livre 3).

禮 佛 發 願 文
Li fo fa yuen oen.

Vœux en l'honneur du Bouddha.

Par Jan chan-chi, de Yi-chan.

Feuillets 77 à 79.

— LXXXVII (livre 3).

讚觀音文

Tsan koan yin oen.

Éloge de Koan-yin.

Feuillet 79.

— LXXXVIII (livre 3).

禮觀音文

Li koan yin oen.

Traité en l'honneur de Koan-yin.

Par Ta-hoei kao chan-chi.

Feuillets 79 à 81.

— LXXXIX (livre 3).

祈禱觀音文

Khi tao koan yin oen.

Prière à Koan-yin.

Feuillets 81 et 82.

— XC (livre 3).

在家誦經回向

Tsai kia song king hoei kiang.

Vœux pour la récitation des sūtra à domicile.

Feuillets 82 et 83.

— XCI (livre 3).

六根偈。法身偈

Lou ken kie. Fa chen kie.

Gāthā des six sens. Gāthā du dharmakāya.

Feuillets 83 et 84.

— XCII (livre 3).

爲臨終人念佛式。靈前通用

Oei lin tchong jen nien fo chi.
Ling tshien thong yong.

Règles pour la méditation du Bouddha au moment de la mort.

Feuillets 84 et 85.

— XCIII (livre 3).

念佛弥陀讚

Nien fo mi tho tsan.

Éloge d'Amitābhabuddha.

Feuillets 85 et 86.

— XCIV (livre 3).

西方淨土讚

Si fang tsing thou tsan.

Éloge de la Terre Pure.

Feuillet 86.

— XCV (livre 3).

晨朝功德讚

Tchhen tchao kong tę tsan.

Puṇya stotra pour le matin.

Feuillet 86.

— XCVI (livre 3).

消災讚

Siao tsai tsan.

Éloge à propos de la destruction du malheur.

Feuillet 86. — Cf. n° 6136, art. VI.

— XCVII (livre 3).

藥師讚

Ya chi tsan.

Bheṣajyagurustotra.

Feuillets 86 et 87. — Voir plus haut, art. LXIII.

— XCVIII (livre 3).

佛寶讚。法寶讚。僧寶讚

Fo pao tsan. Fa pao tsan. Seng pao tsan.

Buddharatnastotra. Dharmaratnastotra. Saṅgharatnastotra.

Feuillets 87 et 88.

— XCIX (livre 3).

釋迦讚

Chi kia tsan.

Çākyastotra.

Feuillet 88.

— C (livre 3).

觀音讚

Koan yin tsan

Avalokiteçvarastotra.

Feuillet 88.

— CI (livre 3).

地藏讚

Ti tsang tsan.

Kṣitigarbhastotra.

Feuillet 89.

— CII (livre 3).

熾盛讚

Tchhi cheng tsan.

Tejaḥstotra.

Feuillet 89. — Cf. n° 6136, art. IV.

— CIII (livre 3).

求生西方十六觀門讚

Khieou cheng si fang chi lou koan men tsan.

Éloge des seize degrés du dhyāna pour chercher à renaître au Paradis occidental.

Feuillets 89 et 90.

— CIV (livre 3).

送佛讚

Song fo tsan.

Éloge pour prendre congé du Bouddha.

Feuillet 90.

A la fin date et lieu de gravure : Leng-yen seu (1662).

— CV (livre 3).

溈山大圓禪師警策

Koei chan ta yuen chạn chi king tshẹ.

Instructions par Ta-yuen chạn-chi, de Koei-chan.

Feuillets 1 à 7. — Cf. n° 6409, art. XLV.

Grand in-8. 1 vol. demi-rel., au chiffre de la République Française.
Nouveau fonds 4092.

6408. — I.

沙門日用

Cha mẹn ji yong.

Manuel quotidien des bonzes.

Règles, prières, définitions. Par Hong-tsan Tsai-san, de Koang-tcheou. Préface par Khai-ting, élève de l'auteur (1671). Texte annoté; liste des mots difficiles (1671).

2 livres.

— II.

比丘受戒錄

Pi khieou cheou kiai lou.

Sur les devoirs des bhikṣu.

Par Hong-tsan Tsai-san.

21 feuillets. — Voir n° 6401, art. IV.

Grand in-8. Bonne gravure. 1 vol. demi-rel., au chiffre de la République Française.
Nouveau fonds 4082.

6409. 禪門日誦

Chan mẹn ji song.

Office quotidien des bonzes.

Frontispice (1 feuillet double); puis texte, figures, tableaux.

朝時課誦

Tchao chi khoo song.

Office du matin.

— I.

大佛頂首楞嚴神咒

Ta fo ting cheou leng yen chen tcheou.

Mahābuddhoṣṇīṣa çūraṅgama dhāraṇī.

16 feuillets. — Cf. n° 6407, art. LVI.

— II.

千手千眼無礙大悲心陁羅尼

Tshien cheou tshien yen oou 'ai ta pei sin tho lo ni.

Sahasrabāhu sahasrākṣapratihata mahākāruṇikahṛdaya dhāraṇī ; alias : Mahākāruṇika mantra.

2 feuillets. — N° 6407, art. LVII.

— III.

如意寶論王陁羅尼

Jou yi pao loẹn oang tho lo ni.

Padmacintāmaṇirāja dhāraṇī.

1 feuillet. — Cf. Bunyiu Nanjio 1394, 1402, 1437 ; n° 6407, art. LVIII.

— IV.

消災吉祥神咒

Siao tsai ki siang chen tcheou.

Āpadvināça çrī dhāraṇī.

1/2 feuillet. — N° 6407, art. LIX.

— V.

功德寶山神咒

Kong tẹ pao chan chen tcheou.

Guṇa ratnagiri dhāraṇī

1/2 feuillet. — N° 6407, art. LX.

— VI.

佛母準提神咒

Fo mou tchoẹn thi chen tcheou.

Buddhamātṛkā cundī devī dhāraṇī.

1/2 feuillet. — N° 6407, art. LXI.

— VII.

聖無量壽決定光明王陁羅尼

Cheng oou liang cheou kiue ting koang ming oang tho lo ni.

Āryāmitāyurniçcitaprabhāsarāja dhāraṇī.

feuillet. — N° 6407, art. LXII.

VIII.

藥師灌頂眞言

Yo chi koan ting tchen yen.

Bheṣajyagurvabhiṣeka dhāraṇī.

1/2 feuillet. — N° 6407, art. LXIII.

— IX.

觀音靈感眞言

Koan yin ling kan tchen yeṇ.

Avalokiteçvara anubhava mantra

1/2 feuillet. — N° 6407, art. LXIV.

— X.

七 佛 滅 罪 眞 言

Tshi fo mie tsoei tchen yen.

Saptabuddha pāpa dhvaṃsana mantra.

1/2 feuillet. — N° 6407, art. LXV.

— XI.

往 生 淨 土 神 咒

Oang cheng tsing thou chen tcheou.

Dhāraṇī pour renaître en Sukhāvatī.

1/2 feuillet. — N° 6407, art. LXVI.

— XII.

善 天 女 咒

Chạn thien niu tcheou.

Sudevī mantra.

2 feuillets et demi. — Cf. Bunyiu Nanjio 958, 959; n° 6407, art. LXVII.

— XIII.

般 若 波 羅 蜜 多 心 經

Pan jẹ po lo mi to sin king.

Prajñāpāramitā hṛdaya sūtra.

1 feuillet. — N° 5733, art. II.

— XIV.

起 佛 偈

Khi fo kie.

Gāthā en l'honneur du Bouddha.

1 feuillet.

— XV.

回 向 文

Hoei hiang oen.

Sur l'application des mérites à toutes les créatures.

Par Jạn chạn-chi, de Yi-chan.

3 feuillets.

— XVI.

念 佛 讚

Nien fo tsan.

Éloges.

1 feuillet.

— XVII.

觀 無 量 壽 佛 經 上 品 上 生 章

Koan oou liang cheou fo king chang phin chang cheng tchang.

Amitāyur dhyāna sūtra, chap. I, verset de la naissance supérieure.

1 feuillet. — N° 5813, art. II.

暮 時 課 誦
Mou chi khoo song.

Office du soir.

— XVIII.

佛 說 阿 彌 陀 經
Fo choẹ 'o mi tho king.

Sukhāvatyamitavyūha sūtra.

6 feuillets. — N° 5734, art. III.

— XIX.

禮 佛 懺 悔 文
Li fo tchhan hoei oen.

Confession et repentir en l'honneur du Bouddha.

7 feuillets.

— XX.

蒙 山 施 食 文
Mong chan chi chi oen.

Office de Mong-chan pour la nourriture des esprits affamés.

5 feuillets. — N° 6407, art. LXXII.

— XXI.

廻 向 文
Hoei hiang oen; alias :

小 淨 土 文
Siao tsing thou oen.

Application des mérites à toutes les créatures.

Par Tsheu-yun tchhan-tchou.

2 feuillets. — Cf. n° 6407, art. LXXXIV.

— XXII.

西 方 讚
Si fang tsan.

Éloge du Paradis occidental.

1 feuillet. — Cf. n° 6407, art. XCIV.

— XXIII.

善 導 和 尙 示 臨 垂 入 觀 文
Chạn tao hoo chang chi lin tchhoei jou koan oen.

Méditation avant le sommeil par le bonze Chạn-tao.

1 feuillet. — N° 6406, art. VII.

Ici finit l'office du soir.

— XXIV.

祝 聖 儀
Tchou cheng yi.

Service pour l'empereur.

Texte et notes.

1 feuillet. — Voir plus bas, art. XXXI.

— XXV.

祝韋馱儀

Tchou oei tho yi.

Service en l'honneur de Veda ārya bodhisattva.

Texte et notes.

2 feuillets.

— XXVI.

祝伽藍儀

Tchou kia lan yi.

Service en l'honneur du saṅghārāma.

Texte et notes.

2 feuillets.

— XXVII.

祝祖師儀

Tchou tsou chi yi.

Service en l'honneur des bodhisattva et patriarches.

1 feuillet.

— XXVIII.

祝監齋儀

Tchou kien tchai yi.

Service en l'honneur des saints, des kinnara rāja, etc.

1 feuillet.

— XXIX.

諷華嚴經起止儀

Fong hoa yen king khi tchi yi.

Rituel pour la récitation de l'Avataṃsaka sūtra.

7 feuillets.

— XXX.

禮華嚴文

Li hoa yen oen.

Traité en l'honneur de l'avataṃsaka.

Par Soei chan-chi, de Ta-hong-chan, à Soei-tcheou.

2 feuillets. — N° 6407, art. LXXXIII.

— XXXI.

嚴淨儀

Yen tsing yi; alias :

祝聖文

Tchou cheng oen.

Rituel pour l'empereur.

5 feuillets. — N° 6407, art. LXXVII.

— XXXII.

獻十供讚

Hien chi kong tsan.

Éloge à propos des dix offrandes.

2 feuillets.

— XXXIII.

經 讚．懺 讚
King tsan. Tchhan tsan.

Éloges à propos de divers sūtra et de diverses confessions.

6 feuillets.

— XXXIV.

三 寶 讚．大 悲 讚
San pao tsan. Ta pei tsan.

Triçaraṇa stotra, etc.
Éloge en prenant refuge près
des Trois Joyaux, etc.

3 feuillets. — Cf. nº 6223; Bunyiu
Nanjio 1467.

— XXXV.

毘 尼 咒
Phi ni tcheou.

Vinaya dhāraṇī (?).
9 formules.

— XXXVI.

齋 佛 儀
Tchai fo yi.

Rituel de l'upoṣadha.

3 feuillets. — Cf. nº 6407, art.
LXXIX.

— XXXVII.

齋 天 儀
Tchai thien yi.

Rituel en l'honneur des deva.

7 feuillets.

— XXXVIII.

二 時 臨 齋 儀
Eul chi lin tchai yi.

Rituel des deux temps proches
de l'upoṣadha.

2 feuillets. — Cf. nº 6407, art.
LXXX.

— XXXIX.

佛 頂 尊 勝 大 陀 羅 尼
Fo ting tsoen cheng ta tho lo ni.

Sarvadurgatipariçodhanoṣṇīṣa
vijaya dhāraṇī.

3 feuillets. — Nº 5987, art. IX.

— XL.

普 庵 大 德 禪 師 釋 談 章 神 咒
*Phou 'an ta tę chạn chi chi than
tchang chẹn tcheou.*

Dhāraṇī de Ta-tẹ chạn-chi de Phou-'an.

3 feuillets. — N° 6407, art. XLIX.

— XLI.

二佛神咒
Eul fo chen tcheou.

Dhāraṇī des deux Bouddhas.

Avec d'autres invocations à la suite.

5 feuillets. — N° 6407, art. L.

— XLII.

念佛起止儀
Nien fo khi tchi yi.

Rituel pour la récitation des prières.

2 feuillets.

— XLIII.

回向文
Hoei hiang oen; alias :

淨土文
Tsing thou oen.

Textes pour l'application des mérites aux créatures.

4 feuillets. — Cf. n° 6407, art. LXXIV.

— XLIV.

禮觀音文
Li koan yin oen.

Textes en l'honneur de Koan-yin.

Plusieurs sont de Ta-hoei Kao chan-chi.

3 feuillets.

— XLV.

潙山大圓禪師警策
Koei chan ta yuen chan chi king tshẹ.

Instructions par Ta-yuen chạn-chi, de Koei-chan.

Avec lecture des caractères difficiles.

6 + 3 feuillets. — Cf. n° 6407, art. CV.

Suit la date : 1723, à la bonzerie de Hai-tchhoang, avec le nom du bonze Sin-kou.

— XLVI.

監齋
Kien tchai.

Calendrier des fêtes anniversaires.

2 feuillets.

— XLVII.

六十甲子看受生經欠錢數目

Lou chi kia tseu khan cheou cheng king khien tshien chou mou.

Liste par années du cycle de lecture des sūtra et des donations et donateurs.

4 feuillets.

— XLVIII.

釋迦世尊本傳

Chi kia chi tsoẹn pẹn tchoan.

Vie annotée du Bouddha.

3 feuillets.

— XLIX.

佛經緣起

Fo king yuen khi.

Sur la propagation du bouddhisme en Chine.

Avec annexe en petit texte.

6 feuillets.

A la fin : compilé par le bonze Mẹ-tchhi (1792).

Grand in-8. Papier blanc. 1 vol. demi-rel., au chiffre de Louis-Philippe.
Nouveau fonds 645.

6410. 沙門日用錄

Cha mẹn ji yong lou.

Manuel quotidien des bonzes.

Publié de nouveau par le bonze Kou-yun. Texte avec notes. Édition de Hai-tchhoang.

35 feuillets.

Petit in-8. Papier blanc. 1 vol. demi-reliure.
Nouveau fonds 95.

Cinquième Section : TRAITÉS ENCYCLOPÉDIQUES

6411-6413. 經律異相

King lin yi siang.

Extraits de sūtra et de vinaya.

Encyclopédie méthodique du bouddhisme (en 40 classes), par Seng-min, Pao-tchhang et autres religieux (516). Préface de Pao-tchhang ; table très détaillée. Édition de Hoa-tchheng seu (1612).

5o livres. — Bunyiu Nanjio 1473.

Grand in-8. Bonne gravure ; frontispice (1 feuillet double). 3 vol. demi-rel., au chiffre de la République Française.
Nouveau fonds 4o96 à 4o98.

6414-6415. 諸經要集
Tchou king yao tsi.

Extraits importants des sūtra.

Encyclopédie en 30 classes par Tao-chi Hiuen-yun, religieux de Si-ming seu (656-660). Préface de l'auteur. Édition de Leng-yen seu (1660).

20 livres. — Bunyiu Nanjio 1474.

Grand in-8. Bonne gravure. 2 vol. demi-rel., au chiffre de la République Française.

Nouveau fonds 4099, 4100.

6416-6421. 法苑珠林
Fa yuen tchou lin.

Encyclopédie bouddhique.

Formée d'extraits d'auteurs, réunis par le même religieux. Préface par Li Yen Tchong-seu, de Long-si (668). Lecture des caractères difficiles. Édition de la bonzerie de Miao-tę, du Tshing-liang chan (1590, 1591).

120 livres (2 livres pour la table; en tout 100 sections). — Cat. imp., liv. 145, f. 4. — Bunyiu Nanjio 1482.

Grand in-8. Frontispice (1 feuillet double). 6 vol. demi-rel., au chiffre de la République Française.

Nouveau fonds 4103 à 4108.

6422-6427.
Fa yuen tchou lin.

Même ouvrage. Édition de la même date; le frontispice (1 feuillet double) est différent.

In-4. 6 vol. demi-rel., au chiffre de Napoléon III.

Nouveau fonds 1223 à 1228.

6428. 法藏碎金錄
Fa tsang soei kin lou; alias :

晁氏寶文堂
Tchao chi pao oen thang.

Notes sur le bouddhisme.

Par Tchao Hiong, surnom Ming-yuen, nom posthume Oen-yuen, de Chan-yuen, docteur en 980. Portrait de l'auteur avec éloge au verso. Édition donnée par les descendants de l'auteur Tchong-tchho et Tseu-kien. Préface de l'auteur (1031). Notice sur l'auteur datée de 1546.

10 livres. — Cat. imp., liv. 145, f. 8.

Grand in-8. Papier blanc, gravure ancienne. 1 vol. demi-rel., au chiffre de la République Française.

Nouveau fonds 351.

6429-6430. 大藏一覽
Ta tsang yi lan.

Résumé méthodique du Mahā-piṭaka.

第四卷

Indiquant le sens général des sūtra cités. Par Tchhen Chi de Ning-tę; édition revue par Yao Choęn-yu de Sieou-choei. Préface pour la présente réédition par Tchhen Yi-tien de Sieou-choei (1614).

10 livres. — Cat. imp., liv. 145, f. 18.

Grand in-8. 2 vol. demi-rel., au chiffre de la République Française.
Nouveau fonds 4210, 4211.

6431. 正法眼藏

Tcheng fa yen tsang.

Études sur le piṭaka

Par Tsong-kao Ta-hoei chan-chi, de King-chan. Préface de la présente réédition par le bonze Yuen-tchheng, de Hien-cheng seu (1616). Introduction (1616) par Li Ji-hoa Tchou-lan kiu-chi.

3 livres (6 sections).

Grand in-8. 1 vol. demi-rel., au chiffre de la République Française.
Nouveau fonds 4243.

6432. 醒世錄

Sing chi lou.

Exposition méthodique des principes bouddhiques.

Relatifs à la doctrine et à la pratique, d'après les textes. Par

Siu Tchhang-tchi Kin-tcheou, de Oou-yuen; avec préface de l'auteur (1652).

8 livres.

Grand in-8. 1 vol. demi-rel., au chiffre de la République Française.
Nouveau fonds 4212.

6433. 六道集

Lou tao tsi.

Sur les six règnes de l'univers.

Par le bonze Hong-tsan Tsai-san de Pao-siang-lin, à Nan-hai. Avec introduction par l'auteur (1679). Préface par Li Long-piao de Tong-hoan (1682), etc. Texte avec notes, lecture des caractères difficiles.

Règne des deva, thien tao, livre 1.
Règne des hommes, jen tao, livre 2.
Règne des asura, 'o sieou lo tao, livre 2.
Règne des preta, koei tao, livre 3.
Règne des animaux, tchhou cheng tao, livre 4.
Règne infernal, ti yu tao, livres 4 et 5.

Grand in-8. 1 vol. demi-rel., au chiffre de la République Française.
Nouveau fonds 4031.

6434.

Lou tao tsi.

Même ouvrage, avec les mêmes préfaces. Réédition de Hai-tchhoang seu (1796).

In-4. Papier blanc. 1 vol. demi-rel., au chiffre de Louis-Philippe.

Nouveau fonds 627 A.

Sixième Section : TRAITÉS DIVERS

6435. 肇論
Tchao loen.

Le traité de Seng-tchao.

Auteur : Seng-tchao, de Tchhang-'an, disciple de Kumārajīva. Préface par Hoei-ta, bonze de Siao tchao-thi seu. Texte et pièces annexes. Édition de 1585.

3 livres. — Cf. Bunyiu Nanjio, 1627.

Grand in-8. Caractères grêles. 1 vol. demi-rel., au chiffre de la République Française.

Nouveau fonds 4132.

6436. 肇論新疏
Tchao loen sin sou.

Commentaire du Tchao loen.

Par Oen-tshai († 1302). Édition de Tchhoan-yi 'an, à King-chan.

2 livres (incomplet). — Bunyiu Nanjio 1627.

Grand in-8. Gravure grêle. 1 vol. demi-rel., au chiffre de la République Française.

Nouveau fonds 4146.

6437. 肇論新疏游刃
Tchao loen sin sou yeou jen.

Commentaire du Tchao loen sin sou.

Par le même.

3 livres (paraît complet). — Bunyiu Nanjio 1628.

Grand in-8. Caractères grêles. 1 vol. demi-rel., au chiffre de la République Française.

Nouveau fonds 4165.

6438. — I.

八識規矩頌纂釋
Pa chi koei kiu song tsoan chi.

Explication du Pa chi koei kiu song.

Par Koang-yi, de Khoang-chan (époque des Ming). Préface par le vieillard de Han-chan (1622). En frontispice, portrait ; au verso, éloge par le vieillard de Han-chan.

33 feuillets. — Cf. n° 6299, art. II et IX.

— II.

大乘百法規矩纂釋

Ta cheng po fa koei kiu tsoan chi; alias :

大乘百法明門論

Ta cheng po fa ming men loen.

Explication du Çatadharma vidyādvāra çāstra.

Par Koang-yi. Préfaces par Tchheng Khai-yu (1631), par le vieillard de Han-chan (1622), par Lieou Khi-siang Tchong-'an, du Ling-nan (1622), par Fang Yuen, de Mo-ling (1622).

54 feuillets. — Cf. n° 6299, art. III.

Grand in-8. 1 vol. demi-rel., au chiffre de la République Française.

Nouveau fonds 4156.

6439. 翻刻八識規矩略說

Fan kho pa chi koei kiu lio choe.

Explication des règles de la connaissance, nouvelle édition.

Traité attribué à Fong-tseu ; préface contemporaine de l'auteur par le bonze de Han-chan (1614) ; préface pour la présente réédition (1792) ; planches explicatives.

— I.

八識規矩頌

Pa chi koei kiu song.

Éloge des règles de la connaissance.

3 feuillets. — Cf. n° 6299, art. II.

— II.

Pa chi koei kiu.

Règles de la connaissance.

2 feuillets.

— III.

八識規矩頌略說

Pa chi koei kiu song lio choe.

Explication du Pa chi koei kiu song.

25 feuillets. — Cf. n° 6299, art. IX.

Grand in-8. Papier blanc. 1 vol. demi-reliure.

Nouveau fonds 634.

6440. 六祖大師法寶壇經

Lou tsou ta chi fa pao than king.

Sūtra prononcé par le sixième patriarche.

Préface impériale sans date ; préface pour la réédition (1695) par Tchhen Tsi-lin Oou-chang tao-jen. Préface (1056) par Lang Kien. Édition de Hai-tchhoang ; à la fin, liste des donateurs.

— I.

六祖大師緣起外紀

Lou tsou ta chi yuen khi oai ki.

Vie du sixième patriarche.

Hoei-neng, de la famille Lou, de Sin-tcheou ; nom personnel Hing-thao (638-713).

4 feuillets.

— II.

Lou tsou ta chi fa pao than king.

Recueilli par Fa-hai, disciple du patriarche.

68 feuillets. — Bunyiu Nanjio 1525.

— III.

又紀

Yeou ki.

Autre mémorial.

Récit de miracles.

2 feuillets.

In-4. Papier blanc. 1 vol. demi-rel., au chiffre de Louis-Philippe.
Nouveau fonds 639.

6441. 護法論

Hou fa loen.

Traité sur la protection de la Loi.

Composé vers 1170 par Tchang Chang-ying Oou-tsin kiu-chi. Préface (1171) par Tcheng Hing Te-yu Oou-'ai kiu-chi, de Nan-kien. Lecture des caractères difficiles. Préface par Song Lien, de Kin-hoa, et postface par le bonze Lai-fou, de Hang-tcheou, pour la réédition de 1374. Édition de Hai-tchhoang seu.

1 livre. — Bunyiu Nanjio 1502.

In-4. Belle impression sur papier blanc. 1 vol. demi-reliure.
Nouveau fonds 632.

6442. — I.

顯密圓通成佛心要集

Hien mi yuen thong tchheng fo sin yao tsi.

Traité sur la pensée de la transformation en Bouddha.

Par le bonze Tao-koei, de la bonzerie Kin-ho de la montagne Oou-thai. Préface par Tchhen Kio. Texte annoté. Lecture des caractères rares.

2 livres. — Bunyiu Nanjio 1477.

— II.

供佛利生儀

Kong fo li cheng yi.

Rituel pour procurer les offrandes aux Bouddhas et les avantages divers aux êtres vivants.

Texte avec notes et formules en transcription et en caractères hindous. A la suite postface du bonze Sing-kia. Liste des caractères rares. Édition de Leng-yen seu (1634).

10 feuillets (le dernier est manuscrit).

— III.

密咒圓因往生集

Mi tcheou yuen yin oang cheng tsi.

Recueil destiné à assurer la renaissance au moyen des causes parfaites.

Recueil de formules magiques. Gravé aux frais de Tcheou Lin-tchi de Oou-kiang (1614). Collection formée par les bonzes Tchi-koang, de Kan-tshiuen, et Hoei-tchen, de Oou-thai-chan ; traduite et publiée par Kin-kang tchhoang, de Lan-chan. Préface par Ho Tsong-cheou (1200). Le recueil s'ouvre par des prescriptions pour la récitation rituelle des mantra ; suit la collection des formules ; texte en transcription, stances, notes (ci-dessous, 1 à 33).

Bunyiu Nanjio 1478.

1. 金剛大輪明王咒

Kin kang ta loẹn ming oang tcheou.

Vajra mahācakra vidyārāja mantra.

Feuillet 4.

2. 淨法界咒

Tsing fa kiai tcheou.

Mantra de la loi pure.

Feuillet 5.

3. 文殊護身咒

Oen chou hou chen tcheou.

Mantra de Mañjuçrī.

Feuillet 5.

4. 一字輪王咒

Yi tseu loẹn oang tcheou.

Ekākṣaracakrarāja mantra.

Feuillet 5. — Cf. Bunyiu Nanjio 1024, 1434 ; n° 6134.

5. 三字總持咒

San tseu tsong tchhi tcheou.

Dhāraṇī en trois caractères.

Feuillet 6.

6. 七俱胝佛母心大准提咒

Tshi kiu tchi fo mou sin ta tchoen thi tcheou.

Cundī devī mantra.

Feuillet 7. — N° 5987, art. III.

7. 大佛頂白傘蓋心咒

Ta fo ting po san kai sin tcheou.

Mahabuddhoṣṇīṣa sitātapatra hṛdaya mantra.

Feuillet 8. — Cf. Bunyiu Nanjio 1016.

8. 大寶樓閣根本咒

Ta pao leou ko ken pen tcheou.

Mahāmaṇi vimāna mūla mantra.

Feuillets 10. — Cf. Bunyiu Nanjio 535.

9. 大寶樓閣心咒

Ta pao leou ko sin tcheou.

Mahāmaṇi vimāna hṛdaya mantra.

Feuillet 11. — Cf. Bunyiu Nanjio 535.

10. 大寶樓閣隨心咒

Ta pao leou ko soei sin tcheou.

Mahāmaṇī vimāna anuhṛdaya mantra.

Feuillet 12. — Cf. Bunyiu Nanjio 535.

11. 功德山陀羅尼咒

Kong te chan tho lo ni tcheou.

Guṇagiri mantra.

Feuillet 12. — Cf. n° 6407, art. LX.

12. 不動如來淨除業障咒

Pou tong jou lai tsing tchhou ye tchang tcheou.

Dhāraṇī du tathāgata immobile qui écarte les obstacles.

Feuillet 12.

13. 釋迦牟尼滅惡趣王根本咒

Chi kia meou ni mie 'o tshiu oang ken pen tcheou.

Dhāraṇī de Çākyamuni qui éteint le mal.

Feuillet 13.

14. 佛頂無垢淨光咒

Fo ting oou keou tsing koang tcheou.

Vimalaçuddhaprabhāsa mantra.

Feuillet 14. — Nᵒ 6115, art. IV.

15. 佛頂尊勝咒。尊勝心咒

Fo ting tsoen cheng tcheou. Tsoen cheng sin tcheou.

Sarvadurgatipariçodhanoṣṇīṣa vijaya mantra.

Deux dhāraṇī. — Cf. nᵒ 5987, art. VII à IX.

Feuillet 15.

16. 觀自在菩薩六字大明心咒

Koan tseu tsai phou sa lou tseu ta ming sin tcheou.

Avalokiteçvara bodhisattva ṣaḍakṣara mahāvidyā hṛdaya mantra.

Feuillet 16. — Cf. nᵒˢ 5987, art. VI (14); 6357, art. CXIII.

17. 文殊菩薩五字心咒

Oen chou phou sa oou tseu sin tcheou.

Mañjuçrī bodhisattva pañcākṣara hṛdaya mantra.

Feuillet 17. — Nᵒ 6221, art. II.

18. 觀自在菩薩甘露咒

Koan tseu tsai phou sa kan lou tcheou.

Avalokiteçvara bodhisattvāmṛta mantra.

Feuillet 17. — Cf. nᵒ 6221, art. V.

19. 藥師瑠璃光佛咒

Yo chi lieou li koang fo tcheou.

Bheṣajyaguru vaiḍūryaprabhāsa buddha mantra.

Feuillet 18. — Cf. nᵒ 6103.

20. 阿彌陀佛根本咒

'O mi tho fo ken pen tcheou.

Amitābha buddha mantra.

Feuillet 19. — Cf. nᵒˢ 5734, art. III; 5813.

21. 阿彌陀佛心咒

'O mi tho fo sin tcheou.

Amitābha buddha hṛdaya mantra.

Feuillet 20. — Cf. ci-dessus.

22. 阿彌陀佛一字咒

'O mi tho fo yi tseu tcheou.

Amitābha buddhaikākṣara mantra.

Feuillet 20. — Cf. ci-dessus.

23. 無量壽王如來一百八名咒

Oou liang cheou oang jou lai yi po pa ming tcheou.

Amitāyūrājatathāgata nāmāṣṭaçataka mantra.

Feuillet 21. — Cf. Bunyiu Nanjio 815, 816.

24. 智炬如來心破地獄咒

Tchi kiu jou lai sin pho ti yu tcheou.

Jñānolka tathāgata hṛdaya naraka dhvaṃsana mantra.

Feuillet 22. — Cf. nº 6210, art. II.

25. 毗盧遮那佛大觀頂光咒

Phi lou tchẹ na fo ta koan ting koang tcheou.

Vairocana buddha mahābhiṣeka prabhāsa mantra.

Feuillet 22. — Cf. nº 6146, art. IX.

26. 金剛薩埵百字咒

Kin kang sa too po tseu tcheou.

Vajra sattva çatākṣara mantra.

Feuillet 23. — Cf. Bunyiu Nanjio 1442.

27. 十二因緣咒

Chi eul yin yuen tcheou.

Dvādaça nidāna mantra.

Feuillet 23. — Cf. nº 6407, art. XLI.

28. 摩利支天母咒

Mo li tchi thien mou tcheou.

Mārīcī devī mantra.

Feuillet 24. — Cf. nº 5861, art. VIII (3); 6142, art. II et III.

29. 請雨咒

Tshing yu tcheou.

Mahāmegha mantra.

Feuillet 24. — Cf. nᵒˢ 6087; 6107, art. II à IV; 6214, art. V.

30. 截雨咒

Tsie yu tcheou.

Mantra pour arrêter la pluie.

Feuillet 25.

31. 截雹咒

Tsie po tcheou.

Mantra pour arrêter la grêle. Feuillet 25.

32. 心咒
Sin tcheou.

Hṛdaya mantra.

Feuillet 25.

33. 數珠功德法
Chou tchou kong tẹ fa.

Sur le mérite du rosaire.

Feuillets 25 et 26. — Cf. n° 6110, art. VIII et IX.

Lecture des mots difficiles. Édition de Hoa-tchheng seu au King-chan (1614).

Grand in-8. 1 vol. demi-rel., au chiffre de la République Française.
Nouveau fonds 4093.

6443. 辯僞錄
Pien oei lou.

Réfutation du taoïsme.

Recueil formé sur ordre impérial par le bonze Siang-mai (1291). Préfaces de Tchang Po-choẹn et du bonze Koei-ki-siang, de Siue-khi. Édition de Kia-hing (1661).

5 livres. — Bunyiu Nanjio 1607.

Grand in-8. 1 vol. demi-rel., au chiffre de la République Française.
Nouveau fonds 4322.

6444. 三教平心論
San kiao phing sin loẹn.

Traité impartial sur les trois religions.

Par Lieou Mi Tsing-tchai (dynastie des Yuen). Préface de 1324. Liste des caractères difficiles. Édition de Leng-yen seu (1651).

2 livres. — Bunyiu Nanjio 1643.

Grand in-8. Bonne gravure. 1 vol. demi-rel., au chiffre de la République Française.
Nouveau fonds 4155.

6445. 折疑論
Tchẹ yi loẹn.

Traité contre le doute.

Traité par le religieux Tseu-tchheng, surnom Yen-mei, nom littéraire Miao-ming, de Pa-ling, bonze dans la période Tchi-tcheng (1341-1368). Préface (1351), par Po-choei Khiu-phan. Commentaire par un religieux occidental, Chi-tseu (Siṃha). Édition de Tsi-tchao 'an (1608, 1609).

1 + 5 livres. — Bunyiu Nanjio 1634.

Grand in-8. Bonne gravure; les feuillets 6-15 du livre 4 sont manuscrits. 1 vol. demi-rel., au chiffre de la République Française.
Nouveau fonds 4134.

6446. — I.

大明仁孝皇后夢感佛說弟一希有大功德經

Ta ming jen hiao hoang heou mong kan fo choe ti yi hi yeou ta kong te king.

Buddhabhāṣita paramārtha sudurlabha mahāguṇa sūtra, reçu en songe par l'impératrice Jenhiao, des Ming.

Préface par l'impératrice (1403). Texte du sūtra. Postfaces (1407) par le prince héritier Kao-tchhi, par le prince de Han, Kao-hiu, par le prince de Tchao, Kao-soei. Postface impériale (1579). Gravé de nouveau par ordre de l'impératrice douairière Tsheu-cheng siuen-oen. A la bonzerie de Tsi-tchao, à King-chan (1602).

2 livres. — Bunyiu Nanjio 1657.

— II.

Ta ming jen hiao hoang heou mong kan fo choe ti yi hi yeou ta kong te king.

Double.

Grand in-8. Bonne gravure. 1 vol. demi-rel., au chiffre de la République Française.

Nouveau fonds 271.

6447. 緇門崇行錄

Tchi men tchhong hing lou.

Préceptes de conduite pour les bonzes.

Par Tchou-hong, de Hang-tcheou, avec préface de l'auteur (1585); postface par Kin-pien, de Hai-tchhoang (1683). Réimpression de la bonzerie de Hai-tchhoang (1808).

10 sections.

Petit in-8. Papier blanc. 1 vol. demi-rel., au chiffre de Louis-Philippe.

Nouveau fonds 62.

6448. 天樂鳴空

Thien lo ming khong.

Dissertations sur divers points de doctrine.

Par Pao Sing-tshiuen, originaire de Thien-lo, district de Chan-yin, vivant en 1574. Vie abrégée de l'auteur; introduction à l'ouvrage par Oang Khi-long (1648). Préface de l'auteur, postnom Tsong-tchao, surnom Thien-kou (1610). Préface par Kao Yeou-seu Nien-tsou. Liste des donateurs.

3 livres.

Grand in-8. 1 vol. demi-rel., au chiffre de la République Française.

Nouveau fonds 4179.

6449. 雲棲法彙。戒殺放生文

Yun tshi fa hoei. Kiai cha fang cheng oen.

Collection bouddhique de Yun-tshi : traité défendant de tuer les animaux et prescrivant de les mettre en liberté.

Par Tchou-hong, de la bonzerie de Yun-tshi, à Hang-tcheou. Préface par Yen Nou, de Hai-yu.

25 feuillets.

Petit in-8. Papier blanc. 1 vol. demi-reliure.
Nouveau fonds 90.

6450. 重刻憨山大師觀老莊影響論

Tchhong kho han chan ta chi koan lao tchoang ying hiang loen.

Discussion comparative du bouddhisme et du taoïsme, nouvelle édition.

Par Tę-tshing. Préface (1708) par Kou-yun, de Hai-tchhoang. Édition de Hai-tchhoang.

21 feuillets.

Petit in-8. Papier blanc. 1 vol. demi-reliure.
Nouveau fonds 71.

6451. 千松筆記

Tshien song pi ki.

Notes de Tshien-song.

Préface sans nom d'auteur ni date établissant une comparaison entre le Bouddha et Lao-tseu.

— I.

Tshien song pi ki.

Discussion de l'enseignement bouddhique et taoïste.

13 feuillets (gravure médiocre).

— II.

楞嚴擊節序

Leng yen ki tsie siu.

Préface du Traité sur le Çŭraṅgama.

Sans auteur ni date.

Feuillets 1 à 3. — Cf. n° 5991 et suivants.

— III.

金剛正眼

Kin kang tcheng yen.

Examen du Vajra.

Conçu dans le même sens que les articles précédents. Préface (1630) écrite au monastère Tshien-song, sans nom d'auteur.

Feuillets 3 à 8 (gravure en caractères carrés). — Cf. n° 5728 et suivants.

— IV.

雜錄
Tsa lou.

Mélanges.

Recueil préparé par un disciple.

Feuillets 1 à 11 (gravé en caractères cursifs).

— V.

楞嚴擊節
Leng yen ki tsie.

Traité sur le Çūraṅgama.

Feuillets 1 à 38 (caractères carrés). — Voir art. II.

Grand in-8. 1 vol. demi-rel., au chiffre de la République Française.
Nouveau fonds 4181.

6452. — I.

歸戒要集
Koei kiai yao tsi.

Traité de la triple profession de foi et des commandements.

Par Hong-tsan Tsai-san, de Ting-hou chan. Préface de l'auteur (1663). Texte annoté. Édition de Toan-tcheou, au Koang-tong (1663).

3 livres.

— II.

古林如禪師語錄
Kou lin jou chan chi yu lou.

Propos et œuvres du bonze Kou-lin Jou.

Portrait de l'auteur, Ki-jou, de la famille Phan, de Chang-hai, né en 1632. Préface de 1670 ; préface par Lo Tchen-sing, de Sieou-choei (1673). Vie du bonze Ki-jou datée de 1680, par Tshiuen-sou, Tshiuen-oei et autres. Édition de Leng-yen seu.

4 livres.

— III.

因明入正理論解
Yin ming jou tcheng li loen kiai.

Explication du Hetuvidyā nyāyapraveça çāstra.

Par le bonze Tchen-kiai, de Tsoei-li. Postface par l'auteur (1590).

32 feuillets. — Cf. n° 6299, art. I.

— IV.

宗鏡錄引百法論鈔略節
Tsong king lou yin po fa loen tchhao lio tsie.

Extraits du Çatadharma çāstra dans le Tsong king lou.

Édition de Miao-tẹ 'an, au Oou-thai chan (1590).

Feuillets 35 à 42. — Cf. Bunyiu Nanjio 1489 ; n° 6299, art. III.

— V.

金剛經受持感應錄
Kin kang king cheou tchhi kan ying lou.

Effets miraculeux du Vajra sūtra.

Par Toan Tchheng-chi Ko-kou, de Lin-tchi († 863). Préface rapportant des faits de 801. Extraits du Pao ying ki, du Fa yuen tchou lin, du Koang yì ki.

1ʳᵉ section.

金剛經鳩異
Kin kang king kieou yi.

Collection de faits merveilleux du Vajra sūtra.

13 feuillets.

2ᵉ section.

宋太平廣記報應部
Song thai phing koang ki pao ying pou.

Section des effets miraculeux, du Thai phing koang ki.

2 livres.

Extraits du Thai phing koang ki, du Fa yuen tchou lin, etc. Table des matières pour chaque section.

Cf. nᵒˢ 5728 et suivants ; 6416 à 6427.

Grand in-8. 1 vol. demi-rel., au chiffre de la République Française.
Nouveau fonds 4193.

6453. 觧惑編
Kiai hoẹ pien.

Traité pour dissiper les doutes.

Exposé des faits annonçant le bouddhisme ou manifestant son influence, d'après les écrits et l'histoire de l'antiquité jusqu'aux Ming ; avec textes annexes. Lecture des caractères difficiles. Par Hong-tsan Tsai-san. Préface par son disciple Yin Yuen-tsin, de Tong-hou. Édition de 1683.

4 livres.

Grand in-8. 1 vol. demi-rel., au chiffre de la République Française.
Nouveau fonds 4159.

6454.
Kiai hoẹ pien.

Même ouvrage avec des différences de disposition ; même préface. Lecture des caractères difficiles. Édition de Hai-tchhoang (1808).

2 livres.

Grand in-8. Belle impression sur papier blanc. 1 vol. demi-rel., au chiffre de Louis Philippe.

Nouveau fonds 625.

6455. 天然和尚同住訓略

Thien jan hoo chang thong tchou hiun lio.

Instructions abrégées pour la vie en commun, par le bonze Thien-jan.

L'auteur a vécu de 1608 à 1688. Gravé à la bonzerie de Lei-fong par Kin-ying.

61 feuillets.

Petit in-8. Papier blanc, gravure médiocre. 1 vol. demi-rel., au chiffre de Louis-Philippe.

Nouveau fonds 103.

6456. 菜根譚
Tshai ken than.

Traité moral.

En langue parlée, par Hong Ying-ming; préfaces de 1775 et 1810; gravé à la bonzerie de Hai-tchhoang.

58 feuillets.

Petit in-8. Papier blanc. 1 vol. demi-reliure.

Nouveau fonds 84.

6457. 持驗
Tchhi yen.

Préceptes et exemples de piété.

Gravé à la bonzerie de Hai-tchhoang (1797).

12 feuillets.

Petit in-8. Papier blanc. 1 vol. demi-reliure.

Nouveau fonds 640.

6458. 佛說天中北斗古佛消災延壽妙經
Fo choe thien tchong pe teou kou fo siao tsai yen cheou miao king.

Sūtra prononcé par le Bouddha sur les calamités écartées et la longévité prolongée par le moyen du Bouddha de la Grande Ourse.

Texte peut-être taoïste. Éloges au début et à la fin. Publié à Hai-tchhoang seu (1835).

In-4. Papier blanc. 1 vol. en paravent couverture rouge; dans 1 étui in-4 demi-rel., au chiffre de Louis-Philippe.

Nouveau fonds 139.

6459. 佛說大藏正教血盆經
Fo choe ta tsang tcheng kiao hiue phen king

Sūtra du vase de sang.

Texte occupant le bas des pages ; en haut, illustrations avec légendes. Frontispice, 1 feuillet double. Sans nom de traducteur.

Cf. n° 6407, art. LII.

Petit in-8. Papier blanc. 1 vol. en paravent couverture rouge ; dans 1 étui, demi-rel., au chiffre de Louis Philippe.
Nouveau fonds 135.

6460.

Fragment d'un ouvrage bouddhique, texte et commentaire.

In-4. Papier blanc. 1 vol. en paravent, cartonnage.
Nouveau fonds 4933.

6461.

Idoles chinoises.

Objets dépendant du culte bouddhique. Peintures sur étoffe, fond bleu uni, montées sur carton jaune.

25 peintures.

In-folio. 1 vol. couverture soie.
Département des Estampes, Oe 39.

Septième Section : ÉCOLE DHYĀNA

6462. — I.

禪源諸詮集都序

Chạn yuen tchou tshiuen tsi tou siu; alias :

禪那理行諸詮集

Chạn na li hing tchou tshiuen tsi.

Introduction aux explications sur le dhyāna.

Par Tsong-mi, bonze de Koeifong. Préface de Phei Hieou. Préfaces pour des rééditions par Yen Oou-oai Oei-ta (1303), Teng Oenyuen (1303), Kia Jou-tcheou. Édition de Tsi-tchao 'an (1607).

2 livres (4 sections). — Bunyiu Nanjio 1647.

— II.

八識規矩補註

Pa chi koei kiu pou tchou.

Commentaire du Pa chi koei kiu.

Par Phou-thai Lou-'an fa-chi, avec préface de l'auteur (1511). Le commentaire a pour objet douze vers attribués à Hiuen-tsang. Lecture des mots rares. Édition de Miao-tẹ-'an (1590) réédition (1681).

2 livres. — Nᵒˢ 6299, art. II et IX ; 6302, art. IX ; 6438, art. I.

— III.

大乘百法明門論解
Ta cheng po fa ming men loen kiai.

Commentaire du Mahāyāna çatadharma vidyādvāra çāstra.

Par Khoei-ki, de l'époque des Thang ; revu par Phou-thai, des Ming. Postface de ce dernier (1511). Tableau résumé de l'ouvrage. Édition de Miao-te-'an (1590) ; réédition de 1669.

2 livres. — Cf. nᵒˢ 6299, art. III ; 6438, art. II.

Grand in-8. Bonne gravure, frontispice (1 feuillet double). 1 vol. demi-rel., au chiffre de la République Française.
Nouveau fonds 4190.

——————

6463. 萬善同歸集
Oan chan thong koei tsi.

Traité sur la fin unique des diverses sortes de bonté.

Par Yen-cheou chan-chi († 975), de Yong-ming. Lecture des mots rares. Édition de Leng-yen seu (1663).

6 livres. — Bunyiu Nanjio 1655.

Grand in-8. 1 vol. demi-rel., au chiffre de la République Française.
Nouveau fonds 4158.

6464.
Oan chan thong koei tsi.

Même ouvrage. Préface (1733). Lecture des caractères difficiles. Édition de Hai-tchhoang.

6 livres.

In-4. Papier blanc. 1 vol. demi-rel., au chiffre de Louis-Philippe.
Nouveau fonds 238.

——————

6465. — I.
永明智覺禪師唯心訣
Yong ming tchi kio chan chi oei sin kiue.

Un seul cœur, traité par Tchi-kio chan-chi, de Yong-ming.

Auteur : Yen-cheou.

12 feuillets. — Bunyiu Nanjio 1652.

— II.

智覺禪師定慧相資歌
Tchi kio chan chi ting hoei siang tseu ko.

Chant de la connaissance intuitive par Tchi-kio chan-chi.

Feuillets 13 à 15.

— III.

警世
King chi.

Avertissement au monde.

Feuillets 15 à 17.

— IV.

宗鏡錄序
Tsong king lou siu.

Préface pour le Tsong king lou.

Lecture des termes difficiles. Édition de Tsi-tchao 'an (1609).

Feuillets 17 à 23. — Cf. Bunyiu Nanjio 1489.

— V.

禪宗決疑集
Chan tsong kiue yi tsi.

Résolution de doutes à propos de l'école Dhyāna.

Par Tchi-tchhe (dynastie des Yuen). Lecture des caractères difficiles. Réédition de 1692.

26 feuillets. — Bunyiu Nanjio 1653.

— VI.

黃檗山斷際禪師傳心法要
Hoang po chan toan tsi chan chi tchhoan sin fa yao.

Principes de la transmission du cœur, d'après les instructions de Toan-tsi chan-chi à Hoang-po chan.

Recueillis par Phei Hieou, de 842 à 848. Préface de 857.

17 feuillets. — Bunyiu Nanjio 1654.

— VII.

黃檗斷際禪師宛陵錄
Hoang po toan tsi chan chi oan ling lou.

Mémoires de Oan-ling au sujet de Toan-tsi chan-chi.

Édition de 1667.

Feuillets 17 à 29.

Grand in-8. Bonne gravure. 1 vol. demi-rel., au chiffre de la République Française.
Nouveau fonds 4274.

6466. 冥樞會要
Ming tchhou hoei yao.

Étude sur l'école Dhyāna.

Rédigée par le bonze Tsou-sin, de Hoang-long 'an, à Liu-chan (époque des Song); une notice non datée, signée Te-hong, indique que cet ouvrage est un résumé des Tsong king lou, préparé à Long-chan (1086-1093), par Pao-kio.

4 livres. — Comparer Bunyiu Nanjio 1489 (Tsong king lou).

Grand in-8. Papier blanc, illustré, bonne édition. 1. vol. demi-rel., au chiffre de la République Française.
Nouveau fonds 578.

6467. 禪林寶訓
Chạn lin pao hiun.

Instructions précieuses de l'école Dhyāna.

Recueil de morceaux très courts, réunis par les bonzes Miao-hi et Tchou-'an (période Choẹn-hi 1174-1189); complété par Tsing-chạn, bonze de Tong-oou. Préface de Tsing-chạn. Lecture des mots difficiles. Édition de Miao-tẹ-'an au Oou-thai chan (1590).

4 livres. — Bunyiu Nanjio 1638.

Grand in-8. Bonne gravure; les feuillets 23 et 24 du livre 4 sont manuscrits. 1 vol. demi-rel., au chiffre de la République Française.
Nouveau fonds 4229.

6468. 禪林寶訓筆說
Chạn lin pao hiun pi choẹ.

Commentaire sur le Chạn lin pao hiun.

Texte et commentaire par Tchi-siang, de Yun-fong en Tchhou, avec préface de l'auteur (1706); préface du Chạn lin pao hiun, par Tsing-chạn. Réédition de Hai-tchhoang (1744).

3 livres. — Cf. nº 6467.

Grand in-8. Papier blanc, bonne gravure. 1 vol. demi-rel., au chiffre de Louis-Philippe.
Nouveau fonds 105.

6469-6471. 禪宗頌古聯珠通集
Chạn tsong song kou lien tchou thong tsi.

Collection de vers à l'éloge des patriarches de l'école Dhyāna.

Formée par les religieux Fa-ying (1174-1189), puis Phou-hoei (1295-1318). Préface non datée par Fong Tseu-tchen. Préfaces de Phou-hoei (1318); de Tsing-kiai (1392); de Tchang Loẹn (1179); de Fa-ying (1175). A la fin postface (1321?) par Thien-thong Yun-sieou. Edition de Hing-cheng oan-cheou chạn-seu (1596, 1597).

40 livres. — Bunyiu Nanjio 1660.

Grand in-8. Bonne gravure, frontispice (1 feuillet double). 3 vol. demi-rel., au chiffre de la République Française.
Nouveau fonds 4225 à 4227.

6472-6473.
Chạn tsong song kou lien tchou thong tsi.

Double.

Livres 6 à 10, 16 à 20, 26 à 35 (feuillets dégradés).

Grand in-8. 2 vol. cartonnage.
Nouveau fonds 4687, 4688.

———

6474. — I.

寶王三昧念佛直指

Pao oang san mei nien fo tchi tchi.

Guide pour la méditation du Bouddha (ratnarāja samādhi).

Par le bonze Miao-hie qui vivait à la fin de la période des Yuen. Préface pour la réédition par Tchi-hiu (1650). Note et exhortation (1395). Postface de Tchhẹ Tsing-tchi (1651).

2 livres.

— II.

眞妄心境圖說

Tchen oang sin king thou chọe.

Figure et légendes du cœur vrai et du cœur pervers.

2 feuillets.

Ensuite liste des donateurs.

Grand in-8. 1 vol. demi-rel., au chiffre de la République Française.
Nouveau fonds 4010.

6475. — I.

古德禪師眞心直說

Kou tẹ chạn chi tchen sin tchi chọe.

Entretien avec le vrai cœur, par Kou-tẹ chạn-chi.

Auteur : Tchi-no (époque des Yuen). Préface sans date. Postface (1447) par Khieou Mọng-thang.

15 sections. — Bunyiu Nanjio 1649; voir n° 6476, art. II.
21 feuillets.

— II.

紫栢大師心經論

Tseu po ta chi sin king lọen.

Traité sur le Hṛdaya sūtra, par Tseu-po ta-chi.

L'auteur vivait aux xvie et xviie siècles. Texte en caractères cursifs.

3 feuillets.

— III.

般若波羅蜜多心經直指

Pan jẹ po lo mi to sin king tchi tchi.

Explication du Prajñāpāramitā hṛdaya sūtra.

Par le bonze Tchhoan-cheng, de Lei-fong.

10 feuillets. — Cf. n° 5733, art. II.

Grand in-8. Papier blanc. 1 vol. demi-reliure.

Nouveau fonds 83.

6476. — I.

高麗國普照禪師修心訣

Kao li koę phou tchao chạn chi sieou sin kiue.

Sur la culture du cœur, traité du bonze coréen Po-tjyo.

L'auteur vivait à l'époque des Yuen. Édition de Tsi-tchao-'an (1602).

14 feuillets. — Bunyiu Nanjio 1648.

— II.

眞心直說

Tchen sin tchi choę.

Entretien avec le vrai cœur.

Même ouvrage qu'au n° précédent, art. I. Préface sans date; préface pour une réédition par Oen-ting (1469).

1 livre. — Bunyiu Nanjio 1649.

— III.

誡初心學人文

Kiai tchhou sin hio jen oen.

Avertissement aux fidèles du cœur.

Traité de 1205, par Ro-nap, de Tjo-kyei-san, en Corée; note par Tchi-no.

Feuillets 22 à 24.

— IV.

皖山正凝禪師示蒙山法語

Hoan chan tcheng ying chạn chi chi mong chan fa yu.

Instructions religieuses adressées à Mong-chan par le bonze Tcheng-ying, de Hoan-chan.

Feuillets 24 et 25.

— V.

東山崇藏主送子行腳法語

Tong chan tchhong tsang tchou song tseu hing kio fa yu.

Instructions de Tong-san Tchhong-tsang-tchou en accompagnant un voyageur.

Feuillets 25 et 26.

-- VI.

蒙山和尙示眾語

Mong chan hoo chang chi tchong yu.

Sermon du bonze Mong-chan.

Avec postface (1447) par le bonze Ta-thien-kiai Mong-thang. Édition de Tsi-tchao 'an (1606).

Feuillets 26 et 27.

— VII.

寶藏論
Pao tsang loẹn.

Ratna piṭaka çāstra.

Par Seng-tchao, disciple de Kumārajīva. Édition du Neng-jen chạn-yuen, à Oou-lin (1594).

25 feuillets. — Bunyiu Nanjio 1650.

Grand in-8. Bonne gravure. 1 vol. demi-rel., au chiffre de la République Française.

Nouveau fonds 4290.

6477. — I.

普照禪師修心訣
Phou tchao chạn chi sieou sin kiue.

Même traité qu'au n° précédent, art. I.

20 feuillets.

— II.

緇門警訓
Tchi mẹn king hiun.

Instructions pour les bonzes.

Comprenant :

1. 大唐慈恩法師出家箴
Ta thang tsheu 'en fa chi tchhou kia tchen.

Préceptes pour les bonzes, par Tsheu-'en fa-chi (époque des Thang).

Feuillets 21 et 22. — Cf. n° 6478, art. XX.

2. 永明智覺壽禪師垂誡
Yong ming tchi kio cheou chạn chi tchhoei kiai.

Préceptes donnés par Tchi-kio chạn-chi, de Yong-ming.

Auteur : Yen-cheou.

Feuillets 22 à 24. — Cf. n° 6478, art. XXVIII.

3. 終南山宣律師賓主序
Tchong nan chạn siuen liu chi pin tchou siu.

Ordre des hôtes, par le maître du vinaya, de la montagne de Tchong-nan.

Feuillets 24, 25. — Cf. n° 6478, art. LXXXVIII.

4. 禪月大師大隱龜鑑

Chạn yue ta chi ta yin koei kien.

Le miroir mystérieux, par Chạn-yue ta-chi.

Feuillets 25, 26. — Cf. n° 6478, art. XXXV.

Réédition de Hai-tchhoang (1793).

Petit in-8. Papier blanc. 1 vol. demi-reliure.

Nouveau fonds 81.

6478. 緇門警訓

Tchi mẹn king hiun.

Instructions pour les religieux.

Pour l'auteur Jou-pa, voir n°ˢ 6555-6556. Préface pour une réédition (1470) par King-long, bonze de Tshing-phing chan à Oou-lin. Édition de Leng-yen seu (1634).

Bunyiu Nanjio 1644.

— I (livre 1).

潙山大圓禪師警策

Koei chạn ta yuen chạn chi king tshẹ.

Instructions de Ta-yuen chạn-chi, de Koei-chan.

Feuillets 1 à 5. — Cf. n° 6481.

— II (livre 1).

明教嵩禪師尊僧篇

Ming kiao song chạn chi tsoẹn seng phien.

Traité du respect des religieux, par Ming-kiao Song chạn-chi.

Feuillet 5 et 6.

— III (livre 1).

孤山圓法師示學徒

Kou chạn yuen fa chi chi hio thou.

Instructions aux disciples, par Yuen fa-chi, de Kou-chan.

Feuillets 6 à 8.

— IV (livre 1).

勉學

Mien hio.

Encouragement à l'étude.

2 sections.

Feuillets 8 à 12.

— V (livre 1).

姑蘇景德寺雲法師務學十門

Kou sou king tẹ seu yun fa chi oou hio chi mẹn.

Les dix études auxquelles on doit s'appliquer, par Yun fa-chi, de King-tę seu, à Kou-sou.

10 sections.

Feuillets 12 à 18.

— VI (livre 1).

上封佛心才禪師坐禪儀

Chang fong fo sin tshai chạn chi tsoo chạn yi.

Sur la contemplation, par Fo-sin Tshai chạn-chi, de Chang-fong.

Feuillets 18 et 19.

— VII (livre 1).

長蘆慈覺頤禪師坐禪儀

Tchhang lou tsheu kio yi chạn chi tsoo chạn yi.

Sur la contemplation, par Tsheu-kio Yi chạn-chi, de Tchhang-lou.

Feuillets 19 et 20.

— VIII (livre 1).

勸參禪文

Khiuen tshan chạn oen.

Traité pour conseiller la contemplation.

Feuillets 20 et 21.

— IX (livre 1).

自警文

Tseu king oen.

Traité relatif à la vigilance sur soi-même.

Feuillets 21 et 22.

— X (livre 2).

龍門佛眼遠禪師坐禪銘

Long mẹn fo yen yuen chạn chi tsoo chạn ming.

Sur la contemplation, par Fo-yen Yuen chạn-chi, de Long-mẹn.

Feuillet 1.

— XI (livre 2).

三自省察

San tseu sing tchha.

Triple examen de soi-même.

Feuillets 1 et 2.

— XII (livre 2).

鵝湖大義禪師坐禪銘

'O hou ta yi chạn chi tsoo chạn ming.

Sur la contemplation, par Ta-yi chạn-chi, de 'O-hou.

Feuillets 2 et 3.

— XIII (livre 2).

廬山東林混融禪師示眾

Liu chan tong lin koẹn yong chạn chi chi tchong.

Sermon par Koẹn-yong chạn-chi, de Liu-chan.

Feuillet 3.

— XIV (livre 2).

藍谷信法師自鏡錄序

Lan kou sin fa chi tseu king lou siu.

Sur l'examen de soi-mème, par Sin fa-chi, de Lan-kou.

Feuillet 3 à 6.

— XV (livre 2).

釋難文

Chi nan oen.

Solution de difficultés.

Feuillets 6 et 7.

— XVI (livre 2).

梁高僧俌法主遺誡小師

Liang kao seng tchheng fa tchou yi kiai siao chi.

Défenses laissées par Tchheng fa-tchou, bonze éminent des Liang.

Feuillets 7 et 8.

— XVII (livre 2).

右街寧僧錄勉通外學

Yeou kiai ning seng lou mien thong oai hio.

S'appliquer à la science extérieure, traité par un fonctionnaire bonze de Yeou-kiai-ning.

Feuillets 8 et 9.

— XVIII (livre 2).

晉支遁禪師座右銘

Tsin tchi toẹn chạn chi tsoo yeou ming.

Pièce gravée à la droite du trône, par Tchi-toẹn chạn-chi, des Tsin.

Feuillet 9.

— XIX (livre 2).

周京師大中興寺道安法師遺誡九章

Tcheou king chi ta tchong hing seu tao 'an fa chi yi kiai kieou tchang.

Neuf défenses laissées par Tao-'an fa-chi, de Ta-tchong-hing seu, à la capitale des Tcheou.

Feuillets 9 à 13.

— XX (livre 2).

大唐慈恩法師出家箴

Ta thang tsheu 'en fa chi tchhou kia tchen.

Préceptes pour les religieux, par Tsheu-'en fa-chi.

Feuillet 13. — Cf. n° 6477, art. II (1).

— XXI (livre 2).

南嶽法輪寺省行堂記

Nan yo fa loẹn seu sing hing thang ki.

Mémorial de la salle Sing-hing, de Fa-loẹn seu au Nan-yo.

Par Tchao Ling-king Tchhao-jạn kiu-chi.

Feuillet 14.

— XXII (livre 2).

周渭濱沙門亡名法師 息心銘

Tcheou oei pin cha mẹn oang ming fa chi si sin ming.

Sur le repos du cœur, par un religieux anonyme des bords de la rivière Oei, sous les Tcheou.

Feuillets 14 et 15.

— XXIII (livre 2).

洞山和尙規誡

Tong chan hoo chang koei kiai.

Règles et défenses de Tong-chan hoo-chang.

Feuillets 15 et 16.

— XXIV (livre 2).

慈雲式懺主書紳

Tsheu yun chi tchhan tchou chou chen.

Adresse à des notables, par Tsheu-yun Chi tchhan-tchou.

Auteur : Tsoẹn-chi.

Feuillet 16.

— XXV (livre 2).

願文

Yuen oen.

Vœu.

Feuillets 16 et 17.

— XXVI (livre 2).

圭峯密禪師座右銘

Koei fong mi chạn chi tsoo yeou ming.

Pièce gravée à la droite du trône, de Koei-fong Mi chạn-chi.

Feuillet 17.

— XXVII (livre 2).

白楊順禪師示眾

Po yang choẹn chạn chi chi tchong.

Sermon de Po-yang Choẹn chạn-chi.

Feuillet 17.

— XXVIII (livre 2).

永明智覺壽禪師垂誡

Yong ming tchi kio cheou chạn chi tchhoei kiai.

Préceptes donnés par Tchi-kio chạn-chi, de Yong-ming.

Feuillets 17 à 19. — Cf. n° 6477. art. II (2).

— XXIX (livre 2).

八溢聖解脫門

Pa yi cheng kiai thoo mẹn.

La sainteté résultant des huit vertus.

Feuillet 19.

-- XXX (livre 2).

大智照律師比丘正名

Ta tchi tchao liu chi pi khieou tcheng ming.

Sur le vrai nom des bhikṣu, par Ta-tchi Tchao liu-chi.

Feuillets 19 et 20.

— XXXI (livre 2).

捨緣銘

Chẹ yuen ming.

Sur le sacrifice de soi-même.

Feuillet 20.

XXXII (livre 2).

座右銘

Tsoo yeou ming.

Inscription gravée à la droite du trône.

Feuillets 20 et 21. — Voir **art.** XVIII, XXVI.

— XXXIII (livre 2).

規繩後跋

Koei cheng heou po.

Postface aux règles.

Feuillet 21.

— XXXIV (livre 3).

撫州永安禪院僧堂記

Fou tcheou yong 'an chạn yuen seng thang ki.

Mémorial de la salle de l'assemblée, de la bonzerie de Yong-'an, à Fou-tcheou.

Par Oou-tsin kiu-chi.

Feuillets 1 et 2.

— XXXV (livre 3).

禪月大師大隱龜鑑

Chạn yue ta chi ta yin koei kien

Le miroir mystérieux, par Chạn-yue ta-chi.

Feuillets 2 et 3. — Cf. n° 6477, art. II (4).

— XXXVI (livre 3).

右街寧僧錄三教總論

Yeou kiai ning seng lou san kiao tsong loẹn.

Traité des trois religions, par un fonctionnaire bonze de Yeou-kiai-ning.

Feuillets 3 à 5. — Cf. plus haut, art. XVII.

— XXXVII (livre 3).

傳禪觀法

Tchhoan chạn koan fa.

Procédés du dhyāna.

Feuillets 5 et 6.

— XXXVIII (livre 3).

洪州寶峯禪院選佛堂記

Hong tcheou pao fong chạn yuen siuen fo thang ki.

Mémorial d'une salle de la bonzerie de Pao-fong à Hong-tcheou.

Par Tchang Chang-ying, au sujet d'une salle fondée par l'empereur en 1102-1106.

Feuillets 6 à 8.

— XXXIX (livre 3).

三祖鐘智禪師信心銘

Sạn tsou tchong tchi chạn chi sin sin ming.

Inscription du cœur fidèle, par Tchong-tchi chạn-chi.

Feuillets 8 et 9.

— XL (livre 3).

戒定慧三學

Kiai ting hoei san hio.

Les trois doctrines de çīla, morale, samādhi, méditation, prajñā, sapience.

Extrait du Piao tsong.

Feuillets 9 et 10.

— XLI (livre 3).

釋法四依

Chi fa seu yi.

Explication des quatre appuis de la loi.

Feuillets 10 et 11.

— XLII (livre 3).

戒唯佛制不通餘人

Kiai oei fo tchi pou thong yu jen.

Les préceptes des Bouddhas n'atteignent pas jusqu'aux autres hommes.

Tiré du Hing tsong.

Feuillet 11.

— XLIII (livre 3).

撮略諸文以嘆戒法

Tshoo lio tchou oen yi than kiai fa.

Extraits célébrant les commandements.

Tiré du Piao tsong.

Feuillets 11 et 12.

— XLIV (livre 3).

佛在世時偏弘戒法

Fo tsai chi chi phien hong kiai fa.

A l'époque des Bouddhas, étendre les commandements.

Feuillet 12.

— XLV (livre 3).

示僧尼戒相廣畧

Chi seng ni kiai siang koang lio.

Instruction aux religieux et religieuses sur les caractères de la moralité.

Feuillets 12 et 13.

— XLVI (livre 3).

度尼教意

Tou ni kiao yi.

Instructions pour la consécration des religieuses.

Tiré du Ye sou.

Feuillet 13.

— XLVII (livre 3).

尼八敬法

Ni pa king fa.

Huit signes de respect des religieuses.

Feuillets 13 et 14.

— XLVIII (livre 3).

出家超世

Tchhou kia tchhao chi.

Quitter la famille et franchir le monde.

Tiré du Ye sou.

Feuillets 14 et 15.

— XLIX (livre 3).

沙彌五德

Cha mi oou ṭẹ.

Les cinq vertus des çrāmaṇera.

Tiré du Fou thien king (Puṇyakṣetra sūtra).

Feuillet 15. — Cf. Bunyiu Nanjio 383.

— L (livre 3).

三衣興意

San yi hing yi.

Sur les trois vêtements du religieux.

Extrait du Sarvāstivāda.

Feuillets 15 et 16. — Cf. nᵒˢ 6258 et suivants.

— LI (livre 3).

引示袈裟功能

Yin chi kia cha kong neng.

Sur le pouvoir du kaṣāya.

Extrait du Ta pei king.

Feuillets 16 et 17. — Cf. nᵒ 5972.

— LII (livre 3).

大教永斷繪綿皮物

Ta kiao yong toan tseng mien phi oou.

Interdiction perpétuelle des soieries, des étoffes moëlleuses, des fourrures.

Extrait du Yang kiue king.

Feuillet 17. — Cf. Bunyiu Nanjio 621, 622 (Aṅgulimālya sūtra).

— LIII (livre 3).

舉現事以斥妄行

Kiu hien chi yi tchhi oang hing.

Élever les offices présents pour écarter la conduite perverse.

Feuillet 18.

— LIV (livre 3).

示衣財體如非

Chi yi tshai thi jou fei.

Les vêtements, la richesse sont comme non existants.

Tiré du Ye sou.

Feuillets 18 et 19.

— LV (livre 3).

示敬護三衣鉢具法

Chi king hou san yi po kiu fa.

Sur le respect du précepte concernant les trois vêtements et le pātra.

Feuillets 19 et 20.

— LVI (livre 3).

示 開 制 本 緣
Chi khai tchi pęn yuen.

Cause première de l'explication des prescriptions.

Extrait du Piao tsong.

Feuillet 20.

— LVII (livre 3).

鉢 制 意
Po tchi yi.

Précepte relatif au pātra.

Extrait du Seng khi.

Feuillets 20 et 21. — Cf. n° 6272, art. I.

— LVIII (livre 3).

坐 具 教 意
Tsoo kiu kiao yi.

Précepte relatif au siège (ni-ṣīdana).

Feuillets 21 et 22.

— LIX (livre 4).

漉 囊 教 意
Lou nang kiao yi.

Précepte relatif au filtre.

Feuillet 1.

— LX (livre 4).

引 大 教 說 淨 以 斥 倚 濫
Yin ta kiao choę tsing yi tchhi yi lan.

Adopter de la grande doctrine les explications sur la pureté pour écarter tout principe faux.

Extrait du Ti tchhi loęn.

Feuillets 1 et 2.

— LXI (livre 4).

八 財 不 淨 長 貪 壞 道
Pa tshai pou tsing tchhang than hoai tao.

Sur l'impureté des richesses.

Feuillet 2.

— LXII (livre 4).

勸 廣 開 懷 利 隨 道 擁
Khiuen koang khai hoai li soei tao yong.

Sur le mépris des avantages personnels.

Tiré du Seng oang phien.

Feuillet 3. — Cf. n° 6238.

— LXIII (livre 4).

辯燒身指大小相違

Pien chao chen tchi ta siao siang oei.

Sur les incinérations.

Feuillets 3 à 5.

— LXIV (livre 4).

律制雜學以妨正業

Liu tchi tsa hio yi fang tcheng ye.

Sur les préceptes de discipline.

Feuillet 5.

— LXV (livre 4).

解行無實反輕戒律

Kiai hing oou chi fan khing kiai liu.

Sur le mépris des commandements.

Feuillets 5 et 6.

— LXVI (livre 4).

歸敬三寶興意

Koei king san pao hing yi.

Sur le recours au triratna.

Extrait du Koei king yi; non indiqué à la table de l'ouvrage.

Feuillets 6 et 7.

— LXVII (livre 4).

求歸三寶功益

Khieou koei san pao kong yi.

Avantages du recours au triratna.

Extrait du Koei king yi; non indiqué à la table.

Feuillets 7 et 8.

— LXVIII (livre 4).

列示三寶名相

Lie chi san pao ming siang.

Sur le nom et la forme des trois joyaux.

Tiré du Koei king yi; non indiqué à la table.

Feuillets 8 et 9.

— LXIX (livre 4).

三寶住持全由解法

San pao tchou tchhi tshiuen yeou kiai fa.

Sur la garde du triratna.

Feuillet 9.

— LXX (livre 4).

明理三寶功高歸之益大

Ming li san pao kong kao koei tchi yi ta.

Sur le mérite de comprendre le triratna et d'y recourir.

Tiré du Koei king yi.

Feuillets 9 et 10.

— LXXI (livre 4).

住持三寶

Tchou tchhi san pao.

Garder le triratna.

Feuillets 10 et 11.

— LXXII (livre 4).

化相三寶

Hoa hiang san pao.

Transformer et considérer le triratna.

Feuillets 11 et 12.

— LXXIII (livre 4).

仁宗皇帝讚三寶文

Jen tsong hoang ti tsan san pao oen.

Éloge du triratna par l'empereur Jen tsong.

Feuillets 12 et 13.

— LXXIV (livre 4).

大慧禪師看經回向文

Ta hoei chan chi khan king hoei hiang oen.

Vœu de Ta-hoei chan-chi en lisant les sūtra.

Auteur probable : Ta-hoei Phou-kio (milieu du xiiᵉ siècle).

Feuillet 13.

— LXXV (livre 4).

懶菴樞和尙語。四句偈

Lan 'an tchhou hoo chang yu. Seu kiu kie.

Propos et gāthā de Lan-'an Tchhou hoo-chang.

Feuillets 13 et 14.

— LXXVI (livre 4).

示比丘忖己德行受食

Chi pi khieou tshoen ki te hing cheou chi.

Instruction recommandant aux bhikṣu de réfléchir sur eux-mêmes.

Feuillets 14 et 15.

— LXXVII (livre 4).

示比丘慎勿放逸

Chi pi khieou chen oou fang yi.

Instruction recommandant aux bhikṣu d'être attentifs.

Extrait du Tseng yi 'o han king.

Feuillet 15. — Cf. Bunyiu Nanjio 543.

— LXXVIII (livre 4).

菩薩三事無厭

Phou sa san chi oou yen.

Sur les bodhisattva.

Extrait du Tchi loen.

Feuillet 15. — Cf. nᵒˢ 5789-5793.

— LXXIX (livre 4).

戒定慧

Kiai ting hoei.

Çīla, samādhi, prajñā.

Feuillets 15 et 16. — Cf. plus haut, art. XL.

— LXXX (livre 4).

誡觀壇越四事從苦緣起出生法

Kiai koan than yue seu chi tshong khou yuen khi tchhou cheng fa.

Sur la renaissance en échappant aux causes de misère par l'effet de la charité et de la contemplation.

Feuillets 16 et 17.

— LXXXI (livre 4).

誡觀末法中校量心行法

Kiai koan mo fa tchong kiao liang sin hing fa.

Sur l'exercice de la conscience.

Feuillets 17 et 18.

— LXXXII (livre 4).

誡觀破戒僧尼不修出世法

Kiai koan pho kiai seng ni pou sieou tchhou chi fa.

Recommandations aux religieux et religieuses qui ne cherchent pas à sortir du monde.

Feuillet 18.

— LXXXIII (livre 4).

誡觀六難自慶修道法

Kiai koan lou nan tseu khing sieou tao fa.

Sur le perfectionnement moral.

Feuillets 18 et 19.

— LXXXIV (livre 4).

戒賢論師祈禱觀音文

Kiai hien loen chi khi tao koan yin oen.

Prière à Koan-yin.

Feuillets 19 et 20.

— LXXXV (livre 4).

永嘉眞覺禪師發願文

Yong kia tchen kio chạn chi fa yuen oen.

Vœu de Tchen-kio chạn-chi, de Yong-kia.

Feuillets 20 à 23. — Cf. art. CI.

— LXXXVI (livre 4).

隨州大洪山遂禪師禮華嚴經文

Soei tcheou ta hong chan soei chạn chi li hoa yen king oen.

Sur l'Avataṃsaka sūtra, par Soei chạn-chi, de Soei-tcheou.

Feuillets 23 et 24.

— LXXXVII (livre 4).

桐江瑛法師觀心銘

Thong kiang ying fa chi koan sin ming.

Sur l'esprit de contemplation, inscription par Ying fa-chi, de Thong-kiang.

Feuillet 24.

— LXXXVIII (livre 5).

終南山宣律師賓主序

Tchong nan chan siuen liu chi pin tchou siu.

Ordre des hôtes, par (Tao)-siuen, maître du vinaya, de la montagne de Tchong-nan.

Feuillets 1 et 2. — Cf. n° 6477, art. II (3).

— LXXXIX (livre 5).

東山演禪師送徒弟行脚

Tong chan yen chạn chi song thou ti hing kio.

Adieux à des disciples par Yen chạn-chi de Tong-chan.

Feuillets 2 et 3.

— XC (livre 5).

石屋珙禪師送慶侍者回里省師

Chi oou kong chạn chi song khing chi tchẹ hoei li cheng chi.

Adieux à des disciples, par Kong chạn-chi.

Cet article n'est pas marqué à la table.

Feuillets 3 et 4.

— XCI (livre 5).

結 制 小 參

Kie tchi siao tshan.

Avis sur les règlements.

Article non marqué à la table.
Feuillets 4 et 5.

— XCII (livre 5).

上 堂

Chang thang.

Discours dans la salle d'assemblée.

Feuillet 5.

Manquant à la table, qui porte à la place des articles XC à XCII l'ouvrage suivant :

漢 顯 宗 開 佛 化 法 本 內 傳

Han hien tsong khai fo hoa fa pẹn nei tchoan.

Histoire de l'introduction du bouddhisme par Ming ti.

— XCIII (livre 5).

中 峯 和 尙 遺 誡 門 人。 誡 閒

Tchong fong hoo chang yi kiai mẹn jen. Kiai hien.

Conseils de Tchong-fong hoo-chang à ses disciples et aux oisifs.

Feuillet 5 à 7, 7 et 8.

— XCIV (livre 5).

千 嵓 長 禪 師 示 衆

Tshien yen tchhang chạn chi chi tchong.

Sermon de Tchhang chạn-chi, de Tshien-yen.

Feuillet 8.

— XCV (livre 5).

天 衣 懷 禪 師 室 中 以 淨 土 問 學 者

Thien yi hoai chạn chi chi tchong yi tsing thou oen hio tchẹ.

Questions de Hoai chạn-chi à ses disciples au sujet de la Terre Pure.

Feuillet 9.

— XCVI (livre 5).

大 智 律 師 警 自 甘 塗 炭 者

Ta tchi liu chi king tseu kan thou than tchẹ.

Avertissement de Ta-tchi liu-chi à ceux qui se contentent des vanités.

Feuillet 9. — Voir plus haut, art. XXX.

— XCVII (livre 5).

永明壽禪師戒無證悟人勿輕淨土

Yong ming cheou chạn chi kiai oou tcheng oou jen oou khing tsing thou.

Il ne faut pas mépriser la terre pure, conseils par Cheou chạn-chi de Yong-ming.

Auteur : Yen-cheou.

Feuillets 9 et 10.

— XCVIII (livre 5).

慈雲式懺主三衣辯惑篇

Tsheu yun chi tchhan tchou san yi pien hoẹ phien.

Discussion sur la question des trois vêtements, par Tsheu-yun Chi tchhan-tchou.

Feuillets 10 à 13. — Voir art. XXIV et L.

— XCIX (livre 6).

長蘆慈覺頤禪師龜鏡文

Tchhang lou tsheu kio yi chạn chi koei king oen.

Miroir mystérieux par Tsheu-kio Yi chạn-chi, de Tchhang-lou.

Feuillets 1 à 5. — Voir art. VII.

— C (livre 6).

慈受禪師示眾箴規

Tsheu cheou chạn chi chi tchong tchen koei.

Règles pour tous par Tsheu-cheou chạn-chi.

Feuillets 5 à 7. — Voir art. CXIX.

— CI (livre 6).

笑翁和尚家訓

Siao oong hoo chang kia hiun.

Instructions domestiques de Siao-oong hoo-chang.

Feuillets 8 et 9.

— CII (livre 6).

黃龍死心新禪師小參

Hoang long seu sin sin chạn chi siao tshan.

Traité par Seu-sin Sin chạn-chi, de Hoang-long.

Feuillets 9 à 12.

— CIII (livre 6).

褒禪山慧空禪院輪藏記

Pao chạn chan hoei khong chạn yuen loẹn tsang ki.

Mémorial du cakrapiṭaka de la bonzerie de Hoei-khong, dans la montagne Pao-chạn.

Par Yang Kie Oou-oei kiu-chi.

Feuillet 12.

— CIV (livre 6).

慈照聰禪師住襄州石門請查待制爲撰僧堂記

Tsheu tchao tshong chạn chi tchou siang tcheou chi mẹn tshing tchha tai tchi oei tchoan seng thang ki.

Tsheu-tchao Tshong chạn-chi, à Siang-tcheou, prie le tai-tchi Tchha de composer un mémorial pour la salle d'assemblée.

En date de 1009.

Feuillets 12 et 13.

— CV (livre 6).

應菴華禪師荅詮長老法嗣書

Ying 'an hoa chạn chi ta tshiuen tchang lao fa seu chou.

Réponse et explications de Ying-'an Hoa chạn-chi.

En date de 1162.

Feuillets 13 et 14.

— CVI (livre 6).

怡山然禪師發願文

Yi chan jạn chạn chi fa yuen oen.

Vœu de Jạn chạn-chi, de Yi-chan.

Feuillets 14 à 16.

— CVII (livre 6).

開善密菴謙禪師荅陳知丞書

Khai chạn mi 'an khien chạn chi ta tchhen tchi tchheng chou.

Réponse de Mi-'an Khien chạn-chi à Tchhen tchi-tchheng.

Feuillet 16.

— CVIII (livre 6).

司馬溫公解禪偈

Seu ma oen kong kiai chạn kie.

Gāthā expliquant la contemplation, par Seu-ma Oen kong.

Six pièces de 18 caractères, développant une pensée de Oen-tchong-tseu.

Feuillet 17. — Cf. n° 3488, art. X.

— CIX (livre 6).

仰山飯
Yang chan fan.

Repas du Yang-chan.

Par Yuen Tchong-ta; extrait du Yuen hou pou oai tsi.

Feuillets 17 et 18.

— CX (livre 6).

白侍郎六讚偈並序
Po chi lang lou tsan kie ping siu.

Six éloges, par Po chi-lang.

Extrait du Tchhang khing tsi.

Feuillets 18 et 19.

— CXI (livre 6).

天台圓法師自誡
Thien thai yuen fa chi tseu kiai.

Avertissement pour soi-même, par Yuen fa-chi, de Thien-thai.

Feuillets 19 et 20.

— CXII (livre 7).

芙蓉楷禪師小參
Fou yong kiai chan chi siao tshan.

Traité de Kiai chan-chi, de Fou-yong.

Feuillets 1 et 2.

— CXIII (livre 7).

黃蘗禪師示眾
Hoang pe chan chi chi tchong.

Sermon de Hoang-pe chan-chi.

Feuillets 3 et 4.

— CXIV (livre 7.)

徐學老勸童行勤學文
Siu hio lao khiuen thong hing khin hio oen.

Encouragement à l'étude, de Siu hio-lao.

Feuillets 4 et 5.

— CXV (livre 7).

月窟清禪師訓童行
Yue khou tshing chan chi hiun thong hing.

Conseils aux enfants, de Yue-khou Tshing chan-chi.

Feuillets 5 et 6.

— CXVI (livre 7).

山谷居士黃太史發願文
Chan kou kiu chi hoang thai chi fa yuen oen.

Vœu de Hoang Chan-kou kiu-chi.

Feuillets 6 et 7.

— CXVII (livre 7).

雲峯悅和尙小參語

Yun fong yue hoo chang siao tshan yu.

Traité de Yun-fong Yue hoo-chang.

Feuillets 7 et 8.

— CXVIII (livre 7).

月林觀和尙體道銘

Yue lin koan hoo chang thi tao ming.

Sur la réalisation de la connaissance, inscription par Yue-lin Koan hoo-chang.

Feuillet 8.

— CXIX (livre 7).

慈受深禪師小參

Tsheu cheou chen chạn chi siao tshan.

Traité de Tsheu-cheou Chen chạn-chi.

Feuillets 8 à 10. — Voir plus haut, art. C.

— CXX (livre 7).

汾州大達無業國師上堂

Fẹn tcheou ta ta oou ye koẹ chi chang thang.

Discours dans la salle d'assemblée, par Oou-ye koẹ-chi, de Fẹn-tcheou.

Extrait du Tchhoan teng.

Feuillets 10 à 12. — Cf. nᵒˢ 953-954.

— CXXI (livre 7).

法昌運 (alias 遇) 禪師小參

Fa tchhang yun (alias yu) chạn chi siao tshan.

Traité par Fa-tchhang Yun (ou Yu) chạn-chi.

Feuillets 12 à 14.

— CXXII (livre 7).

古鏡和尙回汾陽太守

Kou king hoo chang hoei fẹn yang thai cheou.

Réponse de Kou-king hoo-chang au préfet de Fẹn-yang.

Feuillets 14 et 15.

— CXXIII (livre 7).

雪竇明覺禪師壁間遺文

Siue teou ming kio chạn chi pi kien yi oen.

Traité laissé par Siue-teou Ming-kio chạn-chi.

Feuillets 15 et 16.

— CXXIV (livre 7.)

范蜀公送圓悟禪師行腳

Fan chou kong song yuen oou chạn chi hing kio.

Adieux de Fan Chou-kong à Yuen-oou chạn-chi.

Yuen-oou Fo-koo chạn-chi vers 1133.

Feuillet 16.

— CXXV (livre 7).

保寧勇禪師示看經

Pao ning yong chạn chi chi khan king.

Exhortation à lire les sūtra, par Pao-ning Yong chạn-chi.

Feuillets 16 et 17.

— CXXVI (livre 7).

大智照律師送衣鉢與圓照本禪師書

Ta tchi tchao liu chi song yi po yu yuen tchao pẹn chạn chi chou.

Lettre à Yuen-tchao Pẹn chạn-chi pour lui envoyer un vêtement et un bol à aumônes ; de Ta-tchi Tchao liu-chi.

Feuillet 17 et 18. — Voir plus haut, art. XCVI.

— CXXVII (livre 7).

釋門登科記序

Chi mẹn teng khoo ki siu.

Mémorial et ordre des bonzes qui ont passé les examens.

Feuillets 18 et 19.

— CXXVIII (livre 7).

顔侍郎荅雲行人書

Yen chi lang ta yun hing jen chou.

Réponse de Yen chi-lang à Yun hing-jen.

Feuillets 19 à 22.

-- CXXIX (livre 7).

陳提刑貴謙荅眞侍郞德秀書

Tchhen thi hing koei khien ta tchen chi lang tẹ sieou chou.

Réponse de Tchhen Koei-khien à Tchen Tẹ-sieou.

Tchen Tẹ-sieou (1178-1235).

Feuillets 22 à 24.

— CXXX (livre 8).

慈受禪師訓童行

Tsheu cheou chạn chi hiun thong hing.

Vingt préceptes pour les enfants, par Tsheu-cheou chạn-chi.

Feuillets 1 à 3. — Voir art. CXIX.

— CXXXI (livre 8).

勉僧看病

Mien seng khan ping.

Exhortation aux bonzes de soigner les maladies.

Feuillet 3.

— CXXXII (livre 8).

大慧禪師禮觀音文

Ta hoei chạn chi li koan yin oen.

Prière à Koan-yin par Ta-hoei chạn-chi.

Feuillets 3 et 4. — Voir plus haut, art. LXXIV.

— CXXXIII (livre 8).

天台智者大師觀心誦經法

Thien thai tchi tchẹ ta chi koan sin song king fa.

Sur la récitation des sūtra avec l'esprit de contemplation, par Tchi-tchẹ ta-chi de Thien-thai.

Feuillet 4 à 6. — Cf. n° 6508.

— CXXXIV (livre 8).

觀心食法

Koan sin chi fa.

Sur la nourriture et l'esprit de contemplation.

Feuillet 6.

— CXXXV (livre 8).

大智律師三衣賦

Ta tchi liu chi san yi fou.

Description en prose rythmée des trois vêtements, par Ta-tchi liu-chi.

Feuillets 6 et 7. — Cf. plus haut, art. CXXVI.

— CXXXVI (livre 8).

鐵鉢賦

Thie po fou.

Description en prose rythmée du pātra en fer.

Feuillets 7 et 8.

— CXXXVII (livre 8).

坐具賦

Tsoo kiu fou.

Description en prose rythmée du siège (niṣīdana)

Feuillet 8.

— CXXXVIII (livre 8).

漉囊賦

Lou nang fou.

Description en prose rythmée du filtre.

Feuillet 8.

— CXXXIX (livre 8).

錫杖賦

Si tchang fou.

Description en prose rythmée du bâton (khakkhara).

Feuillets 8 et 9.

— CXL (livre 8).

賾禪師誡洗麵文

Tchẹ chạn chi kiai si mien oen.

Traité de Tchẹ chạn-chi pour défendre de laver la farine.

Par Tsong-tchẹ, avec préface de l'auteur (1100). 40 préceptes de 28 caractères (4 heptasyllabes).

Feuillets 9 à 14. — Cf. n° 6515, art. XII.

— CXLI (livre 8).

辨才淨法師心師銘

Pan tshai tsing fa chi sin chi ming.

Sur le maître du cœur, par Pan-tshai Tsing fa-chi.

Feuillet 14.

— CXLII (livre 8).

唐禪月大師座右銘并序

Thang chạn yue ta chi tsoo yeou ming ping siu.

Pièce par Chạn-yue ta-chi, des Thang.

Extrait du Chạn-yue tsi.

Feuillets 14 et 15. — Voir art. XXXV, XXXII.

— CXLIII (livre 8).

吉州龍濟山友雲鑑和尚蛇穢說

Ki tcheou long tsi chan yeou yun meou hoo chang chẹ oei choẹ.

Sur l'impureté du serpent par Yeou-yun Meou hoo--chang, de Long-tsi chan à Ki-tcheou.

Feuillets 15 et 16.

— CXLIV (livre 8).

大慧禪師荅孫知縣書

Ta hoei chẹn chi ta soẹn tchi hien chou.

Réponse de Ta-hoei chẹn-chi à Soẹn tchi-hien.

Feuillets 16 à 20. — Voir art. CXXXII.

— CXLV (livre 8).

佛鑑懃和尚與佛果勤和尚書

Fo kien khin hoo chang yu fo koo khin hoo chang chou.

Lettre de Fo-kien Khin hoo-chang à Fo-koo Khin hoo--chang.

Feuillets 20 et 21.

— CXLVI (livre 8).

荅投子通和尚書

Ta theou tseu thong hoo chang chou.

Réponse à Theou-tseu Thong hoo-chang.

Feuillets 21 et 22.

— CXLVII (livre 9).

隋高祖文皇帝勅文

Soei kao tsou oen hoang ti tchhi oen.

Édit de Kao-tsou des Soei.

En date de 590.

Feuillet 1.

— CXLVIII (livre 9).

晉王受菩薩戒疏

Tsin oang cheou phou sa kiai sou.

Exposé du prince de Tsin pour recevoir les commandements des bodhisattva.

Le prince de Tsin devenu plus tard l'empereur Yang; pièce de 591.

Feuillets 1 à 3.

— CXLIX (livre 9).

婺州左溪山朗禪師召永嘉大師山居書

Oou tcheou tso khi chan lang chạn chi tchao yong kia ta chi chan kiu chou.

Lettre de Lang chạn-chi, de Tso-khi chan, à Oou-tcheou, au religieux de Yong-kia, pour l'inviter à se retirer dans la montagne.

Feuillet 3.

— CL (livre 9).

永嘉荅書

Yong kia ta chou.

Réponse du religieux de Yong-kia.

Signée Hiuen-kio (époque des Thang).

Feuillets 3 à 6.

— CLI (livre 9).

天台圓法師懺悔文

Thien thai yuen fa chi tchhan hoei oen.

Formule de confession, par Yuen fa-chi, de Thien-thai.

Feuillets 6 et 7. — Voir art. CXI.

— CLII (livre 9).

發願文

Fa yuen oen.

Vœu.

Feuillets 7 et 8.

— CLIII (livre 9).

荆溪大師誦經普回向文

King khi ta chi song king phou hoei hiang oen.

Vœu général pour la récitation des sūtra, par le maître de King-khi.

Feuillet 8.

— CLIV (livre 9).

芭蕉泉禪師示眾

Pa tsiao tshiuen chạn chi chi tchong.

Instruction par Tshiuen chạn-chi, de Pa-tsiao.

Feuillet 8.

— CLV (livre 9).

龍門佛眼禪師十可行十頌并序

Long mẹn fo yen chạn chi chi kho hing chi song ping siu.

Éloges des dix actions convenables, par Fo-yen chạn-chi, de Long-mẹn.

Dix éloges de 4 heptasyllabes chacun.

Feuillets 8 à 10. — Voir plus haut, art. X.

— CLVI (livre 9).

示禪人心要

Chi chạn jen sin yao.

Préceptes pour les contemplatifs.

Feuillet 10.

— CLVII (livre 9).

誡問話

Kiai oen hoa.

Contre les conversations (calomnieuses).

Feuillets 10 et 11.

— CLVIII (livre 9).

大隋神照真禪師上堂

Ta soei chen tchao tchen chạn chi chang thang.

Discours dans la salle d'assemblée, par Chen-tchao Tchen chạn-chi, époque des Soei.

2 sections.

Feuillets 11 à 13.

— CLIX (livre 9).

雲峯悅和尚室中舉古

Yun fong yue hoo chang chi tchong kiu kou.

Sur l'antiquité, par Yue hoo-chang, de Yun-fong.

Feuillet 13. — Voir art. CXVII.

— CLX (livre 9).

金陵保寧勇禪師示眾

Kin ling pao ning yong chạn chi chi tchong.

Instruction par Pao-ning Yong chạn-chi, de Kin-ling.

Feuillets 13 et 14. — Voir art. CXXV.

— CLXI (livre 9).

古德渴熱行

Kou tẹ kho jẹ hing.

Traité par Kou-tẹ.

Feuillet 14.

— CLXII (livre 9).

覺範洪禪師送僧乞食序

Kio fan hong chạn chi song seng khi chi siu.

Kio-fan Hong chạn-chi en en-voyant les religieux mendier leur nourriture.

Feuillets 14 et 15.

— CLXIII (livre 9).

爲僧不預於十科事佛徒消於百載

Oei seng pou yu yu chi khoo chi fo thou siao yu po tsai.

Le bonze qui n'est pas prêt aux dix prescriptions, se consume en vain au service du Bouddha pendant cent ans.

Extrait du Kao seng tchoan.

Feuillets 15 et 16. — Cf. Bunyiu Nanjio 1490.

— CLXIV (livre 9).

或菴體禪師上堂

Hoẹ 'an thi chạn chi chang thang.

Discours dans la salle d'as-semblée, par Hoẹ-'an Thi chạn-chi.

Feuillet 16.

— CLXV (livre 9).

示衆。小參。結座。眞淨文禪師頌。靈芝

照律師頌。古德垂誡。勉看經

Chi tchong. Siao tshan. Kie tsoo. Tchen tsing oen chạn chi song. Ling tchi tchao liu chi song. Kou tẹ tchhoei kiai. Mien khan king.

Instructions, éloges, etc.

19 pièces de 4 heptasyllabes. Par divers auteurs, dont l'un est mentionné à l'art. CLXI.

Feuillets 16 à 18.

— CLXVI (livre 9).

勉應緣

Mien ying yuen.

Exhortation à s'accorder avec les causes.

Feuillet 18.

— CLXVII (livre 9).

勉住持

Mien tchou tchhi.

Exhortation à la fermeté.

Feuillet 18.

— CLXVIII (livre 9).

洞山和尚自誡

Tong chan hoo chang tseu kiai.

Avertissement à soi-même, par Tong-chan hoo-chang.

Feuillets 18 et 19. — Voir art. XXIII.

— CLXIX (livre 9).

雪峯存禪師入閩

Siue fong tshoẹn chạn chi jou min.

Entrée au pays de Min de Siue-fong Tshoẹn chạn-chi.

Feuillet 19.

— CLXX (livre 9).

宏智禪師示衆

Hong tchi chạn chi chi tchong.

Instruction de Hong-tchi chạn-chi.

Feuillet 19.

— CLXXI (livre 9).

省病僧

Sing ping seng.

Religieux examinant les maladies.

Feuillet 19.

— CLXXII (livre 9).

大慧和尙示徒

Ta hoei hoo chang chi thou.

Instruction de Ta-hoei hoo-chang à ses disciples.

Feuillet 19. — Voir art. CXLIV.

— CLXXIII (livre 9).

龐居士頌

Phang kiu chi song.

Éloge de Phang kiu-chi.

Feuillets 19 et 20.

— CLXXIV (livre 9).

自保銘

Tseu pao ming.

Inscription sur la protection de soi-même.

Par Oou-tso, de Kou-sou.

Feuillet 20.

— CLXXV (livre 9).

上竺佛光照法師示小 師正吾

Chang tchou fo koang tchao fa chi chi siao chi tcheng oou.

Instruction au siao-chi Tcheng-oou donnée par Fo-koang Tchao fa-chi, de l'Inde supérieure.

Feuillets 20 et 21.

— CLXXVI (livre 9).

圭峯禪師示學徒委曲

Koei fong chạn chi chi hio thou oei khiu.

Instruction de Koei-fong chạn-chi à son disciple Oei-khiu.

Feuillet 21. — Voir art XXVI.

— CLXXVII (livre 9).

登厠規式

Teng tsheu koei chi.

Règles relatives aux latrines.

Feuillets 21 à 24.

— CLXXVIII (livre 9).

大智律師入厠垂訓

Ta tchi liu chi jou tsheu tchhoei hiun.

Instructions relatives aux latrines, par Ta-tchi liu-chi.

Feuillet 24. — Voir art. CXXXV.

— CLXXIX (livre 10).

讚佛傳法偈

Tsan fo tchhoan fa kie.

Éloge sur la prédication de la loi par le Bouddha.

Feuillet 1.

— CLXXX (livre 10).

禪林妙記前序

Chạn lin miao ki tshien siu.

Préface au mémorial de Chạn-lin (école Dhyāna).

Par Hiuen-tsẹ, religieux de Si-ming seu.

Feuillets 1 à 4.

— CLXXXI (livre 10).

漢顯宗開佛化法本內傳

Han hien tsong khai fo hou fa pẹn nei tchoan.

Voir art. XCII; d'après la table des matières, le présent article fait partie du livre 5 et les articles XC à XCII devraient prendre place ici.

Feuillets 4 à 7.

— CLXXXII (livre 10).

商太宰問孔子聖人

Chang thai tsai oen khong tseu cheng jen.

Questions posées à Confucius par le ministre Chang.

Chang, postnom Phi.

Feuillet 7.

— CLXXXIII (livre 10).

鍾山鐵牛印禪師示童行法晦

Tchong chan thie nieou yin chạn chi chi thong hing ʃa hoei.

Instructions aux enfants par Thie-nieou Yin chạn-chi, de Tchong-chan.

Texte semblant postérieur aux Thang.

Feuillets 7 à 9.

— CLXXXIV (livre 10).

撫州永安禪院新建法堂記

Fou tcheou yong 'an chạn yuen sin kien ʃa thang ki.

Mémorial de la construction de la salle de la loi, à la bonzerie Yong-'an, de Fou-tcheou.

Par Oou-tsin kiu-chi.

Feuillets 9 à 11. — Voir art. XXXIV.

— CLXXXV (livre 10).

宋文帝集朝宰論佛教

Song oen ti tsi tchhao tsai lọen ʃo kiao.

Oen-ti, des Song, expose la doctrine bouddhique à sa cour.

Fait de l'année 452 ou 453.

Feuillets 11 à 13.

— CLXXXVI (livre 10).

後漢書郊祀志

Heou han chou kiao seu tchi.

Notice sur le culte, de l'histoire des Han postérieurs.

Extraits.

Feuillet 13.

— CLXXXVII (livre 10).

杭州淨慈寺守一法眞禪師掃 (alias 帚) 地回向文

Hang tcheou tsing tsheu seu cheou yi ʃa tchen chạn chi sao (thi) ti hoei hiang oen.

Vœu de Cheou-yi Fa-tchen chạn-chi, de Hang-tcheou.

Feuillets 13 et 14.

— CLXXXVIII (livre 10).

隨州大洪山靈峯寺十方禪院記

Soei tcheou ta hong chan ling fong seu chi fang chạn yuen ki.

Mémorial de Ling-fong seu, dans la montagne Ta-hong, à Soei-tcheou.

En date de 1102.

Feuillets 14 à 17. — Voir art. LXXXVI.

— CLXXXIX (livre 10).

唐修雅法師聽誦法華經歌

Thang sieou ya fa chi thing song fa hoa king ko.

Chant pour la récitation du Saddharma puṇḍarīka sūtra, par Sieou-ya fa-chi, époque des Thang.

Feuillets 17 et 18.

— CXC (livre 10).

梁皇捨道事佛詔

Liang hoang chẹ tao chi fo tchao.

Édit de l'empereur des Liang contre le taoïsme et en faveur du bouddhisme.

En date de 504.

Feuillets 18 et 19.

Grand in-8. Bonne gravure. 1 vol. demi-rel., au chiffre de la République Française.
Nouveau fonds 4085.

6479. 禪關策進

Chạn koan tshẹ tsin.

Introduction à l'importance du dhyāna.

Recueil de passages de sūtra, d'instructions, d'œuvres diverses, formé par Tchou-hong Lien-tchhi ta-chi, de Yun-tshi, avec quelques notes ; préface par Tchou-hong (1600). Table des matières. Liste des donateurs. Édition de Chạn-khing 'an, à l'intérieur de Leou-mẹn.

3 sections.

Petit in-8. 1 vol. demi-rel., au chiffre de Napoléon III.
Nouveau fonds 1137.

6480. — I.

黃蘗無念禪師復問

Hoang pẹ oou nien chạn chi fou oen.

Réponses à des questions par Hoang pẹ Oou-nien chạn-chi.

Préface par Yuen Tsong-tao Oou-sieou kiu-chi ; préface primitive (1612) par Kou Khi-yuen Toẹn-yuen kiu-chi. Œuvres recueillies par le bonze Ming-oen.

3 livres.

— II.

黃蘗無念禪師醒昏錄

Hoang pẹ oou nien chạn chi sing hoẹn lou.

Œuvres morales diverses de Oou-nien chạn chi.

Édition de Kin-ling (1625).

Livres 4 et 5 (manque le livre 6).

Grand in-8. 1 vol. demi-rel., au chiffre de la République Française.

Nouveau fonds 4240.

6481. 潙山警策句釋記

Koei chan king tshẹ kiu chi ki.

Instructions de l'école de Koei-chan avec commentaires.

Commentaires par Hong-tsan Tsai-san, de Hou-chan, et par son élève Khai-hiong. Préface (1660) par Koo-yi. Tableau résumant l'ouvrage. A la fin, notice (1670) par Tchheng Ji-cheng Kiun-tsin, nom religieux Khai-tchoẹ. Lecture des caractères difficiles.

2 livres. — Cf. n° 6478, art. I.

Grand in-8. 1 vol. demi-rel., au chiffre de la République Française.

Nouveau fonds 4178.

6482.

Koei chan king tshẹ kiu chi ki.

Même ouvrage; édition de Hai-tchhoang, plus petite, imitée de la précédente.

Grand in-8. Papier blanc. 1 vol. demi-rel., au chiffre de Louis-Philippe.

Nouveau fonds 646.

6483. 翻刻初參要訣

Fan kho tchhou tshan yao kiue.

Conseils sur le dhyāna, nouvelle édition.

Par le solitaire Ta-yen, de Lo-chạn 'an; réédition de la bonzerie de Hai-tchhoang (1742), d'après une première édition de Hang-tcheou. Caractères cursifs, style semi-parlé.

15 feuillets.

Petit in-8. Papier blanc. 1 vol. demi-reliure.

Nouveau fonds 92.